Revenue Law—
principles and practice

Revenue Law—principles and practice

Fifteenth edition

Chris Whitehouse BA, BCL(Oxon), BA(Lond)
Barrister

with

Loraine Watson BA, BCL,
Solicitor,
Lecturer in Law, Brunel University

Natalie Lee LLB
Barrister,
Lecturer in Law, Southampton University

and also with a contribution by

Paul Blakeley FRICS, ACIArb
Partner
Napier Blakeley Winter

Butterworths
London, Dublin and Edinburgh
1997

United Kingdom	Butterworths, a Division of Reed Elsevier (UK) Ltd, Halsbury House, 35 Chancery Lane, LONDON WC2A 1EL and 4 Hill Street, EDINBURGH EH2 3JZ
Australia	Butterworths Pty Ltd, SYDNEY, MELBOURNE, BRISBANE, ADELAIDE, PERTH, CANBERRA and HOBART
Canada	Butterworths Canada Ltd, TORONTO and VANCOUVER
Ireland	Butterworth (Ireland) Ltd, DUBLIN
Malaysia	Malayan Law Journal Sdn Bhd, KUALA LUMPUR
New Zealand	Butterworths of New Zealand Ltd, WELLINGTON and AUCKLAND
Singapore	Malayan Law Journal Pte Ltd, SINGAPORE
South Africa	Butterworth Publishers (PTY) Ltd, DURBAN
USA	Michie Butterworth, CHARLOTTESVILLE, Virginia

A CIP Catalogue record for this book is available from the British Library.

ISBN 0 406 894949

Acknowledgments
Cartoon on the cover of the fifteenth edition is by Mel Calman
© S. & C. Calman
  The quotation in **In Memoriam** is taken from T S Eliot's *The Hollow Men*.

Typeset by Kerrypress, Luton, Beds
Printed and bound in Great Britain by Mackays of Chatham plc, Chatham, Kent

In memoriam

Preface to the fifteenth edition

This fifteenth edition is the first that has been published under a Labour government and, in tax as elsewhere, the time is surely ripe for a new start. Hopefully the redraft of the tax legislation will lead the way and will be accompanied by some simplification in the taxes themselves: one thinks in particular of the labyrinthine complexity of the capital gains tax (and all for so little return!) Lest our hopes are raised too high, it is worth recalling the comments of an earlier taxpayer:

> 'Whoever hopes a
> faultless tax to see
> Hopes what ne'er was, is
> not, and ne'er shall be'.[1]

In passing and to prove how ahead of his time Mr Pope was, he also produced a prophetic couplet for the tax avoidance industry:

> 'Oh! What a tangled web we weave,
> When first we practice to deceive!
> But when we've practised quite a while
> How vastly we improve our style'.[2]

The ever-increasing fiscal jungle has, for the professional adviser, been accompanied by ever-tighter regulations and increased duties of care. This dual process came together (as it were) in *Hurlingham Estates Ltd v Wilde & Partners* [1997][3] in which Lightman J castigated a solicitor for his tax illiteracy. In ringing tones he asserted that:

> 'It is to be expected that an intelligent layman, in the sense of a person unfamiliar with the law of taxation ..., would not have imagined that there was any risk of [   ] incurring any such liability since it was agreed that [   ] should occupy a neutral non-profit, non-loss making role in the transaction. On the other hand I would expect any reasonably competent solicitor practising in the field of conveyancing or commercial law to be aware of this concealed trap to the unwary. It is a matter he should have in mind for any transaction involving the grant of a lease and a related payment by the lessee to the lessor.'[4]

In an ideal world he cannot be wrong.

Thanks are due this year to Rajni Boswell of Tolley Publishing for unstinting labours; to Sara Maccallum for revising the section on corporate groups and to Charles Suchett-Kaye for updating the VAT chapters.

The law is stated as at 15 September 1997.

CJW
8 Gray's Inn Square

---

[1] Alexander Pope.
[2] See further, "Taxation", 19 December 1996.
[3] 1997 STC 627.
[4] The concealed trap lay in TA 1988 s 34.

Extracts from the Preface to the first edition

Dr Johnson considered that 'the only end of writing is to enable readers better to enjoy life or better to endure it'. Our hope is at least to achieve this latter result since there is much to be endured and often little to be enjoyed in the subject of taxation. Yet it is also a subject rich in character and absurdities as one would expect of a wholly man-made system. It has a homogeneity all of its own and is a fascinating study of man's ingenuity both in devising a tax and avoiding it. To a few people then, a study of Revenue law may even prove enjoyable.

In writing this book we have tried to explain the principles and practical application of the tax system in simple language and have followed our belief that Revenue law can be made more comprehensible and human by the use of numerous examples. No advantage is gained from a mere recitation or paraphrase of statutory material. However, the course that we have adopted, necessarily in places, involves the expression of opinions on provisions whose obscurity may yet try the intellects of the House of Lords.

. . .

For the inevitable errors and omissions that remain, the responsibility is ours, although in the long tradition of joint authors we will probably argue that where they exist they are in the sections written by the other!

CJW
ES-B
College of Law
Chancery Lane

Contents

Section 5 Business enterprise, stamp duty and VAT

PART B PRACTICE AND PLANNING

PART C APPENDICES

Table of statutes

References in this Table to *Statutes* are to Halsbury's Statutes of England (Fourth Edition) showing the volume and page at which the annotated text of an Act may be found.

Paragraph numbers preceded by a Roman numeral are to paragraphs of the Appendices.

Table of cases

Paragraph numbers preceded by a Roman numeral are to Appendices.

References and abbreviations

All statutory references are given in the text.
The standard abbreviations are as follows:

ACT	Advance corporation tax
A&M	Accumulation and maintenance trust
BES	Business Expansion Scheme
CAA	Capital Allowance Act 1990
CGT	Capital gains tax
EIS	Enterprise Investment Scheme
ESC	Extra statutory concession
FA (year)	Finance Act (year)
FII	Franked investment income
IHT	Inheritance tax
IHTA 1984	Inheritance Tax Act 1984
IRC	Inland Revenue Commissioners
LPA 1925	Law of Property Act 1925
LS Gaz	Law Society Gazette
MIRAS	Mortgage Interest Relief at Source
MCT	Mainstream corporation tax
PAYE	Pay As You Earn
PET	Potentially exempt transfer
PR	Personal representative
PYB	Preceding year basis
SA 1891	Stamp Act 1891
SDRT	Stamp Duty Reserve Tax
SI	Statutory Instrument
SP	Statement of Practice
STI	Simon's Tax Intelligence
SWTI	Simon's Weekly Tax Intelligence
TA 1988	Income and Corporation Taxes Act 1988
TCGA	Taxation of Chargeable Gains Act 1992
TMA 1970	Taxes Management Act 1970
TLATA 1996	Trusts of Land and Appointment of Trustees Act 1996
VAT	Value added tax
VATA 1994	Value Added Tax Act 1994
WDA	Writing down allowance

References to the Manuals produced by the Inland Revenue are to the relevant manual (eg IM is Inspector's Manual; CG is to the Capital Gains Tax Manual) followed by the relevant paragraph number.

Any other abbreviations in the text are defined there.

PART A PRINCIPLES

Section 1 Introduction

Chapters

1 UK taxation—structure and philosophy

'*Singleton J*—Your appeal must be dismissed. I will pass you back your documents. If I might add a word to you, it is that I hope you will not trouble your head further with tax matters, because you seem to have spent a lot of time in going through these various Acts, and if you go on spending your time on Finance Acts, and the like, it will drive you silly.
Mrs Briggenshaw—I will appeal to the higher court.
Singleton J—I cannot stop you, if I would. The advice which I gave you was for your own good, I thought. That is all.'
(*Briggenshaw v Crabb* (1948) 30 TC 331.)

[**1.1**]

I THE UK TAX PICTURE

1 Taxes in general

Taxes imposed in the UK may be classified in various ways. A tripartite division might be adopted into taxes on income, on capital and on expenditure. Alternatively, and arguably more satisfactorily, the classification might be into direct and indirect taxes. This book is concerned with the following direct taxes:

income tax (Chapters 3-13)
capital gains tax (CGT) (Chapters 14-20)
inheritance tax (IHT) (Chapters 21-27)
corporation tax (Chapters 28-30)
stamp duty (Chapter 32)

and there are also two chapters on VAT (an indirect tax: Chapters 33-34).

It omits indirect taxes such as car tax and customs and excise duties, as well as such direct taxes as petroleum revenue tax and the council tax. In principle, the distinction between direct and indirect taxes is that a direct tax is borne by the taxpayer and is not passed on to any other person, whereas an indirect tax is passed on by the payer so that the burden of the tax is ultimately borne by another, eg VAT which although paid by the businessman, is passed on to the customer.

[**1.2**]

2 What is a tax?

The basic features of a tax may be simply stated. *First*, it is a compulsory levy. *Secondly*, it is imposed by government or, in the case of council tax, by a local authority. *Finally*, the money raised should be used either for public purposes or, if the purpose of the tax is not to raise money, it should encourage social justice within the community (CGT, for instance, was specifically intended to have that effect). So to describe the main features of a tax is not, however, to define the concept. Taxes shade off into criminal fines and into levies imposed for other purposes; water rates, for instance, are probably not taxes since they are paid to the water authority and are not used for general public purposes. So far as the distinction between fines and taxes is concerned, the line is often blurred. HLA Hart in *The Concept of Law* (Oxford, 1975) commented that:

> 'Taxes may be imposed not for revenue purposes but to discourage the activities taxed, though the law gives no express indications that these are to be abandoned as it does when it "makes them criminal". Conversely the fines payable for some criminal offence may, because of the depreciation of money, become so small that they are cheerfully paid. They are then perhaps felt to be "mere taxes", and "offences" are frequent, precisely because in these circumstances the sense is lost that the rule is, like the bulk of the criminal law, meant to be taken seriously as a standard of behaviour.'

[1.3]

3   The purpose of taxation

The primary object of taxation is, and always has been, to raise money for government expenditure. The twentieth century has witnessed increasing expenditure on social welfare whilst the use of taxation both as an economic regulator and for the promotion of the public good (or to discourage certain forms of conduct) may also be discerned in the legislation of this century. Thus, alterations to the rate of VAT can affect the level of economic life in the community as much as adjustments to the money supply and credit regulation. The various tax incentives afforded for gifts to charities may be seen as the promotion of public good and altruism; whilst the duties levied on tobacco and alcohol may be seen as bordering on moral control.

Traditionally, the Conservative party has favoured indirect taxation and the provision of incentives to business and to the higher rate taxpayer. The Labour party has inclined towards direct taxation and to increased social welfare. There is little statistical evidence to suggest that taxation is or has been used as an engine to achieve a dramatic shift in the ownership of wealth.   [1.4]

4   Statistics

Who should pay the bill? Apportioning the burden of taxation fairly amongst the community can turn into the more radical contention that tax should operate as a method for effecting a redistribution of wealth or even the confiscation of wealth above a certain level. One striking feature of the statistics of direct taxation is that the vast proportion of the total yield is from income tax: receipts of income tax in 1995–96 amounted to 70.2% of the total sum raised by direct taxes; corporation tax 24.3% and CGT 0.82%. Ten years earlier the comparable figures were 63.6% (income tax); 19.2% (corporation tax); and 1.6% (CGT). The figures for corporation tax are particularly striking: with the substantial cut in the tax rate and the removal of first year capital allowances in 1984, the tax yield from companies increased from £8,341 million in 1984–85 to £21,495 million in each of 1989–90 and 1990–91. From that peak, the yield fell—to £14,887 million in 1993–94—doubtless indicating the depth of the recession although £23,570 million was collected in 1995–96 and £25,700 million is predicted for 1996–97.

IHT (including its now defunct predecessors, estate duty and capital transfer tax) accounts for 1.56% of the total tax raised: as compared to estate duty which in its final year (1974–75) produced 2.38%. In fact receipts have more than trebled in the period from 1974–75 to 1995–96 and a continued rise is likely as surviving spouses die so that estates exempt on death of the first spouse fall into the charge to tax. Receipts from lifetime transfers have fallen from a peak of £33.9 million in 1986–87 to £10.9 million in 1991–92 and £12 million in 1992–93: this coinciding with the cutback in the tax base which has resulted (generally) in only those lifetime transfers made within seven years of the transferor's death being taxed. Stamp duty, a tax with strikingly low collection costs, raised 2% of the total in 1995–96.

The costs of collection, expressed separately in pence per pound for the major taxes for the last five years, are shown in the table below (taken from the Report of the Board of Inland Revenue for the year ending 31 March 1995).

Costs of collection of the major taxes

	1990/91	1991/92	1992/93	1993/94	1994/95	1995/96
Income tax	2.17	2.46	2.42	2.44	2.14	2.05
Corporation tax	0.58	0.82	0.93	1.05	0.77	0.73
Petroleum revenue Tax/APRT	0.33	NA	2.14	0.82	0.40	0.36
Capital gains tax	2.10	3.80	3.91	5.90	3.62	4.10
Inheritance tax/ Capital transfer tax/estate duty	2.24	2.07	2.16	1.90	2.58	2.50
Stamp duties	0.30	0.36	0.50	0.34	0.31	0.35
All taxes	1.70	2.06	2.09	2.14	1.81	1.70

The overall cost of collection fell by 0.11p in 1995/96 to 1.70p per pound.

DLT (now repealed) required collection costs of 6.3p and was a striking illustration of a tax of great complexity but disappointing yield.

The Inland Revenue's contribution to central government tax revenue has fallen as receipts from Customs and Excise have increased: for 1995–96 it contributed 54.6% of the total as against 64.1% in 1974–75 (the equivalent figures for Customs and Excise were 43.12% and 33.5%). In his 1996 Budget Speech, former Chancellor, Kenneth Clarke announced that an extra 2,000 staff would be deployed in the next three years to counter tax evasion and avoidance: additional tax yield was estimated at £2 billion.   **[1.5]–[1.20]**

II FEATURES OF THE SYSTEM

1 Legislation

a) *Interpretation*

Fiscal legislation is complex and detailed. In part this is inevitable since, above all, tax legislation should be certain: persons should know whether they are or are not subject to tax or duty on a particular transaction or sum of money. It has always been held to be a cardinal principle that in a taxation matter the burden lies upon the Crown to show that tax is chargeable in the particular case. In a famous passage, Rowlatt J in *Cape Brandy Syndicate v IRC* (1921) expressed this rule as follows:

> '... It is urged ... that in a taxing Act clear words are necessary in order to tax the subject. Too wide and fanciful a construction is often sought to be given to that maxim, which does not mean that words are to be unduly restricted against the Crown, or that there is to be any discrimination against the Crown in those Acts. It simply means that in a taxing Act one has to look merely at what is

clearly said. There is no room for any intendment. There is no equity about a
tax. There is no presumption as to a tax. Nothing is to be read in, nothing is
to be implied. One can only look fairly at the language used . . .'

The question of making allowance for the intendment of Parliament is not
clear cut: in *Re Sutherland & Partners' Appeal* (1994), for instance, Nicholls VC
refused to accept one interpretation of the legislation on the grounds that
'Parliament cannot have intended [it]' whilst the same judge in *Elf Enterprise
Caledonia Ltd v IRC* (1994) concluded that 'the taxpayers' construction of the
language leads to a result Parliament could not have intended'.

Where the meaning of the statute is clearly expressed, the court will not
consider any contrary intention or belief of Parliament or, indeed, any contrary
indication by the Revenue. Illustrations of provisions apparently used against
the expressed wishes of their authors include *Page v Lowther* (1983) in which
an anti-avoidance section (now TA 1988 s 776) was used as a charging provision
(see [**8.108**]) and *Leedale v Lewis* (1982) where a provision that was intended
to give relief was held not to do so.   [**1.21**]

b) *Legislative simplification*

FA 1995 s 160 required the Inland Revenue to prepare a report on tax
simplification. That report—*The Path to Tax Simplification*—was published in
December 1995 along with a background paper including examples of rewritten
tax legislation (particularly worthy of study is the redrafted Rent-a-Room
legislation). Over the same period work was undertaken in the private sector
by, *inter alia*, the Tax Law Review Committee of the IFS who produced an
interim report in November 1995. Examples of rewritten legislation were
published in October 1996 and the first tranche will be ready for enactment
in the 1997–98 parliamentary session (for the composition of the steering
committee charged with overseeing the project, see STI (1996) p 2098). [**1.22**]

c) *Use of Hansard*

The principles of statutory interpretation have, to some extent, been eroded
by the House of Lords decision in *Pepper v Hart* (1993). Speaking for the majority
(the Lord Chancellor, Lord Mackay, dissented), Lord Browne-Wilkinson
accepted that the courts could look at Hansard for guidance on the interpretation
of a statute in limited situations:

> 'I therefore reach the conclusion, subject to any question of parliamentary privilege,
> that the exclusionary rule should be relaxed so as to permit reference to parliamentary
> materials where:
> (a) legislation is ambiguous or obscure, or leads to an absurdity;
> (b) the material relied on consists of one or more statements by a minister or
>   other promoter of the bill together, if necessary, with such other parliamentary
>   material as is necessary to understand such statements and their effect;
> (c) the statements relied on are clear.'

In the *Elf Enterprise* case referred to above, the court held that Inland Revenue
Press Releases could *not* be used as an aid to statutory interpretation whilst
in *IRC v Willoughby* (1995) the Parliamentary Debates of 1936 (when the
forerunner of what is now TA 1988 s 739 was introduced) were considered
to be of no value given that:

> 'Whatever might have been the intention of Ministers in 1936, the Court had
> decided in 1948 and again in 1969 that the words used by Parliament manifest
> a different intention. Yet in 1952 and again in 1970 the same formula is used
> and notwithstanding the changes made in 1969. In these circumstances it must
> be assumed that the original intention, whatever it was, was superseded by an
> acceptance of the decisions of the Courts' (*Morritt LJ*).

Much of the complexity of recent tax legislation has been prompted by the growth of the tax avoidance industry. Whilst tax evasion is unlawful, the avoidance of tax is both lawful, and, on a relatively minor scale, widely practised. The growth of larger scale schemes, often devoid of all commercial reality, has inevitably prompted anti-avoidance legislation. **[1.23]**

2 Role of the courts—the 'new approach'

Avoidance schemes have also affected judicial interpretation of the tax statutes with certain judges being prepared to look beyond the words to the underlying purpose and beyond the form of the transaction to its substance. The 1970s saw the development of a flourishing tax avoidance industry with many of the schemes marketed being wholly divorced from reality but obtaining a tax advantage because of the precise wording of the relevant legislation. Seeking to take away this advantage in the old way, for instance by relying upon the canons of statutory construction and the use of limited anti-avoidance legislation, was felt by some to be inadequate and there were those who felt that the Revenue should have new weapons at its disposal. Hence the development of 'the new approach' to tax avoidance schemes in the House of Lords and, in particular, in the speeches of the Law Lords in *Furniss v Dawson* (1984). Apart from illustrating that in certain circumstances it is the substance of the transaction which determines whether or not tax is chargeable, the case also showed an acceptance by the House of Lords that the courts can and should bolster up taxing statutes with judge-made law. Lord Scarman stated that:

'I am aware, and the legal profession (and others) must understand, that the law in this area is in an early stage of development. Speeches in your Lordships' House and judgments in the appellate courts are concerned more to chart a way forward between principles accepted and not to be rejected, than to attempt anything so ambitious as to determine finally the limit beyond which the safe channel of acceptable tax avoidance shelves into the dangerous shallows of unacceptable tax evasion. The law will develop from case to case. Lord Wilberforce in *Ramsay's* case referred to "the emerging principle" of the law. What has been established is that the determination of what does, and what does not constitute unacceptable tax evasion is a subject suited to development by judicial process. Difficult though the task may be for judges, it is one which is beyond the power of the blunt instrument of legislation.'

His approach marked a radical departure from established tradition and contrasted strikingly with the views of Rowlatt J quoted above.

After 1984 there was something of a reaction against this 'new approach'. Quite apart from doubts over the constitutional legality of judge-made fiscal legislation, many objected to the uncertainty generated by cases such as *Furniss v Dawson*. A discernible swing back towards more traditional views could be observed in later cases and notably in the speeches of the House of Lords in *Craven v White* (1988) and *Fitzwilliam v IRC* (1993). In the former Lord Oliver, for instance, first played down the symbolic aspects of the *Dawson* case as follows:

'It has been urged, in the course of the argument, that in *Dawson* this House crossed the Rubicon and that your Lordships should not be astute to confine the bridgehead thus created. That event, of course, constituted a declaration of war upon the Republic of Italy and I confess that I do not find the analogy drawn from so partisan an exercise an altogether happy one. I do not, however, quarrel with the general proposition, but before embarking even upon a reconnaissance into Republican territory it is at least desirable to test what the bridge will support by an analysis of the means by which the crossing was effected.'

and then concluded that:

'It has been said in the course of argument on the present appeals that *Dawson* is "judge made law". So it is, but judges are not legislators and if the result of a judicial decision is to contradict the express statutory consequences which have been declared by Parliament to attach to a particular transaction which has been found as a fact to have taken place, that can be justified only because, as a matter of construction of the statute, the court has ascertained that that which has taken place is not, within the meaning of the statute, the transaction to which those consequences attach.'

Taking the *Dawson* case back into the realm of statutory interpretation undoubtedly flew in the face of what was said in the case itself but could be seen as an attempt to reassert traditional values.

Recently the wheel has turned again, however, with a fresh House of Lords in *IRC v McGuckian* (1997) applying the doctrine and using language redolent of the heady days of 1984. Lord Cooke, for instance, said:

'I suspect that advisers of those bent on tax avoidance, which in the end tends to involve an attempt to cast on other taxpayers more than their fair share of sustaining the national tax base, do not always pay sufficient heed to the theme in the speeches in the *Furniss* case, especially those of Lord Scarman, Lord Roskill and Lord Bridge of Harwich, to the effect that the journey's end may not yet have been found.'

(see further Chapter 36).   [1.24]

3 Practice

Given the volume of legislation, it is not surprising that some provisions may impose hardship and cause unforeseen results in individual cases. As a result the Revenue operates a system of extra-statutory concessions (ESC) and publish Statements of Practice (SP).

An ESC is a relaxation which gives taxpayers a reduction in tax liability to which they would not be entitled under the strict letter of the law: by contrast an SP explains the Revenue's interpretation of legislation and the way in which it is applied in practice (of course the taxpayer may disagree and is free to argue for a different interpretation before the courts!)

The current ESCs are set out in the booklet IRI and comprise over 200 concessions, the effect of which is that tax is not charged despite the case falling within the provisions of a taxing statute. Take for instance the ESC that permits miners to enjoy free coal or, alternatively, an allowance in lieu (ESC A6). The coal or cash allowance would undoubtedly be charged as emoluments under the rules of Schedule E were it not for the concession. More recently, the Revenue has stated that if an employee is occasionally required to work late, and either public transport has ceased or it would not be reasonable to expect the employee to use it, he will not be subject to income tax on the benefit that he receives if his employer sends him home by private transport, eg by taxi (see ESC A66). It needs to be remembered that the published concessions are prefaced by a warning that 'a concession will not be given in any case where an attempt is made to use it for tax avoidance'. Thus in *R v IRC, ex p Fulford Dobson* (1987) an attempt to take advantage of a CGT concession, which, in certain cases, excluded from charge gains realised by a non-resident from the date of his departure from the UK, failed since the relevant asset had been transferred to the non-resident by his spouse with the sole object of benefiting from that concession.

The fairness of concessions is open to question as is their constitutional legality. In a pungent judgment Walton J expressed the objection to ESCs as follows:

'I, in company with many other judges before me, am totally unable to understand upon what basis the Inland Revenue Commissioners are entitled to make extra-statutory concessions. To take a very simple example (since example is clearly called for), upon what basis have the commissioners taken it upon themselves to provide that income tax is not to be charged upon a miner's free coal and allowances in lieu thereof? That this should be the law is doubtless quite correct: I am not arguing the merits, or even suggesting that some other result, as a matter of equity, should be reached. But this, surely, ought to be a matter for Parliament, and not the commissioners. If this kind of concession can be made, where does it stop: and why are some groups favoured against others? . . .

. . . This is not a simple matter of tax law. What is happening is that, in effect, despite the words of Maitland, commenting on the Bill of Rights, "This is the last of the dispensing power", the Crown is now claiming just such a power . . .' (*Vestey v IRC (No 2)* (1979).)

By contrast, in the *Fulford Dobson* case mentioned above, the judge (McNeill J) accepted the existence and indeed the necessity for extra-statutory concessions, concluding that they fell 'within the concept of good management or of administrative common sense' and that they could fairly be said to be made 'within the proper exercise of managerial discretion'.

SPs set out the view that the Revenue takes of a particular provision and should be treated with caution since they may not accurately state the law (see, for instance, *Campbell Connelly & Co Ltd v Barnett* (1992)). Thus, the CGT consequences that ensue when trustees exercise a dispositive power have been set out in a series of Revenue Statements. The first (SP 7/78) was withdrawn as a result of *Roome v Edwards* (1981); its successor (SP 9/81) suffered a similar fate after *Bond v Pickford* (1983); and current Revenue thinking is found in SP 7/84 (issued in October 1984).

There is an argument against inviting the Revenue to express views upon the meaning to be given to particular provisions since in cases where the Revenue indicates that tax is chargeable, it places professional advisers in a difficult position. Do they advise their clients that the Revenue is wrong and that the House of Lords are bound to accept the taxpayer's arguments or do they advise prudence in the face of the risk of protracted and expensive litigation?   **[1.25]–[1.40]**

III CONCLUSIONS

Tax is often seen as an ephemeral area: as a part of law devoid of principle and subject to the whims of politicians. In part this view is true; the annual (sometimes biannual) Finance Act often effects considerable changes. The underlying principles do, however, remain and it is usually only the surface landscape that is altered. The bedrock of income tax, for instance, can be traced back to 1803, whilst although the tax on gifts (now IHT, formerly CTT) is of more recent origin, it is based upon a relatively simple conceptual structure. In understanding tax law the golden rule must be to ignore the form in favour of the substance. Given that the whole edifice is man-made and is designed to achieve practical ends, it should also follow that it is fully comprehensible. There is nothing here of the divine and, in the last resort, one should follow the approach of Lord Reid in the House of Lords in *Fleming v Associated Newspapers Ltd* (1972):

'On reading it [now TA 1988 s 577(10)] my first impression was that it is obscure to the point of unintelligibility and that impression has been confirmed by the able and prolonged arguments which were submitted to us . . . I have suggested what may be a possible meaning, but if I am wrong about that I would not shrink from holding that the subsection is so obscure that no meaning can be given to it. I would rather do that than seek by twisting and contorting the words to give to the subsection an improbable meaning. Draftsmen as well as Homer can nod, and Parliament is so accustomed to obscure drafting in Finance Bills that no one may have noticed the defects in this subsection.'

[1.41]

2 Administrative machinery

I GENERAL STRUCTURE

The government departments responsible for administering UK taxes are the Inland Revenue and Customs and Excise. VAT is under the management of the Commissioners of Customs and Excise and is considered in Chapter 33. Other taxes considered in this book, namely income tax, corporation tax, CGT, IHT and stamp duty, are under the 'care and control' of the Inland Revenue, which is headed by a small number of higher civil servants known as the Commissioners of Inland Revenue ('the Board'). The Board answers to the Treasury and, therefore, to the Chancellor of the Exchequer.

Below the Board, the structure of the Inland Revenue is complex (see 137th Report of the Board of Inland Revenue at p 13) and at present is subject to change, partly due to the introduction of self-assessment. It was the case that the country was divided into tax districts headed in each case by an inspector of taxes who first assessed the taxpayer's tax liability; the tax that was due was then collected by a collector of taxes. Inspection and collection are now being brought together as Taxpayer Service Offices. This will be most taxpayers' main point of contact. However, for each district there will also be a Taxpayer District Office dealing with local companies and local collection and enforcement. Both the inspectors and collectors of taxes are full-time civil servants appointed by the Revenue.

In practice, the different taxes are not all administered together. Income tax, corporation tax and CGT are administered from the Revenue's head office in the Strand (although delegated to districts) under TMA 1970. IHT is administered on a daily basis by the Capital Taxes Office in Nottingham, Edinburgh and Belfast (IHTA 1984). Stamp duty, which requires little administration, is under the supervision of the Controller of Stamps (Stamp Duties Management Act 1891).

This chapter considers the administration of income tax, corporation tax and CGT; the procedures for IHT (which are similar) and for stamp duty are dealt with in the appropriate chapters on those taxes.   [2.1]–[2.20]

II ASSESSMENT AND COLLECTION OF TAX

1 Background to reform

The accountability of the Inland Revenue to the tax-paying public at large (if it is to have any real meaning) must rest upon the premises that the system of taxation which it administers can clearly be understood and that the way in which it is administered is simple and fair. In part satisfaction, at least of the first of those premises, major changes have been made over the last decade or so, one example being the removal of covenants from the tax system.

As far as the second premise is concerned, the 1980s and 1990s have seen (and continue to see) efforts being made towards the reform of the machinery of administration. The greatest effort was revealed by the Chancellor of the Exchequer in his March 1993 Budget Speech when, in response to two Consultative Documents, he outlined his proposals for introducing measures for reforming the system for assessing personal tax. The essence of the reform is that those taxpayers who used to be required to make an annual tax return (for example, and in the main, those self-employed persons assessable to tax under Cases I and II of Schedule D) are now allowed to work out their own tax bill. Assessment on a 'preceding year' basis for the self-employed is being abolished, so that all taxpayers will pay tax on income on a current year basis. This allows for the final change: taxpayers receive one tax statement dealing with all their income from whatever source and one tax bill. These changes, described by the Inland Revenue as 'paving the way for the most fundamental reform of personal tax administration in almost 50 years', apply from the tax year 1996–97 onwards. Self-assessment will reduce the costs of tax administration in the public sector; it should, however, be noted that the costs to the private sector, reflected either in the taxpayer's own time or the amount expended in employing a professional adviser, are bound to increase. Certainly those taxpayers liable for VAT and responsible for their own VAT bills would concur with that statement.

Self-assessment is optional and for personal taxpayers first applies to tax returns for the year 1996–97 whereas the new Schedule D rules marking a switch to the current year basis of assessment (see Appendix I) come into effect in either the following year, 1997–98, for existing sources (with 1996–97 being a transitional year) or, for new sources, from the tax year 1994–95.   **[2.21]**

2   **Returns**

In order that the Revenue may make assessments to tax, it must necessarily be in receipt of the relevant information. Such information is gathered in two ways: first from the taxpayer himself by requiring him to furnish details of his income and gains; and, secondly, from other sources such as banks, public authorities etc.

Taxpayers who do not receive a tax return but have taxable income must notify the Revenue unless they fall within the exceptions in TMA 1970 s 7(3)–(7). The time limit for so doing is six months from the end of the relevant tax year, so that a return can be issued and completed within the normal time limits.

A taxpayer in receipt of a return has the option to 'self-assess'. If a taxpayer choses to self-assess he has until 31 January following the end of the tax year to submit his return (or three months from the date of the issue of the return if it is issued after 31 October); if a taxpayer does not wish to self-assess he must submit his return to the Revenue by 30 September after the year of assessment (or two months from the date of issue of the return, if that is after 31 July) (TMA 1970 ss 8 and 9). The basic tax return will be the same in both cases: the only real difference in the systems is that those opting for self-assessment must add up the figures! Self-assessment already applies in some circumstances and for an example of a self-assessed return, see IHT Form 200 in Appendix II.

Under the old system the return was merely the means by which the taxpayer provided the Revenue with information: the Revenue calculated the tax due and issued an assessment and the tax then became payable. Under the new system the return still operates as a source of information but it *also* fulfils the function that used to be fulfilled by the assessment, ie it creates a debt payable by the taxpayer. The due date for payment of (the balance of—see 6 below) the tax due is the filing date for the self-assessed return: the liability to pay tax arises on submission of the return without the Revenue having to take any further action. This principle applies also where there has been an election *not* to self-assess: the Revenue's calculation of the tax due is treated as if it were a self-assessment for this purpose and the liability to pay is created by their issuing a notice of the tax payable.

All relevant figures will be needed for the self-assessment form to be completed: accordingly business accounts made up to (say) 30 March must be ready before the following 31 January. For partnerships, each partner will need to include his share of the adjusted partnership profit. Trustees are subject to the same rules as individuals.

Some documentary evidence will have to be submitted with the return (s 8) and there is a new duty to preserve the records which were needed to complete the return properly (s 12B). Generally, this duty can be fulfilled by retaining copy documents but FA 1996 s 124 required that certain original documents be retained (eg evidence of tax paid outside the UK). The plan to impose an absolute obligation to retain original vouchers showing tax deducted from dividend payments was abandoned—presumably because it was realised how many untidy individual taxpayers would technically become liable for the (up to) £3,000 fine for failing to do so! The introduction of a penalty for failing to keep proper records may prove very onerous but there are hints that, at least in the early years, it will not automatically be imposed (see *Taxation*, 20 February 1997, p 594) and that, in any event, the maximum £3,000 will only be charged 'in the most serious cases' (see Inland Revenue Booklet *Self-assessment — A General Guide to Keeping Records*).

TMA 1970 s 115A permits the electronic lodgement of returns from the introduction of self-assessment: this came into force on 1 March 1997 for returns by individuals, trustees and partnerships (SI 1997/57).

There are a series of penalties to ensure compliance with the above duties. Section 7 imposes a penalty if liability to pay tax is not notified in time, although since this is based on the tax payable on 31 January in the year following that in which the tax liability arose (see 6 below), it can in fact be avoided by paying the tax due on that date. Section 93 imposes an automatic fixed penalty of £100 if a return is not filed on time, with a further £100 fine if it still has not been filed six months later (the fine will be reduced if the balancing payment due is less than the penalty). The second fixed fine can, however, be overtaken by the Revenue successfully applying to the commissioners for leave to impose a daily penalty of up to £60. An application might be made if the Revenue considers a substantial amount of tax is probably payable—the fixed penalty might not then give sufficient encouragement to file the return! If a return is not filed within 12 months of the filing date, a penalty related to the amount of tax due can be imposed.

The Revenue has another weapon in its armoury if a return is not filed: it can estimate the tax due (s 28C). To replace the estimated figure with an accurate one, the taxpayer merely has to file the return; he does not have to lodge a formal appeal as under the old system. [2.22]

3 Discovery assessments and agreements with taxpayer

Whilst the Revenue will not generally be issuing assessments under the self-assessment regime, they do retain the power to make 'discovery assessments' under a revised s 29. The principle is that the Revenue should be able to make assessments to prevent loss of tax, although the right to do this is limited if the taxpayer has already self-assessed and there has not been negligence or fraud (the Revenue considers that these limitations reflect the decision in *Scorer v Olin Energy*—see below—and has issued a paper on the new discovery and disclosure rules (see Press Release of 31 May 1996)). In the absence of case law on the new s 29, it is perhaps worth noting some cases on the old version.

An assessment can only be made if there is a 'discovery'. Under the old version, it was held that this 'discovery' need not be of new facts; it can be simply a discovery that the wrong conclusion was drawn from the same facts (*Cenlon Finance Co Ltd v Ellwood* (1962)) or that an arithmetical error had been made (*Vickerman v Mason's Personal Representatives* (1984)).

If a taxpayer appeals against an assessment or other decision of the Revenue, he may come to an agreement with the inspector that the original assessment or decision was after all correct or that it be varied. Such agreement has the same effect as if the commissioners had so determined the appeal (TMA 1970 s 54 and see *Tod v South Essex Motors (Basildon) Ltd* (1988)). The precise relationship between this provision and the power to raise an extra assessment to give effect to a 'discovery' was considered by the House of Lords in *Scorer v Olin Energy Systems Ltd* (1985) (and see SP 8/91). The case involved the making of an additional assessment, after a s 54 agreement had been reached, because loss relief had been given erroneously to the taxpayer. In rejecting the extra assessment, the court held that, as the accounts submitted on behalf of the taxpayer set out all the facts relevant to the claim for loss relief, the Revenue was bound by the agreement entered into:

> 'The situation must be viewed objectively, from the point of view of whether the inspector's agreement to the relevant computation, having regard to the surrounding circumstances including all the material known to be in his possession, was such as to lead a reasonable man to the conclusion that he had decided to admit the claim which had been made.' (Lord Keith)

It should be stressed that, apart from s 54, the Revenue are not legally bound by an agreement (eg compromise) made with the taxpayer and nor can estoppel be raised against the Revenue in such cases (for an illustration, see *R v IRC, ex p Preston* (1985), where full disclosure of all relevant facts was not made). Accordingly, a taxpayer who is concerned to ensure that his case will not be reopened should appeal against the contentious assessment or decision and provided he produces all the material facts to the Revenue, any subsequent agreement under s 54 will be binding. The ordinary law of contract applies to s 54 agreements which are therefore capable of rectification (*R v Inspector of Taxes, ex p Bass Holdings Ltd* (1993)) and may be vitiated by mutual mistake (*Fox v Rothwell* (1995)). **[2.23]**

4 Revenue enquiries

Obvious errors in self-assessed returns can be corrected by the Revenue and the taxpayer can also correct his return within 12 months of the filing date (TMA 1970 s 9). This section cannot be relied upon to amend a return once the Revenue have given notice that they intend to enquire into it.

Under the new system there is a formal statutory procedure allowing the Revenue to enquire into the accuracy of a return (ss 9A and 19A). The power extends to any return, so some enquiries will be made on a random basis, whereas others will arise because of specific queries on a particular return.

The Revenue have been given extensive audit powers: notice of any such enquiry must be served on the taxpayer within 12 months after the filing date or up to 15 months after the return was actually filed. An 'audit' for these purposes can range from the raising of one or two queries to a full-scale investigation.

The Revenue can obtain information about a person's income from sources other than the taxpayer, eg from an employer the names of employees and details of payments to them (TMA 1970 s 15); from traders (and certain others) details of payments made for services to persons other than their employees, eg commissions and 'backhanders' (TMA 1970 s 16); from banks, names of customers to whom they have paid interest in the tax year on a deposit account (TMA 1970 s 17); from persons paying interest gross (eg the Director of National Savings) the names of recipients of the interest and the amounts paid (TMA 1970 s 18); from government departments and other public authorities details of payments for services and the payment of grants and subsidies; finally, from lessees and other occupiers of land details of rent and other payments made for the use of the land (TMA 1970 s 19).

A new power to request information and documents from the taxpayer has been given by s 19A. In addition, the Revenue have wide powers to obtain information about a person whose affairs are under enquiry. For instance, under TMA 1970 s 20, that person, or a third party, can be required to produce relevant documents (or written answers to questions, in the case of the taxpayer). Before the tax inspector can make a formal order requiring either the taxpayer or third party to provide the appropriate documents, he must first make an informal request for that information and, secondly, obtain the consent of a General or Special Commissioner for a formal order to be given. The exercise of the power is thus limited by the requirement for independent supervision (for a discussion of the role of the inspector and his duty to lay all relevant information before the Commissioner, see *R v IRC, ex p T C Coombs & Co* (1991)).

A 'tax accountant' (see TMA 1970 s 20A) who has been convicted of a tax offence or who has been subject to a penalty for making or assisting in making an incorrect tax return, can be required with the consent of a circuit judge or, in certain circumstances, the Board's authority, to produce any documents in his possession or under his authority regarding the tax affairs of any client past or present. The issue of whether this provision should be widened, as the Revenue would like to do, is currently subject to an independent inquiry.

The power to demand information from third parties is limited in situations where the information is 'privileged'. Legal professional privilege may, for instance, be available for documents in the possession of a barrister, advocate or solicitor (TMA s 20B(8)) but copies of documents made for the purpose of obtaining legal advice will only be privileged if the original document would be privileged. The claim of privilege is not available in relation to notices issued to a legal adviser *in his capacity as taxpayer*, see *R v IRC, ex p Taylor (No 2)* (1990) and although accountants are protected from disclosing audit papers and tax advice, the Revenue remain entitled to the facts essential to an understanding of the taxpayer's return and accounts (see SP 5/90). Personal records which are excluded from police search powers and journalistic material are likewise protected.

In cases where there are reasonable grounds for suspecting that an offence involving 'serious fraud' has been, is being, or is about to be committed, a tax inspector may request a circuit judge for a warrant to enter private premises (if necessary by force) to search for and remove documents which he reasonably believes to be evidence of such fraud (other than privileged documents (TMA 1970 s 20C and *R v Inland Revenue Board, ex p Goldberg* (1989)). This power is extremely wide. No particular offence need be specified in the warrant other than 'serious fraud' (for an illustration of this power see *IRC v Rossminster Ltd* (1980)). Further, the occupier of the premises has no right to be informed of the precise grounds on which the warrant was issued although he is entitled to a list of the items removed and must be allowed reasonable access to them whilst they are in the possession of the Revenue.

Given the width of the power in s 20 it has been recognised that it must be closely controlled. In a very unusual case (where the court felt it necessary to state formally its objections to the Revenue's behaviour following an interim injunction to stop a search, even though there were not to be contempt proceedings), the High Court suggested legal advice should be available when difficult circumstances arise (*R v IRC, ex p Kingston Smith* (1996)). In *R v O'Kane and Clarke, ex p Northern Bank Ltd* (1996), the court quashed notices given by the Revenue to a bank in relation to its customers, on the basis that the notices were too widely drafted (amounting in effect to 'fishing expeditions' and requiring information as well as documents) and too onerous to comply with but see *R v IRC ex p Ulster Bank Ltd* (1997).

Section 28A sets out the formal procedure for terminating an enquiry and amending the return but this can also be done informally, as under the old system. If no audit notice is served the tax return is final subject only to the Revenue's powers of discovery (see TMA 1970 s 9A and [2.23]).   **[2.24]**

5 **Penalties**

Tax offences may attract monetary penalties. Such a penalty is, of course, in addition to the tax itself and any interest thereon. Penalties for failure to notify liability or file a return on time are discussed at [**2.22**]. There are also penalties for submitting incorrect information.

The penalty for submitting an incorrect return, declaration, statement or account for income tax or CGT is 100% of the tax (ie the difference between the amount of tax payable and the lesser amount which would have been payable on the return or accounts as submitted) (note, however, the power given by s 9 to correct errors or mistakes in the return). The maximum penalty for fraudulently or negligently supplying incorrect information or documents in response to a requirement under specified statutory provisions is now £3,000 and a similar penalty may be imposed on a person who assists in or induces the preparation or delivery of an incorrect return or accounts.

The time limit for commencing penalty proceedings is generally six years from the date when the offence was committed except for penalties linked to the amount of tax lost (eg those levied for incorrect returns) where proceedings can be commenced at any time within three years of the final determination of the amount of tax in question. A person who has assisted in the preparation of an incorrect return may be subject to penalty proceedings at any time in the following 20 years (see generally TMA 1970 s 103).

The bankruptcy of the taxpayer does not preclude the Revenue from claiming maximum penalties (see *Re Hurren, ex p Trustee v IRC* (1982)).

In a change of previous practice the Revenue will seek monetary penalties for any offence which the taxpayer may have committed but which has not been brought before the criminal courts, and it may now seek penalties where the taxpayer has been negligent even though acquitted of any criminal intent. The Board will not, however, take steps to recover civil monetary penalties on the basis of fraud in respect of an offence which has been brought before the criminal courts (SP 2/88).

EXAMPLE 2.1

Tax was underpaid because of the taxpayer's fraud in 1976–77. If the assessment only becomes final in May 1992, the Revenue have until May 1995 to raise penalties, even though the offence was committed more than six years from the date of the assessment.

As the Revenue still have power to make 'discovery assessments' under s 29(3) (see [**2.23**]), they have the consequent right to impose penalties (known as 'surcharges') if tax is found to be due. Penalties (surcharges) can also be imposed under s 59C if the result of an enquiry is that additional tax is due. [**2.25**]

6 Payment of tax

In most cases tax will be paid in three equal instalments: two being estimated on the basis of the previous year's tax (the payment dates being 31 January in the year of assessment and 31 July following) with a final balancing payment (or refund) on 31 January following the end of the tax year.

EXAMPLE 2.2

In 1998–99 Tim opts for self-assessment. His tax for that year will be paid as follows:
(1) half estimated tax—based on his tax liability for 1997–98—due on 31 January 1999;
(2) remaining half due on 31 July 1999;
(3) submission of tax return showing 1998–99 income due 31 January 2000. With this return should be enclosed the payment of the balance (if any) of income tax due for 1998–99 (together with any CGT liability: note that this is not paid in instalments on the basis of estimates) and also together with the first instalments of tax for the year 1999–2000 calculated on the basis of that return.

So far as interim payments of tax based on the previous year's income are concerned, if the taxpayer believes that his current year's income is lower he can reduce the payments provided that he makes a claim specifying the reason for that reduction (s 59A). Although the Revenue cannot oppose this, it can, however, impose a penalty if the claim to reduce the instalment was made fraudulently or negligently.

If the taxpayer's return shows tax as due and it is not actually paid in accordance with s 59B, then s 59C imposes a penalty (known as a 'surcharge').
[**2.26**]

7 Postponement of tax pending appeal

Where a taxpayer disagrees with an amendment to his self-assessment (under s 28A) or other assessment, he must inform the inspector within 30 days of his intention to appeal and the amount of tax he considers excessive. If he fails to do so the whole amount becomes payable as if there were no appeal (TMA 1970 s 55). This provision prevents a taxpayer from postponing his payment of tax by instituting an appeal which he then abandons before the hearing. If the taxpayer and inspector are unable to agree on the amount of tax which is at issue on the appeal, the commissioners decide the matter (TMA 1970 s 55(5)). Only the amount of tax which depends on the outcome of the appeal is postponed until the appeal is heard. In the meantime the collector of taxes is not entitled to seek payment of the amount postponed under s 55(5) but only of the balance (which is payable within 30 days of the agreement or the commissioners' decision under s 55(5)—see *Parikh v Back* (1985)).

On a further appeal to the High Court, the amount of tax as determined by the commissioners remains payable. If the court's decision results in an increased tax liability, this additional tax becomes due in accordance with a revised notice of assessment issued after the hearing. [**2.27**]

8   Interest on tax due and refunded tax

Interest will be automatically charged under s 86 where the tax due is paid late. Interest can be charged on interim payments as well as on the final balancing payment. Interest is also payable on penalties and surcharges which are not paid by the due date (ss 59C(6), 69 and 70).

In cases where there has been an appeal against the assessment and all or part of the tax has been postponed under s 55, the due and reckonable date for interest purposes is usually six months from the date when the tax *was* due, thereby ensuring that the taxpayer obtains no advantage (in terms of total interest payable) from making an appeal against an assessment.

The taxpayer should be further dissuaded from a frivolous appeal by s 86(3) which provides that where the result of an appeal is that additional tax becomes due, interest shall be charged on that sum as if it were postponed tax contained in the original notice of assessment (ie the reckonable date is six months from the date when the original tax was due).

Where tax has been overpaid or penalties or surcharges unnecessarily paid, the refund will carry interest from the date the tax was paid (see TA 1988 ss 824 and 826 and TCGA 1992 s 283, as amended by FA 1997). Repayments will generally be made automatically provided that the tax overpaid exceeds a *de minimis* figure (see SP 6/95). This repayment supplement is not itself taxable! A claim for repayment must generally be made within six years from the end of the tax year in question: exceptionally this period will be extended (ESC B41 and see *Tax Bulletin*, 1995, p 246 and 1996, p 291, for the Revenue's requirements as to the documents to be produced when a repayment claim is made).   **[2.28]**

9   Collection of tax

Once the amount of tax due has been finalised the collectors of taxes have wide powers to collect the tax (but see *Re Selectmove Ltd* (1995) on restrictions on the collectors' power to agree to a proposal to pay arrears of tax in instalments). If the taxpayer fails to pay the collector can levy distress (TMA 1970 ss 61, 62) or, if the taxpayer is an employee, arrange for the tax to be deducted at source under PAYE. Alternatively, the tax charged can be recovered in the magistrates' court, the county court or the High Court, depending on the sum involved (TMA 1970 ss 65–67).

The insolvency of the taxpayer is no bar to the Revenue pursuing the debt, although under the Insolvency Act 1986 the former preference given to the Revenue was abolished, so that they rank as unsecured creditors, except where their claim is for 'quasi-trustee debts' (ie for arrears of PAYE and VAT where the taxpayer acts as collector for the Revenue). In the case of such quasi-trustee debts the preference is limited, in the case of PAYE, to sums owed in the 12 months, and, for VAT, in the six months, prior to the insolvency.

The Revenue have made public (*Tax Bulletin*, 1995, p 245) their (apparently long-established) practice of not pursuing their 'legal right to recovery for the full amount where it would be unconscionable to insist on collecting the full amount of tax assessed and legally due'—a practice known as 'equitable liability'. This practice will be operated if the taxpayer can demonstrate clearly that the liability assessed is greater than it would have been if the documents had been submitted at the right time and acceptable evidence of the correct liability is produced. Operation of the practice will depend on the particular circumstances and it would be very unusual for any taxpayer to benefit from the practice more than once. Taxpayers should not, therefore, *rely* on it applying to them (see further ESC A19).   **[2.29]**

10 **Back duty**

A back duty case arises when the Revenue discovers that a taxpayer has evaded tax, usually by not disclosing his true income, by supplying inaccurate or incomplete information, or by claiming reliefs and allowances to which he is not entitled. The Revenue often discovers this from 'tip-offs' that it receives about the taxpayer, or by a 'confession' from the taxpayer himself. On discovering a back duty case the Revenue can commence criminal proceedings, and/or make assessments for the lost tax plus interest and/or claim penalties. What the Revenue chooses to do in any case depends largely on the degree of co-operation of the taxpayer. Criminal proceedings are rarely taken (the odds are roughly one in fifteen hundred); and the Revenue prefers to reach some settlement with the taxpayer. Its wide discretion in this area is aided by TMA 1970 s 105 which enables the Revenue to tell the taxpayer that it may accept a pecuniary settlement and that it is influenced by a full confession. Despite these inducements, statements made by the taxpayer are admissible in evidence, and any settlement creates a contractual debt for which the Revenue can sue (see *IRC v Nuttall* (1990)).

Small back duty cases are dealt with by local inspectors who have the power to agree settlements. In larger cases the approval of the head office is required before any settlement can be reached. When arriving at a settlement, the factors that the Revenue considers include the amount of tax lost, interest payable,

'*I didn't think you people could reopen a case after a five-year period.*'

penalties available, the co-operation of the taxpayer and, most importantly, the need for uniformity in cases of a similar nature.   [**2.30**]

a) *Criminal proceedings*

Prosecutions can be brought against the taxpayer under the Perjury Act 1911; for forgery; for conspiracy to defraud; or under the Theft Act 1978 for evasion of a liability by deception or false accounting. Company officers can be made liable for such offences if committed by the company. *R v Charlton* (1996) involved the prosecution of a professional adviser for 'cheating the public revenue' and has caused much concern among the professions.

Generally, it appears that criminal prosecutions are on the increase (see *Taxation*, 20 February 1997, p 569) but the Revenue will often not prosecute in cases of fraud provided full disclosure is made and full facilities afforded for investigation into the taxpayer's affairs (known as the '*Hansard*' treatment because this practice of the Board was explained in an answer to a parliamentary question). [2.31]

b) *Assessments for lost tax plus interest*

The normal time limit for making an assessment to tax is, in the case of income and capital gains tax, five years after 31 January following the relevant tax year and in the case of corporation tax, six years after the end of the relevant accounting period (TMA 1970 s 34(1)). There is an extended time limit for assessments to recover tax lost through fraudulent or negligent conduct (TMA 1970 s 36). For income tax and capital gains tax the limit is 20 years after 31 January following the relevant tax year and for corporation tax the limit is 21 years after the relevant accounting period. In cases where the defaulting taxpayer had carried on a business in partnership, there may be an extra assessment on the other individuals who were at that time his partners (but based only on their (revised) share of the partnership profit — see *Tax Bulletin*, August 1996, pp 339 and 340). A taxpayer assessed on the basis of fraudulent or negligent conduct is entitled to his full allowances and reliefs for the year in question even though the time limit for claiming them has expired.

A number of cases (pre-dating the 1989 legislative changes) illustrate the operation of back duty assessments. In *Kovak v Morris* (1985), for instance, persistent failure by the taxpayer to supply tax returns was held to amount to 'wilful default': today it would amount to negligent conduct. A particularly graphic illustration of what was then wilful default and today would be classified as negligent conduct, was afforded by the case of *Pleasants v Atkinson* (1987) in which the taxpayer's accountants purported to deduct, in arriving at the profits of his trade as a property developer, money which was actually expended on his private residence. The commissioners were entitled on these facts to conclude that, although the taxpayer was himself innocent of wilful default, his agent (the firm of accountants) was guilty and furthermore it was not necessary to prove any additional requirement, such as personal enrichment, in order to explain that breach of duty. Accordingly, in this case the taxpayer was assessed in 1981 on profits under-declared for the year 1972-73 (see TMA 1970 s 36(1) which refers to the conduct of a person 'acting on his (ie the taxpayer's) behalf').

For a back duty assessment to be made on a deceased taxpayer's PRs it must be made within three tax years of the 31 January following the year of death for fraudulent or negligent conduct by the deceased in any of the six years up to and including the year of his death (TMA 1970 s 40). Thus, if the deceased died in the tax year 1995-96, the Revenue has until 30 January 2000 in which to assess his PRs for loss of tax because of his fraudulent or negligent conduct in the years from 1989-90 to 1995-96. An assessment is 'made' for these purposes when the certificate of assessment is signed in the assessment book and not when the notice of assessment is received by the taxpayer (TMA 1970 s 40 and *Honig v Sarsfield* (1986)).

In *Baylis v Gregory* (1987) the Court of Appeal had to consider the position when a taxpayer was assessed to CGT, but, because of a typing error, that assessment was stated to be for 1974-75 whereas it should have related to 1975-76. This error went unnoticed until the time limit for making an assessment for 1975-76 had passed. When it was noticed by the inspector he made a note in his records that the assessment for 1974-75 was vacated. On these facts, the court decided, *first*, that the 1974-75 assessment had not been properly cancelled since notice had not been given to the taxpayer, but, *secondly*, that it could not be treated as referring to 1975-76. The correct procedure was for a proper assessment to be made for that year but as the relevant time limit had passed the taxpayer in the particular case could not be taxed on gains realised in 1975–76.

Interest is, of course, charged on tax paid late. The provisions have been made more complicated by the introduction of self-assessment, with different dates for when interest starts to run depending on the nature of the debt (ie is it a late payment on account or does it arise from an amendment to a self-assessment?)—see TMA 1970 s 86.   [2.32]–[2.50]

III APPEALS

Appeals by taxpayers against assessment or other actions of the Inland Revenue are usually made, in the first instance, to the Revenue themselves. Statistics reveal that under the old system (when every taxpayer received an assessment from the Revenue) there were roughly 5 million appeals made annually in England and Wales against those assessments and, of these, about 4 million were settled by agreement between taxpayers and the Revenue. The remaining 1 million were listed for hearing as 'delay cases' (see [2.55]), although the majority were settled and only about 50,000 remained to be determined by the commissioners on the grounds of the failure on the part of the taxpayers to provide the necessary information. Of these, about 5,000 used to prove contentious, with 500 requiring a formal hearing (for the distinction between delay cases and contentious appeals see IR Press Release dated 22 February 1990: [1990] STI 170).

One of the reasons for introducing self-assessment was to reduce the number of appeals. Under the old system estimated assessments (to encourage dilatory taxpayers) were all too common and there had to be a formal appeal against an estimated assessment to avoid having to pay the estimated liability. Under the new system, if a self-assessment return is not filed on time, the Revenue will 'determine' the tax due (s 28C) but, in order to replace that determination, all the taxpayer has to do is file a self-assessed return; in fact there is *no* right of appeal against a determination. Thus self-assessment will reduce the number of appeals arising merely because there has been a delay in the taxpayer fulfilling his statutory duties—although, of course, disputes about pre 1996–97 assessments will be working their way through the courts for several years. On the other hand, the self-assessment legislation introduces new rights of appeal (eg against the Revenue's right to call for documents under s 19A) which will, no doubt, compensate the commissioners for losing the 'delay' cases!

If an appeal cannot be settled by agreement, it is then set down for hearing by the General or the Special Commissioners. Both bodies are appointed by the Lord Chancellor (TMA 1970 ss 2, 4). The General Commissioners are part-time unpaid laypersons appointed locally for a district, like lay magistrates, and are assisted by a clerk who is usually a solicitor (TMA 1970 s 3). The Special Commissioners, who are 'overseen' by a Presiding Special Commissioner chosen by the Lord Chancellor, must be barristers, advocates or solicitors of at least ten years' standing (TMA 1970 s 4). To some extent the taxpayer can appeal to whichever of the two bodies he prefers: however, complicated appeals involving technical questions of law will usually be heard by the Special Commissioners with the more routine appeals coming before the General Commissioners.

In some circumstances an application for judicial review may be the taxpayer's best (or only) way of having a Revenue decision scrutinised by the courts and this is considered briefly at 5 below.   [2.51]

1   **Structure of appeals**

At the first level, an appeal is heard either by a panel of General Commissioners or by a single Special Commissioner unless the Presiding Special Commissioner directs otherwise (TMA 1970 s 45). From the decision of the commissioners, either the taxpayer or the inspector may appeal on a point of law to the High Court although certain appeals from decisions of the Special Commissioners may be referred directly to the Court of Appeal (TMA 1970 ss 56, 56A).

Unless the appeal is referred directly to the Court of Appeal under s 56A there is a right of appeal from the High Court to the Court of Appeal and, with leave, to the House of Lords. Alternatively, use may be made of the 'leapfrog' procedure under the Administration of Justice Act 1969 to appeal directly to the House of Lords.

In general, the taxpayer can appeal to either the General or Special Commissioners although the latter will not hear 'delay' cases (see [**2.55**]). The Revenue may only insist on a case being referred to General Commissioners under TMA 1970 s 31(5)—thereby ignoring any election by the taxpayer to have the matter heard by the Special Commissioners—in delay cases. In certain other cases, eg appealing an assessment by the Board, the taxpayer has no choice and the appeal must be to the Special Commissioners. Where the appeal involves difficult questions of law the taxpayer often chooses the Special Commissioners. In back duty cases, he may be better off with the General Commissioners whose business experience and local knowledge may help him.

The taxpayer must make his appeal to the commissioners within 30 days of the action which is the subject of the appeal (TMA 1970 s 31) and in Schedule D cases he must specify the grounds of appeal. The commissioners may discharge, reduce or increase the amount of tax payable (TMA 1970 s 50).

Where the taxpayer elects for the Special Commissioners, this election may be disregarded at any time before the determination of the appeal by agreement between the parties or, failing agreement, by a non-appealable direction of the General Commissioners given after hearing the parties (TMA 1970 s 31(5A)).

Once started, an appeal cannot be withdrawn except with the agreement in writing of the inspector (TMA 1970 s 54 and see *Beach v Willesden General Comrs* (1982)). However, an appeal which is started before the General Commissioners may, on agreement with the Special Commissioners, be transferred to them (TMA 1970 s 44(3A)). The general principles of court procedures apply to the hearing at which the Crown is usually represented by the inspector and the taxpayer may appear in person or be represented by a barrister, solicitor or accountant. Prior to 1 September 1994, proceedings before both bodies were in private: hearings before Special Commissioners will now usually be in public (SI 1994/1811 reg 12).

The commissioners can call before them and examine on oath any person other than the taxpayer himself. However, legal aid is not available and the General Commissioners have no power to award costs. Following a Consultative Document published in November 1991 entitled *Procedural Rules for General and Special Commissioners*, by virtue of TMA 1970 ss 56B–56D (inserted by F(No 2)A 1992 Sch 16, para 4) the Special Commissioners now have the power to award costs where either party has acted 'wholly unreasonably' and to publish their decisions. Decisions have been published since 1994: anonymity is given if all or part of the hearing was in private (see *Y Co Ltd v IRC* (1996)).

In November 1996 the Tax Law Review Committee published an interim report on reform of the tax appeals system. The Committee would like to see a two-tier tribunal, covering all taxes, with the same procedural rules applying to each tier and a reduction in the number of courts involved in the appeal hierarchy. The Report has generally been favourably received but it remains to be seen whether and when parliamentary time will be found to effect any changes. [2.52]

2 Law or fact?

The difficult borderline between points of law and questions of fact and the role of the appellate courts was discussed by Lord Radcliffe in *Edwards v Bairstow & Harrison* [1956] AC 14 at 35:

> 'I think that the true position of the court in all these cases can be shortly stated. If a party to a hearing before commissioners expresses dissatisfaction with their determination as being erroneous in point of law, it is for them to state a case and in the body of it to set out the facts that they have found as well as their determination. I do not think that inferences drawn from other facts are incapable of being themselves findings of fact, although there is value in the distinction between primary facts and inferences drawn from them. When the case comes before the court, it is its duty to examine the determination having regard to its knowledge of the relevant law. If the case contains anything *ex facie* which is bad law and which bears upon the determination, it is, obviously, erroneous in point of law. But, without any such misconception appearing *ex facie*, it may be that the facts found are such that no person acting judicially and properly instructed as to the relevant law could have come to the determination under appeal. In those circumstances, too, the court must intervene. It has no option but to assume that there has been some misconception of the law and that this has been responsible for the determination. So there, too, there has been error in point of law. I do not think that it much matters whether this state of affairs is described as one in which there is no evidence to support the determination or as one in which the evidence is inconsistent with and contradictory to the determination or as one in which the true and only reasonable conclusion contradicts the determination. Rightly understood each phrase propounds the same test.' (The difficult borderline between questions of fact and law has been considered by the courts in the *Ramsay* line of cases: see, for instance, the judgment of Vinelott J in *Countess Fitzwilliam v IRC* (1990).)

It follows that a decision of the commissioners will not be reversed simply because an appeal court would have come to a different conclusion on the particular facts. The Schedule E case of *Glantre Engineering Ltd v Goodhand* (1983) illustrates the importance of the commissioners' finding of fact. Once they had concluded that the payment in question was an emolument (a finding of fact), the taxpayer was left with the burden of showing that such a finding was inconsistent with the only reasonable conclusion to be drawn from the evidence. Such cases as these must, therefore, be regarded with extreme caution when seeking to find a precedent for a certain line of argument. The 'case stated' procedure, not surprisingly, has been criticised insofar as it allows for the ingenious advocate to dress up as law what are, in reality, pure facts.

When a rehearing before the commissioners is ordered, fresh evidence may not be adduced unless there are special circumstances. In *Brady v Group Lotus Car Companies plc* (1987), for instance, such evidence was allowed because the taxpayer had deliberately misled the commissioners in a material matter and that deception might have affected their decision. [2.53]

3 Appealing the commissioners' decision

Prior to 1 September 1994, the same procedure applied whether a party was appealing a decision of the General or Special Commissioners. For either party to appeal he had to express immediate dissatisfaction with the commissioners' decision, and within 30 days thereof formally require the commissioners to state a case, ie to prepare a summary of their findings and the reasons for their decision. Within 30 days of receiving the case stated the appellant had to transmit it to the High Court (TMA 1970 s 56(4)). This requirement was mandatory so that any breach of its requirements rendered the appeal invalid (*Valleybright v Richardson* (1985)). By contrast, the two requirements, *first*, that an appellant must express immediate dissatisfaction with the commissioners' decision (TMA 1970 s 56(1)), and *secondly* that as soon as the case stated is transmitted to the High Court the appellant must inform the other party of that fact and furnish him with a copy (TMA 1970 s 56(5)) were directory only. Accordingly, failure to comply with either requirement would not necessarily deprive the defaulting party of the right to appeal (*Hughes v Viner* (1985)).

Statutory instruments issued in July 1994, coming into effect on 1 September 1994, introduced divergent practices (SIs 1994/1811, 1812 and 1813). There is now a statutory right to ask both bodies to review their decisions (see reg 19 of SI 1994/1811 and reg 17 of SI 1994/1812). A person dissatisfied with the final decision of the General Commissioners no longer has to express his dissatisfaction immediately: he must merely serve a notice on the Clerk requiring the Tribunal to state and sign a case. The Case Stated procedure has, however, been abolished in relation to decisions of the Special Commissioners. The Tribunal now has to reduce its decision to writing and this is sent to both parties. Either party who is dissatisfied may then appeal to the High Court (or in certain circumstances the Court of Appeal) and it is for that party (rather than the Commissioners under the Case Stated procedure) to identify the points of law to be considered by the appellate court.   [2.54]

4   Special procedure for certain income tax appeals

The majority of income tax appeals under the old system were the result of 'best of judgment' assessments raised simply because of the taxpayer's delay in returning his income, particularly his business profits ('delay appeals'). In an attempt to reduce the large number of delay appeals and the consequently huge administrative costs, the Revenue introduced a specific procedure for income tax appeals (excluding Schedule E) against assessments where the amount of tax paid on account under TMA 1970 s 55 is thought to be reasonable, the source of the income is continuing, and the tax charged is £10,000 or less. Appeals are not listed for a hearing until two years' accounts are outstanding whereupon all the 'two-year appeals' will be listed at the same time after the June following the second year (IR Press Release 25 January 1983).   [2.55]

5   Judicial review

Generally a taxpayer does not have an alternative remedy if the legislation gives him a right of appeal. Lord Templeman in *Preston v IRC* (1985) indicated that this general principle is often not too restrictive because the High Court, on hearing appeals from the commissioners, 'can then correct all kinds of errors of law including errors which might otherwise be the subject of judicial review proceedings'.

Despite this general principle, over time it has become clear that in some areas judicial review of decisions is available. The right might arise because there is no appeal mechanism (for instance, there used to be no appeal procedure to test the validity of notices given under TMA 1970 s 20) but more usually because the courts are willing to apply general administrative law requirements in the tax arena. So, for instance, the *Matrix-Securities* case (1994) referred to at [2.82] was, in fact, a judicial review case: the taxpayer argued that the Revenue's withdrawal of its advance clearance of the scheme was so unfair as to amount to an abuse of power. Although judicial review claims may be based on alleged illegality or irrationality (eg *R v IRC, ex p Mead and Cook*

(1992) where the taxpayers challenged the Revenue's decision to prosecute them and not other fraudulent taxpayers, allegedly guilty of very similar offences) or on the claim that the Revenue had acted for an improper motive, many cases are, in essence, based on the claim that the Revenue has acted unfairly. In *Preston* the House of Lords held that unfairness which arose because 'the conduct of the commissioners is equivalent to a breach of contract or breach of representation' could entitle the taxpayer to relief. In *R v IRC, ex p Unilever plc* (1996), the Revenue's conduct did not amount to a clear unambiguous and unqualified representation, as required in *Preston*. However, on what were unique facts, the Court of Appeal concluded that failure by the Revenue to give the taxpayer clear and general advance notice that they would rely on the statutory time limit to reject the taxpayer's loss relief claims, when over a 20 year period they had allowed claims made out of time, was so unfair as to amount to an abuse of power. In reaching this decision the Court of Appeal indicated that there was a wider principle underlying the decision in *Preston*—unlawfulness derives from its being 'illogical or immoral or both for a public authority to act with conspicuous unfairness and in that sense abuse its power'. It remains to be seen, however, whether and to what extent the House of Lords will adopt this principle; and whether the test of 'conspicuous' unfairness will prove more or less limiting than the *Preston* test. In any event it should be noted that *Unilever* was a 'model taxpayer' and perhaps taxpayers whose hands are not entirely clean will have to establish a more traditional basis for claiming that the Revenue's unfairness amounted to an abuse of power.   [2.56]–[2.80]

V REFORM

1 Taxpayers' Charter and Revenue Adjudicator

In August 1991 the new Taxpayer's Charter was launched setting out the standard of service to be expected of the Inland Revenue and Customs and Excise. Subsequently the Revenue introduced three new codes of practice in support of the Charter (dealing with the conduct of tax investigations, the conduct of inspections of employers' PAYE records and compensation for serious delays or mistakes) and more recently issued a Code of Practice for the Provision of Information and Advice (see [2.82]). As icing on the cake, the Revenue has appointed an independent adjudicator, to be known as the 'Revenue Adjudicator'. The Adjudicator's function is to examine complaints from taxpayers. She is not responsible for hearing appeals on matters of law, such appeals continuing to rest with the commissioners; she is instead concerned with the manner in which the Revenue conducts a taxpayer's affairs, for example, whether there has been excessive delay, any error or any discourtesy. Unless the circumstances are exceptional, the Revenue will normally accept the Adjudicator's decision.

The Adjudicator's third Annual Report was published in October 1996 covering the period to 31 March 1996. 2,507 complaints about the Revenue were received (compared to 1,615 in the first year but 2,581 in the second year). Most requested help in dealing with the Revenue (for instance in obtaining a tax repayment) and these were normally resolved quickly. Others involved in-depth investigations and some resulted in compensation being paid to the taxpayer. The Adjudicator also supervises Customs and Excise and the Contributions Agency.

As part of the drive to make the Revenue's operating procedures more transparent (pursuant to the Charter) it has started publishing extracts from the manuals provided to its Inspectors. Some of these are being published commercially, with an updating service provided, and at considerable expense. Others (for instance the guidelines on Employee Share Schemes) are published as booklets available directly from the Inland Revenue.   **[2.81]**

2   **Rulings by the Revenue**

In certain situations a clearance procedure is laid down in the legislation which enables the taxpayer to obtain a formal ruling from the Revenue on whether a proposed transaction falls within a particular legislative provision (see, for instance, the detailed advance clearance procedure laid down in TA 1988 s 707 in relation to the 'transactions in securities' legislation). In other cases the Revenue has been known to give informal 'rulings' and it is thought that, provided that all relevant facts and circumstances have been disclosed by the taxpayer, such rulings will operate to prevent the Revenue from subsequently reopening the matter. This was confirmed in the House of Lords speeches in *Matrix-Securities Ltd v IRC* (1994), although those speeches failed to provide clear guidance on precisely what the taxpayer must do to ensure that the Revenue is bound by the ruling which is given (but see the letter from the Deputy Chairman of the Inland Revenue in STI 1994, p 729 and now the Code of Practice for the Provision of Information and Advice (available from local tax enquiry centres)).

The issue in that case was whether the Revenue was acting unfairly when it decided to revoke a clearance obtained from the relevant tax inspector. That clearance had stated that capital allowances would be available on the basis that property was being bought (by a unit trust promoted by Matrix) for some £95 *million*, despite the fact that the scheme, by various circular transactions, resulted in the vendor of the property retaining only £8 *million*, being its market value. The House of Lords unanimously considered that the Revenue was acting fairly in revoking the clearance although this conclusion was reached by a number of different routes: these included the degree of factual disclosure that was provided in letters seeking the clearance; a failure to highlight the legal issues involved; and the identity of the person from whom the clearance was sought.

Following *Matrix*, the Revenue issued a Consultative Document proposing a *post transaction* ruling system. The document was not particularly well received because it proposed that in order to make a Revenue ruling binding very extensive information would have to be given—including on the relevant law and the taxpayer's opinions of how the transaction should be taxed (thus making the system of little value to the 'man in the street'!). In September 1996 the government announced that it would introduce a 'comprehensive scheme' to cover the provision of post-transaction rulings in 1997. In November 1995 a Consultative Document on *pre-transaction* rulings was published and again, as may be expected, it proposed that strict criteria would have to be satisfied before the ruling bound the Revenue. It also envisaged excluding certain transactions (most notably those that may involve tax avoidance) and charging for rulings. In September 1996 it was announced that a general formal scheme will not be introduced because of concerns about charging; the amount of information that would have to be supplied; and its impact on informal arrangements. However, consideration of the feasibility of introducing a 'products rulings' system continues (ie a pre-transaction ruling where a new product (eg a savings plan) is to be sold and it is not possible to identify the relevant taxpayers and, in any event, their identity would not affect the ruling).   **[2.82]**

3 Tax law rewrite

Readers of the rest of this book will soon discover how complex are many of the statutory provisions, often all but incomprehensible unless the reader is aware of the perceived problem the particular provision was designed to address. In principle, therefore, the current project to simplify tax legislation must be welcomed. The aim of the exercise is to make the legislation easier to understand—not review the underlying policies. In practice, any staggered introduction of the rewritten legislation (and other practicalities) may create new problems. Nevertheless the project proceeds: a Consultative Document was published in July 1996 and in December members of a Steering Committee were appointed and the Revenue published a paper entitled 'The Tax Rewrite: Plans for 1997' (Also see [**1.22**]).   [**2.83**]

Section 2 Income tax

Chapters

3 General principles

'... No one has ever been able to define income in terms sufficiently concrete to be of value for taxation purposes ... where it has to be ascertained whether a gain is to be classified as an income gain or a capital gain, the determination of that question must depend in large measure upon the particular facts of the particular case.' (Abbott J in *Oxford Motors Ltd v Minister of National Revenue* (1959) 18 DLR (2d) 712.)

'In principle, there is little economic difference between income and capital gains, and many people effectively have the option of choosing to a significant extent which to receive. And, insofar as there is a difference, it is by no means clear why one should be taxed more heavily than the other. Taxing them at different rates distorts investment decisions and inevitably creates a major tax avoidance industry.' (Nigel Lawson, Budget Speech, 15 March 1988.)

[**3.1**]

I HISTORY

Income tax is sometimes referred to as the 'tax which beat Napoleon'. Such claims amount to a gross exaggeration although it is true that the tax was first introduced in 1799 by Pitt the Younger as a wartime measure. Pitt's tax was not wholly innovatory; there had always been a tradition of direct taxation even if that taxation had been applied spasmodically. The origins of income tax may be seen in the land tax and in the Triple Assessment of 1798.

Early yields were disappointing; estimates predicted a yield of £10m in the first year, but under £6m was actually raised. Although the tax was repealed when peace with France was concluded in 1802, it was reintroduced by Addington when hostilities recommenced in the following year. Addington included two basic changes which have survived more or less intact: *first*, a requirement that returns should be of income from particular sources and not just a lump sum; and *secondly*, provisions for deduction of tax at source.

The final cessation of hostilities in 1816 led to the repeal of the tax with the resulting financial deficit being made good by increased yields from Customs and Excise. Income tax was brought back, this time for good, by Peel in 1842. It was not revived because of its own inherent merits, but as a way to simplify and reduce the tariff, as a first step towards the repeal of the Corn Laws in 1846.

By the end of the century, the tax, although an accepted part of the fiscal landscape, raised less than either customs or excise. The twentieth century with the extraordinary demands of war and welfare transformed the picture. By the end of the 1914–18 War, the income tax yield was some £585m as compared with the pre-war figure of £34m and the complexity of the modern tax had been established with earned income relief, supertax, a range of personal allowances, and a primitive system of capital allowances. The process was accelerated by the 1939–45 War with the yield rising from £371m in 1938 to £1,426m in 1945. PAYE was improved in 1943 and the tax avoidance industry maintained a steady growth.

Today, the flood of income tax legislation shows little sign of diminution; the statutory material was consolidated in 1952, in 1970, and such was the output of Parliament again in 1988 (TA 1988). A further consolidation is needed although this presumably will be overtaken by the complete redraft of the legislation (see [**1.22**]).   [**3.2**]–[**3.20**]

II   STATUTORY BASIS OF THE TAX

1   **The statutes and case law**

The authority for imposing taxation is Act of Parliament and, in the case of income tax, the statutory basis is TA 1988 as amended by later Finance Acts. TMA 1970 deals with the administration of the tax. The legislation on capital allowances (see Chapter 35) was reconsolidated in the Capital Allowances Act 1990.

The meaning of the statute is primarily a question for a judiciary which ranges from commissioners to the House of Lords. Many concepts are not defined by statute (eg what is a trade? what is an income receipt/expense?), many provisions are obscure, and it is the role of the judiciary to resolve such difficulties and of case law to fill the gaps. It is questionable whether it should be the job of the courts to create judge-made law to deal with sophisticated avoidance schemes but it is a task, which over the last decade or so, they have undertaken with varying degrees of enthusiasm (see *Furniss v Dawson* (1984) and note increasing caution in later cases such as *Craven v White* (1988) and *Fitzwilliam v IRC* (1993)).   [**3.21**]

2   **Years and rates**

The income tax year runs from 6 April to the following 5 April and is termed the 'year of assessment' or simply the 'tax year'. It is referred to by reference to both the calendar years that it straddles—hence, the year of assessment beginning on 6 April 1997 is referred to as the tax year 1997–98. The curious starting date for the year (6 April) is explicable, as is so much of income tax, on historical grounds. 5 April was adopted as the terminal date because it was one of the old quarter days which marked the end of a period of account: (1985) BTR 56.

The tax needs annual renewal by Parliament. The annual Finance Act traditionally received the Royal Assent in late July or early August. By virtue of the Provisional Collection of Taxes Act 1968, however, the budget resolutions (such as the rates of tax) are given limited statutory force until the passage of the Act.

In his 1992 Budget Speech, Norman Lamont commented:

> 'Each year the Budget for this country is presented in two parts. In the autumn, the Chancellor announces the Government's spending plans for the coming financial year. And in March he sets out the Revenue measures necessary to pay for them.
> Many have criticised this uniquely British institution . . .
> In my view the current system is not only illogical, it has also had a number of highly undesirable consequences. Over the years the separation of public expenditure from taxation and the announcement of tax proposals in isolation has

intensified the pressure for special reliefs and contributed to the excessively complex tax system we have now. The time has come for reform.

I therefore intend that next year's Budget will be the last Spring Budget. From then on the annual Budget will be in December and will cover not just taxation but also expenditure. The Budget in December 1993 will contain the Government's proposals for both revenue and expenditure in 1994–95. It will also include spending plans for the subsequent two years.'

The annual Finance Bill is therefore currently presented to Parliament in January and receives Royal Assent in late April or early May although the new Labour government is minded to return to Spring Budgets. **[3.22]–[3.40]**

III THE SCHEDULES

1 The source doctrine

The Schedules

Schedule	Source	Basis of assessment
A	Profits from a business of letting land in UK	Income of the current year of assessment
D		
Case I	Profits of a trade in UK	
Case II	Profits of a profession or vocation in UK	The income of the accounting period ending in the tax year or income of the current year of assessment
Case III	Interest, annuities and other annual payments	
Case IV	Securities out of the UK	
Case V	Possessions out of the UK (but excluding foreign employment)	
Case VI	Annual profits or gains not falling under Cases I–V and not charged by virtue of any other Schedule; and certain income directed to be so charged	Income of the current year of assessment
E Cases I, II and III	Offices, employments and pensions (both 'home' and foreign). Also, chargeable benefits under the social security legislation	Income of the current year of assessment
F	Dividends and certain other distributions by companies	Income of the current year of assessment

Income tax is levied according to the source of the income and the four Schedules (see table above) exhaustively list the various sources. Schedule B which imposed a charge on commercial woodlands was abolished as from 6 April 1988 and Schedule C, which taxed income from public revenue dividends, from 6 April

1996. Each Schedule has its own rules for determining the amount of income and the available deductions (if any). Schedule A, for instance, taxes the profits of a business of letting property including isolated or casual lettings. The charge is on rents and other receipts which arise as a result of the ownership of land (or of an interest therein) but the landlord may deduct expenses such as repairs to the property.

In arriving at the income of a taxpayer it is, therefore, necessary to discover what sources of income he possesses and then, by applying the rules of the relevant Schedules, to calculate the income arising under each. It follows, as a general principle, that *tax is charged only so long as a taxpayer possesses the source of the income*. Tax avoidance opportunities that would thereby exist are, however, often prevented by the legislation. For instance, although the sale of trading stock after the permanent cessation of the relevant trade would not on general principles fall within Case I (because the source—the trade—had ceased when the sale occurred), there is express provision which brings into the tax net the value of stock unsold at the date of the discontinuance. Any loss of revenue is thereby prevented. Tax avoidance by judicious use of the source doctrine remains possible for non-UK domiciliaries taxed on the remittance basis (see Chapter 13) but *Example 3.1*, below, illustrates a situation where the source doctrine left a gap in the tax net which was closed, in this case by FA 1989.

[**3.41**]

EXAMPLE 3.1

B, having been employed by G Ltd for 20 years, is transferred together with all the other employees to the employment of G Ltd's parent company in the tax year 1988–89. The trustees of a fund for the benefit of employees of G Ltd including B accordingly brought that trust to an end and made distributions to B in the following tax year (ie in 1989–90). Although that distribution may be an emolument (see Chapter 5) because it was paid after B's employment had ceased and could not be attributed to any year of that employment, there was no source of income in the year of receipt and therefore no liability to income tax (see *Bray v Best* (1988)). In the course of changing the charge to tax under Schedule E to the receipts basis, FA 1989 also widened the tax net to include emoluments received *after* an employment had ceased. Accordingly, payments of the type received in *Bray v Best* will now be 'treated as emoluments for the last year of assessment in which the employment was held' (TA 1988 s 19(1) para 4A: inserted by FA 1989).

2   The mutually exclusive rule

The Schedules are mutually exclusive with the result that the Revenue cannot assess income to tax under any Schedule other than the one to which that income is properly attributable (*Fry v Salisbury House Estate Ltd* (1930)). The same principle applies to the taxpayer who may not deduct expenses attributable to a different Schedule nor opt to have his income taxed under a different Schedule (*Mitchell and Edon v Ross* (1962)). So far as Schedule D is concerned there is authority for the view that the Revenue can choose between the different Cases in the rare situations when an overlap between them exists (*Liverpool and London and Globe Insurance Co v Bennett* (1913)).

[**3.42**]

EXAMPLE 3.2

(1) Roger lets several properties to university students and works full time in the management of the properties. Tax must be charged under Schedule A (which applies to rent and other receipts from land), not under Schedule D Case I, because there cannot be a trade of letting properties (see *Griffiths v Jackson* (1983) [**8.23**]).

(2) A firm of solicitors acted as secretary for a number of companies. The profits from the profession of solicitors are assessed under Schedule D Case II; remuneration from the office of company secretary is, however, charged under Schedule E (*IRC v Brander and Cruickshank* (1971) see **[5.21]** and ESC A37 for the tax treatment of directors' fees received in such cases).

3 What is income?

Income is not defined in the legislation. Furthermore, any definition is a matter for acute debate by both economists and philosophers. How, therefore, does the tax operate if the subject matter of the tax (income) is not defined? The answer is that income for this purpose means all the sums calculated under the four Schedules. Hence, a sum of money falling under one of the Schedules is subject to tax (and is, therefore, 'income'), whilst a sum which escapes the Schedules is untaxed (and may, therefore, be termed 'capital'). Critics of income tax (notably the Meade Committee in its report in 1979 on the Structure and Reform of Direct Taxation) argue that it is the distinction between capital and income which has been used to greater effect than many other devices to avoid tax.

Because of the tax avoidance possiblities 'income' is widened in certain cases so that capital sums (notably premiums under Schedule A and golden handshakes and restrictive covenant payments under Schedule E) are deemed to be income for the purposes of the tax. This results in a divergence between those income tax rules and ordinary principles of trust law which identify what sums are income. Take, for instance, TA 1988 s 686 which imposes an additional charge on income received by discretionary or accumulation trusts: see generally **[11.21]**. Because the section is limited to 'income arising to the trustees' this has been construed as limited to income 'in a trust sense' and hence it does not catch profits which are of a capital nature (eg lease premiums) albeit that those profits are deemed to be income for basic rate purposes in the hands of the trustees.

EXAMPLE 3.3

Augustus gives Oxfam £100 every Christmas. Despite the regular nature of the payment it is not income in Oxfam's hands because it does not fall within any of the Schedules. Were he to covenant the sum each year, however, it would become income because it is an annual payment falling within Schedule D Case III. If Augustus had given a one-off sum of at least £250 under the Gift Aid provisions (see FA 1990 s 25 as amended) the payment would be treated in the same way as a covenant (ie as income in Oxfam's hands). (Note: just because the sum is income it does not follow that Augustus is worse off. Indeed, there are tax advantages from payments to charity by deed of covenant or through the Gift Aid scheme; see Chapter 42.)

Although the lack of a definition of income does not generally cause problems, difficulties do arise when the Schedule prescribes that only income receipts are subject to tax or only income expenses can be deducted (as under Schedules A and D Cases I and II where the tax is levied on the profits that remain after income deductions have been taken from income receipts). The meaning of 'income' has accordingly been debated all too frequently before the courts and the various tests that have been suggested for resolving the problem are considered in Chapter 6.   **[3.43]**

4 Computation—charges, allowances and rates

I INTRODUCTION: STAGES OF THE INCOME TAX CALCULATION

Only income as defined by the Schedules is subject to income tax. The tax is levied at three rates; a lower rate of 20%, a basic rate of 23% and a single higher rate of 40%. It may be collected either by direct assessment, or by deduction at source. The following steps are involved in calculating the taxpayer's income and in working out his tax bill for the year:

Step 1 Calculate the individual's 'statutory income', ie the income which is taxable under the rules of the various Schedules and Cases.

Step 2 Calculate the taxpayer's charges on income, ie certain payments which the taxpayer is bound to make, such as certain interest payments.

Step 3 Deduct charges on income from statutory income to obtain 'total income' (TA 1988 s 835).

Step 4 Deduct (certain) personal reliefs from total income to obtain 'taxable income'.

Step 5 Calculate income tax at lower, basic and higher rate on the taxable income.

Step 6 Deduct any relief attributable to investments in the enterprise investment scheme and venture capital trusts and then allowances and reliefs which attract relief at 15%.

Step 7 From the total tax calculated in *Step 5* deduct any income tax which has been collected at source.

Step 8 Calculate basic rate tax on any charges on income from which the individual has deducted tax when making the payment.

   The result of *Step 7* plus *Step 8* is the final amount of tax payable. All these steps involve terms requiring explanation, and the various stages in the income tax calculation will now be considered in detail.   **[4.1]–[4.20]**

II   STATUTORY INCOME *(Step 1)*

1   **General**

Statutory income consists of the taxpayer's income from all sources calculated according to the rules of the particular Schedule or Case under which it arises and after deducting expenses appropriate to the particular Schedule or Case. Since the income tax year runs from 6 April to 5 April following, the income tax assessment (the 'basis of assessment') should logically be on the statutory income of an individual for that period (ie on a current year basis). Historically Schedule D operated on a 'preceding year' basis: a practice which has now ceased with the introduction of self-assessment. For years up to 1996–97 the taxable profits of a trade, for instance, assessable under Schedule D Case I were deemed to be the profits of the accounts which ended in the previous tax year.   [**4.21**]

EXAMPLE 4.1

Mack, a trader (Schedule D Case I), makes up his accounts to 30 June 1994 showing receipts of £12,000. Certain deductions may be made (for instance, £2,000 paid by Mack in salaries to employees). As a result, Mack included £10,000 of Schedule D Case I income in his statutory income for the year of assessment 1995–96 (this was the preceding year basis).

For the tax year 1996–97 Mack was subject to the transitional rules whereby the tax charge was a 12-month average of profits earned in the year to 30 June 1995 and 30 June 1996 (ie $^{12}/_{24}$ of the total of those two years' profits was taxed).

For 1997–98 *et seq* Mack is taxed on profits of the accounting year which ends in the tax year: ie profits to 30 June 1997.

2   **Income received after deduction of tax**

a) *General*

Some income is received and enters the statutory income calculation gross: ie without having suffered any tax. The tax on that income is collected by direct assessment. For certain types of income, however, tax is deducted at source. In such cases, the payer of the income is obliged to act as a tax collector by deducting from the payment an amount of tax and handing it to the Revenue. If the recipient is not liable to income tax (or is only liable at lower rate), he will usually (although not always because in some cases the tax credit is non-repayable) obtain a repayment from the Revenue of the tax deducted. If, however, he is liable to higher rate tax, a further assessment will be necessary.

Accordingly, any sum received after deduction of tax is normally grossed up to discover the greater sum from which the tax was deducted. The resulting (gross) figure must be entered in the recipient taxpayer's calculation of statutory income to discover his tax liability. The tax that has already been paid on this income is credited against his tax bill.   [**4.22**]

b) *Savings income*

Dividends and other company distributions (falling under Schedule F) were placed in an anomalous position as a result of changes made in FA 1993. Paid with a tax credit of 20% (equivalent to the lower rate of income tax having been deducted at source) they were treated as forming the top slice of the individual's income. Provided that did not result in a liability at the higher rate of 40%, the credit was treated as satisfying the taxpayer's basic rate liability (so that no further tax was charged).

FA 1996 extended this treatment to interest and other savings income (see TA 1988 s 1A). Basic rate tax must still be deducted in the case of annual payments (typically covenanted payments to charity) and annuities, rents paid to foreign landlords and patent royalties. [**4.23**]

EXAMPLE 4.2

Austin (with other statutory income of £10,000) receives debenture interest (Schedule D Case III) of £800 from which basic rate (20%) tax has been deducted and handed to the Revenue by the paying company. Austin must include the 'grossed-up' amount of the dividend in his statutory income calculation for the year to work out whether the tax deducted is correct.

To gross up multiply the net interest received by $\dfrac{100}{100 - R}$ where R is the rate at which tax was deducted (which in this case is 20%) ie:

$$800 \times \frac{100}{100 - 20} = 800 \times \frac{100}{80}$$
$$= £1,000 \text{ (gross interest—therefore tax paid is £200)}$$

Austin's statutory income is:

Other sources	£10,000
Schedule D III interest	£ 1,000
Statutory income	£11,000

When the tax due on this income is calculated, Austin can deduct the £200 tax deducted at source by the company. If his liability to tax is for less than £200, he can reclaim from the Revenue the amount for which he is not liable.

c) *Illustrations*

The main examples of income received after deduction of tax at source are:
(1) trust income received by a beneficiary after deduction (normally) of basic rate tax;
(2) emoluments assessable under Schedule E from which tax (at the appropriate rate) is deducted under the PAYE system;
(3) annuities and certain other annual payments, assessed under Schedule D Case III, from which basic rate tax is deducted, eg maintenance payments paid under obligations entered into before 15 March 1988;
(4) income arising from deposit accounts, received after deduction of lower rate tax (see [**4.26**]). [**4.24**]

d) *Irrecoverable tax credits*

Certain forms of income are treated as though they have already suffered income tax when received but that tax is irrecoverable. The main examples are:
(1) Foreign income dividends: TA 1988 s 246D. Tax of 20% treated as paid.
(2) Stock dividends: TA 1988 s 249. Tax of 20% treated as paid.
(3) Loans to participators which are waived: TA 1988 s 421. Tax of 20% treated as paid.

An individual receiving a stock dividend of £80 is therefore treated as if tax of £20 had been paid on an income of £100. However, if he does not pay income tax there is no refund of this sum: if he is a higher rate taxpayer further tax of £20 will be payable (being a liability of £40 on the income of £100 less the £20 credit). F(No 2)A 1997 introduced major changes in the taxation of company distributions: pension funds in receipt of such income are now unable to recover the tax credit and this rule will be extended to individuals and charities from 6 April 1999. **[4.25]**

3   Interest paid by building societies and banks

a) *Background*

Building societies and other deposit-takers (notably banks) were, formerly, subject to income tax at a special rate (the 'composite' rate) and the interest paid to depositors was treated as having suffered basic rate income tax (TA 1988 s 476). Accordingly, the investor had to gross up the sum received in order to calculate his income tax bill and, depending upon his personal circumstances, the interest could be taxed at the higher rate of tax. Where, however, the investor was not subject to income tax (eg because an infant with unused personal allowances), he was unable to obtain a refund from the Revenue for the basic rate tax credited as paid.

Largely to ensure that the average married woman with small savings was not over-taxed and doubtless to prevent wealthier married women from investing in offshore deposit accounts where interest is paid gross, the composite rate scheme was abolished with effect from 6 April 1991. The current system involves interest being paid net of lower rate income tax and non-taxpayers then being entitled to obtain a recovery of this tax on submitting the appropriate claim (TA 1988 s 480A). However, to avoid the necessity for a multiplicity of such claims, there are arrangements whereby non-taxpayers are able to complete a certificate to that effect and then receive interest gross. **[4.26]**

b) *Deposit-takers and 'relevant deposits'*

Deduction of tax at source must be applied in respect of 'relevant deposits' by any deposit-taker who falls within the statutory list. The list includes any recognised bank, the National Giro Bank, any trustee savings bank, any local authority and specified credit and finance companies (see eg SI 1987/1224 and 1987/2127). The National Savings Bank is not included. 'Relevant deposits' are widely defined to include deposits which are held by any person for the benefit of UK resident individuals or deposits where the person entitled to the interest receives it in the capacity of personal representative (PR). Whether the deposit is maintained for private or business purposes is irrelevant; it may, therefore, be held for a partnership of individuals. **[4.27]**

c) *Exclusions*

Excluded from the definition of relevant deposits are those held for companies, associations and charities. There are specific exclusions for 'qualifying time deposits' with a nominal value never falling below £50,000 and, more significantly, when the interest is payable to a person ordinarily resident outside the UK (so long as that person completes a declaration of non-residence: TA 1988 s 480B). A deposit denominated in a foreign currency can constitute a relevant deposit. **[4.28]**

4   Taxation of husband and wife: independent taxation (from 6 April 1990)

Independent taxation of husband and wife has resulted in a married couple being taxed as separate individuals. Formerly the income of a married woman living with her husband had generally been taxed as his income for all purposes. This was the only situation where the income of different persons was aggregated: minor children, for instance, have been taxed independently of their parents for many years. An election for separate assessment under TA 1988 s 283 was possible but did not affect the total tax bill, merely apportioning that bill between the couple. More important therefore was the election for separate taxation of the wife's earnings under TA 1988 s 287 but this only provided for earned income to be taxed separately as her own. [**4.29**]

5 **Earned and investment income**

With the abolition (as from 1984–85) of the surcharge on investment income above a certain limit, the distinction between earned and investment income is relevant only in relatively few situations (most importantly in calculating 'pensionable earnings').

Under TA 1988 s 833 'earned income' falls into two main categories:
(1) All income chargeable under Schedule E which is derived from an office or employment including income from pensions (see Chapter 5).
(2) 'Any income which is charged under Schedule D and is *immediately derived* by the individual from the carrying on or exercise by him of his trade, profession or vocation, either as an individual or, in the case of a partnership, as a partner personally acting therein.'

The borderline between earned and unearned income is not always easy to draw. The phrase 'immediately derived' has been strictly construed by the courts (see, for instance, *Northend v White, Leonard and Corbin Greener* (1975) and *Bucks v Bowers* (1970) and, more recently, *Koenigsberger v Mellor* (1993) where the court held that the income must be earned by 'personal exertions'). Generally, income under Schedule D Cases I and II is earned income, whereas that assessable under Schedule A (rent), Schedule D Case III (such as interest and trust income), Schedule D Case IV (foreign securities, such as dividends), Schedule F (dividends from UK companies), and Schedule D Case VI is investment income. Rent from 'furnished holiday lettings' is specifically treated as earned income (see [**8.61**]). [**4.30**]–[**4.40**]

EXAMPLE 4.3

Winnie owns a honey shop and is chargeable for 1997–98 on £20,000 profit. He also receives rent of £300 from letting a garage.

Calculation of statutory income for 1997–98:

	Investment £		*Earned* £
Profits from shop (Schedule D Case I)			20,000
Rent (Schedule A)	300		
Statutory income	£300	+	£20,000

Winnie's statutory income for the year is £20,300 from which various deductions will be made before tax is chargeable.

III CHARGES ON INCOME *(Step 2)*

1 **General**

Charges on income are amounts which fall to be deducted in computing total income. Thus, they are deductible from the individual's statutory income and technically may be deducted from investment income first. The 'amounts which fall to be deducted' are not defined, but consist of certain transfers of income which the taxpayer is obliged to make. The theory is that such income ceases to be that of the payer and becomes the income of the payee so that the payer should not be taxed on it. Charges are, therefore, deducted before personal reliefs because the latter cannot be deducted from income which is not the taxpayer's.

Charges on income comprise: certain annual payments made for *bona fide* commercial reasons; covenanted payments to charity and certain interest payments.

Formerly maintenance payments and medical insurance premiums for the over 60s were deductible in arriving at total income. With effect from 6 April 1994, however, relief for the latter was limited to the basic rate (23%) being given as a reduction in total tax liability (see *Step 6*, below) and in the case of policies taken out or renewed on or after 2 July 1997 the relief has now been ended altogether. Maintenance payments up to £1,830 are restricted to relief at 15% (see *Step 6*): if relief is available for payments in excess of that sum under pre-15 March 1988 arrangements (as to which see Chapter 41) that excess continues to be deductible as a charge.   **[4.41]**

2   **Annual payments**

The meaning of an annual payment is discussed in Chapter 10. As a result of FA 1988 and FA 1995 relatively few annual payments qualify as charges on income, namely covenanted payments to charity and pre-15 March 1988 maintenance payments. In such cases payments are treated for tax purposes as part of the income of the person (the payee) to whom they are paid.

Although the above annual payments constitute a charge on the payer's income and, accordingly, are free of tax in his hands, the payer is used as an agent to collect basic rate tax on the amount paid (see TA 1988 ss 3, 348, 349). The annual payment is, therefore, added back to the payer's income for this purpose. To recompense himself, he is allowed to deduct and retain from the payment a sum equal to tax at basic rate on that payment. A Gift Aid payment is treated as a covenant for these purposes : see FA 1990 s 25(6) and **[40.84]**.   **[4.42]**

EXAMPLE 4.4

Viola has statutory income of £26,300. She has covenanted to pay the NSPCC (a registered charity) the sum of £1,000 pa (an annual payment). Under TA 1988 s 348 Viola may deduct from the gross payment of £1,000 a sum equivalent to basic rate tax on that figure (ie £230). She, therefore, pays £770 and retains £230.

The income on which she is subject to tax (before deducting personal reliefs) is:

	£
Statutory income	26,300
Less: charge on income (gross)	1,000
Total income	£25,300

From this Viola may deduct her personal allowance and she will be taxed on the balance. In addition, however, she must pay tax at 23% (ie £230) on the covenanted payment.

Notice that the charity receives the sum of £770 after deduction of basic rate income tax at source with a tax credit for the £230 deducted by Viola. As charities are not generally subject to income tax, the NSPCC can reclaim this £230 from the Revenue. (The tax reliefs available to charities are discussed in Chapter 42.)

3 Certain interest payments

An individual obtains income tax relief for certain interest payments by deducting them from his statutory income as a charge. Certain other interest payments are deductible in computing income from a particular source only (eg interest payments made for the purposes of a trade are deductible in computing the profits of that trade under Schedule D Case I and interest payments paid in connection with the letting of property under Schedule A). Most interest payments, however, receive no tax relief. The ordinary bank overdraft, credit card interest, and hire purchase interest payments, to take three typical instances, receive no relief.

The rules governing the deductibility of interest are complex (the provisions are contained in TA 1988 ss 353–366 as amended by FA 1994 and FA 1995). The interest must be payable on a loan made for one of the qualifying purposes dealt with below. However, the old requirements that it must be either annual interest chargeable as the payee's income under Schedule D Case III, or must be payable in the UK on a loan from a bank, or from a person *bona fide* carrying on business as a member of a UK Stock Exchange or as a UK discount house were removed by FA 1994. Interest paid for a qualifying purpose now obtains relief without regard to the character of the interest or the status of the lender. As a general rule, interest that is eligible for tax relief is paid gross and is deductible from the payer's statutory income as a charge. For exceptional cases where income tax must be deducted at source by the payer of the interest see [**10.82**]. [**4.43**]

Loans to acquire an interest in a close company (TA 1988 ss 360, 361, 363) An individual may obtain income tax relief for the interest paid on a loan to acquire ordinary share capital in close trading companies (it has to be shown that the company exists wholly or mainly for the purpose of carrying on a trade: see *Lord v Tustain* (1993)) and on a loan raised to lend money to such a company so long as it is used wholly and exclusively for the business of the company (or of an associated company which is likewise a qualifying close company; note that relief continues to be available even if the company ceases to be close). To qualify for relief, the borrower has to show *either* that he is a shareholder and works for the greater part of his time in the management or conduct of the company *or* that he controls more than 5% (a 'material interest') of the ordinary share capital (in the latter case the borrower need not work for the company).

To calculate whether the individual has the necessary material interest, shares of associates must generally be aggregated with his own shares. 'Associates' include an individual's relatives, partners, trustees of a settlement which he created, and trustees of a settlement holding shares for the benefit of that individual. However, unappropriated shares held by trustees under an approved profit sharing scheme and shares in which the individual has an interest only under an employee benefit trust are not included in deciding whether he has a material interest in the company (see generally TA 1988 s 360A).

To the extent that the borrower recovers any capital from the company during that time (eg by repayment of ordinary share capital), he is treated as having repaid the loan and the amount of interest available for relief is reduced accordingly. Relief is not withdrawn if the company subsequently ceases to be close (see SP 3/78). It is not possible to obtain double tax relief by using the loan to purchase shares qualifying for relief under EIS (Enterprise Investment Scheme: see [**4.122**]). [**4.44**]

EXAMPLE 4.5

Gatty Ltd is the family trading company of the Gatty family. Sam Freebie, a full-time working director owning no shares in the company, borrows £5,000 from his bank to subscribe for ordinary shares. He will own a 4% shareholding and tax relief is available on the interest he pays. If, however, Jack Floor, the caretaker of the company's factory, were to subscribe for a similar number of shares no relief will be available because he is not concerned in the management or conduct of the company.

Loan to acquire an interest in a partnership (TA 1988 s 362)   Interest relief is available to an individual on a loan used to purchase a share in a partnership or to contribute capital or make a loan to the partnership, if it is used wholly and exclusively for the business purposes of the partnership. Relief is available only if, from the application of the loan to the payment of interest, the individual has been a member of the partnership (otherwise than as a limited partner) and has not recovered any capital from the partnership. As a result payments of interest on borrowings to finance the business can be relieved in one of two ways: either under s 353 as described or, alternatively, as a deduction in the partnership accounts. The s 353 deduction has the attraction of enabling the interest to be set against the total income of the individual rather than against the profits of the firm only. Anti-avoidance rules were introduced to deal with the so-called 'transitional year' aimed at preventing the refinancing of businesses through new personal loans (see Appendix I).

Where the partnership is subsequently incorporated into a close company and the loan remains outstanding, relief continues to be available so long as relief would be available under the close company provisions considered above if the loan were a new loan taken out on incorporation.   [**4.45**]

Loan to acquire an interest in a co-operative (TA 1988 s 361)   Relief is available for interest payments made on a loan to acquire an interest in a co-operative, or to be used wholly and exclusively for the business of that body or a subsidiary. A co-operative is defined as a common ownership enterprise or a co-operative enterprise within the meaning of the Industrial Common Ownership Act 1976 s 2. Relief is available only if the individual shows that from the application of the loan to the payment of the interest he has worked for the greater part of his time as an employee in that co-operative or in a subsidiary thereof.   [**4.46**]

Loan to invest in an employee-controlled company (TA 1988 s 361)   Relief is available for interest payments on a loan taken out by an individual to acquire ordinary shares in an employee-controlled company (which must be a UK resident unquoted trading company). An employee-controlled company is one where full-time employees own more than 50% of the ordinary share capital and voting power of the company. When an employee owns more than 10% of the issued share capital, the excess is treated as not being owned by a full-time employee. Other conditions for relief are that the shares must be acquired within 12 months of the company becoming employee-controlled and that the taxpayer or his spouse must be full-time employees of the company from the time when the loan is applied to the date when interest is paid. Furthermore, in the year of assessment in which the interest is paid the company must either first become employee-controlled or be such a company for at least nine months. Accordingly, interest relief will be withdrawn when the company ceases to be employee-controlled. To the extent that the individual recovers any capital from the company, the same rule operates as for close companies and partnerships (see above).   [**4.47**]

Loan to purchase plant or machinery (TA 1988 s 359) Where a partner or a Schedule E employee borrows money to purchase a car or other items of machinery or plant for which capital allowances are available, he can claim interest relief on that loan for up to three years after the end of the tax year when the debt was incurred. (Note that for a sole trader interest on such loans is a deductible business expense.) **[4.48]**

Loans used to purchase land occupied for business purposes by a partnership or company Where an individual takes out a loan to purchase land occupied by a partnership (of which he is a partner) or a company (of which he is a director) relief for interest paid on that loan may be available, depending upon the precise arrangements entered into. Consider the following permutations.

Case 1: Felix purchases land with the aid of a loan and allows his partnership to use the land for business purposes. Felix is paid a rent for the use of the land which is sufficient to cover his interest payments. Felix will obtain tax relief by setting the interest payments against the rent received; see further **[8.43]**. The rent paid by the partnership is a deductible business expense.

Case 2: as in *Case 1* save that the interest payments are made by the partnership and no rent is paid to Felix. The interest payments will be deemed to be rent for the use of the land and, as such, will be a deductible business expense of the partnership. Felix, however, will not be taxed on that sum because he may deduct the interest for which he is liable (TA 1988 s 355). In *R v Inspector of Taxes, ex p Brumfield* (1989) a partnership borrowed money which in turn it allowed one of the partners to use, interest free, towards the purchase of a plot of land. That land, which was acquired in the name of the individual partner, was then used rent free by the partnership. On these facts the court held that the statement of practice was inapplicable: the interest was not a deductible business expense of the partnership and the loan had not been taken out in the name of the individual partner as required in *Case 2*.

Case 3: assume that Felix allows the land to be used by a company (Felix Ltd) of which he is a director. If rent is paid to Felix it will be a deductible expense of the company and Felix will be able to set the interest that he pays against that rent (ie as in *Case 1* above). If the interest payments are made by the company, however, those sums will be taxed as part of Felix's remuneration under Schedule E and will be a deductible expense of the company. No question of interest relief will, therefore, arise.

Case 4: Felix borrows money to purchase land which is used by either a company or partnership as in *Cases 1–3*. Felix pays interest on the loan and no rent is paid for the use of the land. No interest relief is available.

Given these permutations the following conclusions are suggested.

First, *Case 4* leaves Felix in the disadvantageous position of paying interest without qualifying for tax relief thereon.

Secondly, when the company discharges the interest payments Felix may be taxed on those sums without any set-off for the interest which he is liable to pay. Were the company to pay him the same sum as rent, the deduction of interest ensures that Felix will pay no income tax on that sum.

Finally, Felix's possible entitlement to retirement relief in each case should be considered. To the extent that rent is paid (or, in the above cases, deemed to be paid) his retirement relief on the ultimate disposal of the land will be restricted. **[4.49]**

Loan to pay inheritance tax (TA 1988 s 364) PRs are eligible for interest relief on a loan used by them to pay IHT attributable to personal property situated in the UK to which the deceased was beneficially entitled and which has vested in them. The relief is limited to a 12-month period. **[4.50]**

Loan to purchase a life annuity (TA 1988 s 365)   Interest relief is available at the basic rate only on a loan not exceeding £30,000 taken out by a person aged 65 or over in order to purchase an annuity on his life provided that at least nine-tenths of the loan proceeds are used to buy the annuity and that the annuity is secured on land in the UK (or Republic of Ireland) in which he has an interest and uses as his only or main residence at the time when the interest is paid. The relief is given by way of an income tax reduction in those cases where it is not covered by MIRAS (see *Step 6*, below).   [**4.51**]

4   Loans for the purchase of a main residence and the MIRAS scheme (TA 1988 ss 354–358 and 367–378)

Prior to FA 1988, interest relief was available in three circumstances.

First, on a loan to acquire a main residence or develop land for use as a main residence.

Secondly, on a loan to improve a main residence.

Thirdly, on a loan to purchase a main residence for use by one or more dependent relatives.

In the first situation FA 1988 made important changes in the allocation of relief when more than one purchaser is involved but in the second and third situations it withdrew the relief altogether.

The value of the relief that remains has been progressively reduced: as from 6 April 1991 it was only available against income tax at the basic rate: as from 6 April 1994 it was further restricted by being given only at the 20% lower rate and as from 6 April 1995 the relief has been given at only 15%. A further reduction to 10% will come into effect from 6 April 1998.

For most lenders tax relief is available through MIRAS (Mortgage Interest Relief at Source) under which these changes are easily accommodated; for loans outside MIRAS relief is given by a reduction in tax (see *Step 6*).

This section first considers the availability of relief when a main residence is purchased or land developed for use as such and then looks briefly at the other situations where relief has now been withdrawn.   [**4.52**]

a) *Conditions for relief on a loan to purchase a main residence*

Interest is eligible for tax relief if it is paid on a loan by the owner of an estate or interest in land in the UK or the Republic of Ireland for the purpose of acquiring or developing the land for use as his only or main residence. Land includes a caravan or houseboat. Expenditure on purchase includes the cost of any legal fees and stamp duty attributable to the purchase. Land is developed for these purposes if a new building, which is not part of an existing residence, is erected on land which immediately before that development began had no building on it (TA 1988 s 355(2B)). The following conditions must be satisfied for a borrower to qualify: [**4.53**]

Ownership   The interest payments must be made by the person owning the interest in the land and not, for instance, by his rich mother-in-law. If the borrower dies, his PRs are not generally entitled to claim the relief against estate income (for exceptional circumstances where relief may continue to be available on a transitional basis see [**4.63**]).   [**4.54**]

Qualifying purpose   The loan must be used for the 'qualifying purpose' (viz the acquisition or development of land) either when it is obtained or within a reasonable time (thought to be six months) thereafter.   [**4.55**]

EXAMPLE 4.6

Fred takes out a loan of £20,000 in October to build a modern bungalow for use as his main residence on land which he owns in Norfolk. However, the work cannot be started until the spring and in the meantime Fred invests the money in shares. The interest on this loan will not be eligible for tax relief. Fred should, therefore, repay the loan out of the sale proceeds of the shares and take out a new loan to be used for the building work.

Only or main residence   The land must be used as the only or main residence of the borrower. Whether land is used as a person's 'only or main residence' is a question of fact and degree and, if the borrower has more than one residence, he cannot choose which is to be treated for income tax purposes as the main residence (compare the CGT exemption, [**16.61**]). The amount of time spent in the residence is only one of the facts to be taken into account. In *Frost v Feltham* (1981) the taxpayer was the tenant and licensee of a public house in Essex which he was required by the terms of his employment to occupy (to some extent the actual decision in this case has been overtaken by the rules on job-related accommodation introduced after the case was decided and which are considered below). He bought a house in Wales with the aid of a mortgage on which he successfully claimed interest relief even though he only visited the house irregularly; the deciding factor was his intention to use the house as his main residence.

> 'If someone lives in two houses the question which does he use as the principal or more important one cannot be determined solely by reference to the way in which he divides his time between the two. I can test that by reference to an example far removed from the facts of this case and the conditions of our own times. In his "Lives of the Lord Chancellors", Lord Campbell tells how Lord Eldon was often prevented by the burdens of his office from visiting his estate in Encombe in Dorset for long periods at a time. Sometimes he was only able to get down there for three weeks or so in the year, for the partridge shooting in September. True it was that Lord Eldon also had a good house in Hamilton Place, but it could not really have been suggested that he did not use Encombe as his principal or more important residence.' (Nourse J in *Frost v Feltham*.)

In practice, the Revenue takes the view that the accommodation should be furnished and more or less in a state of readiness for permanent occupation if relief is to be available. Temporary absences of up to one year are ignored. So too is an absence of up to four years caused by the borrower having to move elsewhere in the UK or abroad because of his job. In practice, he can string together several four-year periods provided that he returns for a period of three months between each (ESC A27).

Where the taxpayer is required by his employment to live in job-related accommodation, he can claim relief for interest paid on another property, even though it is not his main residence, provided that at the time of the payment it is used by the borrower as a residence (for instance at weekends); or he intends to use it in due course as his only or main residence, for instance after the job ends: TA 1988 s 356. The accommodation is job-related if it fulfils the conditions laid down in TA 1988 s 145. This relaxation of the residence rule for job-related accommodation also applies to interest paid by the self-employed taxpayer or his spouse who is bound, under a contract made at arm's length, to carry on his business on the land of another and to occupy property provided by that person except where the accommodation is provided either by a company in which he or his spouse has a material interest or by his or his spouse's firm (TA 1988 s 356(3), (5)).   **[4.56]**

£30,000 limit   When a main residence is purchased by a single taxpayer relief is available to him for interest on a qualifying loan of up to £30,000. Hence, insofar as the loan exceeds £30,000 the interest on the excess is disallowed. If the borrower has more than one qualifying loan, they are aggregated for the purpose of the £30,000 limit and interest on earlier loans is relieved before interest on later ones. ('Top-ups' involving a higher rate of interest should be signed first, therefore, although, if it is part of a single contract to purchase, the Revenue would treat both loans as made on the same day.)

EXAMPLE 4.7

Balthazar has two loans subject to different interest rates—loan 1 is for £25,000 at 12.5% pa and loan 2 (taken out after the first loan) is for £10,000 at 15% pa.
    Balthazar's interest qualifying for relief in a full tax year would be:

		£
£25,000 at 12.5%	=	3,125
£10,000 at 15% $\times \dfrac{30,000 - 25,000}{10,000}$	=	750
Total interest relief		£3,875

If the two loans were replaced by a single loan, or if both loans were taken out on the same day, the higher interest rate charged on the second loan would be spread evenly thereby enhancing the relief available, ie:

(a) *Total interest paid*

		£
£25,000 at 12.5%	=	3,125
£10,000 at 15%	=	1,500
		£4,625

(b) *Total interest relief*

$$£4,625 \times \frac{30,000}{35,000} \qquad = \quad £3,964$$

   In the case of bridging loans, to which TA 1988 s 354 applies, each residence is treated separately for determining the £30,000 ceiling (see [**4.59**]).
   TA 1988 s 355(5) prevents relief in the case of artificial transactions; in particular, where the vendor and purchaser are husband and wife.   [**4.57**]

'Negative equity' (TA 1988, s 357A-C)   These provisions enable relief to be available where an existing mortgage is not repaid on a move but is resecured on the new home. Formerly interest on that loan ceased to qualify since the loan was not used to purchase the property which is now the borrower's home.   [**4.58**]

The residence basis   For loans taken out before 1 August 1988 to purchase the borrower's main residence, the £30,000 limit applied to each borrower although spouses were treated as one person for these purposes and therefore only entitled to a single relief. As a result unmarried couples could obtain twice as much interest relief as a married couple and accordingly for loans taken out on or after that date (see TA 1988 s 356C(3) for when a loan is made for these purposes) the £30,000 limit on relief is given *per residence* irrespective of the number of borrowers (the 'residence basis'). The available relief must be divided between the various borrowers as illustrated in the following examples:

EXAMPLE 4.8

Cain and Abel have qualifying loans on their main residence of £30,000 and £50,000 respectively. On the assumption that the loans were taken out:

(1) *Pre-1 August 1988:* Cain and Abel will both be entitled to interest relief on a loan up to £30,000 so that Cain will obtain full relief for the interest that he pays whilst Abel will be left with no relief on £20,000 of his loan.

(2) *On or after 1 August 1988:* the £30,000 limit is shared equally between Cain and Abel so that both will get relief on a loan of up to £15,000. Accordingly, Cain will be left with no relief on a loan of £15,000 and Abel with no relief on a loan of £35,000.

Dividing up the £30,000 qualifying amount equally, as in *Example 4.9*, may result in a borrower being allocated an amount which exceeds his loan. In such cases the excess is re-divided between the other borrowers whose loans exceeded their original allocation.

EXAMPLE 4.9

Sing, Sang and Song have jointly purchased a main residence so that, *prima facie*, each is entitled to interest relief on a loan of £10,000. Assume, however, that Sing's loan was £6,000, Sang's loan £22,000, and Song's loan £18,000.

Sing can therefore only use £6,000 of his allocated £10,000 whilst Sang and Song will receive no relief on loans of £12,000 and £8,000 respectively. Accordingly, the unused portion of Sing's allocation (£4,000) will be transferred to the others so that Sang gets an extra relief of £2,400 (ie $\frac{12,000}{20,000} \times £4,000$) while Song gets an extra £1,600 ($\frac{8,000}{20,000} \times £4,000$).

If a husband and wife jointly purchase property with other borrowers they are treated as separate persons for the purposes of calculating each borrower's share of the £30,000 limit and once this computation is made the normal rules for allocating interest relief between spouses, discussed at [**40.28**], apply. [**4.59**]

b) *Exceptions where relief is given despite non-occupation of the property*

In the following cases interest relief is available despite the fact that the property is not used as the only or main residence when the loan is acquired.

First, when the property becomes the main residence within 12 months after acquiring the loan (TA 1988 s 355(1)). This caters for property which requires substantial improvement before it can be occupied.

Secondly, where the taxpayer has obtained bridging finance, he will continue to receive interest relief on the loan on his old property for 12 months after acquiring a 'new loan' on the new property which he occupies as his main residence, provided that the new loan is acquired for a qualifying purpose and that he intends to sell the old property (TA 1988 ss 354(5), 357). Notice that the 'new loan' will not itself qualify for relief unless the new property is actually used as the individual's only or main residence; an intention to do so does not suffice (see *Hughes v Viner* (1985)). The 12-month period may, by concession, be extended if the taxpayer can show that he has been unable to sell the old property. In this situation, the loans are not aggregated and each loan is considered separately in applying the £30,000 ceiling. The relief for delay in occupying a new house and for bridging finance will often be useful when a couple get married. FA 1993 extended this relief to cases where the borrower moves into rented or other accommodation (whether in the UK or elsewhere) and to borrowers aged 65 and over for interest on a loan used to purchase a life annuity (see [**4.51**]) who leave their home but are unable to sell it.

Special rules apply to exempt from tax the benefit where an employee has to move house because of his employment and receives a bridging loan or a reimbursement of net loan interest from his employer (see [**5.150**]). In this case the reimbursement will not be taxed but, of course, the employee will not be allowed to deduct the interest from his taxable income!   [**4.60**]

EXAMPLE 4.10

In the following cases Hugh and Wilma (H and W) are newly-weds. Assume that the loans referred to are for a qualifying purpose and do not (individually) exceed £30,000.

Case A   H pays interest on loan 1 on a house which before marriage was his main residence. After marriage, it becomes the matrimonial home. H continues to receive interest relief.

Case B   As in *Case A* above, except that H and W take out a new loan, loan 2, to purchase a house which becomes the matrimonial home. H continues to receive interest relief on loan 1 (as well as on loan 2) for 12 months from obtaining loan 2 so long as he intends to sell his original house.

Case C   H and W both have loans (1 and 2) on houses acquired before their marriage. They take out another loan, loan 3, on a house which becomes the matrimonial home. By concession they will continue to receive interest relief on loans 1 and 2 (as well as on loan 3) for 12 months from taking out loan 3.

Case D   As in *Case C* above except that H and W do not acquire a new house, but occupy W's existing house as the matrimonial home. TA 1988 s 354(5) cannot apply to this situation because H and W have not taken out a 'new' loan. However, by ESC A35 they continue to receive relief on loans 1 and 2 provided that the property which is not the matrimonial home is sold within 12 months of H ceasing to live there.

Case E   As in *Case C* above except that H and W occupy another property as their matrimonial home without taking out a new loan. H and W lose interest relief on loans 1 and 2 once they cease to occupy those properties. Neither para 6, the concession, nor ESC A35 apply to these facts.

c) *Method of obtaining tax relief—the MIRAS scheme (TA 1988 ss 369–379)*

Tax relief for interest payments is generally given under the so-called MIRAS scheme so that the interest payments can be ignored in computing the taxpayer's income tax liability. Prior to 6 April 1991 relief was also available against income tax at the higher rate and this was given by permitting the taxpayer to deduct the gross interest payment as a charge on his income.

MIRAS covers the majority of mortgage interest payments because it applies whenever:
(1) a 'qualifying borrower' (basically all individuals);
(2) makes a payment of relevant loan interest, which is defined as interest paid in the UK after 5 April 1983 on a loan made for a qualifying purpose; and
(3) the payment is to a 'qualifying lender'. This term covers all bodies who normally make such loans (eg building societies, local authorities and housing associations).

Lenders are also obliged to apply MIRAS to new loans which exceed £30,000 so that tax relief at source is given on that part of the loan which is within the limit (TA 1988 s 373).

EXAMPLE 4.11

Sebastian, who has taxable income of £13,400, pays £200 relevant loan interest to the Dodgy Building Society each month. He satisfies his obligation to the building society by paying them each month:

	£
Gross payment	200
Less: sum equivalent to tax at 15%	30
Payment to building society	£170

The building society recover the amount deducted by Sebastian (ie £30) from the Revenue (s 369(6)). Sebastian's income tax liability for the year on his income of £13,400 is calculated in the usual way ignoring the interest payment which has been relieved at source.

The operation of MIRAS does not increase the cost of mortgages since, instead of tax relief, the borrower obtains a reduction in the interest payments made. However, there is a timing difference, in that the payer will pay less to his lender each month, thereby increasing his cashflow. MIRAS is positively advantageous to the taxpayer in the (unlikely) circumstances that his personal allowances exceed his income left after deducting the interest payments. Before the introduction of MIRAS the result would have been a loss of personal allowances, but now unused allowances can effectively be set against income on which the taxpayer would otherwise be subject to income tax (see TA 1988 s 369(4), which was designed to compensate for the abolition of the mortgage option scheme).

EXAMPLE 4.12

Bertrand, a single man, has income for 1997-98 of £3,000 and pays relevant loan interest of £3,000 for the year. Therefore, he pays the lender £2,550 and retains £450 (giving him relief at 15%).

But he has unused allowances of £4,045 so that by s 369(4):

	£
Sum assessed under s 369(3)	3,000
Less: unused allowance	4,045
Sum taxed	Nil

This may be contrasted with the position of Bertrand in 1982-83 (ie before the introduction of MIRAS) when, assuming the same figures, he would have paid no income tax since his interest payments (£3,000) would have been deducted from his income (£3,000). His personal reliefs for the year would have been wasted. In 1982-83 Bertrand would have made gross payments to the lender of £3,000 instead of £2,550 under MIRAS. As a result, Bertrand is better off under the MIRAS scheme by £450.

A taxpayer is not subject to UK income tax if he is working abroad and his emoluments from the employment are subject to the 100% foreign income deduction, TA 1988 s 193(1). Nevertheless, the MIRAS scheme can still apply to interest payments made by such a taxpayer, provided that the loan is for a 'qualifying purpose'; this will be the case where, for example, the borrower is required by his job to be absent from the UK for up to four years because such absence does not prevent the property from being his only or main residence for the purpose of claiming income tax relief (see ESC A27). **[4.61]**

EXAMPLE 4.13

(1)   Adam is an engineer. He has bought a house in the UK with the aid of a mortgage for £35,000 from the Roxy Building Society who (as it is a pre-April 1987 loan) have not elected to have MIRAS applied to that loan.

  (i)   *Whilst he is working in the UK:* interest is paid gross and Adam obtains relief in his PAYE coding or assessment.

  (ii) *He is absent from the UK on a two-year contract in the Middle East:* Adam satisfies the requirements of ESC A27 so that the property remains his main residence. However, his earnings in the Middle East attract no UK income tax because of the 100% deduction (above) and Adam has no other UK income. Accordingly, he must continue to pay the interest gross and will obtain no tax relief thereon.

(2)   Take the same facts as in (1) but assume that the Roxy Building Society have opted to bring loans over £30,000 within MIRAS. As long as the loan remains outstanding, Adam will pay interest on the relevant portion net (ie after deduction of basic rate tax). Thus he will continue to receive relief whilst he works abroad even though he has no UK taxable income.

d) *Loans for home improvements*

Interest formerly qualified for relief if the loan was used for the improvement of the main residence of the borrower, his dependent relative, or his former or separated spouse. An improvement involved expenditure of a capital nature rather than mere maintenance or repair and the relief was only given if the loan was so used within a reasonable time of being made. In practice, over 85% of such loans were taken out for improvements which did not involve any extension to the property (most were for the installation of double glazing or central heating). This relief is not available for interest paid on loans taken out after 5 April 1988. Relief continues to be given for interest paid on qualifying loans taken out on or before that date although it will not be available in the case of a replacement loan taken out subsequently.   **[4.62]**

e) *Dependent relatives*

Similarly, interest paid on loans taken out for the purchase of property used as the main residence of a dependent relative or former or separated spouse of the borrower formerly qualified for tax relief. Although the relief was not limited to the provision of a single house for all dependent relatives (so that theoretically so long as the borrower had enough dependent relatives a number of houses could be purchased) in practice, the £30,000 ceiling on relief, which applied per borrower, meant that it was unlikely that more than one such residence would attract relief. Interest relief was also withdrawn for interest paid after 5 April 1988 subject, however, to continuation of relief where the relevant loan was made before 6 April 1988. This transitional relief will be available so long as the property remains occupied by the same dependent relative or spouse who was in occupation on 6 April 1988.

Relief had also been available for interest paid by personal representatives of a deceased borrower when the relevant property had been used by the deceased as his main residence at the date of death if, at the time when the personal representatives paid the interest, it was occupied as the main residence of a dependent relative of the deceased. Relief ceased in this case as well unless the deceased had died before 6 April 1988 and the property concerned was occupied by the relative as his main residence before that date.   **[4.63]**

5 Training (FA 1991 ss 32–33 amended by FA 1996)

The costs incurred by an individual in respect of a qualifying course of vocational training qualify for tax relief at basic and higher rates. Basic rate relief is given by deduction from the study and examination fees paid (in the same way as MIRAS relief) whilst tax relief at the higher rate is given on a claim being submitted to the individual's tax office. Relief is given whether or not the individual obtains the qualification! Detailed administrative arrangements are set out in SI 1992/746 and the qualifying courses are those leading to National Vocational Qualifications at levels 1–5 (these qualifications being accredited by two government supported bodies: the National Council for Vocational Qualifications in England, Wales and Northern Ireland and the Scottish Vocational Education Council). 16, 17, and 18-year-olds receiving full-time education at school are excluded. Because of the way in which relief is given (at source by deduction from the fees) it will be available even for the trainee with no taxable income: hence unemployed people retraining with a view to returning to work will be able to obtain some benefit from the new relief. FA 1996 extended the relief to most full-time courses of between four weeks and one year which are intended to retrain for employment whether or not there is a link with NVQs and SVQs. *However*, only trainees aged 30 and over can benefit (especially those taking specified courses such as MBAs). The intention of the change is to put those paying for their own retraining on an equal footing with those paid for by a (former) employer (see TA 1988 s 589 and [5.119]).   [4.64]

6 Class 4 national insurance and pension contributions

Prior to 6 April 1996 one-half of the Class 4 national insurance contributions paid by a self-employed person each year was deductible in arriving at his total income (TA 1988 s 617(5)). Although not strictly a charge on income, this sum was deducted at this stage of the income tax calculation. As a simplification measure this deduction was withdrawn for the tax year 1996–97 and as a *quid pro quo* the Class 4 rate was cut.

Although an employer cannot deduct the national insurance contributions that he makes for his employees in arriving at his total income, these sums will be an allowable expense of the business (see [6.128]). An employee's contributions do not qualify for relief from income tax.

Appendix IV discusses the provision of both occupational and personal pensions. In general terms, contributions by an employee or, in the case of a personal pension, the relevant individual, are deductible from his income for lower, basic and higher rate purposes.   [4.65]–[4.80]

IV TOTAL INCOME *(Step 3)*

Charges are deducted from income before any other deductions and the resultant sum is 'total income'. Insofar as charges exceed statutory income, the unabsorbed charge receives no tax relief and cannot be carried forward to a future year. After charges, the individual deducts personal reliefs from total income to arrive at his taxable income. However, losses may be available and will be deducted before personal reliefs. Notice that it is the total income figure before any such deduction that is used to calculate (where applicable) the age allowance and (where available) the one-sixth for life assurance premium relief (see [4.151]).   [4.81]

Loss relief (TA 1988 ss 380–381)

Sometimes losses arising under a particular Schedule are deductible only in computing profits from the same source. Such losses, therefore, affect the calculation of the individual's statutory income by reducing income from that source.

EXAMPLE 4.14

Anita receives a salary as a lecturer (Schedule E) of £14,000 pa. She also owns a house in Chelsea which she rents to nurses from the Chelsea Hospital. In the current tax year her allowable expenses on the property under Schedule A exceeded her Schedule A rental income by £1,000. Her statutory income for the current year is:

	£
Schedule E	14,000
Schedule A (loss £1,000)	Nil
Statutory income	£14,000

Anita cannot deduct her £1,000 Schedule A loss from income from any other source. All she can do is carry the loss forward to a subsequent year and deduct it from Schedule A profits of that year. Thus, if in the following year her rental income exceeds her allowable expenses under Schedule A by £2,000, Anita's statutory income is:

	£	£
Schedule E		14,000
Schedule A: profit	2,000	
Less: loss c/f	1,000	
		1,000
Statutory income		£15,000

Where the individual makes a loss in his trade, profession or vocation, however, he may choose to deduct that loss from his total income before deducting personal reliefs (see TA 1988 ss 380–381 and [**7.41**]). The danger with claiming this loss relief is that it may so reduce total income that personal allowances are unused. [**4.82**]–[**4.100**]

EXAMPLE 4.15

Andrew is a barrister (Schedule D Case II) and a part-time lecturer (Schedule E) with a salary for the current year of £14,000 pa. He pays £1,000 pa to charity by deed of covenant. In the current tax year he makes a loss in his first year at the bar of £5,000 which he chooses under TA 1988 s 380 to deduct from his total income. His income tax calculation (in part) for the current tax year is as follows:

	£
Schedule E	14,000
Schedule D (loss £5,000)	Nil
Statutory income	14,000
Less: charge on income	1,000
Total income	13,000
Less: loss (TA 1988 s 380)	5,000
	£8,000

Andrew has £8,000 income from which he can deduct his personal reliefs.

V PERSONAL RELIEFS (TA 1988 s 256) *(Step 4 or Step 6)*

1 General

Individuals resident in the UK can deduct certain personal reliefs from their total income. The availability of the reliefs depends not on the type of income involved, but on the taxpayer's personal circumstances. He must claim his reliefs each year by completing the section headed 'Allowances' in the income tax return. If personal allowances exceed the total income of the taxpayer, the surplus is unused and cannot be carried forward for use in future years. The position of a taxpayer who makes interest payments falling within the MIRAS scheme and who has surplus allowances has already been discussed at [**4.61**].

Prior to 6 April 1994 *all* personal reliefs operated by way of deduction from total income. From that date, however, certain allowances and reliefs have been given by subtracting from the individual's total tax liability 20% of the allowance for 1994-95 and only 15% of the allowance for 1995-96 and subsequent years (see further *Step 6*, below).

A summary of the personal reliefs available for 1997-98 is set out below. Since 1983-84, certain reliefs (marked with a ●) are linked to increases in the Retail Prices Index between December preceding the year of assessment and the previous December.

- Personal allowance: £4,045
- Personal allowance (age 65-74)* £5,220
- Personal allowance (age 75 and over)* £5,400
- Married couple's allowance £1,830
- Married couple's allowance (age 65-74)*† £3,185
- Married couple's allowance (age 75 and over)*† £3,225
- Additional personal allowance (for a single person who has responsibility for a child)† £1,830
- Widow's bereavement allowance† £1,830
- Blind person's relief £1,280
- Income limit for age-related allowances £15,600

> *These allowances are reduced if the taxpayer's income exceeds the income limit.
> †Allowances where relief is restricted to 20% in 1994-95 and 15% in 1995-96 *et seq.*

In certain situations non-UK residents may claim personal reliefs in respect of their UK income (see TA 1988 s 278 and [**13.71**]). [**4.101**]

2 The reliefs

Personal allowance (TA 1988 s 257(1)) The personal allowance (for 1997-98, £4,045) is available to all taxpayers resident in the UK including minor children. The allowance can be set against any form of income but any surplus is wasted since it cannot be used in any other tax year nor transferred to any other taxpayer. [**4.102**]

The married couple's allowance (TA 1988 s 257A) This relief (£1,830 for 1997-98) can be claimed by a man who is married and living with his wife for *any part* of the tax year. The use of the allowance and how it is divided between the married couple is considered at [**38.24**]. For these purposes a couple are treated as living together unless they are separated under a court order, written deed, or are in fact separated in such circumstances that the separation is likely to be permanent. Accordingly this allowance cannot be claimed by a husband who though separated from his wife continues to maintain her: see further [**41.6**].

The availability of (one!) higher married allowance in a case where the man had two wives was confirmed in *Nabi v Heaton* (1983) but in *Rignell v Andrews* (1990) a taxpayer who had lived with the same woman for 11 years and who treated her as his common law wife was considered not to be married and therefore not entitled to a higher allowance.   [**4.103**]

Additional personal allowance (TA 1988 s 259)   This is also known as the single parent family allowance, which as the name suggests is intended to alleviate the financial position of the 'one-parent' family. Relief is £1,830 for 1997–98 and is available to a woman who is not *throughout* the tax year married and living with her husband and to a man who is either not married or not living with his wife for the whole or any part of the tax year. To qualify for the relief the taxpayer must have a 'qualifying child' living with him for the whole or part of the year of assessment. A *qualifying child* is one who is:

(1) born in that tax year; or
(2) under the age of 16 at the start of the tax year; or
(3) over 16, but attending a full-time educational course or undergoing vocational training with an employer for at least two years;

and who is:

(a) the taxpayer's own natural legitimate or legitimated issue (including a stepchild and adopted child under 18 at the date of adoption); or
(b) any other child born in, or under 18 at the beginning of the year and maintained at the taxpayer's expense for the whole or part of the year (legal custody is not required).

Only one allowance is available to any one taxpayer, regardless of the number of qualifying children that he may have. When more than one person is entitled to the allowance (for instance, because they each maintain the child for a part of the year) the one allowance is apportioned between them, but not more than £1,830 can be received in total.

A claimant need not be living alone to receive the allowance provided that the above conditions are fulfilled. Cohabitees, who have produced more than one offspring, were formerly both entitled to a full allowance in respect of one child, provided that they could convince the Revenue that they were each separately responsible for the maintenance of one child. However, cohabitees are restricted to only one allowance which will be given in respect of the youngest child.

A married man entitled to the married couple's allowance may claim the additional personal allowance if his wife was totally incapacitated mentally or physically throughout the tax year and there are qualifying children. There is no equivalent increase in allowances where the husband is similarly incapacitated.   [**4.104**]

Age allowance (TA 1988 s 257(2))   Personal allowances increase with the age of the taxpayer:

(1) *up to 65* the personal allowance and (if appropriate) the married couple's allowance are available;
(2) *between 65 and 75* a higher allowance is available and for taxpayers aged over 75 the allowances are further increased.

The higher allowances are given by reference to the tax year in which the 65th or 75th birthday falls—curiously they are available even if the taxpayer dies before that birthday!

The personal allowance depends solely on the age of the relevant taxpayer. From £4,045 it increases to £5,220 (for taxpayers aged 65-74 in the tax year) and then to £5,400 (for those aged 75 and over in the tax year).

By contrast the level of the married couple's allowance depends on the age of the *elder spouse* in the relevant tax year. The allowance rises from £1,830 to £3,185 (where the elder spouse is aged 65-74) and finally to £3,225 (elder spouse 75 and over).

These higher allowances for taxpayers aged 65 and over are subject to an income limit: this limit (currently £15,600) is the same for all taxpayers, male and female, married and single. Provided that the taxpayer's total income (see [**4.81**]) is below this figure *full allowances are due.* However, if total income exceeds £15,600 then the age-related allowances are reduced by half the difference between the taxpayer's total income and the limit (ie the reduction is £1 of allowance for every £2 of income above £15,600). At worst, this reduction will wipe out the higher allowances: no taxpayer, however, will have his personal allowance reduced below the level for those aged under 65 (ie £4,045 for the current year). So far as the married couple's allowance is concerned, the reduction is calculated solely by reference to the husband's total income and the allowance will only be reduced *after* the husband's higher personal allowance has been wiped out. At worst, the reduction will leave the husband with the basic married couple allowance of £1,830. Note, finally, that married couples cannot transfer any unused part of their income limits to each other. [**4.105**]

EXAMPLE 4.16

(1) Fred is 50; his wife, Wilma, is 73. Fred has income of £8,000 pa; Wilma £15,900.
  (a) Fred is entitled to a personal allowance of £4,045. Wilma, because of her age, will qualify for an allowance of £5,220 but this will be reduced as follows:

  Wilma's income above £15,600: £300
  One-half of the excess above £15,600: £150.
  Reduce full allowance by £150 = £5,070.

  (b) The married couple's allowance will be calculated by reference to Wilma's age and so will be £3,185. Despite Wilma's income, this allowance will not be reduced since Fred's income is below the £15,600 limit.
(2) Robert is aged 78 with an income of £18,500; his wife, Alison, is aged 68 with an income of £3,000.
  (a) Alison will be entitled to a personal allowance of £5,220 of which £2,220 will be wasted.
  (b) Robert's personal allowance of £5,400 will be reduced to the basic allowance of £4,045 because his income exceeds the £15,600 threshold by more than £2,710. The married couple's allowance (given by reference to Robert's age) of £3,185 will also be reduced—in this case by £95 to £3,090 because Robert's surplus total income after reducing his personal allowance exceeds the threshold by £190 (ie total income of £18,500 will have been reduced by £2,710 thereby reducing Robert's personal allowance and leaving an excess of £95 to reduce the married couple's allowance).

Widow's bereavement allowance (TA 1988 s 262) Where a married man dies in a year of assessment in which he was living with his wife, his widow is entitled to an additional allowance both in the year of his death and in the following year provided she has not remarried before then. This allowance is £1,830 for 1997-98 and widows with dependent children are also entitled to the single parent allowance (see above). [**4.106**]

Blind person's allowance (TA 1988 s 265(1), (2))   A taxpayer who is a registered blind person for the whole or part of the year of assessment receives an additional relief (for 1997–98) of £1,280. If a husband and wife are both registered blind they can each claim the blind person's allowance and if they are living together either can transfer any surplus allowance to the other.   **[4.107]**

Child benefit   As from April 1979, the mother (usually) has received tax-free child benefit for each child who is under 16, or under 19 and receiving full-time education at a recognised educational establishment. There are no child tax allowances.   **[4.108]-[4.120]**

VI   METHOD OF CHARGING TAXABLE INCOME

1   **Rates of tax** (*Step* 5)

Income tax is charged on an individual's taxable income for 1997–98 at the following rates:

	Income band
On the first £4,100 at 20% (lower rate)	£1–£4,100
On the next £22,000 at 23% (basic rate)	£4,101–£26,100
On the remainder at 40% (higher rate)	Excess over £26,100

Since 1982–83 increases in the rate bands have been linked to the increase in the Retail Prices Index between the December before the year of assessment and the previous December. The indexed rises are, however, subject to a negative resolution of Parliament (ie they occur 'unless Parliament otherwise determines'; TA 1988 s 1(4)). Prior to 1988–89 a relatively complex rate structure existed with the top rate being 60%; from that year until 1991–92 there were only two rates of tax (the basic 25% and the higher 40% rate); 1992–93 witnessed the introduction of the 20% lower rate band. F(No 2)A 1997 introduces an (almost!) unbelievably complex structure for the taxation of dividends paid on or after 6 April 1999.

It should be remembered that where payments are *made by* the taxpayer under deduction of tax at source (eg annual payments to charity and certain interest payments) those payments are added back to the taxpayer's taxable income for basic rate tax purposes, thereby effectively increasing the figure chargeable to basic rate tax above £26,100. When payments are *received by* the taxpayer after deduction at source, the tax due from the payee will be reduced by the tax already paid on his behalf by the payer. 15% of the amount of certain allowances and reliefs are deducted from the tax due and this is considered in the next section.   **[4.121]**

EXAMPLE 4.17

Brian has a statutory income for 1997–98 of £40,000. He makes covenanted payments to charity of £3,000 pa and is entitled to a personal allowance of £4,045. His income tax calculation is as follows:

	£
Statutory income	40,000
Less: charge on income	3,000
Total income	37,000
Less: personal reliefs	4,045
Taxable income for basic and higher rates	£32,955

Tax payable:	£
First £4,100 at 20%	820
Next £22,000 at 23%	5,060
Balance of £6,855 at 40%	2,742
Add back for basic rate tax only payment	
to charity £3,000 × 23%	690
	£9,312

2   Enterprise Investment Scheme (EIS): FA 1994 s 137; Sch 15 amended by FA 1995 reviving TA 1988 ss 289–312

The Business Expansion Scheme (BES) came to an end on 31 December 1993; EIS is in a sense a replacement although the tax relief that it affords is less generous and the scheme is more closely targeted in an attempt to avoid some of the pitfalls which affected BES.   **[4.122]**

a) *The relief*

EIS applies to new shares issued in qualifying companies on or after 1 January 1994 and provides income tax relief at 20% (only!) on qualifying investments of up to £100,000 in any tax year. To calculate the available relief an individual's taxable income is arrived at by deducting charges on income and those allowances which afford relief at the highest rate (ie the personal allowance and the blind person's allowance). EIS relief is then given *after* venture capital relief (see **[4.131]**) but *before* those allowances attracting relief at only 15%.

Any gain made by an investor on the eventual disposal of his qualifying shares, provided that these are held for five years, is exempt from CGT. If the shares are sold at a loss (on cost) the cost of the shares is treated as reduced by the EIS relief given (TCGA 1992 s 150A). Subject to that, if the loss cannot be offset against CGT gains, relief can be obtained under TA 1988 s 574 against the taxpayer's income.

EXAMPLE 4.18

Eddy Investor puts £100,000 into an EIS investment in June 1994. In the tax year 2000/2001 he sells the shares for either (a) £150,000 or (b) £50,000. His tax position is as follows:
(1) *The original investment:* EIS relief at 20% was available so that Eddy's net investment cost was £80,000.
(2) *The sale for £150,000:* Given that the shares have been owned for five years the gain is tax free.
(3) *The sale for £50,000:* A capital loss of £50,000 minus £20,000 (being the EIS relief) is available for offset against Eddy's chargeable gains in 2000/2001 failing which against his income under TA 1988 s 574.

A form of carry-back relief is available for shares issued before 6 October in the tax year. This enables the lower of one-half of the investment or £15,000 to qualify for relief in the preceding tax year subject to the limits for that year not being exceeded.   **[4.123]**

EXAMPLE 4.19

Argent makes the following investments:

9 December 1993	X Ltd	£30,000
9 July 1994	Y Ltd	£24,000
1 October 1994	Z Ltd	£86,000

His tax position is as follows:

Tax year 1993-94: BES relief was limited to investments of up to £40,000 pa. EIS was introduced as from 1 January 1994 but relief for the tax year 1993-94 was restricted to the BES level for all investments made during that year. Accordingly whilst the December investment qualifies for BES relief at 40% Argent can only carry back relief of £10,000 for his investment in Y Ltd. This will then attract 20% EIS relief in 1993-94.

Tax year 1994-95: Assuming that £10,000 of the Y Ltd investment is carried back to 1993-94, EIS relief is available on the remainder of the Y Ltd investment and all of the investment in Z Ltd.

b) *Qualifying individuals*

EIS relief is available to individual investors who are liable for UK income tax, whether or not they are actually resident in the UK, who are not connected with the company (it is not available to trustees or companies). Broadly an individual is so connected if he, or an associate of his, is an employee or paid director of the company; or if he and his associates possess more than 30% of the capital (including loan capital) or voting power of the company (see amended ESC A76 dealing with subscriber shares). For these purposes an associate excludes brothers and sisters but otherwise has a close company meaning (see [**28.92**]) whilst a director is not debarred from the relief if the only payments that he receives from the company are for travelling and other tax deductible expenses. Relief will not therefore be available in the case of management or employee buy-outs (see generally TA 1988 s 291). Certain individuals (commonly called 'business angels') will, however, qualify for the tax relief even though they are connected with the company by being paid directors. (They must not, however, be connected with a company or its trade at any time *before* the shares were issued.) Precisely how these rules on business angels are intended to operate is far from clear: the drafting in FA 1994 leaves much to be desired! IR 137 (a booklet published in the Inland Revenue's Business Series) comments that:

> 'the "business angel" must have subscribed for and been issued with the shares on which income tax relief is to be claimed before the first day for which he or she receives payment as a director ... the remuneration must be reasonable for the services ... perform[ed]. What qualifies as reasonable remuneration in any particular case depends on the facts. The level of remuneration will not be challenged unless there are grounds for supposing that it is excessive in the circumstances.'
>
> **[4.124]**

c) *Qualifying company*

The relevant company must be unquoted; it must not be controlled by another company and must not have an unqualifying subsidiary. It can be a holding company only if its subsidiaries qualify. It need not be UK resident. The company must exist wholly for the purpose of carrying on one or more qualifying trades and generally must do so for three years from the date of issue of the shares or from the commencement of the qualifying activity (whichever is later). **[4.125]**

d) *Eligible shares*

These must be issued on or after 1 January 1994 and during five years from the date of the issue there can be no preferential rights to the dividends or to the company's assets on a winding up, and there must be no right to redeem the shares. The shares must be fully paid and there must be no loans connected with those shares (see SP 3/94). Qualifying companies can raise up to £1m a year through the scheme: in the event that they raise more, EIS relief is not given on the excess. **[4.126]**

e) *Qualifying activities*

Although the company need not be incorporated or resident in the UK, it must carry on trading activities wholly or mainly in the UK if it is to qualify (see SP 3/94). Those activities must either be carried on or intended to be carried on and actually carried on within two years of the date of issue of the shares. Broadly speaking the categories of qualifying trade are the same as those under BES. Accordingly certain activities are prohibited including dealing in shares, securities or land; dealing in goods otherwise than in the course of an ordinary trade or wholesale or retail distribution; banking or other financial activities; provision of legal or accountancy services and leasing. Unlike BES, property development and farming is permitted. However, the BES trade which attracted most investment (the letting of residential property on assured tenancies) is not permitted under EIS.

Under BES there was a restriction which disqualified a company if *at any time* the value of its interests in land was greater than one-half of the value of the company's assets as a whole. In defence of this land and buildings rule it was argued that a trader should not be involved in property investment: he should rent his assets on short-term leases. This rule was carried over into EIS but it was abolished with effect from 29 November 1994. **[4.127]**

f) *Anti-avoidance*

TA 1988 s 289(6) contains an anti-avoidance rule founded on the experience of BES. It provides that relief is not given to an individual in respect of any shares unless those shares are subscribed for and issued for *bona fide* commercial purposes and not as part of a scheme or arrangement the main purpose of which (or one of the main purposes of which) is the avoidance of tax. **[4.128]**

g) *Double relief*

Reinvestment relief is not available for investment in EIS shares and nor can EIS shares be replacement assets for roll-over relief on the disposal of shares to an ESOP (TCGA 1992 s 164M). Interest relief is not available on loans to acquire EIS shares (see **[4.44]**).

However, FA 1995 enables an investor to defer a chargeable gain arising on *any* disposal if he subscribes for EIS shares in a period beginning one year before and ending three years after the disposal (TCGA 1992 s 150A–C: Sch 5B effective for disposals made on or after 29 November 1994: reinvestment relief is considered at **[16.121]**). Given that income tax relief at 20% applies to the investment the investor may qualify for total initial tax relief of up to 60%. The deferred gain will be brought into charge in certain circumstances: for instance, if the company ceases to qualify under the EIS legislation; if there is a disposal of the shares; or on a change in the residence status of the investor (Sch 5B para 3). **[4.129]**

h) *'Sharpening the focus'*

In his 1997 July Budget the Chancellor, Gordon Brown, announced that the focus of EIS (and the VCT scheme (see below)) would be sharpened to exclude arrangements where a substantial part of the return to investors is guaranteed or which are backed by property and so do not carry a sufficient level of risk. Changes to deal with guaranteed exits are to be introduced in the 1998 Finance Bill but taking effect from 2 July 1997 (although the change will not affect individuals who had already subscribed for EIS shares). So far as asset-backed schemes are concerned the list of excluded activities is to be amended after the government has considered the matter.   [**4.130**]

3 Venture capital trusts (TA 1988 ss 42AA and 332A; TCGA 1992 ss 151A, B; Sch 5C all inserted by FA 1995 s 71)

a) *Background*

The then Chancellor (Kenneth Clarke) announced in his 1993 November Budget that he proposed, subject to consultation, to introduce a further measure to assist small business by channelling investment into unlisted trading companies (the definition of which mirrors that in the EIS legislation). His proposal was to establish a new type of quoted investment company (called a venture capital trust: 'VCT'). Investors' dividends and gains on shares held in the VCT (which would be quoted on the Stock Exchange) would be free of income tax and CGT. The intention of using a VCT was to enable the investors' risk to be spread across a number of different companies. The original Consultation Document (published in March 1994) was not well received.   [**4.131**]

b) *FA 1995*

In the light of the adverse reaction the Chancellor announced substantial improvements to the original proposals in his 1994 Budget speech. As a result tax reliefs introduced by FA 1995 are as follows.   [**4.132**]

Income tax Individual investors are exempt from tax on dividends received from shares in a VCT (whether the shares have been acquired by subscription or purchase) and are also entitled to relief at 20% for investment in *new* ordinary shares in a VCT (this relief is limited to investments of up to £100,000 in any tax year and requires the shares to be retained for five years). The investment relief is given in priority to other deductions and reliefs available to the taxpayer which are given in terms of a tax offset (such as EIS relief). To the extent that full relief is not available it is not possible to carry forward any unused portion.   [**4.133**]

Capital gains The individual investor is exempt from CGT on disposals of ordinary shares in a VCT (whether the shares were acquired by subscription or purchase and so that losses will equally not be allowable) so long as the VCT was and has remained approved by the Revenue throughout; the consideration paid for the shares was eligible for income tax relief, and the disposal takes place on or after 6 April 1995. In addition (as with EIS) reinvestment relief may be available to an individual who after 5 April 1995 has crystallised a chargeable gain. That gain can be deferred either in whole or part by matching it against a subscription for eligible shares in a VCT subject to the £100,000 limit: that investment must take place within a qualifying period of 12 months before and 12 months after the chargeable event. This two-year period may straddle three tax years so that it may be possible to shelter a gain of up to £300,000. When both income tax and CGT reinvestment applies to a subscription for shares, the investor may therefore qualify for total initial tax relief of up to 60%.   [**4.134**]

The venture capital trust It must be quoted on the Stock Exchange and, in general, will enjoy the same exemption from corporation tax on its capital gains as investment trusts (TCGA 1992 s 100(1)). At least 70% of the investments of VCTs must be in unquoted trading companies with not more than 15% in any one company or group of companies. The investments may include both equity and loans with a minimum term of five years but at least 30%

of the investments must be in new ordinary shares. VCTs will initially have up to three years to meet the 70% unquoted trading company and 30% ordinary share requirements: investments in unquoted trading companies held by VCTs at a time when such companies become quoted may be treated as investments in unquoted trading companies for up to a further five years. Finally, there are requirements about the size of the companies in which VCTs may invest to qualify for tax relief: broadly speaking the value of the relevant company's assets (for this purpose the gross assets of a group of companies would be taken) immediately before the issue of the relevant holding must not exceed £10m.

The following example (taken from the IR Press Release of 4 January 1995) illustrates how the VCT rules operate. **[4.135]**

EXAMPLE 4.20

Mr Smith acquires existing VCT shares for the value of £30,000 on 1 May 1996. He is entitled to relief on distributions and CGT relief on disposals of those shares. He also subscribes £100,000 for new venture capital trust shares issued on 1 October 1996. He is entitled to relief on distributions and relief on disposals for £70,000 of that subscription. He can claim income tax relief on investment on the full £100,000 subscription. In addition, he can claim deferral relief in respect of his subscription for new shares on 1 October 1996 if he reinvests the chargeable gain accruing from the disposal of any asset between 1 October 1995 and 1 October 1997.

c) *'Sharpening the focus'*

Similar changes are envisaged to those considered above in connection with EIS (see [4.130]). In particular, the government is looking at 'protected VCTs' where a substantial part of their investments are in the form of guaranteed loans which greatly reduces the risk to the investor (see generally IR Press Release dated 2 July 1997). **[4.136]**

4 The 'income tax reduction' attributable to certain allowances and reliefs

Allowances From 6 April 1994 the following allowances attract tax relief by means of a reduction in the individual's total tax liability equal to a percentage of the value of the allowance. Initially 20%, the deduction is now (for 1997–98) at 15% of the allowance.

Allowance	*Value (£)* (1997–98)	*Reduction (£)* @ 15%
Married couple	1,830	274.5
Age related: 65–74	3,185	477.75
Age related: 75 and over	3,225	483.75
Widow's bereavement allowance	1,830	274.5
Additional personal allowance	1,830	274.5
Maintenance payments (save for pre-March 1988 agreements where the excess is not restricted)	1,830	274.5

[4.137]

Relief for interest   Mortgage interest relief is currently given at 15% (reduced to 10% from 6 April 1998) with the adjustment generally taking effect through the MIRAS system. Interest payments will not enter the calculation of a taxpayer's total income but instead his income tax liability will be reduced by 15% of the qualifying interest. Where relevant the reduction attributable to interest relief will be made before that attributable to the married couple's allowance (since if the latter allowance is unused in whole or in part the excess may be transferred to the other spouse). Elderly people who use a loan to buy a life annuity continue to qualify for tax relief at 23%. Again, this relief is now given as an income tax reduction in the rare cases where it is not within the MIRAS scheme.   **[4.138]**

Private medical insurance   Income tax relief was given for premiums paid by an individual under an 'eligible' private medical insurance contract. Contracts were only eligible if the person or persons insured were aged 60 or over when the payment was made and UK residents or, alternatively, a married couple both UK residents with at least one of them being 60 or over. If the contract was eligible, tax relief was then given to *whoever* made the payments. Accordingly, a wealthy son could obtain the relief on insurance taken out for his elderly parents. The actual mechanics of giving the tax relief were that the payer obtained relief by handing over reduced premiums to the insurer (in the same way as with MIRAS relief). Relief was limited to the basic rate and was given in terms of tax as a reduction in that individual's total tax liability. F(No 2)A 1997 abolished the relief in respect of payments on policies taken out or renewed on or after 2 July 1997.   **[4.139]**

EXAMPLE 4.21

In 1996–97 Viola had income from her employment (Schedule E) and from trading (Schedule D Case 1) amounting in all to £27,500. When tax on this sum was calculated she was entitled to obtain a reduction equivalent to 20% of the gross premiums payable on an eligible medical insurance contract which had been taken out for the benefit of her elderly parents. Accordingly if the gross premiums payable amounted to £100 per month (ie £1,200 pa) her tax liability was reduced by £288.

3   Dates for payment of tax

The due date for the payment of tax is 31 January following the year of assessment but with two interim payments falling due on 31 January in the year of assessment and 31 July immediately following that year (TMA 1970 Part VA).

   Tax is collected under the PAYE system of Schedule E at basic and higher rates on a current year basis (TA 1988 s 203). If the taxpayer's only source of income is from Schedule E, the correct amount of tax can be collected under this system necessitating no further adjustment. Otherwise, where the taxpayer has other sources of income, either too much or too little tax may be deducted, thereby necessitating an adjustment.   **[4.140]**

4   Specimen income tax calculation

Applying the steps listed at **[4.1]** it is now possible to calculate an individual's income tax liability for a tax year.   **[4.141]–[4.150]**

EXAMPLE 4.22

Benjamin has the following income for 1997–98:

		£
(i)	Lecturer (Schedule E)	12,000
(ii)	Author (Schedule D Case II)	3,000
(iii)	Part-time barman (Schedule E)	9,000
(iv)	Rents from houses (Schedule A)	11,000
(v)	Dividends (Schedule F) from Tenko Ltd (gross—including tax credit of £400)	2,000

Benjamin is married to Bertha. He is liable to make interest payments of £3,000 pa to the Wonky Building Society and £1,000 pa to the RSPCA (a registered charity).

	£
Schedule E	21,000
Schedule D Case II	3,000
Schedule A	11,000
Schedule F	2,000
Step 1: Statutory income from all sources	37,000
Step 2: Deduct charges on income:	
Annual payment	1,000
Step 3: Total income	36,000
Step 4: Deduct personal relief:	
Personal allowance	4,045
Step 5: Taxable income for lower, basic and higher rates	£31,955

	£
Tax chargeable at *Step 5:*	
First £4,100 at 20%	820
Next £22,000 at 23%	5,060
Balance of £5,855 at 40%	2,342
Tax on £31,955 at lower, basic and higher rate	8,222
Step 6: Deduct 15% of	
additional allowance (£1,830)	274.5
	7,947.5
Step 7: Give credit for tax deducted at source, ie from	
the dividends	400
	7,547.5
Step 8: *Add back for basic rate tax only sums paid to the RSPCA:	
ie £1,000 at 23%	230
Total tax due	£7,777.5

Notes: (1) Tax would have been deducted at source under the PAYE system in respect of the employment. Credit would be given for this tax in *Step 7*, thereby affecting the actual tax due from Benjamin by direct assessment. Nevertheless, Benjamin is actually liable (howsoever it is collected) for tax of £7,777.5 in 1997–98.

(2) The interest paid to the Wonky Building Society falls within the MIRAS scheme. With the restriction of tax relief to 15% the result is that, because Benjamin's payments to the building society are net of the tax relief, he has obtained full tax relief. Accordingly these payments can be ignored in the tax computation.

(3) The dividends are treated as the top slice of Benjamin's taxable income and accordingly suffer tax at the 40% higher rate with a credit limited to 20%.

(4) The married couple's allowance is only given tax relief at the 15% rate: hence it is deducted as shown at *Step 6*.

VII MISCELLANEOUS MATTERS

1 Life assurance premium relief (TA 1988 ss 266, 267, 273, 274)

a) *Premium relief on 'old' policies*

Tax relief is available for premiums paid by a UK resident on a 'qualifying' life assurance policy made *before* 14 March 1984 (TA 1988 ss 266–267). The relief is given by allowing the policyholder to deduct and retain 12½% of the premium, provided that the total annual premiums payable do not exceed the greater of £1,500 and one-sixth of his total income. The insurer reclaims the deduction from the Inland Revenue. The relief is not available for policies made after 13 March 1984, nor for those made before that date where the holder subsequently alters the policy to increase the benefits secured or to extend the term. In such cases premiums will be paid without the 12½% deduction.

The proceeds of a qualifying policy are not normally subject to income tax.   [4.151]

b) *Treatment of non-qualifying policies*

The typical example of a non-qualifying policy is the single premium insurance bond. Not only is no relief available on the sum invested, but any gain realised by the policyholder, net of premiums paid, which he obtains on encashment (eg on surrender or death) may be subject to income tax at higher rate (but not basic rate) subject to top slicing relief. He can make annual tax-free withdrawals. These withdrawals are allowed up to the value of the original investment so long as they do not exceed 5% of the premium paid for each year of the policy (ie the tax-free withdrawals cease after 20 years). Single premium bonds therefore provide shelter for income in the case of higher rate taxpayers.

The rate of corporation tax on the relevant profits (both income and capital) of a life assurance company is equal to the basic rate of income tax (23% in 1997–98). The policyholder is not charged on those accumulating profits.   [4.152]

c) *The Consultative Document*

This document—entitled 'Reform of policy holder taxation'— was published in November 1996 and envisages a wholly new approach. The closing date for comments was 30 April 1997.   [4.153]

2 Exemptions from income tax

There are a number of exemptions from income tax including the following. It should also be noted that a number of items are exempted from tax by virtue of Revenue Extra-Statutory Concessions (see pamphlet IR 1).   [4.154]

a) *Exempt organisations*

Certain organisations are exempt. In particular, the Crown is not within the tax legislation, whilst charities are generally (see Chapter 42) exempt from income tax in respect of:

(1) income from land and investment income provided that it is applied for charitable purposes only; and

(2) trading profits applied purely for charitable purposes where either the trade is part of the main purpose of the charity, or the work is carried out mainly by the beneficiaries (for instance Christmas cards made by the handicapped and sold for their benefit: TA 1988 s 505).

Foreign diplomats and members of overseas armed forces stationed in the UK are exempt (TA 1988 ss 322–323). **[4.155]**

b) *Exempt income*

Some of the more important items that are exempt from income tax include:
(1) scholarship income in the hands of the scholar (TA 1988 s 331 : and see *Walters v Tickner* (1992));
(2) certain social security benefits, namely: income support payments (other than those taxable under TA 1988 s 151); family credit; housing benefit; child benefit (TA 1988 s 617(2)). In addition, certain benefits are excepted from the Schedule E charge including: maternity allowance; widow's payments; invalidity benefit; and attendance and mobility allowances (TA 1988 s 617(1)). Notice, however, that maternity pay, statutory sick pay and unemployment benefit are all taxable under Schedule E (TA 1988 s 150). FA 1996 introduced provisions whereby individuals who take out insurance to protect themselves against financial losses caused by accident, sickness, disability, infirmity or unemployment are not taxed on any benefits received;
(3) interest on National Savings Certificates and schemes (TA 1988 s 326);
(4) the first £70 of interest each year from ordinary accounts at the National Savings Bank;
(5) interest on damages for personal injuries or death (TA 1988 s 329 *ff* and, as a result of changes in FA 1995 and FA 1996, the victim can receive a tax-free annuity for his life instead of a capital sum);
(6) gross income up to £4,250 pa from renting a room: see **[8.46]**. **[4.156]**

c) *PEPs, TESSAs and SAYE*

Personal Equity Plans (PEPs) These are a tax incentive aimed at encouraging saving through the purchase of shares and unit trusts (now TA 1988 s 333). This personal equity plan (PEP) permits resident individuals to invest up to £6,000 pa with an authorised PEP manager. The resulting fund may be invested in equities listed on a UK stock exchange or dealt in on AIM or similar shares in EU companies, in corporate bonds; convertibles; preference shares in sterling eurobonds issued by qualifying companies and (subject to certain restrictions) placed in unit trusts. To qualify for the full £6,000 general PEP limit, unit and investment trusts must hold at least half their assets in UK ordinary shares and similar shares in EU companies. Unit and investment trusts not satisfying this requirement ('non-qualifying trusts') may qualify for an annual PEP investment of up to £1,500 if they hold at least half their assets in UK ordinary shares or similar shares listed on a stock exchange anywhere in the world, provided that the exchange is recognised by the Inland Revenue.

Although the initial investment in a PEP attracts no tax relief (contrast EIS and venture capital trusts), the following tax advantages are conferred.

First, no income tax is charged on income arising from the investment (eg dividends).

Secondly, no CGT is charged on the disposal of the investment nor on a switch of investments within the PEP. Given the relatively small sums that may be invested in the PEP, relief from CGT is the major attraction for taxpayers although with a current annual exemption of £6,300 only individuals who have already exhausted that exemption will benefit. It should be remembered that PEP fund managers will deduct a management charge (usually about 3% of the sum invested).

Up to £3,000 pa can be invested in a single company PEP ('a corporate PEP') as well as investing £6,000 in one or more other companies ('the general PEP'). Accordingly, up to £9,000 pa is available for PEP investment. **[4.157]**

Tax exempt special savings accounts (TESSAs)   The relative success of PEPs encouraged the introduction of tax exempt special savings accounts (TESSAs: FA 1990 s 28). The intention was to stimulate savings in (largely risk free) interest bearing accounts with banks and building societies (now including 'European Authorised Institutions'). Adult individuals, and for this purpose husband and wife are separate individuals, can open one TESSA account with either a bank or building society in which interest earned on the sum deposited will be free from income tax *provided that* the savings are left in the account for five years. Maximum permitted savings over the five-year period are £9,000 but this figure may be arrived at in a variety of ways since the scheme is intended to be flexible. For instance, the individual can make regular savings of up to £150 month or, alternatively, deposit up to £3,000 in the TESSA in year 1 with up to £1,800 in each of the following three years and then up to £600 in year 5.

The sums involved are hardly startling—for a basic rate taxpayer the saving will be less than £100 pa. Once the five-year time period has ended the account ceases to qualify for tax relief with the result that interest subsequently earned will become subject to tax in the normal way.

An advantage of TESSA is that although the capital must remain frozen in the account during the five-year period, interest earned in any one year (less a sum equivalent to the basic rate income tax for that year) may be withdrawn. Assume, for instance, that interest of £200 is credited to the account in June 1996: £160 may then be withdrawn without giving rise to any tax penalty. The saver is not therefore deprived of all benefit from his investment during the five-year qualifying period. The retention of an amount equal to the basic rate tax on interest earned in each year is, in a sense, security in case the investment should cease to qualify for relief under TESSA. Of course, if the investment continues so to qualify for the full five-year period, the retained amount of interest will then be handed to the taxpayer in full. By contrast,

however, if the investment ceases to qualify (eg if capital is withdrawn or an excessive amount of interest withdrawn) the result will be an immediate cancellation of the tax advantages and the saver may then find himself in a worse position than would have been the case if he had made a non-TESSA investment since all the interest credited to the date of cancellation will immediately be subject to income tax *at the rates in force in the year of cancellation.* Not only is there a risk that rates may have risen since the interest was earned, but, in addition, taxing all the interest in a single year may result in the taxpayer becoming subject to higher rate liability. Should the taxpayer die during the five-year qualifying period the TESSA will end but without any tax charge arising. Investors who have held a TESSA for the full five-year period can open a second account with the full amount of the capital deposited in the first TESSA (excluding, however, any accumulated interest).

This form of saving prompts comparisons with PEPs. An important difference is that, unlike a PEP, a TESSA investment does not involve the investor in any management charges. There is, of course, nothing to stop an individual making both investments and, taking the limit of investments in PEPs at £9,000 pa (both corporate and general PEP), the maximum tax-free investment that can be made in both plans over the next five years is as follows:
Under the PEP — £9,000 × 5 = £45,000
Under TESSA — £9,000 over five years   [**4.158**]

Save As You Earn (SAYE)   SAYE contracts were first introduced in 1969 and allowed a fixed monthly saving of between (only!) £1 and £20 for five years (for SAYE share option schemes the monthly investment permitted is £250). As compared with TESSA investments, the sum invested (maximum £1,200 over five years) was relatively derisory and no interest could be withdrawn during the five-year period. Instead the investor received at the end a tax-free bonus equivalent to the interest earned over the period and this bonus was doubled if the sum was not withdrawn for a further two years. With the intention of simplifying the tax incentives for reliefs given that SAYE has largely been superseded by new schemes (especially TESSA) 'ordinary' schemes were abolished as from 29 November 1994. Existing contracts will continue with full tax relief and tax relief will still be available for SAYE sharesave schemes (ie contracts linked to approved employee share option schemes (see Chapter 39)).   [**4.159**]

Individual Savings Accounts (ISA)   This was announced by the Labour government in the July 1997 Budget—what information there is being contained in a Press Release of 2 July 1997. The intention is to 'build on' the experience of TESSAs and PEPs and for the new account to provide a tax favoured environment for savings. It is envisaged that the new scheme will be in place by 6 April 1999 when the current rules permitting tax credits to be repaid to individuals in respect of company distributions cease (for the change in corporate taxation.   [**4.160**]

5 Schedule E—offices and employments

I INTRODUCTORY

The emoluments derived from an 'office or employment', after deducting any allowable expenditure, are charged to income tax under one of the three Cases of Schedule E (TA 1988 s 19(1)). Tax is levied on a receipts basis and is usually collected at source under the PAYE system. Insofar as the Cases of Schedule E involve a foreign element, the matter is considered in Chapter 13. This chapter will be limited to the charge under Case I which applies when the person holding the office or employment is resident and ordinarily resident in the UK.

Schedule E is of crucial significance in the income tax system since it raises, mainly through PAYE, some 75% of total income tax per annum. High rates of tax led to the proliferation of fringe benefits designed to minimise tax or avoid the PAYE net and give the employee a cashflow advantage. Accordingly a characteristic feature of the Schedule has been regular legislation seeking to close loopholes in its operation. It is now an area where detail has come to swamp principle.

Another important development that has affected this area in recent years has been the substantial increase in employers' national insurance contributions charged in respect of higher paid employees (see Chapter 37, Appendix A for rates). This has provided a further incentive to employers to reward their employees not by wage increases (which will attract increased employer national insurance contributions) but, instead, by fringe benefits which used not, generally, to be subject to the contribution. Recent changes have, however, limited the scope of this benefits in kind exemption.

Lower contributions payable by the self-employed as well as perceived tax advantages encouraged taxpayers to argue that they were self-employed rather than employees. In turn, the Revenue has sought to broaden the Schedule E net to catch workers who had traditionally been taxed as self-employed: such attempts have been met with fierce opposition.   **[5.1]–[5.20]**

II   OFFICE OR EMPLOYMENT

1   Meaning of 'office'

The term '*office*' is not statutorily defined but it was described by Rowlatt J in *Great Western Rly Co v Bater* (1920) as 'a subsisting, permanent, substantive position which had an existence independent from the person who filled it, which went on and was filled in succession by successive holders . . .'. Although this dictum has been approved in cases over the years, in *Edwards v Clinch* (1981) the emphasis on permanence and continuity was played down by the House of Lords in favour of the requirement of some degree of continuance and of a position with an existence independent of the individual holding it. In that case a civil engineer who received *ad hoc* appointments as a planning inspector was held not to be an office-holder because the position had no independent existence but lapsed when the particular assignment was completed. Mr Clinch was appointed to execute a task not to perform a certain *type* of work (an office).

This distinction was relied on by the Court of Session in *IRC v Brander & Cruickshank* (1971) (affirmed by the House of Lords) in a case dealing with the difficulties which arise when a taxpayer acquires an 'office' by reason of his particular profession: eg solicitor partners (taxable under Schedule D Case II) often acquire trusteeships. Each office will be separately assessed under Schedule E and not taxed under Schedule D, unless that office is acquired as an integral part of the trade or profession. In practice, the Revenue allows partnerships which receive directors' fees to enter those fees in their Schedule D Case II assessment so long as the directorship is a normal incident of the profession and of the particular practice; the fees form only a small part of total profits; and under the partnership agreement the fees are pooled for division amongst the partners (see ESC A37).

Typical examples of office-holders include trustees, PRs, company secretaries and auditors. It is generally assumed that a company director, whether full-time and salaried or part-time and in receipt of fees, is an office-holder under Schedule E (*McMillan v Guest* (1942)). Often the directorship will continue regardless of the person who occupies it; but it may still be an office, it appears, even if it is created for a particular person (see *Taylor v Provan* (1974), cf *Edwards v Clinch* (1981)).   [5.21]

2   Employed or self-employed?

The term '*employment*' is not statutorily defined. It connotes a position where there is a written or implied contract of service. If the taxpayer works for more than one person, the difficulty is to know whether he holds a number of separate employments (taxable under Schedule E) or is making a series of engagements carried out as part of a trade, profession or vocation. The basic division is between a contract of service (Schedule E) and a contract for services (Schedule D). Cooke J in *Market Investigations Ltd v Minister of Social Security* (1969) identified the relevant factors as follows:

> 'a contract of service may exist even though the control does not extend to prescribing how the work shall be done ... the most that can be said is that control will no doubt always have to be considered although it can no longer be regarded as the sole determining factor; and that factors, which may be of importance, are such matters as whether the man performing the services provides his own equipment, whether he hires his own helpers, what degree of financial risk he takes, what degree of responsibility for investment and management he has, and whether and how far he has an opportunity of profiting from sound management in the performance of his task.'

This test as to whether the person is 'in business on his own account' forms the basis of the Revenue's view of the factors that have to be taken into account in deciding whether a person is self-employed (see Inland Revenue booklet IR 56). However, issues of control and integration can still be important. The main problems arise when a taxpayer works for more than one person, either consecutively or concurrently.

In *Davies v Braithwaite* (1931), for instance, an actress who entered into a series of separate engagements to appear on film, stage and radio was held to be taxable under Schedule D. Rowlatt J looked at her total commitments during the year and, as the number was considerable, decided that each was a mere engagement in the course of exercising her profession: compare *Fall v Hitchen* (1973) where the taxpayer was employed as a professional ballet dancer by Sadlers Wells under a contract which only allowed him to take other work with their consent (which was not to be unreasonably withheld). Pennycuick V-C looked at the characteristics of the contract in isolation and held that the taxpayer was taxable under Schedule E; undoubtedly one reason for the decision was that the taxpayer had only one contract which provided for a first call on his time.

The Revenue, adopting this approach of looking at each contract in isolation, tried to bring persons traditionally taxed under Schedule D (eg actors) within Schedule E. However, the courts have recently reverted to taking an overview and in *Hall v Lorimer* (1994) the Revenue's attempt to recategorise technical workers in the film industry as Schedule E taxpayers, whatever the number and nature of their engagements each year, was successfully resisted. The Court of Appeal felt that the duration of each engagement and the number of people by whom Mr Lorimer was engaged were of critical importance. The Court said that in these types of case the question of whether the taxpayer was 'dependent on or independent of a particular paymaster for the financial exploitation of his talents may well be significant' and that this was a more useful test than the 'business on own account' one since persons who exercise a profession or vocation will often do so 'without any of the normal trappings of a business'. Thus, although the taxpayer only supplied his own expertise, he could still be treated as self-employed.

Other successes before the Commissioners suggest that self-employed status may be established even where the number of contracts are few, provided there is other evidence of self-employment, including that the worker does not have the protections normally given to an employee (eg sick pay or holiday entitlement) (see *Taxation*, 16 February 1995, p 450 and 20 April 1995, p 68).

IR 56 (May 1995) indicates that the Revenue is now beginning to accept that an overview is required: it states that 'for each engagement the whole picture needs to be looked at in the light of all the facts'. However, it exhibits a marked reluctance to adopt the *Hall v Lorimer* (1994) test: it suggests that the 'business on own account' test has to be applied to *each* job when the taxpayer works for more than one person and only admits the possible influence of other criteria if the taxpayer provides 'services to *many* different persons' and does not 'work regularly for one person to the exclusion of all others'. Lightman J's decision in *Barnett v Brabyn* (1996) underlines the need for greater subtlety. In that case the taxpayer's situation not only lacked the factors identified in *Market Investigations* above, but Mr Barnett also worked only for one employer and their relationship involved many factors indicating employment, including receipt of holiday pay. However, the court felt that the taxpayer's contractual right to work as much or as little as he liked (which right he did in fact exercise) and the parties' agreement that he should be self-employed (as to which, see [**5.23**]) were sufficient to ensure that status. The Revenue's latest summary of the law (Tax Bulletin, April 1997, pp 405–413) suggests they now accept this need. [**5.22**]

3   Taxing a partner

An equity partner in a business is self-employed and, therefore, assessable under Schedule D Case I or II. Difficulties may arise, however, as to the status of a salaried partner. Whether he is an employee or is self-employed does not necessarily depend upon the labels used or whether his salary is taxed at source under PAYE though in a non-partnership case, *Barnett v Brabyn* (1996), Lightman J stated that whilst the parties' agreement on status 'cannot contradict the effect of a contract as a whole and must be disregarded if inconsistent with the substantive terms or general effect of the contract as a whole, when the terms and general effect of the contract as a whole are consistent with either relationship, the parties' label may be decisive'.

In *Stekel v Ellice* (1973), although the agreement referred to 'salaried partner' and a 'fixed salary', it was, in substance, a partnership agreement rather than a contract of employment. However, in *Horner v Hasted* (1995) the fact that the rules of the ICAEW prevented a firm of accountants from appointing a non-qualified person as a partner (and that his being a partner would therefore have breached various statutory rules) and that the firm, therefore, went out of its way technically to preserve Mr Horner's employment status (for instance, by paying employers' national insurance contributions) significantly influenced Lightman J in confirming his employment status when otherwise he had a 'status in the firm equivalent to that of a partner', including receiving a 'salary' that was a share of the profits, attending and voting at partners' meetings and being held out to clients as a partner! Accordingly, provided that the partnership determines the new partner's status in advance and drafts the agreement accordingly, its terms are likely to be conclusive unless there is strong factual evidence to the contrary (*BSM (1257) Ltd v Secretary of State for Social Services* (1978)). If the partners are in any doubt on the matter, they should seek confirmation of status from the Revenue.   **[5.23]–[5.40]**

III   ARE THE EMOLUMENTS FROM EMPLOYMENT?

1   Introduction

TA 1988 s 19 taxes emoluments from an office or employment. 'Emoluments' are partially defined in TA 1988 s 131 as including 'all salaries, fees, wages, perquisites and profits whatsoever'. This is wide enough to cover benefits in kind as well as cash payments and the limits imposed on the meaning of the term by the courts are discussed in Section V. This section considers when it can be said that a receipt by an employee is 'from' his employment (the term 'employee' will be used to cover office-holders as well).   **[5.41]**

2   General principles

In *Hochstrasser v Mayes* (1960) Upjohn J said that in order for a payment received by an employee to be a profit arising from his employment 'it must be something in the nature of a reward for services past, present or future'. In the same case Lord Radcliffe stated:

> 'While it is not sufficient to render a payment assessable that an employee would not have received it unless he had been an employee, it is assessable if it has been paid to him in return for acting as or being an employee.'

The essence of these two statements is that a payment is not taxable merely because it relates to the existence of a contract of employment—there must be some additional factor to bring the payment within the tax net. The *Mayes* case itself related to a scheme whereby if an employee was transferred within the group, ICI would buy his house at a fair valuation and would also reimburse any capital loss on the sale. Mr Mayes was reimbursed following a move—he would not have received that money unless he was an employee of ICI but that was not sufficient to make it taxable.

The difficulty arises in categorising the additional element that is required to bring a payment within the tax net. The courts have been fairly consistent in their requirement that the payment must be a 'reward for services'. Lord Templeman in *Shilton v Wilmshurst* (1991) (for the facts see [**5.43**]) said:

> 'Section [19] is not limited to emoluments provided in the course of the employment; the section must therefore apply first to an emolument which is paid as a reward for past services and as an inducement to continue to perform services and, second, to an emolument which is paid as an inducement to enter a contract of employment and to perform services in the future. The result is that an emolument "from employment" means an emolument "from being or becoming an employee". The authorities are consistent with this analysis and are concerned to distinguish in each case between an emolument which is derived "from being or becoming an employee" on the one hand and an emolument which is attributable to something else on the other hand, for example, to a desire on the part of the provider of the emolument to relieve distress or to provide assistance to a home buyer.'

In *Mairs v Haughey* (1993), the House of Lords reaffirmed that payments to compensate for loss or to relieve distress are not taxable under TA 1988 s 19, certainly if they are only payable in certain circumstances after the employment comes to an end (the relative significance of these factors was not explained in the judgment). The case involved payments made to employees to give up their contingent rights under a non-statutory redundancy scheme but in reaching its decision the Lords also considered whether the redundancy payments themselves would have been taxable. Lord Woolf delivering the judgment of the House held that they would not have been and said that 'a characteristic of a redundancy payment is that it is to compensate or relieve an employee for what can be the unfortunate consequences of becoming unemployed'.

The decision in *Mairs* was that a certain type of payment (which was not a 'reward for services', which was only payable in certain circumstances and then only after the termination of employment) was not an emolument from employment within TA 1988 s 19. No view was expressed on whether any payment which is not a 'reward for services' *can* fall within s 19. The significance of the Court of Appeal decision in *Hamblett v Godfrey* (1987) is still, therefore, unclear. In that case the court held that a payment of £1,000 made to each employee of GCHQ who relinquished his right to join a trade union was taxable. This decision was seen as indicating a payment could be taxable even if it was not paid as a reward for services. Sir Nicholas Browne-Wilkinson in the Court of Appeal in *Shilton v Wilmshurst* (1990) thought that there was a wider principle behind the 'reward for services' test which also caught the *Hamblett v Godfrey* payment: to be taxable a payment must be 'referable to the performance of the services under the relevant contract of employment and nothing else ...'. However, Lord Hutton CJ in the Northern Ireland Court of Appeal in *Mairs v Haughey* (1992) thought that *Hamblett v Godfrey* did not depart from previous authorities because the payment 'was held to be made in return for Miss Hamblett continuing to be an employee at GCHQ'—Neill LJ had stated:

> 'It is plain that the taxpayer received her payments as a recognition of the fact that she had lost certain rights as an employee, *and* by reason of the further fact that she had elected to remain in her employment at GCHQ' (italics added).

Lord Hutton CJ's explanation would remove one obstacle to a general acceptance of the 'reward for services' test. However, his explanation was not accepted by Carnwath J in *Wilcock v Eve* (1995) (for the facts see [**39.27**]) who stated that taxable emoluments are not limited to those 'in the nature of a reward for continuing services'. Payments for loss of rights 'intimately connected with employment' (as in *Hamblett v Godfrey*) will also be taxable although those for losses suffered in some other capacity (as in *Hochstrasser v Mayes*) will not. The actual decision was that as the benefit received on exercising an option would not have been taxable under s 19, the *ex gratia* payment made in recognition of the loss of that benefit was also not taxable; these propositions are supported by *Abbott v Philbin* (1961) (see [**39.27**]) and *Mairs v Haughey* (1993) (see [**5.65**]) and it is felt that the judge's more general consideration of the scope of Schedule E is therefore *obiter dicta*. Even so, it indicates the debate is alive and the Revenue are likely to continue to press for the wider test enunciated in *Hamblett v Godfrey* (the August 1996 *Tax Bulletin*, in an article giving the Revenue's views on payment in lieu of notice, does indeed state 'tax case law shows that [emoluments include] payments which are not strictly a reward for services, for example, compensation paid for the loss of the protection of certain employment law rights').

On a different point, the redundancy payments in *Mairs* were payable under the 'conditions of employment': it was not clear whether the written contracts of employment referred to the scheme. In *Comptroller-General of Inland Revenue v Knight* (1973), Lord Wilberforce, delivering the opinion of the Privy Council said:

> 'Where a sum of money is paid under a contract of employment it is taxable, even though it is received at or after the termination of the employment: see, for example, *Henry v Foster* (1931).'

Lord Woolf in *Mairs* stated that this was only 'an agreed general proposition' which is 'subject to exceptions'. Therefore, although Lord Woolf's statement is not part of the *ratio decidendi* of *Mairs* (since there was no finding that the redundancy payments would have been 'paid under a contract of employment'), it seems likely that the fact that a payment is provided for in the contract of employment will no longer be decisive of its taxability.   [**5.42**]

3   Third party payments

Tips will normally form part of an employee's taxable emoluments and in some businesses form a substantial part of take-home pay. In such cases the payment is made by a third party rather than by the employer. In *Shilton v Wilmshurst* (1991) the House of Lords decided that such payments could amount to emoluments even if the third party did not have an interest in the performance of the employment contract. The case concerned Peter Shilton, the former England goalkeeper, who on his transfer from Nottingham Forest to Southampton received a payment of £75,000 from Nottingham Forest. Deciding that this sum was an emolument Lord Templeman stressed that:

> 'there is nothing in [the section] or the authorities to justify the inference that an "emolument from employment" only applies to an emolument provided by a person who has an interest in the performance by the employee of the services which he becomes bound to perform when he enters into the contract of employment ... so far as the taxpayer is concerned, both the emoluments of £80,000 from Southampton and £75,000 from Nottingham Forest were paid to him for the same purpose and had the same effect, namely, as an inducement to him to agree to become an employee of Southampton.'
>   [**5.43**]

4   Past services

The debate about past services does not, of course, relate to the normal case where salary is paid in arrears. What is in issue is the taxability of a payment which relates to a period of employment for which payment has already been received.

Upjohn J in the *Mayes* case ([**5.42**]) envisaged that rewards for past services would be taxable. However, Lord Templeman, in the passage from *Shilton* quoted above at [**5.42**], indicated that rewards for past services will only be taxable if they are *also* 'an inducement to continue to perform services'.

In *Brumby v Milner* (1976) the House of Lords held that payments made from an employee trust when it was wound up, to employees who were still in employment, were taxable. In *Bray v Best* (1989) payments in similar circumstances were made to *former* employees. Lord Oliver said:

'Although before the Special Commissioners and High Court the taxpayer had contested that the sum paid constituted an emolument from his employment, the decision ... in *Brumby v Milner* ... effectively precludes further argument on this point and the question has not been pursued either before the Court of Appeal or before your Lordships.'

There is some difficulty in reconciling the idea that the payments in *Bray v Best* were emoluments from employment with Lord Templeman's statement in *Shilton v Wilmshurst*; there *may* also be an argument that the payments were capital in nature and therefore not taxable (see Lord Woolf's comments quoted at [**5.65**]). [**5.44**]–[**5.60**]

IV PROBLEM CASES

1 **Introduction**

Applying the general principles discussed in Section III can be particularly difficult in the relation to the types of cases discussed in this section. [**5.61**]

2 **Gifts**

There is a basic distinction between a payment which is a reward for services and which is, therefore, taxable under s 19 and one which is made in appreciation of an individual's personal qualities, which is not so taxable. Various factors are relevant in drawing this distinction.

First, whether the payment is made once only or whether it is recurring (in the former case it is more likely to escape tax).

Secondly, whether it is made to only one employee or to a whole class of employees. In *Laidler v Perry* (1966), for instance, all the employees received a £10 voucher at Christmas instead of the turkey that they had received in previous years. The employees were taxed on the cash value of the voucher.

Thirdly, if the payment is by the employer there is a strong presumption that it is an emolument, whereas if it is from a third party, it is easier to show that it is a gift for personal qualities. However, tips are generally regarded as being in return for services and so taxable, even though made voluntarily by someone other than the employer. In *Calvert v Wainwright* (1947), a taxi driver was taxable on tips received from customers although the court suggested that a particularly generous tip from a special customer (eg at Christmas) might escape tax (see also *Blakiston v Cooper* (1909)).

Fourthly, a payment to which the employee is entitled under the terms of his contract of employment will usually be taxable as a part of his emoluments, although this is subject to exceptions (see [**5.42**]).

EXAMPLE 5.1

(1) Ham has played cricket for Gloucestershire for many years. At the end of his distinguished career the county grants him a benefit match (ie he is entitled to all the receipts from a particular game). The benefit is a tax-free testimonial paid for Ham's personal qualities (see *Seymour v Reed* (1927)). *Compare*:

(2) Mercenary plays as a professional in the Lancashire League and under the terms of his contract is entitled to have the 'hat passed round' (ie a collection taken) every time he scores 50 runs or takes five wickets in an innings. The sums that he receives will be taxed as emoluments because he is entitled to them in his contract of employment (see *Moorhouse v Dooland* (1955)).

Finally, the gift rules overlap with the benefit in kind rules. In deciding whether tax is chargeable under Schedule E, the gift rules should be applied first and then the benefit in kind rules (see Sections V and VII of this chapter). A gift connected with the termination of an employment is considered at **[5.69]**.   **[5.62]**

EXAMPLE 5.2

Free Range Ltd gives all its employees a 25lb turkey at Christmas. In deciding whether tax is charged, (1) apply the gift rules (ie is the turkey given in return for services or is it for personal qualities?); then (2) apply the benefit in kind rules (ie is the turkey convertible into money; if not, is it caught by TA 1988 ss 153–168 in the case of 'higher paid' employees and directors?). If it is decided that the benefit is a gift, no tax is charged on lower-paid employees, although ss 153–168 may catch others. If it is decided that it is in return for services, tax may be charged under s 19 on all employees, if the general benefit in kind rules are satisfied; even if those rules are not satisfied, 'higher paid' employees may still be taxable. It is likely in this example that tax would be chargeable.

3   Inducement payments

Shilton v Wilmshurst (1991) (see **[5.42]** and **[5.43]**) illustrates that payments which are made (even by a third party) for 'being or becoming an employee' are taxable. However, payments made to compensate the taxpayer for some sacrifice that he has made by taking up an employment are generally not taxable because they are not in return for services. In *Jarrold v Boustead* (1964) an international rugby union player was not taxable on a £3,000 signing-on fee paid to him when he turned professional. The payment was not an emolument but was to compensate him for permanent loss of his amateur status.

The same principle was applied in *Pritchard v Arundale* (1971) where a chartered accountant was not taxed on a large shareholding transferred to him in return for signing a service contract as managing director of the company. The benefit was held to accrue to him, not for future services as managing director which were to be adequately rewarded, but as compensation for loss of his professional status as a chartered accountant. It may also be noted that the shares were to be transferred in return for the taxpayer's signing the service contract. Hence, even if he had died without performing any services for the company, the shares would have been transferable to his estate. Further, they were given by a third party not by the new employer (see also *Vaughan-Neil v IRC* (1979): **[5.70]**).

In *Jarrold v Boustead* (1964) Lord Denning MR said that a church organist appointed for seven months at £10 per month would not be taxable on £500 paid to him in return for giving up golf *for the rest of his life*. On the face of it, this is difficult to reconcile with *Pritchard v Arundale* but perhaps the following conclusions can be supported:

(1) Mr Arundale had been the senior partner in a firm of chartered accountants. Although he could have resumed his status as a chartered accountant on leaving the employment, his age (48) in practice made it 'most unlikely' that he would 'be able to pick up his former profession as soon as his other activities' ended; the organist in Lord Denning's example could never again play golf on a Sunday. In both cases, therefore, the compensation was, in effect, for a permanent loss to the taxpayer. If the loss is merely restricted to the period of the contract, the payment is likely to be viewed as advance remuneration.

(2) Mr Arundale was fully rewarded for his services under the contract. It seems likely that £10 per month was a reasonable payment, in 1964, for an organist. If the salary is not fair remuneration, again the payment is likely to be viewed as advance remuneration.

In *Glantre Engineering Ltd v Goodhand* (1983) an inducement payment made to a chartered accountant was held to be an emolument as the taxpayer failed to show that he had provided consideration in return for the payment since he was merely moving from one Schedule E employment to another. Once the taxpayer fails to show that he has been permanently deprived of something akin to amateur status or the status of being a partner, it must follow that the payment is a reward for future services in the new employment. Even if the employee can show that the payment is not taxable under general principles, consideration should be given as to whether s 313 could apply, given the width of its wording (see [5.70]).   [5.63]

4 Compensation for other losses

Compensation for loss caused to the employee may escape tax even when not paid as part of an inducement payment. The cases discussed at [5.42] illustrate that compensation paid for a personal loss suffered by an employee (for instance, compensation for loss on the sale of a house as in *Hochstrasser v Mayes* (1960)) will usually not be taxable under TA s 19 (although s 154 could apply in the case of 'higher paid' employees and directors—see Section VII of this chapter).

EXAMPLE 5.3

Num Ltd paid its employee, Sid, £1,000 to compensate him for the anguish he suffered as a result of his wife running off with the milkman. The company may argue that the payment is necessary and, therefore, a deductible expense because otherwise Sid may suffer a mental and physical collapse. Further, the payment may be non-taxable in Sid's hands as compensation for his suffering rather than a reward for services.

[5.64]

5 Payments on variation of terms of employment

Payments are sometimes made to employees when a benefit is withdrawn. With very few exceptions the courts have held that such payments are taxable whether they were gratuitous—because the employee had no right to the benefit which had been removed—or could be seen as compensation for breach of contract on the employer unilaterally withdrawing a contractual right.

Where the employee is to receive a smaller salary in the future, as in *Cameron v Prendergast* (1940) and *Tilley v Wales* (1943), the lump sum is taxable. In *Bird v Martland* (1982) compensation was paid following withdrawal of company cars (which did not cause a breach of contract); in *McGregor v Randall* (1984) a contractual right to receive commission was withdrawn: in both cases the compensation was taxable.

Lump sum compensation payments have, however, been held not to be taxable where the taxpayer gave up a contingent right which would have provided him with a benefit *after* his employment had ceased; as in *Hunter v Dewhurst* (1932) where compensation was payable under the articles of association when a director gave up his office; and in *Tilley v Wales* (above) where the taxpayer was (also) entitled to a pension on retirement.

There is some difficulty in reconciling these two groups of cases. In *Mairs v Haughey* ((1993): see [**5.42**]), Lord Woolf said that a 'payment made to satisfy a contingent right to a payment derives its character from the nature of the payment which it replaces'. On this basis, sums paid to 'buy out' the employees' contingent rights to redundancy payments under a non-statutory redundancy scheme were not taxable, since the redundancy payments themselves would not have been taxable. This suggests that if the benefit itself would have been taxable, then a lump sum compensation payment following its withdrawal would also be taxable. However, the Northern Ireland Court of Appeal held in *Mairs* (1992) that 'even if a payment under the enhanced redundancy scheme was taxable, a payment to secure the termination of [the employee's] rights under the scheme would not be taxable as an emolument from the employment' on the basis of *Hunter v Dewhurst* (above). Although not necessary to the decision, Lord Woolf in *Mairs* indicated that he was not:

> 'persuaded that this aspect of the Court of Appeal of Northern Ireland's decision was incorrect or that *Hunter v Dewhurst* was wrongly decided. This is because for the Revenue to succeed, the Revenue would have to establish, contrary to my provisional view, that the lump sum payment was in the nature of an income payment before it could begin to qualify as being chargeable to tax under Schedule E.'

This is a novel approach: the income/capital distinction has generally been considered irrelevant to the issue of taxability under Schedule E. Given the novelty of the approach and that this was only his provisional view, Lord Woolf's statement should not be relied on too heavily. However, if the capital/income distinction did become important, it could be argued that all compensation payments for withdrawn benefits fall outside s 19, though it is hard to imagine the courts willingly acceding to taxable salary being converted into non-taxable lump sums.

Even if such payments fall outside s 19 they may be caught by other charging provisions. The Revenue have in the past argued that TA 1988 s 313 applies if the employee gives any sort of undertaking not to sue for breach of contract (but see now [**5.70**]). In the case of 'higher paid employees' (see [**5.141**] ff) consideration should be given to the applicability of TA 1988 s 154: see *Mairs v Haughey* (1992) in the Court of Appeal (but note that the case was unusual because the deeming provision in s 168(3) did not apply). If neither of these apply, the payment may still fall within TA 1988 s 148 (see [**5.122**]) as being in connection with a change in the emoluments of an employment. It is possible that s 148 could apply even where, as in *Mairs v Haughey*, the right given up was not a right to taxable emoluments of the employment: this would depend on the width which a court was willing to give to the words of s 148. If no income tax provisions apply, TCGA 1992 s 22 (capital sums derived from assets) needs to be considered carefully when rights are being surrendered.   [**5.65**]

6   Payments after the termination of employment

a) *General*

A payment made after the termination of employment is, *prima facie*, not an emolument from that employment. However, it may be an emolument if it is in the nature of 'deferred remuneration': further, as a general proposition, a payment made under the contract of employment will be taxed in full, even though it is paid because of the termination of the employment. In *Dale v de Soissons* (1950), followed in *Williams v Simmonds* (1981), a director's service agreement provided for him to be paid £10,000 if it should be prematurely terminated. The taxpayer argued that the payment was not in return for services. It was held, however, that as the payment was one to which he was contractually entitled, it was an emolument. This general proposition is, however, subject to exceptions (see Lord Woolf in *Mairs v Haughey* (1993)—[**5.42**] and [**5.67**]). In view of the generous taxation of non-contractual payments on a termination of employment ([**5.122**]), it will generally still be advisable to omit such compensation clauses from contracts of employment.

This Section is concerned with the applicability of s 19 to various types of 'problem cases' but whenever the issue of the taxability of termination payments (or benefits provided to employees after termination) arises, consideration should be given to the possible application both of the benefits in kind legislation (if it applies when the employment has terminated) and of TA 1988 s 313 or s 596A. If none of these provisions apply, the benefit or payment will normally be taxable under s 148 and able to benefit from the £30,000 exemption given by s 188. [**5.66**]

b) *Payments in lieu of notice*

If correct notice is given to the employee and he works out that period or remains employed but on 'garden leave', payments that he receives are emoluments under general principles. If the employer terminates the contract and makes a payment in lieu of notice, then tax is not payable under general principles (as the payment is seen as damages for breach of contract (see *Henley v Murray* (1950)). However, if the employment contract obliges or permits the employer to make a payment in lieu of notice on terminating the employment, it was generally thought that the payment would be taxable under general principles as paid 'under the contract of employment'. Since the House of Lords in *Mairs v Haughey* (1993) indicated that this rule is subject to exceptions, the fact that the contract provides for a payment in lieu may no longer be decisive of its taxability (see [**5.42**]); further, there appears to be an argument that such a provision is void because it, in effect, excludes the right to statutory minimum periods of notice under (now) the Employment Rights Act 1996 (see *Personal Tax Planning Review*, vol 4, p 25). In either case, such payments *may* escape s 19 as having characteristics similar to those which enabled the House to hold that non-statutory redundancy payments, due under the 'conditions of employment', were not taxable. The Revenue's resistance to these arguments is clear from *Tax Bulletin*, August 1996, and the Special Commissioners in *Thorn EMI Electronics Ltd v Coldicott* (1996) supported their position by holding that payments under a right reserved in the employment contract were emoluments. [**5.67**]

c) *Redundancy payments*

Statutory redundancy payments can only be taxed under s 148 (TA 1988 s 580(3)). Following the House of Lords decision in *Mairs v Haughey* (1993), the Revenue accepts that lump sum payments under non-statutory schemes will also only be taxable under s 148 provided they are made on a genuine redundancy (as defined (now) in the Employment Rights Act 1996 s 139) and are genuinely made to compensate for the employment lost through redundancy (SP 1/94). Advance clearance for schemes can be obtained. Presumably genuine one-off redundancy payments will be taxed in the same way but the SP does not mention them. In either situation, the Revenue will have to be convinced that no part of the payment is what it refers to as a 'terminal bonus' (the Revenue will seek to tax those under s 19) and that the employee is not really 'retiring' (in which case it will seek to apply SP 13/91—see d) below).   [**5.68**]

d) *Ex gratia payments on termination*

In contrast to payments for redundancy or breach of contract these may be made as a testimonial or present to the employee—to the employee as an individual rather than in return for services rendered (see [**5.62**]). An *ex gratia* payment made to an employee on termination of employment will not be taxable under general principles (see *Cowan v Seymour* (1920) but note the comments at [**5.66**] on the possible applicability of other charging provisions). Further, the Revenue treatment of lump sum payments made on termination due to retirement or death was modified by SP 13/91 (and see also [1992] STI 869 and 1005). Lump sum payments of this nature *may* now be subject to the rules governing payments by retirement benefits schemes. The Pension Schemes Office has the power to approve *ex gratia* schemes; if approved, the payment will be wholly tax free (on the conditions for approval, see [**IV.9**]): if the payment is made under an unapproved retirement benefits scheme, it will be taxable in full under s 596A without the benefit of any £30,000 exemption, since s 148 only applies if the payment is not otherwise taxable.   [**5.69**]

7   Payments for entering into restrictive covenants (TA 1988 s 313)

The tax treatment of restrictive covenant payments made to former employees has undergone substantial revision over the years. Formerly, the sum paid escaped tax in the hands of the employee since it was thought not to be a reward for services performed under his contract and usually it was not provided for under the contract itself (*Beak v Robson* (1943)). For the employer, the sum would usually be non-deductible in arriving at his profits since it would be of a capital nature (*Associated Portland Cement Manufacturers Ltd v Kerr* (1946): see [**6.115**]). However, it was accepted that if the restriction imposed on the employee was for a relatively short period, then the payment by the employer was tax deductible.

Legislation was introduced (now TA 1988 s 313 and FA 1988 s 73) as a result of which all restrictive covenant payments are now fully taxed in the hands of the employee and always deductible by the employer in arriving at his profits.

Limitations on the ambit of s 313 are illustrated by *Vaughan-Neil v IRC* (1979) which involved the payment of £40,000 to a barrister to induce him to leave the planning bar and work for a company. This sum was not taxed. It was not a reward for services, being in effect a compensation payment (see *Pritchard v Arundale* [**5.63**]), nor was it caught by s 313 because the barrister had given no undertaking to the company not to practise at the bar. His inability to do so was not caused by accepting the particular terms of employment but rather by accepting the employment itself; the payment was merely recognition that the job would prevent his practising at the bar.

On the other hand, some Revenue officers argued that s 313 had a wide ambit and applied where an employee agreed, on receiving a compensation payment, to give up his right to claim damages. The uncertainty has now been resolved by SP 3/96 stating that when an employee expressly or impliedly agrees on receipt of a capital sum to give up his legal claims, that sum will *not* be taxed under s 313. Sums paid for other restrictive undertakings continue to be taxed even if contained in a settlement agreement.   [**5.70**]

8 Unearned income

A payment may be taxable under Schedule E even though it would, in other circumstances, be treated as unearned income.

David O'Leary, like Shilton, was a professional footballer. He was domiciled in Eire and entered into an arrangement, designed to avoid income tax, with his employers, Arsenal FC. An offshore trust was established with O'Leary as life tenant and the sum of £266,000 was loaned interest free repayable on demand to that trust by Arsenal. The income produced by this sum (£28,985 pa) was payable to O'Leary but, so it was argued, because the sum fell to be taxed under Schedule D Case V and because O'Leary was non-UK domiciled tax would not arise unless and until that sum was remitted to the UK (see [13.33]). Once O'Leary ceased to be employed by Arsenal the loan would be repaid. Vinelott J decided, contrary to the taxpayer's submissions, that the annual interest was correctly assessed as an emolument. He commented:

> 'The fallacy which I think underlies Counsel for the taxpayer's submission can be shortly stated. If an employer lends money to an employee free of interest or at a favourable rate of interest and if the employee is free to exploit the money in any manner he chooses his employment cannot be said to have been the source of the income derived from the exploitation; the employer is the source of the money and the taxpayer is assessable to tax under Schedule E on the benefit to him of obtaining the loan on the terms on which the loan was made; but if the loan is repayable on demand that benefit cannot be quantified and form the basis of an assessment under Schedule E [but see [5.150]]. By contrast if an employer were to lend money to a bank on terms that interest was paid to the employee until further order the interest paid to him while he remains an employee would almost inevitably be taxable as an emolument of his employment ... (*O'Leary v McKinlay* (1991)).

[5.71]–[5.90]

V WHAT IS AN EMOLUMENT?

1 Introduction

This Section considers the general principles to be applied in considering whether a particular receipt by an employee constitutes an 'emolument'. These general principles apply to all employees. For employees earning £8,500 or more per year and (most) directors there is a special statutory regime which will usually bring a benefit into charge even if it is not an emolument under general principles. However, that regime often only applies if the benefit is not otherwise chargeable to tax, so even for those employees and directors it is important to establish whether the receipt is taxable under general principles. It is also important to establish what is the taxable value of a benefit under general principles: the special regime may seek to bring a larger amount into the tax net and will, therefore, apply even though the benefit *is* caught under general principles.

Employee incentives, in the shape of share schemes, employee trusts and profit related pay, are considered in Chapter 39. Pension schemes are considered in Appendix IV. [5.91]

2 Money or money's worth

There are two basic principles as to the taxability of benefits in kind.

First, a benefit in kind is taxable in the hands of the employee only if it is convertible into money. In the case of *Tennant v Smith* (1892) the House of Lords, in interpreting what is now s 131, held that the benefit of a house which the employee was required by his employment to occupy but which he could not assign or sublet did not constitute an emolument since it was not convertible into money. The test is whether the benefit *could* be converted; it is irrelevant whether the employee actually converts it into money. Consider, for instance, a British Rail season ticket which cannot be sold because it is non-assignable, but which can be converted into cash by surrender.

Although in *Abbott v Philbin* (1961) Lord Reid stated 'if a right can be turned to pecuniary account that in itself is enough to make it a perquisite', the Special Commissioner in *Bootle v Bye* (1996) thought that this was not intended to apply 'regardless of whether any payment obtainable would be heavily depreciated'. He accordingly held that a right to receive a payment if the employing company was sold (an event over which the taxpayer had no control) was not a perquisite as, realistically, any payment would in no way reflect the right's intrinsic value. It will be interesting to see whether higher courts adopt this novel approach.

Secondly, if the benefit is an emolument, tax is levied on the value of the benefit to the employee: this is taken to be its secondhand value. In *Wilkins v Rogerson* (1961) the company arranged with Montague Burton that each employee would be permitted to obtain clothes of up to £15 in value. The contract provided for payment directly by the company. When the Revenue sought to tax an employee on a suit costing £14.50 the court held that the benefit was convertible into money, because the taxpayer could sell the suit, but that he could only be taxed on the secondhand value, estimated at £5 (see also *Jenkins v Horn* (1979), where this test operated to the taxpayer's disadvantage).

The practical application of these two principles can cause problems. For instance, the provision of a non-convertible benefit, such as the free use of a car, is not chargeable whereas the provision of money to enable the employee to purchase such a benefit is an emolument (see *Bird v Martland* (1982)). A further problem is that it may be difficult to decide whether particular facts involve the rules on benefits in kind or not. This is illustrated by the case of *Heaton v Bell* (1970) where a company operated a scheme under which its employees were offered the use of fully insured company cars. If they accepted the offer they thereupon received reduced wages. An employee could withdraw from the scheme on giving 14 days' notice whereupon he would revert to his original wage. The House of Lords by a majority of four to one held that an employee who joined the scheme was entitled to his original unamended wage and that he had merely chosen to spend a portion of that wage on the hire of a car (but see Lord Reid's dissenting judgment). Thus tax was charged on the full wage since what the taxpayer chooses to spend his wages on is not tax deductible! Three members of the House also considered that, if the full wage was not taxable, then the car was a taxable benefit in kind because, even though the right to use the car could not be assigned, it could be converted into money by withdrawing from the scheme and receiving the original wage again.   **[5.92]**

EXAMPLE 5.3

Simon is employed as a butler at a wage of £10 pw. He is required to 'live in' and 50p is deducted per week for board and lodging. Simon is assessed to tax on £10 pw (see *Machon v McLoughlin* (1926)). Compare the case of Rosie who is employed as a housemaid and is paid a weekly wage of £9.50. She is required to live in but is not charged for board and lodging. She is taxed on £9.50; the board and lodging is a non-convertible benefit in kind which, therefore, escapes tax under s 19.

3 Discharge of liability

Difficulties may also arise when the employer discharges debts incurred by his employee. In *Nicoll v Austin* (1935) a managing director told his employer company that he would have to sell his imposing house, where he entertained potential customers, because he could no longer afford to pay for its upkeep. To prevent the sale, the company paid the outgoings on the house and the employee was taxed on this sum as if he had been given the money to pay the bills himself. Similarly in *Richardson v Worrall* (1985) payment for petrol using an employer's credit card was held taxable since it discharged the taxpayer's liability to the garage. **[5.93]**

EXAMPLE 5.4

(1) Employees are given £14.50 to buy clothes to wear to work. The sum is an emolument (cf *Wilkins v Rogerson* (1961)).
(2) Employees choose clothes and they send the bills to the employer for payment. As the debt has been incurred by the employee tax will be charged in accordance with *Nicoll v Austin* (1935).

4 Expenses

If a lower-paid employee receives an 'expense allowance' it will be presumed to be a reimbursement of expenditure unless the Revenue can show it to be an emolument; higher paid employees and directors will have to prove actual deductible expenditure (see **[5.142]**). Where an employee incurs expenses which the employer reimburses, those reimbursements will not be taxed as emoluments provided that the employee could have deducted the money he spent from his Schedule E income as an expense of the employment (see TA 1988 s 198 and Section VIII below for a discussion of what expenditure is deductible and **[5.142]** for the position of higher paid employees and directors). In such cases it can be said that the employee has derived no personal profit from the reimbursement (in the sense that he is no better off) and, in addition, no practical purpose would be served by deciding that the reimbursement is an emolument but then permitting the employee to reduce that emolument to nil by setting off an equivalent expense.

In *Pook v Owen* (1970) a doctor holding a part-time hospital appointment who had to attend the hospital several times a week was reimbursed two-thirds of his travelling expenses. It was held that the reimbursements were not emoluments because he was no 'better off' as a result of them. They were (partial) repayments of actual expenditure which would have been deductible in arriving at the emoluments of the taxpayer.

In other cases, however, reimbursements have been held not to be emoluments even though the relevant expenditure would not have been deductible by the employee under s 198. Thus, in *Donnelly v Williamson* (1982), a teacher, who was reimbursed for travelling expenses incurred in attending out-of-school functions, was not taxable on the reimbursements. The court held that they were not emoluments because they were not derived from her employment (she attended the functions voluntarily) and that they were a genuine attempt to compensate her for actual expenditure. Compare *Perrons v Spackman* (1981) where a mileage allowance paid by the council to one of its rent officers was held to be an emolument because it contained a profit element.

If it is accepted that there is no correlation between the reimbursement rules and the test for deductibility of expenditure under Schedule E, exactly what expenses may be reimbursed is not clear. Presumably, the expense must be directly connected with the employment, since the reimbursement of, eg, the employee's private gas bill will be taxed as an emolument (*Nicoll v Austin*, [**5.93**]).

> **EXAMPLE 5.5**
>
> Justinian, a lowly paid law lecturer, attends a legal conference and his University employers refund the cost of the conference which he had paid. The reimbursements are not emoluments taxable under s 19. If the University had instead paid for the conference so that he had received a benefit in kind Justinian would be taxed on it if it was convertible. If Justinian had borne the expenses himself he would have been unable to deduct them from his emoluments under TA 1988 s 198 (see [**5.172**]).

TA 1988 s 200A provides a specific exemption where an employer reimburses (or pays directly for) incidental expenses (eg for newspapers) incurred by an employee during overnight absences, up to an allowable maximum (currently £5 for stays in the UK and £10 for those abroad): such expenditure would not normally be deductible under s 198 as it would not be necessarily incurred in the performance of the employee's duties. The exemption applies to round sum allowances, paid 'wholly and exclusively for the purpose of being used for defraying' such expenses, up to the limit. If the maxima are exceeded, the exemption does not apply to *any* part of the payment; nor does it apply if the costs of the employee's travel to his overnight rest place are not deductible.

TA 1988 ss 200B–D, inserted by FA 1997, provide an exemption from a Schedule E charge where the employer (or a third party — for instance, when a manufacturer organises training for a retailer's staff) pays or reimburses the cost of 'work-related training' or 'related costs'. These provisions replace ESC A63: consequent changes to the national insurance contribution rules that may be needed are under consideration.   [**5.94**]–[**5.110**]

VI   BENEFITS IN KIND—ALL EMPLOYEES

The following benefits, which are not convertible into cash or which would have a low convertible value, are specifically taxed as emoluments under Schedule E for *all* employees and generally for all office-holders.   [**5.111**]

1   Living accommodation (TA 1988 ss 145 and 146)

Following the introduction of TA 1988 s 146A by FA 1996, these charges apply even if the employee was offered a lower cash alternative to the accommodation. Of course, if the cash offered was *higher* than the amount taxable under ss 145 and 146, that higher amount will be taxed!

The 1995 Budget did, however, bring some good news. Where employer-provided accommodation is in multiple occupation, theoretically each employee could be charged on the full value of the accommodation. However, ESC A91 limits the total amount chargeable on the accommodation to what it would have been if it was occupied by one employee. The amount chargeable on each employee will depend on 'all the relevant facts'.   [**5.112**]

a) *The s 145 charge*

If an employer provides his employee with living accommodation, the employee is taxed under TA 1988 s 145 on the value to him of that accommodation less any sum that he actually pays for its use. In *Stones v Hall* (1989) the court concluded that the provision of services in return for accommodation was, for the purposes of s 145(1), neither the payment of rent nor the making good of the cost to the company of providing that accommodation. Accordingly, the taxpayer was charged on the value of the accommodation.

The value is the higher of the annual value of the premises (defined in TA 1988 s 837 as the rateable value—see IR Press Release of 19 April 1990 on the effect of the abolition of rates) and the rent paid by the employer for that accommodation (TA 1988 s 145(2)). As a result, tax under s 145 is frequently on a nominal sum since the annual value bears little relationship to the rent that would be received if the property were actually let and, if the employer owns the premises, the alternative charge cannot apply. As domestic rating lists will become increasingly outdated, the government announced in 1990 that it was reviewing the long-term basis of the s 145 charge (with a view to introducing new rules in the future) but changes have not yet been made.

[**5.113**]

b) *The additional s 146 charge*

Special rules apply in cases where the cost of providing the accommodation exceeds £75,000 (s 146). Broadly, the employee will in such circumstances be charged to tax on an additional emolument calculated by applying the official rate of interest (as under beneficial loans—see [**5.150**]) to the excess by which the actual cost of providing the accommodation exceeds £75,000. That actual cost will usually be the cost of acquiring the property.

EXAMPLE 5.6

Giles, the managing director of Clam Ltd, sells to the company his house in Chelsea for its market value of £160,000. He is granted an option to buy the property back in ten years' time for its present value. The annual value of the house is £750 and Giles continues to live in the property. Giles is assessed to tax under Schedule E on an emolument of £750 pa plus (say) 7% of £85,000 (£160,000 – £75,000) ie £5,950 pa.

ESC A91 removes a potential double tax charge here also. Even when the charge under s 145 is based on the open market rent, a charge can sometimes arise under s 146. Typically this will be the case if the accommodation is overseas when the 'annual value' for s 145 purposes is taken by the Revenue to be the open market rent. In such cases the s 146 charge will not apply (for a discussion of whether these provisions do in any event apply to overseas properties, see *Taxation*, 29 February 1996, p 543 and 14 March 1996, p 628).

[**5.114**]

c) *Exemptions*

The charge under TA 1988 s 145 does not catch the provision of ancillary services such as cleaning, repairs and furniture. However, if the employee is higher paid or a director who falls within s 167(1), tax is charged under s 154 on the cost to the employer of providing the services less any amount paid by the employee for those services (but note that there is a cap on the taxable amount if the employee is in 'representative accommodation'—s 163).

No charge arises under TA 1988 s 145 for 'representative occupation'. This means occupation falling within s 145(4), ie accommodation which is:

(1) necessary for the proper performance of the employee's duties (eg a caretaker and see *Tennant v Smith* (1892) at [**5.92**]); or

(2) customary for the better performance of the employee's duties (eg a policeman who occupies a police house adjacent to the police station); or

(3) where there is a special threat to his security and special security

arrangements are in force as a result of which he resides in that accommodation.

A director who falls within the provisions of TA 1988 s 167(1) cannot be a representative occupier under (1) or (2) above (s 145(5)).

In *Vertigan v Brady* (1988) the owner of a nursery site near Norwich provided his 'right-hand man' with a rent-free bungalow some three miles from the nursery. That employee was in direct charge of the plants and their propagation and was on standby at all hours during the week and on two out of three weekends to make adjustments to the heating and ventilation of the greenhouses. He was able to reach the nursery within five minutes of leaving the bungalow. There was evidence that he had been unable to obtain council accommodation in the area when he took the job and could not afford to buy a house in the vicinity. The court decided that the benefit of the rent-free accommodation constituted a taxable emolument since the exception for accommodation which was customarily provided ((2) above) did not apply. What was customary depended upon three main factors: statistical evidence (how common was the practice?); how long had the practice existed (a custom does not grow up overnight!); and whether the relevant employer accepted the customary practice. In this case, although statistical evidence showed that approximately two-thirds of all key nursery workers were provided with rent-free accommodation, there was insufficient evidence to show that the practice had become so normal as to be an established custom.   [5.115]

d) *Shadow directors*

Whether ss 145–146 are capable of applying to shadow directors has long been a matter of debate: the issue is especially important when a non-UK domiciliary purchases a UK house for personal occupation through a foreign company. If it can be shown that he is a shadow director of that company, can he then be assessed on benefits derived from occupying the property? (See generally *Law Society's Gazette*, 12 and 19 July 1989.) A Special Commissioner case suggests that the answer is 'no' on the basis that these sections apply to offices and employments but not to the 'deemed' office of a shadow director (see *Private Client Business*, 1994, p 227) but this is not the Revenue's view (SE 2205).
                                                                      [5.116]

2   Vouchers and credit tokens (TA 1988 ss 141–144)

An employee or office-holder who (or whose family) receives a benefit in the form of a voucher or credit token may be charged to tax thereon.

Where he receives a non-cash voucher (ie a voucher or similar document which can be exchanged for goods or services) he is taxed on the cost to the employer of providing the voucher rather than on its exchange value. Cheque vouchers (ie a cheque provided for an employee to be used by him to obtain goods or services) are similarly charged as emoluments. Section 141 contains some specific exemptions (eg non-cash voucher used for car parking near place of work) and various ESCs provide further relief: eg A2 (first 15p of luncheon vouchers).

Where the employee receives a cash voucher, ie a voucher which can be exchanged for a sum of money not substantially less than the cost to the person providing it, he is taxed on its exchange value (s 143).

Where the employee receives a credit token (including a credit card) he is taxed on the cost to the employer of providing the goods, money and services obtained by the use of that credit token (TA 1988 s 142).

The charge under s 141 or s 142 is reduced if the employee could have claimed a tax deduction if he had paid for the goods or services himself or if the voucher or token was used for 'incidental overnight expenses' up to the permitted maximum (see [**5.94**]). [**5.117**]

3 **Other benefits**

a) *Sick pay and permanent health insurance*

Sick pay is a taxable emolument for all employees and office-holders whether paid by the employer, a Friendly Society, an insurance company or a third person if it is paid as a result of arrangements entered into by the employer (TA 1988 s 149). Where an employer runs a sick pay scheme to which both employer and employee contribute, the employee is not taxed under Schedule E on sums paid to him or his family to the extent that the sums reflect contributions made by the employee. Similarly, if the employee receives *income* benefits under a permanent health insurance policy which he has taken out then, provided the cost of the insurance premiums was not met by the employer, benefits will be exempt from tax provided that they are only paid while the individual is sick or disabled (including payments during convalescence or rehabilitation and income 'top-ups' following sickness etc): TA 1988 s 580A and B, inserted by FA 1996; and see *Tax Bulletin*, December 1996, p 377, on the types of insurance benefits not covered by the exemption and when and how gross payments can be received.

Statutory sick pay and maternity payments are taxable under s 150. [**5.118**]

b) *Training*

If an employer pays certain costs for employees attending educational courses full-time at universities or technical colleges etc, any benefit which would otherwise be chargeable to tax under Schedule E is not treated as an emolument (SP 4/86 reissued 18 November 1992 ([1992] STI 991)). Where an employer meets the cost of a qualifying training course undertaken by his employee or former employee to retrain the latter in skills needed for a new job or self-employment, that cost will not be treated as an emolument of the employee (s 588). The employee must leave that employment within two years of completing the course and must not be re-employed by that employer within the two years thereafter (s 589) (see further [**4.64**]). [**5.119**]

c) *Outplacement counselling*

When employees are made redundant employers sometimes arrange 'outplacement counselling' for them. This is a service provided by a third party to help the employee: for instance, by providing counselling to help him adjust to the redundancy or providing assistance in the preparation of his CV. TA 1988 s 589A exempts the provision of these services from income tax and gives the employer a statutory deduction for their cost. [**5.120**]

d) *Relocation costs*

The taxation of benefits provided to a relocating employee is complex.

If the employer offers a guaranteed reselling price ('GSP') scheme (which normally involves the employer or a relocation company buying the house and then selling it) then, even if the price paid is no more than the market value of the property, other costs incurred by the employer could be taxable under TA 1988 s 154 (eg his legal costs). However, by ESC A85 many of these costs will be ignored (see [**5.147**]).

Benefits not covered by the ESC, whether or not arising under a GSP scheme, may be relieved under TA 1988 ss 191A, 191B and Sch 11A—but only 'eligible' expenses and benefits are relieved and the maximum relief is limited to £8,000.

Reimbursement of a capital loss is not covered. The Revenue's view is that if the employer (or relocation company) pays more than the market value, the difference is taxable under Schedule E (*Tax Bulletin*, May 1994, pp 122–124) but this does not seem essentially different from the employee selling to a third party at a loss and being reimbursed by his employer, as in *Hochstrasser v Mayes* (1959) (see [**5.42**]). It is not clear whether the Revenue considers that the House of Lords would reverse its previous decision or that the situation would be likely to arise only where s 154 applied and compensation would be taxable thereunder. Even the latter view is not uncontroversial, particularly if the payment was not made by the employer (see the Northern Ireland Court of Appeal's discussion of the scope of s 154 in *Mairs v Haughey* (1992)).   [**5.121**]

4   Termination payments (TA 1988 ss 148 and 188)

Lump sum payments, not taxable under general principles (see [**5.66**]–[**5.69**]) or specific charging provisions formerly escaped tax (the payment was often called a 'golden handshake'). TA 1988 s 148, however, applies a special scheme of taxation to 'any payment (not otherwise chargeable to tax) in connection with the termination of the holding of an office or employment or any change in its functions or emoluments'. Crucially, the first £30,000 of any payment falling within s 148 is exempt from tax (see s 188(4)). Section 148 is very wide and includes payments made by a person other than the employer to someone other than the employee (eg to his spouse or PRs) and catches golden handshakes (*ex gratia* payments), compensation and damages for wrongful dismissal and redundancy payments which are not otherwise taxable. Section 148 extends to payments in kind, eg the receipt by a dismissed employee of a company car as compensation. What is the position where continuing benefits (such as use of a car or cheap loan) are provided to ex-employees? There has been some debate as to whether the benefits in kind legislation applies (see [**5.145**]). In *George v Ward* (1995) the Special Commissioner held the use of a car to be taxable under s 148 (but it seems that no attempt was made to assess the benefit under s 157). The Revenue's view seems to be that s 148(3) applies. This can cause problems. Strictly the value of the right to receive future benefits should be taxed in the year of termination (s 148(4)). However, such rights are difficult to value, particularly if it is not known how long the employee will enjoy the benefit; and if the enjoyment period is shorter than that originally envisaged, there is no mechanism for refunding any excess tax paid. The Revenue have, therefore, given the taxpayer the right to choose an alternative approach, under which the continuing benefit will be taxed in the year of receipt (its value to be calculated in accordance with s 596B) (see [1997] STI 381 and Tax Bulletin, June 1997, p 427) until s 148 is amended. A consultative document is expected in late 1997.

Vinelott J's decision in *Nichols v Gibson* (1994) suggested that s 148 is even wider than generally supposed. An employee received a termination payment on the last day of his employment, being 6 April, the first day of a year of assessment during which he was neither resident nor ordinarily resident in the UK and did not perform any duties here. He argued that the payment was not taxable because at the time of receipt he did not fall under any of the cases of Schedule E in s 19(1) para 1. The court held that the charge under s 148 was independent of s 19(1) para 1 and, therefore, the fact the taxpayer did not fall thereunder was irrelevant: the payment was taxable. This view was upheld by the Court of Appeal (1996) (see (1996) BTR 619 for criticism of this decision).

Section 148 does not apply (TA 1988 s 188 and Sch 11) to:

(a) payments otherwise chargeable to tax under Schedule E (for instance, payments caught by *Dale v de Soissons*—see [**5.66**]);

(b) payments charged to tax under TA 1988 s 313;

(c) benefits received under approved retirement benefits schemes;

(d) payments because of death, injury or disability; and

(e) certain payments for foreign service.

Exclusion (d) was considered in *Horner v Hasted* (1995). Section 188(1)(a) exempts, inter alia, a payment 'made on account of disability of' an employee. Lightman J's view was that it has to be established as an objective fact that there was a 'relevant disability' (which, reflecting SP 10/81, he considered to be one affecting the employee's ability to perform his duties) and as a subjective fact that the disability was the motive for the payment.

Lump sum benefits from unapproved pension schemes used to be excluded from the s 148 charge by s 188(1)(c) provided the employee had been taxed on the employer contributions. This now only applies to benefits provided under schemes established before 1 December 1993 and not varied on or after that day (FA 1994 s 108(6)). Lump sum benefits provided under other schemes will escape s 148 (and ss 19 and 596A) if they satisfy the requirements of s 596A(8), as amended by FA 1994 s 108(5) (see generally [**IV.15**]).

By concession, payments of legal costs of a former employee or office-holder will not be taxed under s 148, provided certain criteria are met (for instance, that the payment is made directly to the employee's solicitor) (ESC A81 and see also [1993] STI 1414 and 1422 and *Tax Bulletin*, November 1993, p 101 and October 1994, p 170).

That part of any payment which exceeds the £30,000 exempt slice is taxed in full. Two or more payments made in respect of the same office or employment or made by the same or associated employers are aggregated for this purpose.

EXAMPLE 5.7

During the year 1997–98, A (a single woman without dependent children) has the following income:

	£
Earnings from employment	25,000.00
Other income	nil
Lump sum on termination of employment	80,000.00
Personal allowances	4,045.00

Tax payable disregarding the termination payment:

Taxable income:	25,000.00
Less:	4,045.00
	20,955.00

Tax payable:	first £4,100 at 20%	820.00
	remaining £16,855 at 23%	3,876.65
		£4,696.65

Tax payable including the termination payment:
(1) Calculate taxable slice: £80,000 – £30,000 exempt = £50,000

(2) Calculate tax at marginal rate on £50,000 as follows:

	£
first £5,145 at 23% =	1,183.35
remaining £44,855 at 40% =	£17,942.00
	£19,125.35

Final liability is £4,696.65 + £19,125.35 = £23,822

The exemption for the first £30,000 of a termination payment taxable under s 148 can cause problems when assessing the damages payable for breach of the employment contract. *British Transport Commission v Gourley* (1956) and subsequent cases are concerned with the assessment of damages awarded by the courts in tort and breach of contract. The cases are not concerned with the tax treatment of the sum once it has been awarded. Damages in tort for personal injury are not taxed, but damages for breach of contract and, in tort, for financial loss may be subject to charge if they represent compensation for lost profits (see *London and Thames Haven Oil Wharves Ltd v Attwooll* (1967) [**6.83**]) especially when they are payable on the termination of an employment contract, (in certain circumstances a disposal of contractual rights may attract CGT: see [**14.7**]).

Damages should compensate the innocent party for a breach of contract; they should not normally penalise the contract breaker. Hence, if an employment contract has been broken, the damages should reflect the fact that, had the employee performed the contract, he would only have been left with the benefit of a net sum after payment of tax. Therefore, the damages awarded should be computed by reference to that net sum. Obviously this will adequately compensate the plaintiff so long as the damages are not themselves taxed; if they are, the net sum will be insufficient.

It could be argued that once a payment is subject to charge (as terminal payments are by virtue of s 148), there is no room for the application of the *Gourley* rule and a gross sum should be paid. The courts, however, have distinguished between terminal payments of less than £30,000 and those in excess of £30,000. A payment below £30,000 is free of tax and, therefore, the amount awarded should be calculated on *Gourley* principles (see *Parsons v BMN Laboratories* (1963)). *Lyndale Fashion Manufacturers v Rich* (1973) shows that the calculation should proceed as if the damages formed the highest slice of the recipient's income for the year (see *Law Society's Gazette*, 1983, p 346). If the net damages exceed £30,000 (after making the appropriate *Gourley* deduction), those damages must be increased by a sum equal to the estimated income tax that will be charged on the award under TA 1988 s 148. This final net award will represent as realistically as possible the actual loss suffered (*Shove v Downs Surgical plc* (1984) and see (1984) MLR 471 where the conflicting decisions of the courts are discussed).

Terminal payments caught by TA 1988 s 148 are treated as earned income in the year when the job is lost (not the year when the money is paid in cases when the two are different—see s 148(4)). Tax must be deducted under PAYE on the amount above £30,000. If the payment is made before delivery of Form P45, the deduction should be in accordance with the employee's code for the relevant period. If made after delivery of Form P45, tax should be deducted at the basic rate (Income Tax (Employments) Regulations, SI 1993/744, reg 24). If the PAYE rules would result in the deduction of an excessive amount of tax it may be possible to agree with the inspector of taxes that a lesser sum be paid or, alternatively, if the tax has already been deducted, that an interim repayment be made.

Problems may arise when the employee is also a substantial shareholder in the employer company and the payments are made on the change of ownership of that company. In such cases, a payment, ostensibly for termination of his service contract, may be challenged on the grounds that it represents partial consideration for the shares transferred. To the extent that the challenge is successful the payment will not be deductible as a business expense of the company and will not qualify for the £30,000 exemption (see *James Snook & Co Ltd v Blasdale* (1952)). To avoid this danger it is desirable to separate, so far as possible, arrangements for the share sale from the question of compensation for loss of office.   [**5.122**]-[**5.140**]

VII   BENEFITS IN KIND—'HIGHER PAID EMPLOYEES'

1   **General outline**

a) *Who is caught by these rules?*

The relatively lenient rules applicable to lower paid employees will not be applied to employees falling within TA 1988 ss 153–168 which catch any

employee with emoluments of at least £8,500 pa. The origin of the special
legislation taxing directors and employees earning above an income threshold
goes back to 1948 when, because of the then threshold, the rules only applied
to very senior employees. When the legislation was redrafted in 1976, they
were referred to as 'higher paid employees'. However, the threshold of £8,500
has not been raised since 1979 and the idea that these rules only apply to
senior employees has become increasingly absurd since £8,500 is well below
the national average of full-time earnings. In fact, the provisions now apply
to the great majority of employees. Not surprisingly, therefore, FA 1989 deleted
all reference to 'higher paid employees' and the previous government accepted
the general principle that '*all* employees should pay income tax on the whole
of their earnings whether received in cash or in kind'. Given such a categorical
statement, it remains something of a mystery why these special rules remained
confined to employees with earnings of £8,500 and above!

To determine whether the employee has emoluments of £8,500, it is assumed
that the employee is within the special rules; those rules are therefore applied
in valuing the benefits and only if the resultant figure for emoluments is below
£8,500 is he taxed as lower paid.

EXAMPLE 5.8

Aziz receives a salary of £8,100 pa and an expense allowance of £400 (which is
taxed as an emolument for a higher paid employee). He is treated as receiving
emoluments of £8,500 pa and is, therefore, within the special rules.

Sections 153–168 also apply to a director whose emoluments are less than
£8,500 pa *unless* he has no material interest in the company (ie he does not
control more than 5% of the ordinary share capital) and either works full-
time for the company, or the company is non-profit making or a charity (TA 1988
s 167(5)).

The Special Commissioner in *Jacobs v Templeton* (1995) held that benefits
'provided' to *future* employees in the tax year before the employment commenced
were not caught by s 154. This point was not considered by the High Court
(because it interpreted 'provided' differently—see [**5.142**]): also note that the
relationship between s 19(1) para 4(a) and ss 154(1) and 168(2) has not been
considered by the courts.   [**5.141**]

b) *The purpose of the special rules*

The object of the general charging provision of TA 1988 s 154 is to tax all
benefits (other than those specifically excluded or charged elsewhere) 'provided
by reason of the employment' by any person (not just the employer) to the
employee or his family *and whether or not convertible into cash*. Generally, the cost
incurred in providing the benefit is treated as an emolument, subject to a
deduction for any payment made by the employee (TA 1988 s 156). In *Rendell
v Went* (1964) the managing director of a company had a car accident and
was prosecuted at the Old Bailey for dangerous driving. The company paid
for the best available legal services for him and he was acquitted. He was
taxed on the cost to the company of providing the legal services (a non-convertible
benefit in kind) although he did not request the benefit and could have found
cheaper services elsewhere.

In *Templeton v Jacobs* (1996) the court held that a benefit was 'provided'
to an employee when the benefit in question became available to be enjoyed
by the taxpayer (not when the employer had done everything it had to do
to secure the provision of the benefit, as had been held by the Special
Commissioner (1995)).

When the benefit is provided at the cost of the employer it is normally deemed to be provided by reason of employment (TA 1988 ss 154(3) and 168(3)). If the benefit is provided at the cost of a third party, it must be shown that it was provided 'by reason of employment'. The Northern Ireland Court of Appeal in *Mairs v Haughey* (1992) thought these words were wider than the word 'therefrom' in s 19 (accepting that s 19 imposed a 'reward for services' test) and that the question to be asked is 'what enabled [the employee] to enjoy the benefit?' (but note the comments of Carnwath J in *Wilcock v Eve* (1995) if s 19 has a wider scope).

Finally, the purpose of s 154 is to bring 'benefits' into the tax net and the Court of Appeal in *Mairs v Haughey* (1992) indicated that not every payment by an employer to an employee will be caught. In particular, they stated that a 'fair bargain' (in that case reasonable compensation for the employees surrendering rights under a non-statutory redundancy scheme) was not within s 154.

Under s 153, if the employee receives an expense allowance or a reimbursement of expenses he has incurred, he is taxed on it in full as an emolument unless he can claim any allowable expenses (s 153(2)). This forces the employee to justify his expenses. An exemption for round sum allowances for, or reimbursements of actual expenditure on, 'incidental overnight expenses', up to the permitted maximum, was introduced by FA 1995 (see [**5.94**]).   [**5.142**]

EXAMPLE 5.9

Andy has a salary of £9,000 pa and an expense allowance of £4,000 pa. He is taxed on emoluments of £13,000 pa unless he can deduct any expenses under s 198.

c) *The cost of providing the benefit*

TA 1988 s 156 provides as follows:

'(1) The cash equivalent of any benefit chargeable to tax under section 154 is an amount equal to the cost of the benefit, less so much (if any) of it as is made good by the employee to those providing the benefit.

(2) Subject to the following subsections, the cost of a benefit is the amount of any expense incurred in or in connection with its provision, and (here and in those subsections) includes a proper proportion of any expense relating partly to the benefit and partly to other matters.'

In *Pepper v Hart* (1992) the taxpayers were assistant masters at Malvern School and they each had one or more sons in attendance at the school under a concessionary fees scheme. Payments equal to 20% of the normal school fees were paid and it was accepted that these more than covered any *direct additional expense* resulting from the boys' presence in the school. The issue before the courts was whether s 156 was solely concerned with 'additional direct expenses' or did it also involve a rateable proportion of the expenses incurred in providing the school facilities that were enjoyed generally by *all* the boys? The House of Lords held that, in the case of in-house benefits, the cost of the benefit to the employer for the purposes of TA 1988 s 156 is the additional (or marginal) cost and not a *pro rata* share of all the costs of the employer. The House of Lords reached this decision by taking into account statements made by the Financial Secretary to the Treasury during Standing Committee debates on the Finance Bill 1976. The House's acceptance of the admissibility of excerpts from Hansard in certain circumstances has much wider implications than merely resolving the dispute in this case. However, we do know that taking Hansard into account here changed the result: the House would have found 4:1 in favour of the Revenue if the argument based on Hansard had not been raised.

If an employee sells an asset to his employer for its market value, there could still be a charge under s 154 for the employer's other acquisition costs (eg legal fees). ESC A85 relieves an employee from charge if the costs would normally have been incurred by any buyer. **[5.143]**

d) *Are cash payments caught?*

The wording of s 156 would seem to indicate that s 154 does not apply to cash payments. However, the Court of Appeal in *Wicks v Firth* (1982) held that it did apply to cash benefits (the House of Lords did not have to decide the point) and this approach was also taken by the Northern Ireland Court of Appeal in *Mairs v Haughey* (1992). **[5.144]**

e) *Do the rules apply after termination?*

Employers sometimes provide benefits to former employees—for instance, a redundant employee may still have a cheap mortgage; a retired employee may still have his private medical insurance premiums paid. In some cases, these benefits may be taxable under the unapproved pension schemes legislation (ss 596A and 596B), given the wide meaning of 'relevant benefits' (and note SP 13/91—see **[5.69]**). If not, could such benefits be taxed under the benefits in kind legislation?

Pensions, lump sums and 'other like' benefits provided to the employee, or his family or dependants, on his death or 'retirement' cannot be so taxed as a result of s 155(4). In relation to other benefits, the wording of the various provisions suggests they cannot apply in a year of assessment when the taxpayer has not been employed at all (although note that the relationship with s 19(1) para 4(a) has not been considered by the courts); there is some dispute as to whether specific provisions can apply for the remainder of the year of assessment after termination of employment (see the discussion in *Taxation*, 18 August 1994, p 500 and 10 November 1994, p 141, but note that the opening words of the sections in Chapter II often differ). In any event, certain termination payments *may* escape s 154 as being 'fair bargains' (see **[5.142]**). If ss 153–168 do not apply, s 148 will usually do so: s 148 is to be amended to put the taxation of continuing benefits on a fairer basis (see **[5.122]**). **[5.145]**

f) *Special rules for use of an asset*

When the benefit consists of the *use* of an asset owned by the employer, the cash equivalent included in the employee's emoluments is the higher of the actual cost to the employer in providing the asset (eg the cost of hiring it) and the 'annual value' of the use of the asset (s 156(6) and (7)). In the case of land, its annual value is the rent that it might be expected to fetch on a yearly letting and will usually be the rateable value (see TA 1988 s 837). For any other asset, the annual value is 20% of its market (capital) value when it is first put at the employee's disposal (TA 1988 s 156(6)).

If assets which have previously been used or have depreciated are *given* to an employee, the cash equivalent is the market value of the asset *at the date of transfer* less any sum paid by the employee (TA 1988 s 156(1) and 156(3)). If, however, the employee had previously had the use of the asset, he is taxed on its market value *at the date when he first used it* less the sum of the annual value(s) on which he has already been taxed (TA 1988 s 156(4)).

Whenever an employer transfers an asset to an employee, the former's CGT position should be considered in the light of TCGA 1992 s 17 given that the Revenue has withdrawn its former concessionary treatment whereby that section was not applied if the employee paid less than market value and was taxable under Schedule E on the difference (*Tax Bulletin*, December 1994, p 181). **[5.146]**

EXAMPLE 5.10

On 6 April 1995, Mr C Rash was given by his employer the use of a hi-fi system costing £2,000. In October 1997 the employer transferred the system to Mr Rash free of charge when its market value was £800.

Market value at the date when first used by Mr Rash, ie cost	£2,000
*Benefit in kind in 1995–96: 20% × £2,000	£ 400
*Benefit in kind in 1996–97: 20% × £2,000	£ 400
Benefit in kind in 1997–98: £2,000 – £800 (£400 + £400)	£1,200

*If the employer had rented the system at £500 pa, this higher figure would be taxed as an emolument.

2   Exemptions from the charge

Certain benefits are exempted from charge under TA 1988 s 154 by s 155 namely:

(1) certain benefits provided in relation to a company car or van (s 155(1)—see [**5.148**]);

(2) car parking space near workplace (s 155(1A)) (and note that the payment or reimbursement of expenses incurred for such a space is excluded from Schedule E by s 197A and this may include roadside parking meters — *Taxation*, 4 July 1996, p 376);

(3) employers' payments in relation to 'incidental overnight expenses', up to the permitted maximum (s 155(1B)—see [**5.94**]);

(4) accommodation, supplies or services provided to the employee 'in premises occupied by' the provider and used by the employee purely in performing his work; for instance, the provision of an office or secretarial services (s 155(2)) — note Jonathan Parker J's view in *Templeton v Jacobs* (1996) that the mere payment of rent by the employer did not mean it was 'occupying' the relevant premises for the purposes of s 155(2));

(5) certain works to living accommodation provided by reason of employment (s 155(3));

(6) a pension, lump sum (or similar benefit) for the employee or his family or dependants on his death or retirement (s 155(4)—see Appendix IV);

(7) meals in any canteen in which meals are provided for employees generally (s 155(5)); in practice, this provision is generously construed to enable different categories of staff to enjoy separate dining rooms (hence, 'two tier' canteens) and it may be possible to use outside restaurants as a 'canteen' in the absence of 'in-house' facilities;

(8) the provision of medical treatment, or insurance against the cost of such treatment, outside the UK where the need for the treatment arises because the employee is performing his job outside the UK (s 155(6))—the cost of providing medical insurance within the UK is a taxable benefit for higher paid employees and directors under s 154.

Nursery facilities ceased to be a taxable emolument from 6 April 1990 (TA 1988 s 155A). The facilities may be provided either at the workplace or elsewhere by the employer and either alone or jointly with other persons. Neither is there any charge when similar provisions are available for older children after school. Relief from the charge is not, however, available if the employer provides cash to enable his employee to pay for nursery facilities nor, indeed, if the employer directly pays nursery fees to a third party. Similar costs incurred by a self-employed taxpayer do not qualify as deductible expenditure nor can an individual employee deduct the costs of a nanny or child help in the home!

Section 156(8) effectively provides an exemption from the s 154 charge where the employee would have been able to claim an income tax deduction if he had incurred the expenditure on which he is to be taxed. ESC A85 relieves the employee from a charge on the incidental expenses incurred by his employer in buying an asset from him (provided these are costs which would not normally be met by a seller).   **[5.147]**

3 Specific benefits

a) *Vehicles and fuel (TA 1988 ss 157–159AC, 168–168G and Sch 6)*

These provisions tax employees and directors on the benefit that they derive from a firm or company car or van which is available for their private use. Tax is not, therefore, charged if the employee can prove that he was forbidden to use the vehicle for private use and did not so use it (*Gilbert v Hemsley* (1981) and see s 168(6)). A lower-paid employee will not be taxed on this benefit because it is not convertible into cash.

The legislation distinguishes between two categories of car and van: the pooled car or van and all others. A pooled vehicle is one which is made available to different employees; is normally garaged overnight at the employer's premises; and any private use is merely incidental to its business use (TA 1988 ss 159 and 159AB—and see SP 2/96 and FA 1996 s 108 particularly in relation to the position when a pooled car is used for chauffeur-driven home to work journeys for a senior employee and IR 480 for a discussion of what is 'merely incidental' private use). When these conditions are satisfied the benefits of using pooled cars or vans are not taxable.

If a non-pooled car is available for the private use of an employee or his family or household, he is taxed on the cash equivalent of the car as fixed by statute (TA 1988 s 157 and Sch 6).

These provisions were extensively amended by FA 1993 because it was thought that the old system substantially undertaxed the private use of a company car. From 6 April 1994 the charge is usually based on 35% of the list price of the car and accessories (the Revenue apparently takes the list price as the manufacturer's one, not the dealer's—see *Taxation*, 19 December 1996, p 353; note the exemption for accessories provided for the disabled in s 168AA). The market value will be taken if the car is 15 years old or more and worth £15,000 or more, if this is higher than the list price (s 168F). In any case, there is a cap on the value of a car of £80,000. The cash equivalent will be reduced by one-third if the employee does at least 2,500 business miles per year and by two thirds if he does at least 18,000 business miles, provided the employee 'was required by the nature of his employment' to use the car that much (see *Henwood v Clarke* (1997) on how the threshold mileage (proportionately reduced) has to be applied to each car if more than one car is made available during the tax year). There will be a (further) reduction of one-third if the car is four years old or more at the end of the year.

In order to avoid these increased charges (and Class 1A national insurance contributions) some employers offered a (low) cash alternative, so that under *Heaton v Bell* (1970) (see **[5.92]**) the employee would be taxed on (and the employer's national insurance contributions based on) the salary foregone (under TA 1988 s 19). Now s 157A means that the mere fact that a cash alternative is offered will not make the use of a company car taxable under s 19. The employee will pay tax on what he actually receives—the car, or the cash.

Vans available for private use are taxed under separate provisions—s 159AA and AB and Sch 6A. Basically, the cash equivalent is £500 if the van is less than four years old at the end of the year and £350 if aged four or more years. There are special provisions to deal with shared vans.

Generally, any benefit received from the private use of a 'heavier commercial vehicle' is exempt from tax, provided the employee's use of the vehicle is not wholly or mainly private use (s 159AC).

The amount of tax payable can be reduced if the employee is required to make a payment for the private use of the vehicle or it is unavailable for at least 30 days (Sch 6 paras 6, 7 and 9); or if the employee makes capital contributions (s 168D). Reliance on any of these provisions is not straightforward (see generally *Taxation*, 29 June 1995, p 321). For instance, any payments must clearly be for the private use and so a payment for insurance premiums, required by the agreement with the employer, did not reduce the cash equivalent in *IRC v Quigley* (1995) because they were made 'in exchange for the insurance of the vehicle, not for the use of it'.

Problems also arise where contributions are made in order to receive a more expensive car. While the Revenue may allow these to be deducted from the cash equivalent if the agreement is properly worded (see *Tax Bulletin*, November 1991, p 3), it is easy not to satisfy the (literally interpreted) words of Sch 6 para 7 (see *Brown v Ware* (1995)). It is not even certain that monthly contributions will count as capital payments for the purpose of s 168D (but see *Taxation*, 13 July 1995, p 381).

Finally, the Revenue interprets 'unavailability' in para 6 strictly so the fact that the employee is out of the country for three months and cannot in fact then use the car does not seem sufficient (*Taxation*, 17 August 1995, p 532).

There is a separate scale charge on the provision of petrol for private use in an employer's car (TA 1988 s 158). The provision of a personal chauffeur for an employee is a taxable benefit under TA 1988 s 154 (but see the comment on pool cars above). The employee is not taxed on other benefits provided in connection with the car such as insurance, road fund tax and a car parking space provided by the employer (TA 1988 s 155), although mobile phones made available in connection with cars, vans and even 'heavier commercial vehicles' may be taxed (s 159A(8)—see [**5.149**]).   [**5.148**]

b) *Mobile telephones (TA 1988 s 159A)*

From 1991–92 employees have been subject to tax on *every* mobile telephone provided by their employer. The tax benefit is currently fixed at £200 per telephone but this level of charge will be kept under review and may be increased by statutory instrument. There is no charge in cases where there is no private use of the telephone by the employee nor where the employee is required to reimburse the employer for the full cost of any private use (and does so!) (see IR Booklet 480 for the Revenue's interpretation of the 'full cost'). Introducing this charge in the 1991 Budget Speech Norman Lamont commented as follows:

> 'I turn now to one of the great scourges of modern life: the mobile telephone. I propose to bring the benefit of car phones into income tax and simplify the tax treatment of mobile phones by introducing a standard charge on the private use of such phones provided by an employer ... I hope that as a result of this measure, restaurants will be quieter and roads will be safer.'

[**5.149**]

c) *Beneficial loan arrangements (TA 1988 ss 160–161)*

Interest-free (or cheap) loans to employees are not caught under TA 1988 s 154: if the loan is repayable on demand, the benefit cannot be quantified (see quote from *O'Leary v McKinlay* (1991) at [**5.71**]); in any event, if the money comes from the employer's own funds, then foregoing the opportunity to earn interest may not be a 'cost' to the employer within s 154. Accordingly, s 160 provides that where a relevant employee or director obtains a loan by reason of his employment, either interest free or at a low rate of interest, he is taxed on the cash equivalent of that loan. This is defined as the difference between interest for the year calculated at the 'official rate' and any interest actually paid by the employee. From 6 April 1991 the official rate has been kept in line with typical mortgage rates but does not generally change in response to movements of less than ½% in such rates. A beneficial loan is obtained by reason of employment if it falls within Part I of Sch 7.

Prior to FA 1996, outstanding 'non-qualifying' loans between the lender and borrower had to be aggregated when calculating the cash equivalent but s 107 of that Act limits this to loans by a close company to a director thereof. The same section also simplifies the procedure for electing the alternative method of calculating the amount of interest that would have been payable during the year at the official rate of interest (Sch 7 para 5). With the introduction of self-assessment employers are obliged to calculate the cash equivalent of benefits and these changes are aimed at simplifying this duty.

Section 160 applies whenever a benefit is obtained because of an interest-free loan and it is not necessary to show that the employee derived any advantage therefrom. In *Williams v Todd* (1988) a district inspector of taxes was taxed on an interest-free loan paid as 'a douceur to soften the financial and other disadvantages he had suffered as a result of his compulsory removal from Wigan to the more expensive South': he was taxable on the benefit.

EXAMPLE 5.11

Day, an employee of Digday Ltd, borrows £25,000 in order to purchase a suite of Italian furniture. He pays interest at 2% pa and the capital is to be repaid on demand. For 1997–98 Day has received an emolument equal to:

	£
Interest at official rate (say) 7% of £25,000	1,750
Less: interest paid at 2% pa	500
Taxable emolument	£1,250

A loan to a relative of the employee is also taxed under TA 1988 s 160 unless the employee can show that he derived no benefit from it (s 161(4)).

If a loan to a relevant employee or director is released or written off, he is treated as receiving an emolument equivalent to that amount, even if the release is made on (or after) the termination of his employment (unless the termination is due to his death) (s 160(3) and s 161(6)). 'Golden handshakes' given in the form of the release of a loan will not have the benefit of the £30,000 exemption under TA 1988 s 148 (see [**5.122**]) and should, therefore, be avoided.

There is no charge to tax where the aggregate amount of all beneficial loans outstanding at any time in the tax year does not exceed £5,000; or if the aggregate 'non-qualifying' loans does not exceed this amount (s 161(1)). This enables small loans (eg to buy a season ticket) to escape the tax net even if the employee has a larger 'qualifying' loan (eg a cheap mortgage). Loans provided on the same terms as loans made to the general public in the ordinary course of the employer's business are generally exempt (ss 161(1A) and (1B) and *Tax Bulletin*, August 1994, p 157 for the Revenue's interpretation of the provisions): this avoids an employee being subject to a tax charge if the rate of interest normally charged by his employer is less than the official rate. Any sums advanced by the employer to cover expenses that will be necessarily incurred in the employment will not be taxed under s 160 provided that the sum advanced is less than £1,000 and that the advance is spent within six months (SP 7/79).

Prior to FA 1995 any loan which replaced one taxable under s 160 was also taxable thereunder. This blanket rule has been replaced and it is now possible for the employer to transfer the loan to a commercial lender (in particular to a subsidiary of such a lender which has been set up to provide this facility and which would not fall within the general exemption for commercial lenders because it does not deal with the public), which would provide the replacement loan on arm's length terms, without s 160 continuing to apply (see the new s 160(3A) and the amendments to Sch 7 para 4, effected by FA 1995 s 45).

There has always been a problem meshing the s 160 charge with the provisions which give relief for 'qualifying loans' (basically loans on which interest is eligible for relief under s 353(1)—see s 161(1C)) when the employee uses the loan for a qualifying purpose. The problem was exacerbated when mortgage interest relief was restricted to 25% by FA 1991, leading to complicated provisions that were in Part IV of Sch 7. If the same approach had continued these provisions would have become even more complex (and would have applied to more employees) with the restriction of mortgage interest relief to 20% in 1994: basic rate employees would have had to pay tax at 5% on the benefit of the employer loan and 40% taxpayers at 20%. FA 1994 therefore adopted a new approach. Whatever the loan is used for, the employee pays tax under s 160. To the extent the loan is used for a qualifying purpose, the employee is deemed to have paid interest (at the official rate) and can claim relief accordingly.

EXAMPLE 5.12

Day receives a further loan from his employer of £100,000 to purchase a house. The loan is interest free.

	£
Taxable emolument under s 160:	
£100,000 × 7%	7,000

Tax relief under s 353:

$$\left(£7,000 \times \frac{£30,000}{£100,000} \right) \times 20\% \qquad \underline{420}$$

$$\underline{\underline{£6,580}}$$

The benefit of a cheap or interest-free bridging loan provided when an employee has to move house because of his job may be exempted from tax: see TA 1988 s 191B and Sch 11A.   **[5.150]**

d) *Shares (TA 1988 s 162)*

If partly paid shares are issued to an employee or director to whom TA 1988 Chapter II Part V applies, then a notional loan charge, based on the difference between the price paid and the market value of the shares at that time, can arise under TA 1988 s 162. Further charges can arise if the amount payable is written off or if an employee sells shares acquired by reason of employment for more than they are then worth. Section 162 is considered in detail at **[39.23]**.   **[5.151]**

e) *Scholarships*

Scholarship income is exempt from tax (TA 1988 s 331). However, scholarships awarded to the children of higher paid employees and directors are taxed as emoluments of the parents unless not more than 25% of the total payments from the fund are to children of employees (whether or not higher paid or directors) and the award is fortuitous, ie not resulting from the employment (TA 1988 s 165: see further [1984] STI 62).   **[5.152]**

f) *Returns*

Employers are required to make an annual return in respect of each higher paid employee and director on IR Form P11D detailing all benefits, including expense allowances, and payments made to that employee. The employer can, however, apply for a blanket dispensation from having to include routine items such as travelling, hotel expenses and any other type of expense (other than round sum allowances) which need not then be included in Form P11D, nor in the employee's income tax return (TA 1988 s 166 and IR 69: revised 1992). **[5.153]**

4   Conclusions on the treatment of benefits in kind

The present system is neither logical nor fair and presents a bewildering range of alternatives. Consider, for instance, the following example.   **[5.154]-[5.170]**

EXAMPLE 5.13

Rod wants his computer operator, Julie, to work overtime two evenings per week. Her salary is £4,500 pa. He plans to provide her with meals or a meal allowance on those two evenings. So far as Rod is concerned, the sum that he expends will be a deductible business expense, but for Julie taxation under Schedule E depends upon how the provision is made:
(1)   If Rod, the employer, pays a cash allowance, that sum is an emolument.
(2)   If Rod pays the bill incurred by Julie, that sum is an emolument (*Nicoll v Austin* (1935)).
(3)   If Rod gives Julie a voucher exchangeable at a restaurant, the cost incurred by Rod in providing the voucher is an emolument.
(4)   If Julie buys the food herself and is reimbursed, it may be that there is no charge (see *Donnelly v Williamson* (1982)).
(5)   If the employer has an arrangement with the restaurant so that food is provided and the expense is directly met by the employer there is no charge (see *Wilkins v Rogerson* (1961)).
If Julie earned £8,500 pa then those methods of provision which escape tax for lower paid employees will be caught by s 153 or s 154.

VIII   DEDUCTIBLE EXPENSES

Tax under Schedule E is charged on emoluments after deducting allowable expenditure. Allowable expenditure is defined in TA 1988 s 198, which draws a distinction between travelling and other expenses. However, the Revenue's treatment of subsistence expenses incurred during an employee's temporary absence from his normal place of work follows their treatment of his travel expenses, rather than being based on the general rules relating to other expenses (*Tax Bulletin*, May 1994, p 130).

Following a consultative document on employee travel and subsistence, FA 1997 s 62 amends s 198 to simplify and make fairer the rules relating to travel expenses (it is expected that the Revenue's approach to subsistence costs will alter in line with these changes). The fundamental change is that where the employee is obliged to *attend* somewhere other than his normal workplace in the performance of his duties (as opposed to being obliged to *travel* there in such performance, as under the current rules) a deduction for the travel may be claimed, even if he does not set off from his normal workplace (or, indeed, does not have one). However, *any* claim to a deduction for travel expenses (i.e. even one allowable under the current rules) will be reduced by any consequent saving in 'ordinary commuting' costs. Consultation will continue through the 1997-98 tax year, with s 62 not coming into force until 6 April 1998. These changes will, therefore, be considered in more detail in the next edition of this book. **[5.171]**

1 **Expenses other than travelling expenses**

Expenses will be deductible only if incurred '... wholly exclusively and necessarily in the performance of the said duties ...'. These provisions may be contrasted with the more generous expenditure rules of Schedule D Cases I and II (see [**6.111**]).

Three requirements must be satisfied if an expense is to be deductible: *first*, it must be incurred 'in performing' the duties. No deduction is allowed for expenses which enable the employee to prepare for his duties or to be better equipped to carry them out. In *Shortt v McIlgorm* (1945), for instance, the taxpayer could not deduct the fee that he paid to an employment agency (contrast TA 1988 s 201A allowing agents' fees paid by actors and other theatrical artists taxed under Schedule E to be deducted). In *Simpson v Tate* (1952) a medical officer could not deduct the cost of joining learned societies which would enable him to perform his duties better (note the partial reversal of this decision by TA 1988 s 201). The House of Lords adopted a similarly strict approach in *Fitzpatrick v IRC (No 2)*; *Smith v Abbott* (1994) which concerned expenses incurred by journalists in purchasing newspapers and journals. The House held that when a journalist reads newspapers and periodicals he is *preparing* to perform his duties efficiently but not actually acting 'in the performance of' his duties. Parts of Lord Templeman's speech indicate that the House was to some extent influenced by the amount of tax that would be lost if the journalists' claims were allowed:

'If a journalist or other employee were allowed to deduct expenses incurred by him in his spare time in improving his usefulness to his employer, the imposition of income tax would be distorted and the amount of the expenses claimed by the individual would depend only on his own choice ... if each [journalist] spends £1,000 a year the total deduction for 30,000 journalists will be £30m a year ... the principle of the decision in the present cases does not apply only to journalists; the ramifications of [a] decision in their favour would be enormous.'

This contrasts with the approach of Nolan LJ in the Court of Appeal in *Smith v Abbott* (1993):

'The submission that the reading by the taxpayers of other newspapers and periodicals could only reasonably be regarded as a means of adding to their general qualifications seems to me to ignore the short-lived and almost ephemeral nature of the benefits which they thus acquired.

The purpose which their reading was designed to serve, and did serve, was the production of the next edition of the *Daily Mail* or the *Mail on Sunday*. In these circumstances, the reading seems to me to constitute preparation for a particular assignment.'

Secondly, the expense must be 'necessarily' incurred in the performance of the duties. This is an objective test: the expenditure must arise from the nature of the employment and not from the personal choice of the taxpayer (see Lord Blanesburgh in *Ricketts v Colquhoun* (1926) as clarified by Lord Wilberforce in *Owen v Pook* (1970)). Nor is it sufficient that the employer requires the expenditure—the nature of the duties must require it. In *Brown v Bullock* (1961) a bank manager was required by his employer to join a London club. He could not deduct his subscription because it was not necessary for the performance of his duties. It seems odd that the employer is not allowed to decide what is necessary to the particular office or employment!

The *third* requirement is that the expense should be incurred 'wholly and exclusively' in the performance of the duties. This same requirement is found in Schedule D Cases I and II (see [**6.117**]).

Few expenses will satisfy all three conditions. However, the harshness of TA 1988 s 198 is, in practice, mitigated in relation to various employments by a number of Revenue concessions (for instance, the flat rate allowance for the cost of tools and special clothing, ESC A1) and by certain statutory deductions (for instance, fees for joining certain professional bodies and learned societies: TA 1988 s 201 and see [1997] STI 9).

There are other statutory deductions. Since 6 April 1992 a person can claim relief for certain payments for a 'qualifying course of vocational training' under FA 1991 s 32, unless relief can be claimed under any other income tax rule. The relief can be claimed by deducting basic rate tax from the payment: the recipient then reclaims the tax deducted from the Revenue. The courses for which relief can be claimed were extended by FA 1994 s 84 and FA 1996 s 144 but the persons who can claim the relief has been restricted and in some cases is limited to those who are at least 30 years old. Since 6 April 1995 a person can claim relief if he pays the premiums on liability insurance or pays uninsured work-related liabilities, even for payments made after employment has ceased (at least if made before the end of the sixth year of assessment following that in which the employment ceased) (FA 1995 ss 91 and 92, the former introducing a new TA 1988 s 201AA—and see *Tax Bulletin*, October 1995, p 257 for the Revenue's interpretation of these provisions). An innovation, designed to encourage charitable giving, is the so-called 'payroll deduction scheme'. So long as a recognised scheme is operated by their employer, employees can make donations to the charity of their choice up to a maximum amount of £1,200 pa. These sums are deductible expenses for the employee and, as a novel feature, are paid gross to an approved charitable agent which then distributes the sums to the charity of the employee's choice (TA 1988 s 202). [5.172]

2 Travelling expenses

If travelling expenses are to be deductible they must be 'necessarily' incurred 'in the performance' of the duties (or be 'expenses of keeping or maintaining a horse to perform the same ...'): there is no 'wholly and exclusively' requirement. The expense of travelling to work is not deductible because it is incurred before, rather than in, the performance of the duties (but note ESC A4). In contrast, travelling between places of work is deductible.

EXAMPLE 5.14

(1) Sally is employed as a lecturer by the Midtech University and gives seminars at both branches of the University which are two miles apart. Her travelling costs between both branches are deductible.

(2) Jim works as a postman and as a barman in a local pub. The cost of travelling between the sorting office and the pub is not deductible since Jim has two different jobs and is not therefore travelling between centres of work in the course of a single employment.

The requirement that travelling expenditure be 'necessarily incurred' has been considered in three House of Lords cases. In *Ricketts v Colquhoun* (1926) the travelling expenses of a barrister to and from Portsmouth where he had been appointed Recorder were not deductible. In *Owen v Pook* (1970), a general medical practitioner was allowed to deduct the expenses of travelling to a hospital where he held a part-time appointment, because some of the functions of that post were performed at his home so that he was travelling between two centres of work. Finally, in *Taylor v Provan* (1974) a Canadian director of Bass Charrington was allowed to deduct his travelling expenses to the UK because he performed part of his duties at places outside the UK. What emerges from these cases is that travelling expenses for getting to work will not be deductible since where a person resides is his personal choice and therefore the expenses of travelling to work will not satisfy the objective test established by the courts (see [**5.172**]). Further, a job will not be treated as having two centres just because the taxpayer *chooses* to perform some of its functions at his home. In *Miners v Atkinson* (1997) the court agreed with the extreme interpretation given to this rule by the Special Commissioner: even if it is an objective requirement of the job that duties are performed at home, if the duties could be performed equally well wherever the taxpayer lived, then doing the work at that precise address should be treated as a matter of personal choice and, therefore, the costs of travelling thereto and therefrom are not deductible (for a criticism of the Special Commissioner's reasoning see *Taxation*, 27 April 1995, p 79). This decision is in line with the Revenue's view that it is extremely difficult to establish home as a place of work except where the employee has a 'travelling appointment' (paras 2.13 and 2.14 of the consultative document). Problems of deductibility caused by this interpretation of the cases will to some extent be alleviated by the enactment of FA 1997 s 62 (see [**5.171**]).

Travelling expenses raise two further problems. *First*, allowable expenditure has to be reasonable. In *Marsden v IRC* (1965) an Inland Revenue investigator could not deduct the full cost of travelling by car to perform his duties because he could have used a cheaper form of transport. This is not to say that the cheapest form must always be used, since the matter is one of fact and degree and allowance must be made for the inconvenience of certain forms of transport and for the dignity of the employee or office-holder. Presumably, a company director will not be consigned to the local bus service! For expenditure to be reasonable, the shortest route does not necessarily have to be taken, if the longer route is taken for a good business reason (see IR 480 para 8.4). *Secondly*, the relationship between the rules for deductibility of expenditure and the taxation of reimbursements should be carefully noted (see [**5.94**]). In the case of higher paid employees and directors such reimbursements are automatically treated as emoluments (TA 1988 s 153).

Finally, it may be that the decision of the House of Lords in the employment law case of *Smith v Stages* (1989) will mark a relaxation in the courts' view of when an employee will be travelling in the course of performing the duties of his employment. The Law Lords held that an employee who was travelling back home from a place of work to which he had been temporarily assigned, was still acting 'in the course of his employment' so as to render his employer vicariously liable for the employee's negligence. Were this decision to be applied in the context of deductible expenditure under Schedule E, it would suggest that if an employee has several places of work not only would expenditure on travel between those places be deductible but so also would the cost of travelling from home to the first place of work, provided that it is not the employee's regular or normal place of work.   [**5.173**]–[**5.190**]

IX   BASIS OF ASSESSMENT AND PAYE

Prior to 1989–90 tax was charged under Schedule E on a current year basis and was levied on emoluments when earned. Accordingly the date of payment was strictly irrelevant to the tax charge. Inevitably this led to problems of referring payments back to the tax year when earned: for instance directors are frequently voted bonuses long after the relevant tax year for which they performed the services. To tidy this area up and to correct certain other defects in the Schedule E legislation, FA 1989 altered the basis of assessment under Schedule E from the earnings to the *receipts basis*.   [**5.191**]

1 General principle

Emoluments are subject to charge when they are received rather than when they are earned and, not surprisingly, this rule is backed-up by a detailed definition of when a payment is received for these purposes (TA 1988 s 202A). In the case of directors, for instance, payment is made when the sum is credited in the company's accounts or records—hence crediting the director's account with that sum will constitute a payment for these purposes (TA 1988 s 202B). [**5.192**]

2 Position of employer

Inevitably, if the employee is to be assessed on the receipts basis rather than the earnings basis, the question which then arises is how the employer should be treated. To permit him to deduct emoluments when they are earned even though he has not yet paid them would lead to an imbalance between the deductibility rules under Schedule D Cases I and II as compared with the emolument rules under Schedule E.

Accordingly, it is provided in FA 1989 s 43 that an employer can only deduct the sum in question from his accounts if that sum is actually paid either *during* the period of account (the same definition of payment as above) or *within nine months* thereafter; the same rule is applied by s 43(11) to 'potential emoluments' — sums reserved in the accounts of the employer or held by an intermediary (for instance, an employee trust) with a view to their becoming actual emoluments. Sums earned but not paid until more than nine months after the end of a period of account will therefore be deducted not in that period but in the accounting period when paid. [**5.193**]

EXAMPLE 5.15

Jason, a self-employed builder, makes up his accounts to 31 December each year. He employs Lumpy as his bricklayer. In 1996 he pays Lumpy £20,000 and at the end of the year (because of cashflow problems) owes him £15,000. £7,000 of this sum he pays in June 1997 and the balance in October. He submits his accounts to the Revenue (showing £35,000 as a deductible expense) in April 1997.
(1) The £20,000 paid to Lumpy is a deductible expense in 1996.
(2) The £15,000 unpaid when the accounts are submitted will be presumed not to be paid within nine months of the end of the accounting period and will therefore be *disallowed* in 1996: however the £7,000 subsequently paid within that period will result in an adjustment to the 1996 accounts if a claim is made.
(3) The remaining £8,000 will be deducted in the 1997 accounts.
(4) Lumpy will be assessed on the £15,000 in 1997–98 (year of receipt).

3 The source doctrine

One of the hallowed principles of income tax (see [**3.41**]) is that a charge can only be made if the source of the income is continuing. This principle has, of course, been much modified by statute. Thus, the possibility of a barrister ceasing to practise and at some time during his peaceful retirement receiving arrears of fees which, because the source of the fees had ceased, escaped tax, has long since gone under the post-cessation receipts rules. More recently, the case of *Bray v Best* (1988) (see *Example 3.1*) revealed an unsuspected gap in the Schedule E legislation on this matter.

This gap has now been closed and if an emolument is paid to an employee before his employment commences, it will be treated for the purposes of s 19 as an emolument of the first year of that employment: if paid after the employment has ceased it will be related back to the last year of employment. Accordingly, should the facts of *Bray v Best* recur in the future, the distribution payment will be related back to the last year of the employment. Note, however, that this change merely extends the source doctrine to catch the payment: the tax itself will still remain charged in the year of receipt. The principle that tax is charged in the year of receipt but that the source of the income must be determined in the year when it is earned, applies in the facts of the following example.   [5.194]

EXAMPLE 5.16

(1) In 1996–97 Bert is resident and ordinarily resident in the UK. His job ceases and in 1997–98 he becomes non-resident (taking a job as a Eurocrat in Brussels). A bonus paid in 1997–98 in relation to the UK job is taxed under Schedule E Case I and is *taxed in year of receipt*.

(2) Take the opposite case: ie in 1996–97 Henri is non-UK resident; his job ceases; he comes to the UK in 1997–98 when he receives a bonus in respect of 1996–97. He is not subject to UK tax since he was outside the tax net when the money was earned.

4   Directors

A major purpose of the new rules was to deal more satisfactorily with the tax treatment of directors' emoluments. In this connection the term 'director' is widely defined to include 'shadow directors' and the Revenue generally takes the view that all directors fall to be taxed under Schedule E. Former practice which enabled certain directors to be self-employed under Schedule D will no longer be followed.   [5.195]

5   The collection machinery of PAYE

a) *The scope of the provisions*

Tax is collected by a sophisticated method of deduction at source operated by the employer and known as the PAYE system (TA 1988 s 203). The employer is required to 'deduct' tax when he makes a payment (which is treated as made when it is treated as received by the employee (see s 203A, mirroring s 202A [5.192])). There are difficulties in establishing that there has been a 'deduction' when no actual payment is made at the time of the deemed payment, particularly when money is never actually handed over but a credit is merely given against drawings already made on a director's loan account. In *R v IRC, ex p McVeigh* (1996) May J was prepared to hold there had not been a deduction when a 'net' sum had been credited to a director's loan account to wipe out his drawings because there was no 'pre-existing entitlement to gross pay': the employer merely entering the tax and national insurance due on this net sum in the company's ledgers was not sufficient to count as 'deduction'.

The system generally applies to all income assessable under Schedule E. Prior to FA 1994, tax could not generally be collected under the PAYE system if the employer (and, if different, the person who paid the employee) were outside the UK. FA 1994 s 133 introduced detailed and far-reaching provisions (TA 1988 ss 203C–203E) to widen the PAYE net.

Section 203C provides that if the employer (or, if applicable, the person paying the emoluments on behalf of the employer) is not subject to the Income Tax (Employments) Regulations 1993, SI 1993/744 ('the PAYE Regulations') (as to which, see *Clark v Oceanic Contractors* (1993), discussed at [13.51]), and does not collect PAYE voluntarily, then the person for whom the employee 'works' (in the UK) is treated as making the payment and is, therefore, required to operate PAYE. Typically this will catch the employee seconded to a UK branch or subsidiary. Section 203D deals with the situation where a non-UK resident employee is liable to UK income tax under Schedule E Case II on his UK earnings because he performs part of his duties here. The employer now needs to apply to the Revenue for a direction agreeing 'what part of his remuneration is liable to UK income tax'; if no direction is applied for, the employer must operate PAYE in respect of the entire salary. Section 203E enables the Revenue to subject a person for whom an employee works (but who is not his employer) to the PAYE Regulations even if the actual employer is taxed in the UK and therefore subject to the PAYE regulations. The Revenue can direct that person to operate PAYE 'if it is likely that income tax will not be deducted or accounted for in accordance with the Regulations'.

Before 1975, workers supplied through agencies who were self-employed could escape tax on earnings on a particular assignment by disappearing once it was completed. Accordingly, TA 1988 s 134 (originally introduced in that year), provides that where a worker receives remuneration under a contract with an agency to render personal services under supervision to a client he is taxable under Schedule E; the agency therefore has to operate PAYE (*Brady v Hart* (1985) and, on the supervision requirement, see *Bhadra v Ellam* (1988)).

Certain workers (such as entertainers) are excluded from the operation of the section and special rules also apply to self-employed persons working in the construction industry.　　　　　　　　　　　　　　　　　　　　　　　　　　　**[5.196]**

b) *Exclusions from the provisions*

Benefits in kind are generally excluded from the PAYE net on the basis that there is no payment (but see the Budget Press Release IR24 (30 November 1993) for some situations which the Revenue considered fell within the then current provisions). However TA 1988 ss 203F–203L (introduced by FA 1994) impose PAYE where assessable income is provided in the form of 'tradeable assets' or by way of assets for which trading arrangements exist; PAYE is also imposed where non-cash vouchers and credit tokens which may be exchanged for such assets (or money, in the case of credit tokens) are obtained and where cash vouchers to which s 143(1) applies are received. Regulations provide how and when the employer is to account for PAYE on these 'notional payments' (see SI 1994, 1212, Tax Bulletin, February 1997, p 385 and c) below). Payment by assigning trade debts are to be caught by these provisions with effect from 2 July 1997 (see [1997] STI 915).

Regulations exclude certain benefits from the scope of these provisions (eg cash vouchers used to defray expenses if the amount for which the voucher can be exchanged would not, if it had been paid directly by the employer to the employee, have been taxable except under s 153; most shares received through approved employee share schemes or on exercise of any option granted before 27 November 1996 (see **[39.21]**—SI 1994/1212 as amended by SI 1996/2969).

Another exclusion derives from the House of Lords decision in *IRC v Herd* (1993). It was held that any payment 'only part of which is assessable to income tax under Schedule E' is excluded from the system because there is no machinery for distinguishing the part that is taxable from the part that is not. In such a situation there is no obligation on the payer to operate PAYE in relation to the taxable part. This type of situation might arise (as it did in *Herd*) where an employee sells shares acquired by reason of his employment and part only of the purchase price is taxable under Schedule E (for instance, under TA 1988 s 162(6)—see **[39.23]**).

The decision in *IRC v Herd* (1993) cast doubt on the practice under which employers operated PAYE on part of an employee's remuneration where the other part was not subject to UK tax (because he performed some of his duties abroad and was not resident or not ordinarily resident). TA 1988 s 203D was therefore introduced by FA 1994 s 126 to deal with this situation (see [**5.196**]). It also led to a debate on the PAYE position when cash payments (taxable under TA 1988 s 135) were made in return for surrender of employee share options (eg on a takeover) where the option had been granted under seal. The Revenue has now confirmed such payments fall outside the PAYE net (see [1995] BTR 532).   [**5.197**]

c) *Coding and accounting for tax due*

PAYE is an effective tax collection system which reduces the opportunity and incentive for tax evasion. Each employee has a code which represents his allowances for the tax year. This amount is taken into account when calculating the amount of tax to be deducted at source. PAYE can be used to collect underpayments of tax by the employee in previous years by reducing (or withholding completely) allowances in the current year: FA 1996 s 126 permits regulations to be made to deal with the problems this would otherwise cause under the self-assessment regime.

On 6 April 1993 a system of 'K' codes was introduced. A K code is applied if the employee receives benefits in kind (or has other income not subject to PAYE) the value of which exceeds his personal allowances. The K code is a negative code: normally the code is deducted from emoluments to arrive at the amount subject to PAYE; the K code is *added* to the emoluments, thereby increasing the amount collected. However, all an employee's salary cannot disappear in paying tax on his benefits in kind: tax deducted from any payment cannot exceed 50% of the payment (except where tax is being collected on 'notional payments' (see below)—see *Tax Bulletin*, May 1994, pp 121–122).

For directors and employees earning at least £8,500 pa, the employer must also complete Form P11D giving details of benefits in kind and payments by way of expenses (save, in the latter case, those for which a dispensation has been granted: see explanatory leaflet IR 69); for other employees Form P9D must be completed. A Form P60 must be given to each employee working for the employer on 5 April, giving details of emoluments subject to PAYE and the tax paid and a Form P45 (giving similar details for the tax year to date) is given on cessation of employment. The burden on employers has been further increased by the introduction of self-assessment. For 1996–97 onwards they have to provide certain information to employees so that they can complete their tax returns (see SIs 1995/1284, 1996/804 and 1996/1312).

Prior to 6 April 1996 about 2,500 employers regularly agreed to pay their employees' tax liabilities on minor items—a lump sum was paid for the group. FA 1996 s 110 made statutory these 'settlement agreements'. The detailed rules are set out in the Income Tax (Employments) (Amendment No 6) Regulations 1996 (SI 1996/2631); SP5/96, a leaflet (IR 155) and a statement in the *Tax Bulletin*, December 1996, p 365.

The PAYE Regulations contain a grossing-up requirement where emoluments are paid tax free. Further, in an attempt to ensure that PAYE is operated on remuneration paid to directors, TA 1988 s 164 provides that whenever tax on a director's emoluments should have been deducted in accordance with regulations made under s 203 and the whole, or part, of the amount due was not deducted but was accounted for to the Revenue by a person other than the director then, unless the director makes good the tax paid, he will be treated as receiving a further emolument equal to the amount of tax that has been accounted for to the Revenue. This provision applies to directors falling within the provisions of TA 1988 ss 153–168. FA 1994 introduced a similar provision if an employer is treated as making a 'notional payment' to an employee (generally, a payment treated as made under ss 203B, 203C, 203F–203I: see s 203J(2)(a)) and is, accordingly, required to account for the tax due, if that tax was not deducted from actual payments made and the employee does not make good the amount due within the requisite time (s 144A).

An employer may be liable to interest on tax paid late where he has failed to apply PAYE correctly at the right time. This charge will begin to run 14 days after the tax year to which the tax relates (TA 1988 s 203). In the event of an overpayment of tax in a previous year, this will be corrected either by direct repayment or by set-off against other tax liabilities of that year.

Under the PAYE system the liability of the employer to deduct and account for the correct amount of tax is usually exclusive so that the Revenue cannot assess an employee for unpaid tax. Exceptions are provided for in regs 42(2) and (3) of the PAYE Regulations (amended by the Income Tax (Employments) (Amendment No 2) Regulations 1995 (SI 1995/447) to give the Revenue greater powers). Regulation 42(2), which can be applied by the Revenue if satisfied that the employer took reasonable care to comply with the Regulations and the error was made in good faith, is rarely (if ever) applied. Regulation 42(3), which applies when an employee receives the emolument knowing that the employer has wilfully failed to deduct the proper amount of tax, is often relied on. In *R v IRC, ex p McVeigh* (1996) May J commented that this provision 'would normally operate where the employer had wilfully paid an employee gross and the employee knew this' (see further [**5.196**]).

A heavy burden is placed on the Revenue if reg 42(3) is to be satisfied since not only is actual knowledge on the part of the employee required but also an element of blameworthiness on the part of the employer must be shown. This burden was satisfied in the cases of *R v IRC, ex p Keys and ex p Cook* (1987) where the employees in question were the controlling directors of the employer company which had failed over a number of years to operate PAYE in respect of their salaries.

In *Booth v Mirror Group Newspapers plc* (1992), Hobhouse J held that a one-off payment by a third party made to induce the taxpayer to enter into the contract of employment was within the PAYE system: in such a case the deduction is at basic rate under regs 2 and 20 of the PAYE Regulations. However, although the PAYE Regulations define 'employer' as any person paying 'emoluments', the Revenue does not always apply the Regulations literally (eg to a person paying a tip—see *Tax Bulletin*, 1993, p 85). FA 1994, by introducing s 203B, ensured PAYE will be operated when payments of 'assessable income' are made by an 'intermediary of the employer' (eg trustees of an offshore employee trust). [**5.198**]

6 Schedule D—trades and professions

'... take a gang of burglars. Are they engaged in trade or an adventure in the nature of trade? They have an organisation. They spend money on equipment. They acquire goods by their efforts. They sell the goods. They make a profit. What detail is lacking in their adventure? You may say it lacks legality, but it has been held that legality is not an essential characteristic of a trade. You cannot point to any detail that it lacks. But still it is not a trade, nor an adventure in the nature of trade. And how does it help to ask the question: If it is not a trade, what is it? It is burglary and that is all there is to say about it.' (Lord Denning in *Griffiths v Harrison* (1963) but contrast the profits of prostitution which are derived from a trade: see *IRC v Aken* (1990).)

[6.1]

I INTRODUCTION

Tax is charged under Schedule D Case I on the annual profits or gains arising to a UK resident from a trade carried on in the UK or elsewhere and under Case II from a profession or vocation (TA 1988 s 18). These Cases, therefore, charge the self-employed and apply equally to sole traders, trading partnerships, sole practitioners, and professional partnerships. (For partnerships, see Chapter 31.) Generally, the same principles operate under both Case I and Case II so that the two Cases may be treated together. The following differences should, however, be noted:

(1) An isolated transaction may be a trade (under Case I), but it can never be the exercise of a profession or vocation (under Case II) and so may attract income tax only under Schedule D Case VI (Chapter 9).
(2) Certain capital allowances are available only to traders (see Chapter 35).
(3) The rule in *Sharkey v Wernher* (**[6.95]**) applies only to traders.

In most cases it will be clear whether the taxpayer is self-employed or whether he is an employee holding a post or office under Schedule E (but see **[5.22]**).   **[6.2]–[6.20]**

II WHAT IS A TRADE?

1 The problems involved

'Trade' is not defined. According to TA 1988 s 832(1) it 'includes every trade, manufacture, adventure, or concern in the nature of a trade'. This provision, although generally unhelpful, indicates that a single adventure may constitute a trade (see eg *Martin v Lowry* (1927) below). In *Ransom v Higgs* (1974) Lord Wilberforce considered that a trading transaction would usually exhibit the following features:

> 'Trade normally involves the exchange of goods or services for reward ... there must be something which the trade offers to provide by way of business. Trade moreover presupposes a customer.' ([1974] 3 All ER at 964.)

In the absence of a satisfactory statutory definition the meaning of trade must be sought from the voluminous case law in this area. The Final Report of the Royal Commission on the Taxation of Profits and Income (1955: Cmd 9474) concluded that there could be no single test but suggested certain objective tests ('the badges of trade').

Before considering these 'badges of trade', two general matters should be noted in connection with the case law. *First*, when the case is concerned with whether a taxpayer carried on a trade or not, caution needs to be exercised in citing it as precedent since the findings of the commissioners are decisions of fact which will rarely be overturned on appeal (see *Edwards v Bairstow and Harrison* (1956): [**2.53**]). The appeal court is often and reluctantly forced to conclude that facts exist to justify the findings of the commissioners. *Secondly*, before the introduction of CGT in 1965, the question whether or not a person engaged in a trade was of fundamental significance. If he had, any profit was charged under Case I; if not income tax was inapplicable so that the resultant (capital) profit escaped tax altogether. Since 1965 the choice is not between a charge under Case I and no tax, but, normally, is between paying income tax and CGT or, for companies, corporation tax on their income and capital profits. The imposition of CGT at income tax rates has further blurred the importance of the distinction between capital gains and income profits. [**6.21**]

2   The 'badges of trade'

The Royal Commission identified six 'badges' designed to determine whether or not the purchase and resale of property is a trading transaction.   [**6.22**]

The subject matter of the transaction   Property which neither yields an income nor gives personal enjoyment to its owner is likely to form the subject matter of a trading transaction. Other property (typically land, works of art, and shares) may be acquired for the income and/or enjoyment which it provides.

In *Rutledge v IRC* (1929), the taxpayer was a businessman connected with the film industry. Whilst in Berlin he purchased one million toilet rolls for £1,000 which he resold in the UK at a profit of approximately £11,000. The Court of Session held that the taxpayer had engaged in an adventure in the nature of a trade so that the profits were assessable under Case I. They stressed that such a quantity of goods must have been intended for resale. Similarly, in *Martin v Lowry* (1927), the gigantic speculation involved in purchasing and reselling 44 million yards of government surplus aeroplane linen, at a profit of £1,600,000, amounted to a trade largely because of the nature of the subject matter and the commercial methods employed to sell it.

The purchase and resale of land causes more difficulty since owning land in quantity does not raise a presumption that trading is intended. In *IRC v Reinhold* (1953), for instance, despite the taxpayer having bought four houses over two years, admittedly for sale, the Court of Session concluded that 'heritable property is not an uncommon subject of investment' and that the taxpayer was not trading.

Similar difficulties arose in *Taylor v Good* (1974) where the taxpayer was held not to be trading when he resold at a considerable profit, because he had obtained planning permission, a house which he had purchased with the original intention of living in. The Court of Appeal took the view that a person intending to resell property is entitled to take steps to ensure that he obtains the best possible price for it. In particular, the court decided that the house did not become his trading stock merely because he had applied for planning permission before the sale:

> 'If you find a trade in the purchase and sale of land, it may not be difficult to find that properties originally owned (for example) by inheritance, or bought for investment only, have been brought into the stock in trade of that trade. But where, as here, there is no question at all of absorption into a trade of dealing in land or lands previously acquired with no thought of dealing, there is no ground at all for holding that activities such as those in the present case, designed only to enhance the value of the land in the market, are to be taken as pointing to, still less as establishing, an adventure in the nature of trade.' (Russell LJ 1974 STC 148 at 155.)

The definition of a trade was further limited in this area in *Marson v Morton* (1986). The taxpayer was a potato merchant and on advice from an estate agent friend, purchased (in July 1977) land suitable for development. He paid £65,000: £35,000 out of his own resources and £30,000 on a mortgage arranged by the estate agent. At the time of the purchase the taxpayer said that he intended to make a medium to long-term investment in the land. However, in September 1977, and on advice from that same estate agent, the land was sold for £100,000. Both the commissioners and Sir Nicholas Browne-Wilkinson VC held that the taxpayer was not trading and that land could be held as an investment even though it produced no income. The following passage from the judgment is especially worthy of note:

> 'In 1986 it is not any longer self evident that unless land is producing income it cannot be an investment. The legal principle, of course, cannot change with the passage of time: but life does. Since the arrival of inflation and high rates of tax on income, new approaches to investment have emerged putting the emphasis in investment on the making of capital profit at the expense of income yield. For example, the purchase of short dated stocks giving capital yield on redemption but no income has become commonplace. Similarly, split level investment trusts have been invented which produce capital profits on one type of share and income on another. Again, institutions now purchase works of art by way of investment. In my judgment those are plainly not trading deals; yet no income is produced from them. I can see no reason why land should be any different and the mere fact that land is not income producing should not be decisive or even virtually decisive on the question whether it was bought as an investment.'

[6.23]

Length of ownership This is a weak 'badge' because the presumption that, if property is sold within a short time of acquisition, the taxpayer has traded will often be rebutted on the facts. **[6.24]**

Frequency of similar transactions Repeated transactions in the same subject matter point to a trade. Since a single adventure may amount to a trade this 'badge' will be applicable only in circumstances where that would not otherwise be the case. In *Pickford v Quirke* (1927) the court held that although a single purchase and resale by a syndicate of four cotton mills did not amount to trading, the series viewed as a whole did. Hence, subsequent transactions may trigger a Case I liability on earlier transactions (see also *Leach v Pogson* (1962) in which the founding and subsequent sale of 30 driving schools consecutively, was held to be trading). **[6.25]**

Work done on the property When work is done to the property in order to make it more marketable, or when an organisation is set up to sell the asset, there is some evidence of trading (see *Martin v Lowry* (1927): compare *Taylor v Good* (1974)). In *Cape Brandy Syndicate v IRC* (1921) three individuals engaged in the wine trade who formed a syndicate and purchased some 3,000 casks of Cape brandy which they blended (with French brandy), recasked, and sold in lots over an 18-month period were held to be trading.   **[6.26]**

Circumstances responsible for the realisation   A forced sale to raise cash for an emergency raises a presumption that the transaction is not a trade. Sales by executors in the course of winding up the deceased's estate and by liquidators and receivers in the administration of an insolvent company will often fall into this category (see *Cohan's Executors v IRC* (1924) and *IRC v The 'Old Bushmills' Distillery Co Ltd* (1927) and see **[6.30]**).   **[6.27]**

Motive   If the transaction was undertaken in order to realise a profit, that is some evidence of trading. The absence of a profit motive does not prevent a commercial operation from amounting to a trade, however (see, for instance, dividend stripping and for the effect of fiscal motives, *Ensign Tankers (Leasing) Ltd v Stokes* (1992)) and, conversely, the mere fact that an asset is purchased with the intention of ultimate resale at a profit will not of itself lead to a finding of trading. Often the subject matter involved will be decisive. In *Wisdom v Chamberlain* (1968) the taxpayer (a comedian) who bought £200,000 of silver bullion as a 'hedge' against an expected devaluation of sterling and three months later sold it realising a profit of £50,000 was held to be trading. His claim that he had made no profit, but rather that the pound had fallen in value, was rejected.   **[6.28]**

3   Mutual trading

No man can trade with himself (but see the rule in *Sharkey v Wernher* **[6.95]**). Thus, when persons join together in an association and jointly contribute to a common fund for their mutual benefit, any surplus received by the members on a division of that fund is tax free (*New York Life Insurance Co v Styles* (1889)). If the association trades with non-members, however, the profits attributable to that activity are taxable. In *Carlisle and Silloth Golf Club v Smith* (1913), fees paid by visitors for the use of the club facilities were held to be trading receipts. TA 1988 s 491 prevents the mutual trading rules from being used to avoid tax, by imposing a charge on the return of surplus assets in circumstances when the original contributions were tax deductible.   **[6.29]**

4   Trading after a discontinuance

The realisation of assets after the permanent discontinuance of the business is not trading. Hence, in *IRC v Nelson* (1938) income tax under Case I was not charged when a whisky broker, who because of ill health had closed his business, sold the entire business including the stock in trade. By contrast, a sale of stock *with a view to* the cessation of trading (a 'closing-down sale') is chargeable because the trade is still continuing (see *J & R O'Kane & Co Ltd v IRC* (1922)).

Special rules operate for the valuation of trading stock held at the date of cessation of a business (TA 1988 s 100, see **[6.92]**).   **[6.30]–[6.40]**

III MEANING OF 'PROFESSION' AND 'VOCATION'

In common with 'trade', neither 'profession' nor 'vocation' are statutorily defined. 'Profession' has been judicially described as involving 'the idea of an occupation requiring either purely intellectual skill or manual skill controlled by the intellectual skill of the operator' (see Scrutton LJ in *IRC v Maxse* (1919)). This definition can be misleading, because a person exercising an occupation in those terms (such as a solicitor) may, as a question of fact, be an employee assessable under Schedule E (see [**5.22**]). As already mentioned, a profession is unlike a trade in that it involves an element of continuity. Hence, casual profits and fees arising from an isolated transaction are taxed under Schedule D Case VI.

'Vocation' has been judicially defined by Denman J in *Partridge v Mallandaine* (1886) as '. . . the way in which a man passes his life'. This definition is somewhat unhelpful, but the term embraces self-employed bookmakers, jockeys, authors and photographers.   [**6.41**]-[**6.60**]

IV COMPUTATION OF PROFITS

1 **The accounts**

Tax under Cases I and II is on the 'annual profits of the trade, profession or vocation' (TA 1988 s 18). 'Annual' in this context means of an income, as opposed to of a recurring, nature (*Martin v Lowry* (1927)). From the profit and loss account income profits are calculated as income receipts less income expenditure. For instance, a trader whose income receipts are £40,000 and income expenses £25,000 has income profits of £15,000 (£40,000 - £25,000).

The taxpayer's profits as shown in his accounts must be agreed for tax purposes with the inspector of taxes. Accounts prepared for commercial purposes and according to standard accountancy practice will rarely show the taxable profits. Some items which have been deducted in the accounts may not be deductible for income tax purposes (such as entertainment expenses: see [**6.118**]). Other items are treated differently for taxation purposes: expenditure on a capital asset, for instance, is written off annually over the life of the asset as depreciation under standard accounting practice but is deductible for income tax purposes only if it falls within the system of capital allowances (see Chapter 35). As a result the taxpayer's accounts must be adjusted by adding back deductions which are not allowable and, where appropriate, by making permitted deductions (such as capital allowances).   [**6.61**]

2 **The different bases**

In drawing up accounts for taxation purposes, the taxpayer must use one of three bases: the earnings; the cash; or the bills delivered (the cash and bills delivered bases are known as the 'conventional' bases).   [**6.62**]

a) *The earnings basis*

Profits are calculated by deducting the expenses incurred during the accounting period from the income earned during that period. It is irrelevant whether the expenses have been paid or the income received. If accounts are rendered on this basis stock in trade and work-in-progress must be valued (see [**6.90**]).

EXAMPLE 6.1

Jasper runs a bookshop in Covent Garden. He makes up his accounts each year to 31 December. For the year ending in 1997 his sales of books amount to £25,000, although he has not received payment from a valued customer, Leo, for a set of Dickens (sold for £5,000); nor from the Astery Gallery for a set of art books sold for £3,500. His expenditure incurred during the year includes rent and rates on the bookshop of £3,000; staff wages, heating and lighting of £6,000; and expenditure on books (trading stock) of £13,000. Out of this incurred expenditure, Jasper owes rates of £1,000 and an electricity bill of £250. He further owes some £2,500 on the books purchased. He estimates that he owns stock at the end of the year which cost him £6,000. His opening stock was valued at £4,000. Jasper's accounts, computed on an earnings basis, will be:

	£	£
Total sales		25,000
+ closing stock		6,000
		31,000
Less: total of:		
Opening stock	4,000	
Rent/rates	3,000	
Stock bought	13,000	
Wages, lighting etc	6,000	
	26,000	
Jasper's taxable profit		£5,000

Note: In drawing up the account it is irrelevant that £3,750 of the incurred expenditure is unpaid and that customers owe £8,500.

Recent cases (notably *Gallagher v Jones* (1993) and *Johnston v Britannia Airways Ltd* (1994)) have stressed the importance of ordinary commercial accountancy in computing the profits of a taxpayer (see the illustration in *Example 6.2* below). Such practice, in the absence of statute or case law to the contrary, is persuasive but not determinative of the matter (see generally *BTR*, 1995, No 5 and see IM 354 *et seq*).

A sum cannot be treated as earned, or an expense as incurred, until all the conditions precedent to earning or incurring it have been fulfilled by the trader (see *J P Hall & Co Ltd v IRC* (1925)). This does not mean, however, that the legal date for payment must have arisen. Thus, where goods are supplied or services rendered in year 1 which are not to be paid for until year 2, the price (even if it has to be estimated) must be included in the accounts for year 1. If the figure proves to be inaccurate, the assessment for year 1 generally may be reopened (*IRC v Gardner, Mountain and D'Ambrumenil Ltd* (1947)).

This doctrine of relating back gives rise to two difficulties; *first*, if the goods or services are never paid for, the bad debt cannot be related back to the year when the goods were supplied, but is deductible only in the year when it is shown to be bad (see [**6.124**]); and *secondly*, if the estimated payment was agreed between the Revenue and the taxpayer at the time as being correctly stated, the accounts cannot subsequently be adjusted if the amount proves inaccurate. Any adjustment will have to be made in a subsequent account when the error is discovered (see IM 357: current accountancy practice is to recognise any receipt as a current year item rather than by way of a 'prior year adjustment').

Profits and losses which have not accrued cannot be anticipated and nor can future expenses. A provision for contingent liabilities is, however, permissible provided that they are capable of sufficiently accurate computation: ie the accountancy method must be adequate to arrive at a true picture of the profits for the relevant period (*Southern Railway of Peru v Owen* (1956) and *Johnston v Britannia Airways Ltd* (1994)). **[6.63]**

EXAMPLE 6.2

(1) Gazza installs central heating equipment and enters into long-term maintenance contracts. In return for a fixed annual sum he maintains the equipment for seven years. Most of the maintenance work is undertaken in the final two years and as a matter of accountancy practice the business defers part of the annual payment until these later years. That practice will be followed in the absence of a statutory provision to the contrary or contrary judicial interpretation.

(2) Sid began trading in hiring out narrow boats. He entered into a leasing arrangement in relation to three such boats under which he was required to make substantial initial payments. As a result his first accounts showed a substantial trading loss. The Court of Appeal held that the profit and loss computation had to be made according to accepted principles of commercial accountancy and not on the basis that distorted the trading results. Accordingly the expenditure was to be spread evenly over the period to which it related (see *Gallagher v Jones* (1993)).

(3) Aircraft engines must receive a major overhaul every 17,000 flying hours (effectively every three to four years) to obtain a certificate of airworthiness. The taxpayers made provision for those costs in its annual accounts on the basis of the average cost of overhaul per hours flown multiplied by the hours flown in the relevant accounting period. The Special Commissioners accepted that this method of accounting complied with the concept of prudence in SSAP 2 and gave a full and fair picture of the profits and this was upheld by Knox J (*Johnston v Britannia Airways Ltd* (1994)). The alternative method, preferred by the Revenue, involved writing off the expenses of a major overhaul over the following three to four years (capitalise and amortise) and was rejected.

b) *The cash basis*

Profits are calculated by deducting payments actually made from sums actually received during the accounting period ('cash in minus cash out'). This basis presents a misleading picture of the state of the business when the taxpayer gives and receives credit, and carries trading stock. Further, it can be manipulated by the taxpayer to reduce his taxable profits. **[6.64]**

EXAMPLE 6.3

Justinian, a barrister, makes up his accounts to 31 December each year. For 1997 he received fees of £12,000 and is owed a further £50,000; and he has paid bills of £5,000, but owes a further £4,000. On a cash basis his accounts show a profit of £7,000 (£12,000 - £5,000), but that profit would be reduced to £3,000 were he to pay off all his outstanding liabilities on 31 December.

c) *The bills delivered basis*

Profit is calculated on this basis by deducting bills received from bills sent out during the accounting period. Unlike the earnings basis, this does not involve the taxpayer in valuing work-in-progress and is, therefore, particularly appropriate for solicitors and accountants. **[6.65]**

d) *Choice of basis*

Although there is no statutory authority stating whether the Revenue or the taxpayer can insist on using a particular basis, in practice the basis has to be agreed with the Revenue. As a general principle, the accounts should be drawn up on the basis which presents an accurate picture of the state of the business during the year. Most self-employed persons render accounts on the earnings basis, although solicitors, for instance, are usually allowed to change to the bills delivered basis after their first three years provided that they agree to bill clients regularly. The Revenue is reluctant to accept the cash basis except, for example, for authors whose royalties are earned only when received and for barristers, who cannot sue for their fees. Once the Revenue has assessed the taxpayer on one basis, it cannot supplement that assessment by an assessment on an alternative basis (see *Rankine v IRC* (1952)).

The taxpayer may, however, change his basis for a later period. On a change from the earnings (or bills delivered basis) to the cash basis, the taxpayer may suffer the penalty of a double charge to tax, because in year 1 he is taxed on the earnings basis on sums owed (or on sums billed) and in year 2 (on the cash basis) he is taxed on that same money when received. Although there is no relief against this double charge, the taxpayer may as a corollary obtain a benefit because the same expenses may be deducted in years 1 and 2.

On a change from the cash to the earnings or bills delivered basis, the taxpayer could profit, because in year 1 (on the cash basis) he is taxed only on receipts, whereas in year 2 (on the earnings basis) he is taxed on sums earned. Earnings not received in year 1, therefore, formerly escaped tax altogether; they are now taxed as post-cessation receipts.   [**6.66**]

3   Post-cessation receipts and expenses (TA 1988 ss 103–110)

a) *Receipts*

TA 1988 s 103 provides that where profits were calculated on the earnings basis, sums received in respect of the trade, profession or vocation after its discontinuance, which would not otherwise be charged to income tax because the source of the income no longer exists, are taxed under Schedule D Case VI. For this purpose, a debt released after a discontinuance is treated as a receipt (TA 1988 s 103(4)). Certain sums are excluded; in particular, receipts on the transfer of stock or work-in-progress in order to avoid an overlap with TA 1988 ss 100 and 102 (see TA 1988 s 103(3) and [**6.92**]).

Where profits were assessed on the cash basis, TA 1988 s 104 imposes a similar charge to tax on post-cessation receipts, except that sums received for the transfer of work-in-progress after a discontinuance are brought within the charge. Section 104 also catches receipts that would otherwise escape tax on a change from the cash to the earnings basis.

Receipts charged under s 103 or s 104 are taxed as earned income under Schedule D Case VI, generally in the year of receipt or, if the taxpayer elects, in the year of discontinuance so long as that discontinuance has not occurred more than six years before the receipt.   [**6.67**]

b) *Expenses*

Under TA 1988 s 105 expenditure that would have been deductible if the trade had not discontinued may be offset against post-cessation receipts. If there were no post-cessation receipts such expenditure formerly went unrelieved. This position was improved by FA 1995 (inserting new s 109A into TA 1988) in respect of certain specified items of expenditure including the cost of remedying defective work or goods; payment of damages in respect of such defective work or services and legal or other expenses and insurance premiums paid to insure against such costs. Such expenditure must be incurred no later than seven years from the date of discontinuance and must be wholly and exclusively incurred for the relevant purpose. The expenditure provisions also apply to debts of the business which are, after discontinuance, shown to be bad. The relief must be claimed and is given against income of the year of assessment in which the expenditure is incurred with, if the taxpayer so wishes, a claim that if there is insufficient income then the excess be treated as an allowable capital loss of the same year. Expenditure that remains unrelieved may neither be carried forward nor back under these provisions: it is not entirely lost, however, since it may attract relief against subsequent post-cessation receipts in the normal way under TA 1988 s 105. **[6.68]–[6.80]**

V TRADING RECEIPTS

To be a 'trading receipt' a sum must possess two characteristics. **[6.81]**

1 The sum must be derived from the trade

If the payment is in return for services or goods the payment is a trading receipt, whereas if it is made voluntarily in recognition of some personal quality of the taxpayer it is not (compare the rules for Schedule E: [5.62]). In *Murray v Goodhews* (1976), for instance, Watneys took back tied tenancies (mainly pubs) from their tenant traders as they fell vacant and made *ex gratia* lump sum payments to the traders which were held not to be trading receipts; they were paid voluntarily by Watneys to acknowledge the good relationship with the traders and to maintain their good name. (As to whether the payments were deductible expenditure of the payer, Watneys, see [6.112].) By contrast, in *McGowan v Brown and Cousins* (1977) the taxpayer, an estate agent, found sites for a company for which he was paid a low fee because it was expected that he would handle the subsequent lettings for the company. The company, however, found another agent to do the letting and 'paid off' the taxpayer with £2,500. This was held to be a trading receipt: it was a reward for services even though paid in pursuance of a moral rather than a legal obligation.

In *Higgs v Olivier* (1952) Laurence Olivier starred in the film of *Henry V* which did not achieve instant commercial success. As a result, the film company paid him £15,000 not to be involved in any film for 18 months. The payment was held not to be a receipt of his profession but compensation for not exercising that profession and, therefore, escaped tax. It might today attract a CGT charge as a capital sum derived from goodwill: see [14.7].

A payment which is not in return for services or goods may nevertheless be a trading receipt if it is intended to be used in the taxpayer's business. Thus, in *Poulter v Gayjon Processes Ltd* (1985), a government subsidy paid to encourage a shoe manufacturer to retain persons in employment was held to be a taxable trading receipt (see also *Ryan v Crabtree Denims Ltd* (1987)). In *Donald Fisher (Ealing) Ltd v Spencer* (1989), compensation paid by an agent whose negligence had resulted in the taxpayer becoming liable to pay substantially increased rent on its business premises was held to be a trading receipt. In the course of his judgment, subsequently upheld in the Court of Appeal, Walton J stated that:

> 'If compensation is received which is in substance payable in respect of either the non-receipt of what ought to have been received or the extra expense which would not have been incurred if all had gone properly, it seems to me that the principle is exactly the same.'

[6.82]

2   The sum must be income not capital

The difficulty of determining whether payments are income receipts (taxable under Case I or II) or capital receipts (when the only possible liability is to CGT) was forcibly expressed by Greene MR in *IRC v British Salmson Aero Engines* (1938):

'. . . in many cases it is almost true to say that the spin of a coin would decide the matter almost as satisfactorily as an attempt to find reasons'.

A number of tests have been suggested. The classic test is the distinction between a sale of the fixed capital of the business and of its circulating capital. Sale of the circulating capital produces income receipts. The defect with this test is that the classification of the asset (is it fixed or circulating?) depends upon the particular trade.

EXAMPLE 6.4

(1)   Koob, a bookseller, owns a freehold bookshop in Covent Garden. The books are his circulating capital (his stock in trade) so that the sale proceeds are trade receipts. The bookshop is his fixed capital, the sale of which would give rise to a CGT liability.

(2)   Seisin buys vacant premises in Covent Garden which he renovates and sells as bookshops. He is trading in the sale of bookshops which are his circulating capital so that the receipts are income receipts.

Other tests are but variations on the original theme and contain the same defect. For example, whether the expenditure brings into existence an enduring asset for the benefit of the trade (capital) or not, and the 'trees and fruit' test (the tree is the capital producing the fruit which is income).

The case law is considerable and characterised by subtle distinctions. Many involve compensation receipts where the question is, usually, whether the receipt is for the loss of a permanent asset (capital), or is in lieu of trading profits (income). In *London and Thames Haven Oil Wharves Ltd v Attwooll* (1967), the taxpayer owned jetties used by oil tankers. A tanker crashed into and badly damaged a jetty. The taxpayer received compensation of £100,000, £80,000 to rebuild the jetty (capital) and £20,000 to compensate him for lost tanker fees (income). In *Lang v Rice* (1984) the taxpayer ran two clubs in Belfast until they were destroyed by bombings. He did not resume trading thereafter and received compensation from the Northern Ireland Office for, *inter alia*, 'consequential loss'. The Revenue argued that the payment was a once and for all capital payment to compensate the taxpayer for the permanent loss of his business (in effect, a payment for goodwill). The Northern Ireland Court of Appeal held, however, that the payment was designed to compensate the taxpayer for loss of profit during the period that would elapse before business could be resumed. Accordingly, the fact that business did not recommence had no effect on the nature of the payment. An air of some unreality pervades this decision since, as the premises had been totally destroyed and the taxpayer held only a short lease, there was never any question of the business being resumed.   [6.83]

The decided cases will be considered under six headings:

Restrictions on activity   If, as part of his trading arrangements, the taxpayer agrees to restrict his activities in return for payments made to him, the payments are trade receipts. In *Thompson v Magnesium Elektron Ltd* (1944), the taxpayers manufactured magnesium which required chlorine, a by-product of which is caustic soda. ICI agreed to supply the chlorine at below market value and paid the taxpayers a lump sum to prevent them from making their own chlorine and caustic soda, sales of which would compete with those of ICI. The sum was a taxable receipt paid as compensation for profits that the taxpayers would have made on the sale of caustic soda. In *IRC v Biggar* (1982), a payment to a farmer, under EC regulations, to compensate him for changing from milk to meat farming was a trade receipt (it was compensation for lost profits). **[6.84]**

Sterilisation of an asset A payment for the permanent restriction on the use of an asset is capital even though the sum is computed by reference to loss of profits. In *Glenboig Union Fireclay Co Ltd v IRC* (1922), fireclay manufacturers who received compensation for the permanent loss of their right to work fireclay under neighbouring land were held to have received a capital sum. If the compensation is for the temporary loss of an asset, however, it is a trade receipt. Hence, in *Burmah Steamship Co Ltd v IRC* (1931), repairers of a vessel over-ran the contractual date for completion of the work and paid compensation for the lost profits of the owners. The payments were trade receipts. **[6.85]**

EXAMPLE 6.5

Hercules arranges to have his new cargo ship built in a Liverpool shipyard by 31 December 1997. The agreed price is £2m, but this is to be reduced by £10,000 per day if the ship is not ready on time. The ship is delivered ten days late, so that the price is reduced by £100,000. Although this reduction is calculated on the basis of Hercules' lost profits, it would seem that he has not received a sum in lieu of trading receipts.

Cancellation of a business contract or connection When a taxpayer receives compensation for the cancellation of a contract, the nature of the receipt depends upon the significance of the cancelled contract to the business. If it relates to the whole structure of the profit-making apparatus, the compensation is capital. Thus in *Van den Berghs Ltd v Clark* (1935) a Dutch and an English company (both manufacturing margarine) had contracted to trade in different areas so as to avoid competition. The Dutch company cancelled the contract, which had 13 years to run, and paid £450,000 in compensation. It was held to be a capital receipt because the contract had provided the means whereby profits were produced; the English company had, therefore, lost the equivalent of a fixed asset of the business (see also *Whitehead v Tubbs Elastics Ltd* (1984)).

If, however, the contract is merely one of many and of short duration, the compensation received is income. In *Kelsall Parsons & Co v IRC* (1938) the taxpayer was a manufacturers' agent who had contracts with different manufacturers and received commission on a sale of their products. One such contract was terminated a year early and the manufacturer paid £15,000 compensation. It was held to be a trade receipt. The contract was the source of profits and the compensation equalled the estimated profit that the taxpayer would have made. Likewise in *Rolfe v Nagel* (1982) a payment to compensate a diamond broker for a client transferring his business elsewhere was taxable as a payment in lieu of profits. **[6.86]**

Appropriation of unclaimed deposits and advances Sums are often received from customers as deposits to be used later in part payment towards the price of goods supplied. If they can be forfeited, because of the customer's failure to take delivery of the goods, they are trade receipts in the year of payment (*Elson v Price's Tailors Ltd* (1962)). If at the time of receipt, a deposit is not a trade receipt, however, it does not later become one by appropriation, unless its nature has been changed by statute. Thus in *Morley v Tattersall* (1938), deposits taken by auctioneers remained clients' money and were not trading receipts even though unclaimed and appropriated by the auctioneers. Contrast *Jays the Jewellers Ltd v IRC* (1947) where pawnbrokers' pledges, although originally customers' money, became trading receipts when rendered irrecoverable by statute.   **[6.87]**

Sale of information ('know-how')   Where a trader disposes of know-how but continues to trade, any receipt is a trading receipt (TA 1988 s 531(1)), but where he disposes of know-how as one of the assets of his business which he is selling as an entity, it is treated as a sale of goodwill. In the latter case liability will be to CGT, unless the trader elects to treat the sum as a trading receipt (TA 1988 s 531(2)(3)). Any sum received as consideration for a restriction on the vendor's freedom of activity (following a sale of know-how) is treated as a payment for know-how (TA 1988 s 531(8)).   **[6.88]**

Release of debts   A debt owed by the trader which has been deducted as a trade expense and later released, becomes a trade receipt in the year of its release (TA 1988 s 94). This provision does not, however, apply to debts released as part of a voluntary arrangement under the Insolvency Act 1986 Part I (ie such debts are *not* treated as receipts of the debtor's trade).   **[6.89]**

EXAMPLE 6.6

Bill, a greengrocer, obtains lettuces from his brother Ben who runs a market garden. In 1996–97 he incurs debts of £3,000 to Ben which on the earnings basis is a trading expense. In 1997–98 Ben agrees to forgo the debt because of the critical state of Bill's business, so that the £3,000 will be a trading receipt in Bill's 1997–98 accounts.

3   Valuation of trading stock

a) *Why value stock (work-in-progress)?*

When the taxpayer calculates his profits on the earnings basis, he must value his unsold stock at the end of the accounting period, otherwise he could spend all his receipts on the purchase of new stock, thereby increasing his deductible expenses and reducing his taxable profits to nil. The same principle applies to unbilled work-in-progress.

EXAMPLE 6.7

In year 1 Zac, a trader, buys 10,000 units of stock at £1 each. During the year he sells 5,000 units at £2 each.

	£
Receipts (sales)	10,000
Less: Expenses (purchases)	10,000
Profit	£ Nil

The trader appears to have made no profit whereas, in fact, his profit is £5,000. Therefore, at the end of the accounting year, his unsold (closing) stock must be treated as a receipt of the trade (ie it is treated as if he had sold it). Hence, the account becomes:

	£
Sales	10,000
Plus: Value of closing stock	5,000
	15,000
Less: Purchases	10,000
Profit	£5,000

At the start of the next accounting period the stock-in-hand (opening stock) or work-in-progress, must be entered into the accounts for that year at the same figure (ie £5,000 from *Example 6.7*) as an expense in order to avoid the stock being taxed twice. **[6.90]**

EXAMPLE 6.8

Continuing *Example 6.7*, in year 2, Zac has opening stock of 5,000 units valued at £1 each. His purchases during the year are 15,000 units of stock at £1 each and he sells 10,000 units at £2 each.

	£
Sales	20,000
Plus: Closing stock	10,000
	30,000
Less: Purchase	15,000
Profit	£15,000

Failure to value opening stock as an expense produces too much profit (£15,000): his true profit is only £10,000:

	£	£
Sales		20,000
Plus: Closing stock		10,000
		30,000
Less: Opening stock	5,000	
Purchases	15,000	20,000
Profit		£10,000

b) *Method of valuation*

Each item of unsold stock must be valued at the lower of its cost price and market value. This follows from *IRC v Cock Russell & Co Ltd* (1949) which, in effect, allows losses but not profits to be anticipated: ie the trader can apply 'cost' to items that have increased in value and 'market value' to items that have fallen in value. 'Cost' is the original acquisition price; 'market value' means the best price obtainable in the market in which the trader sells—for instance, a retailer in the retail and a wholesaler in the wholesale market (*BSC Footwear v Ridgway* (1972)).

'Cost' is more difficult to calculate where the price of stock has altered during the accounting period so that it is necessary to identify which stock is left. The only method acceptable to the Revenue is for the trader to treat the stock sold as the stock first bought ('first in first out' ie 'FIFO'). This rule is applied despite evidence that goods were sold on the basis of last in first out ('LIFO').

Unlike stock, work-in-progress cannot be valued as individual items. Instead, it is usually valued by adding to 'direct costs' (such as labour) a proportion of indirect overhead expenses (the 'on-cost' method). However, the taxpayer is allowed to value work-in-progress at direct cost only (see *Duple Motor Bodies v Ostime* (1961)). Because of the difficulty of valuing work-in-progress, professional persons often prefer to draw up their accounts on the bills delivered basis. **[6.91]**

c) *Valuation on a discontinuance (TA 1988 ss 100–102)*

On discontinuance of a trade (which includes a deemed discontinuance under TA 1988 s 337) the rule in *IRC v Cock Russell* does not apply and trading stock unsold must be entered into the final accounts at the amount realised on its sale or transfer or at market value (TA 1988 s 100 and *Moore v R J Mackenzie & Sons Ltd* (1972)). A similar rule applies to work-in-progress. This provision is designed to prevent tax avoidance by the taxpayer discontinuing his business, entering his unsold stock at cost in the final accounts and then selling it privately at a tax-free profit.

Where the stock is sold to another UK trader for valuable consideration so that it will appear in his accounts for tax purposes anyway tax could be avoided by a manipulation of the price. Typically where the parties are connected an under-value might be agreed in order to ensure a loss for the vendor which could be relieved against past profits of his business. Alternatively the sale could be at over-value in order to absorb losses of the vendor and, in effect, to pass losses to the purchaser. FA 1995 s 140 (inserting new provisions into TA 1988 s 100) provided that disposals between connected persons (the basic definition in TA 1988 s 839 being widened for these purposes) will be taken to be for the amount which would have been realised if the sale had been at arm's length. This 'arm's length rule' can be excluded by joint election of the parties if the arm's length value exceeds both (a) the actual price paid, and (b) the acquisition value of the stock. If an election is made arm's length value will be replaced by the greater of (a) and (b) (see further IM 570a *et seq*).   [**6.92**]

EXAMPLE 6.9

Aldo ceases trading and sells his stock of CDs to his great rival Baldo and his stock of 'vinyls' to his son Caldo. Both Baldo and Caldo carry on business in the UK and so far as the sale to Baldo (an unconnected person) is concerned, the actual sale price will be taken. The arm's length rule will apply to the Caldo sale unless that produces a figure which is higher than both the actual sale price and Aldo's acquisition costs in which case the joint election referred to above may be made.

4   Gifts and dispositions for less than market value

A trader has no duty to make the maximum profit and normally tax is assessed according to the actual sum received on a disposal of his stock. There are, however, certain exceptions to this rule.   [**6.93**]

Transfer pricing (TA 1988 s 770 ff)   This legislation applies to transactions between UK investment companies, multi-national companies and partnerships: see [**28.44**].   [**6.94**]

Rule in Sharkey v Wernher (1956)   If an item of trading stock is disposed of otherwise than in the ordinary course of the taxpayer's trade, it must be brought into account as a trading receipt at its market value at the date of the disposal. In *Sharkey v Wernher* (1956) the taxpayer carried on the trade of a stud farm. She also raced horses for pleasure and she transferred five horses from the stud farm to the racing stable. The House of Lords held that the market value as opposed to the cost price of the horses at the date when they left the stud farm must be entered in the accounts of the trade as a receipt.

EXAMPLE 6.10

(1)   Rex is a diamond merchant and on the occasion of his daughter's wedding he gives her his choicest diamond which cost him £80,000 and has a market value of £110,000. As the disposal is not a trading transaction, the market value (£110,000) is a trading receipt. The result is that Rex is treated as making

a taxable profit of £30,000 on the stone. (There is no distinction between the trader using the goods himself and giving them away to a friend or relative: see *Petrotim Securities Ltd v Ayres* (1964).)

(2) Company A sells securities for which it had paid £400,000 to an associated UK trading company (company B) for £200,000. The securities then had a market value of £800,000. The following points should be noted:

    (i) TA 1988 s 770 is inapplicable since the purchaser company is a UK resident trading company.

    (ii) The sale will be caught by the rule in *Sharkey v Wernher* which applies to both gifts of trading stock and to sales at under-value (see *Petrotim v Ayres* (1964)).

    (iii) The recipient of trading stock caught by the rule in *Sharkey v Wernher* is treated as receiving the goods for their market value. Hence, company B is treated as having paid £800,000 for the securities (see *Ridge Securities Ltd v IRC* (1964)).

    (iv) In extreme cases both the purchase and the resale may be expunged from the accounts of the trader if neither constitutes a genuine trading transaction (see the Y transaction in *Petrotim v Ayres* (1964)).

The market value rule is subject to two major qualifications. *First*, it is only appropriate when the disposal of stock is not a genuine trading transaction. So long as the disposal can be justified on commercial grounds the general principle remains that a trader is free to charge what he likes for his goods.

EXAMPLE 6.11

Cutthroat runs a hi-fi business. In an attempt to encourage custom he gives away a cassette player (market value £40) to any customer who purchases goods costing more than £250. The gift is a commercial disposition and outside the scope of *Sharkey v Wernher*. Accordingly, Cutthroat is not required to enter the market value of the player as a trading receipt.

Secondly, the rule does not apply to professional persons (Case II taxpayers). In *Mason v Innes* (1967), Hammond Innes, the novelist, began writing *The Doomed Oasis* in 1958 and incurred deductible travelling expenses in obtaining background material. When the manuscript was completed in 1960 he assigned it to his father in consideration of natural love and affection when it had a market value of about £15,000. Innes was taxed under Case II and rendered accounts on the cash basis. When the Revenue sought to tax the market value of the copyright as a receipt of his profession the Court of Appeal held that the market value rule was limited to traders and to dispositions of trading stock. The fact that Innes was assessed on the cash basis was a further, but not the decisive reason, for excluding the rule. In rejecting the Revenue's argument, Lord Denning MR said:

'Suppose an artist paints a picture of his mother and gives it to her. He does not receive a penny for it. Is he to pay tax on the value of it? It is unthinkable. Suppose he paints a picture which he does not like when he has finished it and destroys it. Is he liable to pay tax on the value of it? Clearly not. These instances ... show that ... *Sharkey v Wernher* does not apply to professional men.'

[6.95]–[6.110]

EXAMPLE 6.12

Lex is a partner in the solicitors' firm of Lex, Lax & Lazy and he purchases a house in Chelsea. All the conveyancing work is done by his firm free of charge. The rule in *Sharkey v Wernher* does not apply.

VI   DEDUCTIBLE EXPENSES

1   **Basic principles**

An expense will be deductible in arriving at the taxpayer's profits under Cases I and II only if:

(1) It is an income and not a capital expense.

(2) It is incurred wholly and exclusively for the purpose of the trade, profession or vocation.

(3) Its deduction is not prohibited by statute (see generally TA 1988 s 74).

Deductible expenses are allowed under Schedule D only by implication from the charging section which imposes tax on 'profits' and from TA 1988 s 74 which contains a list of prohibited deductions. Generally, the rules for deductible expenditure under Schedule D are more generous than under Schedule E (see TA 1988 s 198 and [**5.171**]).

A distinction is drawn between expenses incurred in earning the profits (which may be deductible) and expenses incurred after the profits have been earned, which are not deductible. For example, the payment of income tax is an application of profit which has been earned and is, therefore, not deductible (*Ashton Gas Co v A-G* (1906)). Other taxes, however, such as rates and stamp duty, may be paid in the course of earning the profits and so may be deductible.

The professional costs involved in drawing up the trader's accounts and fees paid for tax advice are, in practice, deductible, but expenses involved in contesting a tax assessment are not. In *Smith's Potato Estates Ltd v Bolland* (1948), Viscount Simonds stated that:

> '... His [the trader's] profit is no more affected by the exigibility to tax than a man's temperature altered by the purchase of a thermometer, even though he starts by haggling about the price of it.'

[**6.111**]

2   **The expense must be income not capital**

General   Similar tests are applied in classifying expenditure as income or capital as in deciding whether a receipt is income or capital (see [**6.83**]). Hence, a distinction is drawn between the fixed and the circulating capital of the business. A payment is capital if it is made to bring into existence an asset for the enduring advantage of the trade (see *British Insulated and Helsby Cables v Atherton* (1926)). The asset may be intangible as in *Walker v Joint Credit Card Co Ltd* (1982) where a payment by a credit card company to preserve its goodwill was held to be a capital payment.

A once and for all payment, even though it brings no enduring asset into existence, is more likely to be of a capital nature than a recurring expense. In *Watney Combe Reid & Co Ltd v Pike* (1982), *ex gratia* payments made by Watneys (the brewers) to tenants of tied houses to compensate them for the termination of their tenancies were held to be capital, because their purpose was to render capital assets (the premises) more valuable.   [**6.112**]

Employee payments are generally deductible in computing the profits of the employer, so long as they are paid in the interests of the business. In *Mitchell v B W Noble Ltd* (1927), a company deducted the sum of £19,500 paid to a director to induce him to resign. It was held to be in the interests of the company to get rid of him and to avoid undesirable publicity by encouraging him to 'go quietly'. For similar reasons, the House of Lords in *Lawson v Johnson Matthey plc* (1992) decided that the sum of £50m was a deductible revenue expense being paid to save its business (by removing an obstacle to successful trading).

It was not, as the lower courts had concluded, a sum paid to get rid of a burdensome capital asset (which would itself have been capital).

Problems may arise when the payments in question are linked to the cessation of the business; in particular, such payments may not satisfy the 'wholly and exclusively' test (discussed below at [**6.117**]). In *O'Keeffe v Southport Printers Ltd* (1984), however, payments made to employees in lieu of notice were deductible by the employer since they were incurred as part of the orderly conduct of the business prior to its termination. [**6.113**]

'I hardly think it's worth claiming for your work clothes, Mabel.'

Employee trusts   In *Heather v PE Consulting Group* (1978) payments made by a company to a trust created in order to acquire shares in that company for the benefit of employees and to prevent outside interference in the affairs of the company were deductible expenses because, *inter alia*, they encouraged the recruitment of well-qualified staff (see also *Jeffs v Ringtons Ltd* (1985)). Not all payments to employee trusts will be deductible, however, and it was partly to deal with this uncertainty that special provisions were introduced for ESOPs (employee share ownership plans). If such a trust is established all payments by the company to the trustees will be deductible business expenditure. These payments may then be used by the trustees to repay both interest and capital on external borrowings (see further [**37.62**]). [**6.114**]

Restrictive covenants   *Associated Portland Cement Manufacturers Ltd v Kerr* (1946) involved payments to two retiring directors in return for covenants that they would not compete with the company for the rest of their lives. The payments were held not to be deductible. It was a capital expense being a payment to enhance the company's goodwill. The tie was for life in the *Kerr* case: had the covenant been for a shorter period the expenditure might have been of an income nature (and therefore deductible). To prevent the making of restrictive covenant payments instead of salary increases (which could result in the deduction of the payment by the employer even though it was not fully taxed in the hands of the employee), TA 1988 s 313 now provides, *inter alia*, that such payments are tax deductible by the employer and taxed in the hands of the employee in *all* cases (see [**5.70**]).   [**6.115**]

Capital allowances   Although capital expenditure is not generally deductible and there is no deduction for depreciation as such, tax relief may be given in accordance with the rules governing capital allowances (see Chapter 35). When there was a first year allowance for plant and machinery of 100% it was often a matter of indifference to the taxpayer whether a particular item of expenditure was of an income or of a capital nature. If income, it could be deducted in arriving at the profits of the business; if capital, then, so long as the item in question constituted plant or machinery, the system of capital allowances produced much the same result. As only a writing-down allowance is now available, the taxpayer will be concerned to argue, wherever possible, that the expense is of an income nature so that it can immediately be deducted in full.   [**6.116**]

3   Expense must have been incurred 'wholly and exclusively' for business purposes (TA 1988 s 74(a))

The courts have generally interpreted the requirement strictly, so that the *sole* reason for the expenditure must be a business purpose. In *Bentleys, Stokes & Lowless v Beeson* (1952), Romer LJ explained the requirements that have to be satisfied for an expense to be deductible as follows:

> 'it is quite clear that the purpose must be the sole purpose. The paragraph says so in clear terms. If the activity be undertaken with the object both of promoting business and also with some other purpose, for example, with the object of indulging an independent wish of entertaining a friend or stranger or of supporting a charitable or benevolent object, then the paragraph is not satisfied though in the mind of the actor the business motive may predominate. For the statute so prescribes. Per contra, if, in truth, the sole object is business promotion, the expenditure is not disqualified because the nature of the activity necessarily involves some other result, or the attainment or furtherance of some other objective, since the latter result or objective is necessarily inherent in the act.'

Dual purpose expenditure is not deductible and there are numerous cases where this rule has been strictly applied. In *Caillebotte v Quinn* (1975) a self-employed carpenter worked on sites 40 miles from home. He ate lunch at a nearby café which cost him 40p per day instead of the usual 10p which it cost him at home. His claim to deduct the extra 30p per day as an expense was disallowed on the grounds that he ate to live as well as to work so that the expenditure was incurred for dual purposes. Similarly, in *Prince v Mapp* (1970) a guitarist in a pop group could not deduct the cost of an operation on his little finger because he played the guitar partly for business, but partly for pleasure (but contrast *McKnight v Sheppard* (1997) in which legal expenses incurred at disciplinary hearings of the taxpayer—a stockbroker—were held deductible). In *Mallalieu v Drummond* (1983) the House of Lords held that expenditure on clothing to be worn in court by a female barrister was not deductible. Although she only wore the clothes for business purposes and that was her sole conscious purpose when she purchased the garments, Lord Brightman concluded that 'she needed the clothes to travel to work and clothes to wear at work ... it is inescapable that one object though not a conscious motive, was the provision of the clothing that she needed as a human being'. (In practice, the cost of protective clothing is deductible and the Revenue has concluded 'clothing and tool allowances' with a number of trade unions.)

The same test for deductible expenditure is applied whether the business is run as a sole trade or partnership. In *MacKinlay v Arthur Young McClelland*

Moores & Co (1990) the Court of Appeal had allowed a partnership to deduct removal costs paid to encourage two partners to move house: in one case from London to Southampton, in the other from Newcastle to Bristol. In both cases the move was desirable from the point of view of the firm's business and neither partner would have agreed to move had his relocation expenses not been borne by the firm. This decision was not easy to reconcile with earlier authorities and its reversal by the House of Lords was scarcely surprising. Their Lordships restated the principles underlying the rules governing deductible expenditure and stressed that the same rules applied to individuals and to unincorporated partnerships (see [**31.3**]).

The 'dual purpose' cases show that it is not possible to split a purpose: ie if the taxpayer incurs the expenditure for two purposes, one business and the other personal, none of the expenditure is deductible. It may, however, be possible to split a payment into a portion which is incurred for business purposes and a portion which is not. This approach was apparent in *Copeman v Flood* (1941) where the son and daughter of the managing director of a small private company were employed as directors at salaries of £2,600 each pa. The son was aged 24 and had some business experience, but the daughter was only 17 and incompetent. Although both performed duties for the company, the Revenue successfully claimed that the entire salary was not an expense incurred by the company 'wholly and exclusively' for business purposes. Lawrence J remitted the case to the commissioners for them to decide, as a question of fact, to what extent the payments were deductible expenses of the trade. He accepted that the expenditure could be apportioned into allowable and non-allowable parts (see also *Earlspring Properties Ltd v Guest* (1994) and contrast *Abbott v IRC* (1996)).

In practice, payments are regularly split in this fashion when a car is used both for business and private use and when a business is run from the taxpayer's home and he claims to deduct a proportion of the overheads of the house. If the 'wholly and exclusively' test is satisfied there is no further test—based on the expenditure being 'sufficiently connected' with the business—to be satisfied (*McKnight v Shepperd* (1997)). [**6.117**]

4 Deduction of the expense must not be prohibited by statute

The deduction of expenses under Cases I and II is permitted by implication because TA 1988 s 74 contains a list of expenses which are stated not to be deductible. For instance, under s 74(1) no deduction is allowed for any sum 'recoverable under an insurance or contract of indemnity' whilst expenditure incurred for private as opposed to business purposes is made non-deductible by s 74(b). The deduction of business gifts and entertainment expenses is severely curtailed by TA 1988 s 577 which is drafted widely enough to catch hospitality of any kind (TA 1988 s 577(5)). A number of exceptions are permitted; the entertainment of *bona fide* members of staff is permitted (TA 1988 s 577(5); and it does not even have to be reasonable!); small gifts carrying conspicuous advertisements are permissible (TA 1988 s 577(8)), whilst there is an exception for the provision of that which it is in the ordinary course of the taxpayer's trade to provide (TA 1988 s 577(10) and see *Fleming v Associated Newspapers Ltd* (1972) where the House of Lords struggled to make sense of this all but incomprehensible provision). [**6.118**]

5 Illustrations of deductible expenditure

Expenditure in heating and lighting business premises, rates on those premises and the wages paid to employees are obvious examples of allowable expenditure.

Other expenditure may be more problematic, as the examples considered below show.   **[6.119]**

Rent paid for business premises   TA 1988 s 74(c) accepts that rent is deductible and it may be apportioned if part of the premises is used for non-business activities. An individual's private house may, of course, be used in part for business purposes and a portion of the overheads may be claimed as allowable expenditure. So long as no part of the house is used exclusively for business purposes the full CGT main residence exemption will still be available (see [**16.72**]).

When the taxpayer pays a premium in return for the grant of a lease, a portion of the premium (corresponding to the portion that is taxed under Schedule A; see [**8.85**]) may be deducted as an expense (TA 1988 s 87).   **[6.120]**

Sale and leaseback arrangements   Specific provisions were enacted to deal with the problems caused by sale and leaseback, and surrender and leaseback arrangements. The attraction of such schemes stemmed from booming land values which encouraged the owner of the land (or of an interest therein) to sell (or surrender) it, thereby realising a capital sum, and immediately to take a leaseback of the same property. TA 1988 s 779 prohibits the deduction of rent in excess of a commercial level and in certain circumstances TA 1988 s 780 imposes a charge to income tax on a capital sum received in return for surrendering a lease which has less than 50 years to run, when a leaseback for a term not exceeding 15 years is taken.   **[6.121]**

EXAMPLE 6.13

Jake runs a pub on leasehold premises in Covent Garden. The lease has 30 years to run and property values have recently boomed in that area. The landlord offers Jake £50,000 to surrender the existing lease and agrees to grant him a new seven-year lease at a dramatically increased rent:

(1) The new rent will be deductible save for any excess above a commercial rent.
(2) A portion of the capital sum received by Jake will be subject to income tax and the balance may be subject to CGT (Jake has disposed of a chargeable asset).

Repairs and improvements   Sums expended on the repair of business assets are deductible (TA 1988 s 74(d)). The cost of improvement is not, however, allowable being capital expenditure (TA 1988 s 74(g)). The borderline between the two is a difficult factual question which depends upon the nature of the asset and the importance of the work in relation to it (see *Lurcott v Wakely and Wheeler* (1911) on the duty to repair and *O'Grady v Markham Main Colliery Ltd* (1932)).

The cost incurred on initial repairs carried out to a business asset may cause difficulties. In *Law Shipping Co Ltd v IRC* (1924), a vessel purchased for £97,000 was in such a state of disrepair that a further £51,000 had to be spent before it could obtain its Lloyd's Certificate. The Court of Session disallowed most of the subsequent expenditure; as Lord Cullen stated:

'It is in substance the equivalent of an addition to the price. If the ship had not been in need of the repairs in question when bought, the appellants would have had to pay a correspondingly larger price.'

By way of contrast, in *Odeon Associated Theatres Ltd v Jones* (1972) subsequent repair work on a cinema which had been purchased in a run-down condition after the war, was allowed. There are three points of distinction from the *Law Shipping* case: *first*, the cinema was a profit-earning asset when purchased despite its disrepair; *secondly*, the purchase price was not reduced because of that disrepair; and *thirdly*, the Court of Appeal accepted that the expenses were deductible in accordance with the principles of proper commercial accounting. (For the precise significance of the evidence of accountants, see *Heather v PE Consulting Group* (1978) and [**6.63**].)   [**6.122**]

Pre-trading expenditure   Under TA 1988 s 401 income expenditure incurred in the seven years before a trade, profession or vocation commences is treated as incurred on the day on which the business commences. The problem of identifying when a business commences trading is considered at [**I.26**]. [**6.123**]

Bad debts   Bad debts are deducted when shown to be bad (TA 1988 s 74(j)); if later paid they are treated as a trading receipt for that later year. These rules have been amended in the case of voluntary arrangements under the Insolvency Act 1986 Part I. The release of a trade debt in such circumstances is fully deductible by the creditor (even if the debt could not be shown to be 'bad') and does not give rise to a taxable receipt in the hands of the debtor.   [**6.124**]

Damages and losses   In *Strong & Co of Romsey Ltd v Woodifield* (1906) damages paid to an hotel guest injured by the fall of a chimney from the building were not deductible. Lord Loreburn, somewhat unsympathetically, observed that 'the loss sustained by the appellants . . . fell upon them in their character not of traders but of householders' whilst Lord Davey rejected the claim because 'the expense must be incurred for the purpose of earning the profits'. Had the guest suffered food poisoning from the hotel restaurant any compensation would have been deductible! In practice, the *Strong v Woodifield* case will be avoided by the trader carrying insurance to cover compensation claims; further, the premiums that he pays for such insurance will be deductible.

Theft by employees causes particular difficulties. Petty theft by subordinates, so that money never finds its way into the till, will result in reduced profits for tax purposes, but defalcations by directors will not be similarly allowable (*Curtis v Oldfield* (1933); *Bamford v ATA Advertising* (1972)).   [**6.125**]

Work training and outplacement counselling   The costs of training an employee in skills relating to present or future duties of his job are deductible. In addition, the costs of retraining an employee or former employee for a new job with another employer (or for self-employment) are in certain circumstances deductible (see further [**5.119**]: TA 1988 ss 588–589). Training costs incurred by a self-employed person are deductible in computing his profits, provided the costs are incurred wholly and exclusively for the purposes of his trade or profession (TA 1988 s 74). The provision of outplacement counselling services to employees who are made redundant is not a taxable benefit for that employee and the costs are deductible by the employer (TA 1988 s 589A and B: see also [**4.64**]).   [**6.126**]

Expenditure involving crime   A payment (such as a bribe) which involves the commission of a crime is not deductible and nor is a payment made as a result of blackmail (such as a payment made under duress to terrorist groups): TA 1988 s 577A.   [**6.127**]

Travelling expenses   The cases establish two general propositions. *First*, that the cost of travelling to the place of business is not deductible; and *secondly*, that the cost of travelling in the course of the business is deductible. In *Horton v Young* (1971), for instance, a labour-only sub-contractor who operated from his home was entitled to deduct expenses incurred in collecting his team of bricklayers and travelling to the building site.   [**6.128**]

EXAMPLE 6.14

Wig is a barrister who travels into chambers each day from his home in Isleworth. He also travels from chambers to courts in the London area.

(1)   The cost of travelling from Isleworth to chambers is not deductible because chambers is his base. It does not matter that he does a substantial amount of work at home and that he claims a deduction for a portion of the expenses of the house (see *Newsom v Robertson* (1953)).

(2)   Expenses in travelling from chambers to court are deductible (contrast *Horton v Young* (1971): travelling between two centres of work).

(3)   If he were regularly to go from Isleworth to a case at Bow Street Magistrates' Court and then on to chambers could he deduct all the travelling expenses? The difficult case of *Sargent v Barnes* (1978) in which a dental surgeon was unable to deduct travelling expenses to collect false teeth from a laboratory on his way to work, suggests that the answer is no, although it should be noted that the laboratory was not a place of work whereas the court is. A claim for travelling from the court to chambers might, therefore, succeed.

National insurance contributions   Contributions paid by an employer on behalf of his employees are a deductible business expense. The employer cannot, however, deduct his own contributions.   **[6.129]–[6.140]**

VII   RELIEF FOR FLUCTUATING PROFITS

The profits earned from certain businesses are so irregular that it would be unfair to tax them all in the year of receipt. Instead, they are deemed to have been received over a longer period ('averaged').   **[6.141]**

1   Farmers and market gardeners

TA 1988 allows farmers and market gardeners to compare the profits of two consecutive years of assessment and, if the profits of either year are nil or one is less than 70% of the other, the profits of both years are equalised. ('Profit' means profit before deducting loss relief and capital allowances.) The relief is tapered where the profits in one year are between 70% and 75% of the other. The trader must claim the relief within two years of the end of the second year of assessment and he may not claim it for his opening or closing years.   **[6.142]**

EXAMPLE 6.15

A farmer's profits in Year 1 are £600 and in Year 2 £16,000. £600 is less than 70% of £16,000. Therefore profits are equalised and in years 1 and 2 he is taxed on profits of £8,300 (£16,600 ÷ 2).

2   Authors and artists

Two provisions afford relief to authors who receive lump sums for copyright or royalties. TA 1988 s 534 provides that lump sums received for royalties within two years of the work's first publication, or for the assignment of copyright or in respect of non-returnable advances, may be spread back and taxed over either two or three years depending upon the length of time spent by the author in producing the work. This relief applies in respect of literary, dramatic, musical and artistic works.

By TA 1988 s 535, any sum received for the assignment of a copyright more than ten years after publication can be spread forward and taxed over a maximum of six years depending on the duration of the assignment. Special provisions apply where the author dies or retires within that six-year period. Commissions, fees and similar payments received by a painter, sculptor or other artist for a sale of his work can be spread back over two or three years (TA 1988 s 538).   **[6.143]**

3 **Inventors**

Similar provisions apply to lump sums received by inventors for the exploitation of their patents. By TA 1988 s 524, a sum received in return for patent rights is spread over the year of receipt and the next five years. By TA 1988 s 527, sums received for the use of a patent for a period of at least six years may be spread back over six years.   **[6.144]–[6.160]**

VIII   BASIS OF ASSESSMENT

The rules are considered in Appendix I.   **[6.161]**

7 Losses

I INTRODUCTORY

1 General

Whenever an individual, partnership or company makes a loss (ie where allowable expenses in an accounting period exceed taxable receipts) there are two repercussions.

First, any year of assessment using as its basis period one in which the loss was incurred will have a nil tax assessment.

Secondly, the loss is, in tax terms, an asset which may be used to cancel out or relieve tax assessments of that or other years so that the taxpayer will either pay less tax or be able to reclaim tax which he has previously paid. Losses are, however, personal to the taxpayer. They are not in any sense an asset which can be bought and sold.   **[7.1]**

2 Companies

When the loss is made by a trading company it is not available for use by individual shareholders (even in a 'one man' company). Hence, when it is proposed to start a business and early losses are anticipated the advantages of income tax relief for the losses must be weighed against the protection of limited liability (see [**37.46**]). In the past, companies have been bought for their tax losses. The provisions of TA 1988 s 768, however, now prevent this from happening save in cases where (broadly speaking) the same business is carried on in the company before and after the change in ownership (see [**28.64**]).   **[7.2]**

3 Loss relief under Schedule A

The loss reliefs available for the landlord are discussed at [**8.44**]. It should be noted, however, that losses under this Schedule are 'ring fenced': ie they can only be set against profits from the Schedule A business. A similar rule operates for losses arising under Schedule D Case VI (see Chapter 9) which are only offsettable against Schedule D Case VI income.   **[7.3]**

4   Losses in a trade profession and vocation

This chapter concentrates on the loss reliefs available under Schedule D Cases I and II. When seeking to apply relief under these provisions it is important to realise that the loss may be eligible for relief under more than one provision and that the choice will usually rest with the taxpayer. Certain reliefs must be set against the taxpayer's earned before unearned income. The reliefs apply, with some modification, to members of a partnership in respect of their share of any business losses.   **[7.4]**

5   Self-assessment and the current year basis

Formerly Case I and Case II profits were assessed on a preceding year basis whereas losses were relieved on a current year basis. As a result the switch to assessing profits on a current year basis (see further Appendix I) has not necessitated major changes in the loss relief rules: some changes were, however, inevitable and some simplification has been achieved. Capital allowances, for instance, are now deducted as a trading expense rather than as a deduction from assessable profits (CAA 1990 s 140). Inevitably where the basis periods for two years overlap, the loss is only counted once in the first of those years (see IM 3351).   **[7.5]–[7.20]**

II   RELIEF UNDER TA 1988 s 385: CARRY-FORWARD

A loss which is sustained in carrying on a trade, profession or vocation can be carried forward under s 385 and set off against the first available profits of the same trade, profession or vocation without time limit. The loss must be deducted as far as possible from the earliest subsequent profits with the result that the taxpayer may lose his personal allowance. The subsequent profits may include any balancing charge under the capital allowance legislation and are net of any capital allowances given in that later year.

EXAMPLE 7.1

Scrooge's accounts are as follows:

Accounting period

Year to 31 December 1997	£2,000 profit
Year to 31 December 1998	(£6,000) loss
Year to 31 December 1999	£1,600 profit
Year to 31 December 2000	£3,600 profit
Year to 31 December 2001	£4,000 profit

The income tax assessments are:

Tax year	*Taxable profit (loss)*
	(£)
1997–98	2,000
1998–99	(6,000)
1999–2000	nil (£1,600–£6,000 loss)
2000–01	nil (£3,600–£4,400 loss)
2001–02	3,200 (£4,000–£800 loss)

Scrooge would lose the benefit of his personal allowance in 1998–99, 1999–2000 and 2000–01 if he had no other income against which to set it.

When a business receives income which has already been taxed at source (eg dividends) any loss brought forward under s 385 can be used against that taxed income and a repayment claim made (TA 1988 s 385(4)).

In calculating the loss to be carried forward under s 385, certain items may be treated as losses. For instance, by s 387 an annual payment which is made wholly and exclusively for the purpose of the business and assessed under TA 1988 s 349 (because the taxpayer has no income) and which cannot be relieved because there are no profits against which to set it, may be treated as a loss for s 385. The same principle applies to unrelieved interest payments (TA 1988 s 390).

EXAMPLE 7.2

Oliver makes a loss of £10,000 in his accounting year ended 31 July 1997 and is expected to make a loss in the year to 31 July 1998. He makes an annual payment each year on 1 June of £1,000. In 1997–98 there will be a nil assessment on his business profits, but under TA 1988 s 349 the Revenue requires Oliver to pay basic rate income tax on £1,000 at 23% (£230). As he made a loss of £10,000 and has paid out £1,000 in total, Oliver's loss to be carried forward under s 385 is £11,000.

Losses can only be carried forward under s 385 against future profits from the *same* business. Thus, if the nature of the business changes in a future year, there can be no carry-forward of losses. In *Gordon and Blair Ltd v IRC* (1962) brewing losses could not be carried forward against bottling profits. Similarly, if the business ceases, there can be no carry-forward, although special rules operate on a change of partners (see Appendix I).

There are two major drawbacks to loss relief under s 385. *First*, it is only available against profits from the same business and not against any other income of the taxpayer. *Secondly*, the relief is not immediate. Even assuming that the business makes profits in the future, loss relief may not be obtained for some years (see *Example 7.1*). In inflationary times, this delay renders the loss relief less valuable in real terms (cp TA 1988 s 380). **[7.21]**

The move to the current year basis of assessment has not necessitated substantive changes in this section. The claims procedure has, however, been simplified: under the new rules a single claim is all that is necessary which will establish the amount of the loss. The time limit for making this claim is that laid down in TMA 1970 s 43 (ie five years and ten months from the end of the year in which the loss arose): once an effective claim has been made the loss will then be carried forward and utilised each year until extinguished without the need for any further claim. **[7.22]–[7.40]**

III RELIEF UNDER TA 1988 s 380: CARRY-ACROSS

Under the recast s 380(1)(a) trading losses may be set against the taxpayer's total income of the year when the loss arises and (see s 380(1)(b)) of the *preceding year*. It is possible to choose the year in which the loss is to be set off—for instance, the claim may indicate that the loss is to be allowed in the preceding year. If the claim is for relief in both years, the claim for relief in the current year takes precedence over that for the preceding year (s 380(2)); claims for relief must generally be made within 12 months from 31 January following the end of the tax year in which the loss arose.

EXAMPLE 7.3

Confused makes his account up to 5 October each year. For the year to 5 October 2000 a loss of £24,000 is suffered; for the previous year a loss of £18,000.

(i) *The loss of £18,000*
Given that these accounts are the basis period for tax year 1999–2000, loss relief may be claimed as follows:

(a)   against Confused's other income for 1999–2000 under s 380(1)(a); or
(b)   against his income for 1998–99 (under s 380(1)(b)).

He may choose the year in which relief is given in the claim: viz by stipulating that the loss is to be relieved in (or as far as possible in) 1998–99.

(ii) *The loss of £24,000*
The rules are the same with the qualification that if relief is claimed for both a loss in the current year and a loss in the preceding year, the current year is given priority. Accordingly if relief was claimed for the £18,000 loss in 1999–2000 that would take priority over a claim to relief for the £24,000 loss in that year.

Certain restrictions are placed on the availability of s 380 relief in order to prevent a taxpayer indulging in a 'hobby' trade. TA 1988 s 384 denies the relief unless the taxpayer can show that the loss-making business was run on a commercial basis with a view to profit (although a reasonable expectation of profit is conclusive evidence of this: for a recent illustration, see *Wannell v Rothwell* (1996)). By TA 1988 s 397, a farmer or market gardener will automatically lose the relief if he incurs a loss in each of the preceding five years unless he can show that any competent farmer or market gardener would have made the same losses. The moral here is 'let your losses be those of the reasonable man or make a profit every sixth year!' (See ESC B5 for the permitted deduction of maintenance expenses in the case of owner-occupied farms not farmed on a commercial basis.)   **[7.41]–[7.60]**

IV   RELIEF AGAINST CAPITAL GAINS (FA 1991 s 72)

The fusion of the rates of income tax and CGT in 1988 did not involve a joining together of the taxes themselves. As a general principle, therefore, the two remain distinct so that income losses cannot generally be offset against chargeable gains and nor can capital losses be offset against income. To some extent these divisions are blurred so far as company taxation is concerned: trading losses can be set against a company's 'profits' of the same accounting period and, to the extent unrelieved, against profits of one previous accounting period and for corporation tax purposes 'profits' includes the company's chargeable gains (TA 1988 s 393(2) and see [**28.47**]).

However, trading losses of an individual can be offset against his capital gains in the tax year when the loss arises and in one preceding year. The following matters are particularly worthy of note concerning this relief:

(1)   The relief depends upon an election being made by the taxpayer and this claim for relief may only be made if a claim is also submitted under TA 1988 s 380 (ie to set the loss against the taxpayer's other income). Capital gains may only be used to the extent that the trading loss cannot be made good against the taxpayer's other income for the year (this is 'the relevant amount').

(2)   Relief is obtained by setting the trading loss against the amount which

would otherwise be subject to a CGT charge—ie after deducting current year and losses carried forward—but *disregarding for this purpose the taxpayer's annual exemption* (this is referred to as 'the maximum amount'). This rule exactly mirrors that for CGT losses which must also be set against gains for the year when the loss is incurred even if the effect is that the taxpayer loses any benefit from his annual exemption (see [**14.91**]). For these purposes the trading losses are treated as an allowable capital loss made in that year.

(3) To the extent that full relief is not available in the year when the trading loss is incurred, any unrelieved balance may then be carried back and set against gains in the immediately preceding tax year in accordance with the s 380 procedure. [**7.61**]–[**7.80**]

EXAMPLE 7.4

Curious' tax position for 1997–98 is as follows:

	£
Taxable income	50,000
Trading losses	75,000
Chargeable gains	120,000
Allowable capital losses (current year)	30,000
(brought forward)	25,000
Annual exemption	6,500

He makes claims under s 380(1)(a) and s 72(1) in respect of the trading loss.

(i) *Assessable income:* reduced to nil (hence a loss of personal allowances) and the 'relevant amount' for s 72 is £25,000.

(ii) *The 'maximum amount':* £120,000 – (£30,000 + £25,000) = £65,000. Accordingly relief is not restricted.

Hence £25,000 of trading losses are treated as allowable (capital) losses. Curious' gains for the year are therefore £40,000.

V RELIEF FOR LOSSES IN THE EARLY YEARS

1 TA 1988 s 381: initial loss relief

A business will often make losses in its early years and TA 1988 s 381 provides relief where a loss is sustained in the year of assessment in which the business is first carried on, or in any of the next three years of assessment, as an alternative to relief under TA 1988 ss 380, 385 and FA 1991 s 72.

The relief is obtained by a set-off against the taxpayer's total income of the three years of assessment preceding the year of loss. The set-off is against earlier years before later years and in each year is against the taxpayer's earned before unearned income. The effect of the relief is to revise earlier income tax assessments and to obtain a tax refund. Section 381 is available to individuals (including partners) for a maximum of four years only and is not available to a limited company. Therefore, where early losses are envisaged, it may be worth starting as a sole trader (or partnership) and at a later stage incorporating the business (see Chapter 37).

Section 381 relief requires a specific election by 31 January in the second tax year following the year of assessment in which the loss is sustained. Relief is denied unless it can be shown that the business was carried on on a commercial basis with a view to profit (TA 1988 s 381(4)). Further the relief cannot be extended to eight years by the taxpayer transferring the business to his spouse after the first four years (TA 1988 s 381(5)).   **[7.81]**

EXAMPLE 7.5

Fergus began business as a sole practitioner on 1 July 2000. His results for the first two year of assessment was:

2000–01: loss £23,600 (ie 1 July 2000–5 April 2001)

Before beginning his own business, Fergus was employed as an assistant solicitor. He also has income from dividends. This other income comprised:

	Salary (Schedule E)	Dividend (Schedule F)
1997–98	£9,600	£6,000
1998–99	£10,000	£6,400
1999–2000	£12,000	£7,000
2000–01	—	£4,000

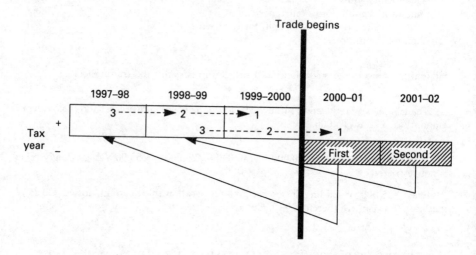

The position is as follows:

1997–98	£
Schedule E income	9,600
Dividend income	6,000
Less: 2000–01 loss carried back (part)	£(15,600
Revised assessment	NIL

1998–99	
Schedule E income	10,000
Less: 2000–01 loss carried back	8,000
	2,000
Dividend income	6,400
Revised assessment	£8,400

1999–2000	
Schedule E income	12,000
Schedule F income	4,000
No revision of assessment of	£16,000

2000-01
Schedule D income   Nil
No revision of assessment of   NIL

---

2 Relationship of s 381 with ss 380 and 385

As with s 380, relief under s 381 requires a specific election. The election need only be made for one year of loss, but, once made, that loss must be carried back against the taxpayer's income in the earlier years without limit, which may result in a loss of personal allowances.

Sections 381 and 380 are alternatives so that the same portion of any loss cannot be relieved under both sections (ie twice). Where, however, relief has been given as far as possible under one section, any surplus loss remaining can be relieved by a specific election under the other section (see *Butt v Haxby* (1983)). Any surplus loss still unrelieved will then be carried forward under s 385.

EXAMPLE 7.6

Angus begins trading on 1 August 1997 and in the period to 5 April 1998 makes a loss of £15,000. His income in the preceding three years (1994–95 onwards) amounted to £10,000. If Angus elects for s 381 relief he will have wasted his personal allowances in the preceding years. He will be left with an unrelieved loss of £5,000 which can be relieved under s 380 against any other income which he may have in 1997–98 and (by a further election) in 1998–99. To the extent that relief is not given under s 380, the surplus loss will be carried forward under s 385.

Which relief the taxpayer chooses will depend upon the facts. Section 381 relief is advantageous when the taxpayer has a large pre-trading income, since it will ensure a cash refund. Alternatively, if his other income/gains in the year(s) of loss is large, relief under TA 1988 s 380/s 72 may be more attractive. Changes in income tax rates are an important factor to bear in mind.

[7.82]–[7.100]

VI RELIEF FOR LOSSES IN THE FINAL YEARS

1 TA 1988 s 386: transfer of a business to a company

The general rule is that loss relief is personal to the taxpayer who sustains the loss; it cannot be 'sold' with the business or otherwise transferred. Thus, if a business is incorporated, any unabsorbed loss of the old business which ceases to trade cannot be carried forward under s 385 by the company. However, TA 1988 s 386 provides that where the business of a sole trader or a partnership is transferred to a company and the whole or main consideration for the transfer is the allotment of shares to the former proprietor, he can set his unabsorbed losses against income which he receives from the company for any year throughout which he owns the shares allotted to him and during which the company continues to trade. He will normally be able to set the losses against either dividends on the shares or salary if he is a director or employee of the company in the order of earned before unearned income. The Revenue has confirmed that even if the vending agreement refers to a cash consideration provided that shares are taken relief is available (IM 3551) and that this relief will be allowed provided that the taxpayer keeps shares which represent more than 80% of the consideration received for the business (IM 3552).

EXAMPLE 7.7

Evans sells his business to a company in return for an allotment of shares on 30 September 1997. His unused losses from the trade amount to £4,200.

In the period from 1 October 1997 to 5 April 1998, he receives a salary of £3,000 and dividends (gross) of £400 from the company. In 1998–99 he receives a salary of £5,000 and dividends of £600. Evans obtains relief under s 386 as follows:

	Total income £	*Losses* £
1997–98		
Unabsorbed Schedule D Case I loss		(4,200)
Salary	3,000	
Dividends	400	
	3,400	
Less s 386 relief	(3,400)	3,400
	Nil	(800)
1998–99		
Salary	5,000	
Less s 386 relief	(800)	800
	4,200	
Dividends	600	
	£4,800	

Relief under s 386 is given automatically (as an extension of s 385) as if the original business had not ceased and as if the income derived from the company were profits of that business. However, for all other purposes the business has discontinued and, if the taxpayer wants relief for his business loss in the year of discontinuance under s 380(1), or terminal relief under s 388 (see [**7.102**]), he must make a specific election to that effect. Section 386 relief is, of course, given to the individual taxpayer who sustains the loss and affords no relief for losses made by the newly formed company.   [**7.101**]

2   TA 1988 s 388: terminal loss relief

If a loss is sustained in the last 12 months of a business, the unabsorbed loss of that period, so far as not otherwise relieved (eg under TA 1988 s 380/s 72, in the year of discontinuance) may be relieved by set-off against the business profits in the year of cessation and of the three years of assessment preceding the one in which the business terminates. Relief is given as far as possible against later rather than earlier years. A terminal loss is defined as one sustained in the year of assessment in which the trade discontinued together with such proportion of any loss sustained in the previous year beginning 12 months before the discontinuance (if in either case there was a profit then nil is entered in calculating the terminal loss). For the purpose of this calculation capital allowances are deducted as a business expense.

The loss includes (i) any annual payments charged under TA 1988 s 349, (ii) any unrelieved interest payments so long as they are incurred wholly and exclusively for the purposes of the business.

If profits of a preceding year are insufficient to absorb the loss, dividends and other income taxed at source in that year (and which are received in the course of carrying on the business) are treated as profits for the purposes of obtaining a repayment of income tax (TA 1988 s 385(4)).

Relief may be claimed under TA 1988 s 388 as an alternative to relief under TA 1988 s 386 (transfer to a company) and any unused loss can be relieved under s 386.   [**7.102**]–[**7.120**]

EXAMPLE 7.8

Dolly closes down her hairdressing business on 5 June 1997. Her results for the four years ending 5 December 1996 and for her final six months of business were:

Accounting period	Profit/loss	Tax years	Original assessments
Year to 5 December 1993	£11,000 profit	1993–94	£11,000
Year to 5 December 1994	£7,000 profit	1994–95	£7,000
Year to 5 December 1995	£3,000 profit	1995–96	£3,000
Year to 5 December 1996	£1,000 profit	1996–97	£1,000
Six months to 5 June 1997	£12,000 loss	1997–98	£nil

The terminal loss is calculated as:

(i) loss in year of discontinuance:

$$\frac{2}{6} \times 12,000 = £4,000$$

plus

(ii) loss in preceding year of assessment:

$$\frac{4}{6} \times 12,000 = 8,000$$

plus

$$\frac{6}{12} \times 1,000 = £nil$$

ie £12,000

That loss is relieved as follows:

Tax year	Fiscal assessment
1997–98	nil
1996–97 ⎫	profits for these years (starting with 1996–97) reduced by the
1995–96 ⎬	terminal loss of £12,000. 1996–97 was a transitional year and
1994–95 ⎭	earlier periods were taxed on a preceding year basis.

VII INVESTMENT IN UNQUOTED CORPORATE TRADES (TA 1988, s 574)

As a general rule, a person who subscribes for shares in a company and later disposes of them at a loss can only claim CGT relief for his loss. In an attempt to stimulate investment in corporate trades, however, TA 1988 s 574 enables the taxpayer to obtain income tax relief for his loss in certain circumstances. Broadly, the section allows an individual who has made a loss on the disposal of shares in a 'qualifying trading company' to deduct the loss from his total income in the year of assessment in which the loss is incurred or against total income of the preceding year (s 574(1)(b)). This relief is hedged about with restrictions:

(1) It is available only to an individual who subscribes for shares in a company for money or money's worth, including one who acquires the shares from a subscribing spouse; it is not available to a subsequent purchaser of the shares.

(2) The disposal giving rise to the loss must be a sale at arm's length for full consideration; or a distribution from the company on a dissolution or a winding up; or a deemed disposal under TCGA 1992 s 24(2) where the shares have become of negligible value.

(3) The company must satisfy the complex requirements of s 576(4) and (5). Basically, it must be an unquoted trading company, resident in the UK,

which does not trade in certain prohibited items such as land or shares and which is not a building society, or a registered industrial and provident society.

If these conditions are satisfied, the allowable loss is calculated on CGT principles and is deducted in priority to relief under TA 1988 s 380 or s 381 from the individual's earned, before unearned, income. This is to the taxpayer's advantage given that trading losses can be carried forward under TA 1988 s 385 whereas capital losses cannot.

The deduction is given in accordance with the s 380 rules, ie against income of the year of assessment in which the loss arises and income of the previous year. A claim must be made by notice given within 12 months from 31 January of the tax year following the disposal. Relief may be claimed against either or both of the income tax years: to the extent that part of the loss is unrelieved the capital gains tax rules apply (see [**14.61**]).

To prevent the taxpayer from obtaining double tax relief on his investment, any income tax relief he received on the acquisition of the shares under the Enterprise Investment Scheme (see [**4.122**]) must be deducted from the base value of the shares when calculating an allowable loss for CGT and therefore, for s 574.   [**7.121**]

8 Land

I INTRODUCTORY: SCHEDULE A REMODELLED

As part of the move to self-assessment the Chancellor in his 1994 Budget Speech announced measures to reform and simplify the income tax treatment of income from land. As a result the system of taxing such income originally introduced in 1963 was swept away in the case of individuals as from 6 April 1995. In its place a new Schedule A charges *profits of a business of letting property* which include isolated or casual lettings, income from furnished lettings and certain lease premiums. Inherent in these changes were radical alterations in the treatment of interest payments made by a landlord.

Having said all this, in practice the old Schedule A rules were much modified and to some extent it is true to say that the new rules amount to a statutory recognition of practices which had already developed (for the transitional provisions see [1995] SWTI 250). Note also that these changes have only been made for income tax purposes: companies generally remain subject to the old Schedule A regime which was felt to be more beneficial in two respects. *First*, interest paid by companies may be deducted against profits generally (see [**28.52**]) and, *secondly*, management expenses may in practice be flexibly relieved for investment companies (see [**28.66**]). In both cases this flexibility would be lost under the new rules which limit the deduction of interest to Schedule A income.   [**8.1**]–[**8.20**]

II APPLICATION OF CASE I PRINCIPLES

1 Ambit of Schedule A

FA 1995 s 39 inserted a new Schedule A for income tax purposes with effect from tax year 1995–96. Paragraph 1(1) of TA 1988 s 15 provides:

> 'Tax under this Schedule shall be charged on the annual profits or gains arising from any business carried on for the exploitation, as a source of rents or other receipts, of any estate, interest or rights in or over any land in the United Kingdom.'

The following matters should be noted.

First, the tax is not levied by reference to income produced from individual properties but instead looks at *all* properties owned by the individual under the umbrella of a 'Schedule A business'.

Secondly, that business includes isolated transactions provided that they are entered into 'for the exploitation of a right in or over land'. (Insofar as the term 'a business' implies continuous activities, it is therefore something of a misnomer.) As a result a sum paid on the sale of a lease originally granted at an under value and which formerly fell within the income tax charge under Schedule D Case VI (see [**8.83**]) is now caught by these rules.

Thirdly, rents from furnished lettings which were formerly taxed under Case VI are also now within the Schedule A net.

Finally, 'other receipts' not just rent are caught, by the Schedule although given that the charge is on *annual* profits or gains, it is only receipts of an *income* nature that are caught (subject to the special rules in TA 1988, ss 34–36 governing lease premiums: see [**8.81**] ff).   [**8.21**]

EXAMPLE 8.1

(1) Rustic sells turves from his land: he falls within Schedule A and the payments are of an income nature being received for the exploitation of rights in UK land (*Lowe v J W Ashmore Ltd* (1971)). Contrast the position of Campo who received a 'one-off' payment in return for a licence to tip. This payment is of a capital nature and therefore outside the Schedule A rules; see *McClure v Petre* (1988) in which Browne-Wilkinson VC concluded that:

'The substance of the present matter is that the payments were received by the taxpayer as consideration for a once and for all disposal of a right or advantage appurtenant to the land; namely the right or advantage of using it for dumping. Immediately before the licence was granted, the value of the land itself included the value of the right to turn it to advantage by using it for dumping. After the licence that right or advantage had gone forever in return for a lump sum. True the acreage of land and the taxpayer's interest remain the same; but it was shorn of this valuable advantage. It was in truth a realisation of part of the value of the freehold. That strikes me as a disposal of a capital nature...'

(2) Junius lets flats and the tenants pay a service charge aimed at recouping Junius's costs of maintenance, insurance and repairs. These payments fall within Schedule A (see TA 1988 s 24(6)). Contrast the position if Junius provided other services, such as a caretaker, when he would be carrying on a trade and so payments made in return for such services would be assessed under Schedule D Case I (in practice, given that Schedule A is now computed on Case I principles, the only real importance of this distinction lies in the treatment of Case I income as earned for the purpose of, eg, Junius' pension entitlement (see generally *Fry v Salisbury House Estate Ltd* (1930)).

2   The income is unearned

The concept of the 'Schedule A business' is limited in that although the tax charge is computed on Schedule D Case I principles, the income is not itself treated as earned income (as made clear in *Example 8.1(2)* above). As a result income tax benefits associated with earned income (notably pension entitlement) and the CGT business reliefs do not apply. Special rules, however, apply to 'furnished holiday lettings' in the UK (see [**8.61**]). Whether property lettings qualify for IHT business property relief is considered elsewhere (see [**23.45**]).
                                                                            [**8.22**]

3   Lettings outside Case I

The changes have not affected a line of cases decided in the early 1980s, such as *Webb v Conelee Properties Ltd* (1982), in which the court held that there was no such trade as 'the letting of properties producing a rent' since that is precisely what is chargd to tax under Schedule A and the taxpayer had conducted no other activities which could have amounted to a trade. Similarly, in *Griffiths v Jackson* (1983), income from letting furnished flats or bed-sitting rooms to students was held to be income from land and not assessable under Schedule D Case I (see also *Gittos v Barclay* (1982)). Unless a landlord can establish that either he is running an hotel or guest house (both trades taxed under Case I) or can bring himself within the holiday letting provisions, then all his income from land (apart from separate service charges) will be taxed as the unearned income of a Schedule A business.   [8.23]

4 Exclusions from the Schedule A charge

Paragraph 2 in s 15 expressly excludes certain income from the Schedule A charge: namely, yearly interest; profits and gains arising from mines, quarries and certain other concerns such as markets, tolls, bridges and ferries (which by TA 1988 s 55 are taxed under Schedule D Case I); mineral rent and royalties (taxed half as income under Schedule D and half as capital) and miscellaneous receipts of income from, for instance, way-leaves or tolls, in which cases the income is received after basic rate income tax has been deducted at source by the payer under TA 1988 s 119 (and see TA 1988 s 120 (as amended by FA 1997 s 60) in relation to payment for wayleaves for electricity cables, telephone lines etc).   [8.24]–[8.40]

III CHARGEABLE PERSONS AND COMPUTATION

1 Chargeable persons

Section 21(1) provides for the tax to be charged on and paid by 'the persons receiving or entitled to the income in respect of which the tax is directed by the Income Tax Acts to be charged' whilst s 21(2) provides for the tax to be computed on 'the full amount of the profits or gains arising in the year of assessment'.

The tax can therefore be levied on any person who is entitled to a net sum (wide enough presumably to include life tenants under settlements of land). Income for these purposes refers to net profits and gains not gross receipts. Section 21(2) makes it clear that the tax charge itself is calculated on the accruals (or earnings) basis.   [8.41]

2 Computation: accountancy practice

So far as computation is concerned, s 21(3) provides for the Case I rules to apply and s 21(4) states that:

> 'All the businesses and transactions carried on or entered into by any person or partnership, so far as they are businesses or transactions the profits or gains of which are chargeable to tax under Schedule A shall be treated for the purposes of that Schedule as, or as entered into in the course of carrying on, the one business.'

As a result, Schedule A profits must be computed on the basis of standard accountancy practice which will, in the absence of express statutory provision, decide what is a taxable receipt and what is an allowable expense. In place of the concept of 'permitted deductions' which formerly applied for Schedule A purposes, reference is now made to the general principle that deduction is available for items of expenditure incurred wholly and exclusively for the purpose of the Schedule A business provided that the particular type of expenditure does not fall within the prohibited list in, for instance, TA 1988 s 74 (eg capital expenditure incurred in the making of improvements or acquiring the premises: see s 74(1)(f) and (g)).   [8.42]

EXAMPLE 8.2

Julia acquires a Fulham flat for letting. It is in a rundown condition and she expends substantial sums restoring it to its former glory. These sums will be deductible expenses provided that the purchase price for the property was not substantially less than if the property had been in a proper state of repair and provided that the property was capable of letting without repair works having to be carried out (see generally the cases of *Law Shipping Co Ltd v IRC* (1924) and *Odeon Associated Theatres Ltd v Jones* (1971) discussed at [**6.121**]).

3   Interest payments

Prior to 6 April 1995 interest payments could be deducted by landlords if they satisfied the detailed rules laid down in TA 1988 ss 353–368. Broadly speaking, the interest had to be on a loan used to acquire an estate or interest in land or in improving or developing the land or buildings (hence loans used for the maintenance or repair of property did not generally qualify). In addition, the relevant land had to be let at a commercial rent for a period of at least 26 weeks during the year of assessment and available for letting (or used as the taxpayer's main residence) at other times. Even if relief was available it was limited to the income produced by the particular property.

The new rules in this area are truly revolutionary, permitting deduction for interest payments 'wholly and exclusively' expended for the Schedule A business in computing the profits of that business. Linking interest payments to rent from a particular property is no longer necessary: indeed the particular property acquired by means of the relevant loan may be sold but relief will continue provided that the Schedule A business continues.   [**8.43**]

EXAMPLE 8.3

Jennie borrows substantial sums to acquire property A, to renovate property B and to re-roof property C. During the year, despite her best endeavours, property A remains unlet whilst property C is sold. Property B is let throughout the year. Jennie is carrying on a Schedule A business and all the interest payments are deductible in computing her profit.

4   Losses

The former restricted loss relief rules have been marginally improved but the general principle remains that losses incurred in a Schedule A business can only be off-set against future profits of that business (TA 1988 s 379A). Relief against other income is only available in two cases—*first*, losses resulting from claims to capital allowances and, *secondly*, for 'agricultural expenses' incurred in connection with the management of an agricultural estate. There is no right to carry back unrelieved Schedule A losses. The Case I rules for bad debts and pre-business expenditure apply.   [**8.44**]

5   Capital allowances

Capital allowances for machinery and plant used in the management of property will be given as if it were used for the purposes of a Schedule A business (ie as a Schedule A expense, as part of the profit calculation). Capital allowances in respect of expenditure on leased plant and machinery will also be given as a trading expense: TA 1988 s 32(1A), however, prevents relief being given under Schedule A where it is already available under CAA 1990 s 61 or s 67. As capital allowances are not available for plant or machinery let in a dwelling house the renewals basis or the wear and tear allowances for furnished lettings are maintained (see SP A19). Under the renewals basis the entire cost of replacing the asset may be deducted in arriving at the profits from the lettings in the year when that expense is incurred. The alternative method, the allowance for depreciation, permits the deduction of (usually) 10% of the gross rent less water rates each tax year that the premises are let. Once a taxpayer has claimed allowances on one of these two bases, the practice is for that basis then to continue for that taxpayer. [**8.45**]

EXAMPLE 8.4

Rakeman is the landlord of furnished premises the rent from which is £10,000 in 1997–98. During that tax year, his total expenses comprising the costs of managing, maintaining and repairing the premises (including the decoration of two rooms and water rates of £800) amount to £6,000. His profit is, therefore, £4,000 (£10,000 − £6,000). In addition, however, Rakeman spent £6,500 on refurbishments (buying new carpets and new kitchen and bathroom units). If Rakeman claims the renewals basis he has further deductible expenditure in 1997–98 of £6,500 leaving him with no Schedule A taxable income, but instead a loss of £2,500 (£10,000 − (£6,000 + £6,500)) which he can set against other Schedule A income in that year or in future tax years. Alternatively, under the depreciation basis, Rakeman can claim a 10% deduction of £920 calculated on gross rent less water rates (ie 10% × (£10,000 − £800)) which he can treat as a further deductible expense to leave him with a taxable profit for 1997–98 of £3,080 (£10,000 − (£6,000 + £920)). Under this basis, he will continue to claim a 10% deduction in each tax year during which the premises are let.

6 Rent-a-room (F(No 2)A 1992 s 59, Sch 10 and SI 1996/2953)

Designed as a tax incentive to encourage owner occupiers and tenants who have a spare room in their home to let it out, gross annual rents not exceeding £4,250 are exempt from income tax. The following conditions must be satisfied:

(1) relief is available to *individuals* on a letting of *furnished* accommodation;
(2) the letting income must be taxed under either Schedule A or Schedule D Case I (the latter only applying if substantial services are provided by the landlord);
(3) the letting must be in the individual's '*only or main home*' in the '*basis period*' (ie in the current year in the case of an assessment under Schedule A or preceding year basis for Schedule D Case I income);
(4) the gross income limit of £4,250 will be halved if more than one person lets rooms in the same house and husband and wife may so arrange matters that the income is either wholly the wife's or wholly the husband's;
(5) the individual can elect for this exemption not to apply (he may wish to do so, for instance, in order to claim loss relief for the relevant period);
(6) if gross annual receipts exceed £4,250, the individual can choose either to pay tax in the normal way (on gross receipts less actual expenses) or, alternatively, on gross receipts less £4,250 (this is termed 'the alternative basis'). An election must be made on or before the first anniversary of the 31 January next following the year of assessment for which it is made (or such later date as the Board may allow) if the alternate basis is to apply. Such election remains in force until withdrawn. [**8.46**]–[**8.60**]

IV FURNISHED HOLIDAY LETTINGS

TA 1988 ss 503–504 provide for income from furnished holiday lettings in the UK to be treated as trading income and for the CGT business reliefs to be available. The provisions apply to lettings by individuals and by companies. The new Schedule A rules do not affect these provisions and owners of property suitable for letting as holiday accommodation are advised to satisfy the conditions of s 503 wherever possible so that full (rather than restricted) loss relief is available; the income qualifies as earned for pension purposes and the CGT reliefs are available.   **[8.61]**

Definition   The accommodation must be available for letting to the public commercially as furnished holiday accommodation for at least 140 days in the tax year and must be actually let for at least 70 days. These periods need not be continuous and accordingly both winter and summer holiday accommodation may qualify. To ensure a 'genuine' holiday letting, it must not 'normally' (undefined) be let to the same person continuously in any seven months of the year (but including the 70-day period above) for more than 31 days. In the remaining five months of the tax year, therefore, the landlord may do what he wishes with the property, eg let it continuously; keep it empty; go into occupation himself. The above requirements will however normally exclude student accommodation. The letting of caravans is included, insofar as it is not taxed as a trade under Schedule D Case I, but not the letting of sites (taxed under Schedule A) nor residential caravans for long-term occupation (IR Press Release [1984] STI 386).

The term 'holiday' accommodation is undefined; if the above conditions are satisfied, it will be deemed to be a holiday letting (see eg *Gittos v Barclay* (1982) where these requirements were satisfied). Letting means occupation by a person other than the landlord and includes granting a licence to occupy.

Whether the accommodation qualifies as a holiday let in any tax year is judged on the facts of that year (for company landlords, the financial year). However, where the letting begins in a tax year (eg on 1 August 1997), it may qualify as a holiday let for that year if it satisfies the above requirements within the following 12 months (ie between 1 August 1997 and 31 July 1998). Likewise, a letting which ends in a tax year, must satisfy the necessary conditions during the previous 12 months.   **[8.62]**

Tax treatment   The income profits for the whole year will be assessed under Schedule A, but treated as trading profits for the purposes specified in TA 1988 s 503(1) and, therefore, receive most of the benefits of an assessment under Schedule D Case I. Thus, the income is earned income. The tax is payable in two equal instalments in January and July as under Case I.

For CGT purposes the letting is treated as a trade in any year when it satisfies the above conditions or would do so but for the fact that the property is under construction or repair. Thus, roll-over (replacement of business assets) relief (TCGA 1992 s 152 ff); hold-over relief on a gift of business assets (TCGA 1992 s 165); and retirement relief (TCGA 1992 s 163) may be available on a disposal (see generally Chapter 16). However, a landlord who claims roll-over relief and occupies the property himself may not claim the main residence exemption against the entire gain on a subsequent disposal. In such a case the rolled-over gain is chargeable and the exemption applies only to any remaining gain. No special relief is given from IHT and property lettings do not qualify for business property relief (see **[23.45]**).

EXAMPLE 8.5

'Seaview' is purchased for £40,000 in 1988 and let as furnished holiday accommodation until 1994. It is then sold for £60,000 and the proceeds used in the purchase of 'Belvedere' for £85,000 which is also let. In 1996 the landlord takes possession and lives there until 2000 when he sells it for £145,000.

In 1994, the gain on 'Seaview' is rolled over into the purchase of 'Belvedere' giving it a base cost for CGT of £65,000. On the sale of 'Belvedere' in 2000 the gain is £80,000 of which £20,000 (rolled over from 'Seaview') is chargeable. The remaining gain is apportioned between the period of occupation which is exempt (ie 4/6 = £40,000) and the let period (ie 2/6 = £20,000) which is chargeable, unless eliminated under TCGA 1992 s 223(4) (see [**16.72**]).

If, instead, 'Belvedere' is sold in 1996 at the end of the season for £115,000, the gain of £50,000 might be eliminated by any retirement relief available to the landlord (he must show that the disposal is of a business or part of a business).

Where the same landlord lets several 'qualifying' properties, they are taxed as one trade. Should one or more properties qualify as furnished holiday lettings in the tax year and others not, because they fail to satisfy the 70-day requirement, the landlord can claim, within two years of the end of the relevant tax year, for the days of letting to be averaged between all or any of the properties thereby enabling all the properties to qualify. Thus, if property A is let in 1997–98 for 90 days and properties B and C for 50 days each respectively, A and B or A and C can be averaged so that two properties qualify; there are insufficient letting days for all three to qualify.   [**8.63**]–[**8.80**]

V THE TAXATION OF PREMIUMS UNDER SCHEDULE A (TA 1988 ss 34–39)

1 Introductory

A premium is a capital sum paid by a tenant to a landlord in connection with the grant of a lease. To understand the taxation of premiums, it should be noted that the original Schedule A was introduced before CGT so that a landlord could have avoided paying any tax by extracting a capital sum from the tenant instead of rent. Accordingly, certain premiums are deemed to be income and so chargeable to income tax. Insofar as a premium is not chargeable as income it may be subject to CGT. As CGT is now charged at income tax rates, the importance of the distinction between the taxes has been reduced although not wholly removed. For instance, when a landlord is entitled to substantial interest relief or has incurred deductible expenditure, he may want any premium to be taxed as rent.   [**8.81**]

2 The charge (TA 1988 s 34)

If a lease is granted for a period not exceeding 50 years and the consideration includes a premium, a proportion of that premium is treated as additional rent taxable under Schedule A. This proportion is the amount that is left after deducting 2% of the premium for each complete year of the lease other than the first. The effect of the 2% discount is that the amount of premium charged to income tax falls with the length of the lease. For a one-year lease all the premium is taxed and for a 50-year lease 2%.

EXAMPLE 8.6

Lease 16 years; premium £3,000.

Discount 2% of £3,000 over 15 years = $£3,000 \times \dfrac{2}{100} \times 15 = £900$

Chargeable slice: £3,000 – £900 = £2,100

The grant of a sub-lease of 50 years or less will, as a general rule, be taxed in the same way as the grant of a head lease. If, however, a premium on the grant of the head lease was taxed under Schedule A, this is taken into account when taxing any premium on the grant of the sub-lease (TA 1988 s 37).   [**8.82**]

3 Anti-avoidance provisions

There are elaborate provisions designed to prevent the charge to income tax on premiums from being circumvented.

First, a landlord cannot avoid the TA 1988 s 34 charge by disguising the length of the lease. If its length can be extended by an option to renew or shortened by an option to surrender or to terminate, those options will be taken into account only insofar as they are likely to be exercised (TA 1988 s 38).

> **EXAMPLE 8.7**
>
> L grants a lease to T for 60 years at a premium of £20,000 and a rent of £1,000 pa for the first ten years and thereafter at an annual rent of ten times the then market rent. T has an option to surrender the lease after ten years. For the purposes of Schedule A this is treated as a ten-year lease since the tenant is likely to exercise the option to surrender in view of the penal increase in the rent after ten years.

Secondly, where a landlord, instead of taking a premium on the grant of a lease for 50 years or less, requires the tenant to make improvements to the premises, the amount by which the value of the landlord's reversion is increased as a result of those improvements is treated as a premium (TA 1988 s 34(2)). This provision does not, however, apply if the tenant is required to make improvements to another property of the landlord; if the obligation is not imposed by the lease; or if the expenditure would have been a deductible expense of the landlord.

> **EXAMPLE 8.8**
>
> Property is let from 1 June 1997, for seven years. Under the terms of the lease the tenant is required to carry out certain structural alterations as a result of which the value of the landlord's interest in the premises is increased by £2,000.
>
> | | |
> |---|---:|
> | Increase: | £2,000 |
> | *Less:* discount: $\frac{2}{100} \times £2,000 \times 6$: | £240 |
> | Included in 1996–97 Schedule A profits: | £1,760 |

Thirdly, TA 1988 s 34(4) and (5) charge 'delayed premiums' as income. If a premium becomes payable at some date during the currency of the lease or the tenant has to pay a sum for the waiver or variation of any terms of the lease, the sum is treated as a premium and in both cases the premium is taxed in the year of receipt as a premium for the then unexpired period of the lease. If a tenant has to pay a sum for the surrender of a lease it is taxed as a premium on a lease running from the date of commencement to the date of surrender.

Fourthly, the assignment of a lease, which has been granted at an undervalue is charged under TA 1988 s 35. The charge under s 34 could be circumvented by a landlord granting a lease to, say, his spouse or to a company which he owns. No premium would be charged on the grant but the lease could then be assigned to the intended tenant and a premium taken. Section 34 only applies to a premium paid on the grant of a lease not on its assignment. However, s 35 provides that, when a lease is granted for less than its market premium, tax is charged under Schedule A on assignors of the lease up to the amount of premium foregone by the landlord and to the extent that such assignors have made a profit on that assignment.

EXAMPLE 8.9

A grants B a 21-year lease at a premium of £2,000 although he could have charged £3,000. Therefore, the 'amount foregone' is £1,000. A is chargeable under Schedule A on the premium that he actually receives.

Two years later B assigns the lease to C charging a premium of £2,800. B receives £800 more than he paid; that is within the 'amount foregone'.

B is, therefore, chargeable under Schedule A on:

$$£800 - \left(\frac{2}{100} \times 20 \times £800 \right) = £480$$

Notice that the 'amount foregone' still outstanding is £200 and that the period of the lease remains at the original length (viz 21 years) for the purpose of discounting. Two years later C assigns the lease to D charging a premium of £3,200. He has received £400 more than he paid but only £200 of that is caught under TA 1988 s 35 since that exhausts the 'amount foregone' by A. C is chargeable, therefore, under Schedule A on:

$$£200 - \left(\frac{2}{100} \times 20 \times £200 \right) = £120$$

An assignee should, therefore, ensure (so far as possible) that the lease was not granted at an undervalue, and if necessary should take advantage of the clearance procedure under TA 1988 s 35(3).

The *final* anti-avoidance provision prevents the grant of a lease from being disguised as a sale (TA 1988 s 36(1)). If D sells land (freehold or leasehold) to E with a right to have the property reconveyed to him in the future, any difference between the price paid by E and the reconveyance price payable by D is treated as a premium on a lease for the period between the sale and the reconveyance and is taxed under Schedule A.

TA 1988 s 36(3) extends TA 1988 s 36(1) so that if D sells land to E with a right for him (or a person connected with him) to take a leaseback of the property in the future, any difference between the price paid by E and the aggregate of the premium (if any) payable on the grant of a lease by E, together with the value of the reversion in E's hands, is treated as a premium on a lease for the period between the sale and leaseback and is taxed under Schedule A. So as not to prejudice a commercial sale and leaseback, this provision does not apply where the leaseback is within one month of the sale.   **[8.83]**

EXAMPLE 8.10

D sells land to E for £40,000 with a right to take a 20-year lease of the property after 11 years for a premium of £8,000. The value of E's reversionary interest subject to the lease is £2,000. There is a deemed premium under TA 1988 s 36(3) of £30,000 (£40,000 – (£8,000 + £2,000)) on a lease of 11 years. D is chargeable under Schedule A on:

$$£30,000 - \left(\frac{2}{100} \times £30,000 \times 10 \right) = £24,000$$

4   Premium payable in instalments

If the premium is payable in instalments, tax is charged on the total of the instalments in the tax year when the first instalment is payable. Exceptionally the tax may be paid by instalments over the shorter of the period of the instalments of the premium and eight years if the taxpayer can satisfy the Revenue that to pay the tax in one lump sum would cause him 'undue hardship' (undue hardship is not defined, but the Revenue considers the resources made available by the particular transaction in permitting payment by instalments in relation to *bona fide* commercial transactions: TA 1988 s 34(8)). This claim must be made within the tax year following the one when the first instalment of the premium became payable. **[8.84]**

5   Relief for traders paying a premium on trading premises (TA 1988 s 87)

Rent is an allowable deduction from the trading income of a trader (TA 1988 s 74). If a trader is granted a lease of business premises for 50 years or less at a premium, he can treat a portion of the premium as an annual rent and deduct it from his trading income. This portion is the amount of the premium that is charged to income tax in the landlord's hands under Schedule A divided by the unexpired term of the lease. The rest of the premium is a capital expense.

A premium paid by a trader who takes an assignment of a lease is not allowable as a deduction from trading income unless the premium is caught by s 35. **[8.85]**

> **EXAMPLE 8.11**
>
> L grants T a lease of business premises for ten years at an annual rent of £100 and a premium of £10,000.
>
> L is chargeable under Schedule A on £8,200 of the premium (see TA 1988 s 34). The yearly equivalent of this sum, £820 (£8,200 ÷ 10), can be treated by T as additional rent so that each year he can deduct rent of £920 (£820 + £100) from his trading receipts.

6   Position of trusts

Lease premiums received by trustees are a capital receipt as a matter of general law. Hence whilst the trustees will run a Schedule A business so that basic rate income tax will be charged on the income deemed to arise from the premium, that deemed income will not be subject to the 'surcharge' under TA 1988 s 686 and, in the case of interest in possession trusts, will not lead to a higher rate liability in the hands of the life tenant. **[8.86]-[8.100]**

VII   TA 1988 s 776 AND THE DEVELOPMENT OF LAND

1   Transactions in land and s 776

The section was formerly headed 'Artificial Transactions in Land' and s 776(1) states that it was enacted to prevent the avoidance of tax by persons concerned with land or its development. However, the relevant transaction need not be *artificial* and a tax avoidance motive is not an essential precondition for liability (*Page v Lowther* (1983): see **[8.108]**). Capital sums falling within the terms of the section are brought within the income tax charge. **[8.101]**

2   Trading under Schedule D Case 1

Section 776 does not apply if the taxpayer engages in a trading transaction subject to an income tax charge under Schedule D Case I. In such cases land will be trading stock and all sums derived therefore will be subject to income tax. The definition of a trade has been restrictively interpreted in *Marson v Morton* (1986) in which the judge stated that:

> 'the mere fact that land is not income producing should not be decisive or even virtually decisive on the question whether it was bought as an investment'.

However, land originally acquired for a non-trading purpose (eg investment) may subsequently be appropriated to trading stock. At this point a CGT charge may arise under TCGA 1992 s 161 although this can be avoided by the election to transfer the land at no gain/no loss (see [**14.117**]). Whether such appropriation occurs will depend on the facts of each case. In *Taylor v Good* (1974), discussed at [**6.23**], the house in question did not become trading stock merely because the taxpayer had applied for planning permission before the sale:

> 'If you find a trade in the purchase and sale of land, it may not be difficult to find that properties originally owned (for example) by inheritance, or bought for investment only, have been brought into the stock in trade of that trade. But where, as here, there is no question at all of absorption into a trade of dealing in land or lands previously acquired with no thought of dealing, there is no ground at all for holding that activities such as those in the present case, designed only to enhance the value of the land in the market, are to be taken as pointing to, still less as establishing, an adventure in the nature of trade.' (Russell LJ)

By contrast, in *Pilkington v Randall* (1966) land was held in a will trust for a brother and sister absolutely. It was sold at different times and roads and drains were constructed prior to the sales. Furthermore, the brother bought parcels of the land from his sister. He was held to be trading. At first instance, Cross J stated:

> 'I do not think that one can lay down hard and fast rules, such as that the construction of roads and sewers and the installation of services can never be enough to make the case one of embarking upon a trade. One has to look at the whole picture and say whether the amount of money spent on the development before sale and the objects for which and the circumstances in which the money was spent are such as to make it reasonable to say that what was inherited has changed its character and become part of the raw material or stock in trade of a business.'

In the Court of Appeal, Danckwerts LJ likewise stated that there was no general proposition of law to the effect that whenever a property owner develops his land by making roads and laying sewers and selling plots he can never be carrying on a trade:

> 'This would be opening the door very wide to modern property developers. I think the highest it can be put is that usually in such circumstances the property owner is not carrying on a trade, but whether in the particular case he is or is not doing so must depend on the facts of the particular case. It is essentially a question of fact and degree.'

It is apparent from the foregoing cases that how the land was originally acquired by the taxpayer is an important factor in determining whether he is trading. If by *inheritance* or *gift* the Revenue will have to show that it has at some point been appropriated to trading stock. On the other hand, if acquired *by purchase* the taxpayer's motive at that time will be relevant. If it is clear that it was acquired as an investment, again the burden will be on the Revenue to show that at a subsequent stage it was appropriated to trading stock. Furthermore, if land was originally acquired as an investment, the mere act of obtaining planning permission prior to a sale will not by itself result in an appropriation of the land to trading stock. Generally the taxpayer is entitled to get the best possible price for the land (*Taylor v Good*, above).

Care needs to be exercised if, as a prelude to sale to a developer, the taxpayer decides to acquire adjacent parcels of land. Such extra parcels will have been acquired purely for resale and there is a risk therefore that the taxpayer will be treated as a trader (and not just in relation to those portions but also in relation to the previously owned land). The purchase of small areas of land should not create problems: the taxpayer will be seen as merely taking steps to obtain the best possible price for his existing land as in *Taylor v Good. Pilkington v Randall* may be distinguished in that the amount of land acquired was large and the taxpayer undertook various preparatory works. Having said this, it will be advisable, whenever practicable, to arrange for the developer to acquire any extra land that will be needed for the development.   **[8.102]**

3   **The effect of falling within s 776**

The section converts a gain which would otherwise be of a capital nature (and therefore in the case of an individual subject to CGT) into an income profit subject to tax under Schedule D Case VI for the chargeable period in which that gain is realised (s 776(3)). The gain is to be computed by such method as is 'just and reasonable' in all the circumstances (s 776(6)) so that CGT computational rules will not necessarily apply.

The effect of taxing the gain as income is that for an *individual* the maximum rate of charge is 40%. In the case of a *company* the rate of tax is either 31% or 21%: accordingly it may be advantageous to shelter the gain in a company. If the gain is realised by *trustees*, income tax will be charged at basic rate (23%). If there is an interest in possession, as a matter of trust law the capital sum will not belong to the life tenant and it is not thought that there is any provision in the Taxes Act which would enable the s 776 income to be taxed as that of the beneficiary. In general, therefore, gains realised through the medium of a trust will escape income tax at the top rate of 40% (subject to an exception where the trust income is deemed under the tax legislation to be that of the settlor: see further Chapter 11).

There remains a danger that trusts falling within TA 1988 s 686 will be subject to tax at 'the rate applicable to trusts' and hence taxed at 34%. That section applies in two situations. *First*, to 'income which is to be accumulated'. These words are not thought appropriate to catch a sum which remains, for trust purposes, capital. *Secondly*, the section applies to income 'which is payable at the discretion of the trustees' and it is arguable that a sum treated as income by s 776 will fall within these words if the trustees of a settlement have a power to pay or advance capital to beneficiaries. Accordingly, there is a danger of an income tax charge in such cases at the 34% rate on s 776 gains. As against this construction of s 686, it is arguable that the word 'income' is used throughout the provision in a purely trust sense and will not apply to capital sums deemed to be income under the tax legislation. Certainly, the Revenue is not known to have taken the point that payments caught by s 776 may fall within the provisions of s 686.

Because the gain is taxed as income under Schedule D Case VI it is unearned income and although it may be reduced by Case VI losses it cannot be reduced by pension contributions nor by Case I losses.   **[8.103]**

4   **When does s 776 apply?**

The following requirements must be satisfied:

Requirement I
Either:
(a) the land or property deriving its value from land is acquired with the sole or main object of realising a gain from disposing of the land etc (s 776(2)(a)); *or*
(b) land is held as trading stock (s 776(2)(b)); *or*
(c) the land held is developed with the sole or main object of realising a gain from disposing of the land when developed (s 776(2)(c)).

Requirement II
A gain of a *capital* nature is obtained.

Requirement III
The gain is obtained from a *disposal of the land*.

Requirement IV
That gain must be obtained *either*
(a) by the person who acquired, held or developed the land or any connected person(s); *or*
(b) as a result of a scheme or arrangement which has allowed a gain to be realised by an indirect method by any person who is a party to or concerned in the arrangements or the scheme.   **[8.104]**

5   Comments on Requirement I

If land is held as trading stock or obtained with the main purpose of selling at a profit, that profit will be subject to tax under Case I in the majority of cases (see [**8.102**]). However, a disposal of land is widened in s 776(4) to include transactions, arrangements, and schemes concerning the land or property deriving its value from the land as a result of which there is a disposal of the land or control over the land. Hence, it is likely that s 776(2)(a) will apply in cases where the land (or more likely property deriving its value from the land) is acquired with the intent of transferring control over the land by some indirect means.

An owner-occupier who decides to develop his land will naturally fall within s 776(2)(c). It is provided in s 776(7) that the relevant gain is that arising after the intention to develop is formed. Apart from the difficulties of determining when this occurs, the formation of this intention may result in the land becoming trading stock within 2 above with the result that any charge will arise under Case I (see also s 777(11)). The owner-occupier who sells his land for development by a third party will not normally fall within this provision unless he stipulates for some future payment linked to the value of the land after it has been developed (see [**8.108**]).   **[8.105]**

6   Comments on Requirement II

As the gain must be of a capital nature, the section does not catch trading gains nor other gains of an income nature. Hence, if land is let (a disposal) there will be no charge under s 776 if rent only (assessable under Schedule A) is payable. Thus s 777(13) provides that a 'capital amount' means a sum which (apart from these provisions) does not fall to be included in the calculation of a person's income for the purposes of the Taxes Acts. A trading gain made by an overseas trust or company and not subject to UK tax under the Taxes Acts may, therefore, amount to a gain of a capital nature for these purposes (see *Yuill v Wilson*, [**8.110**], below).   **[8.106]**

7   Comments on Requirement III

For a charge under s 776 to arise there must be a disposal of land. 'Disposal' is not defined but it may include the disposal of shares in a land company and an interest in a company, partnership, or trust which is wound up.

Land is also deemed to be disposed of if, as a result of arrangements and schemes falling within s 776(4), there is an effective disposal of the land itself or control over the land. It is a moot point whether the letting of land at a rack rent is a disposal. Given that the value of the property in the hands of the taxpayer is unchanged, it may be argued that such a lease does not involve any disposal of land. As against that view, such a letting does confer rights in land on the tenant.

For tax to be imposed it is also necessary for a gain to be *realised*. Under s 777(13) this will only occur when a person can effectively enjoy or dispose of money or money's worth. In the case of the right to future sums the question is, therefore, whether such sums can be valued and treated as part of the disposal proceeds (see *Yuill v Wilson* (1980)). A further disposal for the purposes of s 776 will occur when sums become quantifiable (see *Yuill v Fletcher* (1984)).   [**8.107**]

8   Comments on Requirement IV

The person who holds or develops the land may be caught as may a person connected with him (for 'connected persons' see TA 1988 s 839). In addition, a gain realised through a scheme or arrangement by an indirect method, or as a result of a series of transactions, will lead to a s 776 charge on any person concerned in that scheme or arrangement. In such cases, tax is imposed to the extent of the gain realised by the particular individual as can be seen by the case of *Winterton v Edwards* (1980). In that case L was the prime mover in a complicated tax avoidance scheme and owned all the shares in the relevant property company except for two small holdings owned by W and B. He acquired two sites outside the company for development and when W and B protested at this he arranged to give them a share in any sale proceeds from the land. Section 776 assessments on W and B were upheld because, although they were not parties to L's various transactions, they were *concerned in* the transactions as a result of their small interests in the proceeds of sale. Hence, if one person intends to realise a gain within s 776 (in this case both acquiring and developing land with the intention of realising a gain on its disposal) other persons may then be caught, even though they lack that intention, if they participate in the arrangement (see also *Page v Lowther*, below).

The phrase 'scheme or arrangement' is wide enough to catch a vendor or landowner who retains a share of the ultimate development profits. In *Page v Lowther* (1983), trustees owned four houses forming a site suitable for redevelopment. They granted a 99-year lease to the developers who in turn granted underleases of new dwellings when constructed at premiums payable partly to the trustees and partly to the developers. In all, the trustees received premiums totalling £1.2m. On these facts, the Court of Appeal held that the expression 'an arrangement or scheme' had no sinister overtones so that the grant of the lease by the trustees to the developers was such an arrangement. Further, the grant of the underlease was a disposal (albeit not by the trustees) in return for a capital sum so that the trustees were held liable on their share under s 776. The Court of Appeal did not accept that the duty of the trustees to obtain the best possible price afforded any defence to them. The case is authority for the proposition that the section is not limited to artificial transactions nor need tax avoidance be a proven motive on the part of the taxpayer (see [**8.101**]). For the rate of tax charged on the trustees, see [**8.103**].   [**8.108**]

9   Shares in landholding companies

There is a disposal of land if a controlling interest over it is disposed of (s 776(4)). Hence the disposal of a controlling shareholding in a landowning company is treated as a disposal of the land.

The further requirement, that a gain of a capital nature must be obtained from the disposal by a person owning that land *or by any connected person* may be satisfied when shares in a landowning company are sold if the vendor controls that company. In such a case he will then be a connected person (s 839(6)). If two or more shareholders act together their interests may be aggregated in order to determine whether they have control for these purposes: the agreement of a number of minority shareholders to sell their shares may amount to an 'arrangement' under s 776(4).

There is an exemption from charge under s 776(10) when land is held as trading stock by a company and there is a disposal of the shares in that company *provided* that the land is subsequently disposed of by the company in the normal course of its trade in order to ensure that all opportunity of profit in respect of that land arises to the company. To take advantage of this exemption it is normal when selling a property dealing company to obtain from the purchaser a warranty that the trading stock (ie the land) will be sold in the normal course of the trade. However, it is obviously difficult to draft such warranties and the vendor remains very much in the hands of the purchaser. It should also be noted that this exemption does not furnish any defence when a scheme or arrangement has been entered into.   **[8.109]**

10   Providing an opportunity

A gain may be obtained for another person (eg under s 776(7) trusts are treated as distinct entities from the beneficiaries). In general, a gain is obtained in such circumstances if the opportunity of making that gain is transmitted by premature sale or otherwise (s 776(5)): eg if B allows value to pass out of his land into A's land whereupon A makes a gain falling within the section, all or part of that gain may be attributed to B (s 776(8)). In such cases B is given a right of recovery against A for the tax that he suffers (under s 777(8)(a)) although this may prove to be worthless if A is a non-resident.

The opportunity of making a gain is not presumably transmitted merely because land is sold even when it is possible that a gain will be made in the future. As the following case illustrates, however, it is no defence to claim under this section that the land was transferred for full consideration.

In *Yuill v Wilson* (1980), Mr Yuill, who controlled various UK companies, arranged for land to be sold to Guernsey companies who thereupon obtained planning consent for redevelopment and sold the land back to a Yuill UK company at a substantial profit. This profit constituted a gain of a capital nature (see **[8.106]**) and Mr Yuill was treated as a person who indirectly furnished the opportunity for the making of that gain. It was Yuill personally who was subject to charge not the companies which he controlled and which actually transferred the land to the Guernsey company. Note also that all these transactions were at market value. It is somewhat surprising that sales at full value can be regarded as a transfer of an opportunity to make a gain simply because at some later date the market value of the land increases.

Does an outright sale of land with the benefit of planning permission constitute the transmission of an opportunity? It is generally thought that the answer to this question is no so long as the sale is a genuine transaction (ie not to a connected person) for which full consideration is paid. The wording of the Act does not state this in terms although it may be argued that 'premature sale or otherwise' must imply some element of under-value.   **[8.110]**

11   Typical situations

First, a landowner may sell his land for a capital sum at a time when there is obviously development potential. That sale will not usually be a trading transaction (assuming that there are no other trading factors present) and s 776 will also be inapplicable assuming that it is on arm's length terms to an unconnected person (see **[8.110]**).

Secondly, the landowner may obtain planning permission and then sell the land. This is not usually trading (see *Taylor v Good*, [**8.102**]) and s 776 will not apply if the sale is at arm's length etc (see [**8.110**]).

Thirdly, the landowner may develop his own land. On an eventual disposal of the land or an interest therein he will be subject to an income tax charge either as a trader or under s 776. In both cases his gain will be computed from the time when the intention to develop was formed. If a landowner buys extra land with a view to developing the enlarged site he may then become a trader (*Pilkington v Randall*, see [**8.102**]). Similarly, there is a risk of trading if agreements are entered into with an adjacent landowner (such agreements may even result in the formation of a trading partnership) although a mere agreement to find a single purchaser for two parcels of land should not have this result.

Finally, a vendor or landowner who intends to sell but who wishes to obtain a slice of any future development profits runs the risk of falling within *Page v Lowther* (see [**8.108**]). In this case the courts proposed a fairly general test for the applicability of s 776: for instance 'has a gain of a capital nature been derived from the relevant disposal?' (which will usually be the leasing of the developed site) and 'did the (original landowner) obtain any gain from the disposals effected by the under-leases?'   [**8.111**]

12   Possible ways of avoiding s 776 but still obtaining 'a slice of the action'

A vendor could insert a covenant against development into the contract of sale and subsequently agree to release this in return for a capital sum. Although this arrangement may offer advantages when there is no immediate prospect of the purchaser wishing to develop the land it is impractical if that is his immediate intention. Furthermore, such restrictions may not be commercially acceptable to the purchaser.

Alternatively, provision could be made in the original sale agreement for a further sum to be payable based on a proportion of the market value of the land after it has been developed. Arguably this does not constitute a gain of a capital nature derived from a disposal of land falling within s 776(2)(c) and the other sub-sections ((a) and (b)) are inapplicable. Further, even if this sum is calculated by reference to rents achieved, it is thought that the capital sum is still not derived from a *particular disposal*.

There are two major objections to this arrangement. *First*, the developer may find it unacceptable since it imposes an obligation on him to pay a capital sum unrelated to moneys received for letting the developed site. (Thus it will be payable even if he fails to let or sell that site.) *Secondly*, it has been suggested that the arrangement involves the landowner in trading. This view may be doubted: if it is correct it is difficult to see why *Page v Lowther* was argued under s 776 since the arrangements in that case would be trading transactions.

A further possibility is to shelter the gain by transferring the land to a trading company. This operation should be carried out before any development is undertaken and the result will then be that the land is held as trading stock so that any profit from the development will be an income receipt of that company (but taxed, at most, at 31%) and therefore a gain of a capital nature will not have been obtained. This arrangement depends upon the existence of a suitable company and there is obviously a risk of a s 776 charge if the shares in that company are subsequently sold for a capital sum (see [**8.109**]).

As an alternative sheltering device, ensure that any gain is realised by trustees. Only the basic rate of tax (23%) will be payable unless s 686 can be invoked by the Revenue (see [**8.103**]).

Finally, ensure that a capital sum is not received from a disposal of the developed land. Assume, for instance, that the purchaser/developer agrees that he would only take a rack rent (not premiums) on lettings of the developed site. For s 776 to apply in this case, a capital sum received by the taxpayer would have to fall within sub-s (2)(c). Under that provision it is necessary for land to be developed 'with the sole or main object of realising a gain from disposing of the land when developed'. It is arguable that the grant of leases at a rack rent is not a disposal (see [**8.107**]) and furthermore, that the receipt of rents will not amount to the realisation of a *gain* for the purpose of the subsection. The difficulties with this arrangement are, *first*, will the purchaser agree to accept only a rental return? And *secondly*, the original vendor remains entitled on the properties being let to a capital sum based upon a multiple of the rental value. Thus, it is arguable that *Page v Lowther* may apply since he will then have obtained a capital sum from a disposal of the developed land, albeit that that sum was paid by the original purchaser not the sub-lessee.   [**8.112**]

13 Other matters

Although there is a clearance procedure under s 776(11), opinions vary as to whether it should be used. In *Page v Lowther*, for instance, clearance was refused, the scheme went ahead and was then challenged. There are those who feel that applying for clearance merely puts the Revenue on notice. Unlike the other clearance procedures (eg under TA 1988 s 707 and TCGA 1992 s 138) the application must be made to the local tax office: ie the matter is considered at a much lower level where there is obviously a temptation simply to issue a blanket refusal giving no reasons.

Section 776 applies to non-UK residents if all or any part of the land is situated in the UK (s 776(13)). When the person entitled to the consideration is not resident in the UK the Revenue can require the payer to deduct income tax at the basic rate from the consideration and pay it over to the Revenue (s 777(9)). This can apply even if the recipient is not the taxable person but the Revenue obviously needs to know about the transaction in advance and this will not normally be the case unless the consideration is payable by instalments. It is not entirely clear whether s 776 can apply to land situated outside the UK since the declaration in s 776(13) is ambiguous on this point. Section 776 does not apply to a gain arising to an individual on the disposal of his principal private residence which is exempt from CGT (TCGA 1992 s 222 ff), or (generously) which would be exempt from CGT were it not that the property was acquired with the intention of making a gain on its disposal (TCGA 1992 s 223(3)).   [**8.113**]

14 The importance of s 776 after FA 1988

Before FA 1988, it was important for a development to be structured outside s 776 in order that income tax at a top rate of 60% was avoided. Now that CGT is charged at income tax rates and the top rate has been reduced to 40%, the importance of the section is reduced. There remain, however, good reasons for seeking to ensure, in many cases, that the profit remains subject to CGT but there will now be circumstances when it is to the taxpayer's advantage to fall within s 776: eg when he has substantial unused personal allowances or unused loss relief. In some circumstances a lower income tax rate may be applicable. Take, for instance, the case of a settlement in which part of the property is held on discretionary or accumulation trusts falling within s 686. Capital gains made by such a settlement are taxed at 34% whereas if a s 776 gain is realised by the trustees the rate is (probably—see [**8.103**]) 23%.   [**8.114**]

9 Schedule D Case VI—residual

I   Scope   [**9.1**]
II Basis of assessment   [**9.21**]
III Territorial scope   [**9.41**]

I SCOPE

Schedule D Case VI is a residual or sweeping-up case. The charging provision of Case VI is TA 1988 s 18(3), which provides for tax to be charged on 'any annual profits or gains not falling under any other case of Schedule D and not charged by virtue of Schedule A or E'. Apart from this general charge, certain categories of income are specifically charged under Schedule D Case VI.   [**9.1**]

1 The general charge (TA 1988 s 18(3))

Although potentially wide, catching any profits not otherwise charged to income tax, the ambit of Schedule D Case VI has been limited by the courts in a series of cases which are not always consistent. In common with Schedule D Cases I and II, the word 'annual' in s 18(3) means of an income nature rather than recurring each year. Capital receipts are not, therefore, caught. In *Scott v Ricketts* (1967) £39,000 was paid voluntarily to an estate agent (in addition to his fee) to persuade him to withdraw from participating in a property development scheme. It was held that the payment was a capital receipt and so not taxable under Schedule D Case VI.

The expression 'annual profits and gains' is construed *ejusdem generis* with other profits and gains under Schedule D. Accordingly, gifts, gambling winnings and findings do not constitute profits under Case VI. An isolated purchase and sale of property as in *Jones v Leeming* (1930) where rubber estates were acquired for resale at a profit is either 'an adventure in the nature of a trade', in which case the profit is a trading receipt taxable under Schedule D Case I, or a capital transaction. But in neither case is Schedule D Case VI relevant.

The major example of profits falling within Case VI is those realised from the performance of casual services, which are neither derived from an office or employment, nor from a profession or vocation under Schedule D Case II because the element of regularity is missing (see [**6.41**]). However, the profit must be substantially derived from the performance of services rather than from the sale of property although this distinction is sometimes difficult to draw. In *Hobbs v Hussey* (1942) a solicitor's clerk (who was not an author by vocation) contracted with a newspaper to write his memoirs and then to assign the copyright; the payment that he received was taxable under Schedule D Case VI since it was substantially in return for the performance of services. The fact that there was a subsidiary sale of property (the copyright) was irrelevant and did not make the payment a receipt of capital (see also *Housden v Marshall* (1958) and *Alloway v Phillips* (1980)). By contrast, in *Earl Haig's Trustees v IRC*

(1939), trustees who owned the copyright in the Earl's diaries allowed an author to use the diaries to write a biography in return for a half share of the profits from the book. This payment was not taxable under Schedule D Case VI since it was not a payment for services, but a capital receipt from the part-disposal of an asset (the diaries).

A payment that is partly in return for services and partly for the sale of property, will, it appears, be wholly taxable under Schedule D Case VI unless it can be apportioned. In *Hale v Shea* (1964), a payment to a retiring partner for future services (income) and for his share of the partnership assets (capital) was all taxed under Schedule D Case VI.

The payment must be made under an enforceable contract for ascertainable services, otherwise it is a gift and escapes income tax. Thus, in *Dickinson v Abel* (1969) a farm was owned by a trust and the taxpayer was a relation of a beneficiary. Because of this family connection, prospective purchasers offered him £10,000 if they managed to buy the farm for £100,000 or less. The taxpayer never agreed to provide services, but merely 'made the introduction' and eventually received £10,000. This payment was held to be a gift and escaped tax under Schedule D Case VI (see also *Scott v Ricketts* (above)). Notice, however, that once there is a contract for services, any receipt under it will be taxable even though it is not received for the particular services contracted for (see *Brocklesby v Merricks* (1934)). For other examples of payments for isolated services which are outside the normal business of the taxpayer and caught by Schedule D Case VI see *Ryall v Hoare* (1923) (payment of commission by a company to one of its directors for guaranteeing the company's overdraft) and *Lyons v Cowcher* (1916) (commission received from an isolated act of underwriting an issue of shares).

Casual profits received from activities which are analogous to a trade but which lack a fundamental characteristic may be caught by Schedule D Case VI. In *Cooper v Stubbs* (1925) profits received by a cotton broker from dealings in 'futures' were taxable under Schedule D Case VI as the profits of speculation rather than of trade. Today dealings in commodity and financial futures, traded options and financial options which are not part of a trade taxed under Schedule D Case I, will be charged to CGT rather than to income tax under Schedule D Case VI (TA 1988 s 128). There are also cases where the profits from stud fees have been taxed under Schedule D Case VI rather than Schedule D Case I (see for instance *Leader v Counsell* (1942)). It is difficult to see why these cases were not assessed under Case I, which catches single speculations as well as regular trading operations.   **[9.2]**

2   Specific charges

The categories of income specifically charged under Case VI include:

(1) Payments received for 'know-how' if not taxed as a trade receipt or as a capital gain (TA 1988 s 531(4); see Chapter 6).

(2) Certain receipts after a change of accounting basis and post-cessation receipts (TA 1988 ss 103–104; see **[6.67]**).

(3) Income from certain settlements which is taxed as that of the settlor (for example, under TA 1988 s 660A; see Chapter 11).

(4) Transactions in securities (TA 1988 ss 703–709; see **[36.62]**).

(5) Transfer of assets abroad (TA 1988 ss 739–740; see **[13.111]**).

(6) Certain transactions in land (TA 1988 s 776; see **[8.101]**).

(7) Gains on the disposal by UK investors of a material interest in an offshore fund (TA 1988 ss 757–764; see below).

(8) Non-trading exchange gains/losses (see Appendix V).

(9) By ESC A94 the profits (and losses) of theatre backers (angels).   **[9.3]**

3 Investment in offshore 'roll-up' funds (TA 1988 ss 757-764)

These sections seek to prevent UK residents from avoiding a charge to income or corporation tax by an investment in offshore 'roll-up' funds. Typically, the investment is in a non-UK resident company or unit trust which does not distribute income, so that the eventual return to the investor would only be charged to CGT (TA 1988 s 739 (see [**13.114**]) will not apply given that the income does not arise because of the taxpayer's investment in the fund). The legislation only applies to entities that are 'collective investment schemes' within the Financial Services Act 1986.

TA 1988 s 761 ensures that, subject to three conditions being satisfied, there will be a charge to income tax under Schedule D Case VI or to corporation tax on any gain accruing to a UK resident (including a trustee). The conditions are, *first*, that he must dispose of a material interest (ie one realisable within seven years after investment; see s 759); *secondly*, in an 'offshore fund' (see s 759); and, *thirdly*, on or after 1 January 1984, *except* where the fund has obtained Revenue clearance for each accounting period as a 'distributor' of its income (ie it distributes at least 85% of its income before permitted allowances: see TA 1988 Sch 27). Funds with very low gross income (no more than 1% of the average value of the fund's assets for the year in question) no longer need to incur the administrative cost of distribution in order to satisfy the 'distribution test'.

Death is treated as a disposal; there is no indexation allowance; and hold-over relief has never been available. Finally, s 759 ensures that normal trading ventures or consortia are not caught by any of the above provisions. The Revenue's views on the interpretation of this legislation are set out in SP 2/86.

The tax charge under Case VI is on the amount of the income arising at the time of the disposal: resident individuals, trusts and companies are all chargeable and *all* trusts are subject to the 34% rate of tax (TA 1988 s 764). [**9.4**]-[**9.20**]

II BASIS OF ASSESSMENT

Tax is calculated under Schedule D Case VI on all profits or gains actually received (not receivable) in the current year of assessment: ie on a strict tax year basis (TA 1988 s 69). There are no express rules for deductible expenses, but the words 'profits or gains' imply a surplus of income after deducting expenses. A loss that is made on one Schedule D Case VI transaction can only be used against profits from other Case VI transactions in the same tax year and any surplus carried forward against profits from Case VI transactions in future years (TA 1988 s 392). There is no set-off against income from other sources (cp the loss rules under Schedule D Cases I and II).

Whether Schedule D Case VI income is treated as earned or unearned income depends on its source. Casual profits from services, for instance, are earned income, whereas rent from furnished lettings (other than furnished holiday lettings) is, generally, unearned. [**9.21**]-[**9.40**]

III TERRITORIAL SCOPE

The usual principles apply (see TA 1988 s 18 and Chapter 13). Thus, in *Alloway v Phillips* (1980) a Canadian resident contracted with an English newspaper to provide information about her husband Charles Wilson, the Great Train Robber. She was taxed under Schedule D Case VI on the £39,000 that she received, since the source of her income was her rights under the contract (a *chose in action*) which was enforceable and situated in the UK. [**9.41**]

10 Schedule D Case III—annual payments

I INTRODUCTORY

1 General

Schedule D Case III charges income tax in respect of:

> '(a) any interest of money, whether yearly or otherwise, or any annuity or other annual payment, whether such payment is payable within or out of the United Kingdom, either as a charge on any property of the person paying the same by virtue of any deed or will or otherwise, or as a reservation out of it, or as a personal debt or obligation by virtue of any contract, or whether the same is received and payable half-yearly or at any shorter or more distant periods, but not including any payment chargeable under Schedule A, and
> (b) all discounts, and
> (c) income from securities which is payable out of the public revenue of the United Kingdom or Northern Ireland.' (TA 1988 s 18(3) amended by FA 1996.)

Income under Schedule D Case III is often termed 'pure income' because it is not normally reduced by any deductible expenses; it is pure profit. Annuities and annual payments are sometimes referred to as settlements of income since they can operate to reduce the income of the payer and increase that of the payee. Hence, the payer may be seen as settling an income sum on the payee.

Income tax is charged under Case III on the person receiving or entitled to receive the income in question (in the case of payment by cheque the sum is received when it is credited to the account of the recipient; see *Parkside Leasing Ltd v Smith* (1985)). If the payment is not made at all there is no liability to tax (*Woodhouse v IRC* (1936)), but, if it is paid late, the rate of tax deducted and the time limits for a repayment claim are determined in the case of a payment falling under TA 1988 s 348 by reference to the year when the payment fell due (*IRC v Crawley* (1987), **[10.66]**).

In *MacPherson v Bond* (1985) a bank held a charge on the taxpayer's deposit account as security for a loan to a company. The taxpayer had not personally guaranteed this loan and accordingly interest earned on the deposit account and which was credited to it could not be said to reduce his personal liability. In the event, the company debt finally absorbed the whole of the deposit account plus interest but as Vinelott J explained:

'Even before the liability of the company to the bank had been finally determined ... the taxpayer's only prospect was that he would in time become entitled to repayment of so much of the deposit as was not required to meet the company's liability to the bank and to interest on that part of the deposit. The crediting of interest on the whole of the deposit could therefore be aptly described as a mere book entry: a matter of convenience of accounting for the bank.'

On the facts of this case, because the taxpayer was not entitled to the interest, he was not subject to any tax charge thereon. By contrast, if the security is backed up by a personal guarantee, interest credited to the account is not then a mere book entry but can be seen as reducing the sum payable by the taxpayer under the guarantee. It will therefore be subject to income tax in the hands of the taxpayer as it arises even though he does not actually receive it! (*Dunmore v McGowan* (1978); *Peracha v Miley* (1990) and on the general position of receipts and payments under guarantees see *Taxation*, 1992, p 157.)   **[10.1]**

2   Basis of assessment

FA 1994 inserted a new TA 1988 s 64, effective from 6 April 1994 for new sources of income and from 6 April 1997 for existing sources (with transitional rules for 1996–97). It provides that income assessable under Case III is charged to tax on the actual income of the fiscal year rather than (as had been the case) on the income of the preceding year (in effect, therefore, it puts the taxation of interest etc. on to a strictly fiscal year basis).   **[10.2]–[10.20]**

II   TERMINOLOGY

1   Interest

'Interest' is not statutorily defined, but was described as 'payment by time for the use of money' (per Rowlatt J in *Bennett v Ogston* (1930)). More precisely interest:

'may be regarded either as representing the profit the lender might have made if he had had the use of the money, or conversely, the loss he suffered because he had not that use. The general idea is that he is entitled to compensation for the deprivation' (*per* Lord Wright in *Riches v Westminster Bank Ltd* (1947) 28 TC at 189).

Interest generally presupposes the idea of a debt to be repaid. The *Riches* case established that interest awarded by the court under the Law Reform (Miscellaneous Provisions) Act 1934 fell within the Schedule D Case III charge (today the award is under either the Supreme Court Act 1981 s 35A or the County Courts Act 1984 s 69).

EXAMPLE 10.1

Bigco Ltd executes a debenture deed in favour of Mr Big who has made a secured loan to the company of £10,000. The deed provides for repayment of the loan together with a 'premium' of £2,000 by the end of 1997 and interest at 10% pa on the full redemption figure (£12,000) until 1997. The interest falls within Schedule D Case III and the repayment of £10,000 is a capital sum. The so-called 'premium' may be seen as deferred interest or, alternatively, as a capital sum paid as compensation for the capital risk taken by Mr Big.

The true nature of the payment is a matter of fact and the terms used by the parties are not conclusive (see *Lomax v Peter Dixon & Son Ltd* (1943) and *Davies v Premier Investment Co Ltd* (1945)). So long as the rate of interest charged is commercial, it is likely that the sum on which the interest is calculated will be treated as capital and will escape both income tax and CGT unless the debt is a 'debt on a security' within the meaning of TCGA 1992 s 132 (see TCGA 1992 s 251 and [**16.44**]).

Finally, it should be noted that if the principal debtor defaults so that the moneys are paid under a contract of indemnity the sum will still be taxed as interest; if paid by a guarantor, the position is unclear (see *Re Hawkins, Hawkins v Hawkins* (1972) on indemnities and contrast *Holder v IRC* (1932) on guarantors). [**10.21**]

2 Discounted securities

The legislation in FA 1996 (as amended by FA 1997) concerning loan relationships provides in Sch 13 for income tax under Schedule D Case III to be charged on profits realised from 'relevant discounted securities'. In simple terms a relevant discounted security is one where the amount payable on redemption would (or might) constitute a 'deep gain' (ie the issue price is less than the amounts payable on redemption by the 'relevant percentage'). A profit may be realised in the year of transfer (defined as any sale, gift, exchange 'or otherwise' and it is specifically provided that on death the individual is treated as transferring the security for market value immediately before death) or redemption and the taxed profit is the proceeds of transfer or redemption less the amount paid on acquisition together with relevant costs. In the event that a loss is sustained (calculated in the same way as a profit) the taxpayer may claim to set that loss against his income for the year. [**10.22**]

3 Annuities

Annuities fall into two broad categories. First, a purchased annuity usually arising from a contract with an insurance company under which a capital sum is paid in return for a right to income (an annuity) for a stated period of time. Secondly, annuities payable under an instrument; for instance, an annuity that is bequeathed in a will. The changes made by FA 1988 in the treatment of annual payments (see [**10.44**]) do not affect annuities. [**10.23**]

4 Other annual payments

'Other annual payments' comprise a residual category, although the term is wide enough to include an annuity. Hence, all annuities may be described as annual payments but not all annual payments as annuities. For reasons that will be discussed at [**10.44**]-[**10.60**], TA 1988 s 347A takes most annual payments out of the tax system. There are, however, some exceptions to this, and it is thus still relevant to discuss the main features of annual payments. These were laid down by Jenkins LJ in *IRC v Whitworth Park Coal Co Ltd* (1958):

'(1) To come within the rule as an "other annual payment" the payment in question must be *ejusdem generis* with the specific instances given in the shape of interest of money and annuities...

(2) The payment in question must fall to be made under some binding legal obligation as distinct from being a mere voluntary payment...

(3) The fact that the obligation to pay is imposed by an order of the court and does not arise by virtue of a contract does not exclude the payment...

(4) The payment in question must possess the essential quality of recurrence implied by the description "annual"...

(5) The payment in question must be in the nature of a "pure income" profit in the hands of the recipient.'

[**10.24**]

The following matters should be borne in mind when applying the above propositions:

A legal obligation (propositions (2) and (3))   The legal obligation must arise from a contract, a court order, or a deed of covenant. Gifts, therefore, are not annual payments. However, it does not matter that the payments are not of the same amount each year nor that the payments are contingent (*Moss Empires Ltd v IRC* (1937); contrast *British Commonwealth International Newsfilm Agency Ltd v Mahany* (1963)).

EXAMPLE 10.2

(1) Willie has two rich uncles, Feisal and Kemal, and they each wish to give him £1,000 every Christmas. Feisal is a very precise man and executes a deed of covenant to pay Willie £1,000 every year on 25 December. Kemal merely hands over a cheque each year.

   The £1,000 paid under covenant by Feisal is an annual payment which, if entered into before 15 March 1988 is within Schedule D Case III, whereas the gift from Kemal is not (and is not Willie's income despite its recurrent quality).

(2) Aunt Lucy covenants to make Paddington's income up to £3,000 pa for the rest of his life. In some years she has to pay him money, in other years not. The sums are still annual payments although the amount paid each year varies.

Income sums paid to a beneficiary by the trustees of a discretionary trust fund are annual payments falling within Case III.   **[10.25]**

The payment must be 'annual' (proposition (4))   A payment is 'annual' if it is recurrent or is capable of recurrence. Payments made at intervals of less than a year will still be 'annual' provided that they may continue beyond a year.

Only payments which are income in the hands of the recipient are included (see for instance *Martin v Lowry* (1927) for the meaning of 'annual profits' under Schedule D Case I). Payments may, therefore, be annual income payments; or they may represent instalments of a capital sum; or they may represent part income and part capital (in the latter case the income element will usually be interest on a debt which is being repaid in instalments). The interest element of any payment will be subject to charge under Schedule D Case III.

In considering whether payments constitute capital and/or income, the form of the document drawn up by the parties is not conclusive and a payment may represent a capital expenditure of the payer, but an income receipt for the payee and (presumably) *vice versa*.   **[10.26]**

EXAMPLE 10.3

Denis wants to sell his dental practice (which is worth £30,000) to Flossie and retire. The contract could be drawn up in a variety of different forms, eg:

(1) Flossie is to pay the purchase price of £30,000 over five years, at £6,000 pa. Each payment is a capital sum (see generally *IRC v Ramsay* (1935)).

(2) Flossie is to pay by instalments as in (1) above, but is to pay five instalments of £6,250 (so that the total sum to be paid will be £31,250). Each payment probably represents a capital and an income element and must accordingly be dissected. £6,000 is an instalment of capital and £250 interest on the unpaid balance (see *Secretary of State in Council of India v Scoble* (1903)).

(3) Denis agrees to be paid by Flossie either 15% of the profits of the business each year for the rest of his life or £1,000 pa whichever is the higher. Denis is in effect purchasing a life annuity so that the payments each year will be

income in his hands (see *IRC v Church Comrs for England* (1977): s 656—see [**10.101**]—does not apply by reason of s 657(1)); Flossie's payments are instalments of capital (see *IRC v Land Securities Investment Trust Ltd* (1969)).

The payment must be pure income profit in the hands of the recipient (proposition (5)) If the income is to be pure profit to the recipient, he must not have incurred allowable income expenditure in return for the payment. This proposition prevents any attempt to disguise trading receipts as annual payments (see Scrutton LJ in *Howe v IRC* (1919)).

The rule is relatively easy to apply in the case of payments to traders. Far more difficult is the position when the payments are to a charity (consider for instance *IRC v National Book League* (1957) and *Campbell v IRC* (1970)). It would appear that a payment will still fall within Schedule D Case III in cases where the recipient promises something in return so long as that promise does not relate to the provision of goods or services, ie does not involve expense (see, eg, Lord Upjohn in the *Campbell* case: 'pure profit' had no relation to 'pure bounty').

EXAMPLE 10.4

Jason pays £4,000 under a deed of covenant that is to last for ten years and was entered into on 1 January 1988 with his old public school in return for the school agreeing to take Jason's son who is a dunce. It is further agreed that Jason will pay the full fees for his son's education (see the discussion in *Campbell v IRC* (1968) 45 TC at 427). The payment represents pure income profit to the school since the counter-stipulation costs it nothing. The position would be different if fees were not paid by Jason, when the annual payment would be treated as a payment in return for the son's education.

Because a mere counter-stipulation is not enough to deprive payments of the quality of pure income profit, priority booking given by theatre or opera companies and private viewing days by art galleries to friends will not prevent covenanted payments from satisfying the pure income profit test. By contrast, the provision of reduced priced tickets for performances may well have this effect (see *Taw and Torridge Festival Society v IRC* (1959) which decided that benefits worth almost 25% of a membership subscription could not be ignored as insubstantial). As a result of this decision Revenue practice has been to ignore benefits worth *less than* 25% but to treat payments as not satisfying the 'pure income profit test' where the benefits are worth 25% *or more*. These rules were relaxed to a limited extent by FA 1989 s 59 which provided that in the case of deeds of covenant made in favour of heritage and conservation charities, the benefit of free entry to view the charities' property will not disqualify the payment from being pure income profit. This change was limited to specific charities and the only benefit which is ignored is the right of free entry to the charities' property.   [**10.27**]-[**10.40**]

III   THE TAXATION OF ANNUITIES AND 'OTHER ANNUAL PAYMENTS'

One of the characteristic features of Schedule D Case III, although not applicable to all payments chargeable thereunder, has always been that basic rate income tax is not directly assessed on the recipient but, rather, is deducted and collected at source from the payer by virtue of TA 1988 ss 348 and 349 (and s 3). Both s 348 and s 349 are designed to achieve the same objective: under both, the

Revenue collects basic rate income tax from the payer on the annual payment and the payer is permitted to deduct that sum from the amount paid to the payee. Generally, therefore, the payee will receive a net sum together with a credit for the basic rate income tax which has been deducted at source and paid to the Revenue on his behalf (note that TA 1988 s 3 specifically provides that deduction from annuities and annual payments is made at the basic rate: this is unaffected by the existence of the lower rate: contrast, however, payments of interest from which only the 20% rate is deducted). If he is not liable to pay income tax (because his income is below the taxable threshold) he will be entitled to repayment by the Revenue of the basic rate tax already paid on his behalf. The payee will be assessed directly to higher rate tax, if that is appropriate in the circumstances. It follows that he is not entitled to claim that he has been underpaid because of the deduction at source by the payer (TA 1988 ss 348(1)(d) and 349(1)). The scheme of deduction at source used also to apply to payments of yearly interest as well as to annuities and other annual payments. Nowadays, most payments of interest are outside the scheme (see further [10.83]). [10.41]

1   Annual payments in tax planning

It is useful at this stage to emphasise the necessity for distinguishing between the person on whom the burden of taxation falls on the one hand and, on the other, the person from whom it is collected. In the case of annuities and annual payments, historically the payer was looked upon as having alienated that part of his income representing the annuity or annual payment. This meant that such payments were, in effect, deductible in computing the total income of the payer, the burden of both basic and higher rate tax thereby falling on the payee. Further, whilst higher rate tax was assessed directly upon the payee, basic rate tax was collected from the payer.

It can now be understood why annual payments have been used over the years for the purposes of avoiding or minimising tax. A taxpayer, subject to the higher rates of tax, would assign a part of his income, eg by deed of covenant, to a taxpayer who paid no income tax at all, such as a charity, or to one who paid at the lower rates of tax. This can be illustrated by reference to *IRC v Duke of Westminster* (1936), in which case gardeners were paid by the Duke, their employer, by means of a deed of covenant in lieu of wages, with the advantageous tax result that the Duke escaped paying higher rate taxes on the covenanted sums. [10.42]

EXAMPLE 10.5

Taking the tax year 1987–88 for illustration purposes, assume that Homer was then subject to income tax at the highest rate: 60%. He paid his son Hiram an allowance of £400 pa. Hiram had no other income. At Homer's marginal rates the total cost in gross terms of that allowance was £1,000 (since £1,000 – [60% × £1,000] = £400).

As an alternative, Homer could have covenanted to pay Hiram £1,000 pa. As an annual payment the result would have been:
(1) Homer's income is reduced by £1,000 (ie he does not pay 60% tax on that sum).
(2) Homer pays basic rate tax at source under (now) TA 1988 s 348.
(3) Hiram receives a net sum and reclaims (because of his unused allowances) the tax paid at source by Homer.

The total cost to Homer is the same (£1,000), but Hiram receives an extra £600 and the Revenue loses £600 of tax.

2 Anti-avoidance and TA 1988 Part XV

The ability to avoid tax in this way was lessened over the years by the enactment of provisions (found in TA 1988 Part XV) designed to prevent:
(1) short-term covenants not capable of lasting for more than six—or in the case of charities, three—years (see [10.47]);
(2) revocable settlements (including covenants);
(3) assignment of income to the infant unmarried child of the settlor (see [11.62]);
(4) covenants to trustees who do not distribute income.

The statutory provisions covering these situations were simplified by FA 1995 and amended provisions inserted as ss 660A, 660B of TA 1988 (see [11.61]).

The result of these provisions is that if a taxpayer, for example, entered into a deed of covenant which could last for only, say, five years, or covenanted in favour of his infant daughter, the annual payment made under the covenant in each of the examples would remain that of the payer for both basic and higher rate tax purposes. There would therefore be no ensuing tax advantages, nor the need for applying TA 1988 ss 348 and 349 (deduction at source).

Other annual payments not caught by these provisions were nevertheless limited in their effect by a provision that the taxpayer should be subject to excess liability (ie the difference between the higher rate and the basic rate of income tax) on the payment. So, if in 1987 a taxpayer executed a seven-year covenant in favour of, say, his niece, while the recipient, the niece, would bear the burden of basic rate tax (collected at source from the payer), the taxpayer would be liable for any excess liability on the covenanted sum.

Certain annual payments were specifically left unscathed by the anti-avoidance legislation, the payer bearing no liability for either basic or higher rate tax, with the basic rate being collected from him on behalf of the recipient under TA 1988 ss 348 and 349. Such payments are set out in TA 1988 s 660A and, in particular, include covenanted payments to charity, maintenance payments made under a settlement or court order by one party to a marriage for the benefit of the other (but see below [10.44] and [10.45], and annual payments made for *bona fide* commercial reasons in connection with a trade, profession or vocation.   [10.43]

3 Taking annual payments outside the tax net: TA 1988 s 347A

Despite the legislature's best endeavours, annual payments continued to be used for tax avoidance purposes, notably covenants by grandparents in favour of their grandchildren for the payment of school fees and by parents in favour of their adult children to support them during their time at college or university.

Thus it was that by virtue of FA 1988 s 36 (now TA 1988 s 347A), most annual payments by individuals were taken outside the tax net altogether. Because of these changes, s 348 and s 349 have lost much of their impact, as have the anti-avoidance provisions in TA 1988 Part XV. There are exceptional cases, however, where the annual payment remains effective (see [10.45]–[10.60]) and in respect of which tax will continue to be collected at source under TA 1988 ss 348 and 349, with the anti-avoidance rules remaining of importance. It should also be borne in mind that the TA 1988 Part XV provisions are concerned with capital as well as income settlements. This breadth of coverage is inevitable since, if it is desired to stop a particular income settlement from attracting fiscal benefit, it is necessary to cover a settlement of income-producing assets (ie capital) which might otherwise achieve the same result. The provisions in the context of capital settlements are considered in Chapter 11.

FA 1988 s 36 (now TA 1988 s 347A) provides that:

'(1) A payment to which this section applies [ie any annual payment made by an individual with only limited exceptions] shall not be a charge on the income of the person liable to make it, and accordingly—

(a)   his income shall be computed without any deduction being made on account of the payment, and

(b)   the payment shall not form part of the income of the person to whom it is made or of any other person.'

The result is that the majority of annual payments now fall wholly outside the tax system. The section is, however, subject to the following exceptions.   [**10.44**]

a) *Existing obligations*

In the context of annual payments, an existing obligation means a binding obligation arising under a deed executed, or a written agreement made, before 15 March 1988 and received by an inspector of taxes before the end of June 1988. Whilst existing maintenance obligations continue to be taxed under Case III (see TA 1988 s 660A(8) and [**41.7**]), the 'simplified' rules enacted in s 660A have severe implications for payments under non-charitable covenants made prior to 15 March 1988. By the omission of any specific reference to them, under the new rules such payments are treated as the income of the settlor for all *tax* purposes. The result is that the settlor will no longer be entitled to the basic rate tax relief, and recipients who are either non-taxpayers or lower rate taxpayers will be unable to claim repayment of any tax deducted. It may be presumed that the thinking behind this was that most seven-year covenants made under existing obligations would have run their course by April 1995. However, it cannot be assumed that there do not exist non-charitable covenants made prior to 15 March 1988 which may last for longer than seven years and, to the extent that some do, these provisions amount to retrospective legislation.   [**10.45**]

b) *The annual payment must be made by an individual*

TA 1988 s 347A is limited to annual payments made by individuals. Annuities, whether purchased or payable out of a deceased's estate, are therefore unaffected and, similarly, the beneficiary of a discretionary trust who receives income payments from the trustees will continue to be assessed under Case III.   [**10.46**]

c) *Covenanted payments to charity*

These payments are expressly excluded from the section. Accordingly, Case III will continue to apply to such payments so that, provided the relevant deed of covenant is drafted to avoid TA 1988 s 660A (so that it must be capable of lasting for more than three years and must not be revocable by the settlor for four years—see TA 1988 s 347A(7)). A deed of covenant which, mistakenly, fails to satisfy the requirements of TA 1988 s 347A(7) will not be rectified in order to avoid TA 1988 s 660A unless there is clear evidence to establish that the document did not give effect to the intention of the covenantor at the time the deed was executed—see *Racal Group Services Ltd v Ashmore* (1995)). The sum paid will be a charge on the income of the payer; will be paid subject to deduction of basic rate income tax under s 348; and will be taxed as the income of the charity which may therefore reclaim the basic rate tax deducted at source.   [**10.47**]

d) *Bona fide commercial payments*

Annual payments made for *bona fide* commercial reasons in connection with a trade, profession or vocation continue to fall within Case III. The main example of such payments is annuities payable under partnership agreements to outgoing partners—see [**31.14**]. [**10.48**]

e) *The payment of interest*

These major changes only applied to annual payments: accordingly, the tax treatment of interest continued unchanged. [**10.49**]-[**10.60**]

IV THE MACHINERY OF TAX COLLECTION FOR ANNUITIES AND 'OTHER ANNUAL PAYMENTS' (TA 1988 ss 348–350)

1 The operation of TA 1988 s 348 for the payer

Section 348 will apply 'where any annuity or other annual payment [subject to the changes made by FA 1988: see [**10.44**]] charged with tax under Case III of Schedule D, not being interest, is payable wholly out of profits or gains brought into charge to income tax . . .'. It is, therefore, confined to the payer who has income ('profits and gains') on which he is subject to income tax. It cannot apply to companies as they do not pay income tax. When the payer satisfies these requirements, it is presumed (in the absence of contrary evidence) that the payment is made out of his income.

> **EXAMPLE 10.6**
>
> Wilbur, with an income of £10,000 pa from investments, covenants to pay his favourite charity, The Otter Protection Society (TOPS) £1,000 pa for the next ten years.
>
> *Step 1:* Wilbur is permitted under s 348(1)(c) to deduct from the £1,000 a sum equal to the basic rate tax thereon. Hence, at present rates, Wilbur can deduct £230 (23% × £1,000). He will, therefore, give TOPS £770 together with a certificate showing that tax has been deducted (TA 1988 s 352; the appropriate form is IR 185).
>
> *Step 2:* Wilbur's income is reduced from £10,000 to £9,000 because the covenanted sum operates as a charge on his income (he is settling £1,000 pa on TOPS). It, therefore, follows that his 'total income' is £9,000 (TA 1988 s 835) and that he can set his personal allowances only against that sum (TA 1988 s 276). Wilbur's own tax will, therefore, be calculated on the taxable income that is left.
>
> *Step 3:* In addition, Wilbur is also charged on the covenanted sum at the basic rate of income tax (see TA 1988 s 3).
>
> The result is that the total cost of the covenant to Wilbur is £1,000 since he handed £770 to TOPS at *Step 1* and £230 to the Revenue at *Step 3*.

As Viscount Simon explained in *Allchin v Coulthard* (1943), by deducting the tax from the covenant at source (*Step 1*) 'the payer recoups himself for the tax which he has paid or will pay on the annual payment'. It is, therefore, in the interests of the payer to make the deduction of tax and does not directly concern the Revenue since it will collect the basic rate tax under TA 1988 s 3 at *Step 3* in any event. Hence, s 348(1)(c) *permits* the payer to make the deduction, but does not compel deduction. The whole process in *Example 10.6* may be represented diagrammatically thus:

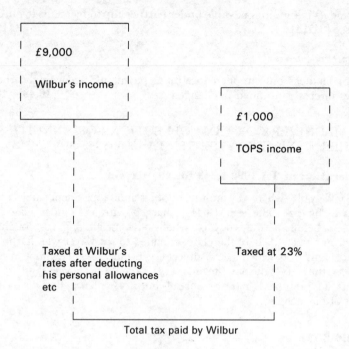

If Wilbur's taxable income had been such that he was liable to higher rate income tax, because the covenant that he executed was in favour of a charity, he would not be subject to any excess liability (see TA 1988 s 660A(9)).   **[10.61]**

2   The operation of TA 1988 s 349 for the payer

TA 1988 s 349 provides as follows:

> 'Where:
> (a) any annuity or other annual payment charged with tax under Case III of Schedule D, not being interest, ... is not payable, or not wholly payable, out of profits or gains brought into charge to income tax, the person by or through whom any payment thereof is made shall, on making the payment, deduct out of it a sum representing the amount of income tax thereon...'

Section 349 will apply when the payer has no income or insufficient income to cover the amount of the annual payment and when he is not subject to income tax. Annual payments made by companies are, therefore, payable subject to the deduction of income tax under s 349. Unlike under TA 1988 s 348, deduction from the covenanted sum is compulsory.

As soon as a relevant annual payment is made there is an obligation on the payer to notify the Revenue who will then assess him to basic rate income tax on the annual payment. The annual payment net of basic rate income tax is made to the recipient who receives a certificate of tax deducted on Form IR 185.

Under s 349 tax may be collected from agents of the payer (on the dangers of being held liable as an agent see *Rye and Eyre v IRC* (1935)). This difference in collection machinery from that under s 348 is necessary because the payer will not normally be subject to income tax when a s 349 payment is made. It will not, therefore, be possible to collect the basic rate tax on the annual payment at the same time as the rest of his income tax.   **[10.62]**

EXAMPLE 10.7

Wilbur (see *Example 10.6*) falls on hard times and receives no income. He remains bound by his covenant to pay TOPS £1,000 pa. When he makes the next annual payment:

Step 1: Wilbur should deduct the basic rate tax (£230) on that annual sum and pay TOPS £770 only.

Step 2: In accordance with s 350(1) Wilbur should notify the Revenue that the payment has been made. He will, therefore, be liable to pay income tax of £230.

The total cost of the covenant is, therefore, £1,000, made up of £770 paid to TOPS and £230 to the Revenue.

3 The position of the recipient

The position of the recipient of an annual payment falling under Case III is broadly the same whether that payment is made under TA 1988 s 348 or s 349. He will have income under Schedule D Case III equivalent to the gross value of the payment (not just of the sum that he actually receives) and will be given a tax credit equal to the basic rate income tax deducted at source by the payer. Accordingly, he may be entitled to reclaim that tax (eg if the recipient is a charity and is exempt from paying income tax or, in the case of a recipient who has unused personal allowances); or, the tax may exactly discharge his tax liability; or, he may be liable to extra income tax at the higher rate. This third possibility (more tax owed by the recipient) is comparatively rare and is only likely to arise in respect of maintenance payments under existing obligations (see [**41.7**]) or annual payments made for bona fide commercial reasons in connection with a trade, profession or vocation (see [**10.48**]).   [**10.63**]

EXAMPLE 10.8

Watson received £770 from Holmes in respect of an annuity of £1,000 payable under a partnership agreement on his retirement. He is also given an IR 185 certificate of tax deducted.

Watson's income under Schedule D Case III is £1,000 and he has a credit for income tax paid of £230. Therefore, his tax position will be as follows:
(1) If he is subject to tax at the basic rate (ie if he has no unused allowances or charges and has used up his lower rate band), there is no further liability to tax and no question of a refund.
(2) If he has no other income and so has available personal allowances he can reclaim the £230 tax paid on his behalf by Wilbur. If he had (say) £200 of unused allowances he would have taxable income of £800 (£1,000 – £200) on which tax at 20% would be £160. As the tax credit of £230 exceeds his tax liability by £70, he can obtain a refund of £70 of the tax deducted at source.
(3) If he has other income so that he is paying income tax at the top rate (currently 40%), he will be liable to excess liability on the annuity, ie the difference between the higher and basic rates of tax. On present rates, such excess liability would be 17% × £1,000.

4 Principal problems arising in connection with the deduction of tax at source

a) *The effect of failure to deduct tax at source*

The payer of an annual payment falling within Case III is allowed to deduct tax from the payment under s 348 and bound to do so under s 349. Failure to do so will not lead to any penalty. It will not generally concern the Revenue when the payment is made under s 348 since it will assess the payer to tax on the whole of his income without distinguishing the annual payment and if it fails to recover tax from the payer in a case where s 348 applies, the payee may be assessed.

Where there is a failure to pay the tax under s 349, however, the Revenue will seek to recover the sum either from the payer or by direct assessment from the payee. When an assessment is made upon the recipient the burden is on him to show that he was only paid a net sum. If he discharges that burden he cannot be assessed to tax (see eg *Hume v Asquith* (1969)).

Failure to deduct tax will of course affect the parties *inter se*. In general, if the payee has been overpaid, that over-payment cannot be reclaimed or corrected from later payments; it is a payment made under a mistake of law and the excess is treated as a perfected gift which cannot be undone (*Re Hatch* (1919)). There are a few exceptions to this general principle: if the mistake is one of fact recovery is possible (*Turvey v Dentons (1923) Ltd* (1953)); if the basic rate of tax increases after the payment, the excess can be recovered (TA 1988 s 821), but it appears that under-deductions cannot be recouped from later payments made in that tax year (*Johnson v Johnson* (1946) explaining *Taylor v Taylor* (1938) and see *Tenbry Investments Ltd v Peugeot Talbot Motor Co Ltd* (1992)). There is of course nothing to stop a recipient who has been overpaid from reimbursing the payer!   **[10.64]**

EXAMPLE 10.9

Wilton has income of £5,000 for the tax year 1997–98. He makes an annual maintenance payment of £1,000 to his former wife, Jean, under an arrangement entered into in 1987 from which he fails to deduct basic rate income tax.
(1) The Revenue may assess Wilton under the s 348 machinery.
(2) If Wilton fails to pay, the Revenue may assess Jean. Note that in the event of Wilton paying the tax, Jean's income is £1,000 with a credit for £230 tax paid. The extra £230 that she has received is ignored; it is a tax-free gift.

b) *The use of formulae*

TMA 1970 s 106(2) provides that 'every agreement for payment of interest . . . or other annual payment in full without allowing any such deduction shall be void'. The parties may not, therefore, agree not to operate ss 348 and 349. If s 106(2) is infringed, the instrument is void only as to the provision seeking to oust the deduction machinery. The section is also limited in that it only applies to 'agreements', so that payments under court orders and wills are outside its terms (see Chapter 12).

Despite s 106, the parties will often wish to ensure that a fixed sum is paid each year to the recipient regardless of fluctuations in the basic rate of income tax. Say, for instance, that Felix is making annual payments to the charity, Hope, and wants to ensure that it receives £770 each year. Whilst the basic rate is 23%, a covenant to pay £1,000 pa would achieve this result. Were the basic rate to rise to 35%, however, Hope would only receive £650. Indeed, with the reduction in the basic rate of tax to 23% for 1997–98, a payment of £760 which, for the previous tax year, represented £1,000 less tax at 24% will, from 6 April 1997, represent £987.01 less tax at 23%. As it is not possible to agree to pay £770 and not to deduct tax, the only way of achieving what Felix wants is to use a formula in the covenant. The standard formula would be that 'Felix agrees to pay Hope such sum as will after deduction of income tax at the basic rate for the time being in force leave £770'. This takes effect as an undertaking to pay the gross sum which after deducting the appropriate income tax leaves Hope with £770. What the charity receives is, therefore, constant; what will vary with the rate of tax is the sum paid to the Revenue and, therefore, the total cost of the covenant to Felix.

An alternative formula would be to promise Hope £770 'free of tax', which takes effect as an undertaking to pay such sum as after deduction of income tax leaves £770 (*Ferguson v IRC* (1969); a similar rule applies to court orders that are so worded). One danger if such a formula is employed is that it is arguable that a promise to pay £770 free of tax means that the recipient should in any event end up with neither more nor less than £770. It follows that if the recipient is liable to higher rate income tax on the annual payment the payer must reimburse him for that tax, whilst conversely, any repayment of tax should be returned to the payer (the rule in *Re Pettit* (1922); see Chapter 12 and [**41.8**]).   [**10.65**]

c) *Which section applies: TA 1988 s 348 or s 349?*

Difficulties will arise, for instance, if an annual payment falls due in a year when the payer has no income, and is finally paid in a year when he does have taxable income and vice versa (see generally *Luipaard's Vlei Estate and Gold Mining Co Ltd v IRC* (1930) and ESC A16). Which section applies is of considerable significance; it will, for instance, determine the ownership of the sum deducted from the annual payment since, under s 348, it belongs to the payer whereas under s 349 it should be handed to the Revenue. In general, if the payer has taxable income for the appropriate year, it is presumed that the payment is made out of that income. This provision is normally advantageous to the taxpayer as the following example illustrates.

EXAMPLE 10.10

Hank has taxable income of £10,000 for 1997–98 and pays £1,000 pa for four years under a deed of covenant in favour of a charity which he entered into in 1995.

(1) *If s 348 operates* Hank will be assessed to income tax on £4,100 at 20% (£820) and £4,900 at 23% (£1,127) and in addition to 23% on £1,000 (£230). (£9,000 is Hank's income and £1,000 is that of the charity.) The total sum payable to the Revenue will be £2,177.

(2) *If s 349 operates* Hank will be assessed on £4,100 at 20% and £5,900 at 23% (£2,177) together with £1,000 at 23% (£230). The total sum payable to the Revenue will be £2,407.

The presumption that s 348 applies if income is available is displaced when the payer has secured some fiscal or other advantage from charging the payment to capital (as in *Birmingham Corpn v IRC* (1930)), or where he has made a deliberate decision to charge the sum to capital (see, for instance, *Chancery Lane Safe Deposit and Offices Co Ltd v IRC* (1966)). In such cases, despite the availability of income profits, s 349 will be applied.

In making an annual payment under TA 1988 s 348 the payer should deduct tax at the basic rate in force when the payment fell due and not at the rate when it was actually paid. Accordingly, in calculating the income of the payee, the covenanted sum will be treated as his income of the tax year in which it fell due and not of that in which the payment was made (if the two are different). In *IRC v Crawley* (1987) payments under a charitable covenant were made in arrears and, although the charity made a claim for repayment of tax deducted under TA 1988 s 348 within six years of the payment being made, the claim was refused because it was made more than six years after the date when the payments had fallen due. Vinelott J agreed with the Revenue's argument in the case that:

'the payer on making an annual payment deducts tax at the rate in force at the date when the payment became due or at the date of payment according to whether the payment is or is not made out of profits or gains brought into charge to tax. In estimating the total income of the payee the income is deemed to be the income of the year by reference to which the tax was deducted.'

[**10.66**]

5   Payments outside the tax net—TA 1988 s 347A

The result of taking the majority of annual payments outside the tax system is illustrated in the following example: [**10.67**]-[**10.80**]

EXAMPLE 10.11

On 20 June 1997 Toby, with an income of £50,000, entered into a deed of covenant to pay £1,000 pa to his nephew, Jacques. Jacques has no income. The sum falls outside Case III with the following result:
(1) Toby is taxed on £50,000 without any deduction for the annual payment. As the payment has to be discharged out of taxed income, the gross cost to Toby (in 1997–98) is therefore £1,667.
(2) The sum of £1,000 is paid over to Jacques and is not taxed in his hands.
(3) Jacques has no income so that his personal allowances remain unused.

V   TAXATION OF INTEREST PAYMENTS

1   Tax relief for payment of interest

Tax relief for the payment of interest is only given in certain limited cases (see [**4.43**] ff). Formerly, to attract relief in such cases interest had either to be 'annual' chargeable to tax under Schedule D Case III or, alternatively, payable in the UK or Eire on an advance from a bank carrying on business in those countries. These restrictions were removed by FA 1994 s 81 (amending TA 1988 s 353) and this change was of particular assistance to non-UK residents with foreign borrowings. Depending upon the purpose for which the loan was taken out, interest is accorded different tax treatment:
(1) payment of interest in respect of, eg, a bank overdraft or credit card interest, receives no tax relief;
(2) payment of interest made, eg for the purposes of a trade, receives relief by allowing the payment as a deduction in computing the profits of that trade under Schedule D Case I;
(3) payment of interest which qualifies under TA 1988 ss 354–364 receives relief in the form of a 'deduction or set-off' of the interest payable from or against the borrower's taxable income of the year in which the payment is made. This deduction or set-off operates in a similar fashion to a charge on income, so that relief for the interest paid will be given, where appropriate, against lower, basic or higher rates of tax (TA 1988 s 353 (1B));
(4) payment of interest which qualifies for relief under TA 1988 ss 354, 355(1)(a), 356, 358, 365 and which is not covered by the MIRAS scheme receives relief by means of a deduction from any tax liability of the payer arising in the year in which the payment is made. The amount of the deduction is a percentage of the qualifying interest payment, 15% for 1997–98. The interest payment is not treated as a charge on income and is included in calculating the payer's taxable income (TA 1988 s 353(1A));
(5) payment of interest within the MIRAS scheme, under which relief is given by deducting from the payment an amount equal to 15% of the payment for 1997–98. The payment is not treated as a charge on income and is

included in calculating the payer's taxable income (TA 1988 ss 369, 369(1A)). **[10.81]**

2 Source of the interest

The availability of tax relief for payments of interest (and the existence of an obligation to deduct tax at source from the payments) may depend on whether the interest falls within Case III which requires there to be a UK source. Factors to be considered in deciding whether this is the case were discussed in *Westminster Bank Executor & Trustee Co (Channel Islands) Ltd v National Bank of Greece SA* (1968) and subsequently enumerated by the Inland Revenue in the *Tax Bulletin*, November 1993, at p 100 as follows:

'The factors considered relevant in that case (leading to the conclusion that the income involved did not have a UK source) were

● there was an obligation undertaken by a principal debtor which was a foreign corporation

● the obligation was guaranteed by another foreign corporation with no place of business in the UK

● the obligation was secured on lands and public revenues outside the UK

● funds for payments by the principal debtor of principal or interest to residents outside Greece would have been provided either by a remittance from Greece or funds remitted by debtors from abroad (even though a cheque might be drawn in London).

Although the Greek Bank case was concerned with income which turned out not to have a UK source, inferences can be drawn from that case about the factors which would support the existence of a UK source and we regard the most important as

● the residence of the debtor, ie the place in which the debt will be enforced

● the source from which interest is paid

● where the interest is paid, and

● the nature and location of the security for the debt.

If all of these are located in the UK then it is likely that the interest will have a UK source.' **[10.82]**

3 Deduction of tax at source

TA 1988 ss 348 and 349 do not generally apply to interest payments. It is only in the relatively few cases falling within TA 1988 s 349(2) that lower rate tax must be deducted at source and, in accordance with TA 1988 s 349(2), the payer is put under a duty to notify the Revenue that the payment has been made. This subsection covers the payment of yearly interest chargeable to tax under Schedule D Case III and which is paid either:

(1) by a company or local authority otherwise than in a fiduciary or representative capacity, eg debenture interest; or

(2) by or on behalf of a partnership of which a company is a member; or

(3) by any person to another person whose usual place of abode is outside the UK.

Generally, interest must be 'yearly' if these provisions are to operate. The distinction between 'yearly' and 'short' interest depends upon the degree of permanence of the loan. The crucial question is whether it is stated, or expected, that the loan will last, or is capable of lasting for 12 months or longer (see *Tax Journal*, 30 March 1995, p 14).

Even if the payment falls within one of the three categories of interest payments listed in s 349(2), it must still be paid gross if it is:

(1) paid in a representative or fiduciary capacity;

(2) payable on an advance from a bank if the person beneficially entitled to the interest is within the charge to corporation tax on that interest (TA 1988 s 349(3)(A));

(3) interest paid on quoted Eurobonds in certain circumstances (TA 1988 s 124; SP 8/84);

(4) interest paid from on direction from FICO consistent with terms of a double tax treaty;

(5) payable under a group election under TA 1988 s 247 (see [**30.81**]).

[**10.83**]-[**10.100**]

VI   MISCELLANEOUS MATTERS

1   Purchased life annuities (TA 1988 s 656)

Purchased life annuities were formerly taxed as income with no allowance being given for their capital cost. TA 1988 s 656 now permits the amount of any annuity payment which falls within its scope to be dissected into an income and a capital amount. The capital amount in each payment is found by dividing the cost of the annuity by the life expectancy of the annuitant at that time, calculated according to government mortality tables. The balance is treated as income taxable under the rules of Schedule D Case III.

Generally, s 656 does not apply if the annuity is already given tax relief (as is the case with purchased annuities for a fixed term of years which have always been dissected in a similar fashion); or, if the annuity was not purchased by the annuitant but by a third party (eg if it was purchased as the result of a direction in a will); or, if the premiums qualified for tax relief under TA 1988 s 266, s 273 or s 619 when they were paid or if the annuity is payable under approved personal pension arrangements.

For 1996–97 and subsequent tax years, the rate at which tax will be deducted at source on the payment of a purchased life annuity is the lower rate of 20%. In respect of other annuities (apart from those to which PAYE applies), the rate is 23%.   [**10.101**]

2   Patents and copyrights

Patent royalties are payable subject to the deduction of basic rate tax (23% for 1997-98) under the provisions of TA 1988 ss 348 and 349. Such payments may be annual payments, but will usually fall within Schedule D Cases I and II as receipts of a trade or profession. There are 'spreading provisions' in certain cases where lump sums are received (TA 1988 ss 524; 527, see [**6.144**]).

Copyright royalties do not fall within ss 348 and 349 and are payable without deduction of tax. The recipient will be taxed under either Schedule D Case II (if a professional author) or otherwise under Schedule D Case VI. Again, spreading provisions are available for certain of these lump sum payments (TA 1988 ss 534 and 535; see [**6.143**]).   [**10.102**]

11 Trusts and settlements

Possible reforms of the income tax and CGT treatment of UK resident trusts were canvassed in an Inland Revenue Consultative Document in March 1991. The general aim of the review was to find a way of bringing the taxation of trusts into line with the taxation of individuals. Due, in the main, to the concern expressed that tax might fall more heavily on certain beneficiaries than on others, the Financial Secretary to the Treasury announced in March 1993 that the central proposals were not to be implemented, although some of the more detailed proposals were still being considered. The simplification of TA 1988 Part XV provisions (see [**11.61**]) in FA 1995 may be seen as part of that continuing review.   [**11.1**]

I   GENERAL PRINCIPLES

1   Trustees' liability at basic rate

Trustees are subject to basic rate income tax under the appropriate Schedule on all the income produced by the fund regardless of their own personal tax position and that of the beneficiary. For this reason, they are not allowed to deduct their personal allowances (the trust income is, after all, not their property) nor those of any beneficiary. A beneficiary, entitled to the income under the terms of the trust, may claim a credit for the tax paid by the trustees—see [**11.41**].

The theory behind this system of taxing trustees is that, although they are not beneficially entitled to the income, they receive it in their fiduciary capacity and are thus entitled to it on the basis that they can sue for it. Furthermore, as a policy matter, it is essential to levy income tax on the trustees since otherwise, were income to be accumulated as it arises (and thereby turned into capital), rather than distributed, it would escape income tax altogether.

Expenses incurred in administering the fund may not be deducted in computing the tax liability of the trustees and are, therefore, paid out of taxed income.   [**11.2**]

EXAMPLE 11.1

(1) The trustees of the Jenkinson family trust run a bakery. The profits of that business will be calculated in accordance with the normal rules of Schedule D Case I and be subject to basic rate income tax in the trustees' hands.

(2)   A and B, trustees of the Joel family settlement, farm trust land in partnership with Sir Joel (head of the family) who owns adjacent land. Normal rules of partnership taxation apply (see Chapter 31) and as the trustees have entered the partnership agreement *qua* trustees any change in their composition will not lead to a cessation for the purposes of the Schedule D deemed discontinuance rules. In the event of losses arising the relevant proportion may be set against other trust income.

2   Direct assessment and deduction at source

Where trustees, for example, carry on a trade, assessment to tax is made upon them directly; where, however, they receive investment income arising, for example, under Schedule D Case III or Schedule F, tax will have been deducted at source. In the case of dividends paid after 5 April 1993 and other savings income after 5 April 1996, the value of the credit is at the lower rate of 20% (which will, however, discharge the trustees' basic rate liability). Other savings income includes distributions from authorised unit trusts, interest from gilts and other securities including corporate bonds and interest from banks and building societies (see [**4.23**]).

From 6 April 1999 the tax credit on dividends will be reduced to 10%. This will continue to satisfy the basic rate liability of the trustees, but that credit will be irrecoverable by any beneficiary and to ensure that discretionary and accumulation trusts are not prejudiced a reduced rate of charge will apply to dividend income (see further [**11.24**]).

The normal self-assessment rules apply to trustees, but note that every person who was a trustee when the income arose or who subsequently becomes one is responsible for making trust returns etc (TMA 1970 s 7(9)). However anything done by one trustee satisfies the liability of all and penalties can only be recovered once (from a person who was a trustee when the penalty was triggered). Trustees are generally required to complete the new Trust and Estate Tax Return (which has superseded Forms 1, 31 and 32): there is, however, no requirement on bare trustees to complete a self-assessment tax return or to make any payment on account (see (1997) SWTI, p 88).   [**11.3**]

3   Exceptions: when trustees are not accountable

It was noted earlier that trustees are liable to income tax because they are entitled to receive the income; it follows, therefore, that where the trust income accrues directly to a beneficiary, the trustees will not be assessed on that income. Of some doubt is a possible second exception to the general liability of trustees to income tax, namely that where trustees receive income, they may nevertheless escape assessment on the ground that the beneficiary for whose benefit the income accrues is not liable to income tax. Even if such exception should exist, its scope is limited and would appear to apply only where there is no liability to tax because, for example, of non-residence or charitable status and not where the income is untaxed merely because of the personal allowances of the beneficiary.   [**11.4**]

4   Buy-back of shares from trustees

FA 1997 Sch 7 para 3 provides that the relevant part of the sum received on a buy-back of shares is taxed as if it were income falling within s 686 (which is discussed below). As this provision applies to *all* trusts the effect is to impose a special charge on trustees of (for instance) interest in possession trusts.

[**11.5**]–[**11.20**]

II TRUSTS WHERE THE TRUSTEES ARE LIABLE TO 'THE RATE APPLICABLE TO TRUSTS' (TA 1988 ss 686–687)

1 The charge imposed by TA 1988 s 686

The 'rate applicable to trusts' Trustees are not liable to income tax at the higher rate (nor at the lower rate) because they are not individuals. Prior to 6 April 1993, there was, however, a special surcharge of 10% which applied to income arising in certain trusts after deducting administrative expenses. As a result of the changes made to the taxation of dividends by FA 1993, trustees of such trusts are now liable to income tax at a single flat rate, 34% for 1997–98 (thus remaining the same as for 1996–97 in spite of the cut in the basic rate of tax to 23%), irrespective of the source of that income (TA 1988 s 686(IA)). The trustees receive dividends and other types of savings income (see [**11.3**]) net of tax at the lower rate of 20% together with a tax credit matching that lower rate of tax. They will thus have a further 14% to pay on the grossed-up value of the dividends. (Note that for 1997–98, a 34% CGT rate also applies to these trusts: see [**14.85**].) [**11.21**]

Which trusts are caught? TA 1988 s 686(2) provides as follows:

'This section applies to income arising to trustees in any year of assessment so far as it—
(a) is income which is to be accumulated or which is payable at the discretion of the trustees or any other person (whether or not the trustees have power to accumulate it); and
(b) is not, before being distributed either—
  (i) the income of any person other than the trustees, or
  (ii) treated for any of the purposes of the Income Tax Acts as the income of a settlor; and
(c) is not income arising under a trust established for charitable purposes only . . .; and
(d) exceeds the income applied in defraying the expenses of the trustees in that year which are properly chargeable to income (or would be so chargeable but for any express provisions of the trust).'

Trusts which contain a power for trustees to accumulate income, and trusts which give the trustees a discretion over the distribution of the income are caught. The result is to increase the cost of accumulating income in such trusts.

EXAMPLE 11.2

(1) Magnus is a wealthy individual who pays income tax at the highest rate (currently 40%). He creates a settlement of income-producing assets on discretionary trusts for his children giving the trustees power to accumulate the income for 21 years. Under the general principles discussed above, the income which was accumulated would suffer tax at only 20% (if it was dividend or savings income) or 23% (instead of 40% in Magnus' hands) and would subsequently be paid out as capital and so be free from any further income tax. As a result of s 686, however, the trustees have to pay an extra 14% or 11% rate of tax respectively (making a 34% rate in all) so that the attractions of the settlement to Magnus are reduced (although not wholly removed).
(2) Trustees of a discretionary trust have income of £10,000 and incur administrative expenses of £1,000. Their income tax assessment will be:

	£
Trust rate on £9,000 (34% × £9,000)	3,060
Basic rate on £1,000 (23% × £1,000)	230
Total tax liability	£3,290

For the position when dividends are included in the trust income see [**29.87**].

Section 686(2)(a) was considered in *IRC v Berrill* (1982) where the settlor's son was entitled to the income from the fund unless the trustees exercised a power to accumulate it. Vinelott J held that s 686 applied since the income was 'income . . . which is payable at the discretion of the trustees'. 'Discretion' is wide enough to cover a discretion or power to withhold income. The phrase 'income which is to be accumulated' in para (a) presumably refers to income which the trustees are under a positive duty to accumulate. A mere power to accumulate is not sufficient, although it will usually mean that the income 'is payable at the discretion of the trustees' within para (a).

In *Carver v Duncan* (1985) trustees paid premiums on policies of life assurance out of the income of the fund as they were permitted to do under the trust deed. The House of Lords held that the payments did not fall to be deducted under s 686(2)(d) which was limited to expenses which were properly chargeable to income under the general law. As the life assurance premiums were for the benefit of capital they should, as a matter of principle, be borne by capital and accordingly, the express authority in the instrument did not bring the sums within the section.   [**11.22**]

Exclusions   The surcharge will not apply to income which is treated as that of any person other than the trustees. This will be the case, as explained in *Tax Bulletin*, December 1996, where the beneficiary has 'a complete right' to receive the capital without having to satisfy any conditions, ie where the beneficiary has 'an indefeasibly vested interest in capital'. Any income arising to the trust in such circumstances is to be treated as the beneficiary's income so long as he is alive or unless and until the trustees exercise an overriding power of appointment in respect of that income in favour of another. This will also be the case where a beneficiary has a vested interest in the income (eg a life tenant). These cases must be contrasted with the *Pilkington* settlement (see Chapter 24), in which the income of a life tenant could be taken from him after it had arisen by the exercise of a power to accumulate it. Accordingly, it would be subject to the surcharge as the income still 'belongs' to the trustees.

The surcharge does not apply to trusts where the anti-avoidance provisions of TA 1988 Part XV operate to deem the income to be that of the settlor (see [**11.61**]). Prior to 6 April 1995, this exception applied to *all of the income* so deemed. Section 686(2)(b) (inserted by FA 1995) now provides that it applies only to income so treated *before it is distributed*. Under the rules in TA 1988 s 660B (see [**11.62**]), income will only be treated as that of the settlor for income tax purposes if it is actually paid to or for the benefit of the settlor's unmarried minor child. In the event of a distribution out of a discretionary or accumulation trust in favour of such a child, TA 1988 s 687, as amended by FA 1995, provides that it will be treated as a payment net of the additional and basic rate tax.   [**11.23**]

Miscellany   A number of other points should be noted: *first*, s 686 does not apply to the income of an estate of a deceased person during administration (though it may, of course, apply to a subsequent will trust).

Secondly, from 6 April 1996, TA 1988 ss 481, 482 provide for the deduction at source of the lower rate of income tax (20% for 1997–98) from bank interest on deposits belonging to accumulation and discretionary trusts. If the trustees make a declaration that they are not resident in the UK and have no reasonable grounds for believing that any beneficiary of the trust is either an individual who is ordinarily resident in the UK, or a company which is resident in the UK, bank interest may continue to be paid gross (see [**4.28**]). Concern has been expressed over the width of the definition of 'beneficiary' for these purposes. The Revenue's view, as stated by the Financial Secretary to the Treasury, is that the term 'beneficiary' will extend only to those identified as beneficiaries under the terms of the relevant trust deed *at the time of the declaration.* It will not include somebody who might become a beneficiary at a later date under a power to add to the class of beneficiaries and who might be a UK resident.

Thirdly, prior to 6 April 1993, non-resident discretionary trustees were not liable for basic rate income tax on dividends paid by a UK company (TA 1988 s 233(1)(a)) and the additional rate of 10% which was chargeable was charged on the actual amount of the dividends received. After 5 April 1993, the trustees are liable at the single flat rate of 34% on the value of the dividends *notionally grossed up* at the lower rate of 20%. They are treated as having paid tax at the lower rate and will thus be liable for a further 14% (TA 1988 s 233(1A)). Since there is no credit for the lower rate tax, it follows that there can be no repayment of any such income tax (see [**13.78**] and for 'excluded income' see [**13.71**]).

Fourthly, the additional rate is imposed on 'income' and because this term is not defined it is limited to income in a trust sense: hence the various provisions in the tax legislation deeming capital sums to be income do not apply. For instance, a premium paid on the grant of a lease for less than 50 years (as to which see [**8.81**]). Likewise, if a company bought back its own shares from discretionary trustees in circumstances where the payment was taxed as a distribution, the sum received by the trustees was capital and not subject to the surcharge. This 'loophole' has, however, been stopped and the additional rate now applies in such cases, as a result of FA 1997 Sch 7 para 3 (see [**11.5**]).

Finally, dividends paid to trustees from 6 April 1999 carry an irrecoverable credit of 10% (instead of the current 20%). To ensure that discretionary trustees do not suffer extra tax as a consequence the additional rate will be reduced to 25% so that the position is largely neutral:

Dividends pre-6 April 1999		£	*Position from 6 April 1999*		£
Dividend		80			80
Tax credit (20%)		20	(10%)		8.89
Income		100			88.89
s 686 tax (34%)		34	(25%)		22.22
After tax income		£66			£66.67

[**11.24**]

2 The charge imposed by TA 1988 s 687

The purpose of s 687 is to impose a charge to income tax on income payments made at the trustees' discretion. Section 687(2) provides that:

> 'The payment shall be treated as a net amount corresponding to a gross amount from which tax has been deducted at the rate applicable to trusts for the year in which the payment is made; and the sum treated as so deducted shall be treated, so far as not set off under the following provisions of this section, as income tax assessable on the trustees.'

The set-off referred to allows the trustees to deduct from the tax payable the tax that has been charged at the rate applicable to trusts under s 686 on income when it arose.

EXAMPLE 11.3

In 1997–98 the trust produces £2,000 income. The income tax assessment (at 34%) will be for £680. In 1998–99 the trustees in the exercise of their discretion pay a net sum (£1,300) to a beneficiary. In that year the rate applicable to trusts is (say) 50%. The net payment must be grossed up in accordance with s 687(2) as follows:

$$£1,300 \times \frac{100}{100 - 50*} = £2,600$$

*The grossing-up formula deducts the rate of tax in force in 1998–99 from 100.

Hence, the tax liability is £1,300 which can be reduced by setting off the £680 paid in 1997–98. £620, therefore, remains payable.

While it is the trustees who are assessed to tax under s 686 and, where applicable, s 687, where a discretionary payment is made to a beneficiary the income tax paid by the trustees under those provisions is treated as having been paid by the beneficiary.

It is thought that s 687 does not apply to income payments made by non-UK resident trustees to UK beneficiaries. Although the section is not on its face limited to UK trustees, it is expressed to apply instead of the sections imposing a charge to tax at source under Schedule D Case III, and income from overseas trusts falls not under this Case of Schedule D but under Case V. Further, the phrasing of ESC B18 proceeds upon the assumption that s 687 does not apply to confer a tax benefit on a UK beneficiary who receives such income (see [13.15]).   [11.25]–[11.40]

III   THE TAXATION OF BENEFICIARIES

1   Taxing a beneficiary who is entitled to trust income

General rule   A beneficiary who is entitled to the income of a trust as it arises (or is entitled to have it applied for his benefit) is subject to income tax for the year of assessment in which that income arises, even if none of the money is paid to him during that year (*Baker v Archer-Shee* (1927)). The sum to which the beneficiary is entitled is that which is left in the trustees' hands after they have paid administration expenses and discharged their income tax liability. The beneficiary is, as a result, entitled to a net sum which must be grossed up at the basic rate of income tax in order to find the sum which enters his total income computation and to a credit for some of the income tax paid by the trustees; not, it should be noted, for the full amount in cases where management expenses have been deducted (*Macfarlane v IRC* (1929)). When a beneficiary is entitled to dividends or receives other savings income the value of the credit passed on to him by the trustees is at the lower rate of 20% (see [11.3] and *Taxation*, 24 February 1994, p 444).

Depending upon his other income and allowances, a beneficiary may be entitled to reclaim all or some of the tax paid by the trustees. Alternatively, he may be liable for tax at the higher rate. The income that he receives from the trust will be unearned even if it arises from a trade run by the trustees (see *Fry v Shiels' Trustees* (1915) and TA 1988 s 833(4) but note also *Baker v Archer-Shee* (1927) which indicates that if a beneficiary is entitled to the income as it arises, he will be taxed according to the rules of the Schedule appropriate to that source of income).   [11.41]

EXAMPLE 11.4

Zac is entitled to the income (which does not include any dividends or other savings income (see [**11.3**])) of a trust fund. In 1997–98 £6,000 is produced and the trustees incur administrative expenses (properly chargeable against income) of £1,000. The trustees are taxed at 23% on the income of £6,000. The balance of the income available for Zac will be:

	£	£
Gross income		6,000
Less: tax	1,380	
expenses	1,000	2,380
		£3,620

Zac, is, therefore, taxed on £3,620 grossed up by tax at 23% ie:

$$\frac{£3,620 \times 100}{77} = £4,701.30$$

He will be given a credit for that portion of the basic rate tax paid by the trustees which is attributable to £4,701.30 ie £1,081.30, but does not receive a credit for the rest of the tax paid by the trustees (£1,380 – £1,081.30 = £298.70) and the result is that management expenses have been paid out of taxed income so that the total cost of these expenses is £1,298.70. (An alternative way of dealing with management expenses is considered at [**11.50**]. For the position when trustees receive dividends, see [**29.87**].)

What is income? 'Income' for these purposes will not (in the absence of express provision to the contrary — as has been introduced for company buy-backs) include items which are capital profits under trust law although income tax may have been charged on them in the hands of the trustees: eg premiums treated as rent under TA 1988 s 34 and capital sums received on a disposal of land under TA 1988 s 776.　　　　　　　　　　　　　　　　　　　　　　　**[11.42]**

Demergers and enhanced scrip dividends　In recent years corporate demergers and the provision of enhanced scrip dividends (as an alternative to a cash dividend) have become commonplace. In both cases the trustees must decide whether what is received is *income* and so belongs to the life tenant or is available for distribution/accumulation under their powers or is capital. The law in this area is far from satisfactory and the problems are explored at [**29.121**] ff.

　　　　　　　　　　　　　　　　　　　　　　　　　　　　　　　[11.43]

2　Taxing an annuitant

An annuitant under a trust is not entitled to income of the trust as it arises; he is taxed under Schedule D Case III on the income that he receives. Not being a purchased life annuity, as basic rate income tax will be deducted from the annuity by the trustees under TA 1988 s 348, an assessment for basic rate tax on the beneficiary will be precluded. He has a tax credit for the basic rate tax deducted at source in the usual way.　　　　　　　　　　**[11.44]**

3　Taxing a discretionary beneficiary

A discretionary beneficiary has no right to a specific amount of income but is merely entitled to be considered. Any payments that he receives will be charged as his income under Schedule D Case III (they are annual payments since they may recur) and he will receive a credit for the tax paid by the trustees and attributable to that payment. As the trust is discretionary, that tax will be at a rate of 34% (TA 1988 s 686). The effect of s 686 is to encourage trustees to distribute income to beneficiaries who are subject to income tax at less than 34% so that all or a part of the surcharge can be repaid.

Once an irrevocable decision has been taken by the trustees to retain income as a part of the capital of the fund, the sum accumulated loses its character as income and is treated in the same way as the original fund, ie as capital. It follows, therefore, that the income tax suffered by that income (at 34%) is irrecoverable and that no further income tax will be charged on the accumulations when they are eventually paid out to the beneficiaries as capital (although such distributions may have CGT and IHT consequences). In deciding whether it is more advantageous to accumulate income or to pay it out to beneficiaries under their discretionary powers, trustees need to consider, *inter alia*, the tax position of the individual beneficiaries.   **[11.45]**

EXAMPLE 11.5

Trustees receive trust income (not including company dividends or other savings income) of £10,000. There are three discretionary beneficiaries (all unmarried), Ding, Dang and Dong. Ding has no other income and has an unused personal allowance; Dang is a basic rate taxpayer; and Dong is subject to tax at a marginal rate of 40%. The trustees are deciding whether to pay income to any one or more of the beneficiaries or whether to accumulate it. The following tax consequences will ensue:

(1) The trustees are subject to 34% tax on the trust income (ie £3,400 tax).
(2) If the trustees decide to pay all the income to Ding (who has no other income) he will be entitled to a partial repayment of tax as follows:

	£
Income (Schedule D Case III)	10,000
Less: personal allowance	4,045
Total income	£ 5,955

Income tax	
£4,100 at 20%	820.00
£1,855 at 23%	426.65
Less: tax credit	3,400.00
Tax refund	£(2,153.35)

(3) If the trustees pay the income to Dang (the basic rate taxpayer), he will not be entitled to a refund of any basic rate tax, but, depending upon the amount of his other income, he may obtain a refund of such part of the rate applicable to trusts as exceeds the basic rate of tax.
(4) If the trustees pay the income to Dong (the higher rate taxpayer), extra tax will be levied as follows:

	£
Income	£10,000

Tax at 40%	4,000
Less: tax credit	3,400
Tax owing	£ 600

(5) If the trustees accumulate the income, the £3,400 tax paid will be irrecoverable and the net income of £6,600 will be converted into capital.
     Ideally, the trustees will avoid payments to Dong, will consider appointing all or part of the income to Ding and Dang and accumulate any balance.

4 **The dangers of supplementing income out of capital**

The problem Capital payments will not generally be subject to income tax. If a beneficiary is given a fixed amount of income each year and is entitled to have that sum made up out of capital should the trust fail to produce the requisite amount of income, however, such 'topping up' payments will be taxed as income in the hands of the beneficiary (see *Brodie's Will Trustees v IRC* (1933) and *Cunard's Trustees v IRC* (1946)). **[11.46]**

EXAMPLE 11.6

(1) The settlor's widow is given an annuity of £4,000 pa; the trustees have a discretion to pay it out of the capital of the fund if the income is insufficient. The widow will be assessed to income tax on the payments that she receives whether paid out of income or capital since they will be annual payments (TA 1988 s 349 will apply to the extent that there is insufficient income in the trust and they are paid out of capital).

(2) The settlor's widow is given an annuity of £4,000 pa and, in addition, the trustees have the power 'to apply capital for the benefit of the widow in such manner as they shall in their absolute discretion think fit'. Any supplements out of capital will now escape income tax since the widow has an interest in both income and capital, and payments out of capital will, therefore, be treated as advances of capital rather than as income payments.

Stevenson v Wishart In the past the Revenue sought to argue that payments made out of trust capital could be taxed as income in the hands of the recipient beneficiary even when the payments were not paid in augmentation of an income interest. This argument was based on its view that the income nature of the payment in the hands of the recipient could be discovered by looking at the size, recurrence, and purpose of the payments. *Stevenson v Wishart* (1987) provided a test case for this view since the discretionary trust income was there paid out in full each year to a charity and capital sums were then paid to one of the beneficiaries who had suffered a heart attack. The purpose of the payments was to cover medical expenses and the cost of living in a nursing home. The Revenue's view that these sums were paid out for an income purpose and were therefore subject to income tax was rejected both at first instance and by the Court of Appeal. Fox LJ stated that:

> 'There is nothing in the present case which indicates that the payments were of an income nature except their recurrence. I do not think that is sufficient. The trustees were disposing of capital in exercise of a power over capital. They did not create a recurring interest in property. If, in exercise of a power over capital, they chose to make at their discretion regular payments of capital to deal with the specific problems of the beneficiary's last years rather than release a single sum to her of a large amount, that does not seem to me to create an income interest. Their power was to appoint capital. What they appointed remained capital.'

The Court of Appeal did stress the exceptional nature of nursing home payments. Fox LJ, for instance, stated that such expenditure, although involving day-to-day maintenance, was emergency expenditure of very substantial amounts which would usually fall outside normal income resources. It may be, therefore, that if the expenditure was not of an emergency nature the court would consider the payments to be income. A typical example is the payment of school fees out of a trust fund where the Revenue has argued for a number of years that lump sum payments can be taxed as the income of the recipient beneficiary in the year when that payment is made (see LS Gaz, 1982 p 692 and LS Gaz, 1984, p 3382). **[11.47]**

Current position   It is understood that the Revenue currently treat advances or appointments out of trust capital as capital in the hands of the recipient beneficiary unless the payments in question fall within one of the following three categories. *First*, when they are designed to augment income as in the *Brodie* case; *secondly*, if the trust instrument contains a provision authorising the use of capital to maintain a beneficiary in the same degree of comfort as had been the case in the past (the *Cunard* case); and, *finally*, if the capital payment in question really amounts to an annuity (see *Jackson's Trustees v IRC* (1942)).   [11.48]

5   The effects of Trustee Act 1925 s 31

The effects of s 31 (which may be excluded by the trust instrument) can be dealt with in two propositions: *first*, if an infant has a vested interest in the capital of a fund and the income is accumulated with the capital, the income belongs to the infant. Hence, the charge under s 686 is inapplicable since the income is that of a person other than the trustees ([11.23]); were the infant to die, both capital and income accumulations would belong to his estate. *Secondly*, if an infant has a vested interest in income only, eg to Albert for life where Albert is seven, the trustees will accumulate that income with the capital of the fund. Were the infant to die the accumulations would not pass to his estate. In this case s 31 has a divesting effect and for income tax purposes the accumulating income is subject to the TA 1988 s 686 surcharge because it does not belong to a beneficiary as it arises. In *Stanley v IRC* (1944) it was stated that 's 31 has effected a radical change in the law. The beneficiary is, in fact, for all practical purposes in precisely the same position as if his interest in surplus income were contingent'.   [11.49]

EXAMPLE 11.7

(1) Shares are settled for Amanda absolutely. She is aged six. Income produced by the shares (dividends) will be taxed as Amanda's income and grossed up at 20% with a credit for the lower rate tax deducted at source.

   If, instead, the fund was held for Amanda contingent upon her attaining the age of 21, the surcharge would apply to the income, as it is not Amanda's, and only sums paid out to her by the trustees in the exercise of their powers of maintenance would be taxed as her income (in which case she would, of course, have a credit for the 34% tax paid by the trustees). When Amanda becomes 18 she will be entitled to the income by virtue of s 31 (despite her interest remaining contingent until 21).

(2) Shares in a settlement are held on trust for Barbara (aged six) for life with remainder to her Uncle Silas. As Barbara, the life tenant, has only a vested interest in income the trustees will be liable for tax at 34% (in fact the dividends will have already suffered lower rate deduction at source). Barbara will not be subject to tax on the income and will not, therefore, be able to reclaim any of the tax paid by the trustees, except to the extent that income is applied for her maintenance.

Note: it may be possible to obtain income tax advantages without succession disadvantages by giving an infant a vested interest in income and a contingent interest in capital. If IHT could pose a problem on the death of that infant a 'bucket trust' could be set up (see LS Gaz, 1984, p 2938).

6   The taxation of management expenses

Management expenses, as already discussed, are deductible in calculating the excess liability to tax arising from the difference between the rate applicable to trusts (currently 34%) and the lower rate of 20% (if the income is savings income) and the basic rate of 23% (if it is any other income). They are not deductible for basic rate purposes and the beneficiary is only entitled to the income that is left after deducting those expenses. Where a beneficiary has unused allowances (and, hence, will obtain a refund for any income tax paid by the trustees) the treatment of trustees' expenses results in a partial loss of that refund. A settlor should, therefore, give trustees a power to charge all expenses to capital or, in the absence of such a clause, trustees should consider paying the whole income to the beneficiary in return for an undertaking by him to reimburse the trustees for their expenditure. If the beneficiary entitled to the income is a higher rate taxpayer, however, the effect of the management expense rules is that he will be treated as entitled to less income, so that less tax will be paid and it will, therefore, be cheaper if the expenses are paid out of the trust income. **[11.50]-[11.60]**

EXAMPLE 11.8

Assume that the beneficiary has no other income and unused allowances.
(1) Expenses borne by the trustees

	£
Gross income from a trust of, say, land	1,000
Less: tax at 23%	230
	770
Less: expenses paid by trustees	100
Net income of beneficiary	670

Gross income of beneficiary $\left(£670 \times \dfrac{100}{77} \right) = £870.13$

Tax refund (23% × £870.13)	200.13
Income retained by beneficiary	£ 870.13

(2) Contrast (1) with the case where the whole income is given to the beneficiary:

	£
Net income of beneficiary	770
Tax refund	230
Income received by beneficiary	1,000
Less: management expenses	100
Income retained by beneficiary	£ 900

IV THE ANTI-AVOIDANCE PROVISIONS

1 Introductory

Prior to 15 March 1988, a wealthy individual paying income tax at a top rate of 60% who wished to transfer a part of his income, eg to a grandchild, could have done so in one of two ways. *First*, by entering into a deed of covenant (ie an income settlement); or, *secondly*, by transferring capital assets that produce the required amount of income to trustees to hold for the benefit of the chosen grandchild for a stated period. Inevitably, therefore, the legislation which sought to restrict the efficacy of covenants was also drafted so as to deal with capital settlements. Income settlements were generally rendered tax ineffective by TA 1988 s 347A so that the choice open to the wealthy taxpayer is whether or not to create a capital settlement. FA 1989 contained further provisions aimed at preventing what were essentially covenant arrangements being dressed up as capital settlements.

When the anti-avoidance rules operate, the provisions generally deem the income of a capital settlement to be that of the settlor and enable him to recover from the trustees any tax that he suffers on that income in excess of the basic rate. The term 'settlement' is widely defined for these purposes to include any 'disposition, trust, covenant, agreement, arrangement or transfer of assets'. However, although for the purposes of the general law a settlement can be established even though created for consideration, liability under Part XV depends upon there being some element of bounty (see, for instance, *IRC v Plummer* (1979)).

The *Consultative Document on Trusts* recognised the need for simplification in this area where rules had developed in a piecemeal fashion since 1992 (so that considerable overlap existed) and many had become obsolete. This simplification was brought into effect by FA 1995.

The statutory provisions can be divided into three areas:
(1) rules which apply where the unmarried minor children of the settlor receive a benefit from the settlement ([**11.62**]);
(2) rules which apply where the settlor or his spouse has retained an interest in the settlement or where the settlor transfers income not capital ([**11.63**]);
(3) rules which apply where the settlor or his spouse or minor child have received a capital payment or benefit from the settlement ([**11.69**]).

It is important to realise that 'settlement' is widely defined for the purposes of this legislation to include 'any disposition, trust, covenant, agreement, arrangement or transfer of assets' (TA 1988 s 660G(1)) and 'settlor' has a similarly wide meaning as well as including reciprocal settlors (TA 1988 s 660(G)(2)).

[**11.61**]

2   **Benefits received by unmarried infant children from parental settlements (TA 1988 s 660B)**

The provisions are based largely on the previous legislation (TA 1988 ss 663–664), with the effect that any payments of income made to or for the benefit of the settlor's own unmarried infant child will be treated as the income of the settlor. It should be stressed that the rules only apply where income (or, in certain cases, capital—see below) is *actually paid* to or for the benefit of the child. The rules will apply to settlements whenever made, but where the total income paid to the child under such a settlement does not exceed £100 in any year, it will not be treated as that of the settlor. If income is accumulated under a capital settlement in favour of unmarried infant children, the income is not treated as that of the settlor, but payments of capital out of the fund will be treated as the income of the settlor to the extent that they can be matched against any available undistributed income.

There will be taken to be available retained or accumulated income so long as the total amount of settlement income arising since the settlement was made is more than the aggregate of:
(1) the amounts treated as income of the settlor or a beneficiary;
(2) payments to other beneficiaries;
(3) payments of expenses properly charged to income (TA 1988 s 660B(2), (3)).

EXAMPLE 11.9

Darien settles shares for the benefit of his three children: Amien, Darien Jr and Arres in equal shares contingent upon them attaining the age of 21. They are all infants and unmarried. If the income of the fund is £10,000 pa the income tax position is as follows:
(1) The trustees will be liable for income tax at a rate of 34% on that income (TA 1988 s 686).
(2) If the balance of the income (after the payment of tax) is accumulated, it

will not be treated as the income of the settlor. Hence, so long as the income is retained in the trust no further income tax is payable.

(3) If any of the income is paid to a child, it is treated as income of Darien. Say, for instance, that £1,320 is paid to, or for the benefit of, Amien. The result will be that Darien's income is increased by £2,000 (£1,320 grossed up at 34%). He has a tax credit for the £680 tax paid by the trustees (TA 1988 s 687). If he is charged to further income tax on that sum, TA 1988 s 660D contains tax recovery provisions that will enable him to claim a refund from the trustees or from any other person to whom the income is payable (in this case Amien, Darien Jr and Arres, although recourse would only be had to the beneficiaries to the extent that they had received income). If Darien is subject to a marginal rate of income tax of 40% the result is:

	£
Deemed income	2,000
Darien's tax (highest rate) at 40%	800
Less: tax credit (tax paid by trustees)	680
Tax owing	£ 120

(4) TA 1988 s 687 did not allow for the settlor of a *non-resident* trust to claim credit against his income tax liability arising under TA 1988 s 660B for income tax paid by the trustees. That position was changed by ESC A93.

(5) If all the net income (£6,600) is distributed amongst the three beneficiaries it is treated as Darien's income. Once the income treated as that of the settlor (together with any payments to other beneficiaries and payment of expenses properly charged to income) exceeds the aggregate amount of income which has arisen under the settlement since it was made, any further distributions to the beneficiaries will be capital advancements and thus *not* treated as the income of the settlor.

(6) This settlement is an accumulation and maintenance trust for IHT purposes (see Chapter 26); but this does not bestow any income tax advantages.

(7) It should be noted that references to 'payments' include payments in money *or money's worth*. Thus a non-cash distribution *in specie* will be caught (TA 1988 s 660B(6)).

Three other general matters should be noted. *First*, that income covenants by the settlor/parent in favour of trustees will be ineffective annual payments in accordance with the rules discussed in Chapter 10. *Secondly*, 'child' is widely defined to include 'a stepchild, an adopted child, and an illegitimate child' (TA 1988 s 660B(6)), but does not include a foster child. *Finally*, the definition of settlement includes a transfer of assets (TA 1988 s 660I(1); and see *Thomas v Marshall* (1953)).

If the settlor is not the parent of the infant beneficiary, TA 1988 s 660B is not applicable; grandparental settlements may, therefore, be advantageous from an income tax point of view. Even if the settlor is the parent, so long as he retains no interest in the settled property (within the meaning of TA 1988 s 660A—see [**11.63**]) and the income is accumulated, there will still be an income tax saving if the parent is subject to income tax at the higher rate of 40%. In particular, notice the income tax saving where capital is settled for an infant absolutely as illustrated in the following example: [**11.62**]

EXAMPLE 11.10

Dad's marginal rate of income tax is 40%. He settles shares, which produce an income of £1,000 gross, upon trust for his infant daughter absolutely. The income is accumulated.

(1) If Dad had received the income, the income tax payable would have been £400, so that he would have been left with £600.

(2) As the income is settled upon trust for his daughter absolutely, the income

will be treated as belonging to her so long as it is accumulated. As a result, she will be able to set her allowances against the income which will result in no income tax being charged. (The rate applicable to trusts does not apply because the income belongs to a beneficiary.) The sum of £1,000 is, therefore, retained in the settlement. However, there must be no payments out of the fund until the daughter attains 18 (or marries under that age), otherwise the sums paid out will be taxed as Dad's income.

3   Settlements in which the settlor retains an interest

The charging rules, formerly found (in the main) in six sets of provisions, are now encapsulated in TA 1988 s 660A. In outline, the new s 660A provides that where during the life of a settlor any property subject to a settlement, or any 'derived property', can become payable to, or applicable for the benefit of, the settlor or spouse of the settlor in any circumstances whatsoever, the income of the settlement is treated as the settlor's income for all income tax purposes.   [**11.63**]

a) *Inter-relationship with the former rules*

Although s 660A will generally apply to a settlement where the old provisions (found in TA 1988 ss 660, 671–674A and 683–684) previously applied to such a settlement, the inter-relationship between the old rules on revocable settlements and absolute divesting, and the new code on settlements in which the settlor retains an interest, is questionable. In its definition of when a settlor is to be treated as retaining an interest, s 660A resembles the former TA 1988 s 673, but it would appear, in some respects, to be wider in scope. As with the old TA 1988 s 674A, the operation of the rules is not restricted to undistributed income; however, more settlements will be caught than under the former provisions, since the new rules apply to settlements *whenever made*. Moreover, where the old rules (in TA 1988 s 683) treated income as that of the settlor for higher rate tax purposes only, the new rules treat it as the settlor's for *all* income tax purposes, although the settlor may claim reimbursement from the trustees of any tax paid in respect of that income. The result, then, of these new provisions is that beneficiaries whose settlements were not caught under the former rules but who will now come within the new code, will no longer be able to claim repayment of tax if they are non-taxpayers or lower rate taxpayers. By the same token, taxpaying beneficiaries will no longer have to pay tax on income which as a result of the changes will be treated as that of the settlor. Settlors are under an obligation to notify their tax office of any liability under these provisions even if they do not normally receive a tax return. In certain other aspects, the circumstances in which a settlor is to be treated as having retained an interest are narrower (by the exclusion of certain remote possibilities of reversion to a settlor—see [**11.67**]). This means that some settlements to which the former rules applied will now be excluded from the rigours of the new ones.   [**11.64**]

b) *Retention of benefit*

Section 660A provides that if property or any derived property is, or will or may become, payable to or applicable for the benefit of the settlor or his spouse in any circumstances whatsoever, then the income from that property is taxed as his for all income tax purposes.   [**11.65**]

EXAMPLE 11.11

Jasper wishes to make provision for his son, Jonas, who is going up to Cambridge to read law. A covenant to pay Jonas £1,000 pa so long as he is studying law is, since FA 1988, ineffective for tax purposes. Accordingly, Jasper proposes to settle ICI shares on trust for Jonas for so long as he is reading law at Cambridge with a provision that thereafter the shares will revert to him. Because the property will revert to the settlor on the ending of Jonas' university career, Jasper will be taxed on the income. The section does not apply in cases where there has been an absolute divesting: hence were the property to pass on Jonas finishing his law studies to, eg, Jasper's daughter, the income would then fall outside the provision and be taxed as that of Jonas so long as he was studying law. Where Jasper has retained an interest but subsequently ceases to do so by whatever means, TA 1988 s 660A will then cease to treat the income of the settled property as his for income tax purposes.

c) *Benefit to spouse*

The settlor is treated as having an interest in settled property if his spouse is capable of benefiting from it unless that benefit derives from an outright gift made to the spouse (see TA 1988 s 660A(6)).

EXAMPLE 11.12

In January 1997 Popeye settled property on trust for his wife, Olive, for life, with remainder to his children. Because a benefit from the settlement is being received by the spouse of the settlor (and there is no outright gift to that person) the income will be taxed as Popeye's under s 660A.

In *Pearce v Young; Scrutton v Young* (1996) the spouses of two directors who ran a tooling company were allocated preference shares in the company by special resolution. This arrangement constituted a 'settlement'. In the subsequent three years, they received dividends amounting to more than 30% of the net profits of the company. The spouses has no voting powers and, apart from the preferential rights to dividends, their only other entitlement was to repayment of the sums subscribed for the preference shares in a liquidation of the company. Accordingly, although the allotment of the preference shares did amount to an outright gift to the spouses, it was property which was 'wholly or substantially a right to income', and Sir John Vinelott thus concluded that the dividends on the shares were caught by the anti-avoidance provisions. The key point in the decision was the absence of rights, apart from the right to income, attaching to the preference shares. He observed, '[A]s a matter of strict legal principle, the preference shares were assets distinct from the income derived from them . . .'; in other words, preference shares do give rights in the capital. However, he continued by saying that 'in reality they could never have been realised'. The decision has to be read in the context of this particular anti-avoidance legislation and, for a similar scheme to succeed, it will be necessary to ensure that greater rights attach to the shares, eg by making the preference shares convertible.

TA 1988 s 660A(3) restricts the definition of a spouse of the settlor. It does not include a widow or widower, so that a possibility of benefit for the widow or widower of the settlor will not cause the income of the settled property to be taxable as the settlor's (and see *Lord Vestey's Executors v IRC* (1949)). In a similar fashion, s 660A(3)(a) excludes a prospective spouse, and s 660A(3)(b) a separated spouse. TA 1988 s 660A(8) has carried forward an exception for settlements made by one party to a marriage to provide for the other after divorce or separation, where the income is being paid to that other. So, on the break-up of a marriage, one party to the marriage can make a settlement to provide for the other under which the income is paid to that other, but under which the settled property may revert to the settlor, without the income paid to the other party being taxed as the settlor's.   [**11.66**]

d) *When the settlor is not to be regarded as retaining an interest*

Exceptions are provided by TA 1988 s 660A(4) for the possibility of a settlor becoming entitled to settled property on a disposition, bankruptcy or death by or of beneficiaries, or on the death of his own child or children over the age of 25 where the child has, for example, a life interest. Moreover, the settlor will not be regarded as retaining an interest while there is a living beneficiary under the age of 25 during whose life the settled property cannot be paid to or applied for the benefit of the settlor except in the events mentioned above (TA 1988 s 660A(5)).   [**11.67**]

> **EXAMPLE 11.13**
>
> Tybalt settles property upon trust for such of his three children as attain the age of 25 and if more than one in equal shares absolutely and subject thereto for the benefit of the settlor.
>
> As a result of s 660A(5) Tybalt is not treated as having retained an interest in the fund. Even if the children took only life interests so that the property would revert to Tybalt on death he is not taxed on the income (TA 1988 s 660A(4)(d)).

e) *Non-domiciled settlors*

The former provision (TA 1988 s 681), whereby a non-domiciled or non-resident settlor would not be charged on the income of a settlement if he would not be taxable on the income if it were his own, is reproduced. In other words, a non-domiciled settlor cannot be taxed on foreign income accumulated overseas even if he had an interest in the settlement. *However*, it is provided that if such income is subsequently remitted to the UK in a year of assessment in which the settlor is resident in the UK, it is to be treated as income arising *in that year* and chargeable to tax as the settlor's income. This appears to impose a new charge to tax in that although the income might have arisen in a year when the settlor had *no* connection with the UK, it will be taxed if there is a remittance after the settlor has acquired such a connection (TA 1988 s 660G(4) and *Tax Journal* 30 March 1995, p 9).   [**11.68**]

4   Receipt of capital benefits (TA 1988 ss 677–678 as amended)

a) *The current law*

The purpose of this provision is to prevent the settlor obtaining any benefit from a settlement in which the income may be taxed at a lower rate than that which would have applied had the settlor retained the income. In effect, capital payments to the settlor (or his spouse) from the fund are matched with undistributed income of the fund and taxed as the settlor's income under Schedule D Case VI. The sum is grossed up at the rate applicable to trusts but the settlor is entitled to a credit for tax paid by the trustees—although not to any repayment! There are no provisions enabling the settlor to recover any tax that he may have to pay.

A 'capital sum' covers any sum paid by way of loan or a repayment of a loan and any sum paid otherwise than as income and which is not paid for full consideration in money or money's worth (TA 1988 s 677(9)). A capital sum is treated as paid to the settlor if it is paid at his direction, or as a result of his assignment, to a third party (TA 1988 s 677(10)).

The capital sum will only be caught by s 677 to the extent that it is less than, or equals, the income available in the settlement; this means the undistributed income of the fund from any relevant year: ie any year of assessment after 1937–38. Any excess will not be charged in the year of receipt but it may be charged later if income becomes available in any of the next 11 years (TA 1988 s 677(1)(b)).

EXAMPLE 11.14

The undistributed net income of a settlement is as follows:

Year 1   £10,000
Year 2   £ 2,500
Year 3   £15,000
Year 4   £ 6,000
Year 5   £ 7,000

In year 3, the trustees lend the settlor £45,000. That loan is a capital sum and, therefore, the settlor is charged to income tax in year 3 on that sum to the extent that it represents available income. As the available income is £27,500 (years 1–3) he will be taxed on £27,500 grossed up at 34%—ie on £41,666.67. He will not be subject to basic or additional rate tax on that income so that if his marginal rate is 40% he will be taxed at 6% (40% – 34%).

The remaining £17,500 is carried forward to be taxed in succeeding years when income becomes available; in year 4, for instance, £6,000 is available. If the loan is repaid, there will be no further charge on available income in subsequent years, but any tax paid during the loan period cannot be recovered (s 677(4)).

Section 677 also applies to a capital sum received by the settlor from a body corporate connected with the settlement. Generally, a company will be connected with a settlement if it is a close company and the participators include the trustees of the settlement (TA 1988 s 682A). The width of s 677 and its somewhat capricious nature (see for instance *De Vigier v IRC* (1964)) means that settlements will often contain a clause prohibiting the payment of capital sums to the settlor or his spouse.   **[11.69]**

b) *Proposed change*

The 1995 Finance Bill as originally published contained new provisions which would have replaced ss 677–678 with rules applying wherever loans were made between a settlor and his trust and vice versa (both directly and via companies). As a result of widespread criticism these proposals were dropped: the government was said to be 'reconsidering the position'.   **[11.70]**

5   **General conclusions**

(1) With the demise of the income settlement, the transfer of income-producing capital assets has assumed greater importance. So long as the settlor is prepared to sever all interest in the property settled, the anti-avoidance provisions considered above need not cause problems in the majority of cases. Particularly attractive settlements include those made by grandparents on their infant grandchildren under which use is made of the grandchild's personal allowance to ensure that income in the settlement is effectively tax free. By contrast, parental settlements in favour of the settlor's own infant unmarried children are less attractive since (unless the settlement falls within *Example 11.10*) the income must be accumulated if it is not to attract tax at the settlor's rate. Hence, the settlement income will suffer an irrecoverable 34% charge. Given a top rate of income tax of only 40%,

a saving of 6% may not justify the expenses involved in creating and running the relevant trust.

(2) The Part XV provisions involve 'looking through' a settlement and treating the income as that of the settlor: similar provisions are found in the CGT treatment of UK resident trusts and more draconian provisions in the case of non-resident trusts.

(3) Part XV is capable of applying to foreign as well as UK trusts. For instance, in a case where assets are transferred to non-resident trustees, these provisions need to be considered as, of course, does TA 1988 s 739. It is common for the Revenue to base a claim for tax on both sets of provisions stated in the alternative.   **[11.71]**

12 Estates in the course of administration

Personal Representatives ('PRs', meaning both executors and administrators) are under a duty to administer a deceased's estate. From the point of view of taxation this involves:

(1) Settling the deceased's outstanding tax liabilities to the date of death. Although this chapter is concerned primarily with income tax, notice that there may also be an outstanding CGT liability (see Chapter 15) and that the PRs cannot obtain a grant of probate until any IHT, payable on their application for a grant, has been accounted for (see Chapter 22).

(2) Liability to income tax on any income produced during the administration period. In addition, the PRs may incur a CGT liability (see Chapter 15) and the original IHT bill may require adjustment as a result of events happening after the death (see [**22.54**]).

It is also necessary to consider the liability of beneficiaries to tax on any income distributed to them from the estate.   [**12.1**]

I   THE DECEASED'S INCOME

The PRs are liable for any income tax owed by the deceased (TMA 1970 s 74(1)). They should report the death to the appropriate inspector of taxes and complete an ordinary income tax return on behalf of the deceased for the period from 6 April preceding his death to the date of death, and for earlier tax years (if necessary!). In computing the income tax of the deceased, normal principles operate and full personal allowances are available for the year of death.

Any outstanding income tax is a debt of the estate thereby reducing the value of that estate for IHT purposes. Conversely, any repayment of income tax will swell the assets of the estate and may increase the IHT bill on death. Failure to make the appropriate returns means that the Revenue can assess the PRs, at any time within three years after 31 January following the year of assessment in which he died, for any tax that is owing for a period that is within six years of the date of death (TMA 1970 s 40). An assessment is made for these purposes when the inspector authorised to make assessments signs the certificate contained in the assessment books kept at the relevant district (*Honig v Sarsfield* (1986)).   [**12.2**]

EXAMPLE 12.1

A died on 28 September 1997 (tax year 1997–98). If the Revenue assesses his PRs on 2 January 1999 (tax year 1998–99) they can relate it back to the tax year 1992–93.

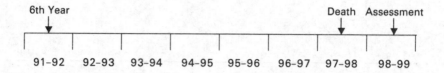

1   Dividends

Dividends received before the deceased's death form part of the deceased's income. For IHT purposes the quoted securities in the deceased's estate must be valued at death; if that quotation was 'ex div' (ie it did not include the value of a declared dividend) the dividend that is to be paid must be added to the value of the security. This problem does not arise when the shares were valued at death 'cum div' since the quotation includes any accruing dividend to date.

If the dividend is paid after the death but relates to a period partly before and partly after death, it may have to be apportioned (Apportionment Act 1870 s 2) for succession purposes.

However, whether or not the dividend is apportioned for succession purposes any dividend paid after the deceased's death is treated as the *income of the estate and not of the deceased* and must not be included in the deceased's tax return (*IRC v Henderson's Executors* (1931)). This rule follows from the fact that as the dividends were never owed to the deceased they never became a part of his income. Only in cases where a dividend is declared due before death, but paid after that death will it be taxed as the deceased's income (see, for instance, *Re Sebright* (1944) and contrast *Potel v IRC* (1971)). Similarly, certain other investment income paid after death but relating to the period before death (for instance bank deposit interest) should be apportioned for succession purposes, but included as estate income for tax purposes. This may lead to some double taxation in that the income which is deemed for succession purposes to accrue before death is charged both to IHT (as part of the deceased's estate on death) and also to income tax in the hands of the PRs and beneficiaries. TA 1988 s 699 affords some relief against such double taxation but only to an absolutely entitled residuary beneficiary who is a higher rate taxpayer (see **[12.54]**).   **[12.3]**

EXAMPLE 12.2

T died on 30 May 1997 leaving his residuary estate (including 1,000 shares in B Ltd) to his brother B absolutely. On 15 June 1997 B Ltd declared a dividend on those shares of £400 (£500 gross) in respect of the year ending on 30 June. The dividend was paid on 28 July 1997.

Of this dividend 11/12 (£458.33) is deemed to have accrued before T's death and will be reflected in the value of the shares in T's estate which will have been valued 'cum div'. It will thus be taxed as part of the capital in T's estate.

However, for income tax purposes the whole dividend is taxed as the income of the estate, albeit with some relief for double taxation against any higher rate liability of B under TA 1988 s 699.

2   Trust income

Where the deceased was a life tenant under a trust, any income which was received by the trustees before his death is treated as his income and must be included in the PRs' tax return to the date of death. If income was paid to the trustees after the death but is attributable in part to the period before death tax is payable according to the actual apportionment. Any income that is apportioned to the deceased life tenant is taxed as the income of the estate—and not of the deceased (*Wood v Owen* (1941)).

Income that is apportioned to the deceased life tenant forms an asset of his estate, thereby increasing his IHT liability. This may result in an element of double IHT because the apportioned income will affect the value of the trust assets on which the trustees pay IHT on the life tenant's death. This double taxation is avoided by deducting the apportioned income from the value of the settled assets.

EXAMPLE 12.3

T who died on 30 June 1997 was life tenant of a trust. Included in the settled assets was debenture stock in Blank Ltd. On 31 December 1997 B Ltd paid the trustees the annual interest of £80 (£100 gross). This interest was apportioned by the trustees as to half (£40) to T and half (£40) to the remainderman X. The £40 apportioned to the deceased is estate income. Notice, also, that the £40 besides forming an additional asset of T's estate for IHT purposes also swells the value of the trust fund on which the trustees pay IHT at T's rates (see [**25.23**]). To avoid the £40 being charged twice to IHT, it is deducted from the value of the settled assets. (If T's free estate passed to a residuary beneficiary absolutely, the latter may be entitled to relief under TA 1988 s 699 above.)

If the Apportionment Act 1870 is excluded so that all the income is paid to either a subsequent life tenant or a remainderman, income tax follows the actual apportionment made. That income, therefore, is not taxed as part of the deceased's estate.   [**12.4**]

3   Sole traders and partners

As from tax year 1997–98 (in all cases) and from 6 April 1994, in the case of businesses commencing on or after that date, the discontinuance rules apply: see [**I.64**] and [**I.93**].   [**12.5**]

4   The surviving spouse: ESC A7

If a business or a source of untaxed interest or income from abroad is left to a surviving spouse the normal cessation rules (under Schedule D Cases I–V) are not, in practice, applied unless claimed either by the PRs or the spouse. Accordingly, the closing year rules under Cases I and II will not operate in the case of a business but, even so, losses and capital allowances for which the deceased had not obtained tax relief may not be carried forward. On 4 April 1995 the Inland Revenue announced the withdrawal of this concession with effect from 6 April in the case of businesses commencing on or after 6 April 1994: for businesses or other sources already in existence on that date withdrawal will not be effective before 6 April 1997 (the precise date is to be announced). With the introduction of the current year basis of assessment the precise profits of the business are taxed over its lifetime so that the concession (which aimed to prevent unfairness) becomes redundant.   [**12.6**]–[**12.20**]

II   THE ADMINISTRATION PERIOD

1   **Duration of administration**

The administration period is the period from the date of death until the date when the residue is ascertained and ready for distribution. Until that time no beneficiary is entitled to the income or to any property comprised in the estate and, accordingly, is not liable to income tax unless income is actually distributed to him. Identifying precisely when completion of the administration of the estate occurs can present problems: for the position in Scotland see TA 1988 s 702(a) and for the position elsewhere see, for instance, *IRC v Pilkington* (1941) and *Prest v Bettinson* (1980) and the IR Manual CG 30840 considering claims that an administration has continued for a prolonged period. The question is also of importance in CGT given that during administration a rate of 23% applies: see [**15.61**]).   [**12.21**]

2   **Taxing PRs during administration**

During the administration period, the PRs are liable, in a representative capacity, to income tax on all the income of the estate computed in the usual way. This liability is to pay tax at either lower rate (20%) or basic rate (23%) depending upon the type of income involved. Dividends and savings income, for instance, is taxed at lower rate whilst rents and sums equivalent to interest paid in respect of a solicitor's undesignated client account is taxed at basic rate.

Some income received by the PRs will already have borne tax: in such cases the PRs have no further tax to pay. Generally such income falls into three categories:

(1)   income which has borne tax at basic rate;
(2)   income which has borne tax at lower rate (eg dividends and interest paid by banks and building societies);
(3)   income bearing non-repayable basic or lower rate tax (eg a foreign income dividend: see [**29.46**]).

The main examples of income on which PRs are directly assessed are:

(a)   rents from property;
(b)   foreign source income;
(c)   interest (eg from National Savings) which is paid gross.   [**12.22**]

3   **Interest relief**

Tax relief is available, for one year from the making of the loan, for interest on a loan raised to pay the IHT payable on delivery of the PRs' account, which is attributable to personal property owned beneficially by the deceased and which vests in his PRs, provided that the loan is on a loan account not merely by way of overdraft (TA 1988 s 364). Relief is given against the income of the estate for the year in which the interest is paid but where that income is insufficient relief may be given against income of the preceding year and then against the future income of the estate.   [**12.23**]

4   **Trading**

When the PRs carry on a business after the death of a sole trader in order to sell it as a going concern or to transfer it to a beneficiary, they must pay basic rate tax on any profits calculated in the usual way. Hence, they can deduct business expenses (TA 1988 s 74) and claim loss relief (normally under TA 1988 s 380, s 385 or FA 1991 s 72; s 381 does not apply)   [**12.24**].

5 Apportionments

Dividends and certain other income received by the PRs after the death in respect of a period wholly or partly before death is taxed as the income of the estate whether or not it is apportioned for succession purposes. Similarly, trust income received by the trustees after the deceased life tenant's death and apportioned to him is taxed as the income of the estate (see [12.4]).

When property which produces no income is left to persons in succession (eg to A for life, remainder to B) part of the capital sum realised on the sale of that property may be treated as income under the rule in *Re Earl of Chesterfield's Trusts* (1883) since, otherwise, the life tenant would receive nothing. Such equitable apportionment involves no income tax liability for the PRs (or the beneficiaries) because the apportionment is of a capital sum.   [12.25]-[12.40]

III TAXATION OF DISTRIBUTIONS TO BENEFICIARIES

1 The basic principles

Income received by the PRs suffers the equivalent of basic rate tax either by deduction at source or by direct assessment in their hands. From this taxed income the PRs deduct administration expenses chargeable against income, leaving a net sum available for distribution to beneficiaries entitled to the income from the estate. In the days when income was taxed at basic and higher rate only the position was straightforward. As already explained, however, the current position offers a variety of possibilities with PRs receiving savings income (including dividends) with a credit of only 20% whilst other dividends have non-reclaimable tax credits. These different types of income fall to be divided between beneficiaries as is just and reasonable having regard to their different interests (TA 1988 s 701(3A)(a)). Which type of income are administration expenses deducted against? The legislation leaves the matter open, but the best approach will normally be to set expenses first against income carrying a non-reclaimable lower rate credit, then against income bearing tax at lower rate and finally against basic rate income (this order is accepted by the Inland Revenue).

If the PRs have a discretion whether to deduct administration expenses from income or capital they should consider the tax position of the beneficiary (if any) entitled to the income. When that beneficiary has a large income, they should deduct their expenses from income so as to reduce his income and, therefore, his tax bill. Conversely, if the beneficiary has only a small income, they should deduct expenses from capital so as not to prejudice any claim that he may have for a repayment of basic rate tax.   [12.41]

2 General legatees

A general legatee is a person who is entitled to a sum of money (a pecuniary legacy) not charged on any particular fund. This sum is capital and the legatee is generally not entitled to any income unless:

(1) the will directs the PRs to pay him interest; or

(2) the legacy remains unpaid at the end of the executor's year, in which case he is entitled to interest at 6% pa in the absence of a contrary direction; or

(3) the legacy is a 'statutory legacy' arising on intestacy (eg to a surviving spouse) in which case he is entitled to interest at 6% pa from the date of death to the date of payment.

Interest is paid gross by the PRs and the legatee is assessed directly to tax under Schedule D Case III on the interest in the year of receipt. If that interest is neither claimed nor paid, there is no income to be assessed in the beneficiary's hands (*Dewar v IRC* (1935)). Once a sum has been set aside to pay the legacy it may, however, be too late to disclaim the income (*Spens v IRC* (1970)).

[**12.42**]

3 Specific legatees

A specific legatee is entitled to a particular item of property and to any income produced by it as from the date of death. Therefore, once the PRs vest the legacy in the beneficiary, any income from it which arose during the administration period is related back and taxed as the legatee's income for the tax year(s) when it arose. It will have suffered the equivalent of basic rate tax either through deduction at source or as a result of direct assessment on the PRs. Accordingly, the net income will be passed to the beneficiary together with a tax deduction certificate completed by the PRs.   [**12.43**]

EXAMPLE 12.4

A died in September 1997 leaving his 1,000 shares in B Ltd to his nephew T. A dividend of £80 is paid in respect of the shares in January 1998. The administration is completed and the shares vested in T in May 1998 together with the dividend and tax credit for the £20 tax which has been deducted. T must include the £100 in his income tax return for the tax year 1997–98 (when the dividend was paid) and not 1998–99 (when T received it).

4 Annuitants

a) *Definition*

An annuity is a pecuniary legacy payable by instalments. The payments are income from which the PRs must deduct basic rate income tax (under TA 1988 s 348 or, if the payment is out of capital, s 349). The net sum will be paid to the annuitant who will be given a certificate of tax deducted.

Modern wills rarely provide for the payment of an annuity.   [**12.44**]

b) *Use of formula*

A testator may want the annuitant to receive a constant sum despite fluctuations in the tax rates. The two methods most commonly employed are:
(1) The testator provides for the payment of 'such sum as will after deduction of income tax at the basic rate for the time being in force leave (say) £77 pa'.
      The PRs must pay £77 grossed up at the current basic rate, but they are not liable to indemnify the annuitant against any higher rate income tax for which he may be liable. Conversely, if the annuitant can reclaim all or any of the basic rate tax paid, he need not account for it to the PRs.
(2) If the testator provides for the payment of '£77 pa free from income tax' this imposes an obligation on the PRs to pay such sum as after deducting basic rate income tax leaves £77. However, it also means that the annuitant can recover from the PRs any higher rate tax that he may have to pay on the annuity and any basic rate tax that he reclaims must be repaid to the PRs. In effect, he will never be left with more nor with less than £77 (see *Re Pettit, Le Fevre v Pettit* (1922)).   [**12.45**]

c) *Setting aside a capital sum and purchased life annuities*

An annuitant can insist on a capital sum being set aside to provide for his annuity (thereby creating an interest in possession trust for IHT purposes: see Chapter 24). If the capital in the estate is insufficient he can demand that the actuarial value of the annuity be paid to him, abated if necessary (*IRC v Lady Castlemaine* (1943)). This capitalised annuity is not subject to income tax either in the PRs' or in the annuitant's hands.

If the will directs the PRs to purchase an annuity for the beneficiary, he will be charged to income tax on the full amount of each annual payment and cannot claim relief under TA 1988 s 656 which taxes only the income element (see [**10.101**]). The beneficiary should therefore demand that the PRs give him the appropriate capital sum so that he can buy the annuity himself and claim s 656 relief. [**12.46**]

d) *Beware top-ups!*

Where there is insufficient income in the estate to pay the annuity in full, the will may direct the PRs to make up the income from capital. If they do so, that capital is treated as income from which basic rate tax must be deducted (*Brodie's WT v IRC* (1933)). The unfortunate result of such 'top-up' provisions is to convert capital into income and it is, therefore, better to give the PRs a discretion to make good any shortfall in the annuity by capital advances (see [**11.48**]). [**12.47**]

5 Residuary beneficiaries

A beneficiary may have a limited or an absolute interest in residue. A limited interest exists where he is entitled to income only, eg if the will leaves residue to 'my wife for life, remainder to my children', the wife is entitled only to income from the estate. An absolute interest exists when the beneficiary is entitled to both the income and capital of the residue, as where the residue is left to 'my wife absolutely'.

With the introduction of self-assessment the tax treatment of residuary beneficiaries was radically altered ('simplified' was the word used in the relevant Press Release of 29 November 1994) in order to 'make it easier for them to self assess'. These rules applied to estates in the course of administration on 6 April 1995 as well as to new estates. [**12.48**]

a) *Beneficiary with a limited interest in residue*

Any income paid to the beneficiary during the administration period will be paid net of tax deducted by the PRs. The beneficiary must gross up these sums as part of his total income in the year of receipt for the purposes of his excess liability or to obtain a repayment of tax (as appropriate). [**12.49**]

Position prior to 6 April 1995
When the administration was completed, the total net income payments of the period were aggregated and deemed to have been paid out to the beneficiary at a uniform rate over the administration period. This often necessitated adjustments to his original income tax liability. [**12.50**]

Position from 6 April 1995 ('the receipt basis')
FA 1995 inserted a new s 695(3) into TA 1988 and amended s 695(2) with the result that:
(1) sums paid out during the administration are deemed for all tax purposes to be income of the recipient in the tax year in which paid; and

(2) on completion of administration any sum paid is treated as being the income of the beneficiary in the tax year in which the administration ends.

This switch to the 'receipts basis' was intended to simplify the position in anticipation of the introduction of self-assessment. The result is that the total income paid to a beneficiary in the tax year equals his estate income for that year.   [**12.51**]

EXAMPLE 12.5

Mandy died on 6 March 1996 leaving her residuary estate to Shirley for life remainder to Jemima. The net income of the estate was:

Tax year	*amount*
	(£)
1995–96	3,000
1996–97	10,000
1997–98	1,000
Total	£14,000

Payments made to Shirely were:

Tax year	*amount*
	(£)
1995–96	nil
1996–97	9,000
1997–98	5,000
Total	£14,000

Shirley is taxed on the payments in the tax years of receipt, ie in 1996–97 and 1997–98.

Note: If at the end of administration there is an undistributed income balance that is deemed to have been paid to the beneficiary in the tax year when the administration ended (this being the one exception to the receipts basis). For instance if the administration of Mandy's estate had been complete on 4 April 1997 the undistributed income balance of £5,000 would be taxed on Shirley in 1996–97 even though she did not receive it until the following tax year.

b) *Beneficiary with an absolute interest in residue*

Such a beneficiary is entitled to receive both income and capital from the estate. He can, of course, only be charged to income tax insofar as any payments that he receives represent income. FA 1995 introduced provisions similar to those considered above in relation to limited interests in residue. The result is that:

(1) Payments during administration are taxed as income up to the amount of the aggregated income entitlement of the beneficiary for the year of assessment in which the sum is paid (see TA 1988 s 696(3) (3A) (3B): 'aggregated income entitlement' means the net income to which the beneficiary is entitled); and

(2) If on completion of administration the beneficiary has not received his full aggregate entitlement to income the shortfall is treated as having been paid to him immediately before the end of the administration period.
                                                                                                [**12.52**]

EXAMPLE 12.6

Simple Simon died on 6 March 1996 leaving his entire estate to Dorothy. Net income arising to the estate was as follows:

Tax year	Net income
	(£)
1995–96	3,000
1996–97	10,000
1997–98	1,000
Total	£14,000

(i) Tax year 1995–96: assuming that no payment is made to Dorothy £3,000 is carried forward to 1996–97. As at 5 April 1996 Dorothy's aggregated income entitlement is £3,000.

(ii) Tax year 1996–97: at 5 April 1997 Dorothy's aggregated income entitlement assuming no payment in 1995–96 is £13,000. As a result if a payment of £63,000 is made to her in this year the first £13,000 is treated as income.

Notes:
(a) The timing of the payment in the tax year is irrelevant: it could for instance occur on 6 April 1996 but nonetheless it is Dorothy's aggregated income entitlement at 5 April 1997 which is crucial.
(b) The rules apply to the payment of 'any sum': it is not possible for the PRs to specify that the payment is 'of capital'. Further the Inland Revenue consider that for these purposes the payment of 'any sum' includes a transfer of assets. They will therefore treat the value of such assets as income up to the amount of the beneficiary's aggregated income entitlement (limited support for this view may be found in TA 1988 s 701(12)).

Position when a multiplicity of beneficiaries
In this situation income arising during administration must be split between beneficiaries in the same proportion as their capital shares (see TA 1988 s 696(2) referring to a 'proportionate part' of the residuary income). A further complexity arises from the different types of estate income: this too needs to be split proportionately between the beneficiaries. Payments are made first from income bearing tax at basic rate before income bearing tax at lower rate and income carrying non-reclaimable credits. [12.53]

EXAMPLE 12.7

Betty's estate is to be divided between Adam (50%); Claude (25%) and Cecil (25%). In 1997–98 the net income of the estate was £15,850 made up of:

dividends	£10,000 (credit for 20%)
rent income	£3,850 (credit for 23%)
FID	£2,000 (credit for 20% non-reclaimable)

(i) Aggregated income entitlement for 1997–98

Type of income	Adam (50%)	Claude (25%)	Cecil (25%)
Basic rate	1,925	962.5	962.5
Lower rate	5,000	2,500	2,500
Non-reclaimable lower rate	1,000	500	500
£15,850	£7,925	£3,962.5	£3,962.5

(ii) Treatment of income distribution in the year

Assume that each beneficiary received one-half of his aggregated income entitlement for the year, the position would be:

	Adam (£)	Claude (£)	Cecil (£)
Receipt	3,962.5	1,981.25	1,981.25
made up of:			
Basic rate income	1,925	962.5	962.5
Lower rate income	2,037.5	1,018.75	1,018.75
Non-reclaimable lower rate	—	—	—

Notes:

(1)   Each beneficiary would carry-forward an aggregated income entitlement to the next tax year: in Adam's case this would be £3,962.5 being comprised of lower rate income of £2,962.5 and non-reclaimable lower rate of £1,000.

(2)   What if tax rates change between receipt of income by PRs and its distribution? TA 1988 s 694(4) provides for income to be paid with the appropriate credit for rates of tax current in the year of payment not in the year of receipt by PRs.

(3)   Each beneficiary is considered separately and a distribution to one beneficiary may not be matched by an equivalent distribution to another in that tax year. For instance the PRs may distribute income to Claude but not to Adam or Cecil in 1997–98. Of course, ultimately income of the estate must be split in the ratio 50:25:25 and so the other beneficiaries shares must be made good in the future.

Relief against a double charge

Income which accrued before death, but is received by the PRs after death, is included in the value of the deceased's estate for IHT purposes and is also taxed as the income of the estate (see [**12.3**]). Some relief against this double taxation is provided by TA 1988 s 699 which allows a reduction in the residuary income for the purposes of any liability to higher rate tax of a residuary beneficiary absolutely entitled to residue. The reduction is of an amount equal to the IHT chargeable on that income at the estate rate and the resultant sum is then grossed up at the basic rate of income tax.   [**12.54**]

EXAMPLE 12.8

X died on 30 April 1997. He left his residuary estate including 1,000 debentures in B Ltd to his daughter D. His PRs received interest of £160 (£200 gross) from B Ltd in November 1997 in respect of that company's accounting year ending 31 October 1997. The whole interest is taxed as the income of the estate but, as half the interest accrued before death, that portion is included in X's estate for IHT purposes. Under TA 1988 s 699 if D is a higher rate taxpayer one-half of the interest is eligible for relief. Assume that the estate rate of IHT is 20%.

	£
Interest (gross)	£200
Sum accrued before death	100
Less: income tax for year of death	20
	£80

	£
The relief is calculated as:	
£80 × 20% (IHT estate rate)	16
Add income tax	5
Grossed-up amount that can be deducted from the residuary income to reduce D's liability to higher rate income tax only	£21

6   **Conclusions on the 1995 changes**

Position of PRs   The move to a payments basis of assessment for residuary beneficiaries means that the date of payment or conclusion of administration is critical: if all payments are bunched in a single tax year this may push the beneficiary into the higher rate of income tax (the Inland Revenue rejected suggestions for the introduction of a system of top slicing).

When deciding upon the timing of distributions therefore PRs should consider whether the bunching or spreading of income over the administration best suits the tax position of the beneficiaries. To do this the PRs will need to know the circumstances of each beneficiary. **[12.55]**

Beneficiaries   Beneficiaries faced with completing an income tax return are given (by TA 1988 s 700(5)) the right to certain information as follows:

'(5) It shall be the duty of a personal representative of a deceased person, if a request to do so is made in writing by a person who has, or has had, an absolute or limited interest in the residue of the estate of the deceased or by a person to whom any of the income of the residue of that estate has been paid in the exercise of any discretion, to furnish the person making the request with a statement in writing setting out—

(a) in respect of every amount which has been, or is treated as having been, actually paid to that person in respect of that interest or in the exercise of that discretion, the amount (if any) deemed under this Part to have been paid to him as income for a year of assessment; and

(b) the amount of any tax at the applicable rate which any amount falling within paragraph (a) above is deemed to have borne;

and, where an amount deemed to have been paid as income to any person for any year of assessment is deemed for any of the purposes of this Part to have borne tax on different parts of it at different applicable rates, the matters to be set out in pursuance of paragraphs (a) and (b) above shall be set out separately as respects each part of that amount.'

[12.56]

Successive interests in residue   TA 1988 s 698 provides for the situation where an interest in the whole or part of the residue is held successively by different persons during the course of administration. In the case of instruments of variation (as to which see **[22.118]**) the result is that provided no distributions have been made to the original beneficiary before the variation all income will be assessed on the new beneficiary. **[12.57]**

13 The overseas dimension

'The [UK resident] is taxed because (whether he be a British subject or not) he enjoys the benefit of our laws for the protection of his person and his property. The [non-UK resident] is taxed because in respect of his property in the United Kingdom he enjoys the benefit of our laws for the protection of that property.' (*Whitney v IRC* (1926) 10 TC 88 at 112.)

The territorial scope of any tax raises both theoretical and practical questions. The UK system, for instance, proceeds on the basis that if an individual is closely connected with the UK he will be subject to UK tax on his property (both income and capital) worldwide. By contrast, an individual who has only a tenuous connection will be taxed on property (income and capital) situated in or arising from the UK and not on other, worldwide, assets. A strong element of practical reality inevitably permeates this area: theoretically the UK could impose a tax on the income of a Chinaman resident in Peking but little revenue would be raised from that source! The practical constraints upon tax collection and enforcement are well illustrated in the House of Lords speeches in *Clark v Oceanic Contractors Inc* (1983): see [**13.50**].

The 'connecting factors' which determine the extent to which the individual should be subject to income tax are residence and ordinary residence and the meaning of these terms will be considered in this chapter. This discussion will also be relevant when the territorial scope of CGT is considered (in Chapter 20); IHT (in Chapter 27); and corporation tax (in Chapter 28). Domicile, which is relevant for income tax and CGT but of prime concern for IHT, will be considered in Chapter 27.

As a general rule, a UK resident is subject to UK income tax on all his income wherever its source, including income arising abroad, whereas a non-UK resident is only liable to UK income tax on income arising to him in the UK. However, a non-domiciled but UK resident individual will only be taxed on foreign income if remitted to the UK.   [**13.1**]

I   RESIDENCE AND ORDINARY RESIDENCE

1   **Residence**

Neither 'residence' nor 'ordinary residence' is statutorily defined and the meaning of these terms has to be sought in decisions of the courts and in the useful guidance booklet published by the Inland Revenue ('Residents and Non-Residents': IR 20, October 1996) and *Tax Bulletin*, May 1994. The dictionary definition of these words has usually been adopted but for taxation purposes

' *"An individual is resident and ordinarily resident in the*
United Kingdom if he is living in the ordinary course
of his life, or for an extended period; also though normally
he lives here, if he is abroad for occasional residence
only; or if he visits the United Kingdom, year by year,
even though his main home is abroad" . . . *who on earth*
wrote this, Harold Pinter?'

questions of residence do not depend upon any mental element (unlike domicile). Hence, the American who finds himself stuck in the UK because of illness may become resident here although his intention is to return to America as soon as he is fit to travel.

A person can be resident in more than one country so that the UK citizen who spends the winter months in Manchester and the summer in the Costa del Sol is probably resident both in the UK and in Spain. Alternatively, an individual may not be resident anywhere as in the case of the travel writer who spends two years exploring North and South America by bus and is therefore continually on the move (or waiting to be on the move!). In this sense, residence contrasts with domicile since a person must always have a country of domicile and the abandonment of a domicile of choice results in the revival of his domicile of origin.

A permanent abode is not necessary for residence in a country so that the individual who moves from UK hotel to UK hotel may be resident here. This proposition may be illustrated by reference to that well-known taxpayer, the homeless tramp:

'Take the case of a homeless tramp, who shelters tonight under a bridge, tomorrow in the greenwood and as the unwelcome occupant of a farm outhouse the night after. He wanders in this way all over the United Kingdom. But will anyone say that he does not live in the United Kingdom?—and will anyone regard it as a misuse of language to say he resides in the United Kingdom?' (Lord President Clyde in *Reid v IRC* (1926).)

Residence and ordinary residence are not decided in a vacuum but in relation to particular tax years and, in general, the individual who is resident for any part of a tax year is treated as being resident for the whole of that year. This proposition, that it is generally not possible to split tax years into periods of residence and non-residence, is made explicit in the CGT legislation where it is provided in TCGA 1992 s 2(1) that CGT is levied if the individual is resident in the UK during *any part* of the tax year.

EXAMPLE 13.1

Alan, resident and ordinarily resident in the UK, goes to live abroad from June 1995 to March 1997. He will be treated as retaining his UK residence in 1995–96 and 1996–97 for both income tax and CGT purposes (see IR 20 at pp 11–12).

As a matter of practice, in certain cases the tax year may be split into a period of residence and non-residence (ESC A11). This is permitted, for instance, when an individual leaves the UK for permanent residence abroad and likewise when an individual comes to the UK for permanent residence. In the former case, UK residence ceases on the day following the day of departure from the UK: in the latter, UK residence is acquired from the day of arrival. A similar splitting of the tax year occurs when an individual leaves the UK to take up full-time employment abroad or to work full time in a trade or profession (IR 20 Chapter 2). [**13.2**]

2 Who is a UK resident?

In the following situations an individual is resident in the UK. [**13.3**]

The '183-day' rule If he spends more than six months here in any one tax year. This rule is derived from TA 1988 s 336 and six months is interpreted by the Revenue to mean 183 days (even in 1996—a leap year!) It is normal practice to ignore days of arrival and departure (IR 20 para 1.2) although this will not apply to the case of the EU national who commutes to the UK to work each day! [**13.4**]

The '91-day' rule A person who has left the UK for permanent residence abroad is regarded as continuing to be resident here if his visits to the UK average 91 days or more per tax year. In addition a regular visitor to the UK becomes resident after four years if his visits during those years average at least 91 days per year. In cases where it is clear that the taxpayer intends to make such visits he is treated as resident either from the date of his first visit or from the date when he forms that intention (if later). For this purpose SP 2/91 provides that 'any days spent in the UK because of *exceptional circumstances beyond an individual's control* (such as illness) are excluded from the calculation'. This SP does not apply for the purpose of computing the six-month (or 183-day) period. [**13.5**]

EXAMPLE 13.2

(1) Barry comes to England from America to study law at London University. The course is to last three years. As Barry will be present in the UK for more than six months in each of those tax years he is UK resident from the date of his arrival.
(2) Ellie comes to the UK on holiday from America. Usually her visit is for one month per annum. She will not be treated as UK resident.

Available accommodation   The individual who had UK accommodation available for his use and who merely set foot in this country (even if he did not visit that accommodation) was treated as UK resident. In *Cooper v Cadwalader* (1904), for instance, an American barrister took a lease on a shooting box in Scotland where he lived for two months each year. He was held to be resident in the UK as was the taxpayer in *Loewenstein v de Salis* (1926) who had the use of a residence belonging to the company which he controlled and which he visited for hunting.

This available accommodation test operated harshly and as a trap for the unwary. An exception was contained in TA 1988 s 335 which enabled the accommodation to be ignored in the case of an individual who worked full time in a trade, profession, vocation, office or employment all the duties of which were performed outside the UK. Full time for these purposes meant a full working day five days a week and duties performed within the UK could only be ignored if their performance was merely incidental to the performance of other duties outside the UK. Precisely what was meant by incidental duties was somewhat unclear: in *Robson v Dixon* (1972), a KLM airline pilot who maintained an English residence was held not to perform merely incidental duties when he landed in the UK (in all, some 38 times out of a total of 811 flights over a period of six years). Undoubtedly where similar duties are performed in the UK to those abroad they cannot be incidental but the overseas employee who returns to the UK for, for example, fresh instructions or fresh stock would be considered to be performing merely incidental duties during that period.

In his 1993 Budget Speech, the then Chancellor, Norman Lamont, announced the removal of the 'available accommodation' test in order to introduce greater fairness for temporary UK visitors. This change was effected by the insertion of a new sub-s (3) into TA 1988 s 336. This provides that in determining whether an individual is in the UK for some temporary purpose only, and not with a view to establishing a UK residence, no regard shall be paid to living accommodation available for that person's use in the UK (see IR 20 Chapter 4).   [**13.6**]

EXAMPLE 13.3

Toki, an international playboy, comes to London each year for 'the season'. If he acquires a flat in town, that will not by itself make him UK resident and, provided that he does not remain in the UK for 91 days in any tax year, he will not become so resident (but for the use of accommodation in deciding whether the individual is a long-term visitor, see IR 20 p 18).

Residence in a previous year

The absence of a person from the UK *throughout* a tax year provides strong evidence that he is not resident in that year. Exceptionally, however, the Revenue will seek to argue that UK residence continues (see IR 20 para 1.2 and *Rogers v IRC* (1879)).

By TA 1988 s 334, a Commonwealth citizen who has been ordinarily resident in the UK and who leaves for *occasional residence* abroad will be treated during his absence as remaining resident in the UK unless he can prove to the contrary. In the case of *Reed v Clark* (1985), it was held that s 334 was a charging provision and was not limited to persons who were out of the UK for part only of a tax year but could equally apply to persons living abroad throughout a year of assessment. In that case, however, the taxpayer (the pop star Dave Clark) left the UK with the deliberate intention of living and working abroad for a limited period in excess of one tax year and then returning to the UK.

On these facts the judge held that his absence could not be described as for the purpose of merely occasional residence abroad so that he was not treated as UK resident under s 334. Occasional residence under this section, the judge concluded, was to be contrasted with ordinary or settled residence.

> 'The presence of a tax avoidance intention may help to show, for instance, why a person went abroad at all or at the particular time he did, how long he intended to remain away, or where his home in fact was in the year of assessment. But residence abroad for a carefully chosen limited period of work there ... is no less residence abroad for that period because the major reason for it was the avoidance of tax. Likewise with ordinary residence.' (Nicholls J, at 346.)

Crucially, therefore, there was a 'distinct break' with the UK in this case: where the individual has *not* become resident or ordinarily resident elsewhere it may be difficult to rebut the presumption that he remains UK resident. [13.7]

3 Acquiring and losing resident status

An individual who comes to the UK with the intention of taking up permanent residence here will be regarded as both resident and ordinarily resident from the date of arrival (so that the tax year is split). By contrast, a short-term visitor will not become UK resident unless he falls within the 91-day rule. The casual UK resident (eg one who spends an isolated six months here) will lose his resident status simply by returning abroad.

If a person goes abroad for full-time service under a contract of employment which requires all the duties of his employment to be performed abroad (with any UK duties being merely incidental) and his absence from the UK extends over a period covering a complete tax year with interim visits to the UK not exceeding six months in any tax year or an average of 91 days per tax year (the average being taken over the period of absence up to a maximum of four years), then he is normally regarded as neither resident nor ordinarily resident in the UK from the day following the date of his departure (on arrivals and departures, see IR 20 Chapters 2 and 3). [13.8]

4 Ordinary residence

Ordinary residence has been held to mean habitual residence: ie a regular choice of abode which is a settled purpose and forms part of the regular order of an individual's life (see, in particular, *R v Barnet London Borough Council, ex p Nilish Shah* (1983)). A person may therefore be resident without being ordinarily resident in the UK and *vice versa* (IR 20 states: 'If you are resident in the UK year after year, you are treated as ordinarily resident here'.)

EXAMPLE 13.4

(1) Bonzo has lived in Hackney for many years. He sells his terraced house and goes on a world cruise for 18 months. He probably ceases to be UK resident (but see [13.7]) but remains ordinarily resident.

(2) Claude, a French journalist, visits the UK for six months in the 1997–98 tax year to study the eating habits of the natives. He becomes UK resident but is not ordinarily resident.

In a number of cases liability to UK tax is *only* imposed on individuals who are ordinarily resident (for instance under TA 1988 ss 739–740) whilst, in other cases, liability arises if the individual is *either* resident *or* ordinarily resident, eg CGT liability under TCGA 1992 s 2(1).

When a person comes to the UK with the intention of visiting the UK regularly for at least four tax years (so that his visits will average 91 days or more per tax year) ordinary residence will be presumed from the outset. Where there is no such intention, SP 17/91 indicates that ordinary residence will commence from 6 April of the tax year after the individual has visited the UK over four years (averaging 91 days per year) if he originally came with no definite plans about the visits that he would make.   **[13.9]**

5 Corporations

Prior to 15 March 1988, a company was resident in the UK (and therefore subject to corporation tax on its worldwide profits) if its central management and control was located in the UK. Central management and control was considered to reside at the place where board meetings were held and not necessarily where the company was incorporated or registered (see *De Beers Consolidated Mines v Howe* (1906) and SP 6/83).

> ### EXAMPLE 13.5
>
> The directors of a Kenyan subsidiary company always held meetings in Kenya but in fact the company was managed, in breach of its articles, by its UK parent company. The company was therefore held to be resident in England since the question was where the actual control and management was located (see *Unit Construction Co Ltd v Bullock* (1959) and see *Untelrab Ltd v McGregor* (1996) in which the Revenue failed to prove that a subsidiary was managed and controlled by its UK parent company).

From 15 March 1988 this control and management test was supplemented by a further test based on the place of company incorporation (FA 1988 s 66). As a result, companies incorporated in the UK *always* remain UK resident even if control and management is exercised abroad (hence, the non-resident UK company has become a thing of the past) unless under the terms of a 'tie breaker' article in a double tax treaty they would be treated as non-UK resident (FA 1994 ss 249–251). Foreign incorporated companies may become resident, as before, if their central management and control is exercised in the UK.   **[13.10]**

6 Partnerships

Non resident partnerships A similar central management and control test applies to partnerships. If the management and control of the business is exercised abroad, the firm is deemed to be non-resident even though individual partners may be resident in the UK and conversely a firm established abroad will be treated as resident in the UK if managed and controlled here (TA 1988 s 112). Given that a partnership is not normally taxed as a separate entity, more important than the residence of the firm is the residence of the individual partners.

It appears that the forerunner of s 112 was aimed at clarifying the source classification of income from foreign controlled partnerships rather than altering the liability to tax of the individual partners. In practice, a foreign source is attributed to profits from foreign trading operations even when the firm also trades in the UK (this being treated as a UK source). This departs from the normal analysis of a trade as a single indivisible source.   **[13.11]**

Fiscal transparency   The UK Revenue authorities will look through a partnership to the residence of its individual members for the purpose of deciding what, if any, is the tax liability of that person. So far as *UK source* income is concerned, individual members of a partnership will be subject to income tax at all rates whether UK resident or not. So far as *non-UK source* income is concerned, however, UK residents will be subject to tax (under Case V when it is a foreign partnership) whereas partners who are non-UK resident will escape UK tax and will suffer tax either in the country where the profits are earned or, alternatively, in the country of their residence. In the case of a trading partnership which is itself managed and controlled in the UK, it is highly unlikely that a trade carried on, for instance, in France would be treated as being carried on wholly outside the UK and therefore the profits will attract tax under Case I of Schedule D and non-resident partners will suffer UK income tax (*Colquhoun v Brooks* (1889)).   [13.12]

7   Trustees and personal representatives

Residence of trustees   The residence of a trust is determined by reference to the trustees and the Revenue always considered that a trust was resident for income tax purposes in the UK if any *one* of them was so resident (cp residence rules for CGT). In *Dawson v IRC* (1989), however, three discretionary settlements (governed by English law) were established between 1946 and 1965 by a family then domiciled and resident in England. In 1969 the family became permanently resident in Switzerland and by 1975–76 of the three trustees only one was UK resident. The assets then consisted primarily of securities in non-UK companies: the certificates were in the name of a Swiss bank and the income was paid into an account at that bank. In line with the practice already mentioned, the Revenue assessed the sole UK trustee to income tax on the whole income of the settlements. All trustee meetings were held in Switzerland and none of the income was remitted to the UK. The House of Lords concluded that the relevant provision in TA 1988 s 18(1)(a)(i) did not result in a tax charge arising since that provision required *all* persons entitled to the income to reside in the UK. Accordingly, it was limited to the case where *all* the trustees were UK resident. Lord Keith accepted that whichever way the decision had gone anomalies would result:

> 'Counsel for the Crown for his part observed that if the taxpayer's argument were correct the foreign income of an accumulation trust administered in England and governed by English law could be made to avoid taxation by the simple expedient of appointing one co-trustee resident abroad. He further maintained that the anti-avoidance provisions of TA 1988 ss 739–745 relating to the transfer of assets abroad could in the case of trusts be side-stepped by a similar expedient. The issue cannot be resolved by a balancing of the anomalies which would arise on either view ... It can be perceived that there will be much to be said for making the liability to tax depend on the centre of administration of the trust and the place of residence of the majority of the trustees as is the position with Capital Gains Tax ... but Parliament has not so far chosen to do that.'   [13.13]

FA 1989 changes   Not surprisingly, FA 1989 ss 110–111 and 151 amended the law in line with the former Revenue practice. Accordingly, when the trustees of a settlement include one UK resident and one non-UK resident (a 'mixed' trust), the trustees will be treated as UK resident *unless* the settlor was neither resident, ordinarily resident, nor domiciled in the UK when he set up the trust or at a later time when he provided funds for the trust. Furthermore, assessments may now be made in the name of any one or more of the trustees. Thus, in the *Dawson* case the sole UK trustee would now be made liable to

UK income tax on the entire overseas income which had not been remitted to the UK.

[13.14]

EXAMPLE 13.6

(1) The de Vere family trust was set up in 1980 when the settlor had no connection with the UK. All the trustees are non-UK resident and therefore the trust will be liable to UK income tax on UK source income *only*. This position was not altered in 1989 provided that there remains at least one non-UK resident trustee: s 110 cannot apply because the settlor had no connection with the UK.

(2) The Walpole trust was set up by UK residents. It has since been exported and currently all the trustees are non-UK resident and there is no UK source income. There is no liability to UK income tax.

(3) As in (2) except that there is now one UK resident trustee. The trust's world-wide income is subject to UK income tax which can be assessed on the UK resident trustee.

Income tax status of trustees   As a matter of general law a trust is not a separate legal entity as is, for instance, a company. For income tax purposes the position is futher complicated by the division between trusts where the beneficiary has an immediate entitlement to the income (where a 'look through' principle is applied so that the trustees are only liable for UK income tax to the extent that the beneficiary is liable) and other trusts (discretionary and accumulation) where liability to UK tax may be imposed directly on the trustees. It is only in the case of such 'other trusts' that the residence of trustees is of critical importance and in this connection it should be borne in mind that income arising in the UK is always subject to UK tax subject only to specific exemptions (for instance, income arising on government securities under FA 1996 s 154). Non-resident trustees do not qualify for 'excluded income' treatment (see [13.71]) if a relevant beneficiary is UK ordinarily resident (FA 1995 s 128(5)). Discretionary and accumulation trusts are subject to tax at 34% on UK source income although the Revenue may experience collection difficulties (on the tax credit available to beneficiaries, see ESC B18).   [13.15]

Personal representatives   FA 1989 s 111 extended the residence rules for trustees to personal representatives and in so doing created an apparent injustice. Assume, for instance, that Dan Dare is an American domiciliary who comes to the UK to work or to start up a business. As it is envisaged that he will stay in this country for a number of years he acquires a house and other assets here and, accordingly, is advised to make a UK will (with UK personal representatives) disposing of this property. The bulk of his assets remain in America and a separate American will disposing of this property is also made. Assume then that Dan dies without having altered these arrangements. Under s 111, UK tax will be imposed on *all the income produced by his estate* passing under *both* wills since under his English will UK resident personal representatives have been appointed. As Dan is resident in the UK the conditions laid down for the operation of the section are satisfied given that the definition of personal representatives includes not just the UK appointees but also (in relation to another country) 'the persons having under its law any functions corresponding to the functions for administration purposes of personal representatives'. The end result appears unjust: surely UK tax should only be charged on UK source income arising under his UK estate? In practice, although no formal statement has been made, it is understood that the Revenue will apply the legislation in this way.   [13.16]

8 Double tax treaties

The standard double tax treaty contains a provision which will determine in which country a person is to be treated as resident. Such treaties proceed upon the assumption that a person will only be resident in one of the two treaty jurisdictions. It is important to realise that although the treaty may therefore lead to the person in question being treated as resident in only one of the two countries, this will only apply for the purposes of the taxes and types of income and gains covered by the relevant treaty. Accordingly, for other purposes, the individual will still be treated as resident in the other country (see generally IR 20 Chapter 10).   **[13.17]–[13.30]**

II TAXATION OF FOREIGN INCOME

1 Schedule D Cases IV and V

Case IV charges income arising from foreign securities; Case V that arising from foreign possessions. 'Foreign possessions' has been given the widest meaning and therefore includes land, shares, interests in foreign partnerships and interests under non-resident discretionary trusts. It is also capable of including foreign securities and so the Inland Revenue can assess income from such securities either under Case IV or Case V (*Butler v Mortgage Co of Egypt Ltd* (1928)).
                                                                                       [13.31]

2 Calculation of liability

a) *The effect of the switch to self-assessment*

Until the introduction of self-assessment the preceding year basis normally applied. From 6 April 1997 a current year basis applies in respect of unearned income (ie on the whole amount arising or received in the tax year). In the case of a trade carried on abroad the assessment is by reference to the accounting period: ie the Case I and II basis period rules apply (see Appendix I). **[13.32]**

b) *Expenses and remittance problems*

Deductible expenses (including travelling expenses if, broadly, the same conditions are met as in the case of an employee working abroad (see below)), capital allowances and losses are calculated as under Case I but loss relief is only given against other foreign (not UK) income. Where, despite the endeavours of the taxpayer, income cannot be remitted to the UK because of foreign laws, executive action abroad, or the non-availability of foreign currency, the payment of tax may be postponed until that problem passes.   **[13.33]**

3 The remittance basis

If the taxpayer is not domiciled or, being a citizen of the Commonwealth or the Republic of Ireland, not ordinarily resident in the UK, then tax is only charged under Cases IV and V on the remittance basis: ie on actual sums received in the UK (TA 1988 s 65(5)). Unless income is actually brought to the UK there is therefore no tax charge and there is no concept of a constructive remittance. It follows that if income is not intermixed with capital then remittance from capital cannot be treated as a remittance of the income. The non-domicilary therefore may arrange for income to be reinvested or spent abroad. If assets are bought out of income and then sold a remittance of the proceeds of sale is treated as a remittance of the original income whilst a remittance will occur if money is used to settle a liability of the taxpayer in the UK: for instance, liability to a credit card company (see *Timpson's Executors v Yerbury* (1936)). TA 1988 s 65(6)-(9) deems a remittance to occur if the taxpayer applies income outside the UK in or towards the satisfaction of any of the following:

(1) the principal or interest on any loan made to him in the UK;
(2) the principal of any loan made to him outside the UK, the proceeds of which are brought to or received in the UK (note that this provision does not cover the payment of interest on such a loan);
(3) the principal of any loan made to satisfy any debt within (1) or (2) above.

The gap noted in (2) above is often exploited: the individual borrows money abroad, spends it in the UK, pays interest on the loan out of foreign income and eventually clears the loan either out of capital or when he has ceased to be UK resident. Such loans may be charged on foreign situs assets provided that these have not been purchased out of foreign income.

A remittance does not occur if, when the income reaches the UK, the taxpayer is no longer entitled to it, and nor does it occur if an asset bought abroad out of income is brought to the UK *in specie*, although a remittance will then occur if the asset is sold while in the UK (*Scottish Provident Institution v Farmer* (1912)).

The remittance rules operate on the basis that the ground of liability is income arising under Case IV or Case V and the measure of liability is income remitted in the preceding year. Accordingly, if the source of the income does not exist in the year of remittance there can be no liability to charge. However, once a liability exists the measure may be income which arose in a period when the taxpayer was not liable to tax, whether by reason of non-residence or otherwise (see IR 20 para 7.20).

The remittance basis provides a valuable element in tax planning for non-domiciled UK residents.

EXAMPLE 13.7

(1) Carlos, domiciled and ordinarily resident in Spain, but resident in England carries on his business in France. Out of the profits of his business he buys a Picasso painting in France which he brings to England. This is property in kind and not a remittance under Case V. Were he to sell the Picasso in the UK, he would be taxable under TA 1988 s 65.

(2) Diego, resident but not domiciled in the UK, arranges for his share of the profits in an overseas firm to be invested abroad. There is no remittance and therefore no UK tax charge. Should he need to remit foreign moneys he will still avoid UK income tax if the remitted sum is capital. He may be able to arrange this by operating a number of separate overseas bank accounts. Assume, for instance, that he receives rents from letting land abroad which are paid into one account and that receipts from disposal of capital assets are paid into a separate account. Remittances from the latter are capital (and not subject to UK income tax though a CGT charge may arise: see Chapter 20) and Diego can compensate for the reduction in this account by arranging for sums in the other (income) account to be invested, for example, in the purchase of replacement capital assets abroad (see generally on how non-UK domiciliaries should bring money into the UK, *Taxation*, 1992, p 441).

If the taxpayer acquires a UK domicile he can no longer take advantage of the remittance basis and previously un-remitted foreign income can be remitted without charge to tax (see *Taxation Practitioner*, December 1992, p 541). **[13.34]**

4 Particular categories of income

a) *Profits of a trade, profession or vocation*

A UK resident is assessed under Schedule D Case I or II on all his profits arising from a trade, profession or vocation ('trade') carried on by him in the UK, despite some of the profits being attributable to overseas business: TA 1988 s 18(3).

For a trader to be assessed under Schedule D Case V, he must be resident in the UK, but the trade must be carried on wholly abroad. This is a question of fact, and for the sole trader who is resident in the UK and who has the sole right to manage and control the business it will be difficult to argue that the trade is wholly carried on abroad (*Ogilvie v Kitton* (1908)).

A UK resident company may, however, be able to show that it is trading wholly abroad (*Mitchell v Egyptian Hotels Ltd* (1915)). Where the company establishes a foreign subsidiary (as opposed to a branch) it is a question of fact whether that subsidiary is carrying on its own trade or acting merely as agent for the parent company. The answer depends upon where the head and brains of the trade are to be found and not on who owns the shares. To avoid the risk of the subsidiary being treated as UK resident it is prudent to ensure that UK resident directors are not in a majority on the subsidiary's board; that the non-resident directors of the subsidiary are men of substance who are capable of independent thought and judgment; and that board meetings (where 'real' decisions and not just 'rubber stampings' occur) should be held outside the UK.

If a non-resident partnership trades in the UK, any UK resident partner will be assessed under Case I on all the UK profits and under Case V on his share of any foreign profits.

EXAMPLE 13.8

Wino and Co, a French partnership, have one partner resident in London who arranges for sales of their wine in the UK. In deciding whether the firm is trading in the UK (so that a Schedule D Case I assessment is appropriate) the precise mechanics of the wine sales are important. If contracts are made in the UK it is likely that a business in the UK is being carried on, whereas if the orders are merely obtained here and the actual contracts are made in France, the firm may merely be trading with the UK so that any assessment to UK tax will be under Case V (see generally the problem of when non-UK residents trade within the UK discussed at [**13.72**]).

Although 'trade' is used here to include professions and vocations, in practice, profits arising from a profession will rarely be taxed under Case V because the individual exercising his profession wholly abroad is unlikely to be a UK resident and hence will escape UK income tax completely (see *Davies v Braithwaite* (1931)).   [**13.35**]

b) *Distributions from companies*

Distributions are charged under Case V unless they relate to a secured debt: eg a debenture (Case IV). The distribution will only be taxable if it is of income. This is decided by applying the local law to see whether or not the *corpus* of the asset is left intact after the distribution: if it is, the payment will be taxed as income; if not, it is capital (*IRC v Reid's Trustees* (1949)). Dividends received from a foreign company are subject to UK tax at *20% only* until the dividend (treated as a top slice of income) brings the recipient into the 40% tax band (for the treatment of dividends generally, see Chapter 29).   [**13.36**]

EXAMPLE 13.9

Ferdinand has Schedule E income of £8,000 and dividends from a Bermudian company (no tax deducted at source) of £27,000 in 1997–98. His tax position is:

	£
Total income	35,000
Less: personal allowance	4,045
	£ 30,955

The tax charge is as follows:

Schedule E	£
£3,955 at 20%	791.00

Schedule D Case V	£
£22,145 at 20%	4,429
£4,855 at 40%	1,942
	£ 6,371

The taxation of foreign dividends at 20% does not apply to income tax under Schedule D Case V charged on the remittance basis. Accordingly, in particular cases there may be attractions in ensuring that the remittance basis does not apply to the income.

c) *Income from land and unsecured loans*

This income is taxable under Case V. The treatment of receipts from overseas land was altered by TA 1988 s 65(2A) (inserted by FA 1995) which provided for such income to be computed in accordance with the new Schedule A rules. The same deductions in arriving at profits will be made and lease premiums and analogous receipts will be taxed (interest paid on a loan to acquire the property may for instance be deducted in arriving at the Case V income). However a UK Schedule A business is wholly separate thereby preventing losses on one being offset against the other.   **[13.37]**

d) *Income from a foreign trust*

If a UK resident beneficiary has an absolute right to all or part of the income of the foreign trust (one where the trustees are non-UK resident and the assets are abroad), he is taxed under Case V on the income as it arises and whether or not he receives it (*Williams v Singer* (1921)). Similar principles apply to a discretionary beneficiary in whose favour the trustees have exercised their discretion to appoint income.

Of course, in appropriate cases tax may be charged on a UK settlor under TA 1988 Part XV (see **[11.61]**); or under TA 1988 s 739 (see **[13.111]**) or under TA 1988 s 740 in respect of capital payments which are derived from income.   **[13.38]**

e) *Income from a foreign partnership*

In *Padmore v IRC* (1987) it was held that a UK resident partner was not subject to income tax under Schedule D Case V on his share of the profits of an overseas partnership because of the wording of the Jersey double tax treaty. The decision was reversed retrospectively and the present position is that such treaties do not affect the taxation of a partner's share of overseas profits or gains (see TA 1988 s 112(4), (5)).   **[13.39]**

f) *Miscellany*

Certain pensions (see [**13.49**]) and alimony ordered by a foreign court are taxed under Case V. [**13.40**]

g) *Coming to the UK*

In cases where an individual becomes UK resident and ordinarily resident during the course of a tax year there are complex rules which identify the overseas investment income which thereupon becomes subject to UK tax. Professional advice should be taken *before* becoming UK resident (see generally IR 20 para 7.17 ff). [**13.41**]

5 Employment income (Schedule E)

The three Cases of Schedule E tax the emoluments, wherever earned, of a person resident or ordinarily resident in the UK (TA 1988 s 19(1) but see *Nichols v Gibson* (1996) establishing that TA 1988 s 148 is an independent charging provision not subject to the restrictions of Cases 1–III.

The expression '*foreign emoluments*' used in all three Cases means the emoluments of a person not domiciled in the UK whose employer is not a UK resident (TA 1988 s 192). The employee may be resident or ordinarily resident in the UK (such as a French domiciled journalist employed by a French newspaper in England as their foreign correspondent). When an individual is in receipt of foreign emoluments and the duties of the relevant employment are performed wholly outside the UK, those emoluments are taxed on a remittance basis. To ensure that tax is charged on the remittance basis, it is therefore necessary to establish *first*, that the duties of the office are performed wholly outside the UK; *secondly*, under a contract of employment with a non-resident employer; and, *thirdly*, that the individual is not domiciled in the UK. In the case of a new arrival to the UK who will perform duties both abroad and in the UK, it is essential that the overseas duties should be carried out under a separate contract of employment. Care needs to be taken in drafting the terms of any such contract since the Revenue has power to ensure that the emoluments are not artificially weighted in favour of the overseas contract. [**13.42**]

a) *Individual resident and ordinarily resident: Case I*

Where a person is resident and ordinarily resident in the UK, but is required by his employment to perform duties wholly or partly outside the UK, he is charged on all his emoluments under the usual principles of Schedule E (see Chapter 5) with the following limited relief. [**13.43**]

Long absence (TA 1988 s 193; Sch 12) Where the duties are performed wholly or partly abroad during a qualifying period of absence of at least 365 days the employee can deduct 100% of the emoluments earned during that period. This 365-day period is unlikely to fall within one tax year—if it did, the employee would probably be regarded as non-resident so that Case I would not apply and he would not be liable to UK tax on his foreign earnings (see SP 18/91 which makes it clear that a period of non-UK residence does not count as part of the 'qualifying period' for the purposes of this relief). Accordingly, when it straddles tax years, the 100% deduction is given against so much of the total emoluments of that year as were earned during the part of the qualifying period falling within that year (see *Example 13.10*).

A qualifying period of 365 days means that the employee must be abroad for a *continuous* period of 365 days although a period abroad will be continuous for these purposes unless visits back to the UK exceed 62 consecutive days for any single period, or one-sixth of the total days in the period from leaving the UK to returning to the UK for the next visit (see *Example 13.10*). The period of permitted intervening days is increased from 62 to 183 and the permitted fraction from one-sixth to one-half in the case of seafarers (TA 1988 Sch 12 para 3(2A)).

Terminal leave spent abroad will count as a qualifying period; if spent in the UK it will not (see *Robins v Durkin* (1988): days spent in the UK during the employment but after the period of absence from the UK had ended cannot be included in the 365-day qualifying period). Some duties (such as reporting back to base in the UK) can be regarded as incidental to overseas duties but the days so spent in the UK nevertheless count as 'days in the UK' in calculating the one-sixth and 62-day rules.

TA 1988 Sch 12 para 2 contains anti-avoidance provisions which apply whenever the duties of that employment or any other 'associated employment' held by the employee are not performed wholly abroad as would be the case if the intervals between periods of absence were spent performing duties in the UK. This is to prevent an abuse of the relief by the loading of emoluments onto the foreign duties. Employments are 'associated' if they are with the same employer or with different companies in the same group (see para 2(3) and *Platten v Brown* (1986)). It may, therefore, be advantageous for the employee to have a separate service contract for his duties abroad.

In applying this relief, TA 1988 Sch 12 para 6 provides that, if overseas duties are merely incidental to a main UK employment, they are deemed to be performed in the UK. Even where the duties are performed substantially abroad, any duties in the UK will be taken into account in calculating the relief (TA 1988 s 132(2), (3)).   **[13.44]**

EXAMPLE 13.10

(1) A spends 300 days abroad before returning to the UK for 65 days. He then goes abroad for a further 300 days. A does not have a qualifying period of 365 days' absence because, although his period in the UK does not exceed one-sixth of the total, it exceeds 62 days.

(2) A has the following periods of absence from, and presence in, the UK.

	Period	Days
1	Absent from UK	70
2	Present in UK	8
3	Absent from UK	105
4	Present in UK	26
5	Absent until final return	160
	Total days	369

A has a qualifying period of 365 days which is not broken by the two periods in the UK. Period 2 can be amalgamated with 1 and 3 because eight days is less than one-sixth of that total period of 183 days (from leaving the UK to the next visit). Presence in the UK on 34 days (2 and 4) is less than one-sixth of the final total period of 369 days.

EXAMPLE 13.11

Wanderer is employed as the export sales manager of Worldwide Enterprises plc. He is absent from the UK on a sales promotion campaign in the Far East from 1 October 1996 to 31 December 1997 (458 days). During this period he returned to the UK to visit his mother for 21 days in 1996–97 and 30 days in 1997–98.

His salary in 1996–97 was £16,000 and in 1997–98 £18,000. His duties are performed wholly abroad:

The whole period qualifies for the 100% deduction.

	1996–97 £	*1997–98* £
Salary	16,000	18,000
Less: relief for overseas duties		
1996–97 100% × $\left(£16,000 \times \dfrac{188}{365}\right)$	8,241	
1997–98 100% × $\left(£18,000 \times \dfrac{270}{365}\right)$		13,315
Schedule E assessment	£7,759	£4,685

b) *Emoluments for duties performed in the UK: Case II*

Where a person is resident, but not ordinarily resident in the UK, or is neither resident nor ordinarily resident, he is assessed under Case II on emoluments for duties performed in the UK only (see [**13.73**]). [**13.45**]

c) *The remittance basis of Schedule E: Case III*

Case III applies to an employee who is resident (whether or not ordinarily resident) in the UK to tax emoluments which would otherwise escape tax under Cases I or II, but only if the emoluments are remitted to the UK.

Hence, Case III applies in two instances. *First* where the emoluments received in the UK are foreign emoluments and the duties of the employment are performed wholly abroad (so that neither Case I nor Case II can apply). *Secondly,* where the emoluments received in the UK are for duties performed abroad (so that Case II cannot apply) and the employee, although resident, is not ordinarily resident in the UK (so that Case I cannot apply).

Remittances, for Schedule E, are governed by TA 1988 s 132(5) and, basically, bear the same meaning as for Schedule D Case V (see [**13.34**] and TA 1988 s 65). Remittances under Schedule E are, however, assessed on a current year basis and will be subject to tax even if the emoluments are for some previous year or the employment has ceased (TA 1988 s 202A(2)).

Where an employee, resident but not ordinarily resident, in the UK is potentially liable under both Cases II and III in respect of emoluments paid partly in the UK and partly abroad from a single employment performed inside and outside the UK, any emoluments paid in, enjoyed in, or remitted to the UK will only be taxed under Case III to the extent that they exceed the Case II emoluments for the year (SP 5/84). The emoluments assessable under Case II must be computed 'in a reasonable manner', ie on a time basis by reference to working days. [**13.46**]

d) *Place of work*

In deciding whether the duties of an employment are in substance performed wholly abroad, merely incidental duties performed in the UK are ignored (TA 1988 s 132(2)). This is a question of fact, and the rule is restrictively construed (see *Robson v Dixon* (1972)). However, such incidental duties are included in calculating whether the employee is entitled to the deduction for long absence in Case I (TA 1988 s 132(3)).

By TA 1988 s 132(4) specific duties are always deemed to be performed in the UK; in particular Crown employments and certain duties of seamen and aircrew. The rules regarding the latter are, however, relaxed in applying the Case I long absence deduction. Generally, crews of ships and aircraft will be treated as performing their duties abroad in respect of any part of a voyage that does not begin *and* end in the UK.

For the purposes of income tax generally, areas designated under the Continental Shelf Act 1964 are regarded as part of the UK (eg workers on oil rigs in the UK sector of the North Sea are deemed to work in the UK). **[13.47]**

e) *Deductible expenses*

Expenses (typically travel and subsistence) may be incurred by the employee, in which case the question of their deductibility arises, or, alternatively, if borne by the employer they may be treated as an emolument of the employee. After two consultative documents the rules were relaxed and the following matters should be noted.

First, in cases where the employment is performed partly in the UK and partly abroad by a UK resident the expenditure incurred on all business journeys (including travel outside the UK) is a deductible expense under the normal rules of Schedule E (a similar rule applies to the self-employed taxpayer who can deduct these expenses under the rules of Schedule D).

Secondly, the non-UK resident (eg the individual who works abroad throughout the tax year) and the taxpayer entitled to the long absence deduction will not suffer UK tax on reimbursements by their employer for travelling etc expenses incurred during those periods. For the Case I taxpayer who is wholly employed abroad, however, such expenses (and reimbursements) will not be excluded from tax under the usual rules of Schedule E (because they will not be 'necessarily incurred' in the performance of the employment duties). TA 1988 ss 193–194 therefore provide that he can deduct his costs of travelling to and from the UK to take up or leave the employment. If the expenses of board and lodging incurred in carrying out the duties abroad are paid or reimbursed by the employer, the employee will be entitled to a deduction so that those payments will not be emoluments. In addition, where he spends 60 or more continuous days outside the UK, the expenses of travel of his spouse and children under 18 are not taxable if met by his employer (limited to two trips in each year of assessment). Any number of other journeys made by the employee between the place of work and the UK can be paid for by the employer without such payments being taxed as emoluments (though notice that the employee cannot deduct the costs of such journeys where he pays for them).

Finally, the travelling expenses that are available to expatriate (ie non-UK domiciled) employees working in the UK broadly mirror the provisions discussed above for UK residents who work abroad. Accordingly, so long as the employer bears the cost of (any number of) journeys undertaken between the employee's usual place of abode and the UK such sums will not be taxed as emoluments and there are similar provisions to those already discussed for visits by spouses and children. Notice, however, that the reliefs for expatriates are limited to a period of five years from the date of his arrival in the UK (TA 1988 s 195). **[13.48]**

f) *Foreign pensions and annuities*

Foreign pensions and annuities are taxed under Schedule D Case V on 90% of the income arising (TA 1988 s 65(2)). However, such income will be taxable under Schedule E if it is payable in the UK through a department or agent of a Commonwealth government. **[13.49]**

g) *Collection of tax*

Tax on Schedule E emoluments is generally collected at source from the employer under the PAYE system (TA 1988 s 203 and see Chapter 5). Accordingly where an employer is resident in the UK he must as a general rule operate PAYE in respect of all his employees assessable under Schedule E, except for those entitled to a 100% deduction when emoluments can be paid gross.

The application of TA 1988 s 203 to a non resident employer, whose employees were assessable under Schedule E, was considered in *Clark v Oceanic Contractors Inc* (1983). In that case a non resident company made payments abroad to employees engaged in performing duties in the UK sector of the North Sea and so within the UK for the purpose of liability under Schedule E (TA 1988 s 830(5)). The House of Lords held that s 203 applied to the employer company so that it should have operated PAYE in respect of the payments. When employees are assessable under Schedule E, the only limit on the territorial scope of s 203 is whether it can effectively be enforced. It will, therefore, apply to the non resident employer who maintains a 'trading presence' in the UK. This was so in the *Oceanic* case: the company carried on activities in the UK and in the UK sector of the North Sea; was liable to corporation tax on its profits; and had an address for service in the UK.

If Schedule E emoluments are paid overseas by a non-UK resident employer with no trading presence in the UK, it appears therefore that the employer cannot be made to deduct tax under s 203 on making the payments. In these circumstances, the Revenue is empowered to collect the tax from the relevant employees, in four equal instalments, by direct assessment under the 'direct collection' method (TA 1988 s 205 and SI 1993/744).   **[13.50]–[13.70]**

III TAXATION OF THE FOREIGN TAXPAYER

The following general rules apply to an individual who is not resident in the UK:

(1) He is not charged to UK income tax on foreign source income.

(2) So far as *earned income* is concerned, tax is charged on UK pensions and employments where the duties are carried on in the UK (see Schedule E Case II: **[13.73]**). Tax is also charged on the profits of a trade or profession which is not carried on wholly outside the UK (see **[13.72]**).

(3) For *investment income*, with the exception of UK rental income (as to which see **[13.75]**), the general rule is that the tax charge is limited to the tax (if any) deducted at source ('excluded income': see FA 1995 s 128). Note:

   (a) If the taxpayer has other fully taxed UK source income any personal allowances to which he is entitled (as to which, see below) will be first set against excluded income (although not so as to result in any tax refund).

   (b) If, however, the taxpayer is resident in a country with which the UK has a double tax treaty, then he may be entitled to exemption or relief from tax on UK investment income (although not on income from land).

   (c) These rules do not apply to non-resident trustees when a 'relevant beneficiary' (broadly speaking, one who is or may be entitled to income) is ordinarily resident in the UK (FA 1995 s 128(5), (6)).

Non residents are entitled to personal allowances in the circumstances set out in TA 1988 s 278 (as amended by FA 1996). Under that section allowances are given, *inter alia*, to Commonwealth citizens: citizens of a state within the European Economic Area ('EEA') and residents of the Isle of Man or Channel Islands.   **[13.71]**

1   **Profits of a trade, profession or vocation**

As an application of the source doctrine, the foreign taxpayer will be taxable under Schedule D Case I on the profits of any trade carried on *within* as opposed to *with* the UK. For these purposes, however, maintaining an administrative or representative office as opposed to a branch in the UK will not *per se* constitute trading within the UK. The same principle applies to the exercise of a profession or vocation although the exercise of either in the UK would normally render the taxpayer UK resident (TA 1988 s 18(1)(a)(iii)).

The majority of cases in this area have been concerned with the sale of goods by a non-resident to a person in the UK. The courts have tended to say that the trade is carried on in the place where, under English law, the contract is made. This is the place where acceptance of the offer is communicated. In general terms, acceptance by post occurs at the place of posting, whereas acceptance by any other form (eg by telex) occurs at the place where acceptance is received. Accordingly, the non-resident who telexes his acceptance of an order to a UK customer is in danger of trading within the UK, whereas the non-resident who posts his acceptance to such a customer from outside the UK would appear to be merely trading with the UK. However, the place where contracts are made is only one (albeit important) factor to be considered and is of greater significance where the trade consists simply in the purchase and resale of goods. The better test is probably whether the trading operations which give rise to the profits take place in the UK (*Firestone Tyre and Rubber Co Ltd v Lewellin* (1957): see further [**13.35**]). It is likely, for instance, that if land in the UK is acquired, developed and then sold the trade will take place in the UK irrespective of when the contract of resale was entered into.

When a trade is carried on within the UK, the profits are computed under the normal rules for Schedule D Case I. The tax charge is limited to the profits from the part of the trade carried on in the UK measured on an arm's length basis.

When a foreign taxpayer is assessed to tax under Schedule D Case I, the tax can be levied on the branch and agency within the UK through which the trade is being carried on although certain agents, eg independent brokers, are excepted from this provision (FA 1995 ss 126–127, Sch 23 and see *Willson v Hooker* (1995)).

So far as non-resident companies are concerned, even if they are trading within the UK, there will be no liability to UK corporation tax unless that trade is carried on through a branch or agency. If that is not the case the liability will be to income tax at basic rate not corporation tax (TA 1988 s 6(2)(b)). In the latter case, as the company will not have any UK presence, the UK Revenue may be presented with insurmountable problems of tax collection.   [**13.72**]

2   **Employment income**

The foreign taxpayer is assessed under Schedule E Case II on emoluments he receives for duties performed in the UK. Case II, in effect, treats the UK duties as a source of income which would otherwise escape tax completely. If the emoluments are foreign emoluments, some relief from tax may be available in appropriate cases (see [**13.42**]).   [**13.73**]

3   **Non-resident entertainers and sportsmen**

The UK has encountered difficulties (also experienced by other countries) in securing tax payments from non-resident entertainers and sportsmen and women (eg tennis players, golfers, actors and pop stars) who only pay short visits to the country and who have often left before tax can be assessed and collected. Accordingly, a withholding tax was introduced by TA 1988 ss 555–558; SI 1987/530. In general, the payer of the moneys is obliged to make returns to the Revenue at quarterly intervals and to account for basic rate income tax which he should deduct from the payment made to the entertainer. There is a *de minimis* provision which ensures that these rules do not operate if the total payments made in the tax year to an entertainer do not exceed £1,000. **[13.74]**

4 Income from land in the UK (TA 1988 s 42A; SI 1995/2902)

Profits from letting property in the UK are subject to income tax at lower, basic and higher rates as appropriate. With the introduction of self-assessment the rules governing the collection of tax were altered with effect from 6 April 1996:

(1) *Position of the landlord*: A non-resident landlord (including a person whose usual place of abode is outside the UK) can apply to the Financial Intermediaries and Claims Office (FICO) for approval that the rental income can be paid gross. FICO must be satisfied that his tax affairs are up to date; or that he has never had UK tax obligations; or that he does not expect to be subject to UK tax (see further IR booklet 140).

(2) *Position of tenants and agents*: In the absence of any agreement with FICO that the rent should be paid gross a tenant paying rent direct to his landlord should deduct tax at the basic rate and account for that to the Revenue (TA 1988 s 43 applying s 349).

The burden is on the tenant to know the landlord's usual place of abode: if the tenant fails to deduct tax from an instalment of rent the right to deduct is lost and cannot be made good out of later rent payments (*Tenbry Investments Ltd v Peugeot Talbot Motor Co Ltd* (1992)). A repayment to the landlord may be made in the event of the tax deducted exceeding (for instance, because of deductible expenses) the landlord's liability.

In cases where an agent is employed to collect the rent, that agent is responsible for making a tax return and then liable to pay the relevant tax (under TMA 1988 s 78). In appropriate cases allowable deductions will mean that no tax is due.

(3) *Deductible expenses*: Letting agents must pay tax at basic rate on rental income less deductible expenses: by contrast tenants must account for basic rate tax on all rent directly paid to the landlord together with basic rate tax on rental income paid to third parties which is not a deductible expense. In general an expense can only be deducted when the letting agent/tenant can reasonably be satisfied that it is allowable in computing the profits of the landlord's letting business (SI 1995/2902 regs 9(4), 8(2)). Note also that deduction is only permitted if the expense is borne by the tenant/letting agent and not if it is directly paid by the landlord.

(4) *Assessment on the landlord*: The tax deducted at source by a letting agent/tenant will usually not be identical to the landlord's liability so that adjustments will be needed. For instance (as already noted), letting agents cannot deduct expenses paid by the landlord and landlords who are individuals may be subject to the higher rate of income tax whilst discretionary trustees may suffer the additional rate of tax for trusts. A non-resident company is normally subject to income tax at basic rate on its profits from UK lettings.

[13.75]

5 Interest from UK banks and building societies

Interest can be paid gross provided that an appropriate declaration is made that the taxpayer is not ordinarily resident in the UK (TA 1988 s 481(5)(k)). **[13.76]**

6   **UK government securities**

Tax is not chargeable on certain government securities owned by persons not ordinarily resident in the UK ('Free of Tax to Residents Abroad'—FOTRA— securities: FA 1996 s 154, Sch 28).   **[13.77]**

7   **Dividends paid by UK companies**

The general rule is that a non-UK resident is not entitled to a tax credit in respect of a qualifying distribution (TA 1988 s 231(1)). This position is, however, modified in many double tax treaties: see, for instance, *Steele v European Vinyls Corpn (Holdings) BV* (1995). Currently litigation is being mounted by Hoechst and Pirelli SpA on the basis that the tax credit provisions of s 231 contravene the non-discrimination provision and freedom of establishment articles of the EC Treaty. The Hoechst litigation also includes the claim that a UK subsidiary of an EU parent should be entitled to pay dividends gross as is the case if there is a UK parent.

The following example illustrates the operation of treaty relief:

EXAMPLE 13.12

This example shows the effect that the half-ACT refund (provided for, for instance, in the US/UK Treaty) has in relation to the payment of a dividend by UK Co to its American parent out of UK profits of (say) £100,000, assuming that all of the profits will be distributed.

	£
UK subsidiary's profits	100
UK corporation tax at 31%	(31)
Profits available for dividend	69
Dividend	(69)
Profits retained	Nil

UK corporation tax liability discharged by:

ACT paid on dividend (ie 69 × ¼)	17.25
Mainstream corporation tax paid later	13.75
Tax credit for shareholder $\left(\text{ie } 69 \times \dfrac{20}{80} \right)$	17.25

US parent receives:

Cash dividend	69
½ tax credit = 50% of 17.25	8.625
	77.625
Less: 5% withholding on £77.625	3.88
Cash received	£73.745
Effective UK tax rate	26.255%

Changes to take effect in April 1999—in particular the reduction in the credit to 10%—will, in effect, remove the benefit of treaty relief.

[13.78]–**[13.90]**

IV   DOUBLE TAXATION RELIEF

Overseas income may be taxed in its country of origin and if UK tax is also chargeable on the same income, the taxpayer is entitled to relief in one of three ways.

First, the UK has a number of double taxation agreements (treaties) with foreign countries. They differ in details, but generally provide that certain categories of income will be taxed in only one of the countries concerned (usually where the taxpayer is resident). Other income will be taxable in both countries, but with a credit for one amount of tax against the other.

Secondly, if there is no treaty in force, 'unilateral relief' is given under TA 1988 s 790. This takes the form of a credit against the UK tax equal to the foreign tax paid (see SP 7/91). Whereas a double tax treaty specifies the taxes which are covered by the agreement, s 790 relief is limited to taxes which are similar to UK taxes against which the relief is claimed (see, for instance, *Yates v GCA International Ltd* (1991) and SP 7/91).

Thirdly, if neither of the above applies, unilateral relief may be given under TA 1988 s 811 by way of deduction (from the foreign income which is assessable to UK tax) of the amount of foreign tax paid. Relief by deduction is less advantageous to the taxpayer than relief by credit.   **[13.91]–[13.110]**

V   ANTI-AVOIDANCE LEGISLATION: TRANSFER OF ASSETS ABROAD (TA 1988 ss 739–746)

1   **General**

a) *The mischief*

A person who is neither resident nor ordinarily resident in the UK cannot be assessed to UK income tax on income which arises from a source outside the UK. Accordingly, an individual resident in the UK could seek to avoid UK income tax by transferring income-producing assets to a non-UK resident who is not subject to UK income tax. The relevant wording in TA 1988 s 739(1) is as follows:

> '. . . the following provisions of this section shall have effect for the purpose of preventing the avoiding by individuals ordinarily resident in the United Kingdom of liability to income tax by means of transfer of assets by virtue or in consequence of which, either alone or in conjunction with associated operations, income becomes payable to persons resident or domiciled outside the United Kingdom.'

EXAMPLE 13.13

(1)   Toby, a UK resident, owns land in Barbados which produces a substantial income. He transfers it to a non-UK resident company in return for an allotment of shares and is subsequently loaned money by the directors of that company.

(2)   Toby also owns shares in a German company which he transfers to a non-UK resident trust. As one of the beneficiaries he is then advanced capital by the trustees.

To prevent such arrangements, TA 1988 s 739 provides that if an individual who is ordinarily resident in the UK transfers assets so that as a result of that transfer, or of associated operations, income becomes payable to any person resident or domiciled outside the UK and the transferor has either power to enjoy that income (TA 1988 s 739(2)) or receives a capital sum (TA 1988 s 739(3)), the income of the non-UK resident is taxed as that of the transferor under Schedule D Case VI. The scope of the legislation (formerly TA 1970 s 478) was restricted as a result of the House of Lords decision in *Vestey v IRC* (1980) to the original transferor of the assets or his spouse. As a result, fresh legislation (now s 740) was introduced to 'fill the gaps'.   **[13.111]**

b) 'Individuals ordinarily resident in the UK'

The Revenue always argued that the legislation was capable of applying even if the transfer occurred at a time when the individual was not ordinarily resident in the UK. In *IRC v Willoughby* (1997), however, the House of Lords held that the section could not apply if the transferor was non-UK resident when he made the transfer. Giving the House of Lords judgment, Lord Nolan concluded that:

> 'The crucial words, as it seems to me, are those in sub-s (1) which state that the section is to 'have effect for the purpose of preventing the avoiding by individuals ordinarily resident in the United Kingdom of liability to income tax by means of transfer of assets', coupled with the identification, in sub-s (2), of 'such an individual' as the subject of lability. What can the words 'such an individual' refer to save for an individual of the kind described in sub-s (1), that is an individual ordinarily resident in the United Kingdom seeking to avoid liability by means of transfers of assets? Although the point was not determined in *Vestey*, the view there taken that the individual to be charged must be the individual who made the transfer seems to me to lead inevitably to the conclusion that the individual concerned must be the only type of transferor with which the section is concerned, and that is a transferor ordinarily resident in the United Kingdom. At the risk of seeming over-confident in expressing an opinion about language which has been constructed in diametrically opposite senses by your Lordships' House in the past, I woud say in the light of *Vestey* that this is the natural and plain meaning of the words used.
>
> I accept that in consequence the immigrant tax avoider who makes his dispositions before taking up residence in this country would escape liability under the section. I would for my part find it fruitless to speculate whether this consequence was foreseen and accepted, or arose through inadvertence. I would not, in any event, regard it as sufficiently astonishing in itself to cast doubt on what I have described as the natural meaning of the words used . . .'

Even before the House of Lords judgment the law was changed by FA 1997 s 81 in respect of income arising on or after 26 November 1996 irrespective of when the transfer took place: as a result the section now applies irrespective of the residence of the transferor at the time of the transfer.   **[13.112]**

c) Motive

An individual will avoid liability under these sections if he can prove *either* that the transfer or associated operation was not made for the purpose of avoiding any tax (s 741(a)) *or* that it was a *bona fide* commercial transaction the purpose of which was not to avoid tax (s 741(b)). There is no clearance procedure and the onus of proof is on the taxpayer. In *IRC v Willoughby* (1997) the court accepted that if the overall objective was not tax avoidance the motive defence could apply even if the objective was achieved in a tax efficient manner. In the course of rejecting the Revenue's submission that a tax avoidance motive must attach to an investor who invested in a personal portfolio bond with a non resident life office, Lord Nolan commented:

> 'it would be absurd in the context of s 741 to describe as tax avoidance the acceptance of an offer of freedom from tax which Parliament has deliberately made. Tax avoidance within the meaning of s 741 is a course of action designed to conflict with or defeat the evident intention of Parliament'

If a motive of the taxpayer is to avoid any UK tax, the defence will not apply: by contrast, avoiding foreign tax falls within the *bona fide* commercial transaction defence! (*IRC v Herdman* (1969)) and, putting the matter beyond doubt, FA 1997 s 81 inserting new s 739(1A)(b).   **[13.113]**

2 Liability of the transferor (TA 1988 s 739)

a) *General*

Two factors are essential to the operation of s 739.

First, there must be a transfer of assets by an individual. This means a transfer of property or rights of any kind but also includes the creation of those rights so that the incorporation of a company or formation of a partnership may be caught. In *IRC v Brackett* (1986), the taxpayer, by entering into a contract of employment with a Jersey company, fell within the section since rights created under that contract were assets and, as 'transfer' included the creation of rights, those assets were transferred to a non-UK resident person. The assets need not be situated in the UK.

Secondly, as a result of the transfer, either alone or together with associated operations, income must become payable to a non-UK resident or non-UK domiciled person. The person to whom the income becomes payable need not be non-resident at the time of transfer (*Congreve v IRC* (1948)). 'Person' includes a corporation and, for these purposes, a corporation incorporated outside the UK is always considered non-resident (TA 1988 s 742(8); the UK does not include the Channel Islands or Isle of Man).

'Associated operations' is widely defined in s 742(1) and case law. Basically, any operation (except death) which is carried out by any person (not necessarily the transferor) is capable of being an associated operation, provided only that, together with the transfer, it results in income becoming payable in accordance with the section (for a case where this did not happen see *Fynn v IRC* (1958)). Whether the operation has this result is judged objectively without regard to the intention of the person effecting the operation.

EXAMPLE 13.14

(1) Sam settles overseas property on a UK trust. Subsequently overseas trustees are appointed so that the trust becomes non-UK resident. Income produced in the trust may be taxed as Sam's under s 739.

(2) A transfers assets to a company resident in the UK. Subsequently it becomes non-UK resident and receives income from the assets which A has the power to enjoy. The removal of the company overseas is an associated operation which may trigger s 739 (*Congreve v IRC* (1948)). Thus, an otherwise innocent transaction may be brought within the section.

(3) A transfers assets to a UK resident company, B Ltd, in consideration for an allotment of shares. Some years later B Ltd sells the assets to a non-resident company, C Ltd, in return for shares in C Ltd. The transfer by B Ltd to C Ltd is associated with the transfer of assets from A to B Ltd although the operations were not contemplated as part of a single scheme at the time of the transfer (*Corbett's Executrices v IRC* (1943)).

(4) A sells foreign investments to an overseas company in return for shares in that company. He makes a will leaving his residuary estate (which includes the shares) to his daughter. The making of the will, although not the death, is an operation associated with the transfer of the assets abroad. Hence, on the death of A the daughter becomes entitled to dividends on those shares and falls (today) within s 740 (cp *Bambridge v IRC* (1955)).

If there has been a transfer of assets resulting in income becoming payable to a non-UK resident, s 739 may then apply if the transferor has the power to enjoy the income (s 739(2)) *or* receives or is entitled to receive a capital sum (s 739(3)).   **[13.114]**

b) *Section 739(2)*

Section 739(2) will only apply if, given that the above conditions are satisfied, an individual ordinarily resident in the UK has 'power to enjoy the income of a person resident or domiciled outside the UK'. The income caught by the section need not be derived directly from the assets transferred, but the power of enjoyment must be held by the transferor or his spouse (*Vestey v IRC* (1980); TA 1988 s 742(9)(a)). An individual has the power to enjoy income if any of the five circumstances in s 742(2) are satisfied. Generally, they apply to any situation whereby the transferor receives, or is entitled to receive, any benefit in any form from the income:

(1) Where he receives a benefit (including a payment in kind) from the use of the income by any person.

EXAMPLE 13.15

A non-resident company uses its income profits to redeem the debentures of a UK resident individual. The capital received is a benefit within (1) because it results from a use of the income (*Latilla v IRC* (1943)).

(2) Where assets that he holds, or which are held for him, increase in value as a result of the income becoming payable to the non-UK resident.

EXAMPLE 13.16

(a) X Ltd, a non-resident company, is in debt to A, a UK resident. When income becomes payable to X Ltd, A's *chose in action* (the debt) increases in value (unless X Ltd had sufficient funds to repay the debt) because X Ltd is more likely to be able to honour its obligations (*Lord Howard de Walden v IRC* (1942)).

(b) As in (a) save that A also owned shares in X Ltd which he transferred to a discretionary trust for the benefit of himself and his family. The section applies because the value of the shares is increased and they are assets held for his benefit.

(3) Where he directly receives, or is entitled to receive, a benefit from the income or the assets representing the income.

EXAMPLE 13.17

(a) C, a UK resident transferor, holds 90% of the issued shares of a non-UK resident company, B Ltd, which gives him the right to a dividend when declared. C is entitled to receive a benefit within (3) (*Lee v IRC* (1941)). Similarly, if, after he has transferred his shares, the directors make a gift to him, C has then received a benefit and it does not matter that the directors were acting *ultra vires*.

(b) Trustees of a non-UK resident trust exercise their discretion to pay income to a UK resident settlor B. B has received a benefit within (3) above.

(4) Where he is a member of a class of discretionary beneficiaries who may become entitled to some of the income as a result of the exercise of a power by any person. Even if the power is never exercised so that the transferor never benefits, he is within (4). Thus, in *Example 13.17(b)*, B has power to enjoy the income whether or not he receives a benefit. This

paragraph also catches the revocable settlement and settlements where trustees have power to appoint absolute or income interests back to the settlor.

(5) Where he can control the application of the income in any way, not necessarily for his own benefit. This does not include a right to direct the investments nor a power of appointment which is concerned with capital rather than income payments (*Lord Vestey's Executors v IRC* (1949)). Thus in *Example 13.17(a)* C has power to enjoy B Ltd's income through his ability to replace the existing directors by virtue of his 90% shareholding (contrast the power to appoint trustees; *IRC v Schroder* (1983)).

When applying these tests regard must be had to the overall effect of the transfer and anything to do with it (TA 1988 s 742(3)).   **[13.115]**

c) *Section 739(3)*

Section 739(3) applies where, in connection with a transfer of assets abroad, the transferor or his spouse receives or is entitled to receive a capital sum, whether before or after the relevant transfer. 'Capital sum' is defined as a sum paid or payable by way of loan; or any sum (not being income) which is paid or payable otherwise than for full consideration in money or money's worth.   **[13.116]**

EXAMPLE 13.18

B, a UK resident, who has transferred income-producing assets to a non-UK resident trust, has power to direct the investments of the trust. He authorises a loan to be made to his son. B falls within s 739(3).

d) *Computation of the income chargeable under TA 1988 s 739(2) and (3)*

When a transferor is caught by s 739(2), he can be assessed to income tax under Schedule D Case VI on the whole of the non-resident's income from any source, not just the income which he has the power to enjoy or the income arising from the assets which he transferred (this aspect of *Congreve v IRC* (1948) was not apparently overruled by the House of Lords in *Vestey v IRC* (1980)).

If s 739(3) applies the transferor can only be assessed on the income arising as a result of the transfer of assets. The assessment is not limited to the amount of the capital sum, however, and includes income arising in the year when the capital sum was paid or payable and *all* such income arising thereafter (see *Private Client Business*, 1995, p 209).

Should the Revenue assess both the transferor and his spouse under either subsection, they cannot tax the same income twice (TA 1988 s 744(1)), but must charge it in such proportions as they consider 'just and reasonable'.

In computing the income of the non-resident which is chargeable under s 739(2) or (3), the transferor is only entitled to such deductions and reliefs as he would have been allowed had he, and not the non-resident, actually received the income (see *Lord Chetwode v IRC* (1977); management charges of a non-resident company were not deductible by a UK resident individual, and see TA 1988 s 743(2)). If, however, the income has already suffered basic rate tax, this will not be collected again from the UK resident (TA 1988 s 743). Section 743(3) provides that a non-UK domiciliary is not chargeable 'in respect of any income . . . if he would not, by reason of his being so domiciled, have been chargeable to tax in respect of it if it had in fact been his income'. The wording may be tortuous in the extreme: the effect, however, is to preserve the remittance basis in full.   **[13.117]**

3   Liability of non-transferors: s 740

This provision was designed to fill the gaps in the legislation revealed by the *Vestey* case. The section has effect where:

'(a) By virtue or in consequence of a transfer of assets, either alone or in conjunction with associated operations, income becomes payable to a person resident or domiciled outside the UK; and

(b) An individual ordinarily resident in the UK who is not liable to tax under s 739 by reference to the transfer receives a benefit provided out of assets which are available for the purpose by virtue or in consequence of the transfer or of any associated operations' (s 740(1)).

The important limitation in s 740 is that such an individual is only assessed to income tax under Schedule D Case VI *to the extent of any benefit that he receives*. It should be realised therefore that the section leaves open planning opportunities. An overseas settlement (from which the settlor and any spouse are excluded) and in which the income is accumulated will be free from UK income tax unless and until benefits are conferred under s 740 (at the very least therefore there will be a deferment in UK tax). The term 'benefit' is not defined except only that it includes a payment of any kind (TA 1988 s 742(9)). A cash advance or the transfer of an asset *in specie* will be caught and the Inland Revenue also considers that the free use of property constitutes a benefit. In general, tax is charged even if the benefit is received and kept abroad. This is subject to limited protection for non-domiciliaries under TA 1988 s 740(5). Broadly speaking, the benefit will remain taxable in such cases unless, *first*, it is received outside the UK and, *second*, all the relevant income is foreign source income which has not been remitted to the UK. If some of the relevant income is UK source income or is remitted then the benefit is taxable to the extent of such income.

The benefit is taxed under Schedule D Case VI as the income of the UK resident in the year of receipt to the extent that it does not exceed the 'relevant income' of the non-resident in the tax years up to and including the year when the benefit is paid. Insofar as it exceeds the relevant income of those years, any excess is carried forward and set against the first available relevant income of future years until it is finally absorbed. The tax charge cannot be relieved by double tax relief.

'Relevant income' means, in relation to an individual, income arising in any year of assessment to the non-resident and which, as a result of the transfer of assets, can be used to provide a benefit to that individual (s 740(3)).

The same income cannot be charged to tax twice (s 744). Therefore, where several beneficiaries receive benefits, the relevant income is allocated amongst them by the Revenue in such proportions as may be just and reasonable. The taxpayer may appeal against the apportionment to the Special Commissioners.

EXAMPLE 13.19

A non-resident discretionary trust has relevant income in three consecutive years of £6,000, £6,000 and £12,000 respectively. It makes payments to two UK resident beneficiaries in *Year* 2. It is assumed that the apportionment provisions would be applied pro rata and not according to the order in which the payments are made.
     The benefits are taxed as follows:

	A £	B £
Year 1		
Benefits paid	Nil	Nil
Relevant income £6,000 (unapportioned)		
	A	B

		£	£
Year 2			
Benefits		6,000	12,000
Relevant income	£6,000		
Plus income brought forward	£6,000		
	£12,000 apportioned	4,000	8,000
Untaxed benefit carried forward		2,000	4,000
Year 3			
Benefits paid		Nil	Nil
Relevant income	£12,000		
	£6,000 apportioned	2,000	4,000
Relevant income carried forward	£6,000	Nil	Nil

In *Year 2* A and B are assessed to income tax under Case VI on £4,000 and £8,000 of their respective benefits. The balance is assessed in *Year 3*.

If the benefit is of a capital nature and results from a capital gain made by the non-resident, the same sum is not charged to both income tax under s 740 and CGT under TCGA 1992 s 87. To the extent that the benefit exceeds relevant income it is charged to CGT, in which case, it cannot be treated as income in a subsequent year under s 740 (TA 1988 s 740(6). **[13.118]**

4 Powers of the Revenue to obtain information (TA 1988 s 745)

The Revenue has wide investigatory powers for the purposes of these sections which are exercisable against a taxpayer, and also against his advisers. They can demand, at 28 days' notice, such particulars as they deem necessary.

A solicitor is exempted from these powers in that he can only be compelled to state that he was acting on his client's behalf and to give the client's name and address. However, he is only exempt to the extent that he is acting *qua* solicitor. Thus, where he acts, eg as a tax consultant, he may not be able to claim the exemption.

A bank is also exempted from providing details of ordinary banking transactions (s 745(5)), except to the extent that it has acted for a customer in connection with either the formation and management of a non-resident company which would be close if resident in the UK and is not a trading company, or the creation or execution of a trust which may be used for schemes under these provisions. The banks' exemption has been narrowly construed in *Royal Bank of Canada v IRC* (1972) and in *Clinch v IRC* (1973) where a 'fishing expedition' was upheld in the courts. Other advisers, eg barristers and accountants, have no exemption from s 745. **[13.119]**

5 Reform

A joint working group of the Revenue and professional experts has been set up to review the whole of the legislation on the transfer of assets abroad. **[13.120]**

Section 3   Capital gains tax

Chapters

14 CGT—basic principles

'It is impossible to draw an unambiguous distinction between "capital" gains and "income" gains and the attempt to do so necessarily results in great uncertainty for the taxpayer because a particular transaction may or may not be found by the courts to fall on one side of the line or the other' (Carter Commission, Canada, 1966).

[**14.1**]

I INTRODUCTION

1 Background

Capital gains tax (CGT) was introduced in the Finance Act 1965 and was first consolidated in the Capital Gains Tax Act 1979 (CGTA 1979) and, more recently, in the Taxation of Chargeable Gains Act 1992 (TCGA 1992). It was largely introduced to tax profits left untaxed by income tax. Income tax, in the much quoted dictum of Lord Macnaghten, was and is a tax on income. Thus, it does not tax the profit made on a disposal of a capital asset. However, since 1965, the taxpayer has been charged to CGT on his gain after deducting any available exemptions and reliefs.

As the then Chancellor of the Exchequer, Mr James Callaghan, in his 1965 Budget speech introducing CGT, explained:

'Yield is not my main purpose ... The failure to tax capital gains is ... the greatest blot on our system of direct taxation. There is little dispute nowadays that capital gains confer much the same kind of benefit on the recipient as taxed earnings more hardly won. Yet earnings pay tax in full while capital gains go free ... This new tax will provide a background of equity and fair play ...'

[**14.2**]

a) *Overlap with income tax*

CGT aims to tax only what is untaxed by income tax and, normally, there will be no CGT on a transaction that is chargeable to income tax. Hence, in the case of certain transactions which might attract both taxes, CGT is chargeable on only so much of the transaction as is not charged to income tax, as, for instance, on the purchase and sale of assets which qualify for capital

245

allowances (see [**35.65**]) and the grant of leases at a premium where part of the premium is assessable to income tax under Schedule A (see [**8.81**]).

There is, however, no general rule against double taxation that prevents the same sum from being subject to two different taxes and in *Bye v Coren* (1986) Scott J (whose judgment was upheld in the Court of Appeal) held that 'whether it is so subject is a matter of construction of the statute or statutes which have imposed the taxes'. TCGA 1992 s 37 will provide relief in most cases since it states that once an income tax assessment has become final in respect of a sum of money the same person cannot be subject to a CGT assessment on that same sum. There is, of course, nothing to prevent the Revenue from raising alternative assessments (eg to income tax and CGT) on the same sum of money (*Bye v Coren*, above and *IRC v Wilkinson* (1992)).   [**14.3**]

b) *The changing face of CGT*

The scope of the tax has fluctuated since its introduction in 1965. The charge on death was removed in 1971 and criticism that the tax was levied on inflationary gains was largely removed by the introduction of an indexation allowance in 1982 and by the rebasing of the tax to 1982 (introduced in FA 1988). This trend towards limiting the scope of the tax was, however, reversed by changes made in FA 1989. These concerned lifetime gifts where the position from 1980 had been that in most cases tax could be postponed by the exercise of a hold-over election (provided for in FA 1980 s 79 as subsequently amended). From 14 March 1989 it has only been possible to make such an election in a limited number of cases (see Chapter 17). As a result, CGT may be charged on a sale of assets which have increased in value by more than the rate of inflation and on a gift of assets where hold-over relief is not available (subject to the value of the asset having increased in the hands of the donor by more than the rate of inflation over his period of ownership). The curious position is therefore that a tax aimed at catching profits may now apply to gifts (deemed profits) whereas the tax intended to catch all gifts (CTT now IHT) will only apply to lifetime gifts which are not potentially exempt or which are made in the period of seven years before the death of the donor!

The yield from CGT represents a mere 0.9% of the total revenue raised in direct taxes. In his 1984 Budget Speech the Rt Hon Nigel Lawson MP acknowledged the 'unfairness and complexity' of the CGT legislation. In his 1985 Budget Speech he declared that the right way to reform the tax was to improve the indexation allowance thereby ensuring that a charge was levied only on real and not inflationary gains. As a result of a number of improvements which he then introduced he felt able to conclude that 'the tax is now on a broadly acceptable and sustainable basis'. Three years later, his views had altered, and a further reform (rebasing the tax from 1982 instead of 1965) was introduced in FA 1988 to remedy the 'manifest injustice' of taxing 'paper profits resulting from the rampant inflation of the 1970s'. It is unfortunate that this apparently elusive quest for justice and fairness always involves further complications to this already over complex tax. The process continues, however, with Gordon Brown announcing in his first Budget (on 2 July 1997) that 'our consultations on capital gains tax will be completed in time for the next Budget'.
                                                                          [**14.4**]

2 **Basic principles**

CGT is charged on any gain resulting when a chargeable person makes a chargeable disposal of a chargeable asset. Tax is charged on so much of the gain as is left after taking into account any exemptions or reliefs and after deducting any allowable losses. The tax is payable on 31 January following the year of assessment (which is on a current year basis: TCGA 1992 s 7). It is, therefore, sensible to make disposals early in a tax year in order to achieve the greatest delay in the payment of tax.

The tax was introduced in 1965 and was not retrospective. Accordingly, it has only taxed gains arising after 6 April in that year. Thus, where an individual acquired an asset in 1960 for £10,000 and sold it in 1970 for £20,000, thereby making a gain of £10,000, only such part of the gain as accrued after 6 April 1965 was charged (see [**14.33**]). For assets owned on 31 March 1982 and disposed of after 5 April 1988, the chargeable gain may be computed on the basis that the asset in question had been acquired in March 1982 at its then market value. This rebasing of the tax is discussed in detail at [**14.34**] and means that gains from 1965 to 1982 have now been removed from the tax charge. [**14.5**]

a) *Who is a chargeable person? (TCGA 1992 s 2)*

Chargeable persons include individuals who are resident or ordinarily resident in the UK; trustees, personal representatives and partners. In the case of partners, each partner is charged separately in respect of his share of the partnership gains (TCGA 1992 s 59, see Chapter 31). Although companies are not chargeable persons for CGT purposes, the corporation tax to which they are subject is levied on corporate profits which include chargeable gains (see [**28.22**]). It should be noted that non-residents are—in general—not taxed on a disposal of UK *situs* assets. [**14.6**]

b) *What is a chargeable asset? (TCGA 1992 s 21(1))*

A number of assets are not chargeable to CGT and the gain on the disposal of certain other assets is exempt from charge (for details see Chapter 16). Apart from these exclusions, however, all forms of property are assets for CGT purposes including options, debts, incorporeal property, any currency (other than sterling), milk quota (*Cottle v Coldicott* (1995)) and property that is created by the person disposing of it (eg goodwill which is built up from nothing by a trader). An asset which cannot be transferred by sale or gift may be within the definition.

In *O'Brien v Benson's Hosiery (Holdings) Ltd* (1979), for instance, a director under a seven-year service contract paid his employer £50,000 to be released from his obligations under the contract. The employer was charged to CGT on the basis that the contract, despite being non-assignable, was an asset under s 21(1) so that the release of those rights resulted in 'a capital sum being received in return for the forfeiture or surrender of rights' (TCGA 1992 s 22(1)(c); see further [**14.112**]).

In *Marren v Ingles* (1980) shares in a private company were sold for £750 per share, payable at the time of the sale, plus a further sum if the company obtained a Stock Exchange quotation and the market value of the shares at that time was in excess of £750 per share. Two years later a quotation was obtained and a further £2,825 per share was paid. The House of Lords held that the taxpayers were liable to CGT calculated on the original sale price of £750 per share plus the value of the contingent right to receive a further sum (their Lordships did not attempt to put a value on it; was it nominal?). That right was a *chose in action* (a separate asset) which was disposed of for £2,825 per share two years later, leading to a further CGT liability (see further [**14.26**]).

A 'right' may be used in both a colloquial and a legal sense. In its wider colloquial sense a right is not an asset for CGT purposes: it must be legally enforceable and capable of being turned into money. In *Kirby v Thorn EMI plc* (1988) the Revenue initially argued that the right to engage in commercial activity was an asset for CGT purposes with the result that if the taxpayers agreed to restrict their commercial activities in return for a capital payment, that sum would be brought into charge to tax. This argument was rejected on the basis that freedom to indulge in commercial activity was not a legal right constituting an asset for CGT purposes. On appeal, the Revenue produced an alternative argument that the taxpayers had derived a capital sum from the firm's goodwill and that therefore the payment in question was chargeable to CGT. In this argument they were successful.   [**14.7**]

c) *What is a chargeable disposal?*

This topic is considered at [**14.111**]ff. 'Disposal' is extended to include cases where a capital sum is derived from an asset (for instance, insurance money paid for the damage or destruction of an asset).   [**14.8**]-[**14.20**]

II   CALCULATION OF THE GAIN

The gain on which CGT is chargeable is found by taking the disposal consideration of the asset and deducting from that figure allowable expenditure (often called the '*base cost*'). The disponer's acquisition cost is usually the main item of expenditure. If the allowable expenditure exceeds the disposal consideration, the disponer has made a loss for CGT purposes which may be used to reduce the gains that he has made on disposals of other assets (see [**14.61**]).

> **EXAMPLE 14.1**
>
> A sells a painting for £20,000 (the disposal consideration). He bought it six months ago for £14,000 (the acquisition cost) and has incurred no other deductible expenses. His chargeable gain is £6,000. If A sold the picture for £10,000 he would have an allowable loss of £4,000.

Inevitably, the calculation of disposal consideration and allowable expenditure is not always as simple as in the above example and the onus is on the taxpayer to establish what (if any) part of the disposal consideration is not within the charge to CGT (see *Neely v Rourke* (1987)).   [**14.21**]

1   **What is the consideration for the disposal?**

a) *General*

Where the disposal is by way of a sale at arm's length, the consideration for the disposal will be the proceeds of sale. For disposals between husband and wife the disposal consideration is deemed to be of such a sum that neither gain nor loss results (TCGA 1992 s 58: a 'no gain/no loss' disposal), irrespective of the actual consideration given.

Where the disposal is not at arm's length, however, the consideration for the disposal is taken to be the market value of the asset at that date. This applies to gifts, to disposals between 'connected persons' (where the disposal is always *deemed* to be otherwise than by bargain at arm's length), to transfers of assets by a settlor into a settlement and to certain distributions by a company in respect of shares (TCGA 1992 s 17(1)(a)). Also, in the case of disposals by excluded persons who are exempt from CGT (including charities, friendly societies, approved pension funds, and non-residents) the recipient is taken to acquire the asset at market value.

EXAMPLE 14.2

(1) Sarah gives her husband a Richard Eurich painting for which she had paid £10,000. He acquires the picture for such sum as ensures neither gain nor loss results to Sarah, ie for £10,000 plus an indexation allowance to the date of the gift (note that when he subsequently sells the painting this allowance cannot be used to create a loss; see further [**14.32**]).

(2) A gives a Ming vase worth £40,000 to the milkman. The consideration for the disposal is taken to be £40,000. If, instead, A sold the vase to his son B for £10,000 (or, indeed, for £60,000), B is a 'connected person' and the consideration for the disposal is taken to be £40,000.

(3) In 1997, A, a resident of Peru, gives a house in Mayfair worth £150,000 and which he had acquired in 1989 for £20,000 to his son B who is a UK resident. A is not chargeable to CGT on his gain of £130,000 because he is an excluded person and B acquires the property at a base value of £150,000.

The market value of the asset is taken to be the disposal consideration whenever the actual consideration cannot be valued or the consideration is services (TCGA 1992 s 17(1)(b)).

EXAMPLE 14.3

A, an antiques dealer, gives B, a fellow dealer, his country cottage worth £40,000 in consideration of B entering into a restrictive covenant with A, whereby he (B) agrees not to open an antique shop in competition with A. The consideration for the disposal is taken to be £40,000.

This market value rule can work to a taxpayer's advantage by giving the recipient a high acquisition cost for any future disposal in a transaction where the disponer is not charged to CGT on the gain (known as 'reverse Nairn Williamson' arrangements). To some extent this is prevented by TCGA 1992 s 17(2) which provides that, where there is an acquisition without a disposal (eg the issue of shares by a company) and either no consideration is given for the asset, or the consideration is less than its market value, the actual consideration (if any) given prevails.   [**14.22**]

EXAMPLE 14.4

A Ltd issues 1,000 £1 ordinary shares to B at par when their market value is £2 per share. The issue of shares by a company is not a disposal. This is, therefore, an acquisition of a chargeable asset by B without a disposal. Were it not for s 17(2), B's acquisition cost of the shares would be £2,000. As it is, B's acquisition cost is what he actually paid for the shares: ie £1,000.

b) *Connected persons*

'Connected persons' for CGT purposes fall into four categories (TCGA 1992 s 286).

(1) An individual is connected with his spouse, his or her relatives and their spouses. Relatives include siblings, direct ancestors (parents, grandparents), and lineal descendants (children, grandchildren) but not lateral relatives (uncles, aunts, nephews and nieces). Marriage continues for the purpose of this provision until final divorce (see *Aspden v Hildesley* (1982)).

(2) A company is connected with another company if both are under common control. A company is connected with another person if he (either alone or with other persons connected with him) controls that company.

(3) A partner is connected with a fellow partner and his spouse and their

relatives except in relation to acquisitions and disposals of partnership assets under *bona fide* commercial arrangements (eg where a new partner is given a share of the assets).

(4) A trustee is connected with the settlor, any person connected with the settlor and any close company in which the trustee or any beneficiary under the settlement is a participator (for the definition of close company and participator see Chapter 28). He is not connected with a beneficiary as such and once the settlor dies ceases to be connected with persons connected with the settlor.   [14.23]

EXAMPLE 14.5

A would like to 'unlock' the unrealised losses which apply to a number of his assets. He disposes of such assets into a trust in which he enjoys a life interest. The result is to crystallise the loss but, because of the connected persons rule, that loss will only be available against gains on disposals between the same parties. Accordingly, A disposes of assets showing a gain to the same trustees. Now the loss can be offset against that gain and, if those assets are immediately sold by the trustees, no chargeable gain will result to them. The settlement may contain a power for the trustees to return the assets to A.

c) *The market value of assets*

Market value is the price for which the asset could be sold on the open market with no reduction for the fact that this may involve assuming that several assets are to be sold at the same time (TCGA 1992 s 272).

The market value of shares and securities listed in The Stock Exchange Daily Official List is taken as the lesser of:

(1) the lower of the two prices quoted for that security in the Daily Official List, plus 1/4 of the difference between the two prices ('quarter-up');

(2) half way between the highest and lowest prices at which bargains were recorded in that security on the relevant date excluding bargains at special prices ('mid-price').

Unquoted shares and securities are valued on a number of criteria including the size of the holding and, therefore, the degree of control of the company.

CGTA 1979 s 151 modified the market value rule in cases where a person acquired assets by a series of transactions from one or more connected persons. It imposed a charge upon the transferor(s) in cases where the value of all the assets transferred was greater when aggregated than when considered separately. This provision proved unsatisfactory (see [1985] STI 3) and was replaced by (now) TCGA 1992 s 19 which applies when assets are fragmented (ie when one transferor makes two or more transfers to connected persons and the transfers occur within six years of each other).

EXAMPLE 14.6

Alf owned a pair of Ming vases which as a pair were worth £100,000 but separately each was worth only £40,000. In January 1997 he gave one to his daughter and in the following July the other to his son.

(1) The disposal to his daughter was for an original market value of £40,000. However, as it is linked to the later disposal to his son the assets disposed of by the two disposals are valued as if they were disposed of by one disposal and the value attributed to each disposal is the appropriate proportion of that value. The market value of both vases is £100,000 and the appropriate proportion is £50,000. (Notice that this revaluation of an earlier transaction will lead to an adjusted CGT assessment.)

(2) The later disposal, occurring within six years, is a linked transaction. Again

the original market value (£40,000) is replaced by the appropriate proportion (£50,000).

(3) Compare the CGT rules on a disposal of sets of chattels (see [**16.23**]) and the IHT associated operations provisions (see [**21.81**]).

(4) With the removal of general hold-over relief in the case of disposals by way of gift these rules are of increased importance. Presumably hold-over relief may continue to apply in the case of earlier disposals (pre the 1989 changes) where the consideration has to be revalued because of a subsequent linked transaction.

Disposals to a spouse are treated as giving rise to neither gain nor loss (TCGA 1992 s 58: [**14.22**]) but may form part of a series in order to determine the value of any of the other transactions in that series. [**14.24**]

d) *Deferred consideration*

Where the consideration for the disposal is known at the date of the disposal (which will normally be the date of contract: TCGA 1992 s 28) but is payable in instalments (TCGA 1992 s 280) or is subject to a contingency (s 48), the disponer is taxed on a gain calculated by reference to the full amount of the consideration receivable with no discount for the fact that payment is postponed. If, in fact, he never receives the full consideration his original CGT assessment is adjusted. [**14.25**]

EXAMPLE 14.7

(1) A bought land five years ago for £50,000. He sells it today for £100,000 payable in two years' time. A is taxed now on a gain of £50,000 despite the fact that he has received nothing and with no discount for the fact that the right to £100,000 in two years' time is not worth £100,000 today. If A had been 'connected' with his purchaser market value would be substituted for the actual consideration under s 17 thereby enabling a 'discount' to be taken into account. (For the CGT position when the purchase price is paid in instalments, see [**14.93**].)

(2) Mucky sells four oil rigs for a consideration of $38.6m payable by instalments over nine years. At exchange rates prevailing at the date of disposal this produced a gain of £6.7m. Taking rates at the time when each instalment was paid, however, Mucky realised a loss of £2.7m. The basic CGT rule for foreign currency transactions is that the gain is to be computed by taking the exchange rate equivalent of the allowable expenditure at the time when it was incurred and the rate equivalent of the disposal consideration at the date of disposal (see *Capcount Trading v Evans* (1993)). Accepting this position, will Mucky succeed in arguing that because of the change in exchange rates part of his consideration was irrecoverable under s 48? Not according to Lloyd J who held that 'consideration' meant what was promised (ie dollars) rather than any sterling equivalent (see *Loffland Bros North Sea Inc v Goodbrand* (1997)).

e) *Marren v Ingles*

It may be that the deferred consideration cannot be valued because it is dependent on some future contingency. In the House of Lords case of *Marren v Ingles* (1980) (see [**14.7**]) part of the payment for the disposal of shares was to be calculated by reference to the price of the shares if and when the company obtained a Stock Exchange listing. The taxpayer's gain on the disposal of the shares could not be calculated by reference to such an unquantifiable consideration. Accordingly he was treated as making two separate disposals. The first was the disposal of the shares. The consideration for this was the payment that the taxpayer actually received plus the value (if any) of the right to receive the future deferred sum (a *chose in action*). The value of the *chose in action* then formed the acquisition cost of that asset. Hence, once the deferred consideration became payable, the taxpayer was treated as making a second disposal, this time of the *chose in action*. He was, therefore, chargeable on the difference between the consideration received and whatever was the acquisition cost of that asset.

The House of Lords did not attempt to value the *chose in action*. In all probability its value would have been nominal, with the result that on the first disposal (of the shares) the gain would have been calculated by reference only to the cash received, whilst on the second disposal (of the *chose in action*) the entire consideration received would constitute a gain. There is no element of double taxation involved in the *Marren v Ingles* situation. Instead, the CGT is collected (in effect) in two instalments with the result that the taxpayer may be better off than A, in *Example 14.7(1)*, above, who is taxed on money years before receiving it. (Where the taxpayer is entitled to retirement relief on the disposal of the shares, however, the relief may not be exhausted on the share disposal and the balance cannot be used against the gain on the disposal of the *chose in action*.)   **[14.26]**

2   **What expenditure is deductible?**

Once the disposal consideration is known, the gain (or loss) can be calculated by deducting allowable expenditure. This is defined in TCGA 1992 s 38 as 'expenditure incurred wholly and exclusively' in: **[14.27]**

Acquiring the asset   The purchase price or market value, including any allowed incidental costs (such as stamp duty), or where the asset was created rather than acquired (eg a painting) the cost of its creation may be deducted (TCGA 1992 s 38(1)(a)). In certain circumstances a deemed acquisition cost will be deducted. This is the case, for instance, when an asset is acquired by inheritance (probate value being the acquisition cost) and when the 1982 rebasing rules apply (market value in 1982 being the acquisition cost: see TCGA 1992 s 38(2)(b)).   **[14.28]**

Enhancing the value of the asset   Expenditure on improvements must be reflected in the state or nature of the asset at the time of its disposal (TCGA 1992 s 38(1)(b)). Thus, in the case of land, the costs of an application for planning permission which is never granted are not deductible, whereas the costs of building an extension are. Also deductible under this head are the costs of establishing, preserving or defending title to the asset (eg the costs of a boundary dispute and, in the case of PRs, a proportion of probate expenses).

In *Chaney v Watkis* (1986) the taxpayer agreed to pay his mother-in-law a cash sum (£9,400) if she surrendered up vacant possession of a house which he wished to sell. Between exchange of contracts on the property and completion this agreement was varied by mutual consent. Instead of the cash sum, the taxpayer agreed to build an extension onto his own home and allow her to occupy it rent free for life. It was held that the cash sum would have been deductible in arriving at his gain on sale of the house if it had been paid (since vacant possession enhanced the value of the house). The same principle applied to a consideration in money's worth (the rent-free accommodation) and the case was remitted to the Commissioners for them to determine the value of this consideration. Two matters are especially worthy of note: *first*, that expenditure incurred post-contract but pre-completion was taken into account and the phrase 'at the time of the disposal' in s 38(1)(b) must be construed accordingly; and, *secondly*, that the taxpayer's mother-in-law was a protected tenant of the property (and had been before he purchased the house) and hence the agreement with her was a commercial arrangement.   **[14.29]**

Disposing of the asset The incidental costs of disposal which are deductible include professional fees paid to a surveyor, valuer, auctioneer, accountant, agent or legal adviser; costs of the transfer or conveyance; costs of advertising to find a buyer and any costs incurred in making a valuation or apportionment necessary for CGT (TCGA 1992 s 38(1)(c)). Expenses incurred in making a valuation and in ascertaining market value include the costs of an initial valuation to enable a tax return to be submitted but do not include costs of negotiating that value with the Revenue nor costs of appealing an assessment (*Caton's Administrators v Couch* (1997)). Other taxes, such as IHT on a gift, are not deductible.

The requirement in TCGA 1992 s 38 that expenditure must be 'wholly and exclusively' incurred makes use of the same test for allowable expenditure as that found for income tax under Schedule D Cases I and II (see [**6.117**]). For CGT purposes, however, the words have been interpreted relatively liberally. In the case of *IRC v Richards' Executors* (1971), PRs who sold shares at a profit claimed to deduct from the sale proceeds the cost of valuing the relevant part of the deceased's estate for probate. The House of Lords held that they could do so even though the valuation was for the purposes of estate duty as well as for establishing title (ie even though the costs were 'dual purpose expenditure').

'Expenditure' within TCGA 1992 s 38 must be something that reduces the taxpayer's estate in some quantifiable way. Thus in *Oram v Johnson* (1980) the taxpayer who bought a second home for £2,500, renovated it himself and later sold it for £11,500 could not deduct the notional cost of his own labour.

On a deemed disposal and reacquisition (see [**18.47**]) notional expenses are not deductible (TCGA 1992 s 38(4)), but actual expenses are. Thus, in *IRC v Chubb's Settlement Trustees* (1971), where the life tenant and the remainderman ended a settlement by dividing the capital between them so that there was a deemed disposal under (now) TCGA 1992 s 71, the costs of preparing the deed of variation of the settlement were deductible (the result of this case is to leave s 38(4) as a prohibition on the deduction of imaginary expenses!).

The deduction of certain items of expenditure is specifically prohibited. For instance, interest on a loan to acquire the asset (TCGA 1992 s 38(3)); premiums paid under a policy of insurance against risks of loss of, or damage to, an asset; and, most important, any sums which a person can deduct in calculating his income for income tax. Additionally, no sum is deductible for CGT purposes which would be deductible for income tax, if the disponer were in fact using the relevant asset in a trade; in effect therefore, no items of an income, as opposed to a capital, nature will ever be deductible. For example, the cost of repair (as opposed to improvement) or of insurance of a chargeable asset, both of which are of an income nature, are disallowed as deductions for CGT.   [**14.30**]

EXAMPLE 14.8

A buys a country cottage in 1990 for £11,000 to rent to high net worth individuals. He spends £6,000 in installing a gold plated bathroom and £4,000 on mending the leaking roof. Over the following five years he spends a further £500 on repairing leaking radiators and £400 on general maintenance. He pays a total of £3,000 on property insurance. He sells it in 1997 for £25,000.

His chargeable gain (ignoring indexation) is:

	£	£
Sale proceeds		25,000
Less:		
Acquisition cost	11,000	
Cost of improvements	6,000	17,000
		£ 8,000

The cost of repairs, maintenance and insurance are not deductible for CGT because they are deductible in computing his income under Schedule A. The insurance premiums are specifically disallowed under TCGA 1992 s 205.

If A had bought the cottage as a second home, his gain on sale would still be £8,000; the other items are disallowed as deductions for CGT because they are of an income nature.

3   The indexation of allowable expenditure

a) *Basic rules*

Before 1982 CGT made no allowance for the effects of inflation on the value of chargeable assets and, accordingly, it taxed both real and paper profits. FA 1982 afforded a measure of relief by introducing an indexation allowance for disposals of assets on or after 6 April 1982 (1 April in the case of companies); FA 1985 made major improvements to that allowance in respect of disposals on or after 6 April 1985 (or 1 April) but FA 1994 introduced restrictions to prevent the allowance from creating a loss. Generally items of allowable expenditure are index-linked (to rises in the RPI), so that the eventual gain on disposal should represent only 'real' profits (see TCGA 1992 ss 53–57).

The indexation allowance is calculated by comparing the RPI for the month in which the allowable expenditure was incurred (ie due and payable) with the index for the month in which the disposal of the asset occurs. Assuming that the RPI has increased, the allowable expenditure is multiplied by the fraction

$$\frac{RD—RI}{RI}$$

where RD is the index for the month of disposal and RI is the index for the month in which the item of expenditure was incurred or March 1982 if later (this fraction, calculated to three decimal places, produces the 'indexed rise' decimal which is published by the Revenue each month). The resultant figure (known as the 'indexation allowance') is a further allowable deduction in arriving at the chargeable gain on disposal of the asset.

As the allowance is linked to allowable expenditure, it follows that, where an asset has a nil base cost (for instance, goodwill built up by the taxpayer) there can be no indexation allowance. ESC D42 makes provision for the situation where a leaseholder acquires a superior interest in the land so that his interests merge and the inferior interest is extinguished.   **[14.31]**

EXAMPLE 14.9

A painting was bought for £20,000 on 10 April 1990 and sold for £100,000 on 30 June 1997. RPI for April 1990 is 300; RPI for June 1997 is 500. The indexed rise is:

$$\frac{(500 - 300)}{300}: \text{ ie } 0.667 \text{ (correct to three decimal places).}$$

Indexation allowance is: £20,000 × 0.667 = £13,340

Therefore, the chargeable gain is:

	£	£
Sale proceeds		100,000
Less:		
Acquisition cost	20,000	
Indexation allowance	13,340	33,340
Chargeable gain		£66,660

Assume that the painting was restored on 12 November 1993 for £2,000. RPI for November 1993 is 400. Indexation allowance is £13,340, as above, plus:

$$£2,000 \times \frac{(500 - 400)}{400} = £500$$

Therefore, the chargeable gain is £64,160 (£66,660 – £2,000 – £500)

b) *The indexation allowance and capital losses*

The indexation allowance cannot create or increase a capital loss: it only operates to reduce or extinguish capital gains (TCGA 1992 s 53(1), (2A)).   **[14.32]**

EXAMPLE 14.10

Alain acquired an asset for £100,000. He disposes of it for £110,000 and his indexation allowance is £15,000. Alain can use £10,000 of the indexation allowance (*only*) thereby wiping out his gain. If he had sold the asset for £90,000 none of the allowance would be used. If he had sold it for £125,000 then the full allowance would be available to reduce the gain to £10,000.

4 Calculation of gains for assets acquired before 6 April 1965

Only gains after 6 April 1965 are chargeable (TCGA 1992 s 35(9)). Thus, for assets acquired before 6 April 1965, the legislation contains rules determining how much gain is deemed to have accrued since that date. Generally, the gain is deemed to accrue evenly over the whole period of ownership (the so-called straight-line method: TCGA 1992 Sch 2 para 11(3)). The chargeable gain is, therefore, a proportion of the gross gain calculated by the formula:

$$\text{Gross gain} \times \frac{\text{period of ownership since 6 April 1965}}{\text{total period of ownership}} = \text{chargeable gain}$$

EXAMPLE 14.11

(The indexation allowance and 1982 rebasing have been ignored.)

	£
A bought a picture on 6 April 1964 for	5,000
He sells it on 6 April 1994 for	19,000
His gain is	£14,000

His chargeable gain is: £14,000 $\times \frac{29}{30}$ = £13,533

In applying this formula, the ownership of the asset can never be treated as beginning earlier than 6 April 1945 (TCGA 1992 Sch 2 para 11(6)) so that if it was acquired before that date it is deemed to have been acquired on that date.

In *Smith v Schofield* (1993) the taxpayer inherited a Chinese cabinet and French mirror (combined value £250) on the death of her father in 1952. She sold both items early in 1987 for a price which, after deducting incidental costs of sale and the deemed acquisition cost, left a net gain of £14,088. That figure had to be further reduced for CGT charging purposes by (1) the indexation allowance which would be calculated on the value of the assets in March 1982, and (2) by the straight-line allowance for chargeable assets owned on 6 April 1965. The House of Lords decided that the indexation allowance must be deducted first, and then time apportionment applied with the result that the chargeable gain was £7,189. Had time apportionment been applied first, thereby reducing the gain to £8,864, and then the indexation allowance deducted in full, the chargeable gain would have been only £6,224. Commenting on the decision, Lord Jauncey had some regrets:

> 'I reached this decision with regret because its effect is that an allowance which was given to offset the effect of inflation on gains accruing from and after 1982 is in part being attributed to notional non-chargeable gains accruing prior to 6 April 1965, a situation which cannot occur where an election of valuation on that date is made. In the present case the effective value of the indexation allowance will be reduced by more than one-third. ... I should be surprised if Parliament had intended such a result.'

These rules are of limited importance in view of the rebasing provisions which are considered in the next section.   [**14.33**]

5   Calculation of gains on assets owned on 31 March 1982 ('rebasing')

The following rules apply to disposals of assets which were owned on 31 March 1982 by the person making the disposal.   [**14.34**]

Basic rule   Assets which the taxpayer owned on 31 March 1982 are deemed to have been sold by that person and immediately reacquired by him at market value on that date. Rebasing requires the taxpayer to incur expenses in agreeing with the Revenue a valuation figure for the relevant asset in March 1982 (TCGA 1992 s 35).   [**14.35**]

EXAMPLE 14.12

Jacques' valuable collection of porcelain cost £12,000 in 1970; it is estimated to have been worth £100,000 on 31 March 1982 and has just been sold for £175,000. In computing Jacques' capital gain arising from his disposal, rebasing to March 1982 will result in a reduction in the gain from £163,000 to £75,000.

Qualifications   In cases where a computation based on the actual costs and ignoring 1982 values would produce a smaller gain or loss, rebasing will not generally apply so that it is that smaller gain or loss which will be relevant. In cases where one computation would produce a gain and the other a loss, there is deemed to be neither.   [**14.36**]

EXAMPLE 14.13

(1) Assume that under rebasing the disposal of an asset would show a loss of £60,000 whereas ignoring 1982 values the loss would be only £35,000. In this case the £35,000 loss will be taken.

(2) Alternatively, assume that the disposal would show a gain of £25,000 if rebasing applied but only £15,000 if it did not. The smaller gain (£15,000) will be taxed.

(3) Under the rebasing calculation there is a gain of £50,000 on the disposal of a chargeable asset: on the alternative calculation ignoring 1982 values, however, there is a loss of £2,000. In this case there is deemed to be neither gain nor loss. (Similarly if the loss had been produced by rebasing and the gain under the alternative calculation.)

(4) Assume that there is a loss of £6,000 if the asset is rebased to 1982 but, on

the alternative calculation, a loss of £20,000. In this case mandatory rebasing will occur with the result that the loss is restricted to £6,000.

The election Because the qualifications discussed above require the taxpayer to keep pre-1982 records and will usually involve alternative calculations, the taxpayer is given an election for rebasing to apply to all disposals of assets which he held on 31 March 1982. This election may be made at any time before 6 April 1990 or (if no election has been made by that time) within two years from the end of the tax year in which the first relevant disposal (ie of assets owned at 31 March 1982) occurs or within such longer period as the Board may allow (see SP 4/92). The election is irrevocable and will apply to all disposals of assets owned on 31 March 1982 by the particular taxpayer (TCGA 1992 s 35(5)). In SP 2/89 the Revenue indicated that it will always exercise its discretion to extend the election time limit to (at least) the date on which the statutory time limit would expire (ie six years) if the first relevant disposal was one on which the gain would not be chargeable (eg a disposal of private cars; chattels which are wasting assets; gilt-edged securities). **[14.37]**

Technical matters A crucial feature of the rebasing rules is the determination of when an asset was acquired by the taxpayer. In exceptional cases, the ownership period of another person can be included in deciding whether the asset was owned on 31 March 1982. These are situations where the disponer acquired the asset as a result of a no gain/no loss disposal which took place after 31 March 1982 and was made by a transferor who had owned the asset before that date.

EXAMPLE 14.14

Doris inherited a gold snuff box on the death of her father in 1977. Its probate value was £10,000. In 1983 she gave it to her husband, Sid, on their wedding anniversary. In March 1982, the box was worth £25,000 and in 1983 £28,000. Sid has just sold the box for £35,000.
(1) The 1983 transfer between spouses was made at no gain/no loss so that Sid is treated as having acquired the box for £10,000.
(2) In calculating the gain on sale, Sid is treated as having held the asset on 31 March 1982 so that the market value at that date (£25,000) will be his allowable base cost.

In certain other situations ownership of an asset may be related back to an earlier date: generally these are cases where the asset is treated as forming part of or replacing an earlier asset. This, for instance, is the case where new shares are acquired on a company takeover under TCGA 1992 ss 135–137 (see Chapter 19).

Where a capital gain is realised on a disposal but tax is postponed, eg under a hold-over election or when roll-over relief is available, there is still a relevant disposal at that time and hence, if that disposal occurred after 1982 but before 6 April 1988 and was of assets held by the disponor on 31 March 1982, simple rebasing was not available. Under TCGA 1992 Sch 4, however, when a gain was deferred on a disposal made between 1982 and 1988 and that gain was attributable (at least in part) to the disposal of an asset acquired before 31 March 1982, the deferred gain will be halved on the eventual disposal of that asset. **[14.38]**

EXAMPLE 14.15

Simpkin, who has been a partner in an estate agency business, sells his interest in goodwill in 1983. The acquisition cost of the goodwill was nil: its value in 1982 was estimated at £85,000. When he sold the goodwill in 1983 he obtained £100,000 which he then rolled over into a farm purchased in 1985 at a total cost of £210,000. As a result of roll-over relief (see [**16.92**]), the base cost of the farm in Simpkin's hands was reduced to £110,000. As the farm was acquired in 1985 there is no question of rebasing. However, on the eventual sale of the farm, one-half of the deferred gain will be ignored so that Simpkin's base cost will be £110,000 + £50,000 (one-half of the deferred gain) = £160,000.

6   Part disposals

General rule   The term disposal includes a part disposal, so that whenever part of an asset or an interest in an asset is disposed of it is necessary to calculate the original cost of the part sold before any gain on it can be computed (TCGA 1992 s 42). This applies, for instance, to a sale of part of a landholding or of part of a shareholding, or to the grant of a lease (for leases see [**14.42**]).

The formula used for calculating the deductible cost of the part sold is:

$$C \times \frac{A}{A + B}$$

Where   C = all the deductible expenditure on the whole asset
A = sale proceeds of the part of the asset sold
B = market value of part retained (at the time when the part is sold).

The indexation provisions are applied in the same way for part disposals as for disposals of the whole, except that only the apportioned expenditure is index-linked. [**14.39**]

EXAMPLE 14.16

Ten acres of land were bought for £10,000 on 1 January 1990. Four acres of land were sold for £12,000 on 1 October 1997 (the remaining six acres are then worth £24,000). RPI for January 1990 is 250. RPI for October 1997 is 340.
Acquisition cost of the four acres sold is:

$$£10,000 \times \frac{£12,000}{£36,000} = £3,333$$

Indexation allowance is: £3,333 × 0.360 = £1,200

Therefore, the chargeable gain is:

	£	£
Sale proceeds		12,000
Less:		
Acquisition cost	4,000	
Indexation allowance	1,200	5,200
		£6,800

Cases when the formula is not used   The part disposal formula need not be used (thereby removing the need to value the part of the asset not disposed of), when the cost of the part disposed of can be easily calculated. In particular, on a part disposal of shares of the same class in the same company the cost of each individual share can be worked out as a fraction of the total number owned by the taxpayer.

Further the rules will not be applied to small part disposals of land (TCGA 1992 s 242) if the taxpayer so elects. Where the consideration received is 20%

or less of the value of the entire holding and does not exceed £20,000 (or is 'small' in the case of a disposal to an authority with compulsory powers of acquisition: see s 243) the transaction need not be treated as a disposal. Instead, the taxpayer can elect to deduct the consideration received from the allowable expenditure applicable to the whole of the land.

Similar principles apply to small capital distributions made by companies (see [19.21] and for the meaning of 'small', see *Tax Bulletin*, February 1997).

[14.40]

7 Wasting assets (TCGA 1992 ss 44–47)

A wasting asset is one with a predictable useful life not exceeding 50 years. If the asset is a wasting chattel (ie an item of tangible movable property such as a television or washing machine), there is a general exemption from CGT. In the case of plant and machinery qualifying for capital allowances there are special rules (see [14.63]). Short leases of land are likewise subject to their own rules; freehold land, needless to say, can never be a wasting asset. The main types of asset subject to the wasting asset rules are:

(1) tangible movable property with the exception of commodities dealt with on a terminal market (TCGA 1992 s 45(4));
(2) options with the exception of quoted options to subscribe for shares in a company; traded options quoted on a recognised stock exchange or recognised futures exchange; financial options and options to acquire assets for use in a business (TCGA 1992 s 146);
(3) purchased life interests in settled property where the predictable life expectation of the life tenant is 50 years or less (TCGA 1992 s 44(1)(d));
(4) patent rights;
(5) copyrights in certain circumstances; and
(6) leases for 50 years or less (other than of land: see below).

On disposal of any of the above assets any gain is calculated on the basis that the allowable expenditure on the asset is written down at a uniform rate over its expected useful life so that any claim for loss relief will be limited. Consistent with the general principles which apply to such assets, it is only the written down expenditure which is entitled to the indexation allowance.   [14.41]

EXAMPLE 14.17

Copyright (21 years unexpired) of a novel is bought for £3,000 on 1 April 1980. The copyright is sold for £2,600 on 1 April 1996. The market value of the copyright in March 1982 (19 years unexpired) is £2,800. RPI for March 1982 is 250; RPI for April 1996 is 350. The gain on disposal is calculated as follows:

Calculate written down acquisition cost:

$$£2,800 - \left(£2,800 \times \frac{14\,\text{years}}{19\,\text{years}} \right) = £737$$

The indexation allowance is:

$$£737 \times 0.4 = £294$$

Therefore, the chargeable gain is:

	£	£
Sale proceeds		2,600
Less:		
Acquisition cost	737	
Indexation allowance	294	1,031
Chargeable gain		£1,569

Note: If rebasing had not applied the gain would be:

Written down acquisition cost:

$$\text{£3,000} - \left(\text{£3,000} \times \frac{16 \text{ years}}{21 \text{ years}} \right) = \qquad \text{£714}$$

Indexation allowance: £714 × 0.4 =   £286

Therefore chargeable gain is:

	£	£
Sale proceeds		2,600
Less:		
Acquisition cost	714	
Indexation	286	1,000
		£1,600

8   Rules for leases of land (TCGA 1992 s 240, Sch 8)

a) *Basic rule*

The grant of a lease out of a freehold or superior lease is a part disposal. The grant of a lease for a 'rack rent' and no premium will not attract any CGT charge. **[14.42]**

b) *CGT on premiums*

The gain is computed by deducting from the disposal consideration (ie the premium) the cost of the part disposed of, calculated as for any part disposal (see 6 above). Included in the denominator of the formula as a part of the market value of the land undisposed of is the value of any right to receive rent under the lease. In *Clarke v United Real (Moorgate) Ltd* (1988), the court held that a premium included any *sum* paid by a tenant to his landlord in consideration for the grant of a lease and therefore caught payments to the landlord covering past and future development costs. It did not, however, catch the value of building works undertaken and paid for by the tenant on the demised premises (see the definition of 'premium' in TCGA 1992 Sch 8 para 10(2)). By contrast the value of work carried out on other premises retained by the landlord will apparently fall within the opening words of TCGA 1992 s 22(1) and so be subject to charge (*Chaloner v Pellipar Investments Ltd* (1996): see **[14.112]**). **[14.43]**

c) *The wasting asset rules*

A lease which has 50 or less years to run is a wasting asset. It does not depreciate evenly over time, however, so that on any assignment of it, its cost is written down, not as described in **[14.41]**, but according to a special table in TCGA 1992 Sch 8 (on the duration of a lease see *Lewis v Walters* (1992) deciding that the possibility of extending the term under the Leasehold Reform Act 1967 should be ignored).

Where a sub-lease is granted out of a lease which is a wasting asset, the ordinary part disposal formula is not applied. Instead, any gain is calculated by deducting from the consideration received for the sub-lease, that part of the allowable expenditure on the head lease which will waste away over the period of the sub-lease. **[14.44]**

EXAMPLE 14.18

A acquires a lease of premises for 40 years for £5,000 (that lease is, therefore, a wasting asset). After ten years he grants a sub-lease to B for ten years at a premium of £1,000.

A's gain is calculated by deducting from the consideration on the part disposal (ie £1,000), such part of £5,000 as will waste away (in accordance with TCGA 1992 Sch 8 para 1) on a lease dropping from 30 years to 20 years.

d) *Income tax overlap*

Any part of a premium that is chargeable to income tax under Schedule A (see Chapter 8) is not charged to CGT. Thus, on the grant of a short lease out of an interest that is not a wasting asset (eg the freehold) there must be deducted from the premium received such part of it as is taxed under Schedule A. The part disposal formula is then applied and in the numerator the sum representing the consideration received on the part disposal is the premium received less that part taxed under Schedule A. **[14.45]**

EXAMPLE 14.19

A buys freehold premises for £200,000. He grants a lease of the premises for 21 years at a premium of £100,000 and a rent. The value of the freehold subject to the lease and including the right to receive rent is now £150,000.

Of the premium of £100,000, 20/50ths is discounted (ie £100,000 × 20 × 2/100) and the balance (ie £100,000 × 30/50) is taxed under Schedule A = £60,000.

A's chargeable gain is, therefore:

	£
Consideration received	100,000
Less: amount taxed under Schedule A	60,000
	40,000

Less: cost of the part disposed of

$£200,000 × \dfrac{£40,000}{£100,000 + £150,000}$: 32,000

Chargeable gain (ignoring indexation) £ 8,000

e) *Tenants and lease surrenders / regrants*

For the position of a tenant who extends his lease, often by surrendering the old lease in return for the grant on a new long lease and payment of a premium, see ESC D39 ([**14.122**]); for the calculation of his indexation allowance ESC D42. A reverse premium received by a tenant as an inducement to enter into the lease will not normally attract a tax charge: see CG 70833. **[14.46]–[14.60]**

III LOSSES FOR CGT

1 **When does a loss arise?**

A loss arises whenever the consideration for the disposal of a chargeable asset is less than the allowable expenditure incurred by the taxpayer (but excluding any indexation allowance).

EXAMPLE 14.20

If an antique desk was bought for £12,000, restored for £1,000 and then sold for £11,000, a loss of £2,000 would result.

Although the disposal of a debt (other than a debt on a security) is usually exempt from CGT, a loss that is made on a qualifying loan to a trader may be treated as a capital loss (see [16.43]).

If an asset is destroyed or extinguished; abandoned, in the case of options that are not wasting assets ([14.116]); or if its value has become negligible (see [14.115]), the taxpayer may claim to have incurred an allowable loss.   [14.61]

2   Use of losses

Losses must be relieved primarily against gains of the taxpayer in the same year, but any surplus loss can be carried forward and set against his first available gain in future years without time limit.

Losses cannot be carried back and set against gains of previous years except for the net losses incurred by an individual in the year of his death (TCGA 1992 s 62(2)). Capital losses cannot generally be set against the taxpayer's income for tax purposes. The only exception is for losses arising as a result of investment in a corporate trade under TA 1988 s 574 (see [7.121]). Similarly, income losses cannot generally be set against an individual's capital gains: although this rule is also subject to an important exception whereby trading losses which cannot be relieved against the taxpayer's income may be set against his chargeable gains for both the year when the loss was incurred and one following tax year (see FA 1991 s 72 and [7.61]).

A loss that is incurred on a disposal to a connected person can only be set against any gains on subsequent disposals to the same person (TCGA 1992 s 18(3)).   [14.62]

3   Restriction of losses: capital allowances

Generally, chattels which are wasting assets are exempt from CGT (see [16.21]). Plant and machinery which are tangible movable property are always classified as wasting assets, but will not be exempt from CGT if they are used in a trade and qualify for capital allowances (accordingly if capital allowances are withdrawn, eg because the asset is never brought into use in the business, the exemption will apply: see *Burman v Westminster Press Ltd* (1987)). Other assets which qualify for capital allowances, such as industrial buildings, are chargeable assets because they are not wasting.

As CGT does not generally overlap with income tax, a gain which is charged to income tax will not be charged to CGT; and a loss will not be allowable for CGT if it is deductible for income tax. Thus, the gain or loss on a disposal of plant and machinery and other assets qualifying for capital allowances is calculated in the usual way (and not written down in the case of wasting assets) and any gain is charged to CGT to the extent that it exceeds the original cost of the asset.

EXAMPLE 14.21

	£
Year 1: Machine bought for	10,000
WDA at 25%	2,500
Year 2: Machine sold for	12,000

There is a balancing charge for income tax of £2,500 (ie to the extent of the capital allowance given—see further Chapter 35). The excess of the sale price over the acquisition cost (£2,000) is chargeable to CGT.

However, it is rare for plant and machinery to be sold at a gain; it is more likely to be sold at a loss, in which case the loss is not allowable for CGT to the extent that it is covered by capital allowances. Capital allowances may reduce a loss to nil, but they cannot produce a gain. **[14.63]–[14.80]**

EXAMPLE 14.22

	£
Machine bought for	4,000
Sold later for	2,000
Capital allowance given of	2,000
Loss for CGT is:	
Disposal proceeds	2,000
Less: acquisition cost	4,000
Capital loss	(2,000)
Credit for capital allowances	2,000
Allowable loss	£ Nil

IV   CALCULATING THE TAX PAYABLE

1   **Rates**

a) *Fusion with income tax*

CGT was formerly charged at a flat rate of 30%. Changes in FA 1988, however, resulted in the abandonment of this single rate and the appropriate rate will now depend upon the identity and circumstances of the disponor. In his 1988 Budget Speech, the Chancellor (Nigel Lawson) explained these changes as follows:

> 'Rebasing the tax so as to produce a fully indexed system makes it possible to bring the taxation of gains closer to that of income. In principle, there is little economic difference between income and capital gains, and many people effectively have the option of choosing to a significant extent which to receive. And, insofar as there is a difference, it is by no means clear why one should be taxed more heavily than the other. Taxing them at different rates distorts investment decisions and inevitably creates a major tax avoidance industry ... I therefore propose a fundamental reform ... I propose in future to apply the same rate of tax to income and capital gains alike ... Taxing capital gains at income tax rates makes for greater neutrality in the tax system. It is what we now do for companies. And it is also the practice in the United States, with the big difference that there they have neither indexation relief nor a separate capital gains tax threshold.'

[14.81]

b) *Individuals*

The rate of CGT is the same as the basic rate of income tax (for 1997–98, 23%), subject to two qualifications:
(1) *qualification 1*: if the taxpayer has no taxable income or if such income falls below £4,100 chargeable gains will, to that extent, be taxed at the lower rate of 20%;
(2) *qualification 2*: if in the year of assessment the taxpayer is liable to higher rate income tax, his capital gains will be charged at that higher rate (for 1997–98, 40%).

CGT is therefore charged at the taxpayer's marginal income tax rate (TCGA 1992 s 4). Accordingly, capital gains realised in a particular tax year may push the individual into a higher rate which will apply to that gain.

The following diagram illustrates the position and shows that gains from non-UK trusts are treated as the lowest slice of a taxpayer's gains:

CAPITAL GAINS	Other gains
	Offshore trust gains under TCGA 1992 ss 86–98A
INCOME	Dividends and other savings income
	Other income (eg earned and rental income)

For many taxpayers linking the rates of income tax and CGT resulted in an increase in the rate of tax applicable to capital gains from 30% (in 1987–88) to 40%.   [**14.82**]

EXAMPLE 14.23

(1) Bill has no income in the tax year 1997–98 but realises chargeable capital gains of £10,000. His rate of tax on those gains is 20% on the first £4,100 and 23% on the remaining £5,900: note that he cannot reduce the gain by deducting his unused personal allowance.

(2) Had Bill's gain been £28,000, CGT would have been charged as follows:
first £4,100 at 20%
next £22,000 at 23%
remaining £1,900 at 40%.

c) *Companies*

Companies are subject to corporation tax, not CGT, but that tax is charged on corporate profits including chargeable gains. The rate of tax charged on such gains is therefore either 21% (small company rate) or 31% (see [**28.21**]).   [**14.83**]

d) *Personal representatives*

PRs are subject to tax at 23%. Accordingly, it may be advantageous for assets to be sold by the PRs rather than by the relevant beneficiary (see [**15.61**]).   [**14.84**]

e) *Trustees*

Trustees are taxed at 23% subject to two main exceptions.

First, if the trust is an accumulation or discretionary settlement, gains realised by trustees are taxed at 34% (TCGA 1992 s 5). For these purposes a trust is treated as accumulation or discretionary where all *or any part* of the income arising to the trustee in a year of assessment is taxed at 'the rate applicable to trusts' under TA 1988 s 686 ([**11.21**]). The settlement is also accumulation and discretionary where all the income of the trustees is treated as that of the settlor but would otherwise have suffered additional rate tax.

The *second* exceptional case is designed to prevent the relatively low rate of charge on settlements from being employed by settlors who would otherwise be subject to CGT at 40%. Accordingly, in cases where the settlor or his spouse has an interest in the settlement, tax is assessed as if the gains had been realised by the settlor and not by the trustees (TCGA 1992 ss 77–78).

A settlor retains an interest for these purposes if:

'(a) any property which may at any time be comprised in the settlement or any income which may arise under the settlement is, or will or may become, applicable for the benefit of or payable to the settlor or the spouse of the settlor in any circumstances whatsoever, or

(b) the settlor, or the spouse of the settlor, enjoys a benefit deriving directly or indirectly from any property which is comprised in the settlement or any income arising under the settlement.'

As can be appreciated these provisions are widely drawn (although not so widely as the 'defined person' provisions that apply to settlors of non-UK resident trusts: see [**20.56**]) so that they could catch, for instance, a situation where money was lent to the settlor by his trustees.   **[14.85]**

EXAMPLE 14.24

(1) Trustees of the Blandings marriage settlement, set up by Lord Blanding in 1986, under which Fiona Blanding is the life tenant, realised chargeable gains of £150,000 in 1997–98. The rate of CGT is 23%.

(2) Trustees of a trust set up by Fiona Blanding for her infant twins, Maxie and Minnie, realised chargeable gains of £150,000 in 1997–98. The rate of tax is 34% since the income will be accumulated by the trustees insofar as it is not paid for the maintenance or education of the twins.

(3) The Blandings family trust now includes interests in possession in 95% of the fund with the remaining 5% being held on the original discretionary trusts. The rate of tax on capital gains realised by the trust is 34% whether such gains can be attributed to the 95% of the fund which is settled on fixed interest trusts or the 5% discretionary rump. Only if separate settlements existed would different rates apply (in which case the fixed interest portion would be subject to a 23% rate whilst gains in the rump would be taxed at 34%). For a contrary view, suggesting that separate funds of a single settlement can be taxed separately, see *Capital Taxes* (1989) p 7.

(4) Solomon wishes to take advantage of the 23% rate which applies to interest in possession trusts. There are two obstacles in his path:
   (i) the creation of the trust may be a chargeable disposal for CGT purposes with hold-over relief not being available;
   (ii) if he (or his wife) retains an interest in the trust future gains will be taxed, not at the 23% rate, but on him and at his rates.

2   The annual exemption

The amount of the annual exemption depends on the capacity in which the person made a gain. The amount is index-linked and as the indexation allowance is also available as soon as expenditure is incurred the result is double relief for the taxpayer.   **[14.86]**

Individuals   The first £6,500 (for 1997–98) of the total gains in a tax year are exempt from CGT (TCGA 1992 s 3).

EXAMPLE 14.25

	£	£
A sells a painting for		17,000
Original cost of painting	8,700	
Indexation allowance (say)	1,000	9,700
Chargeable gain		7,300
Less: annual exemption for 1997–98		6,500
Gain charged to CGT		£800

If the exemption is unused in a tax year it is lost since there is no provision to carry it forward (contrast the IHT annual exemption).   **[14.87]**

Personal representatives   In the tax year of the deceased's death and the two following tax years, PRs have the same annual exemption as an individual. In the third and following tax years they have no annual exemption and so are charged to CGT on all chargeable gains they make (see **[15.62]**).   **[14.88]**

Trustees   Trustees generally enjoy only half the annual exemption available to an individual, ie £3,250 (for 1997–98). Where the same settlor has created more than one settlement the annual exemption is divided equally between them. Four settlements for instance would each have an exemption of £812.50. This is subject to a minimum exemption per trust of one-tenth of the individual's annual exemption, ie £650. Thus, if a settlor creates ten settlements they will each have an exemption of £650.

Where the settlement is for the mentally or physically disabled, the trustees have the same exemption as an individual, ie £6,500 (subject to the same rules for groups of settlements).   **[14.89]**

Husband and wife   Husband and wife are both entitled to a full exemption (see further Chapter 40). Any unused annual exemption cannot be transferred to the other spouse.   **[14.90]**

3   Order of set-off of capital losses

Current year losses must be deducted from current year gains in full.

EXAMPLE 14.26

A makes chargeable gains of £4,000 and incurs allowable losses of £3,000 in the tax year. His gain is reduced to £1,000 and is further reduced to zero by £1,000 of his annual exemption. He is forced to set his loss against gains for the year which would in any event have escaped tax because of the annual exemption.

Unrelieved losses in any tax year can be carried forward to future tax years without time limit though they must be deducted from the first available gains. However, the loss need only be used to reduce later gains to £6,500 (the amount covered by the annual exemption) and not to zero. Losses of one spouse can only be used to reduce the gains of that spouse—they cannot be set against gains of the other spouse.

EXAMPLE 14.27

A makes the following gains and losses:

Tax year	Gain £	Loss £
Year 1	4,000	9,000
Year 2	7,500	3,000
Year 3	12,400	Nil

In Year 1 A pays no CGT and carries forward an unused loss of £5,000. His annual exemption for that year is wasted. In Year 2 A's gain is reduced to £4,500 and he pays no CGT as this is covered by his annual exemption. The £5,000 loss from year 1 does not reduce his gain to zero. It is carried forward to year 3. In Year 3 A can use the £5,000 loss that he is carrying forward from year 1 to reduce his gain to £7,400. After deducting his annual exemption he pays CGT on £900.

The relief enabling trading losses to be offset against capital gains by FA 1991 s 72 is considered at [**7.61**]. [**14.91**]

4 **When is CGT payable?**

a) *General rule*

CGT is assessed on a current year basis and is normally payable in full on 31 January following the year of assessment unless a return is issued after 31 October following the year of assessment and there has been no failure to notify chargeability under TMA 1970 s 7 when the date becomes three months from the issue of the return (TMA 1970 s 59B). Interest is charged on tax remaining unpaid after the due date. [**14.92**]

b) *Payment by instalments*

CGT may be paid in instalments in two cases. *First*, when the consideration for the disposal is paid in instalments over a period exceeding 18 months running from the date of the disposal or later and the taxpayer elects to pay by instalments. The instalments of tax can be spread (in the discretion of the Board) over a maximum of eight years provided that the final instalment of tax is not payable after the final instalment of the disposal consideration has been received (TCGA 1992 s 280).

Secondly, CGT may be paid by ten annual instalments when the gifted property is land; a controlling shareholding in any company; or a minority holding in an unquoted company provided that hold-over relief is not available on the disposal (TCGA 1992 s 281). The outstanding instalments carry interest and become payable in full if the gifted asset is sold unless the original gift was made by an individual to an unconnected donee.

Finally, in a *Marren v Ingles* type case (see [**14.26**]) an incidental result of two disposals having occurred is that tax on the overall gain of the disponor will be paid in two stages. [**14.93**]–[**14.110**]

V MEANING OF 'DISPOSAL'

1 **General**

A 'disposal' is not defined for CGT. Giving the word its natural meaning, there will be a disposal of an asset whenever its ownership changes or whenever an owner divests himself of rights in, or interests over, an asset (eg by sale, gift or exchange). Additionally, the term is extended by the legislation to cover certain transactions which would not fall within its commonsense meaning. Thus, in certain circumstances, trustees of a settlement are treated as disposing of and immediately reacquiring settlement assets at their market value ('deemed disposals': see [**18.43**]).

A part disposal of an asset is charged as a disposal according to the rules considered earlier ([**14.39**]). Death is not a disposal for CGT purposes (see Chapter 15). [**14.111**]

2 **Capital sums derived from assets (TCGA 1992 s 22)**

When a capital sum is derived from an asset there is a disposal for CGT. This is so whether or not the person who pays the capital sum receives anything in return for his payment (see *Marren v Ingles* (1980)).

All legal rights which can be turned to account by the extraction of a capital sum are assets for CGT purposes. The test is whether such rights can be converted into money or money's worth and the mere fact that they are non-assignable does not matter so long as consideration can be obtained in some other way (for instance, by surrendering the right). This is apparent from the case of *O'Brien v Benson's Hosiery (Holdings) Ltd* (1979) (see [**14.7**]). In *Marren v Ingles* (1980) (see [**14.26**]) the right to receive an unquantifiable sum in the future was considered to be an asset, a *chose in action*, from which a capital sum was derived when the right matured.

The rights must, however, be legally enforceable. Thus, a sum derived from a personal agreement, eg by a person to restrict his future activities, is not a disposal because it is not a disposal of an asset (the right to work is not a legal right, although it may be a right of man!). Where a restrictive agreement is entered into by a trader or by a taxpayer exercising a profession it may be argued that a capital sum has been derived from his goodwill (see *Kirby v Thorn EMI plc* (1988)).

Four specific instances of disposals are given in s 22:

(1) where a capital sum is received by way of compensation for the loss of, or damage to, an asset (for instance, the receipt of damages for the destruction of an asset). It should be noted that there is only a disposal where a capital sum is received and so if the receipt is of an income nature, it is charged to income tax and not to CGT: an example is compensation received by a trader for loss of trading profits—see, for instance, *London and Thames Haven Oil Wharves Ltd v Attwooll* (1967) and *Lang v Rice* (1984): [**6.83**]. For compensation payments made under the Foreign Compensation Act 1950 and similar payments see ESC D50.

(2) where a capital sum is received under an insurance policy for loss of or damage to an asset;

(3) where a capital sum is received in return for the forfeiture or surrender of rights. This category includes payments received in return for releasing another person from a contract (*O'Brien v Benson's Hosiery (Holdings) Ltd* (1979)); from a restrictive covenant; but not a statutory payment on the termination of a business tenancy since that sum is not derived from the lease (*Drummond v Austin Brown* (1984));

(4) where a capital sum is received for the use or exploitation of assets, eg for the right to exploit a copyright or for the right to use goodwill created by another person. In *Chaloner v Pellipar Investments Ltd* (1996) Rattee J commented of this provision 'those words are apt to include capital sums received as consideration for the use or exploitation of assets title to which remains unaffected in their owner referred to in the opening words of s 22(1) but are not apt to include capital sums received as consideration for a grant of the owner's title to the assets, whether in perpetuity or for a term of years'. He therefore held that the subsection did not catch consideration in the form of development works paid in return for the granting of a lease (see [**14.43**]).

In the case of disposals falling within (1)-(4) above the time of disposal is when the capital sum is received (see [**14.124**]).

The receipt of a capital sum from an asset under categories (1) and (2) above need not be treated as a disposal or part disposal provided that the asset has not been totally lost or destroyed. Instead, the taxpayer can elect to deduct compensation money from the acquisition cost of the asset thereby postponing a charge to CGT (TCGA 1992 s 23 and see ESC D19). However, this relief, which does not apply to wasting assets, is only available if one of three conditions is satisfied. *First*, the sum must be wholly used to restore the asset. *Secondly*, if the full amount of the capital sum is not used to restore the asset, the amount unused must not exceed 5% of the sum received. Where the sum unused exceeds 5%, the asset is treated as being partly disposed of for a consideration equivalent to the unused sum. *Thirdly*, the capital sum must be small compared with the value of the asset (for the meaning of 'small' see *Tax Bulletin*, February 1997 and [**19.21**]). [**14.112**]

EXAMPLE 14.28

A buys a picture for £20,000 which is now worth £30,000. It is damaged by rain from a leaking roof and A receives £8,000 compensation with which he restores the picture. The £8,000 is deducted from the cost of the asset (£20,000), but it also qualifies as allowable expenditure on a future disposal so that for CGT the cost of the asset remains £20,000 and A is in the same position as if the damage had never occurred.

Assume, however, that A restores the picture for £7,600. The £400 unused does not exceed 5% of £8,000. It is, therefore, deducted from the total allowable expenditure which is reduced to £19,600.

Alternatively, if A received compensation of £1,500 which he does not use to restore the picture, A need not treat this receipt as a part disposal (since the amount is 'small'). Instead, he can elect to deduct £1,500 from his acquisition cost, so that the picture has a base value of £18,500 on a subsequent disposal.

3 Total loss or destruction of an asset (TCGA 1992 s 24(1))

Total loss or destruction of an asset is a disposal for CGT purposes and, where the owner of the asset receives no compensation, it may give rise to an allowable loss equal to the base costs of the taxpayer. Where the asset is tangible movable property, however, the owner is deemed to dispose of it for £6,000 thereby restricting his loss relief. This limitation derives from the fact that gains on such assets are exempt from CGT insofar as the consideration does not exceed £6,000 (see [**16.22**]). As a corollary, therefore, loss relief on the disposal of these assets is not available where the consideration received is less than £6,000.

EXAMPLE 14.29

A buys a picture for £10,000 which is destroyed by fire; A is uninsured. Although the picture is now worthless, A's allowable loss is restricted to £4,000.

Land and the buildings on it are treated as separate assets for these purposes. Where the building is totally destroyed both assets are separately deemed to have been disposed of and reacquired, and it is the overall gain or loss which is taken into account.

Where the taxpayer later receives compensation or insurance moneys for an asset which is totally lost or destroyed, this would appear to be a further disposal for CGT purposes under TCGA 1992 s 22 since it is a capital sum derived from an asset (the right under the insurance contract). In practice, however, the Revenue treats both disposals (ie the entire loss of the asset and the receipt of capital moneys) as one transaction (see also the discussion of this problem by Hoffmann J in *Powlson v Welbeck Securities Ltd* (1986)). If the taxpayer uses the capital sum within one year of receipt to acquire a replacement asset, he may claim to roll over any gain made on the disposal of the destroyed asset against the cost of the replacement asset; this relief does not apply to wasting assets. If only part of the capital sum is used in replacement, only partial roll-over is available (TCGA 1992 s 23(4), (5) and ESC D19).

EXAMPLE 14.30

A buys a picture for £6,000 which is destroyed when its value is £10,000. He receives insurance money of £10,000 and uses it towards the purchase of a similar picture for £12,000. A has made a gain of £4,000 on the original picture (£10,000 – £6,000) on which he need not pay CGT. He may deduct the gain from the cost of the new picture so that his base cost becomes £8,000 (£12,000 - £4,000).

Assume that A buys the new picture for only £7,000 and claims roll-over relief. Amount of insurance money not applied in replacement = £3,000 (£10,000 - £7,000).

His chargeable gain is, therefore, £3,000 and £1,000 is rolled over so that A's base value for the new picture is £8,000 - £1,000 = £7,000.

The same relief applies where the asset destroyed is a building. The gain on the old building can be rolled over against the cost of the new building. Any gain deemed to have been made on the land cannot, however, be so treated and will, therefore, be chargeable.   [**14.113**]

4   Compensation, damages and *Zim Properties*

In *Zim Properties v Proctor* (1985) a firm of solicitors acting for the taxpayer in a conveyancing transaction were allegedly negligent, with the result that a sale of three properties owned by the taxpayer fell through. An action in negligence against the solicitors was eventually compromised and compensation of £69,000 was paid to the taxpayer. Undoubtedly, this was a capital sum, but was it derived from the disposal of an asset? Warner J held that it arose from the right of action against the solicitors which, as it could be turned into a capital sum by negotiating a compromise, was an asset for CGT purposes. Although the ownership of the properties put the taxpayer in the position to enjoy that right of action, the sum was not derived from the properties themselves, because, after receipt of that sum, the taxpayer still owned the properties.

This decision raises a number of difficult problems.

First, not all rights to payment or compensation are themselves 'assets' for CGT purposes. Warner J cited as an example the right of a seller of property to payment of the price. The relevant asset in such a case must be the property itself (contrast, however, *Marren v Ingles*, discussed at [**14.26**]). A further example is shown by *Drummond v Austin Brown* (1984) where a tenant's right to statutory compensation on the termination of his lease under the Landlord and Tenant Act 1954 was not subject to CGT; it was neither compensation for loss of the lease, nor was it derived from that lease (contrast *Davenport v Chilver* (1983) where the right to statutory compensation for confiscated property was held to be an asset). There are also a number of statutory exemptions: eg for damages following personal injury.

Secondly, Warner J held that the asset was acquired at the time when the taxpayer acted upon the allegedly negligent advice, although this matter is not free from doubt (see the House of Lords judgments in *Pirelli v Oscar Faber* (1983)).

Finally, the question of how to calculate the acquisition costs of this asset, namely the taxpayer's right to sue, was left unclear (see also *Marren v Ingles* and *O'Brien v Benson's Hosiery*). Arguably, it was acquired otherwise than by bargain at arm's length, so that the market value (if any) of the right should be taken at the moment of its acquisition (see TCGA 1992 s 17(1), discussed at [**14.22**]: it may be doubted, however, whether the taxpayer is able to satisfy the requirements in s 17(2)(b) and failure to do so would result in a nil acquisition cost). As the purpose of damages is to compensate the plaintiff, the award in such cases needs to be grossed up if the damages themselves will be reduced by taxation.

Some of the difficulties resulting from the *Zim* case have been solved by ESC D33 which affords relief from CGT in two ways.

First, 'where the right of action arises by reason of the total or partial loss or destruction of or damage to a form of property which is an asset for CGT purposes, or because the claimant suffered some loss or disadvantage in connection with such a form of property, any gain or loss on the disposal of the right of action may by concession be computed as if the compensation derived from that asset and not from the right of action'.

EXAMPLE 14.31

(1) Because of the negligence of his land agent, Lord Q's sale of a plot of land to Out of Town Supermarkets Ltd falls through. The agent is forced to pay £70,000 in compensation to Lord Q. Instead of treating this sum as consideration on the disposal of a separate *chose in action* it may be treated as arising on a part disposal of the land itself (see [**14.40**] for the part disposal rules). Accordingly, part of the expenditure attributable to that land may be deducted in arriving at Lord Q's chargeable gain.

(2) Zara, because of the negligence of her solicitor, ends up with less money from the sale of her main residence than would otherwise have been the case. Because the underlying asset (her main residence) is exempt from CGT (see [**16.61**]) any compensation paid by the solicitor will likewise escape tax.

Secondly, if there is no underlying asset. In this case, any gain accruing on the disposal of the right of action will be free from CGT.

EXAMPLE 14.32

Zappy, a wealthy taxpayer, suffers a massive income tax liability because his professional adviser negligently fails to shelter that income from tax by arranging for Zappy to invest in BES and in an industrial building in an enterprise zone. Substantial compensation is therefore paid to Zappy and because there is no underlying form of property which is an asset for CGT purposes, the sum is not subject to charge.

The logic behind this is that as the compensation merely puts the taxpayer into the position he would have been in but for the negligence, there should be no tax charge since the benefit which he was entitled to (a lesser income tax liability) is not itself subject to charge. It should be noted that the *Zim* case has no application to compensation payments which attract an income tax charge (see, for instance, *London and Thames Haven Oil Wharves Ltd v Attwooll* (1967) at [**6.83**]) whilst its application in the context of warranties and indemnities on a company takeover is discussed in Chapter 38.   [**14.114**]

5 Assets becoming of negligible value (TCGA 1992 s 24(2))

Where an asset becomes of negligible value (eg shares and securities in an insolvent company) the taxpayer is deemed to have disposed of and immediately reacquired the asset at its market value (nil) thus enabling him to claim loss relief. This disposal is deemed to occur in the tax year in which the Revenue accepts the claim or at any earlier time specified in the claim provided that (i) the taxpayer owned the asset at that earlier time; (ii) the asset had become of negligible value at that earlier time; and (iii) that earlier time was not more than two years before the beginning of the year of assessment in which the claim is made (*Williams v Bullivant* (1983) and see *Larner v Warrington* (1985)). The Revenue considers that 'negligible' means considerably less than 5% of the original cost (or March 1982 value).

Should the value of the asset subsequently increase, the result of claiming relief under s 24(2) will be that on a later disposal the base value will be nil so that all the consideration received will be treated as a gain and there will be no question of claiming any indexation allowance.   **[14.115]**

6   **Options (TCGA 1992 ss 144–147)**

The grant of an option (whether to buy or to sell an asset) is a disposal, not of a part of the asset which is subject to the option, but of a separate asset, namely, the option itself at the date of the grant. The gain will be the consideration paid for the grant of the option less any incidental expenses (see *Strange v Openshaw* (1983)). In *Garner v Pounds Shipowners & Shipbreakers Ltd* (1997) P Ltd granted an option to M to purchase its land which included a term that P Ltd was to use its best endeavours to obtain the release of a restrictive covenant and would only receive the option fee if it was successful. In the event the covenants were released in return for a payment of £90,000 by P Ltd which the court held was not deductible under TCGA 1992 s 38(1)(a) (since the asset had already been provided) but was to be taken into account in computing the consideration received on the grant of the option.

EXAMPLE 14.33

(1)   A grants to B for £3,000 an option to buy A's country cottage in two years' time for £30,000 which is its current market value. A has made a gain of £3,000 from which he can deduct any incidental expenses involved in granting the option. (This is an option to buy.)

(2)   A pays B £3,000 in return for an option to sell that country cottage to B in two years' time for £30,000. (This is an option to sell.) B has made a gain of £3,000 less any incidental expenses.

If the option is exercised, the grant and the exercise are treated as a single transaction for both grantor and grantee. It is understood that the Revenue will normally apply this treatment provided that the option is of short duration and/or for a relatively small consideration compared with the eventual sum payable on exercise. In other cases they may insist on imposing a tax charge on the grant of the option and then making suitable adjustments if and when it is eventually exercised.

EXAMPLE 14.34

As in *Example 14.33*, assuming that A had deductible expenses of £15,000:
(1)   when B exercises the option and pays A £30,000 for the house, A's gain is:

	£
Proceeds from sale of house	30,000
Consideration for option	3,000
	33,000
Less: deductible expenses	15,000
Chargeable gain	£18,000

B's acquisition cost is £30,000 plus the cost of the option, ie £33,000 (both items will be index-linked from the dates when the expenditure was incurred).

(2)   when A exercises the option and sells the house to B for £30,000, A's gain is:

	£	£
Proceeds of sale		30,000
Less: cost of option	3,000	
deductible expenses	15,000	18,000

Chargeable gain   <u>£12,000</u>

B's acquisition cost of the cottage is only £27,000 (ie £30,000 reduced by the amount that he received for the option).

An option is a chargeable asset so that, if disposed of, there may be a chargeable gain or allowable loss. It will be a wasting asset unless it is an option to subscribe for shares which is listed on a recognised stock exchange; a traded option; a financial option; or it is an option to acquire assets to be used in a trade. The abandonment of an option which is a wasting asset is not a disposal (but notice that a capital sum received for relinquishing an option will be chargeable under TCGA 1992 s 22(3): see *Golding v Kaufman* (1985); BTR, 1985, p 124 and CG 12340). **[14.116]**

7 Appropriations to and from a trader's stock in trade (TCGA 1992 s 161)

There are two cases to consider. *First*, where a trader acquires an asset for private use and later appropriates it to his trade. As a general rule, this is a disposal and CGT is payable on the difference between the market value of the asset at the date of appropriation and its original cost.

EXAMPLE 14.35

A owns a picture gallery. He buys a picture for private use for £5,000 and transfers it to the gallery when it is worth £15,000. He has made a chargeable gain of £10,000. Later he sells the picture to a customer for £30,000. The profit on sale of £15,000 (£30,000 – £15,000) is chargeable to income tax under Schedule D Case I.

However, the trader can elect to avoid paying CGT at the date of appropriation by transferring the asset into his business at a no gain/no loss value (see s 161(3A) for time limits in making the election). When the asset is eventually sold, the total profit will be charged to income tax under Schedule D as a trading receipt. So, in the above example, were A to make the election he would pay no CGT, but instead he would be liable to income tax on a profit of £25,000 (£30,000 – £5,000).

Whether the election should be exercised or not must depend upon the particular facts of each case. CGT may be more attractive as a choice of evils with its annual exemption but income tax, on the other hand, will be paid later (on eventual sale) and the profit so made may be offset against personal allowances or unused capital allowances.

Secondly, where an asset originally acquired as trading stock is taken out for the trader's private use. In this case, there is no election and the transfer is treated as a sale at market value for income tax purposes (see *Sharkey v Wernher* (1956) at **[6.95]**). The taxpayer will have market value as his CGT base cost. **[14.117]**

EXAMPLE 14.36

One of the pictures in A's gallery cost him £6,000. He removes it to hang it in his dining room when its market value is £16,000. He later sells it privately for £30,000.

On the appropriation out of trading stock, A is treated as selling the picture for its market value (£16,000) and the profit (£10,000) is assessed to income tax. The gain on the subsequent sale (£30,000 – £16,000 = £14,000) is chargeable to CGT.

8   **Miscellaneous cases**

Hire purchase agreements   Although the purchaser does not own the asset until he pays all the instalments, the vendor is treated as having disposed of the asset at the date when the purchaser is first able to use it (usually the date of the contract). The consideration for the disposal is the cash price payable under the contract. These transactions rarely give rise to a CGT charge, however, either because the asset is exempt (eg a private car or a chattel worth less than £6,000) or because it is a wasting asset. Further, the contract will normally be a trading transaction falling within the income tax charge (for an illustration where these provisions were held to apply to the sale of a taxi-driver's licences see *Lyon v Pettigrew* (1985)).

In the rare case where there is a CGT charge and the contract is subsequently rescinded there will be repayment of CGT.   **[14.118]**

Mortgages and charges (TCGA 1992 s 26)   Neither the grant nor the redemption of a mortgage is a disposal. Where the property is sold by a mortgagee or his receiver, the sale is treated as a disposal by the mortgagor.   **[14.119]**

Settled property   On the happening of certain events the trustees are deemed to have disposed of the trust assets and immediately reacquired them (see Chapter 18).   **[14.120]**

Value-shifting (TCGA 1992 ss 29–34)   There are anti-avoidance provisions intended to charge a person who passes value to another without actually making a disposal (see **[19.61]**).   **[14.121]**

Lease extensions (ESC D39)   The ESC provides that a tenant who surrenders his lease in return for the grant of a new lease over the same premises does not make a disposal or part disposal of the old lease provided that certain conditions (eg as to the terms of the new lease) are met. It does not address the position of the landlord.   **[14.122]**

Relief for exchanges of joint interests in land (ESC D26)   The relief is along the lines of that in TCGA 1992 ss 247–248 in the case of compulsory acquisitions (see **[16.99]**) and is available when a joint holding of land is partitioned (so that each joint owner becomes a sole owner of part of the land) or when a number of separate joint holdings are partitioned.   **[14.123]**

9   **Time of disposal**

A disposal under a contract of sale takes place for CGT purposes at the date of the contract, not completion, with an adjustment of tax if completion never occurs (TCGA 1992 s 28(1): contrast s 38(1)(b)—see **[14.29]**). If the contract is conditional, the disposal takes place when the condition is fulfilled (s 28(2)). The subsection also provides that when a contract is conditional on the exercise of an option (presumably either a put or call option) the relevant disposal occurs when that option is exercised. In order to decide whether a contract is conditional for these purposes the contract in question has to be construed in order to determine whether any conditions stipulated therein are truly conditions precedent to any legal liability or whether they are merely conditions precedent to completion. In the former case there is a conditional contract for CGT purposes: in the latter, the contract is unconditional (*Eastham v Leigh London and Provincial Properties Ltd* (1971)).

EXAMPLE 14.37

Lord W agrees to grant a lease to Concrete (Development Company) Ltd if they obtain satisfactory planning permission to develop the relevant land as a business park. The contract to grant the lease is conditional on satisfactory permission being obtained and so the relevant part disposal will occur only if and when that happens.

Where a local authority compulsorily acquires land (other than under a contract), the disposal occurs when the compensation is agreed or when the authority enters the land (if earlier). In the case of gifts, disposal occurs when the ownership of the asset passes to the donee (usually the date of the gift). Where a capital sum is derived from an asset, the disposal occurs when the sum is received (TCGA 1992 s 22(2) and see *Chaloner v Pellipar Investments Ltd* (1996)).
[14.124]–[14.140]

VI CAPITAL GAIN OR INCOME PROFIT?

With the linking of the rates of CGT to the income tax rates of the taxpayer, much conventional tax planning designed to ensure that capital profits rather than income were received by a taxpayer, was rendered redundant. A number of anti-avoidance sections, notably TA 1988 s 776, became of reduced importance. The distinction between capital and income receipts remains important, however, and the following are some of the factors to bear in mind. As will be apparent the facts of each individual case will largely determine whether the taxpayer is better off receiving a sum as capital or income.
[14.141]

1 Consequences of realising a capital gain

Tax on the gain will not be due until 31 January of the following tax year and in computing the chargeable gain not only will an indexation allowance be available, but in addition the £6,500 annual exemption may be deducted. Income profits are commonly taxed in the year of receipt without any allowance for indexation or an annual exemption. It is also important to remember that CGT is only levied when a disposal has occurred and therefore it may be possible to arrange disposals in the most advantageous tax year. There is the ability to shelter gain from relief under the reinvestment relief provisions (see **[16.121]**).
[14.142]

2 Taxation of income profits

Receiving a profit as income may be advantageous for the taxpayer in that the sum may be reduced by personal allowances, charges on income, unused losses, and there is the possibility of sheltering part of any sum remaining from income tax, eg by investment in an Enterprise Investment Scheme. To escape from the income tax net, however, it is often necessary to impose unattractive restrictions on the commercial arrangements, eg in the case of approved share option and incentive schemes. Accordingly, given the fusion of the rates of tax, the decision may now be taken that instead of striving to fall within an approved scheme it is more sensible to set up an unapproved scheme albeit that the individual employees are then subject to income tax on the profits that they make (see further **[39.21]**).
[14.143]

15 CGT—death

I   GENERAL

On death the assets of the deceased are deemed to be acquired by the personal representatives (PRs) at their market value at death. There is an acquisition without a disposal: an uplift in the value of the assets but no charge to CGT (TCGA 1992 s 62(1)). Hence, death wipes out capital gains.

EXAMPLE 15.1

Included in T's estate on his death in October 1997 is a rare first edition of 'Ulysses' which T had acquired in 1990 for £10,000. It is worth £100,000 at death. The gain of £90,000 (ignoring indexation) is not chargeable on T's death. Instead his PRs acquire the asset at a new base value of £100,000.

PRs are deemed to have the same residence, ordinary residence and domicile status as the deceased had at the date of death (but note that the remittance basis—which would have been available to a non domiciled deceased in respect of a disposal of non UK *situs* assets—does not apply to PRs): see TCGA 1992 s 62(3); s 65(2).   **[15.1]–[15.20]**

II   VALUATION OF CHARGEABLE ASSETS AT DEATH

The assets of the deceased are valued at their open market value at the date of death. At that time if an asset has been valued for the purpose of calculating a charge to inheritance tax that figure will constitute the CGT acquisition cost of the deceased's PRs (TCGA 1992 s 274). When the IHT related property rules apply the resultant figure may be artificially high (see [21.67]). Section 274 refers to the value of an asset being 'ascertained for the purpose of that [ie IHT] tax'. In cases where the deceased's estate does not attract IHT (eg because it is wholly left to a surviving spouse or where the property qualifies for 100% agricultural or business relief) the value will not have been ascertained and so will not fix the CGT value (see *Tax Bulletin*, April 1995, p 209). There is no reduction in the CGT value because of the availability of business or agricultural property relief.

Where property valued on death as 'related property' is sold within three years after the death, or land is sold within four years of death, or listed securities within one year, for less than the death valuation, the PRs may substitute a lower figure for the death valuation and so obtain a reduction in the IHT paid on death (see [**22.7**]). Not surprisingly, this lower figure will also form the death value for CGT so that the PRs cannot claim CGT loss relief. As an alternative to reducing the estate valuation, the PRs may prefer to claim a CGT loss on the disposal. This would be advantageous where they have made chargeable gains on disposals of other assets in the estate and where no repayment of IHT would result from amending the value of the death estate.

Ideally, for CGT purposes, the PRs want a high value for the assets on death because of the tax-free uplift, whereas in the case of estates where IHT is payable they want as low a value as possible. Generally IHT will take precedence with the result that a low valuation is usually the goal.

[**15.21**]–[**15.40**]

III   CGT LOSSES OF THE DECEASED

Losses of the deceased in the tax year of his death must be set against gains of that year. Any surplus loss at the end of the year of death can be carried back and set against chargeable gains of the deceased in the three tax years preceding the year of death, taking the most recent year first (TCGA 1992 s 62(2)). Any tax thus reclaimed will, of course, fall into the deceased's estate for IHT purposes!

[**15.41**]–[**15.60**]

IV   SALE OF DECEASED'S ASSETS BY PRs

1   **Rate of tax**

A sale of the deceased's chargeable assets by his PRs is a disposal for CGT purposes and will be subject to CGT on the difference between the sale consideration and the (indexed) market value at death. PRs pay tax at a rate of 23%.

[**15.61**]

2   **Deductions and allowances—who should sell an asset?**

The normal deductions for the incidental expenses of sale are available and PRs can deduct an appropriate proportion of the cost of valuation of the estate for probate purposes (*IRC v Richards' Executors* (1971) and see *Administrators of the Estate of Caton dec'd v Couch* (1997)). Although the Revenue publishes a scale of allowable expenses for the cost of establishing title (see SP 8/94), PRs may claim to deduct more than the 'scale' figure when higher expenses have been incurred. For deaths after March 1982, the PRs have the benefit of the indexation allowance. PRs have an annual exemption from CGT of £6,500 in the tax year of death and in each of the two following tax years. Thereafter they have no exemption, so that if it is intended thereafter to sell property in the estate and that sale will result in a chargeable gain, it may be advantageous to vest the asset in the appropriate beneficiary for him to sell. This will ensure that the beneficiary's annual exemption will be available to reduce the chargeable gain. On the other hand, it may be that any remaining gain will then be taxed at the 40% rate rather than at 23% as would have been the case if the PRs had sold the asset. The decision must depend upon the facts of each particular case.

[**15.62**]

EXAMPLE 15.2

(1) Dougall died in May 1993. In June 1997 a valuable Ming vase then worth £100,000 (probate value in 1993 £40,000) is to be sold. Administration of the estate has not been completed. The proceeds of sale will be split equally between Dougall's four children. The following possibilities should be considered:

(a) the PRs could first appropriate the vase to the four children who could then sell it taking advantage of four CGT annual exemptions (£26,000 in all). The resultant gain (say £34,000) will then be divided equally (£8,500 per child) and taxed at the appropriate rate which may be 40%. *Accordingly, maximum tax will be £13,600*; or

(b) the PRs could themselves sell the vase and realise gains of £60,000. No annual exemption will be available but the rate of CGT will be limited to 23%. *Accordingly, the maximum tax bill will be £13,800*.

Note: In appropriate cases PRs may prolong the administration of an estate so that they can eventually sell appreciating assets (typically land with development value) paying tax at only 23% (although note that the Revenue will look closely at such cases: See CG 30840).

(2) Continuing *Example 15.1*, if the PRs sell the book in March 1998 for £130,000, they have made a gross gain of £30,000 from which they can deduct their annual exemption of £6,500 (if unused); the incidental expenses of sale; a proportionate part of the cost of valuing the estate for probate in November 1997; and an indexation allowance, calculated on £100,000 as from October 1997, and on the relevant part of the cost of valuation as from November 1997.

3 The main residence

Where the PRs dispose of a private dwelling house which, both before and after the death, was occupied by a person who is entitled on death to the whole, or substantially the whole, of the proceeds of sale from the house, either absolutely or for life, by concesssion PRs have the benefit of the private residence exemption from CGT (ESC D5 and for principal private residence exemption, see [**16.61**] *et seq*). [**15.63**]-[**15.80**]

EXAMPLE 15.3

Bill and his brother Ben live in Bill's house. On his death Bill leaves the house to Ben who goes on living in it. The property has to be sold by the PRs to pay for Bill's funeral. Any gain will be exempt.

V LOSSES OF THE PRs

Losses made by the PRs on disposals of chargeable assets during administration can be set off against chargeable gains on other sales made by them. Any surplus losses at the end of the administration period cannot be transferred to beneficiaries (*contrast* losses made by trustees which can be passed to a beneficiary when the trust ends: [**18.44**]). Accordingly, when PRs anticipate that a loss will not be relieved, they may prefer to transfer the loss-making asset to the relevant beneficiary so that he can sell it and obtain the loss relief. [**15.81**]-[**15.100**]

VI TRANSFERS TO LEGATEES (TCGA 1992 s 62(4))

On the transfer of an asset to a legatee, the PRs make neither gain nor loss for CGT purposes and the legatee acquires the asset at the PRs' base value together with the expenses of transferring the asset to him (but note that no indexation allowance is available on these expenses). The base costs will in appropriate cases be a fraction of the probate value: for instance, if a 60% shareholding (valued at death as a majority holding) was split between the deceased's four sons each would receive a 15% holding with a base cost equal to one-quarter of the probate valuation of the 60% holding.

EXAMPLE 15.4

The PRs transfer the book (see *Example 15.1*) to the legatee (L) under the will in March 1998 when it is worth £130,000. The cost of valuing the book as a part of the whole estate in November 1997 was £1,000 and the PRs incurred incidental expenses involved in the transfer of the book in March 1998 of £150. L sells the book in July 1999 for £140,000. On the transfer by the PRs to L, no chargeable gain accrues to the PRs and L's base value is:

	£
Market value at death	100,000
Valuation cost	1,000
Expenses of transfer	150
Base cost of L	£101,150

When L sells the book in July 1999 for £140,000 he is charged to CGT on his gain which is £38,850 (£140,000 - £101,150) as reduced by any allowable expenditure that he has incurred, including an indexation allowance on £101,150 from March 1998 to July 1999.

A legatee is defined in TCGA 1992 s 64(2) as any person taking under a testamentary disposition or on intestacy or partial intestacy, whether beneficially or as a trustee. This definition covers only property passing under the will or on an intestacy to a beneficiary and to the extent that a beneficiary contracts with the PRs to purchase a particular asset or to obtain a greater share in an asset he is not taking that asset *qua* legatee (*Passant v Jackson* (1986)). A *donatio mortis causa* is treated for these purposes as a testamentary disposition and not as a gift, so that the donee acquires the asset at its market value on the donor's death and the donor is not treated as having made a chargeable gain.

Difficult questions may arise when a person receives assets under a trust created by will or under the intestacy rules. Does he receive them as a legatee (in which case there is no charge to CGT) or as a beneficiary absolutely entitled as against the trustee, in which case there is a deemed disposal under TCGA 1992 s 71 which may be chargeable (see Chapter 18)? The answer depends upon the status of the PRs (have they turned into trustees at the relevant time?) and the terms of the will (see *Cochrane's Executors v IRC* (1974) and *IRC v Matthew's Executors* (1984)). During the course of administration PRs are the sole owners of the deceased's assets, albeit in a fiduciary capacity (*Stamp Duties Comr (Queensland) v Livingston* (1965)) so that there is no trust of particular assets at that time (although the trustees will own a *chose in action*). Accordingly, if, before the completion of administration or the vesting of assets in themselves as trustees (whichever first occurs), the property ceases to be settled for CGT purposes, it would appear that when it is transferred to the relevant beneficiary he will take *qua* legatee (see *Example 15.5(2)* below and *Marshall v Kerr* (1994) at [**15.123**]).

EXAMPLE 15.5

(1) T dies leaving his house to executors on trust for his three children all of whom are over 18, in equal shares absolutely. Whether the children receive the assets before the administration is completed or after the executors have assented to themselves as trustees does not matter since they take as legatees. For CGT purposes joint ownership does not result in the property being settled (TCGA 1992 s 60: see further Chapter 18).

(2) T dies leaving his property to executors on trust for his widow for life and then for his three children absolutely, all of whom are over 18. If the widow dies *before the executors become trustees*, any distributions to the children will be received by them as legatees since, for CGT purposes, the trust ended on the widow's death. If, however, the widow dies *after* the executors have become trustees, the property is settled, so that the children receive assets as persons absolutely entitled as against the trustees with a consequent deemed disposal under TCGA 1992 s 71 (there will be no charge in this case because the event leading to their entitlement was the death of the life tenant: contrast the position if the interest had terminated *inter vivos*—see Chapter 18).

When the former matrimonial home of the deceased passes to his surviving spouse there is an uplift in the base value of the property on death in the usual way. On a subsequent disposal by that spouse, any gain since death will be exempt from CGT if the house has been occupied as that spouse's main residence. Even if it has not, by TCGA 1992 s 222(7), the deceased's period of ownership is deemed to be that of the surviving spouse in deciding what proportion of the gain (if any) is chargeable (see [**16.75**]).

[**15.101**]–[**15.120**]

EXAMPLE 15.6

T bought a house in 1987 for £50,000. It was his main residence until his death in 1991 when it was worth £150,000. His wife (W) never lived there with him, but became entitled to the house on his intestacy. T's administrators transferred the house to W in 1992. She thereupon occupied it as her main residence for one year and then went abroad until 1997 when she returned and sold the house for £250,000.

For the purpose of the main residence exemption, W can claim that she has occupied the house as her main residence for nine out of the ten years that it has been in the ownership of herself or T, ie:

1987–90 (4 years)	Occupied by T as his main residence
1991–92 (2 years)	Occupation by administrators treated as that of W and occupied by W
1993–97 (4 years)	Abroad from 1993 but last three years of ownership disregarded (TCGA 1992 s 223(1))

W is, therefore, charged on a proportion of the gain:

(1) Sale consideration (£250,000) - base cost (£150,000) = £100,000 (assuming no other allowable expenses).

(2) Fraction chargeable: £100,000 × $^1/_{10}$ = £10,000.

Were it not for s 222(7), she would be charged on a larger proportion of

the gain, ie: £100,000 × $\dfrac{1}{6 \text{ (length of her ownership)}}$ = £16,667

VII   DISCLAIMERS AND VARIATIONS (TCGA 1992 s 62(6))

1   **Basic rule**

Subject to conditions, which are the same as for IHT (see [**22.118**]), any variation of the deceased's will or of the intestacy rules, or any disclaimer, made in both cases within two years of the deceased's death may be treated:

(1) as if it were not a disposal (s 62(6)(a)); and
(2) as if it had been effected by the deceased or, in the case of a disclaimer, as if the disclaimed benefit had never been conferred (s 62(6)(b)).   [**15.121**]

EXAMPLE 15.7

Facts as in *Example 15.1*. L is entitled under T's will to the book worth £100,000. Within two years of T's death L varies the will so that the book (now worth £140,000) passes to his brother B. This need not be a disposal by L. Instead, it can be treated as if T's will had provided for the book to pass to B. Accordingly, B acquires the asset at its market value at death (£100,000) plus any additional expenses of the PRs.

2   **The election (TCGA 1992 s 62(7))**

As with IHT the above treatment does not apply to a variation unless the person or persons making the instrument so elect within six months of the instrument (or such longer period as the Board may allow). The election is couched in identical terms to that for IHT. In many cases, both elections are exercised so that the variation will be read back for both CGT and IHT purposes. This is not necessary, however, since the elections are independent of each other with the result that the IHT election can be exercised without the CGT election and *vice versa*. Careful thought should be given to this problem. Consider the following: [**15.122**]

EXAMPLE 15.8

(1) A will leaves quoted shares worth £100,000 to the testator's daughter. She transfers the shares within two years to her mother (the testator's surviving spouse). The shares are then worth £106,000.

    For IHT the election will be desirable as the result will be to reduce the testator's chargeable estate at death by £100,000 since the shares are now an exempt transfer to a surviving spouse.

    For CGT the election to read the disposal back should *not* be made since, if the daughter makes a chargeable disposal, her gain will be £106,000 – £100,000 = £6,000 which will be covered by her annual CGT exemption. Her mother will then acquire the shares at the higher base cost of £106,000.

(2) A will leaves quoted shares worth £100,000 to the testator's surviving spouse. After they have risen in value to £140,000 she decides (within the permitted time limit) to vary the will in favour of her daughter.

    For IHT it is debatable whether the election should be made. If it is, £100,000 will constitute a chargeable death transfer so that, assuming that the nil rate band has already been exhausted, tax will be charged at 40%. If it is not, the widow will make a lifetime gift of £140,000 which, if she survives by seven years, will be free of all tax. On the other hand, if it is likely that she will only survive her husband by a few weeks, then it will be necessary to consider whether it is better for £100,000 to be taxed as part of her dead husband's estate or for £140,000 to be taxed on her death.

    For CGT the disposal should be read back into the will since otherwise there will be a chargeable gain of £140,000 – £100,000 = £40,000.

3 **Marshall v Kerr (1994)**

a) *The issue*

The testator died in 1977 domiciled in Jersey and Mrs Kerr (UK resident and domiciled) became entitled to one-half of the residuary estate. By a deed of family arrangement executed in January 1978 made before the administration of the estate had been completed, her half share was to be retained by the personal representatives (a Jersey resident company) as trustees for, *inter alia*, Mrs Kerr. In due course gains were realised by those trustees and capital advanced to Mrs Kerr. If the settlement had been created by Mrs Kerr then the rules of TCGA 1992 s 87 would apply and capital payments made to her would attract a CGT charge (see [**20.54**]). Given that she had transferred property to trustees, on general principles she would be treated as the settlor of that trust: but was this conclusion displaced by the deeming provision in s 62(6) whereby if a variation is made within two years of death—provided that the appropriate election is made—it takes effect 'as if the variation had been effected by the deceased'?   [**15.123**]

b) *The taxpayer's argument*

The relevant variation fell within s 62(6) so that it did not constitute a disposal by Mrs Kerr but instead took effect as if it had been effected by the deceased. The trustee therefore received the property as legatee under s 62(4) and was treated as if the PR's acquisition of the asset had been his. The PR acquired the asset at the date of death at probate value (s 62(1)) so that on this analysis the trustee had acquired the asset at the date of death with the result that *at no stage did Mrs Kerr own the property*. Hence she could not be a settlor for the purpose of the s 87 charging provisions with the result that the payments that she received from the trustees were tax free.   [**15.124**]

c) *House of Lords speeches*

The Inland Revenue succeeded in the House of Lords by taking a point not argued in the lower courts. While accepting that s 87 took effect subject to the various deeming provisions contained in s 62 the argument presented before the Lords was that there was nothing in the latter section to prevent Mrs Kerr from being treated as settlor. Lord Browne-Wilkinson analysed matters as follows:

(1) Two assumptions were made in the lower courts neither of which was correct: *first*, that the variation constituted a settlement of assets comprised in the testator's estate and, *secondly*, that those were assets of which the testator was competent to dispose and so were acquired by the PRs under s 62(1).

(2) When the variation was made the estate was unadministered and hence Mrs Kerr did not dispose of specific assets but of a *chose in action*: namely her right to have the estate properly administered. Although an asset for CGT purposes, this was not an asset owned by the deceased, and so was not an asset of which the deceased had been competent to dispose.

(3) The disposal of the *chose* was not itself subject to charge because of s 62(6)(a).

(4) Under s 62(6)(b) the interest of the 'new' beneficiary is deemed to arise under the will of the deceased with the result that:

> 'an asset of which the deceased was competent to dispose at the death which is not sold in the course of the administration but is vested in the varied beneficiaries is deemed to have been acquired by the varied beneficiary as legatee under the Will'.

The 'new' beneficiary is therefore only deemed to acquire *qua* legatee if two conditions are satisfied. *First*, the asset must be one of which the deceased was competent to dispose and, *secondly*, that asset must be vested in the varied beneficiary as legatee. The process of administering the estate cannot be ignored: assets acquired by the PRs during administration are treated as if that acquisition were by the legatee who is not treated as acquiring those assets at death.

(5) Given that Mrs Kerr settled a *chose in action*, it followed that the trustees could not trace their ownership of the settled property to the PRs and thence back to the date of death. There was therefore nothing to displace the general proposition that Mrs Kerr was the settlor of the property. It would appear from the judgment of Lord Browne-Wilkinson that a similar conclusion would be arrived at even if the estate had been fully administered (and see CG 37888).   [**15.125**]

d) *Conclusions from the case*

(1) The judgments were based on technical arguments as to the nature of Mrs Kerr's proprietary interest.

(2) If a variation establishes a UK settlement, TCGA 1992 s 77 will provide that if the settlor retains an interest he is taxed on all gains realised by the trustees. As a result of the House of Lords speeches the settlor will be the original beneficiary (s 77 is discussed at [**14.85**]).

(3) A similar conclusion would be arrived at if the variation established an offshore settlement: as in the *Marshall v Kerr* case itself, it is the original beneficiary who will be treated as the settlor with the result that TCGA 1992 s 86 will apply to the settlement given that the settlor or a 'defined person' is one of the beneficial class (see [**20.56**]).

It should be stressed that in other cases, ie where the variation effects an outright gift, the decision in *Marshall v Kerr* does not create difficulties.

EXAMPLE 15.9

Boris, domiciled in France, leaves his villa in Tuscany and moneys in his Swiss bank account to his son Gaspard, a UK resident. By a variation of the terms of his will made within two years of Boris' death, the property is settled on discretionary Liechtenstein trusts for the benefit of Gaspard's family.

For *IHT* purposes, reading back ensures that the settlement is of excluded property (see [**27.21**]).

For *CGT* purposes, the settlement has been created by Gaspard, a UK domiciliary, so that the charging provisions in TCGA 1992 s 86 ff (see [**20.56**]) will apply.

(4) The case does not affect the IHT treatment of instruments of variation and disclaimer: see *Tax Bulletin*, February 1995, p 194.   [**15.126**]

16 CGT—exemptions and reliefs

In many cases a gain on the disposal of an asset will not be chargeable either because the gain itself is exempt or because the asset is not chargeable. Even if a gain is chargeable, there are various reliefs whereby the tax can be minimised or deferred indefinitely. As already noted at [14.86], there is an annual exemption for an individual whose gains do not exceed £6,500 (for 1997–98) in the tax year; trustees are generally entitled to half of the exemption available to individuals: ie £3,250 (see [14.89]). [16.1]

I MISCELLANEOUS EXEMPTIONS

Exempt assets Certain assets are not chargeable to CGT. The taxpayer, therefore, realises no chargeable gain or, often more significantly, no allowable loss on their disposal.

Non-chargeable assets include sterling (TCGA 1992 s 21), National Savings Certificates, Premium Bonds and Save As You Earn deposits (s 121), and private motor vehicles (s 263). Gains and losses arising on the disposal of investments in a Personal Equity Plan (PEP: see [4.157]) are disregarded. [16.2]

Exempt gains The following gains are exempt from CGT:
(1) damages for personal injuries and betting winnings (s 51 and see ESC D33);
(2) gains on the disposal of decorations for valour unless the decoration was acquired for money or money's worth (s 268);
(3) gains on the disposal of foreign currency obtained for private use (s 269). . A foreign currency bank account is a chargeable asset (a debt) unless the sum in that account was obtained for the personal expenditure of an individual or his family outside the UK (s 252). Where several accounts in a particular foreign currency are owned by the same taxpayer he may treat them as one account so that direct transfers between the accounts will not be chargeable disposals (SP 10/84);
(4) gains on the disposal of gilt-edged securities (s 115): the exemption also applies to futures and options in these instruments;
(5) gains on the disposal of ordinary shares in a venture capital trust are exempt from CGT (see [16.141]). There is also a qualified exemption for shares

acquired under the complimentary enterprise investment scheme (see [**4.122**]);

(6) the disposal of pension rights, annuity rights and annual payments will not generally give rise to a chargeable gain (s 237);

(7) any gain on the disposal of a life policy, a deferred annuity policy, or any rights under such policies, unless the disposal is by someone other than the original beneficial owner and *that person* acquired the interest or right for money or money's worth (s 210 and see *Taxation*, 17 November 1994, p 153); and

(8) gains are exempt if made by such bodies as authorised unit trusts and investment trusts (s 100); and charities, provided that the gain is applied for charitable purposes (s 256).   [**16.3**]

Charities   Disposals to charities and to certain national institutions are treated as made on a no gain/no loss basis (s 257 and see [**42.85**]).   [**16.4**]

Heritage property and woodlands   The exemptions for heritage property are basically the same as for IHT (see Chapter 23).

First, where property of national interest is given (or sold by private treaty) to a non-profit making body (including a charity or other national institution mentioned in s 256) any gain will be exempt from CGT provided that the Treasury so directs (see IHTA 1984 s 26(1)). *Secondly*, any gain on a disposal of such property may be conditionally exempt from CGT in the same way as for IHT (s 258; see IHTA 1984 ss 30, 31). *Thirdly*, the gain on any property that is accepted by the Treasury in satisfaction of IHT is exempt from CGT (s 258(2)(b)).

Consideration received for a disposal of trees (or saleable underwood) is excluded from any CGT computation provided that the disponer is the occupier who manages the woodlands on a commercial basis with a view to profit (s 113).   [**16.5**]-[**16.20**]

II   CHATTELS

1   Chattels which are wasting assets

A gain on the disposal of a chattel that is a wasting asset is generally exempt from CGT, the rationale being that since the taxpayer has enjoyed the use of the chattel, he should not be entitled to claim any loss in respect of it. A wasting asset is one with a predictable useful life of 50 years or less and includes yachts, caravans, washing machines, animals and all plant and machinery, the latter term to include, in the Revenue's view, such assets as antique clocks and watches, and certain vintage cars (see TCGA 1992 s 44 and [**14.41**]).   [**16.21**]

2   Non-wasting chattels

In the case of non-wasting chattels (eg, items of jewellery, antiques etc), if the disposal consideration is £6,000 or less, any gain is exempt and so does not enter the computation of the taxpayer's total gains in a tax year, leaving the annual exemption to be set against other gains (TCGA 1992 s 262(1)). CGT is as a result easier and less costly to administer as there is no need to calculate gains and losses on assets of relatively low value. Insofar as the disposal consideration exceeds £6,000, the chargeable gain is limited to 5/3 of the excess of that consideration over £6,000.

Where a loss is made on the disposal of a chattel and the disposal consideration is *less than* £6,000, the sum of £6,000 is substituted for that consideration so as to limit a claim for loss relief.   [16.22]

EXAMPLE 16.1

(1) A bought a necklace for £4,600 and later sold it for £7,200 so making a total gain of £2,600. The chargeable gain is reduced to 5/3 × £1,200 (£7,200 − £6,000) = £2,000.

(2) A bought a brooch for £8,000 and sold it for £4,600 so making an actual loss of £3,400. He is deemed to have sold it for £6,000 so that his allowable loss is restricted to £2,000 (£8,000 − £6,000).

Note: For the purpose of this Example incidental costs of disposal and the indexation allowance have been ignored: they should, of course, be taken into account in computing the chargeable gain which is subject to reduction.

3 Chattels comprising a set

The taxpayer cannot dispose of a set of articles by a series of separate transactions so as to take advantage of the £6,000 exemption on each disposal. Whether the disposals are to the same person or to connected persons (albeit on different occasions) they are regarded as a single transaction (see also TCGA 1992 s 19 and [14.24]).   [16.23]–[16.40]

EXAMPLE 16.2

A owns three Rousseau paintings which, as a set, have a market value of £30,000. He paid £4,000 for each of the paintings which individually are worth £6,000. He sells all three paintings at different times to his sister B for £6,000 each. He thereby appears to fall within the chattel exemption on each disposal. The Revenue can, however, treat the three disposals as a single disposal of an asset worth £30,000 with a base value of £12,000 so that A has made a chargeable gain of £18,000. (The meaning of 'a set' is not always obvious: a valuable collection of lead toy soldiers, for instance, is arguably not a set and the wording of s 262(4) suggests that at least three articles are required for a set: for the Revenue's views see CG 76632.)

III DEBTS

1 What is a debt?

A debt is a chargeable asset (TCGA 1992 s 21). It is not defined and bears the common law meaning of 'a sum payable in respect of a liquidated money demand recoverable by action' (*Rawley v Rawley* (1876)). It can include a right to receive a sum of money that is not yet ascertained (*O'Driscoll v Manchester Insurance Committee* (1915)) or a contingent right to receive a definite sum (*Mortimore v IRC* (1864)). However, for the purposes of CGT, it cannot include a right to receive an uncertain sum at an unascertained date; there must be a liability, either present or contingent, to pay a sum which is ascertained or capable of being ascertained at the time of disposal (*Marren v Ingles* (1980): see [14.26]).   [16.41]

EXAMPLE 16.3

Barry agrees to sell his Ming vase to Bruce for £15,000 plus one-half of any profits that Bruce realises if he resells the vase in the next ten years. The disposal consideration received for the vase is £15,000 plus the value of a *chose in action*. As that *chose* is both contingent (on resale occurring) and for an unascertained sum (half of any profits) it is not a debt. The *chose* is a separate asset and a CGT charge may arise on its disposal (see [**14.26**]).

2   The general principle

A disposal of a debt by the original creditor, his personal representatives or legatee is exempt from CGT unless it is a debt on a security (see [**16.44**]). 'Disposal' includes repayment of the debt (TCGA 1992 s 251). Since a contractual debt will normally give a creditor merely the right to repayment of the sum lent, together with interest, the disposal of a debt will rarely generate a gain and the aim of s 251 is to exclude the more likely claim for loss relief, particularly where the debt is never repaid. This provision only applies to the original creditor so that an assignee of a debt can claim an allowable loss if the debtor defaults, unless the assignee and the creditor are connected persons (s 251(4)).

If the debt is satisfied by a transfer of property, that property is acquired by the creditor at its market value. Since this could operate harshly for an original creditor who can claim no allowable loss, s 251(3) provides that on a subsequent disposal of the property, its base value is taken as the value of the debt.   [**16.42**]

EXAMPLE 16.4

A owes B £30,000 and in full satisfaction of the debt he gives B a painting worth £22,000. B does not have an allowable loss of £8,000. However, if B later sells the painting for £40,000 he is taxed on a gain of £10,000 only (£40,000 – £30,000).

3   Loans to traders

The harshness of TCGA 1992 s 251 is mitigated by s 253, allowing original creditors to claim loss relief in respect of a qualifying loan. The loan must have become irrecoverable and the creditor must not have assigned his rights. Creditor and debtor must not be married to each other nor be companies in the same group. A 'qualifying loan' must be used by a UK resident borrower *wholly for the purpose of a trade* (not being moneylending) carried on by him and the debt must not be 'on a security'. The relief is extended to include a loss arising from the guaranteeing of a 'qualifying loan' (see s 253(4) and *Leisureking Ltd v Cushing* (1993)).   [**16.43**]

4   Debt on a security

The legislation distinguishes between debts which can normally only decrease in value and those which may be disposed of at a profit. It, therefore, provides that a 'debt on a security' is chargeable to CGT even in the hands of the original creditor (TCGA 1992 s 251).

The term 'debt on a security' lacks both statutory and satisfactory judicial interpretation despite three cases (*Cleveleys Investment Trust Co v IRC* (1971); *Aberdeen Construction Group Ltd v IRC* (1978); *W T Ramsay Ltd v IRC* (1981)). It has a limited and technical meaning and '[it] is not a synonym for a secured debt' per Lord Wilberforce in *Aberdeen Construction Group Ltd v IRC*. The word 'security' is defined in TCGA 1992 s 132(3) as including 'any loan stock or similar security whether of the government of the UK or elsewhere, or of any company, and whether secured or unsecured'. Despite the word '*including*' the Revenue has stated that it regards the definition as exhaustive (see CCAB June 1969 although this is not referred to in CG 53421 which refers to this definition as being 'of limited use').

In *Taylor Clark International Ltd v Lewis* (1997) Robert Walker J concluded that the basic requirement for a debt on security were:

(1) the debt had to be capable of being assigned;
(2) it had to carry interest;
(3) to have a structure of permanence; and
(4) to provide proprietary security.

For the Revenue's views, see CG 53425

With the introduction of a new regime for the taxation of company loan relationships (see [**28.48**]) most debt held by companies has been removed from the capital gains charge: instead profits and losses on such debt together with interest are charged or allowed as income. [**16.44**]

5 Qualifying corporate bonds

Gains on the disposal of a 'qualifying corporate bond' (which includes most company debentures) are exempt from CGT under TCGA 1992 s 117. Losses realised by the original investor may, in certain circumstances, attract relief under s 254. This matter is considered at [**28.76**]. [**16.45**]-[**16.60**]

IV THE MAIN RESIDENCE

The most important exemption for the individual taxpayer, and the one which probably affects more taxpayers than does any other is from any gain made on the disposal of the principal private residence. This exemption, combined with mortgage interest relief (albeit that such relief has now been severely restricted) provides government encouragement for the investment of private capital in home ownership (TCGA 1992 ss 222–226). [**16.61**]

1 When is the exemption available?

The exemption is available for any gain arising on the disposal by gift or sale by a taxpayer of his only or main residence, including grounds of up to half a hectare (or such larger area as is required for the reasonable enjoyment of the dwelling house) (TCGA 1992 s 222). [**16.62**]

2 Meaning of 'dwelling house' and 'residence'

a) *Meaning of a 'dwelling house'*

What qualifies as a dwelling house is a question of fact. In *Makins v Elson* (1977) the taxpayer bought land intending to build a house on it. In the meantime, he lived there in a caravan. He never built the house and later sold both land and caravan at a profit. The caravan was held, on the facts, to be a dwelling house; the most significant of these facts being that it was connected to the mains services as well as to the telephone system and that it was resting on bricks so that it was not movable. In contrast, in *Moore v Thompson* (1986) the court held that since there was no supply of water or electricity, the caravan in question was not a dwelling house. [**16.63**]

b) *'Residence': a degree of permanence*

Although permanent residence is not a *condition* for the application of relief, a distinction has to be drawn between a permanent residence and temporary accommodation. In *Goodwin v Curtis* (1996), the taxpayer had advertised a farmhouse for sale before he had completed his purchase of it. He lived in the farmhouse for just a day over one month until the completion of the sale by him. In agreeing with the Commissioners that the farmhouse could not be said to have been occupied by the taxpayer as his home, Vinelott J said that amongst other factors to be weighed by the Commissioners in deciding whether a particular dwelling house qualifies as a residence are 'the degree of permanence, continuity and the expectation of continuity'.   [**16.64**]

c) *A 'residence': the entity test*

As far as the term 'residence' is concerned, a major problem is whether, in any given situation, two or more units can constitute a single residence. Selling a house with additional accommodation available either for staff or aged relatives is not unusual and there now exists a substantial body of case law, but from which there has failed to emerge any clear or satisfactory guidelines. In *Batey v Wakefield* (1982), the first in the series of cases, a separate bungalow within the grounds of the taxpayer's house and found by the General Commissioner as fact to have been used by a caretaker to enable him to perform the duties of his employment with the taxpayer, was considered by the Court of Appeal to be exempt from CGT on its sale. The court concluded that it was necessary to identify the entity which could properly be described as constituting the residence (the 'entity' test). Fox LJ commented:

'in the ordinary use of English, a dwelling house, or a residence, can comprise several dwellings which are not physically joined at all'.

In his view, the fact that the bungalow was physically separate from the main dwelling house was 'irrelevant'.

This was followed by Vinelott J in *Williams v Merrylees* (1987) who echoed the words of Fox LJ when he summarised the approach to be taken:

'what one is looking for is an entity which can be sensibly described as being a dwelling house though split into different buildings performing different functions'.   [**16.65**]

d) *The curtilage test*

However, in *Markey v Saunders* (1987), Walton J, ignoring the entity test, indicated that two conditions had to be satisfied: *first*, that occupation of the 'secondary' building had to increase the taxpayer's enjoyment of the main house and, *secondly*, that the other building had to be 'very closely adjacent' to the main building. He decided that a staff bungalow some 130 metres distant from the main residence and standing in its own grounds did not satisfy the second of the two conditions and so could not be treated as part of a single residence, with the result that, on its disposal, CGT was chargeable.

The Court of Appeal had the opportunity to review these decisions in *Lewis v Rook* (1992) which concerned the sale of a cottage some 200 yards from the main house which had been occupied by the taxpayer's gardener. Giving the judgment of the court, Balcombe LJ concluded that no building could form part of a dwelling house which included the main house unless the building was 'appurtenant to, and within the curtilage of' the main house (the 'curtilage' test). In applying what he believed to be 'well-recognised legal concepts' in the interpretation of the term 'dwelling house' or 'residence' and rejecting the previous approach of treating the matter as a question of fact, Balcombe LJ concluded that the main residence exemption was inapplicable.

It is a cause for concern that the word 'curtilage' appears nowhere in the CGT legislation, although in other contexts it has been held to mean 'a small area about a building', and that the court appears to be preferring the restrictive approach in *Markey v Saunders* to the flexibility of *Batey v Wakefield* and *Williams v Merrylees*. The very imprecision of the word 'curtilage' ensures that further cases are likely to come before the courts! The first such case, *Honour v Norris* (1992) largely turned on its own facts with the judge rejecting as an 'affront to commonsense' the suggestion that a number of separate flats in a square could constitute a single dwelling house.

Current Revenue thinking in this area was set out in the *Tax Bulletin*, August 1994, p 148 where it is stated:

'Where more dispersed groups of buildings have a clear relationship with each other they will fall within a single curtilage if they constitute an integral whole. In the Leasehold Reform Act case of *Methuen-Campbell v Walters*, quoted with approval in *Lewis v Rook*, the Court held that "for one corporeal hereditament to fall within the curtilage of another, the former must be so intimately associated with the latter as to lead to the conclusion that the former in truth forms part and parcel of the latter". Whether one building is part and parcel of another will depend primarily on whether there is a close geographical relationship between them. Furthermore, because the test is to identify an integral whole, a wall or fence separating two buildings will normally be sufficient to establish that they are not within the same curtilage. Similarly, a public road or stretch of tidal water will set a limit to the curtilage of the building. Buildings which are within the curtilage of a main house will normally pass automatically on a conveyance of that house without having to be specifically mentioned. There is a distinction between the curtilage of a main house and the curtilage of an estate as a whole and the fact that that whole estate may be contained within a single boundary does not mean that the buildings on the estate should be regarded as within the curtilage of the main house.'

(See also CG 64245.)

[16.66]

3 How many residences can qualify for exemption?

Property owned by the taxpayer but used as a residence by a dependent relative   Prior to 6 April 1988, a maximum of two houses qualified for exemption; the only or main residence and a property owned by the taxpayer but used as a residence by a dependent relative rent-free and for no other consideration.

This exemption for dependent relatives does not apply to disposals on or after 6 April 1988 (when mortgage interest relief was similarly withdrawn from dependent relative accommodation, see [**4.63**]). However, transitional relief continues to be available so long as the dependent relative conditions were satisfied either on 5 April 1988 or at any earlier time. Where this relief is claimed, ESC D20 permits payment by the relative of rates and of the costs of repairs to the dwelling house attributable to normal wear and tear without prejudicing the condition that the dwelling house must have been provided free and without consideration. In contrast, any payments made by the occupier towards repayment of a mortgage would lead to a loss of relief.

If qualifying occupation ceased before 6 April 1988 or ceases thereafter, the subsequent re-occupation of the property by a dependent relative will not be included in calculating the amount of any gain which, when the property is sold, is exempt from CGT. [**16.67**]

EXAMPLE 16.5

Thoughtful's widowed mother-in-law has lived since 1980 rent free in a bijou cottage owned by Thoughtful. He does not provide similar accommodation for any other dependent relative.

(1) As an existing arrangement, Thoughtful will continue to be entitled to the

CGT exemption on any disposal of the cottage so long as his mother-in-law continues to live there on the same terms.

(2) If the cottage is sold after 6 April 1988 and a small flat purchased as a replacement, no CGT will be charged on the sale but the flat will not qualify for CGT relief.

(3) If, instead, Thoughtful's mother-in-law ceases to occupy the cottage as her main residence either before or after 6 April 1988 but at some stage thereafter resumes occupation, no CGT exemption will be available to Thoughtful in respect of the gain attributable to his mother-in-law's later period of occupation.

Husband and wife   Husband and wife can have only one main residence whilst they are living together (s 222(6)). For the operation of the election (which is considered below) when a couple marry, see CG 64525.   **[16.68]**

Where the taxpayer has more than one residence   The question of whether a particular property is a taxpayer's 'only or main residence' is sometimes a difficult one to answer. If only one property is occupied by him as a residence the exemption *prima facie* applies to that property. Where the taxpayer has two residences, only the residence which is his main residence can qualify for relief. Any problems that might arise in deciding which of two residences is the main residence are obviated since the taxpayer can elect for one to be treated as his main residence (TCGA 1992 s 222(5)). Of course the election is only available in respect of 'residences' and cannot be used to convert a dwelling house which is not in use as a residence into one for the purpose of obtaining relief (see CG 64486). The election can be back-dated for up to two years to the date when the second residence was acquired and can be varied at any time, the variation also being effective for the two previous years. In *Griffin v Craig-Harvey* (1994), the taxpayer's argument that an election could be made at any time during the period of ownership of a dwelling house to take effect for a period of up to two years prior to the date of the notice, was rejected. Vinelott J held that an election could only be made within two years of the acquisition of a second or subsequent residence. This decision has practical implications for taxpayers owning more than one residence who may find themselves out of time to make the necessary election.

Failure to make an election means that the inspector of taxes will decide which is the main residence, subject to the right of appeal by the taxpayer. The inspector's decision is a question of fact, decided not simply by the periods of time spent in each residence. For a discussion of the courts' approach, see the income tax case of *Frost v Feltham* (1981) [**4.56**]).

An election can and should be made if a taxpayer occupies a property as a residence under a tenancy agreement (but *not* under a licence, where the occupier has only a personal, and not a proprietary, interest) whilst at the same time owning a second property (see further ESC D21).   **[16.69]**

EXAMPLE 16.6

Barber having lived in Spitalfields for many years acquires a luxury flat on the Essex coast in June 1997. At the same time he puts the Spitalfields house up for sale. When that house is sold he intends to rent a *pied à terre* in London.

(1) By June 1999 he should elect whether Spitalfields or the flat is his main residence in respect of the period from June 1997.

(2) The last three years of ownership are ignored in applying the main residence exemption and so if Spitalfields is sold by June 1999 or if he expects it to sell within the following year he should elect for the flat to be his main residence.

(3) When he acquires the rented property in London he will again have two

residences and should therefore elect within two years for the Essex flat to be his main residence.

(4) If, instead of renting a property in London, he moves instead into job-related accommodation under a service occupancy, an election *cannot* be made and relief will remain available for the Esssex flat. This is because his rights, which derive from the contract of service, are personal only and create no proprietary rights in his favour (for residences occupied under licence, see *Tax Bulletin*, October 1994, p 166).

4 Miscellaneous problems

Land used with the house Land of up to half an hectare (or permitted larger area) is exempt only if it is being used for the taxpayer's own occupation and for the enjoyment of his residence. In construing this phrase, it should be noted that the legislation as it relates to the *land* (in contrast to the *dwelling house*) refers to the position at the date of disposal. Thus, a gain made on a disposal of land will not be exempt if the residence has already been sold. In *Varty v Lynes* (1976) the taxpayer sold his house and part of the garden. Later he sold the remaining part of the garden with the benefit of planning permission. It was held that this second disposal was chargeable and the whole gain, including that which had accrued whilst the garden land was occupied by the taxpayer along with the house, was taxed. Had the taxpayer sold the garden before or at the same time as the house, any gain would have been exempt. Brightman J suggested that his construction of s 222(1)(b) created an anomaly in that 'if the taxpayer goes out of occupation of the dwelling house a month before he sells it, the exemption will be lost in respect of the garden'. However, the current Revenue practice as explained in *Tax Bulletin*, August 1994, p 148 is not to apply arguments based upon that *dictum*, so that contemporaneous sales of the house and the garden (even if for development) benefit from the exemption.

What constitutes land for the enjoyment of a principal private residence was considered in *Wakeling v Pearce* (1995). In that case, the taxpayer had cultivated a garden and maintained a washing-line in a field which was separated from her residence by another property not owned by her. The use of the field declined over the years, but it continued in a reduced form until its eventual sale as two building plots. The Special Commissioner held that the field was enjoyed with the residence and that there was no statutory requirement that the land should adjoin or be contiguous with the residence. Following its decision not to appeal against this decision because of the particular circumstances of the taxpayer, the Revenue published their interpretation of the legislation (*Tax Bulletin*, August 1995, p 239). Attributing to the terms 'garden' and 'grounds' their normal, everyday meaning, the Revenue regards a garden as land devoted to cultivation of flowers, fruit or vegetables but that grounds cover 'enclosed land serving chiefly for ornament or recreation surrounding or attached to a dwelling house or other building'. So, where land surrounds the residence and both are in the same ownership, it will qualify for relief unless it is used for other purposes such as a trade or agriculture. Relief will not be lost by reason only of the fact that the land is not used exclusively for recreational purposes or if there is a building on the land, provided that it is not being used for business purposes. Where land is physically separated from the residence, relief cannot be claimed merely by reason of the fact that it is used as a garden and that the two are in common ownership; by the same token, mere separation is not by itself sufficient to deny relief. The practice of the Revenue is to allow a claim in respect of land which can be shown to be 'naturally and traditionally the garden of the residence, so that it would normally be offered to a prospective purchaser as part of the residence'.

[16.70]

EXAMPLE 16.7

Bill is the owner of a village house which he purchased along with a small garden across the road from the residence. He later bought a further one acre of land upon which he built a tennis court. This land is separated from his house by the neighbouring property, and is reached by means of an informal path. Bill has recently sold all of his land, whilst retaining his residence.

It is quite common in villages for a garden to be across the road from the residence. If it can be shown that this was such a village, then Bill could claim relief under TCGA 1992 s 222(1)(b) for this part of his garden, even though separated from his residence, on the ground that it is a garden that would 'normally be offered to prospective purchaser as part of the residence'. The land upon which the tennis court stands is unlikely to qualify for relief. Although Bill may regard it as part of the garden, it was bought because the existing garden was inadequate for a tennis court, and could not be viewed as being 'naturally and traditionally' the garden of the residence.

Sale by trustees   Where trustees dispose of a house which is the residence of a beneficiary who is entitled to occupy it by the express terms of the settlement (TCGA 1992 s 225) or under a discretion exercised by the trustees, any gain is exempt. The latter point was decided in *Sansom v Peay* (1976) and has repercussions for IHT since the Revenue will argue that the beneficiary in whose favour the discretion has been exercised thereby acquires an interest in possession in the settlement (see SP 10/79 and [**24.27**]).   [**16.71**]

Use of a house for a business   If part of the house is used *exclusively* for business purposes, a proportionate part of the gain on a disposal of a property becomes chargeable (TCGA 1992 s 224). However, as long as no part is used exclusively for business purposes no part of the exemption will be lost. Doctors and dentists who have a surgery in their house are advised to hold a party in that surgery at least once a year (and to invite their tax inspector!).   [**16.72**]

Letting part of the property   Where the whole or part of the property has been let as residential accommodation this may result in a partial loss of exemption. However, the gain attributable to the letting (calculated according to how much was let and for how long) will be exempt from CGT up to the lesser of £40,000 and the exemption attributable to the owner's occupation. This relief does not apply if the let portion forms a separate dwelling (TCGA 1992 s 223(4)). The Revenue has stated that the taking of lodgers will not result in a loss of any of the exemption provided that the lodger lives as part of the family and shares living accommodation (SP 14/80).

In *Owen v Elliott* (1990) the taxpayer carried on the business of a private hotel or boarding house on premises which he also occupied as his main residence and argued that he was entitled to relief since taking in hotel guests amounted to 'residential accommodation'. The Court of Appeal accepted this argument and rejected the argument that the occupation had to be by persons making their home in the premises let as opposed to paying guests staying overnight or on holiday. Leggatt LJ stated that:

'The expression "residential accommodation" does not directly or by association mean premises likely to be occupied as a home. It means living accommodation, by contrast, for example, with office accommodation. I regard as wholly artificial attempts to distinguish between a letting by the owner and a letting to the occupant; and between letting to a lodger and letting to a guest in a boarding house; and between a letting that is likely to be used by the occupant as his home and one that is not.'   [**16.73**]

EXAMPLE 16.8

A sells his house which he has owned for 20 years realising a gain of £120,000. He occupied the entire house during the first ten years. For the next six years he let one-third of it and for the final four years the entire property.

	£	£
Total gain		120,000
Less: exemptions		
(i) 10 years' occupation	60,000	
(ii) 6 years' occupation of		
²/₃ (£60,000 × ²/₃ × 6/10)	24,000	
(iii) final 3 years' ownership		
(£60,000 × 3/10)	18,000	102,000
Gain attributable to letting		18,000
Less: exemption (part)		18,000
Chargeable portion		£ Nil

Disposals by PRs   Concessionary relief may be available to PRs (see ESC D5 discussed at [**15.63**]).   [**16.74**]

Disposals by legatees   A spouse who inherits a dwelling house on the death of the other spouse also inherits the other spouse's period of ownership for the purpose of calculating this relief (TCGA 1992 s 222(7)(a); and see ibid, s 62; *Tax Bulletin*, August 1994, p 150 and [**15.101**]). In other cases the beneficial period of ownership begins on the date of death and if the beneficiary does not become resident until a later date the period prior to becoming resident will not qualify for relief (unless falling within the final 36 month period prior to disposal): see *Tax Bulletin*, August 1994, p 151 and [**16.76**].   [**16.75**]

5   Effect of periods of absence

To qualify for the exemption, the taxpayer must occupy the property as his only or main residence throughout the period of his ownership: for these purposes only the period of ownership after 31 March 1982 counts (s 223(7)). As a general rule, therefore, the effect of periods of absence is that on the disposal of the residence a proportion of any gain will be charged. That proportion is calculated by the formula:

$$\text{Total gain} \ \times \ \frac{\text{period of absence}}{\text{period of ownership}}$$

Special rules operate for husband and wife since in deciding whether a house has been occupied as a main residence throughout the period of ownership one spouse can take advantage of a period of ownership of the other (TCGA 1992 s 222(7)(a): see [**15.101**] for an illustration of this rule).

Despite the general rule that absences render part of the gain chargeable certain permitted absences are ignored. These include, by concession, the first 12 months of ownership in cases where occupation was delayed because the house was being built or altered, or up to a period of two years where there are good reasons for exceptional delay (SP D4). More important, the last three years of ownership are likewise ignored and this may prove helpful on a matrimonial breakdown (see generally Chapter 41 and ESC D6). It also means that a taxpayer owning two houses can by careful use of his election obtain a tax advantage, subject of course, to the necessity of making the election within two years of the second or subsequent acquisition (see [**16.69**] and *Example 16.6*).

TCGA 1992 s 223 allows other periods of absence to be ignored provided that the owner had no other residence available for the exemption during these periods and that as a matter of fact he resided in the house *before and after* the absence in question. These periods are:

(1) any period or periods of absence not exceeding three years altogether;
(2) any period when the taxpayer was employed abroad; and
(3) a maximum period of four years where the owner could not occupy the property because he was employed elsewhere.

ESC D3 gives relief when the absence results from a non-owning spouse's employment and the Revenue also accepts that, if the absence exceeds the permitted period in (1)–(3), it is only the excess which does not qualify for the exemption. The requirement that the taxpayer should reside after the period of absence will not apply in (2) and (3) if that is prevented by the terms of his employment (ESC D4). If he is required either by the nature of his employment or as the result of his trade or profession to live in other accommodation ('job-related accommodation'—see [**4.56**]) he will obtain the exemption if he buys a house intending to use it in the future as a main residence. It does not matter that he never occupies it and that it is let throughout, provided that he can show that he intended to live there. He should, of course, be advised to make the main residence election since he is occupying other (job-related) property (unless this occupation derives from his contract of service — see [**16.69**]).   [**16.76**]

6   Expenditure with profit making motive

The exemption does not apply if the house was acquired wholly or partly for the purpose of realising a gain, nor to a gain attributable to any expenditure which was incurred wholly or partly for the purpose of realising a gain (TCGA 1992 s 224(3)). The acquisition of a freehold reversion by a tenant with a view to selling an absolute title to the property would appear to fall within this provision. If so, the portion of the gain attributable to the reversion would be assessable. The Revenue has, however, indicated that expenditure incurred in obtaining planning permission or obtaining the release of a restrictive covenant would be ignored for the purpose of s 224(3). The requirement of motive makes this provision difficult to apply, but the Revenue view is that only where the *primary purpose* of the acquisition was an early disposal at a profit will it be invoked (*Tax Bulletin*, August 1994, p 150). In *Jones v Wilcock* (1996) the taxpayer and his wife had lived in their home for nearly five years. In trying to establish an allowable loss, he argued that the exemption should not apply since he had acquired his home with the object of selling it at a profit. The Special Commissioner rejected this argument, saying that the word 'intention' did not always equate with 'purpose' and that the taxpayer had bought the property in order to provide himself and his wife with a home. An eventual gain was a hope, possibly an expectation, but it was not a 'purpose' within s 224(3).   [**16.77**]–[**16.90**]

V   BUSINESS RELIEFS

1   The problems and the taxes

A number of CGT reliefs relate to businesses both incorporated and unincorporated. Their aim is to enable businesses to be carried on and transferred without being threatened by taxation. This chapter is concerned only with

CGT reliefs: bear in mind a disposal of a business will normally involve other taxes.

The disposal may be by way of gift (including death) or by sale. If by way of *gift*, the relevant taxes will be CGT, income tax and IHT. For CGT, hold-over relief under TCGA 1992 s 165 will usually be available on a lifetime gift; on a death, there will be no CGT. Where the transfer is a *sale*, income tax and CGT may apply.

The CGT business reliefs may apply to a disposal of:

(1) a sole trade/profession;
(2) a part of a trade/profession (eg a partnership share);
(3) shares in a company; and
(4) assets used by a company or partnership in which the owner of the assets either owns shares or is a partner.

In a number of cases relief is given by a deferment of the CGT charge and this is usually done by deducting the otherwise chargeable gain from the acquisition cost of a new or replacement asset (roll-over or hold-over relief). For the Revenue's views on the order of reliefs, see CG 60210. **[16.91]**

2 Roll-over (replacement of business assets) (TCGA 1992 ss 152–159)

Basic conditions for relief Where certain assets of a business are sold and the proceeds of sale wholly reinvested in acquiring a 'new' asset to be used in a business, the taxpayer can elect to roll over the gain and deduct it from the acquisition cost of the new asset. Tax is, therefore, postponed until that asset is sold and no replacement qualifying asset purchased. The new asset must be bought within one year *before* or three years *after* the disposal of the old one, and once it is acquired, it must 'on the acquisition' be taken into use for the purposes of the taxpayer's trade. A gap between the time of acquisition and the time when it is used in the trade will mean that the exemption will not be available (see *Campbell Connelly Co Ltd v Barnett* (1993) and the Special Commissioner's decision in *Milton v Chivers* (1996) holding that while 'on the acquisition' did not imply immediacy, it did exclude dilatoriness).

> ### EXAMPLE 16.9
>
> A makes a gain of £50,000 on the sale of factory 1, but he immediately buys factory 2 for £120,000. He can roll the gain of £50,000 into the purchase price of factory 2 thereby reducing it to £70,000 (actual cost £120,000 minus rolled-over gain of £50,000).

It with be appreciated that the 'new' asset can be acquired before the disposal of the old asset — the Revenue accepts that the requirements are met if 'the old assets, or the proceeds of the old assets, are part of the resources available to the taxpayer when the new assets are acquired'. An important limitation on the relief was, however, confirmed by the Court of Appeal in *Watton v Tippett* (1997) where the taxpayer, having purchased certain freehold land and buildings (unit 1) for a single unapportioned consideration, within 12 months of that purchase sold part of the same land and buildings (unit 1A) and claimed to roll over the gain made on that disposal into the land and buildings retained by him (unit 1B). Rejecting this claim the court held that it was critical to identify the asset acquired and disposed of and unit 1B had not been acquired as such. The position would have been different if two separate properties had been purchased albeit for a single unapportioned consideration given that this could be apportioned under TCGA 1992 s 52(4). **[16.92]**

EXAMPLE 16.10

If A acquires factory 1 (as in the above example), but almost immediately sells part of it, he cannot roll any gain over into the acquisition cost of the remainder of the factory retained by him. It is a part disposal of a single asset; the consideration for that single asset cannot, according to *Watton v Tippett* (above), be apportioned.

If A acquires two adjacent factories (1 and 2) at the same time but under separate contracts, and immediately sells factory 2, A can roll over any gain into the acquisition cost of factory 1: this is *not* a part disposal of a single asset, but rather a disposal of a severable part of the taxpayer's assets, with separate consideration attributable to the 'old' asset (factory 2) and 'other' assets (factory 1). *Note* that s 152 does not as such require 'new' assets to be acquired; rather it refers to the consideration being applied in acquiring *other* assets (and see, for instance, ESC D22 permitting expenditure on improvement to existing assets).

Qualifying assets: The assets must be comprised in the list of business assets in TCGA 1992 s 155. These are land and buildings; fixed plant and machinery; ships; aircraft; hovercraft; goodwill; satellites, space stations and spacecraft; milk and potato quotas and the EU quotas for the premium given to producers of ewes and suckler cows. This list can be added to by Treasury Order. The old and new assets need not be of the same type, however, eg a gain on the sale of an aircraft can be rolled over into the purchase of a hovercraft. Further, although the old asset must have been used in the taxpayer's trade during the whole time that he owned it (otherwise only partial roll-over is allowed), it could have been used in successive trades provided that the gap between them did not exceed three years.   **[16.93]**

EXAMPLE 16.11

A inherited a freehold shop in 1979 when its value was £25,000. The shop was kept empty until 1985 when he started a fish and chip shop. He sold the shop in 1997 for £60,000 and purchased new premises for £75,000. The value of the shop in 1982 was £36,000.

As a result of rebasing, his total gain in 1997 (excluding indexation) is £24,000 and (counting only periods after March 1982) the premises have been used for business purposes during twelve-fifteenths of the ownership period. Hence £19,200 of the gain is rolled over but the balance (£4,800) is taxed.

Occupation for business purposes: The assets that are sold must be occupied as well as used for the purposes of the taxpayer's business. If the property is occupied by his partner or employee, he must be able to show that their occupation is *representative* (ie attributed to him) to obtain the relief. For occupation to be representative it must *either* (1) be essential for the partner or employee to occupy the property to perform his duties; *or* (2) be an express term of the employment contract (or partnership agreement) that he should do so, and the occupation must enable him to perform his duties better. If either of these conditions is proved, the Revenue accept that the property is used for the purpose of the owner's trade (see *Anderton v Lamb* (1981)).

The new asset need not be used in the same trade as the old but can be used in another trade carried on by the taxpayer simultaneously or successively, provided in the latter case that there is not more than a three-year gap between the ceasing of one trade and the start of another (see SP 8/81). There is nothing to prevent the taxpayer from rolling his gain into the purchase of more than one asset or to require him to continue to use the new asset in a trade throughout his period of ownership. ESC D22-25 extend the relief, *inter alia*, to cover improvements to, or capital expenditure to enhance the value of, existing assets;

the acquisition of a further interest in an asset already used for the purposes of the trade; and the partition of land on the dissolution of a partnership. **[16.94]**

Non residents and foreign assets: Relief is not available to a non-UK resident who sells a chargeable asset (ie one used in a trade carried on through a UK branch or agency) and then purchases a new asset which is not chargeable because it is situated outside the UK (TCGA 1992 s 159). Relief is, however, available if he acquires further UK branch or agency assets and is also given to a UK resident who rolls over into the acquisition of a qualifying asset wherever situated (and even though he may be non resident at the time of acquisition: see CG 60253). **[16.95]**

Partnerships, Companies and Employees: This relief is available to partnerships and to companies and it can be claimed for an asset which is owned by an individual and used by his partnership or personal company (for the definition of such a company, see **[16.107]**). In such cases, however, the relief is only available to the individual and the replacement asset cannot be purchased by the partnership or company. Employees may claim the relief for assets owned by them so long as the assets are used (or, in the case of land and buildings, occupied) only for the purposes of the employment. (Note, however, that it is not necessary for the asset to be used *exclusively* by the employee in the course of his employment so that relief may apply even if the asset is provided for the general use of the employer: see SP 5/86.) **[16.96]**

Restrictions on the relief There are certain restrictions on the relief.

First, if the new asset is a depreciating asset (defined as a 'wasting asset'—see **[14.41]**—or one which will become a wasting asset within ten years, such as a lease with 60 years unexpired) the gain on the old asset cannot be deducted from the cost of the new. Instead, tax on the gain is postponed until the earliest of the three following events:

(1) ten years elapse from the date of the purchase of the new asset; or
(2) the taxpayer disposes of the new asset; or
(3) the taxpayer ceases to use the new asset for the purposes of a trade.

ESC D45 exempts from tax gains arising when the new asset ceases to be used in a trade because of the death of the taxpayer.

If, before the deferred gain becomes chargeable, a new asset is acquired (whether the depreciating asset is sold or not), the deferred gain may be rolled into the new asset (see TCGA 1992 s 154).

EXAMPLE 16.12

Sam sells his freehold fish and chip shop for £25,000 thereby making a gain of £12,000. One year later he buys a 55-year lease on new premises for £27,000 and seven years after that acquires a further freehold shop for £35,000.
(1) Purchase of 55-year lease: this lease is a depreciating asset. The gain of £12,000 on the sale of the original shop is, therefore, held in suspense for ten years.
(2) Purchase of the freehold shop: as the purchase occurs within ten years of the gain, roll-over relief is available so that the purchase price is reduced to £23,000.

Secondly, if the whole of the proceeds of sale are not reinvested in acquiring the new asset there is a chargeable gain equivalent to the amount not re-invested and it is only the balance that is rolled over. Accordingly, if the purchase price of the new asset does not exceed the acquisition cost of the old, all the gain is chargeable and there is nothing to roll over (contrast 'reinvestment relief' which requires the gain *only* to be reinvested: see **[16.121]**).

The new asset must, of course, be purchased for use in a business so that if there is an element of non-business user relief will be restricted accordingly.

EXAMPLE 16.13

A buys factory 1 for £50,000 and sells it for £100,000 thereby making a gain of £50,000. A buys factory 2 for £80,000. The amount not reinvested (£20,000, ie £100,000 - £80,000) is chargeable. The balance of the gain (£30,000) is rolled over so that the acquisition cost of factory 2 is £50,000. If factory 2 had only cost £50,000 the amount not reinvested would equal the gain (ie £50,000) and be chargeable.

In *Tod v Mudd* (1987) the taxpayer sold his accountancy practice and with his wife bought premises to carry on business as hoteliers in partnership. The premises were bought as tenants in common with a 75% interest being held by Mr Mudd and 25% by his wife and it was agreed that they would be used as to 75% for business purposes and 25% for private purposes. The partnership agreement stated that the business of the partnership should be conducted on that portion of the premises attributable to Mr Mudd's share. The court held that roll-over relief should be given to Mr Mudd but only on 75% of 75% of the purchase price because his interest as a tenant in common constituted a share in the whole property and not in a distinct 75% portion thereof. Accordingly, because of the way in which this arrangement had been structured, roll-over relief was restricted. There are a number of ways in which matters could have been organised so that full relief would have been given to Mr Mudd. *First*, he could have bought the whole of the new premises for business use and then given 25% to his wife. *Secondly*, he could have purchased an identified and separate portion of the premises (75% thereof) in his sole name and for business use leaving his wife to purchase the remaining portion for private purposes. Finally, the defective arrangement could have been cured had Mr Mudd bought out Mrs Mudd's 25% share within three years of the disposal of his accountancy practice.

If the taxpayer knows that the price of the new asset will be too low to enable him to claim roll-over (or full roll-over) relief and he is married, it may be advantageous to transfer a share in the old asset to his wife before it is sold although this ruse could be challenged under the *Ramsay* principle (Chapter 36).

EXAMPLE 16.14

H buys factory 1 for £50,000 and transfers 2/5 of it to his wife W. The factory is sold for £100,000. H's gain is £30,000 ([3/5 × £100,000]-[3/5 × £50,000]). W's gain is £20,000 ([2/5 × £100,000]-[2/5 × £50,000]).

H's share of the proceeds of sale is £60,000. H then buys factory 2 for £50,000. The proceeds of sale are not wholly reinvested in factory 2 and, therefore, H is charged to CGT on £10,000 (£60,000 - £50,000). The balance of his gain £20,000 (£30,000 - £10,000) can be rolled over, leaving him with a base value for factory 2 of £30,000. H and W between them are taxed on a gain of £30,000 instead of (as in *Example 16.13*) H being taxed on a gain of £50,000.

Finally, roll-over relief should not be claimed where the taxpayer makes an allowable loss on the sale of the old asset since he cannot add this loss to the base value of the new asset. Nor should he claim the relief where the gain does not exceed his annual exemption. Even if his gain does exceed the exempt limit, it may not be worth claiming the relief, as the claim cannot be to hold over only a part of the gain and the effect of reducing the base cost of an asset is to depress the indexation allowance. **[16.97]**

Self-assessment and provisional relief where an intention to reinvest: TCGA 1992 s 153A allows taxpayers to obtain provisional relief in advance of the reinvestment of the proceeds from the sale of the assets. At such time as the conditions for the granting of the relief have been satisfied, the provisional relief will be replaced by that actual relief. **[16.98]**

3 Roll-over relief on compulsory acquisition of land (TCGA 1992 s 247)

This form of roll-over relief is limited to the disposal of land (or an interest in land) to an authority exercising or able to exercise compulsory purchase powers. Any gain arising can be rolled over into the cost of acquiring replacement land. Similar restrictions to those which apply to the replacement of business assets roll-over relief (see **[16.92]**) apply: for instance, the replacement asset must not have a limited life expectancy and, for full relief, all the disposal consideration must be reinvested. Further, reinvestment into property qualifying for the main residence relief is not allowed. The Revenue allows s 247 relief to be claimed by landlords when leasehold tenants exercise their statutory rights to acquire the freehold reversion and, by concession, when two or more persons sever their joint interests in land (or in milk or potato quotas: ESC D26).

No charge arises irrespective of the s 247 concession when persons pool their resources and subsequently extract their shares from the pool. (See *Example 18.3(2)* and the cases there cited.) **[16.99]**

4 Retirement relief (TCGA ss 163–164, Sch 6)

The following conditions must be satisfied:
(1) the disposer must satisfy either an age or ill-health requirement and have owned the property for a minimum period of one year prior to the disposal;
(2) he must make a 'material disposal' or 'other qualifying disposal'; and
(3) the disposal must be of chargeable business assets.
Various aspects of these conditions are considered below. **[16.100]**

a) *The disposer*

Relief is given on all disposals of chargeable business assets (see below) by individuals, and in certain circumstances, by trustees. To be eligible for relief an individual must *either* be at least 50 years of age at the date of the disposal (although he need not retire from business); *or* he must have been forced to retire before that age on grounds of ill health (see TCGA 1992 Sch 6 para 3 for detailed requirements that must be satisfied if ill-health is to be established and notice that the Revenue's decision on the matter is non-appealable).

If either of these conditions is satisfied retirement relief will be available but to obtain the *full* relief, the individual must have owned the appropriate asset for *ten years* prior to its disposal. If this ten-year ownership condition is not satisfied in full the relief is scaled down so that a proportion will be available, provided that the asset has been owned for at least *one year*. Relief may be given on more than one occasion but is limited to the overall maximum.

EXAMPLE 16.15

(1) A retires aged 54 and disposes of his business owned for the previous 12 years. Full relief is available.

(2)   As in (1) except that A is aged 48. No relief is available unless the retirement is on the grounds of ill health; if it is, full relief will be given.

(3)   A retires at 90 having owned a business for nine months. No relief is available because the minimum one-year ownership period is not satisfied.

The relief may also be given in the case of settlements with an interest in possession (other than for a fixed term) provided that the beneficiary (not the trustees) satisfies the appropriate conditions (see further [**16.112**]).   [**16.101**]

EXAMPLE 16.16

(1)   A newsagent's shop was settled in favour of Benny for life. At the age of 61 and after running the business for 25 years Benny retires and the business is sold by the trustees. Maximum retirement relief will be available.

(2)   As in (1) above except that the business was run by the two trustees. The business is sold when they are both over the age of 50, but no relief is available.

b) *The amount of relief*

Retirement relief exempts from charge gains of up to £250,000 and 50% of gains between £250,000 and £1m. Hence, as the following example illustrates, the maximum relief available is for gains of up to £625,000.   [**16.102**]

EXAMPLE 16.17

At the age of 60, Thad, who has been a partner in an estate agency business since 1960, sells his interest in that business realising capital gains of £1.5m. He is entitled to maximum retirement relief calculated as follows:

$$£250,000 + [50\% \times (£1m - £250,000)] = £250,000 + £375,000 = £625,000$$

In situations where the ten-year ownership requirement has not been met, the relief must be reduced proportionately by the following method:

Stage 1:
Calculate the relevant chargeable gains which may attract relief. For this purpose no scaling down is involved.

Stage 2:
Calculate the appropriate percentage of relief to which the taxpayer is entitled. This involves considering the ownership period of the taxpayer as a percentage of ten years. Assume, for instance, that a particular taxpayer has owned the business for three years in which case the relevant percentage is 30%. (Had his ownership period been four years, the percentage would have been 40% and so on: the calculation will be in months and days.)

Stage 3:
Calculate the available amount of 'full relief'. The full relief is available on gains of up to £250,000 and therefore in the example considered the taxpayer will be entitled to a maximum of 30% of that figure, ie £75,000.

Stage 4:
Calculate the appropriate percentage of the upper limit of the half rate relief band. The half rate relief band applies to gains between £250,000 and £1m and it is necessary to calculate what percentage of the upper limit figure (£1m) is available. In the example being considered this will be 30%: ie £300,000.

Stage 5:
The relief available to the taxpayer in the example under consideration is therefore:

(1)   gains within the full rate band: £75,000; plus

(2)   50% of the gains within a half rate band running from £75,000 to £300,000. Hence, maximum relief in this band will be for gains of £112,500;

(3) accordingly, the total gains available for retirement relief in the case of a taxpayer who has owned his business for three years will be £187,500.

To illustrate how these limits operate, assume that the total gains of the taxpayer (arrived at as indicated in *Stage 1* above) are £1m. Retirement relief calculated as above on a three-year ownership period will exempt from charge £187,500 of those gains. Contrast, however, the position if the total gains were only £200,000. Now the available relief would be reduced as follows:

(1) on the relevant portion of the full relief band £75,000 is available (*Stage 3*, above); *plus*

(2) one-half of the gains between £75,000 and £200,000. Notice that the scaled down upper limit (£300,000) is ignored since this figure exceeds the actual gain realised.

Hence, the relief available in this case is limited to £137,500 (ie £75,000 + £62,500).

c) *A material disposal of business assets*

The relief is given on a material disposal of business assets; the meaning of '*a disposal of business assets*' is set out in s 163(2) and '*material disposal*' in TCGA 1992 s 163(3)–(5): given the limitation of the relief to chargeable business assets (as defined) investment activities are excluded.   [**16.103**]

Situation 1:   A disposal of a business or part of a business; hence, a sole trader who sells his business may qualify for the relief, as may a partner (including a limited partner) who sells his share in the partnership assets (see TCGA 1992 s 163(2)(c) and s 163(8)). There is no minimum size of interest which must be owned before relief is available.   [**16.104**]

Situation 2:   A disposal of assets which, at the time when the business ceased to be carried on, were in use for the purposes of that business (see TCGA 1992 s 163(2)(b) and *Clarke v Mayo* (1994) and *Private Client Business*, 1994, p 285 and 1997 at p 147). The conditions for relief must be satisfied at the date when the business ceased (ie on or before that date the individual must have satisfied the age/ill-health requirements and owned the business for a minimum of one year), but the disposal of the asset may occur within a 'permitted period' after that cessation. This period is one year, unless the Revenue by notice in writing allows a longer period in a particular case.

EXAMPLE 16.18

Jock had run a newsagent's business for many years, but on 1 July 1996 he ceased trading because of ill-health. He owned a lease on the shop which he was unable to assign until 1 January 1997. Retirement relief on the disposal of the lease will be available to Jock provided that on 1 July 1996 he is at least 50 or can prove ill-health and that he has owned the business for at least 12 months.

In *Plumbly v Spencer* (1997) farm land was let to the taxpayer's farming company and he disposed of that land at the time when the farming business ceased. Relief under s 163(2)(b) was not available because at the time of the disposal the taxpayer did not own the business (and note that relief for an 'associated disposal' — see [**16.109**] — was likewise unavailable on these facts). These arguments were not considered by the court in *Marriott v Lane* (1996) which was concerned solely with the question: when does a business cease?

Unless the business ceases, relief is not given for a mere disposal of assets. Accordingly, on a disposal by an individual who is continuing in business, it may be necessary to decide whether that disposal is of part of a business (which qualifies for relief) or of assets used in the business (which does not).

In *McGregor v Adcock* (1977) a farmer sold about one-sixth of his farming land with planning permission and continued farming the remainder. His claim for retirement relief failed because it was held that he had sold only a business asset and not a part of the business which continued unchanged after the disposal. For relief to be available, Fox J, in drawing a distinction between the business and the individual assets used in the business, considered that there must be 'such an interference with the whole complex of activities and assets as can be said to amount to . . . a part disposal of the business'.

Subsequently, in *Mannion v Johnston* (1988) a taxpayer who farmed 78 acres sold 17 acres in April 1984 and a further 18 acres in the following December whilst in *Atkinson v Dancer* (1988) the taxpayer owned and farmed 28 acres, farmed a further 67 acres as tenant, and then sold 9 acres in all. Despite doubting whether the above test of Fox J was 'particularly helpful or illuminating', the *McGregor* case was followed and retirement relief refused in both cases. Giving judgment Peter Gibson J concluded that:

'In my judgment it must be implicit in [Fox J's] remarks that changes in activities and assets caused by something other than the sale are irrelevant. It is no doubt often the case that a farmer over [50] will decide to cut down on his farming activities. He may do so in a number of ways. He may decide to stop a particular activity completely; he may reduce the scale of the activity; he may do it simply by stopping to do that which he has done before; or he may sell the assets or undertaking. But unless the change in his activities is attributable to the disposal by way of sale it is simply not material that prior to the sale there had been a connection between the activity that has ceased or been reduced and that which is sold.'

In deciding whether the disposal is of part of a business or merely of assets used in a business, it may become necessary to determine whether a number of disposals can be looked upon as one single transaction. In the *Mannion v Johnston* and *Atkinson v Dancer* judgment, Peter Gibson J said:

'I cannot see anything in s [163] or in the capital gains tax legislation in general which allows or requires such disposals to be treated as one. They are two separate disposals occurring, it may be, in different fiscal years and having separate fiscal consequences accordingly. Unless there may be some evidence to enable the two disposals to be treated as one, such as evidence that they were part of the same transaction, they must be treated separately.'

This principle was followed in *Wase v Bourke* (1996), where the disposal by the taxpayer of a milk quota nearly one year after the sale by him of both his dairy herd and the fattened young cattle, was held to be a separate and distinct disposal of an asset which had been used in, or was part of, a business already disposed of by the taxpayer in previous disposals. A different conclusion was reached in *Jarmin v Rawlins* (1994) which concerned a dairy farmer who owned 64 acres of land and a milking parlour and yard, hay barn, implement shed, cattle sheds and a herd of cattle. He sold, *inter alia*, the milking parlour and yard at auction and between that time and completion of the sale (some three months later) also sold approximately half his cattle. The remainder were then transferred to another farm and eventually sold over a period of time. Following completion the taxpayer ceased dairy farming and thereafter reared and finished store cattle. On these facts retirement relief was held to be available since the sale by auction coupled with the cessation of all milking operations amounted to a disposal of his dairy farming business.

It may be that relief will be available in cases where the taxpayer sells not just the land but assets appropriate to the business which he had carried on on that land. In his comments on the *Dancer* case the judge referred to 'a mere sale of 9 out of 89 acres with *no livestock or equipment or other stock or goodwill or anything else included in the sale*'. It may follow that the cases would have been decided differently if the land had been sold along with (say) a tractor, a plough, a combine harvester, or cattle as appropriate (see also *Pepper v Daffurn* (1993) and *Wase v Bourke* (1996) where the changes in the business occurred before the sale). **[16.105]**

Situation 3: Relief may be available on a disposal of shares or securities in a *'personal company'* (TCGA 1992 s 163(2)(c), (5)–(7)). In this case the business must be owned by a trading company which is *either* the individual's personal company *or* a member of a trading group of which the holding company is the individual's personal company (see **[16.107]** for the definition of 'personal company'): and the individual must be a full-time working officer or employee who is required to devote substantially the whole of his time to the service of that company (or another group company) in a managerial or technical capacity. Although not defined, the Revenue normally requires the individual to work about 30 hours per week to qualify as 'full-time'. The provisions do, however, recognise that the individual may go into a period of semi-retirement before selling his shares. In such a case the ownership period is calculated by reference to the date when the taxpayer ceased to be a full-time officer or employee and, so long as he continues to work at least ten hours a week for the company in a managerial or technical capacity, entitlement to the relief is preserved. (See CG 63620 *et seq*). **[16.106]**

EXAMPLE 16.19

(1) A trading business is incorporated and all the shares in the company are owned by the sole director Rich. On a disposal of those shares relief may be available.

(2) Rich owns all the shares and is the sole director of Head Co Ltd. That company owns all the shares in two trading subsidiaries, Alpha Ltd and Beta Ltd. On a disposal of his shares in Head Co Ltd, Rich may be entitled to retirement relief.

(3) Andrew was employed by his personal company on leaving college at the age of 25 as PA to his father (the managing director). At the age of 40 he inherited 35% of the shares from his mother and was appointed to the board of directors. At 46 he decided to take it easy and ceased to work full time in the business although he retained a seat on the board and continued to work three mornings a week. Four years later in 1996 (aged 50) he disposed of his shares. He will be entitled to retirement relief which has in effect been 'frozen' from his semi-retirement (at the age of 46). Hence as he was a full-time working director in his family company for six years (from 40 to 46) his maximum relief will be limited (the appropriate percentage will be 60%). Because the requirement is that he work in a managerial or technical capacity his period as PA to his father will not be included.

Personal company A personal company is defined in relation to any individual as one in which he exercises at least 5% of the voting rights. This definition (introduced in 1993) replaced the more stringent requirements that had applied in the case of 'family companies'. **[16.107]**

d) *Assets used in an office or employment*

By TCGA 1992 s 164(1), relief may be available on the disposal of an asset which was held for the purposes of an office or employment (other than as an officer or employee of a personal company) exercised by the disponer. Generally, the necessary conditions have to be satisfied with regard to the office or employment. Hence, the office or employment must have been held for at least 12 months before the disposal of the asset; if it terminates before the disposal of the asset the taxpayer must satisfy the age/ill-health requirement at the date of that termination and dispose of the asset within the 'permitted period' (as above, this will normally be 12 months) of that termination.   **[16.108]**

e) *Associated disposals*

Relief is also given on the disposal of a business asset by an individual which had been used by a partnership (in which the disponer was a partner) or by his personal company (an *'associated disposal'*: 164(6) and Sch 6). To qualify for relief the disposal must take place as part of the withdrawal of the individual from participation in the business (ie it must be linked to the disposal of part at least of the taxpayer's share in his personal company or partnership). The qualifying conditions (one-year ownership and age/ill health) must be satisfied in relation to that disposal, but it should be noted that relief on the associated disposal of the asset may be restricted if it was used in the appropriate business for part only of the taxpayer's period of ownership, or if a rent was charged for its use. In such cases relief shall be given against such part of the gain as appears to the Revenue to be 'just and reasonable' (TCGA 1992 Sch 6 para 10; note that, in certain circumstances, interest payments paid on behalf of the disponer may be treated as rent: see **[4.49]**) These restrictions would have prevented relief on the basis of an associated disposal in *Plumbly v Spencer* (1997) (see **[16.105]**) since (1) rent had been paid for the use of the land, and (2) the taxpayer did not dispose of any of his shares in the farming company.   **[16.109]**

EXAMPLE 16.20

A is aged 62 and acquired 60% of the shares in A Ltd at a cost of £40,000 ten years ago. He has been a full-time working director of A Ltd throughout this time. Five years ago A bought land for £100,000 which the company has since used rent free. A gives the shares (now worth £100,000) and the land worth £180,000 to his son.

A is entitled to full relief (he is aged 62 and has owned the shares for ten years) which he can set against his gain on the shares (£60,000) and land (£80,000).

Notes
(1)   Although the disposal of the land must be 'associated' with A's withdrawal from A Ltd, that disposal need not be to the person who obtains A's shares.
(2)   If there is a delay in disposing of the land (eg when it is difficult to find a purchaser), relief will still be available so long as it can be shown that the intention throughout was to dispose of both shares and land.

f) *Duration of ownership*

As stressed above, the relief depends upon the business assets being owned for a minimum of one year prior to disposal and, to obtain full relief, a ten-year ownership period must be satisfied. When full relief is not available on a disposal, but in the preceding ten years a separate (and earlier) business had been carried on by the taxpayer, it may be regarded as the same business as that disposed of, provided that the earlier business did not terminate more than two years before the start of the later business (TCGA 1992 Sch 6 para 14). Provision is made for calculating relief on the later disposal in cases where the earlier disposal qualified for retirement relief (TCGA 1992 Sch 6 para 15).

EXAMPLE 16.21

(1)   Sal, having owned a fish and chip shop for four years, transfers the business to Sal Ltd, in which he owns all the shares. After a further six years Sal

retires aged 60 and sells the shares. Full relief is available since the periods of ownership are aggregated.

(2) Mal, having owned a fish and chip shop for four years, sells the business and goes cruising round the world. One year later he opens a vegetarian restaurant and six years later retires, aged 50, selling that business. Mal can aggregate the ownership periods of the different businesses, subject to the proviso that the extended period cannot begin earlier than ten years before the disposal of the vegetarian restaurant. Accordingly, although aggregation produces a ten-year ownership period Mal can take advantage of only nine years' aggregation.

Aggregation of ownership is also possible where the business assets are transferred between spouses at a time when they are living together. The inter-spouse transfer, if effected *inter vivos*, will be at no gain/no loss (see [**14.22**]), but on a subsequent disposal of the assets the ownership period of the husband and wife may be aggregated. For aggregation to apply an election in writing by the transferee spouse is required and relief is generally limited by TCGA 1992 Sch 6 para 16(4) in cases where the inter-spouse disposal occurred *inter vivos*. [**16.110**]

EXAMPLE 16.22

Jack transfers his ironmonger's business to his wife Jill after he has owned it for five years. After a further three years she disposes of it on attaining the age of 50. Jill may elect to aggregate Jack's five years' ownership with her three years' ownership thereby giving relief calculated on the basis of an ownership period of eight years.

Note: As the disposal occurred *inter vivos*, retirement relief on the disposal by Jill is the lower of (1) relief calculated on the basis of eight years' ownership less the amount of any retirement relief claimed by Jack on disposals up to the time of his disposal to Jill; and (2) the relief available had the later transfer been by Jack; had the earlier transfer to Jill not occurred; and assuming that anything done by Jill in relation to the business had been done by Jack. Assuming that Jack had received no retirement relief up to the date of disposal by Jill, the relief available will, as stated above, be arrived at taking the relevant percentage to be 80%.

g) *Chargeable business assets*

Relief is given only against gains occurring on the disposal of chargeable business assets. Accordingly, gains on other assets (eg private investments) may not benefit from the relief. The appropriate gains are aggregated and relief is then deducted; any remaining gains may be subject to charge (Sch 6 para 6).

When the disposal is of shares in a company, relief is given only against so much of the gain as is related to the chargeable business assets of the company. Such assets will include land, goodwill and plant and machinery which qualifies for capital allowances (see Chapter 35). Cash, debts and stock are not chargeable assets, whilst shares held in another company, although chargeable, are investment not business assets (Sch 6 para 7). In order to calculate the gain that is eligible for retirement relief, first, calculate the total gain on shares and then multiply by the fraction of chargeable business assets (CBA) divided by total chargeable assets (TCA):

$$\text{ie total gain on shares} \times \frac{\text{CBA}}{\text{TCA}} = \text{gain eligible for relief.}$$

EXAMPLE 16.23

A makes a gain of £140,000 on a disposal of shares in his personal company and is entitled to retirement relief of £50,000. If the chargeable business assets of the company are valued at £200,000 and chargeable investment assets at £600,000, the amount of the gain against which retirement relief can be set is:

$$£140,000 \times \frac{\text{CBA}}{\text{TCA}} = £140,000 \times \frac{£200,000}{£800,000} = £35,000$$

Thus, the balance of the gain of £105,000 (£140,000 - £35,000) is chargeable and A has unused retirement relief of £15,000 (£50,000 - £35,000).

If the disposal is of shares in a holding company of a trading group the apportionment is by reference to the chargeable business assets and chargeable assets of every member of the trading group (ie of all the subsidiaries). **[16.111]**

h) *Application to trusts*

As mentioned above, the relief may be available when there is a material disposal by trustees of assets used for the purpose of a business, or of shares in a personal company. Only trusts with an interest in possession may qualify (hence, discretionary trusts are excluded) and the relief is given by reference to the life tenant entitled in possession to the entire fund or to that part of the fund comprising the business assets (TCGA 1992 s 164(3)). There must be a disposal by the trustees of either shares or securities of a company or of assets used, or previously used, for the purposes of a business; and, in the former case, the beneficiary must cease to be a full-time working officer or employee on that disposal: whilst in the latter, the business must cease on the disposal. Accordingly, relief is not available for a part disposal of a business which thereafter continues nor for a part disposal of shares where the beneficiary remains a full-time working officer or employee of the company concerned.

In calculating the amount available for relief, the disposal is treated as being by the beneficiary and in cases where on the same day there is a disposal of business assets by the trustees and by the beneficiary himself the relief available is applied to the beneficiary's own disposal in priority to the trustees' disposal (TCGA 1992 Sch 6 para 13(3)). **[16.112]**

i) *Claiming the relief*

The relief is automatically given, except when the taxpayer has retired because of ill health (when a claim must be made not later than two years after the relevant disposal) or when the disposal is by trustees (when a joint claim by the trustees and beneficiary is necessary). **[16.113]**

5   Postponement of CGT on gifts and undervalue disposals (TCGA 1992 s 165)

This provision is considered in detail in Chapter 17. **[16.114]**

6   Hold-over relief on the incorporation of a business (TCGA 1992 s 162)

This relief takes the form of a postponement of, rather than an exemption from, CGT. It applies when there is a disposal of an unincorporated business (whether by a sole trader, a partnership, or trustees but *not* by an unincorporated association) to a company and that disposal is wholly or partly in return for shares in that company. Any gains made on the disposal of chargeable business assets will be deducted from the value of the shares received (the gain is 'rolled into' the shares) and the relevant assets are acquired by the company at market value (ie there is a 'step-up' in their value). (Note that a similar relief is available for companies which transfer a trade carried on outside the UK to a non resident company: See TCGA 1992 s 140.)

The business must be transferred as a going concern; a mere transfer of assets is insufficient. Further, all the assets of the business (excluding only cash) must be transferred to the company. As only a gain on business assets can be held over, it will be advisable to take investment assets out of the business before incorporation. The Revenue accepts that 'business' has a wider meaning than 'trade': managing a landed estate would, for instance, qualify as a business (see CG 65712).

EXAMPLE 16.24

On the incorporation of a business for shares, there is a gain on business assets of £50,000. The market value of the shares is £150,000. The gain is rolled over by deducting it from the value of the shares so that the acquisition cost of the shares becomes £100,000 (£150,000 - £50,000). The assets are acquired at market value of (say) £150,000.

Where only a part of the total consideration given by the company is in shares (the rest being in cash or debentures), only a corresponding part of the chargeable gain can be rolled forward and deducted from the value of the shares. That part is found by applying the formula:

$$\text{Gain rolled forward} = \text{total gain} \times \frac{\text{market value of shares}}{\text{total consideration for transfer}}$$

In practice the assumption of liabilities by the company is not treated as consideration for this purpose (see CG 65746 and ESC D32).

EXAMPLE 16.25

A transfers his hotel business to Strong Ltd in return for £160,000, consisting of 10,000 shares (market value £120,000) and £40,000 cash. The chargeable business assets transferred are the premises (market value £130,000) the goodwill (market value £10,000) and furniture, fixtures etc (market value £20,000). On the premises and the goodwill A makes chargeable gains of £35,000 and £5,000 respectively.

Thus A's chargeable gain is:

$$£40,000 - \left(£40,000 \times \frac{£120,000}{£160,000} \right) = £40,000 - £30,000 = £10,000$$

and the acquisition cost of the shares is £120,000 - £30,000 = £90,000 (ie £9 per share).

Although s 162 is a mandatory provision and enables the entire gain to be held over, the Revenue accepts that, if the relevant conditions are satisfied, retirement relief may first be deducted so that only the gain remaining is held over under s 162. So long as the company is the taxpayer's family company, retirement relief may subsequently be available on a disposal of the shares.

If it is desired to sell an unincorporated business s 162 may be used to defer any CGT liability on the sale. The business is first incorporated and s 162 ensures that the vendors will not be subject to CGT until they dispose of their shares in that company. As the company acquires the business assets at market value, however (under TCGA 1992 s 17: see [**14.22**]), the trade can immediately be resold to the intended purchaser without any CGT charge (see *Gordon v IRC* (1991)). **[16.115]**

7   Relief on company reconstructions, amalgamations and takeovers

The relief afforded by TCGA 1992 ss 135–137 in respect of 'paper for paper exchanges' is considered in Chapter 38.

If there is a bonus or rights issue so that the existing shareholders are allotted shares or debentures in proportion to their existing holding, the new securities are treated as acquired when the original shares were acquired. The price for this combined holding will then be the sum originally paid for the original shares plus whatever is paid for the new securities (TCGA 1992 ss 127–130). Altering the rights attached to a class of shares or the conversion of securities can similarly be achieved without an immediate charge to CGT (TCGA 1992 ss 133–135). **[16.116]–[16.120]**

VI   REINVESTMENT RELIEF (TCGA 1992 ss 164A–164N AS AMENDED)

1   The relief

FA 1993 introduced what, at first glance, looked like a valuable new category of roll-over relief, designed to encourage individuals to reinvest in a qualifying company ('entrepreneurial relief'). The relief operated to defer a potential charge on a gain arising on a disposal of shares in a company where the gain was rolled over into qualifying replacement shares. The provisions blended elements of retirement relief, roll-over relief and BES, but the relief given was quite distinct from these other forms of relief. Whilst appearing generous, the legislation contained a number of hurdles that had to be overcome before relief was available, and was criticised as being of Byzantine complexity. In the event FA 1994 extended the relief (the enhanced relief being known as 'reinvestment relief') and improvements were subsequently made by FA 1995. Further changes made by FA 1997, although described as a 'relaxation' of the rules, would appear to be restrictive in nature. The current position is that to obtain relief a *chargeable gain* must accrue to an individual (or to trustees) on a *disposal of (any) assets*, and that person must then reinvest in a *qualifying investment* in the *qualifying period* and make the appropriate claim for relief.

The more restricted entrepreneurial relief applied to disposals in the period from 16 March 1993 to 29 November 1993 and is not considered further.
[16.121]

2   A disposal of assets

Reinvestment relief permits *any* chargeable gain to be rolled into a qualifying investment. This has been achieved by allowing for the disposal of *any asset*, in contrast to the previous position which required a 'material disposal' involving the disposal by an individual of shares in his personal company of which he was a full-time working officer or employee. Relief is available on a chargeable gain arising on the disposal of a Qualifying Corporate Bond (see s 164A(2A) and **[16.45]** and **[28.76]**). The relief can also be claimed by trustees in respect of all forms of trust *provided that* the beneficiaries are either individuals or charities (see further *Tax Journal*, 10 March 1994). **[16.122]**

3   A qualifying investment

Relief is available only if within a one-year period before or the three-year period following the disposal (*the qualifying period*) ordinary shares are acquired in a qualifying company. That acquisition may be by subscription for new ordinary shares in a new or existing company or by the purchase of existing ordinary shares (but not by receipt of a gift or inheritance). FA 1994 removed the requirement that at least 5% of the voting shares must be acquired; the only restrictions now are that (1) the asset *disposed of* must not be shares in the qualifying company or shares in a member of the same group as the qualifying company; and (2) where a share acquisition is by subscription, the company or one of its subsidiaries must intend to use the money wholly for the purpose of a qualifying trade (see below).

There is no requirement that the person must work in that company so that a pure investment suffices. However, a major restriction is that the company itself must be 'qualifying' and the basic definition of such a company, largely lifted from the BES/EIS legislation (see [**4.122**]), is 'an unquoted company which exists wholly for the purpose of carrying on one or more qualifying trades or which so exists apart from purposes capable of having no significant effect . . . on the extent of the company's activities'. The following are *excluded* trades: dealing in land, commodities, futures, shares, securities or other financial instruments; dealing in goods other than wholesale or retail distributions; banking, insurance, money lending, debt factoring, hire purchase, financing or other financial activities; leasing or receiving royalties or licence fees; providing legal or accountancy services. FA 1995 removed the previous restrictions on property development and farming companies, whilst FA 1997 inserted the requirement that the trade must be carried on wholly or mainly in the UK.

Formerly reinvestment was also prohibited in a company if more than half the value of the company's assets was represented by land and buildings. This restriction was also abolished by FA 1995 (as it was for the purpose of EIS relief), but the new Labour government has had second thoughts about this matter in the context of venture capital trust and EIS schemes, and is reviewing the availability of tax relief for 'asset-backed' investments (see Press Release of 2 July 1997 commenting, *inter alia*, that 'a number of lower risk activities are already excluded from the schemes, and the Government will be considering whether trading activities involving the exploitation of land and property rights, such as, for example, providing nursing home accommodation, should also be excluded'). If changes are made in these areas, they are likely to be adopted for reinvestment relief as well. [**16.123**]

4 Corporate groups

Formerly a company with subsidiaries could only be a *qualifying company* if *all* the subsidiaries were directly owned and were either occupied in the carrying on of a qualifying trade or in the holding and managing of group property. FA 1997 (inserting new subsection s 164G) now provides that a company will qualify if it is the unquoted parent of a trading group; and a company will be a parent company if it is the principal compamy of the group within the meaning of the CGT group rules (see [**30.21**] and the activities of the group are substantially trading. In determining whether a group's business is substantially trading, certain activities are disregarded. These are holdings in, and loans to, group companies and properties owned for the purpose of group trading activities.

It should be noted (1) that the parent company can only control a company or otherwise have a subsidiary if such company is a *qualifying subsidiary*. A qualifying subsidiary must be a 75% subsidiary; (2) for the purposes of reinvestment relief, a company may be in a CGT group even if it is registered or resident outside the UK. [**16.124**]

5   **The relief**

The familiar principle of roll-over, which allows CGT to be deferred, applies so that the disposal consideration and the consideration for the reacquisition are both reduced.

The amount of the reduction is the *lowest* of:

(1) the chargeable gain on the disposal;
(2) the consideration paid (or market value) for the reinvestment;
(3) the amount specified in the claim.

Crucially therefore, and unlike roll-over relief, the gain is the first part of the proceeds reinvested: accordingly *CGT can be avoided by reinvesting only the gain*. It is possible to claim relief for part only of the gain and this will be desirable if the remainder is covered by the taxpayer's annual exemption and/or retirement relief.   **[16.125]**

EXAMPLE 16.26

Eddie, aged 65, realises a gain of £1 million on the sale of his widget company. He reinvests £100,000 12 months later in the acquisition of ordinary shares in Nuts & Bolts Limited (a qualifying trading company).

		£	£
(i)	Chargeable gain		1,000,000
(ii)	Deduct retirement relief	625,000	
(iii)	Deduct annual exemption	5,800	630,800
(iv)	Maximum reinvestment relief		100,000
	Remaining chargeable gain		£269,200

Notes:

(1) Additional relief will be available if further qualifying investments are made within the three-year period whether in Nuts & Bolts Limited or in another investment.

(2) The claim for reinvestment relief must be made within six years of the end of the tax year to which the claim relates. In practice it is believed that having raised an assessment the Revenue will accept a claim for postponement of tax based on an intention to acquire a new asset.

6   **Anti-avoidance**

FA 1995 contains provisions to ensure that a tax deferral is not converted (at least in part) into an exemption. Under these provisions, the amount of any gains which can be rolled over into a qualifying investment will be restricted to the *acquisition cost* of the qualifying reinvestment.   **[16.126]**

EXAMPLE 16.27

Frank realises a chargeable gain of £140,000 on a disposal of assets. He acquires shares in a qualifying company for £10,000 from his wife, Constance. She had acquired them in 1993 for £60,000.

	£
Chargeable gain	140,000
Reinvestment relief (restricted to cost of acquisition by Frank, ie acquisition by one spouse from another is at disponor spouse's base cost: TGCA 1992 s 58)	60,000
Remaining chargeable gain	£80,000

Notes

(1) But for these provisions, Frank could have claimed maximum reinvestment relief of £100,000. This would have exceeded his acquisition cost, deemed under TCGA 1992 s 58 to be £60,000. Since the acquisition cost cannot be reduced to less than zero, the excess of £40,000 would escape tax altogether on a subsequent disposal of the shares.

(2) The provisions also prevent the same result as in (1) above where the taxpayer rolls the gains on more than one disposal into the acquisition of a single qualifying investment, in which case it is possible for the total amount of rolled-over gains to exceed the acquisition cost of the qualifying investment.

7 Clawback of gain

Relief may be lost for two reasons. *First*, the held-over gain may crystallise early if certain events occur within three years of the investment: for instance, if the acquired shares cease to be eligible shares (ie ordinary shares) or the company in which the reinvestment is made ceases to be a qualifying company (although relief is not withdrawn if it obtains a Stock Exchange listing) or if the person who acquired the holding emigrates. The period of clawback is, however, limited to three years following the date of reinvestment—after that clawback cannot occur so that the tax deferral will then only be terminated on a disposal. Further, a clawed-back gain can be rolled into a further qualifying investment provided that the new holding is acquired within the one-year period before or three-year period after the occurrence of the event which triggered the clawback, or such extended period as the Revenue may agree. The deferred gain crystallises in full immediately before the clawback event but is not retrospective to the date of reinvestment.

Secondly, there will be a clawback of the gain where money is raised by subscription and was (1) intended for use in an existing trade and the money is not used within one year: (2) raised for the purposes of a trade not yet carried on and the trade started up within two years, but the money is not used within one year of the start-up date; and (3) the trade does not start up at all, and the money is not used within one year. In cases (1) and (3), clawback will be awarded if the money is in fact used for the purposes of that *or another* qualifying trade within one year. Where clawback occurs in these circumstances, the deferred gain is treated as accruing to the reinvestor at the expiry of the appropriate time limit. Any gain so clawed-back may itself be rolled into a further qualifying investment.   **[16.127]**

8 Clearance scheme

Procedures have been introduced which enable a company to advise potential investors as to whether an investment would qualify for reinvestment relief and ultimately stimulate further the reinvestment of gains. The company can complete a questionnaire (obtainable from any tax office) containing a list of the key requirements for eligibility. After furnishing the Inland Revenue with details of its activities the company can seek a ruling as to eligibility. Of course the key issue remains eligibility at the date of the investment which—despite this ruling—may not be the case. (See further (1996) SWTI, p 2023). **[16.128]**

9 Importance of the relief

The relief enables a gain on the disposal of *any* asset to be deferred and note that:

(1) the taxpayer can choose how much of the gain is to be covered by the relief;

(2) the reinvestment shares are likely to qualify for 100% IHT business property relief two years after acquisition;

(3) the taxpayer can remain closely involved with the company: eg he can be the sole shareholder and a paid director and he may already have been carrying on the business. In a simple case Ted may liquidate his share portfolio and reinvest the gain for these purposes by incorporating his existing farming business.

(4) Formerly a gain could be sheltered by incorporating an existing business: as a result of FA 1997 changes requiring subscription moneys to be expended for the purposes of the qualifying trade, it is now implicit that the subscription has to be for cash (see *Private Client Business*, 1997, p 150).

Before assuming that the relief offers some kind of general panacea, however, bear in mind the following:

(1) the possibility of an increase in tax rates at the time when the postponed gain is taxed;

(2) sheltering the gain by other methods, eg by realising losses;

(3) possibility of emigration from the UK.   [**16.129**]

10   **Postponement claims and self-assessment**

Unlike roll-over relief it is not possible to make a provisional claim for reinvestment relief. Hence a claim can only be made after a qualifying investment has been acquired (see CG 62218).   [**16.130**]–[**16.140**]

VII   VENTURE CAPITAL TRUSTS

The reasons behind the introduction of this new investment trust, together with the conditions for approval of companies as trusts and the entitlement to income tax relief have been discussed elsewhere (see [**4.131**]). This section is concerned only with the CGT advantages of obtaining approval as a venture capital trust (VCT).   [**16.141**]

The trust itself Chargeable gains realised by the trust are exempt provided that it has not lost its approval (TCGA 1992 s 100(1) as amended).   [**16.142**]

Relief on disposals by investors An individual (aged 18 or over) is exempt from CGT on gains arising from a disposal of ordinary shares in a VCT (whether or not acquired as a new issue) provided that it retains approval until the date of disposal and the shares disposed of were not acquired in excess of the permitted maximum (ie investments not exceeding £100,000 in any tax year—see [**4.132**]). Capital losses are not allowable.   [**16.143**]

Deferred CGT relief on reinvestment in a VCT An individual may claim a deferral of a chargeable gain to the extent that the gain is matched against a qualifying investment in a VCT (which must be a new issue of shares) made within a period of 12 months prior to the chargeable event giving rise to the gain (but not before 6 April 1995) and 12 months after the chargeable event (TCGA 1992 Sch 5C(1)(3)(a)). The maximum amount of the gain that can be deferred is the amount of the qualifying investments (TCGA 1992 Sch 5C(2)). This is a further species of reinvestment relief (see [**16.121**]).

The deferred gain will become chargeable on the happening of certain events, most notably on a disposal of the shares other than to a spouse (TCGA 1992 Sch 5C(3)(1)(a)–(f)) and is assessed for the year in which that chargeable event occurs. Where the investor, or a person who acquired the shares on a disposal within marriage, becomes non-resident while holding the shares, normally the deferred gain becomes chargeable. However, no charge will crystallise if that investor or person becomes non-UK resident more than five years after making the qualifying investment. Apart from this particular instance, there is no time limitation on the deferred gain becoming chargeable.   [**16.144**]

EXAMPLE 16.28

Alex subscribes £50,000 for shares in an approved VCT on 10 May 1995. On 19 June 1996 he realises a chargeable gain of £70,000 accruing from a disposal of chargeable assets, and he subscribes a further £50,000 for new ordinary shares in an approved VCT on 10 March 1997.

Alex is entitled to CGT relief in respect of disposals of *all* the acquired shares (they are within the permitted maximum). In addition, he can claim deferral relief of *£50,000* in respect of his subscription for new shares on 10 March 1997 being a reinvestment made within 12 months after the event causing the chargeable gain.

17 CGT—gifts and sales at undervalue

'Mr Turner has really argued his case on broader lines than I have so far indicated, and has used language, though moderate and reasonably temperate, as to the ways of Parliament in misusing language and in effect "deeming" him into a position which on any ordinary use of the words "capital gains" was impossible to assert. He in effect says "Here is a discreditable manipulation of words. The Statute is not truthful. Words ought to mean what they say".' (Russell LJ in *Turner v Follett* (1973) 48 TC at 621.)

[**17.1**]

I INTRODUCTORY

1 A gift as a disposal at market value

A disposal of an asset, otherwise than by way of a bargain at arm's length, is treated as a disposal at the open market value (TCGA 1992 s 17). A donor is, therefore, deemed to receive the market value of the property that he has given away even though he has in fact received nothing (*Turner v Follett* (1973)). A disposal between connected persons is treated as a transaction 'otherwise than by way of bargain at arm's length' (and hence taxed as a disposal at market value: see TCGA 1992 s 18(2); for the definition of connected persons see [**14.23**]). [**17.2**]

> **EXAMPLE 17.1**
>
> Jackson sells a valuable Ming vase to his son Pollock for £10,000 which is the price that he had paid for it ten years before. The market value of the vase at the date of sale is £45,000. This disposal between connected persons is deemed to be made otherwise than by way of bargain at arm's length so that market value is substituted for the price actually paid and Jackson is deemed to have received £45,000. Pollock is treated as acquiring the vase for a cost price of £45,000.

2 IHT overlap

In addition to being treated as a disposal at market value for CGT purposes, a gift of assets may be chargeable (or potentially chargeable) to IHT. Only limited relief is available against this double charge (see further [**17.26**]).

317

First, in calculating the fall in value of the transferor's estate for IHT purposes, his CGT liability is ignored. IHT is not, therefore, charged on CGT paid by a donor (see [**21.61**]).

Secondly, if the CGT is paid not by the transferor but by the transferee, the amount of that tax will reduce the value transferred for IHT purposes (IHTA 1984 s 165(1)). Normally CGT is paid by the transferor but there is nothing to stop the parties from agreeing that the burden shall be discharged by the transferee.

> **EXAMPLE 17.2**
>
> Mr Big transfers a freehold office block to his daughter Martha Big. Assume that the value of the freehold (ignoring IHT business relief) is £750,000 and that the CGT amounts to £250,000.
> (1) If the CGT is paid by Big the diminution in his estate for IHT purposes is £750,000 (ie it is *not* £750,000 + £250,000).
> (2) If the CGT is paid by Martha the diminution in Big's estate is reduced to £500,000 (ie £750,000 - £250,000).

In certain situations CGT on a lifetime gift may be postponed if a hold-over election is made and these are considered in the following sections.   [**17.3**]–[**17.20**]

II   GIFTS OF BUSINESS ASSETS (TCGA 1992 s 165)

1   **When does s 165 apply?**

There must be a disposal by *an individual* although this includes the deemed disposal made by trustees under TCGA 1992 s 71 on the termination of a trust (see [**18.43**]). The disposal must be 'otherwise than under a bargain at arm's length' and therefore includes both gifts and undervalue sales. The recipient can be any 'person', a term which embraces not just individuals but also trustees and companies.   [**17.21**]

2   **What property is included?**

The section is limited to gifts of business assets, defined as follows (s 165(2)):

> 'an asset is within this sub-section if—
> (a) it is, or is an interest in, an asset used for the purposes of a trade, profession or vocation carried on by—
>   (i) the transferor, or
>   (ii) his personal company, or
>   (iii) a member of a trading group of which the holding company is his personal company, or
> (b) it consists of shares or securities of a trading company, or of the holding company of a trading group, where—
>   (1) the shares or securities are neither listed on a recognised stock exchange nor dealt in on the Unlisted Securities Market, or
>   (2) the trading company or holding company is the transferor's personal company.'

In addition shares dealt in on the Alternative Investment Market (AIM) may attract relief.

It should be noted that *any* asset is included provided only that it is used for the purposes of a trade, profession or vocation (contrast, for instance, roll-over reinvestment relief (see [**16.92**]) which is limited to certain categories of asset). Non-business assets do not attract relief and that part of the gain on a disposal of shares in a company which owns such assets is therefore excluded from relief (the appropriate calculation is similar, although not identical, to that used for retirement relief: see TCGA 1992 Sch 7 and [**16.111**]). Unlike retirement relief, a mere disposal of assets suffices: it is not necessary for the disposal to be of part of a business.

Whether an asset is used for the purposes of a trade may sometimes be a moot point: for instance, would the relief be available on a gift of a valuable Munch oil painting ('The Sick Corpse') which has adorned the offices of a funeral parlour for many years?

Land qualifying (or which would qualify on a chargeable transfer being made) for 100% or 50% IHT agricultural property relief is specifically included as a business asset for these purposes (TCGA 1992 Sch 7).

An individual's 'personal company' has the same meaning as for retirement relief (see [**16.107**]).

These definitions and requirements are modified in the case of business assets owned by trustees. Broadly, the relevant business must either be that of the trust or of a beneficiary with an interest in possession in the settled property and in the case of a disposal of shares in a trading company either that company must not be listed on a recognised stock exchange or dealt in on the USM (or AIM) or, alternatively, at least 25% of the voting rights at the company's General Meeting must be exercisable by the trustees. [**17.22**]

3 The election

Hold-over relief under the section will only be given on a claim being made in the prescribed form by both transferor and transferee (save where the transferee is a trustee when only the transferor need elect: TCGA 1992 s 165(1)). The donor is treated as disposing and the donee as acquiring the asset for its market value at the date of the gift *minus* the chargeable gain which is held over. This postponement of tax continues until the asset is sold since if the donee in turn makes a gift of the asset a further hold-over election is available. In the event of the donee dying still owning the asset, the entire gain is wiped out by the death uplift in value.

Since the election is to hold over a gain which would otherwise be chargeable, in principle it is necessary to agree the amount of that gain with the Revenue so that the election should be accompanied by relevant valuations. In SP 8/92, however, the Inland Revenue published a revised practice whereby computation of the gain (and hence valuation of the asset) is not required. Both transferor and transferee must request this treatment in writing and provide full details of the asset transferred; the date of its acquisition, and the allowable expenditure. Once such a request has been accepted it cannot subsequently be withdrawn. In the majority of cases, taxpayers will be only too happy to avoid the time and trouble (not to mention the expense) involved in agreeing valuations with the Revenue.

EXAMPLE 17.3

(1) Sim gives his ironmonger's business to his daughter Sammy in 1996. For CGT purposes any gain resulting from this gift of chargeable business assets may be held over on the joint election of Sim and Sammy.

(2) Jim settles his ironmonger's business on trust for his son Jack on becoming 30. As in (1) above, s 165 will apply: however in this case only Jim need elect. When the trust ends, eg on Jack becoming absolutely entitled to the business, a further hold-over election may then be made by the trustees and

Jack to postpone payment of tax which would otherwise arise under TCGA 1992 s 71.

(3)   Oliver is the sole shareholder and director of a computer company (ACC Ltd) and owns the freehold site used by the company. He gives away his shares to his four daughters equally and the freehold to his son. Section 165 relief is available to postpone tax on all five gifts since ACC is Oliver's family company.

When the election is made:

'(a) the amount of any chargeable gain which, apart from this section, would accrue to the transferor on the disposal, and

(b) the amount of the consideration for which, apart from this section, the transferee would be regarded for the purposes of CGT as having acquired the asset or, as the case may be, the shares or securities, shall each be reduced by an amount equal to the held-over gain on the disposal.'

This is illustrated in the following example:

EXAMPLE 17.4

Smiley gives Karla shares in his family company worth £35,000. Smiley's allowable expenditure for CGT purposes is £10,000. They make a joint election under s 165 so that the disposal consideration deemed to have been received by Smiley is reduced by the held-over gain: ie £35,000 – £25,000 = £10,000. Hence, Smiley is treated as disposing of the shares for £10,000 and, as his expenses are £10,000, he has made neither gain nor loss. Karla is treated as acquiring the shares for the same consideration, £10,000.

Assume that within 12 months of the gift Karla sells the shares for £41,000 incurring deductible expenses of £2,000. He will be assessed to CGT on a gain calculated as follows:

	£	£
Sale proceeds		41,000
Less:		
Acquisition cost	10,000	
Deductible expenses	2,000	
		12,000
Chargeable gain		£29,000

Notes:

(1)   Of this gain, £4,000 is attributable to Karla's period of ownership (£29,000 – £25,000) and £25,000 represents the gain held over on the gift from Smiley.

(2)   Karla's deemed acquisition costs will include the value of Smiley's indexation allowance. Karla therefore obtains an indexation allowance on an indexation allowance. This result is less striking when it is realised that the RPI itself gives indexation on indexation.

No time limit for making this election is prescribed in the section and hence the general rule laid down in TMA 1970 s 43 (as amended) applies: *viz* the claim must be made within five years from 31 January in the tax year following that in which the disposal occured (ie a period of some five years and ten months). With the introduction of self-assessment the Revenue introduced a standard claim form which *must* be used in all cases (although photocopies of the form will be accepted: see Tax Bulletin, April 1997, s 417).   **[17.23]**

4   The annual exemption and retirement relief

Section 165 operates by postponing the tax charge on 'the chargeable gains which would otherwise accrue to the transferor on the disposal'. The CGT *annual exemption* (see [**14.86**]) is deducted from an individual's 'taxable amount' (TCGA 1992 s 3(1)) which is defined as the total chargeable gains for the year after deducting losses: s 2(2). Accordingly, as the annual exemption is deducted from chargeable gains, it is not possible to combine it with an election under s 165. Either the whole chargeable gain must be held over or be subject to CGT but with the benefit of the annual exemption. Where any gain will not exceed the annual exemption, the s 165 election should not be made: even if the gain just exceeds the exemption it may be preferable to pay a small CGT charge. In appropriate cases it will be possible to obtain the best of both worlds: ie to make two disposals, the first of an asset where the gain is covered by the annual exemption and the second of other business assets where hold-over relief under s 165 is claimed.

Unlike the annual exemption, *retirement relief* operates by reducing the gross gain made by a taxpayer on the disposal of a business or part of a business so that only the balance (if any) remaining is chargeable gain (TCGA 1992 Sch 6 para 6; and see Chapter 16). This relief can therefore be combined with s 165 so that the gain is first reduced by retirement relief and any remaining chargeable gain is then held over.   [17.24]

EXAMPLE 17.5

Magnus gives his greengrocer's business to his daughter, Minima. There is a gain of £90,000 on the value of the chargeable assets transferred. If Magnus is entitled to retirement relief of £40,000, his gain will be reduced to £50,000 (£90,000 – £40,000) and this can be held over if Magnus and Minima make a joint election under s 165.

5 Sales at undervalue

Although s 165 applies both to gifts and sales at undervalue, if the actual consideration paid on a disposal exceeds the allowable CGT deductions of the transferor, that excess is subject to charge. It is only the balance of any gain (ie the amount by which the consideration is less than the full value of the business asset) which may be held over under s 165.

EXAMPLE 17.6

Julius sells shares in his family company worth £25,000 to his brother Jason for £16,500. Julius has allowable deductions for CGT purposes of £11,500. The CGT position is:
(1) Total gain on disposal: £25,000 – £11,500 = £13,500.
(2) Excess of actual consideration over allowable deductions: £16,500 – £11,500 = £5,000.
(3) Gain subject to CGT ((2) above) is £5,000 so that after deducting Julius' annual exemption tax payable is nil.
(4) Balance of gain, £8,500 (ie (1) – (2)) can be held over under s 165.

If the partial consideration is less than the allowable deductions it is ignored so that a CGT loss cannot be created.

If retirement relief is available it is deducted first from any chargeable gain actually realised. Any unused relief is then deducted from the notional gain which arises as a result of treating the disposal as being at market value and any remaining gain may then be held over.   [17.25]

EXAMPLE 17.7

Moira transfers her newsagent's business to her son Michael. The base costs of the chargeable business assets total £50,000; their market value is £225,000. Michael is to pay his mother £100,000. Moira is entitled to retirement relief of £60,000. The CGT position is as follows:

(1) Total gain on disposal: £225,000 – £50,000 = £175,000.
(2) Excess of actual consideration over base cost: £100,000 – £50,000 = £50,000.
(3) Deduct retirement relief from (2). The actual gain is therefore wiped out.
(4) Balance of gain, £125,000 ((1) minus (2)) will be reduced by the remaining £10,000 of retirement relief and so £115,000 will then be held over if a s 165 election is made.

6 The interrelation between hold-over relief and IHT

The overlap between CGT and IHT in the area of lifetime gifts and gratuitous undervalue transfers has already been noted (see [**17.3**]).

When chargeable gains are held over under s 165 the transferee can add to his CGT acquisition costs all or part of the IHT paid on the value of the gift. This principle applies whoever pays the IHT.

EXAMPLE 17.8

Wendy gives shares in her family cookery company ('Cook-Inn & Co') to her daughter, Kim. The chargeable gain arising of £100,000 is held over under s 165 and Kim therefore acquires the shares at a value of £75,000. For IHT purposes the gift by Wendy is a potentially exempt transfer when made and therefore no tax is payable at that stage. Assume, however, that Wendy dies within seven years so that the gift then becomes chargeable and that IHT of £20,000 is paid. Kim can add that sum to her base cost for CGT purposes which therefore becomes £95,000 (£75,000 + £20,000).
Note:
(1) A similar principle applies in the case of lifetime gifts which are subject to an immediate IHT charge.
(2) Although the IHT paid is added to Kim's base cost in order to reduce her gain on a subsequent disposal of the shares, this sum is not an item of deductible expenditure for CGT purposes *and therefore does not benefit from the indexation allowance*.
(3) It may be that Kim has already disposed of the shares before the death of her mother. Nevertheless she is entitled to have her allowable expenditure increased by the IHT resulting from Wendy's death and therefore an adjustment will be made to any CGT paid on the disposal of the shares.

There are two limits on the amount of IHT that can be added to the donee's CGT base cost.

First, the maximum amount permissible is the IHT *attributable to the gift*. This means that if IHT had been paid by the transferor on a chargeable lifetime gift so that 'grossing-up' applied, it is only the IHT charged on the value of the gift received by the donee which can be used (grossing-up is discussed at [**21.102**]: with the introduction of the PET it will now rarely occur).

Secondly, IHT which is added to the transferee's base cost cannot be used to create a CGT loss on a later disposal by the transferee. Accordingly, in *Example 17.11,* above, if Kim were to sell the shares after the death of Wendy for £90,000 she would only be able to use £15,000 of the IHT payable on Wendy's death since this could have the effect of wiping out any chargeable gain and she cannot use the remaining £5,000 to create a CGT loss (TCGA 1992 s 165(9)).   [**17.26**]

7 Non-UK residents

Section 165 hold-over relief is not available if the transferee is neither resident nor ordinarily resident in the UK (TCGA 1992 s 166). This limitation is necessary since disposals by such a person are outside the CGT net! In addition, any held-over gain will be triggered on the subsequent emigration (within six years) of the transferee.

EXAMPLE 17.9

In 1990 Imelda's father gave her shares in the family company. A gain of £80,000 was held over so that she had an acquisition cost of £10,000. In 1995 she took up permanent residence in Spain. The held-over gain of £80,000 becomes chargeable 'immediately before' she ceased to be UK resident at the rates in force in the tax year of emigration.

If the shares had increased in value to £130,000 by 1995, there is no question of charging that increase which is attributable to her period of ownership; any loss would likewise be ignored.

The CGT in such cases is payable primarily by the transferee, but if tax remains unpaid 12 months after the due date it can be recovered from the transferor (TCGA 1992 s 168(7)). In such an event the transferor is given a right to recover a corresponding sum from the transferee (TCGA 1992 s 168(9)) although, if the Revenue has not obtained payment from the transferee, the transferor is unlikely to succeed!

The emigration charge will only operate if the original disposal on which the gain was held over occurred after 5 April 1981 and the emigration occurred within six years after the end of the year of assessment of that disposal (TCGA 1992 s 168(4)). Further, the charge will not apply if the transferee has left the UK because of work connected with his office or employment and performs all the duties of that office or employment outside the UK. He must not dispose of the asset whilst outside the UK (if so the gain is taxed unless the disposal is to a spouse) and must resume UK residence within three years of his initial departure otherwise the gain is taxed (TCGA 1992 s 168(5)).

It will obviously be unnecessary to invoke this emigration charge if, before becoming non-resident, the transferee had made a disposal of the asset (TCGA 1992 s 168(1)(b)). That disposal will either have triggered the held-over gain or, if it was by way of gift and a s 165 election had been made, the asset pregnant with gain will now be owned by another UK resident, so that the Revenue is not threatened with a loss of tax. If that prior disposal was merely a part disposal, so triggering only a part of the held-over gain, the balance will be chargeable on emigration.

An exception to the provision that the transferor who emigrates after the disposal of the asset will not be subject to a charge is when that prior disposal is to the emigrating transferor's spouse. If that spouse had also disposed of the asset, however, resulting in a CGT charge on the gain originally held over, that further disposal will be treated as if it had been by the transferor so that the emigration charge will not apply (TCGA 1992 s 168(3)).   **[17.27]**

8 Other triggering events

Apart from the emigration of the donee, a gain held over on creation of a settlement will become chargeable on the death of the life tenant (this matter is discussed at **[18.48]**). A subsequent sale of the property by the donee will also result in the held-over gain becoming taxable and it should be noted that, because rebasing is not available when the gift was made between 1982 and 1988, there will be a 50% reduction in the amount of the held-over gain which is taxed (see also **[14.38]**).

EXAMPLE 17.10

Diane acquired a business for £10,000 in 1980. By 31 March 1982 its value had increased to £25,000. In June 1986 she gave it to her niece when its value was £40,000 and both entered into a hold-over election. In July 1996 the niece sold the business for £50,000. Ignoring the indexation allowance any incidental expenditure and assuming that the business comprises only chargeable business assets, the CGT position is as follows:

(1) In 1986 the niece acquired the assets at a base cost of £10,000 (ie £40,000 minus the held-over gain of £30,000).

(2) In 1996 her gain on disposal is £40,000 but one-half of the gain held over in 1986 (ie £15,000) is not subject to charge so that the chargeable gain is £25,000 (£40,000 – £15,000).

Note: As a result of TCGA 1992 Sch 4 para 1 the niece's acquisition cost in 1986 is increased to £25,000 thereby affecting the calculation of the indexation allowance.

A subsequent gift of the property will not trigger a charge provided that a further election is made: on the death of the donee any held-over gain is wiped out (though see the special rules when a gain is held over on creation of a settlement: see [**18.48**]).

EXAMPLE 17.11

Boy Sam settled his family company shares on trusts for his companion Justin for life, remainder to his mother, Iris. Under a power in the settlement the trustees advanced the collection to Justin. No CGT arose on the creation of the settlement provided that Boy Sam so elected (in this case an election by the settlor alone sufficed) nor on the deemed disposal under TCGA 1992 s 71(1) resulting from the termination of the settlement when the property was advanced *in specie* to Justin. As in the case of outright gifts, therefore, CGT may be postponed until the assets are sold.   [**17.28**]–[**17.40**]

III   GIFTS OF ASSETS ATTRACTING AN IMMEDIATE IHT CHARGE (TCGA 1992 s 260)

The second situation where hold-over relief is available on a gift or undervalue sale, is if the relevant disposal 'is a chargeable transfer within the meaning of the IHTA 1984' or would be such a transfer but for the availability of the annual exemption. The transfer of business or agricultural property qualifying for 100% relief from IHT is eligible for relief under this provision. The operation of s 260 is considered in this and the following sections. [**17.41**]

1   When is there an immediate IHT charge on inter vivos gifts?

Most lifetime transfers are now PETs which do not attract an immediate IHT charge: in such cases hold-over relief under this section is *not* available *even if* the PET subsequently becomes chargeable because of the death of the transferor within seven years. Consequently relief under s 260 is only available in the following cases:

(1) On a gift between individuals or on the creation of an accumulation and maintenance or disabled trust where such gifts fall outside the definition of a potentially exempt transfer. Such cases are rare: see [**21.41**].

(2) On a gift to or by trustees *which is not a PET*. This category embraces the creation and termination of no interest in possession trusts (typically, the discretionary trust).

Because s 260 specifies that to come within its terms the disposal must be to and by either an individual or the trustees of a settlement, gifts to and by companies (which cannot be PETs) do not attract hold-over relief. (Unless, of course, the gift to a company is of a business asset when relief may be available under s 165 as discussed at [**17.22**].)   [**17.42**]

2   The relief

The hold-over relief afforded by s 260 is broadly the same as that given under s 165. Relief under s 260 does, however, take precedence over the s 165 relief (TCGA 1992 s 165(3)(d)) and this may have attractions when what is contemplated is a transfer of shares in a family company which owns non-business assets since there is no apportionment requirement under s 260 (contrast s 165 [**17.22**] and see *Capital Taxes*, 1990, p 52).

An election is required in the same terms as under s 165; the effect of holding over the gain is the same (ie the asset is disposed of and acquired at market value less held-over gain); the transferee must be either UK resident or ordinarily resident and subsequent emigration may trigger the charge. Unlike s 165 there is, however, no restriction on the type of asset for which relief may be claimed.   [**17.43**]

3   Practical uses of s 260

The main situation where this provision will be employed is when a discretionary trust is either created or ended. In both cases an immediate IHT charge may arise so that the gain on any chargeable asset entering or leaving the trust may be held over. The following example illustrates the various permutations:
                                                                        [**17.44**]–[**17.80**]

EXAMPLE 17.12

(1) Jake transfers his portfolio of stocks and shares (worth £500,000) into a discretionary trust for his family; the transfer results in an immediate IHT charge and therefore any gain on the investments can be held over if Jake (alone) elects under s 260. Note that any IHT paid by Jake (ignoring grossing-up) can be deducted by the trustees in arriving at the CGT charge on a subsequent disposal of the shares (and this sum may be increased should an extra tax charge result from the death of Jake within seven years of establishing his trust).

(2) Joseph establishes his discretionary trust by transferring land worth £215,000 to the trustees. As his first chargeable transfer, IHT will not be payable since it falls within Joseph's nil rate band. Despite this, hold-over relief under s 260 is available since the transfer by Joseph is (strictly) chargeable to IHT albeit at a nil rate. This gives the best of all worlds: no IHT but CGT hold-over. (Note that s 260 also applies if a transfer of value which would otherwise attract an immediate IHT charge is covered by the transferor's annual exemption.)

(3) Thal and Thad, trustees of the Mallard discretionary trust, appoint chargeable assets to Billy Beneficiary. For IHT, an 'exit' charge will arise (see [**26.23**]) and therefore any chargeable gain can be held over on the joint election of Thal, Thad and Billy. Note, however, that an appointment out of such a trust *within three months of its creation* does not give rise to any IHT charge (see [**26.25**]) and therefore CGT hold-over is not available in such a case.

(4) Trustees Tom and Ted in exercise of powers conferred on them by the settlement, resettle the property on new trusts. This is a deemed disposal under s 71(1) for CGT purposes but any resulting gain may only be held over if it is also a chargeable event for IHT. In many cases this will not be the case since the property will be treated as remaining comprised in the original settlement (IHTA 1984 s 81: see [**26.32**]). In particular, this will be the case where trustees of one discretionary trust reappoint the property on new discretionary trusts. By contrast, the termination of a life interest whereupon property becomes

held on discretionary trusts, although chargeable for IHT, is not a deemed disposal for CGT purposes unless (which is unlikely) a new settlement results.

(5)   Mr Wealthy wishes to give his seaside cottage (current value £100,000) to his son but is concerned to postpone the payment of any CGT on that disposal. If he settles the property on discretionary trusts there will be no IHT to pay provided that the transfer falls within his available nil rate band but CGT hold-over relief will be available. Were the trustees subsequently (eg six months later) to appoint the cottage to the son outright, there should still be no IHT charge but again CGT hold-over relief will be available.

IV   THE ACCUMULATION AND MAINTENANCE TRUST

Accumulation and maintenance trusts are the creature of the IHT legislation where they are accorded privileged treatment (see [**26.91**] ff).

In general terms, the *inter vivos* creation of such trusts is a PET so that, unless the assets settled are business property, CGT hold-over relief is not available. The termination of such trusts generally occurs in one of two ways.

First (and the most common), termination is the result of a beneficiary becoming entitled to an interest in possession in the trust fund. Typically this will occur at 18 or 21 with capital vesting at a later age (often 25). The trust therefore continues until this later date albeit that it will already have ceased to qualify as an accumulation and maintenance trust. For CGT purposes the vesting of the income interest does not give rise to a deemed disposal: that occurs on the ending of the settlement (see Chapter 18).

Secondly, the accumulation and maintenance trust may end with the trust assets becoming the absolute property of the beneficiary so that the settlement itself comes to an end. In this case the ending of the trust involves a deemed disposal of the trust property under TCGA 1992 s 71 (see [**18.43**]).

So far as hold-over relief is concerned an election is permissible in the second case—irrespective of the nature of the trust assets—under TCGA 1992 s 260(2)(d). Relief is not, however, available in the more common first case where the beneficiary becomes absolutely entitled to the property on the termination of his prior interest in possession.   [**17.81**]–[**17.100**]

EXAMPLE 17.13

(1)   Property is settled on an accumulation and maintenance trust for Floyd on attaining 18. At 18, Floyd becomes absolutely entitled to the assets; the accumulation and maintenance trust ends, a hold-over election is possible under s 260 (whatever the nature of the settled property).

(2)   Property is settled on accumulation and maintenance trusts for Sid contingent on his attaining the age of 25.

   (i)   *At 18:* Sid obtains an interest in possession under the Trustee Act 1925 s 31. For CGT purposes this does not occasion a deemed disposal and there is no question of any tax charge arising. For IHT purposes the accumulation and maintenance trust has ended, being replaced by an interest in possession settlement.

   (ii)   *At 25:* When Sid becomes absolutely entitled there is a deemed disposal for CGT purposes under TCGA 1992 s 71(1) but hold-over relief will only be available if (or to the extent that) the settled property comprises business assets.

   (iii)   *Is it possible to vary the trusts so that hold-over relief will be available when Sid becomes 25?* Consider the consequences if Sid assigns his life interest to the trustees, providing for it to be held on the trusts of the settlement with the income being accumulated until he attains the age of 25 (does this turn the settlement back into an accumulation and maintenance trust thereby permitting hold-over when Sid becomes 25?). And, alternatively, consider the position if Sid were to settle his capital entitlement (before 25) on discretionary trusts (at 25 does his interest in possession come to an end in favour of a discretionary settlement which, being an immediately chargeable transfer, permits hold-over relief?).

V   MISCELLANEOUS CASES

Hold-over relief under s 260 is also available in the following situations where the relevant transfer is exempt from any IHT charge:
(1)   transfers to political parties under IHTA 1984 s 24;
(2)   transfers for public benefit under IHTA 1984 s 26;
(3)   transfers to maintenance funds for historic buildings under IHTA 1984 s 27 and for disposals out of settlement to such funds;
(4)   transfers of designated property under IHTA 1984 s 30;
(5)   transfers of works of art under IHTA 1984 s 78.

It may also be noted that there are other provisions in the CGT legislation which result in a postponement of tax. Share exchanges under TCGA 1992 ss 135–137 (considered at [**19.3**]) and relief on the incorporation of a business under s 162 (discussed at [**16.115**]) are examples whilst disposals between husband and wife are always taxed on a no gain/no loss basis irrespective of any actual consideration paid ([**14.22**]).   [**17.101**]–[**17.120**]

VI   PAYMENT OF TAX BY INSTALMENTS

1   General rule

CGT must generally be paid on 31 January following the tax year when the disposal occurs and, even if the disponer receives payment in instalments, there is no general right to pay the tax by instalments (see TCGA 1992 s 7 and [**14.93**]).   [**17.121**]

2   Payment by instalments

Section 281 qualifies this general principle but only in the case of gifts of certain property (not, apparently, sales at undervalue) and for deemed disposals of settled property. Broadly, the ability to pay by instalments will only, even in these cases, be available if the relevant chargeable gain could not have been held over under either s 165 or s 260 (notice, therefore, that failure to make the election will not give the right to pay tax by instalments).

The relevant property on which tax may be paid by instalments is land (including any estate or interest in land); a controlling shareholding; and a minority shareholding in a company neither listed on a recognised stock exchange nor dealt in on the Unlisted Securities Market (or AIM). The latter category will include all private companies which do not trade.

The person paying the CGT must give notice if he wishes to pay by instalments: tax is then paid by ten equal yearly instalments starting on the usual payment date (ie 31 January following the tax year of the disposal). Interest is charged on the unpaid CGT and is added to each instalment. The outstanding tax can be paid off at any time and must be paid off if the gift was to a connected person or was a deemed disposal of settled property and the relevant assets are subsequently sold for valuable consideration.   [**17.122**]

EXAMPLE 17.14

In July 1996 Bob gives his seaside cottage to his daughter Thelma. The resulting CGT of £50,000 may be paid by ten equal annual instalments on the appropriate notice being given by Bob (who is to pay that tax). The first instalment of £5,000 falls due on 31 January 1998 and subsequent instalments will carry interest on the unpaid balance of the CGT.

3   Payment by a donee

TCGA 1992 s 282 provides that if a donor fails to pay the tax referable to the gift the Revenue may look to the donee for payment (for a criticism of the drafting of this provision see *PTPR*, vol 4, p 107).   **[17.123]**

18 CGT—settlements

The legislation generally seeks to tax gains which arise (or are deemed to arise) on property comprised in the trust fund and not a disposal of the interests of the beneficiaries. Actual disposals by the trustees and certain deemed disposals may trigger a charge, but disposals of beneficial interests will normally be exempt.   [**18.1**]

I WHAT IS A SETTLEMENT?

'Settled property': the provisions of TCGA 1992 s 60

Definition   'Settlement' is not defined but 'settled property' is 'any property held in trust' (TCGA 1992 s 68) with the exception of certain trusts mentioned in s 60. In the following three situations s 60 provides that, although there is a trust of property, the property is *not* 'settled property' and is treated as belonging to the beneficiary.   [**18.2**]

Nominees and bare trusts   Property is not settled where 'assets are held by a person as nominee for another person, or as trustee for another person absolutely entitled as against the trustee'. The provision covers nomineeships and bare or simple trusts.   [**18.3**]

EXAMPLE 18.1

Tim and Tom hold 1,000 shares in DNC Ltd on trust for Bertram, aged 26, absolutely. This is a bare trust since Bertram is solely entitled to the shares and can at any time bring the trust to an end (see *Saunders v Vautier* (1841)). The shares are treated as belonging to Bertram so that a disposal of those shares by the trustees is treated as being by Bertram and any transfer from the trustees to Bertram is ignored.

Beneficiaries under a disability   Where the property is held on trust 'for any person who would be [absolutely] entitled but for being an infant or other person under a disability' it is not settled.   [**18.4**]

EXAMPLE 18.2

(1) Topsy and Tim hold property for Alex absolutely, aged nine. Because of his age Alex cannot demand the property from the trustees and the trust is not simple or bare. Alex is, however, a person who would be absolutely entitled but for his infancy and he is (for CGT purposes) treated as owning the assets in the fund.

(2) Teddy and Tiger hold property on trust for Noddy, aged nine, contingent upon his attaining the age of 18. At first sight it would seem that there is no material difference between this settlement and that considered in (1) above since, in both, the beneficiary would be absolutely entitled were it not for his infancy. Noddy, however, is not entitled to claim the fund from the trustees because of the provisions of the settlement. Unlike (1) above, Noddy's entitlement is contingent upon living to a certain age, so that, were he to ask the trustees to give him the property, they would refuse because he has not satisfied the contingency. This distinction would be more obvious if the settlement provided that the contingency to be satisfied by Noddy was the attaining of (say) 21 (see *Tomlinson v Glyns Executor and Trustee Co* (1970)). The property in this example is, therefore, settled for the purposes of CGT.

Concurrent interests   Where property is held for 'two or more persons who are or would be jointly [absolutely] entitled' the property is not settled. The word 'jointly' is not limited to the interests of joint tenants, applying to concurrent ownership generally. It does not, however, apply to interests which are successive, but only covers more than one beneficiary concurrently entitled 'in the same interest' (see *Kidson v MacDonald* (1974); *Booth v Ellard* (1980); and *IRC v Matthew's Executors* (1984)).   **[18.5]**

EXAMPLE 18.3

(1) Bill and Ben purchase Blackacre as tenants in common. The land is held on a trust of land, but for the purposes of CGT the property is not settled and is treated as belonging to Bill and Ben equally (*Kidson v MacDonald* (1974)).

(2) Mr T and his family hold 72% of the issued share capital in T Ltd (their family company). In 1995 they enter into a written agreement as a result of which the shares are transferred to trustees and detailed restrictions, akin to pre-emption provisions in private company articles, are imposed. The beneficial interests of Mr T and his family are not, however, affected. Subsequently the shares are transferred out again to the various settlors. In such a 'pooling arrangement' the shares will be treated as nominee property with the result that there is no disposal for CGT purposes on the creation of the trust nor on its termination (cp *Booth v Ellard* (1980) and see *Jenkins v Brown* and *Warrington v Sterland* (1989) in which a similar result was arrived at (surprisingly?) in the case of a pooling of family farms. See further [**16.99**]).

(3) Thal and Tal hold property on trust for Simon for life, remainder to Karl absolutely. Although Simon and Karl are, in common parlance, jointly entitled to claim the fund from the trustees, they are not 'jointly absolutely entitled' within the meaning of s 60. The property is settled for CGT purposes.

Meaning of absolute entitlement   It is the concept of being 'absolutely entitled as against the trustee' which lies at the root of the three cases mentioned in s 60. Section 60(2) provides that:

'It is hereby declared that references in this Act to any asset held by a person as trustee for another person absolutely entitled as against the trustee are references to a case where that other person has the exclusive right, subject only to satisfying any outstanding charge, lien or other right of the trustees to resort to the asset for payment of duty, taxes, costs or other outgoings, to direct how that asset shall be dealt with.'

The various rights against the property possessed by trustees and mentioned in s 60(2) refer to personal rights of indemnity; they do not cover other beneficial interests under the settlement.

EXAMPLE 18.4

Jackson is entitled to an annuity of £1,000 pa payable out of a settled fund held in trust for Xerxes absolutely. The property is settled for CGT purposes (*Stephenson v Barclays Bank Trust Co Ltd* (1975)).

Section 60(2) does not offer any guidance on the question of when a beneficiary has 'the exclusive right ... to direct how [the] asset in [the settlement] shall be dealt with'. Under general trust law beneficiaries will not be able to issue such directions unless they have the right to end the trust by demanding their share of the property (see eg *Re Brockbank* (1948)). Difficulties may arise where one of a number of beneficiaries is entitled to a portion of the fund.

EXAMPLE 18.5

A fund is held for the three daughters of the settlor (Jane, June and Joy) contingent upon attaining 21 and, if more than one, in equal shares absolutely. Jane, the eldest, is 21 and is, therefore, entitled to one-third of the assets. Whether she is absolutely entitled as against the trustees to that share depends upon the type of property held by the trustees. The general principle is that she will be entitled to claim her one third share, but not if the effect of distributing that slice of the fund would be to damage the interests of the other beneficiaries. When the settled assets are land or a substantial private company shareholding this would normally be the result since, in the case of land, the asset will often have to be sold to raise the necessary moneys, and, in the case of shares, the trustees may lose a controlling interest in the company (see *Crowe v Appleby* (1975)).
(1) If Jane is absolutely entitled to her share that portion of the fund ceases to be settled (even though Jane leaves her share in the hands of the trustees).
(2) If the fund consists of land, Jane will not be absolutely entitled; hence, the settlement will continue until all three daughters either satisfy the contingency or die before 21. Only then will the fund cease to be settled since one or more persons will, at that point, become jointly absolutely entitled. (For problems that can arise on a division of a controlling shareholding see *Lloyds Bank plc v Duker* (1987).)

A person can become absolutely entitled to assets without being 'beneficially' entitled (see [**18.61**]).

In deciding whether the class of beneficiaries has closed so that those in existence (who have satisfied any relevant contingency) have become absolutely entitled the medical impossibility of further beneficiaries being born to a living person is ignored. Hence a settlement on the children of A who attain 21 and if more than one in equal shares will remain settled property until the death of A even though he may have become incapable of having further children before that time (*Figg v Clarke* (1996) where the class closing rules were inapplicable). [**18.6**]-[**18.20**]

II THE CREATION OF A SETTLEMENT

1 General rule

The creation of a settlement is a disposal of assets by the settlor whether the settlement is revocable or irrevocable, and whether or not the settlor or his spouse is a beneficiary (TCGA 1992 s 70). If chargeable assets are settled, a chargeable gain or allowable loss will result unless hold-over relief is available (as to which see Chapter 17). **[18.21]**

2   The 'connected persons' rule

As the settlor and his trustees are connected persons (TCGA 1992 s 18(3): see **[14.23]**), any loss resulting from the transfer will only be deductible from a gain realised on a subsequent disposal by the settlor to those trustees. Apart from being connected with the settlor, trustees will also be connected with persons connected with the settlor who will often be beneficiaries. However, it has been confirmed by the Revenue that:

> 'if the settlor dies the connection with the trustees and relatives and spouse of the settlor is broken. Therefore if, for instance, the beneficiaries of the settlement are the children of the late settlor, the trustees are not connected with those beneficiaries, even if one or more of the children are trustees' (*Tax Bulletin*, February 1993, p 56). **[18.22]–[18.40]**

EXAMPLE 18.6

Roger settles his Van Gogh sketch 'Peasant with Pig' worth £200,000. His allowable expenditure totals £50,000. He also settles his main residence. The beneficiaries are his wife Rena for life with remainder to their two children Robina and Rybina. For CGT purposes, the following rules apply:
(1) *Main residence*   This is exempt from CGT.
(2) *The Van Gogh*   This is treated as disposed of for its market value (£200,000) and, hence, Roger has made a gain of £150,000.

III   ACTUAL AND DEEMED DISPOSALS BY TRUSTEES

A charge to CGT may arise as a result of either actual or deemed disposals of property by the trustees. Notice, however, that where trust property is transferred, on a change of trustees, from old to new trustees, there is no charge since trustees are treated as a single and continuing body (TCGA 1992 s 69(1) provided that the trust does not thereby cease to be UK resident: see **[20.51]**).

The relevant rate of CGT depends upon the type of trust and whether or not the settlor has reserved an interest in his trust. In general, a 23% rate will apply but if the trust (in whole or in part) falls within TA 1988 s 686 (a discretionary or accumulation trust) the rate is increased to 34% whilst if the settlor has retained an interest tax is charged at his rate (ie at 20%, 23% or, more likely, 40%). See **[14.85]**.

Trustees are generally only entitled to one-half of the full annual exemption (ie to £3,250 in 1997–98: see **[14.89]**). **[18.41]**

1   Actual disposals and the use of Trust losses

When chargeable assets are sold by trustees normal principles apply in calculating the gain (or loss) of the trustees. If the disposal generates a loss it may be set off against gains of the same year or of future years made by the trustees. If a beneficiary becomes absolutely entitled to trust property, any loss which has accrued to the trustees in respect of that property (including a carried forward loss) and which cannot be offset against trustee gains for that year occurring prior to the beneficiary becoming so entitled is transferred to that beneficiary. If more than one beneficiary becomes so entitled, the loss is apportioned between them (TCGA 1992 s 71(2)). (Note that a trust loss is more favourably treated than losses made by PRs; see [15.81].)   [18.42]

2 The exit charge: TCGA 1992 s 71(1)

a) *The general rule*

Section 71(1) provides for a deemed disposal of the chargeable assets in the trust fund, whenever a person becomes absolutely entitled to any portion of the settled property (an 'exit charge'). The section is a 'deeming' provision and treats the assets in the fund as being sold by the trustees (so that it is trustee rates of CGT which are relevant) for their market value at that date and immediately reacquired for the same value, thereby ensuring that any increase in value in the chargeable assets is taxed (except in the situation discussed below). The deemed reacquisition by the trustees is treated as the act of the person who is absolutely entitled to the fund as against the trustees (see TCGA 1992 s 60(1)).   [18.43]

EXAMPLE 18.7

Shares in Dovecot Ltd are held by trustees for Simone absolutely, contingent upon attaining the age of 25. She has just become 25 and the shares are worth £100,000. The trustees' base costs (including the indexation allowance) are £25,000. She is now absolutely entitled to the fund and the trustees are deemed to sell the shares (for £100,000) and to reacquire them (for £100,000). On that deemed disposal they have realised a chargeable gain of £75,000 (£100,000 – £25,000). The shares are now treated as Simone's property so that if she directs their sale in the future and £107,000 is raised she will have a chargeable gain of £7,000 (£107,000 – £100,000).

b) *Losses*

A loss arising on the deemed disposal which occurs under s 71 will be deducted from gains accruing to the trustees in that same tax year but before the loss is realised. Subject to that, the loss is passed to the beneficiary under s 71(2) as discussed in para [18.42]. How is this rule affected by the existence or otherwise of connected persons? The Revenue has confirmed that the beneficiaries' entitlement to the loss under s 71 is *not* affected by this rule. Indeed, it seems odd that there was ever any doubt about the matter bearing in mind that the utilisation of losses is only restricted if the relevant disposal is to a connected person. On the termination of a trust the legislation provides not for a disposal of the settled property to the relevant beneficiary but rather for a deemed disposal by the trustees. Hence, irrespective of any question of connected persons, the loss will be fully available for offset against prior trustee gains in that year and any balance will pass through to the relevant beneficiary (see *Tax Bulletin*, February 1993, p 56).   [18.44]

c) *Deemed disposal triggered by the death of a beneficiary entitled to an interest in possession: TCGA 1992 s 73*

The termination of an interest in possession because of the death of the beneficiary may result in a deemed disposal by the trustees under s 71(1) if on that occasion the settlement ends (ie a person becomes absolutely entitled to the trust assets). Although there is a deemed disposal and reacquisition, no CGT (or loss relief) is charged (or allowed) on any resultant gain (loss): see [18.48] for the definition of an interest in possession. This corresponds to the normal CGT principle that on death there is an uplift in value but no charge to tax (see Chapter 15; and, for the IHT consequences, Chapter 25).

EXAMPLE 18.8

Property consisting of shares in Zac Ltd is held on trust for Irene for life, or until remarriage and thereafter to Dominic absolutely.
(1) *If Irene dies* There will be a deemed disposal and reacquisition of the shares at the market value by the trustees (TCGA 1992 s 71(1)), but CGT will not be charged. The property henceforth belongs to Dominic.
(2) *If Irene remarries* The life interest will cease with the same consequences as in (1), save that CGT may be chargeable.

If the interest is in a part only of the fund, the death of the beneficiary will result in an uplift in the appropriate portion of each asset in the fund without any CGT charge thereon (TCGA 1992 s 73(2)).

If the death causes the property to revert to the settlor, the 'reverter to disponer' exception applies (see TCGA 1992 s 71(1)(b) and [**25.35**]). The death of the beneficiary in these circumstances does not lead to a charge to IHT and, hence, the normal uplift but no charge provisions of CGT are modified to ensure that there is no double benefit. For CGT therefore the death will cause a deemed disposal and reacquisition, but for such a sum as will ensure that neither gain nor loss accrues to the trustees (a no gain/no loss disposal).

EXAMPLE 18.9

In 1989 Sue settled property on trust for Samantha for life. In 1997 Samantha dies and the acquisition value and allowable expenses of the trustees are then £15,000 (probate value £25,000). There is a deemed disposal and reacquisition by the trustees for £15,000 (to ensure neither gain nor loss).

The above treatment applies to interests in possession which are not life interests but which came to an end on death. For instance, if the income for a trust fund was settled on A until the age of 40 and thereafter the entire fund passed to B and A died aged 35 (see, for the definition of an interest in possession, [**18.48**] below).   [**18.45**]

d) *Hold-over relief and the tax-free death uplift*

Normally, a tax-free uplift occurs when the death of the interest in possession beneficiary gives rise to a s 71(1) disposal. This general rule is, however, subject to one limitation. If the settlor had made an election to hold over his gain when he created the settlement, that held-over gain is not wiped out on the subsequent death of the life tenant but instead is chargeable at that time (TCGA 1992 s 74).

EXAMPLE 18.10

Property was settled on trust for Frank for life with remainder to Brian absolutely. The settlor elected to hold over the gain of £12,000 when he created the settlement. When Frank dies, the *total* gain on the deemed disposal made by the trustees under s 71 is £40,000. The CGT position is:
(1) There will be a tax-free uplift on the death of Frank, but only for gains arising since the creation of the settlement. Of the total gain of £40,000, £28,000 is, therefore, free of CGT.
(2) The remaining £12,000 gain (the gain held over by the settlor) is subject to tax on Frank's death.

The result of s 74 is a partial revival of the CGT charge on death which is explicable as an anti-avoidance measure. Assume that Bertha wished to give her daughter Brenda an asset on which there was a large unrealised capital gain and on a gift of which a hold-over election was available. They could have elected for hold-over relief, but that would have resulted in Brenda taking over the gain. As an alternative, therefore, Bertha could have settled the asset on an aged life tenant, who was expected to die imminently, and given the remainder interest to Brenda. No CGT would have arisen on the creation of that settlement if Bertha elected for hold-over relief and, were it not for s 74, the death of the life tenant would have wiped out all gains leaving Brenda with the asset valued at its then market value.   **[18.46]**

e) *Allowable expenditure on a deemed disposal*

By its very nature a deemed disposal will rarely lead to any expenditure. TCGA 1992 s 38(4) (which prohibits notional expenditure) seems somewhat redundant, especially in the light of *IRC v Chubb's Settlement Trustees* (1971) which permitted the deduction of *actual* expenses incurred upon the partition of a fund (see **[14.30]**). The normal indexation allowance is available to trustees and, once the settlement ends, to the beneficiary.   **[18.47]**

3   **The termination of an interest in possession on the death of the beneficiary, the settlement continuing (TCGA 1992 s 72)**

The death of a life tenant in possession, in cases where the settlement continues thereafter (ie where TCGA 1992 s 71(1) does not operate), results in a deemed disposal and reacquisition of the assets in the fund by the trustees at their then market value (TCGA 1992 s 72). CGT will not normally be imposed, and the purpose of s 72 is the familiar one of ensuring a tax-free uplift.

The termination of a life interest in a part of the fund, where the settlement continues thereafter, results in a proportionate uplift in the value of all the assets (but see SP 11/73).

An interest in possession for these purposes includes an annuity—the relevant provision in s 72(3) is as follows:

'(3) This section shall apply on the death of the person entitled to any annuity payable out of or charged on, settled property or the income of settled property as it applies on the death of a person whose interest in possession in the whole or any part of settled property terminates on his death.

(4) Where, in the case of any entitlement to an annuity created by a settlement some of the settled property is appropriated by the trustees as a fund out of which the annuity is payable, and there is no right of recourse to, or to the income of, settled property not so appropriated, then without prejudice to subsection (5) below, the settled property so appropriated shall, while the annuity is payable, and on the occasion of the death of the person entitled to the annuity, be treated for the purposes of this section as being settled property under a separate settlement.'

EXAMPLE 18.11

Property is held on trust for Walter for life and thereafter for his son Vivian contingently on attaining 25. Walter dies when Vivian is 24. The CGT consequences are:

(1) *Death of Walter*:   There is a deemed disposal of the property under TCGA 1992 s 72; there is a tax-free uplift. The settlement continues because Vivian is not yet 25.

(2) *Vivian becomes 25*:   There is a further deemed disposal under s 71(1) and CGT may be charged on any increase in value of the assets since Walter's death.

As with deemed disposals under s 71(1) on the death of a life tenant the full tax-free uplift on death does not apply to a gain held over on the creation of a settlement which becomes chargeable.   **[18.48]**

4   Conclusions on deemed disposals under TCGA 1992 ss 71 and 72

The ending of general hold-over relief in 1989 had important consequences for settlements. In particular, if it is no longer possible to postpone payment of the tax, it may prove prohibitively expensive to end a settlement. This may be the case with a life interest settlement when it may be preferable to wait for the death: in the case of discretionary trusts, because there remains a chargeable transfer for IHT, it remains possible to hold over any capital gains.

Resettlements of property (considered at **[18.61]**), which were employed in order to obtain a lower rate of CGT, will now be avoided since the act of resettlement will (in most cases) itself trigger a CGT charge. Note, however, that not every change in beneficial interests results in a deemed disposal: for instance, if a life interest terminates, for a reason other than the death of the beneficiary and the settlement continues, there is no deemed disposal for CGT purposes and this is also the case when a beneficiary merely acquires a right to the income of the trust.   **[18.49]–[18.60]**

EXAMPLE 18.12

Property is settled upon trust for Belinda for life or until remarriage, and thereafter for Roger contingent upon his attaining 25. If Belinda remarries when Roger is ten, the CGT position is:

(1) *The remarriage of Belinda*: Belinda's remarriage terminates her life interest, but there is no deemed disposal as Roger is not at that time absolutely entitled to the fund. Hence, there are no CGT consequences.

(2) *When Roger attains 18*: He will become entitled to the income from the fund as a result of Trustee Act 1925 s 31. There is no CGT consequence.

(3) *When Roger attains 25*: There is a deemed disposal under s 71(1), and (unless the property comprises business assets) hold-over relief will not be available.

IV   RESETTLEMENTS

When property is transferred from one settlement into another, different, settlement a CGT charge may arise under TCGA 1992 s 71(1) because the trustees of the second settlement (who may be the same persons as the trustees of the original settlement) become absolutely entitled to that property as against the original trustees (see *Hoare Trustees v Gardner* (1978)).

Exactly when a resettlement occurs as the result of the exercise by trustees of dispositive powers (eg of appointment and advancement) contained within the trust deed is still a matter of uncertainty (see especially *Roome v Edwards* (1981); *Bond v Pickford* (1983); and *Swires v Renton* (1991)). In *Roome v Edwards*, Lord Wilberforce stressed that the question should be approached 'in a practical and common sense manner' and suggested that relevant indicia included separate and defined property, separate trusts and separate trustees although he emphasised that such factors are helpful but not decisive and that the matter ultimately depends upon the particular facts of each case. He contrasted special powers of appointment which, when exercised, will usually not result in a resettlement of property, with wider powers (eg of advancement) which permit property to be removed from the original settlement.

In *Bond v Pickford* (1983), the Court of Appeal distinguished between two types of power:

(1) a power *in the narrower form* (such as a power of appointment); and

(2) a power *in the wider form* (typically a power of advancement).

The distinction depends on whether the trustees are permitted to free settled property from the original settlement and transfer it into a new settlement. In the absence of an express provision enabling them to do this such action would be prohibited because of the principle that trustees cannot delegate.

Powers in the narrower form cannot create a new settlement: so far as powers in the wider form are concerned *their exercise will not necessarily* create a new settlement. In *Swires v Renton* (1991), Hoffmann J stressed that the classic case involving a new settlement would be where particular assets were segregated, new trustees appointed, and fresh trusts created exhausting the beneficial interest in the assets and providing full administrative powers so that further reference back to the original settlement becomes redundant. The absence of one or more of these features leaves open the question whether a new settlement has arisen: the question would then have to be decided on the basis of intention. In the *Renton* case, for instance, despite exhaustive beneficial trusts, the administrative powers of the original settlement were retained and the appointment made other references to it thereby indicating that a new settlement had not been created.

SP 7/84 generally conforms to the recent cases and indicates that the exercise of a power in the wider form will *not* create a new settlement if it is revocable, non-exhaustive, or if the trustees of the original settlement still have duties in relation to the advanced fund.

In order to provide maximum flexibility it is recommended that settlements should have dispositive powers which are in the narrower and wider form so that the trustees can then decide whether it is their wish to create a new settlement or not. **[18.61]–[18.80]**

EXAMPLE 18.13

The Bladcomb family trust was created in discretionary form in 1965 since when 90% of the assets have been irrevocably appointed on various interest in possession trusts with the remaining 10% being appointed on accumulation and maintenance trusts for infant beneficiaries. The various funds are administered by the original trustees of the 1965 discretionary trust. On these facts the property has remained comprised in the original settlement for CGT purposes. Accordingly:

(1) Even if separate trustees are appointed for, for example part of the assets held on interest in possession trusts, the trustees of the original 1965 trust will remain liable for any CGT attributable to that portion of the assets.

(2) Only one annual exemption is available for gains realised in any part of the settled fund (see *Taxation*, 2 October 1987, for how this exemption should be divided between the various portions of the fund).

(3) As 10% of the fund is held on discretionary and accumulation trusts, any capital gains realised by the trustees (in any portion of the fund) are subject to CGT at 34% not 23% (see further **[14.85]**). Although a reduction in the CGT rate applicable to the interest in possession part of the fund would occur if a separate settlement of the two parts occurred, the disposal of the part of the fund passing to new trustees would attract a CGT charge without the benefit of hold-over relief (unless the assets transferred were business property).

V DISPOSAL OF BENEFICIAL INTERESTS

There is no charge to CGT when a beneficiary disposes of his interest provided that it has not *at any time* been acquired for a consideration in money or money's worth other than another interest under that settlement and provided that the trustees are, at that time, UK resident (TCGA 1992 s 76(1): contrast the disposal of an interest in an unadministered estate).

Once a beneficial interest has been purchased for money or money's worth, a future disposal of that interest will be chargeable to CGT. The consideration does not have to be 'full' or 'adequate': ie any consideration however small will turn the interest into a chargeable asset.

When a life interest has been sold, the wasting asset rules (see [**14.41**]) may apply on a subsequent disposal of that interest by the purchaser.

> **EXAMPLE 18.14**
>
> Ron is the remainderman under a settlement created by his father. He sells his interest to his friend Algy for £25,000. No CGT is charged. If Algy resells the remainder interest to Ginger for £31,000, Algy has made a chargeable gain of £6,000 (£31,000 - £25,000).

The termination of the settlement may result in the property passing to a purchaser of the remainder interest. As a result, that purchaser will dispose of his remainder interest in return for receiving the property in the settlement (TCGA 1992 s 76(2)). The resultant charge that he suffers does not affect the deemed disposal by the trustees (and the possible CGT charge) under s 71(1).

> **EXAMPLE 18.15**
>
> Assume, in *Example 18.14*, that Ginger becomes entitled to the settled fund which is worth £80,000. He has realised a chargeable gain of £49,000 (£80,000 - £31,000). In addition, the usual deemed disposal rules under s 71(1) operate.

An exchange of interests by beneficiaries under a settlement is not treated as a purchase so that a later disposal of either interest will not be chargeable.   [**18.81**]–[**18.100**]

VI   NON-UK SETTLEMENTS

The CGT rules that apply to non-resident trusts are dealt with in Chapter 20. If part only of the settled property is appointed to non-resident trustees who realise a chargeable gain and that part is still treated as comprised in the original settlement (see [**18.61**]), the UK trustees of the other part can be made accountable for any CGT.   [**18.101**]

Disposal of beneficial interests in non-resident trusts

TCGA 1992 s 85(1) modifies the basic exemption from CGT for disposals of beneficial interests.   [**18.102**]

a) *Disposals of beneficial interests prior to 19 March 1991*

Two rules applied.

First, if the disposal occurred *after* the trust had become non-resident, the disposal was chargeable to CGT (s 85(1)). This rule continues to apply to disposals on or after 19 March.

Secondly, if the trust became non-resident after the disposal (so that the exemption under TCGA 1992 s 76(1) had applied at the time of the disposal) the effect of the emigration was to *trigger a charge which was payable by the retiring UK trustees*. In a sense, therefore, the exempt gain under s 76(1) was held in suspense (the relevant provision was FA 1981 s 88(2)). Section 88(2) did not apply if, before becoming non-resident, the trustees had disposed of all the assets which were subject to the trusts at the time when the disposal of the beneficial interest occurred. If some of those assets were retained, the chargeable gain was limited to the value of those assets (FA 1981 s 88(3), (4)). If the trustees failed to pay tax under s 88(2) within 12 months of the due date, tax could be recovered at any time in the next five years from the beneficiary who had disposed of his interest, although he was given a right of recovery against the trustees (FA 1981 s 88(5), (6)).

EXAMPLE 18.16

Bloggs, the remainderman in a family trust, disposed of his interest for £50,000 in 1988. In 1990 non-resident trustees were appointed. For CGT purposes:
(1) The original sale by Bloggs was exempt (s 76(1)).
(2) Immediately before the trust became non-resident the UK resident trustees were treated as making a chargeable gain equal to that which had accrued to Bloggs.

So far as the calculation of the tax charge on the disposal is concerned, in many cases there would have been no acquisition cost given that the disponor was an original beneficiary of a settlement created after March 1982. [**18.103**]

b) *Disposals on or after 19 March 1991*

With the introduction of the exit charge on the emigration of a trust (see [**20.53**]), maintaining s 88 intact would have led to the prospect of a double tax charge and so it was repealed where trustees cease to be UK resident on or after 19 March 1991. The s 85(1) charge was preserved but with the addition of the following:

'in calculating any chargeable gain accruing on the disposal of the interest the person disposing of it shall be treated as having:
(a) disposed of it immediately before the relevant time, and
(b) immediately reacquired it, at its market value at that time.' (TCGA 1992 s 85(3))

Although not happily drafted, the purpose of the subsection is to fix the acquisition cost of the disponor at the date when the trustees emigrated (ie his acquisition cost will take into account the gains then realised and subject to UK tax). On first reading, the provision might be thought to impose a second charge at that time but this is not thought to be the case.

An infelicity in the drafting is that the provision is said to be relevant for the purpose of calculating the chargeable gain of the disponor: it should also be relevant in arriving at any allowable loss which he may have suffered!   [**18.104**]–[**18.120**]

EXAMPLE 18.17

The Halibut trust was set up in 1988 with Jason Halibut being entitled to the residue of the trust on the death of his sister, Rose. The trustees became non-UK resident on 20 March 1996 and Jason sold his remainder interest shortly afterwards for £150,000.

Analysis:
(i) Jason has made a chargeable disposal (TCGA 1992 s 85(1));
(ii) in order to compute his chargeable gain (if any) the market value of his interest when the trust became non-resident on 20 March needs to be ascertained.

VII   RELIEF FROM, AND PAYMENT OF, CGT

1   **Payment**

CGT attributable to both actual and deemed disposals of settled property is assessed on the trustees. The rate of tax will, depending on the type of settlement, be charged at either 23% or 34% (see [**14.85**]: in exceptional cases the settlor's rate will apply). If the tax is not paid within six months of the due date for payment, it may be recovered from a beneficiary who has become absolutely entitled to the asset (or proceeds of sale therefrom) in respect of which the tax is chargeable. The beneficiary may be assessed in the trustees' name for a period of two years after the date when the tax became payable (TCGA 1992 s 69(4)).   [**18.121**]

2   **Exemptions and reliefs**

Exemptions and reliefs from CGT have been discussed in Chapter 16, but note the following matters in the context of settled property:

Main residence exemption   May be available in the case of a house settled on both discretionary and on interest in possession trusts (see *Sansom v Peay* (1976)).   [**18.122**]

The annual exemption   Trustees are generally allowed half of the exemption appropriate to an individual (for 1997–98, half of £6,500 = £3,250).   [**18.123**]

Death exemption   As already discussed, the tax-free uplift will be available for trusts with a life interest, but not for discretionary trusts.   [**18.124**]

Retirement relief   Retirement relief may be available for trusts with a life interest: it is not available for discretionary trusts.   [**18.125**]

Roll-over relief   Available only if the trustees are carrying on an unincorporated business.   [**18.126**]

Reinvestment relief   Available if the beneficiaries are either individuals or charities (see further *Tax Journal*, 10 March 1994 and note that trustees *cannot* defer gains by EIS or VCT investment).   [**18.127**]

19 CGT—companies and shareholders

I CGT problems involving companies [**19.1**]
II Capital distributions paid to shareholders [**19.21**]
III The disposal of shares [**19.41**]
IV Value shifting [**19.61**]

I CGT PROBLEMS INVOLVING COMPANIES

1 CGT and corporation tax

Companies and unincorporated associations are not subject to CGT; instead chargeable gains are assessed to corporation tax. Broadly, the principles involved in computing the chargeable gain (or allowable loss) are the same as for individuals but the effective rate of corporation tax charged on the gain is either 21% or 31% (see Chapter 28).

Disposals within a group of companies (as defined) will generally be free of corporation tax. Any charge is held over until either the asset is sold outside the group or until the company which owns the asset leaves the group; see [**30.000**].
[**19.1**]

2 Company reorganisations

The basic principle is that there is neither a disposal of the original shares nor the acquisition of a new holding: instead, the original shares and new holding are treated as a single asset acquired when the original shares were acquired. When new consideration is given on a reorganisation (for instance, on a rights issue) that is added to the base cost of the original shares and treated as having been given when they were acquired (TCGA 1992 ss 126–131).
[**19.2**]

3 Company takeovers and demergers

If the takeover is by means of an issue of shares or debentures by the purchasing company (a 'paper for paper exchange'), CGT on the gain made by the disposing shareholder may generally be postponed until the consideration shares are sold (TCGA 1992 ss 135–137). If the consideration for the acquisition is partly shares and partly cash the latter is treated as a part disposal of the shareholding and s 135 will apply to the balance. There are detailed requirements that must be satisfied concerning the level of control that the purchaser will exercise over the purchased company and the exchange must be effected for *bona fide* commercial reasons and not form part of any scheme or arrangement of which the main purpose or one of the main purposes is to avoid a liability to CGT or corporation tax. An advance clearance may be applied for (TCGA 1992 s 138).

Where the assets of the target company are acquired for a cash consideration, a chargeable gain will result for the target company unless it obtains roll-over relief under TCGA 1992 ss 152–158 (see [**16.92**]). From the point of view of the target's shareholders, failure to obtain this relief would not only lead to a corporation tax charge on the gains raised by the sale of the assets, it would also leave them the problem of what to do with a 'cash shell' company (see further Chapter 38).

TCGA 1992 s 192 contains provisions aimed at facilitating arrangements whereby trading activities of a single company or group are split up in order to be carried on either by two or more companies or by separate groups of companies ('demergers'; see [**38.51**]). [**19.3**]

4   Incorporation of an existing business

TCGA 1992 s 162 affords relief in cases where a business is transferred to a company as a going concern in return for the issue of shares in the company. [**19.4**]–[**19.20**]

II   CAPITAL DISTRIBUTIONS PAID TO SHAREHOLDERS

A capital distribution (whether in cash or assets) is treated in the hands of a shareholder as a disposal or part disposal of the shares in respect of which the distribution is received (TCGA 1992 s 122(1)). 'Capital distribution' is restrictively defined to exclude any distribution which is subject to income tax in the hands of the recipient (s 122(5)(b)). As the definition of a distribution for the purposes of Schedule F is extremely wide (see [**29.2**]) the CGT charge is confined to repayments of share capital and to distributions in the course of winding up.

> **EXAMPLE 19.1**
>
> (1) Prunella buys shares in Zaba Ltd for £40,000. Some years later the company repays to her £12,000 on a reduction of share capital. The value of Prunella's shares immediately after that reduction is £84,000.
>   The company has made a capital distribution for CGT purposes and Prunella has disposed of an interest in her shares in return for that payment. The part disposal rules must, therefore, be applied as follows:
>   (i) consideration for part disposal: £12,000
>   (ii) allocation of base cost of shares:
>
> $$£40,000 \times \frac{A}{A + B} = £40,000 \times \frac{£12,000}{£12,000 + £84,000} = £5,000$$
>
>   (iii) gain on part disposal: £12,000 − £5,000 = £7,000.
> (2) Stanley buys shares in Monley Ltd for £60,000. The company is wound up and Stanley is paid £75,000 in the liquidation. Stanley has disposed of his shares in return for the payment by the liquidator and, therefore, has a chargeable gain of £15,000 (£75,000 − £60,000).
>   If the company had been insolvent so that the shareholders received nothing Stanley should claim loss relief because his shares would have become of negligible value (see TCGA 1992 s 24(2); *Williams v Bullivant* (1983); and [**14.115**]). He has an allowable loss of £60,000.

These rules are also applied when a shareholder disposes of a right to acquire further shares in the company (TCGA 1992 s 123). The consideration received on the disposal is treated as if it were a capital distribution received from the company in respect of the shares held.

Under s 122(2), if the inspector is satisfied that the amount distributed is relatively small, the part disposal rules are not applied but the capital distribution is deducted from the allowable expenditure on the shares. The result is to increase a subsequent gain on the sale of the shares (in effect the provision operates as a postponement of CGT). On that later disposal the indexation allowance will presumably be calculated on the reduced allowable expenditure. For these purposes, a capital distribution has always been treated as small if it amounts to no more than 5% of the value of the shares in respect of which it is made. This test has been retained but a revised approach was announced in the *Tax Bulletin* for February 1997 as a result of *dicta* in *O'Rourke v Binks* (1992) which noted that the purpose of the legislation was to avoid the need for an assessment in trivial cases, an approach that would have regard to the likely costs of carrying out the part disposal computation and the likely tax consequences in each case. As a result, in additon to the 5% test, the Revenue now accepts that s 122(2) can apply in cases where the distribution is £3,000 or less (see CG 57836).

Under s 122(4) where the allowable expenditure is *less than* the amount distributed the taxpayer may elect that the part disposal rules shall not apply and that the expenditure shall be deducted from the amount distributed. In *O'Rourke v Binks* (1992), the Court of Appeal held that the capital distribution must be small for the purpose of this subsection and that what was 'small' was a question of fact for the Commissioners.

On a liquidation there will often be a number of payments made prior to the final winding up and each is a part disposal of shares (subject to the relief for small distributions) so that the shares will need to be valued each time a distribution is made (see SP 1/72).

EXAMPLE 19.2

Mark purchased 5,000 shares in Rothko Ltd for £5,000. The company has now made a 1:5 rights issue at £1.25 per share. Mark is, therefore, entitled to a further 1,000 shares but, having no spare money, sells his rights to David for £250. At that time his 5,000 shares were worth £7,500. As the capital distribution (£250) is less than 5% of £7,500 the part disposal rules will not apply. Therefore, £250 will be deducted from Mark's £5,000 base cost. (NB Mark may prefer the part disposal rules to apply since (i) any gain resulting may be covered by his annual exemption; and (ii) expenditure of £5,000 (rather than £4,750), will then be index-linked for the purpose of the indexation allowance.)

When a company ceases trading, retirement relief may be available to the shareholder provided that the capital distribution by the liquidator does not consist of chargeable business assets. Further, that distribution must be made within one year of the cessation of trading (or such longer period as the Revenue may allow) and any gain on the deemed disposal of the shares under TCGA 1992 s 122 is only eligible for relief in the proportion which the company's chargeable business assets bear to its total chargeable assets. **[19.21]–[19.40]**

III THE DISPOSAL OF SHARES

1 Introduction

a) Pre-FA 1982 system

A disposal of shares is a chargeable event. Before FA 1982, the CGT rules were relatively straightforward and involved treating identical shares as a single asset. This 'pooling' system involved a cumulative total of shares with sales being treated as part disposals from the pool and not as a disposal of a particular parcel of shares. Special rules applied where all or part of a shareholding was acquired before 6 April 1965. **[19.41]**

EXAMPLE 19.3 (*Pre-FA 1982 pooling*)

Low acquires ordinary shares in XYZ Ltd as follows:

Date	Shares	Cost (£)
1966	100	100
1970	60	250
1976	500	400
1978 (1:1 bonus)	660	—
1980 (1:10 rights)	132	132
Total	1,452	£882

In 1980 Low was treated as owning a single asset (1,452 shares) which cost him £882. In 1981 he sold 726 shares for £726, a part disposal of one-half of the holding. His chargeable gain was £726 - £441 (one-half of the total cost of the asset) = £285.

---

b) *FA 1982 regime—operative from 6 April 1982 to 6 April 1985*

Shares of the same class acquired after 5 April 1982 and before 6 April 1985 were not pooled. Instead, each acquisition was treated as the acquisition of a separate asset (TCGA 1992 s 108(1)). A disposal of shares was then matched with a particular acquisition in accordance with detailed identification rules which applied even where the shares were distinguishable from each other by, for instance, being individually numbered. Shares were therefore treated as a 'fungible' asset. These rules were introduced because of the indexation allowance which made it necessary to know whether the shares disposed of had been acquired within 12 months (when no allowance was available) or, in other cases, to calculate the indexation allowance by reference to the original expenditure. The rules also sought to prohibit avoidance and saving schemes and seriously damaged bed and breakfasting arrangements (see **[19.47]**). For disposals by companies the rules were operative from 1 April 1982.

Major changes in the indexation allowance in 1985 enabled a form of pooling to be reintroduced. Although this change is of benefit to both taxpayers and their professional advisers, there are now four different sets of rules that may apply on a disposal of shares or securities:
(1) The new pooling regime (see 2 below).
(2) Rules that apply to shares acquired after 5 April 1965 and before 6 April 1982 (see 3 below).
(3) Rules that apply to shares acquired before 6 April 1965 (pre-CGT holdings); see 4 below.
(4) Special rules that apply to certain types of security only. *First*, certain gilt-edged securities and qualifying corporate bonds are exempt from CGT. *Secondly*, other securities subject to the bond washing provisions, together with certain offshore funds, are excluded from the new pooling provisions introduced by FA 1985 and remain governed by the system introduced in FA 1982.

Identification rules in FA 1985 determine the order of disposal of shares and securities (other than securities falling within (4) above) and these are discussed at 5 below. These complex provisions have not been altered by 1982 rebasing introduced in FA 1988. **[19.42]**

2 **The new pooling rules**

Shares of the same class acquired after 5 April 1982 and still owned by the taxpayer on 6 April 1985 are treated as one asset and further acquisitions of the shares after that date form part of this single holding (TCGA 1992 s 104). There is an indexed pool of expenditure for each class of share and, if shares in the pool were acquired between 1982 and 1985, the initial value of this pool on 6 April 1985 comprises the acquisition costs of the relevant shares together with the indexation allowance (including an allowance for the first 12 months of ownership) that would have been given had the shares been sold on 5 April 1985.

If identical shares are acquired after 6 April 1985 they are added to the share pool with the cost of their acquisition increasing the indexed pool of expenditure (a similar result occurs if a rights issue is taken up).

EXAMPLE 19.4

Silver acquires 10,000 ordinary shares in Mines Ltd for £10,000 in August 1982 and a further 5,000 shares (cost £7,500) in November 1984. Assume 'indexed rise' from August 1982 to April 1985 was 0.25 and from November 1984 to April 1985 was 0.01.

The value of qualifying expenditure and of the indexed pool of expenditure on 5 April 1985 is as follows:

			£
(1)	*Qualifying expenditure*		
	(i)	1982 purchase	10,000
	(ii)	1984 purchase	7,500
			£17,500
(2)	*Indexed pool of expenditure*		£
	(i)	at 0.25 on 1982 purchase	2,500
	(ii)	at 0.01 on 1984 purchase	75
	(iii)	add acquisition costs	17,500
			£20,075

When some of the shares are sold the part disposal rules are applied to both the qualifying expenditure and the indexed pool of expenditure. The indexation allowance is then found by deducting a proportion of the qualifying expenditure from a proportion of the indexed pool. The allowance can only be used (except in the transitional period) to reduce a gain — not to create or increase a loss.

EXAMPLE 19.5

In March 1997 Silver sells 7,500 of the shares for £18,750 (the value of his remaining holding is £18,750). Indexation from April 1985 to March 1997 is 0.15.

(1) *Proportion of qualifying expenditure*

$$\frac{18,750}{37,500} \times £17,500 = £8,750$$

(2) *Proportion of indexed pool*

Indexed pool at March 1997:

$$£20,075 \times 0.15 = £23,086.25$$

$$\frac{18,750}{37,500} \times £23,086.25 = £11,543.125$$

(3)   *Indexation allowance available*

£11,543.125 - £8,750 = £2,793.125

(4)   *Gain*

£18,750 - (8,750 + £2,793.125) = £7,206.875

(*Note*: If shares are acquired by a no gain/no loss disposal (eg if Silver acquired further shares from his wife) the indexation allowance on those shares is added to the indexed pool of expenditure.)   **[19.43]**

3   Shares acquired after 5 April 1965 and before 6 April 1982

Shares and securities of the same class acquired after 5 April 1965 and before 6 April 1982 are treated as a single asset with a single pool of expenditure (hence, they must *not* be aggregated with identical shares subsequently acquired). For the purpose of the indexation allowance and the rebasing rules the market value of the shares on 31 March 1982 will generally be treated as the taxpayer's acquisition cost (TCGA 1992 s 109).   **[19.44]**

4   Shares acquired before 6 April 1965

For unquoted shares any gain is deemed to accrue evenly (the 'straight-line method') and it is only the portion of the gain since 6 April 1965 which is chargeable. The disponer may elect to have the gain computed by reference to the value of the shares on 6 April 1965. This election may only reduce a gain; it cannot increase a loss or replace a gain by a loss. Where different shares are disposed of on different dates the general rule of identification is last in, first out (TCGA 1992 Sch 2 paras 18–19).

For listed shares and securities the general principle is that a gain is calculated by reference to their market value on 6 April 1965 (the rules for ascertaining the market value are laid down in TCGA 1992 Sch 2 paras 1–6). If, however, a computation based upon the original cost of the shares produces a smaller gain or loss, it is the smaller gain or loss which is taken. If one calculation produces a gain, and one a loss, there is deemed to be neither.

As an alternative to the above procedure, the taxpayer may elect to be charged by reference to the market value of either all his shares or all his securities or both on 6 April 1965 (ie pooling on 6 April 1965). The original cost becomes wholly irrelevant and can neither reduce a gain; nor reduce a loss; nor result in neither gain nor loss (TCGA 1992 Sch 2 para 4).

Section 109(4) permits this election to be made within two years after the end of the year in which the first disposal of such securities occurs after 5 April 1985 (31 March for companies). If the election is made, pre-1965 shares are treated either as part of the taxpayer's 1965–82 pool or as forming a separate 1965-82 pool (ie 3 above).   **[19.45]**

5   Identification rules on a disposal of shares

On a disposal of shares the following identification rules operate (TCGA 1992 s 107).

First, shares are identified with shares acquired on the same day (TCGA 1992 s 105).

Secondly, if within a period of ten days securities are acquired, which either constitute a new holding or are added to a new holding (ie **[19.43]**), and subsequently there is a disposal of identical shares, then so far as possible the acquisition and disposal are matched (TCGA 1992 s 107(3)).

Finally disposals are identified with identical shares owned by the taxpayer at the date of disposal on a last in first out (LIFO) basis. Accordingly, new pools ([**19.43**]) are exhausted first, then shares in the frozen, 1965–82 pool ([**19.44**]) and finally, in cases where the appropriate election has not been made, shares acquired before 1965. As a result shares with the largest potential gain (those owned for the longest time) are deemed to be disposed of last. The identification rules must apply even if the disposal shares can be separately identified.   [**19.46**]

6   Effect of the identification rules on bear transactions and bed and breakfasting

Normally, shares will be acquired before they are sold. So far as transactions on The Stock Exchange are concerned, however, the delivery of shares which have been sold need not take place until five days after the sale. Shares may, therefore, be disposed of and later acquired within the same account. This is a 'bear transaction': the aim is to buy at a lower price to fulfil the earlier sale bargain.

A 'bed and breakfasting' arrangement is employed to enable the taxpayer to extract either a gain or loss from his shares without permanently disposing of those shares as the following example shows:

EXAMPLE 19.6

Alberich has unused CGT losses. He owns shares which have an unrealised gain and which he wishes to retain. He sells the shares at close of business one day and repurchases them at the start of business the next. Shares have been 'parked' overnight and the gain extracted. (Notice that 'b & b' transactions might equally be used to extract an allowable loss to set against realised gains.)

As the ten-day provision (discussed above) only matches disposals with acquisitions in the preceding ten-day period it does not affect traditional 'bed and breakfasting' arrangements nor bear transactions. In correspondence with the Institute of Chartered Accountants (see [1985] STI 568) the Revenue considered the possible impact of the *Ramsay* principle (see Chapter 36) on 'bed and breakfasting'. After noting that the share identification rules in FA 1985 had removed some of the restrictions on this operation they stated:

> 'it will remain necessary to make sure that the transactions involved are effective in (for instance) transferring beneficial ownership of the shares. Assets other than shares and securities may need special consideration in this context'.

[19.47]–[19.60]

IV VALUE SHIFTING

Complex provisions designed to prevent 'value shifting' are found in TCGA 1992 ss 29–34. Although the sections are not limited to shares, the commonest examples of value shifting involve shares.

Under s 29 three types of transaction are treated as disposals of an asset for CGT purposes, despite the absence of any consideration, so long as the person making the disposal could have obtained consideration. The disposal is deemed not to be at arm's length and the market value of the asset is the consideration actually received plus the value of the 'consideration foregone'. Instances of value shifting are to be found in the following paragraphs:

[19.61]

Controlling shareholdings (see CG 58853)　Section 29(2) applies when a person having control (defined in TA 1988 s 416) of a company exercises that control so that value passes out of shares (or out of rights over the company) in a company owned by him, or by a person connected with him, into other shares in the company or into other rights over the company. In *Floor v Davis* (1979) the House of Lords decided that the provision could apply where more than one person exercised collective control over the company, and that it covered inertia as well as positive acts.　**[19.62]**

EXAMPLE 19.7

Ron owns 9,900 ordinary £1 shares in Wronk Ltd and his son, Ray, owns 100. Each share is worth £40. At the instigation of Ron a further 10,000 shares are offered to the existing shareholders at their par value (a 1:1 rights issue). Ron declines to take up his quota and all the shares are subscribed by Ray. The value of Ron's shares has been substantially reduced as he now holds a minority of the issued shares. CGT will be charged on him under s 29(2).

Leases　Section 29(4) provides as follows:

> 'If, after a transaction which results in the owner of land or of any other description of property becoming the lessee of the property, there is any adjustment of the rights and liabilities under the lease, whether or not involving the grant of a new lease, which is as a whole favourable to the lessor, there shall be a disposal by the lessee of an interest in the property.' (and see CG 58860).

[19.63]

EXAMPLE 19.8

Andrew conveys property to Edward by way of gift, but reserves to himself in the conveyance a long lease at a low rent. As the lease is valuable, the part disposal will give rise to a relatively small gain. Andrew later agrees to pay a rack rent so that the value of Edward's freehold is increased. When the rent is increased tax is charged on the consideration that could have been obtained for Andrew agreeing to pay that increased sum.

Tax-free benefits resulting from an arrangement   In contrast to s 29, s 30 applies only if there is an actual disposal of an asset. It strikes at schemes or arrangements, whether made before or after that disposal, as a result of which the value of the asset in question (or a 'relevant asset', as defined) has been reduced and 'a tax-free benefit has been or will be conferred on the person making the disposal or a person with whom he is connected; or on any other person'. When it applies, the inspector is given power to adjust, as may be just and reasonable, the amount of gain or loss shown by the disposal (s 30(4)). This widely drafted provision will not operate if the taxpayer shows that the avoidance of tax was not the main purpose, or one of the main purposes, of the arrangement or scheme. Further, it does not catch disposals between husband and wife (within TCGA 1992 s 58); disposals between PRs and legatees; or disposals between companies which are members of a group. A typical situation where the provision could apply is where a parent company of a group arranges for a subsidiary company to pay a dividend or transfer an asset at an undervalue to another group member: for instance distributing unrealised capital gains to other group members. The benefit of the gain is thereby retained within the group and the value of the subsidiary reduced but the distribution itself is untaxed. This arrangement is prevented by an appropriate addition being made to the sale consideration. The provision is not intended to catch distributions out of normal profits and reserves (TCGA 1992 ss 31–34) and see CG 46800.   **[19.64]**

20 CGT—the foreign element

I GENERAL

1 Territorial scope: residence as the connecting factor

An individual who is resident or ordinarily resident in the UK in any year of assessment is taxed on his worldwide chargeable gains made during that year: 'resident' and 'ordinarily resident' have their income tax meanings (TCGA 1992 s 2(1): s 9(1)). There are two qualifications to this general proposition.

First, where the gain is on overseas assets and cannot be remitted to the UK because of local legal restrictions, executive action by the foreign government or the unavailability of the local currency, CGT will only be charged when those difficulties cease (TCGA 1992 s 279).

Secondly, an individual who is resident, but not domiciled, in the UK is liable only to CGT on such gains on overseas assets as are remitted to the UK. For the location of assets, see TCGA 1992 s 275 and note that a non-sterling bank account belonging to a non-UK domiciliary is located overseas (TCGA 1992 s 275 (1)).

A person who is neither resident nor ordinarily resident in the UK is generally not liable to CGT on gains even if resulting from a disposal of assets situated in the UK. A trust is not UK resident if a majority of the trustees are non-resident *and* the trust is administered outside the UK. [**20.1**]

2 'Going non-resident' and ESC D2

In the light of these provisions CGT may be avoided by an individual 'going non-resident': ie acquiring a residence abroad and then disposing of the asset in question. 'Resident' and 'ordinarily resident' have the same meaning as for income tax and as discussed in Chapter 13, a taxpayer is, for instance, always UK resident if present in the UK for 183 days or more in a tax year, whilst absence from the UK for a complete tax year will not necessarily prevent him from being ordinarily resident in the UK.

As with income tax, residence will usually be determined for a complete tax year with TCGA 1992 s 2 providing that tax is levied if the individual is resident in the UK *during any part* of the tax year. It is only by concession that the tax year may be split into a period of residence and non-residence and the relevant provision (ESC D2) provides that:

'When a person leaves the United Kingdom and is treated on his departure as not resident and not ordinarily resident in the United Kingdom he is not charged to CGT on gains accruing to him from disposals made after the date of his departure.'

A taxpayer is treated as non-resident from the day of his departure when he leaves the UK for permanent residence or to take up full-time employment abroad (see [**13.8**]). In *R v IRC, ex p Fulford-Dobson* (1987) a taxpayer obtained permanent employment in Germany and shortly before his departure his wife transferred a chargeable asset into his name (that disposal attracted no CGT because of the no gain/no loss rule: see [**14.22**]). Within four days of leaving the UK the asset was sold and the taxpayer sought to avoid an assessment to CGT by claiming that he fell within the terms of the above concession. The court held, however, that the Revenue could restrict the giving of concessions and, in particular, could refuse to operate the concession 'in any case where an attempt is made to use it for tax avoidance'. If the taxpayer had retained the asset until the following tax year, and then had made the disposal, reliance upon the concession would have been unnecessary since tax would not be chargeable by virtue of TCGA 1992 s 2.

Two other matters should be noticed. *First*, any CGT losses should be realised prior to departure; and, *secondly*, care should be taken to ensure that arrangements with a potential purchaser, made before going non-resident, do not amount to a disposal at that time. Accordingly, careful thought is required before a conditional contract is concluded or put and call options granted.

The Revenue comments as follows:

'There are three circumstances where Capital Gains Tax liability may arise where the date of disposal appears to be after the date of emigration. These are where it can be shown that

1   there was a binding agreement or contract for sale on or before the date of emigration

2   a business was carried on in the UK through a branch or agency in the period from the date of emigration to the date of disposal

3   an attempt has been made to use ESC D2 for tax avoidance' (see CG 25803)

ESC D2 does not apply to trustees nor to gains realised on the disposal of assets of a business carried on in the UK through a branch or agency.

Gains may be taxed both in the UK and in a foreign country. Where the UK has a double taxation treaty with the relevant country, the matter is dealt with under the terms of the treaty. Otherwise, a person may claim unilateral relief from double taxation usually by receiving a tax credit against CGT for the foreign tax paid (TCGA 1992 s 278).   [**20.2**]

3   Coming to the UK and ESC D2

ESC D2 provides as follows:

'A person who is treated as resident in the UK for any year of assessment from the date of his arrival here but who has not been regarded at any time during the period of 36 months immediately preceding the date of his arrival as resident or ordinarily resident here, is charged to CGT only in respect of the chargeable gains accruing to him from disposals made after his arrival in the UK.'

[**20.3**]–[**20.20**]

II REMITTANCE OF GAINS BY A NON-UK DOMICILIARY (see CG 25350 *et seq*)

An individual who is resident or ordinarily resident, but not domiciled, in the UK is chargeable to CGT only on the remitted gains from overseas assets, with no relief for any overseas losses. The definition of remittance is wide and catches a sum resulting from the gains, which is paid, used or enjoyed in the UK or brought or sent to the UK in any form (TCGA 1992 s 12(2)) and a transfer to the UK of the proceeds of sale of assets purchased from the gain. Anti-avoidance provisions in TA 1988 s 65 designed to catch disguised remittances are extended to CGT. The section applies, for example, where a loan (whether or not made in the UK so long as the moneys are remitted to the UK) is repaid out of the overseas gain (see [**13.34**]).

[**20.21**]–[**20.40**]

III CGT LIABILITY OF NON-RESIDENTS

1 **Individuals**

A non-resident individual escapes tax even on disposals of assets situated in the UK *except* where he carries on a trade, profession or vocation in the UK through a branch or agency (TCGA 1992 s 10(1)). In such cases he is taxed on any gain that arises on a disposal of assets used or previously used for the business or held or acquired for that branch or agency (eg a lease of premises). The charge under s 10 cannot be avoided by removing assets from the UK or by ceasing to trade in the UK. In both cases a deemed disposal at market value will occur (compare the deemed disposal which results from the migration of a foreign company. Further, ESC D2 does not apply when disposals of assets used by a branch or agency are made during the year of emigration. Such disposals will therefore continue to be made by a UK resident and to attract a tax charge: in the following tax year disposals will fall under the s 10 charge with a deemed disposal arising on the final cessation of the trade.   [**20.41**]

2 **Companies**

General rule   A non-resident company is excluded from liability to CGT except when it trades in the UK through a branch or an agency. Thus, a non-resident investment company is never liable to CGT.   [**20.42**]

Anti-avoidance   There are provisions designed to prevent UK resident and domiciled individuals from using these rules to avoid the payment of CGT by the formation of non-resident companies. The legislation, in TCGA 1992 s 13, was substantially amended as a result of increasing evidence that its provisions could be circumvented, for instance by the use of guarantee companies. The re-cast section, applicable to disposals on or after 28 November 1995, applies in the following circumstances:

(1) Chargeable gains must accrue to a company which is not resident in the UK but which would be a close company if it were so resident.
(2) The gain is attributed to a 'participator's' interest in the company to the extent of that interest and there is an attribution process which involves looking through multiple layers of intermediate holdings with final attribution being on a just and reasonable basis. 'Participator' has the TA 1988 s 417 meaning as further amplified and will catch all interests in shares as well as the interest of loan creditors. Trustees can be participators but the provisions do not 'look through' to their beneficiaries.

(2) No assessment is made if the participator's interest in the company is less than 5%.

(4) Gains made on the disposal of most assets of a trading company that are used in the trade are not apportioned (TCGA 1992 s 13(5)). Thus, problems really arise only for the shareholder of a non-resident investment or holding company.

(5) Losses made by the non-resident company cannot be used to reduce its gain before apportionment, nor can the losses as such be apportioned except to the extent that a shareholder has had a gain apportioned to him in that tax year and the apportioned loss would eliminate or reduce the gain. A shareholder can be reimbursed by the company for tax paid on apportioned gains without a further charge. Otherwise, he can deduct the tax paid from any gain made on a subsequent disposal of the shares.

(6) Under the former provisions an assessment was discharged if within two years of the relevant disposal the gain was distributed by way of dividend; distribution of capital or on a winding up of the offshore company. That position has now been altered so that on a subsequent distribution the s 13 assessment stands but any tax paid thereon is allowed as credit against any liability arising on the distribution.

EXAMPLE 20.1

In the early 1980s the Wonka family set up a Jersey trust which owned all the shares in a Netherlands Antilles ('NA') company which in turn owned all the issued share capital of a Californian corporation ('CC'). Assume that the latter company owned substantial property interests around Los Angeles which have just been sold showing a substantial gain.
(1) That gain realised by CC may be apportioned to NA: see TCGA 1992 s 13(9).
(2) In turn, the apportioned gain may be further apportioned to the Jersey trust (TCGA 1992 s 13(10)) and to the extent that the trust makes capital payments to UK beneficiaries, those apportioned gains may attract a UK tax charge.

Notice that the provisions whereby the profits of a 'controlled foreign company' including an investment company may be apportioned to its UK resident corporate members do not apply to its chargeable gains (see TA 1988 s 747(6)).   **[20.43]**

3 Trusts

a) *Background*

The CGT treatment of offshore trusts has undergone a number of changes of which the following is a brief summary.   **[20.44]**

From 1965–81   FA 1965 s 42 imposed a charging system for non-UK resident trusts which led to major difficulties and was ultimately abandoned in 1981.   **[20.45]**

From 1981   FA 1981 s 80 introduced a charging system based on capital distributions received by UK domiciled and resident beneficiaries. One consequence was that offshore trusts could be used to defer indefinitely the payment of CGT and, in addition, there was no exit charge when a UK trust migrated. Section 80 (now TCGA 1992 s 87) was supplemented by changes introduced in FA 1991.   **[20.46]**

An exit charge   Since 19 March 1991 an exit charge has been levied on UK trusts which migrate: see TCGA 1992 ss 80–84.   **[20.47]**

Settlor reserving an interest In cases where a 'defined person' can benefit under the trust, gains realised by certain non-UK resident trustees result in a CGT charge on the settlor: TCGA 1992 s 86 and Sch 5. **[20.48]**

The 'interest' charge An interest charge supplements the s 87 charge in cases where capital distributions are not made out of a non-resident trust in which the trustees have realised gains (TCGA 1992 ss 91–97). **[20.49]**

b) *Exporting an existing UK trust*

Why export? Moving a trust offshore has usually been undertaken in order to obtain all or some of the following benefits: protection from a reintroduction of exchange control; deferment of CGT; and deferment of income tax. So long as the settlor and any spouse are excluded from benefit, UK income tax will be avoided unless beneficiaries ordinarily resident in the UK receive a benefit and the trust produces 'relevant income' (TA 1988 ss 739–740 and see **[13.111]**). For CGT, provided a 'defined person', does not have any interest in his trust, TCGA 1992 s 87 will not lead to any UK tax charge so long as capital payments are not made to UK domiciled and resident beneficiaries. Because of the wide definition of 'defined person', however, it is now relatively uncommon for UK domiciled residents to set up new offshore trusts or to export existing trusts. **[20.50]**

When is a trust non-resident? A trust is only non-resident for CGT purposes when a majority of the trustees are neither resident nor ordinarily resident in the UK *and* the general administration of that trust is ordinarily carried on outside the UK (TCGA 1992 s 69(1)). There is a proviso to s 69(1) for professional trustees. Where a person who is resident in the UK carries on a business consisting of or including the management of trusts and acting as a trustee in the course of that business he is treated in relation to the trust as non-resident if the whole of the settled property consists of or derives from property that was provided by someone not at the time of making that provision domiciled, resident or ordinarily resident in the UK.

In blatant cases where a trust is exported and gains are then immediately realised it has always been open to the Revenue to argue that under *Ramsay* principles the appointment of non-resident trustees is an artificial step which can be excised so that the gain is thereby made by the (former) UK trustees and is subject to tax. In this connection ESC D2 (see **[20.2]**) does not apply to trustees and hence the tax year is not split so that the UK trustees may be taxed on gains realised later in the tax year after foreign resident trustees had been appointed. **[20.51]**

Can UK trusts be exported? It is important to ensure, so far as possible, that all beneficiaries agree to the moving of the trust. The equitable rules on the appointment of overseas trustees were set out by Pennycuick VC in *Re Whitehead's Will Trusts* (1971) as follows:

'The law has been quite well established for upwards of a century that there is no absolute bar to the appointment of persons resident abroad as trustees of an English trust. I say "no absolute bar" in the sense that such an appointment would be prohibited by law and would consequently be invalid. On the other hand, apart from exceptional circumstances, it is not proper to make such an appointment, that is to say, the court would not, apart from exceptional circumstances, make such an appointment; nor would it be right for the donees of such a power to make an appointment out of court. If they did, presumably the court would be likely to interfere at the instance of beneficiaries. There do, however, exist exceptional circumstances in which such an appointment can properly be made. The most obvious are those in which the beneficiaries have settled permanently in some country outside the UK and what is proposed to be done is to appoint new trustees in that country.'

This *dictum* would suggest that appointing non-resident trustees is acceptable but usually 'improper'. (Trustee Act 1925 s 36(1) might imply that residence outside the UK for more than 12 months is unacceptable for a trustee whilst s 37(1)(c) may create difficulties given that a non-UK corporate trustee cannot be a 'trust corporation'.) However, since that case it may be that judicial attitudes have changed so that provided that the export can be shown to be for the beneficiaries' advantage (eg in saving tax) the courts are not likely to interfere (see the unreported case of *Richard v Hon A B Mackay* (1987)).

The Inland Revenue itself may not be able to object to the appointment since it does not have *locus standi* but any UK trustee should consider taking indemnities from the new overseas trustees in case beneficiaries at some future date allege that breaches of trust have been committed and seek to set aside the appointment. It is also sensible to include in any trust instrument an express power for the existing trustees to retire in favour of non-resident trustees.

[**20.52**]

c) *The CGT export charge (TCGA 1992 s 80(2))*

When trustees of a UK settlement become neither resident nor ordinarily resident in the UK, they are deemed to have disposed of assets in that settlement and immediately reacquire those same assets. This deemed disposal is closely modelled on that which applies when a person becomes absolutely entitled to settled property (see [**18.43**]) and on the exit charge which is levied when a non-UK incorporated company ceases to be UK resident (TCGA 1992 ss 185-186).

Imposing the exit charge gives rise to a number of problems. When, for instance, does the charge come into effect? Section 80(1) defines the phrase 'relevant time' as meaning any occasion when trustees become non-UK resident provided that *the relevant time falls on or after 19 March 1991*.

A second problem is when do trustees become non-UK resident? A simple view would be that this would occur whenever UK trustees (Alan and Ben) are replaced by, say, two Jersey trustees (Cedric and Desmond). Certainly, if s 80 stood alone, such a simple change in the trusteeship would be 'the relevant time'. However, the section must be read in the light of the rest of the CGT legislation and under s 69(1) it is provided that:

'The trustees of the settlement shall for the purposes of this Act be treated as being a single and continuing body of persons ... and that body shall be treated as being resident and ordinarily resident in the United Kingdom *unless the general administration of the trusts is ordinarily carried on outside the United Kingdom and the trustees or a majority of them for the time being are not resident or not ordinarily resident in the United Kingdom.*'

Replacing A and B with C and D will satisfy part of s 69(1) but there is a 'frequently overlooked' second limb in that provision: namely that the administration of the trust must be conducted outside the UK. Until that occurs, the trustees remain UK resident.

So far as timing is concerned, the deemed disposal is said to take place 'immediately before' the relevant time: accordingly the disponors are the retiring UK trustees who, given that the CGT year cannot generally be split, also remain liable for gains realised by the new trustees in the tax year in which they are appointed (SP 5/92 para 2).

Who is liable to pay the export charge? Because the deemed disposal is by the retiring UK trustees they are primarily responsible. It is therefore important that they retain sufficient assets to cover this liability. TCGA 1992 s 82 further provides that if tax is not paid by those trustees within six months of the due date, any former trustees of that settlement who held office during the 'relevant period' can be made accountable. The relevant period (broadly) means the 12-month period which ends with the emigration (although not back-dated before 19 March 1991). Assume, for instance, that A and B, two professional trustees, retire on 1 January 1996 in favour of two family members. Those family trustees subsequently (on 1 July 1996) retire in favour of two non-UK resident trustees, C and D, such retirement being without the prior knowledge of A and B. On these facts, the appointment of C and D constitutes the 'relevant time' for s 80 purposes and any gain arising as a result of the deemed disposal will therefore be payable on 31 January in the following tax year (ie on 31 January 1998). If not paid within six months of that date the Revenue may demand that tax from all or any of A, B and the family trustees. However, a former trustee can escape liability if he shows that 'when he ceased to be a trustee of the settlement there was no proposal that the trustees might become neither resident nor ordinarily resident in the UK' (s 82(3) and SP 5/92 para 5).

The deemed disposal is of 'defined assets' which (predictably) includes all the assets which constitute the settled property at the relevant time. The term does not include UK assets used for the purpose of a trade carried on by the trustees through a UK branch or agency. This is because such assets remain within the UK tax net even after the trustees become non-resident: hence there is no need to subject them to the deemed disposal (see [20.41]).

Section 81 deals with involuntary exports and imports. Assume that the trustees of a settlement are Adam (UK resident) and Cedric (a Jersey resident accountant) who does all the paperwork and performs the administrative tasks for the trustees. Adam dies with the result that the conditions laid down in s 69(1) are satisfied and the trust ceases to be UK resident. On these facts, there was no intention to export the trust and, indeed, the appointment of a new resident UK trustee will have the effect of reversing the process. Imposing an exit charge in such a case would be unjust and hence s 81 prevents the charge arising *provided that* within six months of Adam's death the trustees of the settlement become again UK resident. Not surprisingly, the exit charge remains in force for those defined assets which are disposed of during the period of non-UK residency (ie between the death and the resumption of residence).

Finally, the converse situation (a non-resident settlement becoming UK resident because of the death of a trustee) is provided for in sub-ss (5)–(7). Reverting to non-resident status within six months of the death will not generally trigger the s 80 exit charge subject only to an exception where the period of UK residence has been used to add assets to the settlement claiming hold-over relief on that transfer. Resuming non-resident status will result in a deemed disposal at market value of such assets.   [20.53]

d) *Taxing the beneficiaries a non-resident trust*

Subject to the special rules which may apply if a 'defined person' has an interest in the settlement (see [20.56]), TCGA 1992 s 87 applies to non-resident trusts in respect of gains made from 1981–82 onwards where the trustees are not resident nor ordinarily resident in the UK during the tax year, but the settlor is domiciled and either resident or ordinarily resident in the UK at some time during the tax year or when the settlement was made. Hence, if the settlor was UK domiciled and resident at the date of the trust's creation the rules of s 87 *always* apply, but if a settlement was originally created by a non-domiciled settlor, who subsequently becomes a UK domiciliary, it will be caught by these rules only for those years when the settlor is UK resident and will cease to be caught on his death. 'Settlement' and 'settlor' are defined as for income tax (see TA 1988 s 660G(1)) and settlor includes the testator or intestate when the settlement arises under a will or intestacy (TCGA 1992 s 87(9)).

When s 87 applies the following rules operate:

First, the trust gains for each year must be calculated ('the amount on which the trustees would have been chargeable to tax ... if they had been resident and ordinarily resident in the UK in the year'). Non-resident trustees are *not* entitled to the benefit of a CGT annual exemption, but the normal uplift in value in the settled assets will occur on the death of a life tenant in possession (see [**18.00**]).

Secondly, in computing this total, gains made in offshore companies may be attributed to the trustees (see TCGA 1992 s 13(10)). It was thought that there was a lacuna in the legislation which existed from 6 April 1988 until it was closed from 6 April 1991. Under TCGA 1992 s 77 special rules apply when a settlor reserves a benefit in a UK settlement. In such cases gains made by the trustees are deemed to be those of the settlor who is accountable for the tax with a right of reimbursement. Under s 87 the computation of gains of non-resident trustees proceeds on the basis of computing the gains which those trustees would have made had they been UK resident and it follows that in cases where the settlor has reserved a benefit trustees would have made no such gains. It was therefore arguable that gains realised by overseas trustees in such circumstances will *never* attract a CGT charge! This 'ingenious argument' was, however, rejected in *de Rothschild v Lawrenson* (1995) by the Court of Appeal who restricted the wording of s 77 to cases where the trustees were *actually* resident in the UK and in fact chargeable to tax.

Thirdly, the gains realised by the trustees will then be attributed to beneficiaries to the extent that they receive 'capital payments'. A 'capital payment' is widely defined (see TCGA 1992 s 97(1) and (2)) to include, *inter alia*, the situation where a beneficiary becomes absolutely entitled to the trust property as well as to 'the conferring of any other benefit'. When a beneficiary is entitled to an interest in possession in the settlement and is provided either with an interest free loan or permitted to occupy trust property rent free it is, however, arguable that he has received no 'benefit' since had interest or rent been charged it would have belonged to him as life tenant.

Fourthly, trust gains are attributed to *all* beneficiaries who receive capital payments as follows. The first beneficiary to receive a payment has attributed to him all the gains then realised by the trustees to the extent of the benefit which he receives. This can produce unfair results: assume, for instance, that Bill and Ben become absolutely entitled to an overseas trust fund worth £200,000 in equal shares when they become 25. The trust fund has realised gains of £100,000 when Ben becomes 25 (Bill will become 25 in a following tax year). *All the gains are attributed to Ben.*

When more than one capital payment is made in a single tax year gains are attributed to the payments *pro rata* (TCGA 1992 s 87(5)). If a capital payment is made at a time when there are no trust gains, subsequent gains may be attributed to that beneficiary (s 87(4)). Finally, if no capital payments are made, trust gains are carried forward indefinitely until such a payment occurs (s 87(2)).

EXAMPLE 20.3

A non-resident discretionary settlement has four beneficiaries, two of whom (A and B) are UK domiciled. Over three years the fund has no income and makes the following net gains and capital payments. No capital payments have been made to the non-UK domiciled beneficiaries.

	£	A £	B £
Year 1			
Capital payments		10,000	5,000
Net gains £6,000 apportioned		4,000	2,000
Capital payments c/f		6,000	3,000
Year 2			
Capital payments		3,000	6,000
Including payments b/f		9,000	9,000
Trust gains	20,000		
Amount apportioned	18,000	9,000	9,000
Gains c/f	£2,000	—	—

	£	A £	B £
Year 3			
Capital payments		15,000	5,000
Trust gains	10,000		
Gains b/f	2,000		
Amount apportioned	£12,000	9,000	3,000
Capital payments c/f		£6,000	£2,000

Fifthly, a capital payment made by trustees may be treated as income in the hands of the beneficiary under the anti-avoidance provisions of TA 1988 ss 739–745 (see Chapter 13). Such payments are charged to income tax up to the trust income for that year; income from previous years is included to the extent that such income has not already been charged to a beneficiary. It is only the excess which is treated as a capital payment for the purpose of the apportionment of trust gains.

EXAMPLE 20.4

The same settlement as in *Example 20.3*, except that the following payments made to A and B over three years are first treated as income under TA 1988 ss 739–745.

	£	A £	B £
Year 1			
Trust payments		20,000	10,000
Trust income	£12,000		
Charged to income tax on A and B		8,000	4,000
		12,000	6,000
Trust gains	£15,000		

	£	A £	B £
Apportioned for CGT		10,000	5,000
Payments c/f		£2,000	£1,000

Year 2	£	A £	B £
Payments b/f		2,000	1,000
Payments made		10,000	11,000
		12,000	12,000
Trust income	30,000		
Charged to income tax on A and B	24,000	12,000	12,000
Income c/f	£6,000	—	—
Trust gains c/f	£12,000		

Year 3	£	A £	B £
Trust payments		10,000	10,000
Trust income	8,000		
Trust income b/f from year 2	6,000		
Charged to income tax on A and B	£14,000	7,000	7,000
		3,000	3,000
Trust gains	4,000		
Trust gains b/f from year 2	12,000		
	16,000		
Apportioned for CGT	6,000	3,000	3,000
Trust gains c/f	£10,000		

Sixthly, a beneficiary who receives a capital payment is subject to CGT on the attributed gains *provided that* he is UK domiciled and resident (TCGA 1992 s 87(7)). Accordingly, a non-UK resident may have trust gains attributed to him *but will not suffer any tax on those gains*. The UK beneficiary will be taxed in accordance with normal rules: ie he may deduct from the attributed gain losses and his annual exemption and the balance will then attract tax at 20%, 23% or 40% as appropriate. In calculating his liability it is believed that the gains will be treated as the *lowest part* of his total gains for the year (thereby enabling them to benefit from the beneficiary's annual exemption and, in appropriate cases, reducing any surcharge: see [**20.55**] and see CG38321 in the context of the charge on the settlor).

Seventhly, if non-resident trustees make losses these will be set off against future overseas gains in the normal way. Note, however, two important qualifications to the general provisions dealing with losses. Such losses do not pass to a beneficiary who becomes absolutely entitled to the trust assets (contrast the position with UK trusts and see TCGA 1992 s 16(3) and s 97(6)). Further, it may be that losses can only be used against gains made by the trustees *at a time when they are non-UK resident*. If a settlement becomes UK resident the realised gains are not wiped out but will be taxed as and when capital payments are made in the usual way.

EXAMPLE 20.5

Bonzo created a non-UK resident settlement in which he is one of the discretionary beneficiaries. Capital payments have not so far been made by the trustees and the gains (losses) of the settlement are as follows:

Tax year	*Gain (loss)* £
1986–87	250,000
1987–88	(75,000)

Assume further that the Bonzo family now wish to import this trust and that there are some assets in the fund showing an unrealised gain and some showing an unrealised loss.

(1) The trust can be imported by the appointment of a majority of UK resident trustees.

(2) The trust has realised gains of £250,000 from 1986–87 which will remain on the settlement 'clock' and so attract a tax charge as and when capital payments are made to UK beneficiaries.

(3) The loss of £75,000 in 1987–88 will (it appears) only be offset against future trust gains if realised by non-resident trustees. Accordingly, it will be desirable for gains to be realised in the tax year before the trust becomes UK resident.

A charge under s 87 can be deferred so long as the trustees avoid making capital payments. The charge can be avoided altogether if such payments are made to a non-UK resident or non-UK domiciled beneficiary. Gains can therefore be washed out of the trust by the making of such payments. **[20.54]**

e) *The supplementary (interest) charge*

The supplementary charge may apply to beneficiaries who receive capital payments on or after 6 April 1992. Because it is intended to be supplementary to the s 87 charge, it will only apply if those beneficiaries are UK domiciled and resident. Accordingly (as with the s 87 charge) this extra levy will *not* apply if *either* the settlor was and has remained non-domiciled or non-resident *or* the recipient beneficiary is non-resident or non-domiciled (TCGA 1992 ss 91–95).

The charge operates as an interest charge on the delayed payment of CGT following a disposal of chargeable assets by non-resident trustees. It is, however, limited to a six-year period and therefore the time covered by the charge begins on the *later* of (a) 31 January in the tax year following the year in which the disposal occurred, and (b) 31 January six years before 31 January in the year of assessment following that in which the capital payment was made. The rate of charge is 10% pa of the tax payable on the capital payment (this percentage may be amended by statutory instrument).

EXAMPLE 20.6

The Moisie Liechtenstein Trust realises capital gains in the tax year 1996–97 and a capital payment is made to a UK domiciled and resident Moisie beneficiary on 1 July 2002.

(1) That beneficiary will be assessed to CGT on the capital payment received (at current rates at, say, 40%).

(2) The interest charge will begin to run on 31 January 1998 at 4% per annum (ie 10% of the ultimate tax charge). The charge itself will apply for the period from 31 January 1998 to 30 January in the year of assessment following that in which the capital payment is made (ie 30 January 2003 so that the interest charge continues to run after the capital payment has been made and the *minimum* level of charge is 20%). In all, five years will be subject to the charge (20%) thereby giving a total tax bill of 60% (at present rates the maximum interest charge is six years at 4% pa = 24% and so the maximum CGT levy is 64%). Note that if the beneficiary does not suffer a CGT charge—for instance because he is able to set capital losses against the gains attributed to him—there is no interest charge.

The precise mechanics governing the supplementary charge are complex, with capital payments being matched first with total trust gains at 6 April 1991 and then on a first-in first-out basis. By way of concession, however, trustees are given at least 12 months in which to distribute gains since the interest charge does *not* apply to gains realised in the same or immediately preceding year of assessment.

EXAMPLE 20.7

(1) In 1996–97 the Cohen Offshore Settlement has accumulated trust gains of £100,000. Although the interest charge begins to run on 31 January 1998 no charge is levied on capital distributions made before 6 April 1998.

To what extent has the charge encouraged the break-up of existing offshore trusts? Much turns on the facts of individual cases but it should be remembered that one way of avoiding the s 87 charge—distributing to non-residents—remains available to 'wash-out' all the potential tax including this interest charge. For the wealthy family, who view their trust as a roll-up fund which they do not need to dip into, a 10% charge may be seen as a relatively small impost given that the deferred tax may be an insignificant percentage of the total offshore fund. Given that income from offshore trusts may be taxed less heavily (at a maximum of 40%) trustees should, in appropriate cases, ensure that income rather than capital is distributed. **[20.55]**

f) *Taxing the settlor when 'a defined person' has an interest in his trust (TCGA 1992 s 86, Sch 5)*

These provisions resemble (although they are more severe!) those in TCGA 1992 s 77 which deals with UK resident trusts. When they apply, gains realised by the trustees, which would have attracted a UK CGT charge had the trustees been resident, are taxed as gains of the settlor and form the top slice of his taxable gains for that year. As in the s 77 rules, the gains are not reduced by a trustee annual exemption whilst losses realised by the trustees (although available to set against future gains which they may make) are not treated as losses of the settlor. The settlor is given a statutory right to recover any tax which he suffers from his trustees: the extent to which this right may be enforced in a foreign jurisdiction is, of course, uncertain (see CG 38321).

In considering the provisions of the Schedule, two key questions need to be answered. *First*, which settlements are caught and, *secondly*, when does a settlor retain an interest for these purposes?

So far as the first question is concerned, the rules apply to 'qualifying settlements' which are defined in Sch 5 para 9 as settlements created 'on or after 19 March 1991'. Old settlements are therefore generally outside the scope of the rules *but* para 9(2) provides that in four situations such settlements may *become* qualifying settlements (see further SP 5/92).

EXAMPLE 20.8

(1) The Jonas Family UK Trust was set up in 1982. In 1996 the trustees become non-UK resident. Not only will that event trigger an exit charge but, in addition, because the settlement was exported after 18 March 1991 it will become a 'qualifying settlement'.

(2) The Popeye Settlement has been resident in Liechtenstein since 1989. In 1996:
   (i) A court order is obtained in Vaduz whereby the beneficial class is widened to include the settlor. This has the effect of turning the trust into 'a qualifying settlement'. By contrast, in settlements where the trustees have always had the power to *add* beneficiaries and exercise that power to add a 'defined person' after March 1991 it is not thought that the terms of the trust have been varied so that it becomes 'qualifying settlement'. (In SP 5/92 it is stated that 'where the terms of the trust include a power to appoint anyone within a specified range to be a beneficiary, exercise of that power after 19 March 1991 will not be regarded as a variation of the settlement'.)
   (ii) The trustees distributed funds to the settlor's spouse who is not a

beneficiary. The effect of what is a breach of trust is to convert the trust into 'a qualifying settlement' since she is now a person who has enjoyed a benefit (and is a 'defined person') and she was not a person who might be expected to have enjoyed such a benefit from the settlement after 18 March 1991.

(iii) On 1 March 1992 Julian Popeye added property to his father's trust. Such an addition, whether by the settlor or another, has the effect of turning the trust into a 'qualifying settlement'. This provision must be watched carefully: it does not apply in cases where there is an accretion to settlement funds (eg where the trust receives dividends or bonus shares from a company in which it has investments) nor if the settlor adds property to discharge the administrative expenses of the trust (to the extent that such expenses cannot be discharged out of trust income: on the meaning of 'administrative expenses' see SP 5/92 para 26). Bear in mind, however, that other additions—*however small and whoever makes them*—have the effect of converting the *entire trust* into a 'qualifying settlement'.

Apart from the settlement needing to 'qualify', the legislation only applies in years when the settlor is *both* domiciled and either resident or ordinarily resident in the UK. Gains realised in other years are not taxed as the settlor's and nor are gains realised in the tax year when the settlor dies.

Turning to the second question, gains will be taxed on the settlor if a 'defined person' benefits or will or may become entitled to a benefit in either the income or the capital of the settlement. Paragraph 2(3) identifies a 'defined person' as follows:

'(a)   the settlor;
(b)   the settlor's spouse;
(c)   any child of the settlor or of the settlor's spouse [no age limit];
(d)   the spouse of any such child;
(e)   a company controlled by a person or persons falling within paragraphs (a) to (d) above;
(f)   a company associated with a company falling within paragraph (e) above.'

The list is formidable (contrast the provisions of s 77(3) in relation to UK trusts) and it is particularly worthy of note that children (including step-children) *of whatever age* are included. The only exclusions of real consequence are the settlor's cohabitee and his grandchildren! A deliberate policy decision was taken not to apply the provisions of s 77 to offshore trusts because it was intended to widen the class of defined persons. Note the trap which exists for a settlor in cases where a UK trust has been created in favour of his children which is then exported. Although the settlor is otherwise excluded from all benefit under the rules of the trust, the effect of the export is to create a qualifying settlement with the result that gains will be taxed as the settlor's since defined persons (his children—even if they are geriatric adults) will or may benefit.   **[20.56]**

g) Offshore trusts: information (TCGA 1992 s 98A, Sch 5A)

FA 1994 widened the information provisions to catch all non-resident trusts, not just those in which a defined person retains an interest. Accordingly, they apply to additions to an existing trust; to the establishment by a UK settlor of a foreign settlement and indeed to a foreign settlement created by a non-UK resident and domiciliary who subsequently becomes resident and domiciled; and, finally, to the export of a UK trust. In all cases details of the date when the settlement was created; name and address of persons delivering the return and details of the trustees must be provided.   **[20.57]**

h) *Disposal of a beneficial interest in an offshore trust*

Disposals of beneficial interests in such cases are subject to charge (TCGA 1992 s 85(1) disapplying s 76(1)).

What happens if the interest of a beneficiary terminates not as a result of any voluntary action on his part but by act of the trustees: eg where a life interest is terminated by the trustees under a power reserved to them in the settlement? In this case it is thought that the termination will not amount to a disposal for CGT purposes since whilst it is true that under the legislation certain involuntary disposals (eg a sale under a compulsory purchase order) are subject to charge (so that a voluntary act on the part of the disponor is not always required) even in these cases there is a transfer of assets as opposed to a mere forfeiture of rights. So far as a forfeiture of rights is concerned there is no disposal unless a capital sum is paid or deemed to be paid on that event (TCGA 1992 ss 22–24). **[20.58]**

Section 4   Inheritance tax

Chapters

Introduction—from estate duty to inheritance tax

Most countries impose some kind of wealth tax. It usually takes the form of a death duty either levied on property inherited or on the value of a deceased's estate on death. In the UK estate duty was introduced in 1894 as a tax on a deceased's property whether passing under a will or on intestacy. Over its long life the tax was extended from its originally narrow fiscal base (property passing on death) to catch certain gifts made in the period before death and at the time of its replacement by CTT it extended to gifts made in the seven years before death. By the 1970s estate duty was, however, widely condemned as an unsatisfactory tax. 'A voluntary tax'; 'a tax on vice: the vice of clinging to one's property until the last possible moment'—were typical descriptions.

In 1972 the Conservative government considered replacing estate duty with an inheritance tax (Cmnd 4930). The idea was that a beneficiary would keep a cumulative account of all gifts that he received on death and pay tax accordingly. Nothing came of this proposal, largely because such a tax would have been too costly to administer and because the Conservative government fell from office.

The Labour government, which came to power in 1974, was committed to achieving a major redistribution of wealth. As a first stage (without any prior consultation) it introduced CTT in the 1974 Budget. This tax had '. . . as its main purpose to make the estate duty not a voluntary tax, but a compulsory tax, as it was always intended to be' (Mr Healey, the then Chancellor of the Exchequer). A proposed wealth tax (Cmnd 5074) was never introduced. In reality CTT, substantially altered during its passage through Parliament in 1974–75, never achieved its espoused redistributive purpose. There was no doubt, however, that in concept it was a brilliantly simple tax which removed the arbitrariness of the old estate duty. All gifts of property, whether made *inter vivos* or on death, were cumulated with earlier gifts and progressive rates of tax applied to that cumulative total.

The advent of Conservative governments in 1979 has seen a steady erosion of the principles underlying CTT. The old idea of a fully comprehensive cradle to grave gifts tax was abandoned in 1981 in favour of ten-year cumulation, thresholds were raised, and a new relief introduced for agricultural landlords. By 1986, as a percentage of GNP, CTT yielded less than one-third of the revenue formerly produced by estate duty.

To some extent, the changes made by FA 1986 merely completed this process. Ten-year cumulation was reduced to seven years and the majority of lifetime gifts made more than seven years before death were removed from charge. As in the days of estate duty, therefore, tax is now levied on death gifts and gifts made within seven years of death. In an attempt to prevent schemes whereby taxpayers could 'have their cake and eat it' (ie give property away but continue to enjoy the benefits from it) there was a further echo from estate duty in the reintroduction of rules taxing gifts with a reservation of benefit. These changes do not amount to a replacement of CTT by estate duty but did represent a welding of certain estate duty rules onto the already battered corpse of CTT. The end result is simply a mess and to call this amalgam an inheritance tax is to confuse matters further since the tax is not levied on beneficiaries in proportion to what they receive from an estate and neither is it a true tax on inheritances since certain lifetime transfers are subject to charge. 'There has been no attempt at reform. The Chancellor has merely given us some reasons for making a shabby handout to the very rich. Not only has he reverted to the old estate duty, he has falsified the label' (Cedric Sandford, *Financial Times*, 26 March 1986).

Capital transfer tax was rechristened inheritance tax as from 25 July 1986 and the former legislation (the Capital Transfer Tax Act 1984) *may* be cited as the Inheritance Tax Act 1984 from that date (FA 1986 s 100). Despite the permissive nature of this provision the new title for this Act will be used in this book and inheritance tax abbreviated to IHT. All references to CTT take effect as references to IHT and, as all references to estate duty became references to CTT in 1975, they now become references to IHT.

As a final curiosity it may be noted that the removal of a general hold-over election for CGT in the 1989 Budget was justified by the then Chancellor (Nigel Lawson) on a somewhat inaccurate view of the current scope of IHT. In his Budget Speech, he stated that:

'the general hold-over relief for gifts was introduced by my predecessor in 1980, when there was still Capital Transfer Tax on lifetime gifts, in order to avoid a form of double taxation. But the tax on lifetime giving has since been abolished, and the relief is increasingly used as a simple form of tax avoidance.'

The bizarre position has now been reached whereby what was intended as a general tax on gifts has been limited (in the main) to gifts on or within seven years of death whilst a tax intended to catch capital profits may now operate to impose a tax charge on any gain deemed to be realised when a lifetime gift is made!

21 IHT—lifetime transfers

For a charge to IHT to arise, either immediately or at a future time, there must be a chargeable transfer. Whether and, if so, when tax is levied on that transfer then depends upon whether it is:

(1) *potentially exempt* in which case IHT will only be charged if the donor dies within seven years of that transfer: otherwise it is exempt.

(2) *chargeable immediately* because it does not satisfy the definition of a potentially exempt transfer. In the event of the transferor dying within seven years of this chargeable transfer a supplemental charge to IHT may arise.

It is proposed to discuss first what is meant by a chargeable transfer and then to consider under what circumstances such a transfer is subject to IHT. [**21.1**]

I DEFINITION OF A 'CHARGEABLE TRANSFER'

The principal IHT charging provision is IHTA 1984 s 1 which states that 'IHT shall be charged on the value transferred by a chargeable transfer'. A chargeable transfer is then defined in IHTA 1984 s 2(1) as having three elements: there must be a transfer of value; made by an individual; which is not exempt. [**21.2**]

1 A transfer of value

A *transfer of value* is defined in IHTA 1984 s 3(1) as any disposition which reduces the value of the transferor's estate and includes certain deemed transfers of value ('events on the happening of which tax is chargeable *as if* a transfer of value had been made'): see IHTA 1984 s 3(4). Examples of deemed transfers of value include the termination of an interest in possession in settled property (see Chapter 25) and transfers of value made by a close company which are apportioned amongst its participators (see [**21.121**]).

369

'*Disposition*' is not defined, but the ordinary meaning is wide and includes any transfer of property whether by sale or gift; the creation of a settlement; and the release, discharge or surrender of a debt.   **[21.3]**

2   Omissions

By IHTA 1984 s 3(3), a disposition includes an omission to exercise a right. The right must be a legal right and the omission must satisfy three requirements:
(1)   The estate of the person who fails to exercise the right must be reduced in value.
(2)   Someone else's estate (or a discretionary trust) must be increased in value (ie contrary to the usual principle, there must be a positive benefit to another).
(3)   The omission must be deliberate which is presumed to be the case in the absence of contrary evidence.

Examples of such omissions include failure to sue on a debt until after the limitation period has expired; failure to exercise an option either to sell or purchase property on favourable terms; and failure by a landlord to exercise his right to increase rent under a rent review clause. The omission will constitute a transfer of value at the latest time when it was possible to exercise the right, unless the taxpayer can show (1) that the omission was not deliberate but was a mistake of fact (eg he forgot) or of law (eg failure to realise that the debt had become statute barred) or (2) that it was the result of a reasonable commercial decision involving no element of bounty (eg failure to sue a debtor who was bankrupt).   **[21.4]**

3   Examples of transfers of value

(1)   A gives his house worth £60,000 to his son B.
(2)   A sells his car worth £4,000 to his daughter C for £2,000.
(3)   A grants a lease of his factory to his nephew D at a peppercorn rent. The factory was worth £100,000; the reversion is worth only £60,000.
(4)   A is owed £1,000 by a colleague E. A releases the debt so that his estate falls in value and E's estate is increased in value.   **[21.5]–[21.20]**

II   WHAT DISPOSITIONS ARE NOT CHARGEABLE TRANSFERS?

1   Commercial transactions (IHTA 1984 s 10(1))

A disposition is not a transfer of value and, therefore, is not chargeable if the taxpayer can show that he did not intend to confer a gratuitous benefit on another. This provision excludes from charge commercial transactions which turn out to be bad bargains. The transferor must not have intended to confer a gratuitous benefit on *any* person.

The onus is on the taxpayer to prove that he had no gratuitous intent. Hence any disposition reducing the value of the transferor's estate may trigger a liability to IHT (by analogy to a crime the disposition may be seen as the *actus reus*) unless the taxpayer can show that he did not have the necessary *mens rea* for the liability to arise, ie that he had no gratuitous intent.

EXAMPLE 21.1

A purchases a holiday in the Bahamas in the name of C. A must show that he had no intention to confer a gratuitous benefit on C which he may succeed in doing if, for instance, C was a valued employee.

In order for a disposition between two *unconnected* persons not to be chargeable, the transferor must show that he had no gratuitous intent and that the transaction was made at arm's length. In the case of a disposition to a *connected* person, in addition to proving no gratuitous intent, the taxpayer must show that the transaction was a commercial one such as strangers might make. A 'connected person' is defined as for CGT (IHTA 1984 s 270: for details see TCGA 1992, s 286 and [**14.23**]) and includes:

(1) relatives, extended for IHT to include uncle, aunt, nephew and niece;
(2) trustees, where the terms 'settlement', 'settlor' and 'trustees' have their IHT meaning (IHTA 1984 ss 43–45, see Chapter 24);
(3) partners (for certain purposes only); and
(4) certain close companies.

EXAMPLE 21.2

T sells his house worth £70,000 to his daughter for £60,000. T will not escape a potential liability to IHT unless he can show that he never intended to confer a gratuitous benefit on his daughter and that the sale at an undervalue was the sort of transaction that he might have made with a stranger (eg that he needed money urgently and, therefore, was prepared to sell at a reduced price).

In *IRC v Spencer-Nairn* (1991) the taxpayer owned a large estate in Scotland. He had little experience of farming and estate management and relied heavily on the family's adviser, a chartered accountant and actuary. In 1975 one of the farms was leased to a Jersey resident company at a rent which was largely absorbed in the costs of repairs and maintenance. The Jersey company almost immediately demanded that the piggery buildings on the farm be replaced at the taxpayer's expense. The adviser obtained a professional report which estimated the cost at in the region of £80,000. As the taxpayer could not afford this the adviser recommended that the farm should be sold. He handled all matters connected with the sale and eventually it was sold for £101,350 to a second Jersey company. The farm was never advertised for sale and the taxpayer accepted this offer on the recommendation of his adviser: interestingly, neither the taxpayer nor the adviser were aware at the time that the company was a 'connected person'.

For CGT purposes the Lands Tribunal for Scotland determined the market value of the farm at £199,000 on the basis that, contrary to the adviser's view, the taxpayer was not liable to pay for the improvements demanded by the tenant. In due course (not surprisingly!) the Revenue raised a CTT assessment on the basis of a transfer of value of £94,000. It was generally accepted that the taxpayer did not have a gratuitous intention: but the Revenue argued that the transfer was not such as the taxpayer would have made in an arm's length transaction with an unconnected person.

For s 10 to be relevant the transferor must be shown to have made a transfer of value (ie he must have entered into a disposition as a result of which his estate has been diminished) and, once that is shown, the taxpayer is then forced into the position of having to prove that he did not intend to make any gift *and* that what he did would satisfy the test of an objective commercial arrangement. The Revenue had taken a restricted view (some would say a minimalistic view!) of the section. In effect it had argued that if there was a substantial fall in the transferor's estate that was the end of the matter. In *Spencer-Nairn* the Lord President dismissed arguments of this nature in summary fashion:

'The fact that the transaction was for less than the open market value cannot be conclusive of the issues at this stage, otherwise the section would be deprived of its content. The gratuitous element in the transaction becomes therefore no more than a factor, which must be weighed in the balance with all the other facts and circumstances to see whether the onus which is on the transferor has been discharged.'

The case is a curiosity in that a substantially higher value had been determined by the Lands Tribunal, largely because of the view it took of the relevant Scottish agricultural holdings legislation. It had concluded that under that legislation the landlord was not obliged to erect the new piggery buildings. Clearly, had this burden rested on the landlord the actual sale price which he received would not have been unreasonable.

In applying the test in s 10 it was accepted by the Revenue that the vendor had no intention of conferring a gratuitous benefit on anyone so that the sole question for the court was whether the sale was such as would have been made with a third party at arm's length. When the court came to apply this test, although it is basically drafted in objective terms, they found it necessary to incorporate subjective ingredients. The hypothetical vendor must be assumed to have held the belief of the landlord that the value of the property was diminished by his obligation to rebuild the piggeries. A wholly unreasonable (and in the event mistaken) belief will not presumably be relevant.

The *Spencer–Nairn* case is unusual in that the parties did not know that they were connected: in a sense therefore they were negotiating *as if* they were third parties on the open market.

'A good way of testing the question whether the sale was such as might be expected to be made in a transaction between persons not connected with each other is to see what persons who were unaware that they were connected with each other actually did' (Lord President Hope).

The following conclusions are suggested:
(1) whether the transferor has a gratuitous intent is entirely subjective;
(2) there can be a sale at arm's length for the purposes of the second limb of s 10 even though the price realised is not approximately the same as the 'market value';
(3) in considering what amounts to an 'arm's length' sale features of the actual sale (such as the reasonably held beliefs of the vendor) must be taken into account—this limb is not a wholly objective test.   **[21.21]**

There are special rules in the following cases:

a) *Reversionary interests*

A beneficiary under a settlement who purchases for value any reversionary interest in the same settlement may be charged to IHT on the price that he pays for the interest (IHTA 1984 s 55(2): for the rationale of this rule see **[25.29]**).   **[21.22]**

EXAMPLE 21.3

Property is settled on A for life, remainder to B absolutely. B has a reversionary interest. A buys B's interest for its commercial value of £50,000. A has made a chargeable transfer of £50,000.

b) *Transfer of unquoted shares and debentures*

A transferor of unquoted shares and securities must show, in addition to lack of gratuitous intent, either that the sale was at a price freely negotiated at that time, or at such a price as might have been freely negotiated at that time (IHTA 1984 s 10(2)). In practice, such shares are rarely sold on an open market. Instead the company's articles will give shareholders a right of pre-emption if any shareholder wishes to sell. Provided that the right does not fix a price at which the shares must be offered to the remaining shareholders, but leaves it open to negotiation or professional valuation at the time of sale, the Revenue will usually accept that the sale is a *bona fide* commercial transaction satisfying the requirements of IHTA 1984 s 10(1).   **[21.23]**

EXAMPLE 21.4

The articles of two private companies make the following provisions for share transfers:
(1) *ABC Ltd*: the shares shall be offered *pro rata* to the other shareholders who have an option to purchase at a price either freely negotiated or, in the event of any dispute, as fixed by an expert valuer.
(2) *DEF Ltd:* the shares shall be purchased at par value by the other shareholders.

Position of shareholders in ABC Ltd: they will be able to take advantage of IHTA 1984 s 10(1) since the price is open to negotiation at the time of sale.

Position of shareholders in DEF Ltd: s 10(1) will not be available with the result that if the estate of a transferor falls in value (if, for instance, £1 shares have a market value of £1.50 at the time of transfer) IHT may be charged *even in the absence of gratuitous intent*. (Note that articles like those of DEF Ltd may also cause problems for business property relief—see **[23.48]**.)

c) *Partnerships*

Partners are not connected persons for the purpose of transferring partnership assets from one to another.   **[21.24]**

EXAMPLE 21.5

A and B are partners sharing profits and owning assets in the ratio 50:50. They agree to alter their asset sharing ratio to 25:75 because A intends to devote less time to the business in the future. Although A's estate falls (he has transferred half of his partnership share to B), he will escape any liability to IHT if there is a lack of gratuitous intent. Assuming that A and B are not connected otherwise than as partners, lack of gratuitous intent will be presumed, since such transactions are part of the commercial arrangements between partners.

2 Other non-chargeable dispositions

Excluded property (IHTA 1984 s 6)   No IHT is charged on excluded property (see Chapter 27). The most important categories are property sited outside the UK owned by someone domiciled outside the UK and reversionary interests under a trust. Although not within the definition of excluded property, business or agricultural property which qualifies for 100% relief will not attract any IHT charge (see **[23.42]** ff).   **[21.25]**

Exempt transfers (IHTA 1984 Part II)   Exempt transfers are not chargeable transfers and hence are not subject to charge (see Chapter 23). Examples are:
(1) transfers between spouses, whether *inter vivos* or on death;
(2) transfers up to £3,000 each tax year;
(3) outright gifts of up to £250 pa to any number of different persons. **[21.26]**

Waiver of remuneration and dividends (IHTA 1984 ss 14, 15)   A waiver or repayment of salaries and other remuneration assessable under Schedule E by a director or employee is not a chargeable transfer provided that the Schedule E assessment has not become final; the remuneration is formally waived (eg by deed) or if paid, repaid to the employer; and the employer adjusts his profits or losses to take account of the waiver or repayment.

Similarly, a person may, in the 12 months before the right accrued (which time is identified in accordance with usual company law rules), waive a dividend on shares without liability to IHT. A general waiver of all future dividends is only effective for dividends payable for up to 12 months after the waiver and must, therefore, be renewed each year (see Chapter 37, *Example 37.5*, for an illustration of when a waiver of dividends will prove advantageous). [21.27]

Voidable transfers (IHTA 1984 s 150)   Where a transfer is voidable (eg for duress or undue influence) and is set aside, it is treated for IHT purposes as if it had never been made, provided that a claim is made by the taxpayer. As a result any IHT paid on the transfer may be reclaimed. Tax on chargeable transfers made after the voidable transfer, but before it was avoided, must be recalculated and IHT refunded, if necessary. [21.28]-[21.40]

III   WHEN ARE LIFETIME TRANSFERS SUBJECT TO IHT? THE POTENTIALLY EXEMPT TRANSFER (PET)

If the taxpayer makes a chargeable *inter vivos* transfer IHT may be charged at once: alternatively the transfer may be potentially exempt (a PET). In the latter case, IHT is only levied if the taxpayer dies within seven years of the transfer: otherwise the transfer is exempt. During the 'limbo' period (being the period of seven years following the transfer or, if shorter, the period ending with the transferor's death) the PET is treated *as if it were exempt* (IHTA 1984 s 3A(5)) so that despite the legislation calling the transfer potentially exempt it would be more accurate to refer to it as potentially chargeable. With the exception of transfers involving discretionary trusts and transfers to companies (and by close companies) the majority of lifetime transfers are PETs.   [21.41]

What is a PET?

A PET is defined in IHTA 1984 s 3A(1). It must satisfy two preliminary requirements: *first*, it must be made by an individual on or after 18 March 1986; and *secondly*, the transfer must, apart from this section, be a chargeable transfer (hence exemptions—such as the annual £3,000 exemption—must be deducted first). If these requirements are satisfied the following transfers then fall within the definition: [21.42]

a) *Outright gifts to individuals*

A transfer which is a gift to another individual is a PET so long as *either* the property transferred becomes comprised in the donee's estate *or*, by virtue of that transfer, the estate of the donee is increased (s 3A(2)). [21.43]

EXAMPLE 21.6

(1) Adam gives Bertram a gold hunter watch worth £5,000: this is a PET.
(2) Claude pays Debussy's wine bill of £10,000. Although property is not transferred into the estate of Debussy, the result of Claude's transfer of value is to increase Debussy's estate by paying off his debt. Accordingly this also is a PET.
(3) Edgar who owned 51% of the shares in Frome Ltd transfers 2% of the company's shares to Grace who had previously owned no shares in the company. Edgar suffers a substantial drop in the value of his estate (since he loses control of

Frome Ltd) which exceeds the benefit received by Grace. The whole transfer
is a PET.

b) *Creation of accumulation and maintenance trusts or trusts for the disabled*

These trusts are discussed in Chapter 26. In both cases, the transfer which
establishes the trust is treated as a PET *to the extent that the value transferred
is attributable to property which by virtue of the transfer becomes settled.*   [21.44]

EXAMPLE 21.7

(1) A settles £100,000 in favour of his infant grandchildren on accumulation and
maintenance trusts. This transfer is a PET.

(2) B settles an insurance policy, taken out on his own life, on accumulation and
maintenance trusts. (This transfer is a PET.) He subsequently pays premiums
on that policy and, although the payments are transfers of value, they do
not increase the property in the settlement and are not, therefore, PETs. B
should, therefore, consider making a gift of that sum each year to the trustees
to enable them to pay the premiums on the policy (alternatively the problem
may be avoided if B's payments are exempt from IHT as normal expenditure
out of income: see [23.3]).

c) *Interest in possession settlements*

As will be seen in Chapter 25, a beneficiary entitled to an interest in possession
is treated as owning (for IHT purposes) the capital of the trust in which that
interest subsists. Hence, the *inter vivos* creation of such a trust is treated as
a gift to that person and the *inter vivos* termination of his interest as a gift
by him to the person or persons next entitled. In *Example 21.8(1)* below, for
instance, Willie is treated as if he had made a gift to Wilma (the next life
tenant). Taking different facts, if on the termination of the relevant interest
in possession the settled property is then held on discretionary trusts, the lifetime
termination of that interest cannot be a PET, since the PET definition excludes
the creation of trusts without interests in possession (see [21.46]).   [21.45]

EXAMPLE 21.8

Wilbur Wacker settles £100,000 on trust for his brother Willie for life, thereafter
to his sister Wilma for life, with remainder to his godson Wilberforce. Wilbur's
transfer is a PET. Subsequently he settles a life insurance policy on the same trusts
and continues to pay the premiums to the insurance company (as in *Example 21.7(2)*,
above). The premiums will be PETs since the more restrictive definition of a PET
in the context of the accumulation and maintenance trust does not apply to fixed
trusts. Assume also that the following events occur:

(1) Willie surrenders his life interest on his fiftieth birthday: this deemed transfer
of the property in the trust is a PET made by Willie.

(2) Wilma purchases Wilberforce's remainder interest for £60,000 (see *Example
21.3*, above); this transfer by Wilma is a PET.

d) *The limits of PETs*

Although the majority of lifetime transfers fall within the PET definition, there
remain two main categories which are immediately chargeable and, because
of the wording of s 3A, there are a number of traps which may catch other
transfers.

(1) The creation of no interest in possession trusts. Hence, a charge may
be levied on the creation of, eg discretionary trusts and, in addition, ten-

year anniversary and exit charges may occur during the life of the trust (see Chapter 26).

(2) 'Where, under any provision of this Act other than s 52, tax is in any circumstances to be charged *as if* a transfer of value had been made, that transfer shall be taken to be a transfer which is not a PET.'

This provision ensures that PETs are limited to lifetime gifts because it excludes the transfer deemed to take place immediately before death and it also means that tax charges will still arise when close companies are used to obtain an IHT advantage (see [**21.121**]).

(3) In the case of accumulation and maintenance and disabled trusts property must be transferred directly into the settlement if the PET definition is to be satisfied (see *Example 21.7(2)*).

(4) Jack pays the school fees of his infant grandson Jude or Simon buys a holiday for his uncle Albert. In neither case does property become comprised in the estate of another by virtue of the transfer, and neither Jude's nor Albert's estate is increased as a result of the transfer. Accordingly, both Jack and Simon have made immediately chargeable transfers of value (by contrast, a direct gift to each donee would ensure that the transfers were PETs).

(5) The reservation of benefit provisions are analysed at [**21.181**] and it should be noted that, when they apply, property which has been given away is brought back into the donor's estate at death. The original gift will normally have been a PET and, therefore, there is a possibility of a double charge to IHT should the donor die within seven years of that gift at a time when property is still subject to a reservation. (This double charge may be relieved by regulations discussed in Appendix III.)   [**21.46**]

e) *CGT tie-in*

CGT hold-over relief continues to be available in cases where a gift falls outside the PET definition provided that it is made *by* an individual or trustees to an individual or trustees (TCGA 1992 s 260). Both the creation and termination of a discretionary trust satisfy this wording so that the CGT that would otherwise be levied on the chargeable assets involved may be held over. By contrast, gifts to close companies do not involve gifts between individuals and trustees so that, unless the property given away is business property within the definition in TCGA 1992 s 165, hold-over relief will not be available (for the CGT position on gifts generally, see Chapter 17).   [**21.47**]

f) *The taxation of PETs*

As already noted there is no charge to tax at the time when the PET is made and for all purposes that transfer is assumed to be exempt unless the transferor dies within the following seven years. There is, therefore, no duty to inform the Revenue that a PET has been made and for cumulation purposes it is ignored. All of this, however, changes if the donor dies within the following seven years: the former PET then becomes chargeable; must be reported; and the transfer must be entered into the taxpayer's cumulative total *at the time when it was made*. As a result, IHT on chargeable lifetime transfers may need to be recalculated (these transfers may in any event attract a supplementary charge). These consequences are illustrated in *Example 21.9* and explained in Chapter 22.   [**21.48**]-[**21.60**]

EXAMPLE 21.9

(1) On 1 May 1991 Ian gave £3,000 to Joyce.
(2) On 1 May 1992 he settled £500,000 on discretionary trusts in favour of his family.
(3) On 1 May 1993 he gave £60,000 to his daughter.
(4) On 1 May 1997 he died.

Ian, therefore, dies within seven years of all three transfers. The transfer in 1991 ((1) above) is, however, exempt since it is covered by his annual exemption (see [**23.2**]).

Transfer (2) was a chargeable lifetime transfer and attracted an IHT charge when made. Because of Ian's death within seven years a supplementary IHT charge will arise (the calculation of this additional IHT caused by death is explained in Chapter 22).

Transfer (3) was a PET. Because of Ian's death it is rendered chargeable and is subject to IHT. Further, Ian's cumulative total of chargeable transfers made in the seven years before death becomes (assuming the non-availability of the £3,000 annual exemption in both 1992 and 1993) £560,000. Had Ian lived until 1 May 2000 this PET would have become an exempt transfer (ie free from all IHT).

IV ON WHAT VALUE IS IHT CALCULATED?

1 General: what is the cost of the gift?

Where an individual makes a chargeable disposition (including a PET rendered chargeable by death within seven years) IHT is charged on the amount by which his estate has fallen in value as a result of the transfer. A person's estate is the aggregate of all the property to which he is beneficially entitled (IHTA 1984 s 5(1)); it includes property over which he has a general power of appointment (IHTA 1984 s 5(2), because he could appoint the property to himself), but not property owned in a fiduciary or representative capacity: eg as trustee or PR.

In theory the transferor's estate must be valued both before and after the transfer and the difference taxed. In practice, it is normally unnecessary to do this since the transferor's estate will only fall by the value of the gift (and, as discussed in *Example 21.10* below, by the costs of making the gift). However, in unusual cases the cost to the transferor of the gift may be more than the value of the property handed over (see *Example 21.12*).

EXAMPLE 21.10

A gives £500,000 to a discretionary trust. His estate falls in value by £500,000 *plus* the IHT that he has to pay, ie £500,000 must be grossed up at the appropriate rate of IHT to discover the full cost of the gift to A (see [**21.102**]).

Were he to give the trust land worth £500,000 his estate falls in value by the value of the property (£500,000) and by any CGT, and costs of transfer (such as conveyancing fees) that A pays. It will also fall by the IHT payable.

However, IHTA 1984 s 5(4) provides that, for the purpose of calculating the cost of the gift, the transferor's estate is deemed to drop by the value of the property plus the IHT paid by the transferor but *not* by any other tax nor by any incidental costs of transfer. Thus, in *Example 21.10*, A's estate falls only by the value of the land and by the IHT that he pays.

Where the donees (the trustees in the above example) agree to pay the IHT, the overall cost of the gift is reduced since A's estate will fall only by the value of the property transferred. The trustees will be taxed on that fall in value.

EXAMPLE 21.11

A gives property worth £50,000 to the trustees. If A pays the IHT, the £50,000 is a net gift and if A is charged to IHT at 20% (rates of tax are considered at [21.101]: for the purpose of this example it is assumed that A has used up his nil rate band and annual exemption for the year) then that rate of tax is chargeable on the larger (gross) figure (here £62,500) which after payment of IHT at 20% leaves £50,000 in the trustees' hands.

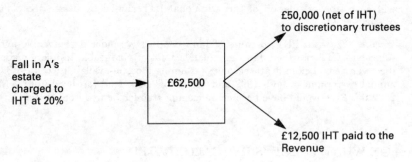

If, in this example, the trustees paid the IHT the result would be:

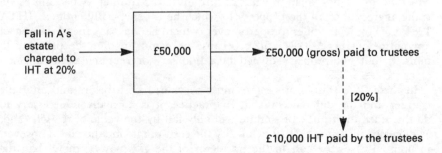

IHT is generally calculated on the fall in value of the transferor's estate not on the increase in value of the transferee's estate. This can work to the taxpayer's advantage, or disadvantage.   [21.61]

EXAMPLE 21.12

Compare

(1) A gives B a single Picasso plate value £20,000; B pays any IHT. In fact, B owns the remaining plates in the set (currently worth £150,000) and the acquisition of this final plate will give B's set a market value of £200,000. Although B's estate has increased in value by £50,000, IHT will only be charged on the fall in value in A's estate (£20,000).

(2) A owns 51% of the shares in A Ltd. This controlling interest is worth £100,000. He gives 2% of the shares to B who holds no other shares. 2% of the shares are worth (say) £2 but A, having lost control, will find that his estate has fallen by far more than £2—say to £80,000. It will be the loss to A (£20,000) not the gain to B (£2) which is taxed.

2 Problems in valuing an estate

Any calculation of IHT will require a valuation of the property transferred (see generally IHTA 1984 Part VI and [**22.3**]). As a general rule it is valued at the price that it would fetch on the open market. No reduction is made for the fact that the sale of a large quantity of a particular asset might cause the price to fall (IHTA 1984 s 160). **[21.62]**

a) *Examples of the value transferred*

Liabilities Incumbrances affecting property (to the extent that they were incurred for money or money's worth) reduce the value of the property (IHTA 1984 s 5(5)). **[21.63]**

> **EXAMPLE 21.13**
>
> A gives his house to his son B. The market value of the house is £80,000, but it is subject to a mortgage to the Halifax Building Society of £25,000 which B agrees to discharge. Hence, the property is valued for IHT purposes at £55,000. (This position will commonly arise when a death gift of a house is made since, in the absence of a contrary intention stated in the will, the Administration of Estates Act 1925 s 35 provides that debts charged on property by the deceased must be borne by the legatee or donee of that property.)

Co-ownership of land If land worth £100,000 is owned equally by A and B, it might be assumed that the value of both half shares is £50,000. In fact the shares will be worth less than £50,000 since it will be difficult to sell such an interest on the open market (see the Lands Tribunal cases of *Wight v IRC* (1984) and *Charkham v IRC* (1997)). Whoever purchases will have to share the property with the other co-owner and in practice a discount of 10–15% is reasonable. (Note that because of the related property rules—see [**21.67**]—there will be no discount when the co-owners are husband and wife.) **[21.64]**

Shares and securities When listed shares and securities are transferred, their value is taken (as for CGT; see Chapter 14) as the smaller of the 'quarter-up' and 'mid-price' calculation.

Valuation of unquoted shares and securities is a complex topic. A number of factors are taken into account, eg the company's profit record, its prospects, its assets and its liabilities. The percentage of shares which is being valued is a major factor. A majority shareholding of ordinary voting shares carries certain powers to control the affairs of the company (it will, for instance, give the owner the power to pass an ordinary resolution). A shareholding representing more than 75% confers greater powers, notably the power to pass special resolutions. Correspondingly, a shareholder who owns 50% or less of the voting power (and, even more so, a shareholding of 25% or less) has far fewer powers (he is a minority shareholder). In valuing majority and substantial minority holdings the Revenue takes a net asset valuation as the starting point and then applies a discount (between 10–15%) in the case of minority holdings.

In the case of shares and securities which were dealt in on the USM, although recent bargains through that market were taken as a starting point, other factors could result in a different value being adopted (see SP 18/80).

When shares are subject to a restriction on their transfer (eg pre-emption rights) they are valued on the basis of a sale on the open market with the purchaser being permitted to purchase the shares, but then being subject to the restrictions (*IRC v Crossman* (1937) and see [**21.69**]). **[21.65]**

b) *Special rules*

IHTA 1984 Part VI Chapter 1 contains special valuation rules designed to counter tax avoidance.   **[21.66]**

Related property (IHTA 1984 s 161)   IHT savings could be engineered by splitting the ownership of certain assets (typically shares, sets of chattels, and interests in land) amongst two or more taxpayers. The saving would occur when the total value of the individual assets resulting from the split was less than the value of the original (undivided) asset. A pair of Ming vases, for instance, would be worth more as a pair than the combined values of the two individual vases. When it is desired to split the ownership of such assets, however, it should be remembered that the transfer needed to achieve this result will normally be potentially chargeable and, as any tax will be charged on the entire fall in value of the transferor's estate, no tax saving may result. Inter-spouse transfers are, however, free of IHT (see **[23.41]**) and hence, were it not for the related property provisions, could be used to achieve substantial savings by asset splitting. To frustrate such schemes the related property rules provide that, in appropriate circumstances, an asset must be valued together with other related property and a proportion of that total value is then attributed to the asset (compare the CGT provisions on asset splitting: **[14.24]**).

EXAMPLE 21.14

X Ltd is a private company which has a share capital of £100 divided into 100 £1 shares. Assume that shares giving control (ie more than 50%) are worth £100 each and minority shareholdings £20 per share. If Alf owns 51% of the shares the value of his holding is £5,100 (£100 per share) but, if that 51% holding were split so that Alf has 25% and Bess 26% the value of those holdings (at £20 per share) would be £500 and £520 respectively.

Suppose that Alf and Bess are married. Alf transfers 26% of the company's shares to Bess. Alf becomes a minority shareholder with shares worth £500 but pays no IHT because transfers between spouses are exempt. Bess also has a minority holding worth £520. If Alf and Bess then each transfer their respective holdings to their son Fred, they may be liable to pay IHT on a value of £1,020, whereas if Alf had transferred his 51% holding to Fred directly he would be potentially liable to tax on £5,100. To prevent this IHT saving Alf and Bess's holdings are valued together as a majority holding worth £5,100. Accordingly, when Alf transfers his 25% holding to Fred this is 25/51 of the combined holding and is valued, therefore, at £2,500 (ie 25/51 of £5,100). Once Alf has disposed of his holding, Bess's 26% holding is then valued in the normal way on a subsequent transfer: ie as a minority holding worth £520 (in certain cases the associated operations rule or the '*Ramsay* principle' might be invoked; see **[21.81]**).

Inter-spouse transfers are the main instance of transfers which attract the related property provisions. However, the rules also catch other exempt transfers (eg to a charity or political party) in circumstances where the transferor could otherwise obtain a similar tax advantage.

EXAMPLE 21.15

As *Example 21.14*, Alf owns 51% of the shares in X Ltd. He transfers 2% to a charity paying no IHT because the transfer is exempt. He then transfers the remaining 49% to Fred. Alf is a minority shareholder and the loss to his estate is only £980 compared with £5,100 if he had transferred the entire 51% holding directly to Fred. Some time later Fred might purchase the 2% holding from the charity for its market value of £40. Unless the two transfers (ie to the charity and to Fred) are more than five years apart, the charity's holding is related to Alf's so that his 49% holding is valued at £4,900 on the transfer to Fred.

The related property rules apply to the deemed transfer on death subject to the proviso that if the property is sold within three years after the death for a price lower than the related property valuation, the property may be revalued on death ignoring the related property rules (see [**22.8**]).   [**21.67**]

Property subject to an option (IHTA 1984 s 163)   When property is transferred as a result of the exercise of an option or other similar right created for full consideration, there should be no liability to IHT.

Where an option is granted for less than full consideration, however, there will be a chargeable transfer or a PET at that time and there may be a further charge when the option is exercised. A credit will be given against the value of the property transferred, when the option is exercised, for any consideration actually received and for any value that was charged to IHT on the grant of the option.   [**21.68**]

EXAMPLE 21.16

(1) Harold grants Daisy an option to purchase his house in three years' time for its present value of £12,000. Daisy pays £3,000 for the option. When Daisy exercises the option three years later the house is worth £25,000.

   Harold has not made a transfer of value and is not liable to IHT since (as the option was granted for full consideration) the house is only worth £12,000 to him.

(2) Assume that Daisy gives no consideration for the option which is worth £3,000. IHT may, therefore, be chargeable on that sum. On the exercise of the option IHT may be payable on £13,000 (£25,000—£12,000) minus the sum that was chargeable on the grant of the option (£3,000). Hence, any charge will be on £10,000.

Property subject to restrictions on transfer   In *IRC v Crossman* (1937) the testator owned shares in a private company the articles of which imposed restrictions on alienation and transfer. By a bare majority the House of Lords held that in valuing those shares for estate duty purposes the basis to be taken was the price which they would fetch on the open market on the terms that a purchaser would be registered as the owner of the shares but would in turn be subject to the restrictions contained in the company's articles of association. As was recognised by Lord Hailsham in the case the view contended for by the executors would have resulted in property which could not be sold in the open market escaping the tax net altogether. The *Crossman* case was subsequently followed by the House of Lords in *Lynall v IRC* (1972) and has been adopted in a series of cases concerning inheritance tax. For instance, in *Alexander v IRC* (1991) a Barbican flat was purchased under the 'right to buy' provisions of the Housing Act 1980. All or part of the discount under that legislation had to be repaid in the event of the flat being sold within five years of its purchase. The taxpayer, however, died in the first year. The Court of Appeal—following *Crossman*—held that for valuation purposes an open market value must be taken and the flat was to be valued on the basis of what a purchaser would pay to stand in the deceased's shoes: ie taking over the liability to repay the discount should he sell the property within the prescribed period. It is inherent in this approach that the valuation thereby obtained may result in a higher figure than would actually be the case if the property were sold by the executors (and it appears that such a sale, even if occurring within four years of death, will not result in revaluation relief under IHTA 1984 s 190: see [**22.10**]).   [**21.69**]

Non-assignable agricultural tenancies   The vexed question of whether a non-assignable agricultural tenancy has any value was decided in the affirmative by the Lands Tribunal for Scotland on *Crossman* principles (see generally [**23.63**]). Once it is accepted that *Crossman* applies the question is merely one of fixing the correct value. In the Scottish case, *Baird's Executors v IRC* (1991), this matter was not argued and the 'robust approach' of the District Valuer in taking 25% of the open market value was accepted. The recent Court of Appeal decision in *Walton v IRC* (1996), confirmed that there can be no hard and fast valuation rule in such cases. The tenancy will not automatically be valued on the basis of a percentage of the freehold value on the assumption that the landlord will always be a special purchaser: in that case the freeholder had no interest in acquiring the tenancy. Evans LJ commented that 'the sale has to take place "in the real world" and that account must be taken of the actual persons as well as of the actual property involved'.   [**21.70**]

Life assurance policies   Life assurance policies normally involve the payment of annual premiums in return for an eventual lump sum payable either on retirement or on death. Special valuation rules, which do not apply on death (see [**22.6**]), are laid down by IHTA 1984 s 167 to prevent a tax saving when the benefit of such a policy is assigned.   [**21.71**]–[**21.80**]

EXAMPLE 21.17

A gives the benefit of a whole life policy effected on his own life to B when its open market value is £10,000. A has paid five annual premiums of £5,000, so that the cost of providing the policy is £25,000 to date. For IHT purposes the policy is valued at the higher of its market value or the cost of providing the policy. As a result tax may be charged on £25,000.

V   'ASSOCIATED OPERATIONS' (IHTA 1984 s 268)

The legislation contains complex provisions to prevent a taxpayer from reducing the value of a gift or the IHT chargeable by a series of associated operations.
   'Associated operations' are defined in IHTA 1984 s 268 as:

'(1) ... any two or more operations of any kind, being—
   (a) operations which affect the same property, or one of which affects some property and the other or others of which affect property which represents, whether directly or indirectly, that property, or income arising from that property, or any property representing accumulations of any such income; or (b) any two operations of which one is effected with reference to the other, or with a view to enabling the other to be effected or facilitating its being effected, and any further operation having a like relation to any of those two, and so on; whether those operations are effected by the same person or different persons, and whether or not they are simultaneous; and "operation" includes an omission.
   (2) The granting of a lease for full consideration in money or money's worth shall not be taken to be associated with any operation effected more than three years after the grant, and no operation effected on or after 27 March 1974 shall be taken to be associated with any operation effected before that date.
   (3) Where a transfer of value is made by associated operations carried out at different times it shall be treated as made at the time of the last of them; but where any one or more of the earlier operations also constitute a transfer of value made by the same transferor, the value transferred by the earlier operations shall be treated as reducing the value transferred by all the operations

taken together, except to the extent that the transfer constituted by the earlier operations but not that made by all the operations taken together is exempt under s 18 (spouse exemption).'

The definition is wide, and the Revenue has issued no general guidelines as to when they intend to invoke it. (Compare similar difficulties caused by the *Ramsay* principle which creates a judicial associated operations rule: see Chapter 36.)   **[21.81]**

The Macpherson case   In *IRC v Macpherson* (1989) trustees entered into an agreement which reduced the value of the settled property and subsequently appointed that property in favour of a beneficiary. The House of Lords held that the two transactions were associated operations and that they formed part of an arrangement designed to confer a gratuitous benefit, this benefit being conferred by the appointment (see further **[25.30]**). The case affords some guidance on what events can be treated as part of a series of operations affecting the same property. Lord Jauncey (in a speech with which the other Law Lords concurred) identified the boundaries of the associated operations provisions as follows:

'If an individual took steps which devalued his property on a Monday with a view to making a gift thereof on Tuesday, he would fail to satisfy the requirements of s 20(4) (now s 10(1)) because the act of devaluation and the gift would be considered together ... The definition in s 44 (now s 268) is extremely wide and is capable of covering a multitude of events affecting the same property which might have little or no apparent connection between them. It might be tempting to assume that any event which fell within this wide definition should be taken into account in determining what constituted a transaction for the purposes of s 20(4). However, counsel for the Crown accepted, rightly in my view, that some limitation must be imposed. Counsel for the trustees informed your Lordships that there was no authority on the meaning of the words "associated operations" in the context of capital transfer tax legislation but he referred to a decision of the Court of Appeal in Northern Ireland, *Herdman v IRC* (1967) in which the tax avoidance provisions of ss 412 and 413 of the Income Tax Act 1952 had been considered. Read short, s 412(1) provided that a charge to income tax arose where the individual had by means of a transfer of assets either alone or in conjunction with associated operations acquired rights whereby he could enjoy a particular description of income. Lord MacDermott CJ upheld a submission by the taxpayer that the only associated operations which were relevant to the subsection were those by means of which, in conjunction with the transfer, a taxpayer could enjoy the income and did not include associated operations taking place after the transfer had conferred upon the taxpayer the power to enjoy income. If the extended meaning of "transaction" is read into the opening words of s 20(4) the wording becomes:

"A disposition is not a transfer of value if it is shown that it was not intended, and was not made in a transaction including a series of transactions and any associated operations intended, to confer any gratuitous benefit..."

So read it is clear that the intention to confer gratuitous benefit qualifies both transactions and associated operations. If an associated operation is not intended to confer such a benefit it is not relevant for the purpose of the subsection. That is not to say that it must necessarily *per se* confer a benefit but it must form a part of and contribute to a scheme which does confer such a benefit.'

The House of Lords in *Macpherson* can be seen to be imposing limits on this apparently wide-ranging provision: limitations in the form of only considering relevant transactions—ie transactions undertaken in relation to the property which are in some way linked together. There is, however, no requirement that the series of transactions must have been pre-planned.   **[21.82]**

The Hatton case   Hatton v IRC (1992) involved a classically simple tax avoidance scheme. Within the space of 24 hours two settlements were created. In the first, the settlor (Mrs C) reserved a short-term life interest; in the second, the reversionary interest in the first settlement was itself settled (by Mrs H) on Mrs C for a further 24-hour period with the property then being held absolutely for Mrs H. The creation of the original settlement by Mrs C involved no loss to her estate (under the relevant legislation she was treated as still owning the property by virtue of her interest in possession: see [**25.1**]). The second settlement was likewise tax free since it involved the settlement by Mrs H of excluded property (the reversionary interest: see now IHTA 1984 s 48 and [**25.61**]). Because the termination of Mrs C's first interest in possession was immediately succeeded by an interest in possession in the second settlement it attracted no tax charge (see now IHTA 1984 s 52(2)). Finally, the termination of that second interest in possession was also tax free since the settled property thereupon resulted to Mrs H, the settlor of that second settlement (see FA 1975 Sch 5 para 4(2): amended to prevent such schemes by FA 1981 s 104(1), now enacted as IHTA 1984 s 53(5)(b): see [**25.34**]).

So far as the associated operations provisions were concerned, the judge concluded that the first settlement was made with a view to enabling or facilitating the making of the second (within the meaning of the associated operations provisions: see IHTA 1984 s 268(1)(b)). Accordingly there was a disposition by associated operations which was treated as a single disposition of property from Mrs C into the second settlement of which she therefore became a settlor (see the definition of a settlement in IHTA 1984 s 43(2): [**24.2**]).

It is not unusual for there to be two or more settlors of a single settlement. In an obvious case A and B would both transfer identified assets into a single trust. Under the IHT legislation, when circumstances require, that property may be treated as comprised in two separate settlements (see s 44(2)). For instance, A might settle £100 and B £50 and the resulting settlement fund could, when appropriate, be split into A's settlement (as to two-thirds) and B's settlement (as to one-third). Chadwick J concluded, however, that there could be circumstances where a division of the settlement property in this way was impractical and so, given that more than one settlor existed, the legislation must, in appropriate circumstances, treat each settlor as having created a separate settlement comprising, in each case, *the whole of the settled property*. This position can be illustrated in the *Hatton* case itself where Mrs C was, by dint of the associated operation rules (and, according to the Special Commissioners, because she was a person who had provided funds directly or indirectly) a person who had settled all the property in the second settlement. Mrs H was also a settlor; she was named as the settlor and had provided property in the shape of her reversionary interest in the first settlement. Given the nature of the property settled by these two settlors, Chadwick J was forced to conclude that each had created a separate settlement of the entirety of the property in the second settlement. Under the settlement created by Mrs C, the reverter to settlor rules did not apply.

This approach (treating each settlor as having established a separate settlement of the entirety of the settled property) would, the judge suggested, also apply to reciprocal settlements. In a simple case A would settle property on X for a limited interest in possession and as a *quid pro quo* B would settle property on Y for a similar interest. In both cases the reverter to settlor provisions would, at first sight, apply on the termination of X and Y's respective interests. Once it is accepted, however, that A is also a settlor of B's trust and *vice versa* (see s 44(1)) that analysis does not hold good. Instead, because B is a settlor of 'A's settlement' on the termination of X's limited interest an IHT charge may arise. The judge viewed the situation as one in which A and B were settlors of two separate settlements rather than accepting the view propounded by the Revenue that B should be seen as 'a dominant settlor' of A's trust.

Presumably the judge's approach would not be applied in cases where a full tax charge would, in any event, arise. Take, for instance, the situation where A as part of a reciprocal arrangement settles property on B's son for life with remainder to B's daughter and B creates a similar trust in favour of A's son and daughter. Although there are reciprocal settlements, on the death of (say) B's son a full tax charge would then arise on the property in 'A's settlement' so that even though the analysis may be that B is also a settlor of the whole of the property in that trust there can surely be no question of imposing a further tax charge on the ending of B's son's interest in possession.

Finally, the analysis is not easy to apply in cases where property is settled on trusts lacking an interest in possession by two settlors, one who has made chargeable lifetime transfers and one who has not. Will the Revenue be able to argue, in appropriate cases, that the former is to be treated as the settlor of the entirety so that in arriving at the IHT charge on the settlement his previous chargeable transfers will be taken into account?   [21.83]

The effects of s 268 applying   It enables the Revenue to tax as one transaction any number of separate transactions (including omissions) which, when looked at together, reduce the value of the taxpayer's estate. The transactions need not be carried out by the same person nor need they be simultaneous. Apparently the lifetime act of making a will can amount to an associated operation although the subsequent death will not be such an operation! (*Bambridge v IRC* (1955)). Intestacy is covered by the reference to an omission.

Section 268(1)(a) is concerned with the channelling of gifts, in particular between spouses (where the transfers are exempt). In such dispositions the transferor is deemed to have made a transfer equivalent to the value of all the operations at the time when the last of them is made. If one of the operations involved a transfer of value by the same transferor, he is entitled to a credit for that value against the aggregate value of the whole operation unless the transfer was anyway exempt because it was made to a spouse (IHTA 1984 s 268(3)).

EXAMPLE 21.18

It is certain that H will die shortly whereas his wife is in good health. Any transfer H makes to his son (S), although a PET, will, therefore, be made chargeable by his death. Accordingly, he transfers £20,000 to his wife (W). W then passes the £20,000 to the son. Under IHTA 1984 s 268(1)(a) the Revenue can claim that the transfers (H to W and W to S) are 'associated'. H is deemed to have made a transfer of value equivalent to the value transferred by all the associated operations, ie £40,000, £20,000 (H to W) and £20,000 (W to S). However, on his death, IHT is only chargeable on £20,000 as his transfer of £20,000 to W is exempt as an inter-spouse transfer. It is unclear whether under s 268(3) IHT could also be charged on her gift of £20,000 to S. The preferable view is no since the one charge on H should cover all the relevant transfers; but assume that H also gives £3,000 to his son which is exempt by his annual exemption (but see the *Hatton* case [21.83]). All three transfers (H to S, H to W and W to S) are associated at the time of the last of them (W to S). Under IHTA 1984 s 268(3) on H's death IHT is not charged on the aggregate value of all three transfers (ie £43,000) but on £20,000 only because he has a credit for any previous (associated) transfers of value (the £3,000 transfer to S) and the inter-spouse transfer of £20,000.

Commenting upon the associated operation provisions, Mr Joel Barnett (then Chief Secretary to the Treasury) stated that they would only be used to attack inter-spouse transfers in blatant tax avoidance cases:

'where the transfer by a husband to a wife was made on condition that the wife should at once use the money to make gifts to others, a charge on a gift by the husband might arise under s 268'. (Official Report, Standing Committee A; 13 February 1975 col 1596.)

The same approach is taken by the Revenue in relation to the possible application of the *Ramsay* principle (see Chapter 36).

Thus, spouses may channel gifts in order to utilise the poorer spouse's exemptions, eg the £3,000 annual exemption and the exemption for gifts on marriage of up to £5,000, and to obtain income tax and CGT benefits resulting from the independent taxation of spouses.

EXAMPLE 21.19

H is wealthy, his wife, W, is poor. Both wish to use up their full IHT exemptions and to provide for their son who is getting married. It would be sensible for the following arrangement to be adopted:
Stage 1   H transfers £11,000 to W which is exempt as an inter-spouse transfer. This will enable W to utilise two years' annual exemption of £3,000 plus the £5,000 marriage exemption.
Stage 2   Both spouses then each give £11,000 to the son.
Section 268 will not be invoked so long as the gift to W is not made on condition that she pass the property to S.

Section 268(1)(b) also enables the Revenue to put two separate transactions together.

EXAMPLE 21.20

(1)   A owns two paintings which together are worth £60,000, but individually are worth £20,000. A sells one picture for £20,000. This is a commercial transaction (s 10(1)) and, therefore, not subject to IHT. A then sells the second picture, also for £20,000, to the same purchaser.

As a result of the two transactions, the purchaser has paid only £40,000 but received value of £60,000 and A's estate has fallen in value by £20,000. The effect of s 268(1)(b) is that the Revenue can put the two transactions together and in appropriate cases tax the loss to his estate (ie £20,000) provided there is a gratuitous intent. Where the transactions are with a connected person the presumption of gratuitous intent will be hard to rebut. If both sales were to a commercial art gallery, however, it is likely that, despite s 268, no tax would be chargeable.

Contrast: assume as above that A owns two paintings but wishes to give one to his son. Accordingly he settles that picture on trust for himself for life, remainder to his son. No IHT is charged on creation of that settlement since A is treated as owning the picture (see Chapter 25). A then surrenders his life interest and as a result tax appears to be chargeable on the value of the picture in the settlement: ie on £20,000 only (IHTA 1984 s 52(1)). Could it be argued by an application of s 268 that A has directly disposed of the picture to his son so that £40,000 is subject to IHT? (Alternatively might the *Ramsay* principle apply to produce that result?)

(2)   A owns freehold premises worth £200,000. A gives the property to his nephew (N) in two stages. He grants a tenancy of the premises to N at a full market rent thereby incurring no potential liability to IHT. Two years later, he gives the freehold to N which being subject to a lease is worth only £100,000. Hence, there is a potential liability for IHT on £100,000 only, although A has given away property worth £200,000.

Under IHTA 1984 s 268(1)(b) the Revenue can tax the overall loss to his estate. IHTA 1984 s 268(2), however, provides an exemption where more than three years have elapsed between the grant of the lease for full consideration and the gift or sale of the reversion.

(3) A wants to give his annual exemption of £3,000 to B each year. Although he has no spare cash, he owns a house worth £30,000. Accordingly, A sells the house to B for £30,000 which is left outstanding as a loan repayable on demand. Each year A releases as much of the outstanding loan as is covered by his annual exemption. After ten years the loan is written off. The house is then worth £40,000 (the scheme is generally known as a 'sale and mortgage back'). A loan which is repayable on demand is not chargeable to IHT (see [21.109]) and the release of part of the loan each year, although a transfer of value, is covered by A's annual exemption.

These may be associated operations under IHTA 1984 s 268(1)(b). The Revenue has intimated that it *might* regard the overall transaction as a transfer of value by A of the asset at its market value (£40,000) at the date when the loan is written off. A would have a credit for his previous transfers of value, ie £30,000 (s 268(3)) and there would, therefore, be a potential charge to IHT on the capital appreciation element only, ie £10,000.

For the Revenue's view in *Example 21.20(3)* to be upheld they would have to show that the donor retained ownership of the house throughout the period of ten years. In support, it could be argued that the transferor's estate must be valued immediately after the disposition and that in the case of a disposition effected by associated operations that means at the time of the last of those operations (see IHTA 1984 ss 3(1), 268(3)). The counter-argument is that the value transferred is the difference between the value of the house immediately before the first stage in the operation (ie £30,000) and the value of the debt after the last operation (nil) so that the loss to the transferor is £30,000 all of which is covered by the annual exemptions.   [21.84]–[21.100]

VI HOW IS IHT CALCULATED?

1 Cumulation and rates of tax

Cumulation Each individual must keep a cumulative account of all the chargeable transfers made by him because IHT is levied not at a flat rate but at progressively higher rates according to that total. It is the cumulative amount which fixes the rate of IHT for each subsequent chargeable transfer. From 18 March 1986 cumulation has only been required over a seven-year period. This restricted period contrasts with the original CTT legislation (in 1975) which had provided for unlimited cumulation (a ten-year period was introduced in 1981).

Rates of tax From 6 April 1997 IHT rates are as follows:

Portion of value		*Rate of tax*
Lower limit	*Upper limit*	*Per cent*
£ 0	£ 215,000	Nil*
215,000	—	40*

* Chargeable lifetime transfers (for instance into a discretionary trust) are charged at half rates (ie at 0% or 20%).

EXAMPLE 21.21

(Ignoring exemptions, reliefs and assuming that current IHT rates apply throughout.)
A makes the following chargeable transfers (ie none of the transfers is a PET):

(1) *June 1991*   £100,000
     Applying the half rates of IHT the £100,000 falls within the nil rate band.

(2) *June 1997*   £160,000
     The starting point in using the table is £100,000 which was the point reached
     by the gift in 1991 and IHT is charged at rates applicable to transfers from
     £100,000 to £260,000:
     ie first £115,000 at nil%
     the final £45,000 at 20%.

(3) *July 1998*   £80,000
     The 1991 gift of £100,000 drops out of the account as it was made more than
     seven years before. IHT is, therefore, charged at rates applicable to transfers
     from £160,000 to £240,000.

The above discussion has been concerned solely with the cumulation of
chargeable lifetime transfers since PETs are presumed to be exempt *unless and
until* the transferor dies within seven years of the transfer. The effect of that
death is to render the PET a chargeable transfer (thereby necessitating the
payment of IHT) and, in addition, a supplementary charge may be levied
on any chargeable transfers made in the seven years before death. In cases
where the deceased taxpayer had made a mixture of chargeable transfers and
PETs in the seven years before death, tax paid on the chargeable transfers
may have to be recalculated because the PETs are converted into chargeable
transfers from the date when they were made.

EXAMPLE 21.22

T makes the following transfers of value:
Year 1 PET of £75,000
Year 2 chargeable transfer of £150,000
Year 4 T dies.

IHT charged on the chargeable transfer in *Year 2* will have been calculated ignoring
the PET made in *Year 1*. Accordingly it will have proceeded on the basis that
T had made no prior chargeable transfers. As a result of his death in Year 4,
however, the PET of £75,000 is made chargeable in *Year 1* so that IHT on the
Year 2 transfer must be recalculated on the basis that when it was made T had
made a prior chargeable transfer of £75,000. Hence it is recalculated using the
IHT rates applicable in *Year 2* from £75,000 to £225,000.

The impact of death on chargeable lifetime transfers and PETs is considered
in Chapter 22.   **[21.101]**

2   **Grossing-up**

As already stated IHT is charged on the fall in value in the transferor's estate.
Accordingly, tax is charged on the value of the gift *and* on the IHT on that
gift, when the tax is paid by the transferor. To understand this principle, take
the example of A, who has made no previous chargeable transfers and who
settles £230,000 on discretionary trusts. IHT payable by A can be calculated
as follows:

Step 1   Deduct from the transfer any part of it that is exempt. A has an available annual exemption of £3,000 (see further [**23.2**]): there is, therefore, a chargeable transfer of £227,000.

Step 2 Calculate the rate(s) of IHT applicable to the chargeable transfer. The first £215,000 falls within the nil rate band and, therefore, IHT is payable only on the balance of £12,000 at 20%.

Step 3 If A pays the IHT on the gift, his estate falls in value by £227,000 plus the IHT payable on the £12,000, ie A is charged on the cost of the gift by treating the £227,000 as a gift net of tax.

Therefore, the part of the gift on which IHT is payable (here £12,000) must be 'grossed up' to reflect the amount of tax payable on the gift by using the formula:

$$\frac{100}{100-R}$$

where R is the rate of IHT applicable to the sum in question. In A's case the calculation is:

$$£12,000 \times \frac{100}{80} = £15,000 \text{ gross.}$$

As a result:
(1) *Position of A:* Gift to trust (£230,000) plus IHT liability (£3,000) means a total cost of £233,000;
(2) *Position of the trust:* Receives from A £230,000.

Once the taxpayer's cumulative total exceeds the nil rate band (currently £215,000) tax is levied (because of the grossing-up computation) at 25% on the excess. For instance, if A gives £50,000 to his close company (a chargeable lifetime transfer) at a time when his cumulative total exceeds £215,000, tax on that transfer, if paid by A, will be 25% × £50,000 = £12,500.   [**21.102**]

3 Effect of the tax being paid by a person other than the transferor

Grossing-up is necessary to establish the cost to a donor of making a gift where the donor is paying the IHT. There is no grossing-up, however, if the tax is paid by any other person. Accordingly, as most lifetime transfers will be PETs, any IHT that is eventually charged will be due after the transferor's death from the donee and it will not, therefore, be necessary to gross up. In such cases the transferee is charged on the gift that he receives (strictly, on the fall in value of the transferor's estate) and the tax will be calculated according to the previous chargeable transfers of the donor.   [**21.103**]

EXAMPLE 21.23

(1) A has made no previous chargeable transfers but has used up his annual exemption. He gives £225,000 to discretionary trustees who agree to pay the IHT due on the chargeable transfer. A has made a chargeable transfer of £225,000, on £10,000 of which IHT is payable at the rate of 20%. If the trustees pay, A's estate falls in value by only £225,000. The trustees are charged to IHT at A's rates. The trustees, therefore, pay IHT at 20% on £10,000 (ie £2,000) so that £500 less tax is paid than if A had paid (he would have paid tax at a rate of 25% on £10,000 = £2,500). However, the trust ends up with less property than if A had paid the IHT: £223,000, instead of £225,000. A further result of the trustees paying the tax is that A's cumulative total of gross chargeable transfers is lower for the purposes of future chargeable transfers, ie £225,000, rather than £227,500.

Compare

(2) If the trustees are to pay the IHT on A's gift to them and A wants them to retain a net sum of £225,000 after paying the tax, A must give a larger sum (£227,500) to enable them to pay the tax of £2,500. The result is that whether donor or donee pays the IHT, the Revenue will receive £2,500 tax and the total cost to A will be the same.

4   Transferring non-cash assets the cheapest way

Where the gift is of a non-cash asset such as land, IHT is calculated as before, but the question of who pays the tax and how much has to be paid will be of critical importance since neither party may have sufficient cash to pay the IHT without selling the asset. If the donor pays the IHT, the value of the gift must be grossed up. In addition, the tax must be paid in one lump sum. If, however, the donee (normally trustees on a chargeable lifetime transfer) pays the tax, there is no grossing-up so that the transfer attracts less IHT. Additionally, in the case of certain assets the tax can be paid by the donee in ten yearly instalments (IHTA 1984 s 227). If the asset is income producing, the donee may have income out of which to pay, or contribute towards, the instalments. Alternatively, the donor can fund the instalments paid by the donee by gifts utilising his annual exemption. The assets on which IHT may be paid by instalments are:

(1) land, whether freehold or leasehold;
(2) a controlling shareholding of either quoted or unquoted shares;
(3) a minority shareholding of unquoted shares in certain circumstances (see [**22.49**]);
(4) a business or part of a business, eg a share in a partnership.

However, in the case of a transfer of land ((1) above), interest on the outstanding tax is charged when payment is made by instalments.   [**21.104**]

EXAMPLE 21.24

A wants to settle his landed estate which is valued at £500,000 on discretionary trusts. A has made no previous chargeable transfers. If A pays the tax (ignoring exemptions and reliefs) the gift (£500,000) must be grossed up so that the total cost to A is £571,250 and the IHT payable is £71,250; A must pay this in one lump sum. If the trust pays the tax, the £500,000 is a gross gift on which the IHT at A's rates is £57,000. Thus, there is a tax saving of £14,250. Further, the trust can pay the tax in instalments out of income from the estate.

5   Problem areas

a) *Transfers of value by instalments (IHTA 1984 s 262)*

Where a person buys property at a price greater than its market value, the excess paid will be a transfer of value (assuming that donative intent is present). If the price is payable by instalments, part of each is deemed to be a transfer of value. That part is the proportion that the overall gift element bears to the price paid.   [**21.105**]

EXAMPLE 21.25

A transfers property worth £40,000 to B for £80,000 payable by B in eight equal yearly instalments of £10,000. Hence, after eight years there will be a transfer of value of £40,000 divided between each instalment as follows:

$$\text{Annual instalment} \times \frac{\text{value of gift}}{\text{price payable}} = £10,000 \times \frac{£40,000}{£80,000} = £5,000.$$

b) *Transfers made on the same day (IHTA 1984 s 266)*

If a person makes more than one chargeable transfer on the same day and the order in which the transfers are made affects the overall amount of IHT payable, they are treated as made in the order which results in the least amount of IHT being payable (IHTA 1984 s 266(2)). This will be relevant where the transfers taken together straddle different rate bands and the donor does not pay the tax on all the transfers. Where this is the case the overall IHT will be less if the grossed-up gift is made first. In other cases an average rate of tax is calculated and applied to both transfers. When a PET made on the same day as a chargeable transfer is rendered chargeable by the donor's death within seven years these rules apply. **[21.106]**

c) *Transfers reported late (IHTA 1984 s 264)*

When a transfer is reported late (for the due date for reporting transfers see **[21.142]**) after IHT has been paid on a subsequent transfer, tax must be paid on the earlier transfer and an adjustment may have to be made to the tax bill on the later transfer. The tax payable on the earlier transfer is calculated as at the date of that transfer and interest is payable on the outstanding tax as from the date that it was due. If there is more than seven years between the earlier and the later transfers, no adjustment need be made in respect of the later transfer since the seven-year limit on cumulation means that the later transfer is unaffected by the earlier transfer. When there is less than seven years between the two transfers the extra tax charged on the later transfer is levied on the earlier transfer in addition to the tax already due on that transfer. The recalculation problems that arise when PETs are chargeable are considered at **[22.23]**. **[21.107]**

d) *Order of making lifetime transfers*

If the taxpayer wishes to make both a chargeable transfer (eg the creation of a discretionary trust) and a PET (eg a gift to a child) the chargeable transfer should be made *before* the PET so that if the latter becomes chargeable it will not necessitate a recomputation of tax on the chargeable transfer (nor, in the case of a discretionary trust, have an effect on the calculation of the tax charged on the settlement: see ([**26.21**])). **[21.108]**

e) *Non-commercial loans*

There are no special charging provisions for loans of property and accordingly (subject only to IHTA 1984 s 29 which ensures that the usual exemptions and reliefs are available) tax will be charged, if at all, under general principles (ie has the loan resulted in a fall in value of the lender's estate?). In the case of money loans it is necessary to distinguish between interest-free loans repayable after a fixed term and loans repayable on demand. If A lends B £20,000 repayable in five years' time at no interest, A's estate is reduced in value because of the delay in repayment and (assuming gratuitous intent) A makes a PET equal to the difference between £20,000 and the value of the right to receive £20,000 in five years' time.

If, instead, A lent B £20,000 repayable on demand with no interest charged, A's estate either does not fall in value because it includes the immediate right to £20,000 or, alternatively, any fall is likely to be *de minimis*. Accordingly, A has not made a transfer of value and there is no question of any charge to IHT. Loans repayable on demand may be employed so that the use of property, and any future increase in its value, is transferred free from IHT to another.

If a commercial rate of interest is charged on a loan, the transaction is not a chargeable transfer since the estate of the lender will not have fallen in value. Further, any interest may (normally) be waived without any charge to IHT by virtue of the exemption for regular payments out of income (see Chapter 23).   [**21.109**]

EXAMPLE 21.26

Jasmine benefits her children without attracting a potential liability to IHT as follows:
(1)   She lends her daughter £100,000 repayable on demand. The money is invested in a small terraced house in Fulham which quickly trebles in value. That increase in value belongs to the daughter who is merely obliged to repay the original sum loaned if and when Jasmine demands it.
(2)   She allows her son to occupy her London flat rent free. The son enjoys the benefit of living there during the winter and lets the property to wealthy summer visitors. As there is no loss to Jasmine's estate the son's benefits are not subject to IHT.

e) *Relief against a double charge to IHT*

In a number of situations there is the possibility of a double charge to IHT:

EXAMPLE 21.27

Gustavus gives Adolphus his rare Swedish bible (a potentially exempt transfer). Two years later the bible is given back to Gustavus who dies shortly afterwards. As a result of his death within seven years the original gift of the bible is chargeable and, in addition, Gustavus' estate on death, which is subject to IHT, includes the bible.

Regulations made under FA 1986 s 104 provide a measure of relief in such cases and are discussed in Appendix III.   [**21.110**]–[**21.120**]

VII   SPECIAL RULES FOR CLOSE COMPANIES

Only transfers of value made by *individuals* are chargeable to IHT (IHTA 1984 s 2(1)). An individual could, therefore, avoid IHT by forming a close company and using that company to make a gift to the intended donee, or a controlling shareholder in a close company could alter the capital structure of the company or the rights attached to his shares, so as to reduce the value of his shareholding in favour of the intended donee.

EXAMPLE 21.28

(1)   A transfers assets worth £100,000 to A Ltd in return for shares worth £100,000. A's estate does not fall in value so that there is no liability to IHT. The company then gives one of the assets (worth £50,000) to A's son B. The company and not A has made a transfer of value.
(2)   A Ltd has an issued share capital of £100 all in ordinary £1 shares owned by A. The company is worth £100,000. The company resolves:
(i)   to convert A's shares into non-voting preference shares carrying only the right to a repayment of nominal value on a winding up;
(ii)   to issue to B a further 100 £1 ordinary shares at par value.
The result is that the value has passed out of A's shares without any disposition by A.

IHTA 1984 Part IV contains (*inter alia*) provisions designed to prevent an individual from using a close company to obtain a tax advantage in either of these ways. For the purposes of IHTA 1984 Part IV 'close company' and 'participator' have their corporation tax meaning (see Chapter 28) except that a close company includes a non-UK resident company which would be close if it was resident in the UK and participator does not include a loan creditor (IHTA 1984 s 102). **[21.121]**

1 Transfers of value by close companies (IHTA 1984 s 94)

When a close company makes a transfer of value, it is apportioned amongst the participators in proportion to their interests in the company, so that they are treated as having made the transfer ('lifting the veil') (IHTA 1984 s 94(1)). Thus, in *Example 21.28(1)* above, A is treated as having made a transfer of value of £50,000. For s 94(1) to apply the company must have made a transfer of value, ie its assets must fall in value by virtue of a non-commercial transaction (IHTA 1984 s 10(1)). The value apportioned to each participator is treated as a net amount which must be grossed up at the participator's rate of IHT. Any participator whose estate has increased in value as a result of that transfer can deduct the increase from the net amount (ignoring the effect that the transfer may have had on his rights in the company). The transfer in these circumstances is a deemed transfer of value and cannot be a PET (see [**21.42**]). IHT is therefore chargeable.

EXAMPLE 21.29

A Ltd is owned as to 75% of the shares by A and 25% by B. It transfers land worth £100,000 to A. By IHTA 1984 s 94, A and B are treated as having made net transfers of value of £75,000 and £25,000 respectively. B will be charged to IHT on £25,000 grossed up at his rate of IHT. A, however, can deduct the increase in his estate (£100,000) from the net amount of the apportionment (£75,000), so that he pays no IHT. If A's shares (and B's) have diminished in value, the decrease is ignored.

Apportionment is not always as obvious as it may seem. For instance, in calculating a participator's interest in the company, the ownership of preference shares is usually disregarded (IHTA 1984 s 96). Further, where trustees are participators and the interest in the company is held in an interest in possession settlement (see Chapter 25) the apportioned amount is taxed as a reduction in the value of the life tenant's estate (IHTA 1984 s 99(2)(a)). In no-interest in possession trusts the apportioned amount is taxed as a payment out of the settled property by the trustees (IHTA 1984 s 99(2)(b)). Finally, where a close company is itself a participator in another close company any apportionment is then sub-apportioned to its own participators (IHTA 1984 s 95).

In two cases no apportionment occurs. *First*, if the transfer is charged to income tax or corporation tax in the donee's hands, there is no IHT liability (IHTA 1984 s 94(2)(a)). *Secondly*, where a participator is domiciled abroad, any apportionment made to him as a result of a transfer by a close company of property situated abroad is not charged to IHT (IHTA 1984 s 94(2)(b)).

EXAMPLE 21.30

(1) A Ltd (whose shares are owned 50% by A and 50% by B) pays a dividend. The dividend is not chargeable to IHT in A or B's hands because income tax is charged on that sum under Schedule F.

(2) A Ltd in (1) above provides A with free living accommodation and pays all the outgoings on the property. If A is a director or employee of A Ltd, these

items are benefits in kind on which A pays income tax under Schedule E (see Chapter 5). If A is merely a shareholder in the company these payments are treated as a distribution by A Ltd and are charged to income tax in A's hands under Schedule F. However, if A was not a member of A Ltd, there would be no income tax liability, so that the participator, B, would be treated for IHT purposes as having made a chargeable transfer of value under IHTA 1984 s 94(1).

(3) An English company, A Ltd, in which B and C each own 50% of the shares, gives a factory in France worth £100,000 to B, who is domiciled in the UK. C is domiciled in France and, therefore, the amount apportioned to him (£50,000) is not chargeable under IHTA 1984 s 94(1).

Participators can reduce their IHT liability on sums apportioned by the usual lifetime exemptions with the exception of the small gifts exemption and the exemption for gifts on marriage. Insofar as the transfer by the company is to a charity or political party it is exempt. Participators are also entitled to 100% business relief if the close company transfers part of its business or shares in a trading subsidiary.

The company is primarily liable for the tax. If it fails to pay, secondary liability rests concurrently with the participators and beneficiaries of the transfer. A participator's liability is limited to tax on the amount apportioned to him; for a non-participator beneficiary it is limited to the increase in value of his estate.   [21.122]

2   Deemed dispositions by participators (IHTA 1984 s 98)

When value is drained out of shares in a close company by an alteration (including extinguishment) of the share capital or by an alteration in the rights attached to shares, this is treated as a deemed disposition by the participators although the section does not deem a transfer of value to have been made. When such a transfer occurs, liability under IHTA 1984 s 98 rests purely on the participators and not on the company. As there is no deemed transfer of value under s 98, such transfers are expressly prevented from being PETs by IHTA 1984 s 98(3) (see *Example 21.31(3)*, below).   [21.123]–[21.140]

EXAMPLE 21.31

(1) Taking the facts of *Example 21.28(2)* above there is no actual transfer of value by A or A Ltd. However, under IHTA 1984 s 98 there is a deemed disposition by A equivalent to the fall in value of his shareholding. From owning all the shares and effectively all the assets he is left with a holding of 100 shares worth (probably) only their face value.

(2) A owns 60% and B 40% of the shares in A Ltd. Each share carries one vote. The articles of association of the company are altered so that A's shares continue to carry one vote, but B's shares are to carry three votes each. There is a deemed disposition by A to B equivalent to the drop in value in A's estate resulting from his loss of control of A Ltd.

(3) Zebadee, the sole shareholder in Zebadee Ltd, arranges for a bonus issue of fully paid preference shares which carry the right to a fixed dividend. He retains the shares but gives his valuable ordinary shares to his daughter. This familiar tax planning rearrangement depends in part upon the gift of the ordinary shares being a potentially exempt transfer. Under s 98(1) the alteration in the share structure is treated as a disposition by Zebadee but as the bonus shares are at that stage issued to him, he does not then make any transfer of value. Accordingly, the subsequent gift of the ordinary shares will be a PET. It is thought that the Revenue will not normally seek to argue that the bonus issue and later gift are associated operations falling within s 98(1)

as an extended reorganisation (so that the gift of the shares is not prevented from being a PET by s 98(3)).

VIII LIABILITY, ACCOUNTABILITY AND BURDEN

1 Liability for IHT (IHTA 1984 Part VII)

The person primarily liable for IHT on a chargeable lifetime transfer of unsettled property is the transferor (IHTA 1984 s 199), although in certain cases, his spouse may be held liable as a transferor to prevent him from divesting himself of property to that spouse so that he is then unable to meet an IHT bill (IHTA 1984 s 203).

> **EXAMPLE 21.32**
>
> H makes a gross chargeable transfer to a discretionary trust of £100,000 and fails to pay IHT. He later transfers property worth £50,000 to his wife W which is exempt (inter-spouse). W can be held liable for H's IHT not exceeding £50,000.

If the Revenue cannot collect the tax from the transferor (or his spouse) it can then claim it, subject to specified limits, from one of the following:

(1) The transferee, ie any person whose estate has increased in value as a result of the transfer. Liability is restricted to tax (at the transferor's rates) on the value of the gross transfer after deducting any unpaid tax.

> **EXAMPLE 21.33**
>
> A makes a *gross* chargeable transfer to discretionary trustees of £40,000 on which IHT at A's rate of 20% is £8,000. A emigrates without paying the tax. The Revenue can only claim £6,400 in tax from the trustees, ie:
>
> | | £ |
> |---|---:|
> | Gross chargeable transfer by A | 40,000 |
> | *Less:* unpaid tax | 8,000 |
> | Revised value transferred | £32,000 |
> | Trustees are liable for IHT at 20% | £6,400 |

(2) Any person in whom the property has become vested after the transfer. This category includes a person to whom the transferee has in turn transferred the property; or, if the property has been settled, the trustees of the settlement and any beneficiary with an interest in possession in it; or a purchaser of the property unless he is a *bona fide* purchaser for money or money's worth and the property is not subject to an Inland Revenue charge. The liability of these persons is limited to tax on the net transfer only and liability is further limited, in the case of trustees and beneficiaries, to the value of the settled property and, in the case of a purchaser, to the value of the property. Also included within this category is any person who meddles with property so as to constitute himself a '*trustee de son tort*' and any person who manages the property on behalf of a person under a disability.

(3) A beneficiary under a discretionary trust of the property to the extent that he receives income or any benefit from the trust. Liability is limited to the amount of his benefit after payment of any income tax.

The liability to pay additional IHT on a gift because of the transferor's death within seven years, and liability to IHT on a PET which becomes a chargeable transfer is considered in Chapter 22.

Quite apart from those persons from whom they can claim tax, the Revenue has a charge for unpaid tax on the property transferred and on settled property where the liability arose on the making of the settlement or on a chargeable transfer of it (IHTA 1984 s 237). The charge takes effect in the same way as on death (see [**22.48**]) except that for lifetime transfers it extends to personal property also. It will not bind a purchaser of land unless the charge is registered and in the case of personal property unless the purchaser has notice of the facts giving rise to the charge (IHTA 1984 s 238).

Once IHT on a chargeable transfer has been paid and accepted by the Revenue, liability for any further tax ceases six years after the later of the date when the tax was paid or the date when it became due (IHTA 1984 s 240(2)). However, if the Revenue can prove fraud, wilful default or neglect by a person liable for the tax (or by the settlor which results in an underpayment of tax by discretionary trustees), this six-year period only starts to run once the Revenue knows of the fraud, wilful default or neglect, as the case may be (IHTA 1984 s 240(3)). When the Revenue is satisfied that tax has been or will be paid, it may, at the request of a person liable for the tax, issue a certificate discharging persons and/or property from further liability (IHTA 1984 s 239).   [**21.141**]

2   Accountability and payment

a) *Duty to account*

An account should only be delivered in respect of a chargeable transfer which is not a PET: in the case of PETs an account is only required if the transferor dies within seven years (IHTA 1984 s 216). Thus, the Revenue need not be notified of a transfer of excluded property or of a transfer that is wholly exempt (eg within the annual exemption or inter-spouse), with the exception of an exempt transfer of settled property which must normally be notified.

In addition, in two situations chargeable transfers are 'excepted' from the duty to account (SI 1981/1440). *First*, where the gift is by an individual and, together with other chargeable transfers in the same tax year, does not exceed £10,000 so long as the gift and other chargeable transfers in the previous seven years do not exceed £40,000 in total; and *secondly* where the value transferred on the termination of an interest in possession in settled property is extinguished by the beneficiary's annual or marriage gifts exemption.

As a general rule, the person who is primarily liable for the IHT must deliver the account. When the transfer is by a close company, nobody is under a duty to account, but in practice the company should do so in order to avoid a charge to interest on unpaid tax.

The account must be delivered within 12 months from the end of the month when the transfer was made or within three months from the date when that person first became liable to pay IHT (if later). In practice the account should be delivered earlier, since the tax is due before this date. Form IHT 100 is used for all lifetime transfers including transfers of settled property on life or death with an interest in possession. Anyone who fails to deliver an account, make a return, or provide information when required may be subject to penalties and the Revenue has a wide general power to obtain information from 'any' person (IHTA 1984 s 219) by means of a notice. The Revenue cannot use this power to compel a solicitor or barrister to disclose privileged information concerning a client, but it can use it to obtain the name and address of a client.   [**21.142**]

b) *Payment of tax*

For all lifetime chargeable transfers of settled or unsettled property made between 6 April and 30 September, the tax is due on 30 April following and for transfers made between 1 October and 5 April it is due six months from the end of the month when the transfer was made (IHTA 1984 s 226). The optimum date to make a chargeable transfer is therefore 6 April which gives a 12-month delay before tax is due.   **[21.143]**

Payment by instalments Generally IHT must be paid in one lump sum. IHTA 1984 s 212 provides that any person liable for the tax (except the transferor and his spouse) can sell, mortgage or charge the property even if it is not vested in him, so that if, for instance, A gives property to B who settles it on C for life, either B, the trustees, or C (if called upon to pay the tax) can sell, mortgage or charge the property in order to do so.

As an exception to the general rule, if the transferee pays the IHT he can elect in the case of certain assets to pay the tax in ten yearly instalments; the first becoming due when the tax is due (IHTA 1984 s 227). This lifetime instalment option is available for the same assets as on death (see **[22.51]**), except for the transfer of a minority holding of unquoted shares or securities within category (4) (relief when the IHT on instalment property amounts to 20% of the total bill). Trustees or beneficiaries who are liable for the tax on transfers of settled property can elect to pay in instalments provided that the property falls within one of the specified classes. Despite this election, the outstanding tax (and any interest due) may be paid at any time and if the relevant property is sold or transferred by a chargeable transfer the tax must be paid at once (IHTA 1984 s 227(4)).   **[21.144]**

Interest Interest is charged on any tax which is not paid by the due date (IHTA 1984 s 233). Where the tax is to be paid by instalments, interest is charged on overdue instalments only, except in the case of land where interest is charged on all the outstanding tax.   **[21.145]**

Satisfaction of tax The Revenue has a discretion to accept in satisfaction of tax (but not interest) any object that is pre-eminent for its national, scientific, historic or artistic interest (see IHTA 1984 s 231 and Chapter 23).   **[21.146]**

Adjustments to the tax bill Subject to a six-year limitation (see **[21.162]**) if the Revenue proves that too little tax was paid in respect of a chargeable transfer, tax underpaid is payable together with interest. Conversely, if too much tax was paid, the Revenue must refund the excess together with interest, which is free of income tax in the recipient's hands (IHTA 1984 s 235).   **[21.147]**

3 Burden of tax

The question of who, as between the transferor and the transferee, should bear the tax on a lifetime transfer is a matter for the parties to decide as discussed above. The decision may affect the amount of tax payable (see **[21.103]**). The parties can agree at any time before the tax becomes due and the Revenue will accept their decision so long as the tax is paid. However, the agreement does not affect the liability of the parties, so that if the tax remains unpaid, the Revenue can collect it from persons liable under Part VII of the legislation (see **[21.141]**.   **[21.148]-[21.160]**

IX ADMINISTRATION AND APPEALS

1 Calculation of liability

IHT is not assessed by reference to the tax year. Instead, when the Revenue is informed of a chargeable transfer of value it raises an assessment called a determination (IHTA 1984 s 221). If it is not satisfied with an account or if none is delivered when it suspects that a chargeable transfer has occurred, it can raise a 'best of judgment' or estimated determination of the tax due. A determination of IHT liability is conclusive against the transferor and for all subsequent transfers, failing a written agreement with the Revenue to the contrary or an appeal.

If the taxpayer disputes the determination he can appeal to the Special Commissioners within 30 days of it (IHTA 1984 s 222). The appeal procedure is basically the same as under TMA 1970 for income tax, corporation tax and CGT, except that an appeal can be made direct to the High Court, thereby bypassing the commissioners, either by agreement with the Revenue or on application to the High Court (as, for instance, occurred in *Bennett v IRC* (1995): see [**23.3**]). In this case, the appeal is not limited to points of law. Appeal then lies in the usual way to the Court of Appeal and, with leave, to the House of Lords (or by the 'leap frog' procedure direct to the House of Lords). The disputed tax is not payable at the first stage of the appeal (IHTA 1984 s 242). However, if there is a further appeal, the tax becomes payable; if this appeal is then successful, the tax must be repaid with interest.

Proceedings for the recovery of IHT can be taken by the Crown under the Crown Proceedings Act 1947 in the High Court. Straightforward cases may be taken in the county court by Inland Revenue staff other than barristers or solicitors (IHTA 1984 s 244).   [**21.161**]

2 Back duty

IHT penalties have not yet been amended in line with the Keith Committee recommendations which have now been implemented for the other taxes. The present position is that if a person is fraudulent (including wilful default) in producing accounts and other information, the penalty is £50 plus twice the difference between the liability calculated on the true and false bases. For negligence, the penalty is £50 plus that difference (IHTA 1984 s 247). Solicitors and other agents who fraudulently produce incorrect information are liable to a maximum penalty of £500 reduced to £250 in cases of neglect (IHTA 1984 s 247(3)(4)).

Proceedings for these penalties may be taken before the Special Commissioners or the High Court within three years of the determination of the correct tax due (IHTA 1984 s 250).

Assessments to recover IHT lost through fraud, wilful default and neglect of a person liable for the tax (which for these purposes includes the settlor in the case of discretionary trusts) may be made up to six years from the discovery of the fraud etc (IHTA 1984 s 240).   [**21.162**]–[**21.180**]

X GIFTS SUBJECT TO A RESERVATION OF BENEFIT

1 Legislative history

It was possible, under the CTT regime, for taxpayers to give away property but at the same time retain the benefit and control of it. Typical arrangements are illustrated in the following example.

EXAMPLE 21.34

(1) Joe creates a discretionary trust and includes himself amongst the beneficiaries.
(2) Arty owns a fine Constable landscape. He transfers legal ownership to his daughter by deed of gift but the picture remains firmly hanging up in his house until his death.
(3) Sam gives his Norfolk farm to his son and continues to live in the farmhouse.

These arrangements were ideal for the moderately wealthy since, although the original transfer might attract tax (to the extent that it was not covered by the annual exemption and the nil rate band) future increases in value of the gifted property occurred outside the transferor's estate whilst, should the need arise (and especially in the schemes illustrated in *Example 21.34(1)*), the property could be recovered by the transferor. The widespread use of such arrangements made it likely that they would be attacked by legislation and the switch from CTT to IHT, which included the introduction of the potentially exempt transfer, made this inevitable. Accordingly, provisions were introduced to deal with property subject to a reservation (see FA 1986 s 102 and Sch 20) which apply to lifetime gifts made on or after 18 March 1986.

The legislation is closely based on earlier estate duty sections and the relevant estate duty authorities are, to some extent, relevant (as was confirmed by Ferris J in the *Ingram* case considered below). A cautionary note should, however, be sounded since there are differences of wording in the new legislation (it has, for instance, been modernised) and a court might therefore be able to distinguish some of the earlier authorities. **[21.181]**

2 IHT consequences if property is subject to a reservation

A gift of property subject to a reservation is treated, so far as the donor is concerned, as a partial nullity for IHT purposes. This is because he is deemed to remain beneficially entitled to the gifted property immediately before his death. It is clear from the wording of s 102(3) that the property only returns to the donor at this precise moment although, if the benefit reserved ceases during the lifetime of the donor, he is treated as making a potentially exempt transfer of the property at that time (a deemed PET). No advantage therefore flows from releasing any reserved benefit just before death. Possible double charges to IHT in this area are dealt with in the regulations discussed in Appendix III. The legislation is widely drafted to catch a benefit reserved in the gifted property itself and a 'collateral advantage' (defined in s 102(1)(b) as 'any benefit to [the donor] by contract or otherwise').

EXAMPLE 21.35

(1) In 1992 A gives his daughter his country cottage (then worth £50,000) in return for an annuity of £500 pa payable for the next four years. The annuity ends in 1996 and A dies in 1997. By stipulating for the payment of an annuity A is reserving a benefit.
   (i) *The original transfer:* in 1992 is a PET. The value transferred will be reduced because of A's annuity entitlement.
   (ii) *On the ending of the annuity in 1996:* A makes a potentially exempt transfer equal to the then value of the cottage. (Note that because this is a 'deemed' PET the value transferred cannot be reduced by A's annual exemption.)
   (iii) *With his death in 1997* both the earlier transfers are made chargeable.
(2) Had A died in 1993 the reservation would be operative at his death so that, in addition to the 1992 PET being made chargeable, the value of the cottage in 1993 forms part of his death estate.
For relief against a double IHT charge, see Appendix III.

As a result of including the property in the deceased's estate immediately before death, it is necessary to value it at that time (and not at the time of the gift). Hence, where a transferor makes a gift with reservation there is no 'asset freezing' advantage. It also follows, of course, that as the value of the property swells the size of the estate, it may increase the estate rate of IHT (see [22.26] for 'estate rate') which is charged on the rest of the estate. Primary liability to pay the IHT attributable to reservation property lies with the donee (who should submit an account within 12 months of the end of the month of death) although the donor's PRs are liable if tax remains unpaid at the end of 12 months from the death. PRs who have made a final distribution of the assets in the estate may therefore be faced with a wholly unexpected claim for more IHT and this matter is considered in detail at [22.47]. It must be stressed that although the gifted property is included in the estate for IHT purposes it does *not* form part of the estate otherwise and hence does not benefit from the CGT uplift on death.   [21.182]

3   When do the reservation rules apply?

First, there must be disposal of property *by way of gift*. To base liability to IHT on the making of a gift does not fit in with the general scheme of the legislation which bases the tax charge upon chargeable transfers of value (see [21.2]). The resultant difficulties perfectly illustrate the problems of attempting to weld legislation from estate duty onto the CTT structure. Obviously, the gift must have been completed (and it should be remembered that the courts have no general power to perfect an uncompleted gift: see *Milroy v Lord* (1862)) but it may be assumed that the reservation provisions apply not just to pure gifts but also to the situation where, although partial consideration is furnished, there is still an element of bounty (see *A-G v Johnson* (1903)). A bad bargain, on the other hand, lacks any element of gift. The distinction between a gift (the basis of the reservation rules) and a transfer of value (the basis for IHT liability) is illustrated in the following example:

EXAMPLE 21.36

(1) Adam owns a pair of Constable watercolours and sells one to his daughter, Jemima. He retains possession of the picture. Each picture is worth £10,000: as a pair they are worth £35,000. Jemima pays Adam £10,000 for the picture.
   (i) There is a *transfer of value* of £15,000 (drop in value of Adam's estate). This transfer is a PET (see [21.43]).
   (ii) Is there a *gift* of property so that the reservation rules apply? As Jemima has paid full value for the picture that she has acquired there is no element of gift so that the rules are inapplicable.
(2) Sam settles property on trust for himself until he is aged 50 and the remainder on discretionary trusts for his family (including Sam). Assume that the trustees have the power to terminate Sam's life interest which they exercise six months after the creation of the trust.
   (i) There is no *transfer of value* when Sam creates the settlement since he is the life tenant (IHTA 1984 s 49(1)).
   (ii) At that time Sam makes a *gift* of the remainder interest and, as a member of the discretionary class, will be treated by the Revenue as reserving a benefit in the gifted property.
   (iii) When his life interest terminates Sam makes a chargeable *transfer of value* but does not make a *gift* (contrast the position if he had voluntarily surrendered his interest). With the cessation of the life interest the fund is now held on discretionary trusts and (see (ii) above) is property subject to a reservation (FA 1986 Sch 20 para 5(1)).

Secondly, the reservation rules apply if full possession and enjoyment of the gifted property is not enjoyed by the donee either at or before the beginning of the *relevant period*. For this purpose the relevant period is the period ending with the donor's death and beginning either seven years before that date or (if later) on the date of the gift.

EXAMPLE 21.37

(1) By deed of gift A gives B the family silver but he retains it locked in a cupboard till death.

(2) A gives full possession and enjoyment of the family silver to B and dies two years later.

(3) Assume in (1) above that the deed of gift was made in 1988 but that A hands over the silver in 1989 and dies in 1997.

(4) A gives the family silver to B in 1988 but borrows it back just before his death in 1997.

in (1) possession of the silver is never enjoyed by B so that there is a gift with reservation and the silver forms part of A's estate on death.

in (2) full possession and enjoyment is obtained at the beginning of the relevant period. (Hence no reservation although there is, of course, a failed PET.)

in (3) full possession and enjoyment is obtained more than seven years before death. (No reservation.)

in (4) although full possession and enjoyment was given to B, the return of the silver to A is important so far as the next requirement is concerned.

Thirdly, the reservation rules apply if the donor has not been excluded from benefit *at any time* during the relevant period. In *Example 21.37(4)* the return of the silver shortly before the donor's death results in the property being subject to a reservation at A's death and, accordingly, it is subject to IHT.

EXAMPLE 21.38

In 1924 the taxpayer created a settlement for the benefit of his infant daughter contingent upon her attaining 30. He was wholly excluded from benefit. In 1938 (just before she became 30) he arranged with her to borrow the income from the trust fund in order to reduce his overdraft. Until 1943 he borrowed virtually all the income: he finally died in 1946 (see *Stamp Duties Comr of New South Wales v Permanent Trustee Co* (1956)). On these facts the Privy Council held that a benefit had been reserved for estate duty purposes and the same would be true for IHT. Notice that the settlor had no enforceable right to the income: he merely made an arrangement with his daughter which she could have revoked at any time.

The requirement that the donor must be excluded from all benefit during the relevant period is comprised in two alternative limbs. Limb I requires his exclusion from the gifted property, whilst Limb II stipulates that he should not have received any benefit 'by contract or otherwise'. The two limbs must be considered separately.

So far as Limb I is concerned, in order to determine whether the donor has been entirely excluded from the gifted property, it is necessary to decide what that property comprises. Estate duty cases point to a distinction of some subtlety between keeping back rights in the property (ie making only a partial gift) and giving the entire property but receiving a subsequent benefit therein from the donee. Once the gift is correctly identified, the donor must be entirely excluded both in law and in fact (see *Example 21.38*).

EXAMPLE 21.39

A father owned two properties on which an informal farming partnership was carried on with his son. Profits were split two-thirds to the father, one-third to the son. The father gave one of the properties to his son, free of all conditions, so that the son could have farmed it independently. In fact both continued to farm the property sharing the profits equally. It was held that the father had not been entirely excluded from the gifted property (*Stamp Duties Comr of New South Wales v Owens* (1953)).

Limb II, that the donor must be excluded from any benefit by contract or otherwise, is sufficiently widely drafted to catch collateral benefits which do not take effect out of the gifted property.

EXAMPLE 21.40

(1) Charlie gives land in Sussex to his son Jasper who covenants, at the same time, to pay Charlie an annuity of £500 pa for the rest of his life. The land is property subject to a reservation (cp *A-G v Worrall* (1895): '... it is not necessary that the benefit to the donor should be by way of reservation' *per* Lopes LJ).

(2) Adam sells his farm to Bertram for £100,000 when its true value is £500,000. As a sale at undervalue there is an element of gift. However, it is not easy to see how the payment of £100,000 can amount to a benefit reserved. The estate duty cases do not go this far and even if it is accepted that there is a reserved benefit, it presumably ceases at the moment when the £100,000 is paid to Adam with the result that there may be a deemed PET on that date. Accordingly, the somewhat absurd result is that on the same day there would be a PET of £400,000 (value of farm less consideration received) and a further PET of £500,000 (value of property in which the reservation has ceased). It is understood that the Revenue will *not* argue that the £100,000 is a benefit reserved.

(3) Claude wishes to give his farm to his son Dada subject to Dada taking over the existing mortgage thereon. If the arrangement is structured in this manner the provision for the discharge of his mortgage would appear to result in Claude reserving a benefit. However, the Revenue has commented, with reference to this example, that 'the gift would be the farm subject to the mortgage and it would be an outright gift'. Were he to sell the farm for the amount of the outstanding mortgage that sale for partial consideration is not thought to involve a reservation (see (2) above); Dada could raise a mortgage on the security of the land; Claude would pay off his existing mortgage and any capital gain resulting from the consideration received (the gift element is subject to the hold-over election under TCGA 1992 s 165) would in many cases be covered by retirement relief (TCGA 1992 ss 163–164).

Although the benefit need not come from the gifted property itself, it must be reserved as part of a linked transaction: a purely accidental benefit in no way connected with an earlier gift is ignored. In determining whether there is such a connection, account must be taken of any associated operations (see FA 1986 Sch 20 para 6(1)(c) incorporating for these purposes IHTA 1984 s 268: see [**21.81**]).

Limb II is concerned with benefits reserved 'by contract *or otherwise*'. According to estate duty authority these words should be construed *eiusdem generis* with contract and, therefore, as requiring a legally enforceable obligation (see the unsatisfactory case of *A-G v Seccombe* (1911)). It seems most unlikely that courts today—in the era of *Ramsay*—would permit obligations binding in honour only to slip through this net, however, and the statutory associated operations rule (discussed above) is couched in terms of conduct (ie what actually happened) not of legal obligation. Indeed, the Revenue has confirmed that 'for IHT purposes [the words 'or otherwise'] should be given a wider meaning than they had for estate duty'. **[21.183]**

4 Exceptions—when the rules do not apply

Certain benefits to the donor are specifically ignored. FA 1986 s 102(1) requires the entire exclusion or *virtually* the entire exclusion of the donor from the gifted property. 'Virtually the entire exclusion' had no predecessor in the estate duty legislation and is apparently designed to cover, for instance, occasional visits by the donor to a house which he had earlier given away (including short holidays! For the Revenue's views on this matter see *Tax Bulletin*, November 1993).

A second exclusion is available where the donor furnishes full consideration for the benefit enjoyed (FA 1986 Sch 20 para 6(1)(a): note that the consideration must be 'full' throughout the donor's period of use—hence rent review clauses should be included in any letting agreement). The gifted property, however, must be an interest in land or a chattel and to come within the exclusion actual occupation, enjoyment or possession of that property must have been resumed by the donor (see *Example 21.43*).

EXAMPLE 21.41

(1) Gift of land but donor is subsequently given shooting/fishing rights or rights to take timber. So long as full (not partial) consideration is furnished there is *no retention* of benefit.

(2) Gift of Ming vase—returned to donor in return for payment of full rent. *No reservation.*

(3) As in (1) save that donor sub-lets his rights. *Outside para 6(1)(a)* since actual enjoyment is not resumed and therefore there is a reservation of benefit.

(4) Gift of shares: donor continues to enjoy dividends and pays full value for that right. *Outside para 6(1)(a)* since the property in question is neither land nor chattels. Hence a benefit is reserved.

A benefit may be ignored on hardship grounds but this provision is restrictive and is concerned solely with the occupation of land by a donor of that land whose circumstances have changed since the original gift and who has become unable to maintain himself for reasons of old age or infirmity. Further, the donee must be related to the donor (or his spouse) and the provision of occupation must represent reasonable provision for the care and maintenance of the donor. **[21.184]**

5 Identifying property subject to a reservation

FA 1986 Sch 20 paras 1–5 contains complex rules for identifying property subject to a reservation and makes provision, in particular, for what happens if the donee ceases to have possession and enjoyment of the property whether by sale or gift; for the effect of changes in the structure of bodies corporate when the original gift was of shares or securities; for the position if the donee predeceases the donor; and finally for the effect of changes in the nature of the property when the original gift was settled.

When property subject to the reservation qualified for agricultural or business relief at the date of the gift that relief may also be available if IHT would otherwise be charged because of the retained benefit (see **[23.55]**). **[21.185]**

6   Reserving benefits after FA 1986

The avowed purpose behind the provisions of FA 1986 was to prevent the 'cake and eat it' arrangements that had flourished in the CTT era. To what extent do the new rules achieve their purpose? If care is taken in drafting the terms of the relevant gift, the retention rules may be inapplicable (see [**21.187**]). When it is necessary to identify the property given away, it may be that there is a defect in the rules of FA 1986 Sch 20 with regard to gifts of cash. Such gifts are expressly excluded from the rules and it is arguable that once the money is spent by the donee there is no property in which a benefit can be reserved (a similar principle applies if property originally given was turned into cash by the donee and that cash was either dissipated or used to purchase a replacement asset). A further apparent loophole relates to inter-spouse transfer (see [**21.191**]) whilst the new rules do not prevent the retention of control over the property given (see [**21.189**]).   [**21.186**]

a) *Drafting: reservation or partial gift ('shearing')*

'[By retaining] something which he has never given, a donor does not bring himself within the mischief of the statutory provisions ... In the simplest analysis, if A gives to B all his estates in Wiltshire except Blackacre, he does not except Blackacre out of what he has given; he just does not give Blackacre' (Lord Simonds in *St Aubyn v AG* (1952)).

[**21.187**]

EXAMPLE 21.42

(1)   A owned freehold land. In 1909, a sheep farming business was carried on in partnership with his six children on it.
1913: he gave the land to his children. The partnership continued.
1929: A died.
What had he given away in 1913? Only his interest in the land subject to the rights of the partnership. Accordingly there was no property subject to a reservation of benefit (see *Munro v Stamp Duties Comr* (1934)).

(2)   In 1934 a father made an absolute gift of grazing land to his son. In 1935 that land was bought into a partnership with, *inter alia*, the father. On the death of the father in 1952 it was held that he had reserved a benefit in the land because of his interest in the partnership. (See *Chick v Stamp Duties Comr* (1958): contrast (1) above in that interest of the father arose *after* the absolute gift.)

(3)   T owns Whiteacre. He grants a lease to a nominee, assigns the freehold reversion to his daughter, and continues to occupy the property. Has T made a partial gift (of the reversion) so that the retention of benefit rules do not apply?
   It should be noted that in *Munro* ((1), above) not only was there a substantial time gap between the grant of the lease and the gift of the freehold but, at the time when the lease was granted, the donor had no intention of making a gift of the freehold: ie it was both prior and demonstrably independent (see also the *obiter dicta* in the *Nichols* case referred to below).
   Doubts about shearing operations which involved the case of a nominee were caused by *Kildrummy (Jersey) Ltd v IRC* (1990), a case decided in the Scottish Court of Session and concerning a stamp duty avoidance scheme. Attempting to avoid duty, the taxpayers formed a Jersey company to which they granted a lease over property which they owned outright: the Kildrummy estate. That Jersey company executed a declaration that the lease was held 'in trust and as nominee for' the taxpayers. Just over one month later the freehold was disposed of to a second Jersey company. The Court of Session decided, unanimously, that the grant of the lease to the nominee company was null and void. Lord Sutherland commented as follows:
   'There is no doubt that it is perfectly competent for a person to enter into a contract with his nominee but such a contract would normally

be of an administrative nature to regulate the relationship between the parties and to describe the matters which the nominees are empowered to do by their principal. A contract of lease, however, is in my opinion of an entirely different nature. It involves the creation of mutual rights and obligations which can only be given any meaning if the contract is between two independent parties.'

b) *Ingram v IRC (1997)*

Lady Jane Ingram transferred property to her nominee on 29 March 1987; the following day (on her directions) he granted her a 20-year rent-free lease in the property and on the next day transferred the property (subject to the lease) to trustees who immediately executed declarations of trust whereby the property was held for the benefit of certain individuals excluding Lady Jane. She died on 3 February 1989.

AT First Instance Ferris J held that the lease was a nullity and the *Kildrummy* case (above) 'subject to minor changes in the terminology in one or two instances, correctly [states] the law of England as well as that of Scotland'. However, Lady Jane had reserved an interest in the property since, as the trustees were volunteers, it would be inequitable for them to claim the legal estate free from the leasehold interest which had purportedly been granted to Lady Jane. She therefore had an interest in equity 'equivalent to that which she thought she had acquired by virtue of these leases and that interest arose simultaneously with the establishment of the trust' and the gift was one of the property subject to that interest:

> 'First Lady Ingram never intended to give the property to the trustees and beneficiaries free from the leasehold interests which it is common ground that she had. Secondly the creation and existence of these leasehold interests was not in any way dependent upon the concurrence of the trustees and the beneficiaries, still less upon the performance by them of some positive act ... Lady Ingram had her leasehold interest from the very same moment that the trustees and beneficiaries had the property subject to those interests.'

He, therefore, held that the gift with reservation rules did not apply.

His judgment has recently been reversed by the Court of Appeal (with Millett LJ dissenting). The majority held:
(1) that a lease granted by a nominee was a nullity (upholding Ferris J);
(2) when the property was conveyed to the trustees they took it free from any lease at law but, being volunteers, subject to an equitable obligation to give effect to Lady Ingram's intention: ie to treat her as if the lease had been valid. Unlike a rentcharge—which was capable of taking effect by way of reservation out of property gifted—a lease was a smaller interest necessarily comprised in the freehold gift. Nourse LJ commented:

> 'The principal right and interest which Lady Ingram would have had against the trustees was a right to possession of the property. That right mirrored the trustees' obligation to afford her possession. That obligation, just like an obligation to grant her a lease had there been one, was one to which the trustees only became subject when the freehold interest was vested in them.'

In a powerful dissenting judgment, Millett LJ held:
(1) that a lease involving a nominee was not a nullity;
(2) the subject matter jof the gift was the freehold reversion expectant upon the lease and not the unencumbered freehold. Even if the original lease granted to Lady Ingram had been a nullity the trustees were obliged to grant an equivalent lease, holding merely the freehold interest (subject to the lease) for the beneficiaries of the trust (contrast the position if the

gift had been made direct to the beneficiaries who were obligated to grant a lease back).

It is likely that the case will be appealed to the House of Lords.

c) *The importance of Ingram*

(1) This is the first case in which the reservation of benefit rules in the overall context of the inheritance tax legislation have been considered in the courts and it provides important guidance on their interpretation. It is notable that the judges all referred to the old estate duty cases considering them to be authoritative.

(2) The Revenue did not seek to impugn arrangements that were called 'vertical severance' but sought to attack the 'horizontal severance' that had been effected by the taxpayer. In simple terms, a vertical severance occurs when A divides his property into two portions (Plot A and Plot B) and makes a gift of Plot A, retaining Plot B. The gift is of Plot A only and so the retention of Plot B does not involve the reservation of any benefit in the gifted property. Horizontal severance involves the division of property into a number of separate limited interests which will take effect in succession to or subject to the other or others. For instance, the creation of a life interest followed by a remainder interest is an example of horizontal severance. In the *Ingram* case the creation of the lease followed by the gift of the freehold reversion amounted to a horizontal severance.

(3) The main authority relied upon by the Revenue, from the Court of Appeal judgment in *Nichols v IRC* (1975), is as follows:

> '. . . a grant of the fee simple, subject to and with the benefit of a leaseback, where such grant is made by a person who owns the whole freehold estate free from any lease, is a grant of the whole fee simple with something reserved out of it, and not a gift of a partial interest leaving something in the hands of the grantor that he has not given. It is not like a reservation or remainder expectant on a prior interest. It gives an immediate right to the rent, together with the right to distrain for it, and, if there be a proviso for re-entry a right to forfeit the lease. Of course where as in *Munro* (ante) the lease, or, as it may have been, a licence coupled with an interest, arises under a prior independent transaction, no question can arise because the donor then gives all he has, but where it is a condition of the gift that a leaseback shall be created, we think there must, on a true analysis, be a reservation of a benefit out of the gift and not something not given at all.'

The Court of Appeal held unanimously that the reference to prior independent transactions was *obiter dicta* given that the donee's obligations under a full repairing covenant and under a covenant to pay tithe redemption annuity amount to a reservation. Crucially therefore the judgments gave no credence to the oft stated view of the Revenue that in all cases the grant of the lease must be both prior (in time) and also independent of the gift of the freehold. At the end of his judgment, Nourse LJ commented:

> 'I desire to emphasise that had the leases been valid then, subject to the application of the *Ramsay* principle, the outcome of this case would have been governed by *Munro* and the Crown's claim would have failed.'

(4) It may for instance be possible to carve out a prior lease without need for any nominee, eg if A owns the property absolutely and grants a lease to himself and Mrs A before gifting the freehold reversion. The validity of that lease is not thought to be in any doubt subject only to the point that covenants in the lease should be joint and several rather than simply joint liabilities.

(5) Alternatively consideration may be given to a reversionary lease

arrangement under which A would grant a lease of 999 years to commence at the earlier of the 21st anniversary of the grant or the day after his death.   [**21.188**]

c) *Settlements*

First, if the settlor reserves an interest for himself under his settlement, whether he does so expressly or whether his interest arises by operation of law, there is no reservation of benefit and he is treated as making a partial gift. The position with regard to discretionary trusts is more problematic. It appears that if the settlor is one of the beneficiaries he is not entirely excluded from the property with the result that the entire fund will be included as part of his estate. In view of the limited nature of a discretionary beneficiary's rights (see *Gartside v IRC* (1968)), it is unlikely that he can be treated as making a partial gift.

Secondly, a danger arises if the settlor is one of the trustees and is entitled to remuneration as trustee. According to the estate duty case of *Oakes v Stamp Duties Comr* (1954) he has reserved a benefit. There is no problem if the settlor/trustee is not entitled to remuneration and therefore it is possible for a donor to retain control over the settled property without infringing the reservation of benefit rules.   [**21.189**]

d) *Benefits which are permitted*

It is only necessary for the property to be enjoyed *virtually* to the entire exclusion of the donor thereby permitting the occasional visit or holiday (see [**21.184**]). More important is the exception where the donor provides full consideration for the benefit retained.   [**21.190**]

EXAMPLE 21.43

(1) Dad gives his farm to Phil but continues to reside in the farmhouse under a lease which requires him to pay a full rent. Dad's continued use of a part of the gifted property does not bring the reservation rules into play.

(2) Elderly parents make unconditional gifts of a share in their house to their children (so that the children become tenants in common with the parents). Assuming that they all reside in the house and each bears his share of the running costs, it appears that the parents' continued occupation or enjoyment of that part of the house which they have given away is in return for similar enjoyment by the children of the other part of the property. Accordingly, the parents' occupation is for full consideration (illustration given in Standing Committee G: Hansard, 10 June 1986, col 425).

The restrictive nature of this illustration is all too obvious: it is assumed, for instance, that the children are occupying the house with their parents. If they lived elsewhere would their *right* to occupy be sufficient to lead to the same result? (Furthermore, if they never lived in the house after the making of the gift can they be said to have assumed 'full possession and enjoyment' of the gifted property?) It appears implicit in the statement that ownership of the house is divided equally between the various tenants in common (or that less than 50% is given away) since otherwise the full consideration argument would seem inapplicable.

Perhaps the major difficulty with the views expressed in the statement is that they appear to proceed upon the premise that the house is divided into 'parts' so that the parents use the children's 'part' in return for letting the children use their 'part'. In reality, of course, the interest of a tenant in common is in the whole property: *he is the owner of an undivided share.* Accordingly, the right of such a tenant to occupy the entire property is derived from the interest retained. As it does not amount to a reservation in the gifted share the full consideration argument becomes irrelevant. If this view is correct, it would follow that the precise interest of a tenant in common (eg does he have a 50% share or only 1%?) becomes irrelevant since whatever the size of the interest it confers a right to occupy the entirety.

e) *Reservation and spouses*

The reservation of benefit rules do not apply in the case of an inter-spouse transfer nor do they prevent the donor from reserving a benefit in favour of his spouse. **[21.191]**

EXAMPLE 21.44

(1) S creates a discretionary trust. He is the unpaid trustee, his wife is one of the beneficiaries. S has not reserved any benefit although it appears that *if* his wife benefits under the trust and *if* he shares that benefit the Revenue will argue that he has not been excluded from enjoyment or benefit in the gifted property.

(2) H settles land on his wife, W, for life and reserves a benefit for himself. Her life interest is terminated after (say) six months by the trustees whereupon the land (burdened by H's reserved benefit) passes to his daughter. H does not fall within the reservation of benefit rules unless the Revenue can successfully argue that there has been an associated operation so that H has made a direct gift with reservation to the daughter.

f) *Post-death variations*

Instruments of variation and disclaimer provide an ideal way of transferring wealth without causing any tax charge to arise and permit the disponor to reserve a benefit in the property.

EXAMPLE 21.45

Father leaves his country cottage to his daughter. She continues to use it for regular holidays and at all bank holidays but transfers it to her son by instrument of variation made within two years of father's death and read back into his will.

The crucial point is that the variation is treated as made by father for *all* IHT purposes so that his daughter has not made a gift of property capable of falling within the reservation of benefit provisions. **[21.192]**

22   IHT—death

I   GENERAL

IHTA 1984 s 4(1) provides that:

> 'on the death of any person tax shall be charged as if immediately before his death he had made a transfer of value and the value transferred by it had been equal to the value of his estate immediately before his death . . .'.

For IHT purposes, therefore, there is a deemed transfer of value which occurs immediately before the death and which must be cumulated with chargeable transfers made by the deceased in the preceding seven years. In addition to causing a charge on his estate at death, the death of an individual also has the effect of making chargeable potentially exempt transfers made in the seven years before death and it may lead to a supplementary IHT charge on chargeable transfers made in that same period. The complex tax computations that may occur on a death are illustrated in Section II after a consideration of what property is included in an estate at death and how that estate is to be valued.   [**22.1**]

1   Meaning of 'estate'

The definition of 'estate' for IHT purposes has already been considered in connection with lifetime transfers (IHTA 1984 s 5(1); see [**21.61**]). On death, however, the estate does not include excluded property (see [**27.21**] for the meaning of excluded property) although it does include property, given away by the deceased, in which he had reserved a benefit up to the time of his death (see [**21.181**]). As the transfer is deemed to occur immediately before the death, the estate includes any equitable joint tenancies of the deceased which pass by operation of law (*jus accrescendi*) at the moment of death.

EXAMPLE 22.1

Bill and his sister Bertha own their home as beneficial joint tenants so that on the death of either that share will pass automatically to the survivor and will not be transferred by will. For IHT purposes the half share in the house will be included in their respective death estates and will be subject to charge (for the valuation of the half share, see [**21.64**]).

The estate at death also includes a gift made before death in anticipation of death and conditional upon it occurring (a *donatio mortis causa*). Hence, although dominion over the property will have been handed over, it is still taxed as part of the deceased's estate at death.   **[22.2]**

2   **Valuation**

a) *A hypothetical sale* (See also [**21.62**] ff)

In general, assets must be valued at 'the price which the property might reasonably be expected to fetch if sold in the open market at that time'. No reduction is allowed for the fact that all the property is put on the market at the same time (IHTA 1984 s 160). This hypothetical sale occurs immediately before the death and if the value has been determined for IHT purposes it becomes the value at death for CGT purposes and, hence, the legatee's base cost (TCGA 1992 s 274: [**15.21**]). Where reliefs reduce the IHT value (notably business property relief) that relief is ignored for CGT purposes. For IHT, low values ensure the least tax payable but will give the legatee a low base cost and so a higher capital gain when he disposes of the asset.   **[22.3]**

b) *Lotting and the Fox decision*

In valuing an estate at death, the system of 'lotting' requires a valuation on the basis that 'the vendor must be supposed to have' taken the course which would get the largest price for the combined holding 'subject to the caveat . . . that it does not entail undue expenditure of time and effort'. For instance, if a taxpayer dies possessed of a valuable collection of lead toy soldiers they would not be valued individually but rather as a collection (see *Duke of Buccleuch v IRC* (1967)). In *IRC v Gray* (1994) the deceased (Lady Fox) had farmed the Croxton Park Estate in partnership with two others and the land was subject to tenancies which Lady Fox, as freeholder, had granted to the partnership. The Revenue sought to aggregate or lot together the freehold in the land with her partnership share as a single unit of property so that the value of Lady Fox's freehold reversion was an appropriate proportion of the aggregate value of that reversion and her partnership interest treated as a single item of property (in effect therefore the reversion was being valued on a vacant possession basis with an allowance for the partnership interests of the other partners). It may be noted that under the partnership deed she was entitled to 92½% of profits (and virtually all the losses). The Court of Appeal reversed the Lands Tribunal, holding that lotting was appropriate since that was the course which a prudent hypothetical vendor would take to obtain the best price. The fact that the interests could not be described as forming a 'natural unit of property' was irrelevant. Hoffmann LJ commented that:

> 'The principle is that the hypothetical vendor must be supposed to have "taken the course which would get the largest price" provided that this does not entail "undue expenditure of time and effort". In some cases this may involve the sale of an aggregate which could not reasonably be described as a "natural unit" . . . . The share in the farming partnership with or without other property, was plainly not a "natural" item of commerce. Few people would want to buy the right to farm in partnership with strangers. Nevertheless [s 160] requires one to suppose that it was sold. The question for the Tribunal was whether, on this assumption, it would have been more advantageous to sell it with the land.'

In many ways this was not a typical case involving the fragmentation of farm land within a family and therefore it should not be assumed that this judgment will apply in such cases: see *Private Client Business* (1994) p 210.   **[22.4]**

c) *Funeral expenses*

Although the general rule is that assets should be valued immediately before death, IHTA 1984 Part VI permits values to be amended in certain circumstances, eg reasonable funeral expenses can be deducted including a reasonable sum for mourning for family and servants and the cost of a tombstone or gravestone: see SP 7/87. The CTO have indicated that 'what is reasonable in one estate may not be reasonable in another and regard has to be had to the deceased's position in life and to the size of the estate. Each case has to be treated on its own merits'. [22.5]

d) *Changes in value resulting from the death*

In certain cases, a change in the value of assets caused by the death is taken into account. [22.6]

EXAMPLE 22.2

(1) A took out a whole life insurance policy for £100,000 on his own life. Its value immediately before death would be equal to the surrender figure. As a result of A's death £100,000 will accrue to A's estate and hence the value of the policy for IHT purposes is treated as that figure (IHTA 1984 s 167(2)).

(2) A and B were joint tenants in equity of a freehold house worth £100,000. Immediately before A's death his joint interest would be worth in the region of £50,000. As a result of death that asset passes to B by survivorship (ie its value is nil to A's estate). In this case it is not possible to alter the pre-death valuation (IHTA 1984 s 171(2)).

e) *Post-death sales*

In three cases the death valuation can be altered if the asset is sold within a short period of death for less than that valuation. Relief is not given merely because the asset falls in value after death; *only if it is sold by bargain at arm's length is the relief available.* Normally the sale proceeds will be substituted as the death valuation figure if an election is made by the person liable for the IHT on that asset (in practice this will be the PRs who should elect if IHT would thereby be reduced). Where such revaluations occur, not only must the IHT bill (and estate rate) on death be recalculated but also, for CGT purposes, the death valuation is correspondingly reduced so as to prevent any claim for loss relief. The three cases when this relief is available are: [22.7]

Related property sold within three years of death (IHTA 1984 s 176) The meaning of related property has already been discussed (see [21.67]). So long as a 'qualifying sale' (as defined) occurs, the property on death can be revalued ignoring the related property rules (ie as an asset on its own). Although the sale proceeds need not be the same as the death value, if the sale occurs within a short time of death the proceeds received will offer some evidence of that value. [22.8]

EXAMPLE 22.3

Sebastian's estate on death includes one of a pair of Constable watercolours of Suffolk sunsets. He leaves it to his son; the other is owned by his widow, Jemima. As a pair, the pictures are worth £200,000. Applying the related property provisions, the watercolour is valued at £100,000 on Sebastian's death. If it were to be sold at Sotheby's some eight months after his death for £65,000, the death value could, if a claim were made, be recalculated ignoring the related property rules. It would be necessary to arrive at the value of the picture immediately before the death.

Quoted shares and securities sold within 12 months of death (IHTA 1984 s 178 ff)   If sold for less than the death valuation the sale proceeds can be substituted for that figure. It should be noted that if this relief is claimed it will affect *all* such investments sold within the 12-month period; hence, the aggregate of the consideration received on such sales is substituted for the death values. Special rules operate if investments of the same description are repurchased. The shares or securities must be listed on the Stock Exchange or dealt in on the USM so that the provisions do not apply to private company shares. Relief is also available in cases where the investments are either cancelled without replacement within 12 months of death or suspended within 12 months of death and remain suspended on that anniversary. In the former case, there is deemed sale for a nominal consideration of £1 at the time of cancellation; in the latter a deemed sale of the suspended investments immediately before the anniversary at their then value.   **[22.9]**

Land sold within four years of death (IHTA 1984 s 190 ff)   The relief extends to all interests in land and is similar to that available for quoted securities. Hence, all sales within the four-year period are included in any election. Exchange of contracts is not a 'sale': see *Jones v IRC* (1997)   **[22.10]**

The 'appropriate person'   In the case of both quoted shares and land, the election to substitute the sale proceeds must be made by the appropriate person who is defined in the legislation as 'the person liable for inheritance tax attributable to (the property)'. This will be the PRs. Obviously the election in such cases will commonly be made if the property is sold for less than its probate value but the section dealing with land is not so limited and therefore the election may appear attractive in the sort of case illustrated in *Example 22.4* where substituting a higher probate value would wipe out a CGT liability: **[22.11]**

EXAMPLE 22.4

MacLeod left his entire estate to his wife Tammy on his death in 1990; it included land valued at death at £10,000. As a result of new regional development plans, the land now has hope value and is worth in the region of £100,000. Accordingly, it is now to be sold. An election to substitute the sale proceeds for the probate value would be beneficial in CGT terms. However, because there is no appropriate person (since IHT is not payable on MacLeod's death), that election cannot be made. Had the land been left to MacLeod's son, Ronnie, and fallen within MacLeod's unused nil rate band an election would then be possible (and desirable if the increased value would still attract IHT at 0%!).

3   Liabilities

a) *General rule*

Liabilities only reduce the value of an estate if incurred for consideration in money or money's worth, eg an outstanding building society mortgage and the deceased's outstanding tax liability (IHTA 1984 s 5(5)).   **[22.12]**

b) *Artificial debts*

In addition to this general requirement, FA 1986 s 103 introduced further restrictions on the deductibility from an estate at death of debts and incumbrances created by the deceased. These provisions supplement s 5(5) in relation to debts or incumbrances created after 17 March 1986. Broadly, their aim is to prevent the deduction of 'artificial' debts, ie those where the creditor had received gifts from the deceased as in the following example:

EXAMPLE 22.5

Berta gives a picture to her daughter Bertina in 1990. In 1992 she buys it back, leaving the purchase price outstanding until the date of her death.
(1) The gift is a potentially exempt transfer and escapes IHT if Berta survives seven years.
(2) The debt owed to Bertina is incurred for full consideration and satisfies the requirements of IHTA 1984 s 5(5). Deduction is, however, prevented by FA 1986 s 103.

Section 103(1) provides that debts must be abated in whole or in part if any portion of the consideration for the debt was either derived from the deceased or was given by *any* person to whose resources the deceased had contributed. In the latter case contributions of the deceased are ignored, however, if it is shown (ie by the taxpayer) that the contribution was not made with reference to or to enable or facilitate the giving of that consideration.

Accordingly, unless property derived from the deceased furnished the consideration for the debt, a causal link is necessary between the contribution of the deceased and the subsequent debt transaction.

EXAMPLE 22.6

(1) In *Example 22.5* the consideration for the debt is property derived from the deceased and therefore the debt may not be deducted in arriving at the value of her estate. (NB: it does not matter that the disposition of the deceased occurred before 17 March 1986 so long as *the debt* was incurred after that date.)
(2) In 1974 Jake gave a diamond brooch to his daughter (Liz). In 1984 she in turn gave the brooch to her sister Sam. In 1988 Sam lends £50,000 to Jake who subsequently dies leaving that debt still outstanding.
     The consideration for the debt was not derived from the deceased and Sam would (presumably) be able to show that, although she received property derived from the deceased the disposition of that property by the deceased was not linked to the subsequent transaction. Had Jake bought the brooch back from Liz in 1988 (leaving the price outstanding as a debt) the consideration for the debt would then be property derived from him so that the debt would not be deductible.

When a debt, which would otherwise not be deductible on death because of s 103(1), is repaid *inter vivos* the repayment is treated as a potentially exempt transfer (a deemed PET). This provision is essential since otherwise such debts could be repaid immediately before death without any IHT penalty. However, the application of this rule when a taxpayer repurchases property which he had earlier given away is a matter of some uncertainty. Take, for instance, the not uncommon case where A, having made a gift of a valuable chattel, subsequently decides that he cannot live without it. Accordingly, he repurchases that chattel paying full market value to the donee. Has A made a notional PET under s 103(5) at the time when he pays over the purchase price or, if the money is paid as part and parcel of the repurchase agreement, did A never incur any debt or incumbrance falling within the section? It is thought that the latter view is correct since if the purchase price is paid at once a debt will never arise.

It is also important to realise that an element of multiple charging could arise from the artificial debt rule (in *Example 22.5*, for instance, the PET is made chargeable if Berta dies before 1997; the debt is non-deductible and the picture forms part of Berta's estate). However, the regulations discussed in Appendix III prevent the multiple imposition of IHT in this case. Finally, although a debt may not be deducted in order to arrive at the deceased's estate for IHT purposes, it must still be paid by the PRs and it is therefore treated as a specific gift by the deceased (see further [**22.52**]).   [**22.13–22.20**]

EXAMPLE 22.7

(1) S settled property on discretionary trusts in 1980. In 1990 the trustees lend him £6,000. This debt is non-deductible. NB: it does not matter when the trust was created.

(2) Terry-Testator borrows £50,000 from the Midshire Bank which he gives to his son. The debt that he owes to the Bank is deductible on his death: in no sense is this an 'artificial debt'.

(3) Terry-Testator lends £50,000 to his daughter (interest free; repayable on demand). She buys a house with the money which increases in value. There is no transfer of value by Terry; the debt provisions are irrelevant, and Terry has not reserved any benefit in the property purchased with the loan.

II   HOW TO CALCULATE THE IHT BILL ON DEATH

Tax is calculated according to the rates set out in the following table:

Gross cumulative transfer (£)	Rate (%) – Death	Rate (%) – Life
0 –215,000	0	0
Above 215,000	40	20

These rates (which came into force on 6 April 1997) will be applied to the estate at death and, in addition, where that death occurs within seven years of a chargeable lifetime transfer or PET made by the deceased the following results occur:

(1) In the case of a *chargeable transfer*, IHT must be recalculated either in accordance with the rates of tax in force at the donor's death if these are less than the rates at the time of the transfer or, alternatively, by using full rates at the time of the transfer. Subject to taper relief, extra tax may then be payable (IHTA 1984 s 7(4), Sch 2 para 2).

(2) In the case of a PET, the transfer is treated as a chargeable transfer so that *first*, IHT must be calculated (subject to taper relief) at the rates current at the donor's death (again provided that these rates are less than those in force at the time when the transfer occurred: otherwise the latter apply: see Sch 2 para 1A), and *secondly*, as the PET must now be included in the total transfers of the taxpayer for cumulation purposes which may necessitate a recalculation of the tax charged on other chargeable transfers made by the donor and, where a discretionary trust is involved, the recalculation of any exit charge. These problems will be considered in order, looking first at the effect of death upon the chargeable lifetime transfers of the deceased and then at the taxation of the death estate. The consequences for discretionary trusts are considered at [**26.22**].   [**22.21**]

1   Chargeable transfers of the deceased made within seven years of his death

As already explained (see [**21.101**]) IHT will have been charged, at half the then death rate, at the time when the transfer was made. In computing that tax, transfers in the seven preceding years will have been included in the cumulative total of the transferor. As a result of his death within the following seven years IHT must be recalculated on the original value transferred at the full rate of IHT in force at the date of death. After deducting the tax originally paid, extra tax may be payable.

Taper relief If death occurs more than three years after the gift, taper relief ensures that only a percentage of the death rate is charged. The tapering percentages are as follows:

(1) where the transfer is made more than three but not more than four years before the death, 80%;

(2) where the transfer is made more than four but not more than five years before the death, 60%;

(3) where the transfer is made more than five but not more than six years before the death, 40%; and

(4) where the transfer is made more than six but not more than seven years before the death, 20%.

EXAMPLE 22.8

Danaos settles £265,000 on discretionary trusts in July 1997 (IHT is paid by the trustees). He dies:

        (1) on 1 January 1999

or   (2) on 1 January 2003

or   (3) on 1 January 2005.

The *original transfer* in 1997 was subject to IHT at one half of rates in force for 1997–98 (see Table, [**22.21**]).

In (1) he dies within three years of the gift: accordingly, a charge at the full tax rates for 1998–99 must be calculated, tax paid in 1997 deducted, and any balance is then payable.

In (2) he dies more than five but less than six years after the gift: therefore only 40% of the full amount of tax on death is to be calculated, the tax paid in 1997 deducted, and the balance (if any) is then payable.

In (3) death occurs more than seven years after the transfer and therefore no supplementary tax is payable.

    If it is assumed that the current rates of IHT apply throughout this period, the actual tax computations are as follows (assuming that the 1997 transfer was the first chargeable transfer of Danaos):

(a) *IHT on the 1997 chargeable transfer is as follows:*

    first £215,000   —   nil

    remaining £50,000 at 20% — £10,000

    total IHT payable by the trustees is therefore £10,000.

(b) *If death occurs within three years:* tax on a transfer of £265,000 at the then death rates is:

    first £215,000   —   nil

    remaining £50,000 at 40% — £20,000

    total IHT is therefore £20,000 which after deducting the sum paid in 1997 (£10,000), leaves a further £10,000 to be paid.

(c) *If death occurs in 2003* the calculation is as follows:

    (i) full IHT at death rates £20,000 (as in (b) above)

    (ii) take 40% (taper relief) of that tax: £20,000 × 40% = £8,000

    (iii) as that sum is less than the tax actually paid in 1997 *there is no extra IHT to pay.*

It should be noted in *Example 22.8* that even though the result of taper relief may be to ensure that extra IHT is not payable because of the death, it does not lead to any refund of the original IHT paid when the chargeable transfer was made: in such cases the taper relief is inapplicable, see IHTA 1984 s 7(5). (The assumption in *Example 22.8* that rates of tax remain unchanged is, of course, unrealistic since the IHT rate bands are linked to rises in the RPI.)

Fall in value of gifted property   If the property given falls in value by the date of death, the extra IHT is calculated on that reduced value (IHTA 1984 s 131). This relief is not available in the case of tangible movables which are wasting assets and there are special rules for leases with less than 50 years unexpired.

EXAMPLE 22.9

In 1997 Dougal gave a Matisse figure drawing worth £265,000 to his discretionary trustees (who paid the IHT). He died in 1998 when the Matisse was worth only £225,000.

(1)   Assuming it was Dougal's first chargeable transfer IHT paid on the 1997 gift was £10,000.

(2)   IHT on death (assume rates unchanged) is calculated on £225,000 = £14,000. Hence extra IHT payable is £nil.

Had the property been sold by the trustees before Dougal's death for £40,000 less than its value when given away by Dougal the extra (death) IHT would be charged on the sale proceeds with the same result as above. If, however, the property had been given away by the trustees before Dougal's death, even though its value might at that time have fallen by £40,000 since Dougal's original gift, no relief is given, with the result that the extra charge caused by Dougal's death will be levied on the full £265,000.

It will be realised that as a result of these rules the *value* of a chargeable lifetime transfer for cumulation purposes is not reduced in the seven-year period since s 131 merely reduces the value that is taxed (not the value cumulated) whilst taper relief is given in terms of the rate of IHT to be charged on that transfer. Hence the full value of the life transfer remains in the cumulative total of the transferor and there is no reduction in the tax charged on his death estate. Further, in cases where the transfer fell within the transferor's nil rate band, taper relief does not assist since it takes effect as a reduction in the tax charge (see further *Private Client Business* (1994) p 3).   **[22.22]**

2   PETs made within seven years of death

The PET becomes a chargeable transfer and is subject to IHT in accordance with the taxpayer's cumulative total at the date when it was made (ie taking into account chargeable transfers in the preceding seven years). The value transferred is frozen at the date of transfer unless the property has fallen in value by the date of death in which case the lower value is charged (the rules concerning the fall in value of assets are the same as those considered at **[22.22]** above). Despite these provisions, which look back to the actual date of the transfer of value, the IHT is calculated by reference to the rates in force at the date of death unless those rates have increased in which case the rates at the time of the transfer are taken (subject to taper relief, as above). **[22.23]**

EXAMPLE 22.10

In October 1993 Zanda gave a valuable doll (then worth £250,000) to her grand-daughter Cressida. She died in July 1997 when the value of the doll was £230,000. Assuming that Zanda had made no other transfers of value during her life, ignoring exemptions and reliefs, the IHT consequences are:

(1)   The 1993 transfer was potentially exempt. However, as Zanda dies within seven years it is made chargeable.

(2)   As the asset has fallen in value by the date of death IHT is charged on the reduced value, ie on £230,000.

(3)   IHT at the rates current when Zanda died is:
first £215,000 = nil

next £15,000 at 40% = £6,000
Total IHT = £6,000.
(4) Taper relief is, however, available since Zanda died more than three years after the gift. Therefore:
£6,000 × 80% (taper relief) = £4,800.

Note: Although IHT is calculated by reference to the reduced value of the asset, for cumulation purposes (and for CGT purposes) the original value transferred (£250,000) is retained.

3 Position where a combination of PETs and chargeable transfers have been made within seven years of death

PETs are treated as exempt transfers unless the transferor dies within the following seven-year period. Accordingly, they are not cumulated in calculating IHT on subsequent chargeable transfers. Consider the following illustration:

EXAMPLE 22.11

In July 1993 Planer gives shares worth £230,000 to his son.
In March 1997 he settles land worth £225,000 on discretionary trusts and pays the IHT himself (so that grossing-up applies: see [**21.102**]).
He dies in February 1998. (Assume no other transfers of value were made by Planer; ignore exemptions and reliefs; current IHT rates apply throughout.)
(1) The transfer in 1993 was a PET.
(2) In calculating the IHT on the chargeable transfer in 1997 the PET is ignored and IHT is £2,000.
The chargeable transfer in 1997 is therefore £227,000 (£225,000 + £2,000).
(3) As a result of his death within seven years the PET is made chargeable and the IHT calculation is as follows:
(a) *On the 1993 transfer* IHT at the rates when Planer died is subject to 60% taper relief (gifts more than four, less than five years before death). Hence IHT at death rates is:
first £215,000 — nil
next, £15,000 at 40% = £6,000
Taper relief at 60%:
£6,000 × 60% = £3,600 (tax due on 1993 transfer)

Note: Primary liability for this tax falls upon the donee (see [**22.25**]). Grossing-up does not apply when IHT is charged, or additional tax is payable, because of death.

(b) *On the 1997 transfer* IHT must be recalculated on this transfer since the transferor has died within seven years, and the former PET must be included in the cumulative total of Planer at the time when this transfer was made. Hence:
(i) cumulative transfers of Planer in 1997 = £230,000
(ii) value transferred in 1997 = £227,000
(iii) IHT at death rates on transfers between £230,000 and £457,000 is £227,000 × 40% = £90,800
Taper relief is not available on this transfer since Planer dies within three years.
Therefore:
deduct IHT paid in 1997:
£90,800 – £2,000 = £88,800
Additional IHT payable on the 1997 transfer is £88,800

Note: The cumulative total of transfers made by Planer at his death (which will affect the IHT payable on his death estate) is £457,000.

The following diagram illustrates how seven-year cumulation operates for PETs and chargeable transfers (CTs) made within seven years of death:

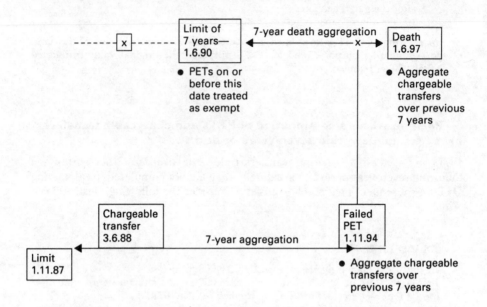

When a PET is made after an earlier chargeable transfer and the transferor dies in the following seven years, tax on that PET will be calculated by including the earlier transfer in his cumulative total. In this sense the making of the PET means that there is no reduction in his cumulative total for a further seven years and the result is that IHT could eventually turn out to be higher than if the PET had never been made ('the PET trap'!).   **[22.24]**

EXAMPLE 22.12

Yvonne made a chargeable transfer of £215,000 on 1 May 1990 and on 1 May 1996 made a gift of £300,000 to take advantage of the PET regime. Unfortunately, she dies after 1 May 1997 (when the 1990 transfer drops out of cumulation) but before 1 May 1999 (when taper relief begins to operate on the PET).

(1) IHT on the former PET (at current rates) is £120,000 since the 1990 transfer forms part of Yvonne's cumulative total in 1996. Tax on the death estate will then be calculated by including the 1996 transfer (the former PET) in Yvonne's cumulative total.

(2) Had Yvonne not made the 1996 PET so that £300,000 formed part of her death estate, tax thereon (ignoring the 1990 transfer which has dropped out of cumulation) is £34,000.

Extra IHT resulting from the making of the PET is therefore £120,000 – £34,000 = £86,000.

4 Accountability and liability for IHT on lifetime transfers made within seven years of death

The donee of a potentially exempt transfer which becomes chargeable by virtue of the subsequent death of the transferor must deliver an account to the Revenue within 12 months of the end of the month of death (IHTA 1984 s 216(1)(bb)). Tax itself is payable six months after the end of the month of death and interest on unpaid IHT runs from that date. There is no question of interest being charged from the date of the PET. Primary liability for the tax is placed upon the transferee although the Revenue may also claim the IHT from any person in whom the property is vested, whether beneficially or not, excluding, however, a purchaser of that property (unless it was subject to an Inland Revenue charge for the tax owing: see generally [**21.141**]).

To the extent that the above persons are not liable for the IHT *or* to the extent that any tax remains unpaid for 12 months after the death, the deceased's PRs may be held liable (IHTA 1984 s 199(2)). An application for a certificate of discharge in respect of IHT that may be payable on a PET may not be made before the expiration of two years from the death of the transferor (except where the Board exercises its discretion to receive an earlier application). If the property transferred qualified for the instalment option (see [**21.144**]) the tax resulting from death within seven years may be paid in instalments if the donee so elects and provided that he still owns qualifying property at the date of death (IHTA 1984 s 227(1A)).

So far as additional tax on chargeable lifetime transfers is concerned the same liability rules apply. Primary liability rests upon the donee although the deceased's PRs can be forced to pay the tax in the circumstances discussed above.

The problems posed for PRs by this contingent liability for IHT on PETs and *inter vivos* chargeable transfers are considered at [**22.47**]. [**22.25**]

5 Calculating IHT on the death estate

(See also Appendix II)

Having considered the treatment of PETs and the additional IHT on lifetime transfers that may result from the death of the transferor, it is now necessary to consider the taxation of the death estate (which includes property subject to a reservation and settled property in which the deceased was the life tenant). To calculate the IHT the following procedure should be adopted:

Step 1 Calculate total chargeable death estate; ignore, therefore, exempt transfers (eg to a spouse) and apply any available reliefs (eg reduce the value of relevant business property by the appropriate percentage).

Step 2 Join the table at the point reached by the transferor as a result of chargeable transfers made in the seven years before death. This cumulative total must include both transfers that were charged *ab initio* and PETs brought into charge as a result of the death.

Step 3 Calculate death IHT bill.

Step 4 Convert the tax to an average or estate rate—ie divide IHT *(Step 3)* by total chargeable estate (arrived at in *Step 1*) and multiply by 100 to obtain a percentage rate. It is then possible to say how much IHT each asset bears. This is necessary in cases where the IHT is not a testamentary expense but is borne by the legatee or by trustees of a settlement or by the donee of property subject to a reservation (see [**22.50**]). If the deceased had exhausted his nil rate band as a result of lifetime transfers made in the seven years before death, his death estate will be subject to tax at a rate of 40% which will be the estate rate.

EXAMPLE 22.13

Dougal has just died leaving an estate valued after payment of all debts etc at £200,000. A picture worth £10,000 is left to his daughter Diana (the will states that it is to bear its own IHT) and the rest of the estate is left to his son Dalgleish. Dougal made chargeable transfers in the seven years preceding his death of £115,000. To calculate the IHT on death:

(1) Join the death table at £115,000 (lifetime cumulative total).
(2) Calculate IHT on an estate of £200,000:

$$\begin{array}{lr} & \pounds \\ \pounds100,000 \times 0\% & 0 \\ \pounds100,000 \times 40\% & \underline{40,000} \\ & \underline{\underline{\pounds40,000}} \end{array}$$

(3)   Calculate the estate rate:

$$\frac{\pounds40,000 \text{ (IHT)}}{\pounds200,000 \text{ (Estate)}} \times 100 = 20\%$$

(4)   Apply estate rate to picture (ie 20% × £10,000) = £2,000. This sum will be payable by Diana.

(5)   Residue (£190,000) is taxed at 20% = £38,000. The balance will be paid to Dalgleish.

Property subject to a reservation and settled property in which the deceased had held an interest in possession at the date of death is included in the estate in order to calculate the estate rate of tax. The appropriate tax is, however, primarily the responsibility of either the donee or the trustees. The IHT position on death can be represented as follows:

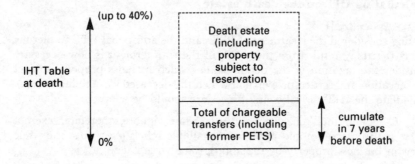

[22.26]–[22.40]

III   PAYMENT OF IHT—INCIDENCE AND BURDEN

If the deceased was domiciled in the UK at the time of his death, IHT is chargeable on all the property comprised in his estate whether situated in the UK or abroad. If he was domiciled elsewhere, IHT is only chargeable on his property situated in the UK.   [22.41]

1   Who pays the IHT on death?

a) Duty to account

The deceased's PRs are under a duty to deliver to the Revenue within 12 months of the end of the month of the death an account specifying all the property that formed part of the deceased's estate immediately before his death and including property:

(1)   in which the deceased had a beneficial interest in possession (eg where the deceased was the life tenant under a settlement); and

(2)   property over which he had a general power of appointment (this property is included since such a power enabled the deceased to appoint himself

the owner so that in effect the property is indistinguishable from property owned by him absolutely).

In practice, the PRs will deliver their account as soon as possible because they cannot obtain probate and, therefore, administer the estate until an account has been delivered and the IHT paid; further, they must pay interest on any IHT payable on death and which is unpaid by the end of the sixth month after the end of the month in which the deceased died (for instance, a death in January would mean that IHT is due before 1 August and, thereafter, interest would be payable). **[22.42]**

b) 'Excepted estates' (SI 1981/880 amended by SI 1996/1470)

No account need be delivered in the case of an 'excepted estate'.

The taxpayer must die domiciled in the UK; must have made no chargeable lifetime transfers; must not have been a life tenant under a settlement; his death estate must not include property subject to a reservation and he must not have owned at death foreign property amounting to more than £30,000. Subject thereto the estate will be excepted if the *gross* value at death does not exceed £180,000. This figure takes account of all property passing under the will or intestacy; of nominated property; and, in cases where the deceased had been a joint tenant of property, the value of the deceased's share in that property.

The Revenue reserve the right to call for an account (on Form 204) within 35 days of the issue of a grant of probate, but if they do not do so, the PRs are then automatically discharged from further liability. **[22.43]**

c) IHT forms

In cases other than b) above, to obtain a grant the PRs must submit an Inland Revenue account (an IHT Form).

IHT Form 202 is a simplified form which proceeds on the assumption that there will be no IHT liability. The deceased must die domiciled in the UK; if he made chargeable lifetime transfers in the seven years before death these must have comprised only cash; quoted shares or securities with a gross value not exceeding £50,000; and have been neither entitled in an interest in possession trust nor have settled property in that seven-year period. The estate must be made up of property situated in the UK only. If these conditions are satisfied IHT Form 202 is then the appropriate form so long as the *net* estate at death does not exceed the current IHT threshold (£215,000) and the *gross* value of the estate (before deducting exemptions and reliefs) does not exceed twice the threshold. For instance, if a millionaire leaves his entire estate to his surviving spouse, although the net estate falls below the threshold (being nil), the gross estate is worth more than twice the threshold and so IHT Form 202 cannot be used. Where the deceased had been a joint tenant at death it is only the value of his share of the property that is included.

If IHT Form 202 cannot be used, either IHT Form 200 or 201 (if the deceased died domiciled outside the UK) must be completed (see Appendix II for a completed IHT Form 200). **[22.44]**

d) Liability for IHT (IHTA 1984 Part VII)

Personal representatives   PRs must pay the IHT on assets owned beneficially by the deceased at the time of death and on land comprised in a settlement which vests in them as PRs. Their liability is personal, but limited to assets which they received as PRs or might have received but for their own neglect or default (IHTA 1984 s 204 and see *IRC v Stannard* (1984) which establishes that overseas PRs or trustees may find that their personal UK assets are seized to meet that liability). If the PRs fail to pay the IHT other persons are concurrently liable, namely:

(1) Executors *de son tort*, ie persons who interfere with the deceased's property so as to constitute themselves executors. Their liability is limited to the assets in their hands (see *IRC v Stype Investments (Jersey) Ltd* (1982)).

(2) Beneficiaries entitled under the will or on intestacy in whom the property becomes vested after death. Their liability is limited to the property that they receive.

(3) A purchaser of real property if an Inland Revenue charge is registered against that property. His liability is limited to the value of the charge.

(4) Any beneficiary entitled to an interest in possession in the property after the death. Liability is generally limited to the value of that property.

[22.45]

Trustees   Where the deceased had an interest in possession in settled property at the date of his death, it is the trustees of the settlement who are liable for any IHT on the settled property to the extent that they received or could have received assets as trustees. Should the trustees not pay the tax, the persons set out in (3) and (4) above are concurrently liable.   [**22.46**]

Contingent liability of PRs   In three cases PRs may incur liability to IHT if the persons primarily liable (the donees of the property) have reached the limits of their liability to pay or if the tax remains unpaid for 12 months after the death. These occasions are, *first*, when a lifetime chargeable transfer is subject to additional IHT because of the death; *secondly*, if a PET is brought into charge because of the death; and finally if the estate includes property subject to a reservation. The following example illustrates the type of problem that may arise:

EXAMPLE 22.14

Mort dies leaving an estate (fully taxed) of £565,000. The PRs are unaware of any lifetime gifts and therefore pay IHT of £140,000 and distribute the remainder of the estate. Consider the following alternatives:

(1) After some years a lifetime gift by Mort of £215,000 which had been made six years before his death and was potentially exempt when made is discovered. Although no IHT is chargeable on that gift the PRs are accountable for extra IHT on the death estate of £86,000; or

(2) A gift of £1,000,000 made one year before Mort's death is discovered. In this case not only will the PRs be accountable for extra IHT of £86,000 as above but in addition if the donee fails to pay IHT on the £1,000,000 gift the PRs will be liable to pay that IHT (limited to the net assets in the estate which have passed through their hands).

Contingent liabilities present major problems for PRs and the following matters should be noted:

(1) Their liability may arise long after the estate has been fully administered and distributed (eg a PET may be discovered which is not only itself taxable but also affects the charge on subsequent lifetime chargeable transfers and on the death estate). It may therefore be desirable for PRs to obtain suitable indemnities from the residuary beneficiary before distributing the estate although such personal indemnities are of course always vulnerable (eg in the event of the bankruptcy of that beneficiary).

(2) The liability of PRs is limited to the value of the estate (as discussed above). However, even if IHT has been paid on the estate and a certificate of

discharge obtained they are still liable to pay the further tax that may arise in these situations.

(3) If PRs pay IHT no right of recovery is given in IHTA 1984 against donees who were primarily liable except in the case of reservation of benefit property (in this situation s 211(3) affords a right of recovery). It is extremely doubtful whether such a right exists under general law. There is, of course, nothing to stop a donor taking an indemnity from his donee to pay any future IHT as a condition of making the PET. Such an arrangement would be expressed as an indemnity in favour of his estate and does not involve any reservation of benefit in the gifted property. Personal indemnities are, of course, vulnerable in the event of the bankruptcy or emigration of the donee.

(4) It will not be satisfactory for PRs to retain estate assets to cover the danger of a future tax liability. Apart from being unpopular with beneficiaries there is no guarantee that PRs will retain an adequate sum to cover tax liability on a PET which they did not know had been made: only by retaining all the assets in the estate will they be wholly protected!

(5) Insurance would seem to be the obvious answer to these problems. PRs should give full information on matters within their knowledge and then seek cover (up to the limit of their liability) in respect of an unforeseen IHT liability arising. It would seem reasonable for testators to give expressly a power to insure against these risks. It is understood that cover can be arranged on an individual basis in such cases with the premium payable ranging from 0.2% up to 2% of the amount of indemnity required. Accordingly in *Example 22.14(2)* the cost would be (at most) 2% × £425,000 = £8,500.

Limited comfort to PRs is afforded by a letter from the Inland Revenue to the Law Society dated 11 February 1991 which states:

'The Capital Taxes Office will not usually pursue for inheritance tax personal representatives who
— after making the fullest enquiries that are reasonably practicable in the circumstances to discover lifetime transfers, and so
— having done all in their power to make full disclosure of them to the Board of Inland Revenue
— have obtained a certificate of discharge and distributed the estate before a chargeable lifetime transfer comes to light.
This statement . . . is made without prejudice to the application in an appropriate case of s 199(2) Inheritance Tax Act 1984.' **[22.47]**

Land In addition to persons who are liable for IHT on death, real property (including a share in land under a trust for sale) is automatically subject to an Inland Revenue charge from the date of death until the date when the IHT is paid (IHTA 1984 s 237(1)(a) and see *Howarth's Ex'ors v IRC* (1997)). **[22.48]**

e) *Payment of tax: the instalment option (IHTA 1984 ss 227–228)*

To obtain a grant of representation, PRs must pay all the IHT for which they are liable when they deliver their account to the Revenue.

In the case of certain property the tax may, at the option of the PRs, be paid in ten yearly instalments with the first instalment falling due six months after the end of the month of death. The object of this facility is to prevent the particular assets from having to be sold by the PRs in order to raise the necessary IHT.

The instalment option is available on the following assets:
(1) land, freehold or leasehold, wherever situate;
(2) shares or securities in a company which gave the deceased control of that

company ('control' is defined as voting control on all questions affecting the company as a whole);

(3) a non-controlling holding of shares or securities in an unquoted company (ie a company which is not quoted on a recognised Stock Exchange) where the Revenue is satisfied that payment of the tax in one lump sum would cause 'undue hardship';

(4) a non-controlling holding as in (3) above where the tax on the shares or securities and on other property carrying the instalment option comprises at least 20% of the tax due from that particular person (in the same capacity);

(5) other non-controlling shareholdings in unquoted companies, where the value of the shares exceeds £20,000 and either their nominal value is at least 10% of the nominal value of all the issued shares in the company, or the shares are ordinary shares whose nominal value is at least 10% of the nominal value of all ordinary shares in the company; and

(6) a business or a share in a business, eg a partnership share.

An added attraction of paying by instalments is that, generally, no interest is charged so long as each instalment is paid on the due date. In the event of late payment the interest charge is merely on the outstanding instalment. Interest is, however, charged on the total outstanding IHT liability (even if the instalments are paid on time) in the case of land which is not a business asset and shares in investment companies. If the asset subject to the instalment option is sold, the outstanding instalments of IHT become payable at once. It should be noted that the definition of 'qualifying property' for these purposes is not subject to the same limitations as business property relief with regard to investment businesses and excepted assets: see [23.53]   [22.49]

Exercising the option: cashflow benefit   If the instalment option is exercised the first instalment is, as already mentioned, payable six months after the month of death. Hence, PRs will normally exercise the option *in order to pay as little IHT as possible before obtaining the grant.* Once the grant has been obtained they may then decide to discharge the IHT on the instalment property in one lump sum. PRs should, however, bear in mind that some IHT will usually be payable before the grant. The necessary cash may be obtained from the deceased's account at either a bank or a building society (building societies, in particular, will commonly issue cheques to cover the initial inheritance tax payable); from the sale of property for which a grant is not necessary; or by means of a personal loan from a beneficiary. If a loan has to be raised commercially, the interest thereon will qualify for income tax relief for 12 months from the making of the loan so long as it is on a loan account (not by way of overdraft) and is used to pay the tax attributable to personal property (including leaseholds and land held on trust for sale: TA 1988 s 364). The Keith Committee rejected suggestions that IHT should generally be payable *after* a grant has been obtained (see Cmnd 9120).

PRs should be advised to exercise the instalment option to defer IHT until after obtaining the grant. Where the IHT is a testamentary expense, the tax can then be paid off in one lump sum. If the residuary legatee objects (it may, for instance, be necessary to sell an asset to pay the IHT), PRs could arrange to vest the residue in that beneficiary and for him to discharge the future instalments. Adequate security should, however, be taken in such cases because if the beneficiary defaults, the PRs remain liable for the outstanding IHT (see *Howarth's Ex'ors v IRC* (1997)). In the case of a specific gift which bears its own IHT and which qualifies for the instalment option, the decision whether to discharge the entire IHT bill once probate has been obtained should be left to the legatee. PRs should not make a unilateral decision (see further [22.52]).

Once PRs have paid all the outstanding IHT they are entitled to a certificate of discharge under IHTA 1984 s 239(2).   [22.50]

Instalments on chargeable lifetime transfers As already discussed, the instalment option may also be available when a chargeable *inter vivos* transfer is made (see [**21.144**]) and when IHT becomes payable on a PET or additional IHT on a chargeable transfer. In these situations, however, further requirements must be satisfied before the option can be claimed. The donee must have retained the original property or, if it has been sold, have used the proceeds to purchase qualifying replacement property (for a discussion of these requirements in the context of business relief see [**23.54**]). Further, when the property consisted of unquoted shares or securities those assets must remain unquoted from the date of transfer to the date of death (IHTA 1984 s 227(1A)). [**22.51**]

2 Allocating the burden of IHT

a) *The general rule*

The Revenue is satisfied once the IHT due on the estate has been paid. As far as the PRs and beneficiaries under the will are concerned, the further question arises as to how the tax should be borne as between the beneficiaries: eg should the tax attributable to a specific legacy be paid out of the residue as a testamentary expense or is it charged on the property (the specific legacy)? The answer is particularly important when specific legacies are combined with exempt or partially exempt residue, since, if the IHT is to be paid out of that residue, the grossing-up calculation under IHTA 1984 s 38 (see [**22.76**]) will be necessary and will result in more IHT being payable.

As a general rule, a testator can, and should, stipulate expressly in his will where the IHT on a specific bequest is to fall. If the will makes no provision for the burden of tax, the general principle is that IHT on UK unsettled property is a testamentary expense payable from residue. Under the estate duty regime land had, in such cases, borne its own duty, but the Scottish case of *Re Dougal* (1981) decided that the IHT legislation drew no distinction between realty and personalty and the matter was put beyond doubt by IHTA 1984 s 211.

EXAMPLE 22.15

In Lyslie's will his landed estate is left to his son and his stocks and shares to his daughter. The residue is left to his surviving spouse. In addition he owned a country cottage jointly with his brother, Ernie.

(1) IHT on the specific gifts of the land and securities is borne by the residue in the absence of any provision to the contrary in Lyslie's will. Note that the spouse exemption therefore only applies to exempt from charge what is left after the payment of IHT on the specific gifts.

(2) IHT on the joint property is paid by the PRs who are given the right to recover that tax from the other joint tenant(s): IHTA 1984 s 211(3).

In drafting wills and administering estates the following matters should be borne in mind:

(1) When drafting a new will, expressly state whether bequests are tax-bearing or are free of tax.

(2) Old wills which have been drawn up but are not yet in force should be checked to ensure that provision has been made for the payment of IHT on gifts of realty. The will may have been drafted on the assumption that such gifts bear their own tax in which case amendments will be necessary.

(3) IHT on foreign property and joint property will always be borne by the beneficiary unless the will provides to the contrary.

Assuming that the will contains a specific tax-bearing legacy, how will the IHT, in practice, be paid on it? As the PRs are primarily liable to the Revenue for the IHT, they will pay that tax in order to obtain probate and either deduct it from the legacy (eg if it is a pecuniary legacy) or recover it from the legatee. For specific legacies of other property (eg land or chattels), the PRs have the power to sell, mortgage or charge the property in order to recover the tax. If they instead (usually at the legatee's request) propose to transfer the asset to him, they should ensure that they are given sufficient guarantees that the tax will be refunded to them. Where the PRs pay IHT which is not a testamentary expense (ie on all tax-bearing gifts; joint property and foreign property), they have a right to recover that sum from the person in whom the property is vested (IHTA 1984 s 211(3)).

Problems can arise for PRs who pay the IHT on specific tax-bearing legacies to which the instalment option applies. If they choose to pay the IHT on such legacies in one lump sum, when they seek to recover that tax from the legatee he can elect to repay them in instalments (IHTA 1984 s 213). Hence, PRs should, after consulting the legatee, elect to pay the IHT on that property by instalments; if they do so, however, and if the legatee defaults in paying the instalments, the PRs remain concurrently liable for the outstanding IHT.

To avoid any dispute, when the PRs have paid IHT which they are entitled to recover from the legatee, they can obtain a certificate from the Revenue which is conclusive as to the amount of tax which they are entitled to recover (IHTA 1984 s 214).

In the three cases mentioned at [**22.47**] PRs are liable to pay IHT if the tax is not paid by the person primarily responsible. As this contingent liability will usually only arise more than 12 months after death, PRs should exercise caution whenever there is a risk of liability. When the tax liability is known, they should retain sufficient assets out of the estate to cover that bill (ie they should not make a final distribution of residue until all IHT resulting from the death has been paid). Otherwise, as discussed earlier, PRs may be placed in an invidious position.   [**22.52**]

b) *IHTA 1984 s 41 and Re Benham's Will Trusts*

As a qualification to the general rules stated above, a chargeable share of residue must always bear its own tax (ie the burden of tax cannot be placed on an exempt slice of residue) and any provision to the contrary in a will is void (IHTA 1984 s 41).

The implications of IHTA 1984 s 41 in the context of a will containing both chargeable and exempt gifts of residence was considered in *Re Benham's Will Trusts, Lockhart v Harker, Read and the Royal National Lifeboat Institution* (1995) in which residue was left as follows:

(1) upon trust to pay debts, funeral and testamentary expenses;
(2) subject thereto 'to pay the same to those beneficiaries as are living at my death and who are listed in List A and List B hereunder written in such proportions as will bring about the result that the aforesaid beneficiaries named in List A shall receive 3.2 times as much as the aforesaid beneficiaries named in List B and in each case for their own absolute and beneficial use and disposal'.

List A contained one charity and a number of non-charitable beneficiaries; and List B contained a number of charities and non-charitable beneficiaries.

By an originating summons, the executor sought, *inter alia*, the opinion of the court on whether, in view of IHTA 1984 s 41 and the terms of the will, the non-charitable beneficiaries should receive their shares subject to IHT, or whether their shares should be grossed up.

On this question, he considered that there were three possibilities:
(1) the non-charitable beneficiaries received their respective shares subject to

IHT, which would mean that they would receive less than the charities; *or*

(2) the non-charitable beneficiaries should have their respective shares grossed up, so that they received the same net sum as the charities; *or*

(3) the IHT was paid as part of the testamentary expenses under clause 3(A), so that the balance was distributed equally between the non-charitable beneficiaries and the charities.

The deputy judge agreed that the third possibility was precluded by s 41. However, he did not agree that the charities should receive more than the non-charitable beneficiaries. The plain intention of the testatrix was that each beneficiary, whether charitable or non-charitable, should receive the same as the other beneficiaries on the relevant list. He concluded that the non-charitable beneficiaries' shares should be grossed up.

In analysing the effect of this case, consider an estate of £100,000 to be divided between wife and daughter (although remember that the problem arises whenever residue is divided between exempt and chargeable beneficiaries: for instance, between relatives on the one hand and a charity on the other).

EXAMPLE 22.16

Assume net residue of £100,000 to be divided equally between surviving spouse and daughter. Estate rate 40%.

(1) *Option 1*: deduct tax on £50,000 and divide balance (£80,000) equally: prohibited by s 41.

(2) *Option 2*: divide equally so that spouse gets £50,000 and daughter's £50,000 then bears tax so that she ends up with £30,000.

(3) *Option 3*: gross up daughter's share so that both end up with the same:

ie $x + \frac{(100 \times)}{60} = £100,000$

$x = £37,500$

Both receive £37,500; gross value of daughter's share is £62,500.

	Spouse (£)	Daughter (£)	Tax man (£)
Option 1	40,000	40,000	20,000
Option 2	50,000	30,000	20,000
Option 3	37,500	37,500	25,000

The difficulty posed by *Benham* lies in the judge's assertion that:

'the plain intention of the testatrix is that at the end of the day each beneficiary, whether charitable or non-charitable, should receive the same as the other beneficiaries . . .'.

On one view the case therefore depends upon its own facts and, in particular, on the wishes of the testatrix. However, the ready inclusion (as a matter of construction) of a grossing-up clause in all cases where:

(1) the residue is left to exempt and non-exempt beneficiaries;

(2) the will provides for them to take in equal shares and there is no evidence that the testator did not intend *Benham* to apply; and

(3) the value of the estate is such that IHT is payable on the chargeable portion of residue;

would go against the existing practice which had been to apply Option 2 in such cases. Two questions therefore arise. *First*, how should wills be drafted in the light of *Benham*? It is important that the whole matter is explained to the testator (with a suitable example to illustrate the fiscal and other consequences of the grossing-up route) and that the will is then drafted *either* to include a statement that chargeable shares of residue bear their own tax *or* to incorporate a full blown grossing-up clause. It is important that the drafting makes it clear whether Option 2 or Option 3 is being adopted. *Secondly*, what is the position with regard to estates which have been fully administered on the basis that no grossing-up clause is to be implied so that chargeable shares bear their own tax? *Benham* purports to state the law as it has always been and so the personal representatives may have incorrectly distributed the residue by over-paying exempt beneficiaries (spouses and charities). Non-exempt beneficiaries who have been underpaid may therefore bring an action against the personal representatives who will not normally be able to recover the value overpaid from the exempt beneficiaries. Two further points should be noted: *first*, although the Revenue is a beneficiary of grossing-up (in that more tax is payable) it accepts that the matter depends on a construction of the particular will and so will not be challenging the interpretation put upon it by the executors. *Secondly*, grossing-up may not always benefit chargeable beneficiaries and there may be cases where both exempt and chargeable beneficiaries receive less and only the taxman is the winner!   [22.53]

3   Cases where the IHT has to be recalculated

In a limited number of instances IHT paid on a deceased's estate will need to be recalculated.   [22.54]

Cases where sale proceeds are substituted for the death valuation   (See [22.7].)
                                                                       [22.55]

As the result of a variation or disclaimer   Such instruments, if made within two years of the death, may be read back into the original will which *may* necessitate a recalculation of the tax payable (see [22.118]).   [22.56]

Discretionary trusts under IHTA 1984 s 144   If broken up within two years of death, tax is calculated as if the testator had provided in his will for the dispositions of the trustees (see [22.114]).   [22.57]

Orders under the Inheritance (Provisions for Family and Dependants) Act 1975   When the court exercises its powers under s 2 of the 1975 Act to order financial provision out of the deceased's estate for his family and dependants, the order is treated as made by the deceased and may result in there having been an under- or over-payment of IHT on death. Any application under this Act should normally be made within six months of the testator's death, so that the PRs will have some warning that adjustments to the IHT bill may have to be made. Further adjustments to the tax bill may be required if the court makes an order under s 10 of the Act reclaiming property given away by the deceased in the six years prior to his death with the intention of defeating a claim for financial provision under the Act. In this case, the deceased's cumulative total of chargeable lifetime transfers in the previous seven years is reduced by the gift reclaimed. This, of itself, may affect the rate at which tax is charged on the deceased's estate on death. Also the value of the reclaimed property and any tax repaid on it falls into the deceased's estate thus necessitating a recalculation of the IHT payable on death.

These rules are bolstered up by a somewhat obscure anti-avoidance provision in IHTA 1984 s 29A. It is relevant when there is an exempt transfer on death (eg to the surviving spouse) and that beneficiary then, in satisfaction of a claim against the estate of the deceased, disposes of property 'not derived from the death transfer'.   [22.58]–[22.70]

EXAMPLE 22.17

A dies leaving everything to Mrs A. Dependant B has a claim against A's estate but is 'bought off' by Mrs A making a payment (out of her own resources) of £150,000.

(1) *In the absence of specific legislation:* the arrangement would probably be a PET by Mrs A to B and so free from IHT provided that Mrs A survived by seven years. Alternatively it could even be argued that there was no transfer of value since the compromise was a commercial arrangement under IHTA 1984 s 10. No IHT was, of course, charged on A's death.

(2) *Position under s 29A:* A's will is deemed amended to include a specific gift of £150,000 to B with the remainder (only) passing to Mrs A. Accordingly a recalculation will be necessary and an immediate IHT charge will arise.

IV PROBLEMS CREATED BY THE PARTIALLY EXEMPT TRANSFER

1 When do ss 36–42 apply?

In many cases the calculation of the IHT bill on death will be straightforward. Difficulties may, however, arise when a particular combination of dispositions is made in a will. IHTA 1984 ss 36–42 provide machinery for resolving these problems with a method of calculating the gross value of the gifts involved and, accordingly, the IHT payable. Consider, first, a number of instances where the calculation of the IHT on death poses no special difficulties: **[22.71]**

Where all the gifts are taxable: eg A leaves all his property to be divided equally amongst his four children. In this case the whole of A's estate is charged to IHT. **[22.72]**

Where all the gifts are exempt: eg A leaves all his property to a spouse and/or a charity. In this case the estate is untaxed. **[22.73]**

Where specific gifts are exempt and the residue is chargeable: eg A leaves £100,000 to his spouse and the residue of £500,000 to his children. Here the gift to the spouse is exempt, but IHT is charged on the residue of £500,000 so that only the balance will be paid to the children. **[22.74]**

Where specific gifts are chargeable but bear their own tax under the terms of the will and the residue is exempt: eg A leaves a specific tax-bearing gift of £300,000 to his niece and the residue to his spouse. The spouse receives the residue after deduction of the £300,000 gift; IHT is calculated on the £300,000 and is borne by the niece. **[22.75]**

Where there are no specific gifts and part of the residue is exempt, part chargeable: eg A leaves his estate to be divided equally between his son and his spouse. As already discussed the chargeable portion of residue must always bear its own tax; any provision in the will to the contrary is void (IHTA 1984 s 41 see **[22.53]** and *Re Benham's Will Trusts* (1995)).

There are bequests where the calculation of the IHT is not so obvious and it becomes necessary to apply the rules in ss 36–42. Taking the simplest illustration, consider a will containing a specific gift which is chargeable but does not bear its own IHT and residue which is exempt, eg A's estate on death is valued at £600,000 and he leaves £275,000 to his daughter with remainder to his surviving spouse. As previously explained, the specific gift of £275,000 will be tax-free unless the will provides to the contrary. The problem which arises is to decide how much IHT should be charged on the specific gift and this involves grossing up that gift. With the simplified IHT rate structure, grossing up has become relatively straightforward and, in the tax year 1997–98, the IHT payable will be two-thirds of the amount by which the chargeable legacies exceed the available nil rate band. Hence, assuming that A has an unused nil rate band of £215,000, tax payable on the daughter's legacy will be two-thirds of £275,000 – £215,000: ie £40,000. As a result:

(1) The gross value of the legacy becomes £315,000 and the daughter receives the correct net sum of £275,000 after deducting IHT at 40% on the amount by which the gross legacy exceeds the available nil rate band.

(2) The £40,000 tax is paid out of the residue leaving the surviving spouse with £285,000. **[22.76]**

Business and agricultural property   When business property is specifically given to a beneficiary that person will benefit from the appropriate relief but in other cases the benefit of the relief is apportioned between the exempt and chargeable parts of the estate (IHTA 1984 s 39A). **[22.77]**

EXAMPLE 22.18

Deceased's estate is valued at £1,000,000 and includes business property (qualifying for 50% relief) worth £600,000. He left a £600,000 legacy to his widow and the residue to his daughter.

	£
Estate	1,000,000
Less: 50% relief on business property	300,000
value transferred	£700,000

(1) Legacy of £600,000 to widow is multiplied by

$$\frac{R \text{ (value transferred)}}{U \text{ (estate before relief)}} = \frac{£700,000}{£1,000,000} = £420,000$$

(2) Accordingly the value attributed to the residue (given to the daughter) is:

$$400,000 \times \frac{R \ (£700,000)}{U \ (£1,000,000)} = £280,000$$

(3) IHT is therefore charged on £280,000.

Notes:

(1) Had relief at 100% been available the taxable sum would have been £160,000.

(2) The lowest tax bill results if the agricultural or business property is specifically given to a non-exempt beneficiary. 'Specific gift' is inadequately defined in IHTA 1984 s 42(1) and the following points may be noted:

   (i) an appropriation of business property in satisfaction of a pecuniary legacy does not count as a specific gift;

   (ii) a direction to pay a pecuniary legacy 'out of' business property is likewise not a specific gift of business property (IHTA 1984 s 39A(6));

   (iii) it is possible to employ a formula to leave business property equal in value to the testator's nil rate band *after* relief at 50%;

   (iv) a defectively drafted will may be cured by an instrument of variation whereby a specific gift of business property is 'read back' into the will.

(3) Difficulties can be caused if a nil rate band clause is used in a will and the estate includes business or agricultural property as illustrated in the following example.

EXAMPLE 22.19

(1) Jill leaves an estate valued at £1 million which includes a controlling shareholding in a private company (qualifying for 100% business property relief) valued at £500,000.

If she leaves the shares to her son Paul by way of specific gift and residue to her husband Jack, no tax is payable.

If she leaves a cash gift of £500,000 to son Paul (this gift to bear its own tax) and residue to husband, the son's gift will attract relief at 50% (being the appropriate part of the business property relief) so its value will reduce to £250,000. After deduction of the nil rate band the taxable value is £35,000 and the tax is £14,000.

(2) Jill instead leaves a will which provides that her son will take 'a cash sum which is the largest amount that can be given without any Inheritance Tax being payable on the transfer of value of my estate which I am deemed to make immediately before my death'. She had anticipated that her son would take £215,000 (being the amount of the nil rate band legacy) although she was aware that if she made chargeable lifetime gifts within seven years of her death, the amount her son would take under the will on her death would be reduced.

With 100% business property relief, however, the amount which her son will take, assuming her nil rate band is unused on death, is £430,000 (which will be reduced by its share of BPR to £215,000, the amount of the nil rate band). The consequence will be that Jill's husband Jack will receive far less than his wife had anticipated when the will was drafted. The effect would be even more dramatic if business property in the estate was worth, say, £800,000. In this case, the cash gift which Paul could take without payment of tax would leave Jack with nothing!

(3) This unintentional result would have been avoided if the will had stated that her son should take:

'a cash sum which is the lesser of:
   (i) the largest amount that can be given without any Inheritance Tax being payable on the transfer of value of my estate which I am deemed to make immediately before my death, and
  (ii) the upper limit of the nil rate band in the table of rates of tax applicable on my death in Schedule 1 to the Inheritance Tax Act 1984.'

2 Effect of previous chargeable transfers on the ss 36–42 calculation

In considering the application of ss 36–42, it has so far been assumed that the deceased had made no previous chargeable lifetime transfers in the seven years before his death. If he has, any specific gift on death must be grossed up taking account of those cumulative lifetime transfers because they may affect the rate at which tax is charged on the estate on death.   **[22.78]**

EXAMPLE 22.20

A's estate on death is valued at £250,000 and he leaves £90,000 tax-free to his son and the residue to a charity. A had made gross lifetime transfers in the previous seven years of £215,000.

The lifetime gifts have wiped out A's nil rate band and therefore IHT on the specific legacy of £90,000 is two-thirds of £90,000 = £60,000. Accordingly, the gross legacy is £150,000 so that the charity is left with £100,000.

3 Double grossing-up

IHTA 1984 ss 36–42 also deal with the more complex problems that arise if specific tax-free gifts are combined with chargeable gifts bearing their own tax, and an exempt residue.

Assume that B makes a specific bequest of £230,000 tax-free to his son, and leaves a gift of £80,000 bearing its own tax to his daughter with residue of £400,000 (before deducting any IHT chargeable to residue) going to his spouse. To gross up the specific tax-free gift of £230,000 as if it were the only chargeable estate would produce insufficient IHT bearing in mind that there is an additional chargeable legacy of £80,000. On the other hand, if the £230,000 were grossed up at the estate rate applicable to £310,000 (ie the two gifts of £230,000 and £80,000) the resulting tax would be too high because the £80,000 gift should not be grossed up. Further, to gross up £230,000 at the estate rate applicable to the whole estate including the exempt residue would produce too much tax because this assumes, wrongly, that the residue is taxable.

The solution provided in ss 36–42 is to gross up the specific tax-free gift at the estate rate applicable to a hypothetical chargeable estate consisting of the grossed-up specific tax-free gift and the gifts bearing their own tax. The procedure, known as double grossing-up, is as follows:

Step 1　Gross up the specific tax-free gift of £230,000 by multiplying excess over nil rate band by $^5/_3$: £15,000 × $^5/_3$ = £25,000.

$$£25,000 + £215,000 = £240,000$$

Step 2　Add to this figure the tax-bearing gift of £80,000 making a hypothetical chargeable estate of £320,000.

Step 3　Calculate IHT on £320,000 using the death table = £42,000. Then convert to an estate rate: viz

$$\frac{£42,000}{£320,000} × 100 = 13.125$$

Step 4　Gross up the specific tax-free gift a second time at this rate of 13.125%:

$$£230,000 × \frac{100}{100 - 13.125} = £264,748.2$$

Step 5　The chargeable part of the estate now consists of the grossed-up specific gift (£264,748.2) and the gift bearing its own tax (£80,000) = £344,748.2.

Step 6　On the figure of £344,748.2, IHT is recalculated at £51,899.28 and the final estate rate is found:

$$\frac{£51,899.28}{£344,748.2} × 100 = 15.05\%$$

Step 7　The grossed-up specific tax-free gift (£264,748.2) is then charged at this rate (15.05%) = tax of £39,855.2.

It should be noted that the IHT on specific tax-free gifts must always be paid from the residue and it is only the balance that is exempt so that the surviving spouse will receive £400,000–£39,855.2 = £360,144.8. The tax-bearing gift of £80,000 will of course be taxed at 15.05%, but the tax (ie £12,040) will be borne by the daughter.

To conclude, ss 36–42 are relevant whenever a tax-free specific gift is mixed with an exempt residue, and, if tax-bearing gifts are also included in the will, then a double grossing-up calculation is required. Logically, to gross up only twice is indefensible since the estate rate established at *Step 6* should then be used to gross up further the £230,000 (ie repeat *Step 4*) and so on and so on! Thankfully, the statute only requires the grossing-up calculation to be done twice with the consequence that a small saving in IHT results!　　　**[22.79]**

4   Problems where part of residue is exempt, part chargeable

So far we have been concerned with a wholly exempt residue. What, however, happens if part of the residue is chargeable? For example, A, whose estate is worth £500,000, leaves a specific tax-free gift of £230,000 to his son; a tax-bearing gift of £80,000 to his daughter; and the residue equally to his widow and his nephew.

The method of calculating the IHT is basically the same as in the double grossing-up example above in that the chargeable portion of the residue (half to nephew) must be added to the hypothetical chargeable estate in *Step 2* to calculate the assumed estate rate. The difficulty is caused because, although IHT on grossed-up gifts is payable before the division of residue into chargeable and non-chargeable portions, the IHT on the nephew's portion of the residue must be deducted from his share of residue after it has been divided (IHTA 1984 s 41). To take account of this, the method for calculating the IHT payable in such cases is amended as follows:

Step 1   Gross up the specific tax-free gift of £230,000 to £240,000.

Step 2   Calculate the hypothetical chargeable estate by adding to the grossed-up gift of £240,000: (1) the tax-bearing gift of £80,000 and (2) the chargeable residue:

	£	£
Estate		500,000
Less: grossed-up gift	240,000	
tax-bearing gift	80,000	320,000
		£180,000

The nephew's share (the chargeable residue) is half of £180,000 = £90,000.
   This results in a hypothetical chargeable estate of:
£240,000 + £80,000 + £90,000 = £410,000.

Step 3   Calculate the 'assumed estate rate' on £410,000:
$$\text{IHT on } £410,000 = 78,000$$
$$\text{Estate rate is } \frac{78,000}{410,000} \times 100 = 19\%$$

Step 4   Gross up the specific tax-free gift at this rate of 19%
$$£230,000 \times \frac{100}{100 - 19} = £283,950.6$$

Step 5   The chargeable part of the estate now consists of:

	£	£
Estate		500,000
Less: grossed-up gift	283,950.6	
tax-bearing gift	80,000	
		£136,049.4

Nephew's share is ½ × £136,049.4 = £68,024.7

Therefore, chargeable estate is
   £68,024.7 + £80,000 + £283,950.6 = £431,975.3

Step 6   Calculate the estate rate on the chargeable estate of £431,975.3

$$\text{IHT on } £431,975.3 = £86,790.12$$
$$\text{Estate rate is } \frac{86,790.12}{431,975.3} \times 100 = 20\%$$

Step 7   The grossed-up specific tax-free gift of £283,950.6 is taxed at the rate of 20% = £56,790.12.

Step 8   The tax-bearing gift of £80,000 is taxed at 20% = £16,000. This tax is paid by the daughter.

Step 9   The residue remaining is £500,000 – (£230,000 + £56,790.12 + £80,000) = £133,209.88. This is then divided:
  Half residue to spouse = £66,604.94
  Half residue to nephew = £66,604.94 less IHT calculated at a rate of 20% on £68,024.7 (ie the nephew's share of the residue at *Step 5*, above). Therefore, the tax on the nephew's share is £13,604.94 so that the nephew receives £53,000   **[22.80]–[22.90]**

V   ABATEMENT

Although ss 36–42 are mainly concerned with calculating the chargeable estate in cases where there is an exempt residue, they also deal with certain related matters:

Allocating relief where gifts exceed an exempt limit   A transfer may be partly exempt only because it includes gifts which together exceed an exempt limit, eg a transfer to a non-UK domiciled spouse which exceeds £55,000. To deal with such cases IHTA 1984 s 38(2) provides for the exemption to be allocated between the various gifts as follows:
(1) Specific tax-bearing gifts take precedence over other gifts.
(2) Specific tax-free gifts receive relief in the proportion that their values bear to each other.
(3) All specific gifts take precedence over gifts of residue.   **[22.91]**

Abatement of gifts   If a transferor makes gifts in his will which exceed the value of his estate, those gifts must be abated in accordance with IHTA 1984 s 37. There are two cases to consider:
(1) Where the gifts exceed the transferor's estate without regard to any tax payable, the gifts abate according to the rules contained in the Administration of Estates Act 1925 and tax is charged on the abated gifts.

EXAMPLE 22.21

A testator's net estate is worth £300,000. He left his house worth £100,000 to his nephew, the gift to bear its own tax, and a general tax-free legacy of £300,000 to a charity. Under IHTA 1984 s 37(1) the legacy must abate to £200,000 to be paid to the charity free of tax. The house will bear its own tax.

(2) Where the transferor's estate is only insufficient to meet the gifts as grossed up under the rules in ss 36–42, abatement is governed by IHTA 1984 s 37(2). The order in which the gifts are abated depends on the general law.   **[22.92]–[22.110]**

VI SPECIFIC PROBLEMS ON DEATH

1 **Commorientes**

Where A and B leave their property to each other and are both killed in a common catastrophe or otherwise die in circumstances such that it is not clear in what order they died, the Law of Property Act 1925 s 184 stipulates that the younger is deemed to have survived the elder. Hence, if A was the elder, he is presumed to have died first so that his property passes to B (assuming no survivorship clause—see below) and IHT will be chargeable. B's will leaving everything to A will not take effect because of the prior death of A so that his assets (including his inheritance from A) will pass on intestacy. IHT would *prima facie* be chargeable. The result is that property bequeathed by the elder would (subject to quick succession relief) be charged to IHT twice. To prevent this double charge, IHTA 1984 s 4(2) provides that A and B 'shall be assumed to have died at the same instant'. Hence, A's estate is charged only once—on his death; it is not taxed a second time on B's death since the gift is treated as lapsing. LPA 1925 s 184 is, therefore, ousted in order to avoid a double charge to IHT, but it still governs the actual destination of the property bequeathed by A and the question of whether the transfer on A's death is chargeable. This may produce bizarre results: **[22.111]**

EXAMPLE 22.22

(1) Fred (aged 60) and his wife Wilma (aged 55) are both killed in a car crash. Fred had left all his property to Wilma, Wilma had left all her property to their son Barnie. According to LPA 1925 s 184, the order of deaths is Fred then Wilma and Fred's property, therefore, passes to Wilma and thence to Barnie. However, the effect of IHTA 1984 s 4(2) is to impose IHT on Fred's death only; ie on the transfer to Wilma which is exempt from IHT, so that Barnie acquires Fred's property free from IHT.

Compare:

(2) Assume that Fred and Barnie are killed in the same crash and that Fred had left his property to Barnie who in turn had left his estate to charity. Although the property passes on Fred's death through Barnie's estate to the charity (which is exempt from IHT), there is a chargeable transfer on Fred's death to Barnie.

2 **Survivorship clauses**

To inherit property on a death it is necessary only to survive the testator so that if the beneficiary dies immediately after inheriting the property, the two deaths could mean two IHT charges. Some relief is provided by quick succession relief (see **[22.113]**), but the prudent testator may provide in his will for the property to pass to the desired beneficiary only if that person survives him for a stated period. Such provisions are referred to as survivorship clauses and IHTA 1984 s 92 states that as long as the clause does not exceed six months there will be (at most) only a single IHT charge.

EXAMPLE 22.23

T leaves £100,000 to A 'if he survives me by six months. If he does not the money is to go to B'.

The effect of IHTA 1984 s 92 is to leave matters in suspense for up to six months and then to read the will in the light of what has happened. Hence, if A survives for six months it is as if the will had provided '£100,000 to A'; if he dies before the end of that period, it is as if the will had provided for £100,000 to go to

B. The result is that two charges to IHT are avoided; there will merely be the one chargeable occasion when the testator dies.

In principle, it is good will drafting to include survivorship clauses. The danger of choosing a period in excess of six months is that IHTA 1984 s 92 will not apply so that the bequest will be settled property to which ordinary charging principles will apply. If a longer period is essential, insert a two-year discretionary trust into the will (see [**22.114**]).   [**22.112**]

3   Quick succession relief (IHTA 1984 s 141)

Quick succession relief offers a measure of relief against two charges to IHT when two chargeable events occur within five years of each other.

For unsettled property quick succession relief is only given on a death where the value of the deceased's estate had been increased by a chargeable transfer (*inter vivos* or on death) to the deceased made within the previous five years. It is not necessary for the property then transferred to be part of the deceased's estate when he dies.

In the case of settled property the relief is only available (and necessary) for interest in possession trusts. It is given whenever an interest in possession terminates and hence can be deliberately activated by the life tenant assigning or surrendering his interest. The earlier transfer in the case of settled property will be either the creation of the settlement or the termination of a prior life interest.

EXAMPLE 22.24

In 1995 S settles property by will on A for life, B for life, C absolutely. In 1996 A dies and in 1997 B surrenders his life interest.

1995   IHT will be chargeable.

1996   Quick succession relief is available on A's death. The chargeable transfer in the previous five years was the creation of the settlement in 1995.

1997   Quick succession relief is available on the surrender of B's life interest. The chargeable transfer in the previous five years was the termination of A's life interest.

The relief reduces the IHT on the second chargeable occasion. IHT is calculated in the usual way and then reduced by a sum dependent upon two factors. First, how long has elapsed since the first chargeable transfer was made. The percentage of relief is available as follows:

100%   if previous transfer one year or less before death
 80%   if previous transfer one–two years before death
 60%   if previous transfer two–three years before death
 40%   if previous transfer three–four years before death
 20%   if previous transfer four–five years before death.

The second factor is the amount of IHT paid on the first transfer. IHTA 1984 s 141(3) states that the relief is 'a percentage determined as above of the tax charged on so much of the value transferred by the first transfer as is attributable to the increase in the estate of the second transferor'. Hence, if A had left £55,000 to B who died within one year of that gift the appropriate percentage will be 100% of the tax charged on the transfer from A to B and if the transfer by A had been his only chargeable transfer and had fallen into his nil rate band the relief is 100% × 0!   [**22.113**]

EXAMPLE 22.25 (assuming current rates of IHT throughout)

(1) *Tax-free legacy/death:* A, who has made no previous chargeable transfers, dies leaving an estate of £430,000 out of which he leaves a tax-free legacy of £215,000 to B. B dies 18 months later leaving an estate of £350,000.

(a)	IHT on A's estate	= £86,000
	Proportion paid in respect of tax-free legacy (50%)	= £43,000
(b)	Quick succession relief 80% × £43,000	= £34,400

		£
(c)	IHT on B's estate	54,000
	Less: Quick succession relief	34,400
	IHT payable	£19,600

(2) Diego gives £25,000 to Madonna in October 1994 (a PET). Madonna dies in July 1996 and Diego in January 1997. As a result of Diego's death, the PET is chargeable and IHT of (say) £5,000 is paid by Madonna's estate.

   (a) QSR at 80% is available—on the tax attributable to the increase in the donee's estate.

   (b) The increase in Madonna's estate is £25,000 – £5,000 = £20,000. IHT attributable to that increase is:

$$\frac{20,000}{25,000} \times 5,000 = £4,000$$

   (c) QSR available on Madonna's death is 80% × £4,000 = £3,200.

4   Flexible will drafting (IHTA 1984 s 144)

If a testator creates, by his will, a trust without an interest in possession, so long as an event occurs on which tax is chargeable (ie a conventional 'exit' charge, see [**26.23**]) *within two years* of his death, the IHT that would normally arise under the discretionary trust charging rules 'shall not be charged but the Act shall have effect as if the will had provided that on the testator's death the property should be held as it is held after the event' (s 144(2)). In other words the dispositions of the trustees are 'read back' into the will. Such a trust enables wills to be drafted with some flexibility and is advantageous where, for example, the testator is dying and desires his estate to be divided between his four children, but is not sure of the proportions. By inserting the two year trust a decision about the final distribution of the estate can be postponed for a further two years.

A typical flexible will involves the testator in settling all his property on discretionary trusts which may be expressly limited to a two-year (or 23-month) period or which may be for the entire perpetuity period. Default provisions will normally provide for property to be divided equally amongst the beneficiaries in the discretionary class should the trustees fail to exercise their dispositive powers within the permitted period. If the trust is ended within two years of death the provisions of s 144 will apply: in other cases if the trust continues beyond that date the usual discretionary trust regime will apply.   [**22.114**]

a) *IHT consequences*

IHT will be charged at the estate rate on the property settled at death but if the ultimate distributions made by the trustees are 'read back' into the will that IHT may need to be recalculated. In *Example 22.26(1)*, for instance, a discretionary trust is ended in favour of the testator's surviving spouse and the reading back provisions result in a repayment of any IHT charged on the death estate. *Example 22.26(2)* reveals an important restriction in the relief afforded by s 144 which only applies if the transfer out of the discretionary trust would otherwise attract a tax charge.   **[22.115]**

EXAMPLE 22.26

A creates a flexible trust in his will and the trustees:

(1) Six months after death appoint the property to A's widow. This appointment is read back to A's death: ie it takes effect as an exempt spouse gift so that there is a resulting IHT repayment.

(2) As in (1) but the appointment is made two months after death. Now there is no question of reading back since there is no charge imposed on events occurring within three months of the creation of a discretionary trust (IHTA 1984 s 64(4), see **[26.25]**). As a result, the original will remains intact, IHT is charged on the entire estate and the spouse exemption is unused. Although this result was never intended the position has been confirmed by *Frankland v IRC* (1996).

b) *Theoretical problems and practical uses of s 144*

Because at the date of death property is left on a discretionary trust, that property is subject to IHT and, in normal circumstances, tax will need to be paid before the personal representatives can obtain a grant of probate. In cases where the trust is ended (as in *Example 22.26(1)*) by appointment to a surviving spouse there will then be a refund of the tax paid but nonetheless the estate may have been put at a cashflow disadvantage. In *Fitzwilliam v IRC* (1993) the testator's residuary estate was settled on trusts which gave the trustees power in the 23 months following the death to appoint amongst a discretionary class of beneficiaries. After the expiration of that period the trustees were to pay the income to the testators widow for the remainder of her life. The executors indicated that they intended to appoint the property to the surviving spouse and the Winchester District Probate Registry therefore accepted that the estate was spouse exempt. This conduct was criticised by the Capital Taxes Office (CTO) but Vinelott J did not join in that criticism and pointed out that because the estate was largely composed of agricultural land and chattels it would have been very difficult for the executors to have paid such a bill. This matter was not raised in the higher courts.

The operation of s 144 was for a time bedevilled by traps. In particular, the Revenue took the view that an appointment could only be made out of a trust when that trust had been properly constituted with the vesting of property in trustees. That by itself was unexceptionable but the Revenue originally considered that this involved either the completion of the administration of the estate or, alternatively, an express assent of property to the personal representatives as trustees before any appointment could be made (see generally *Capital Taxes News*, November 1986, p 147). Helpfully, the CTO have now abandoned this position and accept that such trusts are immediately constituted at the date of the testator's death: see further *Capital Taxes News*, July 1990, p 98.

There is one remaining disadvantage: namely that if an appointment is made out of such a trust which is duly read back under s 144 there can be no question of CGT hold-over relief being available unless the property in the trust qualifies as business assets. There is no equivalent relief to s 144 permitting reading back in CGT legislation.

This trust can be used as an alternative to a survivorship clause. Say, for instance, that the testator wants Eric to get the property if he survives him by 18 months failing which Ernie is to receive it. This cannot be achieved by a conventional survivorship clause (which must be limited to six months; see **[22.112]**). If Eric and Ernie are made beneficiaries of a discretionary trust, however, and the trustees know the testator's wishes concerning the distribution of the fund, there is no risk of a double IHT charge in carrying out his wishes.

Such a trust is attractive as compared with variations and disclaimers. If there is any doubt about who should be given the deceased's estate, it is better to use a trust than to rely upon an appointed legatee voluntarily renouncing a benefit under the will. All the most convincing fiscal arguments will often fail to persuade people to give up property and they cannot be compelled to vary or to disclaim! **[22.116]**

5 Channelling through a surviving spouse

In cases where the testator is survived by his spouse there is a more attractive way of drafting a flexible will. Consider the following illustration.

Lord and Lady Y are both possessed of 'serious money'. Lord Y leaves his property by will as follows:

(1) as to any unused proportion of his nil rate band on accumulation and maintenance trusts for his collection of grandchildren;

(2) as to the residue of his estate on a life interest trust for Lady Y with the trustees having the power to terminate that interest (in whole or in part) at any time once (say) six months have elapsed from the date of Lord Y's death. Although there is a power to advance capital it is understood between Lord and Lady Y that the trustees will in practice exercise their power of termination (probably at different times) and will make appointments of the residuary estate in favour of persons chosen from the wide discretionary class set out in the residuary trust.

Lord Y's will is in standard form: first, he is exhausting his nil rate band and then leaving all his assets to his surviving spouse. On his death, therefore, no IHT will be charged.

The intention, however, is that the trustees will revoke the interest in possession of Lady Y either in whole or in part. The caveat that this should not be done for six months is inserted in an attempt to ensure that that interest has come into effect: ie that Lady Y really has received some benefit under the estate of her dead husband. To some extent therefore the six-month period is an arbitrary choice: some draftsmen prefer a 12-month period whilst others are content with a lesser period. In any event, the intention is that the interest in possession will be terminated and under the current legislation when that occurs (assume, for instance, that the interest is terminated whereupon the property passes on accumulation and maintenance trusts to Lord Y's grandchildren) the effect will be that Lady Y has made a potentially exempt transfer. Provided that she survives for seven years IHT will be wholly avoided. Of course, if she were to die within that time an IHT charge would then result but it should be stressed that this does not worsen the position of the couple. Such a tax charge levied at the full rate of 40% would in any event have arisen if Lord Y had directly left the property to his grandchildren. Accordingly, there is no downside to this arrangement: at best a gift from Lord Y to his grandchildren falls outside the IHT net, at worst the ordinary tax charge results.

The attractions as compared with the s 144 trust are obvious. Had this property been left on a discretionary trust with the beneficiaries including Lady Y and the grandchildren and appointed out to the grandchildren within two years, reading back would have resulted in a tax charge to Lord Y's rates. Restricting the power of revocation until, say, six months have elapsed from death is commonly done in order to avoid any suggestion that Lady Y's interest lacks 'materiality' and so can be ignored. In *Fitzwilliam*, the House of Lords refused to excise an interest in possession lasting one month. **[22.117]**

6 **Disclaimers and variations (post mortem tax planning)**

It will often be desirable to effect changes in a will after the death of the testator, for instance, to rearrange the dispositions with a view to saving tax (and especially IHT) or to provide for someone who is omitted from the will or who is inadequately provided for. In these cases, persons named in the original will reject a portion of their inheritance; hence, they will (usually) be making a gratuitous transfer of value which will either constitute a chargeable lifetime transfer or a potentially exempt transfer. Other taxes too may be important—notably CGT and income tax.

Similar problems arise on an intestacy—indeed the statutory intestacy provisions will often prove even less satisfactory than a will.

So far as both IHT and CGT are concerned certain changes to a will, or to the intestacy rules, are permitted, if made within two years of death, to take effect as if they had been provided for in the original will (for IHT see IHTA 1984 s 142; for CGT, TCGA 1992 s 62(6)-(9): the CGT rules are considered at [**15.121**]). The effect of 'reading back' these changes into the will or amending the intestacy rules is to avoid the possibility of a second charge to IHT.

EXAMPLE 22.27

T by will leaves property to his three daughters equally. He omits his son with whom he had quarrelled bitterly. The daughters might agree to vary the will by providing that the four children take equally and, for the capital taxes, T's original will can be varied to make the desired provision. Hence, no daughter was taxed on the gift of a part of her share to her brother.

To take advantage of these provisions there must be a voluntary alteration of the testamentary provisions; in the case of enforced alterations: eg as a result of applications under the Inheritance (Provision for Family and Dependants) Act 1975, different provisions apply, see [**22.58**].   [**22.118**]

a) *Permitted ways of altering the will or intestacy*

There are two methods of altering the dispositions of a will or intestacy; by disclaimer or by variation. A *disclaimer* operates as a refusal to accept property and, hence, to be valid, should be made before any act of acceptance has occurred (such as receiving any benefit). When a disclaimer is effected the property passes according to fixed rules of law. It is not possible to disclaim in favour of a particular person. Hence, if a specific bequest is disclaimed the property falls into the residue of the will; if it is the residue itself which is disclaimed the property will pass as on an intestacy. Property can also be disclaimed on intestacy. A disclaimer is, therefore, an all or nothing event; it is not possible to retain part and disclaim the rest of a single gift. If, however, both a specific bequest and a share of residue are left to the same person, the benefit of one could be accepted and the other disclaimed.

In a *variation*, the deceased's provisions are altered at the choice of the person effecting the alteration so that the gift is redirected and the fact that some benefit had already accrued before the change (and that the estate had been fully administered) is irrelevant. Any part of a gift can be redirected. Unlike a beneficiary who disclaims, the person who makes the variation has owned an interest in the property of the deceased from the death up to the variation.   [**22.119**]

b) *The IHT rules on variations and disclaimers*

If the following conditions are satisfied the variation or disclaimer is not itself a transfer of value but instead takes effect as if the original will or intestacy had so provided:

(1) The variation or disclaimer must occur within two years of death. In the case of disclaimers it is likely that action will need to be taken soon after the death otherwise the benefit will have been accepted.

(2) The variation or disclaimer must be effected by an instrument in writing (in practice a deed should be used), executed by the person who would otherwise benefit.

(3) In the case of variations, where it is desired to 'read them back' into the original will, an election in writing to that effect must be made to the Revenue (within six months of the variation). This election should refer to the appropriate statutory provisions and must be made by the person making the variation and, where the effect of that election would be to increase the IHT chargeable on the death, also by the PRs. PRs can only refuse to join in the election, however, if they have insufficient assets in their hands to discharge the extra IHT bill (for instance, where administration of the estate had been completed and the assets distributed). No election is necessary in the case of a disclaimer which, assuming that the other requirements are satisfied, is automatically 'read back' into the will.

(4) A variation or disclaimer cannot be for money or money's worth, except where there are reciprocal disclaimers or other beneficiaries also disclaim for the ultimate benefit of a third person.

(5) All property comprised in the deceased's estate immediately before death can be redirected under these provisions except for property which the deceased was treated as owning by virtue of an interest in possession in a settlement (although in this case relief may be afforded by IHTA 1984 s 93) and property included in the estate at death because of the reservation of benefit rules.

EXAMPLE 22.28

(1) A and T were joint tenants. On the death of T, A can redirect the half share of the property that he acquired by right of survivorship taking advantage of IHTA 1984 s 142 (expressly confirmed in *Tax Bulletin*, October 1995, p 254).

(2) T by will created a settlement giving C a life interest. C can redirect that interest under IHTA 1984 s 142.

(3) T was the life tenant of a fund—the property now vests in D absolutely. D cannot take advantage of IHTA 1984 s 142 to assign his interest in the settled property. (Notice, however, that IHTA 1984 s 93 permits a beneficiary to disclaim an interest in settled property without that disclaimer being subject to IHT.)

(4) Mort had been life tenant of a trust fund and on his death the assets passed to his sister Mildred absolutely. He left his free estate equally to his widow and daughter. By a post-death variation the widow gave her half share to the daughter. Assuming that this variation is read back for IHT purposes the extra tax charged on Mort's death will adversely affect the trustees who are not required to consent to the election and are not protected by a deed of discharge (IHTA 1984 s 239(4)).

(5) Father leaves 100,000 shares in J Sainsbury plc to his daughter. She gives those shares to her son, within two years of his death, and reserves a collateral benefit. She elects to read the gift back into the will of her father and as her gift thereupon takes effect *for all IHT purposes* as if it had been made by the deceased the reservation of benefit rules are inapplicable.

(6) Boris, domiciled in France, leaves his villa in Tuscany and moneys in his Swiss

bank account to his son Gaspard, a UK resident. By a variation of the terms of his will made within two years of Boris' death, the property is settled on discretionary Liechtenstein trusts for the benefit of Gaspard's family. For IHT, reading back ensures that the settlement is excluded property (see [**27.21**]). For the CGT position see *Example 15.9*.

In the case of variations, the choice to elect or not to elect is with the taxpayer. A similar election operates for CGT but it is not necessary to exercise both IHT and CGT elections; they can be used separately (see [**15.121**]).

PRs of deceased beneficiaries can enter into variations and disclaimers which can be read back into the original will. Further, the estate of a beneficiary alive at the testator's death can be increased by such a variation or disclaimer (see *Tax Bulletin*, February 1995, p 194).   [**22.120**]

EXAMPLE 22.29

(1) T leaves property to his wealthy brother. The brother wishes to redirect it to grandchildren. An election for IHT purposes is advisable since (a) it will not increase the IHT charged on T's death and (b) it will avoid a second charge at the brother's rates if the brother were to die within seven years of the gift (for which quick succession relief would not be available—see [**22.113**]).

(2) T leaves residue to his widow. She wishes to redirect a portion to her daughter. If the election is made, the IHT on T's death may be increased because an exempt bequest is being replaced with one that is chargeable. If the election is not made, on T's death the residue remains exempt but the widow will make a potentially exempt transfer. If she survives by seven years no IHT will be payable: if she survives by three years tapering relief will apply. Even if the PET becomes chargeable, any IHT may be reduced by the widow's annual exemption (in the year when the transfer is made) and the chargeable transfer may fall within her nil rate band. In cases like this, it will be advantageous to ensure that T's nil rate band is fully used up by a reading back election but, once that has been done, given a single rate of tax (40%), there is no advantage in reading back the variation since the rate of tax on the death of the widow will be the same and, moreover, tax will not be charged at once.

(3) In examples like (2) above a variation may be employed to redirect a posthumous increase in the value of the estate without any IHT charge. Assume for instance that the death estate of £100,000 has increased in value to £225,000. T's widow could vary the will (electing to read the change back) to provide for a specific legacy of £100,000 to herself with the residue to her daughter. Under the provisions of IHTA 1984 ss 36–42 the death estate (£100,000) is attributed to the exempt legacy.

(4) H leaves £1 million to his only daughter, D. His widow, W, dies soon afterwards leaving a small estate to D. D should consider varying H's will so that (say) she retains £215,000 (to use up the nil rate band) and the remainder is left to W. D will then receive that sum from W's estate.

Note: In (4) above the variation is artificial since it is designed solely to reduce the total IHT bill. D is left with all the property. Accordingly it must be vulnerable to attack either under the *Ramsay* principle or on the basis that the dispositions of H's will have not been varied (although it is understood that the CTO do not at present take this point). Were D to redirect the benefit to her own children the variation could not then be attacked as wholly artificial since it would alter the ownership of the property.

c) *Other taxes*

So far as *stamp duty* is concerned variations in writing made within two years after the death are not subject to *ad valorem* duty provided that the appropriately worded certificate is included (see [**32.58**]). No duty is payable on disclaimers which are treated as a refusal to accept, not a disposition of, property.

As regards *income tax* there are no specific relieving provisions for variations and disclaimers. Accordingly, income arising between the date of death and the date of a variation will be taxed in accordance with the terms of the will and the rules governing the treatment of estate income (as to which see Chapter 12). With the new income tax regime (introduced from 6 April 1995) residuary income is taxed only when actually paid to the beneficiary: consequently if no income has been paid to a beneficiary who effects a variation of his entitlement, income tax will be charged only on future distributions to the 'new' beneficiary. To this extent therefore a form of reading back can apply for income tax purposes.

So far as a disclaimer is concerned the Revenue apparently considers that the basic income tax position is the same as for a variation, since the beneficiary's interest under the will remains intact up to the date of the disclaimer (see further *CTT News*, vol 5, p 142: it may be doubted whether this view is consistent with a disclaimer operating as a refusal to accept property).

A variation made by a beneficiary in favour of his own infant unmarried child creates a settlement for income tax purposes within TA 1988 Part XV (see [**11.62**]). Hence, income arising from the redirected property will be assessed as that of the parent (unless accumulated in a capital settlement). A disclaimer will escape these problems, if it is accepted that the property has never been owned by the disclaiming beneficiary. [**22.121**]

d) *Technical difficulties*

A number of technical problems have arisen in connection with instruments of variation. It was argued by the Revenue that for a variation to fall within the IHT relieving provision (IHTA 1984 s 142), the operative clause in the instrument of variation had to state that the transfer of property took effect as a variation to the provisions of a will or intestacy in order to avoid it being construed as a lifetime gift. Accordingly it was suggested that any variation should follow the wording of that section and provide as follows:

> 'The dispositions of property comprised in the estate of the testator (intestate) immediately before his death, shall be varied as follows . . .'

After further advice the Revenue apparently abandoned this view (see *Law Society's Gazette*, 1985, p 1454), but will, nevertheless, require the variation to indicate clearly the dispositions that are subject to it and vary their destination from that provided in the will or under the intestacy rules. Furthermore, the notice of election must refer to the appropriate statutory provisions. This change of position does not indicate that all technical objections to instruments of variation have been dropped and as the Revenue considers that the instrument *itself* must vary the dispositions the use of a deed would appear to be necessary (although a written instrument is sufficient to transfer an existing equitable interest under LPA 1925 s 53(1)(c)).

The second difficulty concerned multiple variations which had been employed (before 1985) in an attempt to avoid *ad valorem* stamp duty. Although this device is no longer necessary it resulted in the Revenue interpreting IHTA 1984 s 142 as permitting only one variation per beneficiary. Again this is a position from which it has retreated, at least in part (see *Law Society's Gazette*, 1985, p 1454); it now considers that an election, once made, is irrevocable and that s 142 will not apply to an instrument redirecting any item or part of any item that had already been redirected under an earlier instrument. Variations covering a number of items should ideally be made in one instrument 'to avoid any uncertainty', although the Revenue accepts that multiple variations by a single beneficiary are not, as such, prohibited.

EXAMPLE 22.30

Under Eric's will £50,000 is left to his brother Wally and £100,000 to his surviving spouse Berta. The following events then occur within two years of Eric's death:

(1)   Wally executes a deed of variation in favour of his own children.
(2)   Berta executes a deed varying £2,500 in favour of her sister Jennie and subsequently a second variation of £47,500 to Jennie.
(3)   Jennie executes a deed of variation of £25,000 in favour of her boyfriend Jonnie.

The variations in (1) and (2) satisfy the requirements of IHTA 1984 s 142 as interpreted by the Revenue and so may be read back into Eric's will, whereas the variation in (3) will not be so treated and, accordingly, will be a PET.

The decision of *Russell v IRC* (1988) confirmed the Revenue's interpretation of the legislation that a redirection of property already varied does not fall within s 142. The deceased had died in 1983 survived by his wife and four daughters. His estate included business assets (Lloyd's underwriting interests) which qualified for business property relief from the then CTT. Under his will, most of the estate passed to his widow and was not therefore subject to a tax charge. As a corollary, however, business property relief was therefore wasted as was the nil rate band. Not surprisingly, therefore, the family decided to vary the dispositions of his will by providing for each daughter to receive a pecuniary legacy of £25,000 to be raised out of the business property. They hoped that by giving away the business property worth £100,000 which would qualify for a reduction in value of 50%, some £50,000 of the testator's nil rate band would thereby be utilised. The Revenue, however, took the view that these legacies were gifts of cash not of qualifying business assets with the result that as no 50% relief was available a tax charge would arise since part of each legacy would then fall outside the nil rate band. Although the family did not accept this, they tried again in 1985 by executing a fresh deed of variation whereby each daughter was to receive instead of a cash legacy a proportionate share of the business assets worth £25,000.

Knox J had to decide whether this second deed was effective to carry out the family's intentions and if not whether the Revenue were correct in their interpretation of the 1983 deed. He decided that under the relevant statutory provision a benefit which had already been redirected once could not be further redirected and read back into the testator's will.

'My principal reason for accepting the Crown's submission that the hypothesis contained in s 142(1) should not be applied to that subsection itself is that this involves taking the hypothesis further than is necessary. No authority was cited to me of a statutory hypothesis being applied to the very provision which enacts the hypothesis. Such a tortuous process would merit a specific reference in the enactment to itself . . .' (Knox J at 204).

Accordingly, on the facts of this case, as there had already been a valid variation in 1983, the further amendment in 1985 could not be read back. Having so decided he then concluded, however, that the Revenue's arguments that the 1983 variation did not have the effect of varying interests in business property was misconceived. He pointed out that the relevant cash gifts could only be satisfied (in this particular case) by resorting to business assets and therefore he was of the opinion that a division of that property by reference to a cash sum should be treated in the same way as a division by reference to a fraction of the assets.

In *Lake v Lake* (1989) Mervyn Davis J held that a deed of variation can be rectified by the court if words mistakenly used mean that it does not give effect to the parties' joint intention. It does not matter that the rectification achieves a tax advantage nor that it is made more than two years after the death. The courts must, however, be satisfied that the deed as executed contains errors: in this case the variation was designed to give legacies to children of the deceased but as the result of a clerical error such gifts were expressed to be 'free of tax'. As residue passed to an exempt beneficiary (the surviving spouse) grossing-up was therefore necessary. The order for rectification substituted 'such gifts to bear their own tax' for 'free of tax' (see also *Matthews v Martin* (1991) and *Schnieder v Mills* (1993)). [**22.122**]

7 IHT and estate duty

Up to 13 March 1975 the estate duty regime operated. The various transitional provisions for estate duty and CTT/IHT are beyond the scope of this book although mention should be made of IHTA 1984 Sch 6 para 2 which preserves for IHT the former surviving spouse exemption. This exemption provided that, for estate duty purposes, where property was left to a surviving spouse in such circumstances that the spouse was not competent to dispose of it (for instance was given a life interest therein) estate duty would be charged on the first death but not again on the death of the survivor. This exemption was continued into the CTT (and now IHT) era by IHTA 1984 Sch 6 para 2 which excludes such property from charge whether the limited interest is terminated *inter vivos* or by the death of the surviving spouse. All too often this valuable exemption may be overlooked and an over-emphasis on the attractions of making PETs may have unfortunate results. [**22.123**]

EXAMPLE 22.31

(1) On his death in 1973, Samson left his wife Delilah a life interest in his share portfolio. She is still alive and in robust health and the trustees have a power to advance capital to her. Estate duty was charged on Samson's death but because of para 2 there will be no charge to IHT when Delilah's interest comes to an end. At first sight, there appear to be advantages if the trustees advance capital to Delilah which she then transfers by means of a PET. However, this arrangement carries with it the risk of that capital being subject to an IHT charge if Delilah dies within seven years of her gift. Accordingly, an interest which is tax free is being replaced by a potentially chargeable transfer.

(2) Terminating Delilah's interest during her life may, however, have other attractions. In particular, the exemption from charge in para 2 is limited to the value of the property in which the limited interest subsists but that property may, by forming part of Delilah's estate, affect the value of other assets in that estate. Assume, for instance, that Delilah owns 30% of the shares in a private company (Galilee Limited) in her own name and that a further 30% are subject to the life interest trust. When she dies she will be treated as owning 60% of the shares: a controlling holding which will be valued as such. Although one half of the value of that holding will be free from charge under para 2, the remaining portion will be taxed. Accordingly, it may be better in such cases for her life interest to be surrendered *inter vivos* even if that operation is only carried out on her deathbed.

23 IHT—exemptions and reliefs

I   Lifetime exemptions and reliefs   [**23.2**]
II   Death exemptions and reliefs   [**23.21**]
III Exemptions for lifetime and death transfers   [**23.41**]

Predictably, although in marked contrast to CGT, whole categories of property are not exempted from the IHT net. Hence, *excluded property*, which is ignored if transferred *inter vivos* and not taxed as part of the death estate, is restrictively defined in IHTA 1984 s 6 (see [**27.21**]).

Exemptions and reliefs apply in a number of situations: some for lifetime transfers only; some for death only; and some for all transfers, whether in lifetime or on death.

The exemptions may be justified on the grounds of necessity—some gifts must be permitted (eg Christmas and wedding presents); or, in the case of reliefs applicable to particular property, because it is desirable that the property should be preserved and not sold to pay the tax bill (eg business and agricultural property where relief up to 100% of the value is available).

The nil rate band (currently £215,000) is not an exempt transfer since transfers within this band are chargeable transfers, albeit taxed at 0%. Accordingly, exemptions and reliefs should be exhausted first so that the taxpayer's nil rate band is retained intact as long as possible.   [**23.1**]

I LIFETIME EXEMPTIONS AND RELIEFS

1 Transfers not exceeding £3,000 pa (IHTA 1984 s 19)

Up to £3,000 can be transferred free from IHT each tax year (6 April to 5 April). To the extent that this relief is unused in any one year it can be rolled forward for one tax year only. There is no general roll-forward since only where the value transferred in any year exceeds £3,000 is the shortfall from the previous year's £3,000 used.

EXAMPLE 23.1

A makes chargeable transfers of £2,500 in 1995–96; £2,800 in 1996–97; and £3,700 in 1997–98.
For 1995–96: no IHT (£3,000 exemption) and £500 is carried forward.
For 1996–97: no IHT (£3,000 exemption) and £200 only is carried forward. The £500 from 1995–96 could only have been used to the extent that the transfer in 1996–97 exceeded £3,000.
For 1997–98: IHT on £500 (£3,200 is exempt).

The relief can operate by deducting £3,000 from a larger gift. Where several chargeable gifts are made in the same tax year, earlier gifts will be given the relief first; if several such gifts are made on the same day there is a *pro rata* apportionment of the relief irrespective of the actual order of gifts. The relief applies also to settlements with interests in possession although in this case it will only be given if the life tenant so elects (see [**25.35**]).

The relationship between the annual exemption and the PET depends on the definition of a PET in IHTA 1984 s 3A:

'a transfer of value . . . which, apart from this section, would be a chargeable transfer (or to the extent which, apart from this section, it would be such a transfer) . . . '.

The position can therefore be stated in two propositions:
(1) a transfer of value which is wholly covered by the annual exemption is not a PET but *an exempt transfer in its own right*;
(2) a transfer of value which exceeds the annual exempt amount is *to that extent a PET*.

EXAMPLE 23.2

(1) In 1997–98 Peta gives her father £2,500. This gift is an exempt transfer.
(2) In the same tax year Beta gives her mother £6,500. Two annual exemptions mean that £6,000 is exempt: £500 is a PET.
(3) Cheeta intends to set up a discretionary trust for his family and to make an outright gift to his sister. He should make the discretionary trust first thereby using up his annual exemption and on a subsequent day make a PET to his sister.

What should a would-be donor do who does not wish to transfer assets/money to the value of £3,000, but at the same time is reluctant to see the exemption lost? One solution is to vest an interest in property in the donee whilst retaining control of the asset (although great care must be taken to ensure that a benefit is not retained in the portion given since a transfer falling within the annual exemption is still a gift for the reservation of benefit rules: see [**21.183**]). Selling the asset with the purchase price outstanding and releasing part of the debt each year equal to the annual exemption may fall foul of the associated operations rules (see [**21.81**]).   [**23.2**]

2   Normal expenditure out of income (IHTA 1984 s 21)

Section 21 provides as follows:
'a transfer of value is an exempt transfer if, or to the extent that, it is shown—
(a) that it was made as part of the normal expenditure of the transferor,
(b) that (taking one year with another) it was made out of his income, and
(c) that, after allowing for all transfers of value forming part of his normal expenditure, the transferor is left with sufficient income to maintain his usual standard of living.'

The legislation does not define (nor indeed seek to explain) 'usual standard of living' whilst the requirement that there must be regular payments out of income makes it impossible to apply this exemption to gifts of anything other than cash. Particular difficulties are presented by requirement (a): what evidence is required to prove that payments (or any payment) constitute normal expenditure? A pattern of payments is presumably required and this is most easily shown where the taxpayer is committed to making a series of payments as, for instance, where he enters into a deed of covenant. In other cases (eg where there is no legal commitment to make a series of payments) it has usually been assumed that a number of payments would have to be made before there was sufficient evidence of regularity.

Bennett v IRC (1995) casts some light on this problem. Mrs Bennett was the life tenant of a will trust established by her late husband, the gross annual income from which was, until 1987, £300 pa. In that year, as a result of the sale of the trust assets, the income of the trust increased enormously and Mrs Bennett (a lady of settled habits) indicated to the trustees that she wished her sons to have surplus trust income above what was needed to satisfy her relatively modest needs. Accordingly in 1989 each of the three sons received a distribution of £9,300 and in the following year £60,000. Mrs Bennett then unexpectedly died. The Inland Revenue contended that the 1989 and 1990 payments were failed PETs: the executors argued that they were exempt under s 21. The court acknowledged that requirements (b) and (c) were satisfied and so the matter turned on the meaning of 'normal expenditure'. This was explained by Lightman J as follows:

> 'the term "normal expenditure" connotes expenditure which at the time it took place accorded with the settled pattern of expenditure adopted by the transferor.
>
> The existence of the settled pattern may be established in two ways. First, an examination of the expenditure by the transferor over a period of time may throw into relief a pattern, eg a payment each year of 10% of all income to charity or members of the individual's family or a payment of a fixed sum or a sum rising with inflation as a pension to a former employee. Second, the individual may be shown to have assumed a commitment, or adopted a firm resolution, regarding his future expenditure and thereafter complied with it. The commitment may be legal (eg a deed of covenant), religious (eg a vow to give all earnings beyond the sum needed for subsistence to those in need) or moral (eg to support aged parents or invalid relatives). The commitment or resolution need have none of these characteristics but nonetheless be likewise effective as establishing a pattern, eg to pay the annual premiums on a life insurance qualifying policy gifted to a third party or to give a pre-determined part of his income to his children.
>
> For expenditure to be "normal" there is no fixed minimum period during which the expenditure should have occurred. All that is necessary is that on the totality of the evidence the pattern of actual or intended regular payment shall have been established and that the item in question conforms with that pattern. If the prior commitment or resolution can be shown, a single payment implementing the commitment or resolution may be sufficient. On the other hand if no such commitment or resolution can be shown, a series of payments may be required before the existence of the necessary pattern will emerge. The pattern need not be immutable; it must, however, be established that the pattern was intended to remain in place for more than a nominal period and indeed for a sufficient period (barring unforeseen circumstances) in order for any payment fairly to be regarded as a regular feature of the transferor's annual expenditure. Thus a "deathbed" resolution to make periodic payments "for life" and a payment made in accordance with such a determination will not suffice.
>
> The amount of the expenditure need not be fixed in amount nor indeed the individual recipient be the same. As regards quantum, it is sufficient that a formula or standard has been adopted by application of which the payment (which may be of a fluctuating amount) can be quantified eg 10% of any earnings whatever they may be, or the costs of a sick or elderly dependant's residence at a nursing home.'

On the basis of this analysis he concluded that the two payments were exempted under s 21. In the later case of *Nadin v IRC* (1997) not only did the payments exceed the taxpayer's income for the year but there was no evidence of a prior commitment or resolution and the payments did not form part of any pattern of expenditure.

EXAMPLE 23.3

A takes out a life insurance policy on his own life for £60,000 with the benefit of that policy being held on a trust for his grandchildren. A pays the premiums on the policy of £3,500 pa. He makes a transfer of value of £3,500 pa but he can make use of the normal expenditure exemption to avoid IHT so long as all the requirements for that exemption are satisfied. Alternatively, the £3,000 annual exemption would relieve most of the annual premium. (It is thought that even if the first premium was paid *before* the policy was settled, the normal expenditure exemption would apply to the value of the policy settled)

Anti-avoidance rules provide that:

(1) The normal expenditure exemption will not cover a life insurance premium unless the transferor can show that the life cover was not facilitated by and associated with an annuity purchased on his own life (IHTA 1984 s 21(2)).

(2) Under IHTA 1984 s 263 (unless the transferor can disprove the presumption of associated transactions, as above) an IHT charge can arise when the benefit of the life policy is vested in the donee. In general, if a charge arises, the sum assured by the life policy is treated as a transfer of value.

These special rules exist to prevent tax saving by the use of back-to-back insurance policies, as in the following example:

EXAMPLE 23.4

Tony pays an insurance company £50,000 in return for an annuity of £7,000 pa for the rest of his life. At the same time he enters into a life insurance contract on his own life for £50,000 written in favour of his brother Ted. The potential advantages are that on the death of Tony the sum of £50,000 is no longer part of his estate and the annuity has no value when he dies but can be used during his life to pay the premiums on the life insurance contract. The insurance proceeds will not attract IHT because they do not form part of his estate and Tony could claim that the premiums amounted to regular payments out of his income and so were free of IHT. The Revenue accepts that such arrangements are effective so long as the policies are not linked and, ideally, are taken out with different companies.

As with the annual exemption, this exemption does not prevent a gift from being caught by the reservation of benefit rules.   **[23.3]**

3   Small gifts (IHTA 1984 s 20)

Any number of £250 gifts can be made in any tax year by a donor provided that the gifts are to different donees. It must be an outright gift (not a gift into settlement) and the sum cannot be severed from a larger gift. The section provides that the transfers of value made to any one person in any one year must not exceed £250: accordingly, it is not possible to combine this small gifts exemption with the annual £3,000 exemption. A gift of £3,250 would, therefore, be exempt as to £3,000 (assuming that exemption was available) but the excess of £250 would not fall under s 20 even if the gift had been structured by means of two separate cheques.   **[23.4]**

4   Gifts in consideration of marriage (IHTA 1984 s 22)

The gift must be made before or contemporaneously with the marriage and only after marriage if in satisfaction of a prior legal obligation. It must be conditional upon the marriage taking place so that should the marriage not occur the donor must have the right to recover the gift (if this right is not exercised, there may be an IHT charge on the failure to exercise that right under IHTA 1984 s 3(3)). A particular marriage must be in contemplation; it will not suffice, for instance, for a father to make a gift to his two year old daughter expressed to be conditional upon her marriage on the fatalistic assumption that she is bound to get married eventually!

The exemption can be used to settle property, but only if the beneficiaries are limited to (generally) the couple, any issue, and spouses of such issue (see IHTA 1984 s 22(4)). Hence, a marriage cannot be used to effect a general settlement of assets within the family.

The sum exempt from IHT is:

(1) £5,000, if the donor is a parent of either party to the marriage. Thus, each of four parents can give £5,000 to the couple.

(2) £2,500, if the transferor is a remoter ancestor of either party to the marriage (eg a grandparent or great-grandparent) or if the transferor is a party to the marriage. The latter is designed to cover ante nuptial gifts since after marriage transfers between spouses are normally exempt without limit (see [23.41]).

(3) £1,000, in the case of any other transferors (eg a wedding guest).

When a gift of property is an exempt transfer because it was made in consideration of marriage, the reservation of benefit provisions do not apply. [23.5]

EXAMPLE 23.5

(1) Father gives son a Matisse sculpture on the occasion of the son's marriage. It is worth £5,000. Possession of the piece is retained by the father but as the transfer is covered by the marriage exemption his continued possession does not fall within the reservation rules.

(2) Mum gives daughter an interest in her house equal to £5,000 when the daughter marries. Although Mum continues to live in the house the reservation rules do not apply.

5 Dispositions for maintenance etc (IHTA 1984 s 11)

Dispositions listed in IHTA 1984 s 11 are not transfers of value so that they are ignored for IHT purposes. The Revenue takes the view that this exemption only applies to *inter vivos* dispositions, because 'disposition' is not adequate to cover the deemed disposition on death. [23.6]

Maintenance of a former spouse (IHTA 1984 s 11(1)(a))   Even without this provision such payments would in many cases escape IHT. If made before decree absolute, the exemption for gifts between spouses (see [23.41]) would operate and even after divorce they might escape IHT as regular payments out of income; or fall within the annual exemption; or be non-gratuitous transfers. What s 11 does is to put the matter beyond all doubt.

Two problems may be mentioned. *First*, maintenance is not defined, so that whether it could cover the transfer of capital assets (eg the former matrimonial home) is uncertain. *Secondly*, if the payer dies but payment is to continue for the lifetime of the recipient, the position is unclear in the light of the Revenue's view that this exemption is limited to *inter vivos* dispositions. [23.7]

Maintenance of children   Provision for the maintenance, education or training of a child of either party to a marriage (including stepchildren and adopted children) is not a transfer of value (IHTA 1984 s 11(2)). The maintenance can continue beyond the age of 18 if the child is in full-time education. Thus, school fees paid by parents escape IHT. Similar principles operate where the disposition is for the maintenance of a parent's illegitimate child (IHTA 1984 s 11(4)). A similar relief is given for the maintenance of other people's children if the child is an infant and not in the care of either parent; once the child is 18, not only must he be undergoing full-time education, but also the disponer must (in effect) have been *in loco parentis* to the child during his minority (IHTA 1984 s 11(2)). Hence, payment of school and college fees by grandparents will seldom escape IHT under this provision.   **[23.8]**

Care or maintenance of a dependent relative   The provision of maintenance whether direct or indirect must be reasonable and the relative (as defined in IHTA 1984 s 11(6)) must be incapacitated by old age or infirmity from maintaining himself (although mothers and mothers-in-law who are widowed or separated are always dependent relatives).   **[23.9]–[23.20]**

II   DEATH EXEMPTIONS AND RELIEFS

1   Woodlands (IHTA 1984 ss 125–130)

This relief takes effect by deferring IHT on growing trees and underwood forming part of the deceased's estate. Their value is left out of account on the death. An election must be made for the relief by written notice given (normally) within two years after the death (s 125(3)). It is not available where the woodlands qualify for agricultural relief (see **[23.58]**) and commercial woodlands will commonly qualify for business property relief (see **[23.42]**). (With the introduction of 100% for 'relevant business property' this relief has become less important.)

To prevent deathbed IHT saving schemes the land must not have been purchased by the deceased in the five years before his death (note, however, that the relief is available if the woodlands were obtained by gift or inheritance within the five-year period). If the timber is transferred on a second death no tax is chargeable on later disposals by reference to the first death (s 126). The relief does not apply to the land itself, but any IHT charged as a result of death can be paid in instalments. The deferred tax on the timber may become chargeable as follows: **[23.21]**

Sale of the timber with or without the land   IHT will be charged on the net proceeds of sale, but deductions can be made for costs of selling the timber and also for the costs of replanting. The net proceeds are taxed according to full IHT rates at the date of the disposal and the tax is calculated by treating those proceeds as forming the highest part of the deceased's estate. Business property relief (at 50%) may be available where the trees or underwood formed a business asset at the date of death and, but for the deferment election, would have qualified for that relief at that time. In such cases the relief is given against the net proceeds of sale (IHTA 1984 s 127).   **[23.22]**

A gift of the timber   Not only is the deferred charge triggered by a gift of the timber, but also the gift itself may be subject to IHT subject to the availability of business relief. In calculating the tax payable on the lifetime gift the value transferred is reduced by the triggered IHT charged on the death and the tax can be paid by interest-free instalments (whoever pays the IHT) spread over ten years (IHTA 1984 s 229).   **[23.23]**

EXAMPLE 23.6

(1)   Wally Wood dies in January 1992 with a death estate of £200,000. In addition, he owns at death woodlands with the growing timber valued at £40,000 and the land etc valued at £30,000. The woodlands exemption is claimed by his daughter Wilma. In 1997 she sells the timber; the net proceeds of sale are £50,000.

    (i)   *Position on Wally's death:* The timber is left out of account. The value of the rest of the business (£30,000) attracts 50% business relief (the relevant level of relief in 1992: see (3) below), so that only £15,000 will be added to the £200,000 chargeable estate.

(ii) *Position on Wilma's sale:* The IHT charge is triggered. The net proceeds are reduced by 50% business relief to £25,000 which will be taxed according to the rates of IHT in force in 1997 for transfers between £215,000 (ie Wally's total chargeable death estate) and £240,000.

(2) As in (1), above except that Wilma settles the timber on her brother Woad in 1997 when its net value is £50,000. The deferred charge will be triggered as in para (ii) of (1), above. IHT on Wilma's gift will be calculated according to IHT rates in force for 1997. She can deduct from the net value of the timber the deferred tax ((1), above) and any IHT can be paid by instalments whether it is paid by her or by Woad.

(3) With the increase in the level of BPR to 100% in 1992, the woodlands election should not be made in such cases today: instead of a partial deferment of charge the business is wholly tax free.

PETs and estate duty Estate duty was not charged on the value of timber, trees, wood or underwood growing on land comprised in an estate at death. Instead, tax was deferred until such time as the woodlands were sold and was then levied at the death estate rate on the net proceeds of sale (subject to the proviso that duty could not exceed tax on the value of the timber at the date of the death). Pending sale, duty was therefore held in suspense and this deferral period only ceased on the happening of a later death when the woodlands again became subject to duty. The introduction of a charge on lifetime gifts with the advent of CTT resulted in this deferral period terminating immediately after the first transfer of value occurring after 12 March 1975 in which the value transferred was determined by reference to the land in question (subject only to an exclusion if that transfer was to the transferor's spouse and therefore exempt from CTT: see FA 1975 s 49(4)). In such cases, the deferred estate duty charge was superseded by a charge to CTT on the transfer value.

With the introduction of the PET it was realised that a transfer of value of woodlands subject to estate duty deferral to another individual would, *prima facie*, be a PET but that the transfer would have the effect of ending the deferral period thereby cancelling any charge to duty without a compensating charge to IHT. Hence, Sch 19 para 46 provides that transfers of value which fall within FA 1975 s 49(4) and thereby bring to an end the estate duty deferral period *shall not be PETs*. Accordingly, such transfers remain immediately chargeable to IHT at the transferor's rates (with the possibility of a supplementary charge should he die within the following seven years). **[23.24]**

EXAMPLE 23.7

On his death in May 1973 Claude left his landed estate to his son Charles. That estate included woodlands valued, in 1973, at £6,000. Consider the tax position in the following three situations:

(1) *If Charles sells the timber in 1997 for £16,000:* The net proceeds of sale will be subject to an estate duty charge levied at Claude's estate rate but duty will be limited by reference to the value of the timber in 1973 (ie it will be charged on £6,000).

(2) *If Charles retains the timber until his death in 1997 when it passes to his daughter:* This transfer of value will end the estate duty deferral period so that the potential charge to duty will be removed. However, the transfer to his daughter will be subject to an IHT charge unless the woodlands deferral election under IHTA 1984 s 125 ff is claimed.

(3) *If Charles makes an inter vivos gift of his estate (including the woodlands) in August 1997 to his daughter:* Such a gift will not be potentially exempt because of para 46. Accordingly, it will terminate the estate duty suspense period, and will result

in an immediate IHT charge levied according to Charles' rates. From the wording of para 46 it is not clear whether any part of this transfer can be potentially exempt or whether the entire value transferred is subject to an immediate charge. Undoubtedly the value of the timber will attract such a charge and likewise it would seem that the value of the land on which the timber is growing will fall outside the definition of a PET (see the wording of FA 1975 s 49(4)). What, however, if the transfer of value made by Charles includes other property, eg other parts of a landed estate which are not afforested? There was a danger that none of the value transferred would be a PET since para 46 is not limited to that part of any transfer of value comprising the woodlands. The injustice is recognised by ESC F15 which states that 'the scope of [para 46] will henceforth be restricted solely to that part of the value transferred which is attributable to the woodlands which are the subject of the deferred charge'.

2   Death on active service (IHTA 1984 s 154)

IHTA 1984 s 154 ensures that the estates of persons dying on active service, including members of the UDR and RUC killed by terrorists in Northern Ireland, are exempt from IHT. This provision has been generously interpreted to cover a death arising many years after a wound inflicted whilst on active service, so long as that wound was one of the causes of death; it need not have been the only, or even the direct cause (*Barty-King v Ministry of Defence* (1979)). Although a *donatio mortis causa* is covered by the exemption it does not apply to lifetime transfers.   [**23.25**]-[**23.40**]

III   EXEMPTIONS FOR LIFETIME AND DEATH TRANSFERS

1   The inter-spouse exemption (IHTA 1984 s 18)

This most valuable exemption from IHT for transfers between spouses is unlimited in amount except where the donor spouse is but the donee spouse is not domiciled in the UK when the amount excluded from IHT is £55,000 (this figure is currently under review). The use of this exemption is considered in different parts of this book and the following points represent a summary of those sections:

(1) For tax planning purposes the lowest total IHT bill is produced if both spouses use up their nil rate bands (see [**40.74**]).

(2) Both should take advantage of the lifetime exemptions. The Revenue will normally not invoke the associated operations provisions to challenge a transfer between spouses even if it enables this to occur ([**21.81**]).

(3) The rules for related property are designed to counter tax saving by splitting assets between spouses (see [**21.67**]).

(4) IHT on a chargeable transfer by one spouse to a third party may be collected from the other spouse in certain circumstances (see [**21.141**]).   [**23.41**]

2   Business property relief ('BPR': IHTA 1984 ss 103–114)

Business (and agricultural property) relief was introduced in order to ensure that businesses were not broken up by the imposition of an IHT charge. BPR takes effect by percentage reduction in the value transferred by a transfer of value and, prior to 10 March 1992, that reduction was at either 50% or 30%. For transfers made on and after that date the levels were increased to 100% and 50% with the result that most family businesses and farms were taken outside the tax net. The relief is given automatically.   [**23.42**]

a) *Meaning of 'relevant business property'*

Business property relief is given in respect of transfers of 'relevant business property' which is defined as any of the following:

(1) *A business:* Eg that of a sole trader or sole practitioner (s 105(1)(a)). A sole trader who transfers a part of his trade falls within this category and this may include a transfer of settled land (of which he is the life tenant) which is used in the business (*Fetherstonehaugh v IRC* (1984)).

(2) *An interest in a business:* Eg the share of a partner in either a trading or professional partnership (s 105(1)(a)).

(3) *Listed shares or securities which gave the transferor control of the company (s 105(1)(cc)):* Control itself does not have to be transferred; the requirement is simply that *at the time of transfer* the transferor should have such control (see [**23.50**]).

(4) *Securities which gave the transferor control of the company (s 105(1)(b)):* Similar comments to those in (3) apply: unquoted shares include shares dealt in on the Unlisted Securities Market and on the Alternative Investment Market ('AIM').

(5) *Any unquoted shares in a company (s 105(1)(bb)).*

(6) *Any land or building, plant or machinery which immediately before the transfer was used by a partnership in which the transferor was a partner or by a company of which he had control (s 105(1)(d)):* Control for these purposes requires a majority of votes (50%+) on all questions affecting the company as a whole (see (3) and (4), above). Hence, an unjust result is produced if the appropriate asset is used by a company in which the transferor owned 25% of the ordinary shares when no relief will be available. Had the asset been used by a partnership, however, irrespective of his profit share relief would be available. Relief is also available if the asset is held in a trust but is used by a life tenant for his own business or by a company which he controls.

The relief is given irrespective of whether a rent is charged for the use of the asset; in practice, however, a nominal rent only should be reserved to preserve CGT retirement relief (see [**16.109**]). [**23.43**]

b) *Amount of relief*

Relief is given by percentage reduction in the value of the business property transferred: ie on the value of assets used for business purposes less liabilities incurred for business purposes (IHTA 1984 s 110(b). The value cannot be increased by charging business debts on non-business property: *contrast* agricultural relief. The chargeable transfer will be of that reduced sum. Business property relief is applied before other reliefs (for instance, the £3,000 *inter vivos* annual exemption). The appropriate percentage depends upon which category of business property is involved.

100% relief is available for businesses, interests in businesses, and all shareholdings in unquoted companies (ie categories (1), (2), (4) and (5), above).

50% relief is available for controlling shareholdings in listed companies (category (3), above) and for assets used by a business (category (6), above). [**23.44**]

EXAMPLE 23.8

Topsy is a partner in the firm of Topsy & Tim (builders). He owns the site of the firm's offices and goods yard. He settles the following property on his daughter Teasy for life: (1) his share of the business (value £500,000) and (2) the site (value £50,000). Business property relief will be available on the business at 100% so that the value transferred is reduced to nil and on the site at 50% so that the value transferred is £25,000.

Notes:
(i) Topsy's total transfers amount to £25,000 which may be further reduced if other exemptions are available.
(ii) IHT may remain payable on business property after deducting the 50% (and any other) relief(s). Whether the chargeable transfer is made during lifetime or on death, it will usually be possible to pay the tax by interest-free instalments (see [**23.51**] for a discussion of the position when IHT or additional IHT is charged because of death within seven years of a chargeable transfer).

c) *The two-year ownership requirement*

In general, relevant business property which has been owned for less than two years attracts no relief (IHTA 1984 s 106). However, the incorporation of a business will not affect the running of the two-year period (IHTA 1984 s 107) and if a transfer of a business is made between spouses on death, the recipient can include the ownership period of the deceased spouse. This is not, however, the case with an *inter vivos* transfer (IHTA 1984 s 108). If the spouse takes the property as the result of a written variation read back into the will under IHTA 1984 s 142 the recipient is treated as being entitled to property on the death of the other spouse. When entitlement results from an appropriation of assets by the PRs this provision would not, however, apply.   [**23.45**]

EXAMPLE 23.9

(1)   Solomon incorporated his leather business by forming Solomon Ltd in which he holds 100% of the issued shares. For business property relief the two-year ownership period begins with the commencement of Solomon's original leather business.
(2)   Solomon set up his family company one year before his death and left the shares to his wife in his will. She can include his one-year ownership period towards satisfying the two-year requirement. If he made a lifetime gift to her aggregation is not possible.
(3)   If Mrs Solomon had died within two years of the gift from her husband (whether that gift had been made *inter vivos* or on death) business relief will be available on her death so long as the conditions for relief were satisfied at the time of the earlier transfer by her husband (IHTA 1984 s 109). A similar result follows if the gift from her husband had been by will and she had made a lifetime chargeable transfer of the property within two years of his death (in this case relief could be afforded under s 109 and, if Mr Solomon had not satisfied the two-year requirement, his period of ownership could be aggregated with that of Mrs Solomon under s 108).

d) *Non qualifying activities*

The relief is not available if a business 'consists wholly or mainly . . . of dealing in securities, stock or shares, land or buildings or making or holding investments' (IHTA 1984 s 105(3)).

For income tax purposes there cannot be a *trade* of 'letting land' (see [**8.23**] although note that the new Schedule A treats all lettings as a business) but the activities of a commercial landlord may amount to a *business* (see *Taxation*, 3 May 1990, p 126). Provided that the letting involved more than merely 'holding investments', BPR had been given by the Special Commissioners in a case involving a commercial landlord who maintained a high quality of service to his professional tenants (embracing primarily cleaning operations and maintenance and decoration) and whose daily activities and obligations far exceeded those normally placed on the holder of an investment. Two recent Special Commissioner decisions have, however, refused BPR holding that the activities of the taxpayer (which included finding tenants and granting leases, exterior painting and repairs, and management) although amounting to a buisness, were part and parcel of the business of making or holding investments and hence did not qualify for relief (*Martin v IRC; Burkinyoung v IRC* (1995)). Section 105(3) incorporates a 'wholly or mainly' test. Accordingly, a business which owns investments — retained for the purpose of the business — will still count as 'relevant business property' provided that the business has not become wholly or mainly one of investment management (see *Brown's Excecutors v IRC* (1996)). In *Hall and Another (Executors Hall deceased)* (1997) the Special Commissioners held that the main business of a caravan park was the receipt of rent and hence was an investment business (and see *Powell and An'or (PRs of Pearce dec'd) v IRC* (1997)).   **[23.46]**

e) *Excepted assets*

Private assets cannot be disguised as a part of the business in an attempt to take advantage of the relief (IHTA 1984 s 112: see the same problem in CGT **[16.111]**)   **[23.47]**

f) *Contracts to sell the business and options*

As it is designed for businesses, relief is not available for transfers of the sale proceeds from a business and the relief does not extend to a business subject to a 'buy and sell' agreement. Arrangements are common in partnership agreements and amongst shareholder/directors of companies to provide that if one of the partners or shareholder/directors dies then his PRs are obliged to sell the share(s) and the survivors are obliged to purchase them. As this is a binding contract, the beneficial ownership in the business or shares has passed to the purchaser so that business relief is not available.

EXAMPLE 23.10

The shares of Zerzes Ltd are owned equally by the four directors. The articles of association provide that on the death of a shareholder his shares *shall* be sold to the remaining shareholder/directors who *must* purchase them. Business relief is not available on that death. If the other shareholders had merely possessed pre-emption rights or if the arrangement had involved the use of options, as no binding contract of sale exists, the relief would apply.

Particular problems may arise to the context of partnership agreements: professional partnerships, for instance, commonly include automatic accruer clauses whereby the share of a deceased partner passes automatically to the surviving partners with his estate being entitled to payment either on a valuation or in accordance with a formula. After considerable uncertainty the Revenue now accept that accruer clauses do not constitute binding contracts for sale and nor do option arrangements (*Law Society's Gazette*, (1996) Sept 4, at p 35).   **[23.48]**

g) *Businesses held in settlements*

For interest in possession trusts the relief is given, as one would expect, by reference to the life tenant. So long as he satisfies the two-year ownership test, relief will be given at the following rates:
(1) *100% relief* for all unquoted shares and for businesses belonging to the trust;
(2) *50% relief* for controlling shareholdings in listed companies held in the trust; and

(3) *50% relief* for the assets listed in (6) at [**23.43**] which are held in the trust and which are either used by the life tenant for his own business or by a company controlled by him. The case of *Fetherstonehaugh v IRC* (1984) concerned the availability of relief when land held under a strict settlement was used by the life tenant as part of his farming business (he was a sole trader absolutely entitled to the other business assets). The Court of Appeal held that 100% (then 50%) relief was available under s 105(1)(a) on the land in the settlement with the result that the subsequent introduction of 50% (then 30%) relief is apparently redundant in such cases. The Revenue now accepts that in cases similar to *Fetherstonehaugh* the maximum 100% relief will be available since the land will be treated as an 'asset used in the business' and, as its value is included in the transfer of value, the land will be taxed on the basis that the deceased was the absolute owner of it.

For trusts without interests in possession the relief is given to the trust so long as the conditions are satisfied by the trustees. The relief will be given against the anniversary charge and when the business ceases to be relevant property (eg when it leaves the trust) relief will again be available on fulfilment of the normal conditions.   [**23.49**]

h) *'Control' for business property relief*

Control is defined in IHTA 1984 s 269(1) as follows:

> 'a person has control of a company at any time if he then has the control of powers of voting on *all questions* affecting the company as a whole which if exercised would yield a majority of the votes capable of being exercised thereon . . .' (IHTA 1984 s 269(1) and see *Walding's Executors v IRC* (1996)).

Hence, control of more than 50% of the votes exercisable in general meeting will ensure that the transferor has 'control' for the purposes of business property relief. A transfer of his shares will therefore attract 100% relief (in a listed company, 50% relief) and a transfer of qualifying assets used by that company, 50% relief. In calculating whether he has control, a life tenant can aggregate shares held by the settlement with shares in his free estate, whilst the related property rules (see [**21.67**]) result in shares of husband and wife being treated as one holding.   [**23.50**]

i) *Relief for minority shareholdings in unquoted companies*

For transfers of value made and other events occurring on or after 6 April 1996 relief at 100% is available for all minority shareholdings in unquoted companies (including companies listed on AIM). Prior to that date relief at 100% was only available for substantial minority shareholdings (ie 25% plus) in such companies with smaller shareholdings attracting only 50% relief. As a result of the change all shares in unquoted companies may now attract 100% relief irrespective of the size of holding: the continuing distinction in the legislation between controlling shareholdings and others remains important where assets are owned ouside the company.   [**23.51**]

j) *Problem areas*

It might be assumed that because of the two-year ownership requirement, both the business property (eg the shares) and control must have been owned throughout this period. This, however, does not appear to be the case for relief under s 105(1)(b) since it is only the shares transferred which must have been owned for two years and control is only required immediately before the relevant transfer. Thus the taxpayer may—for instance as the result of a buy-back—obtain control of the company many years after acquiring his shares.

EXAMPLE 23.11
Of the 100 issued ordinary shares in Buy-Back Ltd Zack owns 40, Jed 40 and the remaining 20 are split amongst miscellaneous charities. Assume that in July 1996 Buy-Back buys Zack's holding. As those shares are cancelled the issued capital falls to 60 shares of which Jed owns 40. Were he to die in September 1996, his shareholding would fall under s 105(1)(b).

In addition to control passing to a shareholder as a result of such extraneous events as a buy-back it may be possible for the partners in a quasi-partnership company to ensure that each obtains control for a short period (eg one month) if that would produce enhanced business relief. **[23.52]**

EXAMPLE 23.12
The shares in ABCD Ltd are owned as to 25% each by A, B, C and D. The shares are divided into four classes in December 1996 which will carry control in January, February, March and April 1997 respectively. In January 1997 A transfers his shares.
(1) As A has control (under s 269(1)) in January 1997 he is entitled to 100% relief under s 105(1)(b) and if, at the same time, he transferred land, which had been used by his company, 50% relief would be available on that transfer.
(2) Might temporary shifts of control be nullified under the *Ramsay* principle? It is arguable that, as the legislation expressly requires control at one moment only (viz immediately before the transfer), that is an end to the matter. It is, however, desirable that A should at the time of transfer actually possess control of the business: ie the other shareholders must accept that A could, if he wished, exercise his voting control over the affairs of the company.

k) *Business relief and the instalment option*

After deducting business property relief at the appropriate percentage, the reduced value of the business (for instance after the deduction of 50% relief) may attract IHT although with the general availability of 100% releif this is currently of reduced importance: note, however, that the option may be valuable where there are excepted assets or where the business is disqualified under the s 105(3) test (see **[23.46]**). This is because of the definition of 'qualifying property' for the purposes of s 227 (the instalment option) and s 234 (interest-free instalments) is wider than for the purposes of BPR. Any value transferred after deduction BPR may also be further reduced. Thus the normal IHT exemptions and reliefs are deducted *after* business relief so that a lifetime gift, for instance, may be reduced by the £3,000 annual exemption. Further, any tax payable may normally be spread over ten years and paid by annual interest-free instalments (see **[22.49]**). This instalment election is only available, in the case of lifetime gifts, if the IHT is borne by the donee: on death the election should be made by the PRs. It should be noted that, although there is a striking similarity between assets which attract business relief and assets qualifying for the instalment option, there are limitations on the availability of instalment relief in the case of a transfer of unquoted shares not giving control (as defined in s 269, **[23.50]**), as the following table indicates:

Relevant business property (IHTA 1984, Pt V, Ch 1)	*Instalment assets* (IHTA 1984, Pt VIII)
s 105 (1)(a): a business or an interest in a business	*s 227*: a business or an interest in a business

Relevant business property	*Instalment assets*
s 105(1)(b): shares etc, giving control	*s 228(1)(a)*: shares etc, giving control
s 105(1)(bb): unquoted shares	*s 228(1)(c)*: unquoted shares with hardship; *s 228(1)(b)*: on death, unquoted shares being at least 20%, of the total transfer; *s 228(1)(d)* and *228(3)*: unquoted shares within the 10% and £20,000 rule; *s 229*: woodlands; and *s 227(2)*: land

These limitations on the instalment option have been defended by the Inland Revenue on the grounds that 'it has been considered inappropriate for the instalment facility to apply in cases involving less than substantial interests in unquoted companies' (see further (1985) 6 *CTT News* 284).   [**23.53**]

l) *PETs and additional IHT—when is relief available?*

When a transferor makes a lifetime chargeable transfer or a PET and dies within seven years, the IHT or extra IHT payable is calculated on the basis that business relief is not available unless the original (or substituted) property remains owned by the transferee at the death of the transferor (or at the death of the transferee if earlier) and would qualify for business relief immediately before the transferor's death (ignoring, however, the two-year ownership requirement). This 'clawback' of relief is somewhat anomalous: relief on death is not similarly withdrawn if the business property is sold by the beneficiary under the will. The instalment option is similarly restricted since it is only available if the original or substituted business property is owned by the transferee at death. Relief is given for substituted property when the entire (net) proceeds of sale of the original property are reinvested within three years (or such longer period as the Board may allow) in the replacement qualifying property (for the position where business property is replaced by agricultural property and *vice versa* see *Tax Bulletin*, 1994, p 182 and [**23.66**]).

EXAMPLE 23.13

(1) Sim gives his ironmonger's business to his daughter, Sammy, in 1994 (a PET) and dies in 1997. Sammy has continued to run the business. Although the PET becomes chargeable because of Sim's death within seven years, 100% relief is available (qualifying property retained by donee).

(2) As in (1) save that Sammy immediately sold the business in 1994.
No business relief is available on Sim's death. The value of the business in 1994 is taxed and forms part of Sim's cumulative total on death.

(3) As in (1) save that Sammy had incorporated the business late in 1994 and had continued to run it as the sole shareholder/director.
Business relief is available on Sim's death (substituted qualifying property).

(4) Sim settles business property on accumulation and maintenance trusts (a PET). At some point before the death of Sim a beneficiary either becomes entitled to an interest in possession in the settled property or, alternatively, absolutely entitled. Has the transferee retained business property in these cases so that the original gift continues to qualify for relief? In the former situation (where a life interest has come into being) common sense would suggest the answer is 'yes' since the property is owned throughout the period by the transferee who in this case would be the trustees. The Revenue disagrees, however, on the basis that under IHTA 1984 s 49(1) the life tenant is treated as owning the capital assets. In the latter case beneficial title has passed to the beneficiary.

Accordingly, *a clawback charge arises in both cases*. If the original settlement had been on interest in possession trusts and by the time of the settlor's death the trustees had advanced the property (under the terms of the trust) to the life tenant there would be no clawback since the life tenant is treated as the 'transferee' throughout.

EXAMPLE 23.14

Jock settles his business (then worth £500,000) on discretionary trusts in 1993 (a chargeable lifetime transfer). He dies in 1997 when the business has been sold by the trustees.

(1) *On the 1997 transfer*: 100% relief is available so that the value transferred is £nil.
(2) *On his death in 1997*: no relief is available so that extra IHT is calculated on a value transferred of £500,000. Note that the result of a withdrawal of relief is that the additional tax is charged on the entire value of the business but this does not alter Jock's cumulative total (*contrast* the effect of loss of relief when the original transfer was a PET: see *Example 23.13(2)*).

There was a technical argument that if the gifted property attracted 100% relief it was an exempt transfer either under IHTA 1984 s 20 (see [**23.4**]) or under s 19 (see [**23.2**]). If so, the transfer could be neither chargeable nor potentially exempt with the result that the clawback rules did not apply! (See *Private Client Business*, 1992, p 7). 'For the removal of doubt' FA 1996 inserted a new sub-s (7A) into s 113A which provided that in determining whether there was a PET or chargeable transfer for the purposes of the clawback rules any reduction in value under the BPR rules was ignored.　　　　　　　　[**23.54**]

m) *Business property subject to a reservation*

Business property subject to a reservation is treated as comprised in the donor's estate at death (if the reservation is still then subsisting) or, if the reservation ceases *inter vivos*, as forming the subject matter of a deemed PET made at that time (see generally [**21.183**]). In both cases business relief may be available to reduce the value of the property subject to charge. Whether the relief is available or not is generally decided by treating the transfer as made by the *donee* who must therefore satisfy the business property relief requirements (FA 1986 Sch 20 para 8). However, for these purposes, the period of ownership of the donor can be included with that of the donee in order to satisfy the two-year requirement.

Any question of whether shares or securities qualify for 100% business property relief must be decided as if the shares or securities were owned by the *donor* and had been owned by him since the date of the gift. Accordingly, other shares of the donor (or related property of the donor) will be relevant in deciding if these requirements are satisfied.　　　　　　　　[**23.55**]

EXAMPLE 23.15

(1) Wainwright gives his ironmonger's business to his daughter Tina and it is agreed that he shall be paid one half of the net profits from the business each year (a gift with reservation).
　(i) At the time of the original gift (a PET) the property satisfied the requirements for business relief. If the PET becomes chargeable as the result of Wainwright's death within the following seven years, relief continues to be available if Tina has retained the original property or acquired replacement property.
　(ii) The business is also treated as forming part of Wainwright's estate on his death under FA 1986 s 102, but business relief may be available to

reduce its value under FA 1986 Sch 20 para 8. Whether relief is available (and if so at what percentage) is decided by treating the transfer of value as made by the *donee*. Accordingly, Tina must satisfy the conditions for relief although she can include the period of ownership/occupation of Wainwright before the gift. (A similar provision applies if the reservation ceases during Wainwright's lifetime so that he is treated as making a PET.)

(2) Assume that Wainwright owns 100% of the shares in Widgett's Ltd and gives 20% of those shares to Tina subject to a reserved benefit. Assuming that he dies within seven years:
  (i) Relief at 100% was originally available under s 105(1)(b) when the gift was made and continues to apply to that chargeable PET if Tina has retained the shares.
  (ii) The shares are treated as forming part of Wainwright's estate because of the reserved benefit. Business relief will be available if Tina satisfies the basic requirements: ie she must have retained the original shares which must still qualify as business property.

Note: Where property attracting 100% relief is transferred by outright gift it may be argued that this is an exempt gift under IHTA 1984 s 20 (see [**23.4**]) with the result that the reservation of benefit rules cannot apply (see FA 1986 s 102(5)(b)).

n) *The consequences of relief at 100%*

For transfers on and after 10 March 1992, 100% relief is available provided that the appropriate conditions are satisfied. This change has had far-reaching consequences. For instance:

(1) It is more important than ever to ensure that full relief is not lost because of a technicality (see [**23.46**]).
(2) Consideration should be given to the structuring of business activity so that the relief is readily available: simple structures are likely to be best and fragmentation arrangements that have been common in the past may prove disadvantageous.
(3) Relief at 100% is equally available in the case of unquoted companies and in the case of sole traders and partnerships.
(4) In contrast to the relief available for heritage property, there is no clawback of the 100% relief on death if the heir immediately sells the assets: if heritage property is or can be run as a business it would be more attractive to use BPR than the heritage exemption.
(5) If lifetime gifts are made and the donor dies within seven years, relief may not be available if the donee has already sold the assets (see [**23.54**]). Because there is no clawback on death taxpayers may be encouraged to delay passing on property qualifying for 100% relief.
(6) If it is feared that the new reliefs will be withdrawn by a future government, a gift of property on to flexible trusts under which the donor retains control as trustee should be considered (note, however, the trap if it is envisaged that the property will be distributed within the first ten years of the trust: see [**26.34**]).
(7) Wills should be reviewed to ensure that property which is eligible for 100% BPR in the hands of the testator but which will not qualify for relief in the hands of the surviving spouse (such as Lloyd's interests or partnership interests where the spouse cannot take on the business activity) are left direct to children.
(8) Business property relief is intended to benefit businesses as opposed to investments but this objective has not been fully achieved. Investment opportunities exist. Investments in limited partnerships may attract 100%

relief and a USM or AIM portfolio, qualifying for relief at 100%, may be attractive.

(9) In some cases it may be worth de-listing: ie turning the fully quoted company back into an unquoted company or one dealt in on AIM because of the higher levels of relief available.

(10) The increased levels of relief are available in the case of gifts made *before* 10 March 1992 if 'an event occurs on or after that date'. Assume that Sim gave his business to his daughter in 1991 (when relief available was at 50%) and that he now dies. If she has retained the business property the value of the failed PET will be reduced to zero by the 100% relief. **[23.56]**

3 Agricultural property relief ('APR': IHTA 1984 ss 115–124)

IHTA 1984 ss 115–124 contain the rules, introduced originally in FA 1981, giving relief for transfers of agricultural property. As with BPR, this relief is given automatically. The old (pre-1981) regime will not be considered save for a brief mention of the transitional provisions. **[23.57]**

a) 'Agricultural property' (IHTA 1984, s 115(2))

Relief is given for transfers of value of *agricultural property*, defined in s 115(2) as follows:

> '"Agricultural property" means agricultural land or pasture and includes woodland and any building used in connection with the intensive rearing of livestock or fish if the woodland or building is occupied with agricultural land or pasture and the occupation is ancillary to that of the agricultural land or pasture; and also includes such cottages, farm building and farmhouses, together with the land occupied with them, as are of a character appropriate to the property.'

This definition includes habitat land and land used for short rotation coppice (this being a way of producing renewal fuel for bio-mass-fed power stations. In simple terms, willow or other cuttings are planted on farmland and, after the first year, are harvested every three years or so and then made into chips which are used as fuel.)

Farm cottages included in the definition of 'agricultural property' must have been occupied for the purposes of agriculture (see s 117(1)); ESC F16 extends relief in such cases to include a cottage occupied by a retired farm employee or his surviving spouse provided that either the occupier is a statutorily protected tenant or the occupation is under a lease granted to the farm employee for his life and that of any surviving spouse as part of his contract of employment by the landlord for agricultural purposes.

Starke v IRC (1995) concerned the transfer of a 2.5 acre site containing within it a substantial six-bedroomed farmhouse and an assortment of outbuildings together with several small areas of enclosed land which was used as part of a medium-sized farm carrying on mixed farming. The court concluded that the relevant property did not constitute 'agricultural land' within the above definition of 'agricultural property'. The decision is hardly surprising but it does point to the dangers of a farmer giving away the bulk of his farm retaining only the farmhouse and a relatively small area of land. Such retained property will rarely qualify for relief (see further on farmhouses, Adrian Baird in *Private Client Business* (1993), p 410 and *ibid* (1995), p 169.) **[23.58]**

b) 'Agricultural value' (IHTA 1984 s 115(3))

It is the *'agricultural value'* of such property which is subject to the relief; defined as the value which the property would have if subject to a perpetual covenant prohibiting its use otherwise than as agricultural property. Enhanced value attributable to development potential is not subject to the relief (although business property relief may apply to this excess value).

The value of agricultural property may be artificially enhanced for the purposes of the relief by charging the costs of acquiring the agricultural property on non-qualifying property (see *Example 23.16*, below; IHTA 1984 ss 5(5), 162(4) and cf business property relief, [**23.44**]). Further, it is not necessary to transfer a farming business or part thereof in order to obtain relief; it can be given on a mere transfer of assets. When milk quota is transferred with land, the value of that quota will normally enhance the value of the land: consequently, relief for agricultural property will be given for the value of the quota as reflected in the agricultural value of the land itself.   [**23.59**]

EXAMPLE 23.16

A farmer owns a let farm qualifying for 50% agricultural relief and worth £1m, subject to a mortgage of £500,000. His other main assets are investments worth £500,000. Were he to die, the value of his estate on death would be £1m made up of the investments plus the farm after deducting the mortgage thereon. Agricultural relief at 50% would then be available on the *net* value of the farm (ie on £500,000) which would reduce that to £250,000 leaving a chargeable death estate of £750,000.

Suppose, however, that before his death the farmer arranged with the appropriate creditor to switch the mortgage from the agricultural land to the investments. The result then would be that on death the value of his estate would, as above, be £1m made up of the value of the farm (£1m) since the investments now, after deducting the mortgage, are valueless. Accordingly, agricultural relief would be available on the entire value of the farm and amounts to £500,000 leaving a chargeable death estate of £500,000.

c) *The level of relief (IHTA 1984 s 116)*

Section 116 provides (subject to the provisions of s 117 which are considered in the next section) that the level of APR is 100% where:

> 'The interest of the transferor in the property immediately before the transfer carries the right to vacant possession or the right to obtain it within the next 12 months.'

This was extended by ESC F17 to cases where the transferor's interest in the property immediately before the transfer *either:*

(1) carried the right to vacant possession within 24 months of the date of transfer; *or*

(2) is notwithstanding the terms of the tenancy valued at an amount broadly equivalent to vacant possession value.

The former situation would cover the service of notices under the terms of the Agricultural Holdings Act 1986 and so-called '*Gladstone v Bower* arrangements' while the second situation would be relevant in cases akin to that of *Lady Fox* (discussed below at [**23.64**]).

With the passage of the Agricultural Tenancies Act 1995 100% relief was extended to landlords in cases where property was let on tenancies beginning on or after 1 September 1995. This applies to all tenancies: ie the relevant tenancy does not have to be a new style business tenancy under the 1995 legislation but includes, for instance, statutory succession rights arising on the death of a tenant (see *Private Client Business* (1996), p 2).

Otherwise the level of relief is at 50%.   [**23.60**]

d) *Ownership and occupation requirements (IHTA 1984 s 117)*

However, relief is not available unless the further requirements of s 117 are satisfied:

's 116 does not apply to any agricultural property unless:

(a) it was *occupied* by the transferor for the purposes of agriculture throughout the period of *two* years ending with the date of the transfer, or

(b) it was *owned* by him throughout the period of *seven* years ending with that date and was throughout that period occupied (by him *or another*) for the purposes of agriculture.' (See *Harrold v IRC* (1996) for when a farmhouse is 'occupied'.) **[23.61]**

EXAMPLE 23.17

(1) Dan started farming in 1982 and died in April 1997. As an owner-occupier he was entitled to APR at 100%.

(2) Bill's farm was tenanted when he acquired it in 1987 but in 1996 the lease was surrendered. In August 1997 Bill died. He was owner-occupier at death but did not satisfy the requirements of s 117(a); assuming that he has owned the farm for seven years, however, s 117(b) will be satisfied so that he will be entitled to 100% APR.

(3) Jack acquired his farm as an investment in 1993 and died in 1997. No APR available.

(4) Tom has owned agricultural land for ten years and has farmed it himself. He wishes to cease the farming operations himself and enters into a share farming arrangement with a neighbouring farmer under which Tom provides the land and the neighbouring farmer provides labour, live and dead stock etc. Tom dies. 100% relief will not be available unless the terms of the share farming agreement are such that Tom could, immediately before his death, serve notice to terminate the arrangements within 12 months.

e) *Trusts and companies*

The relief (at 100% or 50% as appropriate) is available in three further cases: *first*, where agricultural property is held on discretionary trusts (100% relief, if the trustees have been farming the land themselves); *secondly*, where agricultural property is held on trust for a life tenant under an interest in possession trust; and *finally*, where agricultural property is held by a company in which the transferor of the shares has control. 'Control' has the same meaning as for business property relief (see **[23.50]**). To claim the relief the appropriate two or seven-year period of ownership must be satisfied by the company (vis-à-vis the agricultural property) and by the shareholder/transferor (vis-à-vis the shares transferred). **[23.62]**

f) *Technical provisions*

As with BPR there are technical provisions relating to replacement property, transfers between spouses, and succession from a donor. Similarly, a binding contract for the sale of the property results in agricultural relief not being available.

The grant of a tenancy of agricultural property is not a transfer of value provided that the grant is for full consideration in money or money's worth (IHTA 1984 s 16). Hence, it is not necessary for the lessor to show (particularly in the case of transfers within the family) that he had no gratuitous intent and that the transaction was such as might be made with a stranger (see IHTA 1984 s 10(1)). For difficulties that may arise in ascertaining the market value of agricultural tenancies, see *Law Society's Gazette*, 1984, p 2749, *Law Society's Gazette* 1985, pp 420 and 484, *Baird's Executors v IRC* (1991) and *Walton v IRC* (1996) (considered at **[21.70]**). The availability of the relief when extra IHT is payable, or a PET becomes chargeable, because of a death within seven years is subject to the same restrictions as apply for business property relief (see [**23.54**]).   [**23.63**]

g) *Lotting and the Fox decision*

In valuing an estate at death, 'lotting' requires a valuation on the basis that 'the vendor must be supposed to have' taken the course which would get the largest price for the combined holding 'subject to the caveat ... that it does not entail undue expenditure of time and effort' (see further [**22.4**]).

In *IRC v Gray* (1994) the deceased had farmed the Croxton Park Estate in partnership with two others and the land was subject to tenancies which Lady Fox, as freeholder, had granted to the partnership. The Revenue sought to aggregate or lot together the freehold in the land with her partnership share as a single unit of property. It may be noted that under the partnership deed she was entitled to $92\frac{1}{2}\%$ of profits (and losses). The Court of Appeal reversed the Lands Tribunal holding that lotting was appropriate since that was the course which a prudent hypothetical vendor would take to obtain the best price. The fact that the interests could not be described as forming a 'natural unit of property' was irrelevant. The arrangement employed in this case was commonly undertaken (before the introduction of 100% APR) in order to reduce the tax charge on agricultural property. An alternative involved leases being granted to a family farming company and it is likely that the Revenue will seek to apply this decision to those arrangements. As a result of ESC F17 noted in [**23.60**] above transfers in *Fox*-type cases attract 100% relief.   [**23.64**]

h) *Transitional relief; double discounting*

Under the rules which prevailed up to 1981 agricultural property relief was available where L let Whiteacre to a partnership consisting of himself and his children M and N. On a transfer of the freehold reversion (valued on a tenanted, not a vacant possession, basis) 50% relief was available. The ingredient of 'double discounting' consisted of first reducing the value of the property by granting the lease and then applying the full (50%) relief to that discounted value. As a *quid pro quo* the Revenue argued that the grant of the lease could be a transfer of value even if for a full commercial rent.

Double discount is not available under the new system of agricultural relief and the grant of the tenancy will not be a chargeable transfer of value if for full consideration (IHTA 1984 s 16). On a transitional basis, however, where land was let, as in the above example, on 10 March 1981 so that any transfer by L immediately before that date would have qualified for relief, on the next transfer of value, that relief will still apply but at the current level of 100%. (Note that the relief was limited to £250,000 of agricultural value (before giving relief) or to 1,000 acres, at the option of the taxpayer.) The transitional relief will not apply in cases where the pre-10 March 1981 tenancy has been surrendered and regranted but similar transitional relief applies where before 10 March 1981 the land was let to a company which the transferor controlled (IHTA 1984 s 116(2)–(5)).   [**23.65**]

EXAMPLE 23.18

For many years Mary has owned agricultural land which has been let to a family farming company in which she owns 100% of the shares. On her death 50% relief only will be available on the land since she is not entitled to obtain vacant possession (the company being a separate legal entity). If, however, the arrangements had been in place before 10 March 1981 Mary may be entitled to 100% relief under the 'Double Discount Rule' (for instance, if she was a director of the company immediately before 10 March 1981). Relief will only be available up to a maximum of 1,000 acres or land which at 10 March 1981 was worth up to £250,000.

i) *Inter-relation of agricultural and business property reliefs*

Although the two reliefs are similar and overlap, the following distinctions are worthy of note:
(1) Agricultural relief is given in priority to business relief (IHTA 1984 s 114(1)).
(2) Differences exist in the treatment of woodlands, crops, livestock, deadstock, plant and machinery, and farmhouses etc. When APR does not apply consider whether BPR is available.
(3) Agricultural relief is only available on property situated in the UK, Channel Islands and Isle of Man whereas business relief is not so restricted.
(4) In the *Tax Bulletin*, 1994, p182, the Inland Revenue commented that:

   (1) 'Where agricultural property which is a farming business is replaced by a non-agricultural business property, the period of ownership of the original property will be relevant for applying the minimum ownership condition to the replacement property. Business property relief will be available on the replacement if all the conditions for that relief were satisfied. Where non-agricultural business property is replaced by a farming business and the latter is not eligible for agricultural property relief, s 114(1) does not exclude business property relief if the conditions for that relief are satisfied.'
   (2) 'Where the donee of the PET of a farming business sells the business and replaces it with a non-agricultural business the effect of s 124A(1) is to deny agricultural property relief on the value transferred by the PET. Consequently, s 114(1) does not exclude business property relief if the conditions for that relief are satisfied: and, in the reverse situation, the farming business acquired by the donee can be "relevant business property" for the purposes of s 113B(3)(c).'
   [23.66]

j) *Relief at 100%*

Many of the comments made at **[23.56]** in the context of business property relief apply equally to agricultural property. In addition:
(1) there is no longer any attraction in the type of fragmentation arrangements illustrated in the *Fox* case (see **[23.64]**). Maximum relief is available for in-hand land;
(2) in-hand land need not be farmed by the owner himself. He can enter into contract farming arrangements without jeopardising 100% relief provided that these are correctly structured;
(3) the grant of new tenancies after August 1995 will not jeopardise 100% relief: thought should be given to terminating or amending (eg by adding a small area of extra land) existing tenancies so that a new tenancy resulting in 100% relief for the landlord arises;
(4) complex structures should no longer be set up but what should be done with existing structures? The costs of unscrambling may be considerable and it is worth reflecting that, assuming that the value of tenanted land is one half of the vacant possession value, the effect of 50% APR is to reduce the tax rate to 10% of vacant possession value and as that tax can be paid in ten instalments, the annual tax charge is a mere 1%.   **[23.67]**

4 Relief for heritage property (IHTA 1984 ss 30–35 as amended)

In certain circumstances an application can be made to postpone the payment of IHT on transfers of value of heritage property. As tax can be postponed on any number of such transfers, the result is that a liability to IHT can be deferred indefinitely (similar deferral provisions operate for CGT: TCGA 1992 s 258(3)). Tax postponed under these provisions may subsequently become chargeable under s 32 on the happening of a 'chargeable event'. If the transfer is potentially exempt, an application for conditional exemption can only be made (and is only necessary) if the PET is rendered chargeable by the donor's death within seven years.   **[23.68]**

a) *Conditions to be satisfied if IHT is to be deferred*

In order to obtain this relief, *first*, the property must fall into one of two main categories designated by the Treasury:
(1) *Category 1:*   works of art (including pictures, prints and books) which are of 'national, scientific, historic, or artistic interest' and any building of outstanding historic or architectural interest (IHTA 1984 s 31(1)(a)(b)(e)).
(2) *Category 2:*   land of outstanding scenic, historic, or scientific interest (IHTA 1984 s 31(1)(b)).

Secondly, undertakings have to be given with respect to that property to take reasonable steps for its preservation; to secure reasonable access to the public (see *Works of Art: A Basic Guide* published by the Central Office of Information); and (in the case of *Category 1* property) to keep the property in the UK. In appropriate cases of *Category 1* property, it is sufficient for details of the object and its location to be entered on an official list of such assets. In the case of *Category 2* property, concern has been expressed that proper access for the public has not always been secured and that the introduction of 100% agricultural property relief will result in fewer applications for conditional exemption.

The undertaking must be given by 'such person as the Treasury think appropriate in the circumstances of the case'. In practice, this will mean a PR, trustee, legatee or donee.

A *third* requirement exists in the case of lifetime transfers of value. The transferor must have owned the asset for the six years immediately preceding the transfer if relief is to be given. Notice, however, that the six-year requirement can be satisfied by aggregating periods of ownership of a husband and wife and that it does not apply in cases where the property has been inherited on a death and the exemption has then been successfully claimed. As an anti-avoidance provision it is surprising that the six-year requirement is limited to *inter vivos* transfers thereby permitting deathbed schemes.   **[23.69]**

b) *Effect of deferring IHT*

Where relief is given the transfer is a 'conditionally exempt transfer'. So long as the undertakings are observed and the property is not further transferred IHT liability can be postponed. If there is a subsequent transfer, the exemption may be claimed a second time.

Three '*chargeable events*' cause the deferred IHT charge to become payable: *first*, a breach of the undertakings; *secondly*, a sale of the asset; and *thirdly*, a further transfer (*inter vivos* or on death) without a new undertaking. If a further transfer satisfies the requirements for a conditionally exempt transfer, not only will that transfer itself not be chargeable but it will not lead to any triggering of the deferred charge.

In the case where a fresh undertaking is given, but the transfer does not satisfy the other requirements for a transfer of heritage property (eg it is to a spouse or is made before the six-year ownership requirement has been satisfied), no 'chargeable event' occurs (see IHTA 1984 s 32(5)). Thus, any deferred charge is not triggered, but the transfer itself may be chargeable (or potentially chargeable), if not to a spouse.   **[23.70]**

c) *Calculation of the deferred IHT charge*

Calculation of the deferred IHT charge will depend upon what triggers the charge. If there is a breach of undertakings, the tax is charged upon the person who would be entitled to the proceeds of sale were the asset then sold. The value of the property at that date will be taxed according to the transferor's rates of IHT. Where he is alive, this is by reference to his cumulative total at the time of the triggering event (any PETs that he has made are ignored for these purposes even if they subsequently become chargeable); where he is dead, the property is added to his death estate and charged at the highest rate applicable to that estate but at half the Table rates unless the conditionally exempt transfer was made on his death.

EXAMPLE 23.19

In 1992 Aloysius settles a Rousseau painting (valued at £500,000) on discretionary trusts. The transfer is conditionally exempt, but, two years later (when the picture is worth £650,000), the trustee breaks the undertakings by refusing to allow the painting to be exhibited in the Primitive Exhibition in London. If Aloysius is still alive in 1994, IHT is calculated on £650,000 at Aloysius' rates according to his cumulative total of chargeable transfers in 1994. Had Aloysius died in 1994 with a death estate of £1,000,000, £650,000 would be charged at half the rates appropriate to the highest part of an estate of £1,650,000. As can be seen from this example, considerable care should be exercised in deciding whether the election should be made. If the relevant asset is likely to increase in value, it may be better to pay off the IHT earlier assuming that sufficient funds are available.

If the deferred charge is triggered by a sale of the heritage property, the above principles operate, save that it is the net sale proceeds that will be subject to the deferred charge. Expenses of sale, including CGT, are deductible. If there is a disposal of *part* of a property which is conditionally exempt the designation of the *whole* is reviewed: if the disposal has not materially affected the heritage entity then the designation for the remainder stays in force and the IHT charge is limited to the part disposal. However, if the part disposal results solely from the leasehold enfranchisement under the Leasehold Reform, Housing and Urban Development Act 1993 (or Leasehold Reform Act 1967) these rules do not apply: instead there is no review of the retained property and the charge is limited to the part sold.

Calculation of the deferred charge is more complex where it is triggered by a gift of the heritage property since two chargeable transfers could occur; the first on the gift and the second by the triggering of the deferred charge. If the gift is a chargeable event (excluding PETs) the tax payable on that gift is credited against the triggered deferred charge. Where the gift is a chargeable transfer, but not a chargeable event, as the triggering charge does not arise the credit will be available against the next chargeable event affecting that property.

EXAMPLE 23.20

Eric makes a conditionally exempt transfer to Ernie on his death in 1990. Ernie in turn settles the asset on discretionary trusts in 1996 and the trustees do not give any undertaking.

The creation of the settlement is a chargeable transfer by Ernie. IHT will be calculated at half rates in 1996.

The triggered charge: the value of the asset in 1996 will be subject to IHT at Eric's death rates. A tax credit for IHT paid on the 1996 gift which is attributable to the value of the asset is available.

If the trustees had given an appropriate undertaking in 1996, the trust would be taxed as above (the six-year requirement is not satisfied by Ernie). The transfer is not a chargeable event so that no triggering of the conditionally exempt transfer occurs. The tax credit is available if this charge is triggered, eg by the trustees selling the asset.

If a conditionally exempt transfer is followed by a PET which is a chargeable event with regard to the property, IHT triggered is allowed as a credit against IHT payable if the PET becomes chargeable.

Where there has been more than one conditionally exempt transfer of the same property, and a chargeable event occurs, the Revenue has the right to choose which of the earlier transferors (within 30 years before the chargeable event) shall be used for calculating the sum payable.   [**23.71**]

EXAMPLE 23.21

Z gives a picture to Y who gives it to X who sells it. There have been two conditionally exempt transfers (by Z and Y) and the Revenue can choose (subject to the 30-year time limit) whether to levy the deferred IHT charge according to Z or Y's rates.

d) *Settled property*

The exemption may be available for heritage property held in a discretionary trust (IHTA 1984 ss 78, 79). Where it is held in an interest in possession trust, it is treated as belonging to the life tenant and the above rules are applied.   [**23.72**]

e) *Maintenance funds*

IHTA 1984 ss 27, 57(5) and Sch 4 paras 1–7 provide for no IHT to be charged when property (whether or not heritage property) is settled on trusts to secure the maintenance, repair etc of historic buildings. Such trusts also receive special income tax treatment (TA 1988 s 690ff) and, for CGT, the hold-over election under TCGA 1992 s 260 is available.

These funds can be set up with a small sum of money so long as there is an intention to put in further sums later. The introduction of the PET in 1986 has, however, produced a dilemma for an estate owner. He could give away property to his successor as a PET and rely upon living for seven years in order to avoid IHT. Alternatively, he could transfer that property by a conditionally exempt transfer into a maintenance fund. It is not possible to make a gift of the property and then, if the donor dies within seven years, for the donee at that point to avoid the IHT charge by transferring the property into a maintenance fund.

Settled property will be free of IHT on the death of the life tenant if within two years after his death (three years if an application to court is necessary) the terms of the settlement are altered so that the property goes into a heritage maintenance fund (IHTA 1984 s 57A).   [**23.73**]

f) *Private treaty sales and acceptance in lieu*

Heritage property can be given for national purposes or for the public benefit without any IHT or CGT charge arising. Alternatively, the property can be sold by private treaty (not at an auction) to heritage bodies listed in IHTA 1984 s 25(1) and Sch 3. Such a sale can offer substantial financial advantages for the owner. For instance, if conditionally exempt property is sold on the open market, conditional exemption is lost and furthermore a CGT charge may arise. By contrast, a sale by private treaty does not lead to a withdrawal of the exemption or IHT charge, nor is there a liability to CGT. Not surprisingly, because of these fiscal benefits the vendor will have to accept a lower price than if he sold on the open market. The relevant arrangement involves a 'douceur': broadly, the price that he will receive is the net value of the asset (ie market price less prospective tax liability) *plus* 25% of the tax saved.

EXAMPLE 23.22

(taken from '*Capital Taxation and the National Heritage*' (IR 67))

Calculation of the price, with 'douceur' (usually 25% but subject to negotiation), at which a previously conditionally exempted object can be sold to a public body by private treaty.

Agreed current market value (say)		£100,000
Tax applicable thereto:		
CGT @ (say) 30% on gain element, assumed to be £40,000	£12,000	
ED, CTT or IHT exemption granted on a previous conditionally exempt transfer now recoverable @ say 60% on £88,000 (ie market value less CGT)	£52,800	
Total tax	£64,800	£ 64,800
Net after full tax		£ 35,200
Add back 25% of tax (the 'douceur')		£ 16,200
Price payable by a purchaser, all retained by vendor		£ 51,400

The Revenue writes off the total tax of £64,800 (£12,000 + £52,800).
The vendor has £16,200 more than if he had sold the object for £100,000 in the open market and paid the tax. The public body acquires the object for £48,600 less than its open market value.

An asset can be offered to the Revenue in lieu of tax (see IHTA 1984 s 230(1)). Acceptance in lieu of tax has similar financial advantages for the vendor to a private treaty sale. The Secretary of State has to agree to accept such assets and it should be noted that the standard of objects which can be so accepted is very much higher than that required for the conditional exemption.

Under these arrangements the offeror obtains the benefit of any rise in the value of property between the date of the offer and its acceptance by the Inland Revenue, but he has to pay interest on the unpaid IHT until his offer is accepted. As an alternative, therefore, taxpayers can elect for the value of the property to be taken at the date of the offer (thereby avoiding the payment of any interest but forgoing the benefit of any subsequent rise in the value of the property: F(No 2)A 1987 s 97 and see SP 6/87). **[23.74]**

5 Gifts to political parties (IHTA 1984 s 24)

Such gifts are exempt without limit from IHT, whether made during life or on death. There are detailed provisions which deny relief where the gift is delayed, conditional, made for a limited period, or could be used for other purposes (IHTA 1984 s 24(3) (4)). Any capital gain that would otherwise arise can be held over under TCGA 1992 s 260. **[23.75]**

6 Gifts to charities (IHTA 1984 s 23)

Gifts to charities are exempt without limit. As with gifts to political parties detailed provisions deny the exemption if the vesting of the gift is postponed; if it is conditional; if it is made for a limited period; or if it could be used for non-charitable purposes (on charitable gifts, see Chapter 42).   [23.76]

24 IHT—settlements: definition and classification

I Introductory and definitions **[24.1]**
II Classification of settlements **[24.21]**
III Creation of settlements **[24.41]**
IV Payment of IHT **[24.61]**
V Reservation of benefit **[24.81]**

I INTRODUCTORY AND DEFINITIONS

The objective when taxing settled property is to ensure (1) that it is the capital of the settlement which is subject to tax and not just the value of the various beneficial interests and (2) that settled property is taxed neither more nor less heavily than unsettled property. **[24.1]**

1 What is a settlement?

'Settlement' is defined in IHTA 1984 s 43:

'(2) "Settlement" means any disposition or dispositions of property, whether effected by instrument, by parole or by operation of law, or partly in one way and partly in another, whereby the property is for the time being—
(a) held in trust for persons in succession or for any person subject to a contingency; or
(b) held by trustees on trust to accumulate the whole or part of any income of the property or with power to make payments out of that income at the discretion of the trustees or some other person, with or without power to accumulate surplus income; or
(c) charged or burdened (otherwise than for full consideration in money or money's worth paid for his own use or benefit to the person making the disposition), with the payment of any annuity or other periodical payment payable for a life or any other limited or terminable period; . . .
(3) A lease of property which is for life or lives, or for a period ascertainable only by reference to a death, or which is terminable on, or at a date ascertainable only by reference to, a death, shall be treated as a settlement and the property as settled property, unless the lease was granted for full consideration in money or money's worth, and where a lease not granted as a lease at a rack rent is at any time to become a lease at an increased rent it shall be treated as terminable at that time.'

EXAMPLE 24.1

(1) Property is settled on X for life remainder to Y and Z absolutely (a fixed trust; see (2)(a), above).
(2) Property is held on trust for 'such of A, B, C, D, E and F as my trustees in their absolute discretion may select' (a discretionary trust; see (2)(b), above).

473

(3) Property is held on trust 'for A contingent on attaining 18' (a contingency settlement; see (2)(a), above).

(4) Property is held on trust by A and B as trustees for Z absolutely (a bare trust, although for IHT purposes there is no settlement and the property is treated as belonging to Z).

(5) A and B jointly purchase Blackacre. Under LPA 1925 ss 34 and 36 (as amended) there is a statutory trust of land with A and B holding the land on trust (as joint tenants) for themselves as either joint tenants or tenants in common in equity. For IHT purposes there is no settlement and the property belongs to A and B equally (see *Lloyd's Private Banking v IRC* (1997).

(6) A grants B a lease of Blackacre for his (B's) life at a peppercorn rent. This is a settlement for IHT purposes and A is the trustee of the property (IHTA 1984 s 45). Under LPA 1925 s 149 the lease is treated as being for a term of 90 years which is determinable on the death of B.

As discussed at [**18.61**] difficulties have arisen in identifying, for CGT purposes, when property has been resettled (ie when a new settlement has been created out of an existing settlement). Difficulties may also occur when it is necessary to determine whether the settlor has created one or more settlements. There are similar problems in IHT and the definition of 'settlement', set out above, is unlikely to prove of assistance in resolving these problems. In *Minden Trust (Cayman) Ltd v IRC* (1984) an appointment of settled property in favour of overseas beneficiaries was held to amend the terms of the original settlement so that the terms of that appointment read with the original settlement were dispositions of property and therefore a settlement.   [**24.2**]

EXAMPLE 24.2

Each year Sam creates a discretionary trust of £3,000 (thereby utilising his annual exemption) and his wife does likewise. At the end of five years there are ten mini discretionary trusts. As a matter of trust law, and assuming that each settlement is correctly documented, there is no reason why this series should be treated as one settlement. So far as the IHT legislation is concerned the settlements are not made on the same day (see IHTA 1984 s 62); the associated operations provisions (IHTA 1984 s 268) would seem inapplicable (the facts are quite different from those in *Hatton v IRC* (1992) and in no sense is this a series of operations affecting the same property); and the *Ramsay* principle, although of uncertain ambit, could only be applied with difficulty to a series of gifts. The separate trusts should be kept apart (there should be no pooling of property) and each settlement should be fully documented.

2   Settlors and trustees

In the majority of cases it is not difficult to identify the settlor, since there will usually be one settlor who will create a settlement by a 'disposition' of property (which may include a disposition by associated operations; see IHTA 1984 s 272). If that settlor adds further property, this creates no problems in the interest in possession settlement, but difficulties arise if the settlement is discretionary (see [**26.33**]) with further complications if the original property was excluded property and the additional property was not, or *vice versa* (see Chapter 27 and *Tax Bulletin*, February 1997). A settlement may have more than one settlor:

EXAMPLE 24.3

(1) Bill and Ben create a settlement in favour of their neighbour Barum.

(2) Bill adds property to a settlement that had been created two years ago by Ben in favour of neighbour Barum.

IHTA 1984 s 44(2) states that: 'Where more than one person is a settlor in relation to a settlement and the circumstances so require, this Part of this Act (except s 48(4)–(6)) shall have effect in relation to it as if the settled property were comprised in separate settlements.' *Thomas v IRC* (1981) indicates that this provision only applies where an identifiable capital fund has been provided by each settlor. The fund will be treated as two separate settlements in the case of discretionary trusts where both the incidence of the periodic charge and the amount of IHT chargeable may be affected. IHTA 1984 s 44(1) defines settlor (in terms similar to those for income tax purposes) thus:

> 'In this Act "settlor", in relation to a settlement, includes any person by whom the settlement was made directly or indirectly, and ... includes any person who has provided funds directly or indirectly for the purpose of or in connection with the settlements or has made with any other person a reciprocal arrangement for that other person to make the settlement.'

A further problem arises where there is only one settlor who adds property to his settlement; is this for IHT purposes one settlement or two? This question is significant in relation to discretionary trusts (especially with regard to timing and rate of the periodic and inter-periodic charges) and where excluded property is involved in a settlement. As a matter of trust law, there will be a single settlement where funds are held and managed by one set of trustees for one set of beneficiaries, so that such additions will usually not lead to the creation of separate settlements. When it would be advantageous for there to be two settlements, a separate settlement deed with (ideally) separate trustees should be employed (for the Revenue's views on the application of s 44(2) in such cases, see *Tax Bulletin*, February 1997 and *Hatton v IRC* (1992)).

The ordinary meaning is given to the term 'a trustee', although by IHTA 1984 s 45 it includes any person in whom the settled property or its management is for the time being vested. In cases where a lease for lives is treated as a settlement the lessor is the trustee.   **[24.3]–[24.20]**

II CLASSIFICATION OF SETTLEMENTS

1 **The three categories**

Settlements for IHT purposes must be divided into three categories.

Category 1 A settlement with an interest in possession, eg where the property is held for an adult tenant for life who, by virtue of his interest, is entitled to the income as it arises.

Category 2 A settlement lacking an interest in possession, eg where trustees are given a discretion over the distribution of the income. At most, beneficiaries have the right to be considered by the trustees; the right to ensure that the fund is properly administered; and the right to join with all the other adult beneficiaries to bring the settlement to an end.

This category also includes settlements where the property is held on trust for a minor, contingent on his attaining a specified age. As long as the beneficiary is a minor there will be no interest in possession and the settlement will fall into *Category 2*, unless the trust satisfies the requirements for a *Category 3* accumulation and maintenance settlement.

Category 3 Into this category fall special or privileged trusts. They lack an interest in possession, but are not subject to the *Category 2* regime. The main example considered in this book is the accumulation and maintenance trust.

To place a particular trust into its correct category is important for two reasons. *First*, because the IHT treatment of each is totally different both as to incidence of tax and as to the amount of tax charged; and *secondly*, because a change from one category to another will normally give rise to an IHT charge. For example, if a life interest ceases, whereupon the fund is held on discretionary trusts, the settlement moves from *Category 1* to *Category 2*, and a chargeable occasion (the ending of a life interest) has occurred.   [24.21]

2   The meaning of an 'interest in possession'

Normally trusts can easily be slotted into their correct category. Trusts falling within *Category 3* are carefully defined so that any trust not specifically falling into one of those special cases must fall into *Category 2*. Problems are principally caused by the borderline between *Categories 1* and *2* where the division is drawn according to whether the settlement has an interest in possession or not. In the majority of cases no problems will arise: at one extreme stands the life interest settlement; at the other the discretionary trust. However, what of a settlement which provides for the income to be paid to Albert, unless the trustees decide to pay it to Bertram, or to accumulate it; or where the property in the trust is enjoyed *in specie* by one beneficiary as the result of the exercise of a discretion (eg a beneficiary living in a dwelling house which was part of a discretionary fund)? To resolve these difficulties, the phrase an 'interest in possession' needs definition. The legislation does not assist; instead, its meaning must be gleaned from a Press Notice of the Revenue and *Re Pilkington (Pearson v IRC)* (1981) which largely endorses the statements in that Press Notice.   [24.22]

The IR Press Notice (12 February 1976) provides as follows:

> 'an interest in settled property exists where the person having the interest has the *immediate entitlement* (subject to any prior claims by the trustees for expenses or other outgoings properly payable out of income) *to any income* produced by that property as the income arises; but ... a discretion or power, in whatever form, which can be exercised *after income arises* so as to withhold it from that person negatives the existence of an interest in possession. For this purpose a power to accumulate income is regarded as a power to withhold it, unless any accumulation must be held solely for the person having the interest or his personal representatives.
>
> On the other hand the existence of a mere power of revocation or appointment, the exercise of which would determine the interest wholly or in part (but which, so long as it remains unexercised, does not affect the beneficiary's immediate entitlement to income) does not . . . prevent the interest from being an interest in possession.'

The first paragraph is concerned with the existence of discretions or powers which might affect the destination of the income after it has arisen and which prevent the existence of any interest in possession (eg a provision enabling the trustees to accumulate income or to divert it for the benefit of other beneficiaries). The second paragraph concerns overriding powers which, if exercised, would terminate the entire interest of the beneficiary, but which do not prevent the existence of an interest in possession (eg the statutory power of advancement). Administrative expenses charged on the income can be ignored in deciding whether there is an interest in possession, so long as such payments are for 'outgoings properly payable out of income'. A clause in the settlement permitting expenses of a capital nature to be so charged is, therefore, not covered and the Revenue considers that the mere presence of such a clause is fatal to the existence of any interest in possession.   [24.23]

Re Pilkington (Pearson v IRC) (1981)   The facts of the case were simple. Both capital and income of the fund were held for the settlor's three adult daughters in equal shares subject to three overriding powers exercisable by the trustees: (1) to appoint capital and income amongst the daughters, their spouses and issue; (2) to accumulate so much of the income as they should think fit; and (3) to apply any income towards the payment or discharge of any taxes, costs or other outgoings which would otherwise be payable out of capital. The trustees had regularly exercised their powers to accumulate the income. What caused the disputed IHT assessment (for a mere £444.73) was the irrevocable appointment of some £16,000 from the fund to one of the daughters. There was no doubt that, as a result of the appointment, she obtained an interest in possession in that appointed sum; but did she already have an interest in possession in the fund? If so, no IHT would be chargeable on the appointment (see [25.28]); if not, there would be a charge because the appointed funds had passed from a 'no interest in possession' to an 'interest in possession' settlement (*Category 2* to *Category 1*).

The Revenue contended that the existence of the overriding power to accumulate and the provision enabling all expenses to be charged to income deprived the settlement of any interest in possession. It was common ground that whether such powers had been exercised or not was irrelevant in deciding the case. The overriding power of appointment over capital and income was not seen as endangering the existence of any interest in possession (see the second paragraph of the Press Notice at [24.23] above).

For the bare majority of the House of Lords the presence of the overriding discretion to accumulate the income was fatal to the existence of any interest in possession. 'A present right to present enjoyment' was how an interest in possession was defined and the beneficiary did not have a present right. 'Their enjoyment of any income from the trust fund depended on the trustees' decision as to accumulation of income' (per Viscount Dilhorne). No distinction is to be drawn between a trust to pay income to a beneficiary, but with an overriding power to accumulate, and a trust to accumulate, but with a power to pay. Hence, in the following examples there is no interest in possession:

(1) to A for life but trustees may accumulate the income; and
(2) the income shall be accumulated but trustees may make payments to A. [24.24]

3 Problems remaining after *Pilkington*

The test laid down by the majority in the House of Lords established some certainty in a difficult area of law and it is possible to say that the borderline between trusts with and without an interest in possession is reasonably easy to draw; where there is uncertainty about the entitlement of a beneficiary to income, it is likely that the settlement will fall into the 'no interest in possession' regime. In the light of the favourable changes made to the IHT treatment of discretionary trusts in 1982 that may be no bad thing for taxpayers. [24.25]

The following are some of the difficulties left in the wake of *Pilkington*:

Dispositive and administrative powers For there to be an interest in possession the beneficiary must be entitled to the income as it arises. Were this test to be applied strictly, however, even a trust with a life tenant receiving the income might fail to satisfy the requirement because trustees may deduct management expenses from that income, so that few beneficiaries are entitled to all the income as it arises. This problem was considered by Viscount Dilhorne as follows:

'. . . Parliament distinguished between the administration of a trust and the dispositive powers of trustees . . . A life tenant has an interest in possession but his interest only extends to the net income of the property, that is to say, after deduction from the gross income of expenses etc properly incurred in the management of the trust by the trustees in the exercise of their powers. A dispositive power is a power to dispose of the net income. Sometimes the line between an administrative and a dispositive power may be difficult to draw but that does not mean that there is not a valid distinction.'

In *Pilkington* the trustees had an overriding discretion to apply income towards the payment of any taxes, costs, or other outgoings which would otherwise be payable out of capital and the Revenue took the view that the *existence* of this overriding power was a further reason for the settlement lacking an interest in possession. Was this power administrative (in which case its presence did not affect the existence of any interest in possession) or dispositive (fatal to the existence of such an interest)? Viscount Dilhorne decided that the power was administrative. Acceptable though this argument may be for management expenses, is it convincing when applied to other expenses and taxes (eg CGT and IHT) which would normally be payable out of the capital of the fund? In *Miller v IRC* (1987) the Court of Session held that a power to employ income to make good depreciation in the capital value of assets in the fund was administrative. It must be stressed that the House of Lords did not have to decide whether the Revenue's contention was correct or not; Viscount Dilhorne's observations are *obiter dicta* and the Revenue still adheres to its Press Notice ([**24.23**]). Would-be settlors should be advised not to insert such clauses.   [**24.26**]

Power to allow beneficiaries to occupy a dwelling house   This power may exist both in settlements which otherwise have an interest in possession and in those without. The mere existence of such a power is to be ignored; problems will only arise if and when it is exercised. SP 10/79 indicates that if such a power was exercised so as to allow, for a definite or indefinite period, someone other than the life tenant to have exclusive or joint right of residence in a dwelling house as a permanent home, there would be an IHT charge on the partial ending of a life interest. In the case of a fund otherwise lacking an interest in possession, the exercise of the power would result in the creation of such an interest and therefore, an IHT charge would arise. Whether this view is correct is arguable; in *Swales v IRC* (1984), for instance, the taxpayer's argument that the mandating of trust income to a beneficiary was equivalent to providing a residence for permanent occupation (and accordingly created an interest in possession) was rejected by the court. In practice, any challenge could prove costly to the taxpayer, and trustees who possess such powers should think carefully before exercising them (and see *Lloyd's Private Banking v IRC* (1997)).   [**24.27**]

Interest-free loans to beneficiaries   It has been suggested that a free loan to a beneficiary would create an interest in possession in the fund. As the beneficiary becomes a debtor (to the extent of the loan), one wonders in what assets his interest subsists; the moneys loaned would appear to belong absolutely to him. Again, trustees should avoid making such loans and, if need be, the trust should guarantee a bank loan to the beneficiary.   [**24.28**]

EXAMPLE 24.4

The trustees of a discretionary trust lend £10,000 to beneficiary A in 1992. In 1997 he repays that sum in full. If the Revenue's view is correct, the result is that:

(1) In 1992: A has an interest in possession in £10,000. IHT is chargeable.

(2) In 1997: A's interest in possession ceases and as the property is now held on discretionary trusts A has made a chargeable transfer.

Position of the last surviving member of a discretionary class　　If the class of beneficiaries has closed, the sole survivor is entitled to the income as it arises so that there is an interest in possession. When the class has not closed, however, trustees have a reasonable time to decide how the accrued income is to be distributed and, if a further beneficiary could come into existence before that period has elapsed, the current beneficiary is not automatically entitled to the income as it arises so that there is no interest in possession (*Moore and Osborne v IRC* (1984)). Likewise, if the class has not closed and the trustees have a power to accumulate income.　　　　　　　　　　　　　　　**[24.29]–[24.40]**

III　CREATION OF SETTLEMENTS

The creation of a settlement may constitute a chargeable transfer of value by the settlor. If the burden of paying the IHT is put upon the trustees of the settlement, the Revenue accepts that the settlor will not thereby retain an interest in the settlement under the income tax provisions in TA 1988 Part XV (SP 1/82) (see **[11.61]**).

No IHT is charged in the following examples.

EXAMPLE 24.5

(1) S settles £100,000 on trust for himself for life with remainder to his children. As S, the life tenant, is deemed to own the entire fund (and not simply a life interest in it) his estate has not fallen in value.

(2) S settles £100,000 on trust for his wife for life, remainder to his children. S's wife is treated as owning the fund so that S's transfer is an exempt transfer to a spouse.

The *inter vivos* creation of a settlement will be a potentially exempt transfer in the following cases:
(1) If it creates an interest in possession trust.
(2) If the trust satisfies the definition of an accumulation and maintenance or disabled trust.
In other cases (and notably when a discretionary trust is created), there will be an immediate chargeable transfer. Even if the settlement as created contains an interest in possession, the termination of that interest during the lifetime of the settlor and within seven years of the setting up of the trust will trigger the anti-avoidance rules in IHTA 1984 s 54A if a discretionary trust then arises (see **[25.31]**).　　　　　　　　　　　　　　　**[24.41]–[24.60]**

IV　PAYMENT OF IHT

Primary liability for IHT arising during the course of the settlement rests upon the settlement's trustees. Their liability is limited to the property which they have received or disposed of or become liable to account for to a beneficiary and such other property which they would have received but for their own neglect or default.

If trustees fail to pay, the Revenue can collect tax from any of the following (IHTA 1984 s 201(1)):
(1) Any person entitled to an interest in possession in the settled property.

His liability is limited to the value of the trust property, out of which he can claim an indemnity for the tax he has paid.

(2) Any beneficiary under a discretionary trust up to the value of the property that he receives (after paying income tax on it) and with no right to an indemnity for the tax he is called upon to pay.

(3) The settlor, where the trustees are resident outside the UK, since, should the trustees not pay, the Revenue cannot enforce payment abroad. If the settlor pays he has a right to recover the tax from the trust. [**24.61**]–[**24.80**]

V   RESERVATION OF BENEFIT

The creation of *inter vivos* settlements can cause problems in the reservation of benefit area and the following matters are especially worthy of note:

(1) *If the settlor appoints himself a trustee of the settlement*, that appointment will not by itself amount to a reserved benefit. If the terms of the settlement provide for his remuneration, however, there will then be a reservation in the settled property (*Oakes v Stamp Duties Comr* (1954)). One way round this is for the settlor/trustee to be paid an annuity, since such an arrangement will not constitute a reserved benefit and the ending of that annuity will not lead to any IHT charge (IHTA 1984 s 90). Particular difficulties are caused if the settlor/trustee is a director of a company whose shares are held in the trust fund. The general rule of equity is that a trustee may not profit from his position and this means that he will generally have to account for any director's fees that he may receive. It is standard practice, however, for the trust deed to provide that a trustee need not in such cases account for those fees. When the settlor/trustee is allowed to retain fees under the deed it is arguable that he has reserved a benefit in the trust assets within the ruling in the *Oakes* case. The Revenue has, however, indicated that it will not take this point so long as the director's remuneration is on reasonable commercial terms.

(2) *If the settlor reserves an interest for himself under his settlement*, whether he does so expressly or whether his interest arises by operation of law, there is no reservation of benefit and he is treated as making a partial gift (see [**21.189**]).

EXAMPLE 24.6

S created a settlement for his infant son, absolutely on attaining 21. No provision was made for what should happen if the son were to die before that age, and therefore there was a resulting trust to the settlor. The settlor died whilst the son was still an infant and was held to have reserved no benefit. Instead, he was treated as making a partial gift: ie a gift of the settled property less the retained remainder interest therein (*Stamp Duties Comr v Perpetual Trustee Co* (1943); and see *Re Cochrane* (1906) where the settlor expressly reserved surplus income).

The position with regard to discretionary trusts in which the settlor is included in the class of beneficiaries is more problematic. In view of the limited nature of a discretionary beneficiary's rights (see *Gartside v IRC* (1968)) it is unlikely that he can be treated as making a partial gift. The Revenue's view is that in all cases where a settlor is a discretionary beneficiary he will be treated as having reserved a benefit in the entire settled fund despite the fact that he may receive no payments or other benefits under the trust. Although there is some doubt about the correctness of this view, taxpayers face the familiar dilemma in that they would probably have to appeal to the House of Lords to overturn this argument. The insertion of the settlor's spouse as a discretionary beneficiary does not by itself result in a reserved benefit. Were that spouse to receive property from the settlement, however, and that property was then shared with or used for the benefit of the settlor, the Revenue will argue that there is a reserved benefit. Finally, the reservation rules do not apply to an exempt gift to a spouse. Accordingly, and subject to the associated operation rules and the *Ramsay* principle, a reserved benefit may be channelled through a spouse.   [**24.81**]

EXAMPLE 24.7

Bill settles property on his wife Berta for life and subject thereto on discretionary trusts for a class of beneficiaries which includes Bill. Berta's life interest terminates after six months. It is thought that Bill has not reserved any benefit although he is one of the objects of the discretionary trust.

25 IHT—settlements with an interest in possession

I BASIC PRINCIPLES

1 General

The beneficiary entitled to the income of a fund (usually the life tenant) is treated as owning that portion of the capital of the fund (IHTA 1984 s 49(1)). This rule is a fiction since a life tenant normally has no entitlement to capital.

As all the capital is treated as being owned by the life tenant, for IHT purposes it forms part of his estate, so that on a chargeable occasion IHT is charged at his rates. The settlement itself is not a taxable entity (contrast the rules for discretionary trusts), although primary liability for IHT falls upon the trustees.

As the life tenant is treated as owning all the capital in the fund, other beneficiaries with 'reversionary interests' own nothing. IHTA 1984 s 47 defines reversionary interests widely to cover

'a future interest under a settlement, whether it is vested or contingent (including an interest expectant on the termination of an interest in possession which, by virtue of section 50 . . . , is treated as subsisting in part of any property)'.

Generally, reversionary interests are excluded property and can be transferred without a charge to IHT (see [**25.61**]). Despite the breadth of this definition, the term would not appear to catch the interests of discretionary beneficiaries since such rights as they possess (to compel due administration; to be considered; and jointly to wind up the fund) are present rights. Their interests are neither in possession nor in reversion.

The interest in possession trust is unique in having a special charging system based upon the fiction that the fund belongs to the person with the interest in possession. The IHT levy on other settlements operates by treating the settlement as a separate chargeable entity and by (generally) imposing a tax charge at regular intervals. There appears to be no reason why this method, if it achieves its stated object of tax 'neutrality', should not be applied across the board.   [**25.1**]

2 Who is treated as owning the fund?

Life interests   The beneficiary entitled to an interest in possession is treated as being beneficially entitled to the property, or to an appropriate part of that property; if there is more than one beneficiary, it is necessary to apportion the capital in the fund (IHTA 1984 s 50(1)).

A beneficiary who has the right to the income of the fund for a period shorter than his lifetime (however short the period may be) is still treated as owning the entire settled fund. If the settlement does not produce any income, but instead the beneficiary is entitled to use the capital assets in the fund, IHTA 1984 s 49(1) suggests that he is treated as owning those assets. If the use is enjoyed by more than one beneficiary, the value of the fund is apportioned under IHTA 1984 s 50(5) in accordance with the 'annual value' of their respective interests. Annual value is not defined.   **[25.2]**

EXAMPLE 25.1

Bill and Ben, beneficiaries under a strict settlement, jointly occupy 'Snodlands', the ancestral home, which is worth £150,000. This capital value must be apportioned to Bill and Ben in proportion to the annual value of their respective interests. As their interests are equal the apportionment will be as to £75,000 each.

A beneficiary entitled to a fixed amount of income   Difficulties may arise where one beneficiary is entitled to a fixed amount of income each year (eg an annuity) and any balance is paid to another beneficiary. If the amounts of income paid to the two were compared in the year when a chargeable event occurred, a tax saving could be engineered. Assume, for instance, that the annuity interest terminates so that IHT is charged on its value. The proportion of capital attributable to that interest and, therefore, the IHT would be reduced if the trustees switched investments into assets producing a high income in that year. A relatively small proportion of the total income would then be payable to the annuitant who would be treated as owning an equivalently small portion of the capital. When a chargeable event affects the interest in the residue of the income (eg through termination) the trustees could switch the assets into low income producers, thereby achieving a similar reduction in IHT.

IHTA 1984 s 50(3) is designed to counter such schemes by providing that the Treasury may prescribe higher and lower income yields which take effect as limits beyond which any fluctuations in the actual income of the fund are ignored (see SI 1980/1000).

EXAMPLE 25.2

The value of the settlement is £100,000; income £25,000 per annum. A is entitled to an annuity of £5,000 pa; B to the balance of the income. If there is a chargeable transfer affecting the annuity, A is not treated as owning £20,000 of the capital ([£5,000 ÷ £25,000] × £100,000) but instead a proportion of the Treasury 'higher rate' yield. Assume that the higher rate is 15% on the relevant day; the calculation is, therefore:

Notional income = 15% of £100,000 = £15,000.
A's annuity is £5,000; as a proportion of income it is £5,000 ÷ £15,000;
A's share of capital is, therefore, [£5,000 ÷ £15,000] × £100,000 = £33,333.

This calculation is used whenever the actual income yield exceeds the prescribed higher rate. The calculation cannot lead to a charge in excess of the total value of the fund!

When a chargeable transfer affecting the interest in the balance of the income occurs, if the actual income produced falls below the prescribed lower rate, the calculation proceeds as if the fund yielded that rate. If both interests in the settlement are chargeable on the same occasion, the prescribed rates do not apply because the entire fund is chargeable.   **[25.3]**

A lease treated as a settlement When a lease is treated as a settlement (eg a lease for life or lives), the lessee is treated as owning the whole of the leased property save for any part treated as belonging to the lessor. To calculate the lessor's portion it is necessary to compare what he received when the lease was granted with what would have been a full consideration for the lease at that time (IHTA 1984 ss 50(6), 170). **[25.4]–[25.20]**

EXAMPLE 25.3

(1) Land worth £100,000 is let to A for his life. The lessor receives no consideration so that A is treated as owning the whole of the leased property (ie £100,000). The granting of the lease is a potentially exempt transfer by the lessor of £100,000.

(2) As above, save that full consideration is furnished. The lease is not treated as a settlement (see **[24.2]**). No IHT will be charged on its creation as the lessor's estate does not fall in value.

(3) Partial consideration (equivalent to 40% of full consideration) is furnished so that the value of the lessor's interest is 40% of £100,000 = £40,000. The value of the lessee's interest is £60,000 and the granting of the lease is a potentially exempt transfer of £60,000.

II WHEN IS IHT CHARGED?

IHT may be charged on the creation of the settlement and whenever an interest in possession terminates. This event may occur *inter vivos* or on death: in the former case the settlor or beneficiary (as appropriate) will be treated as making a PET provided that the trust fund is not then held on discretionary trusts. There are anti-avoidance rules to prevent the indirect creation of discretionary trusts via short-lived interests in possession (see **[25.31]**). **[25.21]**

1 Creation of interest in possession trusts

If the trust is set up on death the usual IHT charging regime operates (see Chapter 22). If created *inter vivos*, the settlor will make a PET. Under general rules, such a charge will only occur if the settlor dies within seven years; anti-avoidance rules may, however, trigger a charge by reference to the settlor's circumstances when he created the trust if the life interest ends within seven years, at a time when the settlor is still alive and the property then becomes held on trusts without an interest in possession (see **[25.31]** for a discussion of these rules). **[25.22]**

EXAMPLE 25.4

(1) Sam settles property on his daughter Sally for life, remainder to Oxfam. The creation of the trust is a PET and on Sally's death the fund will be exempt from charge.

(2) Sid settles property on a stranger, Jake Straw, for life or until such time as the trustees determine and thereafter the property is to be held on discretionary trusts for Sid's family and relatives. The creation of the trust is a PET; a later termination of Jake's life interest will be a chargeable transfer and may trigger the anti-avoidance rules.

(3) Sam settles property on Susan, his daughter, for life, remainder to her twins at 21. Susan surrenders her life interest when the twins are (i) 17, (ii) 18, (iii) 21.

The creation of the trust is a PET as is the surrender of Susan's life interest. If it is surrendered at (i), the fund is then held for accumulation and maintenance trusts (a PET); if surrendered at (ii), the transfer is to the twins as interest in possession beneficiaries (a PET); while, if surrendered at (iii), the twins are absolutely entitled and so it will be an outright gift which is a PET.

2   The charge on death

As the assets in the settlement are treated as part of the property of the deceased beneficiary at the time of his death, IHT is charged on the settled fund at the estate rate appropriate to his estate. The tax attributable to the settled property must be paid by the trustees. Of course although the trustees pay this tax, the inclusion of the value of the fund in the deceased's estate may increase the estate rate, thereby causing a higher percentage charge on the deceased's free estate.   **[25.23]**

EXAMPLE 25.5

The settlement consists of securities worth £100,000 and is held for Albinoni for life with remainder to Busoni. Albinoni has just died and the value of his free estate is £165,000; he made chargeable lifetime transfers of £50,000. IHT will be calculated as follows:

(1)   Chargeable death estate: £165,000 + £100,000 (the settlement) = £265,000.
(2)   Join table at £50,000 (point reached by lifetime transfers).
(3)   Calculate death IHT (£40,000).
(4)   Convert to estate rate

$$\frac{\text{tax}}{\text{estate}} \times 100: \text{ie } \frac{£40,000}{£265,000} \times 100 = 15.09\%.$$

(5)   IHT attributable to settled property is 15.09% of £100,000 = £1,509.

3   *Inter vivos* terminations

An actual or deemed termination of an interest in possession occurring during the life of the relevant beneficiary is a PET provided that the property is, after that event, held for one or more beneficiaries absolutely (so that the settlement is at an end), or for a further interest in possession or on accumulation and maintenance or disabled trusts. IHT will only be payable in such cases if the former life tenant dies within seven years of the termination. Otherwise (eg where after the termination the fund is held on discretionary trusts) there is an immediate charge to tax.   **[25.24]**

Actual terminations   A charge to IHT may arise if the interest of the life tenant ceases calculated on the basis that the life tenant had made a transfer of value at that time (IHTA 1984 s 52(1)).   **[25.25]**

EXAMPLE 25.6

(1)   £100,000 is held on trust for Albinoni for life or until remarriage and thereafter for Busoni. If Albinoni remarries his life interest terminates and he makes a PET. Accordingly, should he die within seven years, IHT will be charged on the value of the fund at the time when his interest ended.

If Albinoni never remarried, but consented to an advancement of £50,000 to Busoni, his interest ends in that portion of the fund and he makes a PET of £50,000.

Assume that three years later Albinoni surrenders his life interest in the fund, now worth £120,000. This is a further PET; IHT may therefore be charged (if he dies in the following seven years) on £120,000. Notice that in all cases any tax charge is levied on a value transferred which is 'equal to the value of the property in which his interest subsisted' (see s 52(1)). The principle of calculating loss to donor's estate (see **[21.61]**) is inapplicable.

(2) Claude owns 49% of the shares in his family investment company, Money Box Ltd, and is the life tenant under a settlement which owns a further 12% of those shares. The remainder beneficiary under the trust is Claude's daughter. No dividends are paid by the company. The tax position if Claude were to surrender his interest in possession is as follows:

(i) The surrender of a beneficial interest in a settlement is generally free from CGT (TCGA 1992 s 76(1)). Assuming that the settlement ends, there will be a deemed disposal under TCGA 1992 s 71(1).

(ii) For IHT purposes, Claude will make a PET but the value transferred is limited to the value of the shares in the settlement (IHTA 1984, s 52(1)). Thus only the value of a 12% minority holding will be subject to tax in the event of Claude's death within seven years.

(iii) On Claude's death his estate will then comprise only a 49% minority shareholding.

(iv) The merit of this arrangement is that the substantial loss to Claude's estate resulting from his loss of control of the company has not attracted a tax charge: instead, both shareholdings have been valued separately. Surrender of the life interest can occur on Claude's deathbed but the advantages will not, of course, be obtained if the life interest is retained and the 49% holding given away!

Deemed terminations IHTA 1984 s 51(1) provides that if the beneficiary disposes of his beneficial interest in possession, that disposal 'shall not be a transfer of value but shall be treated as the coming to an end of the interest'. The absence of gratuitous intent does not prevent an IHT charge on the termination of beneficial interests in possession. As with actual terminations, the life tenant will normally make a PET so that tax will only be charged if he dies within seven years thereafter. [**25.26**]

EXAMPLE 25.7

(1) Albinoni assigns by way of gift his life interest to Cortot. IHT will be charged as if that life interest had terminated. Cortot becomes a tenant *pur autre vie* and when Albinoni dies Cortot's interest in possession terminates so raising the possibility of a further IHT charge. Both Albinoni and Cortot have made PETs.

(2) If, instead of gifting his interest, Albinoni sells it to Cortot for £20,000 (full value) and the fund was then worth £100,000, Albinoni's interest terminates so that he has made a transfer of value of £100,000. However, as he has received £20,000, he has made a PET equal to the fall in his estate of £80,000 (£100,000 − £20,000: IHTA 1984 s 52(2)).

Partition A partition of the trust fund between life tenant and remainderman causes the interest in possession to terminate and IHT may be charged (if the life tenant dies within seven years) on that portion of the fund passing to the remainderman (IHTA 1984 s 53(2)). [**25.27**]

EXAMPLE 25.8

Albinoni and Busoni partition the £100,000 fund in the proportions 40:60. Albinoni is treated as making a PET of £60,000 (£100,000 − £40,000). The trustees should remember that any IHT will be payable out of the fund to be divided.

Advancements to life tenant/satisfaction of a contingency If all or part of the capital of the fund is paid to the life tenant, or if he becomes absolutely entitled to the capital, his interest in possession will determine *pro tanto*, but no IHT will

be charged since there will be no fall in the value of his estate (IHTA 1984
s 53(2)).   **[25.28]**

Purchase of a reversionary interest by the life tenant (IHTA 1984 ss 10, 55(1))   As
the life tenant is treated as owning the fund, his tax bill could be reduced
were he to purchase a reversionary interest in that settlement. Assume, for
instance, that B has £60,000 in his bank account and is the life tenant of a
fund with a capital value of £100,000. For IHT purposes he owns £160,000.
If B were to purchase the reversionary interest in the settlement for its market
value of £60,000, the result would be as follows: first, B's estate has not fallen
in value. Originally it included £60,000; after the purchase it includes a
reversionary interest worth £60,000 since, although excluded property, the
reversionary interest must still be valued. Secondly, B's estate now consists
of the settlement fund valued at £100,000 and has been depleted by the £60,000
paid for the reversionary interest so that a possible charge to IHT on £60,000
has been avoided.

To prevent this loss of tax, IHTA 1984 s 55(1) provides that the reversionary
interest is not to be valued as a part of B's estate at the time of its purchase
(thereby ensuring that his estate has fallen in value) whilst IHTA 1984 s 10
(see **[21.21]**) is excluded from applying thereby ensuring that the fall in value
may be subject to charge even though there is no donative intent. Hence,
by paying £60,000 for the reversionary interest B has made a PET which will
be taxed if he dies in the following seven years.   **[25.29]**

Transactions reducing the value of the property   When the value of the fund is
diminished by a depreciatory transaction entered into between the trustees
and a beneficiary (or persons connected with him) tax is charged as if the
fall in value were a partial termination of the interest in possession (IHTA
1984 s 52(3)). A commercial transaction lacking gratuitous intent is not caught
by this provision.

In *Macpherson v IRC* (1988) the value of pictures held in a trust fund was
diminished by an arrangement with a person connected with a beneficiary
as a result of which, in return for taking over care, custody and insurance
of the pictures, that person was entitled to keep the pictures for his personal
enjoyment for some 14 years. Although this arrangement was a commercial
transaction, lacking gratuitous intent when looked at in isolation, it was
associated with a subsequent operation (the appointment of a protected life
interest) which did confer a gratuitous benefit so that the exception did not
apply and the reduction in value of the fund was subject to charge.   **[25.30]**

EXAMPLE 25.9

Trustees grant a 50-year lease of a property worth £100,000 at a peppercorn rent
to the brother of a reversionary beneficiary. As a result the property left in the
settlement is the freehold reversion worth only £20,000. The granting of the lease
is a depreciatory transaction which causes the value of the fund to fall by £80,000
and as it is made with a person connected with a beneficiary, IHTA 1984 s 52(3)
will apply and IHT may be levied as if the life interest in £80,000 had ended.
(Contrast the position if the lease had been granted to the brother in return for
a commercial rent.)

4   Anti-avoidance (IHTA 1984 s 54A and s 54B)

a) *When do the rules apply?*

The three prerequisites are that an interest in possession trust is set up by means of a PET; it terminates either as a result of the life tenant dying or by his interest ceasing *inter vivos*; and at that time a no interest in possession trust (other than an accumulation and maintenance settlement) arises. If the termination occurs within seven years of the creation of the original interest in possession trust and at a time when the settlor is still alive, the anti-avoidance rules then apply. [**25.31**]

b) *Operation of the rules*

The IHT charge on the property at the time when the interest in possession ends is taken to be the higher of two alternative calculations. First, the IHT that would arise under normal charging principles: ie by taxing the fund as if the transfer had been made by the life tenant at the time of termination. The rates of charge will be either half rates (when there is an *inter vivos* termination) or full death rates when termination occurs as a result of the death of the life tenant. The alternative calculation involves deeming the settled property to have been transferred at the time of termination by a hypothetical transferor who in the preceding seven years had made chargeable transfers equal in value to those made by the settlor in the seven years before he created the settlement. For the purpose of this second calculation half rates are used. [**25.32**]

EXAMPLE 25.10

In 1997 Sam settles £90,000 on trust for Pam for life or until remarriage and thereafter on discretionary trusts for Sam's relatives and friends. His cumulative total at that time is £200,000 and he has made PETs of £85,000. Pam remarries one year later at a time when she has made chargeable transfers of £50,000; PETs of £45,000; and when the settled property is worth £110,000.

(1) The anti-avoidance provisions are relevant since the conditions for their operation are satisfied.

(2) Normally IHT would be calculated at Pam's rates: ie on a chargeable transfer from £50,000 to £160,000. Alternatively under these provisions the tax may be calculated by taking a hypothetical transferor who has Sam's cumulative total at the time when he created the trust; ie the £110,000 will be taxed as a chargeable transfer from £200,000 to £310,000. In this example the second calculation will be adopted since a greater amount of IHT results. Tax must be paid by the trustees.

(3) Assume that either Sam or Pam died after the termination of the interest in possession trust. This may result in a recalculation of the IHT liability (in this example PETs made by that person in the seven years before death would become chargeable). So far as the anti-avoidance rules are concerned, however, there is no question of disturbing the basis on which the IHT calculation was made in the first place. Hence, as was shown in (2) above, the greater tax was produced by taking the hypothetical transferor and, therefore, the subsequent death of Pam is irrelevant since it cannot be used to switch the basis of computation to Pam's cumulative total. By contrast, the death of Sam may involve additional IHT liability since his PETs of £85,000 will now become chargeable and thus included in the hypothetical transferor's total when the settlement was created.

c) *How to avoid the anti-avoidance rules*

First, if the interest in possession continues for seven years these rules do not apply.

Secondly, they are not in point if the settlement was created without an immediate interest in possession (eg there was an accumulation and maintenance trust which subsequently became an interest in possession trust), or if the settlement was created by means of an exempt transfer (eg if a life interest was given to the settlor's spouse and that interest was subsequently terminated in favour of a discretionary trust).

Thirdly, trustees can prevent the anti-avoidance rules from applying if, *within six months* of the ending of the interest in possession, they terminate the discretionary trust either by an absolute appointment or by creating a further life interest.

Finally, it is always possible to channel property into a discretionary trust by a PET, if an outright gift is made to another individual (a PET) who then settles the gifted property on the appropriate discretionary trusts (a chargeable transfer but taxed at *his* rates). Of course the transferor will have no legal right to force the donee to settle the outright gift.   **[25.33]**

5 Exemptions and reliefs

Reverter to settlor/spouse (IHTA 1984 s 53(3)–(5))   If, on the termination of an interest in possession, property reverts to the settlor, there is no charge to IHT unless the settlor (or his spouse) had acquired that interest for money or money's worth. This exemption also applies when the property passes to the settlor's spouse or (if the settlor is dead) to his widow or widower so long as that reverter occurs within two years of his death (for the CGT position, see **[18.45]**).   **[25.34]**

> **EXAMPLE 25.11**
>
> Janacek creates a settlement of £100,000 in favour of K for life (a PET). When K dies and the property reverts to the settlor no IHT will be charged.
>
> *Contrast the position*, if the settlement provided that the fund was to pass to L on the death of the life tenant, but the settlor's wife had purchased that remainder interest and given it to her husband as a Christmas present. On the death of the life tenant, although the property will revert to the settlor, the normal charge to IHT will apply.

Use of the life tenant's exemptions   The spouse exemption is available on the termination of the interest in possession if the person who then becomes entitled, whether absolutely or to another interest in possession, is the spouse of the former life tenant. In addition, IHTA 1984 s 57 permits the use of the life tenant's annual (£3,000 pa) exemption and the exemption for gifts in consideration of marriage on the *inter vivos* termination of an interest in possession if the life tenant so elects (see IHTA 1984 s 57(3), (4)). The exemptions for small gifts (£250) and normal expenditure out of income cannot be used.

> **EXAMPLE 25.12**
>
> Orff is the life tenant of the fund. His wife and son are entitled equally in remainder. If he surrenders the life interest, there will be no tax on the half-share passing to his wife (spouse exemption). The chargeable half-share passing to his son is a PET and, should it become chargeable because of his death within seven years, the annual exemption and, if surrender coincides with the marriage of the son, the £5,000 marriage gift relief will be available.

Although there the making of a PET is not reported, the appropriate notice should be given to the trustees by the life tenant indicating that he wishes the transfer to be covered by his relevant exemption so that it can then be submitted (if needed) to the Revenue as required by s 57(4).   **[25.35]**

The surviving spouse exemption   The carry-over of this estate duty relief is discussed at [**22.123**]. The first spouse must have died before 13 November 1974 and the relief ensures that IHT is not charged on the termination of the surviving spouse's interest in the property whether that occurs *inter vivos* or on death (IHTA 1984 Sch 6 para 2).   [**25.36**]

Excluded property   If the settlement contains excluded property, IHT is not charged on that portion of the fund (IHTA 1984 ss 5(1), 53(1)).   [**25.37**]

IHTA 1984 s 11 dispositions   If the interest in possession is disposed of for the purpose of maintaining the disponer's child or supporting a dependent relative, IHT is not charged (see [**23.6**]).   [**25.38**]

Charities   Tax is not charged if on the termination of the interest in possession the property is held on trust for charitable purposes.   [**25.39**]

Protective trusts   The forfeiture of a protected life interest is not normally treated as the termination of an interest in possession (see [**26.118**]).   [**25.40**]

Variations and disclaimers   Dispositions of the deceased may be altered after his death by means of an instrument of variation or disclaimer and treated as if they had been made by the deceased. Disclaimers are possible in the case both of settlements created by the deceased (IHTA 1984 s 142) and pre-existing settlements in which the death has resulted in a person becoming entitled to an interest in the settled property (IHTA 1984 s 93). Variations are only permitted for settlements created on death, not for settlements in which the deceased had been the beneficiary.   [**25.41**]

EXAMPLE 25.13

Poulenc, the life tenant of a settlement created by his father, has just died. His brother Quercus is now the life tenant in possession and if he assigns his interest within two years of Poulenc's death, the normal charging provisions will apply. (*Note:* (1) he could disclaim his interest without any IHT charge (IHTA 1984 s 93); (2) see [**22.120**] for problems caused to trustees when other property of the deceased is varied or disclaimed.)

Quick succession relief (IHTA 1984 s 141)   This relief is similar to that for unsettled property (see [**22.113**]). The first chargeable transfer may be either the creation of the settlement or any subsequent termination of an interest in possession (whether that termination occurs *inter vivos* or on death). Hence, it can be voluntarily used (by the life tenant surrendering or assigning his interest) whereas in the case of unsettled property it is only available on a death. The calculation of the relief in cases where there is more than one later transfer is dealt with in IHTA 1984 s 141(4).   [**25.42**]

EXAMPLE 25.14

(1) A settlement is created in January 1993; (2) the life interest ends in half of the fund in March 1995; (3) the life interest ends in the rest of the fund in February 1996. Assume that both PETs become chargeable because of the death of the life tenant within seven years.

Quick succession relief is available at a rate of 60% on event (2); and again at a rate of 40% on event (3). Generally, relief is given in respect of the earlier transfer first ((2) above). To the extent that the relief given represents less than the whole of the tax charged on the original net transfer ((1) above), further relief can then be given in respect of subsequent transfers ((3) above) until relief equal to the whole of the tax (in (1) above) has been given.

Business reliefs In a settlement containing business property that relief is available to the life tenant provided that he fulfils the conditions for relief (IHTA 1984 ss 103–114).

EXAMPLE 25.15

Satie is the life tenant of the settlement. He holds 30% of the shares in the trading company Teleman Ltd, and the trust holds a further 25%. Further, the trust owns the factory premises which are leased to the company. On the death of Satie, IHT business relief is available as follows:

(1) *On the shares*: the relief (assuming that the two-year ownership condition is satisfied) is at 100% on Satie's shares and on those of the fund. The life tenant is treated as having controlled the company since he held 30% (his own) and is treated as owning a further 25% of the shares.

(2) *On the land*: the relief is at 50% since the asset is used by a company controlled by the life tenant. (But see *Fetherstonehaugh v IRC* (1984).)

Similar rules operate for agricultural relief: ie the life tenant must satisfy the conditions of two years' occupation or seven years' ownership (ownership by the trustees being attributed to the life tenant).   **[25.43]–[25.60]**

III   THE TAXATION OF REVERSIONARY INTERESTS

Reversionary interests are generally excluded property so that their assignment or transfer does not lead to an IHT charge.

EXAMPLE 25.16

A fund is settled on trust for A for life (A is currently aged 88); B for life (B is 78); and C absolutely (C, A's son, is 70).

This settlement is likely to be subject to three IHT charges within a fairly short period. The position would be much improved if B and C disposed of their reversionary interests:

(1) B should surrender his interest. Taking into account his age it has little value and is merely an IHT trap.

(2) C should assign his interest to (ideally) a younger person. He might for instance have minor grandchildren and an accumulation and maintenance trust in their favour would be an attractive possibility.

The result of this reorganisation is that the fund is now threatened by only one IHT charge (on A's death) in the immediate future.

In four cases reversionary interests are not excluded property. This is to prevent their use as a tax avoidance device.

First, the sale of a reversionary interest to a beneficiary under the same trust, who is entitled to a prior interest (see **[25.29]**).

Secondly, the disposition of a reversionary interest which has at any time, and by any person, been acquired for a consideration in money or money's worth. (For special rules where that interest is situated outside the UK see **[27.85]**.)

EXAMPLE 25.17

Umberto sells his reversionary interest to Vidor (a stranger to the trust) for its market value, £20,000. If the general rules operated the position would be that:

(1)   Umberto is disposing of excluded property so that no IHT is chargeable.

(2)   Vidor has replaced chargeable assets (£20,000) with excluded property so that were he to die or make an *inter vivos* gift IHT would be avoided.

IHTA 1984 s 48(1)(a) and s 48(3) prevent. The reversion ceases to be excluded property once it has been purchased (even for a small consideration) so that a disposition by Vidor may lead to an IHT charge.

Thirdly, a disposition of a reversionary interest is chargeable if it is one to which either the settlor or his spouse is, or has been, beneficially entitled (IHTA 1984 s 48(1)(b)).

EXAMPLE 25.18

Viv settles property worth £100,000 on trust for his father Will for life (Will is 92). Viv retains the reversionary interest which he then gives to his daughter Ursula. If the general rules were not modified the position would be that:

(1)   The creation of the settlement would be a PET by Viv but the diminution in his estate would be very small (the difference between £100,000 and the value of a reversionary interest in £100,000 subject only to the termination of the interest of a 92 year old life tenant!).

(2)   The transfer of the reversion by Viv would escape IHT since it is excluded property.

IHTA 1984 s 48(1)(b) ensures that the reversion is chargeable so that Viv achieves no tax saving (and, indeed, is left with the danger of a higher IHT bill than if he had never created the settlement since the death of Will is a chargeable event).

Fourthly, the disposition of a reversionary interest is chargeable where that interest is expectant upon the termination of a lease which is treated as a settlement (typically one for life or lives; IHTA 1984 s 48(1)(c)). The lessor's reversion is treated in the same way as a reversionary interest purchased for money or money's worth so that on any disposition of it, IHT may be charged.   **[25.61]**

26 IHT—settlements without an interest in possession

I INTRODUCTION AND TERMINOLOGY

The method of charging settlements lacking an interest in possession is totally different from that for settlements with such an interest. Instead of attributing the fund to one of the beneficiaries, the settlement itself is the taxable entity. Like an individual, a record of chargeable transfers must be kept although, unlike the individual, it will never die and so will only be taxed at half rates. For convenience this chapter will discuss the rules by reference to the discretionary trust which is the most significant 'no interest in possession' settlement. In fact the category is wider than discretionary trusts catching for instance, the settlement in the *Pilkington* case ([**24.24**]) and trusts where the beneficiaries' interests are contingent.

EXAMPLE 26.1

(1) A fund of £100,000 is held upon trust for such of A, B, C, D, E and F as the trustees may in their absolute discretion (which extends over both income and capital) think appropriate. The trust is one without an interest in possession.
(2) Dad settles property on trust for son contingent on his attaining 30. Son is aged 21 at the date of the settlement and the income is to be accumulated until son attains 30. There is no interest in possession.

IHT is charged on 'relevant property' (IHTA 1984 s 58(1)) defined as settled property (other than excluded property) in which there is no qualifying interest in possession, with the exception of property settled on the 'special trusts' considered in Sections V and VI, below.

A 'qualifying interest in possession' is one owned beneficially by an individual or, in restricted circumstances, by a company. If within one settlement there exists an interest in possession in a part only of the settled property, these rules apply to the portion which lacks such an interest.   [**26.1**]-[**26.20**]

II THE METHOD OF CHARGE

The central feature is the periodic charge imposed upon discretionary trusts at ten-yearly intervals. The anniversary is calculated from the date on which the trust was created (IHTA 1984 s 61(1)).

EXAMPLE 26.2

(1) Silas creates a discretionary trust on 1 January 1989. The first anniversary charge will fall on 1 January 1999; the next on 1 January 2009 and so on. If the trust had been created by will and he had died on 31 December 1988, that date marks the creation of the settlement (IHTA 1984 s 83).

(2) He creates (in 1988) a settlement in favour of his wife Selina for life; thereafter for such of his three daughters as the trustees may in their absolute discretion select. Selina dies in 1989. For IHT purposes the discretionary trust is created by Selina on her death (IHTA 1984 s 80) although the ten-year anniversary runs from 1988 (IHTA 1984 s 61(2)).

Apart from the periodic charge, IHT is also levied (the 'exit charge') on the happening of certain events. In general, the IHT then charged is a proportion of the last periodic charge. Special charging provisions operate for chargeable events which occur before the first ten-year anniversary. **[26.21]**

1   The creation of the settlement

This will, generally, be a chargeable transfer of value by the settlor for IHT purposes. The following matters should be noted: *first*, if the settlement is created *inter vivos*, grossing-up applies unless IHT is paid out of the fund (see [**21.102**]).

Secondly, the cumulative total of chargeable transfers made by the settlor forms part of the cumulative total of the settlement on all future chargeable occasions (ie his transfers never drop out of the cumulative total). Therefore, in order to calculate the correct IHT charge it is essential that the trustees are told the settlor's cumulative total at the date when he created the trust. When as a result of the settlor's fraud, wilful default or neglect there is an underpayment of IHT, the Revenue may recover that sum from the trustees outside the normal six-year time limit. In such cases the time limit is six years from the date when the impropriety comes to the notice of the Revenue (IHTA 1984 s 240(3)). Obviously a problem would arise for trustees if at the time when the underpayment came to light they held insufficient assets to discharge the extra IHT bill since they could be made personally liable for the tax unpaid. The Revenue has, however, stated that where the trustees have acted in good faith and hold insufficient settlement assets it will not seek to recover any unpaid tax from them personally (*Law Society's Gazette*, 1984, p 3517).

Thirdly, a 'related settlement' is one created by the same settlor on the same day as the discretionary trust (other than a charitable trust). Generally such settlements should be avoided (see [**26.27**]). The use of 'pilot' trusts is considered at [**26.35**].

Fourthly, additions of property by the original settlor to his settlement should also be avoided (see [**26.33**]). If property is added by a person other than the original settlor, the addition will be treated as a separate settlement.

Problems may arise for the trustees if the settlor dies within seven years of creating the trust. PETs made before the settlement was created and within seven years of his death then become chargeable so that tax on creation of the settlement and the computation of any exit charge made during this period may need to be recalculated. If extra tax becomes payable this is primarily the responsibility of the settlement trustees and their liability is not limited to settlement property in their hands *at that time*. Given this danger it will be prudent for trustees who are distributing property from the discretionary trust within the first seven years to retain sufficient funds or take suitable indemnities to cover their contingent IHT liability. [26.22]

EXAMPLE 26.3

Sumar makes the following transfers of value:
May 1994 £200,000 to his sister Sufi (a PET).
May 1995 £70,000 to a family discretionary trust.
In May 1996 the trustees distribute the entire fund to the beneficiaries and in May 1997 Sumar dies.

As a result of his death, the 1994 PET is chargeable (the resultant IHT is primarily the responsibility of Sufi) and in addition tax on the creation of the settlement must be recalculated.

When it was set up the PET was ignored so that the transfer fell within Sumar's nil rate band. With his death, however, IHT must be calculated, at the rates in force in May 1997, on transfers from £200,000 to £270,000 (tax is £22,000). In addition it is likely that no IHT will have been charged on the distribution of the fund in 1996 and therefore a recomputation is again necessary with the trustees being liable for the resulting tax.

2 Exit charges before the first ten-year anniversary

a) *When will an exit charge arise?*

A charge is imposed whenever property in the settlement ceases to be 'relevant property' (IHTA 1984 s 65). For instance, if the trustees appoint property to a beneficiary or if an interest in possession arises in any portion of the fund, there will be a charge to the extent of the property ceasing to be held on discretionary trusts. If the resultant IHT is paid out of the property that is left in the discretionary trust, grossing-up will apply. A charge is also imposed if the trustees make a disposition as a result of which the value of relevant property comprised in the settlement falls (a 'depreciatory transaction'; see [25.30]: notice that there is no requirement that the transaction must be made with a beneficiary or with a person connected with him).

The exit charge does not apply to a payment of costs or expenses (so long as it is 'fairly attributable' to the relevant property), nor does it catch a payment which is income of any person for the purposes of income tax (IHTA 1984 s 65(5)). [26.23]

b) *Calculation of the settlement rate*

The calculation of the rate of IHT is based upon half the full IHT rates, even if the trust was set up under the will of the settlor. The rate of tax actually payable is then 30% of those rates applicable to a hypothetical chargeable transfer.

Step 1 This hypothetical transfer is made up of the sum of the following:
(1) the value of the property in the settlement immediately after it commenced;
(2) the value (at the date of the addition) of any added property; and
(3) the value of property in a related settlement (valued immediately after it commenced (IHTA 1984 s 68(5)).
No account is taken of any rise or fall in the value of the settled fund and the value comprised in the settlement and in any related settlement can include property subject to an interest in possession.

Step 2 Tax at half rates on this hypothetical transfer is calculated by joining the table at the point reached by the cumulative total of previous chargeable transfers made by the settlor in the seven years before he created the settlement.

Other chargeable transfers made on the same day as the settlement are ignored and, therefore, if the settlement was created on death, other gifts made in the will or on intestacy are ignored (IHTA 1984 s 68(4)(b)).

Step 3 The resultant tax is converted to an average rate (the equivalent of an estate rate) and 30% of that rate is then taken. The resultant rate (the 'settlement rate') is used as the basis for calculating the exit charge.   **[26.24]**

EXAMPLE 26.4

Justinian settles £100,000 on discretionary trusts on 1 April 1997. His total chargeable transfers immediately before that date stood at £125,000. He pays the IHT. If an exit charge arises before the first ten-year anniversary of the fund (1 April 2007) the settlement rate would be calculated as follows:

Step 1 Calculate the hypothetical chargeable transfer. As there is no added property and no related settlement it comprises only the value of the property in the settlement immediately after its creation (ie £100,000).

Step 2 Cumulate the £100,000 with the previous chargeable transfers of Justinian (ie £125,000). Taking the current IHT rates, tax on transfers between £125,000 and £225,000 is £2,000.

Step 3 The tax converted to a percentage rate is 2%; 30% of that rate produces a 'settlement rate' of 0.6%.

c) *The tax charged*

The charge is on the fall in value of the fund. To establish the rate of charge, a further proportion of the settlement rate must be calculated equal to one-fortieth of the settlement rate for each complete successive quarter that has elapsed from the creation of the settlement to the date of the exit charge. That proportion of the settlement rate is applied to the chargeable transfer (the 'effective rate').

EXAMPLE 26.5

Assume in *Example 26.4* that on 25 March 1999 there was an exit charge on £20,000 ceasing to be relevant property. The 'effective rate' of IHT is calculated as follows:

Step 1 Take completed quarters since the settlement was created, ie seven.

Step 2 Take 7/40ths of the 'settlement rate' (0.6%) to discover the 'effective rate' = 0.105%.

Step 3 The effective rate is applied to the fall in value of the relevant property. The IHT will, therefore, be £21 if the tax is borne by the beneficiary; or £21.04 if borne by the remaining fund.

There is no charge on events that occur in the first three months of the settlement (IHTA 1984 s 65(4)) nor, when the trust was set up by the settlor on his death, on events occurring within two years of that death (see **[22.114]**).   **[26.25]**

3   **The charge on the first ten-year anniversary**

a) *What property is charged?*

The charge is levied on the value of the *relevant property* comprised in the settlement immediately before the anniversary (IHTA 1984 s 64). Income only becomes relevant property, and thus subject to charge, when it has been accumulated (see SP 8/86). Pending accumulation it is not subject to the anniversary charge and can be distributed free from any exit charge (see [**26.23**]). The crucial question is, therefore, at what moment is income accumulated? Accumulation occurs once an irrevocable decision to that effect has been taken by trustees, and it may also occur after a reasonable time for distribution has passed (but see *Re Locker* (1977) in which income arising between 1965 and 1968 was still available for distribution in 1977). The legislation gives no guidance on what property is treated as being distributed first: ie if an appointment is made by the trustees out of property comprised in the settlement, does it come out of the original capital or out of accumulations of income? As a reduced charge may apply to property which has been added to the trust (such as accumulated income: see [**26.33**]) this is an important omission (for the approach adopted in practice by the CTO see *Capital Taxes News*, vol 8, May 1989).

The assets in the fund are valued according to general principles and, if they include business or agricultural property, the reliefs appropriate to that property will apply, subject to satisfaction of the relevant conditions. Any IHT charged on such property will be payable in instalments.   [**26.26**]

b) *Calculation of the rate of IHT*

Half rates will be used and, as with the exit charge, the calculation depends upon a hypothetical chargeable transfer.

Step 1 Calculate the hypothetical chargeable transfer which is made up of the sum of the following:
(1) the value of relevant property comprised in the settlement immediately before the anniversary;
(2) the value, immediately after it was created, of property comprised in a 'related settlement'; and
(3) the value, at the date when the settlement was created, of any non-relevant property then in the settlement which has not subsequently become relevant property.

Normally the hypothetical chargeable transfer will be made up exclusively of property falling within (1) above. (2) and (3), which affect the rate of IHT to be charged without themselves being taxed, are anti-avoidance measures. Related settlements are included because transfers made on the same day as the creation of the settlement are normally ignored and, therefore, an IHT advantage could be achieved if the settlor were to set up a series of small funds rather than one large fund. Non-relevant property in the settlement is included because the trustees could switch the values between the two portions of the fund.

Step 2 Calculate tax at half rates on the hypothetical chargeable transfer by joining the table at the point reached by:
(1) the chargeable transfers of the settlor made in the *seven* years before he created the settlement; and
(2) chargeable transfers made by the settlement in the first *ten* years. Where a settlement was created after 26 March 1974 and before 9 March 1982, distribution payments (as defined by the IHT charging regime in force between those dates) must also be cumulated (IHTA 1984 s 66(6)).

Discretionary settlements will, therefore, have their own total of chargeable transfers with transfers over a ten-year period being cumulated (contrast the seven-year period used for individuals). The unique feature of a settlement's cumulation lies in the inclusion (and it never drops out) of chargeable transfers of the settlor in the seven years before the settlement is created.

Step 3   The IHT is converted to a percentage and 30% of that rate is then taken and charged on the relevant property in the settlement.

The highest rate of IHT is 20% (half of 40%). The highest effective rate (anniversary rate) is, therefore, 30% of 20%, ie 6%. Where the settlement comprises business property qualifying for 50% relief, this effective rate falls to 3% and assuming that the option to pay in instalments is exercised, the annual charge over the ten-year period becomes a mere 0.3%. If the property qualifies for 100% business or agricultural relief there is no charge.   **[26.27]**

> **EXAMPLE 26.6**
>
> Take the facts of *Example 26.5* (viz, original fund £125,000, exit charge on £20,000; previous transfers of settlor £125,000). In addition, assume Justinian had created a second settlement of £15,000 on 1 April 1997.
>
> The fund is worth £105,000 at the first ten-year anniversary.
>
> (1) Relevant property to be taxed is £105,000
>
> (2) Calculate hypothetical chargeable transfer
>
> | | £ |
> |--|-----------|
> | Relevant property, as above | 105,000 |
> | Property in related settlement | 15,000 |
> | | £120,000 |
>
> (3) Settlement's cumulative IHT total:
>
> | | £ |
> |--|-----------|
> | Settlor's earlier transfers | 125,000 |
> | Chargeable transfers of trustees in preceding ten years | 20,000 |
> | | £145,000 |
>
> (4) Tax from the table (at half rates) on transfers from £145,000 to £265,000 (£120,000 + £145,000) = £10,000 so that, as a percentage rate IHT is 8.33%.
>
> (5) The 'effective rate' is 30% of 8.33% = 2.5%.
> Tax payable is £105,000 × 2.5% = £2,625.

4   Exit charges after the first anniversary charge and between anniversaries

The same events will trigger an exit charge after the first ten-year anniversary as before it. The IHT charge will be levied on the fall in value of the fund with grossing-up, if necessary. The rate of charge is a proportion of the effective rate charged at the first ten-year anniversary. That proportion is one-fortieth for each complete quarter from the date of the first anniversary charge to the date of the exit charge (IHTA 1984 s 69).

> **EXAMPLE 26.7**
>
> Continuing *Example 26.6*, exactly 15 months later the trustees appoint £25,000 to a beneficiary. The IHT (assuming no grossing-up) will be:
> £25,000 × 2.5% × 5/40 (five quarters since last ten-year anniversary) = £78.12.

If the rates of IHT have been reduced (including the raising of the rate bands) between the anniversary and exit charges, the lower rates will apply to the exit charge and, therefore, the rate of charge on the first anniversary will have to be recalculated at those rates (IHTA 1984 Sch 2 para 3). So long as the IHT rate bands remain linked to rises in the retail prices index (IHTA 1984 s 8) recalculation is likely to be the norm.

No exit charge is levied if the chargeable event occurs within the first quarter following the anniversary charge. **[26.28]**

5 Later periodic charges

The principles that applied on the first ten-year anniversary operate on subsequent ten-year anniversaries. So far as the hypothetical chargeable transfer is concerned the same items will be included (so that the value of property in a related settlement and of non-relevant property in the settlement is always included). The cumulative total of the fund will, as before, include the chargeable transfers of the settlor made in the seven years before he created the settlement and the transfers out of the settlement in the ten years immediately preceding the anniversary (earlier transfers by the settlement fall out of the cumulative total). The remaining stages of the calculation are unaltered. **[26.29]**

6 Technical problems

The basic structure of the charging provisions in IHTA 1984 ss 58–69 is relatively straightforward. The charge to IHT is built on a series of periodic charges with interim charges (where appropriate) which are levied at a fraction of the full periodic charge. **[26.30]**

Reduction in the rate of the anniversary charge If property has not been in the settlement for the entire preceding ten years (as will be the case when income is accumulated during that period) there is a proportionate reduction in the charge (IHTA 1984 s 66(2)). The reduction in the periodic rate is calculated by reference to the number of completed quarters which expired before the property became relevant property in the settlement.

EXAMPLE 26.8

Assume in *Example 26.6* that £15,000 had become relevant property on 30 April 2003.

The IHT charge on the first ten-year anniversary (on 1 April 2007) would now be calculated as follows:

(1) £90,000 (£105,000 – £15,000) at 2.5% = £2,250.
(2) The £15,000 will be charged at a proportion of the periodic charge rate: viz— 2.5% reduced by 24/40 since 24 complete quarters elapsed from the creation of the settlement (on 1 April 1997) to the date when the £15,000 became relevant property. As a result the IHT charged is £15,000 × 1% = £150.

This proportionate reduction in the effective rate of the periodic charge will not affect the calculation of IHT on events occurring after the anniversary, ie any exit charge is at the full effective rate.

The legislation does not contain provisions which enable specific property to be identified. Thus, the reduction mentioned above applies to the value of the relevant property in the fund at the ten-year anniversary 'attributable' to property which was not relevant property throughout the preceding ten years. Presumably a proportionate calculation will be necessary where the value of the fund has shown an increase. Furthermore, if accumulated income is caught by the anniversary charge, a separate calculation will have to be made with regard to each separate accumulation (see SP 8/86: **[26.26]**). **[26.31]**

Transfers between settlements IHTA 1984 s 81 prevents a tax advantage from switching property between discretionary settlements, by providing that such property remains comprised in the first settlement. Accordingly, property cannot be moved out of a discretionary trust to avoid an anniversary charge; property cannot be switched from a fund with a high cumulative total to one with a lower total; and the transfer of property from one discretionary fund to another will not be chargeable.   [**26.32**]

Added property   Special rules operate if, after the settlement commenced (and after 8 March 1982), the settlor made a chargeable transfer as a result of which the value of the property comprised in the settlement was increased (IHTA 1984 s 67(1)). Note that it is only additions by the settlor that trigger these provisions and that it is the value of the fund which must be increased and not necessarily the amount of property in that fund. Transfers which have the effect of increasing the value of the fund are ignored if they are not primarily intended to have that effect and do not in fact increase the value by more than 5%.

> **EXAMPLE 26.9**
>
> Sam, the settlor, creates in 1997 a discretionary trust of stocks and shares in Sham Ltd and the benefit of a life insurance policy on Sam's life.
> (1)   Each year Sam adds property to the settlement, equal to his annual IHT exemption.
> (2)   Sam continues to pay the premiums on the life policy each year.
> (3)   Sam transfers further shares in Sham Ltd.
>   The special rules for added property will not apply in either case (1) or (2), since Sam is not making a chargeable transfer; the first transfer is covered by his annual exemption and the second by the exemption for normal expenditure out of income. The transfer of further shares to the fund, however, is caught by the provisions of IHTA 1984 s 67.

If the added property provisions apply, the calculation of the periodic charge which immediately follows the addition will be modified. For the purposes of the hypothetical chargeable transfer, the cumulative total of the settlor's chargeable transfers will be the higher of the totals (1) immediately before creating the settlement plus transfers made by the settlement before the addition; and (2) immediately before transferring the added property, deducting from this latter total the transfer made on creation of the settlement and a transfer to any related settlement. The settlor should avoid additions, since they may cause more IHT to be charged at the next anniversary and it will be preferable to create a separate settlement.   [**26.33**]

The timing of the exit charge   Assume that a discretionary trust has been in existence for nearly ten years and that the trustees now wish to distribute all or part of the fund to the beneficiaries. Are they better off doing so just before the ten-year anniversary or should they wait until just after that anniversary? Generally, it will be advantageous to distribute *before* an anniversary because IHT payable will be calculated at rates then in force but on historic values: ie on the value of the fund when it was settled or at the last ten-year anniversary. By contrast, if the trustees delay until after the anniversary, IHT (still at current rates) will then be assessed on the present value of the fund. To this general proposition one major exception exists which may well be the result of defective drafting in the legislation. It relates to a fund consisting of property qualifying for either business relief or agricultural relief at 50%. In this situation trustees *should not* break up the fund immediately before the first anniversary.   [**26.34**]

EXAMPLE 26.10

A discretionary settlement was created on 1 January 1988. At all times it has consisted of agricultural property which will qualify for 50% relief. Assume no earlier transfers by settlor and that the value of the property is £500,000 throughout. Consider the effect of agricultural relief if:

(1) *the trustees distribute the entire fund on 25 December 1997*. The distribution occurs before the first ten-year anniversary. The entire value of the property in the settlement immediately after it commenced must be included in the hypothetical transfer of value since there is no agricultural relief reduction. Therefore £500,000 must be included (IHTA 1984 s 111(5)(a)). The rate thus calculated is then applied to the fund as reduced by business relief. Hence, although the amount subject to the charge is only £250,000 (£500,000 minus 50% relief), a higher rate of IHT will apply. (Notice that if 100% relief were to be available in 1997 this trap would not arise.)

(2) *the trustees distribute the entire fund on 3 January 1998*. As the first ten-year anniversary fell on 1 January there will be no exit charge because the distribution is within three months of that anniversary. So far as the anniversary charge is concerned the property subject to the charge will be reduced by 50% relief to £250,000; and for the purpose of calculating the hypothetical chargeable transfer the value of the property is similarly reduced by the relief.

7 Using discretionary trusts

Discretionary trusts are likely to remain attractive in the following situations:

(a) small *inter vivos* discretionary settlements. Notice that two discretionary settlements can be used to create two nil band trusts when the transferor is transferring one and a half times his nil rate band.

EXAMPLE 26.11

A taxpayer transfers agricultural property (qualifying for 50% relief) into two discretionary trusts as follows:

Into Discretionary Trust 1 property which reduces his estate by £107,500 after 50% agricultural property relief.

Into Discretionary Trust 2 property which reduces his estate by £53,750 after 50% agricultural property relief.

In both cases, assume that the agricultural property is sold by the trustees. The result is that the first discretionary trust is worth £215,000 and, in working out any IHT charges, the settlor's cumulative total when the trust was created was nil. The second discretionary trust is worth £107,500 and was set up at a time when the cumulative total of the settlor was £107,500. Accordingly, the two trusts are nil rate band trusts, but remember that to avoid the related settlement rules, they should be created on separate days.

In appropriate cases a settlor can create a number of pilot settlements each with a full nil rate band.

EXAMPLE 26.12

S wishes to put £400,000 into discretionary trusts. He therefore creates four pilot trusts of £10 each on *different days* (so that they are not 'related settlements') and subsequently but *on the same day* pays £99,990 into each trust thus created. The trusts are not related since they are created on different days and each comprises £100,000. As transfers made on the same day are ignored in computing the settlor's cumulative total, that total is either £10 or £20 or £30 when the relevant addition is made. Notice that although each settlement will enjoy a full nil rate band, the transfer of £400,000 into settlement will attract an immediate IHT charge at half rates.

(b) In will drafting the use of the mini (£215,000) discretionary trust remains attractive for the smaller estate (see [**40.74**]).

(c) It is possible to set up discretionary trusts by channelling property through an accumulation and maintenance trust (ie taking advantage of 'children of straw'). [**26.35**]-[**26.50**]

III EXEMPTIONS AND RELIEFS

Many of the exemptions from IHT do not apply to property in discretionary trusts, eg the annual exemption, the marriage exemption, and the exemption for normal expenditure out of income. There is no exemption if the settled fund reverts to either the settlor or his spouse (and note that if the settlor is a beneficiary, or a paid trustee, the reservation of benefit provisions apply). Business and agricultural property relief may, however, be available, provided that the necessary conditions for the relief are met by the trustees. There is no question of any aggregation with similar property owned by a discretionary beneficiary.

Exit charges are not levied in certain cases when property leaves the settlement, eg:
(1) Property ceasing to be relevant property within three months of the creation of the trust or of an anniversary charge or within two years of creation (if the trust was set up on death) is not subject to an exit charge ([**22.114**] and [**26.25**]).
(2) Property may pass, without attracting an exit charge, to such privileged trusts as employee trusts (IHTA 1984 s 75); maintenance funds for historic buildings (IHTA 1984 Sch 4 para 16); permanent charities (IHTA 1984 s 76(1)); political parties in accordance with the exemption in IHTA 1984 s 24 (IHTA 1984 s 76(1)(b); and see Chapter 23); national heritage bodies (IHTA 1984 s 76(1)(c)); and non-profit making bodies approved by the Treasury and holding heritage property (IHTA 1984 s 76(1)(d), (2)). There is no exemption for property passing into an accumulation and maintenance trust.

If a discretionary fund contains excluded property (and property qualifying for 100% business or agricultural relief) the periodic and exit charges will not apply to that portion of the fund. [**26.51**]-[**26.70**]

IV DISCRETIONARY TRUSTS CREATED BEFORE 27 MARCH 1974

Discretionary settlements created before 27 March 1974 are subject to special rules for the calculation of tax which generally result in less tax being charged (see generally IHTA 1984 ss 66–68). [**26.71**]

1 Chargeable events occurring before the first ten-year anniversary

The rate of IHT is set out in IHTA 1984 s 68(6). As the settlement is treated as a separate taxable entity only transfers made by the settlement are cumulated. Such chargeable transfers will either be distribution payments (if made under the regime in force from 1974 to 1982) or chargeable events under IHTA 1984 s 65. Once the cumulative total is known, the rate of tax will be calculated at half rate and the charge will be at 30% of that rate. **[26.72]**

2 The first anniversary charge

No anniversary charge applied before 1 April 1983. Thus, the first trust to suffer this charge was one created on 1 April 1973 (or 1963; 1953; 1943 and so on).

The amount subject to the charge is calculated in the normal way. In calculating the rate of charge, however, it is only chargeable transfers of the settlement in the preceding ten years that are cumulated (as the settlement predates CTT/IHT the settlor has no chargeable transfers to cumulate). Property in a related settlement and non-relevant property in the settlement are ignored. As before, the rate of charge is reduced if property has not been relevant property throughout the decade preceding the first anniversary. The danger of increasing an IHT bill by an addition of property by the settlor (see **[26.33]**) is even greater with these old trusts. If such an addition has been made, the settlor's chargeable transfers in the seven-year period before the addition must be cumulated in calculating the rate of tax on the anniversary charge (IHTA 1984 s 67(4)). The effective rate of charge for the anniversary charge is (as for new trusts) 30% of the rate calculated according to half the table rates. **[26.73]**

3 Chargeable events after the first anniversary charge

The position is the same as for new trusts. The charge is based upon the rate charged at the last anniversary. **[26.74]-[26.90]**

EXAMPLE 26.13

In November 1975 Maggie settled £400,000 on discretionary trusts for her family. The following events have since occurred:
In May 1981: a distribution payment of £100,000.
In May 1984: trustees distribute a further sum of £85,000 (tax borne by beneficiary).
In November 1985: the first ten-year anniversary. The value of relevant property then in the fund is £300,000.
IHT will be charged as follows:
(1) *May 1984*: The distribution is a chargeable event occurring before the first ten-year anniversary. IHT is calculated by cumulating the chargeable transfer of £85,000 with the earlier transfer made by the settlement (the distribution payment of £100,000).
   (Notice that there is no proportionate reduction in the effective rate for exit charges levied on old discretionary trusts before the first anniversary.)
(2) *November 1985*: The anniversary charge will be calculated on the relevant property in the settlement (£100,000). The cumulative total of transfers made by the settlement is £185,000 (£100,000 plus £85,000).

V ACCUMULATION AND MAINTENANCE TRUSTS
(IHTA 1984 s 71)

1 Tax treatment

Inheritance tax Rather than make outright gifts to minor children, property is frequently settled in trust for their benefit. If special treatment were not accorded to such settlements IHT would discriminate between gifts to adults and settled gifts to infants.

EXAMPLE 26.14

Simon makes two gifts: to his brother, Enrico, and to his two month old granddaughter, Frederica.

(1) *The gift to Enrico:* The gift is a potentially exempt transfer (PET) and therefore only subject to IHT if Simon dies within seven years.

(2) *The gift to Frederica:* In view of her age, it is felt necessary to settle the property on trusts which give the trustees the power to maintain Frederica, but which give her no interest in possession. Under general principles, the creation of that settlement will be a chargeable transfer of value and the discretionary trust charging regime will thereupon operate. As a result there would be anniversary charges and, when Frederica obtains either an interest in possession or an absolute interest in the settled fund, an 'exit' charge.

The object of the special provisions is to prevent this double charge. The *inter vivos* creation of an accumulation and maintenance settlement is accordingly a potentially exempt transfer (a PET) and thereafter, so long as the property continues to be held on accumulation and maintenance (A & M) trusts, the ten-year anniversary charge will not apply and there will be no proportionate periodic charge when the property leaves the trust. As a result, the taxation of gifts to children is treated in the same way as gifts to adults.   **[26.91]**

Other taxes   The privileged status of the A & M trust only applies for IHT purposes. So far as the other taxes are concerned, general principles operate. Unless the property settled comprises business assets, CGT hold-over relief is not available on the *inter vivos* creation of the trust and will only be available on its termination if a beneficiary becomes absolutely entitled to the assets on the ending of the accumulation period ([**17.81**]). Capital gains realised by the trustees will be subject to tax at a 34% rate. For income tax, the creation of an A & M trust by a parent on behalf of his own infant unmarried children will result in any income which is distributed being taxed as his under TA 1988 s 660B. Given the nature of an A & M trust, the trustees will suffer income tax at the rate of 34% (TA 1988 s 686).

Accordingly, the IHT attractions of these trusts have to some extent been eroded by their income tax and CGT treatment and it should not be assumed that the A & M trust is always the 'best buy'.   **[26.92]**

2 The requirements of IHTA 1984 s 71

To qualify for privileged IHT treatment, an A & M trust has to satisfy the three requirements considered below. Failure to do so means that the normal charging system applies. When the requirements cease to be satisfied IHT will not be charged save in exceptional cases (see [**26.98**]).   **[26.93]**

3 Requirement 1

'One or more persons (. . . beneficiaries) will, on or before attaining a specified age not exceeding 25, become entitled to, or to an interest in possession in, the settled property or part of it' (IHTA 1984 s 71).

Requirement 1 is concerned with the age at which a beneficiary becomes entitled either to the income from the fund or to the fund itself. The age of 25 is specified as a maximum age limit and this is generously late when one considers that the justification for these rules is to deal with settlements for infant children.

EXAMPLE 26.15

(1) Property is settled upon trust 'for A absolutely, contingent on attaining the age of 18'. A will become entitled to both income and capital at that age so that Requirement 1 is satisfied.

(2) Property is settled upon trust 'for B absolutely, contingent upon attaining the age of 30'. At first sight Requirement 1 is broken since B will not acquire the capital in the fund until after the age of 25. However, the requirement will be satisfied if the beneficiary acquires an interest in possession before 25; B will do so, because the Trustee Act 1925 s 31 (if not expressly excluded) provides that when a beneficiary with a contingent interest attains 18, that beneficiary shall thereupon be entitled to the income produced by the fund even though he has not yet satisfied the contingency.

The requirement that a beneficiary '*will*' become entitled does not require absolute certainty; death, for instance, can always prevent entitlement. The word causes particular problems when trustees possess overriding powers of advancement and appointment (dispositive powers) which, if exercised, could result in entitlement being postponed beyond 25. So long as the dispositive power can only be exercised amongst the existing beneficiaries and cannot postpone entitlement beyond the age of 25, Requirement 1 is satisfied. Accordingly, a power to vary or determine the respective shares of members of the class, even to the extent of excluding some members altogether, is permissible.

EXAMPLE 26.16

Property is held on trust for the three children of A contingent upon their attaining the age of 25 and, if more than one, in equal shares. The trustees are given overriding powers of appointment, exercisable until a beneficiary attains 25, to appoint the fund to one or more of the beneficiaries as they see fit. Requirement 1 is satisfied since the property will vest absolutely in the beneficiaries no later than the age of 25. The existence of the overriding power of appointment is irrelevant since it cannot be exercised other than in favour of the class of beneficiaries and cannot be used to postpone the vesting of the fund until after a beneficiary has attained 25.

The mere existence of a common form of power of advancement will not prevent Requirement 1 from being satisfied (see *Lord Inglewood v IRC* (1983)). However, that such powers can be exercised so as to postpone the vesting of property in a beneficiary beyond the age stated in the trust document and, hence, beyond the age of 25 (see *Pilkington v IRC* (1962)) and they can, in exceptional cases, result in property being paid to a non-beneficiary (as in *Re Clore's Settlement Trusts* (1966) where the payment was to the beneficiary's favourite charity). If the power is so exercised a charge to IHT will result.

The effect of powers of appointment which, if exercised, would break Requirement 1, was considered in an IR Press Release of 19 January 1975 and is illustrated by the following example:

EXAMPLE 26.17

Property is settled 'for the children of E contingent on their attaining 25'. The trustees are given the following (alternative) overriding powers of appointment.

(1) *To appoint income and capital to E's sister F:* The mere existence of this power causes the settlement to break Requirement 1. There is no certainty that the fund will pass to E's children since the power might be exercised in favour of F.

(2) *To appoint income to E's brother G:* The same consequence will follow since the mere existence of this power means that the income could be used for the

benefit of G and, hence, break Requirement 2 (for details of this Requirement see below).

(3) *To appoint capital and income to E's relatives so long as those relatives are no older than 25:* This power does not break Requirement 1 since whoever receives the settled fund, whether E's children or his relatives, will be no older than 25.

It may be difficult to decide whether or not the settlement contains a power of revocation or appointment which will break Requirement 1. In *Lord Inglewood v IRC* (1981), Vinelott J distinguished between events provided for in the trust instrument and events wholly outside the settlor's control:

'the terms of the settlement must be such that one or more of the beneficiaries, if they or one of them survive to the specified age, will be bound to take a vested interest on or before attaining that age ... Of course, a beneficiary may assign his interest, or be deprived of it, by an arrangement, or by bankruptcy, before he attains a vested interest. But he is not then deprived of it under the terms of the settlement, so these possible events, unlike the exercise of a power of revocation or appointment, must be disregarded....' [1981] STC at 318 (see also Fox LJ, in the Court of Appeal, 1983 STC at 138).

EXAMPLE 26.18

Sebag creates a settlement in favour of his second daughter, Juno, under which she will obtain the property if she attains the age of 18. If she marries before that age, however, the property is to pass to Sebag's brother, Sebastian.

This provision in the settlement could operate to deprive Juno of the property in circumstances when, as a matter of general law, she would not be so deprived. The settlement does not satisfy Requirement 1 and so does not qualify for privileged treatment.

Two other matters should be noted in relation to Requirement 1. *First*, even if a trust instrument fails to specify an age at which the beneficiary will become entitled to either the income or capital, so long as it is clear from the terms of that instrument and the known ages of the beneficiaries that one or more persons will in fact become entitled before the age of 25, Requirement 1 will be satisfied (ESC F8).

Secondly, for an A & M trust to be created there must be a living beneficiary at that time. It is possible to set up a trust for a class of persons including some who are unborn ('the grandchildren of the settlor' for instance), but there must be at least one member of the class in existence at the date of creation (IHTA 1984 s 71(7)). If the single living beneficiary dies, the trust (assuming that it was set up for a class of beneficiaries) will remain an A & M trust until a further member of that class is born. If a further class member is never born, it will eventually pass elsewhere and at that stage an IHT charge may arise. **[26.94]**

4   Requirement 2

'No interest in possession subsists in the settled property (or part) and the income from it is to be accumulated so far as it is not applied for the maintenance, education or benefit of such a person' (IHTA 1984 s 71).

There must be no interest in possession and once such an interest arises, the settlement breaks Requirement 2 and ceases to be an A & M trust.

If there is no interest in possession in the income, what is to be done with it? Two possibilities are envisaged by Requirement 2; it can either be used for the benefit of a beneficiary (eg under a power of maintenance), or it can be accumulated. There must be a valid power to accumulate: accordingly once the accumulation period ends Requirement 2 will cease to be satisfied and the settlement will no longer be an A & M trust.

EXAMPLE 26.19

A trust is set up for Loeb, the child of the settlor, contingent on his attaining the age of 25. So long as he is a minor the trustees will have a power to maintain him out of the income of the fund and a power to accumulate any surplus income (Trustee Act 1925 s 31). When Loeb becomes 18 he will be entitled to the income of the fund so that an interest in possession will arise and the settlement will cease to be an A & M trust. The ending of the trust will not lead to any IHT charge.

Care should be taken in choosing the appropriate period if the intention is to accumulate income beyond the minorities of the beneficiaries. Various periods are permitted under LPA 1925 ss 164 and 165 and under the Trustee Act 1925 s 31, but some of them may cause the trust to fall outside the definition of an accumulation and maintenance settlement. In the case of an *inter vivos* trust, for instance, a direction to accumulate 'during the lifetime of the settlor' would mean that an interest in possession might not arise until after the beneficiaries had attained the age of 25; likewise, a provision to accumulate for 21 years when the beneficiaries are over the age of four would be fatal. [**26.95**]

5 Requirement 3

'Either
(i) not more than 25 years have elapsed since the day on which the settlement was made or (if later) since the time when the settled property (or part) began to satisfy Requirements 1 and 2, or
(ii) all the persons who are, or have been beneficiaries are, or were, either grandchildren of a common grandparent, or children, widows or widowers of such grandchildren who were themselves beneficiaries but died before becoming entitled as mentioned in [Requirement 1]' (IHTA 1984 s 71).

Requirement 3 was introduced to stop the A & M trust from being used to benefit more than one generation. There are two ways in which it can be satisfied. First, the trust must not last for more than 25 years from the date when the fund became settled on A & M trusts. The second (alternative) limb of Requirement 3 is satisfied if all the beneficiaries have a common grandparent.

EXAMPLE 26.20

(1) Property is settled for the children and grandchildren of the settlor. As there is no grandparent common to all the beneficiaries, the trust must not last for longer than 25 years if an exit charge to IHT is to be avoided.
(2) Property is settled for the children of brothers Bill and Ben. As there is a common grandparent the duration of the settlement does not need to be limited to 25 years.

There is one case in which two generations can be benefited under an A & M trust since substitution *per stirpes* is permitted where the original beneficiaries had a common grandparent and one of those beneficiaries has died. [**26.96**]

6   Advantages of accumulation and maintenance trusts

No IHT is charged when property from an A & M trust becomes subject to an interest in possession in favour of one or more of the beneficiaries, nor when any part of the fund is appointed absolutely to such a beneficiary (IHTA 1984 s 71(3) (4)). This exemption, together with the exclusion of the anniversary charge (IHTA 1984 s 58(1)(b)), means that once the property is settled on these trusts there should be no IHT liability. Furthermore the *inter vivos* creation of the trust is a PET.

EXAMPLE 26.21

'... to A absolutely contingent on attaining 25'. This straightforward trust will satisfy the Requirements so long as A is an infant. Consider, however, the position:
(1)   *When A attains 18:* he will be entitled to the income from the fund (Trustee Act 1925 s 31) and, therefore, Requirement 2 is broken. No IHT is charged on the arising of the interest in possession.
(2)   *When A attains 25:* ordinary principles for interest in possession settlements apply; A's life interest comes to an end, but no IHT is payable since the life tenant is entitled to all the property (see IHTA 1984 s 53(2)).
(3)   *If A dies aged 19:* IHT will be assessed on the termination of an interest in possession (IHTA 1984 s 51(1)).

As already discussed, there is nothing to prevent an A & M trust from being created for an open class of beneficiaries, eg 'for all my grandchildren both born and yet to be born'. If such a trust is to be created, it is important to ensure that the class of beneficiaries will close when the eldest obtains a vested interest in either the income or capital. Failure to do so will result in a partial divesting of the beneficiary with the vested interest when a further beneficiary is born, and, as a result, an IHT charge. Class-closing rules may be implied at common law (see *Andrews v Partington* (1791)), but it is safer to insert an express provision to that effect.

IHTA 1984 s 71(4)(b) provides that 'tax shall not be charged ... on the death of a beneficiary before attaining the specified age'. It follows that, if the entire class of beneficiaries is wiped out, an A & M trust will cease on the death of the final member, but, whoever then becomes entitled to the fund, no IHT will be payable. When it is necessary to wait and see if a further beneficiary is born, however, this provision will not operate, since it is not the death of the beneficiary which ends the A & M trust in such a case, but the failure of a further beneficiary to be born within the trust period.

EXAMPLE 26.22

(1)   Property is settled upon trust for Zed's grandchild, Yvonne, contingent upon her attaining 18. If she were to die aged 16, the property would (in the absence of any provision to the contrary) revert to Zed and no IHT would be payable.
(2)   Property is settled upon trust for Victor's children contingent upon their attaining 21 and, if more than one, in equal shares. Victor's one child, Daphne, died in 1994 aged 12 and Victor himself has just died.
      No charge to IHT arose on Daphne's death and the property continued to be held on A & M trusts until Victor died when the trust ended with a charge to IHT.

The A & M trust can be drafted to achieve a considerable degree of flexibility. It is common for such a trust to contain the following provisions:
(1)   Primary beneficiaries are present and future grandchildren with a class-closing provision.

(2) The trustees are given a revocable power of appointment among the beneficiaries (inapplicable once a beneficiary has attained 25).

(3) The A & M trust will end with beneficiaries being entitled to interests in possession (not absolute interests) and thereafter such a beneficiary is given power to appoint a life interest to his surviving spouse and divide up the capital as he sees fit between his children. However:

(4) The trustees retain an overriding power to determine the life interest of any beneficiary who has attained (say) 26 and appoint the property in favour of one or more secondary beneficiaries, often called discretionary beneficiaries.

As a result, this kind of settlement includes more than one generation of beneficiaries; has great flexibility; but still qualifies as an A & M trust when set up. **[26.97]**

7 Occasions when an 'exit charge' will arise

It is rare for property to leave an A & M trust otherwise than by appointment to a beneficiary and so long as this happens no IHT is chargeable. Provision is, however, made for calculating an 'exit charge' in the following four circumstances (IHTA 1984 ss 70(6), 71(5)):

(1) When depreciatory transactions entered into by the trustees reduce the value of the fund (IHTA 1984 s 71(3)(b)).

(2) When the 25-year period provided for in Requirement 3 is exceeded and the beneficiaries do not have a common grandparent.

(3) When property is advanced to a non-beneficiary or resettled on trusts which do not comply with the three Requirements.

(4) If the trust ends some time after the final surviving beneficiary has died (see *Example 26.23(2)*).

IHT is calculated in these cases on the value of the fund according to how long the property has been held on the accumulation and maintenance trusts:

0.25% for each of the first 40 complete successive quarters in the relevant period;

0.20% for each of the next 40;

0.15% for each of the next 40;

0.10% for each of the next 40; and

0.05% for each of the next 40.

Hence, on expiry of the permitted 25 years IHT at a rate of 21% will apply to the fund. Thereafter, normal discretionary trust rules will apply, so that five years later there will be an anniversary charge. **[26.98]–[26.110]**

VI OTHER SPECIAL TRUSTS

1 Charitable trusts

If a trust is perpetually dedicated to charitable purposes, there is no charge to IHT and the fund is not 'relevant property' (IHTA 1984 s 58). Transfers to charities are exempt, whether made by individuals or by trustees of discretionary trusts (IHTA 1984 s 76).

IHTA 1984 s 70 is concerned with temporary charitable trusts defined as 'settled property held for charitable purposes only until the end of a period (whether defined by a date or in some other way)' and ensures that when the fund ceases to be held for such purposes an exit charge will arise. That charge (which is calculated in the same way as for A & M trusts; see above) will never exceed a 30% rate which is reached after 50 years. **[26.111]**

2   Trusts for the benefit of mentally disabled persons and persons in receipt of an attendance allowance (IHTA 1984 s 89)

These rules were recast in 1981. As from 10 March 1981, a qualifying trust for a disabled person is treated as giving that person an interest in possession. As a result the IHT regime for no interest in possession trusts does not apply. The *inter vivos* creation of this trust by a person other than the relevant beneficiary is a PET. There are no restrictions on the application of *income* which can therefore be used for the benefit of other members of the class of beneficiaries. This can be particularly useful where the application of income to the 'principal' disabled beneficiary could jeopardise his entitlement to state benefits. At least one half of any *capital* benefits must be paid to the 'principal' beneficiary. A charge to IHT will arise on the death of the disabled person whose deemed interest in possession will aggregate with his free estate in the normal way. Although disabled trusts can also obtain CGT advantages (eg a full annual exemption for the trustees), to qualify the disabled beneficiary must be entitled to at least one half of the income or be the sole income beneficiary (see TCGA 1992 Sch 1 para 1 and (1993) *Private Client Business*, p 161).   **[26.112]**

3   Pension funds (IHTA 1984 s 151)

A superannuation scheme or fund approved by the Revenue for income tax purposes is not subject to the rules for no interest in possession trusts. A benefit payable out of that fund which becomes comprised in a discretionary trust is, however, subject to the normal charging rules; the person entitled to that benefit being treated as the settlor.   **[26.113]**

4   Employee trusts (IHTA 1984 s 86)

These trusts will not in law be charitable unless they are directed to the relief of poverty amongst employees (see *Oppenheim v Tobacco Securities Trust Co Ltd* (1951)). They may, however, enjoy IHT privileges. Their creation will not involve a transfer of value, whether made by an individual (IHTA 1984 s 28) or by a discretionary trust (IHTA 1984 s 75). Once created, the fund is largely exempted from the IHT provisions governing discretionary trusts, especially from the anniversary charge. To qualify for this treatment, the fund must be held for the benefit of persons employed in a particular trade or profession together with their dependants.   **[26.114]**

5   Compensation funds (IHTA 1984 ss 58, 63)

Trusts set up by professional bodies and trade associations for the purpose of indemnifying clients and customers against loss incurred through the default of their members are exempt from the rules for no interest in possession trusts.   **[26.115]**

6   Newspaper trusts (IHTA 1984 s 87)

The provisions relating to employee trusts (above) are extended to cover newspaper trusts such as the Scott Trust (which formerly owned the *Guardian*) and the Telegraph Newspaper Trust (which formerly owned the *Daily Telegraph*).   **[26.116]**

7 Maintenance funds for historic buildings (IHTA 1984 s 77, Sch 4)

IHT exemptions are available for maintenance funds where property is settled and the Treasury give a direction under IHTA 1984 Sch 4 para 1. Once the trust ceases, for any reason, to carry out its specialised function, an exit charge, calculated in the same way as for A & M trusts, occurs.   [26.117]

8 Protective trusts (IHTA 1984 ss 73, 88)

A protective trust may be set up either by using the statutory model provided for by the Trustee Act 1925 s 33, or by express provisions.

These trusts have always been subject to special IHT rules and, as originally enacted, the rules offered scope for tax avoidance (see IHTA 1984 s 73 and *Thomas v IRC* (1981)). Accordingly the rules were changed with effect from 11 April 1978 by providing that the life tenant is deemed to continue to have an interest in possession for IHT purposes despite the forfeiture of his interest (IHTA 1984 s 88). It follows that the discretionary trust regime is not applicable to the trust that arises upon such forfeiture. Should the capital be advanced to a person other than the life tenant, a charge to IHT will arise and on the death of the beneficiary the fund will be treated as part of his estate for IHT purposes (*Cholmondeley v IRC* (1986)). As a result of these rules there is the curious anomaly that, after a forfeiture of the life interest, the interest in possession rules apply to a discretionary trust although it should be borne in mind that ordinary rules apply for other taxes. Thus for income tax a 34% rate applies once the life interest is forfeited and there is no uplift on the death of the principal benficiary.

One cautionary note should be added; this system of charging only applies to protective trusts set up under the Trustee Act 1925 s 33 or to trusts 'to the like effect'. Minor variations to the statutory norm are, therefore, allowed; but not the inclusion of different beneficiaries under the discretionary trust (such as the brothers and sisters of the principal beneficiary) nor a provision which enables a forfeited life interest to revive after the lapse of a period of time. In such cases, the normal rules applicable to interest in possession and discretionary trusts apply (see *Law Society's Gazette*, 3 March 1976 and SP E7).

[26.118]

27 IHT—excluded property and the foreign element

As a general rule, IHT is chargeable on all property situated within the UK regardless of its owner's domicile and on property, wheresoever situate, which is beneficially owned by an individual domiciled in the UK. Any transfer of 'excluded property' is not chargeable to IHT (IHTA 1984 ss 3(2) and 5(1)). The main example of excluded property is 'property situated outside the UK ... if the person beneficially entitled to it is an individual domiciled outside the UK' (IHTA 1984 s 6(1)). In determining whether property is excluded property relevant factors include not only the domicile of the transferor who is the beneficial owner of the property and the situation of the property (*situs*), but also the nature of the transferred property, since certain property is excluded regardless of its *situs* or the domicile of its owner. **[27.1]**

I DOMICILE AND *SITUS*

1 Domicile

a) General rules

An individual cannot, under English law, be without a domicile which connotes a legal relationship between an individual and a territory. There are three kinds of domicile: domicile of origin, domicile of choice and domicile of dependence.

A person acquires a *domicile of origin* at the moment when he is born. He will usually take the domicile of his father unless he is illegitimate or born after his father's death in which case he takes the domicile of his mother. A domicile of origin is never completely lost, but may be superseded by a domicile of dependence or choice; it will revive if the other type of domicile lapses.

A person cannot acquire a *domicile of choice* until he is 16 or marries under that age. Whether someone has replaced his domicile of origin (or dependence) by a domicile of choice is a question of fact which involves physical presence in the country concerned and evidence of a settled intention to remain there permanently or indefinitely (*animus manendi*).

Unmarried infants under the age of 16 (in England and Wales, younger in Scotland) acquire their father's *domicile by dependence* and women who married before 1 January 1974 acquired their husband's domicile by dependence.

[27.2]

b) *Deemed domicile*

If a person's domicile under the general law is outside the UK, he may be deemed to be domiciled in the UK, for IHT purposes only, in one of two circumstances (IHTA 1984 s 267).

First, if a person was domiciled in the UK on or after 10 December 1974 and within the three years immediately preceding the transfer in question, he will be deemed to be domiciled in the UK at the time of making the transfer (IHTA 1984 s 267(1)(a)). This provision is aimed at the taxpayer who moves his property out of the UK and then emigrates to avoid future IHT liability on transfers of that property. In such a case he will have to wait three years from the date of emigration for his property to become excluded property under IHTA 1984 s 6(1) see *Re Clore (No 2)* (1984).

Secondly, a person will be deemed domiciled in the UK if he was resident for income tax purposes in the UK on or after 10 December 1974 and in not less than 17 out of the 20 income tax years ending with the income tax year in which he made the relevant transfer (IHTA 1984 s 267(1)(b)). This provision aims to catch the person who has lived in the UK for a long time even though he never became domiciled here under the general law. Residence is used in the income tax sense (see Chapter 13), and does not require residence for a complete period of 17 years. This is because the Act is concerned with a person who is resident in a tax year and such residence may be acquired if the individual concerned comes to the UK at the very end of that year (eg on 1 April) with the intention of remaining indefinitely in the UK. In such a case, the individual will be resident for the tax year in which he arrived—albeit that it is about to end—and that will count as the first year of residence for the purpose of the 17-year test. Similarly, were he to leave the UK immediately after the commencement of a tax year, he would be treated as resident in the UK in that final tax year. Accordingly, in an extreme case, an individual could arrive in the UK on 1 April in one year, remain for the next 15 years and make a transfer on 10 April in year 17 and yet be caught by the 17-year test, even though only being resident in the UK for a little over 15 years.

EXAMPLE 27.1

(1) Jack who was domiciled in England moved to New Zealand on 1 July 1995 intending to settle there permanently. He died on 1 January 1997 when according to the general law he had acquired a domicile of choice in New Zealand. However, because Jack had a UK domicile and died within three years of losing it, he is deemed under s 267(1)(a) to have died domiciled in the UK. Accordingly, all his property wherever situated (excluding gilts; see below) is potentially chargeable to IHT. Jack would have had to survive until 1 July 1998 to avoid being caught by this provision.

(2) On 5 June 1997, Jim who is domiciled under the general law in Ruritania and who is a director of BB Ltd (the UK subsidiary of a Ruritanian company) gives a house that he owns in Ruritania to his son. By virtue of his job Jim has been resident for income tax purposes in England since 1 January 1974, but he intends to return to Ruritania when he retires. For IHT purposes Jim

is deemed to be domiciled in England under s 267(1)(b); the gift will, therefore, be subject to IHT if Jim dies within seven years.

(3) Boer, resident in the UK but domiciled in South Africa, forms an overseas company to which he transfers the ownership of all his UK property. He has exchanged chargeable assets (UK property) for excluded property (shares in the overseas company).

(4) François, a non-UK domiciliary, owns all the shares in a property dealing company. He converts that share capital into bearer shares holding the relevant certificates offshore. On his death the assets are not UK *situs* (note stamp duty at 1½% is charged on an issue of bearer shares: see [**32.72**]).

[**27.3**]

2 *Situs*

Subject to contrary provisions in double taxation treaties (and special rules for certain property) the *situs* of property depends on common law rules and on the type of property involved. For instance:

(1) An interest in land (including a leasehold estate or rentcharge) is situated where the land is physically located.

(2) Chattels (other than ships and aircraft) are situated at the place where they are kept at the relevant time.

(3) Registered shares and securities are situated where they are registered or, if transferable upon more than one register, where they would normally be dealt with in the ordinary course of business.

(4) Bearer shares and securities, transferable by delivery, are situated where the certificate or other document of title is kept.

(5) A bank account (ie the debt owed by the bank) is situated at the branch which maintains the account. (Special rules apply to non-residents' foreign currency bank accounts: [**27.26**].) [**27.4**]-[**27.20**]

"I'm not complaining Henry, it's just that I always think of sunshine, palm-fringed beaches and villas whenever I think of taxhavens . . ."

II WHAT IS EXCLUDED PROPERTY?

1 Property situated outside the UK and owned beneficially by a non-UK domiciliary (IHTA 1984 s 6(1))

Property falling into this category is excluded regardless of its nature.

Settled property situated abroad will be excluded property if the settlor was domiciled outside the UK at the time when he made the settlement (IHTA 1984 s 48(3)). If the settlor retains an interest in possession either for himself or his spouse, and a discretionary trust then arises on the termination of that interest, an additional test is imposed in determining whether property is excluded property. This test looks at where the settlor or the spouse (if the interest was reserved for him) was domiciled when that interest in possession ended (IHTA 1984 s 82). As this provision only applies where the property is *initially* settled with a life interest on the settlor or his spouse, it may be circumvented if the trust commences in discretionary form and is then converted into a life interest.   [27.21]

EXAMPLE 27.2

(1) Franc, domiciled in Belgium, intends to buy a house in East Anglia costing £500,000. If he buys it in his own name it will be subject to IHT on his death. If he buys it through an overseas company, however, he will then own overseas assets (the company shares) which fall outside the IHT net. Note that if he occupies the house and is a director of the overseas company, the Revenue may seek to tax him on an emolument equal to the value of the property each year under the provisions of TA 1988 s 145 (see [**5.113**] and *Tax Journal*, 12 May 1994, p 12). As an alternative he could buy the property in his own name with a substantial mortgage charged on the house which will have the effect of reducing its IHT value.

(2) Erik, domiciled in Sweden, settles Swedish property on discretionary trusts for himself and his family. He subsequently acquires an English domicile of choice. The settlement is of excluded property for IHT purposes (IHTA 1984 s 48(3)), although the assets would appear to form part of the settlor's estate when he dies because of the reservation of benefit rules in FA 1986 s 102(3), the Revenue accepts that the property remains excluded so that it will not be subject to any charge (*Law Society's Gazette*, 10 December 1986). The position is, however, different if Erik is excluded from all benefit during his life when a deemed PET occurs under s 102(4).

(3) Boris, domiciled in France, died in February 1997 and left his villa in Tuscany and moneys in his Swiss bank account to his son Gaspard, a UK resident and domiciliary. By a variation of the terms of his will made within two years of Boris' death the property is settled on discretionary Liechtenstein trusts for the benefit of Gaspard's family. *For IHT*, reading back ensures that the settlement is of excluded property. *For CGT*, however, although the variation is not itself a disposal, Gaspard is treated as the settlor of the trust and hence the provisions in TCGA 1992 s 86 will apply (see [**20.54**] and *Marshall v Kerr* (1994)).

2 Property which is exempt despite being situated in the UK

Government securities   Certain government securities (gilts) issued before 18 March 1977 and beneficially owned by a person neither domiciled nor ordinarily resident in the UK are exempt from IHT (IHTA 1984 s 6(2)). The deeming provisions of IHTA 1984 s 267 do not apply to such transferors. Such gilts also receive privileged treatment for CGT (see [**16.3**]) and for income tax (TA 1988 s 47). If these securities are settled they will be excluded property if either the person beneficially entitled to an interest in possession (eg a life tenant) is neither domiciled nor ordinarily resident in the UK, or, in the case of a discretionary trust, if none of the beneficiaries are domiciled or ordinarily resident in the UK (IHTA 1984 s 48(4)).

IHTA 1984 s 48(5) contains anti-avoidance provisions:

(1) If gilts are transferred from one settlement to another they will only be excluded property if the beneficiaries of *both* settlements are non-UK resident or domiciled. This prevents gilts from being channelled from a discretionary trust where they were not excluded property (because some of the beneficiaries were UK domiciled and/or resident) to a new settlement with non-domiciled beneficiaries only, where they would be excluded property (as was done in *Minden Trust (Cayman) Ltd v IRC* (1984)).

(2) When a close company is a beneficiary of a trust, any gilts owned by the trust will be excluded property only if all participators in the company are non-UK domiciled and resident, irrespective of the company's domicile. This aims to prevent individuals from using a company to avoid IHT.

This privileged tax treatment only applies to gilts issued before 18 March 1977. Transfers of gilts issued thereafter are chargeable to IHT even if in the beneficial ownership of individuals domiciled and resident outside the UK. **[27.22]**

Certain property owned by persons domiciled in the Channel Islands or Isle of Man Certain savings (eg national savings certificates) are excluded property if they are in the beneficial ownership of a person domiciled and resident in the Channel Islands or the Isle of Man (IHTA 1984 ss 6(3), 267(4)). **[27.23]**

Visiting forces Certain property owned in the UK by visiting forces and staff of allied headquarters is excluded property (IHTA 1984 s 155). **[27.24]**

Overseas pensions Certain overseas pensions (usually payable by ex-colonial governments) are exempt from IHT on the pensioner's death regardless of his domicile (IHTA 1984 s 153). **[27.25]**

Non-sterling bank accounts On the death of an individual domiciled resident and ordinarily resident outside the UK there is no IHT charge on the balance in any 'qualifying foreign currency account' (IHTA 1984 s 157). This exemption does not apply to *inter vivos* gifts of the money in such an account.

[27.26]–[27.40]

For the inter-relationship of excluded property and settlements see below.

III DOUBLE TAXATION RELIEF FOR NON-EXCLUDED PROPERTY

Non-excluded property may be exposed to a double charge to tax (especially on the death of the owner); once to IHT in the UK and again to a similar tax imposed by a foreign country. Relief against such double charge may be afforded in one of two ways.

First, the UK may have a double taxation treaty with the relevant country when the position is governed by IHTA 1984 s 158. The provisions of the treaty will override all the relevant IHT legislation and common law rules regarding the *situs* of property.

Under these treaties, the country in which the transferor is domiciled is generally entitled to tax all property of which he was the beneficial owner. The other country involved usually has the right to tax some of that property, eg land situated there. In such cases the country of domicile will give relief against the resulting double taxation. Most of these treaties also contain provisions to catch the individual who changes his domicile shortly before death to avoid tax.

Secondly, where no double tax treaty exists, unilateral relief is given in the form of a credit for the foreign tax liability against IHT payable in the UK (IHTA 1984 s 159). The amount of the credit depends on where the relevant property is situated; in some cases no credit is available if the overseas tax is not similar to IHT, although some relief is, effectively, given since, in calculating the reduction in the transferor's estate for calculating IHT, the amount of overseas tax paid will be disregarded (IHTA 1984 s 5(3)). This relief is less beneficial than a tax credit because the transferor must still bear the double tax.   **[27.41]–[27.60]**

IV   MISCELLANEOUS POINTS

1   Valuation of the estate—allowable deductions

Certain liabilities of a transferor are deductible when calculating the value of his estate for IHT purposes (see **[22.12]**). However, any liability to a non-UK resident is deductible as far as possible from a transferor's foreign estate before his UK estate. As a result, a foreign domiciliary who is chargeable to IHT on his UK assets cannot usually deduct his foreign liabilities from his UK estate. There are two exceptions to this rule. *First*, if a liability of a non-UK resident has to be discharged in the UK, it is deductible from the UK estate; *secondly*, any liability which encumbers property in the UK, reduces the value of that property.   **[27.61]**

EXAMPLE 27.3

Adolphus dies domiciled in Ethiopia. His estate includes cash in a London bank account, shares in UK companies and a stud farm in Weybridge which is mortgaged to an Ethiopian glue factory. He owes a UK travel company £500 for a ticket bought to enable his daughter to travel around Texas and £200,000 to a Dallas horse dealer. IHT is chargeable on his UK assets. However, the mortgage debt is deductible from the value of his stud farm and £500 is deductible from the UK estate generally. There is no reduction for the debt of £200,000 assuming that he has sufficient foreign property.

2   Expenses of administering property abroad

Administration expenses are not generally deductible from the value of the deceased's estate. However, the expense of administering or realising property situated abroad on death is deductible from the value of the relevant property up to a limit of 5% of its value.   **[27.62]**

3   Enforcement of tax abroad

On the death of a foreign domiciliary with UK assets, the deceased's PRs cannot administer his property until they have paid any IHT and obtained a grant of probate. However, the collection of IHT on lifetime transfers by a foreign domiciliary presents a problem if both the transferor and transferee are resident outside the UK and there is no available property in the UK which can be impounded.   **[27.63]**

4 Foreign assets

If a foreign government imposes restrictions as a result of which UK executors cannot immediately transfer to this country sufficient of the deceased's foreign assets for the payment of IHT attributable to them, they are given the option of deferring payment until that transfer can be made. If the amount that is finally brought into the UK is less than the IHT, any balance will be waived (see ESC F6). **[27.64]–[27.80]**

V FOREIGN SETTLEMENTS, REVERSIONARY INTERESTS AND EXCLUDED PROPERTY

1 Foreign settlements

As a general rule settled property which is situated abroad is excluded property if the settlor was domiciled outside the UK when the settlement was made (IHTA 1984 s 48(3) and see *Tax Bulletin*, February 1997). Therefore, the domicile of the individual beneficiaries in such cases is irrelevant, so that even if the beneficiary is domiciled in the UK, there will be no charge to IHT on the termination of his interest in possession nor on any payment made to him from a discretionary trust. **[27.81]**

EXAMPLE 27.4

Generous, domiciled in the USA, settles shares in US companies on his nephew, Tom, for life. Tom is domiciled and resident in the UK. The property is excluded property, being property situated abroad settled by a settlor domiciled at that time outside the UK, so that there will be no charge to IHT on the ending of Tom's life interest.

If, however, those shares were exchanged for shares in UK companies, the property would no longer be excluded and there would be a charge to IHT on the termination of Tom's life interest.

If Generous had settled those same US shares on discretionary trusts for his nephews, all of whom were UK domiciled, the property would be, for the same reason, excluded property, so that the normal discretionary trust charges will not apply.

2 Reversionary interests

a) *Definition*

For IHT purposes any future interest in settled property is classified as a reversionary interest (IHTA 1984 s 47). The term, therefore, includes an interest dependent on the termination of an interest in possession, whether that interest is vested or contingent. A contingent interest where the settlement does not have an interest in possession is also a reversionary interest for IHT purposes.

EXAMPLE 27.5

Property is settled on the following trusts:
(1) A for life, remainder to B for life, remainder to C. B and C both have reversionary interests for IHT purposes.
(2) A for life, remainder to B for life, remainder to C if he survives B. C's contingent remainder is a reversionary interest for IHT purposes.
(3) To A absolutely contingent upon his attaining the age of 21. A is currently aged six and has a reversionary interest for IHT purposes.

The interest of a discretionary beneficiary is not, however, a 'reversionary interest', being in no sense a future interest. Such a beneficiary has certain present rights, particularly the right to be considered by the trustees when they exercise their discretion and the right to compel due administration of the fund. The value of such an interest is likely to be nil, however, since the beneficiary has no right to any of the income or capital of the settlement. He has merely a hope (*spes*).   **[27.82]**

b) *'Situs' of a reversionary interest*

A reversionary interest under a trust for sale is a *chose in action* rather than an interest in the specific settled assets be they land or personalty (*Re Smyth, Leach v Leach* (1898)). In other cases the position is unclear; but by analogy with estate duty principles it will be a *chose in action* if the settled assets are personalty; but an interest in the settled assets themselves if they are land. Since a *chose in action* is normally situated in the country in which it is recoverable (*New York Life Insurance Co v Public Trustee* (1924)), in some cases the reversionary interest will not be situated in the same place as the settled assets.   **[27.83]**

c) *Reversionary interests—the general rule*

A reversionary interest is excluded property for IHT (IHTA 1984 s 48(1); see **[25.61]**) with three exceptions designed to counter tax avoidance:
(1)   Where it was purchased for money or money's worth.

EXAMPLE 27.6

There is a settlement on A for life, remainder to B. B sells his interest to X who gives it to his brother Y. X has made a transfer of value (a PET) of a reversionary interest (which can be valued by taking into account the value of the settled fund and the life expectancy of A).

(2)   Where it is an interest to which the settlor or his spouse is beneficially entitled.
(3)   Where a lease for life or lives is granted for no or partial consideration, there is a settlement for IHT (IHTA 1984 s 43(3)) and the lessor's interest is a reversionary interest (IHTA 1984 s 47). Such a reversionary interest is only excluded property to the extent that the lessor did not receive full consideration on the grant (see IHTA 1984 s 48(1)(c) for valuation of the lessee's interest in possession and IHTA 1984 s 170 for the valuation of the lessor's interest).   **[27.84]**

EXAMPLE 27.7

L grants a lease of property worth £30,000 to T for £10,000 for T's life. T is treated for IHT purposes, as having an interest in possession and, therefore, as absolute owner of two-thirds of the property (£30,000 - £10,000). L is treated as the owner of one-third of the property (because he received £10,000). Therefore, one-third of his reversionary interest is not excluded property.

d) *Reversionary interests—the foreign element*

Under IHTA 1984 s 48(1) a reversionary interest (with the three exceptions above) is excluded property regardless of the domicile of the settlor or reversioner or the *situs* of the interest. Where the settled property is in the UK, but the reversionary interest is situated abroad (see **[27.83]**) and beneficially owned by a foreign domiciliary, the interest probably is excluded property in all cases under the general rule of IHTA 1984 s 6(1).

However, the status of a reversionary interest in settled property situated outside the UK is cast into some doubt by virtue of IHTA 1984 s 48(3) to which s 6(1) is expressly made subject (IHTA 1984 s 48(3)(b)). Section 48(3) states:

> 'where property comprised in a settlement is situated outside the UK
>
> (a) the property (but not a reversionary interest in the property) is excluded property unless the settlor was domiciled in the UK at the time the settlement was made; and
>
> (b) section 6(1) above applies to a reversionary interest in the property, but does not otherwise apply in relation to the property.'

This provision appears to exclude the operation of s 48(1) by saying that a reversionary interest in settled property situated abroad is only excluded property (under the general rule in s 6(1)) if it is itself situated abroad and owned by a foreign domiciliary.

However, it is thought that s 48(3) only prevails over s 48(1) in cases of conflict and that there is no conflict here since the words 'but not a reversionary interest' in s 48(3)(a) mean that whether a reversionary interest is excluded property depends not on the *situs* of the settled property nor on the settlor's domicile, but on the general rule in s 48(1).

In summary, therefore, a reversionary interest is always excluded property regardless of *situs* or domicile with three exceptions (see [**25.61**]). Even if the interest falls within one of the exceptions, it will still be excluded property if the interest (regardless of the whereabouts of the settled property) is situated outside the UK and beneficially owned by a foreign domiciliary (IHTA 1984 s 6(1)); or if the reversionary interest is itself settled property, is situated abroad and was settled by a foreign domiciliary (IHTA 1984 s 6(1) and s 48(3)). **[27.85]**

Section 5   Business enterprise, stamp duty and VAT

Chapters

28 Corporation tax

'The major reform of business taxation, which I introduced in 1984, and which was completed in 1986, has given us one of the lowest corporation tax rates in the world. This has encouraged overseas companies to invest in Britain and, most important of all, has greatly improved the quality of investment by British firms. It is a crucial part of an environment in which company profitability has recovered to its highest level for some twenty years. It has succeeded in its objectives.'
(Chancellor of the Exchequer, the Rt Hon Nigel Lawson MP, Budget Statement 15 March 1988.)

[**28.1**]

I INTRODUCTION

Corporation tax was introduced by FA 1965 and applies to all resident bodies corporate including authorised unit trusts and unincorporated associations (see, for instance, *Blackpool Marton v Martin* (1990) in which an unincorporated members' club was liable to corporation tax) but not to partnerships or local authorities. It is levied on the profits of a company which are made up of both income profits, computed according to income tax principles, and capital profits which will be assessed in accordance with CGT rules. The 1965 legislation was substantially amended by FA 1972 (with effect from 1 April 1973); it is common to refer to the system in force from 1966 to 1973 as the *classical* system and that introduced in 1973 (and still in force) as the *imputation* system.

The classical system had two main features. *First*, dividends, and company distributions generally, were not allowed as deductions in arriving at profits; instead they were payable out of net profits and were further subject to income tax (and, if relevant, to surtax) in the hands of the recipient. *Secondly*, a special category of company, the close company, was subjected to special rules designed to frustrate the use of small companies in tax planning schemes.

The Conservative government (1970-74) introduced changes in the operation of corporation tax. The special penalties suffered by close companies were reduced but, most significantly, the imputation system fundamentally altered the rules dealing with the taxation of distributions. The new system was designed to achieve parity in the taxation of a company's profits whether those profits were retained or distributed to shareholders, since the classical system had resulted in the double taxation of distributions, first as profits of the company and then as dividends in the hands of the shareholder. The cornerstone was advance corporation tax (ACT) which is generally payable on all company distributions. ACT serves a dual purpose since it represents a payment of corporation tax for the company and income tax for the recipient shareholder.

Although the imputation system has been retained, subsequent Finance Acts, and notably F(No 2)A 1997, have removed a number of basic features leaving behind a mess. The major reduction in the rates of corporation tax in 1984 combined with the abolition of the 100% first year capital allowance (see Chapter 35) resulted in Inland Revenue statistics showing a dramatically increased tax yield from companies as compared with earlier years.

[28.2]–[28.20]

II   GENERAL PRINCIPLES—RATES OF TAX

The tax is charged by reference to financial years (FY) which run from 1 April to 31 March and are referred to by the calendar year in which they commence. Hence, FY 1997 means the financial year running from 1 April 1997 to 31 March 1998. Where companies are wound up, the rate charged during their final financial year is that fixed for the preceding financial year (TA 1988 s 342(2)). The special rate for small companies is discussed at **[28.23]**.

In tabular form the rates are as follows:

Financial year	*Rate (%)*
1983	50
1984	45
1985	40
1986–89	35
1990	34
1991–96	33
1997	31

Corporation tax is charged on a current year basis on the company's profits of the financial year. Therefore, where a company's accounting period straddles two financial years the profits must be apportioned on a time basis (TA 1988 s 8(3)).

EXAMPLE 28.1

Grr Ltd makes up its accounts to 31 December. For the years ended 1991 and 1992 its trading profits were £2,000,000 and £1,600,000 respectively. The rate of corporation tax for FY 1990 is 34%; for 1991 33% and for 1992 33%.

The tax will be calculated as follows:

(1)   *Profits of £2,000,000 apportioned:*
January 1991–April 1991:
3/12 of £2,000,000 = £500,000 taxed at 34% (FY 1990)
April 1991–December 1991:
9/12 of £2,000,000 = £1,500,000 taxed at 33% (FY 1991)
(2)   *Profits of £1,600,000 apportioned:*
January 1992–April 1992:
3/12 of £1,600,000 = £400,000 taxed at 33% (FY 1991)
April 1992–December 1992:
9/12 of £1,600,000 = £1,200,000 taxed at 33% (FY 1992)

The tax is payable within nine months after the end of the accounting period on which it was assessed or (if later) within one month from the making of the assessment. Hence, in *Example 28.1* the tax will normally be due by 30 September in each year. **[28.21]**

1 Capital gains

The capital gains of a company are included in its profits and charged to corporation tax at the rate in force for the relevant financial year.

As a result the corporation tax rate on a gain realised in FY 1997 will be 31% (unless the 21% small company rate applies: see **[28.23]**). Unlike individuals, companies are not entitled to an annual exemption. **[28.22]**

2 The small company rate

A measure of relief from the full corporation tax rate is provided by the small company rate which, for FY 1997, is 21%, less than the basic rate of income tax (TA 1988 s 13). This rate applies to any company (other than a close investment-holding company—see **[28.99]**) whose profits, both income and capital, do not exceed £300,000 in the accounting period. The 21% rate offers an advantage to the small company since it is significantly less than the 40% higher rate which may apply to an individual's income and capital gains.

Where a company's profits exceed £300,000 but not £1,500,000 tapering relief is available, the effect of which is (for FY 1997) to impose corporation tax at the rate of 35.5% on profits above £300,000 but below £1,500,000. This avoids a sudden leap to the full rate of corporation tax. The corporation tax definition of a small company is purely related to its profits for a financial year and for this purpose profits include franked investment income (see **[30.81]**).

If a company wishes to take advantage of TA 1988 s 13 it must submit an appropriate claim which in practice requires a clear indication in the company's return that the profit should be charged at the small companies rate or that marginal relief is appropriate. Any such statement should also indicate whether or not there are associated companies (see SP 1/91, ESC C9 and, for the position of holding companies, SP 5/94).

Changes in the small company rate and in the definition of the small company may be tabulated as follows:

Financial year	Small company rate (%)	Profit limit (£)	Higher limit (£)	Taper (%)
1988	25	100,000	500,000	37.5
1989	25	150,000	750,000	37.5
1990	25	200,000	1,000,000	36.25
1991	25	250,000	1,250,000	35
1992	25	250,000	1,250,000	35
1993	25	250,000	1,250,000	35
1994–1995	25	300,000	1,500,000	35
1996	24	300,000	1,500,000	35.25
1997	21	300,000	1,500,000	33.5

EXAMPLE 28.2

(1) Zee Ltd makes up its accounts to 31 March each year. For the year ending 31 March 1997 the company had trading profits of £80,000 and had made chargeable gains of £42,000.

The profits of Zee Ltd for corporation tax purposes are:

	£
Trading (ie income) profits	80,000
Chargeable gains	42,000

Chargeable profits　　　　　　　　　　　　　　　　　　　　　£122,000

Zee Ltd will, therefore, qualify for the small companies rate so that corporation tax will be charged as follows:

Chargeable profits (£122,000) at 21% = £25,620

(2) Were the income profits of Zee Ltd to be £280,000 then, with the addition of chargeable gains (£42,000), the small companies threshold of £300,000 would be exceeded by £22,000 so that a form of tapering relief would apply as follows:

(i) Corporation tax payable:
£322,000 (ie £280,000 + £42,000) × 31%　　　　　　　　£99,820

(ii) Less tapering relief (TA 1988 s 13(2)):
(upper relevant amount – profits) × statutory fraction

ie (£1,500,000 – £322,000) × $\frac{1}{40}$　　　　　　　　　£29,450

(iii) Total tax ((i) – (ii))　　　　　　　　　　　　　　　£70,370

Two points should be stressed in connection with the small companies rate.

First, anti-avoidance provisions exist to prevent the fragmentation of a business amongst associated companies in an attempt to create a whole series of small companies. (TA 1988 s 13(3)).

EXAMPLE 28.3

X Ltd has three wholly owned subsidiaries. The companies are associated and hence the lower and uppers limits for each company are divided by one plus the number of associated companies. The lower and upper limits for each company in the X Group are therefore £75,000 and £375,000.

Secondly, although tapering relief (also known as the marginal rate) applies where profits fall into the range £300,000 to £1,500,000, this does not mean that the tax on profits in excess of £300,000 is at a rate below 31%. This is because the purpose of tapering relief is to increase gradually the average rate of corporation tax from the 21% payable by a company with profits of £300,000 to the 31% payable by a company with profits of £1,500,000. To achieve this result the rate applicable to the slice of profits between £300,000 and £1,500,000 has to *exceed* 31%. At present this marginal rate is 33.5% calculated as follows:

Tax on £300,000 at 21%　　　　　　　　　　　=　　　£63,000
Tax on £1,500,000 at 31%　　　　　　　　　　=　　　£465,000
Difference (£465,000 – £63,000)　　　　　　　=　　　£402,000

Therefore, £402,000 corporation tax has to be raised on profits falling between £300,000 and £1,500,000 (ie on £1,200,000).

Hence, as a percentage, tax on £1,200,000 will be:

$$\frac{402,000}{1,200,000} \times 100 = 33.5\%$$

Thus, continuing *Example 28.2(2)* (above):

Corporation tax of £70,370 on profits of £322,000 can be analysed as:

		£
First £300,000 of profits at 21%	=	63,000
Final £22,000 of profits at 33.5%	=	7,370
		£70,370

In determining whether tapering relief is available dividends received from other UK companies (franked investment income: 'FII') are taken into account (see [**29.81**] for the meaning of FII and for an illustration of how this affects tapering relief).

The fact that a company's profits may just exceed £300,000 thereby attracting this relatively high marginal rate of 33.5% on the excess over £300,000 is of practical significance when considering how much money the directors of family companies should take by way of remuneration (or how much should be paid into the company's pension scheme). The marginal corporation tax rate exceeds the basic rate of income tax so that it may be advantageous to pay out such moneys in the form of salaries in cases where the directors are not liable to income tax at rates exceeding 21% or by making increased contributions to the company pension scheme. Thus, in *Example 28.2(2)* above, the directors of Zee Ltd should consider paying themselves increased salaries or bonuses of £22,000 before 31 March 1998. In this way, the company's taxable profits for that accounting period will be reduced to £300,000 which (taxed at 21%) results in a tax saving of £7,370 (£70,370 - £63,000) (see further Chapter 37). [**28.23**]-[**28.40**]

III   HOW TO CALCULATE THE PROFITS OF A COMPANY

Profits of a company are defined as including both income profits and capital gains (TA 1988 s 6(4)(a)). [**28.41**]

1   **Income profits**

a) *General principles*

Generally, income profits have to be computed in accordance with the income tax rules that apply in the year of assessment in which the company's accounting period ends (TA 1988 s 9). Each class of income will, therefore, be calculated under the Schedules that apply for income tax. Thus, a trading company having no other income will compute its profits in accordance with the rules of Schedule D Case I so that the rules for what expenditure is deductible by individuals and partnerships (discussed at [**6.111**]) apply equally to companies. Accordingly, the salaries and fees paid to its directors and employees will be allowable expenses under TA 1988 s 74 but note that TA 1988 s 337(2)(b) prohibits the deduction as an expense (excepted in the case of insurance companies), of annual payments and annuities. Such payments must be relieved, if at all, as charges on income (see [**28.55**]). In arriving at the profits of a company under Schedule A (income from land) the pre-6 April 1995 rules must be applied (see [**8.1**]. A problem in the case of a corporate group may arise from the assumption that it represents a single commercial entity. This is not the case for tax purposes and so an expense may be non-deductible in the hands of the paying company if that expense was incurred for 'dual purposes': eg to benefit other group members (see *Vodafone Cellular Ltd v Shaw* (1997) and [**6.117**]). [**28.42**]

b) *Foreign exchange gains and losses and financial instruments for managing interest rate and currency risk*

FA 1993 ss 125–170 and Schs 15–18 set out a framework for the taxation of exchange gains and losses of companies and FA 1994 ss 147–177 and Sch 18 provide a similar framework for interest rate and currency contracts: see further Appendix V. [**28.43**]

c) *Transfer pricing (TA 1988 ss 770–773)*

These sections are aimed at transfer-pricing arrangements entered into by multi-national corporations and provide that on a sale between 'associated' bodies, the Revenue can substitute market value for the sale price if the sale is at an undervalue (TA 1988 s 770(1)). These provisions aim to prevent a UK vendor company realising a tax deductible loss and the buyer company a profit which might be free from tax or charged at a lower rate than that applicable to the vendor. It, therefore, does not apply if the buyer is a resident UK trader.

For similar reasons, market value can be substituted where a sale is at an over-value, unless the seller is a UK resident trader (TA 1988 s 770(2)).

Bodies are associated for this purpose if one controls the other or both are controlled by a third party (for the definition of 'control' see TA 1988 s 840).

In the case of sales between UK companies (which are outside the provisions), the transaction may fall within the rule in *Sharkey v Wernher* (1956) (see [**6.95**]).

It should be noted that, in addition to sales, the section applies to 'lettings and hirings of property; grants and transfers of rights, interests or licences and *the giving of business facilities of whatever kind*' (TA 1988 s 773(4)). In *Ametalco UK v IRC* (1996) the italicised words were held to encompass an interest-free loan made by a UK company to its USA parent.

The Board of Inland Revenue must give a direction before the taxpayer's profits can be adjusted: the Revenue's normal practice is to give effect to directives at the conclusion of a transfer-pricing enquiry by incorporating adjustments into the taxpayer's 'open' tax assessment (this procedure was accepted by the Court of Appeal in *Glaxo Group Ltd v IRC* (1996) and see *Tax Journal* (1996) 4 April).

For the UK Revenue's attitude is the OECD Transfer Pricing Guidelines and for the operation of the mutual agreement procedure, see *Tax Bulletin*, October 1996, p 353. It has been decided to bring transfer pricing within the self-assessment framework but because of concerns at the requirement to self assess on the basis of arm's length pricing, draft legislation and a consultative document will be issued during 1997.   [**28.44**]

d) *Employee trusts*

Payments into employee trusts may constitute deductible expenditure if they are of an income nature (see *Heather v P E Consulting Group* (1978), discussed at [**6.114**]). If the trust qualifies as a statutory 'ESOP' deduction will *always* be given even if the payments are of a capital sum (ESOPs are discussed in Chapter 39).   [**28.45**]

e) *Franked investment income and income taxed at source*

In calculating income profits no account is taken of dividends and other distributions received by one UK company from another (*franked investment income:* TA 1988 s 208). The utilisation of such income is considered at [**29.81**]. Notice, however, that franked investment income (FII) is included in the profits of a company for the purpose of discovering whether the small companies rate is applicable and calculating how much tapering relief is available, although this income is not then taxed (TA 1988 s 13(7) and see *Example 29.24*).

When income is received by a company net of income tax deducted at source (eg building society interest, debenture interest and annuities received by companies), the gross income is included in the profits of the company and a credit is given against the corporation tax payable for the tax deducted at source.

EXAMPLE 28.4

Lexo Ltd makes up its accounts to 31 March each year. The accounts for the period ending 31 March 1998 show the following:

		£
Trading profit		260,000
Profit from lettings		40,000
Building society interest received:		
net	£60,000	
plus tax credit	£15,000	
Gross		75,000
Total profits		£375,000

	£
Corporation tax payable:	
£300,000 at 21% + £75,000 at 33.5%	88,125
Less building society tax credit	15,000
	£73,125

Notes:
(1) The trading profit is calculated according to the rules of Schedule D Case I, for 1997–98, and the profit from lettings according to the old Schedule A (ie the pre-April 1995 rules).
(2) Building society interest is not franked investment income, but is treated in the same way as other sums received subject to deduction of income tax at source. If the tax credit exceeded the corporation tax payable, the excess would be repaid to the company.

Income tax principles are relevant only in determining the amount of the company's income profits—other enactments of that legislation are not relevant. Thus the preceding year rules and the opening and closing year provisions of Schedule D have no application to companies and there is no question of any personal reliefs or allowances applying. The system of capital allowances applies to companies with suitable modifications (see Chapter 35). The specific difficulties that may arise when an existing business or partnership is converted into a company are dealt with in Chapter 38.   [**28.46**]

2 Capital gains

A company's chargeable gains are computed in the same way as for an individual. Hence, the definition of chargeable assets and the occasions when a disposal occurs are common to both individuals and companies. The annual exemption (currently £6,500) is not available for disposals by companies. A disposal between companies in the same group is treated as giving rise to neither gain nor loss until either the asset is disposed of outside the group or until the recipient company leaves the group (see [**30.102**]). A disadvantage suffered by a company and its shareholders is that on any capital gain realised by the company there may be an element of double taxation since not only will the company suffer corporation tax on the gain, but the shareholder whose shares may have increased in value as a result of the capital profit (albeit after tax) will suffer CGT when he disposes of those shares.

EXAMPLE 28.5

Saloman Ltd (a small company wholly owned by John Saloman) makes a chargeable gain of £100,000. It will suffer corporation tax of £21,000 (21%) on that gain. Saloman's shares will have increased in value by, say, £79,000 so that were he to sell them he would suffer CGT at (say) 40% of (ignoring exemptions and reliefs) £31,600. Effectively, therefore, the corporate gain has been subject to tax at 52.6% (21% paid by the company and 31.6% by Saloman). If Saloman Ltd were not a small company this percentage would be 58.6% (31% paid by the company and 27.6% by Saloman). Consider, as an alternative, extracting the profit by the payment of a dividend: see *Example 37.8*.

Vesting appreciating assets in private companies may, therefore, be tax inefficient and it may be better for the shareholder to retain those assets and lease them to the company (see [**37.63**]).   [**28.47**]

3   Taxation of a company's loan relationships

a) *Rules before 1 April 1996*

The tax treatment of loans and securities for corporate borrowers and lenders varied; sometimes the rules were to be found in the corporation tax treatment of income and sometimes in the treatment of chargeable capital gains. For instance, interest, discounts and premiums (ie the cost of borrowing money) was taxed/relieved under the income code whereas profits or gains from holding loans and securities (except for financial traders) fell within the chargeable gains code. Gains on simple sterling bonds (qualifying corporate bonds: see [**28.76**]) were exempt and losses on such instruments were 'nothings'. Within the income code there were distinctions between interest on loans for trading and non-trading purposes; yearly interest as opposed to short-term interest, and discounted securities.   [**28.48**]

b) *Principles of the new regime (FA 1996 ss 80–105, Schs 7–15)*

The intention is to remove the distinctions in the tax treatment of the various types of loans and securities bringing all 'loan relationships' within the corporation tax code on income. This is achieved on the basis of the existing accounting treatment in the company's statutory books (see FA 1996 ss 85ff for authorised accounting methods).   [**28.49**]

c) *Meaning of 'loan relationship' (FA 1996 s 81)*

A loan relationship can arise in one of two ways:
(1) Where a company is either a debtor or creditor in respect of a money debt which arose from a transaction for the lending of money. A money debt is defined as a debt which falls to be satisfied by the payment of money or the transfer of rights under a debt which itself is a money debt.
(2) Where a company issues an instrument as security for a money debt. This is not intended to cover all debts evidenced in writing (such as ordinary trade creditors and debtors): rather the test is whether the instrument was issued in return for cash.

  The new regime does not apply to shares nor to any debt arising from rights conferred by shares (for example rights to a dividend or share capital) nor to gains or losses arising by reference to fluctuations in the value of securities which are convertible/exchangeable into shares and where there is (at the date of issue) more than a negligible likelihood that the conversion etc right will be exercised and the securities are not issued at a deep discount. Also excluded are trade debts including debts arising on the purchase of property or other goods or on the supply of services (hence the straightforward bad debt for goods supplied will be relieved under his trading account as an expense of the business).

However, interest paid on a money debt which is not within the new regime (typically on a late payment of a trade debt) is caught and a similar treatment applies where interest is imputed on a debt, for instance as a result of a court award. **[28.50]**

d) *Extent*

The new regime covers all profits, gains and losses including those of a capital nature arising as a result of a company's loan relationships and related transactions. Certain charges and expenses incurred by the company for the purpose of its loan relationships are taken into account: such as those incurred in bringing a loan relationship into existence; in entering into or giving effect to a related transaction and in making any payments under a loan relationship. In addition, relief is available for abortive expenditure incurred in connection with loans.

However, interest or a discount which is treated as a distribution for income tax purposes is excluded (for the definition of a 'distribution', see **[29.2]**ff). **[28.51]**

e) *Trading profits, losses and expenses*

When a loan relationship is entered into for the purposes of a trade any profits and gains are taxable and interest charges, expenses etc are deductible in computing the company's trading profits (FA 1996 s 82(2)). This means that there is no significant change to the treatment of bank interest paid on a loan raised for trading purposes although commitment fees, commission and interest are all now relievable on an accruals basis. **[28.52]**

f) *Non-trading profits, losses and expenses (FA 1996 s 83)*

If the loan relationship is entered into for non-trading purposes any profits, gains and interest receivable are taxed under Schedule D Case III and losses, interest payable, expenses and charges are tax deductible (FA 1986 s 82(5) (6)). For each accounting period it is necessary to calculate the aggregate of non-trading credits less non-trading debits. If in any period the debits exceed the credits tax relief is available as follows:

(1) As a deduction against the total profits of the company (ie which arise from any source) for the same accounting period. This relief is given before setting off trading losses for the same period or non-trading deficits carried back from a later period.

(2) By way of group relief against the current profits of other group companies in the corresponding accounting period (for group relief see **[30.41]**).

(3) By carry-back against profits from non-trading loan relationships of the company for the three previous years taking later years before earlier ones but with an embargo on carrying back earlier than 31 March 1996.

Finally, deficits which cannot be relieved as above can be carried forward against non-trading profits in subsequent accounting periods. **[28.53]**

g) *Intra-group loans*

Although there are no new rules specifically applying to intra-group loans there are provisions dealing with connected parties which will be relevant in this situation. Because of the accruals basis it is not possible to achieve any timing benefit by having group lender and borrower companies with different accounting periods. **[28.54]**

4 **Deducting charges on income**

a) *What are charges on income?*

Charges on income are defined as annuities and annual payments and such other payments as are mentioned in TA 1988 s 348 (such as patent royalties, mining rents and royalties and payments for easements).

TA 1988 s 337A (inserted by FA 1996) makes it clear that interest payments cannot be deducted as charges on income: rather any deficit on a company's loan relationships must be dealt with in accordance with the rules in FA 1996 (as to which see [**28.52**]).   [**28.55**]

b) *Deduction against profits*

> '... any charges on income paid by the company in the accounting period, so far as paid out of the company's profits brought into charge to corporation tax shall be allowed as deductions against the total profits for the period as reduced by any other relief from tax other than group relief'.

It follows that such charges may be set against all the company's profits, including chargeable gains. As the charges reduce profits any deductions made in calculating those profits cannot be deducted a second time as a charge (TA 1988 s 338(2)). As s 338(1) refers to sums actually paid, it is important for a company to organise, so far as possible, its payments which constitute charges on income to be made at the end of one accounting period rather than at the beginning of the next in order to obtain the earliest possible tax relief. Where charges exceed the total profits for the year, the excess will still qualify for a measure of tax relief (see [**28.60**]; contrast the position of individual taxpayers who obtain no relief).   [**28.56**]

c) *Restrictions on the deductibility of charges*

The permitted charges can only be deducted if (TA 1988 s 338(5)):
(1) the payment is to be borne by the company so that no deduction is allowed where a right to reimbursement exists;
(2) the payment must be charged to income in the company's accounts;
(3) the payment, except for certain payments to charity, must be made under a liability incurred for valuable and sufficient consideration.   [**28.57**]

EXAMPLE 28.6

Zeus Ltd makes the following covenanted payments (TA 1988 s 338(5)):
(1) £5,000 pa to the Society to Promote Antiquarian Studies (a registered charity).
(2) £8,000 pa to the trustees of a trust fund set up by the company to educate the children of its employees and to provide evening classes in arts and crafts for its employees.

The payment of £5,000 pa: will be a charge on income so long as it is capable of lasting for more than three years (TA 1988 s 339(8)). The charity will obtain a full tax rebate so that basic rate income tax (deducted at source by the company under TA 1988 s 349) will be refunded.
The payment of £8,000 pa: is not a charitable payment (see *Oppenheim v Tobacco Securities Trust Co Ltd* (1951)) and will only be an allowable charge if incurred for suitable consideration. In *Ball v National and Grindlay's Bank Ltd* (1973) the Court of Appeal concluded that at the time when the covenant was made it must be possible to show that the company was receiving adequate consideration for the payments. Such consideration could be in the form of money or money's worth including an obligation to the company. Hence, it is likely that the £8,000 would *not* be deductible as a charge since it will not suffice to show that there was some

business advantage in making the payment, and no consideration in money or money's worth is being received by the company. Such payments do not offer tax advantages, therefore, and the company might be advised to avoid the use of annual payments altogether and to argue that the costs of establishing and maintaining the trust are allowable business expenses and, therefore, deductible under TA 1988 s 74 in arriving at profits (see TA 1988 s 337(2)(b)).

d) *One-off charitable donations*

TA 1988 s 339 replicates for companies the Gift Aid provisions for individuals (see [**42.84**]). Money donations to charities not in the form of covenanted payments may be deducted as a charge provided that, as in the case of covenanted payments, income tax at the basic rate is deducted by the paying company. In the hands of the charity the payment is treated as if it were made under covenant so that the basic rate income tax can be reclaimed.

There is no upper limit on the amount: in the case of close companies there is a *minimum* level of £250 after deducting income tax. Although there are provisions to deny relief when a benefit is received by a connected person, the Revenue accepts that the wholly owned trading subsidiary of a charity can make payments to the charity falling within s 339.   [**28.58**]

5 Loss relief

Different relieving provisions apply depending upon the type of loss which the company has made. In all cases, however, it is only the company (or exceptionally another company in the same group: see [**30.41**]) which is entitled to the relief and never the members of the company. The loss is thus 'locked into' the company and this is a matter of some significance in deciding whether to commence business as a company or partnership (see [**37.46**]).

Losses are deducted from the appropriate profits of the company in priority to charges on income.   [**28.59**]

a) *Relief for trading losses: 'carry-forward' (TA 1988 s 393)*

A trading loss can be carried forward and set against trading profits from the *same* trade in the future.

A claim for relief must be made within six years of the end of the accounting period in which the loss was incurred. Relief is given by reducing the trading income of the succeeding accounting period or periods. In cases where such trading income is insufficient to absorb the full loss, interest and dividends received by the company may be treated as trading income for the purpose of loss relief (TA 1988 s 393(8)) provided that such income would have been taxed as trading income if tax had not been assessed under other provisions. Dividends received by a company whose trade involves dealing in shares fall into this category but in *Nuclear Electric plc v Bradley* (1996) it was held that income produced by moneys set aside (although not placed in a segregated fund) for meeting future liabilities could not be treated as trading income:

'Whether income from investments held by a business is trading income must ultimately depend upon the nature of the business and the purpose for which the fund is held. At one end of the scale are insurance companies and banks part of whose business is the making and holding of investments to meet current liabilities. It has been suggested that tour operators might fall into this category but without a good deal more information I do not feel able to express an opinion on this matter. At the other end of the scale are businesses of which the making and holding of investments form no part. In between these two ends there will no doubt fall other types of businesses whose position is not so clear. However in this case it is absolutely clear that the business of NE was to produce and supply electricity. The making of investments was neither an integral nor any part of its business.

Furthermore the investments which it did make were in no sense employed in the business of producing electricity during the year of assessment.' (Lord Jauncey)

Unrelieved charges on income may be carried forward as a trading expense but only to the extent that the charge was made 'wholly and exclusively for the purposes of the trade' (TA 1988 s 393(9)). Thus, any charges not so made should be relieved against current year profits first, leaving only those payments to be carried forward which satisfy the 'wholly and exclusively' test.   **[28.60]**

EXAMPLE 28.7

Hee Ltd had the following corporation tax computation:

	£
Schedule D Case I profit	6,000
Chargeable gains	1,500
	7,500
Less charges on income (total £8,500) limited to	7,500
Taxable profits	£ Nil
Unrelieved charges	£1,000

If all the charges had been laid out wholly and exclusively for Hee Ltd's trade then £1,000 can be carried forward as a loss under s 393(1). But if only £500 had been so expended, the remaining £500 is unrelieved.

b) *Relief for trading losses against current and previous profits (TA 1988 s 393A)*

A company may set its trading loss against profits of the same accounting period. As the relief sets the loss against other profits it follows that *all* current profits can be used, including capital gains.

EXAMPLE 28.8

Haw Ltd's accounts for the financial year show the following: a trading loss of £6,000; rental income of £5,000; chargeable gains of £3,000; and charges on income of £1,000. The corporation tax computation would be:

	£
Schedule A	5,000
Chargeable gains	3,000
	8,000
Less trading loss	6,000
	2,000
Less charges on income	1,000
Profits for corporation tax	£1,000

Where a loss cannot be relieved, or cannot be fully relieved, against profits of the same accounting period a claim may be made to carry that loss back against profits of the accounting period falling within the previous 12 months. The company must have been carrying on the same trade in the earlier period and the claim has to be made within two years of the end of the accounting period in which the loss was incurred (TA 1988 s 393A(10) subject to the Board's discretion to extend that period). Any claim for loss relief will take effect before charges on income are deducted but *after* any loss made in that earlier year.

EXAMPLE 28.9

How Ltd prepares its accounts to the year ended 31 May. Its accounts show the following:

	Trading profits (losses) £	Charges on income £
Year to 31 May 1998	(12,000)	Nil
Year to 31 May 1997	(6,000)	1,000
Year to 31 May 1996	5,000	1,000
Year to 31 May 1995	25,000	Nil
Year to 31 May 1994	30,000	Nil

In respect of the year ended 31 May 1997 a claim for s 393A relief would result in the following corporation tax computation:

	£
Profits of 1997	Nil
Profits of 1996	5,000
Less: 1997 losses	5,000
Taxable profits for 1996	Nil

As a result of the claim:
(1) Any tax paid on the 1996 profit will be recovered.
(2) The loss relief absorbs all of the profits for 1996. The charges on income (£2,000 for 1996 and 1997) will not obtain tax relief unless carried forward as trading losses under provisions already discussed (see [**28.60**]). The unrelieved loss of £1,000 may be relieved under s 393.
(3) part of the tax paid for 1994 will be recovered.

A number of technical points should be made in connection with the relief under s 393A.

First, s 393A was amended by F(No 2)A 1997. Formerly it had enabled the carry back of losses for a three year period and this is still the case with a terminal loss (see s 393A(2A)). The change is effective for accounting periods ending on or after 2 July 1997 (the old rules apply to earlier losses: note that *Example 28.9* assumes that the new rules apply to the entire loss).

Secondly, on a claim being made a terminal loss will be set against profits of earlier accounting periods falling in the previous three years. It is not possible to claim to set the loss against a particular year in that three-year period: rather it must be offset against *later* periods first. A 1996 loss, for instance, will be offset against 1995; then 1994, and, finally, against the 1993 accounting period.

Thirdly, capital allowances may increase the loss to be relieved under s 393A although it should be noted that capital allowances carried forward from an earlier period do not qualify. [**28.61**]

c) *General restrictions on the availability of trading loss relief*

There are restrictions on the availability of trading loss relief under TA 1988 s 393 and s 393A. [**28.62**]

A commercial purpose The trade must be carried on commercially with a view to the realisation of a gain if s 393A relief is to be available. Carry-forward (s 393) relief will, however, always apply. [**28.63**]

Acquiring a tax loss company   TA 1988 ss 768 and 768A prevent the use of losses in certain circumstances where, after the loss has been incurred, there has been a substantial change in the ownership of the company's shares. *The purpose of these provisions is to stop the practice of purchasing companies in order to utilise their accumulated tax losses or their past profits* (and note that FA 1995 s 135 extended these provisions to cover the sale of investment companies with surplus management expenses: see [**28.69**]).

There are two relevant factors to be considered in deciding whether loss relief is unavailable:

(1) whether there has been a substantial change of ownership; and

(2) what has happened to the business of the company.

TA 1988 s 769 contains detailed rules setting out what constitutes a substantial change in ownership; basically it amounts to a change in the beneficial ownership of more than 50% of the ordinary share capital.

So far as the business of the company is concerned the rules in s 768 apply if either:

(1) there is a change in the ownership accompanied by a major change in the nature or conduct of the trade and both changes occur within a three-year period (for the interpretation of 'major' see *Willis v Peeters Picture Frames Ltd* (1983); *Purchase v Tesco Stores Ltd* (1984) and SP 10/91, revised 1996); or

(2) a change in ownership follows a period when the trade carried on by the company has become small or negligible and only after that change of ownership has there been any considerable revival.

In the latter case no time period is prescribed.

The Revenue accepts that a major change does not occur if changes are introduced to increase its efficiency; to keep pace with developing technology; or to rationalise the business by withdrawing unprofitable items. Revised SP 10/91 provides the following illustrations of what does and does not amount to a 'major' change:

'*Examples where a change would not of itself be regarded as a major change*

(a) A company manufacturing kitchen fitments in three obsolescent factories moves production to one new factory (increasing efficiency).

(b) A company manufacturing kitchen utensils replaces enamel by plastic, or a company manufacturing time pieces replaces mechanical by electronic components (keeping pace with developing technology).

(c) A company operating a dealership in one make of car switches to operating a dealership in another make of car satisfying the same market (not a major change in the type of property dealt in).

(d) A company manufacturing both filament and fluorescent lamps (of which filament lamps form the greater part of the output) concentrates solely on filament lamps (a rationalisation of product range without a major change in the type of property dealt in).

(e) A company whose business consists of making and holding investments in UK quoted shares and securities makes changes to its portfolio of quoted shares and securities (not a change in the nature of investments held).

Examples where a major change would be regarded as occurring

(f) A company operating a dealership in saloon cars switches to operating a dealership in tractors (a major change in the type of property dealt in).

(g) A company owning a public house switches to operating a discotheque in the same, but converted, premises (a major change in the services or facilities provided).

(h) A company fattening pigs for their owners switches to buying pigs for fattening and resale (a major change in the nature of the trade, being a change from providing a service to being a primary producer).

(i) A company switches from investing in quoted shares to investing in real property for rent (a change in the nature of investments held).'

[**28.64**]

Corporate reconstructions When a company ceases to carry on a trade (eg when the trade is sold) that trade is treated as ceasing even though it may, in fact, continue by being carried on by another company (TA 1988 s 337(1)). So far as losses are concerned, the result is that the carry-forward relief ceases to be available, although carry-back relief may be claimed.

Of course, where a reconstruction has occurred as a result of which the trade passes from one company to another and both companies are under common control, these consequences would be economic nonsense and penalise the parties concerned. Thus, TA 1988 s 343 contains provisions which operate in such circumstances to permit losses and capital allowances to be carried forward from the predecessor to the successor company.

There are restrictions on the amount of loss which can be carried forward *when the transferor company is insolvent at the time of the transfer*. Broadly, if the successor company fails to take over all the liabilities of the transferor (as when part only of the trade—the successful part!—is being hived-down into a new 'clean' company) and the transferor has insufficient assets to cover them, the losses which can be transferred are reduced by the amount by which the predecessor's 'relevant liabilities' exceeded its 'relevant assets'.

For s 343 to apply the same person or persons must, at any time within the period of two years after the change, directly or indirectly, own the trade (or not less than a three-quarter share in it) and must have owned that trade or the same interest therein within the period of one year before the change. Ownership is normally determined by reference to the ordinary share capital which is, however, given by TA 1988 s 832 a wider definition than its normal meaning and includes all issued share capital except shares which carry a fixed rate dividend and no other interest in the profits of the company.

The normal hiving-down operation satisfies these requirements although restrictions on the amount of loss that can be carried forward have removed some of its attractions: when only a part of the transferor's trade is transferred (as in the typical hive-down) apportionments must be made to determine what fraction of the loss can be carried forward.

The successor company can amalgamate the predecessor's trade with another enterprise already carried on, although, in this situation, the carried-forward loss relief will only be available against future profits arising from the old trade (*Falmer Jeans v Rodin* (1990)).

[**28.65**]

EXAMPLE 28.10

The ordinary share capital of Zee Ltd and Pee Ltd is owned as follows:

	Zee Ltd	*Pee Ltd*
Alan	10	8
Ben	6	12
Claud	30	40
Dennis	29	20
Others	25	20

A transfer of a trade from Zee Ltd to Pee Ltd would fall within s 343 since the 75% common ownership test is satisfied albeit that the relevant shares in Pee Ltd are owned by the same persons in different proportions.

d) *Relief for income losses other than trading losses*

Schedule D Case VI losses may be set against Schedule D Case VI income for either the current year or first available future accounting period (TA 1988 s 396). In the case of losses under Schedule A special relieving provisions provided for in that Schedule apply: remember that the changes made in 1995 do not apply to companies so that it is the older provisions which are in point (see the twelfth edition of this book at [**8.14**]). [**28.66**]

e) *Relief for capital losses*

Losses which would be deductible in computing liability to CGT can be set against the first available chargeable gains made by the company. Such losses cannot be offset against income profits. [**28.67**]

6   Management expenses

a) *The basic rule*

Investment companies can deduct sums paid out in management expenses (such as salaries and general office expenditure) from their total profits. If such expenditure is unrelieved, it can be carried forward and offset in future years, but not back to a previous accounting period. Unrelieved charges can likewise be carried forward and treated as management expenses in future years so long as such charges were incurred 'wholly and exclusively for the purpose of the company's business' (TA 1988 s 75(3)). The term 'investment company' is defined as including:

> 'any company whose business consists wholly or mainly in the making of investments and the principal part of whose income is derived therefrom . . .' (TA 1988 s 130).

In effect the company's main activity must therefore be to hold investments from which income in the form of rents, interest and dividends is received. There must be a 'business' with a financial return.

Hence, authorised unit trusts and savings banks (with the specific exclusion of a trustee savings bank as defined under the Trustee Savings Bank Act 1981) are included. It follows that before 2 July 1997 the relief was often given by setting the expenses against the franked investment income of the company (see [**29.84**]). For companies whose business consists of managing land, expenses involved in administering that land will be deductible from the Schedule A profits, whereas the general running costs of the company will be management expenses. Difficulties may arise in obtaining a deduction for expenses such as brokerage and stamp duty relating to the sale of investments which may be classified as part of costs of purchasing and selling (ie as being of a capital nature). Trading companies do not, of course, require a provision dealing with management expenses since such sums will be deducted in arriving at the Schedule D profits. [**28.68**]

b) *Sales of surplus management expenses companies*

FA 1995 extended TA 1988 s 768 (see [**28.64**]) to sales of investment companies with surplus management expenses. As with the existing rules dealing with trading losses there has to be a change in the ownership of the company and the management expenses can no longer be carried forward to periods beginning after that change in a number of situations. In addition to those which apply for trading losses there is an additional provision designed to prevent the purchaser pumping cash into the acquired company which would be invested to produce income against which the management expenses could be set.   [**28.69**]

c) *The division between investment and trading companies*

A *trading company* exists 'wholly or mainly' for the purpose of carrying on a trade; in practice the Revenue considers, in doubtful cases, that this phrase means more than 50% and will look at turnover, net profits, net assets and management time to see if this requirement is met. When a holding/subsidiary structure is used the holding company will often be an investment company albeit that its main function is to hold shares in trading subsidiaries. Of course a company may fit in neither the trading nor investment category: in *Tintern Close Residents Society Ltd v Winter* (1995), for instance, a residents' company—which owned and managed common property such as gardens, roads, footpaths etc—and whose main source of income was membership subscriptions was considered not to be an investment company (it was obviously not a trading company!). As a result the claim to deduct management expenses was disallowed (see also *White Horse Drive Residents Association Ltd v Worsley* (1997) and contrast *Cook v Medway Housing Society Ltd* (1997)).

The trading/investment division is important in that:
(1) There is a different computation of taxable profits.
(2) Reliefs from capital taxes (CGT and IHT) may be available only to shareholders in trading companies: see, for instance, retirement relief for CGT and business property relief for IHT.   [**28.70**]-[**28.74**]

IV RAISING FINANCE

1 The sources of company finance

There are two major sources of corporate finance. Money can either be raised by an allotment of *shares* so that the contributors become members of the company and will generally expect to receive dividends on those shares. Alternatively, money can be borrowed with the company creating *debentures* and paying interest to the debenture holders.

Interest may attract tax relief under the provisions of FA 1996 (see [**28.48**]) but dividends are not deductible in arriving at the company's profits. As a result of the imputation system a full double charge to tax is avoided but all the corporation tax suffered by the company is not credited to the shareholders and so there remains a discrimination in favour of debentures and against raising funds by a share issue (see Chapter 29).   [**28.75**]

2 Qualifying corporate bonds

Certain loans to traders which prove to be irrecoverable qualify for capital gains loss relief (TCGA 1992 s 253; [**16.43**]). The majority of company loans, however, do not fall within this provision since they are 'debts on security' which are excluded from that section. Until 14 March 1989 this did not matter since relief was separately available for losses incurred by such investors under TCGA 1992 s 251 (relief for debts on security: see [**16.44**]). From that date the law in this area has suffered a series of changes. With the new rules on loan relationships ([**28.48**] above) it is important to appreciate at the outset that the rules for companies on the one hand and individuals and trusts on the other are different. For companies relief (or tax charge) is now generally given in the company's income computation so that the CGT rules do not apply. The following discussion is therefore concerned with the position of individuals and trusts.

First, qualifying corporate bonds ('QCB') have since 1986 been wholly exempt from CGT. Gains are therefore tax free and no relief is available for losses. The original definition of a QCB involved a sterling denominated bond, debenture or loan stock whether secured or unsecured but restricted to securities which were *either* themselves quoted on the UK Stock Exchange *or* dealt in on the USM *or*, alternatively, which were issued by a body with other securities so quoted (or dealt in).

Secondly, FA 1989 widened the definition of a QCB to embrace such securities *whether or not issued by a quoted body*. The consequence was to extend the definition to include virtually all company securities. As a result, the disposal of such securities was wholly exempt from CGT with the result that losses incurred on that disposal were not tax allowable. Not surprisingly, attention was focused on the definition of a QCB in order to draw up an agreement which fell *outside* that definition but which still amounted to a debt on security thereby enabling loss relief to be available under TCGA 1992 s 251.

Two devices were commonly employed. *First*, a QCB must be 'expressed in sterling and in respect of which no provision is made for conversion into or redemption in a currency other than sterling' (TCGA 1992 s 117(1)(b)). Accordingly, provisions for redemption in another currency or by reference to another currency could be included to take the bond outside the QCB definition. An *alternative* lay in the requirement that to be a QCB the debt in question must 'represent and have at all times represented a normal commercial loan' (TCGA 1992 s 117(1)(a) and, for the definition of a normal commercial loan, TA 1988 Sch 18 para 1). Providing a right of conversion into shares would ensure that the test was *not* met so that the security was not a QCB.

Thirdly, the next stage in the drama (tragedy?) was the introduction, in 1990, of what is now TCGA 1992 ss 254–255. Whilst leaving QCBs free from any capital gains charge these sections provided that a capital loss arising on the disposal of such bonds attracted tax relief in certain restricted circumstances:

(1) the bonds themselves must be held or issued after 14 March 1989;
(2) the allowable loss is restricted to the taxpayer's actual loss with no account being taken of any indexation allowance;
(3) relief is only available to the original investor who must show that he has not assigned any right to recover any outstanding amount of the principal of the loan;
(4) a claim has to be made that the value of the bond has become negligible;
(5) were the debt not a debt on security it would qualify for relief under s 253 (loan to trader). Accordingly, the money lent must have been used by the borrower wholly for the purposes of a trade carried on by him.

Finally, special rules exist to deal with the situation where a gain is 'rolled into' a qualifying corporate bond. Assume, for instance, that Toby sells his company to Vulture Ltd in consideration for an issue of securities in Vulture which fall within the definition of a QCB. Toby's gains on the disposal of his shares can be rolled into the replacement securities by virtue of TCGA 1992 ss 135–137 (see [**19.3**]). If the replacement securities are QCBs, special rules in TCGA 1992 s 116 apply as a result of which the postponed gain will be triggered on a subsequent disposal of the QCB. In effect the gain is held in suspense and will arise *even if* the QCB is sold at a loss or is written off. Toby may therefore realise nothing on his QCB and yet be left with a tax liability. To add insult to injury, relief under TCGA 1992 s 254 will not be available even if the security has become of negligible value because the loan in question will not have been used wholly for trading purposes (rather it enabled Vulture Ltd to acquire Toby's company). If Toby dies still owning the QCB the suspended gain will pass to his personal representatives and fall into charge when they dispose of the bond. The Revenue has, however, confirmed that the deferred charge can be avoided if a disposal is made to a charity within TCGA 1992 s 257. There will be no charge on the gift by the donor nor on the subsequent disposal of the bonds by the charity. **[28.76]**

3 Financing a UK subsidiary ('thin capitalisation')

Prior to 29 November 1994 there were no express provisions in the UK tax legislation which denied relief for interest paid by companies that were thinly capitalised (basically which had debt levels disproportionate to their share capital). The nearest equivalent was TA 1988 s 209(2)(e)(iv) which treated interest paid by companies in certain cases as being a distribution. This provision, broadly speaking, applied where the borrower was a 75% subsidiary of a non-resident lender *or* where the lender was non-resident and both it and the borrower were 75% subsidiaries of a third non-resident company *or* the borrower and a non-resident lender were 75% subsidiaries of a UK resident third company where less than 90% of the borrower's shares were directly held by a UK resident company. Under these provisions all interest payments were treated as distributions: ie they did not simply strike out 'excessive' payments. In practice the position was commonly governed by double tax treaties but this did not leave matters in a satisfactory state since some treaties did not contain any override and in other cases the override did not apply where 'a special relationship' existed between borrower and lender (and it was on the basis of this that thin capitalisation claims were usually submitted by the Revenue). TA 1988 s 808A, inserted by F(No 2)A 1992, clarified the interpretation of the 'special relationship' provisions specifying that certain factors had to be taken into account regardless of the wording in the particular treaty.

FA 1995 s 87 repealed s 209(2)(e)(iv) and in its place are rules which apply where both of two conditions are satisfied: either the borrower is a 75% subsidiary of the lender or both are 75% subsidiaries of a third company *and* the whole or any part of the interest paid is greater in amount than would have been paid between unconnected companies. When these new rules apply only the *excessive amount* of the interest is treated as a distribution (s 209(2)(da)) and see *Tax Bulletin*, June 1995, p 218. Whilst much depends on the business sector of the company concerned, the assets which might provide security, cashflow and the general state of the economy, the Revenue is known to favour a debt: equity ratio of 1:1 and income cover of 3:1.

[28.77]-[28.90]

V CLOSE COMPANIES

Companies controlled by one person or by a small group of individuals could be operated so as to secure tax advantages unavailable to the individual taxpayer or to the larger corporate taxpayer. As a result there have been special rules since 1922 aimed at preventing such arrangements. FA 1965 introduced a relatively fierce regime for the closely controlled company but since that date a relaxation in the provisions has occurred: most recently, for instance, FA 1989 removed the statutory apportionment of income provisions providing instead for 'close investment companies' (as defined) to be subject to the full rate of corporation tax even if they would otherwise qualify as small companies.

[28.91]

1   **What is a close company?**

The definition of a close company is:

> 'one which is under the control of five or fewer participators, or of participators who are directors' (TA 1988 s 414(1)).

Hence, it may be either director-controlled (irrespective of the number of directors involved) or controlled by five or fewer participators. In addition it may be close if it satisfies the winding-up test in s 414(2).   **[28.92]**

a) *The meaning of 'control'*

A person (or two or more persons taken together) is deemed to have control of a company if:
(1) he can exercise control over the company's affairs, in particular by possessing or acquiring the greater part of the share capital or voting power; or
(2) he possesses or is entitled to acquire:
   (a) such part of the issued share capital as would give him a right to the greater part of the income of the company if it were all to be distributed; or
   (b) the right to the greater part of the assets available for distribution among the participators on a winding up or in any other circumstances.

In deciding whether a person has control there must be attributed to him any rights vested in his nominees, his associates and companies controlled by him or his associates. A 'nominee' is a person holding assets for another.   **[28.93]**

b) *The meaning of 'participator', 'associate' and 'director' (TA 1988 s 417)*

'*Participator*' is defined as a person having a share or interest in the capital or income of the company and includes a person who is entitled to acquire share capital or voting rights and loan creditors (but not a bank lending in the ordinary course of its business; TA 1988 s 417(1), (9)).

'*Associate*' of a participator includes: (1) any person related to him as spouse, parent, remoter forebear, sibling, child or remoter issue, and as partner; (2) the trustees of any settlement set up by him or by any person related to him; and (3) fellow beneficiaries under a trust of the company's shares or entitled to shares in the company under the will of a deceased shareholder (TA 1988 s 417(3)).

'*Director*' is defined as a person who occupies that post; any person in accordance with whose instructions the directors act; and a manager paid by the company who, with his associates, owns or controls 20% of the company's ordinary share capital (TA 1988 s 417(5)).   **[28.94]**

c) *Companies which are not close*

The following companies which would otherwise fall within the above definition are treated as not being close companies:
(1) any non-resident company;
(2) companies which are registered industrial and provident societies;
(3) companies controlled by or on behalf of the Crown;
(4) companies which would be close companies save for the fact that they are controlled through the beneficial ownership of their shares by one or more companies which are not close companies (therefore, the subsidiary of a non-close company is normally not a close company): note, however,

s 414(6) which provides that the UK subsidiary of a foreign parent will be close if the parent would be close were it UK resident;

(5) companies whose shares have been listed and dealt in on a recognised stock exchange during the preceding 12 months, provided shares carrying at least 35% of the voting power are beneficially held by the public. Shares are not held by the public if (*inter alia*) they are held by a director of the company or his associates and the exception does not apply when the principal members (ie the five members who hold the greatest voting power in the company, but excluding any who hold less than 5% of the voting power) possess more than 85% of the total voting power. [**28.95**]

d) *Illustrations of the definition*

Most small private companies will be close. Where there are fewer than ten shareholders the company must be close since five or fewer shareholders must control it. In other situations the matter may require some thought! [**28.96**]

EXAMPLE 28.11

Aviary Ltd has an authorised and issued share capital of 60,000 ordinary shares of £1 each. Each share carries one vote. The shares are held as follows:

	Ordinary shares
Mr A Robin, Chairman	5,000
Mr B Raven, Managing Director	2,800
Mr C Crow, Director	2,400
Mr D Hawk, Director	4,400
Mr E Thrush, Director	2,200
Mr F Robin, son of A Robin	1,800
Mr G Magpie, Sales Manager	3,600
Mr H Magpie, father of G Magpie	3,000
Mrs J Eagle, sister of G Magpie	3,000
Mrs K Wren, sister of G Magpie	2,400
Sundry small shareholders	29,400
	60,000

Is Aviary Ltd a close company? It will be necessary to consider voting control and to discover whether it is either a company controlled by five or fewer participators or a company controlled by directors who are participators.

Participator/holding		5 largest shareholdings	Shareholdings of all 'directors'
G Magpie—Sales Manager	3,600		
Add: associate holdings:			
H Magpie—father	3,000		
Mrs J Eagle—sister	3,000		
Mrs K Wren—sister	2,400		
	12,000	12,000	12,000
A Robin—Chairman	5,000		
Add: associate holding:			
F Robin—son	1,800		
	6,800	6,800	6,800

Participator/holding	5 largest shareholdings	Shareholdings of all 'directors'
D Hawk—Director	4,400	4,400
B Raven—Managing Director	2,800	2,800
C Crow—Director	2,400	2,400
E Thrush—Director	—	2,200
Total shares	28,400	30,600

Although not controlled by five or fewer participators, Aviary Ltd is a close company because it is controlled by its directors. Notice that for this purpose, Mr G Magpie, the sales manager, is treated as a director because with his associates he holds 20% of the company's shares (TA 1988 s 417(5)).

2 Special rules that apply to close companies

a) *Extended meaning of 'distribution' (TA 1988 s 418)*

Close companies are treated as making distributions when they incur expenses in providing living accommodation or other benefits in kind for a participator or his associates. This rule does not apply in cases where the benefit is subject to taxation under the provisions of TA 1988 ss 153–168 (see [**5.141**]), and is designed to catch benefits conferred upon shareholders and debenture holders who are neither directors nor higher-paid employees of that company. The normal rules which govern the taxation of distributions apply (see Chapter 29). [**28.97**]

EXAMPLE 28.12

DB Ltd, a close company, provides free holidays costing £1,500 each for Barry, a director, Barney, a shareholder and Betty, a debenture holder.
(1) *Barry's holiday* The cost will be a deductible business expense of DB Ltd. Barry will be assessed under the Schedule E rules on the benefit of £1,500 which he has received.
(2) *Barney's and Betty's holiday* In neither case will the expense be charged under Schedule E but, as both are participators, the expense will be treated as a distribution. Hence, DB Ltd will be required to pay ACT on the expense incurred (in each case this will amount to ¼ of £1,500 = £375) and Barney and Betty will each have income under Schedule F of £1,875.

b) *Loans to participators and their associates (TA 1988 s 419)*

A close company which makes a loan to a participator or his associate is obliged to pay to the Revenue tax on that loan at the rate of ACT then in force. However, the loan itself is not a distribution. The sum received by the Revenue is not ACT and the borrower is not entitled to any tax credit. The payment to the Revenue may best be described as a 'forced' loan so that, if the participator repays the sum lent, the Revenue will repay the sum that they received. If, however, the loan is either released or written off, the sum held by the Revenue is likewise forfeited and, in addition, the participator will be assessed to income tax at higher rates (if applicable) on the amount of the loan grossed up at the lower rate for the year of release (for the meaning of a release in this context see *Collins v Addies*; *Greenfield v Bains* (1992)). He will not be liable to the basic rate charge but cannot reclaim any tax. It follows that loans can be used to defer higher rate tax but not ACT. The company will receive no credit against its corporation tax bill for the sum paid to the Revenue. The company must notify the Revenue of the making of such a loan within nine months from the end of the accounting period in which it is made and tax payable under TA 1988 s 419 is due within 14 days thereafter. Tax is not assessable if the loan has been repaid at the time of assessment.

EXAMPLE 28.13

In April 1996 Simco Ltd lends £80,000 to Mr Needy, a shareholder. In 1997 it releases the debt of Needy.
(1) *Tax position in 1996* Simco Ltd will pay the Revenue £20,000 (20/80 of £80,000). This sum is not ACT. Mr Needy suffers no tax consequences.
(2) *Tax position in 1997* The Revenue will keep the £20,000. (The company will never get ACT relief for this sum.) Needy will be subject to income tax at higher rate on the loan (£80,000) grossed up by the lower rate of income tax for 1997 (20%). Hence, he will be taxed on £100,000; and if it is assumed that he is subject to a 40% rate of tax, he will be required to pay further tax of £40,000 − £20,000 = £20,000.

These provisions also catch debts owed to the company, save for the situation where goods or services have been supplied in the ordinary course of the business of the company and the period of credit is either normal or does not exceed six months. Debts assigned to the company are likewise treated as loans but the misappropriation of a company's funds does not create a debt since the necessary consensus is lacking (*Stephens v Pittas* (1983)).

The rules do not apply to loans made in the ordinary course of a company's business of moneylending nor to loans not exceeding £15,000 to someone who works full-time for the company and who does not have a material interest in it (a material interest is normally 5% of the ordinary shares). Exceptionally, it may be advantageous to accept a charge under s 419 since the effective charge for the loan may be less than the income tax rate that would apply were the sum paid as remuneration or dividends.

Two other points must be mentioned. *First*, if the loan is to a director or higher paid employee, income tax may be charged, under TA 1988 s 160, on interest forgone; and *secondly*, loans to directors are, in general, prohibited under the Companies Act 1985 s 330. **[28.98]**

c) *Statutory apportionment and close investment holding companies*

One of the main reasons for the introduction of special rules for close companies was to prevent the hoarding of profits within a company in order to avoid high rates of income tax. For accounting periods beginning on or before 31 March 1989 this was achieved through the use of statutory apportionment. This deemed 'relevant income' (which included certain annual payments and interest expenses) to have been distributed to the shareholders so that income tax could be charged on this deemed income as if there had been a normal qualifying distribution. The most effective way to avoid apportionment was, therefore, to distribute profits.

In his 1989 Budget Speech the then Chancellor, Nigel Lawson, declared that:

> 'The rules for the so called apportionment of close companies' income are notoriously complex, taking up some 20 pages of impenetrable legislation. These rules are no longer needed and I propose to abolish them. I believe that family businesses in particular will welcome this substantial simplification.

> I do, however, have to guard against the avoidance of tax on investment income by channelling it through a closely controlled investment company.'

As a result, the Close Investment Holding Company ('CIC') was born. The original Finance Bill legislation was, after being greeted with universal disbelief (which arose both because of what was proposed and because of the ineptitude of the drafting), withdrawn and significantly watered down provisions eventually introduced in FA 1989 s 105. In essence, these rules only apply to close companies which are not trading companies or members of a trading group and for these purposes a company will be trading if it exists wholly or mainly for the purposes of trading so that it will not necessarily have to trade in every accounting period in order to satisfy the test. Companies which deal in land, shares or securities are trading companies for these purposes and a company carrying on property investment on a commercial basis will likewise be treated as a trading company and therefore will not be a CIC.

The consequence of being a CIC is that the small companies rate of corporation tax (currently 21%) will not be available: instead the company will suffer corporation tax at the main rate of 31%.   **[28.99]**–**[28.120]**

VI   THE OVERSEAS DIMENSION

A company which is resident in the UK is liable to corporation tax on all its profits wherever arising (TA 1988 s 8(1)). A non-resident company is liable to corporation tax only if it trades in the UK through a branch or agency and liability will then be restricted to the chargeable profits from that branch or agency (TA 1988 s 11). A non-resident company trading in the UK but not through any branch or agency, cannot be assessed to corporation tax but will automatically be subject to UK income tax: in such cases, as the company will probably not have any UK presence, the UK Revenue may have problems of tax collection. Any charge under the CGT rules will only arise on the trade assets of non-resident persons who are trading through a branch or agency in the UK (TCGA 1992 s 10).   **[28.121]**

1   **The meaning of 'residence'**

Formerly, companies were treated as UK resident and taxed accordingly if their central management and control was situated in the UK. The law developed in a series of cases and where precisely management and control is exercised is a factual question of some difficulty. Generally, of course, such powers will be vested in the board of directors, so that the problem becomes one of identifying where the board exercises its powers (see, for instance, *Untelrab Ltd v McGregor; Unigate Guernsey Ltd v McGregor* (1996)). Two general points should be stressed. *First*, that the overseas country where the company was incorporated is usually of small significance when it is a question of establishing UK residence. *Secondly*, it is possible under English law for a company to be 'dual resident', namely resident in more than one country (for the Revenue's views on the meaning of residence, see SP 6/83).

From 15 March 1988 this residence test has been supplemented by an additional test based upon the place of company incorporation. As a result, UK incorporated companies will *always* be taxed as UK resident irrespective of where central management and control is exercised *subject to the qualification* (introduced in 1994) that 'dual resident' companies that would not be regarded as UK resident under the 'tie-breaker' provisions of a double tax treaty are not treated as UK resident. Subject to this qualification, there is now therefore a dual test in operation as a result of which a company will be UK resident if *either* it was incorporated here *or*, in the case of companies incorporated abroad, its central management and control is located here (SP 1/90 sets out the Revenue's views on these rules). UK incorporated companies which were non-resident immediately before 15 March 1988 and were then carrying on business were deemed to become UK resident on 15 March 1993. **[28.122]**

EXAMPLE 28.14

(1) Styx Ltd, a UK incorporated company, was trading on 15 March 1988 and, because its management was located in Liechtenstein, was then taxed as a non-UK resident. It became UK resident on 15 March 1993 whereupon its worldwide profits fell into charge to UK corporation tax.

(2) Aster Ltd is incorporated in the UK on 16 March 1988 and is managed and controlled from Liechtenstein. It is taxed as a UK resident corporation.

(3) Rambo Ltd is incorporated in Panama and controlled by directors resident in the UK. It is taxed as a UK resident company.

2 *Tax consequences of ceasing to be UK resident

Subject to the 'tie-breaker' provisions, a UK incorporated company cannot lose its UK residence. In the case of overseas companies, however, if central management and control becomes located elsewhere, UK residence will cease and in that event a tax charge will arise on the unrealised gains of the company immediately prior to its change of residence. FA 1988 s 105 deems the company to have disposed of all its assets at market value immediately before it migrates and to have immediately reacquired them: any claim for roll-over reinvestment relief on the deemed proceeds of such assets is excluded (note that if the tax is not paid within six months from becoming payable it may be collected from other persons: TCGA 1992 s 191).

EXAMPLE 28.15

On 1 August 1997 Rambo Ltd (see *Example 28.14*, above) ceases to be UK resident. At the relevant time it owns chargeable assets worth £200,000 on which its allowable expenditure is £50,000. Immediately before its change in residence it is deemed to sell the assets for £200,000, immediately reacquiring them, and thereby realising corporation tax profits of £150,000 in Financial Year 1997.

The company must inform the Revenue in advance of its intention to cease UK residence (see SP 2/90 for the procedure to be followed) and this should be done by notice in writing specifying the time when this change will occur and should include a statement of UK tax payable together with particulars of how that tax is to be paid. The tax in question will include any PAYE for which the company is liable. If such tax remains unpaid for more than six months, it may then be recovered from, *inter alia*, a controlling director or another company in the same group. Failure by the company to comply with the notification procedures before ceasing to be UK resident may lead to a penalty on both the company and certain other persons: the maximum amount payable being equal to the tax unpaid at the time when the company ceased to be resident. **[28.123]**

3 Taxing resident companies

All profits wherever made by a UK resident company will be charged to corporation tax subject to any available double taxation reliefs. Any credit for foreign tax must be set against corporation tax on the UK company's foreign income or gains in priority to ACT (TA 1988 s 797(4): for the problems that this can cause as a result of surplus ACT see [**29.44**]).

When a trade is to be carried out by a UK company in a foreign country there are three possible methods of operation available.

First, the trade may be with that country so that there is no trading presence within the country and foreign tax is avoided (typically a representative office is established in the foreign country).

Secondly, a branch may be opened overseas which, from a UK tax point of view, results in any profits being subject to corporation tax. It also means that loss relief will be available and that problems of leaving the UK are avoided. Double tax relief permits the set-off of foreign tax against UK corporation tax on the profits of the branch either by virtue of a double tax treaty with the relevant country (TA 1988 s 788) or by unilateral relief (TA 1988 s 790). If a foreign branch is incorporated by the formation of a subsidiary company in the foreign jurisdiction it is possible to postpone the payment of UK tax on capital gains that would otherwise result: see TCGA 1992 s 140.

EXAMPLE 28.16

Accounting period to 31 March 1997

	£
UK profits	2,000,000
Overseas branch profit (income and gains)	100,000
(overseas tax paid £25,000)	
	£2,100,000
Corporation tax (33%)	693,000
less relief	25,000
UK tax payable	£668,000

Notes:
(1) Double tax relief cannot exceed the amount of corporation tax attributable to the foreign income or gains; hence the maximum relief in this example is 33% of £80,000 = £26,400.
(2) Double tax relief is set against corporation tax on overseas income or gains in priority to ACT; limited relief is available for unused ACT although this may be of little use to the UK company (see [**29.45**]).

Thirdly, a subsidiary non-resident company may be formed with the result that corporation tax is generally avoided on profits until they are distributed to the UK by way of dividend. The attractions are obviously considerable when the tax rates in the overseas country are low in comparison with those in the UK and TA 1988 ss 747–756 contain provisions to prevent tax avoidance by the use of controlled foreign companies.   [**28.124**]

4   Controlled foreign companies ('CFCs')

The legislation enables the Board to apportion chargeable profits amongst all persons with an interest in the CFC and to assess a UK resident company holding such an interest, provided that at least 10% of the profits would be apportioned to it. These provisions only apply if the CFC is under UK control and is resident in a 'low tax' area, defined as one where the tax is less than three-quarters of what would have been charged in the UK (for FY 1997 at rates of less than 24.75%). Even then, the CFC's chargeable profits (as to which see *Bricom Holdings Ltd v IRC* (1997) 97 STC 1179) must exceed £20,000. There are provisions to ensure that a charge will only arise where a CFC is used with the object of avoiding tax (see *Tax Bulletin,* October 1995 for this 'motive' test in relation to holding companies) and to exclude CFCs which pursue an 'acceptable distribution policy', or carry on 'exempt activities'. So far as the former is concerned changes in FA 1996 mean that trading companies have to distribute 90% of their taxable profits less capital gains and foreign tax. The provisions do not catch chargeable gains which may be apportioned amongst UK shareholders under TCGA 1992 s 13 when the overseas company is 'close' (see [**20.43**]). The Revenue issues a list of those countries in which residence and the carrying on of a business will not trigger a charge under the legislation and there is a clearance procedure (see STI (1994) p 1343).

With the introduction of self-assessment, a Consultative Document was issued proposing that the Revenue would not in future give a direction; that the 'acceptable distribution' test would go and that the profits of the CFC would be taxed on a current basis albeit with a 20% discount. As a result of representations the government has now decided that whilst the CFC legislation will be brought within the self-assessment framework the 'acceptable distribution' test will be retained (IR Press Release, 26 November 1996). [**28.125**]

5 Taxing non-UK resident companies

Companies not resident in the UK are subject to corporation tax on income arising from a trade carried on in the UK through a branch or agency. The crucial factor in establishing a liability to UK tax is, therefore, whether a trade is carried on within the UK or not (see further Chapter 13). Other income arising from a UK source may be charged to income tax in the non-resident company's hands (TA 1988 s 6(2)). Hence, a property investment company with no branch or agency in the UK, but owning land in the UK, would be assessed to income tax on the profits arising from that land.

Capital gains will be chargeable only if they arise from property associated with the trade carried on by the branch or agency (TA 1988 s 11(2); TCGA 1992 s 10). In the case, therefore, of a non-resident property company owning land in the UK, no chargeable gain will arise on a disposal of its capital assets. A UK resident subsidiary of an overseas company is a separate legal entity from the overseas company and will be subject to UK tax on its worldwide income. If a UK branch or agency is transferred to a UK resident company in the same worldwide group as the transferor company, a tax charge can be postponed if a joint election is made by both companies (TCGA 1992 s 172). [**28.126**]

6 Taxing non-resident shareholders of resident companies

The tax credit and franked investment income provisions (as to which see SP 2/95) only apply to a resident shareholder. Therefore a non-resident is not (subject to the provisions of a double tax treaty) entitled to any tax credit (TA 1988 s 231 but see further [**29.64**]). The non-resident's income tax liability is limited to the tax deducted at source (FA 1995 s 128). [**28.127**]-[**28.140**]

VII PAY AND FILE

1 Introduction

Following recommendations made in the Keith Committee Report (Cmnd 8822) designed to streamline the machinery for the assessment and collection of corporation tax, F(No 2)A 1987 ss 82–91 amended TMA 1970 by introducing a new system ('pay and file') for company returns. It applied to accounting periods ending on or after 1 October 1993. [**28.141**]

2   **The operation of pay and file**

a) *Payment of tax and filing returns*

The pay and file system is based on self-assessment. A company is required to pay its corporation tax—or at least what the company calculates to be its liability—within nine months of the end of its accounting period. Companies are required to complete the tax return CT 200 and deliver it to the Revenue within 12 months of the end of the period to which the return relates. The return includes a corporation tax computation which enables the company to calculate its own liability. When filing its return a company must deliver computations showing how the figures in the return were calculated and a copy of its audited accounts for the period.

Under pay and file, claims for group relief, capital allowances and repayments of income are made by way of a completed tax return. If a company wishes to alter any of these claims or to revise the corporation tax calculation, a new form of amended return (CT 201) must be used. Alterations to these details will not be accepted in any other form.

The requirement to make a return under pay and file is not automatic—a company is only required to make such a return if a form is sent to it. However, a company which is liable to pay corporation tax in respect of an accounting period must notify the Revenue of this fact within 12 months of the end of that accounting period. Furthermore, the company must pay its estimated corporation tax liability by the normal due date (ie nine months after the end of the accounting period).   **[28.142]**

b) *Interest*

Although tax returns under pay and file need not be filed until up to 12 months after the end of the relevant accounting period, the normal due date for payment of corporation tax remains nine months after the end of the accounting period. Interest will run as from this date if the tax has not been paid. Interest on any overpayment or underpayment will also be calculated from the due date. Not surprisingly, the interest on overpayments will not be as high as the interest on underpayments, and the rates of interest are closely linked to market rates.   **[28.143]**

c) *Late and incorrect returns (TMA 1970 s 94)*

If a completed return is not delivered to the Revenue within the 12-month period, the following rapidly escalating penalties are automatically imposed:

Return filed within 12 months	:	no penalty
Return filed within 15 months	:	£100
Return filed within 18 months	:	£200
Return filed within 24 months	:	£200 + 10% of unpaid tax
Return filed outside 24 months	:	£200 + 20% of unpaid tax

Companies which are guilty of persistent failure to make returns are subject to more severe penalties since if a penalty has been levied in respect of both of the two previous accounting periods, and the return for the third period is also late, the flat rate penalties become £500 (instead of £100) and £1,000 (instead of £200).   **[28.144]**

EXAMPLE 28.17

A Ltd makes up its accounts to 31 October each year. Its corporation tax return for the year ended 31 October 1995 is submitted on:
(1) 15 November 1996; or
(2) 15 March 1997; or
(3) 15 January 1998: no tax was unpaid on 1 May 1997; or
(4) 15 January 1998: £1,000 tax was unpaid on 1 May 1997, but was paid by 10 June 1997.
    The penalties levied under each of these alternatives are:
(1) £100 (£500 if the returns for the previous two accounting periods were also late);
(2) £200 (£1,000 if the returns for the previous two accounting periods were also late);
(3) £200 (or £1,000—notice no tax-related penalty is due);
(4) £400 (or £1,200—a tax-related penalty (20% × £1,000) is added to the flat rate penalty).
    For the purposes of calculating penalties, 'unpaid tax' means the amount owing after 18 months, account being taken of credit for income tax withheld, but not for any surplus ACT carried back unless it is a surplus carried back for less than two years.

EXAMPLE 28.18

B Ltd did not file its corporation tax return for the accounting period ended 31 October 1993 until 15 June 1996. The final corporation tax due was £1 million which was paid as follows:

(1) ACT credit on dividend paid during 1993	£400,000
(2) CT paid on the normal due date (1 August 1994)	£300,000
(3) ACT carried back (on dividend paid in 1994)	£ 80,000
(4) ACT carried back (on dividend paid in 1996)	£200,000
(5) CT paid when accounts finally agreed in 1997	£ 20,000
	£1,000,000

Any tax-related penalty will be based on £220,000 being:	
(4) ACT carried back for more than two years	£200,000
(5) CT unpaid on 1 May 1994	£ 20,000
	£220,000

If a company negligently or fraudulently files a false return, penalties can be up to 100% of the tax lost.

d) *Assessments*

A final assessment will be issued by the Revenue once a company's liability has been agreed. Companies are entitled to repayments of income tax deducted at source before their final liability is agreed. The use of estimated assessments is limited under pay and file to situations where the Revenue believes that, for example, a return understates the true liability.   **[28.145]**

3 **Anti-avoidance: company purchase schemes**

When the ownership of a company changes hands and that company fails to pay corporation tax for any period before the date of the change, in appropriate circumstances the tax may be assessed on any person who had control of the company before the change (or any company which that person controlled: see TA 1988 s 767A and s 767B inserted by FA 1994). The relevant circumstances are similar to those which apply in relation to carry forward losses under TA

1988 s 768 (see [**28.64**]) and typically involve the vendor first stripping out trading assets to another group company then selling the company to a purchaser who strips out the remaining cash assets thereby leaving the company unable to pay its tax liabilities.   [**28.146**]

29 Company distributions and shareholders

The term 'a distribution' is widely defined to catch not just the payment of dividends but any method of bleeding off the company's profits to its members.

For the company, a distribution is not deductible in arriving at its profits for corporation tax: rather distributions are paid out of taxed profits.

For individual shareholders the gross amount of the distribution is treated as income falling under Schedule F.

Corporate shareholders are treated as receiving an amount of 'franked investment income'.   [29.1]

I MEANING OF A DISTRIBUTION (TA 1988 Part VI Chs II and III)

The intention is to catch not just the most obvious methods of paying profits to shareholders (such as a dividend), but also all payments and transfers by a company to its members other than repayment of capital subscribed. The main instance of a distribution is a dividend (including a capital dividend); other examples are discussed below.   [29.2]

1 Any distribution out of the assets of the company which is made in respect of shares except insofar as it is a repayment of capital or equal to any new consideration received

When sums are returned to shareholders on a reduction of capital, they will not be treated as distributions provided that they do not exceed the original amount subscribed (including any premium paid on the allotment of the shares). Payments to members on a winding up are expressly excluded from the definition of a distribution (such sums will usually be liable to CGT in the hands of the shareholders). The issue of bonus shares is not itself a distribution, but a repayment of share capital in the ten years following that issue will be a distribution up to the amount paid up on the bonus issue.   [29.3]

EXAMPLE 29.1

U Ltd has a share capital of 100 ordinary £1 shares. It makes a 1:1 bonus issue by capitalising £100 of reserves. Later it repays the shareholders 50p per share on a reduction of capital. Each shareholder is treated as receiving a distribution on the reduction in capital.

Position of a shareholder: Originally, he owned one £1 share. After the bonus issue, he owns two £1 shares. After the reduction in capital, he owns two 50p shares and has £1 in cash. The shareholder is in the same position as if he had received a £1 dividend and is taxed as such.

2   A reduction of share capital followed by a bonus issue

Essentially, this is the same operation as above and has similar taxation consequences. These consequences will not follow if the gap between repayment and the bonus issue exceeds ten years; so long as the bonus issue is not of redeemable shares, and so long as the company is not a closely controlled company within TA 1988 s 704. In addition, the bonus issue cannot be regarded as a distribution if the repaid share capital consisted of fully paid preference shares.   **[29.4]**

EXAMPLE 29.2

As in *Example 29.1*, U Ltd has a share capital of 100 £1 shares. It makes a reduction of share capital by repaying 50p per share. It then issues 100 50p bonus shares (ie a 1:1 issue).

Position of a shareholder: Initially, he held one £1 share. After the repayment of capital, he owns one 50p share and has 50p in cash. After the bonus issue, he owns two 50p shares and has received 50p in cash. Hence, he has shares of identical aggregate par value to the one share held at the start and has received a 50p payment from the company which will be treated as a distribution.

3   The issue of bonus redeemable shares and bonus securities

A bonus issue of redeemable shares (ie shares which the company has express authority or an obligation to redeem in the future) and of securities is a distribution. Unlike the other examples of a distribution, however, this is a *'non-qualifying'* distribution. The taxation consequences of this are considered at **[29.101]**, but it should be noted that this category is unique in being the one distribution where the company is not, at the time of the distribution, paying out money to shareholders, but is entering into a commitment to do so in the future. Hence, the issue represents a potential rather than an immediate charge on profits. The value of the distribution will, in the case of shares, be the nominal value together with any premium payable on redemption. In the case of other securities, it will be the amount secured together with any premium payable on redemption. When redeemable shares and securities are redeemed, the redemption will normally be a qualifying distribution.   **[29.5]**

4   A transfer by a company to its members of assets or liabilities which are worth more than any new consideration furnished by the member

The excess of any assets or liabilities transferred by a company to its members over any new consideration furnished by the members is a distribution. **[29.6]**

5 Certain interest payments (see generally CT 1552)

Interest payments geared to the profits of the company (irrespective of the reasonableness of the rate) or excessive interest (that which exceeds a reasonable commercial return) may be treated as distributions by TA 1988 s 209(2)(d), (e)(iii). Interest payments on bonus securities and on securities which are convertible whether directly or indirectly into shares in the company (unless listed on the Stock Exchange) are distributions. These rules do not apply if the payment is to another company within the corporation tax charge.

For the position of interest payments made to an overseas parent by a connected company see TA 1988 s 209(2)(da) discussed at [**28.77**] (and see *Tax Bulletin*, issue 17, at p 218). [**29.7**]

EXAMPLE 29.3

Zee Ltd borrows £50,000 from Mr Con at a rate of interest of 20% pa. A reasonable commercial rate would be 12%. The company pays £10,000 pa to Con of which £6,000 is deductible from profits for corporation tax purposes. That sum is also interest for TA 1988 s 349(2) so that lower rate tax should be deducted at source. The excess (£4,000 pa) is a distribution on which ACT is payable and Con will be assessed on the gross amount under Schedule F.

6 'Equity loans'

Equity loans are perpetual debt instruments issued by UK resident companies. The term itself is defined in TA 1988 s 209(2)(e)(vii) and (9). A typical illustration is a security with no fixed date for redemption. The UK formerly taxed payments under the instrument as 'interest' but the above provisions now reclassify such payments as distributions. Holding companies chargeable to UK corporation tax are generally unaffected (TA 1988 s 212). [**29.8**]

7 The stock dividend option (see CT 1700)

TA 1988 s 249 provides that where paid up shares are offered to shareholders instead of a cash dividend, those shares will be treated as income in the shareholders' hands (see further [**29.130**] for a consideration of the enhanced stock dividend). [**29.9**]

8 Special rules for close companies

The provision by a close company of a benefit for a participator is treated as a distribution: see [**28.97**] [**29.10**]-[**29.20**]

II DISTRIBUTIONS AND COMPANY BUY-BACKS

The Companies Act 1985 ss 159–181 allows companies (so long as authorised by their articles of association) to purchase their own shares. Generally, such purchases must be paid for out of distributable profits, but private companies can use capital. As already discussed, any payment to a shareholder in excess of the sum paid on the original allotment of the shares is treated as a distribution, unless the repayment occurs on a winding up of the company. With the intention of avoiding a tax discrimination on buy-backs TA 1988 s 219 provides that, in certain circumstances, when shares are bought back, moneys received by a shareholder will not be treated as a distribution so that any profit made will be charged, if at all, to CGT. Accordingly, shares sold to the company will be treated no differently from sales to any other person. However, s 219 is restrictive, so that in some cases there will still be a distribution. For the section to apply the following conditions must be satisfied.   [29.21]

1   The purchasing company

The purchasing company must not be listed on the official list of a stock exchange but its shares may be dealt in on the USM or AIM. It must be either a trading company or the holding company of a trading group.   [29.22]

2   The vendor of the shares

The vendor may be an individual, a trustee, the PR of a deceased shareholder, or a company. He should be resident and, if an individual, ordinarily resident in the UK. Normally, the shares must have been owned for at least five years and it is not possible to aggregate different ownership periods (hence settlor/trustees and trustees/beneficiaries must each satisfy the five-year period). In the exceptional cases of husband/wife and of the deceased/his PRs and legatees aggregation is permissible and in the latter case the aggregated ownership period need only be three years.

The vendor must either dispose of all his shares in the company or, at least, 'substantially reduce' his shareholding. The Revenue takes the view that a holding will only be substantially reduced if the shareholder reduces his fractional interest in the company's issued capital by at least 25% and is not left with a dominant (at least 30%) holding of the issued shares. In calculating these fractions, spouses and associates are treated as one person. As any transactions in the same shares within 12 months of the sale will form part of the same transaction, it follows that shares must not be repurchased from the company within a period of one year. In determining whether a substantial reduction has been achieved it should be remembered that shares bought back by the company are cancelled.   [29.23]

EXAMPLE 29.4

Buy-back Ltd has an issued share capital of 200 £1 shares. Adam owns 120 of the shares and sells 90 of them to Buy-back Ltd.

Adam's fraction before sale	$120/200 = 0.6$
Adam's fraction after sale	$30/110 = 0.27$
	$75\% \times 0.6 = 0.45$

Accordingly, Adam has substantially reduced his shareholding and is not left with a dominant holding of issued shares.

3   The reason for the sale

There are two permissible reasons. First, the purchase by the company must benefit its trade (or that of a 75% subsidiary) and not be part of a scheme designed to enable the shareholders to participate in the company's profits without receiving a dividend or otherwise to avoid tax. The requirement that the purchase must be a 'benefit to the trade' is not an easy test to apply. For instance, the buying out of dissident shareholders is certainly for the benefit of the company but that, presumably, is not the same unless it can be shown that the continued dissension was harming the management and, therefore, the trade of the company. In practice, the Revenue has stated (see SP 2/82) that it will expect the requirement to be satisfied in such cases and in cases where the vendor shareholder is 'genuinely' giving up his entire interest of all kinds in the company.

EXAMPLE 29.5

(1) It is proposed that WW Ltd (an unquoted trading company) purchases the shares of Mr Wam, one of the original founders of the company in 1980. He is willing to sell a 60% holding but wishes to keep a small (5%) holding for sentimental reasons. Mr Wam is retiring in favour of a new management team. The transaction will be for the benefit of the trade of WW Ltd and, the other conditions being satisfied, the payment for the shares will not be a distribution.

(2) Sal is the sole shareholder in Sal Ltd, an unquoted trading company. Profits amount to £100,000 for the present accounting period and Sal Ltd plans to use them to purchase 50% of Sal's shares. This scheme will not be within the provisions of TA 1988 s 219 because:

    (i) it would appear to be a scheme designed to pass the profits to Sal without declaring a dividend;

    (ii) Sal is not substantially reducing her holding since she will still own all the shares in Sal Ltd;

    (iii) the purchase is not for the benefit of Sal Ltd's trade.

The second permitted reason for the sale of the shares is where the whole, or substantially the whole, of the proceeds of sale are to be used by the recipient in discharging his IHT liability charged on a death. The money must be so used within two years of death and it has to be shown that the IHT cannot be paid without undue hardship unless the shares are sold back to the company. In this case the above requirements as to the vendor of the shares do not apply. The IHT need not be owing in respect of the shares.　　　　**[29.24]**

EXAMPLE 29.6

(1) Sam inherits the family residence on his father's death. Under the terms of the will it is to bear its own IHT which can be raised by the sale of Sam's shareholding in Sham Ltd (a trading company which is not listed). The only alternative would involve the sale of the family house. If the shares are sold to Sham Ltd the purchase moneys will not be treated as a distribution.

(2) Sue inherits 30% of the share capital of Carruthers Ltd. She does not want the shares and arranges for the company to buy them back. Although this arrangement falls outside the relief for hardship on a death, there will be no distribution since such a payment will be for the benefit of the trade (see SP2/82).

4　Position if the vendor is a UK company

If the vendor of the shares is a UK company the position can be summarised as follows:

First, assuming that s 219 applies so that the payment is not taxed as a distribution it will be taxed as a chargeable gain in the ordinary way.

Secondly, if the payment does not satisfy the s 219 requirements it will then be treated as a distribution and hence, in the hands of the vendor company, as franked investment income. Accordingly, it would be attractive for such buy-backs to fall outside s 219 since the vendor would not only escape corporation tax on the sale proceeds but would, in addition, be entitled to an ACT credit. It was not entirely surprising, therefore, that the Revenue issued SP 4/89 which provides as follows:

'If the purchase of its own shares by a company resident in the UK gives rise to a distribution, and a shareholder receiving such a distribution is itself a company, the distribution is included in the consideration for the disposal of the shares for the purposes of the charge to corporation tax on chargeable gains. In the Inland Revenue's view the effect of TA 1988 ss 208, 345(3) is that the distribution does not suffer a tax charge as income within the terms of [TCGA 1992 s 37(1)].'

The result is that corporation tax will be charged on a capital gain but the Statement has attracted a welter of criticism (see, for instance, *Taxation*, 21 September 1989).   [**29.25**]

EXAMPLE 29.7

KP Ltd owns 500 shares in SJ Ltd which it acquired at par for £1 each in March 1988.

SJ Ltd buys the shares back for £10 each in June 1995.
(1) If the purchase is within s 219 KP Ltd's tax position would appear to be as follows:

	£
Sale proceeds for CGT	5,000
Less: price paid by SJ Ltd	500
Capital gain (ignoring indexation)	£4,500

(2) If the purchase is outside s 219, KP Ltd's tax position would appear to be as follows:

	£
Consideration received	5,000
Net distribution (£5,000 – £500)	4,500
Plus: ACT paid thereon	1,125
Franked investment income	5,625

Note: If SP 4/89 is correct KP Ltd will have realised the same chargeable gain as in (1) above.

5   Advantages if the distribution rules apply

When the distribution rules apply, it is only the excess of the purchase proceeds over the amount originally paid to the company for the shares that is treated as a distribution. As the sum is treated as a distribution must then be ignored in calculating the vendor's CGT position, it is possible for him to make a CGT loss whilst selling the shares at a profit.

EXAMPLE 29.8

Risker subscribed for 200 shares in BB Ltd paying the par value of £1 per share. He sold the shares two years ago to Tusker for £500 and BB Ltd has now bought the shares for £950 Assuming that the sale is taxed as a distribution Tusker's tax position is as follows:

	£
Total consideration received	950.00
Net distribution (£950 – £200)	750.00
Plus: ACT thereon paid by BB Ltd	187.50
Gross dividend (subject to Schedule F income tax)	£937.50
Sale proceeds for CGT purposes (£950 – £750)	200.00
Price paid by Tusker	500.00
CGT loss	£300.00

As a result of the harmonisation of rates of income tax and CGT, the position of the individual shareholder must also be considered to see if there is a real benefit to be derived from the use of s 219. If the purchasing company is able to set all the ACT on a distribution against its mainstream corporation tax (MCT), the company itself may be better served by keeping the buy-back outside s 219. **[29.26]**

EXAMPLE 29.9

Alfie Ltd has an issued share capital of £20,000 comprising 20,000 £1 ordinary shares allotted at par. Harry, a higher rate taxpayer, owns 10,000 shares. The company wishes to buy Harry's shares for £5 each in the accounting year ended 31 July 1997 during which it made profits of £200,000.

Company's tax position

(1) If the purchase is within s 219:

	£
Profits	200,000
MCT (at 21%)	42,000
Net profits	£158,000

	£
Cost of buying Harry's shares	50,000
Remaining profit	£108,000

(2) If the purchase is taxed as a distribution:

		£
Profits		200,000
MCT at 21%	42,000	
Less: ACT on buy-back	10,000	32,000
		£168,000

ACT on buy-back	10,000
Net profits	£158,000

Harry's tax position

(1) If purchase is within s 219:

	£
Sale proceeds for CGT	50,000
Less: original issue price	10,000
Chargeable gain (ignoring indexation)	40,000
CGT @ 40%	£16,000

(2) If purchase is a distribution:

	£
Net distribution (£50,000 – £10,000)	40,000
Plus tax credit	10,000
Gross distribution	50,000
Tax @ 40%	20,000
Less: ACT credit	10,000
Tax payable	£10,000

6 FA 1997 provisions treating distributions on a buy-back as a FID

FA 1997 s 69 and Sch 7 provide that distributions resulting from a purchase by a company of its own shares are treated for all purposes as foreign income dividends (FIDs are discussed at [**29.46**]. The effect is to deny a repayment of the tax credit in respect of such distributions: income tax at lower and basic rate, however, continues to be treated as paid. With the general rules taking away any right to recover the tax credit (effective from 6 April 1999) these rules will thereupon cease to apply. The legislation also provides that when trustees dispose of shares by way of buy-back the 34% rate of tax applies to the resultant distribution irrespective of the nature of the trust (see FA 1997 Sch 7 para 3: the reason for this change was that as a matter of trust law receipts of a share sale were treated as capital and hence did not attract either a higher rate charge in the hands of the life tenant or an additional charge under TA 1988 s 686)   [**29.27**]

7 Clearances and stamp duty

Whenever the buy-back of shares is proposed, advance clearance can be obtained for the scheme and the same application (sent in duplicate) can be used for a clearance under TA 1988 s 707 (see [**36.65**]). Similarly, if the arrangement is designed to fall outside TA 1988 s 219, negative clearance can be obtained. A useful article in *Tax Bulletin*, February 1996, at p 281 comments on various matters that are commonly overlooked or misunderstood when applying for a clearance.

No instrument of share transfer is necessary on a buy-back but the return that must be made by the company to Companies House (Form 169) is subject to stamp duty 'as if it were an instrument transferring shares on sale' (FA 1986 s 66). Accordingly, *ad valorem* duty at ½% is charged. (Note that the redemption of redeemable preference shares is outside the section and free from duty.)   [**29.28**]–[**29.40**]

III TAXATION OF 'QUALIFYING DISTRIBUTIONS' IN THE HANDS OF THE COMPANY

The taxation of distributions is governed by the imputation system. The central feature is ACT which represents, for the company making the payment, a partial discharge of its corporation tax bill. The shareholder is given a credit for this ACT so that he will receive his dividend together with a credit for income tax purposes. The rules to be considered in this section apply to all qualifying distributions. For convenience, the following examples will concentrate on the most common form of distribution, the cash dividend.
                                                                                       [**29.41**]

1 The payment of a dividend

A company is obliged to pay ACT to the Revenue when it pays a dividend to its shareholders (an interim dividend is paid when actually made: a final dividend is paid on the date when it is declared due and payable). For the purpose of collecting ACT the calendar year is divided into quarters and at the end of each quarter (ie on 31 March, 30 June, 30 September and 31 December) the company must make a return indicating what dividends have been paid in the three-month period just ended. If dividends have been paid, the appropriate ACT should be paid within 14 days of the end of the quarter except where the company has franked investment income available to cover the distribution that it makes. In such a case ACT need not be paid.

Prior to 6 April 1993 the rate of ACT was determined in accordance with the following fraction (TA 1988 s 14(3)):

$$\frac{I}{100 - I}$$

where I was the basic rate of income tax for the year of assessment beginning in the financial year for which the rate of ACT was to be fixed. For the financial year 1992, therefore, the rate of ACT was:

$$\frac{25}{100 - 25} = \frac{25}{75}$$

EXAMPLE 29.10

On 1 February 1993 Zed Ltd pays total dividends of £75,000 to shareholders. This should appear in the quarterly return on 31 March 1993 and within 14 days thereof the sum of £25,000 (25/75 of £75,000) should be paid as ACT to the Revenue.

For dividends paid between 6 April 1993 and 5 April 1994, the ACT rate was reduced from 25% to 22.5% and, after 5 April 1994, the rate fell to 20%. TA 1988 s 14(3) has therefore been amended for 1993–94 and subsequent tax years so that 'I' in the above fraction became for the financial year 1993 22.5 and for any subsequent financial year the lower rate of income tax. For 1997 therefore the fraction is:

$$\frac{20}{100 - 20} = \frac{1}{4}$$

EXAMPLE 29.11 (continuing *Example 29.10*)

If Zed Ltd pays £75,000 in dividends in both February 1994 and February 1995, ACT payable with the March return will be:
  (i) In 1994 £21,774 (22.5/77.5 (or 9/31) × £75,000);
  (ii) In 1995 £18,750 (20/80 × £75,000).

The reduction in the ACT rate provided cashflow benefits for companies and some (limited) assistance to those companies which suffer from surplus ACT problems (see [**29.44**]). [**29.42**]

2 The use of ACT by the company

The corporation tax that companies pay nine months after the end of the accounting period (see [**28.21**]) is known as mainstream corporation tax (MCT). ACT paid on dividends can be deducted from the MCT bill on all profits of that period, including chargeable gains (TA 1988 s 239(1)). Profits for this purpose means the income and capital profits of the company less charges on income, allowable income and capital losses, and management expenses.

EXAMPLE 29.12

Assume that Zed Ltd's accounts (see *Example 29.10*) made up to 31 March each year show a constant profit level of £1m made up of income profits of £750,000 and capital profits of £250,000 and that the company pays dividends totalling £75,000 each year. The MCT bill in the financial years 1992, 1993 and 1994 is:

	1992	*1993*	*1994*
£1m taxed at 33%	330,000	330,000	330,000
Less: ACT on dividends of £75,000	25,000	21,774	18,750
Balance payable by the following 1 January	305,000	308,226	311,250

Zed Ltd's total corporation tax bill is £330,000 which will be paid in two instalments (the ACT portion and the MCT balance). Had no dividends been paid to shareholders during the accounting year, there would have been no ACT payable and the MCT bill would have been £330,000 payable by the following 1 January: ie nine months after the end of the accounting period.

In the financial year 1997 the MCT rate fell to 31% with the result that:

£1m taxed at 31%	=	£310,000
Less: ACT on dividends of £75,000	=	18,750
Balance payable		£291,250

Thus, the payment of a dividend will not, unless full ACT set-off cannot be claimed (see [**29.44**]), increase the total corporation tax charged. It merely, as its name suggests, results in an advanced payment of that tax.　　　　[**29.43**]

3　The problems of surplus ACT

There will be surplus ACT when the company pays dividends in a year in which it has made no profits.

EXAMPLE 29.13

The accounts of Eve Ltd for the period ended 31 March 1998 show no profits, but during that year dividends of £75,000 were paid out of distributable profits made by the company in the previous accounting period. The corporation tax position is:

(1)　ACT of £18,750 paid on the dividends;

(2)　there is no MCT liability for the financial year 1997 to be reduced by the ACT paid;

(3)　accordingly, the company has surplus ACT of £18,750.

Surplus ACT also occurs where distributions exceed the 'permitted level' because there is a ceiling on the amount of MCT that can be cancelled by ACT. The maximum ACT set-off is the amount of ACT which would have been paid if the dividend declared together with ACT thereon equalled the profits for the year. In practical terms this is equivalent to the ACT rate of (for financial year 1997) 20% on the profits, so that for small companies (taxed at 21%) the MCT bill can be reduced to 1%.

EXAMPLE 29.14

Xerxes Ltd pays dividends of £2,400,000 in September 1997. During the same accounting period it has profits of £1,500,000. This disparity between dividend and profits can be explained (as in *Example 29.13*, above) by assuming that the company paid out past accumulated profits. For corporation tax purposes:

(1)　ACT of £600,000 (20/80 of £2,400,000) is paid on the dividend;

(2)　MCT at 31% on the £1,500,000 profits is £465,000. This cannot wholly be wiped out by ACT of £600,000. Instead, the maximum ACT available will be £300,000 (20% of £1,500,000) since:

Dividends of £1,200,000 plus ACT thereon of £300,000 equals the profits (£1,500,000) for the year.

Hence, Xerxes Ltd will have surplus ACT of £300,000 (£600,000 – £300,000) and the total corporation tax bill will be:

$$
\begin{array}{ll}
& \text{\pounds} \\
\text{ACT} & 600,000 \\
+ \text{ MCT} & \underline{165,000} \quad (\text{\pounds}465,000 - 300,000) \\
& \underline{\underline{\text{\pounds}765,000}}
\end{array}
$$

An alternative way of explaining how much ACT can be set off against MCT on profits is to say that the rate of MCT can be reduced from 31% to 11% at the most, or, in the case of small companies, from 21% to 1%.

A further situation where surplus ACT arises is when a UK company has foreign subsidiaries and receives distributions from them which have borne foreign tax. Any foreign tax credit must be set off *first* against UK corporation tax on that foreign income and ACT is then available to set off against any residue subject to the normal ACT limit (TA 1988 s 797(4)(a)). In cases where a UK company distributes much of its profit and receives a high proportion of income from a non-UK source, it is likely to have a permanent surplus ACT problem.   [**29.44**]

EXAMPLE 29.15

Titus Ltd's profits are all derived from overseas income taxed abroad at the rate of 36%.

	£
Profit (gross)	2,000,000
*(Foreign tax credit	720,000)
Dividend paid	750,000
ACT paid (¼ × £750,000)	187,500
MCT (31% × £2,000,000)	
= £620,000 minus foreign credit*	nil
Total UK tax (surplus ACT)	187,500

4   The set-off of surplus ACT

A company can carry back surplus ACT and set it against MCT on all its profits (including capital profits) in the preceding six years taking the most recent period first (TA 1988 s 239(3)). A refund of corporation tax will only result if the permitted level of set-off has not been reached in those years. If a surplus still remains it can then be carried forward without time limit and set off against MCT on future profits in the first year when the full quota of dividends has not been paid.

EXAMPLE 29.16

The following represents the dividends paid and profits made by a company during eight consecutive accounting periods (assuming a 33% rate of corporation tax throughout with an ACT fraction of 25/75).

(a)	(b)	(c)	(d)	(e)	(f)	(g)
			ACT	*MCT*	*Maximum set-off*	*Amount unused in year*
			(25/75 ×(b))	*(33% × (c))*	*(25% × (c))*	*((f)–(d))*
	Dividend	*Profit*				
	£	£	£	£	£	£
Year 1	Nil	200,000	Nil	66,000	50,000	50,000
Year 2	75,000	100,000	25,000	33,000	25,000	—
Year 3	75,000	100,000	25,000	33,000	25,000	—
Year 4	37,500	100,000	12,500	33,000	25,000	12,500
Year 5	Nil	50,000	Nil	16,500	12,500	12,500

Year 6	15,000	40,000	5,000	13,200	10,000	5,000
Year 7	375,000	100,000	125,000	33,000	25,000	—
Year 8	37,500	60,000	12,500	19,800	15,000	2,500

In year 7 the ACT is £125,000 which can only be partially offset against the MCT bill for the year. MCT at £33,000 (33% × £100,000) can be reduced by the maximum set-off of £25,000 to £8,000, but no further, leaving surplus ACT of £100,000 (£125,000 – £25,000).

Uses of surplus ACT
(1) Carry-back to years 6, 5, 4 and 1 relieving £5,000, £12,500, £12,500 and £50,000 respectively and leaving surplus ACT of £20,000 (£100,000 – £80,000).
(2) Carry-forward £20,000 to future years without time limit using the first available profits but subject to the permitted level of set-off in each year. In year 8 the surplus can be further reduced to £17,500 (£20,000 – £2,500).

There is a two-year time limit for claiming the relief. This limit is relevant for the actual making of a claim: the settlement of the amount of that claim may, however, take much longer. To what extent can claims be adjusted in the light of events occurring outside the two-year period? In part this question boils down to the difference between amending an existing claim (or fleshing out the details) and submitting a new, out-of-time (and therefore ineffective) claim. The matter arose in *Procter & Gamble v Taylerson* (1990) where the taxpayers, having claimed to carry back surplus ACT, subsequently incurred substantial trading losses. The original claim had been to carry back the surplus to the 1978 accounting period. Losses, however, arose in 1982 (after the amount of that claim had been agreed with the Revenue) and because these losses could also be carried back the taxpayers then sought to amend the ACT claim to include a carry-back to 1977. The Court of Appeal held that such an adjustment amounted to a new claim which, being outside the two-year time limit, was ineffective. The decision leaves open the extent to which events arising whilst the claim is unsettled can be taken into account. It is notable that the amount of the claim had been agreed by the time the losses were incurred. Balcombe LJ commented:

> 'While I would be prepared to accept that the letter may be regarded as a claim to carry back ACT, ... subject to adjustments in matter of detail, ... the letter cannot be construed ... as a claim to carry back the whole surplus of ACT of whatever amount and whenever and however that surplus might arise.'

[29.45]

5 Foreign income dividends and international headquarter companies

The reductions in the ACT rate for the tax years 1993–94 and 1994–95 alleviated the surplus ACT problem but did not solve it and hence the government produced a Consultative Document (*Surplus ACT: Proposals for Reform*— March 1993) which was intended to deal with the situation illustrated in *Example 29.15*. This resulted in legislation in the form of FA 1994 s 138 and Sch 16.

The paying company   The provisions inserted as TA 1988 ss 246A–246Y enable UK resident companies to declare a foreign income dividend (FID) to be paid out of foreign source profits. To obtain this treatment the company must make an election to the inspector no later than the date when the dividend is paid. This election can be withdrawn before payment but not thereafter. The dividend itself must be paid in cash and the shareholder cannot be given any election to decide whether the dividend is to be paid, the form it will take, and nor can he be given an option to be paid by another company.

The company itself cannot pay more than one dividend on shares of the same class and elect for only one to be a FID. It cannot pay a FID to one shareholder and an ordinary dividend to the others. The paying company must deduct ACT on the FID which it may then recover (see s 246N and s 246P for these complex rules and note there are matching requirements in s 246J and s 246K). **[29.46]**

The shareholder A FID does not carry any tax credit. Accordingly, although an individual shareholder is treated as receiving a dividend grossed up at the lower rate of income tax, no repayment claim can be made. This represents the major disadvantage of a FID. There is no liability to basic rate nor to lower rate income tax but the FID is treated as the highest slice of an individual's income and may therefore attract a tax charge at higher rate. As far as the corporate shareholder is concerned a FID does not count as a franked payment: in an accounting period a company will, however, only have to pay ACT if the FIDs that it makes exceed the FIDs that it receives. In the event that it receives more FIDs than it pays the excess is carried forward and treated as a FID received in the next accounting period. **[29.47]**

International Headquarters Companies (IHC) The advantage enjoyed by an IHC is that it does not have to pay ACT on the FIDs that it makes: this represents a cashflow benefit as against the normal position. The definition of an IHC is found in s 246S: in essence the UK company must be wholly owned, either directly or through any number of intermediate holding companies, by another company which is foreign held (at least 80% of its share capital being owned by non-UK residents) throughout the accounting period. **[29.48]**

Deemed FIDS FA 1997 s 69 and Sch 7 deems certain company distributions to be FIDs in order to prevent any repayments of the tax credit to the recipient shareholder (see further [**29.27**]). **[29.49]**

The abolition of FIDs As from 6 April 1999 no election may be made to treat any dividend as a FID. The rules for international headquarter companies remain unaltered. These changes result from the major amendments in the imputation system which are considered further at [**29.66**]. **[29.50]**–**[29.60]**

IV TAXATION OF INDIVIDUALS (AND CHARITIES) WHO RECEIVE DISTRIBUTIONS

1 **Position before 6 April 1993**

Dividends and other distributions received by UK shareholders are assessed to income tax under Schedule F on the gross sum: ie on the dividend actually paid together with the appropriate tax credit (TA 1988 s 231). Prior to 6 April 1993 the tax credit was equal to the rate of ACT when the company paid the dividend and, because ACT was linked to the basic rate of income tax, the credit discharged a shareholder's liability for that sum so that it was only if he was subject to the higher rate of income tax that a further income tax charge arose. Non-taxpayers were entitled to a refund of the tax credit. **[29.61]**

EXAMPLE 29.17 (*Position before 6 April 1993*)

Cam, Mem and Bert are three shareholders in Fromage Ltd and each receives a dividend of £75 in the income tax year 1992-93. Cam has no other income and unused personal allowances; Mem is a basic rate taxpayer; and Bert is subject to income tax at the highest rate (40%). Each has an income of £100 under Schedule F and each receives a tax credit for £25.

Cam, who has unused personal allowances, will be able to reclaim the £25 tax credit.

Mem has had the correct amount of tax deducted at source, having used all her personal allowances and exhausted her lower rate of income tax.

Bert will be subject to extra tax of £15 (40% of £100 = £40, less his tax credit of £25).

2 Position from 6 April 1993 to 6 April 1999

This relatively straightforward system altered in the case of dividends paid from 6 April 1993. The value of the tax credit fell to 20% of the dividend plus the tax credit so that, in the case of a dividend of £75, the credit became £18.75 instead of £25. This reduced credit matches the income tax charge at lower rate on the total of the dividend plus the credit. If matters had been left there, shareholders would have suffered an additional charge at both higher and basic rate. However, income chargeable under Schedule F which does not exceed the higher rate threshold (£26,100 for 1997–98) 'shall ... be charged ... at the lower rate instead of the rate otherwise applicable to it'. Dividend income (and, from 1996–97, other savings income: see TA 1988 s 1A inserted by FA 1996 s 73 and [**4.23**]) is accordingly taxed at the lower rate of 20% up to the higher rate threshold.   [**29.62**]

EXAMPLE 29.18

This example considers the position of three types of shareholder: the basic rate, higher rate and non-taxpayer and contrasts the receipt of a net dividend in 1997–98 with the position if a net dividend of the same amount had been received in 1992–93.

Adam Shareholder (basic rate taxpayer)

	£
Net dividend received	75.00
Add: tax credit @ 20% (75 × 20/80)	18.75
Dividend plus credit	93.75

No further tax payable: tax liability at special rate of 20% for basic rate taxpayer to match tax credit.

No change from the position in 1992–93.

Bertie Shareholder (higher rate taxpayer)

	£
Net dividend received	75.00
Add: tax credit @ 20%	18.75
Dividend plus credit	93.75
Total liability (£93.75 × 40%)	37.50
Less: credit	(18.75)
Tax payable	£18.75

Increase in his tax bill of £3.75.

Non-taxpayers

(i) Polly Pension Fund

	£
Net dividend received	75.00
Add: tax credit @ 20%	18.75
Dividend plus credit	93.75
Refund	18.75
Reduction in refund of	£6.25

(ii) Carrie Charity

As for Polly Pension Fund, except that transitional relief was given over a four-year period as follows, phasing in reduced 20% credit. Additional refunds were made to charities worth:

1/15 of dividend for 1993–94
1/20 of dividend for 1994–95
1/30 of dividend for 1995–96
1/60 of dividend for 1996–97

	£
For instance, net dividend received 1996/97	75.00
Value of credit (refund)	18.75
Add: additional payment (1996–97)	
1/60 × £75	1.25
Total sum received	£95.00

This gave an effective credit of 24% for 1993–94 reducing to 23% for 1994–95, 22% for 1995–96 and 21% for 1996–97. Then, and in line with other shareholders, 20% for subsequent years.

3   Dividend income is taxed as the highest part of an individual's income

As has already been discussed, dividends attract a tax credit at only 20% but this will satisfy an individual's liability to tax at the basic rate. An individual liable to tax at the higher rates will suffer a tax charge on the difference between that higher rate and 20%. Accordingly, it is crucial to know whether the dividend income falls into charge at the higher rate or not and the legislation provides that dividend income and other savings income is treated as the top slice of an individual's income. The consequences are illustrated in the following example.   **[29.63]**

EXAMPLE 29.19

Debbie has earned income (after deducting her personal allowance and any reliefs) of £25,450 and now receives a dividend (net) of £75:

	£
Other income	26,050.00
Dividend received (gross)	93.75
Total taxable income	£26,143.75

Dividend taxed as the highest slice of that income so that:

First £50 taxed at 20% (tax to pay nil)
Remaining £43.75 taxed at 40% (tax to pay £8.75)

Debbie's tax position can be represented thus:

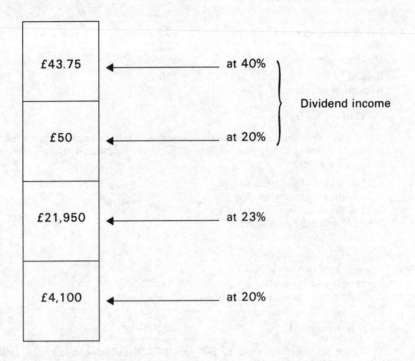

4   Dividends received by non-UK residents

The position of non-UK residents who receive a dividend is as follows:
(a) there is no withholding tax deducted from the dividend;
(b) there is no entitlement to any tax credit (contrast the position of UK resident shareholders whose credit, as already discussed, corresponds to the rate of ACT: TA 1988 s 231);
(c) there is no further UK tax liability.

Limiting the tax credit to UK residents may in the future be challenged as contravening the non-discrimination (art 6) and freedom of establishment (arts 52 and 58) provisions of the EC Treaty. For non-residents able to rely on the standard UK double tax treaty article the above position is modified: as illustrated in the following example they receive the dividend *plus* a repayment of one-half of the tax credit *less* a 5% withholding tax on the aggregate dividend plus half tax credit.   **[29.64]**

EXAMPLE 29.20

This example shows the effect that the half-tax credit refund has in relation to the payment of a dividend by UK Co to its American parent out of UK profits of (say) £100,000, assuming that all of the profits will be distributed.

	£
UK subsidiary's profits	100
UK corporation tax at 31%	(31)
Profits available for dividend	69
Dividend	(69)
Profits retained	Nil

UK corporation tax liability discharged by:

ACT paid on dividend (ie 69 × ¼)	17.25
MCT paid later	13.75

Tax credit for shareholder $\left(\text{ie } 69 \times \dfrac{20}{80}\right)$ 17.25

US parent receives:

Cash dividend	69
half-tax credit = 50% of 17.25	8.625
	77.625
Less: 5% withholding on 77.625	3.88125
Cash received	73.74375
Effective UK tax rate	26.25%

5   Conclusion on the current taxation of dividends

As already noted, ACT is the pivot of the imputation system. For the company, it is an advance payment of corporation tax. For the individual shareholder, part of the ACT is used as the measure for a tax credit which discharges his liability to basic rate income tax. For all companies an element of double charge remains since the shareholder is not given a credit for all the ACT paid by the company. The residual MCT liability is 11% or, in the case of small companies, 1%. The advantage of raising money by debentures, given that the interest is tax deductible by the company, is considered in Chapter 37.   [**29.65**]

EXAMPLE 29.21

Maximum tax liability on a distribution of all corporate profits for shareholders and company:

		£
	Company profit	1m
(a)	CT (at 31%)	310,000
	Net profit	£690,000
	Distributed net profit	690,000
(b)	ACT (¼ × £690,000)	172,500
	Shareholder tax credit	172,500
(c)	Gross dividend	£862,500
	Income tax at 40% on (c)	345,000
	Less: tax credit	172,500
(d)	Income tax bill	£172,500

Total tax payable is:	
ACT (b)	172,500
MCT (a)-(b)	138,500
IT (d)	172,500
	£483,500
Net profit remaining after all tax	£516,500
(Effective tax rate = 48.35%)	

6   **Position from 6 April 1999**

In the case of distributions made on or after 6 April 1999, F(No 2)A 1997 makes the following changes:
(1) the tax credit is reduced to 10% (and the fraction (see [**29.42**]) now called the 'tax credit fraction' becomes one-ninth;
(2) individuals will not be entitled to a repayment of any tax credit;
(3) as a result charities will cease to be entitled to recover tax credits but they will receive compensation from the government as a percentage payment of their dividend income over a transitional period as follows:

Tax year	Percentage of dividend income (%)
1999–2000	21
2000–01	17
2001–02	13
2002–03	8
2003–04	4

(4) although these provisions concerning repayment of tax credits do not apply to non resident shareholders the reduction in the tax credit to 10% coupled with the imposition of a withholding charge (as in the UK/US Treaty considered at [**29.64**]) will in effect deny a refund of any credit.
(5) individuals subject to tax at either lower or basic rate will have no further liability since the 'Schedule F ordinary (tax) rate' applicable in such cases has been set at 10% (TA 1988 s 1B inserted by F(No 2)A 1997). Higher rate taxpayer's will also receive compensation for the reduction in the tax credit with 'The Schedule F upper rate' being set at 32.5%. As the following table indicates they will therefore be no worse off as a result of the change:

	To 5 April 1999 £		From 6 April 1999 £
UK dividend		80.00	80.00
Tax credit	(20% of income) 20.00		(10%) 8.89
Income		100.00	88.89
Higher rate tax	(40%) 40.00		(32.5%) 28.89
After tax income		60.00	60.00

[**29.66**]–[**29.80**]

V   TAXATION OF OTHER PERSONS WHO RECEIVE DISTRIBUTIONS

1   **UK companies**

a) *No tax liability on distributions*

Dividends and other distributions received by one UK company from another are not generally subject to corporation tax in the recipient's hands. The sum paid, together with the ACT thereon, is known as *franked investment income* (FII: TA 1988 s 208).   [**29.81**]

b) *Refund of tax credit*

Formerly a recipient company could only be able to obtain a refund of the tax credit if *either* that distribution was expressly exempt from tax *or* if the recipient was wholly exempt from corporation tax or was exempt on all its income save for trading income (see TA 1988 s 231(2)—eg a charitable company). For the majority of companies, therefore, there was no question of a tax refund. As from 2 July 1997, F(No 2)A 1997 took away the right of pension funds to any refund of tax credits. For other companies who may obtain a refund of credits (notably charitable companies) entitlement to a refund continues until 6 April 1999 when it ceases in line with the rules already considered for individuals and unincorporated charities. **[29.82]**

c) *Utilisation of tax credit to frank distributions*

FII may be used to 'frank' the receiving company's own distributions paid in the accounting period when the FII is received. Hence, ACT will not be payable on such distributions and, if already paid in an earlier quarter of the accounting period, will be refunded (TA 1988 s 241). If FII is not fully used in an accounting period, any surplus can be carried forward (without time limit) and used to frank future distributions. **[29.83]**

EXAMPLE 29.22

During the accounting period ending 31 March 1998 Sellco Ltd has profits of £1,000,000. It receives dividends of £80,000 from Buyco Ltd (another UK company) and itself pays out dividends of £150,000 during the year.
(1) Sellco has FII of £80,000 + £20,000 = £100,000
(2) On paying the £150,000 dividend it can offset the ACT paid on the FII to reduce its ACT liability:

	£
Dividend	150,000
ACT payable (at 20%)	30,000
FII set-off	20,000
Balance of ACT owing	£ 10,000

(3) Profits for the year are £1,000,000 (and do not include FII) so that the MCT liability will be:

	£
MCT at 31%	310,000
Less: ACT	10,000
Balance owing	£300,000

(4) In effect Sellco can pass dividends through to its own shareholders.

d) *Using FII to obtain loss relief*

The second use to which an FII tax credit could be put prior to 2 July 1997 was to obtain partial loss relief (TA 1988 s 242(1)). If a company in any year had trading losses or charges on income or management expenses which exceeded the profits of that year, any surplus FII received in that year could, if a claim was made by the company, be treated as if it were profits liable to corporation tax and the tax credit was recovered directly from the Revenue. 'Surplus FII' excluded FII carried forward from an earlier year (TA 1988 s 242(9)).

EXAMPLE 29.23

Investaco Ltd received dividends of £40,000 for the accounting year ended 31 March 1997. It has unrelieved management expenses of £80,000. It may obtain a repayment as follows:

	£
Surplus FII (40,000 × 100/80)	50,000
Less: management expenses	50,000
Corporation tax payable	£ Nil

The refund of tax paid is £10,000 (the tax credit at 20% accompanying the dividend of £40,000).

Notes:
(1) Some loss relief (£10,000) has been obtained at once.
(2) The relief is only partial, however, since, had the expenses of £50,000 been set against profits subject to corporation tax at 33% (the rate for the financial year 1996), the tax saving would have been not £10,000 but 33% × £50,000 = £16,500. To ensure that full relief was available compensating adjustments were made in later accounting periods to ensure that the balance of the loss relief was then given (TA 1988 s 242(5)).

F(No 2)A 1997 removed this relief by providing that no claims could be made in respect of any accounting period beginning on or after 2 July 1997. As a result the only use to which FII may now be put is to frank a company's own distributions.   **[29.84]**

e) *Taper relief and FII*

As noted at **[28.23]**, in determining whether tapering relief is available to a company its FII is taken into account. Broadly, tapering relief is not available on the profits of a company insofar as those profits include FII, other than FII received from a member of the same group of companies. Accordingly, if the profits of a company include FII the tapering relief calculation will be as follows: **[29.85]**

EXAMPLE 29.24

HN Ltd makes up accounts to 31 March each year. For the year ended 31 March 1998 the company has trading profits of £300,000 and receives FII of £200,000 from another (non-group) UK company (ie £160,000 + £40,000 tax credit).

The corporation tax calculation is as follows:

(i)   Tax at 31% on £300,000   £93,000
      (the dividend income is ignored at this stage)
(ii) *Less:* tapering relief calculated as follows:
      (upper relevant amount − profits) × statutory fraction × *basic profits/profits*

      '*basic profits*' means profits subject to corporation tax;
      '*profits*' means basic profits plus FII, ie:

$$(1,500,000 - 500,000) \times \frac{1}{40} \times \frac{300,000}{500,000} = £15,000$$

(iii) Total tax ((i)−(ii)) = £78,000

2   Trusts and estates

a) *Interest in possession trusts*

The relevant beneficiary receives the tax credit on dividend income at the reduced rate of 20% and the income is taxed in his hands in the same way as with an individual directly entitled. Accordingly, any additional liability depends upon the level of that beneficiary's taxable income. As with discretionary trusts (see [**29.87**]), expenses of the trust, so far as properly chargeable against income, are set against savings income (including dividends) in priority to any other form of income. For distributions from 6 April 1999 the position is set out in [**29.88**]   [**29.86**]

b) *Discretionary trusts*

Discretionary trustees are taxed at a single flat rate of 34% on the gross dividend (ie on the dividend together with the accompanying tax credit). In the case of dividend income this will involve the payment of an extra 14% tax. Any beneficiary receiving a discretionary payment will then receive trust income with a tax credit for 34%. A basic rate taxpayer will be entitled to a refund of 11% but will not receive any refund for the extra 3% tax suffered by the trust on the dividend income:

> **EXAMPLE 29.25**
>
> Assume that the Bloggs discretionary trust receives net dividends totalling £75: ie gross dividend income of £93.75. The liability of the trustees to tax at 34% (£31.87) will be reduced by the credit (£18.75) leaving tax payable of £13.12. If the entire income is distributed to a beneficiary subject to income tax at the basic rate, his total trust income will be £93.75 including the tax credit of £31.87. He will receive a refund of £10.31 (£31.87 - £21.56) but the remaining tax paid by the trustees (£2.81) is irrecoverable.

Expenses properly chargeable against the income of a discretionary trust result in that income being charged only at the basic rate of tax. If the trust receives dividend or other savings income, that income is deemed to be used to discharge those expenses before any other income (which is beneficial in preventing an extra tax charge at 14% on that income).   [**29.87**]

> **EXAMPLE 29.26**
>
> Discretionary trustees receive dividend income of £2,000 and other (non savings) income of £16,000. They have expenses of £900. The position for 1997-98 is that expenses are deducted from the dividend income leaving £1,100 (net). That sum, grossed up at 20%, is £1,375 which—along with the £16,000 other income—is taxed at 34%. Extra tax payable on the dividends is £192.50 (£467.50 - £275).

c) *Distributions received by discretionary trusts from 6 April 1999*

As already explained the tax credit is reduced to 10% but (as with individuals) this will not result in extra tax being charged on discretionary trusts because a special tax rate will apply to distributions. The rate is 25% which will mean that such trusts will be (slightly!) better off.

	To 6 April 1999 £		After 6 April 1999 £	
Net dividend		80.00		80.00
Tax credit	(20%)	20.00	(10%)	8.89
Gross dividend		100.00		88.89
Tax at relevant rate	(at 34%)	34.00	(at 25%)	22.22
After tax income		66.00		66.67

(For the tax position when a payment is made to a beneficiary, see *Taxation*, 17 July 1997, p 425.)   [**29.88**]

c) *Non-resident discretionary trusts*

The rules for non-residents considered at [**29.64**] apply to discretionary trusts provided that no relevant beneficiary is UK resident (FA 1995 s 128(5), (6)).　　　　　　　　　　　　　　　　　　　　　　　[**29.89**]-[**29.100**]

VI　TAXATION OF 'NON-QUALIFYING' DISTRIBUTIONS

An issue of bonus redeemable shares or securities is a non-qualifying distribution (TA 1988 s 209(2)(c)). The two main features of qualifying distributions (the payment of ACT by the company and a tax credit for the shareholder) do not apply to non-qualifying distributions. Instead, the distribution is taxed in two stages: *first*, the issue of the securities has no tax effect on the issuing company and, so far as the recipient is concerned, no assessment to basic rate income tax. It follows that the only tax consequence will be an assessment on the shareholder for any higher rate income tax calculated at his higher rate for that year less the tax credit. *Secondly*, when the shares are redeemed, the redemption will be a qualifying distribution with the normal taxation consequences (see [**29.41**] and [**29.61**]), save that, if the shareholder is then liable for income tax at the higher rate, a deduction is made for any higher rate tax which he originally paid on the non-qualifying distribution.

[**29.101**]-[**29.120**]

EXAMPLE 29.27

Stage (1)　Shareholder Sam has a taxable income of £25,500. He receives bonus redeemable shares whose redemption value is £750. His income tax liability will be calculated by adding £750 to his other income and calculating tax on that £750 at the highest portion of that total. His taxable income is £26,850 (£26,100 + £750). The tax rate applicable on the top £750 is 40%. Therefore:

	£
Higher rate tax (40%) on £750	300
Less: tax credit (20% × £750)	150
Income tax owing	£150

Stage (2)　When the shares are redeemed and Sam is paid £750 assume that his other taxable income is still £26,100 and the bands and rates of tax are unchanged. The tax position is as follows:

(1)　the company will pay ACT of £187.50 on the capital distribution;
(2)　Sam's income under Schedule F will be £937.50 and he will have a tax credit for £187.50;
(3)　Sam's income tax bill will be calculated thus:

	£
Tax on £937.50 at highest rate (40%)	375
Less: tax credit	187.50
	187.50
Deduct: higher rate paid on non-qualifying distribution	150
Income tax owing	£ 37.50

VII　EXEMPT DISTRIBUTIONS AND SCRIP DIVIDENDS

1　Demergers and the ICI test case

The general topic of demergers is considered in Chapter 38 where a distinction is drawn between 'direct' and 'indirect' demergers. From a tax point of view, provided that the requirements of TA 1988 ss 213–218 are satisfied (see [**38.51**]), the transfer of shares in the demerged company to the shareholders is not treated as a distribution for the purposes of Schedule F and, for CGT purposes, the distributed shares are treated as a company reorganisation (TCGA 1992 s 127 and s 192(2)). If the shareholder sells the shares in either company, the original cost of the shares is apportioned between the shares in the distributing company and the demerged company. In principle, therefore, demergers can be effected without the necessity for a liquidation and without attracting fiscal penalties. Unfortunately the statement that demergers leads to no fiscal penalties is not the case in certain situations where the shares are owned by trustees (see generally *Tax Bulletin*, October 1994, p 162). To understand why problems arise it is first necessary to consider the background trust and company law.   **[29.121]**

a) *Company and trust law*

Hill v Permanent Trustee of New South Wales (1930), a Privy Council case, confirmed that a company can only part with its assets to its shareholders by way of a distribution of profits unless it is in liquidation or making an authorised reduction in share capital.

> 'A limited company not in liquidation can make no payment by way of return of capital to its shareholders except as a step in an authorised reduction of capital. Any other payment made by it by means of which it parts with moneys to its shareholders must and can only be made by way of dividing profits. Whether the payment is called "dividend" or "bonus" or any other name, it still must remain a payment on division of profits ... Moneys so paid to a shareholder will (if he be a trustee) *prima facie* belong to the person beneficially entitled to the income of the trust estate. If such moneys or any part thereof are to be treated as part of the corpus of the trust estate there must be some provision in the trust deed which brings about that result. No statement by the company or its officers that moneys which are being paid away to shareholders out of profits are capital, or are to be treated as capital, can have any effect upon the rights of the beneficiaries under a trust instrument which comprises shares in the company.' (Lord Russell)

In the simple direct demerger, a company first declares a dividend out of distributable profits and then satisfies that dividend by an allocation of shares in the demerged company. As a matter of general law following on from the above statement the demerged shares will be income in the hands of the recipient so that if they are owned by trustees of an interest in possession trust those shares will belong to the life tenant. The consequences for the trust fund may be startling: when Thomas Tilling made a distribution, for instance, (which was considered by the courts in the case of *Re Sechiari* (1950)) the effect was to reduce the price of the company's shares by 77%. A windfall for income beneficiaries and a glaring injustice for those interested in the capital of the fund!   **[29.122]**

b) *The position of trustees on the assumption that the demerged shares are income*

On commonsense grounds and in the interests of 'doing equity' between the beneficiaries, trustees may wish to ensure that the trust capital is not depleted as the result of a proposed demerger.

The trustees could dispose of their shareholdings *before* the dividend is declared and demerger occurs and the trustees could subsequently buy back shares in either or both of the demerged companies. The acquired shares would then form part of the capital of the settlement. However, the sale of the original shares may be fiscally unsatisfactory (triggering a CGT charge) and commercially undesirable.

The decision to sell may itself raise difficulties for the trustees: the deprived life tenant may argue that the decision was motivated solely to prevent him receiving income from the trust. It is thought that such arguments will not succeed and that the trustees will have a defence based on their duty to review investments and ensure that a fair balance is maintained between income and capital. But the matter is not wholly free from doubt.

Alternatively, it is possible that the life tenant will agree that the shares should be added to the capital of the settlement. Were he to do so, however, not only might he suffer a CGT charge (disposing of shares which have become his property) but, in addition, he would add property to the settlement and so become, to that extent, a settlor himself.   [29.123]

c) *Tax position if the shares are trust income*

By way of background, an individual who receives demerged shares, provided that the necessary conditions are met, will obtain an exempt distribution so that there will be no question of any income tax liability. The shares will be treated as one with his original holding for CGT purposes so that any CGT charge will be postponed until a disposal occurs.   [29.124]

Trustees of life interest trusts   Under principles established in *Baker v Archer-Shee* (1927): see [11.41], all income (including therefore the demerged shares if treated as income) belongs to the life tenant and, again assuming that the relevant conditions are satisfied, that will be an exempt distribution. For CGT purposes the position is not so straightforward and two approaches are possible. The shares could be treated as part of the trust fund to which the life tenant then became absolutely entitled. This raises the prospect of a charge under TCGA 1992 s 71. Alternatively, because the life tenant is treated as owning income as it arises (subject only to the trustees' lien for costs) it could be argued that the distributed shares never became trust property so that s 71 is not in point. After initial doubts the Revenue has now accepted that the shares belong to the life tenant as a result of the *Archer-Shee* case so that TCGA 1992 s 71 is not in point (see *Tax Bulletin*, October 1994, p 164).

Celebrating the fact that a charge under s 71 will not arise may, however, be premature. In the first place, the base costs of the trust cannot be apportioned to the life tenant and so will now be attributed only to the original shares (despite the diminution in their value flowing from the demerger). Accordingly, the trustees may realise a loss when those shares are sold (the oddness of this result in the case of direct demergers is well illustrated in *Private Client Business*, 1995 p 128). Turning to the life tenant, what is the base cost of the shares that he has received? The Revenue has concluded that in the case of a *direct demerger* the allowable cost to the life tenant is the market value of the demerged shares as a result of TCGA 1992 s 17(1): see [14.22]. The disposal by the company would be the corresponding disposal for the purpose of s 17(2) (see *Tax Bulletin*, October 1994, p 162). In the case of an *indirect demerger*, however, there is no corresponding disposal (because the issue of shares is not a disposal); accordingly the life tenant has no allowable cost.

As compared with individual shareholders, therefore, the life tenant may be placed at a CGT disadvantage in the case of indirect demergers (following the ICI test case (see [29.128]) it is, however, likely that such shares will be capital and so not belonging to the life tenant).

If the terms of a settlement provide for the payment of an annuity and for the balance of the income to be paid elsewhere the above analysis does not hold good. The *Archer-Shee* case cannot apply: the shares become part of the trust funds and a CGT charge under s 71 may arise when they are paid out to a beneficiary.   [29.125]

Discretionary and accumulation trusts where the demerged shares are accumulated The trustees receive the shares as an exempt distribution so that there is no liability to tax under TA 1988 s 686. For CGT purposes, the shares are treated as part of the trustees' original shareholding in the usual way. Although the shares are 'income' in the trustees' hands, provided that they exercise their powers to accumulate there are no further fiscal consequences. [**29.126**]

Discretionary and accumulation trusts where the shares are paid out to a beneficiary Because the shares have been received as income by the trustees, if those shares (or their cash equivalent) are paid to a beneficiary the rules of TA 1988 s 687 will be in point. Given that the trustees received an exempt distribution, no s 686 credit will be available so that (subject to any unused credit) the payment is likely to attract an income tax charge at 34%. If the shares (rather than any cash equivalent) are paid out to a beneficiary, for CGT purposes a charge under TCGA 1992 s 71 may arise in addition to any income tax liability. A hold-over election is, however, generally available when property ceases to be held on discretionary trusts (see [**17.41**]). [**29.127**]

d) *The ICI test case: are demerged shares income after all?*

The ICI demerger was 'indirect': the bio-chemical part of ICI's business was transferred to a new company (Zeneca plc) and the shares in that company were transferred directly to the ICI shareholders. *Sinclair v Lee* (1993) considered the position of trustees of an interest in possession will trust in receipt of Zeneca shares. The Vice-Chancellor concluded, very much on the facts of the particular case, that the Zeneca shares formed part of the capital of the fund and that the *Hill* line of cases could be distinguished.

The judgment is deeply disappointing. Whilst it is true that ICI, for its own tax reasons, chose to effect its demerger by the 'indirect' method, to concentrate on that as a way of escaping from the manacles of precedent is hardly satisfactory. There should be no difference between the case where a shareholder receives as a distribution shares which had been owned by his company (the so-called direct demerger) and that where the company instead procures the issue of shares by a third party (as occurred in the *ICI* case). Having said that, there are *dicta* towards the end of the judgment that could, in the future, be used as ammunition against a mechanical application of the *Hill* decision:

> 'In the last analysis, the rationale underlying the general principles enunciated in *Hill's* case is an endeavour by the law to give effect to the assumed intention of the testator or settlor in respect of a particular distribution to shareholders. When the inflexible application of these principles would produce a result manifestly inconsistent with the presumed intention of the testator or settlor, the court should not be required to apply them slavishly. In origin they were guidelines. They should not be applied in circumstances, or in a manner, which would defeat the very purpose they are designed to achieve.'

Sadly, the result of the judgment is to make future cases necessary and, probably, inevitable. [**29.128**]

e) *Where are we now?*

Some of the recent demergers have been carried out by the direct route, others by the indirect. In 1991, for instance, Racal Electronics plc distributed its shareholding in Racal Telecom plc to its shareholders (a direct demerger) whereas in the following year it demerged the Chubb Group by the indirect route. It is interesting to consider the position of an interest in possession trust owning Racal shares. In the first case the Racal Telecom shares should have been handed over to the life tenant whereas in the second we now know that the shares form part of the trust capital. How many trustees got it right? How many simply assumed—without even addressing the problem—that the shares must be added to the trust capital? And how many have retained the shares waiting for the matter to be cleared up? The best that can be said of *Sinclair v Lee* is that it solves half the problem.

Finally, the generally favourable tax treatment for interest in possession trusts in the case of direct demergers does not necessarily apply where the settlement is governed by foreign law. This will only be the case where the relevant law treats a life tenant as deriving his income directly from the trust investments in accordance with *Baker v Archer-Shee* principles.   **[29.129]**

2   Scrip dividends

The enhanced scrip (or stock) dividend   The stock dividend option has been considered at **[29.9]** and **[29.101]**. In the absence of any element of 'enhancement' the shares are income in the hands of trustees. The main features of the spate of recent scrip offers are that the scrip dividend offered as an alternative to the cash dividend which is otherwise payable is worth something in the region of 50% more than the cash dividend; and, in addition, shareholders are offered the possibility of converting the scrip into cash by an immediate sale. A recent scrip offer illustrates all these points: the net cash dividend of 16.75p per existing share was well exceeded by the scrip offer of 25.125p per share and, if the shareholder wished to sell this scrip, the company had arranged a sale price of 23.87p per share.   **[29.130]**

Tax treatment   Why the recent flood of scrip offers? The attraction for the company is that because it is not a distribution the scrip shares do not attract any advance corporation tax thereby offering immediate benefits for companies suffering from surplus ACT problems (TA 1988 s 230(a)). In addition, the company retains the equivalent cash dividend, obtains an improved financial ratio and may (subject to the Companies Act requirements being met) buy back the shares in the future without ACT becoming payable (TA 1988 s 230(b)). For the shareholder there is no question of liability to income tax at the basic rate; the higher rate taxpayer, however, must gross up 'the appropriate amount in cash' at 20% and is then subject to an additional tax charge (TA 1988, s 249(4), (5) and (6)). This year the rate is 25% of 'the appropriate amount in cash'. These rules apply to:

(1) individual shareholders;
(2) trustees of discretionary or accumulation trusts; and
(3) life tenants who are entitled to receive the scrip dividend (see further on the position of interest in possession trusts **[29.132]**).

'The appropriate amount in cash' is defined in TA 1988 s 251 as meaning in the case of enhanced scrip dividends the market value of the scrip at the relevant date (relevant date meaning either the date of first listing or, for unlisted companies, the due date of issue). For shareholders who are not taxpayers (pension funds, charities etc) the disadvantage of the scrip issue has always been that it is not possible to obtain a repayment of the tax credit. However, at the current level of enhanced scrip dividend, such institutions may still be better off taking the scrip whilst pension funds, of course, are now unable to obtain a refund of the dividend tax credit in any event. For CGT purposes, if the scrip option is exercised the new shares are pooled with the shareholder's existing shareholding and the base cost increased by the addition of 'the appropriate amount in cash' (TCGA 1992 s 141).   **[29.131]**

EXAMPLE 29.28

Jenni, a higher rate taxpayer, and an ordinary shareholder in Wizzo Ltd, opts to take an enhanced scrip dividend. Instead of receiving a cash dividend for £80 she accepts paid up shares having a value of £120. Her tax position is:

(1) *Income tax*: The appropriate amount in cash (£120) must be grossed up at 20% (to £150) and Jenni will then be subject to an income tax charge at the higher rate on this amount (ie to a tax charge of £30). See TA 1988 s 249(4).

(2) *CGT*: The shares are pooled with her existing holding under the reorganisation rules and the appropriate amount in cash (£120) is added to her base cost: see TCGA 1992 s 141.

Notes:

(i) The same rules will apply if the shares had been received by trustees of an accumulation or maintenance trust save that for the purpose of the income tax charge the rate applicable to trusts (34%) would give an income tax liability of £21.

(ii) Similarly if the shares had been treated under an interest in possession trust as belonging to the life tenant the above rules apply subject to the caveat that for CGT purposes under TCGA 1992 s 142 the shares are treated as acquired for a base cost equal to the appropriate amount in cash. Where under the terms of an interest in possession trust, the shares are either treated as capital or, alternatively, the value is split between the life tenant and capital the position is set out in the following paragraph.

Interest in possession trusts (and see SP 4/94) As with demergers it is interest in possession trusts which pose problems for scrip dividends. Traditionally trustees have opted for cash rather than scrip: at the current level of enhancement, however, trustees should at least consider whether to take the scrip. If they do so, a familiar problem arises: are the shares income (and so the property of the life tenant) or must they be added to the capital of the trust? The normal non-enhanced scrip dividend will be treated in the same way as a cash dividend and so belong to the life tenant. In cases of enhanced value, however, there is some authority that the value of the scrip must be apportioned with the life tenant being entitled to the value of the cash dividend. Hence although the shares themselves are added to the trust capital the trustees must raise this sum and pay it to the life tenant (and so they may find it necessary to sell the shares). This was the result in *Re Malam, Malam v Hitchens* (1894). (Contrast, however, *Bouch v Sproule* (1887) in which the shares were allocated to capital and the *Hill* line of cases where they were treated as income.) Presumably the theory underlying apportionment is that the element of enhancement must be attributed to the value of the existing shares (and so treated as a form of capital reorganisation: see further *Law Society's Gazette*, July 1993, p 17).

The tax treatment must depend on how the shares are treated as a matter of trust law (this is expressly recognised by the Revenue in SP 4/94 and a similar rule applies in the case of non-UK trusts). There are therefore three possibilities:

(1) *Shares treated as trust capital*: No income tax liability arises and, for CGT purposes, the issue is a reorganisation in TCGA 1992 s 126 (see [**19.2**]) and the trustees are treated as acquiring the shares for nil consideration.

(2) *Shares treated as income*: The beneficiary with the interest in possession is treated as entitled under TA 1988 s 249(4) and taxed in the same way as an individual shareholder: see [**29.131**].

(3) *A Malam apportionment*: The income tax position of the life tenant in a *Malam* type case is (according to SP 4/94) that he will be taxed on the income when it is paid out to him by the trustees under TA 1988 s 349 and, as the trustees have no tax credit on the scrip dividend, basic rate

income tax must be accounted for by those trustees and the usual credit passed to the life tenant. The life tenant will be treated as receiving income equivalent to the cash dividend plus a tax credit (at the basic rate) and this will be income taxable under Schedule D Case III. The treatment applies whether the payment is made out of the proceeds of sale of the shares, out of other capital of the trust or by a distribution of some of the shares comprised in the scrip issue.

So far as the trustees' tax position on receipt of the shares is concerned, there is no question of any further income tax liability arising, since TA 1988 s 249(6) only applies to trustees who are subject to the additional charge under TA 1988 s 686. It has no application to interest in possession trusts. For CGT purposes, the scrip falls outside the provisions which enable the base cost of the shareholding to be increased to reflect the 'appropriate amount in cash'. Accordingly, shares retained by the trustees will be pooled with their existing holding but with a nil acquisition cost. These startling results arise because the relevant legislation proceeds on the assumption that the shares must belong to the life tenant in such cases who would be liable for higher rate income tax but would also be credited with an uplifted CGT base. If some of the shares are transferred to the life tenant there is a part disposal for CGT purposes.

EXAMPLE 29.29

The trustees of the Dari Will Trust accept an enhanced scrip dividend from ABC plc under which, instead of receiving a cash dividend worth £80, they receive shares to a value of £120. The trustees decide under the terms of the trust that they are obliged to distribute the value of the cash dividend to the life tenant.
(1)   The life tenant will receive £80 together with a credit for the basic rate income tax deducted at source (ie £106.66 in all). The trustees must, according to SP 4/94, pay income tax to the Inland Revenue under TA 1988 s 349 of £24.53.
(2)   So far as the scrip dividend is concerned the trustees will not suffer any income tax liability thereon and the shares will be pooled with the existing holding albeit at a nil base cost. Were the shares to be sold by the trustees a gain of £120 would result and accordingly they would face a CGT liability of £27.6. On these particular facts therefore the trustees would be out of pocket as a result of accepting the scrip dividend since their costs total £80 + £24.53 + £27.6 = £132.13!

In the *Malam* case, Stirling J decided that 'the proceeds of the realisation of the shares should be applied in payment first of the dividend (to which the tenant for life is entitled . . .) and the balance ought to be applied as capital'. Pending sale of the shares, the life tenant would have a charge upon those shares equal to the value of the dividend. The Revenue's view—that the life tenant is to be treated as receiving income falling under Schedule D Case III—is not free from doubt. It is arguable that any 'compensation' payment by the trustees does not constitute income and so escapes the income tax net altogether.   **[29.132]**

30 Corporate groups

I OPERATING STRUCTURES

Assume that Ron and Ed plan to set up in business together: Ron is a chef of renown and Ed has run (with some success) a hamburger chain. A corporate structure, rather than a partnership, is considered appropriate. A single company with two divisions—the catering/food production portion and the restaurant outlet—is one possibility. From a tax and risk perspective there will then be a single accountable entity (the company: the fact that it is run as two separate divisions is purely for internal management purposes). Forming two separate companies—Ron Ltd and Ed Ltd—with different shareholdings may well not be what the two want and so this is a situation where a group structure may be advantageous. A holding company—with shares owned 50:50 by Ron and Ed—may own two subsidiaries, Ron Ltd and Ed Ltd. From a risk and tax perspective there are then three separate legal entities: accordingly the insolvency of the restaurant project, for instance, will not necessarily bring down Ron Ltd nor the holding company.

Commercially, therefore, groups of companies have obvious attractions: different enterprises can be segregated into different corporate units each with its limited liability and separate identity. Each trade will, to a greater or lesser extent, have a separate management and, in the event of a decision to sell any part of the enterprise, the appropriate company can be sold to the purchaser. From a taxation point of view, however, and despite the various reliefs considered below, forming a group may be disadvantageous because the various grouping provisions do not cause all the companies to be treated as one for tax purposes and, accordingly, certain reliefs are restricted. One obvious, but nevertheless significant, problem with using groups which is sometimes overlooked is the application of the small company's rate of tax to the members of the group. Where the companies are 'associated', the upper and lower limits for each associated company for calculating whether taper relief is available are divided by the number of associated companies plus one. This can lead to the loss of tapering relief and hence a failure by the group as a whole to take full advantage of the small companies rate of corporation tax. Two companies are associated if they are under common control or if one has control of the other (TA 1988 s 13). If the two companies form a group, it may be possible to try and manipulate profits within the group in order to minimise tax payable. If the group overall has profits below the lower limit for small companies, it is usually best that they are distributed evenly around the group in order to avoid them falling within the marginal relief band.   **[30.1]**–**[30.20]**

EXAMPLE 30.1

Fred Ltd has one wholly owned subsidiary Barney Ltd. Both companies make up their accounts to 31 March and for the year ending 31 March 1997 both have taxable profits of £150,000. The lower limit for each company is £150,000 (£300,000 ÷ 2) and therefore both are taxed at 24%, making £72,000 tax payable in total.

If Fred Ltd had profits of £250,000 and Barney Ltd profits of £50,000, the position would be different. Fred Ltd has profits falling within the marginal band and therefore pays tax of £71,250 and Barney Ltd pays £12,000—making a total of £83,250.

II   WHAT IS A GROUP?

A group of companies, as defined in TCGA 1992 s 170, comprises at least a parent company (a holding company) which controls another company known as a subsidiary. Groups may consist of any number of interlocking companies; a company for these purposes includes an industrial and provident society; a trustee savings bank; and a building society (TCGA 1992 s 170(9)). Commercially, a group may be regarded as a single entity; so far as the law is concerned, however, they are generally treated as separate legal entities. The tax legislation to some extent accords with commercial reality in conferring a number of useful reliefs upon companies in a group. These reliefs depend upon the structure of the group: some for instance are available to '51% groups'; some to '75% groups' and 'consortia'; some to '100% consortia', whilst provision is made for the case where a company is both a member of a group and either one of the joint owners of a consortium company or is jointly owned by a consortium.

A '51% group' exists where at least 51% of the ordinary share capital of one company is beneficially owned, directly or indirectly, by another company; and a '75% group' where at least 75% of the ordinary share capital of one company is so owned (TA 1988 s 838). Certain privileges may be available even if the 75% or 51% group requirement is not satisfied, in cases where a company is owned by a consortium of corporate members. A company is owned by a consortium if 75% or more of the ordinary share capital is beneficially owned by companies of which none owns less than a 5% share and none owns 75% or more.

One problem that may arise in the group area is that a payment which by its nature is a revenue payment (and which should therefore be deductible from trading profit as an allowable expense) could be disallowed if it is felt to be for the benefit of the trade of the group as a whole rather than wholly and exclusively for the trade of the particular taxpayer company: see *Vodaphone Cellular Ltd v Shaw* (1997). As Millett LJ observed:

'The trade of a parent company is for tax purposes distinct from the trade of its subsidiary. The two companies are separate taxable persons, and the trade or business of one is not the same as the trade or business of the other, however closely it may affect it.'   **[30.21]**–**[30.40]**

III GROUP AND CONSORTIUM RELIEF (TA 1988 s 402)

1 When is relief available?

Group relief applies to 75% groups and to consortia. In addition to the requirements as to the ownership of share capital, certain economic ownership tests must also be met. TA 1988 s 413(7)-(10) provides that for group relief to be available the parent company must also be entitled to not less than 75% of the profits available for distribution and not less than 75% of the assets on a winding up. For consortium relief a consortium member's interest in the consortium company is taken as the lowest of the percentage share capital and entitlement to profits and assets on a winding up.   **[30.41]**

2 The EU dimension

The group relief legislation requires the surrendering company and the claimant to be UK resident. EU companies benefit from arts 52 and 58 of the Treaty which provide for freedom of establishment. The restrictions in the UK legislation is to be tested in the courts in cases involving *Hoechst UK* and *Pirelli UK*. So far as consortium relief is concerned, *ICI v Colmer* (1996) involved two UK resident companies each owning half the shares in a holding company with a number of wholly owned trading subsidiaries, the majority of which were non-UK resident (although a minority were resident in the EU). The Revenue contended that the holding company did not fall within the definition in TA 1988 s 413(3)(b) because it was implicit that the subsidiary trading companies had to be UK resident. As a matter of UK law the House of Lords were disposed to accept this analysis but in view of the EC Treaty (and the articles noted above) this case was referred to the European Court of Justice.   **[30.42]**

3 Operation of the relief

EXAMPLE 30.2

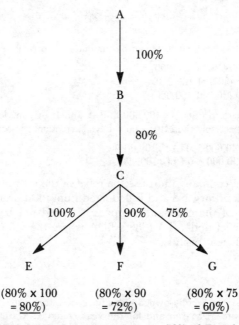

A, B, C and E form a 75% group. A only owns 72% of F and 60% of G. The latter two companies cannot, therefore, form part of a 75% group with A. However, C, E, F and G form a further group.

The relief enables any of the items deductible from total profits (generally charges on income, trading losses, and management expenses; see TA 1988 s 403) to be surrendered to another company in the group or consortium except that such items may not be surrendered by a dual resident investing company to another member of a UK group (TA 1988 s 404). Generally, however, these amounts can be used to reduce the taxable profits of the 'claimant' company on being given up by the 'surrendering' company. It is not necessary to make a payment for group relief but if one is made it is ignored in computing profits and losses of both companies for tax purposes.

The amount of available loss or expense which it is possible to surrender is the amount generated in the part of the accounting period of the surrendering company which overlaps with the accounting period of the claimant company. However, the maximum loss which may actually be surrendered is restricted to the profit of the claimant company made in its overlapping accounting period. F(No 2)A 1997 introduced provisions to ensure that only a loss attributable to a particular overlapping period can be surrendered.

The relief is more restrictive in the case of consortia since losses may be surrendered to the consortium members only in proportion to their percentage shareholdings in the consortium company and by the consortium members to the consortium company only up to their percentage share in the profits.

EXAMPLE 30.3

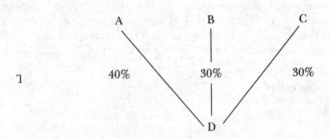

1

D makes a loss of £60,000. It can be surrendered to A, B and C as follows:

A = £24,000 (40% of £60,000)
B = £18,000 (30% of £60,000)
C = £18,000 (30% of £60,000).

If D had made profits of £100,000 and A and B had made losses of £50,000 and £40,000 respectively then they could have surrendered losses to D as follows:

From A = £40,000 (40% of £100,000)
From B = £30,000 (30% of £100,000).

The claimant company must use the relief in the year of surrender; it cannot be carried back or forward and is deducted from total profits after any charges on the income of the claimant company. It need not be surrendered in full (contrast loss relief under TA 1988 s 393A where the full loss must be relieved if there are sufficient profits). **[30.43]**

EXAMPLE 30.4

Little Ltd is the wholly-owned subsidiary of Large Ltd. Both companies make up accounts to 31 March and for the year ended 31 March 1997, Little Ltd has trading losses of £20,000 and Large Ltd profits of £400,000. All the loss could be surrendered to Large Ltd resulting in the profits being reduced to £380,000. Alternatively, Little Ltd might carry back all or a part of the loss under TA 1988 s 393A and merely surrender the balance. If Large Ltd were to pay £5,000 for the surrender, that sum would be ignored for tax purposes.

4 The *European Vinyls Case* and FA 1997

In *Steele v EVC International* (1996) ('the *European Vinyls* Case') the court held that a shareholders' agreement providing for the constitution and control of a jointly owned company caused the shareholders to be connected to each other for the purposes of TA 1988 s 839(7).

It was feared that this case, although not directly concerned with consortium relief, could have had a serious impact on its availability in the case of consortia where the owners had agreed to implement a policy for the company and especially in joint ventures. This is because if all the owners of the company are deemed to be connected, they are each deemed to own 75% of the shares so there will be no consortium (see definition above). The Inland Revenue confirmed in the *Tax Bulletin*, December 1996 that where members of a consortium had entered into an ongoing agreement to operate the consortium company in accordance with their collective will the case would be applied to consortia and could deny relief. As a result FA 1997 s 68 (arguably retrospectively) was enacted to disapply the connected persons test of s 839(7) in the context of claims for consortium relief. **[30.44]**

5 Claims

A claim for relief must be made within a two-year period but there were formerly no specific statutory provisions which prescribed the form and contents of any such claim.

In the light of the House of Lords' speeches in *Gallic Leasing Ltd v Coburn* (1991) the Revenue exercised its powers under TMA 1970 s 42(5) to require claims for group relief to be made in writing specifying the identity of the claimant company; the accounting period of the claimant company for which relief is claimed; the identity of the surrendering company (or companies); the relevant accounting period(s) of each surrendering company; amounts claimed in respect of each surrendering company; and the total amount of profits of the claimant company to be covered by group relief. **[30.45]**

6 Tax avoidance

TA 1988 s 409 contains provisions to prevent tax avoidance through the use of group relief in an accounting period when a company joins or leaves a group or consortium (eg the setting of losses of existing members against profits made by an incoming member before entry). Generally, profits and losses of the company will continue to be time-apportioned between the two parts of that period, but if this works unreasonably or unjustly (eg where the profits are uneven) such other methods shall be used as may be just and reasonable.

Similarly, TA 1988 s 410 is designed to prevent artificial manipulation of the group relief provisions: in particular, the forming of groups on a temporary basis and in order to obtain the relief. Under the terms of this section a company will not be regarded as a member of a group if '*arrangements*' are in existence for the transfer of that company to another group or for any person to take control of the company but not the other companies within the group (for the meaning of 'arrangements' see SP 3/93; ESC C10 and on the general interpretation of this section *Pilkington Bros Ltd v IRC* (1982)). Relief is not available during any period when such arrangements are in force. In *Shepherd v Law Land plc* (1990), for instance, arrangements (an option to purchase the shares of the subsidiary company) came into existence on 6 January 1983 and ceased five weeks later on 11 February 1983 (the option was never taken up). In the accounting period ending 31 March 1983 group relief was therefore not available for that five-week period.

In *J Sainsbury plc v O'Connor* (1991) a joint venture company (Homebase) was formed by Sainsbury's and a Belgian company in which Sainsbury's held 75% of the issued share capital and the Belgians the remaining 25%. There was, in addition, a cross-option agreement whereby 5% of that share capital could be acquired by the Belgians. The options were not exercisable for a five-year period and, in the event, were never exercised. Did their existence prevent Sainsbury's being entitled to group relief? The Court of Appeal decided that they were so entitled: *first*, because mere existence of the options did not deprive Sainsbury's of their beneficial ownership in the relevant shares: accordingly they satisfied the 75% test. *Secondly*, because the existence of the options did not amount to arrangements which affected the rights of the relevant shares within the test for such arrangements laid down in TA 1988 Sch 18. Not surprisingly, amending legislation was introduced, with effect from 15 November 1991, whereby 'arrangements' was extended to include changes in the ownership of shares (such as options to buy and sell).   **[30.46]–[30.60]**

IV   ACT SURRENDER (TA 1988 s 240)

Within 51% groups a parent which has surplus ACT arising as a result of a dividend payment may surrender all or part of that surplus to a subsidiary. The recipient company may then use the surrendered ACT against its own corporation tax bill provided that the recipient was a subsidiary of the parent throughout the accounting period in which the ACT was paid. The subsidiary company may not carry back any surrendered ACT against profits of the previous six years. However surrendered ACT is set off in priority to the subsidiary company's own ACT which may itself be carried back (TA 1988 s 240(4)).
    [30.61]–[30.80]

V   DIVIDENDS AND CHARGES (TA 1988 s 247)

Charges on income (for instance interest payments) may be paid gross (without deducting basic rate income tax) between companies in a 51% group or 75% consortium (although in the case of consortia, interest may only be paid gross by the consortium company to a consortium member and not vice versa). As a general rule, the payee is taxed on the payment under Schedule D Case III on the date when that payment is credited to his account which is not necessarily the same date as the date of the payment (see *Parkside Leasing Ltd v Smith* (1985) at **[10.1]**). The new loan provisions now require an authorised accruals basis of accounting when there is a connection between the parties (FA 1996 s 87 and **[28.54]**). Dividends (but not other distributions) can also be paid without ACT so long as both payer and recipient agree (the sum is called 'group income': see TA 1988 s 247). So far as the recipient company is concerned, it will not be entitled to a tax credit and the sum it receives will not be franked investment income. There is, of course, nothing to stop ACT being paid and a credit given in the normal way; this may be advantageous when the recipient company wishes to make a dividend payment outside the group and so will wish to receive franked investment income.   **[30.81]–[30.100]**

VI CAPITAL RELIEFS

1 What is a group for these purposes?

For chargeable gains purposes, a group consists of a principal company and all its 75% subsidiaries. If any of those subsidiaries also have 75% subsidiaries they are included within the group provided they are effective 51% subsidiaries of the principal company (TCGA 1992 s 170). **[30.101]**

EXAMPLE 30.5

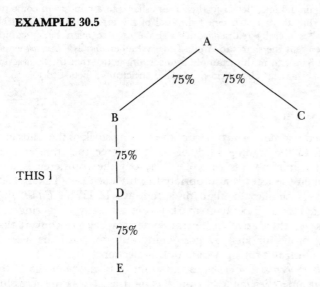

THIS 1

A, B, C and D form a s 170 group. E is not in the group as it is not a 51% subsidiary of A the principal company.

2 Intra-group transfers

The transfer of an asset within a group is treated as being for such consideration as ensures that neither gain nor loss results (TCGA 1992 s 171). The result is, therefore, to hold over any gain and any tax is postponed until the asset is disposed of outside the group or until the company owning the asset leaves the group (TCGA 1992 s 178). A potential purchaser of a company should, therefore, check whether the company will be subject to such 'exit' charges in the event of its leaving its existing group, or whether any company in a group he acquires has any member company with such a potential 'exit' charge. However, the charge will not arise on a company leaving a group more than six years after the intra-group transfer. **[30.102]**

3 Sub-groups

Where two or more companies which are associated (ie which between themselves would form a group) leave the group at the same time no exit charge arises on assets which they acquired from each other. TCGA 1992 s 179(2A) may apply to reinstate the exit charge in situations where after the sub group has left the original group the recipient company of the earlier intra-group transfer leaves the subsequent group. **[30.103]**

4　Triggering a loss

The 'exit' disposal under TCGA 1992 s 178 may be deliberately triggered, usually in order to crystallise a capital loss as the following example illustrates.　　　　　　　　　　　　　　　　　　　　　　　　　　　**[30.104]**

EXAMPLE 30.6

Alpha Ltd transfers a chargeable asset showing a capital loss to subsidiary company Beta Ltd which has realised capital profits. TCGA 1992 s 171 ensures that the transfer is at no gain/no loss. Beta Ltd then issues shares to a non-group company (Omega Ltd) so that there is a deemed disposal of the asset under TCGA 1992 s 178 and the loss is thereby realised which can be used to offset Beta's capital gains. Omega then sells the shares to Alpha Ltd. (Whether *Furniss v Dawson* would deny tax relief to Beta Ltd in this example is uncertain; notice that the transaction has resulted in a permanent change in the capital structure of Beta Ltd.)

5　Trading stock tie in

If the asset transferred had not formed part of the trading stock of the transferor but is appropriated to the trading stock of the transferee the transfer itself is covered by the no gain/no loss rule of s 171; but the transferee is then given an election when the asset is appropriated to his stock (see TCGA 1992 s 173: this election is similar to that discussed at **[14.117]**). *Either* that appropriation is taxed as a disposal at market value thereby triggering any capital gain (or loss) *or*, alternatively, the transferee may elect to convert that gain into a trading profit (or loss) by postponing any tax until the asset is sold. *Example 14.35* illustrates the operation of this election.

In *Coates v Arndale Properties Ltd* (1984) an attempt to take advantage of the election to obtain group relief for a loss on a capital asset was unsuccessful. The House of Lords concluded that the transferee never acquired the asset as trading stock because it was immediately resold to another member of the same group. Hence, the transaction was not covered by the election. This 'constructional' approach to a tax relieving provision may be contrasted with the House of Lords decision in *Furniss v Dawson*: see further **[36.22]**. In *Reed v Nova Securities Ltd* (1985) the House of Lords were again concerned with the question of when assets are acquired as trading stock and concluded that not only must those assets be of a kind which were sold in the ordinary course of the company's trade but also that they were acquired with a view to resale at a profit.　　　　　　　　　　　　　　　　　　　　　　　　**[30.105]**

6　Capital losses

The group relief provisions do not provide for the pooling of capital losses. Accordingly, it is common for chargeable assets to be transferred within the group (taking advantage of TCGA 1992 s 171 which prevents any chargeable gain arising: see above) to enable these losses to be utilised.　　　　**[30.106]**

EXAMPLE 30.7

Subsidiary company Alpha intends to sell land to P, but will realise a capital gain of £80,000 on that sale. Assume that another subsidiary company (Beta) has unused capital losses of £100,000. The land could be sold to Beta for full value and then resold by Beta to P.

(1) *on the sale to Beta:* the disposal is on a no gain/no loss basis irrespective of the actual consideration paid (TCGA 1992 s 171: above). No gain is, therefore, realised by Alpha.

(2) *on the sale to P:* the gain of £80,000 is realised by Beta, which can use its losses to avoid any corporation tax charge.

7 Anti-avoidance

In *News International v Shepherd* (1989) Vinelott J held that the acquisition of a loss-making company to which the parent then transferred shares for sale on the Stock Market did not involve a composite transaction so that the *Ramsay* principle was inapplicable. Crucially, in that case the terms of the actual sale had not been arranged before the intra-group transfer. It did not matter that the subsidiary was acquired for the express purpose of utilising its unrelieved losses. The *News International* case reawakened interest in the acquisition of a company by a group in order to take advantage of its capital losses. Not surprisingly, therefore, FA 1993 inserted a new section (s 177A) into TCGA 1992 and a new Sch 7A providing for capital losses brought into a group to be 'ring fenced'. Broadly, these rules mirror the legislation which deals with income losses in similar cases. The rules were, however, widely drafted to catch unrealised as well as realised losses and apply to a loss-making company joining a group at any time on or after 1 April 1987 if gains are realised on or after 16 March 1993 which would otherwise be set against those losses (minor amendments were made by FA 1994: see *Tax Bulletin*, May 1994, p 129). **[30.107]**

8 Roll-over relief

For roll-over or reinvestment relief, trades carried on by companies in a 75% group are treated as a single trade (TCGA 1992 s 175). The Revenue considers that this section means that a chargeable gain made by one group member on a disposal of an asset outside the group can be rolled over into an asset acquired from outside the group by another group member (SP D19).

EXAMPLE 30.8

R Ltd, S Ltd and Q Ltd are members of a 75% group. The following transactions occur:
(1) R Ltd disposes of an office block with a base cost of £100,000 to Q Ltd when its value is £150,000;
(2) Q Ltd sells that asset to T Ltd for £150,000; and
(3) S Ltd acquires a new office block for use in its business for £200,000.
  The taxation consequences of these transactions are:
(1) *The intra-group transfer from R Ltd to Q Ltd* This is treated as being for no gain/no loss so that tax on the gain (£50,000) is postponed. Q's base cost is, therefore, £100,000.
(2) *The sale by Q Ltd to T Ltd* The asset leaves the group so that a chargeable gain of £50,000 arises to Q Ltd.
(3) *The replacement asset purchased by S Ltd* On a claim being made by both companies (Q Ltd and S Ltd) the gain of Q Ltd can be rolled over into the purchase by S Ltd. Hence, S Ltd's base cost of the new asset will be £150,000 (£200,000 – £50,000) and Q Ltd will not be assessed on a gain as a result of the disposal to T Ltd.

In *Campbell Connelly & Co Ltd v Barnett* (1992) doubt was cast on this view:

'It was submitted to me that the inference should be drawn in relation to [s 175(1)] that not only should the trades carried on by members of a single group of companies be treated as a single trade and thereby the same trade but that members of a group of companies should be treated as a single person and thereby the same person. That does not seem possible to me as a matter of construction, given the very startling difference Parliament provided in the clearest possible way in [s 175(3)].' (Knox J whose judgment was affirmed by the Court of Appeal (1994).)

The result was to leave the correct interpretation of s 175(1) in a state of confusion and the Financial Secretary indicated that irrespective of the *Campbell Connelly* case:

> 'The Revenue's practice seems to me to be sensible and to reflect how commercial transactions are commonly organised. We will ensure that it continues to apply. What needs to be done will depend on the outcome of the appeal.' (See STI (1992) p 834.)

As from 29 November 1994 this view was given statutory effect: relief is available provided that the disposing and acquiring companies are members of the group at the time of *their own* transaction. They do not have to be members of the group at the time of both events.   **[30.108]**

9 'Roll around' relief

FA 1995 contained provisions preventing roll-over relief from being available where a company which had realised a gain on disposal of an asset acquired a replacement asset from another group member (this commonly being referred to as 'roll around' relief). The replacement asset was acquired on a no gain/no loss basis so that the amount deemed to be invested was linked to the original cost to the group of the asset (together with any indexation allowance). Nonetheless this device could be used to shelter a gain and had the merit of avoiding the payment of cash outside the group. (See TCGA 1992 s 175(2C).)   **[30.109]**

10 Group property companies

Roll-over relief is limited to trading companies and so, as a matter of strict law, was not applied to non-trading companies within a group which held assets for use by the trading companies. In fact, relief was extended by means of ESC D30: this concession has now been given statutory force by FA 1995 and that company is now treated as if it were carrying on the 'group trade' in relation to disposals or acquisitions used wholly for the purposes of the group trade (TCGA 1992 s 175(2B)). It is thought that the non-trading company may hold assets used by non-group members and that this will not jeopardise the above relief although such assets will not themselves be eligible for roll-over relief.   **[30.110]**

11 Compulsory acquisition of land

TCGA 1992 s 247 applies when land is compulsorily acquired to enable the vendor to roll over his gains into the acquisition of other land (see **[16.99]**). FA 1995 extended this relief to the situation where the replacement land is acquired by a company in the same capital gains group as the company which made the compulsory disposal.   **[30.111]**

12 Linked transactions

The CGT rules in TCGA 1992 ss 19-20 dealing with assets disposed of in a series of linked transactions (see **[14.24]**) do not apply to transactions between companies in the same (75%) group which, under TCGA 1992 s 171, give rise to neither gain nor loss. Thus such transactions do not count as part of any linked series (contrast the situation where there is a transfer between spouses). Special provision is, however, made for the following case. **[30.112]**

EXAMPLE 30.9

Asset 1 is transferred by a series of intra-group transfers from Slim Ltd to Short Ltd; then to Tall Ltd and finally from Tall Ltd to a connected outsider Wilbur. Asset 2 is transferred directly by Slim Ltd to Wilbur. So long as Wilbur is connected with both Tall Ltd and Slim Ltd the disposal of Asset 1 is treated as having been made by Slim Ltd to him and hence can be linked to the disposal of Asset 2. Any increase in the tax chargeable on the disposal of Asset 1 remains the liability of Tall Ltd (TCGA 1992 s 19(6)).

13 Roll-over claims

In exercise of its powers under TMA 1970 s 42(5) the Revenue has determined the form of a roll-over claim: claims under s 175(2A) must be made jointly by the two companies involved (IR Press Release, 29 November 1994).
[30.113]–[30.140]

VII DEPRECIATORY TRANSACTION AND VALUE SHIFTING (TCGA 1992, s 176, ss 30–34)

Anti avoidance provisions within the legislation may apply to prevent the exploitation of the rules for transfer of assets around groups to secure a tax advantage. TCGA 1992 s 176 operates to restrict allowable capital losses made on a disposal of shares by a group member following an earlier depreciatory transaction which resulted in the value of the share being reduced.

TCGA 1992 ss 30–34 deal with value shifting and operate to both restrict allowable losses and increase capital gains in certain circumstances. The rules can apply where dividends are paid out of profits artificially created by intra-group asset transfers, or where an intra-group asset transfer takes place for less than both cost and market value and is followed by the sale of shares in the transferor company. For the rules to apply a scheme has to be carried out to reduce the value of an asset materially and some person must secure a tax-free benefit. **[30.141]–[30.160]**

EXAMPLE 30.10

Bigco Ltd intends to sell its subsidiary Smallco Ltd for £5,000. The base cost of the Smallco shares is £1,000 which would give Bigco a gain of £4,000 (ignoring indexation). Before the sale Smallco transfers one of its assets which has a market value of £2,000 to Bigco for £500. Smallco had a base cost for the asset of £1,000.

As a result of the transfer Smallco is only worth £3,500 and on the sale Bigco makes a gain of £2,500. At the same time Bigco sells the asset for £2,000 making a gain of £1,000 (as Bigco took over Smallco's base cost). The total gain made by Bigco has been reduced from £4,000 to £3,500, the value shifting rules would be applied to increase the gain.

(If it could be shown that the asset was transferred for *bona fide* commercial reasons and not as part of a scheme to avoid tax, the value shifting provisions would not apply.)

VIII SCHEMES OF RECONSTRUCTION

Assume that Alpha Ltd, with a wholly-owned subsidiary Beta Ltd, now acquires all the issued share capital in a further UK company, Gamma Ltd. It then desires to merge the businesses of Beta Ltd and Gamma Ltd by liquidating Gamma once its assets have been transferred to Beta. The simplest and most tax efficient way of achieving this result would be for a scheme of reconstruction falling within the Companies Act 1985 s 582 to be implemented. This would involve the transfer of Gamma Ltd's business to Beta in return for an issue of shares by Beta to Alpha Ltd followed by the liquidation of Gamma. The transfer of the undertaking will be governed by TCGA 1992 s 139 since it falls within a scheme of amalgamation or reconstruction. Under this provision no corporation tax will arise on the transfer of chargeable assets which are rolled over into the new company. Equally, the transfer should not attract an *ad valorem* stamp duty charge since the relevant instrument will fall either under FA 1930 s 42 (a transfer between associated companies) or FA 1986 s 75 (an amalgamation). The issue of the further shares by Beta to Alpha will be governed by TCGA 1992 s 136 which ensures that so far as Alpha is concerned the old shares are treated as merged with the new. Accordingly, no charge will arise at this point and the whole operation should be submitted in advance for clearance. **[30.161]–[30.180]**

IX   VAT

Corporate bodies within common control may obtain a single or 'group' VAT registration with the result that supplies of goods or services within the group are not subject to VAT (VATA 1994 s 43). This will be particularly attractive when one or more companies in the group make exempt supplies and suffer restrictions on the recovery of input tax. The decision of the High Court in *C & E Comrs v Kingfisher plc* (1994) determined that the effect of the grouping provisions went further than merely allowing a number of VAT entities to account for VAT under a single registration (as Customs had contended) and created a single taxable entity.

Registration is in the name of a 'representative member' who becomes liable for VAT in respect of all group companies. Each individual company, however, remains jointly and severally liable for the tax payable by the representative. Companies may join and leave a group, generally on 90 days' notice. To qualify, companies must be resident or have an established place of business in the UK; 'control' depends on majority voting rights.

Customs may refuse an application to form a group or an application by any company to join or leave a group if they perceive a VAT avoidance motive. FA 1996 contains further provisions giving Customs extensive powers to counter VAT avoidance using the group registration rules. Certain powers are retrospective.

These anti-avoidance provisions arose out of a VAT avoidance scheme involving the exploitation of the grouping provisions. The scheme involved mitigating irrecoverable input tax by making substantial prepayments for goods whilst supplier and customer were within a group and then actually supplying the goods once the supplier had left the group. Following the decision of the Court of Appeal it appears the scheme did not in fact work and therefore the anti-avoidance provisions may now be a matter of overkill (see *Thorn Materials Supply Ltd v Commissioners of Customs and Excise* (1996)) **[30.181]–[30.200]**

X   STAMP DUTY

Conveyance or transfer duty is not charged on an instrument by which one company transfers property to an associated company. The detailed requirements are in FA 1930 s 42 (as amended) which requires that one of the companies in question must beneficially own, directly or indirectly, at least 75% (by nominal value) of the ordinary share capital of the other, or a third company beneficially owns, directly or indirectly at least 75% of the ordinary share capital of each (in general terms the relief accords with group relief: see [**30.41**]). The grant of a new lease from one group company to another qualifies for relief in the same way as an assignment.

FA 1967 s 27(3) contains provisions to prevent abuse of the s 42 relief; of particular note is the requirement that the transaction in respect of which relief is sought must not form part of an arrangement whereby the transferor's interest in the transferee's share capital will be reduced below 75%. It is therefore necessary to apply for adjudication of the instrument effecting the transfer. The claim to intra-group relief is made by a statutory declaration by an officer of the company.   [**30.201**]

31 The taxation of partnerships

I   Income tax   [**31.2**]
II Capital gains tax   [**31.31**]
III Inheritance tax   [**31.51**]

Unlike companies and unincorporated associations, a partnership, whether trading or professional, is not subject to special rules of taxation. The ordinary principles of income tax, CGT and IHT have to be applied to each partner individually. A partnership is therefore 'fiscally transparent'. The position is, however, different for VAT with a partnership for that purpose being treated as a separate taxable entity (VATA 1994 s 45).   [**31.1**]

I INCOME TAX

For the purposes of assessing and collecting income tax a partnership has to some extent been treated as a separate entity. A trading partnership is taxed under the rules of Schedule D Case I, a professional partnership under Schedule D Case II. Although under the self-assessment rules, which now apply, there are no longer partnership assessments (so that individual partners are required to include their share of partnership profits in their own tax return) a partnership return is still required to enable the calculation of the partnership profits to be dealt with centrally (TMA 1970 s 12AA–AB.). These matters are considered in detail in Appendix 1.   [**31.2**]

1 How to calculate the profits of the partnership

a) Contrast the sole trader/practitioner

The procedure for calculating the profits of a partnership under Schedule D Cases I and II is basically the same as for the sole trader or practitioner (see Chapter 6). As an illustration, *C Connelly & Co v Wilbey* (1992) confirmed that legal expenses incurred to protect a partner's interest in the partnership were not deductible as trading expenses.

In *MacKinlay v Arthur Young McClelland Moores & Co* (1989) the Court of Appeal allowed a partnership to deduct removal costs paid to encourage two partners to move house: in one case from London to Southampton, in the other from Newcastle to Bristol. In both cases the move was desirable from the point of view of the firm's business and neither partner would have agreed to move had his relocation expenses not been borne by the firm. Slade LJ explained the Court of Appeal decision and distinguised the *Mallalieu* case (see [**6.117**]) as follows:

> 'The analogy between the case of expenses incurred by a sole trader of which he is the beneficiary and the case of expenses incurred by a partnership, of which

one partner is the beneficiary, is a misleading one. Section 74(a) . . . directs attention to the object of the *spender*, not the recipient. In the first of those two cases it is impossible to differentiate between the objects of the taxpayer *qua* spender and *qua* beneficiary; . . . in the second case, where the payer and the beneficiary are not the same, it is clearly possible to evaluate the objects of the payer in incurring the expenditure separately and distinctly from those of the beneficiary . . . The Revenue [must] ascertain the purpose of the expenditure at least primarily by what was referred to in argument as the "collective purpose" of the partnership in incurring it.'

Not surprisingly, the House of Lords reversed the Court of Appeal decision and, in so doing, restated the principles underlying the rules governing the deduction of business expenditure. Their Lordships held, first, that there was no difference for these purposes between a partnership—even a large professional body run by a management committee on corporate lines—and a sole practitioner. In both cases, to be deductible, expenditure must be 'wholly and exclusively laid out or expended for the purposes of the trade, profession or vocation'. Only in very limited situations is an English partnership a separate entity for tax purposes and the speeches of the Law Lords emphasised again that tax rules applicable to individuals must apply to unincorporated bodies. In some cases this is easier said than done: for instance, the application of CGT principles to partnerships is far from straightforward, as will be discussed later.

A second principle to emerge from the speeches was that (in the words of Lord Oliver) 'a partner working in the business or undertaking of the partnership is in a very different position from an employee'. Crucially, he is also a proprietor and accordingly any money which he withdraws from the business whether in the form of a share of profits, 'salary', or interest on partnership capital, must be treated as a share of profits. This matter will be discussed later. It remains, however, an over-simplification to assume that *no sums* paid out by the firm to a partner can amount to a deductible business expense for the firm. Rent, for instance, paid to a partner who leases premises to his firm (provided, of course, that the sum involved is not excessive) will be deducted by the firm and attract a Schedule A income tax charge in the hands of the recipient partner. The removal expenses considered by the House of Lords in *Arthur Young* did not fall into a similar category.   [**31.3**]

b) *The basis of assessment*

Generally, and the matter is essentially one of Revenue practice, trading partnerships will be assessed on the earnings basis. Professional partnerships will be required to render accounts on the earnings basis for the first three years, but thereafter may be permitted to change to either the bills delivered basis (so long as they give an undertaking to bill clients regularly) or even to the cash basis. The cash basis is particularly advantageous for an expanding business because the increase in debtors (unpaid bills) is ignored.   [**31.4**]

c) *Arriving at a firm's taxable profit*

Although standard accounting practice as amended by the appropriate tax statutes is applied in arriving at the taxable profit (see Chapter 6), a number of specific matters merit comment: [**31.5**]

Salary paid to partners   How a partner's salary is taxed depends on whether he is a partner or merely an employee of the firm. The terms employed by the parties themselves are not decisive of the matter; it is the substance of the relationship between them, as determined from the partnership agreement that needs to be considered (see *Stekel v Ellice* (1973) discussed at [**5.23**]). Notice, however, that the Revenue's usual practice is to assess salaried partners under Schedule E. In view of the relatively high level of national insurance contributions payable by an employer in respect of his higher paid employees (see [**37.44**]), the firm should consider carefully how it wishes new 'partners' to be taxed and draft the partnership agreement accordingly.

If the individual is an employee the salary paid is a deductible partnership expense on which he should be assessed under Schedule E, with tax deducted at source under the PAYE machinery. If the individual is a partner, however, the salary is not an allowable expense of the firm but an agreed profit-sharing method. Hence, the firm's accounts must show the profits as including salaries paid to partners which are then taken into account when apportioning those profits amongst the partners. [**31.6**]

EXAMPLE 31.1

Balthazar, Mountolive and Justine are in partnership sharing profits in the ratio 3:2:1 after deducting salaries agreed at £1,000, £2,000 and £3,000 respectively. In the year ended 31 December 1997 the business profits (after deducting salaries) were £12,000.

For 1997–98 the curent year basis applies (see Appendix I) and the assessment will be on £18,000 (the Revenue treating the salaries as a profit-sharing method) attributed to the partners as follows:

Balthazar:	£1,000 (salary) plus £6,000	(3/6 × £12,000) =	£7,000
Mountolive:	£2,000 (salary) plus £4,000	(2/6 × £12,000) =	£6,000
Justine:	£3,000 (salary) plus £2,000	(1/6 × £12,000) =	£5,000
	£6,000 (salaries) + £12,000	(balance of profits) =	£18,000

This profit will be divided between the partners in accordance with their profit sharing arrangements in the year ended 31 December 1997.

Interest paid to partners Partners may be paid interest on capital they contribute to the firm. As with salaries, the interest is not a deductible expense, but is treated as a profit sharing method. Hence, the profits must be adjusted by adding back the interest and the share of each of the partners in the profits then calculated. [**31.7**]

Rent paid to a partner Where premises are owned by one partner and leased to the firm, any rent paid will be an allowable deduction from the firm's profits, unless it is exorbitant; the partner concerned will be taxed on that rent as unearned income under Schedule A. It may be more attractive for the premises to be let to the partnership at a nominal rent and for the partner to receive his payment in the form of an increased share of the profits. This will not of course be tax deductible by the firm, but the partner concerned will have the benefit of an assessment under Schedule D Case I or II (rather than Schedule A) and, potentially, full CGT retirement relief on an eventual disposal of the premises (see [**16.109**]).

When the partner has taken out a loan for the purchase or improvement of the premises, the interest on which may qualify for income tax relief, care must be taken to obtain that relief and, at the same time, preserve full retirement relief on those premises (see *R v Inspector of Taxes, ex p Brumfield* (1989) discussed at [**4.49**]). Thus if he receives rent from the firm or if the firm discharges the interest payments ('deemed rent') income tax relief will be obtained by setting the interest due against the rent (or deemed rent) but retirement relief will be restricted. Of course, if the premises belong to all the partners they cannot let those premises to the firm since a person cannot let property to himself (see *Rye v Rye* (1962)). [**31.8**]

Losses   Losses incurred by the partnership will be apportioned between the partners in the same way as any profits, each partner dealing with his share of the loss under the normal relieving provisions (see Chapter 7). In the case of a limited partner (whether an individual or a company), loss relief is restricted to the amount which that partner has at risk in the partnership (see TA 1988 s 117 reversing *Reed v Young* (1986)).   **[31.9]**

2   Interest relief on loans to acquire a share in a partnership

Tax relief is available for interest on money which is borrowed to acquire a share in a partnership, or to be used by the firm, or to acquire machinery or plant to be used by the firm. The relief operates by enabling the borrower to deduct the interest as a charge on his income (TA 1988 ss 362, 359(1),(2); see **[4.45]**). In contrast, where the firm borrows money, any interest paid is a deductible business expense (TA 1988 s 74; see **[6.117]**).   **[31.10]**

3   Changes in the partnership

Partnership changes are considered in detail in Appendix I.   **[31.11]**

4   Leaving the partnership

a) *Consultancies*

An outgoing partner may be retained as a consultant whereupon he will often be paid a substantial fee in return for relatively minor duties. For income tax purposes, the consultant is not a partner so that any sum paid to him by the firm will be a deductible business expense under Schedule D assuming that it can be justified according to the 'wholly and exclusively' test (see **[6.117]** *Copeman v Flood* (1941); and *Earlspring Properties Ltd v Guest* (1995)). The consultant will normally be occupying a Schedule E office or employment so that PAYE must be operated and he may benefit from joining the firm's pension scheme for a few years. In some cases he may be able to establish that he is exercising a profession or vocation and should, therefore, be assessed under Schedule D Case II. This argument is more likely to succeed where the individual holds consultancies with several different bodies, or where he is not paid a 'salary' but an *ad hoc* fee each time advice is given. In view of the heavy national insurance contributions payable in respect of highly paid employees (see **[37.44]**) the firm should consider whether it will be preferable to retain the individual as a partner with a reduced profit share rather than as a consultant.   **[31.12]**

b) *Payment of annuities by continuing partners*

Professional partnership agreements may make provision for the payment of annuities to retiring partners in consideration for the outgoing partner surrendering his share of the firm's goodwill and of its capital assets (see **[31.34]** ff). It is largely a matter of commercial expediency whether such annuities are to be payable and if so for how long and for what amount. The recipient would probably prefer an annuity linked to the profits of the business (eg 10% of the net profits) rather than a fixed sum, as this should offer 'inflation proofing'. The following income tax provisions should be noted: **[31.13]**

Position of paying partners   It is usual for the cost of an annuity to be borne by the partners in the same proportion as they share the profits. They are treated as making fully effective annual payments which means that the payments are deductible from their income as a charge on income and should be paid net of basic rate income tax. The annuity will be a tax-effective settlement of income provided that it is payable under a partnership agreement to a former member of that partnership, or his widow or other dependants (where the partner is dead the annuity must not be payable for more than ten years) and is payable under a liability incurred for full consideration (TA 1988 s 347A(2), s 660A(9)). The annuity will also be a fully effective annual payment if it is paid in connection with the acquisition of a share in the business of the outgoing partner.

The partnership agreement will often provide for any incoming partner to take over the cost of an appropriate share of the annuity and that, should the firm cease to exist, the outstanding years of the annuity are to be valued and treated as a debt owed by the partnership at the date of its cessation. **[31.14]**

Position of the recipient The recipient will be taxed on the annuity under the rules of Schedule D Case III with a credit for basic rate tax deducted at source. The annuity will be taxed in his hands as earned income to the extent that the amount payable does not exceed one-half of the average of that partner's best three years' profits out of the last seven; any excess is unearned income (TA 1988 s 628). Those profit figures are index-linked. Hence, where he is paid a fixed annuity the proportion treated as earned income may vary from year to year.

If the annuity is payable after the recipient's death to a widow(er) or dependants, they may have problems enforcing the payments should the continuing partners default (see *Beswick v Beswick* (1967)). **[31.15]**

EXAMPLE 31.2

The partnership agreement of Falstaff and Co provides for retiring partners to be paid an annuity for ten years after retirement amounting to 10% of the annual net profits of the firm earned in the preceding accounting year.

Hal retires as a partner on 5 April 1997. His share of the profit (index-linked) in the last seven years before his retirement is as follows:

1996–97	£20,000*	1992–93	£11,000*
1995–96	£14,000*	1991–92	£ 8,000
1994–95	£ 8,000	1990–91	£ 9,000
1993–94	£ 7,000		

In the tax year 1997–98 Falstaff & Co's net profits amount to £90,000. The continuing partners will pay Hal £6,750, ie 10% × £90,000 = £9,000 less basic rate income tax deducted at source under TA 1988 s 348. Hal must enter the gross amount of the payment (£9,000) in his income tax calculation for 1997–98 with a tax credit for £2,070 (basic rate tax deducted at source).

The £9,000 is treated as earned income in Hal's hands up to a limit of £7,500 (being half the average share of his taxable profits in the best three of the last seven years before retirement (ie 1996–97; 1995–96; 1992–93)). The balance of £1,500 is treated as unearned income.

c) *Retirement annuities and personal pension schemes*

In addition to or instead of (b) above, partners as self-employed individuals should provide for their retirement by taking out insurance. Prior to 1 July 1988, such insurance had to take the form of a retirement annuity contract approved by the Inland Revenue under TA 1988 s 619. However, in order to bring retirement provision for the self-employed into line with that available to employees, TA 1988 ss 630–655 required both employees who contract out of occupational pension schemes and partners who

provide for their retirement after the same date to enter new personal
pension scheme arrangements. Pensions are considered further in Appendix IV.
[31.16]-[31.30]

II CAPITAL GAINS TAX

1 **General**

The application of CGT principles causes difficulties which are exacerbated
by the failure of the legislation to make express provision for the treatment
of partnerships. It is necessary to apply rules designed for individuals to firms
and rely on the Revenue Statements of Practice SP D12; SP 1/79; and SP 1/89
which do not have the force of law and are a poor substitute for proper legislation
in this field.

In applying the CGT legislation to partnerships the general principle is that
CGT is triggered by a disposal of a chargeable partnership asset which is treated
as made by the individual partners in the proportions in which they own the
asset surpluses and is determined primarily by the partnership deed (TCGA 1992
s 59). In the absence of any specific agreement, such entitlement follows the profit
sharing arrangements. Often, however, the asset surplus entitlement will be different
from the profit sharing ratio to reflect the partners' contributions to the capital
of the business. All too often it is uncertain whether a particular asset is partnership
property or owned by one of the partners and merely used, often without any
formal arrangement being entered into, by the firm (see, in relation to milk quota,
Faulks v Faulks (1992)).   [31.31]

EXAMPLE 31.3

(1) Flip & Co, a trading partnership, has three partners, Flip, Flap and Flop,
     who share asset surpluses in the ratio 3:2:1. In 1990 the firm acquired a valuable
     Ming vase for a base cost of £60,000; they sell it subsequently for £180,000.
     The gain of the firm (ignoring any incidental costs of disposal and the indexation
     allowance) is £120,000. CGT must be calculated separately for each partner:

     Flip owns 3/6 of the asset and, therefore, has a base cost of £30,000 and
     is entitled to 3/6 of the sale proceeds (£90,000); his gain is £60,000 (ie he
     is entitled to 3/6 of the partnership gain).
     Flap's base cost is 2/6 of £60,000 (£20,000) and his share of the proceeds
     is 2/6 of £180,000 (£60,000) so that his gain is £40,000.
     Flop's base cost is 1/6 of £60,000 (£10,000) and his share of the proceeds
     is 1/6 of £180,000 (£30,000) so that his gain is £20,000.

(2) Assume that the Ming vase is given to Flip in recognition of his 25 years'
     service with the firm. It is worth £180,000 at the date of the gift. The position
     of Flap and Flop is basically unchanged and they have made gains of £40,000
     and £20,000 respectively. Tax may be postponed by an election under TCGA
     1992 s 165 if the donors and Flip agree (see [**17.23**]). In that event Flap will
     dispose of his 2/6 share for £20,000 and Flop his 1/6 share for £10,000.
     The position of Flip is that since he is given the asset he is not treated
     as making a disposal of his original 3/6 share in the asset (see SP D12, para 3).
     Hence, the only difficulty is to discover Flip's base cost. Under general
     principles it will be:

	£	
	30,000	(cost of original 3/6 share)
plus	60,000	(market value of Flap's 2/6 share at date of gift)
plus	30,000	(market value of Flop's 1/6 share at date of gift)
	£120,000	

The result is that Flip's own gain (£60,000) is held over until such time as he disposes of the vase.

If an election is made under TCGA 1992 s 165 Flip's base cost becomes:

	£	
	30,000	(as above)
plus	20,000	(balance after deducting held-over gain on Flap's share)
plus	10,000	(balance after deducting held-over gain on Flop's share)
	£60,000	

2 Changing the asset surplus sharing ratio

CGT may be triggered when the asset surplus sharing ratio is altered.

Old partners	New partners	Old asset surplus sharing ratio	New asset surplus sharing ratio
(1) AB	ABC	1:1	1:1:1
(2) AB	AB	1:1	2:1
(3) ABC	ABD	1:1:1	2:2:1

In all the above cases there has been a change in the entitlement to asset surpluses (and, therefore, to the beneficial ownership of the capital assets). No asset has been disposed of outside the firm, but there has been a disposal of a share of the assets between the partners.

In (1), above, A and B formerly owned the assets equally; C now joins the firm and is entitled to 1/3 of the asset surpluses. A and B have each made a disposal of 1/3 of their original share in the assets. A, for instance, is now entitled to 1/3 instead of 1/2 or, to put the matter another way, they have together made a disposal of 1/3 of the total assets to C. In (2), although the partners remain the same, the sharing ratio is altered so that B is making a disposal to A of 1/3 of his share of the assets. In (3), C is disposing of a 1/3 share in the assets amongst the continuing partners, A, B and D (A and B each acquire an extra 1/15 of the assets and D 3/15).

Such changes in the sharing ratio are likely to occur principally in three cases: (i) on the retirement or expulsion of a partner; (ii) on the introduction of a new partner; and (iii) on the amendment of the original agreement. It should be noted that the mere revaluation of an asset in the accounts of the firm has no CGT consequences since the revaluation is neither a disposal of an asset nor of a share in assets. (Compare the individual taxpayer who is not assessed to CGT merely because his Ming vase has risen in value from £50,000 to £75,000.)

Whether CGT will be assessed on the disponer depends upon whether he is paid for the share in the asset that he transfers, or whether an adjustment is made to his capital account in the firm by crediting it for that share so that no money is actually paid to him. The CGT position in the latter case will turn upon whether the relevant asset had been revalued in the firm's balance sheet. In some cases, however, the relevant assets may not have been revalued in the accounts. Therefore, on the disposal, the disponer's capital account will not be credited with any gain. For CGT purposes, there has been neither gain nor loss so that no CGT will be payable. This is an example of a no gain/no loss disposal (and is treated as such for the purposes of rebasing and indexation, see SP 1/89) and results in the postponement of payment of any CGT.

EXAMPLE 31.4

(1) Fleur and Camilla have been in partnership sharing profits and asset surpluses equally. The only substantial chargeable asset of the business is the freehold

shop which cost £40,000 in 1990. Fleur now sells her share to Charlotte for £75,000.

Fleur has made a disposal of her half share in the asset and her gain (ignoring any incidental costs of disposal and the indexation allowance) will be:

	£
Consideration received	75,000
Less: base cost (50% of £40,000)	20,000
Gain	£55,000

(2) Slick and Slack are in partnership owning asset surpluses in the ratio 2:1. The main capital asset is the firm's premises which cost £30,000 in 1988 and have recently been revalued at £75,000. The two partners have the following interests in this capital asset:

	Slick	*Slack*
	£	£
Original expenditure	20,000	10,000
Share of increased value	30,000	15,000
	£50,000	£25,000

Sloth joins the firm and Slick disposes of 1/2 of his share to Sloth with the result that the sharing ratio becomes 1:1:1. The capital account of Slick will be credited with the value of the share transferred and ultimately he will be paid that sum of money. Slick has thus disposed of 1/3 of the asset (or 1/2 of his share) which has a value of £25,000. That sum will be credited to his capital account with the result that he will have made a gain (ignoring the indexation allowance) for CGT purposes of £25,000 (consideration for the share disposed of) less £10,000 (base cost of the share disposed of) = £15,000.

Slick will be assessed to CGT on this gain despite the fact that he may not be entitled to receive the £25,000 until the firm is dissolved or until he leaves it. So far as the incoming partner Sloth is concerned, he will acquire a 1/3 share of the capital asset, of a value of £25,000, and that figure will be his base cost (it will often be the capital sum that he will pay into the firm on becoming a partner).

(3) If in (2) above Slick and Slack had never revalued the premises (which appear in the accounts at their original cost price of £30,000) on the disposal to Sloth, Slick will be treated as transferring half of his share for its book value (£10,000) with the result that he will have made no gain. Correspondingly, Sloth's base cost will be £10,000 so that he is acquiring an asset pregnant with gain.

A failure to revalue an asset, with a subsequent transfer of it at cost, might be viewed as a gift to the incoming partner so that market value should be substituted for the share transferred. In *Example 31.4(3)* this would produce a gain for Slick of £15,000 (£25,000 - £10,000). However, although partners are generally connected persons, they are not so treated in respect of transfers of partnership assets (TCGA 1992 s 286(4)). Hence, the presumption of gift will not apply unless the partners are connected in some other capacity, eg parent and child, and even in those circumstances the Revenue states that 'market value will not be substituted ... if nothing would have been paid had the parties been at arm's length' (SP D12, para 7). In all cases, therefore, there will be no question of market value being substituted *so long as the transaction can be shown to be one entered into at arm's length*. Normally, the commercial nature of the arrangement will be assumed. Where there are connected persons, however, the onus is on the taxpayer to show that identical transactions would have been made with a stranger. This onus will usually be discharged by showing that the incoming partner was assuming a large share of responsibility for the running of the business and, thus, furnishing consideration for his share of the assets.

If the bounty element is so great that the transfer must be treated as a gift, the Revenue has stated that 'the deemed disposal proceeds will fall to be treated in the same way as a payment outside the accounts'. In such a case any CGT can be postponed by the parties electing to hold over the gain under TCGA 1992 s 165. **[31.32]**

EXAMPLE 31.5

Jake and Jules are brothers and are in business together sharing profits equally. The chargeable assets of the firm cost a total of £20,000 and are now worth £200,000 although they have not been revalued in the firm's books. Jake now transfers his 50% share to his two sons, Jason and Jasper. For CGT Jake's base cost is £10,000 (1/2 of £20,000). As those assets have not been revalued, they will be passed at that value to his sons. CGT will not be payable.

Should the Revenue successfully claim (as is likely) that the arrangement did not amount to an arm's length bargain, Jake, Jason, and Jasper could make an election under TCGA 1992 s 165 to hold over Jake's gain.

3 Goodwill

Goodwill is a chargeable asset for CGT purposes. Thus, the disposal of the whole or part of a firm's goodwill may be an occasion of charge to CGT. Problems have arisen in recent years (especially with regard to professional partnerships) when the existing partners decided not to charge future incoming partners for any share of the firm's goodwill and, therefore, to write off the goodwill in the partnership's balance sheet. On the question as to whether those partners who originally paid for a share of that goodwill (usually on becoming partners in the firm) can then claim immediate CGT loss relief, the following principles may be suggested.

First, on an actual disposal of the goodwill, whether on retirement or to an incoming partner, provided that its value has been written off in the partnership's balance sheet, an allowable loss for CGT purposes may be claimed by the disposing partner.

EXAMPLE 31.6

Alfie is a partner in Cockney Films & Co. When he joined the firm in 1989 he paid £10,000 for a share in the goodwill. The firm has decided to write off goodwill since incoming partners will no longer be expected to pay for a share of it. When he retires and a new partner, Slicker, joins there will be no payment for Alfie's share of goodwill and Alfie will have made a loss for CGT purposes of £10,000 (being the difference between what he originally paid for the asset and the consideration received on its disposal; for the CGT treatment of losses see [14.91]).

Secondly, at the time when the goodwill is written off in the balance sheet, the partners may wish to claim immediate loss relief under TCGA 1992 s 24(2) which allows a claim for loss relief when 'the inspector is satisfied that the value of an asset has become negligible'. The Revenue does not agree that the mere writing off of goodwill has this result but takes the view that goodwill retains its value even though no longer paid for by incoming partners or shown in the firm's balance sheet, on the grounds that if the business were sold, the consideration would include a sum for goodwill. Whether this fact should influence the valuation of an individual partner's share in circumstances where he could not unilaterally receive consideration for it is most debatable. The law in this area is not settled, with a few inspectors apparently allowing loss claims. **[31.33]**

4 Payment of annuities

When a partner leaves the firm any annuity payments that he receives from the continuing partners will be subject to income tax ([**31.13**]) and, in addition, their capitalised value may be treated as consideration for the disposal of a share of the partnership assets (TCGA 1992 s 37(3)) and CGT levied on any resultant gain. In SP D12 the Revenue has indicated when this will be the case:

> 'The capitalised value of the annuity will only be treated as consideration for the disposal of his share in the partnership assets, if it is more than can be regarded as a reasonable recognition of the past contribution of work and effort by the partner to the partnership. Provided that the former partner had been in the partnership for at least ten years an annuity will be regarded as reasonable for this purpose if it is no more than two-thirds of his average share of the profits in the best three of the last seven years in which he was required to devote substantially the whole of his time to acting as a partner.
>
> For lesser periods the following fractions will be used instead of the two-thirds:

Complete years in partnership	Fraction
1–5	1/60 for each year
6	8/60
7	16/60
8	24/60
9	32/60'

Where the partner receives both an annuity and a lump sum, the Revenue's view is that:

> 'If the outgoing partner is paid a lump sum and an annuity, the Revenue will not charge CGT on the capitalised value of the annuity provided that the annuity and one-ninth of the lump sum together do not exceed the relevant fraction of the retired partner's average share of the profits' (SP 1/79).

The lump sum will, therefore, always be charged to CGT and it may cause the capitalised value of the annuity to be taxed.   [**31.34**]

EXAMPLE 31.7

(1) Charles and Claude agree to pay their partner, Clarence, who retires on 5 April 1998 after 18 years as a partner, an annuity of £3,000 pa for the next ten years. His share of the profits in the last seven years of the partnership was as follows:

Tax year	Profits £	Tax year	Profits £
1997–98	5,000	1993–94	2,000
1996–97	10,000*	1992–93	4,000
1995–96	14,000*	1991–92	5,000
1994–95	12,000*		

The annuity does not exceed two-thirds of Clarence's average share of profits in the best three years (those asterisked) of the last seven years before retirement, ie ⅔ × £36,000 divided by 3 = £8,000. Therefore, no CGT is paid on the capitalised value. (Note that for income tax purposes the annuity will be earned income in Clarence's hands up to £6,000; ie ½ × £36,000 divided by 3.)

Contrast the position if Clarence had been paid an annuity of £9,000 pa. As the permitted £8,000 figure is exceeded the entire capitalised value of that annuity will be subject to CGT.

(2) Assume that, in addition to the annuity (in (1)), it is agreed that Clarence is to receive a lump sum of £54,000. His CGT position is as follows:

　(i) the annuity will be subject to income tax;

(ii) the lump sum (£54,000) will be subject to CGT insofar as it represents consideration for a disposal of chargeable assets; and

(iii) the capitalised value of the annuity will also be included for CGT purposes since the annuity (£3,000) plus 1/9 of the lump sum (£6,000) exceeds the 2/3 limit of £8,000.

5 Reliefs

CGT reliefs have been considered in detail earlier. Those of particular relevance to partnerships are: **[31.35]**

Hold-over relief under TCGA 1992 s 165 gifts of business assets. **[31.36]**

Roll-over (reinvestment) relief (TCGA 1992 s 152 ff) This is of particular importance and the extension of the relief in two circumstances should be noted. *First,* it applies to assets which are owned by an individual partner and used by the firm, so long as the entire proceeds of disposal are reinvested in another business asset used by the firm or used in a new trade carried on by the partner. *Secondly,* where land (or another qualifying asset) is partitioned between the partners it is treated as a new asset for the purpose of this relief provided that the firm is dissolved immediately afterwards (see ESC D23). **[31.37]**

Retirement relief The relief will apply when a partner disposes of his share of the business. By TCGA 1992 s 164(6), the relief is extended to cover the disposal of an asset owned by a partner provided that it is used by the firm at that time and that its disposal is associated with the disposal of his partnership share (see [**16.109**], *Example 16.20*). For these purposes it is sufficient if the disposal represents merely a partial withdrawal from the business.

Since the payment of an actual or deemed rent to the individual partner operates to deny full relief, a partner who wishes to keep an asset in his name, whilst allowing the firm to use it, should ensure that he is paid for its use by an increased share of the profits rather than by a payment of rent. **[31.38]**

Roll-over relief (TCGA 1992 s 162) This relief is available on the incorporation of a partnership. **[31.39]–[31.50]**

III INHERITANCE TAX

As with CGT, there are few specific references in the IHT legislation to partnerships. General principles, therefore, operate and gratuitous transfers of partnership assets or interests therein may be treated as transfers of value by the individual partners (see *Example 31.8*).

Normally, the share of a retiring partner in the firm will pass to the continuing partners. There is no risk of an IHT charge where full consideration is paid, and, even where that is not so, IHT will be avoided if (as is usually the case) the transfer is a commercial transaction within IHTA 1984 s 10(1) (see [**21.21**]).

EXAMPLE 31.8

Big & Co has 20 partners all equally entitled to profits. The following changes are to occur:
(1) Partner Zack is retiring and is to receive an annuity for his share of the assets. His share of goodwill is to pass automatically under the partnership deed to the continuing partners.
(2) Partner Uriah is to devote less time to the business and will receive a reduced share of the profits (including capital profits). At the same time, partner Victor

is to be paid an increased profit share to reflect his central position within the firm.

(3) Partner Yvonne is retiring and her place is to be taken by her daughter Brenda. No payment is to be made by Brenda.

The IHT consequences of these transactions are as follows:

(1) *Zack*   There is no risk of an IHT charge since consideration is given for his assets (there may not even be a fall in value in his estate). Regarding the automatic accrual of goodwill, it is generally thought that the estate duty case of *A-G v Boden* (1912) is still good law for IHT. Thus, mutual covenants by the partners that goodwill shall pass to the surviving partners on death or retirement without any cash payment will make the transfer of goodwill non-gratuitous within IHTA 1984 s 10(1). This principle should apply even where the other parties are, or include, connected persons since it should be possible to show that identical arrangements would have been made with partners who were not so connected.

(2) *Uriah*   The loss to Uriah's estate is the result of a commercial bargain since he is being allowed to devote less time to the business; IHT is not, therefore, potentially chargeable. Likewise, increasing the profit sharing ratio of Victor is merely a recognition by the other partners of his commercial necessity to the firm.

(3) *Yvonne*   The new partner is a connected person and it will be hard to justify this arrangement on commercial grounds as it would not have been entered into with a stranger. On that basis, IHT will be assessed on the fall in value of Yvonne's estate if she dies within seven years after the transaction.

The major IHT reliefs applicable to trading and professional partnerships will be business property relief, agricultural relief, and the instalment option (see Chapter 23). Three points of particular relevance to partnerships should be repeated: *first*, on a transfer of assets held outside the firm and consisting of land, buildings and machinery or plant, business property relief at 50% may be available. If the asset is owned by the partnership, however, the full 100% relief may apply. *Secondly*, the IHT business reliefs are not available where a partner's share is subject to a binding contract of sale at the time of transfer. Therefore, if it is desired to ensure that on the death or retirement of a partner his share shall pass to the survivors whilst at the same time preserving IHT business property relief, the partnership deed should avoid either imposing an obligation on the remaining partners to purchase his share or even providing for his share to accrue automatically to them. Instead the deed should give the surviving partners *an option* (only) to purchase that share (see **[23.48]** and *Law Society's Gazette*, 4 September 1996, at p 35. *Finally*, in *Gray v IRC* (1994), the Revenue succeeded before the Court of Appeal in lotting the deceased's freehold interest in a landed estate with her share in a farming partnership which owned a lease over the land. The case represents a considerable extension of the old authorities, especially with regard to the rejection of any requirement that to be lotted for valuation purposes property must form a 'natural unit'. It may turn out, however, that the actual decision turned on particular facts since the other partners were not members of the family and had no wish to continue in the business, being only too willing to sell their partnership shares to the hypothetical purchaser of the entire estate (see **[23.64]** and (1994) *Private Client Business*, issue 4).   **[31.51]**

32 Stamp duty

'The law upon the subject of stamps is altogether a matter positivi juris. It involves nothing of principle or reason but depends altogether upon the language of the legislature.' (Taunton J in *Morley v Hall* (1834).)

[**32.1**]

I INTRODUCTION

The first stamp duties were introduced in 1694 during the reign of William and Mary and they have since remained a permanent feature of the fiscal landscape. The cardinal feature of stamp duty and one which distinguishes it from the other direct taxes is that it is strictly a charge on instruments and not on either transactions or on persons. This originally simple structure has, however, been eroded gradually over the years by the growth of both charges to and exemptions from duty.   [**32.2**]

1 Reform

In response to a government Consultative Document issued in 1983 ('The Scope for Reforming Stamp Duties'), FA 1985 removed much dead wood and effected a significant simplification of the tax. In addition to reducing the rate of *ad valorem* duty on sales of shares and marketable securities, FA 1986 broadened the base of the duty to include instruments (executed in connection with, for example, company takeovers) which had previously enjoyed an exemption. It also introduced the stamp duty reserve tax (SDRT) which levied duty on certain transactions where no stamped document existed. The SDRT, in reality, was a new tax, levied on transactions rather than instruments and was related to stamp duty only insofar as it could be avoided (or duty collected repaid) if a duly stamped instrument was produced within six years of the transaction.

Further major reforms were envisaged in FA 1990. Duty was to be removed from all transactions in shares to coincide with the introduction of paperless dealing under the Stock Exchange's new share transfer system ('Taurus'). FA 1991 went further in proposing the abolition of stamp duty charges on *all* property *other than* land and buildings.

In the event the collapse of Taurus means that none of these changes are to be implemented at present and nor are they likely to be in the near future, given the government's cash shortage.   [**32.3**]

2   General structure of the duty

The present system of stamp duties depends primarily upon the Stamp Act 1891 and the Stamp Duties Management Act 1891 as amended by subsequent Finance Acts. The interaction of stamp duty with VAT is addressed in SP 11/91. For stamp duty purposes the consideration on sale is the gross amount inclusive of VAT. By contrast stamp duty never forms any part of the consideration for VAT.

Stamp duty (as mentioned above) is conceptually straightforward. It is levied upon any 'instrument' (the term includes 'every written document') which falls within one of the 'Heads of Charge' (analogous to the income tax Schedules) and is not covered by an exemption. Thus, if a transaction can be effected without a written instrument or without coming within one of the heads of charge, duty will be avoided.

EXAMPLE 32.1

Alonzo agrees to sell his country estate to his cousin, Bonzo, for £100,000. Stamp duty at the *ad valorem* rate of 1% will be charged on any instrument of transfer but if the matter is 'left in contract' (ie if no such instrument is executed) duty is avoided.

Notes:

(i)   An exchange of contracts does not give rise to duty since it involves a contract for the sale of the legal estate in property which is outside the ambit of the tax (*IRC v Angus & Co* (1889); *Wimpey v IRC* (1975)).

(ii) However, a contract for the sale of an equitable interest falls within SA 1891 s 59 (see [**32.69**]). Given that on exchange of contract the purchaser would normally acquire on equitable interest in the property, care must be taken to ensure that there is an intention to complete the transaction in due course otherwise it could be argued that on a true construction of the contract what was being sold was only an equitable interest (see *Peter Bone Ltd v IRC* (1995)).

(iii) Subject to the points made in (ii) above matters can be left in contract indefinitely and there is nothing to prevent all the purchase moneys being paid on exchange. If and when completed, duty (at rates then current) will be charged on the purchase price.

The amount of stamp duty to be paid depends upon each individual head of charge, but the sum will be either a fixed duty of (usually) 50p or an *ad valorem* duty which will be calculated (usually) by reference to the value of the transaction recorded in the instrument (rounded up to the nearest £100). SA 1891 s 15 requires an instrument to be stamped within 30 days after its execution or 'after it has been first received in the UK in case it is first executed at any place out of the UK'. The liability relates to any property situated in the UK or to any matter or thing done or to be done in the UK. Hence the residence of the parties is irrelevant but it would appear that no documents executed outside the UK needs to be stamped unless and until it is brought into the UK.

[**32.4**]

3   Going offshore

As will be apparent from the above, the execution and retention of a document overseas may provide a way of deferring payment of duty without any penalty. *Parinv (Hatfield) Ltd v IRC* (1996) involved a typical arrangement:

(1)   the parties agreed a sale of UK land;

(2)   the contract provided that completion would be by way of a declaration of trust;

(3) it would appear therefore that the agreement was to sell an equitable interest, dutiable under SA 1891 s 59 (se [**32.69**]) and so the contract was executed and kept offshore. Similarly the declaration of trust in favour of the purchaser was executed and kept offshore;

(4) the vendor/trustee executed a transfer in favour of the purchaser which was presented as being subject to 50p duty only, being a conveyance or transfer not on sale (see [**32.53**]).

The Court rejected this approach holding that the transfer was dutiable as a conveyance on sale. This conclusion was arrived at on the basis of a consideration of the background documentation which was surely inadmissible given that the transfer contained on its face all necessary information for stamping. The judgment has been heavily criticised and an appeal is pending (see *Tax Bulletin*, issue 30). **[32.5]–[32.20]**

II ENFORCEMENT AND ADMINISTRATION

1 Who is accountable for duty?

The legislation does not directly state who is accountable for the duty. The main sanction for non-payment is that, unless properly stamped, no document executed in the UK or relating to any property that is situated in the UK, will be admissible in evidence in any civil proceedings (SA 1891 s 14(1) and see *Fengl v Fengl* (1914)). Unstamped documents are admissible in criminal proceedings; failure to stamp does not involve any criminal liability; and an agreement between the parties not to stamp the instrument does not amount to a criminal conspiracy. In some cases fines are imposed for offences in relation to stamp duty. **[32.21]**

2 Date for stamping

Technically an instrument should be stamped before execution. In practice, however, the Revenue permits stamping within 30 days after execution without imposing any penalty. A deed is executed when delivered or, if later, when the conditions subject to which it was delivered are satisfied (FA 1994 s 239). Late stamping is permitted subject (normally) to the payment of a penalty of £10 and, where the duty exceeds £10, interest at 5% pa from the date of execution up to a maximum of the unpaid duty. In certain cases, the penalty is equivalent to the stamp duty payable and the legislation names the person who is liable for the penalty—in the case of a conveyance on sale for instance it is the transferee or purchaser (SA 1891 s 15(2)). **[32.22]**

3 Administration

The administration of stamp duty is under the Commissioners of Inland Revenue but the day-to-day work of administration is carried out, in England and Wales, by the Controller of Stamps, and, in Scotland, by the Controller (Stamps) Scotland. In the event of a dispute there will normally be an adjudication followed by the stating of a case by the commissioners with a hearing in the Chancery Division of the High Court. There is a right of appeal to the Court of Appeal and, ultimately, to the House of Lords. Unlike other taxes the taxpayer has to pay the assessed duty before the appeal is heard. **[32.23]**

4 Adjudication

If required to do so the commissioners must state whether, in their opinion, any executed instrument is subject to a stamp duty charge and if so must state the amount of duty chargeable (the *adjudication* process: SA 1891 s 12). Adjudication may be voluntary, in which case the individual will be asking the commissioners to confirm that no duty is payable on the instrument, or, alternatively it may be necessary to ascertain the correct duty to be paid. In certain cases, however, legislation makes adjudication compulsory to ensure that the correct amount of duty is paid or to ensure that an instrument is covered by an exemption from duty (eg where there is a company reconstruction and exemption from duty is sought: see [**32.82**]). Such instruments are deemed not to have been properly stamped unless adjudicated bearing a stamp to that effect.

The process of adjudication is an essential step in the appeals procedure and it also provides the best means by which a third party can be satisfied as to the correctness of the stamp duty paid.   [**32.24**]

5 Produced stamps

In three cases instruments must be produced to the commissioners. In general, production should be within 30 days of execution and the obligation lies upon the transferee or lessee. Such instruments will then be impressed with a produced stamp (a 'PD' stamp) which is quite independent of any stamp denoting duty or any adjudication stamp. Penalties for failure to produce are the same as those which apply on failure to stamp. Such instruments are:

(1) a transfer on sale of a fee simple of land;
(2) a lease (or agreement for a lease) of land for a term of seven years or more;
(3) a transfer on sale of a lease as in (2) (FA 1931 s 28 Sch 2).

Originally this information was necessary for the assessment of the land tax imposed by FA 1932. With the abolition of that tax in 1934 the provisions were left unrepealed since they are useful to valuers in assessing compensation claims in compulsory purchase cases. In an attempt to speed up domestic conveyancing transactions FA 1985 s 89 and SI 1985/1688 provide that transfers of registered land below the stamp duty threshold (currently £60,000) should be exempted from these requirements. Accordingly, in these cases the appropriate instrument of transfer should be sent directly to the Land Registry along with the particulars delivered form.   [**32.25**]–[**32.40**]

III   THE OCCASIONS OF CHARGE

For an instrument to be chargeable to stamp duty it must fall within one of the heads of charge. If it falls within more than one head, the Revenue, although only entitled to one of the duties, can choose the head that will produce the higher duty (*Speyer Bros v IRC* (1908)). Where several instruments are employed to carry out the same transaction, it is only the principal instrument of conveyance that is charged to *ad valorem* duty. The other instruments can only be charged with the 50p miscellaneous conveyance duty which cannot exceed the *ad valorem* duty payable in respect of the principal instrument (SA 1891 s 58(3)).   [**32.41**]

1 Conveyance or transfer on sale (SA 1891 Sch 1)

This head of charge covers the conveyance or transfer on sale of any property and the duty charged is *ad valorem* at a rate for shares and securities of 50p per £100 or part of £100 of the consideration: ie 1/2%. For other property the rate in the case of most transfers made on or after 8 July 1997 is:

(1) if the consideration is £60,000 or less, *nil*;
(2) if the consideration exceeds £60,000 but does not exceed £250,000, *1%*;
(3) if the consideraion exceeds £250,000 but does not exceed £500,000, *1 1/2%*
(4) if the consideration exceeds £500,000, *2%*.

In all cases if a reduced rate of duty is claimed an appropriate certificate of value must be included.

The certificate must state that the transaction effected by the instrument does not form part of a larger transaction or series of transactions in respect of which the amount or value or aggregate amount or value of the consideration exceeds £60,000 if the nil rate is claimed; £250,000 if the 1% rate is claimed and so on. Little guidance is given as to the meaning of 'a series of transactions'. Take, for instance, the sale of four properties from A to B each for £60,000. Assuming that there are four separate transactions, none would attract duty. Treated as one transaction, however, duty at 1% is charged. If the transactions are simultaneous they must amount to a single operation; even if not, such a series of conveyances may have all the hallmarks of an associated operation.

EXAMPLE 32.2

(1) Jason agrees to buy a plot of land for £40,000 on which a house, costing £30,000, is to be built. No duty is paid because the land is below the £60,000 threshold. Stamp duty is not charged on a building contract (since it is not a conveyance or transfer).

(2) Foolish pays £70,000 for a plot of land together with a completed house thereon. He is subject to £700 duty (1% × £70,000).

Note: The Revenue's attitude to the purchase of new houses and to building contracts generally is set out in SP 8/93 which replaced previous Statements published in 1957 and 1987 (SP 10/87). It applies when, at the date of the contract of sale or lease of a building plot, building work has not commenced or has been only partially completed on the site but that work has started or been completed at the time when the conveyance or lease is executed. It is not concerned with the situation where there is a contract for sale of a new house and that is implemented by a conveyance of the whole property. Broadly the position is as follows:

(1) 'Where there is a contract for a conveyance or lease of land and, as a separate transaction, a further contract for building works, stamp duty on the conveyance or lease will be calculated without regard to the further contract.'

(2) 'Where within a single transaction there are separate contracts for the sale or lease of a building plot, and for building works on that plot, the stamp duty charged depends on whether the contracts are genuinely independent. *If the contracts are independent*, duty will be charged on the price paid or payable for both the land itself and for any building that is on the land at the time the instrument is executed, including partly completed buildings. *If the contracts are not independent*, stamp duty will be charged on the total price for the land and *completed* buildings.'

Amendments made by this SP were prompted by the High Court decision in *Prudential Assurance Co Ltd v IRC* (1993).

The reduced rates are not operated on the 'slice system' so that once the consideration exceeds (say) £60,000 (whilst not exceeding £250,000), it is all taxed at 1%. Furthermore the nil rate cannot be used on instruments which transfer shares and other marketable securities (FA 1963 s 55(2)), presumably because larger transactions could easily be split into £60,000 slices. **[32.42]**

Meaning of 'sale' 'Sale' is not defined but there will need to be a vendor, a purchaser, and normally a money consideration (although there is no requirement that the consideration must be adequate). Duty is charged on the amount or value of the consideration and where it is in sterling, there will be no problem. If the consideration is in foreign currency, duty is charged on the sterling equivalent at the rate of exchange applying on the date of execution of the instrument (FA 1985 s 88).

Special provisions operate where the consideration is to be paid over a number of years (SA 1891 s 56). *First*, where the payments are for a definite period not exceeding 20 years the charge is on the total of all those payments (SA 1891 s 56(1)). *Secondly*, if the payments are to last in perpetuity; or for a period exceeding 20 years; or for a period of indefinite length which is not terminable on death, the charge is on the amount payable during 20 years starting with the date of the sale (SA 1891 s 56(2)). For a discussion of the meaning of 'a payment for a period' see *Blendett Ltd v IRC* (1984) and *Quietlece Ltd v IRC* (1984). *Thirdly*, if the payments are to last during a life or lives, duty is charged on the total amount payable during the 12 years from the date of the instrument. The payer's age is irrelevant (SA 1891 s 56(3)).

EXAMPLE 32.3

(1) If the consideration is £10,000 pa payable for eight years, duty will be charged on £80,000 (SA 1891 s 56(1)).
(2) If the consideration is £10,000 pa payable so long as the recipient lives in London, duty will be charged on £10,000 × 20 = £200,000 (SA 1891 s 56(2)).
(3) £10,000 pa is payable during the life of the payer. Duty is charged on £10,000 × 12 = £120,000 (SA 1891 s 56(3)).

These rules for instalment payments apply only to periodic payments which are 'new' requirements and part of the bargain for sale; they do not apply to payments which are naturally a part of the property sold (as, for instance, a payment of rent on the creation of a lease).   [**32.43**]

Unascertainable consideration and the contingency principle If there is a specified *maximum* consideration provided for, then *ad valorem* duty is charged on that amount even though there may be little practical likelihood of it being paid. If there is no maximum sum stated but a minimum figure, *ad valorem* duty is charged on the minimum figure with a 50p charge on the unidentified larger sum. If, however, there was no maximum nor minimum figure the consideration was wholly unascertainable with nothing to stamp. In the case of a lease £2 duty was payable: otherwise duty of 50p (see *Coventry City Council v IRC* (1978); *LM Tenancies 1 v IRC* (1996) and for leases, see [**32.61**]. This so called contingency principle has been amended by FA 1994 s 242 in the case of transfers of any interest in land or the grant of any lease by providing that if the consideration or any part of the consideration could not be ascertained at the time of execution of the instrument, market value is to be taken for stamp duty purposes.

The Revenue's view on the relationship between s 242 and the situation where a maximum or minimum sum is agreed between the parties is as follows:

'The ascertainable figure produced by the contingency principle may be a maximum or minimum, or a basic sum which is subject to future variation. But a minimum figure which was merely a nominal figure inserted in a lease to avoid Section 242, or which did not represent the agreed consideration or rent, would not satisfy Section 242(3)(a) as it would not be a minimum rent for the purpose of the contingency principle as formulated by Lord Radcliffe in the Independent Television Authority case. We consider that for this purpose a minimum rent must be an amount genuinely agreed between the parties as such, i.e., as an amount which is contemplated by the parties and accepted by the landlord as compensation for the use and occupation of the premises by the tenant(s). It is therefore necessary to consider all the facts in order to ascertain the true nature and intended purpose of the instrument (Oughtred v IRC [1958] Ch 678 page 688; [1960] AC 206). (See *Tax Bulletin*, 1995, p 236.) **[32.44]**

Meaning of 'consideration' Although the consideration for a sale will normally be money, for stamp duty purposes stock or marketable securities and debts and other liabilities are treated as sale consideration (SA 1891 s 55, s 57). In an exchange involving land or an interest in land, FA 1994, s 241 widened the definition of consideration to include the market value of the property taken in exchange (see **[32.49]**).

EXAMPLE 32.4

(1) Julie sells her house to Samantha for £40,000. In addition Samantha agrees to repay Julie's overdraft of £30,000 (a similar result would occur if Samantha took over the outstanding mortgage on the property: see SP 6/90 discussed below). The consideration furnished for stamp duty will be £40,000 + £30,000 = £70,000.

(2) Julie sells her lease to Jane in consideration for the transfer of 100 £1 shares in F Ltd. The consideration for stamp duty will be the shares. Generally, the shares will be valued in accordance with the procedure adopted for CGT (see TCGA 1992 s 274 and SP 18/80). Although the shares constitute the consideration for the conveyance of the house, the converse is not the case so that the transfer of the shares themselves will attract only 50p duty.

Subject to the rules on exchanges involving land, if consideration other than money, stocks, shares or the assumption of liabilities is furnished, the transaction will not be treated as a sale for stamp duty purposes. In *IRC v Littlewoods Mail Order Stores Ltd* (1963), for instance, the exchange of a freehold reversion for a leasehold interest in the same property was not treated as the sale of the freehold in exchange for the rent reserved by the lease. **[32.45]**

Transfers of property subject to a debt (SP 6/90) Does the transfer of mortgaged property amount to a sale for the purposes of *ad valorem* duty? The SP draws a contrast between the following cases:

Case 1 The transferee of mortgaged property covenants (either in the transfer or separately) to discharge the debt or indemnify the transferor. The transfer is a sale with the consideration being the amount of the debt.

Case 2 As in *Case 1*, except that the transferor covenants to pay the debt so that no liability is assumed by the transferee. The transfer is a voluntary disposition and can be certified under Category L of the 1987 Regulations (see **[32.60]**.

Case 3 If there is no express covenant or undertaking by either party the Revenue will imply a covenant by the transferee (except in Scotland). This implied covenant will arise even if the mortgaged property is in joint names and transferred to one of the joint holders and even if both parties were jointly liable on the mortgage.

Case 4 If chargeable consideration unrelated to the debt is given by the transferee for the mortgaged property the conveyance is then subject to *ad valorem* duty as a sale on the aggregate of that consideration and the debt whether or not liability for that debt has been assumed by the transferee.

[32.46]

Assents Certain assents are treated as sales: for instance, an assent by a deceased's

PRs in favour of the person to whom the deceased, prior to his death, had contracted to sell property (*GHR Co v IRC* (1943)). Formerly, sale duty was also charged when property was appropriated in satisfaction of the surviving spouse's monetary claim on an intestacy and whenever a pecuniary legacy was satisfied by the appropriation of assets with the consent of the beneficiary under the Administration of Estates Act 1925 s 41 (see *Jopling v IRC* (1940)). FA 1985 s 84, however, excluded appropriations in or towards the satisfaction of a general pecuniary legacy and appropriations to a surviving spouse on an intestacy from sale duty and from 1 May 1987 these assents are also free of the fixed 50p duty and the adjudication requirement provided that the appropriate certificate is included (SI 1987/516). Other assents are free of all duty. Therefore property specifically left to a beneficiary under a will is not subject to *ad valorem* duty when it is transferred to that person, nor is property which is appropriated to a surviving spouse in accordance with the intestacy rules.   **[32.47]**

Partnership dissolutions   On the dissolution of a partnership, the division (or partition) of the assets between the partners will not be treated as a sale (*MacLeod v IRC* (1885)) but, if an outgoing partner is 'bought out', the instrument effecting that arrangement will be a sale (*Garnett v IRC* (1899)). A partition document is subject to a fixed 50p duty. The mere withdrawal of partnership capital does not attract any charge and neither does the introduction of cash by an in-coming partner. However, when an in-coming partner pays for an interest in the business, the relevant document may operate as a conveyance on sale. Given these permutations, considerable care should be exercised in structuring both the admission of new partners and the retirement of old partners.

[32.48]

EXAMPLE 32.5

Dave joins the partnership of Bob, Mick & Tom. He contributes capital of £100,000. This by itself will not amount to a sale. If, however, he pays the money to the other partners or they make a simultaneous withdrawal of capital, the deed or instrument of partnership effecting the transaction will be charged as a conveyance or transfer on sale of partnership property to Dave. (For the position when a partnership is incorporated, see Chapter 38.

Exchanges   It has always been important to distinguish sales from exchanges. There was a specific head of charge in the Stamp Act for exchanges which applied to exchanges of real or heritable property (SA 1891 s 73 Sch 1), and which operated as follows.

EXAMPLE 32.6

(1) A exchanges ten shares in Zee Ltd for B's ten shares in Aah Ltd. This is a sale (*Chesterfield Brewery Co v IRC* (1899)).

(2) A exchanges Blackacre for Whiteacre which was owned by B. This is an exchange not a sale and gave rise to fixed duty of 50p. If equality money exceeding £100 was paid by one party to the exchange to the other it was subject to 1% *ad valorem* duty as a sale payable by the purchaser of the property paying the equality money (subject to an exception if the equality money did not exceed £60,000 and the appropriate certificate was included).

FA 1994 s 241 repealed s 73 of the 1891 Act insofar as it applied to exchanges provided that when the consideration for the transfer or vesting of land or the grant of any lease consists of *any* property (not limited to land) and no amount or value is attributed to *that property* on the transfer or vesting of the land, then the market value of that property is subject to *ad valorem* duty. Accordingly, stamp duty is charged on both transfers and an Inland Revenue Press Release of 18 April 1994 (and an article in *Tax Bulletin*, August 1995, p 234) provided guidance on how this operates (as illustrated in the following example):

EXAMPLE 32.7

(1) Bert exchanges his house (worth £100,000) with Daisy for her house (also worth £100,000). Duty of £1,000 is charged on each transfer.
(2) Gerd exchanges his house (worth £50,000) with Franz for his house (worth £50,000). The £60,000 threshold is applied separately to each side of the exchange and as both transfers are within the threshold no duty is payable on either.
(3) Jane exchanges her Putney house worth £100,000 for Jim's Wandsworth house worth £80,000 together with £20,000 (being 'equality money'). The conveyance for the transfer of Jane's house would normally recite that the consideration consists both of Jim's house and the equality money and so will be stamped with duty on £100,000. So far as the transfer of Jim's house is concerned, 'where it is clear from the contract that the intention of the parties to the transaction is that the cheaper property should be transferred for the more expensive property *less* the equality money, the Stamp Office will limit the charge to duty accordingly'. In Jim's case this will mean duty being charged on £80,000 on the conveyance of his house.
(4) Contrast the position when the transaction is set up as a sale. Assume, for instance, that Barry Builder offers a new house for sale for £100,000 and agrees to deal with a buyer who offers him £30,000 in cash and his old house valued at £70,000. Duty at 1% is charged on the sale of the new house: however, the house which Barry Builder receives in part payment is not regarded as a separate sale and so is subject only to the fixed duty of 50p.

It should be noted that an exchange of shares is a sale not an exchange (*Chesterfield Brewery Co v IRC* (1899)) and that two agreements for sale for cash effected by deed of exchange are treated as two separate sale contracts (*Viscount Portman v IRC* (1956)). [32.49]

Sub-sales A purchaser who resells land before it is transferred to him can avoid stamp duty by ensuring that it is transferred directly to a sub-purchaser. The duty is calculated on the sub-sale consideration (SA 1891 s 58(4)(5)). These provisions offer planning opportunities. For instance, the purchaser of land may delay completion relying upon his equitable title that is obtained on exchange of contracts and he may then sell the property to a third party who thus becomes a sub-purchaser. Accordingly, it is that person who is liable for *ad valorem* duty. Similar arrangements may be employed for transfers between companies when the *intra*-group exemption of FA 1930 s 42 is unavailable (see [32.84]).

EXAMPLE 32.8

Selina agrees to purchase Redmeadow from Angela for £80,000. She immediately agrees to resell Redmeadow to Anna for £100,000 and arranges for Angela to convey Redmeadow directly to Anna. Duty will be assessed on Anna on £100,000. No duty will be charged on Selina.
    Instead of the sale of all of Redmeadow to Anna, assume that only one-quarter is resold to her for £25,000. The one-quarter sold to Anna is conveyed directly to her by Angela; the rest is conveyed to Selina. Duty would be charged:
(1) *On Anna* on £25,000 at nil rate.
(2) *On Selina* on three-quarters of her consideration (ie on £75,000).

Note that a partial resale to a connected person would not save any duty, as the operation would be treated as a series of transactions.

To counter an avoidance scheme, SA 1891 s 58(4) and (5) does not apply in respect of sub-sale contracts where the sub-sale consideration is less than the value of the property immediately before the sub-sale. In such a case duty is charged on the price which the property might reasonably be expected to fetch at that time on a sale in the open market. Even before the introduction of this anti-avoidance legislation, the Revenue had begun to challenge the efficacy of this and similar schemes under the *Ramsay* principle (see [**32.67**] and [**36.37**]).   [**32.50**]

'Leaving the matter in contract'   Stamp duty is often avoided by agreeing to transfer the asset and then failing to execute the formal transfer. The contract itself will not normally be subject to duty (for exceptions see SA 1891 s 59) but if it is specifically enforceable (as in the case of land) the purchaser will become the equitable owner of the property by virtue of that agreement. The contract must contemplate that the transaction will be completed. Notice, however, that any attempt to transfer the full legal title (or to recite that the purchaser is the owner of the property) will be subject to duty at the full rate (see, eg, *Oughtred v IRC* (1960)). In the case of a purchase of shares, when the sale is not evinced by a duly stamped instrument, stamp duty reserve tax may be charged on the transaction (see [**32.101**]) and see *Example 32* above).   [**32.51**]

Documents specifically exempted from sale duty under FA 1985   The following dispositions are specifically exempted from *ad valorem* sale duty under SA 1891 Sch 1.
(1) A deed of variation of a deceased person's property made in consideration of the making of a variation in respect of another of the dispositions (see [**32.58**]).
(2) An assent whereby property is appropriated by a PR in or towards the satisfaction of a general pecuniary legacy or in satisfaction of the interest of a surviving spouse on an intestacy (see [**32.47**]).
(3) A transfer of property on matrimonial breakdown (see [**32.59**]).
(4) Company reconstructions not involving any real change in ownership (see [**32.85**]).   [**32.52**]

2   Conveyance or transfer not on sale

a) *General*

In the case of conveyances or transfers of any other kind (ie not on sale) the duty is fixed at 50p. This will include the dispositions considered below and decrees or orders of the court or commissioners whereby property is transferred or vested in any person (SA 1891 s 62). The 1987 Regulations (see [**32.60**]) provide an exemption from the 50p fixed duty in a number of the more common situations where property is transferred otherwise than on sale. There will still be cases, however, where duty remains payable: for instance:
(1) transfer from a beneficial owner to his nominee (including a declaration of trust: see below);
(2) transfer from a nominee to the beneficial owner;
(3) transfer from one nominee to another nominee of the same beneficial owner;
(4) transfer by way of security for a loan or re-transfer to the original transferor on repayment of a loan;

(5) transfer from the trustees of a profit sharing scheme to a participant in the scheme. **[32.53]**

b) *Voluntary dispositions*

Prior to FA 1985, *ad valorem* duty was charged on the value of the property transferred by a voluntary disposition 'as if' it were a conveyance or transfer on sale under F(1909–10)A 1910 s 74. This was not strictly a separate head of charge and the rate of charge was as for a conveyance on sale. FA 1985 s 82, however, abolished the charge to *ad valorem* duty under s 74 in relation to all voluntary dispositions but an adjudication stamp continued to be required together with the fixed 50p duty but those requirements were in turn removed by SI 1987/516 provided that the appropriate certificate is included in the transfer. With the repeal of *ad valorem* duty on gifts, bad bargains and sales at undervalue are charged as 'conveyances on sale' with duty being levied on the actual consideration furnished. **[32.54]**

EXAMPLE 32.9

(1) Junius conveys his house to his son Brutus for £70,000. There is evidence that the open market value of the property is £85,000. *Ad valorem* duty on a conveyance on sale of £70,000 will be charged.
(2) Titan gives his house worth £100,000 to his son Titus. Titus is to discharge the outstanding mortgage on the property of £75,000 in favour of the Rookyu Building Society. *Ad valorem* duty will be charged on a conveyance on sale of £75,000 (the value of the mortgage debt assumed by Titus).

A declaration of trust   Trusts may be created by self-declaration or by transferring the property to trustees to hold for the intended beneficiaries. Instruments which declare trusts are subject to a fixed charge of 50p but the transfer of assets by the settlor to the trustees will not attract duty unless consideration is furnished (when it will be a sale). A trust created by will is not subject to duty. Deeds effecting changes of trustees are not subject to duty provided a certificate is included (Category A of the 1987 Regulations (see **[32.60]** below) and in practice duty is not charged on automatic vestings under the Trustee Act 1925 s 40). **[32.55]**

Orders under the Variation of Trusts Act 1958   When a variation order is made by the courts, there is no longer any requirement to submit a duplicate of the order for stamping (see Practice Direction (Chancery: Stamp Duty on Orders under the Variation of Trusts Act 1958): 3/89). Arrangements will normally involve either a voluntary disposition (falling within Category L) or a declaration of trust attracting a 50p stamp. **[32.56]**

Release and renunciation   Prior to FA 1985 *ad valorem* duty was charged on the release of a life interest in a settlement whereas a fixed duty of 50p only was charged on advancements of capital in favour of remaindermen. It was, accordingly, desirable to ensure that property was advanced to a remainderman rather than passing to him on the surrender of a life interest. As releases are now subject to the fixed 50p duty only, it follows that the stamp duty attractions of advancements have been removed. **[32.57]**

c) *Variations of dispositions of a deceased person*

The CGT and IHT implications of varying or disclaiming dispositions of property of the deceased under his will or under the rules of intestacy are discussed in Chapters 15 and 22 respectively.

Before FA 1985, an instrument of variation was generally liable to *ad valorem* duty as a voluntary disposition and required adjudication, whereas a deed of disclaimer (being a refusal of property) was subject only to the fixed 50p duty applicable to deeds (*Re Stratton's Disclaimer* (1958)). In a very few cases the deed of variation would constitute a sale and be subject, therefore, to *ad valorem* sale duty. FA 1985 provided an exemption from *ad valorem* duty for all deeds of variation and the fixed 50p duty and adjudication requirement were removed by SI 1987/516 provided that the appropriate certificate is included. With the abolition of the fixed 50p duty on deeds neither variations nor disclaimers attract duty although in the former case the certification requirements of SI 1987/516 must be satisfied.　　　　　　　**[32.58]**

d) *Transfers of property on matrimonial breakdown*

Until FA 1985 there was no specific exemption from duty for transfers of property between spouses and former spouses. Thus, any such transfer made on the breakdown of marriage was subject to *ad valorem* sale duty, unless it was made pursuant to a court order or a separation deed when only the fixed 50p duty was charged.

FA 1985 s 83, however, provided that any instrument which transferred property from one party to the marriage to the other was specifically exempt from sale duty and subject to a fixed 50p duty only provided that the disposition was made pursuant to a court order on divorce, nullity or judicial separation; or to a court order made later, but in connection with the divorce or to an agreement made between the parties in connection with the breakdown of that marriage (see **[41.66]**). SI 1987/516 completed the process by removing the 50p duty and adjudication requirement.　　　　　　　**[32.59]**

e) *Stamp Duty (Exempt Instruments) Regulations 1987*

Instruments falling within the categories listed in the Schedule to these Regulations, which are correctly certified, are exempted from the fixed duty of 50p which would otherwise be chargeable and should not be presented at stamp offices for adjudication. The appropriate certificate should be included in, endorsed or attached to, the instrument and should refer to the category in the Schedule under which exemption is claimed. The following is a suggested form of wording for such certificates:

> 'I hereby certify that this instrument falls within category　　　in the Schedule to the Stamp Duty (Exempt Instruments) Regulations 1987.'

The following are the exempt categories:

Category A: The vesting of property subject to a trust in the trustees on the appointment of a new trustee or in the continuing trustees on the retirement of a trustee.

Category B: The conveyance or transfer of property subject of a specific devise or legacy to a beneficiary named in the will (contrast Category D below).

Category C: The conveyance or transfer of property which forms part of an intestate estate to the person entitled on intestacy.

Category D: The appropriation of property in satisfaction of a general legacy of money or in satisfaction of any interest of a surviving spouse in an intestate's estate.

Category E: The conveyance or transfer of property forming part of the residuary estate of a testator to a beneficiary entitled under the will.

Category F: The conveyance or transfer of property out of a settlement in or towards the satisfaction of a beneficiary's interest in accordance with the provisions of the settlement (the relevant interest must not have been acquired for money or money's worth).

Category G: The conveyance or transfer of property on and in consideration of marriage to a party or to trustees to be held on a marriage settlement.

Category H: The conveyance or transfer of property in connection with divorce etc (see above).

Category I: The conveyance or transfer by the liquidator of property which formed part of the assets of the company in a liquidation to a shareholder in satisfaction of his rights on the winding up.

Category J: The grant in fee simple of an easement in or over land for no consideration in money or money's worth.

Category K: The grant of a servitude for no consideration in money or money's worth.

Category L: The conveyance or transfer of property as a voluntary disposition inter vivos.

Category M: The conveyance or transfer of property under a post death variation. **[32.60]**

3 Leases and agreements for leases

a) *Ambit of SA 1891 Sch 1*

Duty is levied in accordance with SA 1891 Sch 1 on the grant of a lease or tack (tack is the Scottish equivalent of lease). To be dutiable the lease must be of land, tenements or heritable subjects; leases of personalty are not included. Likewise, duty is not charged on licences because they do not confer a proprietary interest in the land. An agreement for a lease is charged to duty as if it were a lease: ie for the term and consideration provided (see **[32.67]**). **[32.61]**

b) *Duty on rent and premium*

Stamp duty is charged on both the rent and the premium reserved in a lease. The premium is charged in the same way as if it were the consideration for a sale. Duty is, therefore, *ad valorem* unless the nil rate band applies which it does not if any associated rent payable under the lease averages more than £600 pa. Leases to charities are exempt from duty (FA 1982 s 129). A lease or agreement for a lease for seven years or more must also be produced and stamped with a produced stamp.

In general, fixed duties are charged on short-term leases at low rents and *ad valorem* duty on leases for more than a year and on periodic tenancies. The duty on rent is as follows: **[32.62]**

(i) *Lease for a definite term of less than one year* In the case of a furnished letting for a definite term of less than one year there is no duty if the rent is below £500 pa; if it exceeds £500 pa, duty of £1 is payable. In other cases duty is charged as if the lease were a lease for one year at the actual rent reserved. **[32.63]**

(ii) *Leases for a definite term of at least one year or for an indefinite term*

Term not exceeding seven years or indefinite		
rent not exceeding £500 pa	nil	
rent exceeding £500 pa	50p duty per £50 or part thereof	(1%)
Term exceeding seven years but not 35 years	£1 per £50 or part thereof	(2%)
Term exceeding 35 years but not 100 years	£6 per £50 or part thereof	(12%)
Term exceeding 100 years	£12 per £50 or part thereof	(24%)

(iii) Leases exceeding seven years   The above level of duty on rent is charged on a sliding scale if the rent does not exceed £500 pa (for details see FA 1982 s 128(3)).

Where all or a part of the consideration for a lease for a definite term in excess of one year, or for an indefinite term, is money or stock or security (a premium), duty is charged on the value of that consideration at the rates which apply to a conveyance or transfer on sale. *Ad valorem* duty will, therefore, be charged although the nil rate band will apply (if a certificate of value is included in the lease) unless the rent exceeds £600 pa.   **[32.64]**

EXAMPLE 32.10

(1)   Bos grants Big a ten-year lease at a rent of £250 pa and a premium of £59,000. As the term exceeds seven years, the normal charge on the rent will be at 1%, but since the rent is below £500 pa a sliding scale will apply (currently duty will be £5). So long as the lease contains a certificate of value, duty will be charged at nil% on the premium of £59,000.

(2)   Rac Developers wish to take a 150-year lease on a development site. However, because stamp duty at a rate of 24% would be payable, it is agreed that they will take a 99-year lease with an option to renew for a further 51 years. Duty payable is therefore halved.

c) *Terminology*

The term *'premium'* does not appear in the Act which imposes duty on 'consideration, moving either to the lessor or to any other person, consisting of money, stock or security'. It should be noted, therefore, that the premium, if paid to a person other than the landlord, still attracts duty. Where the tenant is obliged under the terms of the lease to carry out improvements either to the property let, or to any other property of the landlord, the value of such works is not subject to stamp duty.

There is no definition of *'rent'*. It is in essence a payment reserved out of the land, paid by the tenant to recompense the landlord for loss of exclusive possession. Any service charge reserved in addition to rent is assessed as rent. If that charge is unascertained, as where it is a proportion of the costs incurred from time to time, or is dependent upon services provided by the landlord, fixed duty of £2 is payable and the basic rent is subject to *ad valorem* duty.

d) *Operation of contingency principle and FA 1994 s 242*

If the amount of rent is unascertained but the lease stipulates for a maximum rent, that sum attracts duty. In the absence of a maximum figure, a specified minimum rent or a basic rent which is subject to adjustment could be charged (for this so-called 'contingency principle', see *Coventry City Council v IRC* (1978) and **[32.44]**). In the absence of a maximum or minimum rent so that the rent is wholly unascertainable it is taken to be market rent at that time (FA 1994 s 242(4)). A progressive rent is averaged over the term of a lease.   **[32.65]**

EXAMPLE 32.11

Lord grants Serf a ten-year lease. For the first five years the rent is £1,000 pa; thereafter £1,500 pa. The average rent (on which duty is assessed) is £1,250 pa. (Duty will be at £1 per £50—ie £25.) Had the lease merely provided for a rent review at the end of five years, duty would be charged on the actual rent reserved (£1,000).

e) *Duration of a lease*

As duty on rent is determined primarily by the duration of the lease, its length must be identified at the date of execution. In general, any part of a term commencing before the date of execution of the lease is ignored (which can have unfortunate results: see *Example 32.12(4)*). The following rules apply to ascertain the duration of a lease.

First, a lease for a term of years with an option to renew for a further specified period is subject to duty on the original term. *Secondly*, on a lease for a fixed term which can thereafter be determined by notice, the term is taken as the length of the fixed term plus the period that must elapse before determination (FA 1963 s 56(3)). *Thirdly*, a lease for a specified period which may be terminable on an earlier event occurring is treated as a lease for the specified period and not as a lease for an indefinite period. *Fourthly*, leases for life or lives or for a term of years determinable on the marriage of the lessee are treated as leases for 90 years in accordance with the LPA 1925 s 149(6).   [**32.66**]

EXAMPLE 32.12

(1) A ten-year term with an option to renew for a further five years is charged as a ten-year lease.

(2) A seven-year term is granted which may thereafter be determined on giving six months' notice after the expiration of that term. Duty would be assessed on the basis of a lease for seven years six months.

(3) A lease granted for 99 years if A, B and C should live so long is treated as a lease exceeding 35 years and not exceeding 100 (*Earl Mount Edgcumbe v IRC* (1911)).

(4) A 99-year lease begins to run on 29 September 1989, but is only formally executed on 25 March 1990. If the rent charged is £50 pa for the first 33 years; £100 pa for the next 33 years, with £150 pa being charged for the final 33 years, duty will be charged on an average rent of £100.25 pa (ie the average rent taking the length of the lease to be 98½ years). Duty is, therefore, £18 whereas on an average rent of £100 (ie if spread over the actual duration of the 99-year lease) it would have been only £12!

---

f) *Agreements for a lease*

An agreement for a lease for a term of less than 35 years or for an indefinite term has always been charged as a lease for the term and consideration specified in the agreement (SA 1891 s 75(1) and see FA 1994 s 240 dealing with time for presenting agreements for a lease). Accordingly, agreements for a lease for a fixed term in *excess of* 35 years were excluded from duty with the result that a widely used stamp duty avoidance scheme was devised whereby the purchaser of a freehold or long leasehold interest arranged for a nominee to agree to take a lease exceeding 35 years from the vendor. The purchaser then acquired the superior interest for a nominal consideration. In *Ingram v IRC* (1986) it was held that such schemes fell within the *Ramsay* principle and that the lease could therefore be ignored and duty on the entire purchase price charged upon the conveyance of the freehold reversion (the case is discussed at [**36.37**]). Before this decision, FA 1984 s 111 amended the existing legislation by providing that an agreement for a lease for a term exceeding 35 years was to be charged under s 75. The duty paid thereon must be denoted on any conveyance of a freehold or leasehold interest in land against which the agreement is directly enforceable (eg when the agreement is for a sub-lease it need not be denoted on a conveyance of the freehold reversion). The penalty for not stamping any agreement for a lease falls on the 'lessee' (SA 1891 s 11).

A lease later made to carry out (substantially) the terms of the agreement is chargeable on the difference between the duty paid on the agreement and any duty then payable (SA 1891 s 75(2)): however, duty on the agreement for lease is not repayable (eg if the lease is not subsequently granted or if a reduced amount would have been payable on the lease as granted). Leases must either contain a certificate that there was no prior agreement to be stamped or stamped with the appropriate denoting stamp (FA 1994 s 240): otherwise the lease will not be stamped unless it is accompanied by the agreement for lease.   **[32.67]**

g) *Surrenders and regrants*

When a lease is surrendered, the surrender is subject to duty as a conveyance or transfer on sale on any consideration paid by the landlord. If no consideration is paid, the fixed 50p duty is charged. Formerly duty could therefore be avoided by an agreement for surrender being entered into but for the actual surrender to be by operation of law ie—tenant handing over the lease and keys in return for cash—since then there was no document to stamp (a mere agreement not being a conveyance and hence not attracting duty). Not surprisingly FA 1994 s 243 now provides that a written agreement for surrender/renunciation is dutiable as if it were a deed but only, to avoid a double charge, if the surrender/renunciation is not carried out by deed. The Stamp Office considers that a formal agreement is not necessary and that *any document* evidencing the agreement is now stampable.

Where a lease is surrendered and a new lease of the same property granted, the new lease will be assessed on any rent or premium as usual but ignoring the value of the surrendered lease (SA 1891 s 77(1) and see *Tax Bulletin*, August 1995, p 235). Exemption under s 77(1) will not be refused because of minor changes in the property subject to the lease so long as these can be seen as *de minimis*. Similar treatment applies where a variation of a lease takes effect in law as a surrender and regrant.

When a lease on one property is replaced by a lease on another if the relevant document recited that the consideration for the grant of the new lease was the surrender of the old, duty on the grant would be charged, *inter alia*, by reference to the market value of the lease surrendered. So far as the surrendered lease is concerned it is rare for a deed of surrender to be produced for stamping either because the new lease supersedes the old by operation of law or because the document is not produced. Duty is not attracted when a lease expires at the end of its term. For sale and leaseback, see *Tax Bulletin*, August 1995, at p 235.   **[32.68]**

4   **Contracts chargeable as conveyances on sale**

The practice of 'leaving matters in contract' has already been noted (see **[32.51]**). Duty may thereby be avoided on a conveyance of realty so long as the purchaser is prepared to take only an equitable title to the property transferred. In practice this will often be unacceptable so that a formal transfer will be executed and duty paid. When goodwill and equitable interests are sold, however, the contract will be specifically enforceable and, for practical purposes, there would be no need to execute a formal conveyance or transfer. Duty would, therefore, not be paid on such sales (see *IRC v G Angus & Co* (1889)). To ensure that duty is not so easily avoided SA 1891 s 59 provides that:

> 'Any contract or agreement for the sale of any equitable estate or interest in any property whatsoever, or for the sale of any estate or interest in any property except lands, tenements, hereditaments, or heritages, or property locally situate out of the United Kingdom, or goods, wares or merchandise, or stock, or marketable securities, or any ship or vessel, or part interest, share, or property of or in any ship or vessel, shall be charged with the same ad valorem duty, to be paid by the purchaser, as if it were an actual conveyance on sale of the estate, interest, or property contracted or agreed to be sold.'

The provision starts by imposing liability to *ad valorem* duty on all sale contracts but then excludes from its ambit the most common categories of property (eg land and shares) leaving only a residue of assets subject to the duty, principally debts, goodwill, and the benefit of contracts. The asset must be situated in the UK. An agreement for a lease falls outside the section (but see [**32.67**]), but an option to purchase a legal interest in land is an equitable interest and, thus, within the charge (*George Wimpey & Co Ltd v IRC* (1975)). If duty is charged under s 59, a subsequent conveyance or transfer of the property is not subject to further *ad valorem* duty and should be stamped with a denoting stamp (see s 59(3)). In many cases a number of assets are agreed to be sold for one consideration. For stamp duty purposes an apportionment of that consideration amongst the assets will need to be made on Form Stamps 22. The most important transaction caught by SA 1891 s 59 is the sale of a business (see further Chapter 38). [**32.69**]

5 Partitions (SA 1891 s 73 and Sch 1 as amended by FA 1994)

For partitions of any estate or interest in land fixed duty of 50p is charged unless consideration in excess of £100 is given for equality. If so, *ad valorem* duty is charged on that equality money unless the nil rate applies (SA 1891 s 73 and Sch 1). For exchanges or partitions of any other property, fixed duty of 50p is charged on any document as a conveyance or transfer not on sale. It is important that a partition is not drafted as an exchange of beneficial interests (see [**32.49**]).

The severance and partition of an equitable joint tenancy in land is carried out by a notice to sever (LPA 1925 s 36(2); Trusts of Land and Appointment of Trustees Act 1996 s 7) which must be in writing but will not be subject to duty. [**32.70**]

6 Depositary receipts (FA 1986 ss 67-69)

A 1½% charge is normally imposed when UK shares are converted into depositary receipts or transferred to a clearing house for transfer through a computerised settlement system which enables UK shares to be bought and sold without payment of stamp duty. The charge is levied on the consideration paid if the transfer falls under the conveyance or transfer on sale head of charge: otherwise, if shares are deposited by the owner in exchange for a depositary receipt, it is levied on the value of the shares at that time (see further [**32.101**] and see FA 1986 s 97A inserted by FA 1996 s 196). [**32.71**]

7 Other documents subject to stamp duty

In addition to the occasions of charge already considered, *ad valorem* duty is chargeable on certain bearer instruments (see FA 1963 s 59) at varying rates from 1½% of the market value to 10p for every £50 or part thereof of the market value and bonds, covenants or instruments increasing the rent reserved by another instrument are dutiable as a lease in consideration of the additional rent thereby made payable (see SA 1891 s 77(5)). FA 1985 s 85 abolished some 13 of the previous heads of fixed duty, including the residual 50p duty on deeds not chargeable under any other head. Accordingly, the fixed duties that, currently, remain are chargeable in respect of the following documents only:

(1) conveyance or transfer of any other kind - 50p (see [**32.53**]);
(2) duplicate or counterpart of any instrument chargeable with duty (eg a lease) - maximum 50p (see SA 1891 ss 72, 11);
(3) exchange or partition relating to realty where the amount of the equalisation payments does not exceed £100 - 50p;

(4) lease of a furnished letting for a definite term of less than one year where the rent for the whole term exceeds £500 - £1 (see [**32.63**]);
(5) leases not stampable under any other head - £2;
(6) release or renunciation of any property or interest in property and which is not subject to sale duty (eg a partnership share) see [**32.57**] - 50p;
(7) surrender of any kind which is not chargeable to sale duty - 50p;
(8) transfers from a beneficial owner to his nominee and *vice versa* - 50p;
(9) transfers by way of security for a loan or retransfer on repayment - 50p;
(10) transfers from trustees of a profit sharing scheme to a participant - 50p.
[**32.72**]–[**32.80**]

IV EXEMPTIONS AND RELIEFS FROM STAMP DUTY

1 General

Exemption from duty is conferred upon a number of documents, in particular:
(1) wills;
(2) contracts of employment;
(3) transfers to a charitable body, charitable trust or to the trustees of the National Heritage Memorial Fund (FA 1982 s 129);
(4) renounceable letters of allotment with a renunciation period not exceeding six months (although if transferred for value they will attract SDRT, see [**32.101**]);
(5) transfers of gilts and loan stock which cannot be converted into equities (but including loan stock convertible into other, non-convertible, loan stock);
(6) mortgages.   [**32.81**]

2 Exemptions from stamp duty for companies

FA 1986 pursued a policy of reducing the rate of duty on sales of shares and securities from 1% to ½% and of extending the scope of duty in order to preserve 'fiscal neutrality'. Hence a number of transactions which were not subject to duty because they were exempt were brought into charge. Thus, contracts by which a company agrees to buy back its own shares attract duty which is charged on the relevant return to the Registrar of Companies (Form 169). Similarly, the transfer of a renounceable letter of allotment (save where it relates to stock which would itself be exempt if transferred) has been brought into charge. Formerly there were a number of reliefs from duty on company reconstructions and takeovers but these reliefs were generally removed so that duty at ½% became payable. The reliefs in question are as follows:
(1) *FA 1927 s 55* relief on certain reconstructions and amalgamations.
(2) *FA 1985 s 78* relief on 'paper for paper' exchanges.
(3) *FA 1985 s 79* relief on a reconstruction under the Insolvency Act 1986 ss 110, 111.
(4) *FA 1980 Sch 18 para 12* relief on certain demergers.
It should be noted, however, that the substance of FA 1927 s 55 is preserved by FA 1986 s 76 as a relief to ensure that the transfer of an undertaking is subject to duty at ½% and not the full 1% which is normally charged on sales. This new relief differs from the old s 55 in that there is no requirement that the transaction be a reconstruction or amalgamation and, as the shares may be issued to any of the target company's shareholders, it is available to demergers taking the form of a transfer of a trade to a new company. Adjudication is required.   [**32.82**]
The following exemptions from duty remain.

a) A demerger which is effected by a direct distribution of a subsidiary's shares since this is not a conveyance on sale   **[32.83]**

b) Transfers between associated companies (FA 1930 s 42 as amended)

Conveyance or transfer duty is not charged on an instrument by which one company transfers property to an associated company. The detailed requirements are in FA 1930 s 42 which requires that one of the companies in question must beneficially own, directly or indirectly, at least 75% (by nominal value) of the ordinary share capital of the other, or a third company beneficially owns, directly or indirectly at least 75% of the ordinary share capital of each (in general terms the relief accords with group relief: see **[30.41]**). The grant of a new lease from one group company to another qualifies for relief in the same way as an assignment (see FA 1995 s 151 for agreements for lease).

FA 1967 s 27(3) contains provisions to prevent abuse of the s 42 relief; of particular note is the requirement that the transaction in respect of which relief is sought must not form part of an arrangement whereby the transferor's interest in the transferee's share capital will be reduced below 75%. It is therefore necessary to apply for adjudication of the instrument effecting the transfer. The claim to intra-group relief is made by a statutory declaration by an officer of the company.   **[32.84]**

c) Reconstructions where there is no real change of ownership (FA 1986 s 75 and s 77)

Exemption from ad valorem duty is given when, pursuant to a scheme of reconstruction of the target company, the whole or part of its undertaking (s 75), or the whole of its issued share capital (s 77), is acquired by the acquiring company. The registered office of the acquirer must be in the UK and, apart from the assumption of liabilities, the consideration furnished must be shares in the acquirer. These consideration shares must be issued to all shareholders of the target company only (and not to that company itself) and the acquisition must be for *bona fide* commercial reasons and not have any tax avoidance as a main purpose. After the acquisition each shareholder in the target company must hold shares in the acquirer and vice versa and the proportion of the shares of one company held by any shareholder must be the same as the proportion of the shares in the other company held by that same shareholder (ie the shares must be issued on a *pro rata* basis). Any instrument employed to convey or transfer property under such a reconstruction requires adjudication. Given these requirements, which ensure that the undertaking is held by the same shareholders before and after the acquisition, this exemption is extremely limited. A reconstruction under the Insolvency Act 1986 ss 110, 111 may fall within this relief as illustrated below:

Illustration 1

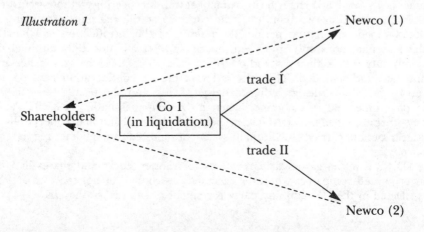

Company 1 is liquidated and its two component trades are split with the ownership being transferred to Newco (1) and Newco (2). Those companies then issue shares to the shareholders of Company 1. This reconstruction qualifies for relief: contrast, however, the following illustration which does not:

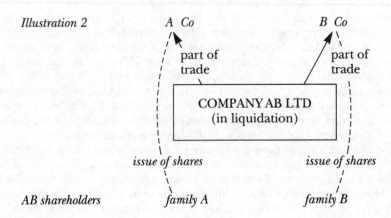

Illustration 2

In *Illustration 2* there is a similar partition but, instead of the shares in the two new companies being divided amongst all the original shareholders, the shares in A Co now pass only to the original shareholders who comprised the A family and the B Co shares to the B family.   **[32.85]–[32.100]**

V STAMP DUTY RESERVE TAX (SDRT)

SDRT is only chargeable on agreements to transfer chargeable securities and ensures that on any purchase of shares duty is payable at ½% even if there is no relevant document to stamp (FA 1986 Part IV). Hence SDRT applies to purchasers unless the sale is evidenced by a duly stamped instrument and, in particular, applies where the shares are registered in the name of a nominee who acts for both buyer and seller and when letters of allotment are transferred. The charge applies to stock, shares, loan capital (generally issued by UK incorporated companies), units in unit trusts together with the right to subscribe for stock, shares or loan capital but does not apply to stocks and shares which are exempt from duty (eg gilt-edged securities); nor to traded options within TCGA 1992 s 144(8); nor to stock or securities subject to charge under the bearer head.

For duty (at ½%) to be payable there must be an agreement to transfer chargeable securities (defined in FA 1986 s 99(3)) for a consideration in money or money's worth and either no instrument of transfer covering all those securities is executed within two months of the contract or the relevant instrument is not stamped within that period. As a result of the introduction of CREST this rule does not apply to agreements made after 30 June 1996 although if stamp duty is subsequently paid on the transfer the SDRT charge is cancelled and tax paid refunded. The duty is levied on the consideration paid or, in cases other than sales at a fixed charge of 50p and the transferee is liable to pay (unless he is a nominee when his principal is liable). CREST (and any other approved paperless system) has a statutory obligation to collect SDRT on transactions carried out within its system or reported through it for regulatory purposes.

SDRT is a charge on all agreements to transfer stocks and shares in UK incorporated companies wherever executed: ie whether or not the transaction is effected in the UK and any party is resident or situated in the UK.

EXAMPLE 32.13

(1) Adam receives a renounceable letter of allotment of shares in Zeta Ltd.
  (i) If he applies to be registered there will be no charge to duty since there has been no transfer of the rights comprised in the letter.
  (ii) If he renounces the rights and transfers the letter of allotment to Bertha who in turn transfers to Charles, SDRT may apply to those transfers.
(2) Bertram buys and sells securities within the same Stock Exchange account or there is a purchase of shares which are registered in the name of a nominee acting for both seller and purchaser. Given that in both cases there is an agreement to transfer chargeable securities for consideration, Bertram is subject to SDRT.

In addition to the principal charge described above, SDRT also applies to shares converted into depositary receipts and to shares put into a clearance system. As it is designed to supplement the charge to duty on depositary receipts (see [**32.71**]), it is charged at a rate of $1\frac{1}{2}\%$ subject to an option, introduced by FA 1996 s 196, enabling as an alternative clearance services to opt for the normal SDRT charges to apply to transactions within the service.   [**32.101**]

33 VAT

I BACKGROUND

'*Taxe sur la valeur adjoutée*', introduced in France in the mid-1950s, provided the model for the system of value added tax (VAT) subsequently adopted by the European Community (EC). The objective of the EC—to establish a common market—required the free movement of goods, persons, services and capital, and as a result necessitated the removal of internal frontiers and the harmonisation of indirect taxes within member states (see the original wording of the EC Treaty art 99). The founder members introduced a common system of VAT in place of their individual turnover taxes by 1 January 1973, and on becoming a member, the UK replaced its existing taxes (purchase tax and selective employment tax) with VAT by FA 1972 (effective from 1 April 1973).

The European Communities Act 1972 s 1 provides for the implementation of Community legislation in UK law and, in particular, for it to take precedence over UK law (direct effect). All regulations and all or part of some directives form part of UK law to be applied by UK tribunals and courts. In cases where UK legislation complies with the relevant Community provision the question of direct effect is irrelevant; by contrast, if Parliament has failed to implement an EC provision or if UK legislation is inconsistent with such a provision, a taxpayer may, but is not obliged, to rely upon direct effect in the UK courts. The Revenue cannot, however, place reliance on EC legislation to remedy a defect in UK legislation.

The EC Sixth Directive (17 May 1977) set out a uniform basis of assessment by, for instance, clarifying transactions within the scope of the tax and abolishing certain derogations permitted by previous EC legislation on VAT (usually on administrative or social grounds). The provisions of the EC Sixth Directive are required to be implemented in all member states' VAT legislation.

[**33.1**]

1 UK legislation and administration

The basic legislation is in the consolidating VATA 1994. Many of the detailed rules are in orders, rules and regulations made by SIs (VATA 1994 s 97). Notices set out the views of Customs on the operation of the legislation and do not generally have the force of law. Certain leaflets or part of them, however, are issued under statutory authority. They include parts of Notice 700 (The VAT Guide), Notice 727 and associated leaflets dealing with retail schemes and Notice 703 in regard to evidence of export. Extra statutory concessions are contained in notices and leaflets (listed and catalogued in Notice No 748).

The Commissioners of Customs & Excise are responsible for the collection and management of VAT (VATA 1994 Sch 11 para 1). Appeals against decisions of the Commissioners on specified matters lie to VAT tribunals (VATA 1994 s 83). Thereafter appeal lies to the High Court (a single judge in the Queen's Bench Division), to the Court of Appeal and, finally, to the House of Lords.

Under the EC Treaty art 77, the European Court of Justice has jurisdiction to give preliminary rulings on matters of the interpretation of EC law referred to it by national courts (which include VAT tribunals) but cannot decide the case. The decision to make a reference is one for the particular national court: an individual has no right of access to the European Court of Justice (on this matter see *Naturally Yours Cosmetics Ltd v C & E Comrs* (1988) where a VAT tribunal obtained a ruling from the European Court of Justice on the meaning of 'taxable amount').   [**33.2**]

2 Mechanics of VAT

VAT is an indirect tax (ie it is levied on consumption rather than on income) which is collected at each stage of a commercial chain.

In *Example 33.1* below a VAT rate of 17½% is assumed throughout and, for the sake of illustration, it deals with a single transaction. In reality, VAT is calculated on turnover during a given period and on inputs during that period, not on particular supplies (see further note (3) to the example).

EXAMPLE 33.1

	Costs (£) (excluding VAT)	Sale (£) (excluding VAT)	VAT (£) on costs (input)	VAT (£) on sale (output)	Paid to Customs (£)
Producer	—	20,000	—	3,500	3,500
Manufacturer	20,000	30,000	3,500	5,250	1,750
Wholesaler	30,000	45,000	5,250	7,875	2,625
Retailer	45,000	58,000	7,875	10,150	2,275
Customer	58,000	—	10,150	—	—
					10,150

Notes:
(1) Each taxable person in the chain must charge VAT on supplies made to customers (outputs). This is termed output VAT and must be accounted for to Customs. So far as VAT on supplies which he has received (inputs) is concerned, this is input tax and can be recovered from Customs provided that it is attributable to a taxable supply made or to be made (VATA 1994 s 26) and appropriate evidence is held. If input tax exceeds output tax the excess can be recovered in full provided, as stated above, that it is attributable to a taxable supply (VATA 1994 s 25(3)). Output tax is only charged on supplies made in the course or furtherance of a business: input tax is only refunded if inputs are used or are to be used for business purposes.
(2) The final tax (£10,150) is wholly borne by the consumer (for VAT purposes this means someone who cannot recover VAT because he is not registered).
(3) The VAT mechanism is intended to ensure that ultimately the VAT paid (£10,150) is exactly 17½% of the taxable value (£58,000). However, since supplies of goods or services which are exempt or outside the scope of VAT may have borne VAT which is not identified and not recoverable, this objective is not always achieved.

In order to ensure that all consumption is taxed, provision exists for the taxation of goods and services imported into the UK in certain circumstances. **[33.3]**

3 Taxable and exempt supplies

The general rule is that all supplies are subject to VAT. However, there are three specific reliefs from the obligation to charge VAT, ie goods or services may be subject to a lower, but positive, rate of VAT such as fuel and power and certain antiques and collectors' items. VAT may also be charged at the zero-rate or a supply may be exempt from VAT. Where a supply is potentially both zero-rated and exempt, zero-rating takes precedence. **[33.4]**

The standard rate applies to most transactions. Currently it is 17½% but, in the past, it has been 8%, 10% and 15%. The rate may be changed by SI upwards or downwards, by up to 25% of the rate then applicable (VATA 1994 s 2(2)). The member states of what is now the European Union (EU) have currently agreed a *minimum standard rate* of 15% subject to review. In practice, changes in the VAT rate have always been made in a Finance Act. **[33.5]**

Zero-rated supplies A supply that is zero-rated is a taxable supply which is taxed at a 0% VAT rate. A person who makes zero-rated supplies is able to recover any input tax incurred in making zero-rated supplies provided he is registered for VAT.

The zero rate was introduced for social and political reasons and covers supplies of food, books and newspapers, and children's clothing. Formerly, zero-rating covered a wider area (in particular, all new construction work) but the European Court of Justice held that some cases were in breach of the Sixth Directive with the result that UK law was amended.

The following heads of supply are zero-rated (see VATA 1994 Sch 8):

Group 1	food
Group 2	sewerage services and water
Group 3	books, newspapers etc
Group 4	talking books for the blind and handicapped and wireless sets for the blind
Group 5	construction of dwellings etc
Group 6	protected buildings
Group 7	international services
Group 8	transport
Group 9	caravans and houseboats
Group 10	gold
Group 11	banknotes
Group 12	drugs, medicine, aids for the handicapped etc
Group 13	imports/exports etc
Group 14	tax-free shops
Group 15	charities etc
Group 16	clothing and footwear **[33.6]**

Exempt supplies By contrast with zero-rating, a business which makes exempt supplies does not charge output VAT on those supplies because they are not taxable, but cannot recover any input VAT relating to them. The following (listed in VATA 1994 Sch 9) are the heads of exempt supply:

Group 1	land
Group 2	insurance
Group 3	postal services

Group 4	betting, gaming and lottery
Group 5	finance
Group 6	education
Group 7	health and welfare
Group 8	burial and cremation
Group 9	trade unions and professional bodies
Group 10	sports/sports competitions and physical education
Group 11	works of art etc
Group 12	fund raising events by charities and other qualifying bodies
Group 13	cultural services etc (effective 1 June 1996)

Businesses which make a mixture of taxable (including zero-rated) and exempt supplies are referred to as *partly exempt;* input VAT directly attributable to taxable supplies is recoverable; that directly attributable to exempt supplies is irrecoverable and that which cannot be directly attributed (eg VAT on overheads) may be recovered in part: see further [**33.82**].

Certain business expenses (such as wages and salaries and local authority rates) are wholly outside the scope of VAT. Not all input tax is recoverable even if attributable to taxable supplies: examples include the cost of entertaining customers; expenses incurred by a company in providing domestic accommodation to directors and their families and expenditure other than for business purposes. There are anti-avoidance provisions preventing VAT being avoided by overcharging on insurance premiums where insurance is supplied in a package with other goods or services liable to VAT. In addition, supplies of goods and services made outside the UK are outside the scope of UK VAT.   [**33.7**]

The VAT fraction   In *Example 33.1* above, note that the purchaser pays a total price of £58,000 + £10,150 = £68,150 for the goods. VAT as a percentage of that gross price is therefore 10,150/68,150 = 7/47. This 'VAT fraction' is used to calculate tax in cases where the price is 'tax inclusive'. It is particularly important at the retail level, where it is common for the price of goods to include VAT. If no mention is made of VAT and the contract does not provide otherwise the consideration paid for the supply is VAT inclusive and the supplier must bear the tax. (See, however, VATA 1994 s 89, which provides that if, after the entering into of a contract, there is a change in the VAT rate (or a change in the VAT liability of a supply) then, unless the contract otherwise provides, the contractual price will be altered to take account of the change.)   [**33.8**]

4   Relationship between VAT and other taxes

CGT   SP 8/73 provides, in the context of CGT, that in cases where VAT paid on the purchase of an asset is recoverable the CGT acquisition cost of the asset will exclude VAT. If no recovery is available the price will be VAT inclusive. On the disposal of an asset, VAT chargeable is ignored in computing the capital gain. Subsequent adjustments to VAT recovery eg under the Capital Goods Scheme [**33.89**]–[**33.100**] are treated as additional capital expenditure or disposal provisions in the period of adjustment   [**33.9**]

Income tax   For income tax purposes, irrecoverable VAT may be deducted as a business expense (see IR Press Release, 7 May 1973) except to the extent that it forms part of the cost of a capital item, in which case, it will be subject to capital allowances, if eligible.   [**33.10**]

Stamp duty The relationship between VAT and stamp duty is set out in SP 11/91. So far as stamp duty is concerned, the consideration on a sale is the price *inclusive* of VAT. By contrast, VAT is *not charged* on stamp duty which is paid by a purchaser direct to the Inland Revenue and not to the supplier.

[**33.11**]-[**33.20**]

EXAMPLE 33.2

Ben, a retailer, acquired a computer from a manufacturer for £23,500 (including VAT). He has just sold it to a customer, Charlie, for £50,000 (excluding VAT).

(1) *VAT:* Ben must charge the customer output tax of £8,750. Input tax of £3,500 is fully recoverable.
(2) *Income tax:* The purchase price, £20,000 net of VAT, is a deductible business expense (TA 1988 s 74). The sale consideration of £50,000 is an income receipt.
(3) *CGT:* Charlie's acquisition cost for CGT purposes is £50,000 + £8,750 (VAT) = £58,750, assuming Charlie cannot recover the VAT.

II TAXABLE PERSONS AND TRANSACTIONS

VAT is charged on *taxable supplies of goods* and *services* made in the UK by a *taxable person* in the course or furtherance of a *business* carried on by him (VATA 1994 s 4(1)). It is possible for a taxable person to make supplies otherwise than in the course or furtherance of his business, eg an individual who sells a private asset or a charity which makes a charitable disposal. Such supplies fall outside the scope of VAT. Goods imported into the UK from outside the EU are also chargeable irrespective of whether they are imported for business purposes and whether the importer is a taxable person. With regard to goods imported from within the EU: see [**34.63**]. Certain services received from abroad are also chargeable but, in this case, only if received by a person for the purpose of his business and on a self-supply basis (see [**33.30**]). By contrast, exports of goods are generally zero-rated and some (although not all) exported services are zero-rated (see [**34.61**]). [**33.21**]

1 A taxable supply

The supply must be made in the UK, which for these purposes means England, Scotland, Wales and Northern Ireland and the territorial sea but not the Isle of Man or the Channel Islands although the Manx VAT system is, in effect, identical with that of the UK. Good title does not have to pass. The transfer of possession of goods in circumstances where it is contemplated that title will pass in the future may be a supply of goods. [**33.22**]

2 A supply of goods

Schedule 4 provides what matters are to be treated as supplies of goods and what are supplies of services; because Sch 4 implements EC VAT law in some cases the definitions are not consistent with established legal practice in other areas. For instance, the production of goods by applying a process to goods belonging to someone else is not, as might be expected, a supply of services but of goods. Similarly, the sale of a freehold interest in land or grant, assignment or surrender of a lease exceeding 21 years is treated as a supply of goods (VATA 1994 Sch 4 para 4) whereas in common legal parlance goods would not normally include land.

Where goods forming part of the assets of the business are disposed of so as no longer to form part of those assets, whether or not for a consideration, there is generally a supply of goods (VATA 1994 Sch 4 para 5(1)).

Where a person ceases to be a taxable person, goods then forming part of the assets of the business carried on by him are deemed to be supplied by him and VAT must be accounted for (VATA 1994 Sch 4 para 8). The rule does not apply to certain items in respect of which input tax was not claimed. The rule also does not apply if on the occasion on which the person ceases to be a taxable trader, the business is transferred as a going concern to another taxable trader (VATA 1994 Sch 4 para 8(1)(a): see [**33.26**]).

Subject to any express provisions in Sch 4 or in any SI, supplies do not include anything done other than for a consideration (VATA 1994 s 5(2)(a)).

[**33.23**]

3 A supply of services

Section 5(2)(b) states that 'anything which is not a supply of goods but is done for a consideration . . . is a supply of services'.   [**33.24**]

EXAMPLE 33.3

(1) Monopoly supplies heating and lighting to X & Co. A supply of *goods* (Sch 4 para 3).

(2) X & Co assign the remaining 30-year term on their lease to Fred. A supply of *goods* (Sch 4 para 4).

(3) Big and Bob jointly own a stallion. Big sells his undivided share to Breeder & Co. A supply of *services*. Contrast the position if Big and Bob sold the horse to Breeder & Co (ie both shares were sold at the same time) when this would be a supply of *goods* (Sch 4 para 1).

(4) Shine cleans Big's windows and Taylor makes up a suit with Big's cloth. Shine is supplying *services*; Taylor *goods* (Sch 4 para 2).

(5) Concrete hires tools and machinery (a supply of *services*); it also sells goods on hire purchase (a supply of *goods*) (Sch 4 para 1(2)).

(6) A, a publisher, gives a glossy calendar to a valued customer as a goodwill gesture. As an exception to the general rule in Sch 4 para 5(1) that the transfer of goods out of a business is a supply, even if no consideration is furnished, a gift of goods made in the course or furtherance of the business is not regarded as a supply provided that the cost of the goods—the calendar—to A does not exceed £15 (VATA 1994 Sch 4 para 5(2)(a)).

(7) Sel sells power tools. One Saturday he borrows an item of trading stock for his own use. This is a supply of services and VAT will be charged on the cost of supplying the power tool (VATA 1994 Sch 4 para 5(4) and Sch 6 para 7).

4 Composite and multiple supplies

A taxable person may supply a combination of goods or services as part of what is nominally a single transaction. Where the liability of the individual supplies of goods and services would be the same as the liability of the goods or services regarded as a single package, no problems arise. However, disputes frequently arise as to whether there is a single (composite) supply or several different individual supplies, even though there is apparently a single consideration. Examination of this complex area of VAT is beyond the scope of this chapter. In essence the test of whether or not two identifiable supplies within a single transaction should be regarded as a single supply or not depends on whether they can be regarded as 'dissociable' from each other (see *EC Commission v UK* [1988] STC 251).   [**33.25**]

5 Transfer of a business as a going concern (VATA 1994 s 49)

When the provisions of the VAT (Special Provisions) Order 1995 (SI 1995/1268) are satisfied, certain supplies of assets of a business as a going concern are treated as neither supplies of goods nor services and no VAT is chargeable on the consideration. This is not a matter of choice: if the conditions are satisfied and the vendor charges VAT in error, the purchaser is not entitled to recover the amount as input tax.

The conditions are that the assets must be used by the transferee in carrying on the same line of business as the transferor with no significant break (refurbishment or redecoration is acceptable); if the transferor is registered for VAT the transferee must likewise either be registered or become registered and where the assets form part only of the business, that part must be capable of separate operation. Where land is included in the transfer, certain other conditions may have to be satisfied (see [**34.36**]).

Where the rules apply the transferee will become responsible in relation to the assets transferred for any future input tax adjustments under the Capital Goods Scheme (as to which see [**33.89**] and *Example 33.10*).

When assets are acquired as a transfer of a going concern and the assets are used exclusively to make taxable supplies, the VAT incurred on the costs of acquiring those assets should be attributed to those taxable supplies and is recoverable in full.   [**33.26**]

6 A taxable person

A taxable person is one who is either registered or required to be registered (VATA 1994 s 3). If the taxable supplies are, or will be, in excess of a ceiling (usually adjusted annually) the taxpayer is required to register with Customs and Excise by submitting Form VAT 1 to, usually, his local VAT office (VATA 1994 Sch 3). The registration requirement is laid on the *person* rather than the business. An individual may therefore operate several businesses but will have only one VAT registration: by contrast a company is a distinct entity from its proprietors (for group registration, see [**33.52**]). For VAT purposes a partnership is treated as a separate taxable entity (VATA 1994 s 45).
                                                                       [**33.27**]

7 A business

Supplies must be made in the course or furtherance of a business (VATA 1994 s 4(1)). Section 47 (predictably) states that a business 'includes any trade, profession or vocation'. 'Business', however, has a wider meaning than either trade or profession (cp [**23.45**]) and there is no requirement of profit motive. The EC Sixth Directive uses the term 'economic activity' (art 4) which is probably a wider term than 'business'. In *C & E Comrs v Lord Fisher* (1981), Gibson J identified the following indicia which should be considered in determining whether the activities carried on amounted to a business:

(1) whether the activity is a 'serious undertaking earnestly pursued' or 'a serious occupation not necessarily confined to a commercial or profit making undertaking';

(2) whether the activity is an occupation or function actively pursued with reasonable or recognisable continuity;

(3) whether the activity has a certain measure of substance as measured by the quarterly or annual value of taxable supplies made;

(4) whether the activity was conducted in a regular manner and on sound and recognised business principles;

(5) whether the activity is predominantly concerned with the making of taxable supplies to consumers for a consideration;

(6) whether the taxable supplies are of a kind which, subject to differences of detail, are commonly made by those who seek to profit by them.

The letting of property on a continuing or regular basis is a business activity.

In *C & E Comrs v Morrison's Academy Boarding Houses Association* (1978) the company ran boarding houses for students of Morrison's Academy. It was in all respects carrying on an activity within the ordinary meaning of the word 'business' save that it charged rents which would produce neither profit nor loss and reserved its accommodation for students of the Academy. It was decided that it supplied services in the course of a business. By contrast, in *Three H Aircraft Hire v C & E Comrs* (1982) the court decided that although a single adventure could constitute a business or trade under other areas of the law it did not amount to a business activity for VAT purposes.

The taxable supply must be made in the course *'or furtherance'* of a business and activities which would not normally be thought of as falling in the normal course of a business may be taxable (such as the sale of assets to assist in the financing of the business).   **[33.28]**

8   The value of a supply

VATA 1994 s 2 provides that VAT is charged on the value of the supply, determined in accordance with the Act.

Section 19(2) states that if the consideration for a supply is money 'its value shall be taken to be such amount as, with the addition of the tax chargeable, is equal to the consideration'. Accordingly, if £117.50 is paid for a supply taxable at the standard rate, the value of that supply is £100. If there is a supply made for no consideration (eg a gift) or for a consideration not wholly in money (eg an exchange) the value of the supply is 'such amount in money as, with the addition of the tax chargeable, is equivalent to the consideration' (VATA 1994 s 19(3)). Remember, however, that first there must be a supply and if services are performed for no consideration there is generally no supply for VAT purposes.   **[33.29]**

EXAMPLE 33.4

(1) A supplies goods to B for £1,762.50 inclusive of VAT. The value of A's supply is £1,500 being £1,762.50 minus the relevant VAT determined in accordance with the VAT fraction (see **[33.8]**): ie £262.50. A is responsible for the payment of this VAT to Customs.

(2) A supplies goods to B who as a quid pro quo replaces A's existing windows. So far as A is concerned, the value in money of the work done by B (less VAT: see s 19(3)) is the consideration for his supply. For B, it is the value of A's goods.

(3) Silas, a solicitor, gives free tax advice to Mr Big, a local businessman, in the hope of obtaining Big's commercial business. No consideration is furnished and there is no supply of services for VAT. Contrast the position if Mr Big had, in return, agreed to drop a negligence claim against Silas (this would constitute consideration so that there would be a taxable supply).

9   The reverse charge and self-supply

A number of occasions arise where a UK taxable person is required to account for VAT as if he had made a supply of goods or services to himself. Output tax is accounted for to Customs and the taxable person may recover such tax in the usual way if he can attribute it in whole or in part to a taxable supply. One such charge arises under VATA 1994 s 8 where a UK taxable person receives certain services from abroad (see [**34.66**]). This method of accounting for VAT is termed '*a reverse charge*'.

EXAMPLE 33.5

Paul receives legal advice from the lawyers Antonio and Carreras (Madrid) on the requirements of Spanish company law. He is charged £10,000. Paul is deemed to supply himself with these services so that output VAT of £1,750 is payable. That same sum is also treated as input tax for Paul although it is not available for offset against the output tax on the deemed supply (VATA 1994 s 26(1)).

The 'reverse charge' is also applied to goods which are acquired by a business from another EU member state [**34.64**].

Goods produced for internal use in a business, or trading stock appropriated for such use, may also lead to a VAT charge. Such cases are referred to as '*self-supplies*' and the Treasury have powers to make orders that VAT should apply as if the relevant goods or services had been both supplied to a person for the purpose of his business and supplied by him in the course or furtherance of that business (VATA 1994 s 5(5)).

Orders have been made in the case of stationery produced by a firm's own printing department (this charge only applies to exempt or partially exempt traders: SI 1995/1268) and to motor dealers who acquire new cars for resale and then appropriate a car for use in the business. In such cases the dealer is put in the same position as any other trader buying a new car for use in his business (ie he suffers output tax on the conversion to own use and input tax is not generally recoverable) (VAT (Cars) Order, SI 1992/3122). An order has also been made in the case of businesses which carry out their own in-house construction works other than for a consideration (Self-Supply of Construction Services Order, SI 1989/472).

EXAMPLE 33.6

Bonzo Bank produces stationery which it uses for the purpose of its business. It is treated as making a supply of services and must account for output VAT.

Finally, a charge known as the 'developer's self-supply charge' may in some circumstances arise under VATA 1994 Sch 10 paras 5 and 6 although this provision has been abolished with effect from 1 March 1995 save for transitional provisions: see [**34.33**].   [**33.30**]

10 Place and time of supply

Place of supply   VAT only applies to supplies made in the UK (VATA 1994 s 1).

In the case of a supply of *goods* which are located in the UK, the supply is deemed to be in the UK so that UK VAT is chargeable (VATA 1994 s 7(2)). If those goods are exported the supply is then generally (see [**34.61**]) zero-rated. Goods supplied outside the UK and which do not enter the UK fall outside the UK VAT net.   [**33.31**]

Services The basic rule is that services are treated as being supplied in the place where the supplier belongs, which need not be the same place as where the services themselves are performed (on the concept of 'belonging', see VATA 1994 s 9). See, however, [**34.65**] for the many exceptions to this rule.   [**33.32**]

Time of supply   The time of supply (the *tax point*) determines both the rate of tax and the accounting period into which the supply falls. The general rule in case of *goods* is that this is the time when they are removed by the customer or, if not removed, when they are made available to him (VATA 1994 s 6(2)). In the case of *services* it is the time when they are performed (VATA 1994 s 6(3)). If, before goods are supplied or services are performed, a tax invoice is issued or payment made, however, this will bring forward the time of supply (VATA 1994 s 6(4)). Furthermore, the general rules for time of supply may be overridden by statutory instrument (see especially VAT Regulations 1995, SI 1995/2518 Part IV).   **[33.33]**–**[33.50]**

III   REGISTRATION, ACCOUNTING FOR TAX AND PENALTIES

1   Registration requirements (VATA 1994 Sch 1)

A person must be registered if:
(1) at the end of any month the value of his taxable supplies over the *previous 12 months* exceeds £48,000 (£49,000 from 1 December 1997) exclusive of VAT; or
(2) at any time there are reasonable grounds for believing that the value of the taxable supplies that *he will* make in the next 30 days will exceed £48,000 (£49,000 from 1 December 1997) exclusive of VAT.

Customs must be notified within 30 days of the end of the relevant month or within 30 days after the date on which reasonable grounds first existed. Registration can be avoided if Customs are satisfied that, although taxable turnover in the previous 12 months exceeded £48,000, it will not exceed £46,000 in the next 12 months (£49,000 and £47,000 respectively from 1 December 1997).

A business, which is required to be registered because it exceeds the registration limits, can be exempted from the requirement to be registered if it makes zero-rated supplies and its input tax would exceed its output tax (VATA 1994 Sch 1 para 14).

A business which is not required to register under the above rules may still do so on a voluntary basis if it can satisfy Customs that it is making taxable supplies by way of business (VATA 1994 Sch 1 para 9(a)). This may be helpful for small businesses desiring to recover input VAT. Voluntary registration cannot be retrospective by more than three years.

A person, who is able to satisfy Customs & Excise that he is carrying on activities preparatory to the making of taxable supplies (eg a feasibility study) is entitled to be registered for VAT (see *Merseyside Cablevision Ltd v C & E Comrs* [1987] VATTR 134 (VATA 1994 Sch 1 para 9(b))).

For the purposes of the registration rules bear in mind that taxable supplies include zero-rated as well as standard-rated supplies but not exempt supplies.

Failure to register does not enable a person to escape his obligations. Registration will be back-dated when notification is made outside the prescribed time periods and the person will be required to account for output tax from the earlier date whether he has in fact charged it to his customers or not. Penalties may be payable (see **[33.64]**).

A business, which is not required to be registered under the provisions clause because, for example, it only makes exempt supplies, may nevertheless have to register for VAT if it receives supplies of goods from other EU member states where value exceeds £48,000 (£49,000 from 1 December 1997) (VATA 1994 Sch 3 para 1).   **[33.51]**

2   Group registration

Corporate bodies within common control may obtain a single or 'group' VAT registration with the result that supplies of goods or services within the group are not subject to VAT (VATA 1994 s 43). This was particularly attractive when one or more companies in the group made exempt supplies and suffered restrictions on the recovery of input tax. The decision of the High Court in *C & E Comrs v Kingfisher plc* (1994) determined that the effect of the grouping provisions went further than merely allowing a number of VAT entities to account for VAT under a single registration (as Customs had contended) and created a single taxable entity. Following the *Kingfisher* decision FA 1997 amended s 43. Group companies are now effectively prevented from taking advantage of any special VAT status enjoyed by their respective member.

Registration is in the name of a 'representative member' who becomes liable for VAT in respect of all group companies. Each individual company in a group remains jointly and severally liable for the tax payable by the representative. Companies may join and leave a group, generally on 90 days' notice although it is possible for a move by a company to be back-dated to take effect up to 30 days prior to the date of application. To qualify, companies must be resident or have an established place of business in the UK; 'control' depends on majority voting rights.

Customs may refuse an application to form a group or an application by any company to join or leave a group if they perceive a VAT avoidance motive. FA 1996 contains further provisions giving Customs extensive powers to counter VAT avoidance using the group registration rules. Certain powers are retrospective.   **[33.52]**

3   De-registration

Customs may cancel a registration if satisfied that the business was not registrable at the time when it did in fact register (VATA 1994 Sch 1 para 13(2)). A registered 'intending trader' must notify Customs within 30 days if he will not now make taxable supplies, otherwise penalties may be imposed (Sch 1 para 11).

If a business permanently ceases to make taxable supplies it *must* notify customs within 30 days. A business may voluntarily de-register if it is expected that its taxable turnover will fall below £46,000 (£47,000 from 1 December 1997) in the coming year.   **[33.53]**

4   Accounting for VAT

General rule   VAT on supplies of goods and services must generally be accounted for on a quarterly basis with quarterly accounting periods being allocated to the trader at the time of his registration. The tax operates on the basis of self-assessment. Return Form VAT 100 is sent to the taxpayer towards the end of a quarterly period and must be returned completed, together with the tax payable so that it is *received* by Customs by the end of the month following the end of the relevant quarter period. A seven-day extension is allowed if payment is by credit transfer but this has been withdrawn for businesses within the 'payments on account' provisions.

The taxpayer must pay the difference between output and input tax applicable to supplies during the quarter period. Customs will repay excess input tax, normally within ten days of receiving the return (s 25(3)). If a taxpayer has, by mistake, overpaid tax in an earlier period Customs must refund that amount. All claims for refunds of VAT are subject to a three-year retrospective limit.

A taxable person must keep detailed records and accounts for six years, together with full supporting documentation, and these are open to inspection by Customs. Except in cases of fraud there is a three-year limit on Customs' power to assess retrospectively for undeclared VAT.   **[33.54]**

Monthly returns   Businesses likely to enjoy a refund of input tax (typically an export business) may submit monthly returns (SI 1995/2518 reg 25).   **[33.55]**

Monthly payments on account   'Very large' VAT payers (defined as those whose liability in the relevant reference period exceeds £2m in a year) are required to make monthly VAT payments on account in respect of each of the first two months of every quarter. From October 1993, the reference period is the year ending on the previous 31 March, 30 April or 31 May. A business that is within the payments on account scheme may only leave it if its liability falls below £1.6m.   **[33.56]**

Annual returns   Completing four VAT returns per year may present a burden to smaller businesses. As an alternative, such businesses with an annual value of taxable supplies *not exceeding £300,000* may make an annual VAT return. On the basis of the previous year's results, nine monthly payments must be made by direct debit; the final payment (adjusted as appropriate) together with the VAT return must then be made in the two-month period following the end of the year. From 1 April 1996, a business whose turnover does not exceed £100,000 and whose previous year's net VAT liability is less than £2,000 may elect to make three quarterly interim payments (instead of the nine monthly payments).   **[33.57]**

Cash accounting   Businesses whose annual value of taxable supplies does not exceed £350,000 may also be assisted by electing to make VAT returns on a cash basis: ie by reference to output tax collected in the quarter less input tax paid in that same period. In other cases returns are on the basis of invoices issued rather than cash received.   **[33.58]**

Bad debt relief   In general VAT is charged on the basis of invoices issued to customers irrespective of whether payment has been received. VAT relief in respect of bad debts was recast in FA 1990 s 11 (now VATA 1994 s 36) as further amended by SI 1997/1086. With effect from 1 May 1997 the requirements for relief are as follows:
(1) the taxpayer must have supplied goods or services on or after 1 April 1989
(2) for a consideration in money; and
(3) must have accounted for *and paid* VAT on that supply; and
(4) the whole or part of the consideration must have been written off in his accounts;
(5) six months must have elapsed from the date *on which payment became due and payable (SI 1996/2690) or if later the date of supply*; and
(6) *claims must be made within three years and six months of the date on which payment became due or the date of supply, whichevere is the later.*
   The result of a successful claim will be either a reduction in output VAT payable in the relevant quarter or, in appropriate circumstances, a refund of VAT.   **[33.59]**

5   Penalties

The powers of Customs to charge penalties and interest were drastically increased as a result of the Keith Report. In brief the rules are as follows:

Default surcharge (VATA 1994 s 59)   Repeated default in submitting returns (or making the appropriate payment) can lead to a default surcharge. One default can lead to the issue of a surcharge liability notice and further defaults during the operative period of that notice (12 months) will both extend the period for a further 12 months and lead to a surcharge of (at worst) 15% of the tax due for the period of default. The default surcharge may also be applied to the default of a business to make a monthly payment on account ([**33.56**] above).   [**33.60**].

Tax evasion (VATA 1994 s 60)   Where tax is evaded dishonestly a penalty of 100% of the tax sought to be evaded is payable.   [**33.61**]

Misdeclaration penalty (VATA 1994 ss 63 and 64)   This penalty was reformed by FA 1993 Sch 2 para 1 with effect from 1 December 1993 and the new name of 'misdeclaration penalty' is now used in place of the old terms 'serious misdeclaration' and 'persistent misdeclaration' penalty. A penalty is charged when a return is made which understates tax due or overstates tax repayable (and also when a VAT assessment understates the tax due and the taxpayer does not draw this error to Customs' attention). The penalty is equal to 15% of the tax loss but will only apply if the lost tax equals or exceeds (in the case of an incorrect return) whichever is the lesser of £1m and 30% of the gross amount of tax (GAT) for the period (or, in the case of a failure to draw to Customs' attention an understatement of liability in an assessment, the lesser of £1m and the true amount of VAT for the period). The GAT is the aggregate of the correct amount of output tax and the correct amount of recoverable input tax for the period.

A penalty is also charged in the case of repeated errors. Since 1 December 1993 this penalty will only arise if returns for three out of 12 VAT periods contain errors and Customs has issued a penalty liability notice. For a penalty to be chargeable, tax lost because of the inaccuracy must be at least £500,000 or 10% of the GAT for the period (whichever is the lesser). The penalty is 15% of the tax lost.   [**33.62**]

Failure to notify registration (VATA 1994 s 67(1)(a))   A penalty based on a percentage of the tax that would have been charged had correct registration occurred can be charged; for instance, at 5% for delays of up to nine months rising to 15% for delays in excess of 18 months.   [**33.63**]

Penalties for breach of the VAT regulations (VATA 1994 s 9)   There are innumerable possible breaches—such as failure to keep appropriate records—and penalties are calculated on a daily basis.   [**33.64**]

Mitigation (VATA 1994 s 70)   In the case of penalties payable under s 60, 63, 64 or 67 of VATA 1994 and assessed after 27 July 1993, there is a discretion available to Customs (or, on appeal, to the tribunal) to reduce penalties if they see fit. In exercising their discretion, neither Customs nor a tribunal may take account of the insufficiency of funds available to the taxpayer to pay the VAT or any penalty; the fact that there has been no VAT lost as a result of the default or the fact that the taxpayer acted in good faith.   [**33.65**]

Interest (VATA 1994 s 12)   Interest, at a commercial rate, is payable on a VAT assessment and where there has been overdeclaration of input tax or underdeclaration of output tax. By a news release of 7 September 1994 Customs announced their intention not to assess interest where there has been no loss to the exchequer, eg where a company has failed to charge VAT but, had it done so, another would have reclaimed it as input tax.   [**33.66**]

The 'reasonable excuse' defence   This is a general defence to a claim for penalties. Lack of funds and reliance on another do not count (VATA 1994 s 21(1))! The question for the tribunal is one of fact and decisions show little consistency with the apparent honesty of the taxpayer often being decisive. Evidence that Customs had been informed and their advice followed is highly material in establishing the defence. **[33.67]**

Repayment supplements and interest on over-payments In cases where a refund of tax due to the taxpayer has been delayed, he may be eligible for a repayment supplement and there is a statutory right to interest in certain cases of official error. **[33.68]–[33.80]**

IV THE RECOVERY OF VAT, PARTIAL EXEMPTION AND THE CAPITAL GOODS SCHEME

1 The deduction principle

A taxable person is only entitled to deduct the VAT he has incurred from the output tax for which he must account if it was incurred in the course or furtherance of a business and then only if it was incurred in the making of taxable supplies or supplies, which are outside the scope of VAT because they were made outside the UK, if they would have been taxable if made in the UK. **[33.81]**

2 The need for apportionment

A taxable person, who makes a combination of supplies on which recovery is allowed and those where it is not, must carry out an apportionment of any VAT incurred to determine how much is recoverable. Where a taxable person has made any supplies otherwise than in the course or furtherance of his business, he must first carry out an apportionment in order to identify and exclude that VAT from deduction. There are no statutory provisions governing this process. Customs usually suggest a turnover based method but any other reasonable method can be used. The remaining VAT is 'input tax' and is potentially recoverable. **[33.82]**

3 The partial exemption problem

A business which makes a combination of taxable and exempt supplies must carry out a further apportionment. Businesses such as insurance companies, banks and property developers usually make exempt supplies [see **33.7**] and are obviously affected but other businesses, not at first sight affected by the partial exemption problem, may also be caught. Typically, rent received from property may give rise to an exempt output and so 'taint' the business. When a business makes exempt supplies the question is how much input tax should be attributed to those exempt supplies and so be irrecoverable (this is referred to as 'exempt input tax'). For the purposes of this apportionment, supplies which are outside the scope of VAT because they were made outside the UK should be regarded as giving rise to a right of recovery if recovery would have been allowed if they were made in the UK. **[33.83]**

4 The solution (VATA 1994 ss 25 and 26; SI 1995/2518)

As from 1 April 1987 the following rules apply:

First, input tax directly attributable to goods and services exclusively used or to be used in making taxable supplies is fully recoverable;
Secondly, input tax directly attributable to goods and services exclusively

used or to be used in making exempt supplies or in any other non-taxable activity is irrecoverable;

Thirdly, the residual input tax must then relate to both taxable and exempt (or non-taxable) activities (a common example is the cost of VAT incurred on overheads). This remaining tax must be apportioned in accordance with the standard method [see **33.86**] or in accordance with a method agreed with Customs. **[33.84]**

5 **Apportionment methods**

A variety of methods are possible. Regardless of whether the standard (ie turnover based) method or a special method is used, however, since 1 December 1994 if input tax is incurred partly in relation to certain exempt financial supplies (such as the issue of shares) which are incidental to the taxpayer's business and partly in relation to other supplies, then the taxpayer can recover only that amount of such input tax used in making taxable supplies (VAT Regulations 1995, SI 1995/2518 reg 102(2)). **[33.85]**

'Standard method' This method (effective from 1 April 1992) attributes residual input tax in accordance with the ratio of taxable outputs to all outputs. The fraction is reduced to a percentage. The fraction must be calculated for each VAT accounting period (monthly or quarterly) using the percentage rounded down to the nearest whole number. At the end of the VAT accounting year (called a 'longer period'), the values must be aggregated and an annual adjustment performed. The percentage is rounded up for the annual adjustment. Certain supplies made by the taxpayer, such as supplies of capital goods, incidental real estate transactions, and self-supplies are ignored for the purpose of this calculation (VAT Regulations 1995, SI 1995/2518 reg 101). The standard method must be used unless and until an alternative method is approved by or imposed by Customs. **[33.86]**

EXAMPLE 33.7

A taxpayer suffers the following input tax:

	£
(i) That attributed to taxable supplies	500,000
(ii) That attributed to exempt supplies	150,000
(iii) Residual input tax	350,000
	£1,000,000

His taxable supplies total £10m and exempt supplies £2m.

To calculate the amount of residual input tax recoverable under the standard method:

(i) calculate (as a percentage) the ratio of taxable supplies to all supplies:

$$\text{ie } \frac{10,000,000}{12,000,000} \times 100 = 83.33\% \text{ (rounded up to 84%)}$$

(ii) multiply residual (or 'non-attributable') input tax by this percentage to obtain input tax recoverable:

$$£350,000 \times 84\% = £294,000$$

Special methods By virtue of SI 1995/2518 reg 102, Customs may approve or direct the use of any other method of apportioning residual input tax but, since 1 December 1994, any supplies of capital goods, incidental real estate transactions and self-supplies must be ignored in making the calculation (SI 1995/2518 reg 101(3)). One alternative way of apportioning residual input tax (the 'input tax' based method which was formerly the standard method) is by employing the fraction:

$$\frac{\text{input tax directly attributable to taxable outputs}}{\text{input tax directly attributable to taxable and exempt outputs}}$$

[**33.87**]

EXAMPLE 33.8

Taking the facts of *Example 33.7* the input tax based method would produce the following:
(i)   multiply residual input tax by the formula. Using the numbering in *Example 33.7* this becomes:

$$(\text{iii}) \times \frac{(\text{i})}{(\text{i})+(\text{ii})}$$

(ii)   tax recoverable is:

$$£350,000 \times \frac{500,000}{650,000} = \underline{£269,230}$$

6 De minimis

The de minimis rules provide that when the exempt input tax of a trader is not more than £625 per month on average or £7,500 pa, and provided this exempt input tax is no more than 50% of all input tax, all input tax shall be treated as attributable to taxable supplies so that the taxpayer is fully taxable and able to recover *all* input tax (SI 1995/2518 reg 106). This test must be applied for each VAT return and again when the annual adjustment is calculated at the end of the year.

In calculating whether the de minimis rules apply, input tax attributable to certain exempt supplies (such as a deposit of money) may be ignored provided the taxpayer's business is not that of a bank or certain other financial institutions. Such input tax may be treated as attributable to taxable supplies and therefore ignored in applying the de minimis rules. This provision is intended to permit small businesses to avoid partial exemption. There are special rules applicable to input tax relating to share issues.   [**33.88**]

7 The Capital Goods Scheme

Rules were introduced from 1 April 1990 to deal with certain capital expenditure incurred by a business. The rules reflect the fact that capital expenditure will normally benefit a business over a period of time, in contrast to income expenditure which is primarily for the benefit of the current period of account.   [**33.89**]

Assets within the scheme   Expenditure on the following assets, incurred on or after 1 April 1990, is within the scheme:

(1)   a computer or item of computer equipment to a value of at least £50,000;
(2)   land or buildings to a value of at least £250,000.   [**33.90**]

Initial deduction   In the year that an asset within the scheme is first acquired, a business calculates the proportion of VAT on the asset, that it is entitled to deduct, in accordance with the usual rules [**33.81–33.88**]   [**33.91**].

Subsequent adjustments   In the second and subsequent 'adjustment intervals', the business must adjust the VAT initially claimed if the extent to which the asset is used for the purposes of the business's taxable supplies is greater or less than the extent to which it was used in the initial period. **[33.92]**

Period of adjustment The number of 'adjustment intervals' depends on the nature of the asset. In the case of an interest in land having more than ten years to run, the VAT deducted is adjusted over ten intervals. There are only five adjustment intervals for computers and interests in land having less than ten years to run. The adjustment interval is the 'longer period' **[33.86]**, normally a year, ending on 31 March, 30 April or 31 May.

Where the asset is sold as part of the transfer of a going concern, an adjustment period will end on the day the asset is transferred. The transferor must then make an adjustment based on the use for that period. The transferee inherits the obligation to make any adjustments over the remaining number of intervals. An adjustment interval will also end where a company leaves or joins a VAT group. Therefore although the adjustment interval is normally a year, it does not have to be and the adjustment period may therefore be less than ten years or five years. **[33.93]**

Making the adjustment At the end of each tax year following the year of acquisition it is necessary to compare the input tax recovery percentage of the business with the recovery percentage in the year of acquisition. If that subsequent recovery percentage is *less* than the initial percentage, input tax has been over-recovered and an amount is payable to Customs; if the then recovery percentage is *greater* than the first year's, a repayment is due from Customs. Special rules apply where the capital item is disposed of during the period of adjustment and F(No 2)A 1997 included anti-avoidance provisions to prevent the artificial manipulation of the disposal price. **[33.94]**–**[33.100]**

EXAMPLE 33.9

Whatto plc purchases a computer for £200,000 exclusive of VAT which is £35,000. The company is partly exempt throughout the following four years but then leases the computer to another business for the fifth year.

Year	% of taxable use	Input tax claims (£)	Adjustment %	Amount of adjustment (£)
1	51	17,850		
2	46		–5	–350
3	49		–2	–140
4	52		+1	+70
5	100		+49	+3,430

Notes:
(1) The adjustment each year is:

$$\frac{\text{total input tax}}{\text{total years (5)}} \times \text{the adjustment percentage}$$

For instance, in *year 2*:

$$\frac{35,000}{5} \times 5\% = £350$$

(2) The total input tax recovered (net of payments made to Customs) is *£3,010*.
(3) Leasing the computer to another person results in 100% taxable user in *year 5*.

EXAMPLE 33.10

X Ltd purchases a new commercial property in June 1990 for £1m plus VAT. It exercises the option to tax and lets out the building. All VAT is therefore recovered. In June 1991 it sells the building to Y Ltd for £900,000 and Y Ltd exercises the option to tax (see [**34.26**]). Because Y buys subject to the existing letting, the sale is treated as the transfer of a business as a going concern so that no VAT is charged. Y Ltd now steps into X Ltd's shoes for the purposes of the scheme. In June 1993, Y Ltd obtains vacant possession of the premises and goes into occupation for the purposes of its own partially exempt business (property investment).

The consequence is that for the last seven years of the ten-year period, the building will not be used for fully taxable purposes and Y Ltd must repay part of the input tax recovered by X Ltd.

34 VAT on property

I INTRODUCTION

The VAT treatment of supplies of land and buildings and construction services changed significantly in 1989. Prior to FA 1989, most transactions in land were exempt from VAT, although there was a significant category of the zero-rated supplies. Only a limited number of supplies were standard-rated.

After FA 1989 the basic rule remains that the grant of any interest in or right over land or any licence to occupy land is *exempt* (VATA 1994 Sch 9 Group 1). The exceptions to this basic rule (which are standard-rated) were, however, extended, and the number of standard-rated transactions has been further increased by the introduction of the 'election to waive exemption' or 'option to tax' by which the person granting an interest in land can convert what would otherwise be an exempt supply of land into a standard-rated supply. The categories of zero-rated supply were reduced.

Customs Notice 742 (dealing with land and property) provides helpful guidance as to their views to property transactions.

Construction services are generally taxable at the standard rate save for certain supplies relating to the construction of new dwellings and other limited categories of residential/charitable buildings and works of alteration to some listed buildings, all of which are zero-rated (see [**34.23**]).   [**34.1**]–[**34.20**]

II LAND, BUILDINGS AND CONSTRUCTION

1 A grant of an interest in, or right over, land (exempt supply)

A grant of an *interest* in land includes a freehold sale as well as the grant, assignment or surrender of a lease.

A grant of a *right over* land includes a grant of mineral rights or easements. Grants of licences to occupy land fall into the exempt category, but must be contrasted with mere licences to use land which are standard-rated. Customs, in their Notice 742, give as examples of the latter: allowing the general public to tip rubbish on your land; shared business premises; and the grant to the general public of admission to premises or events.

EXAMPLE 34.1

(1) On Saturday, Sid pays £5 to watch Richmond RFU. This is not a licence to occupy land: rather it is a licence to go on land and the supply is standard-rated.

On Sunday, he goes fishing on the Thames, paying £15 for a day licence. This is also a standard-rated supply.

(2) Jack sells his freehold interest in two acres of freehold land to Jill and before completion she resells to Eric. Both have disposed of (exempt) interests in land.

In relation to the grant of a lease, the premium or rent payable is consideration for the exempt supply. Unless therefore the landlord has exercised the option to tax, he will not charge VAT on any of these items.

The consideration paid by a landlord to his tenant for the surrender of an interest in land is exempt unless the tenant has exercised the option to tax.

Similarly, in the case of a 'reverse surrender' (being one where the tenant pays the landlord) the supply will be exempt unless the landlord has exercised the option to tax.   [34.21]

2   Standard-rated supplies of land and buildings

The basic rule, already noted, is that grants of interests in or rights over land are exempt. The following are exceptions to this rule, listed in VATA 1994 Sch 9 Group 2.

(1) Freehold sales of new, or uncompleted, commercial buildings or civil engineering works. The legislation does not, in fact, use the term 'commercial building' but refers to a building which is neither designed as a dwelling nor intended solely for a relevant residential or charitable purpose (see [34.23]). Civil engineering works are likewise not defined, but include bridges, tunnels etc. A building or civil engineering work is *new* if it was completed within the last three years. It is treated as completed when the certificate of practical completion is issued or when it is fully occupied, whichever happens first.

EXAMPLE 34.2

(1) Dan Developer completes the construction of an office block on 1 August 1992 and on the same day sells the freehold interest to X-Ray for £5m. VAT at the standard rate is charged.

(2) If on 31 July 1995 X-Ray sells the freehold interest to Mad Mac Burgers for £7.5m, VAT at the standard rate is charged. Had the sale been delayed until 1 August 1995 the supply would have been exempt (unless X-Ray had exercised the option to tax: see [34.26]).

(3) A similar result would follow if X-Ray had effected an immediate sub-sale in favour of Mad Mac and the freehold had been conveyed directly from X-Ray to Mad Mac.

(4) Instead of selling the freehold Dan Developer grants a long leasehold interest at a premium. The grant is an exempt supply (but note that prior to 31 March 1995 Dan Developer would have incurred a self-supply charge: see [34.33]).

(2) A supply made under a development tenancy, lease or licence. This is defined as a tenancy lease or licence of any building constructed, enlarged or extended after 1 January 1992 in respect of which the tenant, lessee or licensee, as the case may be, has incurred a developer's self-supply charge (see [34.33]).

(3) The grant of any interest in, right or licence consisting of a right to take, game or fish except where, at the same time, the grantor also supplies the freehold to the grantee. Where land including the right to take game or fish is leased rather than sold freehold, VAT is chargeable on the proportion of the rent attributable to the sporting rights.

EXAMPLE 34.3

Sid sells his freehold interest in a strip of the River Foul for £75,000. The freehold carries with it mooring and fishing rights. The sale of the freehold is an exempt supply and there is no question of apportioning the price to arrive at a value for the mooring rights or fishing rights.

(4) The provision of accommodation in an hotel, boarding house or similar establishment.
(5) The grant of an interest in, right over or licence to occupy holiday accommodation.
(6) The provision of seasonal pitches for caravans.
(7) The provision of facilities for camping.
(8) The grant of facilities for parking a vehicle except where the facilities are provided in conjunction with domestic accommodation.
(9) The grant of a right to sell and remove standing timber.
(10) The grant of facilities for housing or storage of an aircraft or mooring or storage of a ship, boat or other vessel.
(11) The grant of a right to occupy a box, seat or other accommodation at a sports ground, theatre, concert hall or other place of entertainment.
(12) The grant of facilities for playing sport or participating in physical recreation.
(13) The grant of any right (such as an option) to call for or be granted an interest or right falling within (1) or (3) to (12) above.

Certain of the grants falling within (11) and (12) are nevertheless exempt if made by 'not for profit' bodies.

In addition to these taxable transactions, grants of interests in or rights over land or licences to occupy land which would otherwise be exempt may be converted to taxable supplies if the landowner concerned has exercised the election to waive exemption (the 'option to tax'): see [**34.26**]. [**34.22**]

3 Dwellings, qualifying residential and charitable buildings (zero-rated supplies)

The first grant or assignment of a major interest (defined to mean the freehold or a tenancy for a term certain exceeding 21 years—a lease for a term exceeding 21 years but with an earlier break clause will qualify) in certain qualifying buildings is zero-rated (VATA 1994 Sch 8 Group 5 Item 1).

To qualify, the building subject to the grant or assignment must have been:
(a) a building, constructed by the grantor as a dwelling, number of dwellings or for a relevant residential or charitable person; or
(b) a non-residential building or part thereof, which has been converted by the grantor into a dwelling, number of dwellings or for a relevant residential or charitable purpose.

The conversion of a garage, which was previously occupied with a dwelling, is not zero-rated (VATA 1994 Sch 8 Group 5 Note (8)). Similarly, the conversion of a non-residential building which already contains a residential part, is not zero-rated unless the effect of the conversion is to create an additional dwelling or dwellings or is a conversion for relevant residential use (VATA 1994 Sch 8 Group 6 Note (9)).

EXAMPLE 34.4

(1) Dick, the developer, builds a new house and grants a 99-year lease of it. The premium or first payment of rent is treated as consideration for a zero-rated supply. Further payments of rent are treated as consideration for an exempt supply.

(2) By contrast if he granted a lease for less than 21 years then he would make an *exempt* supply (so that input tax would be restricted).

(3) Fred Archer converts a barn into a dwelling which he then sells. The supply is zero-rated.

A *'dwelling'* includes a garage constructed (or converted) at the same time as the dwelling for occupation with it (VATA 1994 Sch 8 Group 5 Note (3)).

Use for a *'relevant residential purpose'* includes use as a residential children's home or old people's home, residential accommodation for school children or students and certain other similar purposes (VATA 1994 Sch 8 Group 5 Note (4)).

Use for a *'relevant charitable purpose'* means use *either* for something other than a business purpose *or* as a village hall or providing similar social or recreational facilities for a local community (VATA 1994 Sch 8 Group 5 Note (6)).

'Construction' does not include the conversion, reconstruction or alteration of an existing building and a building only ceases to be an existing building when either demolished completely to ground level or when the part remaining above ground level consists of no more than a single facade (or in the case of a corner site a double facade) the retention of which is a condition of a planning or similar permission (VATA 1994 Sch 8 Group 5 Notes (16) and (18)).   **[34.23]**

EXAMPLE 34.5

Fred Flintstone constructs a building. The third floor is designed as a dwelling; the two lower floors as offices. He sells the property to Fred Archer. An apportionment of the consideration must be made: that portion attributable to the supply of the top floor is zero-rated whereas the remainder is standard-rated.

Protected buildings   The first grant of a major interest in a 'protected building' by the person who has substantially reconstructed it is zero-rated provided that the building is intended solely for use as a dwelling, a number of dwellings or for relevant residential or charitable use (VATA 1994 Sch 8 Group 6 Item 1).

There have been a number of cases on the meaning of substantial reconstruction; Customs' views are set out in Notice 708/1. The term 'protected buildings' covers listed buildings and certain other scheduled monuments.

Where there has been a zero-rated supply of a building intended for a relevant residential or charitable purpose and within a period of ten years there is a change of use, the person to whom the zero-rated supply was made is treated as making a taxable supply on which VAT must be accounted for (VATA 1994 Sch 10 para 1).   **[34.24]**

Construction services   Supplies of construction services are generally standard-rated. However, where a builder provides supplies in the course of the construction of a new dwelling or qualifying residential or charitable building, those works are zero-rated (VATA 1994 Sch 8 Group 5 Item 2 and see *Example 34.6*). In relation to listed buildings falling into one of these categories, building works are zero-rated if what is being carried out is an approved alteration (being, generally, an alteration requiring listed building consent) but not if it is a mere repair: VATA 1994 Sch 8 Group 6 Item 2.

Zero-rating is extended to building materials incorporated in a building (VATA 1994 Sch 8 Group 5 Item 4 and Group 6 Item 3). Input tax on materials incorporated in a building which are not building materials is not recoverable (SI 1992/3222 para 6).

DIY builders are able to obtain a refund of VAT incurred on goods used in the construction of buildings which would qualify for zero-rating (VATA 1994 s 35). **[34.25]**

EXAMPLE 34.6

Lucky, a developer, owns Fairacre. He engages Brad, a builder to construct a residence on the land. Brad supplies carpets and fitted bedroom furniture. Subsequently Lucky sells the completed house to Sad.

(1) Brad will zero rate the construction works (a supply in the course of the construction of the dwelling: Group 5 Item 2). Brad can also zero rate building materials. Lucky cannot reclaim the input tax attributable to the carpets and fitted furniture.

(2) Lucky makes a zero-rated supply and can reclaim VAT paid in connection with the project (eg professional fees).

4   Commercial buildings: the election to waive exemption (or option to tax)

A landowner may, in certain circumstances, convert what would otherwise be an exempt supply into a taxable supply by exercising the option to tax (VATA 1994 Sch 10 paras 2–3).

The consequence of the exercising of the option is that all supplies of the land or building made thereafter by that person (subject to any exercise by the taxpayer of the limited right to revoke) are taxable supplies, save to the extent that they relate to a dwelling or a building intended solely for a relevant residential purpose or relevant charitable purpose, other than an office.

Where one company in a VAT group has exercised the option over a building or land, it affects all other companies in the same group.

The main purpose of electing is to enable a landlord who has incurred input tax on the purchase or refurbishment or reconstruction of a non-residential building to recover that tax against a taxable supply (the grant of a lease or other interest in the land or sale of the freehold) which he makes.   **[34.26]**

What is affected by the option?   The option may be exercised over specified land or buildings, or generally over all land and buildings in the taxpayer's ownership.

Where the option is exercised in relation to part of a building, it will affect the whole. For this purpose, buildings linked internally or by a covered walkway and complexes consisting of a number of units grouped around a fully enclosed concourse are taken to be a single building.   **[34.27]**

EXAMPLE 34.7

Lex, a property investor, owns a building which has shop premises on the ground floor, offices on the two floors above and a residential suite on the top floor. He exercises the option to tax. The consequence will be that all rents received thereafter in relation to the ground, first and second floors will be taxable, but the rent attributable to the residential suite will continue to be exempt. The rents will have to be apportioned to calculate the VAT liability.

Mechanics of exercise   In a case where the taxpayer has not previously made any exempt supplies of the land or building concerned, consent of Customs is not required to its exercise and the taxpayer must merely notify Customs in writing of the exercise within 30 days thereafter. Where, however, the taxpayer has previously made exempt supplies of the land or buildings concerned then, from 1 January 1992, he will need prior consent from Customs to exercise the option (before that date no consent was required). Customs will only consent to the exercise if the option to tax if they are satisfied that there will be a fair and reasonable attribution of input tax. Notification must be given to Customs of the exercise of the option within 30 days of exercise. It is important to note that the option to tax must be exercised after the consent is received.   **[34.28]**

Revocation   Prior to 1 March 1995, the option to tax was irrevocable. Since that date the taxpayer may (with the written consent of Customs) cancel the exercise of the option within three months of exercise provided that no VAT has in the meantime become payable or input tax been reclaimed as a result of its exercise and provided also that in the intervening period the land concerned has not been included in a transfer of a business as a going concern. Further, the option may be revoked (again with the written consent of Customs) once at least 20 years have elapsed since its exercise.   **[34.29]**

Output tax   Following exercise of the option, the landlord must account for output tax on all supplies, including rent. Even though a tenant need not have been consulted before the landlord opted, nonetheless he will be liable to pay VAT in addition to the contractually agreed rent following exercise of the option *unless* the lease expressly provides that the agreed rent is to be inclusive of any VAT. This is because VATA 1994 s 89(3) provides that the exercise of the option to tax is equivalent to a change in the tax charged on a supply: see **[33.8]**.   **[34.30]**

EXAMPLE 34.8

(1)   Bill buys a commercial building subject to an existing tenancy. He opts to tax with effect from completion. No consent required since prior to opting he has made no supplies.

(2)   Jim has owned a commercial building for many years and received exempt rents. In August 1991 he obtained vacant possession and applied for planning permission for redevelopment, incurring VAT on professional fees. He opted to tax on 30 September 1991 and was then told he would not recover input tax incurred in August. After 1 January 1992, he can apply for recovery of this tax.

Can the option be exercised?   FA 1997 s 37 restricts the option to tax in situations where an interest in, or works carried out on land or buildings, are a capital item within the Capital Goods Scheme. It applies where the owner makes a grant and he or the person funding his purchase of the property or any person connected to either intends or expects to occupy the property other than mainly for taxable business purposes. There is a transitional period of three years for grants on terms agreed in writing before 26 November 1996.   **[34.31]**

Should the option be exercised?   Given that the main purpose is to enable input tax to be recovered, if little or no such tax has been or is to be incurred there may be no need to exercise the option. Even if substantial input tax is to be incurred the impact of the exercise of the option on lettings and sales of the property must be considered. Exempt or partially exempt tenants (typically banks; insurance companies; building societies; trade unions; charities; schools; and private health care associations) may be unable to recover the whole of the VAT charged to them and may only be willing to pay a lower rent if VAT is imposed. Alternatively, existing leases may be VAT inclusive so that any VAT may be effectively borne by the grantor of the lease. This will in turn deplete the capital value of the property. **[34.32]**

EXAMPLE 34.9

(1) Lenny purchases the fee simple in a newly constructed office block and intends to grant the Bond St Bank a 99-year lease of the premises in return for a substantial premium.

(i) Lenny will suffer input VAT on the price paid for the freehold.

(ii) If Lenny registers for VAT and exercises the option to tax, the Bond St Bank will suffer input VAT on the premium paid and on rent and service charges payable under the lease. As a partly exempt business full VAT recovery will be denied (although non-recoverable VAT will be a deductible business expense for the Bank so attracting 33% corporation tax relief). From Lenny's point of view he is able to offset his input tax on purchase against output tax on the taxable grant.

(2) Jake lets a commercial building to the Dead End School. He has not exercised the option since to date he has not incurred substantial input tax. A major refurbishment will soon be necessary, however, and he may then wish to make the election.

5 The developer's self-supply charge

A developer's self-supply charge arose in relation to buildings, the construction, reconstruction, enlargement or extension of which commenced before 1 March 1995 (VATA 1994 Sch 10 paras 5 and 6).

Article 4.3(b) of the EC Sixth Directive on VAT provides for the treatment of a person who supplies 'building land' as a taxable person. Because the UK has not implemented the provision, a VAT charge arose on land where the land and buildings were supplied by a developer to a user but not where the user owned the land and bought in the construction services. The developer's self-supply charge was intended to rectify this. **[34.33]**

When the charge applies Under the legislation as introduced in 1989, the charge arose only in relation to new commercial buildings (again defined as buildings excluding dwellings or those intended for a relevant residential or charitable purpose) and civil engineering works construction of which commenced on or after 1 August 1989. Under the legislation as amended by the VAT (Buildings and Land) Order 1991, the charge also arose on existing buildings, works of reconstruction on, enlargement or extension which commenced on or after 1 January 1992 (VATA 1983 Sch 6A para 5(8) now VATA 1994 Sch 10 para 5(8)).

The charge originally arose on the first occasion during the period beginning with the day on which the construction (reconstruction, enlargement or extension) was first planned and ending ten years after the completion of the works, on which a person who was a developer either:

(1) made an exempt supply of the building concerned; or
(2) was in occupation of the building for the purpose of his own business when not a fully taxable person.

A developer was widely defined to include any person who either constructs a building, orders it to be constructed or finances its construction with a view either to granting an interest in the building or to occupying it for his own purposes.

If, therefore, a developer constructed a new building and sold it by way of a freehold sale, no self-supply charge could arise because the sale would be compulsorily taxable under VATA 1994 Sch 9 Group 1 Item 1(a). Likewise, if he granted a long lease of the building having first exercised the option to tax the grant would be taxable and no self-supply charge could arise. Only if the developer granted a lease or some other interest in or right over the building without having exercised the option to tax or used it to make exempt supplies himself would the developer's self-supply charge arise.

If construction etc was in progress on 1 March 1995, then the developer can take himself outside the provisions provided he repays any input tax claimed in anticipation of the taxable self-supply and thereafter claims no such input tax recovery; in relation to all other developments subject to the charge. A final charge arose on 1 March 1997 following which the self-supply charge was discontinued.

Where the charge is incurred, the developer is treated as having made a taxable supply to himself and must account for output tax to Customs. VAT on the supply will be input tax to the developer and may be recoverable in part under the normal provisions. If, for example, the developer occupies the building for the purposes of his own partially exempt business, part of the input tax may be recovered under the normal partial exemption provisions. The value of the deemed supply on which tax is charged is, in the case of a new building, the value of all taxable supplies of goods and services (other than any zero-rated supplies) made in connection with the construction of the building and the value of all grants relating to the land on which the building is constructed.   [**34.34**].

Developmental leases   Since 1 January 1992, where the developer who incurs the self-supply charge merely has a lease or licence over the building concerned, he is obliged at the moment when the self-supply charge is incurred to notify his landlord or licensor in writing. From that date, the lease or licence is converted into what is known as a developmental lease or licence (VATA 1994 Sch 9 Group 1 Note (7)). The consequence of this is that the landlord must thereafter charge VAT on part of the rents payable. This is a most unusual provision which means that a supply made by the landlord which would otherwise be exempt becomes taxable as a result of an act, not of the landlord, but of the tenant. The tenancy will continue to be a developmental lease until it expires or is otherwise terminated.   [**34.35**]

6   Application of the transfer of a business rules

At first sight, one would not expect that the simple sale of a building would be treated as a transfer of a business, or part of a business, as a going concern.

However, the exploitation of property by the receiving of rental income amounts to a business for VAT, and so the sale of a let or partially let building could be treated as a transfer of part of that business as a going concern.

Customs' view is that a sale of a let building subject to existing leases can be a transfer of part of a business as a going concern. Under the provisions of the VAT (Special Provisions) Order 1995 (SI 1995/1268), it is necessary, where the sale of the building would otherwise be a taxable supply (because it is the freehold sale of a new commercial building or it is the sale of a commercial building in relation to which the vendor has exercised the option to tax), that not merely is the transferee registered for VAT (assuming that the vendor was a taxable person) but that he has, prior to the date of supply, exercised the option to tax the building and notified Customs of this. Note the impact of the Capital Goods Scheme when a building is purchased under the transfer of business rules: *Example 33.10*.   [**34.36**]–[**34.60**]

III INTERNATIONAL SUPPLIES OF GOODS AND SERVICES

1 General principle

The VAT treatment of the import and export of goods depends on whether or not the movement is between EU countries. Movements to and from non-EU countries are taxed on a destination basis, ie no tax is charged on exports, while VAT is chargeable on import. The treatment of goods movements between EU member states depends on whether or not the person receiving the goods is a taxable person.

The treatment of international services is more complex. First, it is important to note that certain services fall outside the scope of UK VAT because they are regarded as being supplied outside the UK notwithstanding the fact that the supplier is based within the UK. Similarly, services received from abroad may be regarded as supplied within the UK and, in principle, subject to UK VAT.

Second, it should be borne in mind that there is no blanket zero-rating of services to persons outside the UK.

It is also important to note that in the case of both goods imported from within the EU and certain services the liability to account for VAT is shifted to the person importing the goods and services (VATA 1994 s 8). [34.61]

2 Export of goods to countries outside the EU

Under VATA 1994 s 30(6), a supply of goods is zero-rated if Customs are satisfied that the person supplying the goods has (a) exported them to a place outside the EU, or (b) has shipped them for use as stores on a voyage or flight to an eventual destination outside the UK (other than for a private purpose). See VAT Regulations, SI 1995/2518.

It is generally necessary for exports to be made directly to a customer for zero-rating to apply although there is an exception in the case of supplies to export houses in the UK who arrange for the export.

In order to justify zero-rating it is essential to be able to produce evidence of export to Customs such as the airwaybill or shipped bill of lading.

Two different types of retail export scheme are dealt with in the Regulations: one applies to visitors to the UK, the other to UK residents and the crews of ships and aircraft. The taxable person is at risk if the goods are not exported and the safest course for the taxable person is to take a deposit of the VAT and return this to the customer when evidence of export has been provided. [34.62]

3 Import of goods from outside the EU

VAT is currently charged on the import of goods into the UK from outside the EU as if it were customs duty, and this is so whether or not the importer is a taxable person. The UK includes England, Scotland, Wales, Northern Ireland, territorial waters and, for this purpose, the Isle of Man.

Evidence of VAT paid on import (now in the form of a certificate C79) must be obtained by a taxable person and retained as evidence for input tax recovery. VAT paid on import can be recovered as input tax in accordance with normal rules.

VATA 1994 s 21 deals with the value of imported goods.

Payment of VAT on imported goods is due at the time of importation unless the importer or his agent has been approved under a scheme for deferral of tax which enables payment to be deferred until the fifteenth day of the month following import.

Currently, a number of exemptions from the VAT charge on importation apply. Some deal with temporary import only and are dealt with in SI 1984/746. Limited categories of goods are exempted from VAT on import even if permanently imported: see SI 1992/3193.

It is also possible to defer payment of VAT on import by placing the imported goods in a warehouse. Payment of VAT can by this method be deferred until the goods leave the warehouse.   [**34.63**]

4   Transfers of goods between EU countries after 1 January 1993

Where a registered taxable person in the UK despatches goods to a registered taxable person in another EU member state, the supply will normally be zero-rated under regulations made under VATA 1994 s 30(8). No VAT will be paid as the goods cross the frontier. The customer will acquire the goods and will account for VAT on his own VAT return at the rate in force in the country of receipt. Where a UK registered business acquires goods from another EU country, he must now, instead of paying VAT on importation, account for VAT on the goods through his own VAT return.

Where a taxable person in one EU country despatches goods to a person who is not a VAT registered taxable person in another EU country, the supplier will generally charge VAT at the rate in force in the country of despatch. Thus, UK taxable persons who supply goods to customers in the EU who are not registered for VAT may not zero-rate those supplies. In addition, if the goods the supplier despatches to unregistered persons exceeds certain limits, the supplier must register for, and charge, local VAT instead of UK VAT.   [**34.64**]

5   International services

Services are generally treated as made in the UK (and are hence liable to UK VAT) if the supplier 'belongs' in the UK (VATA 1994 s 7(10)). For the place where a supplier belongs see VATA 1994 s 9. This basic rule is, however, modified by the VAT (Place of Supply of Services) Order 1992 (SI 1992/3121) and the VAT (Place of Supply of Services) (Amendment) Order 1996 (SI 1996/2992). With effect from 1 January 1993 for, *inter alia,* certain supplies of transport services and supplies of certain interests in land. This may result in supplies of services made by taxable persons who belong in the UK being treated as made outside the UK and hence being treated as outside the scope of UK VAT. Notwithstanding that such supplies are treated as outside the scope of VAT, a UK taxable person may recover input tax attributable to such supplies if they would be taxable if made in the UK. Equally, it may result in non-UK taxable persons being treated as making supplies of services in the UK and hence being liable to register for UK VAT. Under the Order, services consisting of the transportation of passengers or goods are generally treated as supplied in the country in which the transportation takes place, and the letting or hire of any means of transport for use outside the EU is treated as made outside the UK. In relation to land, any supply of services which consists of the grant, assignment or surrender of an interest in land or a licence to occupy land or any lesser contractual right over land (as well as construction services and services of surveyors etc) is treated as made where the land is situate.

Also under the 1992 Order, supplies of services of a kind listed in VATA 1994 Sch 5, paras 1-8 (including services of consultants, lawyers, accountants etc) and rendered to a person who either belongs outside the EC (but not in the Isle of Man) or who belongs in an EC country other than that in which the supplier belongs and receives the supply for business purposes, are treated as made where the recipient belongs and are so outside the scope of UK VAT unless for use in the UK. Again, a UK taxable person may recover input tax attributable to such supplies if they would be taxable if made in the UK.

EXAMPLE 34.10

(1) Cayco, a Cayman investment company, purchases a building in the UK and grants a five-year lease, having exercised the option to tax the building (see [**34.000**]). The grant is a supply of services made in the UK and Cayco must charge UK VAT.

(2) Lex and Lax (solicitors) provide for Hiram, in the USA, estate planning advice in connection with becoming UK resident and ultimately domiciled. This service is outside the scope of UK VAT; by contrast services in connection with the acquisition of a flat for him in London are standard-rated.

(3) Alternatively, they provide for François, a French resident who is not registered for VAT in France, advice in connection with his personal UK affairs. This service is standard-rated.

A further exception to the general rule relates to the supply of telecommunications services and access to the Internet. In relation to such services provided to UK business customers the place of supply is the UK and the customer is required to declare the VAT due under the reverse charge procedure (see [**34.66**]). Conversely such services provided by suppliers in the UK are outside the scope of UK VAT.

Services rendered by UK taxable persons to persons belonging outside the UK therefore, subject to the above provisions, are standard-rated unless they fall within the categories specified in VATA 1994 Sch 8 Group 7 or would be zero-rated if supplied in the UK, eg air travel, in which case zero-rating will apply. The services under this heading were substantially amended from 1 January 1993 and now comprise only:

(1) the supply of services of work carried out on goods intended for export outside the EU; and

(2) the supply of services comprising the making of arrangements for the export of goods or supply of services outside the EU or for a supply of services detailed in (1) above. [**34.65**]

6 The reverse charge

The 'reverse charge' applies, by virtue of VATA 1994 s 8, where services described as 'relevant services' are supplied by a person who belongs outside the UK to a person who belongs in the UK for the purpose of a business carried on by him. The recipient of the services will be treated as if the services had been supplied by himself to himself and must account for output tax (unless the services fall within an exempt or zero-rated category) and may recover the input tax charged to himself in accordance with normal procedures if it is attributable to taxable supplies he intends to make.

The services within the reverse charge are those set out in VATA 1994 Sch 5 provided that they do not also fall within Sch 9 (exempt services) and comprise:

(1) transfers and assignments of copyright, patents, licences, trade marks and similar rights;

(2) advertising services;

(3) services of consultants, engineers, consultancy bureaux, lawyers, accountants and other similar services; data processing and provision of information (but excluding from this services relating to land);

(4) acceptance of any obligation to refrain from pursuing or exercising any business activity or any such rights as are referred to in (1) above;

(5) banking, financial and insurance services;

(6) the supply of staff;

(7) the letting on hire of goods other than means of transport;

(8) services rendered by one person to another in procuring for the other any of the services mentioned in (1)-(7) above.

(9) any services not of a description specified in paras (1)-(8) above when supplied to a UK VAT registered business.

Anti-avoidance provisions prevent the routing of services tax free via an overseas branch of one of the companies forming a VAT group (see -[33.52]).   **[34.66]**

35   Capital allowances

I INTRODUCTION

In 1878 the Customs and Inland Revenue Act first recognised that fixed assets used in the course of a business and subject to wear and tear should be eligible for an allowance against tax on the capital expenditure incurred.

Capital allowances legislation, which was first consolidated in the Capital Allowances Act 1968, has been the subject of amendment and addition in almost every Finance Act since and was most recently consolidated in the Capital Allowances Act 1990. In November 1996, the Budget introduced proposals, some of which have a significant impact upon capital allowances with effect from 24 July 1996, whilst others took effect from 19 March 1997. There are various anti-avoidance provisions which restrict the extent of certain claims and these are described later in this chapter.

The allowances are available on the capital expenditure incurred on the acquisition of machinery or plant and certain categories of buildings in arriving at taxable profits in the case of corporate taxpayers, or taxable income in the case of individuals. The allowances may also have the effect of replacing a trading profit with an allowable loss which may be carried forward to a future year. However, in order to qualify for capital allowances the expenditure must be of a capital nature and have been incurred by a taxpayer on a qualifying asset (machinery or plant or a prescribed building). In addition, the asset must 'belong to' the taxpayer and be used by him in the course of his trade or business, or produce an assessable income in the case of a lessor.   [**35.1**]-[**35.20**]

II CAPITAL OR REVENUE

Expenditure must be of a capital nature in order to qualify for a capital allowance and it is therefore of prime importance to draw a distinction between capital and income expenditure.

Capital expenditure is, for example, incurred upon the provision of an item of machinery or plant, the construction of a building, or the replacement or renewal of an asset which has reached the end of its useful life. Revenue expenditure, on the other hand, would be incurred in the rental payments on a building, the purchase of consumables, or on the repair or maintenance of an asset, but not in the acquisition of an asset.

There are a number of grey areas of expenditure which fall somewhere between capital and revenue. For example, when does a repair to part of the structure of a building become a replacement or renewal? If it is a repair, the expenditure incurred upon it will qualify as revenue expenditure and may be offset in its entirety against a company's taxable profits or an individual's taxable income. If, however, it involves the renewal of a piece of building fabric it will be capital expenditure, being non-allowable as revenue and non-qualifying as machinery or plant. In some instances the borderline between the two may be difficult to identify. At what point, for instance, does a simple roof repair become a replacement? Each individual case must be judged on its merits.

Wherever possible expenditure incurred on the repair and maintenance of machinery or plant should be claimed as revenue rather than capital, as the former may be offset against profits or income in its entirety.   **[35.21]–[35.40]**

III   PLANT AND MACHINERY

1   **Definition**

The terms 'plant' and 'machinery' have never been defined in legislation, although FA 1994 provided that buildings and structures cannot qualify as plant (excepting buildings and structures which already qualified). These new rules included the addition of Sch AA1 at the end of s 83 of the Capital Allowances Act 1990 which set out a column of assets which would be deemed to be included in the expression 'building' or 'structure' and so fall outside the definition of machinery and plant. There is also a column of assets 'so included', meaning that they are *not* excluded from expenditure on machinery and plant. However, it is important to note that the rules only seek to identify what is *not* plant. Any asset which is outside the new rules (in the column of assets 'so included') remains subject to the existing plant case law and the question of whether it is plant or not will still depend on the facts of the case.

Machinery is easier to define than plant. The *Oxford* dictionary definition of machinery is '*works of a machine*', where machine is defined as '*Apparatus for applying mechanical power, having several parts each with definite function*'. Thus assets with moving parts such as lifts, escalators, pumps, motors and air conditioners can all be regarded as machinery.

Plant, on the other hand, is more difficult to define, notwithstanding the exclusions identified within Schedule AA1, as the plethora of cases in this area bears just testament! The definition of 'plant' has been litigated upon for over 100 years and as well as cases in the UK there is also a variety of relevant case law from countries as far afield as Australia, New Zealand, India, Canada and Ireland. Recent cases, although adopting a more robust view of what constitutes plant and machinery, emphasise that the answer must depend on the particular facts.

The first case to consider the meaning of plant, *Yarmouth v France* (1887), is just as relevant today and has influenced the thinking behind many later judgments. The judgment of Lindley LJ included the following:

> 'There is no definition of plant in the Act: but in its ordinary sense it includes whatever apparatus is used by a businessman for carrying on his business—not his stock-in-trade, which he buys or makes for sale: but all goods and chattels, fixed or moveable, live or dead which he keeps for permanent employment within his business.'

Careful examination of this early *dictum* shows that the apparatus must be used for carrying on the business. This involves a distinction between assets which are used in the course of the trade and those which form part of the setting in which the trade is carried on. This difference was not always clear and has formed the basis of a number of cases, the most notable of which was *Cole Bros Ltd v Phillips* (1982), where an electrical installation was not treated as a single item of plant. General power and lighting were disallowed as these were described as being 'part of the setting' in which the retail trade was carried on, whilst transformers, main switchboard and wiring to specific items of plant were regarded as apparatus with which the retail trade was carried on. Similarly in *Hampton v Fortes Autogrill Ltd* (1980), false ceilings were disallowed as plant as they were not regarded as necessary for the functioning of any apparatus used for the purposes of the trade and were not part of the means by which the trade was carried on. In contrast, a suspended ceiling forming part of an air conditioning duct, such as a 'plenum' system, would be regarded as part of the air conditioning system which qualifies as machinery used in the course of the trade.

It is clear from the *dictum* of *Yarmouth v France*, when it refers to 'goods and chattels . . . which he keeps for permanent employment in the business', that no reference is made to the premises or place within which the business is conducted. Thus, later cases have attempted to identify the 'premises' or 'setting' which are disallowable. The courts have, however, accepted that 'a building or structure could be plant if it was more appropriate to describe it as apparatus for carrying on the business or employed in the business than as the premises or place in or upon which the business was conducted'. Everything turns upon the facts of the individual case. In *IRC v Barclay Curle & Co Ltd* (1969), the majority of the House of Lords held that a dry dock was correctly described as plant since it could be seen as apparatus for carrying on the business of a ship repairer rather than as merely the premises in which that business was conducted. Similarly, in *Cooke v Beach Station Caravans Ltd* (1974), a swimming pool constructed by a caravan owning and operating company for use in connection with a caravan park was plant. In contrast, however, in *Benson v Yard Arm Club Ltd* (1979) the courts rejected the taxpayer's argument that a ship used as a floating restaurant was plant as it attracted business, because it was held that it was merely the place in which the business was conducted. A similar decision applied in *Brown v Burnley Football and Athletic Club Ltd* (1980) where a football stand was considered to be setting rather than plant.

Subsequently, in *Wimpy International Ltd v Warland* (1988), 101 years after *Yarmouth v France*, the analysis of Hoffmann J confirmed that three distinctions derived from that early case served to demonstrate what items were not plant. *First*, anything that is not used for carrying on the business. *Secondly*, stock in trade which is expressly excluded in the Lindley LJ *dictum* which, in any event, lack permanence or which are quickly consumed. *Thirdly*, the apparatus must be used for permanent employment in his business. Hoffmann J explained in the *Wimpy* case as follows:

> 'If the item is neither stock in trade nor the premises upon which the business is conducted, the only question is whether it is used for carrying on the business. I shall call this the 'business use' test. However, under the second distinction, an article which passes the 'business use' test is excluded if such use is as stock in trade. And under the third distinction, an item used in carrying on the business is excluded if such use is as the premises or place upon which the business is conducted.'

In *Wimpy*, Fox LJ identified the difference between the premises in which the trade is carried on and the plant with which the trade is carried on. Where it can be argued that an asset does not become part of the premises, but merely embellishes them, it should qualify as plant. The 'premises test' thus seeks to identify whether an asset is part of the premises. In deciding whether an asset had become part of the premises, Lord Lowry in *IRC v Scottish and Newcastle Breweries* (1982) stated that some of the relevant considerations will be: *first*, whether the asset retains visually a separate identity; *secondly*, the degree of permanence with which the asset is fixed; *thirdly*, the incompleteness of the structure without the asset; *fourthly*, the extent to which the asset is intended to be permanent.

Hoffmann J concluded in the *Wimpy* case that the distinction drawn in earlier cases between expenditure incurred on the setting in which a business is conducted and on the apparatus used in that business was unhelpful, since it was capable of blurring the distinction between the business use test on the one hand and the premises test on the other. Thus in the *Scottish and Newcastle Breweries* case, the items in dispute were wall decor, plaques, tapestries and murals (which were detachable), pictures and metal sculptures used to decorate hotels. All of these were held to be chattels and not integral parts of the premises so that the premises test was irrelevant. The Revenue's argument, that they formed part of the setting of the business and so were not plant, was dismissed by the House of Lords because the chattels satisfied the business use test as they were used to please and attract customers and were therefore for the promotion of the trade. The facts in the *Wimpy* case were similar and again involved the question of whether the premises test should be applied to items which had been added to an original building by way of subsequent improvement. The items consisted mainly of tiling on floors and walls, glass shop fronts, raised and mezzanine floors, staircases and false ceilings. Hoffmann J, in deciding that such expenditure did not qualify for capital allowances, distinguished the *Scottish and Newcastle Breweries* case on the basis that the items in that case were plainly not part of the premises. By contrast, the disputed items in *Wimpy* had, save for one exception, all become comprised in the premises. The one exception was for the expenditure on light fittings, which did qualify for a capital allowance, being regarded as chattels and not an integral part of the building (also referred to in *J Lyons & Co Ltd v A-G* (1944)). The light fittings in *Wimpy* were not simply installed to provide general illumination but were specific to the particular trade since the volume of light was considered by Wimpy to be important in a fast food chain. This contrasts with *Cole Bros*, referred to above, where the lighting was considered to be merely part of the premises or setting in which the trade was carried on.

It is clear from *Scottish and Newcastle Breweries* that items creating atmosphere or ambience can be regarded as plant. However, similar chattel plant to that allowed in the *Scottish and Newcastle Breweries* case, if installed in a different type of building, a shopping centre for example, even though that plant may be regarded as creating atmosphere or ambience, would not be sufficient. A distinction may be drawn insofar as the trade of an hotelier or restaurateur can be regarded as not only providing accommodation and food for their customers, but also an atmosphere in which they enjoy their meal. This atmosphere doubtless has its price, for which the customer pays in the price of his meal. The same would not be true in respect to a shopping centre where generally it could not be said that a consumer pays for the atmosphere in the same way as he might for an hotel or restaurant. The question of atmosphere has since been clarified in CAA 1990 Sch AA1, where column (2) 'Assets so included' in Table 1 refers specifically to '*Decorative assets provided for the enjoyment of the public in the hotel, restaurant or similar trades*'.   [35.41]

2   Building alterations connected with installation of machinery or plant

CAA 1990 s 66 provides that where a person carrying on a trade incurs capital expenditure on alterations to an existing building *incidental* to the installation of machinery or plant for the purposes of the trade, then that expenditure will be treated as if it were expenditure on the provision of that machinery or plant and therefore eligible for capital allowances.

The word *incidental* is defined in the *Oxford* dictionary as 'casual, not essential'. In *IRC v Barclay Curle & Co Ltd* (1969), Lord Reid concluded that *incidental* is a wider word than *necessary*. When new machinery or plant is installed in an existing building, the trade may require more to be done than the mere installation in order that it serves its purpose. Thus alterations connected with the installation of the machinery or plant will qualify for capital allowances.

Under normal circumstances, expenditure incurred on a lift shaft, for example, would not qualify, as the shaft is part of the building and does not satisfy the premises test. Lift shafts are also defined as being part of the expression 'building' in Sch AA1. However, the installation of a new lift in an existing building may well require the construction of a new lift shaft. This could be regarded as being building alterations connected with the installation of the lift and thus fall within the provisions of CAA 1990 s 66 and therefore unaffected by Sch AA1.

Other examples of incidental works might include the formation of access points specifically to accommodate the installation of new plant in an existing building, the underpinning of the foundations of an hotel necessitated by the construction of a new swimming pool in the existing building, or the dropping of a floor construction to accommodate the installation of a new computer system. [**35.42**]

3 Other qualifying expenditure

In addition to plant and machinery and building alterations connected with its installation, capital allowances are available for other miscellaneous items of expenditure. These areas of expenditure are set out in CAA 1990 Chapter VII and include mineral extraction (s 63), thermal insulation (s 67), films, tapes and discs (s 68), fire safety (s 69) and safety at sports grounds (s 70). Those which are most commonly encountered are thermal insulation and fire safety. If a person carrying on a trade or leasing an industrial building incurs expenditure in adding insulation against loss of heat to any industrial building, then the expenditure will be treated as if it were capital expenditure on the provision of plant and machinery and therefore qualify for capital allowances. Similarly, if a person carrying on a trade is served with a notice under s 5(4) of the Fire Precautions Act 1971 to carry out certain works in order to obtain a fire certificate, then the expenditure incurred on carrying out those works will be treated as if it were capital expenditure on the provision of plant and machinery and therefore qualify for capital allowances.

Finally, mention should be made regarding expenditure on safety at sports grounds, which has become particularly important since the Hillsborough disaster and the recommendations of the Taylor Report. This has resulted in football clubs appraising their safety standards with many having to incur substantial expenditure on improving their standards of safety. Where such expenditure is the result of the need to comply with terms and conditions of a safety certificate or the requirements of a local authority, then the expenditure incurred on carrying out those works will be treated as if it were capital expenditure on the provision of plant and machinery and therefore qualify for capital allowances. [**35.43**]

4 Who can claim capital allowances?

a) *Machinery or plant used in the course of a trade*

In order to qualify for capital allowances, the machinery or plant must belong to the taxpayer and be used in the course of his trade or used to produce an assessable income. Under Schedule D Case I or II corporate taxpayers, sole traders and partnerships; employees under Schedule E who purchase machinery or plant 'necessarily provided for use in the performance of the duties', and under Schedule A a landlord who provides machinery or plant for use in the repair, maintenance or management of the property are all entitled to claim.   **[35.44]**

b) *Machinery or plant used otherwise than in the course of a trade*

Capital allowances, however, are not restricted to a taxpayer using machinery or plant in the course of his trade. CAA 1990 s 61 provides that where machinery or plant is *first let* by any person otherwise in the course of a trade and whether or not it is used in the course of the lessee's trade, the capital expenditure incurred by the lessor in providing the machinery or plant will be treated as if it had been provided for the purposes of a trade carried on by the lessor. This is irrespective of any other trade carried on by the lessor at the commencement of the letting. Thus an insurance company, for example, whose trade is insurance, but which invests in and leases property, will be entitled to claim capital allowances on the machinery and plant in that property when it is first let. Similarly, a Schedule A taxpayer who derives rental income from investment property will be entitled to claim capital allowances on the machinery or plant in that property to reduce his taxable rental income.

The provisions of s 61 are particularly important as the majority of capital allowance claims are made upon machinery or plant in investment properties leased otherwise than in the course of a trade, such as by insurance companies under Schedule D or non-resident companies under Schedule A.   **[35.45]**

c) *Tenant's fixtures*

If a lessee of a building incurs capital expenditure on the provision of machinery or plant, which he is required to provide under the terms of his lease, for the purposes of a trade carried on by him (and provided that machinery or plant is not installed or fixed so as to become part of that building or land) then the machinery or plant will be deemed to belong to him, on which he may claim the benefit of capital allowances (CAA 1990 s 61(4)).

In preparing a claim for capital allowances on the machinery and plant in a building it is important to identify the expenditure incurred by the lessor of the building and any lessee. Fixtures will be treated as belonging to the person who incurred the expenditure on the installation of an asset either for use in the trade or for the purpose of leasing other than in the course of a trade, provided that at the time the asset becomes a fixture the person has an interest in the (relevant) land.

In *Stokes v Costain Property Investments Ltd* (1984), Costain installed machinery and plant in a building for which they had an 'agreement to lease'. They were, however, denied capital allowances on their expenditure as, at the time the assets were installed, the term covered by the lease had not commenced and the machinery and plant did not 'belong to' them. Whilst the assets were regarded as belonging to the lessor, they were also unable to claim as the expenditure had not been incurred by them (and see *Melluish v BMI (No 3) Ltd* (1995)).

FA 1985 clarified the entitlements of lessors and lessees: see now CAA 1990 Chapter VI. An interest in land is defined in s 51(1) and includes a fee simple estate or a contract for its purchase; a lease or an agreement for a lease; an easement or an agreement for an easement; a mortgagor's equity of redemption; and a licence to occupy land. As this rule may result in the fixture 'belonging to' two or more persons with different interests in the land at the same time, s 52 lays down an order for priority of entitlement whereby the asset can belong to only one person at a time; generally to the person with the most subordinate interest. [35.46]

d) *Contributions made to capital expenditure*

Where a person contributes a capital sum to expenditure on machinery or plant used for the purposes of a trade carried on by him or by a tenant of land in which he has an interest, and that expenditure would otherwise have been regarded as incurred by another person to whom an allowance would have been made, then the contributor will be entitled to those allowances. [35.47]

> **EXAMPLE 35.1**
>
> A property company owning a shopping centre leases one of the units to a retailer who, under the terms of his lease, is required to fit out that unit in order to carry on his trade. The expenditure incurred on machinery and plant is £50,000 of which the lessor property company contributes the sum of £20,000. The lessor will be entitled to capital allowances on his contribution to expenditure of £20,000 and the lessee on the balance of £30,000.

e) *Non-resident Schedule A taxpayers*

An increasing number of offshore and foreign companies or individuals invest in UK property and are able to make use of capital allowances under CAA 1990 s 61. It is the responsibility of the managing agent acting on behalf of the investor to withhold a sum from the rent in respect of Schedule A tax (currently 23%). In arriving at the appropriate retention he should make allowance for interest payments, management expenses and capital allowances, all of which may be taken into account in calculating the taxable income. [35.48]

f) *Machinery or plant held as stock in trade*

Where machinery or plant is held as stock in trade no capital allowances are available. Thus in the case of a property company, it is important to ascertain whether the property is held in a trading or investment portfolio. Whereas capital allowances will be available on the investment properties they are *not* be available on those held as stock in trade. This will similarly apply to a development company which constructs a building containing machinery and plant for sale and not to produce rental income for the company. The purchaser of that building will, however, be entitled to claim capital allowances, should he qualify, on that part of the purchase price which is attributable to the machinery and plant. [35.49]

g) *Machinery or plant let for use in a residential building*

CAA 1990 s 61(2) specifically *excludes* machinery or plant let for use in a dwelling house. It is, however, worth noting that machinery or plant such as boilers and lifts in the 'common parts' of blocks of flats will be allowable as they are not in the dwelling. [35.50]

5 When may an allowance be claimed?

In the case of a person using machinery or plant in the course of a trade, the allowance will be available against the profits or income of the accounting period in which the expenditure on the asset was incurred, provided the asset belonged to the taxpayer at some time during that period.

Where machinery or plant is used otherwise than in the course of a trade, then allowances will not be available until the machinery or plant on which the expenditure has been incurred is *first let*. Thus, where a vacant building is purchased for lease, the expenditure attributable to the machinery and plant will not be allowable until it is first let. For the purposes of the definition of *first let,* it is generally accepted by the Inland Revenue that the first letting of any of the machinery or plant in the building will entitle the taxpayer to capital allowances on the whole of the expenditure on the machinery and plant in that building.

The date on which expenditure is incurred is usually the date on which the obligation to pay for the asset becomes unconditional (when title will normally pass) even though the agreement may provide a credit period for payment. Where, however, any such credit period exceeds four months from the date when the contract becomes unconditional, the expenditure is incurred only on the latest date by which the payment must be made (CAA 1990 s 159(5)). Furthermore, as an anti-avoidance measure, if the obligation to pay arises earlier than normal commercial usage for that trade and the only or main benefit that results is the bringing forward of capital allowances to an earlier accounting period, the expenditure will be deemed to be incurred on the later date by or on which payment must actually be made.   [35.51]

6   How are the allowances used?

The allowances are deductible from taxable profits in the relevant tax year. If the allowances exceed those profits, or if there are no profits, the unused allowances may be carried forward and set against future profits. Alternatively the taxpayer may elect to treat the surplus as a loss and deduct it from his other income under TA 1988 s 383, or carry it back under TA 1988 s 381 if appropriate (see [**7.81**]). For companies, the effect of TA 1988 s 393(4) is broadly similar to s 383 in that it enables the allowances to be carried back for a period of one year to obtain a refund of tax. For the position under Schedule A, see [**8.45**].   [35.52]

7   How is the amount of qualifying expenditure established?

In order to claim capital allowances, it is first necessary to identify and assess qualifying capital expenditure. Under normal circumstances, such as in the case of the purchase of a printing press, computer or other 'stand alone' identifiable asset, the qualifying capital expenditure is simply established by the actual cost incurred in its acquisition by the taxpayer. Similarly, capital expenditure incurred on machinery and plant in the construction of a new building, or in the alteration or refurbishment of an existing building may be established, in most cases, by identifying those assets qualifying for capital allowances and then abstracting the cost of providing and installing them directly from invoices or priced documentation.   [35.53]

a) *Machinery and plant in purchased buildings*

Establishing qualifying expenditure is not always a case of readily identifying the cost of each asset. In certain instances, such as the purchase of a building containing machinery and plant, the only known cost will be the price paid by the purchaser for the entire building. Within the purchase price of the building the purchaser would have acquired certain assets, such as lifts, heating, sanitary ware, electrical installations, fittings, etc, the cost of which will qualify for capital allowances. CAA 1990 s 150 provides for the apportionment of a consideration. Simply stated, s 150 provides that where the sale of any property includes the sale of other property which qualifies for capital allowances, then the cost of the qualifying machinery or plant will be a *just apportionment of the purchase price properly attributable* to the machinery or plant. Since the majority of capital allowance claims are made on machinery and plant forming part of the acquisition cost of an existing building, the provisions and interpretation of s 150 are particularly important. Unfortunately they are also the most difficult areas of claim to assess.

When a property investor, for example, purchases a freehold interest in a commercial property, he acquires three main assets, namely land, the building and the machinery and plant within the building. In order to establish the capital expenditure incurred upon machinery and plant, it is first necessary to apportion the purchase price between land and buildings. Once this has been achieved, it should be possible to break the purchase price of the building element into its component parts and thus establish the apportionment to machinery and plant. In order to do this the expertise of a property cost consultant will be required, although most are unaware of the broad principles of capital allowances, let alone the detailed legislation and case law surrounding machinery and plant.

Once land cost (and here *cost* should be emphasised as opposed to value) has been established, this must be discounted, since capital allowances are not available on land. An estimate of the reinstatement cost of the building including its machinery and plant split into its component parts may then be used to calculate the equivalent qualifying expenditure in the acquisition, as an apportionment of the purchase price. The detailed procedures, considerations and valuation techniques are beyond the scope of this book, although the Inland Revenue and Valuation Office work to detailed guidelines, the requirements of which would need to be satisfied by the taxpayer.

It should be emphasised that where a claim is made for capital allowances on the qualifying expenditure of machinery and plant in a purchased property under the provisions of s 150, a just apportionment is the *price paid* for the qualifying assets. It is neither the written-down value, market value nor the original cost. **[35.54]**

b) *Restrictions*

The criteria for the amount of qualifying expenditure under the provisions of s 150 are as described in the preceding section. However, there are certain restrictive provisions which may affect the amount of expenditure qualifying for capital allowances. **[35.55]**

c) *Transactions between connected persons and sale and leasebacks*

Where the purchaser of an asset is connected with the vendor or where the purchaser leases the asset back to the vendor (as provided in CAA 1990 s 75), the purchaser will, in the first instance, be restricted to any disposal value brought into account by the vendor, but in any event be restricted in the amount of expenditure qualifying as a capital allowance to the smallest of (CAA 1990 s 76(2)):

(1) the open market value of the machinery or plant;
(2) where capital expenditure was incurred by the seller on the provision of the machinery or plant, the amount of that expenditure;
(3) where capital expenditure was incurred by any person connected with the seller on the provision of the machinery or plant, the amount of that expenditure incurred by that person.

'Open market value' in relation to any machinery or plant, means an amount equal to the price which the machinery or plant would have fetched if sold in the open market. This is not defined any further in the Act, but could be construed as an apportionment of the open market value of the building of which the machinery or plant forms part. However, as this is often difficult to determine, in such cases, the qualifying expenditure is the lesser of (1) or (2). Invariably, and particularly in the case of buildings, the asset is sold by the vendor for a sum greater than that paid by him, resulting in the purchaser being able to claim on a 'just apportionment properly attributable' as provided in CAA 1990 s 150, but restricted to the expenditure incurred by the vendor.

A similar restriction applies where a transaction between parties is one where the sole or main benefit accruing to the parties is the obtaining of an allowance (CAA 1990 s 75). [35.56]

d) *Machinery or plant acquired by a purchaser on or after 24 July 1996*

Where a person has incurred capital expenditure on or after 24 July 1996 on the provision of machinery or plant which has been subject to a claim for capital allowances by any previous owner, then the provisions of the FA 1997 Sch 16 para 4 inserted new s 56B into CAA 1990 which provides that the purchaser will be entitled to claim capital allowances on no greater qualifying expenditure than the disposal value brought into account by any prior claimant. This is the case even where a 'just apportionment' is greater than the disposal value brought into account.

The prior claimant is required to bring a disposal value into account in accordance with CAA 1990 s 24. The disposal value may be less than the price paid by the vendor reflecting depreciation and thus reducing any *balancing charge* (see [**35.65**] on the prior claimant. If a disposal value is not specifically stated or if a *joint election* (see [**35.59**]) has not been made, it is likely that the Revenue would regard the disposal value to be the same as the purchase price. Where more than one of the previous owners had made a claim for capital allowances, then s 56B(5) provides that the purchaser will be restricted to the most recent disposal brought into account.

Where no previous owner has made a claim for capital allowances, even if entitled to do so, then the purchaser will be entitled to an unrestricted claim for capital allowances based upon a just apportionment of his purchase price of the property.

It should be noted that s 56B does not apply where the purchaser acquired the machinery or plant from a vendor who incurred his expenditure before 24 July 1996. In such a case the provisions of CAA 1990 s 59(10) and (11) still apply. These provide that the purchaser will be entitled to claim capital allowances on no greater qualifying expenditure than the disposal value brought into account by the vendor and is less restrictive than s 56B, insofar as it applies only to claims made by a vendor (former owner). In this case where the vendor is a non-taxpayer or not entitled to claim capital allowances such as pension fund, local or central government, charity etc, or where the vendor is a trader or property developer and has held the asset as stock in trade, or where the vendor has been unable to claim due to waving his right to do so, having no taxable profit or income, or has simply disregarded capital allowances, then s 59(10) and (11) will not apply. Under these provisions therefore, it is only the claim of the vendor that is relevant and the purchaser will be entitled to an unrestricted claim for capital allowances based upon a just apportionment of his purchase price of the property, even if a claim was made by any owner prior to the vendor. [35.57]

e) *Machinery or plant acquired by a purchaser before 24 July 1996*

Where a person incurred capital expenditure before 24 July 1996, the provisions of s 56B will not apply. In such a case the provisions of CAA 1990 s 59(10) and (11), as described above, apply in restricting the purchaser to the disposal value brought into account by the vendor.

Where however, the purchaser acquired the machinery or plant before 24 July 1996 from a vendor who incurred his expenditure on such machinery or plant before 12 July 1984 the purchaser will be entitled to an unrestricted claim as described above on a just apportionment of the purchase price of the property, even if a claim for capital allowances had been made by the vendor. In such a case the transaction falls outside the provisions of CAA 1990 Chapter VI. This is subject to any restrictions which might apply due to a transaction between connected persons or sale and leasebacks as described above.

It should be noted that all expenditure incurred after 24 July 1996 which is expenditure incurred under a commitment made by the vendor before 12 July 1984 will no longer be applicable and will no longer be exempt from restriction. **[35.58]**

The effect of capital allowances claims by previous owners under the existing and new legislation

Each horizontal line represents a period of time in the life of properties 1 to 7. The arrows indicate a change of ownership and whether or not a capital allowances claim has been made. The final arrow shows whether or not the claim is restricted for the new owner.

f) *Apportionment of Expenditure by Election*

With effect from 19 March 1997, a vendor who has claimed capital allowances on machinery or plant can enter into a joint election with the purchaser to apportion the sale price of the property to the machinery or plant.

The amount specified in the election cannot exceed either the vendor's claim or the price paid by the purchaser for the whole property. In most cases the cap for the election will be the vendor's claim. The election can be an amount in excess of what the purchaser's apportioned cost of the machinery or plant would be if no election was made.

By allowing an election for the total price paid for the property by the purchaser the Inland Revenue has avoided the need for an apportionment to establish the cap for the election.

Generally the minimum amount specified in the election as being the apportioned cost of machinery or plant would be the notional tax written-down value. However, a lesser amount may be possible where it could be shown that there is no avoidance objective.

The election must be made by notice to the Inland Revenue and, as well as stating the amount fixed by the election, must also contain:

(1) The name of the parties to the election.

(2) Identification of the machinery or plant.

(3) Identification of the relevant land.

(4) Particulars of the interest acquired by the purchaser of the lease granted to him.

(5) The tax district references of the parties to the election.

Unlike an apportionment specified in a contract of sale, an election once made is not negotiable and is irrevocable, binding upon the parties and the Inland Revenue. If the election is higher than the statutory limit, namely the notional tax written-down value (or lower where avoidance is not the objective), then the amount is automatically reduced and treated as if the reduced amount was the original elected figure.

Elections must be made within two years from the date of acquisition, or if the purchaser is acquiring a new lease, two years from the effective date of the lease. In most cases the vendor will have prepared the election for signing at the same time that contracts are exchanged on the property. With this in mind it is important that purchasers consider the implications of an election before signing and satisfy themselves that any potential cost has been taken into account in fixing the purchase price of the property.   [**35.59**]

g) *Agreed sale price of assets between vendor and purchaser without election*

Where there has not been an apportionment of expenditure by election, as described above, and a contract of sale states the sale price of certain qualifying assets which might otherwise have been the subject of an apportionment under the provisions of CAA 1990 s 150, the purchaser is deemed to acquire those assets for the price stated in the contract of sale which becomes the qualifying expenditure for the purpose of capital allowances. Even without an election this could still restrict the purchaser even where no other restriction applies. Where the taxable position of the vendor and the purchaser is affected by an apportionment and a question arises as to the manner in which the sum is apportioned, CAA 1990 s 151 provides that the matter may be referred to the Commissioners. In most unrestricted apportionments, however, under the provisions of s 150 of the Act, the sale price is deemed to be the apportioned price calculated as described above.   [**35.60**]

h) *Leasehold acquisitions*

The foregoing situations refer to acquisitions of freehold interests. Where, however, a purchaser acquires a leasehold interest from a lessor where the interest was created after 11 July 1984 and the lessor was entitled to the benefit of capital allowances, the lessor and the lessee must elect within two years of the date of creation of the lease if the entitlement of the allowances are to be transferred to the lessee, in accordance with the provisions of CAA 1990 s 55(1)(d) and (3). If no joint election is entered into, then the allowances continue to vest in the lessor. Where the lessor is not entitled to claim capital allowances, then the benefit of the capital allowances pass to the lessee without the need for a joint election in accordance with the provisions of CAA 1990 s 56 (see *West Somerset Railway plc v Chivers* (1995)).

Where the leasehold interest was created prior to 12 July 1984 a joint election is not required as the transaction will fall outside the provisions of Chapter VI of the Act. As no two parties can be entitled to claim on the same assets, the lessee will only be entitled to claim if the lessor is unable to claim.

However, should a subsequent transaction take place where the vendor of a leasehold interest disposes of that interest, then the same provisions as described for freehold transactions will apply depending on whether the vendor's expenditure was incurred prior to 12 July 1984 or after 11 July 1984. [**35.61**]

8 The allowances

a) *Writing-down allowances*

Currently capital allowances are available as a writing-down allowance (WDA) at the rate of 25% pa of the 'qualifying expenditure' on a reducing balance basis. The allowances first become available from the end of the chargeable period in which the expenditure was incurred and, in the case of an asset to be leased, when it is first let, as described earlier in this chapter. In the case of individuals the writing-down allowances may be claimed in whole or in part, but in the case of companies the allowances are given automatically unless disclaimed in whole or in part. [**35.62**]

EXAMPLE 35.2

ABC Property Company Ltd acquires a building for investment purposes and incurs, as an apportionment of the purchase price, capital expenditure of £800,000 on machinery and plant, which is leased to its tenants. The company would be entitled to claim writing-down allowances during each year that the machinery and plant remains in its ownership as follows:

	£
Year 1	
Purchase price	800,000
Less: 25% WDA	200,000
Qualifying expenditure transferred to pool	£ 600,000
Year 2	
Less: 25% WDA	150,000
Qualifying expenditure transferred to pool	£ 450,000
Year 3	
Less: 25% WDA (to nearest thousand pounds)	112,000
Qualifying expenditure transferred to pool	£ 338,000

etc, etc . . .

Thus in each of the first three years writing-down allowances of £200,000, £150,000 and £112,000 respectively could be offset against the company's taxable profits. This would continue until the property is sold, when a disposal value would be brought into account (discussed later).

b) *First year allowances*

The first Labour Budget on 2 July 1997 re-introduced a 50% first year allowance for small and medium-sized businesses.

The new rules will apply to expenditure by such businesses on machinery and plant with the exception of motor cars, sea-going ships, railway assets and machinery and plant for leasing. It is particularly important to note the exclusion of machinery and plant for leasing as this will exclude all machinery and plant fixed to a building held for investment purposes. The new rules will apply to all qualifying expenditure incurred in the year ending 1 July 1998.

In order to qualify, a business is classified as small or medium-sized in accordance with the Companies Act definition. In order to qualify a company must satisfy any two of the following conditions:—

(i) Turnover not more than £11.2 million.

(ii) Assets not more than £5.6 million.

(iii) Not more than 250 employees.

Where the company is a member of a group, the group must be small or medium-sized. A first year allowance in such circumstances will also apply to long life assets, where the first year allowances will be doubled to 12%. After claiming a first year allowance the balance is transferred to the pool and then written down at 25% pa on a reducing balance basis as set out in *Example 35.2*.

The rules relating to companies and individuals' rights to claim first year allowances are the same as for writing-down allowances.   **[35.63]**

c) *Pooling*

Reference has been made above to transferring qualifying expenditure to the *pool*. Pooling is simply the principle of pooling the expenditure incurred on a number of assets at the end of each chargeable period to form the basis for the following year's WDA calculation. For certain 'short-life' assets acquired after 31 March 1986, however, a contrary election may be made as discussed later in this chapter.

FA 1997 introduced Sch 14 which allows Schedule A cases (receipt of rents from property investment) to be treated as a trade. This applies to companies in the same way as it applies to individuals.

Capital allowances for expenditure incurred on machinery or plant used in a Schedule A business will not be 'pooled' in the same way as for trades. This means that when a property is acquired, the cost of machinery or plant within the property will be added to a 'pool' of plant expenditure from which writing-down allowances of 25% can be drawn down each year to set against income or corporation tax arising from the Schedule A business. Likewise, property sales will result in the disposal value of the machinery or plant being deducted from the 'pool' in the year of disposal.

These 'pooling' provisions mean that no balancing allowances or charges in respect to machinery or plant will arise on property disposals. Whilst 'pooling' for Schedule A had previously largely been accepted on an unofficial basis by the Inland Revenue, the new rules now make 'pooling' official.   **[35.64]**

d) *Balancing allowances and charges*

In the year when a business terminates and/or the assets are sold there is no WDA; instead the proceeds received on the sale of the machinery and plant are deducted from the qualifying expenditure in the pool. If they are less than the value in the pool, the taxpayer receives a 'balancing allowance' for the difference which is deductible from his profits for the basis period. If the proceeds of the sale are greater than the value left in the pool, the excess is a 'balancing charge' and is taxed as a receipt of the business (this is sometimes referred to as a 'clawback' of capital allowances). This procedure, which also applies to a disposal of a single item of machinery and plant which is not in a pool, ensures that allowances exactly equal the cost of items to the business.

EXAMPLE 35.3

Property company A sells a commercial office development to property company B for £2m and brings into account a written-down disposal value of £250,000 in respect of machinery and plant. However, when it acquired the building two years earlier at a cost of £1.7m, it calculated the cost apportioned to plant at £300,000 for the purposes of capital allowances.

In the first year of owning the plant it claimed a 25% WDA of £75,000 and in the second year a WDA (on the reduced balance) of £56,250. After the second year the balance left in the pool is therefore £168,750. As the disposal value is £250,000 there will be a balancing charge or capital allowances clawback of £81,250 (£250,000 − £168,750).

It can be seen from *Example 35.3* that the more the plant is written down on disposal, the less will be the balancing charge. If company A incurred its capital expenditure acquiring the property prior to 12 July 1984, the disposal value will have no effect on the ability of company B to make an unrestricted claim on an apportionment of the purchase price. If, however, company A acquired the property after 11 July 1984, the expenditure incurred by company B will be subject to the provisions of CAA 1990 s 150 and will be restricted to the disposal value brought into account by company A. In this case therefore, it will be in the best interests of company B to agree as high a disposal value as possible. As a result negotiation of the disposal value between company A and company B may be required to obtain a figure acceptable to both parties. (See [**35.60**].)

Balancing adjustments on the termination of a business or on the disposal of assets may be prevented in two cases where the taxpayer continues to be involved in the running of the business or using the assets. *First*, on a change of partners in a firm (eg when C joins the firm of AB & Co as a partner) there may be a deemed discontinuance (under TA 1988 s 113) of the old firm (AB & Co). Accordingly balancing allowances and charges will be calculated as if the assets were sold for their market value at that time. If, however, there is an election to treat the business as continuing, capital allowances continue as if the new owners had carried on the business and used the assets throughout. *Secondly*, when the transferor and the transferee are connected persons, they can elect not to treat the business as discontinued so that the transferee can take over the allowances of the transferor. This election will normally be used when a business is incorporated. Elections must be made within two years of the date of succession (CAA 1990 ss 77–78).   [**35.65**]

EXAMPLE 35.4

A, who has carried on a trade for many years, owns plant and machinery on which the qualifying expenditure at the end of 1993–94 is £5,000. On 1 June 1994, he transfers the business to A Ltd, a company controlled by him. A and A Ltd may elect for A Ltd to receive the allowances as if there had been no discontinuance. Hence, in financial year 1994, A Ltd receives a WDA on machinery and plant of 25% × £5,000 = £1,250.

e) *Disposal values*

When a taxpayer disposes of machinery and plant, he is required to bring a disposal value into account in accordance with CAA 1990 s 24. From the vendor's point of view, he can dispose of machinery and plant at any price providing that price is agreed with the purchaser. This will enable the vendor to minimise his clawback. However, in order to do so he will need to fulfil two criteria. *First*, the figure at which he wishes to dispose of the machinery and plant must form part of the contract between vendor and purchaser. *Secondly*, the assets to which this figure relates must be clearly set out as an appendix to the contract.

Should the purchaser subsequently disregard the agreement in the contract by claiming a sum greater than that agreed, he could be liable for breach of contract and open himself to legal action by the vendor. However, if the assets to which the disposal value relates are not identified within the contract, then the meaning of machinery and plant could be open to interpretation.

There is no obligation upon the purchaser to enter into a contract which specifies machinery and plant. Indeed, from the purchaser's point of view it would be better if the contract remained silent on this subject. If the vendor purchased the building prior to 12 July 1984, the purchaser will be entitled to a full apportionment under s 150 even if the vendor has made a claim and brought a disposal value into account. However, if the vendor incurred his expenditure after 11 July 1984 and made a claim to capital allowances the purchaser will, of course, be restricted. Under these circumstances the purchaser's maximum entitlement will be either a full apportionment under s 150, or more likely, limited to the disposal value brought into account by the vendor under s 59(10), whichever is the lower. Naturally, the purchaser will want the disposal value to be as high as possible to maximise his claim. If there is no contractual agreement between vendor and purchaser and the apportioned value of machinery and plant is higher than the price paid by the vendor for the same machinery and plant, then the restricted claim under s 59(10) can be no lower than the vendor's purchase price.

Where the vendor has omitted to specify the machinery and plant within the contract of sale, then it will be difficult for him subsequently to justify a disposal value at less than cost if the purchaser's apportionment is higher than the vendor's cost. In such cases, there is no reason why a claim to maximum disposal value should not succeed, irrespective of what the vendor subsequently brought into account.

While vendors are understandably anxious to specify a minimum disposal value, there is no need to become obsessed by the idea. A balancing charge or 'clawback' on disposal is made by adjustment to the pool (balance of unclaimed allowances). This is referred to earlier in this chapter and illustrated in *Example 35.3*. In essence a vendor subject to a balancing charge on disposal will not be required to sign a cheque to the Inland Revenue, the clawback being effected on paper by an adjustment to the pool. This will of course affect the following year's allowance, but this is minimised as the WDA is only available at 25%.

Some inspectors of taxes have stated that there must be an agreement between vendor and purchaser. As stated earlier, there is no obligation in the Act. The Act merely states under s 151 the procedure to be adopted where there is a dispute between vendor and purchaser.   [**35.66**]

f) *Short-life assets (see also SP 1/86)*

In the case of assets acquired after 31 March 1986, the taxpayer may irrevocably elect within two years after the end of the year of acquisition for that asset not to be pooled ('short-life assets'): ie for the WDAs on each short-life asset to be calculated separately from the WDAs on the pool of qualifying expenditure (CAA 1990 s 37). The election is not available for items such as ships, cars, certain leased items and television sets and is intended for (although not specifically limited to) assets with a working life of less than five years. These 'de-pooling' provisions provided some compensation for the abolition of the first year allowance by ensuring that the cost of such an asset can be written off for tax over the same period that it, in fact, depreciates. Thus if a 'short-life' asset is disposed of within five years after the end of the year of acquisition, the disposal proceeds will trigger an immediate balancing allowance or charge for the trader, instead of effecting only a reduction in the overall qualifying expenditure in the pool.

If the asset is not disposed of within that five-year period, the written-down value must then be transferred to the pool.

To prevent the short-life election from being abused by a sale to a connected person within the five-year period, CAA 1990 s 37(8) provides that the purchaser in such a case will be deemed to have made the same election and, therefore, must transfer the asset into his general pool on the same date as the vendor would otherwise have done. The connected vendor and purchaser may, however, elect within two years of the year of sale for the asset to be transferred at its written-down rather than market value, so that the vendor avoids a balancing allowance or charge (CAA 1990 s 37(8)). **[35.67]**

g) *Use for purposes other than trade (CAA 1990 s 79)*

Where expenditure is incurred on an asset not used wholly and exclusively for the purposes of a trade, the asset is kept outside the taxpayer's general pool: it is treated as used in a separate 'notional' trade. Further, if a pooled asset ceases to be used wholly and exclusively for trade purposes, this is treated as a disposal of the asset. Thus, its disposal value reduces the qualifying expenditure in the pool. In these cases WDAs are given on such proportion of the expenditure on the asset (or, where it has come out of a pool, its disposal value) as may be just and reasonable having regard in particular to the extent to which the asset is used for business purposes.

If the asset is disposed of (which includes ceasing to use it for the purposes of the trade at all) its disposal value will give rise to a balancing allowance or charge. **[35.68]**

h) *Long-life assets*

FA 1997 Sch 14 reduced the rate at which writing-down allowances are available on long-life assets from 25% to 6% pa on a reducing balance basis. The definition of a long-life asset is machinery or plant with an effective working life when new of 25 years or more. Section 28B makes it clear that the rules of long-life assets do not apply to expenditure incurred on the provision of machinery or plant which is a fixture in, or is provided for use in, a dwelling house, retail shop, showroom, hotel or office. Whilst these exclusions do not include industrial buildings, it is unlikely that machinery or plant in such buildings will be classified as long-life assets as their economic life had almost certainly been less than 25 years. The 6% rate is aimed at the utilities, such as the power industry, where substantial expenditure is incurred on plant with a long life. **[35.69]**

i) *Expenditure incurred by equipment lessors*

Following the case of *Melluish v BMI (No 3)* (1995) the House of Lords decided that equipment lessors could claim capital allowances for expenditure incurred upon machinery or plant which is leased to non-taxpayers. The Inland Revenue was unhappy by this decision as it meant that future non-taxpayers could indirectly benefit from the value of capital allowances to which they were not entitled by entering into a finance lease with a non-taxpayer who would pass back the value of the capital allowances via reduced finance charges.

As a result of this decision, the FA 1997 introduced a new Sch 1 which changes the rules so that equipment lessors will no longer be entitled to capital allowances for expenditure incurred upon machinery or plant which is a fixture where the equipment lessee is not a taxpayer (eg pension funds, local authorities, charities etc) or where the machinery or plant is for use in a dwelling house.

However, if the machinery or plant can be regarded as chattels, which have only become fixtures for operational purposes, then the equipment lessor will still be entitled to claim capital allowances.   **[35.70]**

9   Motor cars

The allowance for motor cars is restricted because they can (and usually will) be used for private as well as business purposes (CAA 1990 ss 34–36). WDAs (only) are given on motor vehicles used for business purposes. The vehicle must, therefore, be designed to carry goods (eg lorries); or unsuitable for use as a private car (eg taxis and buses); or a hire vehicle which is not hired to any one person for more than 30 consecutive days nor for more than 90 days in any period of 12 months.

Other vehicles qualify for 25% WDA but subject to a maximum allowance calculated on the basis that the original cost was £12,000. Because of this restriction on the WDA for non-business vehicles, they are not pooled but are written down individually so increasing the likelihood of a balancing charge or allowance.

To prevent businesses leasing expensive cars (ie which cost at least £12,000) and circumventing the allowance restriction by claiming the deduction of the whole rental as a business expense, the deduction under TA 1988 s 74 is limited to the proportion that £12,000 plus one-half of the excess above £12,000 bears to the total original cost.   **[35.71]**

EXAMPLE 35.5

Footsore hires a car, which cost £16,000, for business use at a rent of £1,020 for one year. The hire charge that he can treat as a business expense is limited to:

$$\frac{£12,000 + 1/2 \ (£16,000 - £12,000)}{£16,000} \times £1,020 = £892.50$$

10   Hire purchase

The acquisition of machinery or plant on hire purchase is treated as an outright purchase so that capital allowances are granted to the hirer on the capital element of the purchase price as soon as the asset is brought into use in the business. The interest element is a deductible business expense in the year it is paid.   **[35.72]–[35.80]**

IV   INDUSTRIAL BUILDINGS

Capital allowances are available under CAA 1990 Part I for the expenditure incurred upon the construction or purchase of an industrial building or structure used for a *qualifying* purpose. Thus the trade carried on by the occupational tenant is all important.   **[35.81]**

1   Definition

Unlike plant and machinery, an industrial building is defined in detail in the Act. It includes a mill, a factory, a building used for transport and power undertakings, a building used in the manufacture of goods or for subjecting them to a process, or a building used for the storage of goods to be subjected to a process in the course of a trade, or for the storage of goods which in the course of a trade have been the subject of a manufacturing process and not yet delivered to the purchaser—to name but a few (for recent illustrations of the ambit of an 'industrial building', see *Bestway (Holdings) Ltd v Luff* (1997) and *Sarsfield v Dixons Group plc* (1997)). A comprehensive definition is set out in CAA 1990 s 18. Expenditure on acquiring the land itself is not allowed except for the costs of tunnelling, levelling and preparing the land for an industrial building.

In many instances industrial buildings will contain production and administrative offices. Where parts of an industrial building are used for a non-industrial purpose, the full allowance is still available providing expenditure on that part is no more than 25% of the expenditure on the whole building.

Toll roads were specifically brought within the definition of an 'industrial building or structure' by FA 1991 (thereby enabling the costs of construction to be written off over 25 years) and FA 1995 included 'DBFO' roads ('Design, Build, Finance and Operate'). **[35.82]**

2 Form of allowance

a) *Writing-down allowances*

Currently industrial building allowances (IBAs) are available as a writing-down allowance at the rate of 4% pa on a straight-line basis on the original cost of construction, or purchase price (excluding land), in CAA 1990 s 3(2). The allowances commence from the date the building is first brought into use and continue every year the building is used for a qualifying purpose until the cost is written off. The allowances are also available to a landlord where the building is let, providing the tenant uses the building for a qualifying purpose as described above. The landlord in this case is said to hold the 'relevant interest'. **[35.83]**

EXAMPLE 35.6

ABC Property Company Ltd acquires a new industrial building which it lets to Buberlee Mineral Water Company for the storage of their bottled water before it is dispatched to retailers. ABC acquired the building for £2m and following an apportionment calculation in accordance with CAA 1990 s 150, establishes that it has incurred costs of £150,000 on machinery and plant and that the land cost is £500,000. It is therefore entitled to capital allowances on £150,000 at 25% pa on a reducing balance basis and IBAs on £1.35m (£2m – (£500,000 + £150,000)) at 4% pa on a straight-line basis.

---

b) *First year allowances*

Whilst unavailable at the present time, first year allowances have featured at various times since their inception. Most recently they were reintroduced on a temporary basis in FA 1993 when a first year allowance of 20% was available in respect of buildings which (i) qualify for writing-down allowances, (ii) are constructed under a contract and entered into between 1 November 1992 and 31 October 1993, and (iii) are brought into use for the purpose of a qualifying trade no later than 31 December 1994. It is possible to disclaim all or part of this allowance.

After claiming the first year allowance the balance of qualifying expenditure will be available at 4% pa from the tax year in which the building is brought into use. Where expenditure is incurred in the same year in which the building was brought into use both the first year and writing-down allowance will be available, giving a total of 24% in that year. **[35.84]**

c) *Balancing allowances or charges*

Under the provisions of CAA 1990 s 4, when a building is disposed of the qualifying expenditure left on the building is compared with the disposal consideration and a balancing allowance or charge is made. A balancing charge can never recover more than the allowances given, so that if the disposal value exceeds the original cost of the building, the excess represents a capital gain chargeable to CGT.

At the end of 25 years the building will have been written down to nil. A disposal after 25 years will therefore not give rise to a balancing charge or allowance.   [**35.85**]

d) *Purchase of a secondhand industrial building*

Where a secondhand building is purchased whose use is that of a qualifying industrial building, WDAs will be available to the purchaser over the balance remaining of the 25 years on the residue of the expenditure. Where the building had not previously been used as a qualifying industrial building then the whole of the original expenditure will be available to him.   [**35.86**]

EXAMPLE 35.7

Arkwright builds a jute spinning mill at a cost of £1 million in 1980. In 1994 he sells the mill to Hargreaves for £900,000. Hargreaves continues to use the mill for the jute spinning business.

(1) *Position of Arkwright:* He will qualify for allowances between 1980 to 1993 at a rate of 4% pa of £1m. In 1994, at the time of the sale, he would have received WDAs totalling £520,000 and his remaining qualifying expenditure is £480,000.

(2) On the sale to Hargreaves, Arkwright will suffer a balancing charge of £420,000 (£900,000 – £480,000).

(3) *Position of Hargreaves:* He will qualify for WDAs for the next 12 years on the residue of expenditure of £480,000, plus the balancing charge of £420,000, namely on the original cost of £900,000. This is spread evenly over the remaining 12-year period and is not tied to a 4% figure.

EXAMPLE 35.8

Sto Rage Ltd builds a warehouse at a cost of £500,000 in 1987, but does not use it for a qualifying purpose. ABC Property Company Ltd buys the warehouse from Sto Rage in 1994 for £600,000 and lets it to a printing company. ABC will qualify for WDAs for the next 18 years on the whole of the qualifying expenditure of £500,000, provided it excludes the cost of land. This will be spread evenly over the remaining 18-year period and is not tied to a 4% figure.

Note: Both of the foregoing examples ignore the likely presence of machinery or plant, which may be claimed separately at a 25% WDA as described above.

e) *Prohibition of double allowances*

Where expenditure on an industrial building includes expenditure on machinery or plant, writing-down allowances will be available on the machinery or plant at the rate of 25% pa on a reducing balance basis with the balance of the expenditure incurred on the building qualifying for IBAs at the appropriate straight-line rate over the balance of the 25-year period.

Where the expenditure was incurred by the purchaser before 24 July 1996, the basis of calculation to apportion the machinery or plant is based upon an apportionment of the price paid for the building by the purchaser as previously described. However, FA 1997 introduced CAA 1990 s 3(2A)–(2D) dealing with the prohibition of double allowances. The legislation, which is effective for all expenditure incurred on or after 24 July 1996, refers to the situation where a previous owner had not previously claimed capital allowances for machinery or plant in accordance with the rules for machinery or plant, but has instead, included the expenditure within a claim for an industrial building allowance, or indeed, a claim for any other form of allowance. The most common situation, however, applies to an industrial building where a previous owner may have claimed the whole cost of the building, including the machinery or plant as an industrial building allowance rather than to identify the cost of the machinery or plant and claim it separately under the applicable rules. Where this is the case, the purchaser will still be able to claim the machinery or plant separately, but the claim will have to be based on an apportionment of the 'residue of expenditure' incurred on the construction of the building. This means that the purchaser's claim for machinery or plant cannot exceed the original installation cost of the machinery or plant and in some cases could be less.

A claim for machinery or plant under CAA 1990 Part II is only possible if the expenditure has been included in a capital allowances claim under Part I (enterprise zone allowances, industrial building allowances and hotels) or Part VII (scientific research). Where the expenditure on machinery or plant has been included under Part III (dwelling houses let on assured tenancies), Part IV (mineral extraction), Part V (agricultural buildings) or Part VI (dredging) no subsequent claim for machinery or plant can be made.   [**35.87**]

3 **Miscellaneous**

Hotel buildings (CAA 1990 s 7)   Where expenditure is incurred in the construction, improvement or purchase of a hotel, in which there are at least ten letting bedrooms, which offers breakfast and an evening meal and is open for at least four months between April and October ('qualifying hotel' is defined in CAA 1990 s 19), it will be treated as an industrial building and attract WDAs at 4% per annum on a straight-line basis.   [**35.88**]

Enterprise zones (CAA 1990 s 1)   In order to stimulate economic growth and development in certain degenerated areas, the government designated a small number of enterprise zones. Within these areas expenditure on certain industrial buildings, hotels and commercial buildings (CAA 1990 s 21(5) defines) qualifies for 100% initial allowance. Expenditure incurred upon machinery or plant within such buildings will also qualify for the 100% allowance. Where a building in an enterprise zone is sold it will be treated as having a life of 25 years, in much the same way as an industrial building. There will therefore be a balancing charge or allowance on the vendor and the purchaser will be entitled to claim the qualifying expenditure spread evenly over the balance of 25 years.   [**35.89**]–[**35.100**]

V   OTHER CATEGORIES OF EXPENDITURE ELIGIBLE FOR CAPITAL ALLOWANCES

Agricultural or forestry buildings (CAA 1990 Part V)   Allowances are available for capital expenditure by the owner or tenant of agricultural or forestry land used for the sole purposes of husbandry and forestry. The expenditure must be incurred on the 'construction' of, *inter alia,* farm or forestry buildings including farmhouses (for which only one-third of the cost is allowed); farm cottages; fences and walls; and drainage and sewerage works.

The allowance is given at the same rate as an IBA, 4% pa on a straight-line basis. An initial allowance of 20% was available between 1 November

1992 and 31 October 1993. At the option of the taxpayer a balancing adjustment may be made when an agricultural building etc is demolished, destroyed or sold. This election enables the allowance to be brought into line with actual depreciation.   **[35.101]**

Scientific research (CAA 1990 Part VII)   There is a 100% allowance available for expenditure incurred on scientific research, where 'scientific research' is defined as any activities in the fields of natural or applied science for the extension of knowledge. It is unlikely that expenditure incurred by the development division of a company producing a new product merely to improve the company's status and profitability would qualify. However, if that expenditure was incurred to enable a company to research a product which would ultimately benefit mankind, such as a new drug, then such expenditure would qualify as scientific research expenditure.

As from 1 April 1985, the cost of land and houses ceased to be eligible for the allowance and stricter rules were introduced for the recovery of the allowance where an asset is sold.   **[35.102]**

Patents and 'know-how'   The cost of purchasing a patent for use in a business is relieved by an annual WDA of 25% on a reducing balance basis calculated in respect of a separate pool for all patent expenditure. When the final patent in the pool is sold (or expires) any balance then remaining in the pool will give rise to a balancing allowance (see TA 1988 s 528).

The cost of acquiring 'know-how' comprises a separate pool for which an annual WDA of 25% is given on a reducing basis.   **[35.103]**

Residual   Capital allowances are also available for mines and oil wells and mineral rights and for cemeteries and crematoria. There is a WDA on dredging (CAA 1990 Part VI) at 4% pa.   **[35.104]**

Dwelling houses let on assured tenancies (CAA 1990 Part III)   Expenditure incurred on the construction of a dwelling house let on an assured and certain other tenancies, but only where the expenditure concerned was incurred before 1 April 1992, attracts WDAs of 4% pa. Assured tenancies are defined in the Housing Act 1988.   **[35.105]–[35.120]**

PART B PRACTICE AND PLANNING

36 The '*Ramsay* principle', tax planning and anti-avoidance legislation

I INTRODUCTORY

The desire to escape the payment of tax need scarcely occasion surprise. In some cases, this may be achieved either by non-declaration or by the making of a fraudulent return (for example, by deliberately under-declaring), both of which are examples of tax evasion, that is, illegal acts, subject to criminal sanctions. The greater number of situations concern attempts to avoid or minimise the payment of tax, something a taxpayer is legally entitled to do. As Lord Templeman said in *Ensign Tankers (Leasing) Ltd v Stokes* (1992), 'there is no morality in a tax and no illegality or immorality in a tax avoidance scheme'.

In the average case it will amount to no more than a sensible use of the available exemptions and reliefs which are provided in all tax legislation. In other cases, where the sums involved are greater, the methods adopted by the 'tax planning industry' to escape the fiscal net may take on a complexity that is beyond the comprehension of most individuals and may involve schemes which are divorced from reality. The potential tax avoided (or saved) by these schemes is considerable and to combat their effectiveness the Revenue has two main weapons at their disposal. The first is legislative and takes the form of enactments of three types, the first directed at certain transactions, irrespective of whether or not the purpose of the taxpayer is to avoid tax. An example of such legislation is to be found in Part XV of TA 1988 relating to settlements. The second type is directed against specific avoidance schemes and includes the provisions designed to prevent artificial transactions in land which have been considered at [**8.101**], those aimed at combating the transfer of assets overseas at [**13.111**], and the various provisions aimed at transactions in securities, bond washing and dividend stripping at [**36.52**]. The general characteristic of such legislation is that it is designed to deal with a specific problem, normally after it has arisen, but does not purport to prevent new schemes in different areas. Given a sophisticated legal profession, loopholes in such provisions will be exploited and need constant plugging. IHT is unique in having a legislative provision of the third type: a widely drafted associated operations provision (see IHTA 1984 s 268). Surprisingly, this has been little used to date.

The second weapon in the Revenue's armoury is to challenge in the courts the legal efficacy of avoidance schemes. In the past the Revenue won few victories, in part because of the difficulty it had in putting forward the argument that transactions used to avoid tax should be viewed as shams. No matter how artificial a transaction may be, so long as it is genuine and properly implemented, it cannot be ignored as a sham. The main reason for the Revenue's lack of success, however, was to be found in *IRC v Duke of Westminster* (1936). The object of the scheme in that case was to make servants' wages deductible in arriving at the Duke's total income by paying them by deed of covenant. Hence, although there was no binding agreement to that effect, it was accepted that so long as payments were made under the covenant they would not claim their wages. The House of Lords upheld the scheme saying that, in deciding the consequence of a transaction, the courts will look at the legal effect of the bargain which the parties have entered into and not take account of any supposed artificiality.

In the early 1980s, however, the Revenue won some outstanding battles, most importantly before the House of Lords in the leading cases of *WT Ramsay Ltd v IRC, Eilbeck v Rawling* (1981), *IRC v Burmah Oil* (1982) and *Furniss v Dawson* (1984), from which cases there developed what has come to be known as the *Ramsay* principle (named after the first case in the series). At that time, and most notably at the high point of *Furniss v Dawson*, in which case Lord Scarman commented that new law was gradually being developed and that the boundaries remained yet to be fully explored, it was felt that the new principle had sounded the death knell to artificial avoidance schemes. That feeling was given further credence by the high level of hostility shown by the Revenue to such schemes as evidenced by *IRC v Rossminster Ltd* (1980), and it was believed that potential customers would be deterred from purchasing avoidance packages. The status of *Westminster's* case was left unclear by these judgments which showed that modern judicial attitudes to tax avoidance were very different from those prevailing in the 1930s. Indeed, in *Furniss v Dawson*, Lord Roskill considered that 'the ghost of the Duke of Westminster has haunted the administration of this branch of the law for too long'.

The decisions of *Craven v White* (1988) and *Fitzwilliam v IRC* (1993) appeared to cast doubt upon the strength of the *Ramsay* principle, leaving the precise ambit of the 'judicial associated operations rule' uncertain. In the recent case of *IRC v McGuckian* (1997) the House of Lords unanimously reaffirmed the *Ramsay* principle, although applying it to an obvious and elaborate tax avoidance scheme which fell very clearly within the ambit of *Furniss v Dawson*. Crucially, however, the language used by some of their Lordships echoed that used in the mid 1980s: Lord Steyn, for instance, commented 'Given the reasoning underlying the new approach it is wrong to regard the decisions of the House of Lords since the *Ramsay* case as necessarily marking the limit of the law on tax avoidance schemes (even more striking is the extract from Lord Cooke's speech).   [**36.1**]-[**36.20**]

II ARTIFICIAL SCHEMES AND THE '*RAMSAY* PRINCIPLE'

1 The decisions in *Ramsay* and *Burmah Oil*

In both *Ramsay* and *Burmah Oil* the taxpayers sought to obtain the benefits of CGT loss relief, in the former case to wipe out large profits, in the latter to turn a large, non-allowable loss into an allowable one. To achieve this end both adopted schemes involving a series of steps to be carried out in rapid succession according to a prearranged timetable. Once started, it was intended that the schemes should be carried through to their conclusion which would be that a capital loss had been incurred. In reality, a comparison of the taxpayer's position at the start and finish showed that either no real loss was suffered, or, in *Ramsay's* case, that the only loss suffered was the professional fees paid for the implementation of the scheme! The House of Lords decided that such schemes should be viewed not as a series of separate transactions, none of which was a sham, but as a whole; the position of the taxpayer in real terms being compared at the start and at the finish. Thus, the scheme involved no real loss and was self-cancelling. In *Ramsay* Lord Wilberforce expounded this new approach to avoidance schemes and sought to explain the decision in *Westminster's* case:

> 'While obliging the court to accept documents or transactions, found to be genuine, as such, it does not compel the court to look at a document or a transaction in blinkers, isolated from any context to which it properly belongs. If it can be seen that a document or transaction was intended to have effect as part of a nexus or series of transactions, or as an ingredient of a wider transaction intended as a whole, there is nothing in the doctrine to prevent it being so regarded; to do so is not to prefer form to substance, or substance to form. It is the task of the court to ascertain the legal nature of any transaction to which it is sought to attach a tax, or a tax consequence, and if that emerges from a series, or combination of transactions, intended to operate as such, it is that series or combination which may be regarded' ([1981] STC at 180).

In *Ensign Tankers (Leasing) Ltd v Stokes* (1992), the House of Lords applied the *Ramsay* principle to the single composite transaction made up of 17 documents all dated the same day. **[36.21]**

2 Extending *Ramsay*: *Furniss v Dawson*

The case of *Furniss v Dawson* is of fundamental significance in that, by seeking to clarify the conditions necessary for the application of the *Ramsay* principle, the House of Lords seemed effectively to extend that principle. The *Ramsay* and *Burmah Oil* cases both involved circular self-cancelling schemes, the sole object of which was the avoidance of tax. *Furniss v Dawson*, on the other hand, was concerned with the deferment of CGT by channelling the sale of chargeable assets through an intermediary company. The facts of the case are simple. The Dawsons decided to sell shares to Wood Bastow Holdings Ltd ('Wood Bastow') for £152,000. To defer the CGT that would otherwise have been payable, the shares were first sold to a newly incorporated Manx company ('Greenjacket') for the sum of £152,000 which was satisfied by an issue of shares in that company. The purchased shares were then immediately resold by Greenjacket to Wood Bastow for £152,000. The attraction of the scheme was that at no stage did any CGT liability arise: the sale to Greenjacket was specifically exempted from charge under FA 1965 Sch 7 para 6(2) (see now TCGA 1992 s 135(1)), whilst the resale by Greenjacket did not yield any profit to that company (the shares were purchased and sold for £152,000). As the price paid by Wood Bastow was received and retained by Greenjacket the scheme was not circular or self-cancelling: it involved a separate legal entity (Greenjacket) which ended up with the sale proceeds of the shares.

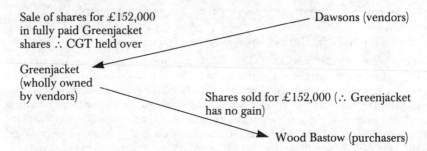

Sale of shares for £152,000
in fully paid Greenjacket
shares ∴ CGT held over

Dawsons (vendors)

Greenjacket
(wholly owned
by vendors)

Shares sold for £152,000 (∴ Greenjacket
has no gain)

Wood Bastow (purchasers)

Before the Special Commissioners, Vinelott J, and a unanimous Court of Appeal, CGT was held not to be payable. The sale proceeds had been paid to Greenjacket and, in the phrase of Slade LJ in the Court of Appeal, the existence of Greenjacket had 'enduring legal consequences'. Before the House of Lords it was accepted that for a *scintilla temporis* legal and beneficial title to the shares passed to Greenjacket. Lord Brightman, however, in the only fully argued speech (which was concurred in by the other Lords) viewed the series of transactions as a pre-planned scheme:

'The whole process was planned and executed with faultless precision. The meetings began at 12.45 pm on 20 December, at which time the shareholdings of the operating companies were still owned by the Dawsons unaffected by any contract of sale. They ended with the shareholdings in the ownership of Wood Bastow. The minutes do not disclose when the meeting ended but perhaps it was all over in time for lunch.'

As its purpose was to obtain a deferral of CGT, he concluded that the scheme should be viewed as a whole, that is as a composite transaction different from the actual transaction entered into by the parties, and that 'the court must then look at the end result. Precisely how the end result will be taxed will depend on the terms of the taxing statute sought to be applied.' Applying that test 'there was a disposal of the shares by the Dawsons in favour of Wood Bastow in consideration of a sum of money paid with the concurrence of the Dawsons to Greenjacket'. The gain on this disposal was subject to CGT. Lord Brightman, in explaining the application of the *Ramsay* principle, set out two basic rules: *first*, there must be a pre-ordained series of transactions (or one single composite transaction); *secondly*, there must be steps inserted which have no commercial purpose other than the avoidance of tax. He stressed that, so long as a pre-planned tax saving scheme existed no distinction should be drawn between the case where the steps were carried out in pursuance of a contract and one where, although the steps were pre-ordained, separate binding contracts only arose at each stage. Although Greenjacket was not contractually bound to resell the shares to Wood Bastow, it was pre-ordained (ie there was an informal arrangement) that this would occur. Hence, 'the day is not saved for the taxpayer because the arrangement is unsigned or contains the magic words "this is not a binding contract"'. In a similar vein, Lord Fraser of Tullybelton considered that 'the series of two transactions ... were planned as a single scheme and ... it should be viewed as a whole'.

It should be noted that not all members of the House of Lords in *Furniss v Dawson* felt that it was possible to lay down precise guidelines for the future operation of the '*Ramsay* principle'. Lord Scarman, in particular, stressed the uncertain extent of the new approach:

'I am aware, and the legal profession (and others) must understand, that the law in this area is in an early stage of development. Speeches in your Lordships' House and judgments in the appellate courts are concerned more to chart a way forward between principles accepted and not to be rejected than to attempt anything so ambitious as to determine finally the limit beyond which the safe channel of acceptable tax avoidance shelves into the dangerous shallows of unacceptable tax evasion. The law will develop from case to case. Lord Wilberforce in *Ramsay's* case referred to "the emerging principle" of the law. What has been established with certainty by the House in *Ramsay's* case is that the determination of what does, and what does not, constitute unacceptable tax evasion is a subject suited to development by judicial process. Difficult though the task may be for judges, it is one which is beyond the power of the blunt instrument of legislation. Whatever a statute may provide, it has to be interpreted and applied by the courts and ultimately it will prove to be in this area of judge-made law that our elusive journey's end will be found.'

A ready acceptance that new law was being created and that this was the proper function of the judiciary was apparent and Lord Scarman in the passage quoted above, appeared to be giving a new meaning to the terms 'tax avoidance' and 'tax evasion'. Such sentiments did not, however, commend themselves to the majority of the House of Lords in later *Ramsay* cases (*Craven v White* and conjoined appeals which are considered in the next section). Lord Goff, for instance, commented that the basis of the *Ramsay* decision was one of statutory construction:

'It would be naive in the extreme to imagine that the principle is not concerned with the outlawing of unacceptable tax avoidance. It plainly is. But it would be equally mistaken to regard the principle as in any sense a moral principle, or having any foundation in morality. It plainly is not. We can see this clearly from Lord Brightman's description of the scheme in *Furniss* as an honest scheme; and I would likewise so describe the schemes in the present three appeals. What the courts have established, however, is that certain tax avoidance schemes, although not shams in the sense of not being what they purport to be, are nevertheless unacceptable because they embrace transactions which are not "real" disposals and do not generate "real" losses (or gains) and so are held not to attract certain fiscal consequences which would normally be attached to disposals or losses (or gains) under the relevant statute. It is these unacceptable tax avoidance schemes which Lord Scarman described as "tax evasion"—a label which is perhaps better kept for those transactions which are traditionally so described because they are illegal.'

[36.22]

3 The limits of the 'Ramsay principle': Craven v White

As already mentioned, Lord Brightman, in *Furniss v Dawson* suggested that there were two basic requirements for the application of the *Ramsay* principle. *First*, there must be a pre-ordained series of transactions (a 'scheme') although there need be no binding contract to carry the entire scheme through, and furthermore the scheme may include the attainment of a legitimate business end. In the *Dawson* case the scheme enabled shares to be sold from the Dawsons to Wood Bastow. *Secondly*, there must be steps in the scheme whose sole purpose is to avoid (or defer) a liability to tax. Such steps may have a 'business effect' but no 'business purpose'. The insertion of Greenjacket was such a step: in the words of Lord Brightman 'that inserted step had no business purpose apart from the deferment of tax, although it had a business effect. If the sale had taken place in 1964 before CGT was introduced, there would have been no Greenjacket'.

The requirements are not, however, easy to apply. Two of their Lordships considered that *Westminster's* case could be distinguished as involving a single and not a composite transaction. Certainly the covenant was a single transaction, but its sole purpose was the avoidance of income tax and it was only entered into on the 'understanding' that the gardeners would not seek to claim their wages. Hence the making of the covenant was a step which had no commercial purpose save for the avoidance of tax. It is arguable, however, that unlike Greenjacket, which was an artificial person under the control of the Dawsons, the gardener's continuing right to sue for his wages serves to distinguish the case. Furthermore, as the covenant was to last for a period of seven years or the joint lives of the parties, it could have continued after the employment had terminated.

Any pre-arranged scheme which involves either tax avoidance, tax deferral or merely the preservation of an existing tax benefit is potentially within the *Ramsay* principle. A single tax-efficient transaction is presumably not since the case does *not* state that persons must so organise their affairs that they pay the maximum amount of tax!

In three conjoined appeals (*Craven v White, Baylis v Gregory*, and *IRC v Bowater Property Developments Ltd*) the House of Lords was faced with the question when does a series of transactions form part of a pre-planned scheme (or alternatively, constitute a single composite transaction)?   [36.23]

a) *Craven v White and Baylis v Gregory*

At first sight the facts of both cases closely resemble those of *Furniss v Dawson*. In *Craven v White* the taxpayers arranged for shares to be sold to J Ltd (see the diagram below) after those shares had first been transferred to M Ltd, an Isle of Man company which had been specially acquired for the purpose. The proceeds of sale were paid to M Ltd and were then loaned to the taxpayers. This loan-back completed the transaction (contrast *Dawson* where it was assumed that the moneys were retained in the Isle of Man company) although the courts did not consider that this final step was of particular significance. Despite the similarities in the two cases, both Peter Gibson J and a unanimous Court of Appeal were not persuaded that the insertion of M Ltd was an artificial step capable of excision and were unable to agree that this case involved a pre-planned scheme. The crucial factor was that the taxpayers were throughout uncertain whether they would succeed in selling their shares to J Ltd, or indeed to any other purchaser (although this was what they desired) and they accepted that they might end up merging their company with the business of a third party, C Ltd. In *Baylis v Gregory*, the taxpayers were negotiating for the sale of their shares in a family company and envisaged that this would be carried out through an Isle of Man company as had been done in *Dawson*. However, the negotiations were broken off and then the Isle of Man company was incorporated and shares exchanged at a time when no other purchaser was on the horizon. This occurred in March 1974 and the shares were not eventually sold until January 1976. On these facts assessments to CGT raised on the basis that there had been a direct share sale by the original proprietors to the ultimate purchaser, were discharged both at first instance and by the Court of Appeal.   [36.24]

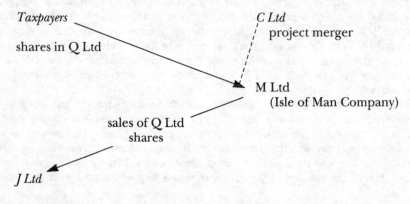

b) *IRC v Bowater Property Developments Ltd*

The case concerned a DLT fragmentation scheme.

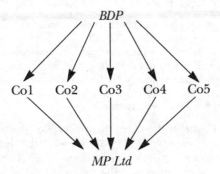

Bowater (BPD) divided the land in question into five slices among five other companies in the group. These companies were chosen because none had used any part of their annual exemption from DLT and the sole object of this transaction was to avoid DLT which would otherwise fall upon BPD if the land was sold, as intended, to MP Ltd. At the time of fragmentation there was a firm expectation that the sale to MP Ltd would proceed although there was no question of any contract being signed at that time and, indeed, some three months later, the projected sale was called off by MP Ltd. It was accepted that the fragmentation was effected without any commercial or business purpose apart from the hope of a tax advantage. In the following year, negotiations were, however, recommenced and the sale duly occurred. Warner J and the Court of Appeal refused to excise the fragmentation step and to treat the sale to MP Ltd as having been effected by BPD. They concluded that there was no pre-arranged scheme: 'in no sense was the second transaction (the sale to MP Ltd) pre-arranged or pre-ordained at the time when the fragmentation was carried out'. **[36.25]**

c) *The House of Lords speeches*

The Law Lords unanimously rejected the Revenue's appeals in two of the cases (*Baylis v Gregory* and *Bowater*) and it was only with regard to the *Craven v White* appeal that Lords Templeman and Goff dissented from their colleagues, finding in favour of the Revenue. Accordingly, a degree of unanimity can be discerned in the speeches and there is no doubt that they mark a significant limitation on the *Ramsay* principle. Having said this, however, the speeches also reveal a considerable level of disagreement on the ambit of that principle and the role of the courts in the area of tax avoidance. At one extreme stand the views of Lord Templeman:

> 'I have read the drafts of the speeches to be delivered in these present appeals. Three of those speeches accept the extreme argument of the taxpayer that *Furniss* is limited to its own facts or is limited to a transaction which has reached an advanced stage of negotiation (whatever that expression means) before the preceding tax avoidance transaction is carried out. These limitations would distort the effect of *Furniss*, are not based on principle, are not to be derived from the speeches in *Furniss*, and if followed, would only revive a surprised tax avoidance industry and cost the general body of taxpayers hundreds of millions of pounds by enabling artificial tax avoidance schemes to alter the incidence of taxation. In *Furniss*, Lord Brightman was not alone in delivering a magisterial rebuke to those judges who sought to place limitations on *Ramsay* ... In my opinion, a knife-edged majority

has no power to limit this principle which has been responsible for four decisions of this House approved by a large number of our predecessors.'

By contrast, Lord Oliver (with whose speech Lords Keith and Jauncey concurred) expressed only limited support for the *Furniss v Dawson* approach:

'I confess to having been a less than enthusiastic convert to *Furniss v Dawson* because I found, initially at any rate, some difficulty in following the intellectual process by which in contra-distinction to the cases which preceded it, it reconstructed the transaction which had taken place in that case in a way which disapplied the specific statutory consequences which, on the face of them, attach to the intermediate transfer which had in fact taken place and which the Special Commissioners had found as a fact was a genuine transaction.'

So far as the actual issue in the case was concerned (viz when a pre-planned series of transactions exists) the majority—Lords Keith, Oliver and Jauncey—adopted a more restrictive view than Lords Templeman and Goff. Lord Jauncey, for instance, suggested the following definition of a 'composite transaction':

'A step in a linear transaction which has no business purpose apart from the avoidance or deferment of tax liability will be treated as forming part of a pre-ordained series of transactions or of a composite transaction if it was taken at a time when negotiations or arrangements for the carrying through as a continuous process of a subsequent transaction which actually takes place had reached a stage when there was no real likelihood that such subsequent transaction would not take place and if thereafter such negotiations or arrangements were carried through to completion without genuine interruption.'

The cases of *Baylis v Gregory* and *Bowater* failed to satisfy such a test whilst in *Craven v White*, at the time of the share exchange, there was a real possibility that the subsequent sale would not occur since negotiations with the prospective purchaser were still continuing and had not been concluded. Accordingly, the majority held that the exchange of shares was a transaction independent from the sale which later occurred.

By contrast with the views of the majority, Lords Templeman and Goff adopted a more flexible approach to the question when a pre-planned scheme exists. Lord Templeman, for instance, expressed himself as follows:

'In *Furniss* ... the transactions formed part of a scheme although the Dawsons had no control, direct or indirect over Wood Bastow and could at no stage oblige Wood Bastow to buy shares in the operating company. But both transactions were part of a scheme which was planned by Dawsons, which in the event was successful and which produced a taxable transaction. Two transactions can form part of a scheme even though it is wholly uncertain when the first transaction is carried out whether the taxpayer who is responsible for the scheme will succeed in procuring the second transaction to be carried out at all. ... if the shadowy, undefined and indefinable expressions "practically certain", "practical likelihood", and "practical contemplation" possess any meanings, those expressions and those meanings are not to be derived from *Furniss*.'

Lord Goff appeared to adopt an even wider test:

'it is not necessary that the details of the second step should be settled at the time when the first step was taken, nor that they should exactly correspond with those planned in advance.'

Even applying the wider tests advocated above, neither *Bowater* nor *Bayliss v Gregory* involved a pre-planned series of transactions: in the former, 'the scheme was frustrated when [the prospective purchasers] abandoned the negotiations' whilst, in the latter, 'the taxpayers placed themselves in a position to escape tax *in the future* but there was no scheme' (Lord Templeman).

As the *ratio decidendi* of the case must be found in the more limited test laid down by the majority, what degree of certainty is necessary for a pre-planned scheme? How sure must the taxpayers be that the scheme which was eventually implemented was always going to be so implemented? From the speeches of the majority, it is possible to extract a number of phrases which define this degree of certainty. They are set out below but it must follow, given the vagueness embraced in such phrases, that room has been left for future disagreements:

'The taxpayers were by no means in a position for all practical purposes to ensure that the sale went through.' (Lord Keith in relation to *Craven v White*)

'a single indivisible composite whole—a concept which may be summed up in homely terms by asking the question whether at the material time that whole is already "cut and dried". ... so certain of fulfilment that it is intellectually and practically possible to conclude that there has indeed taken place one single and indivisible process. ... a degree of certainty and control over the end result at the time when the intermediate steps are taken ... it does seem to me to be essential at least that the principal terms should be agreed to the point at which it can be said that there is no practical likelihood that the transaction which actually takes place will not take place.' (Lord Oliver)

The majority speeches are striking in that they stress that the *Ramsay* principle is, at base, a rule of statutory construction. Lord Oliver, for instance, stated in relation to *Dawson* that 'the question is when is a disposal not a disposal within the terms of the statute'. Such an approach has been used in other tax cases in order to frustrate avoidance schemes: see for instance the decision in *Reed v Nova Securities Ltd* (1985) where on a construction of TA 1970 s 274 it was held that shares were not acquired as trading stock (for an analysis of this 'parallel attack' on trading transactions entered into, in whole or in part, for fiscal reasons, see (1990) BTR 52). It is, however, difficult to fit decisions in the earlier cases and certainly the speeches in *Dawson* into a purely constructional approach. As a simple matter of language, the share exchange carried out in the various cases undoubtedly occurred and involved a disposal of assets. Accordingly, to excise that disposal cannot be a simple exercise in statutory interpretation but must result from a wholly extraneous rule which is more akin to the striking out of a 'sham' transaction. The Court of Appeal in the *Fitzwilliam* case sought to lay this matter to rest. Nourse LJ summarised the position as follows:

'In *Craven v White* each of their Lordships said that the *Ramsay* principle is one of statutory construction. That is without doubt true in the sense that once the single composite transaction has been identified the question is whether it is caught by the taxing statute on which the Crown relies. However, it does not always or even usually involve a question of statutory construction in the sense that the meaning of the statute is in doubt. Usually the question is whether a statute whose meaning is clear applies to the single composite transaction. The principle might equally be described as one of statutory application.'

The approach taken by a majority of the House of Lords in *Fitzwilliam* would appear to support this view which was further considered in the *McGuckian* case (see [36.35] below). Lord Templeman always considered that the type of transactions envisaged by *Ramsay* and *Furniss v Dawson* were akin to sham transactions and should be treated accordingly. In *Matrix-Securities Ltd v IRC* (1994) he commented:

'Every tax avoidance scheme involves a trick and a pretence. It is the task of the Revenue to unravel the trick and the duty of the Court to ignore the pretence.'

The dictionary definition of a 'sham' is a 'trick' or a 'pretence'. **[36.26]**

4   **Further limits of the *Ramsay* principle:** *IRC v Fitzwilliam* **(1993)**

a) *The facts*

The 10th Earl Fitzwilliam died on 21 September 1979 survived by his 81-year-old wife. Under the terms of his 1977 will, and after leaving a number of pecuniary legacies, his residuary estate was settled on a 23-month discretionary trust for a class of beneficiaries including Lady Fitzwilliam and with a provision that in default of exercise and at the end of that period the estate was to be held for Lady Fitzwilliam for life with remainder to her daughter Lady Hastings. The value of the residuary estate was certified at just over £12.4m and accordingly if the trustees exercised their powers to appoint that property away from Lady Fitzwilliam CTT at a rate of 75% would apply. By contrast,

FITZWILLIAM: 'THE SCHEME'

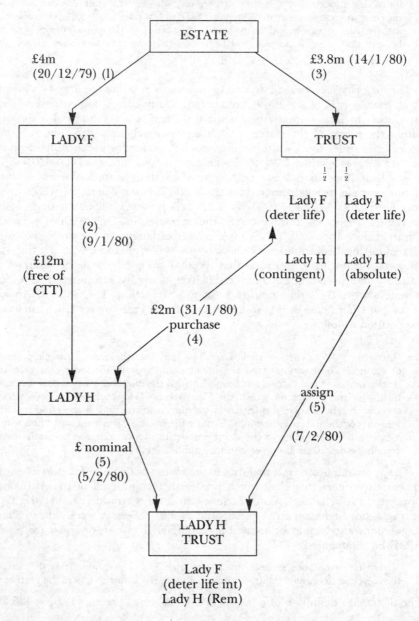

if the property passed to Lady Fitzwilliam no charge would then be imposed although, given her age and then state of health, there was obviously a considerable danger that she too would die in which case the property would on that occasion be taxed at 75%.

CTT was paid on the pecuniary legacies but not on the property comprised in the residuary estate and therefore subject to the 23-month trust. It is usually thought, despite the fact that a surviving spouse is named as one of the beneficiaries, that tax must be paid in such cases albeit that recovery is then possible if the spouse is appointed the property or alternatively takes in default at the end of the 23-month period. In this case, however, CTT was paid only on the pecuniary legacies and, despite criticism from the Revenue, it appears that the Probate Office were consulted and were agreeable to this. Vinelott J did not comment other than to observe that because of the illiquid nature of the estate 'it would in fact have been very difficult for the executors to have delayed probate until a sum sufficient to pay the whole of the CTT had been raised' and the matter was not considered by the higher courts.

The will trustees and two beneficiaries (Lady Fitzwilliam and Lady Hastings) entered into a series of transactions, devised by professional advisers, and intended to mitigate the ultimate CTT bill. The transactions were to a large degree artificial and in some cases circular and the end result was that some £7.8m had been distributed out of the residuary estate—£3.8m to Lady Hastings and £4m to Lady Fitzwilliam—without, it appeared, any CTT liability arising. To assist in understanding how the schemes were structured reference should be made to the diagram above. Part of the scheme rested on a 'plain blunder in the legislation'. **[36.27]**

Step 1

On 20 December 1979 part of the residuary estate to a value of £4m was appointed out to Lady Fitzwilliam. The intention at that time was that land would be appropriated in satisfaction of the appointed sum. **[36.28]**

Step 2

By cheque, back-dated to 9 January 1980, Lady Fitzwilliam gave £2m (free of CTT) to Lady Hastings. At that time lifetime gifts attracted a CTT charge and, unless the tax was paid by the donee, were subject to grossing up. Accordingly, the total cost of this gift to Lady Fitzwilliam was in the region of £5m! **[36.29]**

Step 3

On 14 January 1980 the trustees appointed a further portion of the residuary estate, to a value of £3.8m, on the following trusts. The income was to be paid to Lady Fitzwilliam until her death or until 15 February 1980 (if earlier) whereupon, as to one moiety, the capital was to pass to Lady Hastings absolutely (so that she had a vested remainder interest and this will be referred to as the 'vested moiety') but as to the other moiety the capital was only to pass to Lady Hastings if she was living on the termination of Lady Fitzwilliam's interest in possession (so that as regards this moiety Lady Hastings had a contingent remainder interest: the 'contingent moiety'). Note that the appointment to Lady Fitzwilliam on interest in possession trusts did not result in any CTT liability but that the termination of her interest (which must of course occur *at the latest* in the following month) would! **[36.30]**

Step 4

On 31 January 1980, in consideration for the payment of £2m, Lady Fitzwilliam assigned to Lady Hastings her income interest in the contingent moiety. The CTT consequences of this transaction were that Lady Fitzwilliam thereby made an immediate transfer of value equal in value to one-half of the capital then in the settlement: ie one-half of £3.8m (see FA 1975 Sch 5 para 4(2), now IHTA 1984 s 52(1)). However, by para 4(4) of Sch 5 (now IHTA 1984 s 52(2))—enacted as an anti-avoidance measure—if an interest in possession was assigned for value then CTT was only charged on the excess of the capital value of that interest (one-half of £3.8m) over the consideration paid. Accordingly, as the £2m paid by Lady Hastings exceeded the £1.9m capital value of the interest, no CTT was payable on the assignment by Lady Fitzwilliam.

As a result of the assignment Lady Hastings was now entitled both to an interest in possession in the contingent moiety and, of course, to the capital outright on the termination of that interest in February 1980 provided that she was then alive. Because of the fiction that for CTT/IHT purposes a beneficiary with an interest in possession is treated as owning the underlying capital, there is no tax liability if the interest in possession beneficiary becomes entitled to the underlying capital (IHTA 1984 s 53(2) formerly FA 1975 Sch 5 para 4(a)).

Step 4 did not therefore involve any adverse CTT consequences and, indeed, because of the mutual transfer provisions which existed at this time (see FA 1976 ss 86–87) enabled (so it was argued for the taxpayer) substantial benefits to be obtained. In simple terms the mutual transfer rules enabled a gift to be 'nullified' provided that the value of the gifted property was returned to the donor. Not only was the return transfer free from CTT but the original gift itself was thereupon treated as cancelled. Applying these rules to the present facts it will be recalled that at *Step 2* Lady Fitzwilliam had made a gift of £2m to Lady Hastings on which CTT was payable. At *Step 4* Lady Hastings paid an equivalent sum to Lady Fitzwilliam in return for an assignment of her determinable life interest. Accordingly, and to the extent that the payment by Lady Hastings was a transfer of value, not only would that payment be free from *CTT but it would also have the effect of nullifying the earlier gift at Step 2* which had been made by Lady Fitzwilliam. It is at this stage that the 'plain blunder' in the legislation becomes relevant. FA 1978 s 69(7) had been introduced in order to counter complex tax avoidance schemes and provided that when an interest in possession was purchased then in order to decide whether the purchaser had made any transfer of value the usual principle that the interest in possession was to be valued on the basis of underlying capital must be ignored. Instead, the interest itself must be valued. Applying that principle to these particular facts, Lady Fitzwilliam's interest had a purely nominal value ·so that the £2m paid by Lady Hastings was virtually all gift and could (it was argued) be relieved under the mutual transfer rules.

The end result was that the sum of £2m had been returned to Lady Fitzwilliam (free from any CTT charge) and that some £1.9m had been extracted from the estate and paid to Lady Hastings without any CTT charge. It may be noted in passing that the mutual transfer provisions were repealed with the introduction of IHT in 1986.   [**36.31**]

Step 5

The final step involved Lady Hastings settling a nominal sum on 5 February 1980. Under the terms of the trust Lady Fitzwilliam was entitled to a determinable life interest (the interest determined on Lady Fitzwilliam's death or 15 March 1980, whichever occurred first) with a remainder to Lady Hastings herself. Two days after establishing the trust Lady Hastings assigned her absolute remainder interest (created at *Step 3*, above) to the trustees to be held on the same trusts. The effect of the assignment was that Lady Fitzwilliam's interest in possession did not determine on 15 February 1980 (as would have been the case in the absence of the assignment) but instead continued for a further month. When it did eventually determine the property in the settlement then passed back to Lady Hastings. Accordingly, any CTT charge was avoided by the 'reverter to settlor' exemption (see FA 1975 Sch 5 para 4(5): now IHTA 1984 s 53(3)). [**36.32**]

b) *The House of Lords speeches*

The Lords decided (with Lord Templeman dissenting) against the Revenue's contention that a CTT charge arose on 31 January when the life interest in the contingent moiety came to an end with a further charge on 15 March when the life interest in the vested moiety determined. The following matters are worthy of note:

(1) Initially the Revenue had contended that all five steps formed part of a pre-planned series. That argument was abandoned after Vinelott J (the first instance judge) decided that at the time when the first step was undertaken no decision had been taken as to how matters would proceed. Accordingly, it was not possible to see *Steps 1* to *5* as a pre-planned series. Before both the Court of Appeal and the House of Lords the Revenue therefore decided to argue that only *Steps 2* to *5* were pre-planned. It is difficult not to feel some sympathy with Lord Browne-Wilkinson in the House of Lords when he opined that the whole purpose of the arrangement was to distribute £4m out of the estate to Lady Fitzwilliam and £3.8m to Lady Hastings without CTT being attracted. Perhaps the Revenue should have persisted in its original argument that all five steps were interlinked: as it was the Revenue was forced to argue before the higher courts that it was Lady Fitzwilliam who had made chargeable transfers totalling in all £3.8m.

(2) The House of Lords was unanimous in deciding that *Steps 2* to *5* constituted a pre-planned series. Lord Keith (who gave the leading judgment) said:

'I would accept that *Steps 2, 3, 4* and *5* were preordained in the sense that they all formed part of a pre-planned tax avoidance scheme and that there was no reasonable possibility that they would not all be carried out, notwithstanding the pause while Lady Hastings as an individual took independent legal advice.'

As Lord Browne-Wilkinson commented:

'The device of keeping clients in the dark as to the totality of the scheme . . . is ineffective for tax purposes . . . it is not possible to achieve the result that a scheme is not preordained just by inserting an occasion on which one party is to be separately advised when the only advice that can be tendered in such circumstances is to pursue the scheme or abandon it. If the scheme was carried through that scheme was preordained.'

Accordingly, the *Craven v White* problem did not arise.

(3) Crucial to the majority decision was that although *Steps 2* to *5* constituted a pre-planned series, none of those steps could be wholly excised. Rather the Revenue was forced to rely on all the steps albeit that some were recharacterised (for instance *Step 4* was viewed as a purely gratuitous assignment). As Lord Keith put it:

'The fact of preordainment . . . is not sufficient in itself, in my opinion, to negative the application of an exemption from liability to tax which the series of transactions is intended to create, unless the series is capable of being construed in a manner inconsistent with the application of the exemption ... in my opinion the series in the present case cannot be. The problem for the Crown is that as regards the contingent moiety it has to rely on *Step 3* as creating an income interest in Lady Fitzwilliam until 15 February and on *Step 4* as terminating that interest. As regards the vested moiety it relies on *Step 3* as creating an income interest in Lady Fitzwilliam until 15 February and on *Step 5* as prolonging that interest to 15 March and then determining it. There is no question of running any two or more transactions together as in *Furniss v Dawson* or of disregarding any one or more of them. I am unable to perceive any rational basis on which *Steps 2, 3* and *4* can be treated as effective for the purpose of creating a charge under para 4(2) of Sch 5 to the 1975 Act but ineffective for the purpose of attracting the exemption in para 4(4) and that in para 4(5).'

This crucial part of Lord Keith's judgment was strongly rejected by Lord Templeman. In his view, *Steps 2* and *4* were inserted steps that had no purpose other than the avoidance of CTT on the contingent moiety, and *Step 5* was likewise inserted to avoid tax, in this case on the vested moiety. None of the steps had any commercial purpose although they had 'enduring legal consequences' in that they gave rise, albeit for a very short period of time, to an income interest in favour of Lady Hastings or Lady Fitzwilliam. This question of 'enduring legal consequences' was, of course, fully discussed in Lord Brightman's speech in *Furniss v Dawson*, and yet the distinction therein drawn between *purpose* and *effect* appears to have been ignored by Lord Keith.

(4) Lord Browne-Wilkinson wished to reserve the question whether *Ramsay* was capable of applying to CTT/IHT given the existence of the wide-ranging associated operations provision in IHTA 1984 s 268 (see [**21.81**]):

'This amounts to a statutory statement, in much wider terms, of the *Ramsay* principle which deals with transactions carried through by two or more operations which are inter-related ... it can therefore be argued that there is no room for the Court to adopt the *Ramsay* approach in construing an Act which expressly provides for the circumstances and occasions on which transfers carried through by "associated operations" are to be taxed. It is not necessary in the present case to express any concluded view on this point.'

[**36.33**]

c) *The importance of Fitzwilliam*

The crusading zeal so evident in *Dawson* appeared to leave the House of Lords: can there really be any doubt that the arrangements in *Fitzwilliam* fell within the spirit and intendment of Lord Brightman's test laid down in *Dawson* and which, had Lord Scarman's observations been followed, would have been brought into the tax net? By concentrating on matters of detail the majority of the House of Lords enabled £3.8m to pass tax free to Lady Hastings albeit that the Revenue scarcely helped its own cause by the arguments that it put forward. In circular arrangements (typified by *Ramsay* itself and *Burmah Oil*) the taxpayer's position at the beginning and end of a transaction is compared and tax imposed accordingly. Similarly in *Dawson* intervening steps in a pre-planned scheme were excised to leave the reconstructed transaction. In *Fitzwilliam*, on the basis of treating *Steps 2* to *5* as a pre-planned operation, at the start of that operation Lady Fitzwilliam owned for CTT purposes £3.8m (ie the property in which she was life tenant) but at the end of those steps she did not. In the light of the post-1984 cases it appears that further refinement is needed to the Brightman test if *Ramsay* is to be established on a coherent basis. The requirement that all steps must be pre-planned could, for instance, be widened to include facts like *Fitzwilliam* where, although the precise nature of the later steps was in doubt, it was inevitable that steps aimed at avoiding tax would be undertaken. Similarly, the requirement that there must be an artificial step (ie a step having no 'business purpose') can create difficulties especially where the matter is one of personal—rather than commercial—tax planning. Indeed, it may be that this 'inserted step' requirement is in any event surplus: earlier *Ramsay* cases had suggested that in a pre-ordained series of transactions all that is necessary is to ascertain the real results of the series *as a whole* and then to apply the relevant taxing statute. In this context *Hatton v IRC* (1992) affords an interesting contrast: Chadwick J there excised a short-lived interest in possession commenting that neither of the two settlements involved 'had any practical (business) purpose other than the saving of tax'. Such a power to excise steps whose predominant purpose was to avoid or defer tax would appear to be far more satisfactory: as in *Hatton*, this should enable short-lived life interests (inserted not with a view to giving income to the relevant beneficiary but purely to give 'credibility' to the scheme) to be ignored (see also the dissenting judgment of Millett LJ in *Ingram v IRC* (1997)).

There is a further interesting contrast between the *Fitzwilliam* decision and that in *Hatton* the facts of which are set out at [**21.83**]. Chadwick J concluded in the latter case that the *Ramsay* principle applied. He rejected any suggestion that the taxpayer must have 'control' over the entire operation. In that case the second settlor (Mrs H) could have refused to create her settlement and, indeed, she took separate legal advice (albeit from a recommended adviser who was doubtless familiar with the guidelines of the entire scheme) before doing so. The reality was that a substantial tax liability could only be avoided if the second settlement was created. What actually happened was that legal advice having been taken in England in the morning, the settlement was then established in Jersey in the afternoon and the parties were (in an echo of Lord Brightman's celebrated remark in *Furniss v Dawson*) 'back in England for afternoon tea'! The pre-ordained nature of the arrangement in this case can be contrasted with *Fitzwilliam*. Undoubtedly in *Hatton* the whole operation was planned in advance but, subject to that, it is difficult to distinguish the two cases.

It is possible to see the failure of the House of Lords to adapt *Ramsay* to the facts in *Fitzwilliam* as at root a failure of will. In any event, given the confusing nature of the speeches, it is unlikely that the case will be seen as anything other than a one-off decision on its own facts. Indeed, credence has now been given to this statement by the recent decision in *IRC v McGuckian* (1997). The House of Lords unanimously reversed the Court of Appeal (Northern Ireland) which, relying heavily on the decision in *Fitzwilliam*, had refused to invoke the *Ramsay* or *Furniss* principle to the facts before them.   [**36.34**]

5 Back to basics? *McGuckian* in the House of Lords

The strategy behind the numerous transactions involved was this: to reduce the assets held by a company (B), thus minimising the risk of exposure to a possible wealth tax on its shareholders, namely the taxpayer and his wife. At the same time to avoid an income tax liability on moneys paid out by B by ensuring that the proceeds were received in the form of capital rather than income. The main features of the scheme involved:

(1) the setting up of a trust under which B shares would be held for the benefit of the taxpayer and his wife by a trustee residing outside the jurisdiction; and

(2) a sale by the trustee of their rights to dividends expected to be declared and paid by B. This was in the form of a written assignment between the trustee and the purchaser, and for a consideration which only just fell short (by 1%) of the eventual dividend declared for that year by B.

The trustees were then—so it was argued—in receipt of a capital sum which could not be attributed to the settler under eg TA 1988 s 739. As Lord

Browne-Wilkinson observed, the crucial question was whether the money received by the trustee as consideration for the assignment of the right to the dividends from B was to be treated as the income of the trustee or as capital. As the proceeds of sale, the sum of money would appear to be capital; however, by applying the *Ramsay* principle, the inserted step (the assignment of the right to the dividends) would be excised, leaving the sum of money to be regarded as income.

Unlike the majority of the Court of Appeal (Northern Ireland), Lord Browne-Wilkinson had no difficulty in applying the *Ramsay* principle; in his judgment, 'nothing in this case turns on the exact scope of the *Ramsay* principle. The case falls squarely within the classic requirements for the application of that principle as stated by Lord Brightman in *Furniss v Dawson* . . .'. This was a view shared by Lord Steyn who, although feeling the necessity to analyse the basis of the *Ramsay* decision and to question the literal interpretation of taxation statutes, accepted that the present case was 'a classic case for the application of the *Ramsay* principle'. The inserted step had no commercial purpose apart from the avoidance of income tax, with the consequence that it had to be excised. The other members of the court reached the same conclusion, although the reasoning of each of the four Law Lords who delivered judgments was different in emphasis.

For a case that appears to be so straightforward, it has already attracted considerable comment: criticism has been aimed at the judgments of Lords Steyn and Cooke, who applied the *Ramsay* principles in light of their shared view that tax legislation, like most other legislation, should be interpreted purposively rather than literally. These views may prove to be of great importance in later tax cases, and not even restricted to cases of tax avoidance, but must be viewed as *obiter dicta* in the present case.

Worthy of particular note is the rejection by Lord Browne-Wilkinson of the taxpayer's argument that the *Ramsay* principle can only apply to a series of transactions in the absence of a statutory provision that would reverse the effect of such transactions. He said:

> 'The approach pioneered in *Ramsay* and subsequently developed in later decisions is an approach to construction, viz that in construing tax legislation, the statutory provisions are to be applied to the substance of the transaction, disregarding artificial steps in the composite transaction or series of transactions inserted only for the purpose of seeking to obtain a tax advantage. The question is not what was the effect of the insertion of the artificial steps but what was its purpose. Having identified the artificial steps inserted with that purpose and disregarded them, then what is left is to apply the statutory language of the taxing Act to the transaction carried through stripped of its artificial steps. It is irrelevant to consider whether or not the disregarded artificial steps would have been effective to achieve the tax saving purpose for which they were designed.' (See also Lord Cooke who considered that *Ramsay* was antecedent to or collateral with anti-avoidance provisions.)

Lord Steyn considered the relationship between the *Ramsay* doctrine and the canons of statutory construction noting that two issues were involved: *first*, whether there is a special rule applicable to the construction of fiscal legislation and, *secondly*, whether there is a rule precluding the court from examining the substance of a composite tax avoidance scheme. So far as the former is concerned he rejected a literal in favour of a purposive construction of tax statutes quoting with approval Lord Wilberforce's comment in *Ramsay* that 'there may, indeed should, be considered the context and scheme of the relevant Act as a whole, and its purpose may, indeed should, be regarded'. On the latter issue he noted that 'if it was shown that a scheme was intended to be implemented as a whole, legal analysis permitted the court in deciding a fiscal question to take into account the composite transaction'. On the basis of the foregoing he concluded that:

'The new *Ramsay* principle was not invented on a juristic basis independent of statute ... the principle was developed as a matter of statutory construction.'

The importance of *McGuckian* lies in the language used by the House of Lords in relation to tax avoidance schemes: in terms of clarifying when the principle operates matters are left as unclear as they ever were (see for instance *Piggott v Staines Investments* (1995) which at first glance would appear to fall within the principle but which was not appealed by the Revenue). Thus, in considering *Craven v White*, Lord Cooke noted that it involved facts 'distant from those of the present case' and categorised it as 'a difficult case, partly because of differences of opinion in Your Lordships' House'.   [**36.35**]

6 Parliamentary Statement by the Chief Secretary to the Treasury

Commenting in 1985 on *Furniss v Dawson*, the Rt Hon Peter Rees QC, MP stated that:

'Taken with the decision in *Ramsay's* case, it is now clear that the widespread assumption based on the *Duke of Westminster's* case in the 1930s—that the courts will always look at the form rather than the substance of a transaction or various transactions—is no longer valid.

The House of Lords made it clear that this is an evolving area of law, but the emerging principles do not in any way call into question the tax treatment of covenants, leasing transactions and other straightforward commercial transactions. Nor is there any question of the Inland Revenue challenging, for example, the tax treatment of straightforward transfers of assets between members of the same group of companies. I also assure the House that, in accordance with normal practice, the Inland Revenue will not seek to reopen cases when assessments were properly settled in accordance with prevailing practice and became final before that decision.

The Board of Inland Revenue will also see whether clearance for types of case of special importance or general guidance for the benefit of taxpayers and their advisers can be given. The principle in *Furniss v Dawson* should lead, in future, to greater simplicity in our tax system and will, I hope, enable us in time to prune out provisions which owe their existence to the complexities of a high rate—some might say a confiscatory rate—tax system with a multiplicity of special reliefs.' (HC Deb, Vol 58, col 254.)

This statement was reiterated and, in some respects, added to in an exchange of correspondence between the Board of Inland Revenue and the Institute of Chartered Accountants (see [1985] STI 568 where the correspondence is set out in full). The following matters are particularly significant.

First, that the principle will not be applied retrospectively to cases where assessments have been finalised. It may, of course, be applied to identical cases which arise in the future or are 'in the pipeline', as was evident from the attitude of the Stamp Office to certain pre-FA 1984 conveyancing schemes designed to avoid duty; it took the view that such schemes fell within the scope of *Ramsay* and assessed the transaction accordingly, leaving it up to the taxpayer to challenge their assessment in the courts. Thus, only in a limited sense is *Ramsay* not to be applied retrospectively.

Secondly, there is no intention to upset the treatment of covenants (of less consequence now, in any event and 'straightforward commercial transactions'. So far as covenants are concerned, it is not entirely clear whether *Westminster* involved a scheme or a single transaction (a straightforward covenant), whilst capital (or 'deposit') covenants, which are usually executed in favour of charities, are surely not just simple covenants although expressly excepted from *Ramsay* in the correspondence.

The phrase 'other straightforward commercial transactions' is not particularly helpful: presumably in *Furniss v Dawson*, although the entire transaction was commercial (the sale of shares to Wood Bastow), it was infected by an artificial step (the insertion of Greenjacket) so that it ceased to be 'straightforward'. Lord Brightman considered that the *Ramsay* approach could apply only if steps were inserted 'which have no commercial (business) purpose apart from the avoidance of a liability to tax' ([1984] STC at 166). Nevertheless, whether the insertion of some relatively insignificant business purpose will be sufficient to save a scheme, is uncertain: it remains possible that the law will develop to frustrate schemes where 'the main purpose, or one of the main purposes, is avoidance of liability to (tax) . . .' (as is the case if CGT relief is to be available on a share for share exchange).

Thirdly, the Revenue assumes that *Ramsay* applies generally to all taxes and the *Ingram* decision (see [**36.37**]) offers support for this view. It has been held, for instance, that the doctrine is capable of applying to VAT although it was not invoked since the court decided that the relevant scheme amounted to a single genuine transaction. The particular arrangement was designed to avoid the VAT charge on building alterations which came into effect on 1 June 1984. Accordingly, the taxpayers arranged to be paid in full for the alterations before that date and this was achieved as part of an agreement under which the payment in question was lent back to the customer (under a commercial loan) and was then repaid by instalments equal to the amounts periodically certified as payable by the architects. In effect, therefore, payment for the work did occur after the deadline for the introduction of VAT but, because of the legal arrangements entered into, the taxpayers argued that the late instalments represented the repayment of a commercial loan. This abbreviated summary of the facts reveals the high level of artificiality involved in the case and accordingly the decision of the High Court that *Ramsay* did not apply is somewhat surprising. To categorise the scheme as a single transaction is in itself open to doubt and it was even accepted by the taxpayer that the sole reason for the arrangements was to avoid a VAT liability! (*Customs and Excise Comrs v Faith Construction Ltd* (1989): the Court of Appeal did not need to consider the possible application of *Ramsay*.)

Fourthly, the statement itself envisages some simplification of tax legislation in the wake of the decision in *Furniss v Dawson*. At the time, the presumption was that anti-avoidance legislation would be rendered unnecessary so long as the courts preserved the *Ramsay* principle on a broad basis. Particularly in light of the more recent cases, it will be surprising if the existing provisions are removed from the statute book and one of the most puzzling problems is how to marry the new approach with these statutory provisions (see comments on this matter in *McGuckian*).

Fifthly, the Chief Secretary expressly exempts from *Ramsay* straightforward transfers of assets between members of the same group of companies. For some taxation purposes, groups are looked at as a whole (see, for instance, the group relief and the group income provisions). There is, however, no provision enabling the pooling of *capital* losses and arrangements designed to remedy this gap in the legislation are to be permitted. The intra-group transfer must, however, be 'straightforward': *Shepherd v Lyntress Ltd; News International plc v Shepherd* (1989) provides a graphic illustration of the kind of arrangement which will be attacked. In that case a company which realised a capital loss was acquired as part of the News International Group with the express object of using its loss relief. Chargeable assets pregnant with gain were transferred to the new group member and immediately sold (some on the day of transfer!). That transfer of the assets intra-group did not attract any tax charge and so the eventual gain on sale was available for off-set against the losses. The Revenue, not surprisingly, argued that the whole transaction fell within the scope of *Ramsay*. Vinelott J was unimpressed:

'The Commissioners cannot characterise a series of steps as a single composite transaction unless they have first found facts sufficient to support that inference. In the instant case there is no finding by the Special Commissioners that any step had been taken to place the shares of LWT, News Corporation and Broken Hill [these were the assets pregnant with gain transferred intra-group] for sale through the Stock Exchange at the time when these shares were transferred to Lyntress and Salcombe [these were the "loss" companies]. It is not enough to say that they were transferred with a view to a sale and in order that the gain should be realised by Lyntress and Salcombe. That would be to make the fiscal motive alone a sufficient ground for imposing tax.'

The judge, following *Craven v White*, concluded that there was no reason to suspect that arrangements had been made for the sale of the shares on the Stock Exchange before their transfer to the loss making companies: he stressed that it was doubtful whether such sales would have occurred if the price had collapsed immediately after the transfer (see FA 1993 s 88 for provisions aimed at preventing the acquisition of companies in order to utilise their capital losses). [**36.36**]

7 Stamp duty and the *Ingram* case

It had been argued that there was no room for the application of the *Ramsay* principle to stamp duty because, *inter alia*, it is a duty on documents not transactions. However, in *Ingram v IRC* (1985), Vinelott J held that a stamp duty scheme designed to avoid duty on the purchase of land by splitting the transaction into stages fell within *Furniss v Dawson* and was therefore ineffective. The scheme involved, first, the purchaser agreeing to take a 999-year lease of the property at a premium of £145,000 and small annual rent; secondly, the sale of the property subject to that lease to a company for £500; and finally the resale of the property by the company to the purchaser for £600. As a result of these transactions the taxpayer acquired full title to the land (by merger of the leasehold and freehold interests) but it was intended that the consideration paid for the long lease would escape duty (since agreements for leases exceeding 35 years were excluded from charge under the Stamp Act 1891 s 75) so that only the small sum paid on the transfer of the freehold would be subject to duty.

The judge held that, were it not for the *Ramsay* principle, it was clear that the taxpayer's contentions were correct and that the transfer was what it purported to be—ie of a freehold interest subject to the agreement for the lease which had reduced its value. An application of the *Ramsay* principle, however, required the composite transaction to be 'recharacterised'. Accordingly, the leasehold agreement should be excised as an artificial transaction, leaving the instrument of transfer subject to duty as a transfer of the entire freehold interest at the agreed price (ie £145,600).

Three important matters emerge from this judgment.

First, Vinelott J stated that the principle that, if a document was genuine, the court could not go behind it to some supposed underlying substance (derived from *IRC v Duke of Westminster*) had no application to composite transactions entered into for the purpose of avoiding tax and the result of the new approach of the House of Lords was that many decisions (including some of the House of Lords) needed reappraisal.

Secondly, the view that *Ramsay* had no application in the field of stamp duty was rejected '*after considerable hesitation*'. Although the duty was levied on instruments not transactions, in order to determine the nature of a particular instrument, the court had to ascertain the substance of the transaction effected by it—a task which should be carried out by applying the *Ramsay* principle.

Finally, it is still necessary at the end of the recharacterisation of the transaction to find an instrument to stamp (in this case the final transfer to the purchaser). Had that document not been executed so that the freehold interest (subject to the long lease) was left outstanding in a company (eg one controlled by the taxpayers) would the same result have followed? Presumably, the agreement for the lease could not be stamped because of the express wording of s 75 whereas to impose duty on the transfer of the freehold would ignore the continuing separation of freehold and leasehold interests. Given the apparent willingness of the House of Lords to pierce the corporate veil in tax avoidance cases (as was done in *Furniss v Dawson*), however, such a result is at least possible!

As a postscript note that the avoidance scheme employed is now prevented by FA 1984 s 111 (see [**32.66**]). [**36.37**]

8   'Tax avoidance' versus 'tax mitigation'

Following the Privy Council case of *IRC v Challenge Corpn Ltd* (1986), a distinction appears to have emerged between tax mitigation on the one hand and tax avoidance on the other. In that case, Lord Templeman suggested that income tax is mitigated where a taxpayer reduces his income by incurring a loss or expenditure in fact as well as in appearance. On the other hand, income tax is avoided, where a taxpayer does not reduce his income through suffering a loss or incurring expenditure, but enjoys a reduction in his liability to tax as if he had. If such a distinction can be accepted as a valid one, the question then arises as to how that distinction affects the *Ramsay* principle. Would steps inserted for tax mitigation purposes survive the rigours of the *Ramsay* approach? It was left to the House of Lords in *Ensign Tankers (Leasing) Ltd v Stokes* (1992) to answer this question. Giving the main speech of a unanimous House of Lords, Lord Templeman restated the distinction between avoidance and mitigation and made it clear that if steps were inserted in order to mitigate tax (and thus resulted in an actual loss or the incurring of actual expenditure) then such mitigation would be outside the *Ramsay* principle. However, where steps were inserted to avoid tax, and thus where the taxpayer sought to reduce his liability to tax without incurring any actual loss or expenditure, such steps would come within the principle. [**36.38**]

9   Conclusions

a)   *Applicable to all taxes*

The *Ramsay* line of cases are based on principles of common application. In *Cairns v MacDiarmid* (1983) the taxpayer's claim for income tax relief for interest payments was dismissed by the Court of Appeal on the grounds, *inter alia,* that the scheme fell within the '*Ramsay* principle'. Sir John Donaldson MR concluded that:

> 'The whole transaction was "out of this world". Although no sham, it lacked all reality. It did not even have the reality of *Ramsay's* case in that [the taxpayer] neither paid a fee nor incurred any expenses. But, as in that case, at the end of a series of connected and intended transactions, his financial position was precisely as it was at the beginning!' [1983] STC at 182 (he made similar comments in *Sherdley v Sherdley* but the House of Lords subsequently ruled that *Ramsay* had no application to orders made under the Matrimonial Causes Act).

While Lord Browne-Wilkinson queried the application of *Ramsay* to CTT/IHT (see [**36.33**]), he has been the only member of the House of Lords so to do. Moreover, there seems to be no logical reason to assume that *Ramsay* cannot complement IHTA 1984, s 268 and *vice versa.* However, even if *Ramsay* can apply, there is no suggestion that the Revenue would seek to challenge the normal IHT arrangements between spouses designed to ensure that both make full use of the available exemptions and reliefs and nil rate band of tax. Similar arrangements may be entered into in order to take advantage of the independent taxation of spouses. **[36.39]**

b) *Use by taxpayer?*

Although the majority of the Court of Appeal in *Whittles v Uniholdings Ltd (No 3)* (1996) found that the *Ramsay* principle had no application to the facts of this particular case, two of their Lordships were of the view that it could be applied in favour of the taxpayer in appropriate circumstances (see the judgments of Aldous LJ and Sir John Balcombe). In *Bird v IRC* (1985) Vinelott J at first instance, without expressing a concluded view on the matter, had thought it unlikely that when a taxpayer embarked on a series of transactions designed to avoid tax he could later argue (when those transactions were challenged under anti-avoidance legislation such as TA 1988 s 703 ff) that they should be treated as a fiscal nullity. Further he expressed the view that a party cannot blow 'hot and cold' so that the Revenue could not argue that a scheme fell within TA 1988 s 703 (thereby accepting that all the steps were effective but that the end result was nullified by statute) and, as an alternative, seek to excise certain of those steps under the *Ramsay* approach. **[36.40]**

c) *Options*

The use of options in tax planning needs careful thought in the wake of the *Furniss* decision. It has in recent years become common to spread the sale of land over a number of years by means of options and part of the attraction has been to mitigate the vendor's CGT and (until its abolition in FA 1985) DLT liability by taking advantage of more than one annual exemption. Assume, for instance, that A wishes to sell Blackacre to B and will realise a gain of £12,000 on that sale. Were he to divide Blackacre into two equal portions and agree to sell the first portion in the tax year 1997–98 and, at the same time, grant a call option to purchase the second portion in the following tax year, it would appear that for CGT purposes the land has been disposed of in two different tax years and A will therefore have two annual exemptions available (notice that A could ensure that B is obliged to purchase the land by taking a 'put' option enabling him to require B to purchase the second parcel if he fails to exercise his call option).

There is no doubt that such schemes amount to a pre-ordained series of transactions and arguably the options represent steps which have been inserted purely for the avoidance of tax, since, in the absence of CGT considerations, A would have sold the whole of Blackacre to B in 1997–98. If the steps are excised it may be argued that there was effectively a sale of the land to B at the time when the contract of sale for the first parcel was made and the put and call options taken. Doubts have been expressed about the validity of this argument and if the 'option-step' is excised it is by no means clear that the *Ramsay* doctrine permits the sale of all the land to be treated as occurring in 1997–98. It may be that the Revenue now accepts the efficacy of cross-options—certainly there has still been no challenge raised to the various DLT option schemes—whilst it may be noted that in *J Sainsbury Ltd v O'Connor* (1990) Millett J commented at first instance:

> 'From a commercial point of view, of course, the simultaneous creation of both put and call options puts the parties in much the same position as an unconditional contract of sale would do; but in law the two situations are quite distinct.'

Commercial reasons may, in particular cases, justify the use of options and the *Ramsay* argument is obviously more difficult to sustain when cross-options are not employed but a call option alone is taken by the purchaser.

[**36.41**]

d) *The future*

In addition to the inclusion in FA 1997 and F(No 2)A 1997 of specific measures to reduce the loss to the Exchequer through the avoidance of corporation tax, VAT and PAYE, the Chancellor of the Exchequer, Gordon Brown, announced in his Budget speech in July 1997 that it was his intention to curb generally 'the leakage' and avoidance of direct taxes. He said:

'I have also instructed the Inland Revenue to carry out a wide-ranging review of areas of tax avoidance, with a view to further legislation in future Finance Bills. I have specifically asked them to consider a general anti-avoidance rule.'

Whilst other jurisdictions, most notably Canada, Australia and New Zealand, have introduced a general anti-avoidance provision to combat the ever-increasing amount of tax avoidance, such a measure has never found favour in the UK. It has always been believed that a general anti-avoidance provision would require a significant number of caveats which would, in turn, be likely to cause an increase in tax litigation. No doubt these arguments will be well rehearsed during the consultation stage of the review.   [**36.42**]–[**36.50**]

III   STATUTORY PROVISIONS TO COUNTER TAX AVOIDANCE

1   The legislation

The major provisions that have been enacted in attempts to deal with specific instances of tax avoidance are set out below. In many cases they were designed to prevent the conversion of income profits into capital gains taxed at a lower rate. With the harmonisation in the rates of the two taxes, such provisions are of reduced importance.   [**36.51**]

Transactions in securities   TA 1988 ss 703–709 (originally enacted in FA 1960).   [**36.52**]

Bond washing and dividend stripping   Various provisions deal with these problems, the oldest dating back to FA 1927 with the most recent being in TA 1988 ss 710–728.   [**36.53**]

Transfer of assets overseas   Originally enacted in FA 1936, these provisions were amended in 1981 as a result of *Vestey v IRC* (1980) and again in 1997, partly as a result of *Willoughby* litigation (see Chapter 13).   [**36.54**]

Artificial transactions in land   For TA 1988 s 776 see Chapter 8. Statutory provisions also regulate sale and leaseback transactions (TA 1988 ss 779–784); see Chapter 6.   [**36.55**]

Sale of income derived from personal activities   TA 1988 s 775 (originally enacted in FA 1969) prevents the conversion of future taxable income into capital gains subject to CGT. The avoidance typically involved entertainers who sold their services to a company formed for that purpose and then sold the shares in that company.   [**36.56**]

The use of tax losses and transfer pricing   TA 1988 s 768 (originating in FA 1969) imposes restrictions upon the purchase of tax loss companies (see Chapter 28). Sales at under or overvalue may be subject to challenge under TA 1988 s 770, and under the *Sharkey v Wernher* principle (see Chapter 6).   **[36.57]**

2 Typical avoidance schemes involving securities

A company is a legal entity distinct from its shareholders and, therefore, provides fertile ground for such tax avoidance schemes as dividend stripping and bond washing.   **[36.58]**

Dividend stripping   The simplest illustration of dividend stripping is where A owns A Ltd which has profits available for distribution. A sells the shares to B who is a dealer in securities. A receives a capital sum which reflects the undistributed profits in the company. B will take out the profits from A Ltd (as a dividend) which will be taxed as income but the shares will now be worth less (reflecting the fact that they have been stripped of their dividend). B will, therefore, make a trading loss when he sells the shares which can be set off against the dividend income that B has received (usually under the provisions of TA 1988 s 380). The result is that corporate profits have been extracted free of tax.

The courts were often invited to hold that the purchase and sale of the shares was not a trading transaction. In some cases they decided that it was trading; in others, not (contrast, eg, *Griffiths v J P Harrison (Watford) Ltd* (1962) with *FA and AB Ltd v Lupton* (1971) and see *Coates v Arndale Properties Ltd* (1984) and, for consideration of the effect of fiscal motives, *Ensign Tankers (Leasing) Ltd v Stokes* (1991)). The close company legislation sought to tackle one part of the problem by preventing the accumulation of profits in close companies. In 1960 the problem was attacked with legislation aimed at transactions in securities generally.   **[36.59]**

Bond washing   Dividends only become a taxpayer's income when they are due and payable; when that happens the shareholder can claim the sum from the company as a debt. Usually there is a time gap between declaration and payment which provides an opportunity to wash the shares (or bonds) of their dividend. The washing process usually involves a taxpayer who is subject to no income tax or to lower rates only. Assume, for instance, that shares are owned by A who is subject to income tax at a high rate. When a dividend is declared on his shares he sells them to his cousin, a student with unused personal allowances. A is, therefore, receiving a capital sum for the shares on which CGT rather than income tax will be charged. The dividends are paid to the cousin who suffers little if any income tax thereon. Finally, the shares may be repurchased by A after payment of the dividend. Legislative provisions (notably TA 1988 s 729 and the accrued income scheme discussed below) prevent the most blatant examples of bond washing.   **[36.60]**

3 The accrued income scheme

TA 1988 ss 710–728 are designed to prevent the bond washing of fixed interest securities.

The practice of bond washing involved the conversion of income into capital and resulted in that sum being taxed, if at all, to CGT (with the result that as most fixed interest securities were exempt from CGT if held for 12 months or more, tax was often avoided). Accordingly, these provisions treat interest on securities as accruing on a day-to-day basis between the interest payment dates. On a disposal, therefore, the vendor is subject to income tax under Schedule

D Case VI on the interest accruing from the immediately preceding interest payment date to the date of disposal and the purchaser is treated as owning the income from that date. It follows that when the sale is with accrued interest (*cum div*) the vendor is treated as entitled to extra interest and the purchaser gets relief for a corresponding amount. Conversely, if the sale is without accrued interest (*ex div*), the vendor will obtain relief on an amount equal to the interest to which the purchaser is regarded as entitled. The apportioned sums are treated as received on the day when the interest period ends and are subject to tax under Schedule D Case VI for the chargeable period in which they are received. As a result of these provisions appropriate amendments are made in the computation of any capital gains on the disposal of the securities (gilt-edged securities and qualifying corporate bonds are now generally exempt from CGT) and securities covered by the scheme are excluded from the anti-bond washing provisions which preceded this new legislation.

EXAMPLE 36.1

Elena owns £100,000 in nominal value of Government stock paying interest at 5% pa on 30 June and 31 December. She sells that stock *cum div* to Henrietta on 30 September 1997 for £99,780.

(1) *Elena's tax position*: She is subject to income tax under Schedule D Case VI in 1997–98 on three months' accrued interest (£1,250) for the period from 30 June 1997 (the last payment date) to 30 September 1997 (disposal or settlement date).

(2) *Henrietta's tax position*: Assuming that she retains the stock until 31 December 1997 she will then be subject to income tax on the interest paid as follows:

Interest payment to 31 December 1997	=	£2,500
Deduct accrued interest purchased		
(1 July to 30 September)	=	£1,250
Reduced amount taxable	=	£1,250

(3) Had the sale been *ex div* so that the interest payment of £5,000 to 31 December 1997 was retained by Elena, she would be taxed on £1,250 of that figure and the balance of £1,250 (ie interest from the date of disposal to the date of sale) would be taxed in Henrietta's hands.

The securities caught by these provisions are defined in s 710 and include bearer bonds, UK and foreign securities, and securities whether secured or unsecured issued by governments, companies, local authorities and other institutions. Excluded from the provisions are ordinary or preference shares, National Savings Certificates, certificates of deposit, bills of exchange, Treasury bills, local authority bills and similar instruments. Individuals (including trustees and PRs) resident or ordinarily resident in the UK are within the provisions, but there are specific exclusions for financial traders (whose profits on sale are taxed as income under Schedule D Case I) and for individuals holding securities with a nominal value not exceeding £5,000. For deaths on or after 6 April 1996 transfers on death to a PR are outside the scheme (FA 1996, s 158); from 1 April 1996 the scheme ceased to apply altogether for corporation tax purposes (being replaced by the new code dealing with corporate loan relationships).   [36.61]

4   Transactions in securities (TA 1988 ss 703–709)

These provisions are amongst the most obscure and complex in the tax legislation. Their object is to cancel (for taxation purposes) a tax advantage gained as the result of a transaction in securities. This cancellation will be effected either by an assessment to income tax under Schedule D Case VI at a maximum rate of 40%; or by such other adjustments as may be prescribed by the Revenue, such as the refusal of a tax repayment (TA 1988 s 703(3)). The three conditions which must be satisfied before the provisions of s 703 can be invoked are considered below.   **[36.62]**

There must be a transaction in securities 'Transaction' and 'securities' are given a wide meaning. A transaction apart from covering purchases, sales and exchanges can include the combined effects of a series of operations. Securities include stocks and shares (TA 1988 s 709(2)) and also a secured debt (see *IRC v Parker* (1966)).   **[36.63]**

As a result of the transaction the taxpayer either obtains, or is in a position to obtain, a tax advantage 'Tax advantage' is defined in TA 1988 s 709(1) as 'a relief or increased relief from, or repayment or increased repayment of, tax, or the avoidance or reduction of a charge to tax . . .'. In *IRC v Universities Superannuation Scheme Ltd* (1997) it was held the exemption from tax to which USS was entitled as an approved pension scheme could amount to a 'relief from . . . tax'.

An advantage will arise if money is received in the non-taxable shape of a loan rather than in the (taxable) form of a capital dividend (*Bird v IRC* (1988)). One of the uncertainties raised by the definition is whether a CGT advantage is included; the section was introduced before CGT and the widely held view is that CGT is not included. Where shares are sold, there is the possibility of both a CGT charge and an assessment under TA 1988 s 703. Revenue practice is to give a credit for CGT paid against a liability under s 703 (see *IRC v Garvin* (1981)). In the *Bird* case, assessments under s 703 were reduced because of the corporation tax suffered by the relevant company.

There will be no liability under s 703 if the taxpayer can show that the transaction was carried out for *bona fide* commercial reasons and that obtaining a tax advantage was not one of its main objects (TA 1988 s 703(1)). This is a matter of intention and, as it is a question of fact, the findings of the Special Commissioners on such matters can only be overturned by the court in exceptional cases (*IRC v Brebner* (1967)). In *Clark v IRC* (1978), it was held that this commercial test had to be applied not just to the actual sale of the securities, but in the light of all the relevant circumstances. On the particular facts, the sole purpose of the sale was to enable the taxpayer to raise money for the purchase of a farm and there were sound commercial reasons for that purchase. Fox J decided, therefore, that there was a good defence to an assessment under s 703 (for a recent illustration, see the Special Commissioner's decision in *Marwood Homes v IRC* (1997)).   **[36.64]**

Any one of five circumstances specified in TA 1988 s 704 must be present Paragraph A of TA 1988 s 704 is concerned with the distribution of an abnormal dividend to a person entitled to tax relief thereon and catches the classic dividend stripping operation.

Paragraph B prevents the use of trading losses that may arise for a share dealer on a sale of shares and applies where the value of shares has fallen after the stripping of a dividend.

Paragraph C is aimed at the party to a dividend stripping transaction who receives a capital sum whilst the other party receives an abnormal dividend and catches the original owner of the shares.

Paragraph D covers closely controlled companies whose shares are not dealt in on a UK stock exchange. For transactions entered into on or after 29 April 1996 Paragraph D is limited to companies whose shares are not on the Official List, with the exception of those companies whose securities are traded on the USM until that market closes at the end of 1996. It applies where, in connection with the distribution of the profits of a company, a person receives a consideration which represents the assets of the company available for distribution, or the value of its stock in trade, or is received in respect of future receipts of the company. Unlike Paragraph C, it does not require an abnormal dividend to be paid, nor a resultant fall in value of the securities. The general purpose is to catch cases where the shareholders of a company obtain property which might have been used to pay dividends. It was considered by the House of Lords in *IRC v Parker* (1966), *Cleary v IRC* (1968), *Williams v IRC* (1980), and *IRC v Garvin* (1981).

Finally, Paragraph E overlaps to a large extent with the other paragraphs. It will be relevant when one Paragraph D company acquires another by means of a share exchange and in connection with that transfer a person receives non-taxable consideration in the form of share capital or other security. That consideration must either be, or represent, the value of assets available for distribution by a Paragraph D company.

Where there is a risk that a transaction falls within the scope of s 703, a clearance under TA 1988 s 707 may be obtained. The Revenue has 30 days from the date of the application, or receipt by it of any further information requested, to decide whether to serve a notice on the taxpayer stating that it believes the transaction(s) falls within s 703. If clearance is refused, although the Revenue is under no duty to give its reasons, it will do so in appropriate cases and occasionally grant the taxpayer an interview to clarify the position.

If a notice is served on the taxpayer to the effect that the Revenue believes that his transaction is caught by s 703 he is given by statutory declaration a right of reply within 30 days and if the Revenue decides to continue with the matter a tribunal is set up under TA 1988 s 706 to determine whether there is a *prima facie* case for proceeding further (the taxpayer is not entitled to appear before this tribunal). If a case is found to exist, the Revenue will then serve a notice under s 703(3) indicating how it intends to counter the alleged tax advantage. The taxpayer has a right of appeal against the Revenue's decision to the Special Commissioners.   **[36.65]**

37 Choice of business medium

I   INTRODUCTORY—THE AVAILABLE OPTIONS

When commencing a business the participators will normally have an unrestricted choice between operating through the medium of a company or partnership. The only major legal limitation is that partnerships cannot, save in the case of certain professions, such as accountants and solicitors, be formed with more than 20 partners (Companies Act 1985 s 716). Professions which because of professional regulations cannot operate through the medium of a limited company, may, however, set up a company to service the running of their premises and notably to provide staff, furniture and equipment.

The typical company will be the limited private company and the typical partnership will consist of a number of partners with unlimited personal liability.   [**37.1**]

There are, however, other possibilities such as:

The public company   Its attraction is the ability to raise funds from the public (contrast the restriction on private companies: Companies Act 1985 s 81). In practice, of course, it is unlikely that a new business would commence as a public company since the costs involved are considerable and only in very limited cases would a Stock Exchange listing or permission to deal in the company's shares on the Alternative Investment Market be granted for a completely new enterprise.   [**37.2**]

The unlimited company   This suffers from the disadvantage that the liability of the shareholders is unlimited—hence, they are in the same position *vis-à-vis* creditors as partners (albeit with the convenience of corporate personality). However, the unlimited company need not file the statutory company accounts thus enabling it to preserve a greater degree of secrecy; and it can return share capital to members more easily than can a limited company. Nevertheless, the defect of unlimited liability will in most cases outweigh any advantages.   [**37.3**]

The limited partnership   In practice, these have been few in number. Their creation is regulated by formalities akin to those which have to be satisfied if a company is to be formed and although there can be partners whose liability for the debts of the firm is limited, there must also be at least one general (or unlimited) partner. Furthermore, if a limited partner takes any part in the management of the firm, he loses the protection of his limited liability and becomes a general partner. Thus, a limited partner who has put, say, £10,000 into the firm might be obliged to allow it to be lost by inept management since any attempt to interfere would put at risk the whole of his personal fortune. In recent years the investment and tax planning opportunities afforded to the limited partner have proved attractive to some and with IHT business property relief at 100% this may increase. With increasing concerns amongst professional firms at this unlimited exposure to negligence claims it is likely that the government will produce proposals to modernise the 1907 Limited Partnerships Act during the course of the present Parliament.   **[37.4]**

Partnerships with companies   This hybrid business medium involves an individual joining in partnership with a limited company. If the individual is also a director of the company concerned, making him a limited partner offers attractions since he can participate in the management of the business *qua* director of the company. The particular advantages afforded by the arrangement lie in the regulation of profit sharing ratios to take account of different income and corporation tax rates and to maximise the use of business losses.   **[37.5]**

Any comparison between the major practical alternatives of a partnership or a limited company involves a consideration of both non-tax and tax factors.   **[37.6]–[37.20]**

II NON-TAX FACTORS

1 Limited liability

A limited company is a separate legal entity and is solely liable for its debts and obligations. The shareholders' liability is restricted to the sum that they agreed to put into the business and this liability cannot be increased without their consent (Companies Act 1985 s 16). The limited company offers the ideal vehicle for the individual who wishes to set up in business, but who is not prepared to risk his entire personal fortune in the venture.

> **EXAMPLE 37.1**
>
> Brian is the sole shareholder in Wretched Ltd. The company is in liquidation with total debts of £50,000 and assets of only £20,000. Brian has a personal wealth of £100,000, but the creditors of Wretched Ltd cannot look to Brian for payment of the shortfall other than in exceptional circumstances.

There are exceptions to the principle of limited liability and in certain circumstances the 'veil of incorporation' has been lifted by statute and by the judiciary to make shareholders liable for the company's debts. Although these instances are rare, the director of a private company should be aware that there are circumstances in which he might be liable for the debts of the company. Most notably, a director of a company which has entered insolvent liquidation who is found guilty of wrongful trading under the Insolvency Act 1986 s 214 can be ordered by a court to contribute to the assets of that company.

On a practical level, in order to obtain finance for his company a shareholder/director will often be required to give security for the liabilities of the company by way of a personal guarantee. To the extent that personal guarantees are given, limited liability will be illusory. However, who will demand such guarantees? Major lenders, lease finance companies and landlords, but rarely trade creditors and certainly not customers. [37.21]

2 Corporate personality

A company will never die: it can only be liquidated. The death of a shareholder need not affect the business; the only result will be a transmission of some of the shares of the company. Sole traders and partners enjoy no such advantages, because the assets of the business will be vested in them so that death will disrupt the smooth running of the organisation. Further, from the point of view of simple estate planning, the company provides assets (shares) which are both easy to transfer and easy to divide into separate parcels. A large shareholding can be fragmented between different members of the shareholder's family whereas the ownership of an unincorporated business is not easily divisible.

The existence of a separate legal entity (the company) means that the shareholder/proprietor can enter into legally binding contracts with it (see *Lee v Lee's Air Farming Ltd* (1961)). Normally the shareholder in the small private company will be concerned in the management of the business as a director and will ensure that he enters into a lucrative long-term service contract with the company. Amongst a number of advantages that such contracts offer will be the protection of both statute and common law in the event of the employment being prematurely terminated and preferential treatment for arrears of wages in the event of the company's insolvency.

It is also possible to obtain a valuation advantage by incorporating a business. A 10% partner, for instance, is treated as owning 10% of the firm's assets but a 10% minority shareholder will obtain a substantial discount on the value of his shareholding (because of the very limited rights possessed by such shareholders). Hence incorporating a business may be a useful first step as a prelude to a gift of part of the business. [37.22]

3 Obtaining finance

Companies have advantages when it comes to raising finance. Apart from issuing risk capital in the form of shares, money can also be raised by loans secured by fixed and floating charges. The fixed charge is common to both incorporated and unincorporated businesses (eg the land mortgage), but a floating charge is a unique advantage of companies. It operates as a charge over (usually) the entire undertaking and has the advantage of leaving the company free to deal with the assets of the business as it sees fit save to the extent that the terms of the charge provide otherwise. The floating charge will only crystallise on liquidation or when a default, as specified in the deed of charge, occurs.

How advantageous is the floating charge? This question can only be answered by considering whether creditors will be satisfied with the protection afforded by it and in many cases they will not be. Quite apart from the inherent defects of a non-crystallised charge, the steady addition by statute over the years to the list of preferential creditors on an insolvency has greatly weakened the attractions of such charges. Accordingly, the characteristic feature of company charging in recent years has been the practice of creditors to demand fixed security (see, eg *Siebe Gorman & Co Ltd v Barclays Bank Ltd* (1979) and the growth of *Romalpa* clauses). [37.23]

4 Formality, rigidity and costs

By comparison with the unincorporated business, a company suffers from formality and rigidity and has greater operating costs. A partnership or sole trade can be established with an almost total lack of documentation and formality. A company can be bought 'off the peg' for as little as £140 but the costs of a tailor-made company are usually higher. The obligation to file forms is then a regular feature of a company's life, especially the obligation to file an annual return (with a fee of £32) and to submit annual audited accounts to the Registrar of Companies. Such requirements, however, are probably a small price for the benefits of limited liability and, in practice, the costs of a well-drafted partnership deed may be equal to the expenses involved in company formation.

As an artificial entity, a company must be formed for specific purposes set out in the objects clause of its memorandum of association. Actions in excess of these prescribed objects are ultra vires and, at common law, were void. This difficulty should not be exaggerated since, *first*, objects clauses will generally be drafted in such wide terms that they will embrace all conceivable activities and, *secondly*, as a result of the Companies Act 1989, a company's memorandum may state that the object of the company is to carry on business as a general commercial company (ie any trade or business whatsoever).   **[37.24]–[37.40]**

III   THE TAXATION FACTORS

The formation of a company presents the danger that the company will be taxed as an entity distinct from its members so that double taxation will result. In certain areas specific provisions take away this problem, but elsewhere it remains a major argument against incorporation. Any comparison, however, cannot be just between the taxation of individuals and the taxation of companies, since there is also the need to consider the individual as a director/employee of that company. The topic must, therefore, include some discussion of the pros and cons of being employed as opposed to self-employed.   **[37.41]**

1   Taxation of income profits

a) *Rates of tax*

Income tax on the profits of a partnership or sole trade will never exceed 40% and that level will only be reached when the individual's taxable income exceeds £26,100. Corporation tax will be charged on the profits of the company at either 31% or 21% depending upon whether the company is a small company (see **[28.23]**). Unlike income tax, corporation tax is levied at a flat rate so that in the case of a company taxed at 31% all its profits will be charged at this rate.

For an individual whose taxable income exceeds £26,100, the marginal rate will be 40%, but this will, of course, only apply to the slice of income above £26,100. For small companies whose profits exceed £300,000 but fall below £1,500,000 there is a system of tapering relief and tax on profits which fall within that zone is charged at the marginal rate of 33.5%.

It may be advantageous to ensure that the company avoids making profits taxed at this marginal rate: keeping a company's profits below £300,000 can be achieved by a number of methods: eg paying out additional tax deductible sums to its directors in the form of salaries or bonuses; by making extra contributions to a pension scheme; or by setting up a share incentive scheme for its directors/employees (see *Example 37.3*).   **[37.42]**

b) *National insurance contributions*

The rates for 1997–98 are set out as Appendix A at the end of this chapter. NIC costs must be borne in mind when extra salary/bonuses are paid out to directors and employees.   **[37.43]**

c) *The effect of paying all the profits out as remuneration*

Employees' remuneration is deductible as a business expense of the company (TA 1988 s 74), and will be subject to income tax under Schedule E. The amount paid to a full-time working director is unlikely to be challenged as excessive so that, if all the profits are paid out as remuneration, the company will pay no corporation tax (contrast *Copeman v William J Flood & Sons Ltd* (1941) and *Earlspring Properties Ltd v Guest* (1993) which illustrate that excessive payments to a director's family may be challenged). The only tax charged on the profits will, therefore, be income tax so that the only difference between a shareholder/director who extracts all the profits as salary and the self-employed sole trader lies in the contrasts between Schedule E and Schedule D taxation. The main points of comparison are:

(1) Dates for paying the tax: this is discussed in more detail at [**37.45**] below.
(2) Pension entitlements: the pensions available for employees and for the self-employed are discussed in Appendix IV. It should be remembered that, although the pension choices are now similar in both cases, one advantage for employees is that tax deductible contributions to their pension schemes can also be made by their employer (ie by the company), thus boosting their eventual entitlement under the scheme.
(3) Social security aspects: the salary paid to employees, including directors, attracts Class 1 national insurance contributions payable by both employer (the company) and the employee. [**37.44**]

d) *Dates for paying tax*

For companies, there is a maximum delay of nine months from the ending of the accounting period to the payment of corporation tax. Where company profits are all paid out in directors' fees the tax charge will be under the PAYE system. If a company pays a dividend it will have to pay ACT, an advance payment of its MCT. It should, therefore, delay paying the dividend until as late as possible in its accounting period (see further [**29.42**]).

For individuals the self-assessment regime involves profits for the accounting period ending in the year of assessment being charged on the basis of an estimate using the previous year's profit (this tax is paid in two instalments, on 31 January in the year of assessment and on the following 31 July). A final, balancing, payment is then made the following 31 January. Drawing up accounts to end early in the tax year (eg on 6 April) therefore produces the longest delay before the tax liability is finally settled. [**37.45**]

e) *Trading losses*

The advantages afforded by relief for trading losses generally lie with the unincorporated business. Company losses are 'locked in' so that they cannot be used by the owners to set against their income, and instead relief will only be given when the company makes profits (see [**28.60**]). Prior to FA 1991, the ability to set a trading loss against capital gains in the year in which the loss was incurred was the one real advantage that the company had over the unincorporated trader. However, an unincorporated trader can now set trading losses against capital gains for the year of the loss and one following year (see [**7.61**]). The unincorporated trader is also able to set his trading losses against his other income under the provisions of TA 1988 s 380 and, so far as early losses are concerned, against previous income as a result of TA 1988 s 381. It is often argued that when a new business is likely to show early losses, the ideal is to start that business as an unincorporated trade and then, when profitable, to incorporate. However, if early losses exceed the wildest expectations of the trader the advantage of income tax loss relief will not compensate for the disaster of bankruptcy. Had the loss been realised by a company, of course, limited liability would have protected the proprietors from bankruptcy.   **[37.46]**

EXAMPLE 37.2

Having worked in the Civil Service for many years, Samantha has resigned to open a boutique. She anticipates trading losses in the early years. She has a substantial private income.
(1) If she forms a company to run the business, trading losses can be relieved only against future corporate profits (including capital gains).
(2) If she operates as a sole trader the losses can be set against her private income (and capital gains) for the year of the loss (TA 1988 s 380) or against her income, including that from the Civil Service, in previous years (TA 1988 s 381) or against both (*Butt v Haxby* (1983)).

f) *Interest relief*

Income tax relief is generally available on the interest paid on loans to acquire a share in either a partnership or a close company. To qualify, the taxpayer no longer has to work for the greater part of his time in the business (see generally Chapter 4). Relief is also available on loans raised for the benefit of the close company or partnership. Interest paid on loans to finance the business will usually be a deductible business expense, and from 1 April 1996 companies are subject to new rules whereby all profits and losses (whether as borrowers or lenders) are treated as income with interest payments taxed or relieved as they accrue rather than as they are paid.   **[37.47]**

g) *Corporate investment reliefs*

Various reliefs have been introduced in an attempt to stimulate investment in qualifying trading companies.   **[37.48]**

Loss relief (TA 1988 s 574)   Section 574 is intended to encourage the purchase of shares in unquoted trading companies by allowing a loss on disposal of the shares (including failure of the venture) to be relieved against income (see further **[7.121]**). It is not available for moneys lost in an unincorporated enterprise, but the partner who lends money to the partnership may be able to claim a capital loss under TCGA 1992 s 24 if the partnership defaults and the debt is a debt on a security, or under TCGA 1992 s 253 where the debt is not on security.   **[37.49]**

Enterprise Investment Scheme (TA 1988 s 289)   Subject to detailed provisions being satisfied, tax relief at 20% on the sum invested in a qualifying company is available and the investment may also enable capital gains to be sheltered thereby providing a maximum relief of up to 60%.(see **[4.122]**).   **[37.50]**

Reinvestment relief (TCGA 1992 Part V Chapter 1A)   Gains on the disposal of *any* asset can be sheltered by the acquisition of qualifying shares in qualifying unquoted trading companies (see **[16.121]**). Prescribed companies may also benefit from funds invested via a so-called 'venture capital trust' (see **[4.130]**).   **[37.51]**

h) *Illustrations*

EXAMPLE 37.3

AJ Ltd has taxable profits for the year ended 31 March 1998 of £310,000 after paying its two directors salaries of £23,000 each. To avoid paying corporation tax at 33.5% on profits above £300,000, AJ Ltd pays each of the two directors a further cash bonus of £5,000.

This has the following results (assuming that the directors have no other income and are entitled to the personal allowance).

(1) *Taxation of AJ Ltd*

	£	£
Taxable profit to date		310,000
Less: bonuses to directors (£10,000)		
NIC (@ 10% = £1,000)		11,000
Revised profit for year		£299,000
Corporation tax at 21%		62,790

(2) *Taxation of the directors*

Total income (£23,000 + £5,000)	28,000	
Less: personal relief	4,045	
Taxable income	£23,955	
Income tax payable by each:		
£4,100 at 20%	820	
£19,855 at 23%	4,566.65	
Total income tax paid (2 × £5,386.65)		£10,773.3

(3) Total tax paid (£62,790 + (£5,386.65 × 2))   £73,563.3

Notes:

(a) Dividends cannot be used to reduce profits below £300,000.
(b) Had the bonus payments not been paid, the total tax bill would have been:

(1) *Taxation of AJ Ltd*

	£
Taxable profits	310,000
Corporation tax payable:	
£300,000 at 21%	63,000
£10,000 at 33.5%	3,350
	£66,350

(2) *Taxation of directors*

Total income	23,000	
Less: personal relief	4,045	
Taxable income	£18,955	
Income tax payable by each:		
£4,100 at 20%	820	
£14,855 at 23%	3,416.65	
Total income tax paid (£4,236.65 × 2)		£8,473.3

(3) Total tax paid   £74,823.3

Hence, the extra tax paid if the bonus payments are not made is £74,823.3 – £73,563.3 = £1,260.

(c) In addition the bonus payments will result in an NIC liability for the company of £1,000 (ie £10,000 at 10%).
(On ways to avoid NIC on bonus payments see [**37.61**].)

Example 37.4 shows the advantages of a small company when it is desired to retain profits for use in the business.

EXAMPLE 37.4

Business profits are estimated to be £40,000 in the year ended 31 January 1998 and the proprietor will take £15,000, but leave the remainder in the business to finance expansion.

(1)   If an unincorporated business:

		£
Taxable income (ignoring reliefs)		£40,000

Income tax on £40,000:		
£4,100 @ 20%	820	
£22,000 @ 23%	5,060	
£13,900 @ 40%	5,560	
	£11,440	

NIC		
Class 2	319.8	
Class 4	1,030.20	
	£1,350	

		£
Gross profit:		40,000
Less	11,440	
	1,350	12,790
		£27,210

(2)   If a company with £15,000 paid out as emoluments and the balance retained:

Proprietor:	£	£
Taxable income (ignoring reliefs)		15,000
Tax on £15,000 @ 20% and 23%	3,327	
NIC on £15,000	799.2	4,126.2
Total amount received after tax and NIC		£10,873.8

Company:		£
Total profits:		40,000
Less: remuneration	15,000	
NIC on remuneration	1,500	16,500
Taxable profits		23,500
Corporation tax on £23,500 at 21%		4,935
Retained profit		£18,565

The amount of profits that can be retained in a small company is 79%, ie after paying corporation tax at the rate of 21%. The tax saving in this example of £2,228.8 ((£10,873.8 + £18,565) – £27,210 is extra profits retained for the business.

If the company was not a small company, so that it was paying tax on income and capital profits at 31%, there would be a tax advantage in profit retention if the proprietors were liable to income tax at a rate of 40%, given the NIC position.

If the business is generating profits in excess of the needs of the proprietor(s), the ability to use the lower corporation tax rates to retain profits (as in *Example 37.4*) represents one of the attractions of incorporation. Further, it should be noted that with the disappearance of first year capital allowances, the costs of acquiring plant, machinery and industrial buildings have to be borne out of taxed rather than pre-tax profits. Hence, the retention of profits is a factor of importance in most businesses.   [**37.52**]

2   Extracting cash from the business

One of the drawbacks of a company may occur when the proprietor desires to extract surplus profits for his own benefit. Legal theory—the company is a separate legal entity—means that the extraction will be charged to tax and, as the profits extracted may have already been subject to charge in the company's hands, there is a risk of double taxation. The major methods of 'bleeding off' profits are: [**37.53**]

Paying dividends There is an element of double taxation since although ACT paid on the dividend discharges the MCT bill of the company, full credit is not given to the shareholder for the amount paid in ACT (see [**29.65**] and *Example 29.21*).

Of course a shareholder may waive his entitlement to a dividend before it is declared and it will not then be treated as paid to him since it never becomes due and payable. Accordingly, ACT is not charged on that sum and neither does it enter the income of the shareholder for income tax purposes. Further by IHTA 1984 s 15, it will not be a transfer of value if it is made within one year before the dividend is declared. Hence, two advantageous uses of the waiver may be noted: *first*, it may enable the company to declare a larger dividend on the other shares; *secondly*, it can be employed to enable profits to be extracted by shareholders who are not directors by the latter waiving their dividend and taking their share of the profits as remuneration. Exceptionally the income tax settlement provisions and CGT value shifting rules may pose problems when a dividend waiver is proposed. [**37.54**]

EXAMPLE 37.5

Magna is a higher rate taxpayer with a 75% shareholding in Magna Ltd. His daughter, Minima is the managing director with a 15% shareholding and his son Minimus owns 10% of the shares and is an unemployed sociologist with unused allowances and reliefs. Profits could be extracted from Magna Ltd as follows:

(1) Magna could waive his entitlement to dividends; as a higher rate taxpayer he does not wish to increase his taxable income for the year.

(2) Minima could likewise waive her entitlement to dividends and arrange to receive extra remuneration instead, preferably in the form of extra benefits in kind which will not result in increased NIC for the company.

(3) Minimus could receive a dividend; since he is not employed by the company it is not possible for his share of the profits to be paid as salary.

Interest payments Excessive interest payments, and any attempt to link the interest to the profits of the company, may result in an application of the rules that apply for dividends (see [**29.7**]). Interest payments have to be in respect of *bona fide* loans. [**37.55**]

Lending the profits Apart from restrictions on the making of loans to directors in the Companies Act 1985, the company concerned will usually be close with the result that the provisions of TA 1988 s 419 will apply (see [**28.98**]), so that it must pay notional ACT which will only be refunded when the loan is repaid. In addition, the director/shareholder will suffer Schedule E income tax on the beneficial loan (see [**5.150**]). [**37.56**]

Extracting the profits by selling the shares Profits made by the company will be reflected in the value of the shares. Hence, a sale of the shares will ensure that the profit is obtained by the shareholder. This method of extracting profits suffers from two defects. *First*, there will be double taxation since not only will the company's profit be subject to corporation tax, but also the share sale will be a taxable occasion.

Secondly, the sale of the shares may fall foul of TA 1988 s 703 (see [**36.62**]) so that the gain made will be taxed as unearned income.

In normal circumstances, therefore, extracting profits by sale or liquidation will be less tax efficient than dividends or salary (see Appendix D at the end of this chapter).   [37.57]

EXAMPLE 37.6

Hoco Ltd makes income profits of £100. Corporation tax at 21% is £21 so that £79 is retained by Hoco Ltd. If all the shares are owned by Mr Hoco they would be worth £79 more. Therefore, were he to sell his shares, he would make a gain of £79 subject to (say) 40% CGT = £31.6. The total tax attributable to the company's £100 profit is therefore £52.6 (£21 paid by Hoco Ltd and £31.6 paid by Hoco.) Were TA 1988 s 703 successfully invoked Hoco would be subject to income tax at a maximum rate of 40%.

As can be seen from this example the fusion of the rates of income tax and CGT may remove any advantage to the Revenue from invoking s 703. Advantages in taking a profit as capital gain (rather than as income) do however remain: (see [**14.141**]).

Buy-backs   This topic is considered at [**29.21**]: reference should be made to TA 1988 s 219 and SP 2/82.   [37.58]

EXAMPLE 37.7

Doug is the sole shareholder of Doug Enterprises Ltd, a company which is a 'cash shell' having disposed of its business assets some months ago. It has paid a substantial amount of corporation tax on the gain thereby realised. Doug is willing to transfer some of the shares to his children and would like them to receive at least part of the cash in the company. Doug should consider the following arrangement:

Stage 1: Doug settles shares on discretionary trusts for the benefit, *inter alia*, of his children. CGT hold-over relief is available and IHT may be avoided if the value transferred falls within Doug's nil rate band.

Stage 2: The company then buys back its shares from the trustees. This will be a distribution by the company and the ACT payable may be offset against the corporation tax paid on the profits. So far as the trustees are concerned prior to 5 December 1996 no further income tax charge at the additional rate arose since the sum was received by them as capital. FA 1997 Sch 7 para 3 now provides for the rate applicable to trusts to apply in such cases.

Stage 3: The trustees subsequently distribute capital to the children: no CGT is payable and IHT will be avoided if the transfer falls within the nil band.

Extraction in the form of remuneration   As already discussed, this method avoids any double charge to tax since the sum paid will be deductible for corporation tax and, therefore, subject only to income tax. In the typical private company, where all the shareholders are also full-time working directors, profits are bled off in this fashion. (See *Ebrahimi v Westbourne Galleries Ltd* (1973) for a practical illustration of such a private company and for a salutary lesson in what can happen if things go wrong!) The amount of NIC borne by the company (discussed above) should, however, be borne in mind when fixing levels of remuneration.
                                                                                                  [37.59]

Tax-efficient benefits   Modest savings can be obtained by the provision of certain benefits in kind, for instance:
(1) holiday accommodation or a second home where the cost of the property is less than £75,000 (see [**5.113**]);
(2) assets which directors can use but subject to limitations so that the benefit should be small (for instance, use of a yacht/holiday home etc);
(3) are there still attractions in the company car and company fuel? In extreme

cases the provision of a van as a second car may be attractive since this will result in a significantly lower taxable benefit;

(4) as far as NIC mitigation is concerned the loopholes in this area have been steadily reduced over the years but certain options remain, such as vouchers for goods; pension contributions via a FURBS; and benefits in kind contracted for directly by the company (such as holidays, school fees etc). **[37.60]**

Dividends or remuneration?   The main choice facing proprietors of the private company is, therefore, between dividends and salary. Until recently the payment of salary had obvious attractions: it was fully deductible by the company and was taxed as the earned income of the recipient. The removal of the investment income surcharge combined with the high level of NIC has improved the position of the dividend, however, and removed some of the advantages of paying emoluments.

Bear in mind the following factors:

(1) National insurance contributions are calculated on salary (including any bonuses and commission) but excluding some benefits in kind. Instead of paying extra salary to highly paid employees, the employer should consider providing increased benefits (notably in improved pension arrangements).

(2) Depressing salaries to artificially low levels should be avoided. Pension contributions and entitlement will be affected whilst regular payments of dividends will increase the value of shares in the company which will, in turn, increase the dangers of a high CGT or IHT charge.

(3) Dividends can only be paid in years when the company has accumulated realised profits.

As can be seen from Appendix C at the end of this chapter, dividends are more tax efficient when the marginal corporate tax is 21% and salary bonus more tax efficient when the corporation tax rate is 31%. Of course, if a bonus is paid without incurring employers' NIC that is the most tax efficient in all cases! The different cashflow implications of paying dividends as against a bonus must also be considered and Appendix B shows that the advantage of deferred tax payments in the case of a dividend is significant. However, the NIC-free benefit in kind is still the most effective way of extracting profit. **[37.61]**

3   Capital taxes

a) *General*

Recent changes in the capital taxation of companies have placed the small company in an improved position *vis-à-vis* the unincorporated business.

Sole traders and partners are subject to CGT at a rate of 20%, 23% or 40% with an annual exemption (for 1997–98) of £6,500. For partnerships, the rules for calculating the CGT liability of the individual partners are applied in accordance with SP D/12 (see Chapter 31). So far as companies are concerned, capital gains are taxed at the normal corporation tax rate: ie at either 21% or 31%. Such gains are included in determining whether the small company rate is applicable. In terms of tax rates, therefore, companies may be at an advantage since the individual will usually find that a 40% rate of tax will apply to his gain whereas the company will, at worst, be subject to a 31% rate.

In many cases both individuals and companies will be able to defer a charge by claiming roll-over reinvestment relief under TCGA 1992 s 152 (see **[16.92]**). In other cases, the company should consider disposing of the asset in a year when its trading profits are low so that it may come within the small company's 21% rate of charge (the same advice holds good for individuals but often the basic rate band will have been exceeded by taxable income). Capital profits can be taken out of the company by means of a dividend, the ACT on which can be set against the company's MCT on all its profits. In this way, a shareholder who wishes to realise the capital profit on his shares can avoid the double charge to tax that would otherwise result when he sells those shares (see *Example 37.8*).   [37.62]

EXAMPLE 37.8

In its accounting period ending 31 December 1997, Kafka Ltd, a small company, makes capital profits of £100. K, a basic rate taxpayer, is the sole shareholder/director and wishes to obtain the benefit of this profit.

(1) *Sale of shares:* Kafka Ltd incurs a corporation tax charge of £21 on the £100 of capital profit. Accordingly the net profit of £79 is retained in the company. If K were to sell his shares for a price reflecting this retained profit he would be subject to CGT of £18.17 on the retained profit (ie 23% × £79). Hence, the total tax attributable to the company's £100 capital profit will be £39.17 (£21 corporation tax + £18.17 CGT).

(2) *Payment of dividend:* If, instead of selling his shares, K arranges for Kafka Ltd to distribute the profit by way of dividend the tax position is as follows:

	£
Dividend	79
MCT thereon	21
	£100
K's income (Schedule F)	98.75

No further charge for the basic rate taxpayer

Total tax paid	£21

Hence, K saves tax of £18.17 (ie £38.17 in (1) – £21 in (2)).

b) *Retention of assets outside the business*

Over the years the practice has grown up of keeping appreciating capital assets out of a company. In part, this is to avoid any risk of a double charge to CGT: but undoubtedly the most compelling reason is very often the desire of the owner of the asset to retain all of any future profits made from the sale of that asset! In such a case, therefore, the relevant shareholder will allow the asset to be used by the company, but will retain its ownership.

On its disposal therefore, any gain will be subject to CGT only in the hands of the shareholder. The difficulty is that although a double charge may be avoided, other problems can be created, for instance:

(1) *Retirement relief* can apply to assets used by both partnerships and companies so long as the owner is either a partner or a full-time working director in a personal company (see [**16.109**]).

(2) *IHT business property relief:* Relief may be available if the asset is given away, but only at 50% and, in the case of an asset used by an unquoted company, only if the owner is a controlling shareholder (which limits the relief to those cases where the individual has more than 50% of the company's voting shares). For a partner the relief at 50% is available whatever the size of his share in the partnership (see [**23.43**]). The possibility of 100% relief is a crucial factor which may encourage assets to be held within partnerships and companies.

(3) *Payment for use of the asset:* Apart from such payments being subject to income tax (under Schedule A) they will either prevent retirement relief from applying or restrict the amount of gain which can be wiped out by the

relief. Hence, it may be better for the taxpayer to take, instead, an increased share of the profits or, in the case of a company, a greater salary. If rent is paid the company should obtain a corporation tax deduction (provided that it is not excessive): rent in excess of a market rent paid to a shareholder is treated as a distribution. Interest paid on a loan to acquire property can only be set against Schedule A rental income whereas interest on a loan to purchase shares in, or make a loan to, the company can be deducted from the taxpayer's total income.

(4) *Section 162 relief*: Hold-over relief for CGT on the incorporation of a business will not be available if assets (except cash) are retained outside the company.

(5) *Paying IHT by instalments* is generally not available in the case of assets held outside a company except for land (when interest will be charged on the unpaid IHT). [**37.63**]

c) *VAT and IHT aspects*

If a new commercial building is acquired, the purchaser will have to pay VAT on the purchase price. If this VAT is to be recovered, the purchaser will need to register for VAT and to charge VAT on the rent which he receives. This adds to the administrative burden on the owner and necessitates that he charge rent giving rise to the difficulties referred to above.

For IHT purposes, two comparisons between the company and the unincorporated business should be noted. *First*, the facility to pay the tax by instalments, which is generally available on a transfer of a business or part of a business, is only available on a transfer of shares if that transfer satisfies detailed requirements (see [**23.53**]). *Secondly*, 100% relief encourages simpler structures (see [**23.56**]). [**37.64**]

4 **Stamp duty**

Sales of a business, a part of a business and of shares will at present lead to a stamp duty charge on the instrument of transfer. The nil rate band is not available on a share transfer and duty is accordingly always charged at an ad valorem rate of only ½% per £100 or part thereof. For businesses and shares in a partnership the nil rate may be available and assets that can be transferred by delivery need not be subject to duty (see Chapter 38).
[**37.65**]–[**37.80**]

IV GENERAL CONCLUSIONS

It was often pointed out that, although the non-taxation factors tend to favour incorporation (notably the benefit of limited liability), tax considerations probably favoured the unincorporated trader. Note, however, in particular:

(1) The small companies rate of 21%, which is equivalent to the basic rate of income tax and which encourages the retention of profits (up to £300,000 pa) in the company (see *Example 37.4*).

(2) The top rate of corporation tax (31%) is less than the higher rate of income tax (40%) and applies to both income and capital profits.

(3) Dividends are subject only to a small element of double charge in small companies and deductible in part in the case of other companies.

(4) Interest on loan capital is deductible as a charge on companies' profits.

(5) Retirement relief is usually available on a disposal of shares held in a personal company (including a holding company of a personal trading group).

(6) The danger of an investor being 'locked-into' the private company has been reduced by the 'buy-back' provisions (see [**29.21**]).

(7) Taxpayers are given incentives to invest in corporate trades; notably through the Enterprise Investment Scheme and via CGT reinvestment relief.

Two final points may be mentioned. *First*, questions of commercial 'prestige' favour incorporation: the label 'company director' is more impressive than 'sole trader'! *Secondly*, and by way of a cautionary note, considerable tax reliefs are given to encourage firms to incorporate and new corporate businesses to commence, but the same is not true on disincorporation. A company is easier to get into than to escape from and this is a factor to be remembered when the decision to incorporate is taken.   [37.81]

APPENDIX A: TABLE OF RATES OF NATIONAL INSURANCE CONTRIBUTIONS FOR 1997–98

The table below shows the rates of national insurance contributions for the year 1997–98.

CLASS 1 (EMPLOYMENT)—NOT CONTRACTED OUT

	Employer *% of all earnings*	*Employee*
Weekly earnings bands		
£62 – £109.99	3.0	
£110 – £154.99	5.0	2% of first £62
£155 – £209.99	7.0	(ie £1.24) plus
£210 – £465	10.0	10% of remainder
Over £465	10.0	£41.54 max
Men 65 and over and women 60 and over	as above	Nil
Class 1A – On car and car fuel benefits	10.0	Nil
Class 2 – Self-employed		£6.15 per week
Limit of net earnings for small earnings exemption		£3,480 pa
Class 3 – Voluntary		£6.05 per week
Class 4 – Self-employed on profits		6%
£7,010–£24,180		£1,030.20 max

APPENDIX B: EXTRACTING CASH FROM THE BUSINESS—CASHFLOW CONSIDERATIONS†

Amount of payment (£150,000)	Assumed date	Year ending 31 March 1998		
		Cash flow £	Discount factor*	NPV £
1 Bonus				
Net bonus receipt by individual	1 Jan 98	81,818	1.0000	81,818
Payment of bonus by company	1 Jan 98	(81,818)	1.0000	(81,818)
Payment of PAYE/NIC	14 Feb 98	(68,182)	0.9917	(67,616)
				(67,616)
2 *NIC free payment in kind*				
Net bonus receipt by individual	1 Jan 98	150,000	1.0000	150,000
Payment of bonus by company	1 Jan 98	(150,000)	1.0000	(150,000)
Payment of income tax	31 Jan 99	(60,000)	0.9293	(55,758)
				(55,758)
3 *Dividend-corporation tax at 21%*				
Cash dividend received by individual	1 Jan 98	118,500	1.0000	118,500
Higher rate tax on dividend	31 Jan 99	(29,625)	0.9293	(27,530)
Payment of dividend by company	1 Jan 98	(118,500)	1.0000	(118,500)
ACT on dividend	14 Apr 98	(29,625)	0.9809	(29,059)
MCT	1 Jan 99	(1,875)	0.9346	(1,752)
				(58,341)
4 *Dividend-corporation tax at 31%*				
Cash dividend received by individual	1 Jan 98	103,500	1.0000	103,500
Higher rate tax on dividend	31 Jan 99	(25,875)	0.9293	(24,046)
Payment of dividend by company	1 Jan 98	(103,500)	1.0000	(103,500)
ACT on dividend	14 Apr 98	(25,875)	0.9809	(25,381)
MCT	1 Jan 99	(20,675)	0.9346	(19,323)
				(68,750)

Note:
* Assumes an annual compound rate of interest of 7%

† Supplied by Arthur Lancaster of Ernst & Young.

APPENDIX C: EXTRACTING CASH FROM THE BUSINESS—DIVIDEND v BONUS†

Amount of payment (£150,000)	Year ending 31 March 1998 Corporation tax @ 31%			Year ending 31 March 1998 Corporation tax @ 21%		
	Dividend £	*Bonus* £	*NIC-free bonus* £	*Dividend* £	*Bonus* £	*NIC-free bonus* £
Distributable profits—single company	150,000	150,000	150,000	150,000	150,000	150,000
Corporation tax @ 21%				(31,000)	–	–
Corporation tax @ 31%	(46,500)	–	–			
	103,500	150,000	150,000	118,500	150,000	150,000
Employer's NIC @ 10%		(13,636)			(13,636)	
Employer's NIC avoided	–	–	–	–	–	–
	103,500	136,364	150,000	118,500	136,364	150,000
Tax credit @ 20%	25,875	–	–	29,625	–	–
Individuals taxable income	129,375	136,364	150,000	148,125	136,364	150,000
Employees' NIC*						
Income tax @ 40%	51,750	54,546	60,000	59,250	54,546	60,000
Tax credit	(25,875)	–	–	(29,625)	–	–
Net income tax due	25,875	54,546	60,000	29,625	54,546	60,000
Net income	77,625	81,818	90,000	88,875	81,818	90,000
MCT paid by company	20,675			1,875		
Effective tax rate (%)	48.25	45.54	40.00	40.75	45.54	40.00

Note.
* Assume taxpayer is above the NIC threshold

† Supplied by Arthur Lancaster of Ernst & Young.

APPENDIX D: EXTRACTING CASH FROM THE BUSINESS—CGT ROUTE†

Amount of payment (£150,000)	Year ended 31 March 1998	Year ended 31 March 1998
	Corporation tax at 31%	Corporation tax at 21%
	£	£
Distributable profits	150,000	150,000
Corporation tax at 21%	—	(31,500)
Corporation tax at 31%	(46,500)	—
Net liquidation proceeds	103,500	118,500
CGT @ 40%	(41,400)	(47,400)
Net proceeds	**62,100**	**71,100**
Effective tax rate on return of profits (%)	**58.60**	**52.60**

Note:
Ignore CGT base cost as this is an illustration of effective tax rates on the gain, not the return of capital.

† Supplied by Arthur Lancaster of Ernst & Young.

APPENDIX E: EXTRACTING CASH FROM THE BUSINESS—CASHFLOW CONSIDERATIONS (FINANCIAL YEAR 1999)

Amount of payment (£150,000)	Assumed date	Year ending 31 March 2000		
		Cash flow £	Discount factor*	NPV £
1 Bonus				
Net bonus receipt by individual	1 Jan 00	81,818	1.0000	81,818
Payment of bonus by company	1 Jan 00	(81,818)	1.0000	(81,818)
Payment of PAYE/NIC	14 Feb 00	(68,182)	0.9917	(67,616)
				(67,616)
2 NIC-free payment in kind				
Net bonus receipt by individual	1 Jan 00	150,000	1.0000	150,000
Payment of bonus by company	1 Jan 00	(150,000)	1.0000	(150,000)
Payment of income tax	31 Jan 01	(60,000)	0.9293	(55,758)
				(55,758)
3 Dividend–corporation tax at 21%				
Cash dividend received by individual	1 Jan 00	118,500	1.0000	118,500
Higher rate tax on dividend	31 Jan 01	(29,625)	0.9293	(27,530)
Payment of dividend by company	1 Jan 00	(118,500)	1.0000	(118,500)
ACT on dividend	14 Apr 00	(13,167)	0.9809	(12,915)
MCT	1 Jan 01	(18,333)	0.9346	(17,134)
				(57,579)
4 Dividend–corporation tax at 31%				
Cash dividend received by individual	1 Jan 00	103,500	1.0000	103,500
Higher rate tax on dividend	31 Jan 01	(25,875)	0.9293	(24,046)
Payment of dividend by company	1 Jan 00	(103,500)	1.0000	(103,500)
ACT on dividend	14 Apr 00	(11,500)	0.9809	(11,280)
MCT	1 Jan 01	(35,000)	0.9346	(32,711)
				(68,037)

Note:
* Assumes an annual compound rate of interest of 7%

APPENDIX F: EXTRACTING CASH FROM THE BUSINESS—DIVIDEND v BONUS (FINANCIAL YEAR 1999)

Amount of payment (£150,000)	Year ending 31 March 2000 Corporation tax @ 31%			Year ending 31 March 2000 Corporation tax @ 21%		
	Dividend £	*Bonus* £	*NIC-free bonus* £	*Dividend* £	*Bonus* £	*NIC-free bonus* £
Distributable profits—single company	150,000	150,000	150,000	150,000	150,000	150,000
Corporation tax @ 21%	—	—	—	(31,500)	—	—
Corporation tax @ 31%	(46,500)	—	—	—	—	—
	103,500	150,000	150,000	118,500	150,000	150,000
Employers NIC*	—	(13,636)	—	—	(13,636)	—
Employers NIC avoided	—	—	150,000	—	—	150,000
	103,500	136,364	150,000	118,500	136,364	150,000
Tax credit @ 10%	11,500	—	—	13,167	—	—
Individuals taxable income	115,000	136,364	150,000	131,667	136,364	150,000
Employees NIC*	—	—	—	—	—	—
Income tax @ 40% (32.5% on dividends)	37,375	54,546	60,000	42,792	54,546	60,000
Tax credit	(11,500)	—	—	(13,167)	—	—
Net income tax due	25,875	54,546	60,000	29,625	54,546	60,000
Net income	77,625	81,818	90,000	88,875	81,818	90,000
MCT paid by company	35,000	—	—	18,333	—	—
Effective tax rate (%)	48.25	45.54	40.00	40.75	45.54	40.00

Note:
* Assume taxpayer is above NIC threshold

APPENDIX G: EXTRACTING CASH FROM THE BUSINESS—CGT ROUTE (FINANCIAL YEAR 1999)

Amount of payment (£150,000)	*Year ended* *31 March 2000*	*Year ended* *31 March 2000*
	Corporation tax *at 31%* £	*Corporation tax* *at 21%* £
Distributable profits	150,000	150,000
Corporation tax at 21%	—	(31,500)
Corporation tax at 31%	(46,500)	—
Net liquidation proceeds	103,500	118,500
CGT @ 40%	(41,400)	(47,400)
Net proceeds	**62,100**	**71,100**
Effective tax rate on return of profits (%)	**58.60**	**52.60**

Note:
Ignore CGT base cost as this is an illustration of effective tax rates on the gain, not the return of capital.

38 Incorporations, acquisitions and demergers

Some aspects of business takeovers will be considered in this chapter, although in view of the complexities and technicality of the subject all that is attempted is a general introduction to the problems involved.   [**38.1**]

I TRANSFER OF AN UNINCORPORATED BUSINESS TO A COMPANY

This section is concerned with the problems when an existing unincorporated business is transferred to a limited company. There are a variety of ways in which this might happen, for instance:

(1) The transfer could be to a company formed or purchased 'off the shelf' by the proprietor of the business to take over the running of that business. Normally the transfer will be in consideration of the issue of shares in that new company (see *Salomon v Salomon & Co* (1897)).

(2) The business might be taken over by an existing company in return for shares in the company, cash, or a combination of both. Where cash is received the recipient might then use the moneys to start a new business or he might retire on the proceeds of the sale.   [**38.2**]

1 Income tax

Unincorporated trades are subject to income tax under Schedule D Case I and the result of a company takeover is that the closing year rule will apply. The taxpayer should ensure that he has sufficient cash (from the sale of the business or elsewhere) to meet this bill. Where assets only are sold and the former proprietor continues the same trade, these results do not follow: he will continue to be taxed according to the current year rules.

Termination of a business may lead to a claim for terminal loss relief (TA 1988 s 388(1): see [**7.102**]). As an alternative, where the business is sold to a company wholly or mainly for shares, the taxpayer can elect for any year throughout which he retains beneficial ownership of the shares to set off unrelieved trading losses against income that he receives from the company. The set-off must first be used against salary if the proprietor is employed by the company but any balance can be used to reclaim tax on dividends paid by the company (TA 1988 s 386: see [**7.101**]). The loss cannot, of course, be transferred to the company.

A discontinuance may result in a clawback of capital allowances by a balancing charge. Where the transfer is to a company controlled by the transferor, however, an election can be made by both parties, in the case of machinery and plant, that the trade shall not be treated as discontinued so that the company will take over the tax position of that person. That election must be made within two years of the date of succession.   **[38.3]**

2   **Capital gains tax**

a) *The available reliefs*

Any takeover involves the transfer of chargeable assets to the company with a consequent risk of a CGT charge. A number of reliefs may be available: **[38.4]**

Where the transfer is in return for shares   Hold-over relief under TCGA 1992 s 162 is available and operates to roll any gain on the business assets into the replacement shares. CGT will, therefore, be postponed until the shares are sold. For the relief to apply, all the business assets (except cash) must be transferred to the company. It follows that retention of appreciating business assets prevents s 162 from applying and any attempt to remove those assets from the business prior to its incorporation (eg by transferring them to a spouse) may result in the Revenue applying the *Ramsay* principle to deny s 162 relief. If the consideration is partly shares and partly cash an appropriate portion of the gain will be subject to charge and only the balance will be held over (see [**16.105**]). Special rules operate if part of the consideration furnished is a qualifying corporate bond. If the transferor qualifies for retirement relief in respect of the unincorporated business, the Revenue will permit him to deduct that relief from any gains arising on the incorporation and to hold over any remaining gain under s 162. Alternatively, if retirement relief is either not desired or is unavailable on the incorporation, it may be available on a subsequent disposal of the shares provided that the company is his 'personal company'. For the purpose of the ten-year ownership requirement, aggregation of the ownership of the business and the shares is permitted.   **[38.5]**

A transfer for cash   Roll-over reinvestment relief under TCGA 1992 s 152 may be available if the disponer reinvests the proceeds of sale of permitted assets within the prescribed period. Where the disponer is over 50, retirement relief may be available. Alternatively, general reinvestment relief is available provided that the *gain* is reinvested within the permitted period in qualifying shares (see [**16.121**])   **[38.6]**

A gift to the company   Under TCGA 1992 s 162 all the assets of the business must be transferred to the company. It is possible to postpone the payment of CGT when some assets are to be retained by the transferor and transferee making an election to hold over the gain on the assets transferred under TCGA 1992 s 165. The use of this hold-over election under s 165 should, however, be carefully considered since the effect is to transfer any capital gain in the assets to the company. Accordingly it can lead to a double charge when that gain is ultimately realised (see further Chapter 37 and *Example 38.1*, below).

It may be more efficient in appropriate circumstances for no such election to be made. When retirement relief is available to relieve in whole or in part the gain, that relief is given first with any balance of chargeable gain then being held over (see [**17.45**]). [**38.7**]

The retention of appreciating assets outside the company The double charge which may arise when capital gains are realised by a company means that where a business is incorporated there may be attractions in retaining outside the company assets which are likely to appreciate substantially in value and to allow the company to use or lease those assets. Difficulties will, however, arise if this is done. For instance, TCGA 1992 s 162 will not apply to the incorporation so that, unless retirement relief or hold-over relief is available, gains on the incorporation will be subject to charge. The owner of the asset may, however, be entitled to retirement relief on the eventual disposal of the asset (subject to satisfying the conditions of TCGA 1992 s 164 and Sch 6 para 10) and if he were to sell the asset and reinvest the proceeds, roll-over relief may be available under TCGA 1992 s 157. A gift of the retained asset should attract hold-over relief under TCGA 1992 s 165 and business property relief for IHT at a rate of 50% so long as he controls (within the IHTA 1984 s 269 definition) the company (but note that 100% relief will *not* be available). [**38.8**]

b) *Incorporation under s 162 or s 165*

To obtain relief under s 162, all business assets (except cash) must be transferred to the company: however, to incorporate by using the s 165 route, although this may result in stamp duty savings, leaves other often insurmountable problems. [**38.9**]

EXAMPLE 38.1

Slick intends to incorporate his existing business. Accordingly, Slick Ltd is formed with £100 share capital. Slick then sells to Slick Ltd goodwill (if any) for a nominal sum and other assets at their CGT base cost. The consideration may either be paid in cash or left outstanding as a loan to Slick Ltd. An election under TCGA 1992 s 165 is then made. The following matters should be noted:

(1) Slick is free to retain the ownership of whichever assets he desires (hence avoiding the problems of s 162).

(2) Stamp duty will be charged only on those assets transferred and hence will not apply to the value of debtors if Slick retains title in the debts.

(3) Under s 165 the gain is rolled over against Slick Ltd's base cost of the assets whereas under s 162 it is the base cost of the shares held by the shareholder which is reduced. Section 165 may be attractive since if the postponed gain is realised by Slick Ltd, roll-over (reinvestment) relief may be available. Note, however, that Slick Ltd will obtain the benefit of the CGT indexation allowance only on the base value of the assets transferred. A major problem which may arise if s 165 is used is that the postponed gain may be taxed twice—once on disposal by the company of chargeable assets and the second time when the shares showing an increased value are sold.

3 **Stamp duty**

The sale of a business to a company may involve a charge to stamp duty (see [**32.68**]) unless the contract contains a certificate of value (so that the nil rate applies). Duty will be charged on the land, goodwill, book debts (including VAT), cash in a deposit account, patents, copyright and know-how. It need not be charged on goods, wares and merchandise which can be transferred by delivery. Items such as stock in trade and cash in hand or in a current account must be included in the contract for sale of the business but need not be included in the certificate of value so long as they are not transferred by the instrument of transfer. An apportionment of consideration between the chargeable and non-chargeable assets is made on Stamps Form 22. Duty will, however, be charged on liabilities taken over by a purchaser. **[38.10]**

EXAMPLE 38.2

Yol agrees to sell his business to M Ltd for £49,000. M Ltd further agrees to take over Yol's outstanding liabilities to secured and trade creditors. The state of Yol's business is:

Liabilities	£	Assets	£
Secured creditors	8,000	Freehold	33,000
Trade creditors	12,000	Goodwill	6,000
		Stock	9,000
Excess of assets		Book debts	12,000
over liabilities	49,000	Deposit a/c	9,000
	£69,000		£69,000

M Ltd will purchase the business for a consideration for stamp duty purposes of £69,000, ie £49,000 (purchase price) + £20,000 (liabilities taken over).

Stamp duty will be reduced if the following measures are adopted:

(1) Cash is put into current account before contract.
(2) Yol retains the book debts (£12,000) to pay off trade creditors.
(3) Yol could retain the freehold premises and grant M Ltd a lease or licence to use them. This may not prove satisfactory where the company is not owned by Yol.
(4) The title to the stock does not pass under the conveyance but by delivery.

As a result of taking steps (1), (2) and (4) the consideration for stamp duty is reduced by £30,000 (£9,000 (cash) + £9,000 (stock) + £12,000 (book debts)) from £69,000 to £39,000. As a result no duty is charged provided a certificate of value is inserted into the contract and the appropriate entries made on Form 22. Retention of the book debts means that TCGA 1992 s 162 relief will not be available on the disposal of the chargeable assets.

4 Problems for a purchasing company

Where the business is not being incorporated by the existing owner but instead is being sold to an existing company other difficulties for that purchaser should be noted. For instance, if the business is acquired as a going concern it must be treated separately for corporation tax purposes from any existing trade already carried on. The price paid for items such as land, plant and machinery, and goodwill constitute the purchaser's base cost for the purpose of computing any future capital gains. So far as capital allowances are concerned, a conflict of interest is likely with the vendor being concerned to attribute as small a sum as possible to such assets in order to avoid a balancing charge whilst for the purchaser a high figure will give him a greater capital allowance. The agreed apportionment set out in Form 22 will normally be accepted by the Revenue but will probably only be reached after hard bargaining between the parties. **[38.11]**

5 Other matters

A number of ancillary matters should also be considered on incorporation or sale of a business. The following summarises the more important:

(1) If an existing trade is incorporated, contracts of employment automatically transfer with the business. Where assets alone are sold, however, claims for redundancy will occur if staff are reduced. (See especially the Employment Rights Act 1996 and the Transfer of Undertakings (Protection of Employment) Regulations 1981.)

(2) If the vendor of the business is a director of the purchasing company (this will normally be the case when a business is being incorporated) under Companies Act 1985 s 320 a general meeting of the company will usually have to approve the agreement. If new shares are to be issued it will be necessary to ensure that the company has available shares (if necessary, share capital should be increased: see Companies Act 1985 s 121); that the directors have the power to allot such shares (see Companies Act 1985 s 80); and that any pre-emption provisions in the articles of association have either been satisfied or do not apply to shares issued in return for a non-cash consideration.

(3) So long as the company is registered for VAT before the transfer of the business as a going concern, there will be no charge on the transfer of items which are subject to VAT on the sale of the business (VATA 1994 s 49). VAT may be charged on a mere transfer of assets.

(4) Ensure that all necessary consents are obtained and/or documents amended, eg a landlord's consent to the assignment of a lease.

(5) If the business is sold for cash, the vendor should remember that for IHT purposes, business property relief and the instalment option will not be available on any transfer of value of that cash. An asset which carries a full or partial exemption for IHT is, therefore, being exchanged for cash which enjoys no such exemption.   **[38.12]**-**[38.30]**

II COMPANY ACQUISITIONS

A sale of a company may take one of two different forms. Either the assets of the target company may be purchased; or the shares of that company may be acquired. In the former, the shareholders of the target will be left with a company whose sole asset is cash; in the latter, the shareholders themselves will be left with cash. Alternatively the takeover may be by a share exchange in which case the vendors will be left with shares in the purchaser. On a share acquisition, the purchaser will have acquired the entire enterprise as a going concern and, if a corporate purchaser, will have acquired a subsidiary company. In an assets takeover, the purchaser may simply amalgamate those assets with his existing business so that instead of acquiring a new enterprise he may simply be expanding the existing business.   **[38.31]**

1 **Considerations on an assets sale**

a) *The vendor*

If the vendor company intends to continue in business, an asset sale has the advantage that the vendor company will not be subject to corporation tax on any capital gains realised on prescribed assets if these are rolled over into the purchase of new assets within the permitted time. It is possible to reinvest in a completely different trade (see SP 8/81 and **[16.92]**). A disposal of stock results in a corporation tax charge and a disposal of machinery and plant may lead to balancing charges.

If the company plans to discontinue trading permanently, the consequences are far from satisfactory. The company will be assessed on the capital profits made on the sale. The normal carry-back of losses over one previous year will be available (see **[28.52]**), but carry-forward relief will be lost. Problems will arise if the shareholders wish to extract the cash from the company. The result will be either an income tax charge on a distribution, or a charge to CGT on a liquidation in addition to the tax charge already borne by the company. Retirement relief may be available on a liquidation if the conditions of TCGA 1992 s 164(4) are satisfied. Generally, however, if the vendors plan to discontinue their business, they should not engage in a sale of assets; it is better for them to sell the shares.   [**38.32**]

b) *The purchaser*

The first and most obvious attraction is that the purchaser can select which assets he wants to acquire since he will not be acquiring the entire entity. Secondly, save in respect of employees (which the purchaser will take over if there is a transfer of a business as a going concern), the purchaser will not run the risk of acquiring liabilities which he does not want and/or of which he is not aware. Thirdly, the purchaser will be entitled to capital allowances (for instance, on the purchase of plant and machinery) and to roll-over relief on the purchase of prescribed assets.   [**38.33**]

2   Considerations on a share sale

a) *The vendor*

This will be the preferable solution if the vendors are intending to go out of business. The sale of shares will be a disposal for CGT purposes and, if the requirements are satisfied, retirement relief is available. Because the company is sold, there is no change of owner of the business so that continuity of employment is automatically preserved and all debts and liabilities effectively pass to the purchaser. Needless to say the vendors will normally be required to give certain undertakings and warranties to the purchaser so that there will be some continuing personal liability.

If the purchase moneys are to be paid in instalments, CGT will still be charged on the total sum at once unless the Revenue allows the tax to be paid by instalments (see TCGA 1992 s 280). Where the consideration is partly cash and partly a *chose in action* (eg a proportion of the share price if and when the company goes public as in *Marren v Ingles* (1980); see [**14.7**]) retirement relief will only be available against the cash received and the value of the *chose* (if any); it will not be available on the later disposal of the *chose in action*.

If the vendors intend to stay in business, a share sale may not be recommended since, for CGT, gains on the sale of the shares can only be rolled over into the purchase of replacement shares in a qualifying company ('reinvestment relief': see [**16.121**]). The position of the vendor if consideration for the sale is in the form of shares or loan notes is considered below.   [**38.34**]

b) *The purchaser*

The company is bought *in toto* so that there will be continuity in the business. There will be no tax relief for the purchase of the shares themselves. It is possible to carry forward trading losses suffered by the company prior to the sale of the shares but by TA 1988 s 393(1) these losses may only be set against profits *in the same trade*. If the trade has ceased at any time, carry-forward is not possible even if an identical trade is later restarted. Further, TA 1988 s 768 prevents relief in the event (*inter alia*) of a 'major change in the nature or conduct of the trade' within a period of three years of the sale (see *Willis v Peeters Picture Frames Ltd* (1983) and (revised) SP 10/91; [**28.55**]). The prudent purchaser should, therefore, tread warily for three years before attempting any major revitalisation of the target company.

One headache for the purchaser is to ascertain what skeletons are hidden in the target company's cupboards. To this end, warranties and indemnities will normally be sought. In a typical share acquisition agreement the vendor will be asked to warrant at the time of sale that the company has no undisclosed tax liabilities. Since the function of tax warranties is not only to protect the purchaser against future liabilities but also to extract for the purchaser information about the company, tax warranties normally involve detailed points. For example, the vendor will be asked to warrant that the company has duly and punctually paid all taxes, has operated the PAYE system correctly and has not been involved in any anti-avoidance scheme. It is usual to back up these warranties with a deed of tax indemnity whereby the vendor indemnifies the purchaser against any tax liability of the company which comes to light after the sale but by reference to a pre-completion event and which was not disclosed to the purchaser. As a result of *Zim Properties Ltd v Proctor* (1985) (see **[14.114]**) payments made under such indemnities were thought to be taxable in the hands of the recipient as the proceeds of the disposal of a *chose in action* (ie the right to sue was considered a separate asset). This led to the practice of inserting a 'grossing-up' clause in the deed of indemnity to ensure that the amount payable in the event of a claim would equal the liability under the deed plus the tax payable by the purchaser thereon. However, ESC D27 makes it clear that, *provided that payments under indemnities are made to the purchaser*, they will be regarded as a reduction in the purchase price and therefore not subject to tax (contrast the position if payments are made to the company).

When purchasing a company out of a group special considerations arise. In particular, there may be a CGT clawback charge under TCGA 1992 s 178(3) in respect of assets transferred to the subsidiary by another group company on a no loss/no gain basis under s 171.   **[38.35]**

c) *Pre-sale dividend strip*

The use of a pre-sale dividend to extract value from a subsidiary before its sale is a well-used tax saving device for such dividends can be paid under a group election without ACT. With the equalisation of rates of income tax and CGT, the pre-sale dividend strip has also become popular with individual vendors of private companies as a means of reducing the tax liability on sale: changes in dividend tax credits have, however, increased the cost of this operation for the higher rate shareholder.

EXAMPLE 38.3

SJ Ltd has £400,000 of undistributed profits. The owner, Mr Simon Wise, has been offered £2m for his shares, producing a capital gain of £1.2m which, taxed at 40%, would lead to a CGT liability of £480,000.

If, shortly before the sale, a dividend of £300,000 is paid to Mr Wise and the sale price is reduced to £1.7m, he will suffer a CGT liability of £360,000 on his reduced gain of £900,000 plus higher rate income tax on his gross dividend of £375,000 (ie £375,000 at 40% = £150,000) less the tax credit of £75,000. Thus, Mr Wise will pay tax totalling £435,000, a saving of £45,000.

The target company will be required to account for the ACT payable on the dividend in the usual way within 14 days of the end of the three-month period in which it is paid (see **[29.42]**). However, the ACT can generally be set off against MCT liability for profits made during the accounting period in which the dividend was paid but the amount of set-off is not unlimited and there may be an ACT surplus as a result of a particularly large dividend. This can be carried back up to the six years under TA 1988 s 239 (see **[29.45]**) but a purchaser will be concerned to ensure that this is possible and should also be aware that the company's future dividend policy may be affected by a large pre-sale dividend strip.

FA 1997 s 69 and Sch 7 introduced new rules taxing distributions linked to transactions in securities: these catch the standard pre-sale dividend strip and provide that the distribution is treated as a FID (for the definition of a FID, see [**29.000**]). Sch 7 para 6 provides, however, that this treatment does not apply to 'an excepted pre-sale distribution' defined, *inter alia*, as one made in the period of 14 days before the sale of the company.   [**38.36**]

3   Acquisition by means of a share issue

Shares or assets in the target may be acquired in exchange for an issue of shares in the acquiring company. In such an event:

(1) On a share exchange CGT will not usually be payable by the vendors since a roll-over deferral is available provided that the arrangement is a *bona fide* commercial one and, generally, that more than 25% of the target's shares are owned or acquired by the purchaser (TCGA 1992 s 135). Deferral is also available if the exchange is as a result of a general offer made to the shareholders of the target which is conditional upon the purchaser acquiring control of the target and is for *bona fide* commercial purposes. A clearance can be obtained from the Revenue that these requirements are satisfied. If the old shares qualified for retirement relief whereas the new shares would not it is possible for these provisions to be disapplied and for retirement relief to be available (TCGA 1992 Sch 6 para 2). It is likewise possible to exclude s 135 (in whole or in part) when the vendor wishes to take advantage of reinvestment relief.

(2) *Marren v Ingles* (see [**14.7**]) can present problems in share-for-share transactions where shares in the vendor are transferred to a purchaser in return for an immediate issue of shares in the purchaser together with a future right to further shares (an arrangement sometimes referred to as an 'earn-out' since the further share issue is often made dependent on a future profit target being met). These future shares (ie the deferred consideration) do not fall within TCGA 1992 s 135 and accordingly were not granted a clearance by the Revenue. A number of arrangements were employed to avoid the problems thus posed. Commonly these involved an issue of loan stock by the purchaser which was ultimately converted into shares (ie the deferred shares) in the purchaser. The immediate exchange of shares for convertible loan stock fell within TCGA 1992 s 135 whilst the subsequent conversion of the loan stock was free from CGT under TCGA 1992 s 132. It is understood that clearances were granted when such arrangements were entered into.

In any event, the problems of earn-outs were eased by ESC D27 which provided that:

> 'where an agreement for the sale of shares or debentures in a company creates a right to an unascertainable element (whether or not subject to a maximum) against the purchaser which is acquired by the vendor at the time of disposal and that right falls to be satisfied wholly by the issue of shares or debentures, then, notwithstanding a concurrent right to consideration other than in the form of shares or debentures, the Board are prepared to treat the right to shares or debentures in the hands of the vendor as a security within the meaning of [TCGA 1992 s 132].'

Relief under s 135 was therefore available if the other conditions are satisfied. The concession was not happily worded but it was understood that the Revenue applied it to the extent that the future consideration could only be satisfied by an issue of shares or debentures and therefore ignored the existence of a concurrent or separate right to a cash payment (such right will, of course, not attract relief from CGT). The concession was revised by the insertion of a final paragraph in two situations which extended its ambit. *First*, if the original purchaser was itself subsequently purchased on a share for share basis by another company (not in the same group) and the initial vendors earn-out rights were exchanged for similar rights in the new purchaser and, *secondly*, if there was a subsequent variation in the terms of the original sale agreement (for instance by extension of the earn-out period or to record an agreed settlement). In both cases the original s 135 roll-over was not prejudiced.

FA 1997 s 89 (inserting new TCGA 1992 s 138A) put the extra-statutory concession onto a legislative basis: the legislation is, however, more detailed — for instance it defies 'unascertainable' and it is clear that although the relief is only available if the earn-out is satisfied by paper, there can be two separate earn-outs, one for cash and one for paper.

EXAMPLE 38.4

Jon owns shares in J Ltd which is taken over by P Ltd. For his shares J receives an initial cash sum together with a right to further (deferred) consideration depending on the profits of J Ltd and to be satisfied by an issue of shares in P Ltd (at the time of the takeover the value of the deferred consideration is unascertainable). Jon's CGT position is as follows:

(i)   under general principles the consideration for the disposal of his shares will include the value of the earn-out right (which is a separate asset — see *Marren v Ingles* (1980));

(ii) under s 138A any gain that would have resulted from the value attributed to this right is deferred;

(iii) when the right is satisfied by an issue of shares this can be treated as a conversion of securities so that the charge is further deferred until such time as Jon sells the P Ltd shares;

(iv) if the earn-out is satisfied by an issue of securities in the form of qualifying corporate bonds the new legislation makes it clear that the postponed tax will be charged on the disposal of the qualfying corporate bond.

(3) If assets of the target are transferred in return for shares by way of a *bona fide* commercial arrangement with the target going into liquidation, there will be no corporation tax on the transfer of assets by the target. Instead, the assets will be transferred at no gain/no loss, so that tax will be deferred until the purchaser sells (TCGA 1992 s 139). The shares in the purchaser company received by the vendor's shareholders are not subject to CGT until sold (TCGA 1992 s 136). Clearance is available under both these provisions.

(4) On a share-for-share exchange stamp duty at ½% is payable.   **[38.37]**

4   Acquisition by means of loan notes

The vendor should ensure that the loan arrangements are structured as a debt on security (see **[16.44]**). The paper for paper exchange will fall under the roll-over provisions of TCGA 1992 s 135 and the vendor may be able to spread his gain by encashing the notes in different tax years. There is no question of retirement relief continuing to be available. The vendor should also ensure that the security is not a qualifying corporate bond so that he will be entitled to loss relief in the event of the purchasing company defaulting (see **[28.72]**). When qualifying corporate bonds are issued on a company acquisition it is unlikely that CGT loss relief will be available under TCGA 1992 s 254 since the conditions in the preceding s 253 (loans to traders) will not be satisfied.   **[38.38]–[38.50]**

III   DEMERGERS AND RECONSTRUCTIONS

Splitting up groups of companies or splitting a company into separate parts under separate ownership is the subject of relieving provisions. TA 1988 ss 213–217 takes distributions which are made to achieve a demerger outside the normal income tax treatment of distributions (under TA 1988 s 209) whilst TCGA 1992 s 192(2) prevents the shareholders from suffering any CGT charge by treating the demerged shares as if received on a reorganisation of share capital. It should, however, be noted that the demerger code in TA 1988 does not deal either with the company's CGT position or with stamp duty.

The conditions to be satisfied are technical and cannot be used to separate trades from investments (see generally SP 13/80). In general, three types of transaction constitute a demerger and qualify for advantageous tax treatment:

(1)   A transfer to ordinary shareholders of shares in another company of which the transferor owns at least 75% of the ordinary share capital. This is the so-called '*direct demerger*' in the sense that the shares pass directly to the shareholders of the demerged company and the distributing company may suffer a CGT charge on the distribution.

(2)   Pursuant to an agreement between the transferor company, its shareholders and the transferee company, the transferor declares a dividend *in specie* of part of its undetaking which it transfers to the transferee in return for an issue of shares to the shareholders of the transferor. This and (3) below are '*indirect demergers*' since the trades or subsidiaries pass first to a company which then issues shares to the original shareholders in the demerged company (this was the type of demerger carried out by ICI and considered by the court in *Sinclair v Lee* (1993)). In both cases a CGT charge on the company is prevented by TCGA 1992 s 139.

(3)   An amalgamation of (1) and (2): viz shares in company 1's 75% subsidiary are transferred to company 2 in return for an issue of shares in that company.

Even where a transaction would appear to fall within one of these categories, further criteria have to be satisfied if relief is to be given. Only trading companies and groups are covered, and each entity resulting from any split must be a trading entity. Further, the reason for the split must be to benefit some or all of the trading activities which before the distribution were carried on by a single company and after the distribution by two or more companies. The purpose of the demerger must not be to save tax nor must it be intended as a means of transferring control of the company to a third party. A clearance procedure is available and the form of application is set out in SP 13/80.

The transfer of an 'undertaking' is exempt from stamp duty under FA 1986 s 75 and a direct demerger, because it involves no sale, is not potentially subject to duty.

The demerger procedure may be employed to effect a partition as illustrated in the following example: **[38.51]–[38.70]**

EXAMPLE 38.5

Audivis Ltd carries on, *inter alia*, two separate trades as a result of a merger of two existing businesses (Audi and Vis). Its shareholders are family A and family B who are concerned in the running of the different trades. The merger has failed and so two classes of share are created (A and V shares); a dividend is declared in respect of the A shares which is satisfied by the transfer of the 'Audi' trade to a transferee company which issues shares to the A shareholders. Audivis Ltd then buys back the A shares.

IV MANAGEMENT BUY-OUTS

The distinction between an MBO and an employee buy-out is that in the latter the business is purchased by all or a part of the work force not just by the managers. There are three typical situations when a buy-out may occur; *first*, when a subsidiary (or division) is purchased from a group of companies; *secondly*, when the owners sell the family company or its business; and *thirdly* when a receiver or liquidator sells all or a part of the failed undertaking often by means of a hive-down. As with any takeover the management may purchase either shares of the target company or the assets of the business and similar considerations to those discussed at [**38.22**] apply in deciding which is the most advantageous method for vendor and purchaser.

When the company is purchased (ie a share purchase) the normal indemnities and warranties should be sought by the management team although the vendors will often take the view that if there are 'skeletons in the cupboard' this is a matter of which the managers will have knowledge.

The major difficulties involved in buy-outs relate to the financing of the purchase since the management team will lack sufficient funds to purchase the business out of their own resources. Accordingly the bulk of the finance must be supplied by institutional investors and the target company or business is generally purchased by a newly formed company ('Newco') in which the managers have voting control but in which the majority of the finance has been provided by the institutions (this will normally be in the form of unsecured loan stock and convertible preference shares).

It may be possible to use the assets of the target company to assist in the purchase of its own shares (see the Companies Act 1985, Part V, Chapter VI). The target's assets may for instance be used as security for the institutions' loans after it has been purchased. Alternatively, dividends or loans may be paid to Newco to enable it to discharge interest payments to the institutions (care should be taken to ensure that when Newco is a holding company it has sufficient profits against which to obtain tax relief for the interest payments). Finally, the target could be liquidated after its purchase and its assets transferred up to Newco. This would have the attraction of ending the holding company/trading subsidiary structure but care should be taken to ensure that the transfer of assets does not trigger a CGT charge (see TCGA 1992 s 122). Accordingly, it might be more satisfactory to transfer the business of the target as a going concern at book value and to leave the consideration outstanding on an inter-company loan account. The target would then be left as a 'shell' company.

So far as the managers are concerned, apart from using their own personal wealth to purchase shares in Newco, it will often be necessary for them to raise additional funds by way of loans. Income tax relief may be available on the interest paid on such loans (see generally *Lord v Tustain* (1993) and Chapter 4). Under TA 1988 s 360 relief is given if the taxpayer works for the greater part of his time in the actual management or conduct of the company. When the buy-out is arranged through Newco, it is essential to ensure that it satisfies the test for a close trading company if s 360 relief is to be available (see *Lord v Tustain* (above): a company formed to acquire a business existed for the purpose of carrying on that business). In practice, this means ensuring that 75% or more of its income is derived from trading subsidiaries and the Revenue accepts, that, so long as it is in receipt of the appropriate amount of dividends or income from the target during its first accounting period, this requirement will be treated as satisfied at the time when the managers make their investment. Thus, if at some later date Newco ceases to satisfy the conditions of s 360, relief will not be withdrawn. Relief may alternatively be available under TA 1988 s 361. Newco must be employee-controlled (ie full-time employees should control more than 50% of the ordinary share capital and votes) and it must be an unquoted trading company or the holding company of a trading group. For the purpose of this requirement Newco may qualify even though it has only the one trading subsidiary. If the company ceases to be employee-controlled, however, tax relief is withdrawn. Reference has already been made to the potential income tax liability of managers under FA 1988 ss 77–89 resulting from an acquisition of shares in their capacity as employees (see further Chapter 39). Further, if shares are offered at below market price an income tax liability under the general provisions taxing benefits in kind could arise.   **[38.71]**

39 Employee participation: options, incentives, trusts and profit related pay

'*Right – that takes care of the company reindeer.
Now, about the share option scheme for
the elves . . .*'

I INTRODUCTION

1 **Background**

In recent years there has been a substantial growth in share option and share incentive schemes designed to reward company employees, especially senior management. A major attraction of such schemes is that they bring together the interests of the employee and the company: if the value of the benefit that will be received is related to the performance of the company, the employee and the company have a mutual interest in securing that the company performs well during the period when it is being earned; and if the shares are retained by the employee, that shareholding may be his most valuable disposable asset after his main residence.

Figures showing the take-up for the three types of approved scheme are given in the Inland Revenue Statistics published annually and show that prior to FA 1996 by far the highest number of approved employee share schemes that were being established were discretionary schemes which were usually directed by employers at senior management. The focus of the government's attention had, before then, therefore been directed at encouraging employers to provide schemes for the benefit of *all* employees. However, following widespread concern about the very large benefits being received by some executives under approved discretionary share option schemes, FA 1996 not only introduced changes designed to make the approved 'all employee' schemes more attractive, but also gave effect to previous announcements preventing options granted under discretionary schemes on or after 17 July 1995 being treated as approved (although such schemes can be restructured as 'company share option plans', under which less valuable options can be granted on a discretionary basis—see further [**39.44**]).

Very large gains will, in the future, only be obtainable under unapproved schemes but recent changes to the PAYE and national insurance contributions regimes have made these less attractive both to employers and employees (see [**39.21**]). As the 'carrot' to balance these 'sticks', the previous government announced, in January 1997, its 'Sharematch' initiative: a consultation exercise aimed at adapting existing approved schemes to encourage employees to invest in their employers' shares and employers to match that investment. Little, however, was done pursuant to this initiative before the general election and it is not clear whether the new government will adopt it.

This chapter covers schemes involving shares although there is a brief reference to profit related pay in *Section V*. As some of the schemes discussed in this chapter involve employees purchasing shares, which may lead to their borrowing to finance the acquisition, readers are referred to [**4.44**] for a discussion of the tax relief available for interest paid on loans taken out to acquire shares.   [**39.1**]

2   Taxation of share incentives and options

An individual who is given fully paid shares by his employer receives a taxable emolument if the shares are 'from employment' within TA 1988 s 19, and will suffer income tax on the market value of those shares on the date when he receives them: *Weight v Salmon* (1935). Similarly, an employee who is sold fully paid shares by his employer at an undervalue receives an emolument equal to the difference between the price paid and the market value of the shares at the date of purchase. These types of arrangement, where the employee receives shares not share options, are referred to as *share incentives*.

Various schemes, including the use of *share options*, were introduced by employers in an attempt to circumvent the income tax net. Inevitably, anti-avoidance legislation was then passed in an attempt to widen that net!

There are, however, certain employee share schemes which are given favourable tax treatment. These are the 'approved schemes' and profits made by the employees under such schemes are treated as capital gains, therefore subject to CGT rather than income tax. Although the unification of the rates of income tax and capital gains has reduced the tax advantages of approved schemes, attractions still remain.

On an administrative role, the introduction of self assessment has raised the spectre of an increased number of employees having to self assess and/or make payments on account solely as a result of having received share scheme benefits. The likelihood of this occurring has however, been diminished by a combination of the widening of the PAYE net; exclusions from these two regimes based on the percentage of the income tax liability collected through PAYE; and Revenue practice (see *Tax Bulletin*, October 1996, p 351 and also December 1996 p 374 on valuation of shares in unquoted companies).   [**39.2**]–[**39.20**]

II   UNAPPROVED SHARE SCHEMES

Unapproved schemes are subject to complex income tax treatment. Although this may not result in a tax liability greatly in excess of that under approved schemes (see [**39.111**] ff), it will often result in an employee being subject to tax *before* he has disposed of the shares and thus give rise to cashflow difficulties. Further, whilst unapproved share incentive and option schemes used to be subject to the same beneficial NIC and PAYE regimes as approved arrangements, this has recently changed.

Employers had been paying employees in 'own company shares' to avoid employer national insurance contributions but from 5 December 1996 such shares are within the national insurance contributions net if they are not obtained under an approved scheme and either they are capable of being traded on a recognised investment exchange or 'trading arrangements' exist for them (SI 1996/3031). At the same time contributions also became payable on unapproved options over such shares which are granted at a discount—but as there was no charge on option exercise and discounted options are becoming rarer, this was not likely to have a major effect on companies' attitudes to granting such options. However, a change has recently been announced: the charge is to be on the gain made on the exercise of unapproved options (probably only ones granted after April 1999: more details should be available in the autumn) and this will be a real extra cost for employers (DSS Press Release of 22 July 1997). Pre-December 1996 PAYE regulations were changed to bring 'own company shares' within the PAYE net if they are 'tradeable assets', unless acquired under an approved scheme or on exercising an option granted before 27 November 1996 (SIs 1994/1212 and 1996/2969 and *Tax Bulletin*, February 1997, pp 385 and 386). This further exacerbated potential cashflow problems.

There is likely to be a reassessment of the use of unapproved arrangements in the light of these changes but unapproved schemes do still offer benefits. The key is flexibility: they can be selective in any way the employer wishes (subject to the requirements of EC and UK non-discrimination legislation); they can relate to any type of share; and they can be more flexible in relation to adjustable performance targets.

In December 1994 the Inland Revenue issued a booklet containing the guidance given to its staff on various aspects of employee share schemes, the major part consisting of guidance on the income tax treatment of unapproved schemes. Occasional references are given below to paragraphs in the booklet: SE being to paragraphs in the income tax section; CG being to ones in the CGT section. **[39.21]**

1 Share incentives

Since the issue of fully paid shares at an undervalue would normally give rise to a charge under TA 1988 s 19, companies developed other means of passing value through shares to employees. **[39.22]**

a) *Partly paid shares Shares (TA 1988 s 162)* If shares are issued to a director or employee for less than their market value at that date, the difference between that value and any consideration paid is taxable under s 19. If shares are acquired by a director or employee falling within Chapter II of Part V of TA 1988 and the consideration to be paid is left outstanding as a debt, s 160 may apply to that loan. However, if shares are issued at market value but only part of that price is payable on issue (so that the shares are issued partly paid), the resultant benefit to such a director or employee does not fall within either of the foregoing situations and accordingly has to be dealt with by the special provisions of s 162. If s 162 applies, there is deemed to be an interest-free loan, taxable under s 160, equal to the undervalue.

Broadly, this section applies when a person to whom Chapter II applies acquires shares at an undervalue as a result of a right or opportunity made available because of his employment: undervalue is defined as the difference between the market value of fully paid shares of the same class and the amount (if any) actually paid at the time of issue. It therefore applies in more situations than the issue of partly paid shares, for instance when shares are acquired on exercise of an unapproved option which was granted by reason of Case II or III employment (SE 3601 and 3619). There are also anti-avoidance provisions so, for example, a charge will arise if shares are acquired by a person connected to the employee as a result of the latter's employment. But note the section does not apply to the extent that the acquisition of the shares is already taxed as an emolument under other provisions and that there are strong arguments, particularly in view of the new approach to taxation of beneficial loans introduced by FA 1994 (see [**5.150**]), that if the aggregate value of the notional loan and any actual loans is less than £5,001 or if money borrowed to purchase the shares would have qualified for relief under TA 1988 s 353 (see [**4.43**] ff), no charge arises under s 162 (arguments apparently accepted by the Inland Revenue—see SE 3613 and 3610).

There is some difficulty in deciding which, if any, deeming provision applies for the purposes of deciding whether shares have been acquired 'by reason of . . . employment'. That in Part I of Sch 7 does not seem to apply: s 162 states that s 160 and Sch 7 apply where shares have been acquired by reason of employment and, therefore, seems to exclude the deeming provisions in Part I of that Schedule for the purpose of deciding whether the shares were so acquired. Although it was probably intended that the deeming provision in TA 1988 s 168(3) should apply, there is some difficulty in reconciling its wording with the charging provision in s 162. While SE 3607 makes no reference to any deeming provision when discussing this issue, it might nevertheless be expected that the Revenue would try to rely on s 168(3) and, therefore, in many cases avoid having to prove the connection between the receipt of the shares and the employee's employment. The meaning of the phrase 'in pursuance of a right or opportunity available by reason of his employment' was actually considered by the Court of Session in *IRC v Herd* (1992). The argument centred around whether an opportunity was 'available' by reason of employment when the employee had stipulated that he must receive the shares as a precondition to taking up the appointment: not surprisingly, the court declined to interpret the provision as requiring it to investigate who instigated the idea of providing share benefits to the employee. The Northern Ireland Court of Appeal's consideration of the analogous wording in s 154 in *Mairs v Haughey* (1992) may provide more helpful guidance in cases where no deeming provision applies.

Where shares are acquired in circumstances falling within s 162(1), then even if they were not acquired at an undervalue, there will be a tax charge if they are subsequently disposed of for more than their market value (TA 1988 s 162(6)-(8)). This is to prevent the use of 'stop-loss' protection under which shares acquired under an incentive scheme are bought back by the company if they fall in value.

EXAMPLE 39.1

Sandy, the buying manager of Cosifabrics Ltd, is allotted 10,000 £1 shares in the company in 1995. The market value of the shares is £2.25 each but the shares are issued partly paid and Sandy pays only 50p per share. In 1997 he pays a further 50p per share to the company. The tax position is as follows:

(1) *From 1995 to 1997:* the notional loan per share is £2.25 - 50p = £1.75. This amounts to £17,500 so that interest on that sum at the official rate is treated as an emolument each year.

(2) *After 1997:* the payment of a further 50p per share reduces the notional loan by £5,000 to £12,500. Henceforth, the official rate of interest on that figure is treated as an emolument.

Generally, the deemed loan remains outstanding until either the employee dies (IHT may then be charged on the shares as part of his estate on death);

the 'loan' is repaid (when liability to income tax will cease); or the 'loan' is released or the beneficial interest in the shares is transferred (when tax is charged as if the 'loan' were written off). **[39.23]**

b) *FA 1988 Part III Chapter II*

Under FA 1988 ss 77–89, in certain circumstances income tax is charged on the growth in value of shares owned by employees. There are two main heads of charge: *first*, that attaching to any growth in value arising from the lifting of restrictions; and, *secondly*, that attaching to the growth in value of shares in a 'dependent subsidiary'. FA 1988 s 80 also imposes an income tax charge where a 'special benefit' is received 'by virtue of . . . ownership or interest in the shares' if that benefit is not otherwise chargeable to income tax. Unfortunately, the legislation designed to impose these charges is somewhat vague and imprecise in its application.

The main provisions apply when shares are acquired 'by reason of employment': there are no deeming provisions, so the causal connection must be established. The previous sections in FA 1972 were considered in *Cheatle v IRC* (1982) and *IRC v Herd* (1992) (see **[39.23]** generally on this point). The main area of contention has been whether a director or employee can escape these provisions on the basis that he has acquired his shares as an investor (for instance, on a management buy-out). The Inland Revenue generally opposes any such argument (SE 2908). Shares acquired in pursuance of an offer to the public do, however, escape the charge.

Section 78 imposes a charge when there is an alteration in rights or restrictions which attach to shares in the company which results in shares held by directors or employees increasing in value. The charge is on the increase in value caused by the alteration. It does not arise if the provisions in s 78(5) and (6) apply — provisions designed to exclude the charge where the alteration was not made to benefit specifically employee shareholders. This section also does not apply if the shares held by the directors or employees are shares in a company which was a 'dependent subsidiary' at the time the shares were acquired or is such a company at the time of the alteration: such shareholdings are subject to a more onerous regime.

It is thought that s 78 does not apply to 'equity ratchets' (see SE 2938 but note the caveats: such ratchets are commonly found in management buy-outs).

EXAMPLE 39.2

Alan takes the opportunity in December 1992 to purchase 10,000 'B' ordinary shares in his employer Sad Ltd, which is not a dependent subsidiary. The shares are subject to certain restrictions as a result of which their value is fixed at £5 per share, which Alan duly pays. After five years, in December 1997, the restrictions are lifted so that the shares rank for all purposes as ordinary shares in the company. As a result their value increases to £12. Some six months later, in July 1998, Alan sells the shares for £14 per share. The tax charges levied on Alan are as follows:

(1) *On the lifting of the restrictions in 1997* income tax will be charged (under Schedule E) on the amount by which the shares increased in value as a result of those restrictions being lifted. Accordingly, Alan will be taxed on £7 per share (ie on a total sum of £70,000).

(2) *On the disposal of the shares in 1998* his CGT charge will be computed allowing as a deductible expense both the sum originally paid for the shares (£5 per share) and the sum taxed in 1996 when the restrictions were lifted (a further £7 per share).

Therefore his gain (ignoring indexation and any other available deductions) is £2 per share (ie a total gain of £20,000).

Particular difficulties may arise when groups of companies wish to motivate employees of a subsidiary company by permitting them to acquire shares in that subsidiary rather than in the parent company. Given the comparative ease with which value can be shifted into a subsidiary (resulting in an increase in the value of the subsidiary's shares), the legislation has to make special provision to cover such cases. Broadly, subsidiaries which do not satisfy the requirements laid down in FA 1988 s 86 are 'dependent subsidiaries' and shares allotted therein will attract an income tax charge *either* when the employee sells the shares *or* seven years after he acquires them, *whichever is the earlier.* The charge is on the whole increase in value of the shares and so covers increases resulting from natural growth or attributable to inflation and not just growth arising from shifting value into the subsidiary.   [**39.24**]

c) *Priority share allocations*

When shares in a company are first offered to the public then, particularly on a privatisation, employees are often given priority and discount offers. Under general principles the employees would be taxable on the benefit of the priority allocation: if they receive more shares than they would have done as members of the public, then if the share value at the date of allocation is higher than the price paid, they will have received a benefit by reason of their employment. As a result of FA 1988 s 68, no charge arises merely because of the priority allocation, provided certain conditions are complied with (the statutory provisions are complicated because sub-sections have been added as new ways of packaging shares on privatisations have been devised). However, if the employees pay less for their shares than members of the public, there will still be a Schedule E charge on that discount.   [**39.25**]

d) *Restricted share schemes*

Restricted share schemes involve employees 'receiving' shares subject to a restriction on disposing of them for a certain period and to their being forfeited if the employee leaves service before the end of that period. Normally the shares will be held in trust until the end of the period but the employee would be entitled to receive dividends and instruct the trustees how to vote in the meantime. These schemes have become increasingly popular with companies over the last few years, presumably because they not only act as an incentive to the employee to remain in service but also ensure an immediate identity of interest between him and the company. Further, as companies can make exercisability of unapproved options subject to satisfying performance criteria (with more flexibility than is available in relation to approved options), so shares held under these schemes can also be made subject to forfeiture if such criteria are not met (but see [**39.110**] for the accounting treatment).

The income tax position of the employee is subject to some debate. While *Edwards v Roberts* (1935) might suggest the employee will not be taxed until the end of the period of retention, it is arguable s 19 should apply when he is allocated the shares, with the possibility of a charge under s 78 arising when the restriction ceases (although there would seem to be arguments that this should be treated in the same way as 'equity ratchets'—see [**39.24**]). An immediate charge under s 19 is generally considered undesirable both because the employee would have to raise the money to pay the tax from other sources and because there is no mechanism for the tax to be refunded if the shares are forfeited. Companies therefore aim to construct schemes in such a way that the Revenue will give its *prior* agreement that no charge will arise until actual receipt of the shares.

Introducing a trust into such an arrangement does, of course, create another taxable entity and the general CGT and IHT position would have to be considered carefully.   [**39.26**]

2 Share options

In *Abbott v Philbin* (1961) the House of Lords held that options are subject to income tax on their value (if any) at the time of grant and that any benefit resulting from the exercise of an option (ie because the shares had grown in value during the option period) was not so taxable. Therefore TA 1988 s 135 was introduced.

If, by reason of an employment taxable under Case I of Schedule E, an individual is granted options to purchase shares, he is not taxed on the value of the options *at that time* unless the options are capable of being exercised more than seven years after the grant. However, the whole gain made on the shares will be subject to income tax at the time *when the option is exercised* (credit will be given for any tax which was actually paid on the grant of an option which was capable of lasting more than seven years) (TA 1988 s 135).

EXAMPLE 39.3

John is granted an option to acquire 10,000 shares in a company at 30p per share. The option can be exercised at any time in the next six years and the price of the shares is fixed at their current market value. John pays £10 for the option, which he exercises five years later when the shares are worth 75p. He sells the shares six months later for 85p per share.

(1) There is no income tax charge on the grant of the option since the option period can not exceed seven years.

(2) When the option is exercised, the sum taxed as an emolument is calculated as follows:

Market value of shares at exercise:		
10,000 × 75p		£7,500
Deduct:		
Option price	£10	
Price paid 10,000 × 30p	£3,000	£3,010
Sum assessed to income tax under		
Schedule E		£4,490

Note: Tax is charged on the above sum *despite the fact that the shares have not been sold by the employee.*

(3) On the subsequent sale of the shares any further gain is subject to CGT:

Sale proceeds: 10,000 × 85p		£8,500
Deduct:		
Option price	£10	
Price paid	£3,000	
Sum assessed to income tax	£4,490	
		£7,500
Gain subject to CGT		£1,000

(*Note:* No account is taken of any indexation allowance or other allowable CGT expenses in this example.)

TA 1988 s 19 and *Abbott v Philbin* will continue to apply to the grant of options where they are capable of being exercised more than seven years after grant or where the employment is a Case II or III one; s 162 will normally apply on exercise of the latter options (see [**39.23**]). *Wilcock v Eve* (1995) illustrates another situation where the general charging provisions are relevant. TA 1988 s 135 contains various anti-avoidance provisions—for instance, there is an income tax charge if a payment is made for release of an option taxable thereunder—but it does not apply where an *ex gratia* payment is made following a lapse of options under the rules of a scheme (in this case because the employing company had left the group). The court held that since the gain made on exercising the option would not have been taxable under s 19, the payment made in recognition of the loss of that benefit was also not so taxable (cf the approach of the House of Lords in *Mairs v Haughey* (1994) at [**5.65**]). The court also considered, *obiter*, whether the payment was taxable under s 154. As the payment was not made by the employer, the deeming provision in s 168(3) did not apply and the court held that the payment was not 'by reason of employment': it was not linked to the employment during the year but to the loss of the share options. This decision creates opportunities for abuse that could best be dealt with by extending s 135.

A subsequent increase in the value of shares acquired by an employee under an unapproved option may be subject to income tax, rather than capital gains tax, if the relevant shares were originally issued to the employee subject to restrictions which are then lifted or if the shares are in a dependent subsidiary (see [**39.24**]).　　　　　　　　　　　　　　　　　　　　　　　　　　　　　[**39.27**]

3　Capital gains tax

a) *Share incentives*

Where an income tax charge arises under an unapproved arrangement, the amount on which tax is charged is normally taken into account in calculating the employee's base cost for CGT purposes (TCGA 1992 s 120). If existing shares are transferred to an employee in circumstances giving rise to a charge under TA 1988 s 19, his base cost will be their market value at the time (TCGA 1992 s 17(1)). Does TCGA 1992 s 17(2) mean that the employee's base cost will not be uplifted to market value if he receives *new* shares (ie his base cost will be what he paid for the shares (if anything))? If s 17(2) does have this effect, the employee will pay income tax on the value of the shares (or on the difference between that value and what he paid for them) and will then be subject to a double tax charge. However, the Revenue does not, apparently, consider that s 17(2) applies (see CG 56353 and 56355 but note the position on public offers at CG 56333 ff) on the (rather unexpected) basis, it is understood, that the employee does provide market value consideration since the value of his services are to be taken into account.

Where existing shares are transferred to an employee the transferor will normally be treated as having received market value for them (s 17(1) — but see [**39.61**] in relation to ESC D35 which will often provide relief where the shares are transferred from an employee trust). Where new shares are issued there will not be a disposal.　　　　　　　　　　　　　　　　　　　　　　　[**39.28**]

b) *Share options*

The grant of an option is a disposal for CGT purposes (TCGA 1992 s 144(1)). FA 1996 excludes the market value rule in s 17 (by amending TCGA 1992 s 149A) when calculating the consideration given and received on the grant of the option (but *quaere* whether the Revenue might consider that the value of the employee's services should be taken into account in light of the comments at [**39.28**]: the Revenue's notes to the 1996 Finance Bill did, however, refer to the consideration being 'the amount, if anything, actually paid by the employee for the option'). It appears the amendment is sufficient to exclude a deemed market value consideration even if the option is granted to a connected person (within s 18).

As TCGA 1992 s 144 provides that, when an option is exercised, the grant and the exercise should be treated as one transaction, the Revenue will then discharge any assessment made on the grant (CG 56375). Where existing shares are transferred to an employee on exercise of an option, it is arguable that the deemed market value rule in s 17(1) does not apply because he acquires the shares as option-holder (rather than employee) and through an arm's length bargain. Accordingly, the employee's base cost will be the consideration given for the option plus the price actually paid for the shares and any amount on which he pays income tax which is added to his base cost; the consideration received by the transferor will be calculated by reference to the first two of these (s 144; CG 56378—56399 (to be read in light of the amended s 149A)). If new shares are issued on exercise of the option, there is no disposal and because of the 'one transaction' rule, it appears that the company has no CGT liability, either on payments received on grant of the option or on payments received on its exercise (CG 56377). The employee's base cost is the same as when existing shares are transferred. When the transaction is between connected persons regard should be had to s 18.

Prior to FA 1996 there were concerns about the CGT position when an existing option was released in return for the grant of a new option (for instance, following a takeover). The new TCGA 1992 s 237A excludes the release of the existing option when calculating the consideration received by the grantor of the new right. As far as the employee is concerned, s 237A introduces a roll-over provision, so that his acquisition cost for the new option will be any consideration given for the original option and the new option, and provides that the new option can be disregarded when calculating the consideration received by him for releasing the existing option. **[39.29]**

4 Phantom schemes

So far, references to unapproved schemes have been to schemes which relate to actual shares. If the objective of the employer is to relate pay to performance of the company, then consideration should also be given to *phantom schemes*. These are basically bonuses paid to selected employees which are calculated by reference to the increase in value of the company's ordinary shares. The 'gain' (ie increase in value over the chosen period) is taxed as any other Schedule E emolument in the hands of the employee. From the company's point of view, the advantages include: *first*, the avoidance of the expense of creating a full-blown share option or incentive scheme; *secondly*, the fact that the bonus payments are deductible for corporation tax purposes; and, *thirdly*, the interests of other shareholders are not affected. **[39.30]-[39.40]**

III APPROVED SHARE SCHEMES

1 General requirements

The so-called 'approved schemes' are those share option and share incentive schemes which satisfy the requirements originally contained in FA 1978, FA 1980 and FA 1984. There are three types of approved schemes, being respectively, approved profit sharing schemes, savings related share option schemes and, from 1995, company share option plans (replacing discretionary (executive) share option schemes). As stated above, the basic tax principle is that any profit made by the employees on the disposal of shares acquired under an approved scheme *is subject to CGT and not income tax*.

Many of the conditions which must be satisfied are common to all three types of approved scheme. For example:
(1) *The type of shares* The shares must be ordinary, fully paid-up, non-redeemable shares in the employing company or its parent (or, if the employer is a consortium company, in a member of that consortium). Furthermore, the shares must be quoted on a recognised stock exchange or, if not quoted, must be in a company which is either controlled by

a quoted company or not controlled by any other company. These rules are aimed at preventing manipulation of the value of the shares to be received under the scheme or at least at only allowing this if it also affects shareholders who acquired their shares through other means.

(2) *Restrictions attached to the shares*   Only two kinds of restriction are permitted. *First*, restrictions which attach to *all* shares of the *same class*; and, *secondly*, restrictions imposed by the articles of association requiring shares held by directors or employees to be disposed of *when the holders cease to be directors or employees*. The first is to ensure that, within a class of shares, shares acquired under an approved scheme cannot be disadvantaged; the second recognises that small private companies have a legitimate interest in excluding outsiders from holding shares.

(3) *The exclusion of persons holding a material interest*   An individual who holds a material interest in *either* the company which issues the shares *or* a company which controls the issuing company, is not eligible to participate in an approved scheme. For these purposes, an individual holds a material interest if he either alone, or together with associates, beneficially owns or controls 25% of the ordinary share capital of the company or, in the case of company share option plans, 10% of the ordinary share capital (TA 1988 s 187(3)). 'Associate' means, broadly, a relative or partner or trustee of any settlement in which the employee has an interest. However, an individual who is a beneficiary under an employee trust which owns shares in the company will not have an interest in those shares for these purposes (TA 1988 Sch 9 Part VI). **[39.41]**

2   Approved profit sharing schemes (FA 1978 schemes; now TA 1988 s 186 and Schs 9 and 10)

These schemes are centred on a *trust fund* set up by the employer company. With contributions provided by the employer, trustees acquire shares in the company (either by subscription or purchase) and appropriate these to individual employees (ie shares are held by the trustees for a particular employee). The amount paid into the trust by the employer may (but will not necessarily) vary according to the company's profitability so that a direct link between the performance of the company and the value of the benefit to the employees can be established at the outset and can be maintained throughout the life of the scheme. It should be noted that merely because a scheme exists, the company is not obliged to contribute to it each year.

The conditions for Revenue approval of a profit sharing scheme include the following:

(1) *All* full-time working directors and employees must be given the *right* to participate on equal terms, each time there is an appropriation of shares. Part-time employees must also be able to participate in schemes approved after 30 April 1995 but participation of part-time directors remains at the discretion of the company (FA 1995 s 137). The scheme may, however, specify a qualifying period of employment of up to five years before an employee becomes eligible. Given this extensive right to participate, the allocation of shares is not completely at the trustee's discretion. However, the formula for calculating the number of shares to be appropriated to each participant may take account of such matters as levels of remuneration and length of service.

(2) The market value of shares appropriated to an employee in *any one year* must not *exceed* £3,000 or 10% of the employee's salary for that year, if greater, subject to an *upper limit* of £8,000. If this limit is exceeded, the excess shares do not qualify for any relief.

(3) The shares appropriated must normally be retained by the trustees for *at least two years*.

No tax charge arises on the appropriation or on any subsequent increase in the value of the shares whilst held in the trust. After appropriation, dividends belong to the employee.

Once the retention period has expired, the employee can direct the trustees to sell the shares, although to avoid all income tax liability the shares must not be disposed of until *at least three years* after the appropriation date (reduced from five years by FA 1996). If sold *within three years*, income tax is payable on the *original market value* of the shares (ie at the date of appropriation) (or the sale proceeds, if less).

If the employment ceases because of redundancy, premature retirement caused by ill-health or the attainment of pensionable age or the specified age (depending on when the scheme was approved—see FA 1994 s 100, adding para 3A to TA 1988 Sch 10), and the shares are sold within the three-year period, only 50% of the original market value is charged to income tax.

The employee may, of course, be subject to CGT on his profit (even if free of income tax), taking his acquisition cost for this purpose as the market value of the shares *at the date of their appropriation*. Therefore, if an income tax charge is avoided, the value of the shares at appropriation is received tax free.

These schemes are tax efficient for *employers*, who can deduct sums paid to the trustees as a business expense (or an expense of management) for corporation tax, *provided that* the sums are spent by the trustees in acquiring shares within nine months or are used to pay the trustees' expenses (s 85) but note the comments at [**39.110**]. The employer can also deduct the cost of setting up the scheme provided that the trustees do not acquire shares before approval is obtained from the Revenue (s 84A).

EXAMPLE 39.4

Eric, an employee, is a basic rate taxpayer to whom trustees under an approved profit sharing scheme appropriate shares when their market value is £1,000. His employer pays corporation tax at 31%. At Eric's direction, the trustees sell the shares after 2½ years for £2,000.

(1) The company had transferred £1,000 to the trust and this sum is used by the trustees to subscribe for a new issue of shares by the company. The company obtains tax relief of £310 (31% of £690) so that the net cost is £670. *There is a net inflow of £310 into the company* since the company will have paid out £690, and received £1,000 attributable to its issued share capital account.

(2) When the shares are sold after 2½ years for £2,000 Eric will be subject to income tax—calculated on 100% of the value of the shares when appropriated (£1,000). Assuming that he is a basic rate taxpayer his liability will be £230 (23% of £1,000). There is unlikely to be any CGT liability on the gain of £1,000 (£2,000 – £1,000) because of Eric's annual exemption.

The company has, therefore, incurred a net cost of £690 and the employee has received £1,770 (£2,000 – £230).

Although the limits under a profit sharing scheme seem somewhat prohibitive, it should be noted that by operating a scheme over a five-year period an employee can be appropriated shares with a base cost equal to 10% of his annual salary up to a total over five years of £40,000. It is therefore possible in a large company for a substantial block of shares to be placed in friendly hands. This may be a comfort to the 'bid conscious' quoted company although a scheme created *solely* to block potential predators might be invalid. [**39.42**]

3 Approved savings related share option schemes (FA 1980 schemes; now TA 1988 s 185 and Sch 9)

Savings related schemes, in contrast to profit sharing schemes, are funded by contributions from the employees themselves. These are accumulated in standard

Save As You Earn contracts which are taken out at the time the options are granted. These contracts require a person to save a regular fixed monthly contribution and pay out a tax-free bonus: contracts taken out after 1 April 1993 pay a bonus equal to nine monthly contributions on a five-year contract (equal to 5.53% pa); a seven-year contract receives a bonus equal to 18 monthly contributions (5.87%). The proceeds are used to provide funds for the exercise of the options to acquire ordinary shares in the employer company. The maximum permitted monthly contribution to SAYE contracts is currently £250. Three-year contracts were introduced in 1996 and the minimum monthly contribution was reduced to £5 (from £10) in an effort to attract more participants into these schemes. These contracts pay a bonus equal to three monthly contributions (equal to 5.26% pa).

The *price* of the shares must be fixed at the time *when the employee is granted* the option and must not be less than 80% of the market value of the shares at that time. Generally, the option must not be exercisable until the SAYE contract matures at the end of three, five or seven years. The employee is *exempt from any charge to income tax* on the grant or exercise of the option. The only charge is to *CGT if and when the shares are sold* and in many cases the employee will be able to take advantage of the annual exemption.

To gain approval, the scheme must be open to *all* full-time employees and directors; part-time employees must also be able to participate in schemes approved after 30 April 1995 but participation of part-time directors remains at the discretion of the company (FA 1995 s 137). The scheme may impose a qualifying period of up to five years and it must satisfy detailed conditions set out in TA 1988 Sch 9.

These schemes are attractive because the employee is not required to produce a large sum of money to exercise his option, since sufficient funds will have accrued through the SAYE scheme. This encourages the employee to *retain* his shares, since he is not forced to sell to repay a loan taken out to acquire the shares.   [39.43]

4 Approved company share option plans (FA 1984; now TA 1988 s 185 and Sch 9, amended by FA 1996 ss 114 and 115 and Sch 16)

FA 1984 introduced an approved share option scheme not linked to savings under SAYE. Many more of these schemes were established than all employee schemes precisely because they were *not* all employee schemes and benefits under them could be granted to selected employees, and because the value of the benefits that could be given was much higher. These types of schemes were, therefore, generally known as 'executive share option schemes'. Following extensive concern that *any* tax benefit should be given to schemes under which some executives were receiving very large (and well-publicised) benefits, action has been taken to limit the value of benefits that can be received. This has been done, essentially, by only allowing options granted on or after 17 July 1995 under new or previously approved schemes to benefit from the tax relief if: (a) the value of shares subject to options (whenever granted) held by any one employee (value to be measured at date of option grant) does not exceed £30,000 (the previous limit was *the greater of* £100,000 and four times the employee's 'relevant emoluments'); and (b) the option exercise price is the market value of the shares at date of option grant (there can, therefore, no longer be a discount). Options granted pre 17 July 1995 will also continue to qualify for relief.

While the government's intention was originally to abolish tax relief altogether, this compromise of limiting the benefits that can be provided reflects the fact that some companies use these types of scheme to benefit a wide range of employees, not just senior executives. Participation in company share option plans does, however, remain subject to the company's discretion, although the scheme must only allow 'qualifying' employees (required to work at least 20 hours per week) and 'full-time' working directors (normally required to devote at least 25 hours per week to duties) to obtain rights under it; options may, however, be granted to part-time employees (but not directors) under schemes approved after 30 April 1995 (FA 1995 s 137).

As with savings related schemes under FA 1980, provided the requirements of the legislation are complied with there is *no income tax* charge on the *exercise* of an option to acquire shares in the employer company. The only charge is to *CGT if and when the shares are sold.* The detailed conditions for approval are set out in TA 1988 Sch 9.

To avoid income tax charges on options, they not only have to be granted under an approved scheme but the requirements of s 185 must also be satisfied. The most important requirement in practice, to avoid the charges normally associated with unapproved share schemes, is that:

(1) the option must be exercised between the third and tenth anniversaries of the date of grant; and

(2) at least three years must have elapsed since the employee exercised an option under a discretionary scheme in circumstances giving relief from income tax.

Even if there is no income tax charge on option exercise, the evidence suggests that many option-holders used to exercise their rights and then immediately sell their shares. This was often because the employee needed to borrow in order to finance the exercise of his options. With the new limit on the benefits receivable, it will be interesting to see whether this pattern changes.

[**39.44**]

5 Corporate PEPs

Single-company PEPs were introduced from 1 January 1992 (see [**4.155**]). Shares acquired through an approved all employee scheme can be transferred to a single company PEP without triggering a CGT charge. Up to £3,000 worth of shares can be transferred in each tax year. Once within the PEP there will be no income tax on dividends from, and no CGT on sale of, the shares. [**39.45**]–[**39.60**]

IV EMPLOYEE TRUSTS

1 Unapproved employee trusts

The term 'employee trust' has no statutory definition but, in broad terms, an employee trust is a discretionary trust the actual and potential beneficiaries of which are defined by reference to employment. Such trusts may enjoy favoured treatment for IHT, CGT, income tax and corporation tax. Consequently, they may be used as a tax efficient means of providing not only incentives to employees but also non-contractual benefits for them (eg to those in difficult circumstances).

There are several other important functions of employee trusts. *First*, they offer non-quoted companies the opportunity of creating a market for the sale and purchase of their shares (without such a market, non-quoted companies cannot effectively embark upon any share scheme unless current shareholders or the company itself would be prepared to buy shares from employees wishing to sell). *Secondly*, they can be used to build up a large shareholding in friendly hands so that the company will be protected against any unwanted takeovers and outside interference. *Thirdly*, they promote good relations between employer and employee since they can be viewed as a demonstration of an employer's concern for the welfare of his staff. *Finally*, and in the same way as approved profit sharing schemes (see [**39.42**]), they offer the company further funds at low cost.

Payments by the establishing employer are deductible under normal principles if they are of a revenue (income) nature (see *Heather v P E Consulting Group* (1978): [**6.114**]). Such payments should not be made under a binding legal obligation nor expressed as instalments of a lump sum. The best policy is to make regular payments geared to a variable factor—eg a percentage of profits. For the *timing* of the corporation tax deduction see [**39.110**]; on the effect of the accounting treatment and whilst FA 1989 s 43 (see [**5.193**]) will not generally defer the deduction (see the *Law Society's Gazette*, 4 October 1989), it may be in issue if, for instance, the trust is being used to distribute cash bonuses to a few staff (see *Taxation*, 14 November 1996, p 185). Funding by close companies requires special care in view of IHTA 1984 s 13 and TA 1988 s 419.

Trustees pay tax at 34% on any income received (TA 1988 s 686). By ESC A68, to avoid an effective double tax charge trustees may reclaim tax paid by them when payments made to employees are treated as emoluments (which will normally be the case).

If the trustees distribute shares to employees, the employee will normally be liable to income tax on the market value of the shares and that value will be treated as his base cost for CGT purposes (TCGA 1992 s 17(1)). The trustees will be liable to CGT on the difference between the market value at the date of distribution and their base cost. ESC D35 relieves the trustees from this CGT liability where the employee is liable to income tax on the full market value of the shares (thus removing the double tax charge). The Concession will not operate where shares are used to satisfy options held by employees because payment of the option price will mean the employee will not be taxable on the *full* market value of the shares acquired. Where an employee trust is to be used to supply shares for a share scheme, particularly an option scheme, consideration should be given as to whether establishing the trust offshore would avoid this double tax charge. The CGT treatment of offshore employee trusts has been problematical, particularly after the changes introduced by FA 1991 but the Revenue's view that if there is no element of bounty (as with genuine commercial arrangements) ss 86–87 do not apply is helpful (*Tax Bulletin*, April 1995, p 204).

Transfers of shares or other assets to an employee trust can have CGT consequences for the transferor. TCGA 1992 s 239 will often, at least, prevent the market value rule in s 17 being applied, so that the transferor's gain will be based on the actual consideration received and in the case of close companies it will limit the effect of s 125.

When dealing with trusts, IHT is an additional tax consideration. To qualify for favoured treatment, an employee trust must satisfy the conditions set out in IHTA 1984 s 86 and especially the requirement that *all or most* of the employees of the establishing employer *must be* within the class of potential beneficiaries. If the trust falls outside s 86, or s 13 or s 28 are not satisfied, contributions to the trust may be transfers of value for IHT purposes (eg if the employer is a close company). Further, if s 86 does not apply the trust will be subject to an IHT charge on each ten-year anniversary and an exit charge when capital is distributed (see [**26.114**]). Even if the trust falls within s 86, an exit charge may, in certain circumstances, arise under s 72.   [**39.61**]

2   Employee share ownership plans

FA 1989 introduced the concept of qualifying employee share ownership plans (ESOPs). At the time the only advantage that an ESOP had over a non-statutory employee trust (see [**39.61**] for tax treatment) was a guaranteed corporation tax deduction for company contributions. FA 1991 then permitted a deduction for the costs of establishing an ESOP (TA 1988 s 85A). However, to benefit from these statutory deductions, numerous conditions must be satisfied. The basic conditions to be satisfied for ESOPs established *on or before 3 May 1994* are:

(1) The beneficiaries of the ESOP must include *all* full-time employees who have been working for the company for at least one year (the qualifying period may be up to five years: FA 1989 Sch 5 para 4). No other beneficiaries are permitted (para 4(7)) and therefore part-time workers are excluded as are new employees. Former employees can be beneficiaries for up to 18 months after they have left the company.

(2) The ESOP trustees, within nine months of receipt, must apply the funds for a qualifying purpose: eg in the purchase of shares in the company establishing the trust; in the repayment and servicing of loans taken to purchase shares; in the making of payments to beneficiaries and in the payment of expenses (these are the same requirements as for approved profit sharing schemes).

(3) The ESOP trustees must transfer any securities which they acquire to a beneficiary or to an approved profit sharing scheme within seven years of acquisition (these ESOPs cannot be combined with savings related share option schemes).

(4) The ESOP trustees must be at least three in number and include one person who is a trust corporation, a solicitor or a member of another professional body approved by the Revenue. A majority of the trustees must be persons who are *not*, and have never been, directors of a company within the establishing company's group. However, a majority of the trustees *must be* persons who are employees of the group and who have been elected by a majority of the employees of the group.

ESOPs are able to borrow funds from the employing company or from third parties and, in the latter case, such loans may be repaid by means of tax deductible payments received from the company. Nevertheless, beyond the certainty that all contributions made by a company will be deductible, the qualifying ESOP introduced in 1989 offered no great benefit in comparison with the ordinary employee trust, since its tax position was precisely the same. Indeed, the stringent conditions to be satisfied if the trust was to qualify as an ESOP proved too much of a burden and very few statutory ESOPs were established.

It was widely predicted that the 1990 Finance Act would relax the statutory requirements. In fact, the only change was a provision enabling shareholders who sold their shares to a qualifying ESOP (holding at least a 10% stake in the company either at that time or within 12 months of the sale) to roll over any CGT that would otherwise be payable into the purchase of other chargeable assets acquired within six months of that sale (TCGA 1992 ss 227–235).

The requirements have, however, been relaxed for ESOPs established *after 3 May 1994* (FA 1994 s 102 and Sch 13). The establishing company now has a choice as to the composition of the trustees. Two of those choices allow non-employees to be in the majority as well as easing the process by which employee representatives are selected. Further, for such schemes the retention period has been extended from 7 to 20 years. These changes may remove some of the non-tax objections to ESOPs (and proposed changes to the rules on collective investment schemes in FSA 1986 will remove others) but the tax incentives remain of limited value. Indeed, these ESOPs may have a tax disadvantage compared to an ordinary employee trust since they cannot benefit all employees (those with less than one year's service must be excluded) and may, depending on the circumstances, attract the ten-year anniversary IHT charge (currently at a maximum rate of 6%). However, FA 1996 s 119 has now abolished the rule that employees and directors with less than one year's service must be excluded, for trusts established *on or after 29 April 1996*. As a result of FA 1996 s 120, trusts established on or after that date can also now be used in conjunction with a savings related share option scheme.

FA 1995 s 137 introduced a further change: schemes established *after 30 April 1995* have to include part-time employees (but still cannot include part-time directors) as beneficiaries (though they too may have to satisfy a qualifying period before participation).

A difficulty with the statutory ESOP is to ensure that the relevant trust documentation satisfies the detailed statutory requirements: the Inland Revenue are 'prepared to examine and comment on draft trust deeds submitted to them' (see [1991] STI 13).

There is scope for the involvement of ESOPs in management buy-outs. For practical purposes, the maximum percentage of a company's shares that could be placed in the hands of employees through an ESOP is probably 49%, with 51% owned by the managers. Banks dislike worker co-operatives—something which would arise if the ESOP took control.   **[39.62]–[39.80]**

V   PROFIT RELATED PAY ('PRP') (TA 1988 ss 169–184 and Sch 8)

FA (No 2) 1987 introduced income tax relief for payments received by employees under a registered PRP scheme. Under such a scheme part of an employee's pay fluctuates with the business profits of his employer. The IR Press Release accompanying the introduction of PRP pointed out that:

> 'Two considerable advantages flow from arrangements which relate pay to profits. First, the workforce have a more direct personal interest in the success of their business; and, second, there would be a greater degree of pay flexibility in the face of changing market conditions.'

Registered PRP schemes link payments to profits *not performance*: accordingly PRP is payable under such schemes even if profits remain static; and each employee's entitlement is determined by the scheme rules—there is no discretionary element. Accordingly, the emphasis is not so much on providing incentives as to link salary to profitability so that the employees as a group share in the good and bad times! By the time of the 1996 Budget, the government considered that the income tax relief 'had successfully served its purpose of getting PRP schemes off the ground' and therefore announced it would be phased out.

For accounting periods beginning between 1 April 1991 and 1 January 1998, an employee receives the whole of his PRP tax free subject to a maximum of 20% of his pay or £4,000 (whichever is the lower) (PRP is not, however, free of national insurance contributions and note that the limits on tax free PRP do not restrict the amount of PRP which can be paid, merely the amount of tax relief). Thereafter there will be a gradual reduction of the £4,000 limit until no tax relief will be available on payments made for accounting periods beginning after 31 December 1999. Schemes can still be registered until 31 December 2000 and readers requiring further details of registered schemes are referred to the 14th edition of this book.   **[39.81]–[39.100]**

VI   CHOICE OF SCHEME

1   **Non-tax aspects**

Whenever any commercial transaction is considered it is vital to look at the tax implications from all angles. However, no transaction can or should be entirely tax driven. Thus, an employer should first decide what commercial objective he is seeking by his scheme of employee participation. Set out below is a list of the likely objectives, together with a note of the schemes (approved and non-approved) which may go at least some way towards achieving them. **[39.101]**

a) *Tax efficient bonus scheme*

Depending on considerations of size and selectivity, a PRP scheme can (at least for the moment) provide immediate tax efficient benefits; in the longer term, however, the share related approved schemes are the most efficient schemes to operate. The selectivity offered by company share option plans may be the deciding factor (see h) below). **[39.102]**

b) *Performance related incentives*

Unapproved schemes are better in this regard because targets can be changed and directly related to individual performance. With all approved schemes, targets must be fixed at the outset (although the decision in *IRC v Burton Group plc* (1990) affords some flexibility). If looking to profitability of the company, rather than individual employees, an approved profit sharing scheme, or employee trust, may be preferred, since both enable the amount passing into the trust for the benefit of the employees to be directly related to the company's performance (subject in the former case to the usual limits). **[39.103]**

c) *Reward for growth in share value*

Share incentive schemes or share options may be used and again the selectivity of company share option plans makes them the more attractive of the approved schemes. However, if there are difficulties with Investment Protection Committees (see 3 below), a phantom share option scheme or ESOP/employee trust arrangement might be appropriate. **[39.104]**

d) *Retention of employees*

Long running schemes which cannot be shortened are required. Approved all employee schemes are appropriate because they can be drawn over a long period and made subject to an employee remaining with the company. Unapproved schemes with restrictions on sale could also be used (but the implications of FA 1988 ss 77–89 (see **[39.24]**) may make these unattractive). **[39.105]**

e) *Creation of 'friendly' share holdings*

With company share option plans shares may be sold immediately after exercise of options and it is therefore better to use an employee trust or an approved profit sharing scheme to create a friendly block holding. This has the added benefit of the shares of the employees being 'co-ordinated' through trustees. Alternatively, use a savings related share option scheme because these schemes tend not to result in an immediate sale because the employee does not need to borrow funds to exercise the option. **[39.106]**

f) *Creation of market in non-quoted shares*

An ESOP or ordinary employee trust will be ideal. **[39.107]**

g) *Generation of sense of identity between employees and the company*

Any form of share ownership should promote this and the normal procedure would be to tie this into a long-term commitment as suggested above. The employee trust is particularly useful in this respect. **[39.108]**

h) *Selective employee participation*

One problem with all approved schemes (including ESOPs) is that they must apply to *all* employees (subject to qualifying periods of employment) with the exception of company share option plans. Should that type of scheme be unacceptable, consider an unapproved scheme which provides *total* flexibility on this matter.   **[39.109]**

i) *Accounting treatment*

There have been moves over the last few years to ensure that a company's accounts adequately reflect all its assets and liabilities.

In June 1995, a committee of the Acccounting Standards Board issued a statement dealing with the accounting treatment of employee trusts (UITF Abstract 13). Prior to this, the trust was treated as entirely separate from the company: a company's contributions were immediately set off against its profits (assuming FA 1989 s 43 did not apply—see **[39.61]**); and the trust assets were not treated as assets of the company. The statement changes this treatment to reflect the fact that, in reality, the company normally bears the financial risk if things go wrong. Further, whilst shares which have unconditionally vested in employees (as under an approved profit sharing scheme) belong to them and will not be treated as assets of the company, shares held by the trust to which employees are only conditionally entitled (as under a restricted share scheme) or which are subject to options held by employees will be treated as assets of the company if it can in reality (as will usually be the case) control what happens to those shares. The effect of treating shares held by the trust as assets of the company is that the difference between the book value of the shares and the amount that the trust can expect to receive when an employee finally unconditionally acquires the shares will be written off over the period of the option/restriction.

The effect of consolidating the company with the employee trust will be that contributions to the trust will not necessarily be charged in the accounts when made; and this may have a consequential effect on the timing of the corporation tax deduction. Whilst the Revenue accepts that the change in the accounting treatment will not affect the timing of the corporation tax deduction for contributions to statutory ESOPs (as a result of FA 1989 s 67) (and presumably for those to approved profit sharing scheme trusts which satisfy the requirements of TA 1988 s 85, although this has not been explicitly stated), it does consider that the accounting treatment should govern the timing of the corporation tax deduction for non-statutory trusts (*Tax Bulletin*, February 1997, p 399).   **[39.110]**

2   Tax aspects

Having determined what type of scheme can best meet his commercial objectives, the employer will need to look at the relative tax benefits of the various schemes available. Two main questions need to be asked: *first*, do approved schemes offer real tax benefits in comparison with non-approved schemes; and, *secondly*, if they do, which of the approved schemes are most beneficial?   **[39.111]**

a) *Approved or unapproved?*

So far as share based schemes are concerned, it has been explained that the benefits provided under *approved* schemes will usually be subject only to *CGT* in the employee's hands, and that any charge will arise only if and when the relevant shares are *sold*. By contrast, benefits provided for an employee under an *unapproved* scheme will always be taxed as *income* and charges can arise even *before sale*.

Prior to FA 1988, with a top rate of income tax of 60% as compared with a CGT rate of only 30%, the attractions of approved schemes from an employee's taxation point of view were obvious. Since 1988–89, however, capital gains have been charged at the employee's marginal income tax rate. Accordingly, for higher rate taxpayers, the rate of CGT has been increased and, even with an annual exemption of £6,500, *the taxation of such gains has to some extent been equated with the treatment of income profits.* To this extent, the distinction between approved and unapproved schemes has, therefore, become somewhat blurred.

However, a capital gain rather than an income profit will still be advantageous for the following reasons.

First, the due date for payment of the two taxes differs: emoluments under Schedule E attract an immediate tax charge, whereas any capital gain realised will only fall into charge on 31 January following the tax year in which the disposal occurred. *Secondly,* in arriving at the chargeable gain, an individual will be entitled both to an indexation allowance and to an annual exemption of £6,500. *Thirdly,* the taxation of benefits received under approved schemes is only triggered on the disposal of the shares: accordingly, so long as the employee or director intends to retain the shares over a period of years, no charge will arise. In due course, that individual may be able to arrange for disposals to occur in different tax years (thereby taking advantage of more than one annual exemption) and for disposals to be channelled through his family.   **[39.112]**

b) *Which approved scheme?*

If the employer decides that his overall objectives fit within the structure of an approved scheme, which scheme should be chosen? This question should be answered by looking at the non-tax aspects of the matter, since it will be evident from these factors which is most appropriate.

The main difference between the various approved share incentive schemes lies in the amount of relief available and whether or not benefits can be given on a selective basis.

The only wholly tax-free benefits which can be obtained are those provided under PRP, but the limit imposed upon the amount of PRP and the phasing out of tax relief reduces the attraction of now establishing such a scheme.

The employee trust offers no tax benefit to the employee at all and so, if such a scheme is adopted, it will not be for reasons of saving the employee tax.

From the *employer's* point of view, all cash contributions to whatever scheme, if wholly and exclusively for the purposes of the business and of an income nature, will be tax deductible.   **[39.113]**

3 Other shareholders

The presence of institutional shareholders may be a further factor for a company considering setting up an employee participation scheme to consider. Any listed company will usually feel obliged to follow the rules of the investment protection committees ('IPCs') which impose limits as to the number of shares which can be subject to employee options and, broadly, set the ceiling at 10%. Further, IPCs generally do not accept the use of subsidiaries for share option schemes. For a company approaching this limit, therefore, there will be a need to look to the schemes—approved or unapproved—which do not involve the issue of new shares. The obvious choice is the employee trust, over which, provided the trust purchases existing shares at market value, the IPCs have little control since prior shareholder approval to their establishment would not normally be *required*, although the ABI expects prior shareholder approval to be sought if 5% or more of a company's equity share capital could be held by the trust.

The IPCs' guidelines cover matters other than the number of shares that can be used for employee share schemes, in particular the circumstance when executive share options may be exercised. The IPCs like the exercise of executive options to depend on performance targets being met. In July 1993 the ABI and NAPF issued a joint statement requiring that the exercise of executive options 'should be subject to some realistic measure of the management performance'. By this, they meant that the performance criteria should be linked to significant and sustained improvement in the underlying financial performance of the company. What performance criteria will satisfy this requirement depends on the nature of the company's business—and is, in any event, subject to much debate. The ABI guidelines, reissued in February 1995, contain examples of some of the formulae that have been adopted. It remains to be seen whether the attitude of institutional investors will change if company share option plans are used to spread (their more limited) benefits more widely than executive schemes did.

Finally, in May 1996 the ABI issued 'an outline of the broad principles that institutional shareholders have applied in looking at' long-term incentive schemes (these include restricted share ownership schemes and other arrangements having 'equivalent economic effect'), in view of the Greenbury Code requirement that shareholders in PLCs should give specific approval to such schemes.   [**39.114**]

40 Taxation of the family unit

*'And what are you going to give me to make up
for all those wasted years on a joint assessment?'*

'The present system for the taxation of married couples goes back 180 years. It taxes the income of a married woman as if it belonged to her husband. Quite simply, that is no longer acceptable. . . . the time has come to take action. I therefore propose a major reform of personal taxation with two objectives. First, to give married women the same privacy and independence in their tax affairs as everyone else and second, to bring to an end the ways in which the tax system can penalise marriage. I have decided to introduce, at the earliest practical date, April 1990, a completely new system of independent taxation. . . . The tax system will continue to recognise marriage as it should do. At the same time, from 1990 married women will pay their own tax, on the basis of their own income, and have their own tax return, when one is necessary. There will, of course, be nothing to stop married women from asking their husbands to handle their tax affairs, or vice versa, as before; and many will no doubt do so. But what matters is that, for the first time ever, married women will have the right to complete independence and privacy so far as tax is concerned.' (The Chancellor of the Exchequer, the Rt Hon Nigel Lawson MP, Budget Speech, 15 March 1988.)

[**40.1**]

I   INTRODUCTION

Until 6 April 1990 the income tax system proceeded on the basis that 'a woman's income chargeable to tax shall ... be deemed for income tax purposes to be her husband's income and not to be her income' (see TA 1988 s 279—originally enacted in 1806). This system of aggregation attracted a growing volume of criticism in the 1980s. It had already been considered by two Royal Commissions earlier this century: the Royal Commission on Income Tax in 1920 and the Radcliffe Commission in 1954, both of which concluded in favour of its continuance. In 1980 a Consultative Paper, *The Taxation of Husband and Wife* (Cmnd 8093), aired the problems but produced no obvious alternative. A further consultative Green Paper, *The Reform of Personal Taxation* (Cmnd 9756), was produced in March 1986 and, although it elicited a 'disappointingly thin response', FA 1988 introduced the new system of independent taxation which came into effect on 6 April 1990. This chapter concentrates on this system: details of the tax treatment of spouses prior to this date may be found in earlier editions of this book.   [**40.2**]-[**40.20**]

II   INCOME TAX

1   **Independent taxation of husband and wife** (see generally IR 93)

From 6 April 1990 every taxpayer resident in the UK has been entitled to a personal allowance (£4,045 for 1997–98) that can be set against all types of income, both earned and unearned. The major advance this marks for the married woman is that she now has an allowance to set against her investment income. Under the previous system, whether she had elected to be taxed separately from her husband or had received the Wife's Earned Income Relief, such personal allowances as had been available could only be set against her earned income. Her investment income was always added to her husband's income and taxed at his rates.   [**40.21**]

2   **The married couple's allowance**

a) *Basic requirements*

A man who is married and whose wife is living with him for any part of the tax year is entitled to a married couple's allowance for that year in addition to the personal allowance. The married couple's allowance which, when introduced, represented the difference between the former married man's allowance and the single person's allowance is, for 1997–98, £1,830. In the short term this allowance was retained to ensure that the position of the married couple did not worsen as a result of the introduction of independent taxation.

TA 1988 s 282 defines the phrase 'living with her husband' as follows:

'(1) A married woman shall be treated for income tax purposes as living with her husband unless—
 (a) They are separated under an Order of a Court of competent jurisdiction, or by Deed of Separation, or
 (b) They are in fact separated in such circumstances that the separation is likely to be permanent.'

For income tax purposes, therefore, a marriage ends at the time of actual separation. Continuing to live in the same house will not normally amount to separation, although if the building is divided into two flats which are self-contained, it is likely that the couple will be living apart for income tax purposes (TA 1988 s 257A). In *Holmes v Mitchell* (1991) the husband and wife had ceased to be one household in 1972 and become two households even though they continued to live under the same roof and there was no physical division of the dwelling space. With the husband's subsequent declaration of intent to seek a divorce some ten years later the circumstances of the separation were then such that it was likely to be permanent. **[40.22]**

b) *Restriction of relief from 6 April 1994*

Prior to the year 1994–95, the married couple's allowance was given as a *deduction from the claimant's total income*. Consequently, in appropriate cases, it had the effect of reducing a taxpayer's marginal rate of tax. In contrast, for 1994–95 and subsequent years of assessment, the claimant's entitlement is by way of a *reduction in respect of the income tax liability* arising on his total income; in other words, a tax credit. This tax credit is an amount equal to a percentage of the allowance, 15% for 1995–96 and subsequent years or, if less, an amount which would reduce the claimant's tax liability to nil.

EXAMPLE 40.1

Porgy and Bess are married and living together throughout the tax year 1997–98. Porgy's gross income (all earned) is £35,000; Bess has no income.

Porgy's income tax liability for 1997–98 is computed as follows:

		£
Income		35,000
Deduct: personal allowance		4,045
		£30,955

Income tax liability:	£4,100 at 20% =	820	
	£22,000 at 23% =	5,060	
	£4,855 at 40% =	1,942	7,822.00
Deduct: relief for MCA: £1,830 × 15%			274.50
Net income tax liability			£7,547.50

If, instead, Porgy's income for 1997–98 was only £5,000, his tax liability would have been computed in the following way:

	£
Income	5,000
Deduct: personal allowance	4,045
	955

Income tax liability: £955 at 20%	191
Deduct: relief for MCA: £1,830 × 15% = £274.50	
restricted to £191	191
Net income tax liability	Nil

A claimant's tax liability is determined for this purpose *after* giving effect to any reduction in respect of relief for qualifying maintenance payments (see **[41.3]**), and by excluding tax at the basic rate which the claimant is entitled to deduct or retain out of charges on income (such as a covenanted payment to a charity: see **[10.47]**). Further, any double taxation relief to which the claimant may be entitled either unilaterally or by virtue of a double taxation agreement is ignored. **[40.23]**

c) *Use of the allowance*

The married couple's allowance goes automatically to the husband but, since 1993-94, a married couple has been able to decide how to allocate the allowance between them. Before the beginning of the appropriate tax year *either* the couple can choose to allocate the whole allowance to the wife, *or* the wife may elect that half should be allocated to her. As a consequence of restricting the relief in respect of the allowance in either case, the wife will become entitled to a reduction from her income tax liability of an amount equal to 15% of the allowance or of her allocated portion of the allowance (see [**40.23**]). Any election must be made on a prescribed form and, once made, will continue until revoked by a subsequent election made before the start of the later tax year (see *Taxation*, 21 September 1995, p 641).

For 1994-95 and subsequent years, in cases where the relief afforded in respect of the married couple's allowance cannot be fully utilised, whether by the husband or the wife, because his or her tax liability is insufficient to absorb the allowable percentage reduction, that spouse may give notice that the other spouse should be entitled to an income tax reduction calculated by reference to the unused part of the allowance.

EXAMPLE 40.2

Susan and Nicholas are a married couple living together throughout the tax year 1997-98. Nicholas has a part-time job bringing in £4,500 pa. Susan earns £21,000 pa and has elected to receive half the married couple's allowance. Relief in respect of this allowance will be split between them in the following way.

Nicholas

	£
Income	4,500
Deduct: personal allowance	4,045
	£455
Income tax liability: £455 at 20%	91
Deduct: relief for MCA: £1,830 × ½ × 15% = £137.25	
restricted to £91	91
Net income tax liability	Nil

As Nicholas has used only £91 of the possible £137.25 in reducing his tax liability to nil, the remaining £46.25 should be transferred to Susan to further reduce her income tax liability.

Susan

	£
Income	21,000
Deduct: personal allowance	4,045
	£16,955
Income tax liability: £4,100 at 20% = £820	
£12,855 at 23% = £2,956.65	3,776.65
Deduct: her own share of relief for MCA: £1,830 × ½ × 15% = £137.25	
— plus unused part transferred from Nicholas = £46.25	183.50
Net income tax liability	£3,593.15

By contrast, a husband and wife cannot transfer any part of the personal allowance to each other. If the married couple's allowance has been reduced in the year of marriage (see [**40.26**]) it is that reduced allowance which forms the maximum amount which can be transferred to the other spouse.   [**40.24**]

3 Elderly couples

The increased allowances available in such cases are discussed in Chapter 4.   [**40.25**]

4 Tax in year of marriage

The personal allowance is available to both husband and wife in the year of marriage in the normal way. However the married couple's allowance for the year of marriage is reduced by one-twelfth for each complete tax month before the date of marriage. For example, in the case of a couple marrying on 4 August where there has been no election as to the allocation of the allowance, the man would lose three-twelfths of the married couple's allowance since there are three complete tax months in that tax year during which the couple are not married.

Where a man marries who is already entitled to the married couple's allowance (because of a previous marriage in the same tax year) only one allowance is available.

If a married couple separate in one tax year but are reconciled in a later year, and were not divorced in the meantime, the husband will get the full married couple's allowance in the year of reconciliation. There is no *pro rata* reduction, as there is for the year of marriage (TA 1988 s 257A(6)).   [**40.26**]

5 Death of either spouse

If the wife dies the husband will get the full married couple's allowance for that tax year, in addition to his personal allowance. For subsequent years he will receive only the personal allowance (assuming that he does not remarry).

By contrast, if the husband dies, in addition to her personal allowance the wife will receive, *first*, relief in respect of the additional personal allowance if she has a child living with her after her husband's death; *secondly*, relief in respect of the widow's bereavement allowance for the tax year in which the husband dies and for the following tax year, provided that she has not remarried by the start of that following year; and *thirdly*, any unused relief in respect of the married couple's allowance. The position of a surviving wife can be summarised diagrammatically as shown overleaf.   [**40.27**]

6 Reliefs, limits and exemptions

Mortgage interest relief From 6 April 1990 a husband and wife have shared the mortgage interest relief allowance currently set at £30,000. If the loan is in their joint names, the £30,000 limit will be divided equally between them so that each will receive relief for payments of interest of up to £15,000. If, however, the loan is in the name of only one spouse then that person will get tax relief on the interest paid, up to the £30,000 limit.

It is possible for a married couple not wishing these rules to apply to make a joint election to the effect that the limit of the tax relief will be allocated

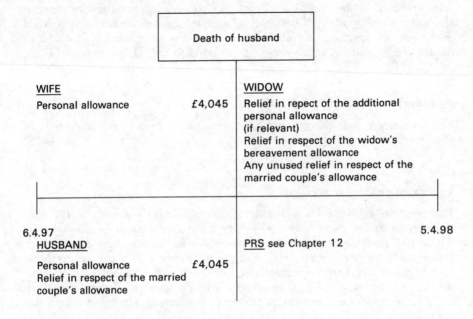

between them *in any way they choose*. In the past this was advisable where one spouse was a higher rate taxpayer, while the other was not, since the relief was more valuable for the spouse paying tax at higher rate. Since the majority of mortgages fall within the MIRAS scheme, and with the reduction in the rate of MIRAS relief, the result is that as relief is given by a deduction from the interest payments of 15% (for 1997–98, reducing to 10% for 1998–99), *there is no longer any advantage in electing to transfer the benefit of the tax relief.*   **[40.28]**

Enterprise Investment Scheme ('EIS')   From 1 January 1994, the Business Expansion Scheme ('BES') was replaced by EIS. As with BES, husband and wife each have their own minimum (£500) and maximum (£100,000 for 1994–95 and subsequent years) limits for EIS relief on qualifying share subscriptions. Inter-spouse transfers do not result in withdrawal of the relief: the transferee spouse is instead treated as the original subscriber for the shares (see Chapter 4).   **[40.29]**

Close company loans   Close companies are exempt from a tax charge on loans to full-time employees without a material interest in their company, and their husbands or wives, if the sum of outstanding loans to the employee and the employee's husband or wife does not exceed £15,000 (TA 1988 s 420). Under independent taxation there are separate £15,000 limits for husband and wife if both are employees of the company and if a loan is made for the first time on or after 6 April 1990.   **[40.30]**

Capital allowances and charges   Capital allowances due by way of discharge or repayment are given against income of a specified class or, on election, against other income for the year or the following year. From 6 April 1990 such allowances can be set only against the income of the person who incurred the expenditure. So far as charges on income are concerned, eg a donation to charity under a deed of covenant or the payment of an annuity, if a married couple are jointly liable to make a payment the amount each person *actually pays* is the amount of his or her charge for tax purposes. If it is unclear how much each person pays the tax office will adopt a 50:50 split.   **[40.31]**

7 Trading losses

The trading loss of one spouse cannot be offset against the income of the other spouse. Instead, any unused loss may be carried forward to set against the income in the following year of the spouse who incurred the loss. **[40.32]**

8 Jointly held property

The advent of independent taxation of husband and wife necessitated the introduction of special rules to determine how income arising from property jointly owned by both spouses should be taxed. Previously, since such income was generally unearned income, it was taxed as the husband's regardless of the beneficial ownership of the property in question. The rules apply to 'income from assets held in the names of a husband and wife who are living together' (TA 1988 s 282A(1)).

The general rule is that such income is treated as income to which husband and wife are entitled equally (TA 1988 s 282A). Thus, if husband and wife have a joint building society account, even if they have contributed to it in unequal proportions, each is treated as owning one half of the interest arising, and taxed accordingly.

The 50:50 rule does not apply to income to which neither spouse is beneficially entitled; to partnership Case I and II Schedule D income; to the income of a married couple who are separated; to the situation where property is held in the name of one party only; or where some other legislation (eg that governing settlements) directs that the income should be taxed in a different way.

It is, however, possible for the general 50:50 rule to be displaced (eg in respect of income to which one spouse only is beneficially entitled or in respect of income to which they are beneficially entitled in unequal shares). For the rule to be displaced an appropriate declaration must be made specifying the shares in which the income is, in fact, beneficially enjoyed by one or both spouses. Any declaration must relate to both the income arising from the property and the property itself, and the income cannot be shared in different proportions from the capital. It has effect in relation to income arising on or after the date of the declaration.

Notice of any declaration must be given to the appropriate tax inspector within the period of 60 days beginning with the date of the declaration and must be made on the prescribed Form 17.

EXAMPLE 40.3

John and Susan jointly own £1,000 10% loan stock in XYZ plc producing annual interest of £100. Each will be taxed on one half of the income. They may enter into a declaration of trust giving John a 1% beneficial interest in the stock and Susan a 99% beneficial interest. If, following that trust, the appropriate declaration is made on Form 17 and submitted to the Revenue within 60 days, as from the date of that declaration Susan will be taxed on 99% of the income and John on 1%.

Some spouses might prefer to rely on the 50:50 rule when, in fact, the asset is owned between them in different proportions. Say, for example, the husband owns an income-producing asset worth £1,000. He might transfer it into the joint names of himself and his wife but only give his wife a 1% beneficial interest in the asset. Nevertheless, if no unequal shares declaration is made, under the 50:50 rule the wife will be taxed on 50% of the income. The husband, however, will own 99% of the asset. **[40.33]**

9 Planning opportunities

The rules offer planning opportunities to many couples. In particular, if one spouse is a higher rate taxpayer and the other is subject to the lower or basic rate only, it will be advantageous for income tax purposes for the former to transfer income-producing assets to the other spouse to ensure that the personal allowance and basic rate band is fully utilised. There may be other advantages (see [**40.58**]). Care must, however, be taken to ensure that any transfer is an outright gift of assets with 'no strings'. Certain gifts will *not* be treated as outright gifts, namely:

(1) a gift not carrying the right to the whole of the income from the property given; or

(2) a gift which is wholly or substantially a right to income (without being a gift of the underlying capital); or

(3) a gift subject to conditions; or

(4) a gift where the property given or any income or property derived from it is or might be paid to or for the benefit of the donor.

In such circumstances, the gift will be treated as a settlement and any income arising treated as the donor's for income tax purposes (TA 1988 s 660A). To be certain that the inter-spouse gift is effective for income tax purposes it is vital to ensure that the gift is outright, incapable of being revoked, unconditional and of matching proportions of income and capital. (For a gift that was considered to be wholly or substantially a right to income, see *Pearce v Young, Scrutton v Young* (1996).)

The above rules do not catch a gift where the donee, of his or her own accord, chooses to apply the income or capital in some way which might benefit the donor and the previous Inland Revenue practice whereby property which might return to the donor following the death of the donee under the donee's will or under the intestacy rules would not, for that reason, fail to be treated as an outright gift is now expressly enacted in TA 1988 s 660A(3)(c).

As noted above, the one way of making an outright gift of unequal amounts of income and capital is to arrange for the capital to be owned jointly, albeit in unequal shares, and then to rely upon the presumption of equality to ensure that half of the income is taxed as that of the spouse with the small capital entitlement.   [**40.34**]–[**40.50**]

III CAPITAL GAINS TAX

1 Separate taxation of gains

The gains of each spouse are calculated separately and each is entitled to an annual exemption (£6,500 for 1997–98).   [**40.51**]

2 Losses

The losses of a spouse can only be offset against his or her own chargeable gains and not set against the gains of the other spouse.   [**40.52**]

3 Inter-spouse transfers (TCGA 1992 s 58)

The disposal of an asset by one spouse to another is treated as being for such consideration as gives rise to neither gain nor loss. This rule operates whether or not any consideration is furnished for the transfer and in spite of the couple being connected persons. Effectively, therefore, gains are held over and the asset will be acquired at the base cost of the disponer spouse together with any incidental costs involved in the disposal. The rule in s 58 applies only as long as the spouses are 'living together' *at any time* during the relevant tax year. The indexation allowance will be included in the deemed consideration.

EXAMPLE 40.4

Jim gives his wife Judy two birthday presents on 1 June 1997, a Ming vase which he acquired from Christie's on 1 April 1987 and a painting by William Roberts acquired on 10 April 1985.

The disposal by Jim will be at no gain/no loss and Judy's base costs will include an indexation allowance on the vase from April 1987 to June 1997 and on the picture from April 1985 to June 1997.

A little publicised legislative change occurred at the time when independent taxation was introduced on to the statute book in 1988. The occasion was used to tidy up a number of the rules dealing with the tax treatment of husband and wife and one such provision (TA 1988 s 282) concerned the question of when a married couple are 'separated' for income tax and CGT purposes. Apart from the well-known situation where they are 'living apart in such circumstances that the separation is likely to be permanent', a couple had also been deemed separated in the case where one was and the other was not resident in the UK during a year of assessment and also when, although both were UK resident, one was absent from the UK throughout the relevant tax year. FA 1988 Sch 3 para 11 repealed this deeming provision with effect from 1990–91. The result is that the couple now remain 'living together' (and therefore taxed as a married couple) in such circumstances. Hence s 58 will apply to inter-spouse transfers of chargeable assets.

Assume, for instance, that the non-resident spouse were to transfer a plot of land in Herefordshire showing a substantial gain to the resident spouse. By virtue of s 58 that land will be acquired at no gain/no loss. *Contrast*, however, the position under the old deemed separation rules. Because the couple were not then living together s 58 was inapplicable. Nonetheless they remained connected persons (because married: see TCGA 1992 s 286) and hence any transfer of chargeable assets would be at market value under TCGA 1992 s 17. Hence a UK resident spouse would have acquired the land at current value so that the gain which had accrued during the ownership of the non-resident would have been tax free. **[40.53]**

4 Retirement relief

Retirement relief is available to both spouses and may be used to ensure that gains of £1,250,000 in aggregate are exempt from charge—TCGA 1992 Sch 6 para 13 as amended (see Chapter 16). **[40.54]**

5 Cohabitees and children

General CGT principles operate for disposals between cohabitees and between parents and their children. In the case of disposals to children the connected persons rules operate with the result that any disposal will be deemed to be made at market value (TCGA 1992 ss 17, 18). **[40.55]**

6 Principal private residence

Only one principal private residence exemption is available where a married couple live together (TCGA 1992 s 222(6)). **[40.56]**

7 Jointly held assets

Where assets are disposed of which were held in joint names of husband and wife, each spouse will be regarded as owning a half share of the asset and charged to CGT accordingly. This is subject to the couple having made a declaration that the asset is held in different shares: in such a case the gain is charged *pro rata* according to their respective shares in the property.

Any declaration that has been made for income tax purposes regarding jointly held property (see [**40.33**] above) will have a corresponding effect for CGT purposes.   [**40.57**]

8 Planning opportunities

If one spouse's annual CGT exemption will not be utilised whilst the other spouse's is fully utilised, it may be worth the couple transferring assets (at no gain no loss under s 58 as discussed above) to the 'poorer' spouse so that both exemptions are used. Similar advice should be given where one spouse has a CGT rate (say 40%) which is in excess of that of the other.   [**40.58**]–[**40.70**]

IV   INHERITANCE TAX

1   General principles

There is no aggregation of spouses' chargeable transfers for IHT purposes. They are treated as separate taxable entities, each entitled to the full exemptions and reliefs. It is immaterial whether they are living together and, unlike the position with respect to income tax and CGT, a couple remain married for IHT until the decree absolute which terminates the marriage. If care is taken with the associated operations ([**21.81**]) and related property ([**21.67**]) rules, transfers between spouses offer an opportunity to mitigate IHT since they are exempt without limit (except where the donee spouse is domiciled abroad, when only £55,000 may be transferred free of IHT). This inter-spouse exemption means that full use may be made of both spouses' exemptions and reliefs and benefits may be obtained by ensuring that the nil rate band (currently £215,000) of each spouse is fully used.   [**40.71**]

2   PETs and the nil rate band

With the introduction by FA 1988 of a simplified structure consisting of only two rates of tax (0% and 40%), the *ideal* IHT planning for spouses should ensure the following: [**40.72**]

1) *Full use is made of PETs*   Whenever practicable, PETs should be employed to transfer wealth *inter vivos* to future generations. The spouse with the greater life expectancy should make the bulk of such transfers in order to minimise the risk of the PET failing. If necessary, property can be transferred from the wealthy to the poorer spouse to enable the transfer to be made without the risk of the associated operations provisions applying (see [**21.81**]).   [**40.73**]

2) *Full use is made of the nil rate band*   In drafting family wills it is desirable to ensure that both spouses fully exhaust their nil rate bands: ie that both make chargeable gifts to, eg, children of £215,000. Above that level there is no IHT advantage in the first spouse to die making further chargeable transfers. Rather he should be advised to leave the balance to his surviving spouse who may then dispose of it to children either by means of PETs or by will. In such cases even if the transfer by the surviving spouse turns out to be chargeable

no extra IHT will arise since all such transfers will fall within the 40% rate band. **[40.74]**

EXAMPLE 40.5

Husband (H) has an estate of £500,000; wife (W) an estate of £84,000.

(1) *If H leaves all to W and dies first:*

IHT on H's death	Nil (spouse exemption)
IHT on W's death	£147,600 (on £584,000).

(2) *Contrast if H leaves £215,000 to his children with remainder only to W:*

IHT on H's death	Nil (on £215,000)
IHT on W's death	£61,600 (on £369,000)

Accordingly, IHT saved is £86,000 (ie 40% × £215,000).

(3) If W dies before H, full use could not be made of her nil rate band (because her estate only amounts to £84,000). It is therefore desirable on these facts for H to make an *inter vivos* transfer so that W has an estate large enough to cover the nil band.

(4) When drafting a family will designed to utilise the nil rate band it is possible to leave a legacy equal to £215,000 (the current nil rate band) or, alternatively, if it is desired to take account of future increases in the threshold of that band, to employ a formula along the following lines:

'I GIVE such sum as at my death equals the maximum amount which could be given by this will without IHT becoming payable in respect of the gift.'

One risk thrown up by employing a formula is that should a future government dramatically increase the nil rate band (eg to £400,000) then the testator might find that his entire estate is going to the children so that inadequate provision is made for his spouse. When the combined estates for the husband and wife are relatively modest (below say £300,000), leaving £215,000 outright to the children on the death of the first spouse may be unacceptable since the couple will probably wish the bulk of the estate to pass to the survivor. The mini-discretionary trust (illustrated in *Example 40.6*, below) provides a halfway house that may be employed in such cases.

EXAMPLE 40.6

Ma and Pa are relatively poor: joint assets below £350,000 including their dwelling house. It is likely that all or at least the bulk of the combined estate will be needed by the survivor and the scope for lifetime planning is non-existent. As discussed above it is desirable that part (at least) of the nil rate band of the first to die is utilised. In this case, however, leaving £215,000 away from the surviving spouse is probably unacceptable since it will be desirable to ensure that the surviving spouse can obtain all the property should the need arise. At the same time, there are advantages of using up the nil rate band in favour of (say) children. One way of achieving both objectives is to set up a discretionary trust, often called a 'mini discretionary trust', of £215,000 in the following terms:

(1) *duration of trust:* the full perpetuity period—say, 80 years;

(2) *beneficiaries:* surviving spouse, children and grandchildren;

(3) *the discretion:* a wide discretion in the trustees to appoint both income and capital during the trust period;

(4) *provision in default:* should there still be unappointed assets at the end of the trust period the amount should be divided in equal shares amongst the living beneficiaries; and

(5) *protection of surviving spouse:* provision that the surviving spouse is to be the

beneficiary with the greatest claim upon the trustees (if desired, the spouse could be appointed a trustee).

Such a trust has the attractions that there will be no IHT payable on creation through the use of the testator's nil rate band; assuming that the rates of IHT remain linked to inflation, subsequent anniversary and exit charges are likely to be nil or very small; and the paramount wish of the testator for flexibility is achieved since, if the need arises, the entire fund can be distributed to the surviving spouse; otherwise full use has been made of the testator's nil rate band.

3   How to leave property to a spouse: outright and limited gifts

A separate problem is whether a spouse gift should be absolute or for a limited (eg life) interest. So far as IHT is concerned, both types of gift fall within the spouse exemption so that the tax is neutral. Accordingly, the decision can be made on non-fiscal grounds.

The *outright gift* has the attraction of flexibility. The surviving spouse is free to use the property for any purpose and may therefore employ it to the best advantage of the family in the future. As a corollary, however, because the assets are given free from all conditions, an imprudent spouse may fritter away the inheritance and leave nothing for the children.

A *life interest* avoids the dangers inherent in the absolute gift by ensuring that the capital assets will eventually pass to persons entitled in remainder (usually children or grandchildren). Giving an interest in income may, however, be inadequate for the needs of the surviving spouse. A sudden emergency requiring a substantial capital outlay, for instance, may arise and if the absolute gift suffers from being too flexible the limited interest may well prove too inflexible!

An alternative to the two major types of gifts considered above is for a limited interest to be conferred on the spouse, but for the trustees of the will to be given a power to advance capital sums to that beneficiary. Such a power can then be exercised should the need arise, bearing in mind that capital sums advanced to the interest in possession beneficiary are free from IHT (IHTA 1984 s 52(2)). Giving only a life interest to a surviving spouse may give rise to a further disadvantage in restricting the ability of that person to pass on the property by means of potentially exempt lifetime transfers. It is true that by including a power to advance capital as set out above, the problem can be partly solved: however, the end result is somewhat cumbrous with the trustee advancing assets to the life tenant in order for that person to make PETs of the same property.

A life interest may, however, be employed *to ensure that the surviving spouse makes a potentially exempt transfer*. Assume, for instance, that a husband wishes the bulk of his estate to pass on his death to his grandchildren on accumulation and maintenance trusts. His wife is much younger but he is concerned that, should he leave the property to her absolutely, it will never find its way to the grandchildren. On these facts the husband should be advised to settle property in his will with his spouse being given an immediate interest in possession. The trustees should then be given the power to terminate the interest (say six months after his death) whereupon the will should provide for the property to be held on the desired trusts for the grandchildren. There is no IHT charged on the husband's death because of the spouse exemption and the subsequent termination of the interest in possession will be a PET by the surviving spouse (see [**22.117**] for a discussion of this flexible method of will drafting as compared with the traditional two-year discretionary trust under IHTA 1984 s 144).   [**40.75**]

4 Cohabitees and children

The general principles of IHT apply to transfers between cohabitees (so that *inter vivos* transfers will be PETs: death transfers chargeable) and between parents and children. In the latter case the connected person rules apply.   **[40.76]**

5 Post mortem adjustments

The rules governing *post mortem* rearrangements (see **[22.118]**) are bolstered up by an anti-avoidance provision in IHTA 1984 s 29A which is relevant when there is an exempt transfer on death (eg to the surviving spouse) and the recipient then, in satisfaction of a claim against the estate of the deceased, disposes of property 'not derived from the death transfer' (see **[22.58]**).   **[40.77]-[40.90]**

V STAMP DUTY

A gift between spouses is (like other voluntary dispositions) exempt from *ad valorem* duty; a sale between spouses is subject to *ad valorem* duty only if it is made otherwise than in connection with the breakdown of the marriage (see FA 1985 s 83, and **[32.59]**). The residual 50p duty and adjudication requirement was removed for instruments executed after 1 May 1987 if the appropriate certificate is completed (Stamp Duty (Exempt Instruments) Regulations 1987 (SI 1987/516)—and see in particular categories H and L of the Schedule).   **[40.91]-[40.110]**

VI ADMINISTRATION

From 1990-91 each spouse's tax affairs have been dealt with separately, not necessarily by the same tax office. It is each spouse's own responsibility to furnish, if required, a tax return in respect of his or her income and gains for the tax year in question.

The Revenue is not permitted to disclose information regarding one spouse's tax affairs to the other without the spouse in question's written permission.   **[40.111]-[40.130]**

VII COMPARISONS IN THE TREATMENT OF SPOUSES AND COHABITEES

The later Thatcher/Lawson years witnessed little short of a revolution in the taxation of married couples and cohabitees. From the vantage point of 1997, it may be concluded that before 1988 cohabitees enjoyed certain tax benefits denied to married couples: thereafter, the pendulum swung to the opposite extreme so that it is now married couples who enjoy benefits denied to cohabitees. It is not the purpose of this section to discuss the rival merits of cohabitation as against matrimony, nor indeed to consider what role taxation should play in influencing the conduct of individuals. It may, however, be suggested that to treat cohabitation on a par with marriage for taxation purposes will be impractical in cases where that relationship is likely to be transitory; in other cases (notably situations falling within the old idea of a 'common law marriage') a different argument may be thought persuasive, albeit that deciding when a temporary accommodation has become permanent may be far from easy! Fewer single people are getting married and those who have tried the experience are increasingly reluctant to repeat it: in both cases couples are opting to live with each other rather than go through the marriage ceremony. Finding a satisfactory tax regime for cohabitees is therefore a growing problem.

Apart from limited and piecemeal changes—such as the restriction of the so-called single parent's allowance to ensure that only one such allowance was available to cohabitees—the major tax changes in recent years were brought about, *first*, by FA 1988 which severely curtailed the tax efficiency of maintenance payments and wholly removed the tax benefits associated with a deed of covenant and, *secondly*, by the introduction of independent taxation for husband and wife. As some compensation for cohabitees it may be noted that varous anti-avoidance rules based upon a test of 'connected persons' will not normally apply to them. In such cases transactions between the cohabiting couple will be taxed in the same way as transactions between strangers. Take, for instance, IHTA 1984 s 10, which is intended to ensure that IHT does not catch the bad bargain (see [**21.21**]). In the case of a transfer between cohabitees, in order to avoid any question of an IHT charge, it is only necessary to show an absence of gratuitious intent on the part of the transferor. It is not necessary to go further, as is the case when the transferee is a connected person, and to show that the transfer in question is one that would have been entered into with a third party. Admittedly this is small beer in the majority of cases where the crucial point in any case where property is transferred between a couple (whether married or otherwise) will be the exemption from charge for inter-spouse transfers.

Consider, however, as a second illustration the CGT rules which apply to tax the settlor on the gains realised by his trustees in cases where he has retained an interest in his trust. For UK trusts, TCGA 1992 ss 77–78 limits the charge to situations where the settlor or his spouse (no mention of other members of the family, nor of cohabitation) can benefit directly or indirectly from property in the settlement (see [**14.85**]). The legislation on offshore trusts goes further: a settlor has an interest if a benefit may be enjoyed by a category of 'defined persons' which also includes children (plus their spouses) and companies controlled by such persons (including any company controlled by that company). Still no mention of the cohabitee!

Turning to specific areas. So far as interest relief for mortgage payments is concerned, a married couple are restricted to one £30,000 mortgage ceiling so that it is not possible for both husband and wife to take out qualifying £30,000 loans. So far as the allocation of relief (now substantially restricted) is concerned, although the presumption is that it will be divided equally between the couple it is possible for relief to be transferred, at the joint election of the parties, from one spouse to the other (but see [**40.28**]).

For loans taken out before 1 August 1988 to purchase a main residence, the £30,000 limit applied to each borrower although spouses were treated as one person and so entitled only to a single relief. Unmarried couples, therefore, could obtain twice as much relief as the married couple. For loans taken out on or after that date this benefit was removed and the £30,000 limit on relief is now given *per residence* irrespective of the number of borrowers. This restriction does not, of course, prevent cohabitees from each owning a property qualifying as their main residence. In such cases, not only will each have an available CGT exemption for that main residence, but in addition both may obtain income tax relief on qualifying loans of up to £30,000. In line with other provisions aimed at tax avoidance which have already been considered, restrictions on which loans qualify for the purpose of income tax relief (in TA 1988 s 355(5)) are aimed at artificial transactions and include situations where vendor and purchaser are husband and wife, or where the purchase involves a settlor (or his spouse) and the trustees of his settlement. Again there is no mention of the cohabitee!

A major area where cohabitees suffer tax disadvantages is that of tax allowances and reliefs. For income tax purposes, the restriction of the single parent allowance has already been noted and the introduction of a uniform personal allowance ('the' personal allowance) for all individuals irrespective of marital status was not accompanied by the immediate removal of all vestiges of the old married order. Accordingly a married couple are still given a special allowance—transferable from the husband to the wife—and increased in amount for 1997–98, although the way in which the relief is now given has substantially reduced its effect (see [**40.23**]). For CGT purposes the annual exempt amount (up to £6,500 for 1997–98) is available to *all* taxpayers (and hence to both husband and wife) whilst for IHT the general exemptions (£3,000 per annum; gifts in consideration of marriage; and normal expenditure out of income) are, of course, available to all. Crucially, however, special reliefs are available to a married couple which enable assets to be transferred *inter se* without the risk of any tax charge. For IHT purposes this relief is unlimited in amount save for the situation where the donee spouse is a non-UK domiciliary (and therefore potentially outside the UK tax net). For CGT purposes, disposals between spouses are treated on a no gain/no loss basis (see TCGA 1992 s 58).

It is the absence of any capital tax relief for transfers *inter se* which is the greatest disadvantage facing cohabitees. Elementary tax planning schemes are, as a result, fraught with difficulties. For income tax purposes, for instance, ensuring that a couple take full advantage of their individual allowances and lower and basic rate tax band will frequently involve an outright transfer of an income-producing asset. In the case of cohabitees, care must be taken to ensure that if that transfer is of a chargeable asset it falls within the transferor's annual CGT exemption whilst, for IHT purposes, if that transfer exceeds the £3,000 annual exemption it will constitute a potentially chargeable transfer. Will drafting for the cohabitor is likewise a problematic exercise: if everything is left to his cohabitee, the estate will be subject to a 40% tax levy once the £215,000 nil rate band has been exhausted. There is no exempt transfer to shelter behind in such cases: no simple channelling operation which can be performed to make any tax liability disappear as in the case of married couples.

A common trap which may arise is as follows. Assume that Terry and June cohabit in No 44 Railway Cuttings, a house which they own as joint tenants. Terry dies without having made a will (a negligent death) with the result that his free estate (ie his property other than his share of Railway Cuttings) passes to his parents. June is not entitled to any property on his intestacy although she could bring an action for reasonable financial provision under the Inheritance (Provision for Family and Dependants) Act 1975 provided she can show that she was financially dependent on Terry. In cases where both cohabitees have had full-time jobs this is unlikely to be the case. To return to the example, assume that the total value of Terry's estate exceeds the IHT nil rate threshold: say, for instance, that Terry's half share in the house is worth £177,000 and that his free estate is likewise worth £177,000. (It may in passing be noticed that in valuing Terry's half share in the house a discount on the basis of the joint occupation should be allowed. Such a discount is not, of course, available in the case of a half share owned by husband and wife because of the related property rules in IHTA 1984 s 161: see [**21.67**].) The IHT bill (£55,600 assuming that Terry had an intact nil rate band) will result in an estate rate of 15.7% and June will be accountable for the £27,800 attributable to Terry's share in the house since the burden of IHT charged on joint property falls on that property. She has received nothing under Terry's intestacy and given that his parents may be unwilling to make any contribution towards the IHT charge on Railway Cuttings, the end result is that unless she can afford to raise a mortgage or alternatively to pay the tax in instalments (with interest) she will end up being forced to sell the house.   [**40.131**]

41 Matrimonial breakdown

Matrimonial breakdown necessarily has tax repercussions, and it used to be an occasion which afforded scope for tax planning. Changes in the tax treatment of maintenance payments by FA 1988 reduced that scope significantly, and it became clear that many traditional arrangements were no longer satisfactory.   [**41.1**]

I INCOME TAX

1 General principles

On the breakdown of a marriage the parties revert to single status. For income tax purposes marriage ends when the parties separate 'in such circumstances that the separation is likely to be permanent'. With the introduction of independent taxation of spouses as from 6 April 1990, both parties will, in any event, have been taxed separately whilst married so that each will have been entitled to the personal allowance (£4,045 for 1997–98) with the couple receiving the benefit of the relief in respect of the married couple's allowance (£1,830 for 1997–98). This relief will continue to be given for the tax year of separation but thereafter each party will normally receive merely the personal allowance. If there are infant children, relief in respect of the additional personal allowance may also be payable to the parent who has custody of those children (see [**4.104**]).   [**41.2**]

2 Effect of FA 1988 on maintenance payments

a) Basic provisions

Under the guise of 'simplifying the tax treatment of maintenance payments' major changes in the treatment of such payments were made by FA 1988. As a result, new maintenance payments were largely removed from the tax system. In particular, payments in favour of children attract no tax relief whilst payments to a former spouse only qualify for tax relief in respect of a maximum £1,830 (for 1997–98).

The importance of these changes went far beyond mere questions of simplification and, although poorer families remained largely unaffected, couples in the middle income bracket suffered because of the withdrawal of relief for payments in favour of children and the severe limitations on the relief in the case of payments to a former spouse. The changes have resulted in a reduction in the amounts paid under maintenance arrangements. For the wealthy, a switch to outright transfers of capital instead of income payments is discernible. [41.3]

b) *Pensions and divorce*

Of considerable interest is the case of *Brooks v Brooks* (1993), where the court held that a pension fund set up by the husband's company during the course of the marriage, and which specifically provided for a pension for his spouse, was a post-nuptial settlement which could be varied by the court in order to provide the wife with an immediate annuity and a pension on the termination of the marriage. In a previous case, *Griffiths v Dawson & Co* (1993), the same judge had held negligent a solicitor, acting on behalf of a wife who was being divorced, for failure to hold up the proceedings in order to investigate any possible rights she might have had in the pension fund related to her husband's employment. Provided that the rules of the pension fund allowed for the other spouse (frequently the wife) to claim such benefits, and provided that the wife was of an age to take advantage of those benefits, these cases seemed to provide an alternative means of providing income for a divorced spouse through contributions paid by the employed spouse which had not suffered tax. The courts now have a duty to consider the loss of pension rights in a divorce settlement and can require the trustees of an occupational pension scheme to make a payment to the other party to the marriage when payment under the scheme becomes due to the party with the pension rights (this is known as 'ear-marking': see Pensions Act 1995 ss 166-167 inserting new ss 25B-D into the Matrimonial Causes Act 1973). In addition, the Family Law Act 1996 made further amendments to these sections to allow pension 'splitting' on divorce as well as 'ear-marking'. such splitting, by taking place at the time of divorce, facilitates a clean-break. However, the 1996 Act changes require further (implementing) legislation. A White Paper, *Pension Rights on Divorce* (Cm 3564), was published in February 1997 but there seems little prospect of implementation in the near future. It will be appreciated that 'splitting' carries a considerable tax advantage with each spouse having allowances/lower rates of tax to set against the income resulting from the split. [41.4]

b) *Old arrangements*

Existing maintenance arrangements (as defined: see [41.7]) continue to benefit from tax relief whether in favour of an ex-spouse or children but the amount in respect of which relief is available is pegged at the level of the maintenance payment in 1988-89. [41.5]

3   Tax treatment of 'new' maintenance payments (TA 1988 s 347B)

Payments of maintenance, whether to spouses or children, have largely been removed from the income tax system with the following three consequences. *First*, the payer is not entitled to deduct the sum paid as a charge on his income and is therefore forced to make the payment out of taxed income. *Secondly*, the sum is paid over gross to the recipient: there is no question of deducting income tax at source. *Finally*, the sum is received free from income tax: ie it no longer falls under Schedule D Case III as an annual payment (nor, in the case of payments arising outside the UK, under Schedule D Case V). Only limited compensation for the payer is offered. Prior to 1994-95, this was obtained by means of a special deduction in computing his total income, thus allowing for relief at his marginal rate of tax. Relief is now given by reducing the payer's tax liability on his total income by 15% (for 1997-98) of an amount equal to the married couple's allowance (£1,830) or, if lower, the actual amount of the maintenance paid. If the payer's income tax liability is insufficient to offset the whole of the reduction, relief is given by reducing the liability to nil; he cannot claim any repayment of tax. In determining what a payer's income tax liability is for this purpose, tax at the basic rate which the claimant is entitled to deduct or retain out of charges on income (such as covenanted payments to charity) is excluded. Further, any income tax reduction to which he may be entitled by reason of married couple's allowance, the additional personal allowance or the widow's bereavement allowance is ignored. It should be noted that this relief is only available in the case of payments to a former or separated spouse: it is not available in the case of maintenance payments made directly to children. The payments must be made under a UK court order or agreement or under court orders of countries which are members of the EU or assessed by the Child Support Agency.　　　　　　**[41.6]**

EXAMPLE 41.1

Under a court order made on 1 July 1991 Eric is obliged to make payments of £2,000 pa to each of his infant children Robert and Rosie and payments of £3,500 pa to his former wife Erica. Eric's income for the year 1997–98 is £35,000.

(1) Eric cannot deduct any of the payments in computing his total income and therefore will have to meet the payments out of income which will have suffered tax at the top rate of 40%.

(2) The sums are not treated as the income of the children nor as the income of Erica so that their personal allowances may be wasted.

(3) Only limited relief is provided by Eric being entitled to a reduction in his income tax liability in respect of payments made to his former spouse only.

	£
Income	35,000
Deduct: personal allowance	4,045
	£30,955

Income tax liability:	£4,100 at 20%	=	£820	
	£22,000 at 23%	=	£5,060	
	£4,855 at 40%	=	£1,942	7,822

Deduct: relief in respect of maintenance payments, subject to a maximum amount of £1,830 = £1,830 × 15%	274.50
Net income tax liability	£7,547.50

4 'Existing obligations'

Maintenance payments made under existing obligations continue to attract income tax relief. The new rules, introduced by FA 1995 Sch 17 which 'tidy up' and 'rationalise' the legislation which taxes the income of settlements as if it were the settlor's income where he retains a benefit or the possibility of a benefit from the settlement, carry forward the exception for settlements made by one party to a marriage to provide for the other after divorce or separation where the income is being paid to that other (see **[11.66]**). Such obligations are defined as follows.

First, an obligation arising under a court order made before 15 March 1988 or before the end of June 1988 so long as the application to court was made on or before 15 March 1988.

Secondly, payments made under a deed executed or written agreement made before 15 March 1988 and received by the appropriate tax inspector before the end of June 1988.

Thirdly, payments under an oral agreement made before 15 March 1988 written particulars of which were received by the tax inspector before the end of June 1988.

Finally, payments made under a court order made on or after 15 March 1988 or under a written agreement made on or after that date where the order or agreement replaces, varies or supplements an order or agreement which falls within the foregoing definition of an existing obligation. Notice that the fourth category above does not contain any time limit: in other words, obligations in force on 15 March 1988 can be varied at any time in the future, although where such variation results in extra payments falling due, tax relief will only be available for extra payments made in the year 1988–89. It may be noted that FA 1988 s 38(3) refers to payments 'due and paid' for 1988–89 for the purpose of these pegging provisions. This appears to mean that where payments were in arrear at the end of 1988–89 those arrears neither qualify for relief from income tax in the year 1988–89 nor count towards the pegged limit for later years *until such time as they are actually paid*. Once they have been so paid they will then count towards the limit for the year in which they were due. In cases where the taxpayer's income was insufficient to entitle him to full relief for 1988–89 payments, the former Revenue practice of allowing relief in subsequent years on the full amount of the payment has now been withdrawn: henceforth, for those claiming under this practice for the first time, relief is limited to payments which attracted relief in 1988–89. Relief will not be withdrawn for those who have benefited from the practice in the past, either in respect of past or future years (*Tax Bulletin*, Issue 15, February 1995). On pegging see *Example 41.4*.   **[41.7]**

5 Tax treatment of payments made under existing obligations

The tax treatment of maintenance payments made before 15 March 1988 depended on whether they were made to a former spouse or to a child. In the former case, so long as the payment was made under a legal obligation (whether that obligation arose by written agreement; deed of covenant; or under a court order) the sum paid was fully deductible by the payer in arriving at his income tax computation and was taxed as the income of the recipient under Schedule D Case III. Technically, the payment constituted a charge on the payer's income with basic rate income tax being collected at source under the provisions of TA 1988 s 348 (see **[10.41]**).

In the case of payments to children, a similar result followed if a court order was obtained directing the payment to be made to the child direct, payments would then constitute a charge on the income of the payer; were made net of basic rate tax; and the recipient child was then entitled to recover income tax deducted at source to the extent of any unused personal allowance. Payments to infant unmarried children not made under a court order, however, did not attract this favourable tax relief since they were caught by TA 1988 s 663 (now TA 1988, s 660B; see **[11.62]**) and were therefore taxed as the income of the payer.

EXAMPLE 41.2

(*How maintenance payments were taxed prior to the 1988 changes*)
By court order dated 1 July 1987, Jason (taxed in 1987–88 at 60% on the top slice of his income) is ordered to pay his former wife Griselda maintenance of £6,000 pa and his infant son Steven £3,000 pa.
(1) Jason can deduct £9,000 from his total income for 1987–88 so that the net cost of the payments to Jason is only 60%.
(2) He will deduct income tax at the basic rate from the payment, handing over only a net sum.

(3) Griselda and Steven are taxed on incomes of £6,000 and £3,000 pa respectively with a credit for the basic rate income tax deducted at source by Jason.

Two other matters are worthy of note in connection with old maintenance payments. *First*, recipients of such payments who were not liable to income tax could claim repayment of the basic rate of tax deducted at source by the payer. Until repayment, recipients could experience a cashflow problem. Thus, in exceptional circumstances such payments were made gross: for this to happen the payments in question had to satisfy the definition of a 'small maintenance payment' (see TA 1988 s 351). *Secondly*, the House of Lords in the case of *Sherdley v Sherdley* (1987) accepted that maintenance payments could be ordered by the court to cover a child's school fees and would then qualify for income tax relief. They further accepted that a custodial father could seek such orders against himself.

FA 1988 provided that payments made under existing obligations continued to receive income tax relief as set out above whether the payments were made to a former or separated spouse or to a child. However, the following matters should be carefully noted.

In 1988-89 the payments continued to be made subject to deduction of basic rate income tax at source (unless the small maintenance provisions applied) and where the payments were to a former spouse that spouse could claim an extra personal allowance of £1,490. (Remarkably, therefore, the position of such a spouse was improved by a Finance Act designed to reduce tax relief on maintenance payments!)

For 1989-90 and following years up to 1994-95, however, payments under existing obligations ceased to be charges on the payer's income. He could, instead, make a claim for relief whereby he would deduct a payment in computing his total income and make the payment gross (ie without deducting basic rate income tax at source). The payment then formed part of the income of the payee, who was directly taxed on the income received under Schedule D Case III. In the case of payments to a former spouse, the extra allowance of £1,720 (equivalent to the amount of the married couple's allowance for those years) continued to be available to the recipient.

For 1994-95 and subsequent years, relief is restricted so that the payer can claim as a deduction in computing his total income only so much of the payment as exceeds an amount equal to the married couple's allowance (£1,830 for 1997-98). The first £1,830 of such payment is treated in the same way as a payment made under an obligation arising after 14 March 1988. This means that whilst the payer can obtain relief at his marginal rate of tax in respect of payments exceeding £1,830, he can only receive relief in respect of the first £1,830 (or the actual amount of the payment, if less) by way of a reduction in his income tax liability of 15% (for 1997-98) of that amount.

EXAMPLE 41.3

Under a court order made in 1987 Julie is obliged to make payments to her former husband Hugo of £7,500 and to her infant child Katie of £2,000 pa. Hugo has no other income and has custody of Katie. Julie's income for the year 1997-98 is £40,000. The tax treatment of these payments in 1997-98 is as follows:

(1) Julie cannot automatically deduct £9,500 as a charge on her income. She will need to submit a claim to obtain income tax relief. She will then be able to deduct £7,670 (the excess over £1,830) in computing her total income. Relief for the first £1,830 is restricted to 15% and is given as a reduction in her income tax liability.

	£
Income	40,000
Deduct: maintenance (£9,500 – £1,830)	7,670
personal allowance	4,045
	£28,285

Income tax liability: £4,100 at 20% = £820	
£22,000 at 23% = £5,060	
£2,185 at 40% = £874	6,754.00
Deduct: relief for first £1,830 of maintenance	
payments: £1,830 × 15%	274.50
Net income tax liability	£6,479.50

(2) The £2,000 received by Katie will be covered by her personal allowance (assuming she has no other income) and is therefore tax free.

(3) The £7,500 received by Hugo will be assessed in the following way:

	£
Income	7,500
Deduct: £1,830 (if claimed) under FA 1988 s 38(5)	1,830
personal allowance	4,045
	£1,625
Income tax liability: £1,625 at 20% =	325
Deduct: relief in respect of additional personal allowance	
(see Chapter 4): £1,830 × 15%	274.50
Net income tax liability	£50.50

It is possible for an election to be made by a person making maintenance payments under existing obligations for the new rules to apply to such payments. Such an election will rarely be of any benefit in the tax year 1997–98: one exception is where the payer of maintenance is non-UK resident and therefore obtains no tax relief on the payments whilst the recipient is subject to UK tax thereon—if the election is made the payments will be free of tax in the hands of the recipient. The election may become beneficial if maintenance payments increase and the pegged limit for relief, discussed above, is less than the maximum amount of relief available under the new rules.

EXAMPLE 41.4

(1) Under an existing obligation created by court order, Samson paid Delilah £15,000 pa and his child £3,000 pa by way of maintenance payments. In 1993–94 payments for the child ceased but the payments to Delilah were increased to £18,000 by an amendment order. The amendment will fall within FA 1988 s 36(5)(b) as being a variation in favour of an existing person and as the pegged sum for 1988–89 is £18,000, this amount is available to cover the extra payment to Delilah. Accordingly the old rules will apply to this increased payment.

Note: This, at first sight, somewhat surprising result is confirmed in *Taxation*, 4 May 1989, p 117 where it is noted—in question 10—that the only limitation is that new recipients cannot be added. It remains, however, something of a moot point whether Delilah in this example would be taxed on the new amount (£18,000) or only on the sum received in 1988–89 (£15,000): see in particular FA 1988 s 38(4).

(2) Under an existing obligation, Frank is ordered to pay his former wife, Sheila, £1,000 pa. In 1997–98 that sum is increased to £3,500 pa. As a result of pegging and the new restriction relief, under the old rules Frank is only entitled to relief by way of a reduction in his income tax liability of 15% of £1,000. However, under the new rules he will be entitled to an income tax reduction of 15%

of £1,830. Will an election be desirable in this case or will the total payment be split so that Frank will get an income tax reduction in respect of a maximum of £1,830 (reduced by the amount of any payments in respect of which Frank is entitled under the old rules) under the new rules in any event?

The election is irrevocable once made and will apply to all maintenance payments made by that payer. Accordingly, in *Example 41.4* if Frank was also obliged to make payments to his infant children it is unlikely that any election would be desirable since the new system affords no relief for such payments.

One problem which may arise is to decide what is to happen in the case of orders and agreements made under the old system involving the payment of a net sum after deduction of tax. Consider, for instance, the payer who is ordered to make payments to his former spouse of £20,000 pa 'free of tax'. In the current tax year will he be obliged to pay £20,000 or £20,000 grossed up by income tax at the current basic rate? If the latter, the sum of £25,974.02 will have to be handed over. As a second illustration, old maintenance arrangements were often in the form of a court order under which (say) a father was obliged to make payments to his infant child of 'such sum as will after deduction of income tax at the basic rate equal (specified) school fees'. Usually that sum was then paid to the school as agent for the child: a somewhat artificial device which seems to have prompted the 1988 changes! Again the problem which arises is whether the father is obliged to hand over merely the school fees for the year or that amount grossed up at the 23% basic rate.

The answer to these questions involves an interpretation of the relevant agreement or court order although the sum handed over is subject to income tax in the hands of the recipient so that the Revenue is involved. Having said that, the taxation of annual payments under Schedule D Case III depends upon income being received rather than mere receivability: income tax is charged on the sum actually handed over (*Dewar v IRC* (1935); *Woodhouse v IRC* (1936)).

The Revenue accepts that the matter turns on the interpretation of the relevant agreement or order and that they have no power to impose their own interpretation since the matter is one for the courts and the parties. In correspondence they have commented that they would accept any 'reasonable interpretation' of the agreement or order. It seems to the authors that they are in no real position to refuse to accept even an unreasonable interpretation!

In the first case above, it is thought that the intention of the order is to provide the former spouse not just with £20,000 but also with the relevant tax credit. Accordingly, the sum to be handed over each year should be grossed up by the current basic rate of income tax. A similar view may be taken in the second case where the intention of the order is again not just to provide for the payment of the school fees but also to cover any income tax liability which might arise thereon or, alternatively, to provide for the enjoyment of the greater sum which would result from a repayment claim.

One final amendment made by FA 1994 affects maintenance payments for persons over 21. Prior to 6 April 1994, the payer was eligible for relief on the full amount of any such payment made under an existing obligation, and the payment was then treated as the income of the recipient and, as such, subject to income tax in his hands. Such a payment made to or for the benefit of a person who reaches 21 after 5 April 1994 will no longer be regarded as made under an existing obligation. The result of this is that the payment will not be treated as the income of the recipient and accordingly the payer will not be entitled to any relief in respect of it. So much for existing orders: in the case of future orders and agreements, the crucial fact to remember is that what limited tax relief is now available (a reduction in income tax liability of 15% of an amount equal to the married couple's allowance which is given to the payer) is only available in the case of orders and payments in favour of a former spouse. *No tax advantage results from obtaining court orders in favour of children.* Orders in the form of the problems discussed above should be avoided. What should now be ordered or agreed is that a gross sum be paid.

[**41.8**]-[**41.20**]

II   CAPITAL GAINS TAX

Disposals between spouses are not subject to CGT and are treated as made for a consideration which will produce neither gain nor loss (see TCGA 1992 s 58 and [**14.22**]). Once the spouses separate this provision ceases to apply and the ordinary rules of CGT operate (but note *Gubay v Kington* (1984)). Hence, a transfer of chargeable assets between spouses after their separation may be subject to CGT (see, for instance, *Aspden v Hildesley* (1982)). It is therefore crucial that the re-organisation of capital assets on the breakdown of a marriage should be arranged, so far as possible, to come within s 58. That section only applies in cases where the disposal is between spouses who 'in that year of assessment' were living together. Accordingly, if assets are not transferred in the year of separation, the no gain/no loss rule will be inapplicable. Although the exemption for inter-spouse transfers is lost in the tax year following separation, the couple remain connected persons until final divorce so that disposals between separation and divorce are deemed not to be bargains at arm's length, but are treated as for a consideration equal to the market value of the property (TCGA 1992 s 18).

For the year 1997–98 husband and wife are each entitled to their own annual CGT exemption (£6,500) and this entitlement will remain unaffected by separation.   [**41.21**]-[**41.40**]

III   INHERITANCE TAX

For IHT purposes marriage continues until the final divorce so that transfers between spouses after separation and before divorce continue to be exempt. After final divorce, the general rules operate, unless the dispositions are exempt under IHTA 1984 s 11 (see [**23.6**]). Maintenance payments fall within s 11 and are, therefore, exempt from IHT. However, s 11 is probably not wide enough to cover maintenance paid by way of a transfer of a capital sum or of a capital asset which may, therefore, be chargeable unless it does not reduce the transferor's estate (eg because it is in satisfaction of outstanding financial claims by the former spouse), or lacks gratuitous intent. In most cases the absence of gratuitous intent ensures no tax charge for transfers between former spouses which result from the breakdown of the marriage (see the statement of the Senior Registrar of the Family Division made with the agreement of the Revenue (1975) 119 SJ 396).   [**41.41**]-[**41.60**]

IV   THE MATRIMONIAL HOME

1   The difficulties

The matrimonial home will often be the only valuable asset owned by a couple so that its destination on divorce poses a number of tax problems. Before considering these, however, it is important to discover who owns the home. One spouse may be the sole owner at law but the other spouse may have acquired an equitable interest in the property either expressly (eg by agreement between the parties in writing) or under a resulting trust arising from that spouse's monetary contribution to the purchase of the property (see eg *Gissing v Gissing* (1971)), or under a constructive trust. A constructive trust may arise in one of two ways. *First*, there may be evidence of an express agreement or an express representation that the property is to be shared beneficially and that the other spouse has acted to his or her detriment in relying on that agreement or representation. *Alternatively* there may be evidence based on the conduct of the parties from which can be inferred a common intention to share the property beneficially, such conduct normally being a direct financial contribution by the spouse who is not the legal owner (*Lloyds Bank plc v Rosset* (1991)). If the house is to be sold on divorce, or its ownership transferred in whole or in part from one (former) spouse to the other, problems of income tax, CGT and (exceptionally) IHT may arise. [**41.61**]

2 Income tax

Usually the property will be subject to a mortgage in favour of either a building society or a bank. To qualify for tax relief on the mortgage the borrower must own an interest in the property and must occupy it as his main residence. Relief for a house occupied by a former or separated spouse was removed by FA 1988. Accordingly, on a marriage breakdown, it is necessary to ensure that both an interest in the house and the mortgage thereon is transferred into the name of the occupying spouse (usually the estranged wife). Building societies and banks will normally be willing to agree to this arrangement provided that they are satisfied that the wife will have sufficient funds to pay the mortgage. In practice, proof that the husband is obliged to make adequate maintenance payments, or that the wife has sufficient alternative funds of her own, will suffice. For the husband this arrangement will be attractive because the wife is entitled to tax relief (albeit limited to 15% for 1997–98 reducing to 10% in 1998–99) on the interest payments so that the sum that he is required to pay as maintenance is less than would have been the case had he directly discharged mortgage payments (which would not have qualified for tax relief).

If the MIRAS scheme applies to the mortgage the borrower is entitled to pay the interest less 15% (for 1997–98) even if he or she has little or no tax liability. Accordingly, to maximise family resources on a marriage breakdown it is necessary to ensure that interest paid by the occupying spouse is within this scheme. It is also important to ensure that the interest falls within the scheme before finalising the maintenance computations. [**41.62**]

EXAMPLE 41.5

Jim and Judy have separated. Jim's income is £25,000. Judy has no income. The matrimonial home is in Jim's name alone and is to be occupied by Judy. It is charged with an outstanding mortgage of £20,000. The alternatives open to Jim and Judy are:

(1) Jim could go on paying the mortgage but would obtain no tax relief on the interest payments which he makes. Accordingly he should be advised to transfer an interest in the house to Judy together with an obligation to discharge the mortgage.

(2) Jim could therefore transfer the entire ownership of the house to Judy and arrange for the mortgage also to be transferred to her. She would then be entitled to the appropriate tax relief and Jim would pay her increased maintenance to cover the total cost of the payments. Care should be taken to ensure that the correct sum is paid: for instance, if the repayments less 15% (for 1997–98) are £140 per month that is the sum which should be paid by way of extra maintenance. Jim will, of course, have the full £30,000 loan relief available should he decide (and should he be able to afford) to buy a further house.

(3) If Jim deserts Judy, she may have to take over the mortgage payments even though the house is registered in Jim's name. Strictly, she should obtain no relief on those payments, since she does not own any interest in the property. By concession, however, relief is allowed (see the pamphlet *Income Tax, Separation and Divorce:* IR 30).

3   CGT

Before separation any disposal of the matrimonial property will be exempt from CGT if it is the spouses' main residence. Once the parties separate, however, an absent spouse who has an interest in the property may incur a CGT liability on a disposal of it. Difficulties principally arise in two cases: assume in each case that the husband owns the house which he has left, and that the wife remains in occupation throughout.   [**41.63**]

Case 1   The house is to be transferred to the wife. This disposal by the husband will not fall within the no gain/no loss rules of TCGA 1992 s 58 since the parties have been separated throughout the relevant tax year. Further, the husband has been absent from the house since the date of separation. So long as the disposal occurs within three years of that date, no charge will arise on any part of the gain (TCGA 1992 s 223(1)), but once that three-year period expires, the proportion of the total gain that is deemed to have accrued from the end of that period may be chargeable (the appropriate calculation is described at [**16.76**]). Any charge is, however, avoided if concession D6 applies:

> 'Where a married couple separate or are divorced and one partner ceases to occupy the matrimonial home and subsequently as part of a financial settlement disposes of the home, or an interest in it, to the other partner, the home may be regarded for the purpose of sections [222 to 224 of TCGA 1992] as continuing to be a residence of the transferring partner from the date his or her occupation ceases until the date of transfer, provided that it has throughout this period been the other partner's only or main residence. Thus, where a husband leaves the matrimonial home while still owning it, the usual capital gains tax exemption or relief for a taxpayer's only or main residence would be given on the subsequent transfer to the wife, provided she has continued to live in the house and the husband has not elected that some other house should be treated for capital gains tax purposes as his main residence for this period.'

Provided that the wife has continuously occupied the house as her only or main residence and the husband has not elected for another house to be his main residence, the disposal of the house may, therefore, occur many years after the separation.   [**41.64**]

Case 2   The house is to be sold. If the sale occurs more than three years after the separation, ESC D6 (because the disposal is not to the wife) is not available, so that there will be a charge on a proportion of the total gain.   [**41.65**]

4   IHT and stamp duty

Transactions involving the matrimonial home will not usually involve IHT. Either the inter-spouse exemption still applies or, after divorce, there is no gratuitous intent (see [**21.21**]). Instruments transferring property between spouses and former spouses as a result of the breakdown of marriage are not subject to *ad valorem* duty whether the transfer is made pursuant to a court order or by the agreement of the parties alone (see FA 1985 s 83). Furthermore, if the appropriate certificate is given there is no fixed 50p duty nor adjudication requirement (SI 1987/516).   [**41.66**]

5 The taxation consequences of typical court orders

In order to consider the taxation implications of four typical court orders dealing with the matrimonial home on divorce, assume throughout that the spouse who has left (H) owns the matrimonial home.   [**41.67**]

a) *The order for outright transfer (the 'clean-break')*

H is ordered to transfer the entire ownership of the house to W (see *Hanlon v Hanlon* (1978)). H may also be ordered to make maintenance payments covering, *inter alia*, any mortgage payments to be made by W.   [**41.68**]

Income tax   W will obtain relief on any mortgage interest payments if she makes them.   [**41.69**]

CGT   The disposal to W attracts no charge if it occurs within three years of separation; if it occurs later, there is no charge if ESC D6 applies.   [**41.70**]

IHT   No charge arises as a transfer pursuant to a court order lacks gratuitous intent.   [**41.71**]

b) *H and W become joint owners of the house with sale postponed*

H is ordered to transfer an interest in the house to W. The couple will be tenants in common. W will be entitled to live in the house to the exclusion of H and the sale will be postponed until (for instance) the children reach 18 (see *Mesher v Mesher* (1980)).   [**41.72**]

Income tax   As W has an interest in the house she will be entitled to mortgage interest relief provided that she makes the payments.   [**41.73**]

CGT   When the half interest in the house is transferred to W the result is as in a) above. On the eventual sale of the house, a proportion of the gain on H's share will be chargeable (corresponding to his period of absence), unless it can be argued that the effect of the order is to create a settlement. Normally, jointly owned land is not settled (TCGA 1992 s 60; *Kidson v MacDonald* (1974) and [**18.2**]). It may, however, be argued that because W has an exclusive right to occupy under the terms of the order the parties are not 'jointly absolutely entitled' since they do not have identical interests in the property. Accordingly, if the property is settled, no CGT will be charged upon its disposal, because it will have been occupied by W 'under the terms of the settlement' (see TCGA 1992 s 225). This is understood to be the current Revenue view.   [**41.74**]

IHT   The property is not settled as there is no succession of interests (IHTA 1984 s 43). Hence if either party died their estate at death would include the half share of the house valued with a discount of (usually) 10–15%.   [**41.75**]

c) *Settling the house*

W is given the right to live in the house for her life, or until remarriage, or until voluntary departure, whichever happens first. Thereafter, the house is to be sold and the proceeds divided equally between H and W (see *Martin v Martin* (1977)).   [**41.76**]

Income tax   W has an interest in the property for the purpose of claiming tax relief on the mortgage payments.   [**41.77**]

CGT   The creation of the settlement will not be chargeable (as in a) above) and on the termination of the life interest although a deemed disposal under TCGA 1992 s 71(1) will occur (see [**18.43**]), no charge to CGT will arise because of either the main residence exemption (TCGA 1992 s 225) or because of the death exemption (TCGA 1992, s 73).   [**41.78**]

IHT   There will be no charge on the creation of the settlement (see [**41.71**]). W has an interest in possession and is, accordingly, deemed to own the house (IHTA 1984 s 50(5) and [**25.1**]). On the ending of her life interest, a charge will not arise on the half share to which she or her estate then becomes entitled. If H is still alive, the other half share is excluded from charge under the reverter to settlor provisions ([**25.35**]). If H dies before W, his reversionary interest in the proceeds of sale is not excluded property, however, and is, therefore, chargeable (IHTA 1984 s 48(1); [**25.61**]) and a further charge will arise when the life interest ends in that half share on W's death since the revertor to settlor exemption does not apply.   [**41.79**]

d) *Outright transfer subject to a charge over the property in favour of the transferor*

H transfers the house to W, but is granted a charge over the property either for a specific sum (as in *Hector v Hector* (1973)), or for a proportion of the sale proceeds (as in *Browne v Pritchard* (1975)). Sale and payment may be postponed until the children attain 18 or until W dies or wishes to leave the house.   [**41.80**]

Income tax   To obtain mortgage interest relief W must make the mortgage payments.   [**41.81**]

IHT   The property is not settled, but belongs to W—no charge.   [**41.82**]

CGT   The transfer to W should not be chargeable on the principles in a) above. On the eventual sale, the position is not entirely clear. If H's charge is for a specific sum, this must be a debt due to H. Therefore, when the house is finally sold and the debt repaid there will be no charge to CGT on the repayment (TCGA 1992 s 251; see [**16.42**]). If the charge is for a proportionate share of the proceeds of sale, however, H's right is not a debt, but a *chose in action*, ie the right to a future uncertain sum; see *Marren v Ingles* (1980) and [**14.7**]. As a result, when the house is eventually sold and a sum of money paid to H, there will be a chargeable disposal of that *chose in action*.   [**41.83**]

e) *Conclusions*

It must be stressed that the taxation factors are not the most important considerations to be borne in mind when considering financial adjustments upon a matrimonial breakdown. The outright transfer may be the ideal for tax purposes, but it leaves the husband with no interest in the former matrimonial home and so deprives him of any capital appreciation. Further, the court has no power to adjust property orders once made, so they must be correct at the start. Finally, a transfer of the house or an interest therein is quite different from a declaration (normally under the Married Women's Property Act 1882) that a woman owns, and has always owned, a share in the asset. No transfer is involved in such cases and the taxation consequences of transfers discussed above are irrelevant.   [**41.84**]

42 Tax treatment of charities

There is a useful Inland Revenue explanatory leaflet (IR 75) and, given the complexity in the definition of charity which is case law based rather than statutory, reference should also be made to standard works on charities such as *Tudor* and *Picarda*.   **[42.1]**–**[42.20]**

I QUALIFYING CHARITIES

(1) Tax reliefs are only available for bodies which are registered as a charity with the Charity Commissioners or, in the case of charities not required to register, which satisfy the Inland Revenue that they are established for charitable purposes only. Educational and other institutions specified in Charities Act 1993 Sch 2; places of worship; charities without a permanent endowment; and charities in Scotland and Northern Ireland fall into the latter category.

(2) The legal definition of charity is complex depending, as it does, on a voluminous body of case law. The roots of the definition may be traced to the preamble to the Charitable Uses Act 1601 which listed those purposes considered to be charitable *at that time*. Subsequent case law has extended that list by reference to the supposed 'spirit and intendment' of the preamble—albeit that judges have frequently confessed that the spirit and intendment of that measure has been stretched almost to breaking point! The end result is that:

> 'The words "charity" and "charitable" bear, for the purposes of English law and equity, meanings totally different from the senses in which they are used in ordinary educated speech, or, for instance, in the Authorised Version of the Bible.' (Lord Hailsham in *IRC v McMullen* (1981).)

(3) Traditionally charities are classified as falling into four categories: for the relief of poverty; for educational purposes; for the promotion of religion; and for other purposes beneficial to the community, although the threadbare nature of this classification is apparent from the final catch-all category. The definition of religion has excited controversy in recent years as has the requirement that charitable trusts must be for the benefit of the public at large or a sufficient section of the public. As a result of this latter requirement a trust to educate the children of employees of a large public company and its subsidiaries was held not charitable (the beneficiaries not comprising a section of the public), nor was a trust for a Carmelite convent

containing 20 contemplative nuns whose activities were not considered by the House of Lords to confer any benefit on an outside world which they never visited. As may be appreciated the case law on the meaning of charity is rich in absurdities!

The charitable purposes do not have to be carried out exclusively in the UK: the Charity Commissioners accept charitable purposes abroad on the assumption that 'the relief of poverty and the advancement of education and religion are charitable in all parts of the world'; but in connection with purposes coming under the fourth head (other purposes beneficial to the community) they take a defensive position and say that there must be a benefit, albeit indirect, to the community of the UK and add that 'it is easier to establish this benefit in relation to Commonwealth than to foreign countries'. Why these distinctions should be drawn is far from clear but the practice of the Charity Commissioners is, of course, crucial since acceptance by them as a charity (and entry on the register) will in turn lead to an acceptance by the Inland Revenue that the organisation qualifies for tax benefits. Theoretically a body may exist for charitable purposes without being registered, but it is highly unlikely that its charitable status will be accepted by the Revenue and, under the Charities Act 1993, the charitable trustees would be in breach of a duty to register and to supply appropriate documents to the Commissioners.

The Charity Commissioners are limited in their operations to England and Wales; in Scotland, a register of charities is maintained by the Inland Revenue. Further, the Commissioners' jurisdiction is restricted to charities which are defined in s 96(1) of the Act as 'any institution, corporate or not, which is established for charitable purposes and is subject to the control of the High Court in the exercise of the Court's jurisdiction with respect to charities'. Overseas charities will, in practice, only come within this definition if a majority of the trustees or the bulk of the funds are subject to the control of the High Court and therefore to supervision by the Attorney General.

As a result of these limitations, charitable purposes carried out through UK resident companies managed by non resident trustees will—unless there are funds in the UK—fail to obtain registration by the Charity Commissioners. Given that the company itself is resident here for corporation tax purposes, the somewhat bizarre result may be that income and profits will attract a tax charge since the tax relief available to charities under Taxes Act 1988 s 505 has a similarly restricted ambit to that confining the Charity Commissioners' jurisdiction. Despite 'charity' being defined in the Taxes Act as 'any body of persons established for charitable purposes only' the House of Lords decided in *Camille and Henry Dreyfus Foundation Inc v IRC* (1956) that these words had to be limited to a body of persons or trusts established for such purposes *in the UK*. In that case a foundation established in the State of New York and which carried on all its activities in the USA was not entitled to exemption (under the forerunner of s 505) for substantial royalties which it received from a company resident in the UK.

(4) English law has generally refused to accept that non-charitable purpose trusts are valid. Amongst the reasons given for this attitude are that in a number of cases the purposes have been so imprecisely drafted that it would be difficult to control the trustees in the exercise of their functions; in other cases the purposes would continue forever and therefore breach the perpetuity rule; whilst certain purposes have been stigmatised as useless or capricious (see, for instance, *McCaig v University of Glasgow* (1907) in which the court set aside a will trust that would have involved building statues of the deceased and other 'artistic towers' at prominent points on

his estate). The unfortunate result of this approach has been that, in general, only charitable purpose trusts are valid and hence the courts have tended to extend the definition of charity to encompass dubious cases in the knowledge that failure to do so would lead to the trusts being held invalid.

(5) The tax reliefs (which will be noted below) are available to all charities. Given that the definition embraces purposes which may be of little benefit to the public, it is debatable whether this position is satisfactory. In 1975 the Expenditure Committee of the House of Commons recommended:

> 'Legislation should be introduced whereby all charities should be required to satisfy the test of purposes beneficial to the community. In the case of those charities formally admitted under one of the other heads, namely the relief of poverty, the advancement of education and the advancement of religion, they should continue to qualify only if they also satisfy the main criteria. We do not believe such a change would affect the great majority of charities in any way; but we do believe it would act as a check to abuse at the fringe.'

In a similar vein, Lord Cross of Chelsea in *Dingle v Turner* (1972) argued as follows:

> 'As Counsel for the Attorney General remarked in the course of argument, the law of charity is bedevilled by the fact that charitable trusts enjoy two quite different sorts of privilege. On the one hand, they enjoy immunity from the laws against perpetuity and uncertainty and though individual potential beneficiaries cannot sue to enforce them, the public interest arising is protected by the Attorney General. If this was all, there would be no reason for the courts not to look favourably on the claim of any "purpose" trust to be considered as a charity if it seemed calculated to confer some real benefit on those intended to benefit by it ... But that is not all. Charities automatically enjoy fiscal privileges which with the increasing burden of taxation have become more and more important and in deciding that such and such a trust is a charitable trust, the court is endowing it with a substantial annual subsidy at the expense of the taxpayer. Indeed, claims for trusts to rank as charities are just as often challenged by the Revenue as by those who would take the fund if the trust was invalid. It is, of course, unfortunate that the recognition of any trust as a valid charitable trust should automatically attract fiscal privileges, for the question whether a trust to further some purpose is so little likely to benefit the public that it ought to be declared invalid and the question whether it is likely to confer such great benefits on the public that it should enjoy fiscal immunity are really two quite different questions. The logical solution would be to separate them and to say ... that only some charities should enjoy fiscal privileges.'

In his 1997 Budget the Chancellor announced that 'the Government will now consult widely on how the tax treatment of charities can be made more appropriate to help charities today'. **[42.21]**–**[42.40]**

II TAX RELIEF ON CHARITABLE INCOME AND GAINS

(1) TA 1988 s 505 and TCGA 1992 s 256 confer relief from income tax; CGT; and corporation tax in respect of:
—rent from land and property;
—interest and dividends;
—covenanted donations;
—single gifts by companies and individuals;
—grants from other charities;
—chargeable gains.
In cases where tax has been deducted at source, the recipient charity is entitled to a refund by application to the Inland Revenue Charities division

(see generally SP 3/87: the special position of charities which receive distributions (including dividends) from companies is discussed in *Example 30.18*). The relevant income must form part of the income of a charity or be applicable, and applied, for charitable purposes only (TA 1988 s 505 and see *Guild v IRC* (1993)).

(2) In addition to the above, a trade carried on by a charity and which produces profits will be exempt from tax provided that *either* the trade carries out a primary purpose of the charity (eg an educational charity running a school) *or* the work is done mainly by beneficiaries of the charity (eg a charity set up to provide work for the disabled).

In those cases where the proposed trade does not satisfy these tests, the device commonly adopted by charities is to incorporate a company to carry out the work and for the profits thereby produced to be covenanted-up to the charity. The result of so doing is that the profits of the company will be kept at zero and the sums received by the charity will not themselves attract tax. Of course before making the payment the company had to estimate its profits for the year and if the payment turned out to be *less than* the profit, the company was left with a corporation tax liability: if *more than* the profit was paid, the excess had to be refunded by the charity (which would also have to pay the Revenue the overpayment in tax refunded). To take away this problem FA 1997 inserted new subsections (7AA)-(7AC) into TA 1988 s 339 which provides that a covenanted donation to charity will be deemed to be a charge on the company's income for the period in which the payment was required to be made provided that (i) the payment was actually made within nine months of the end of that period and (ii) the paying company is wholly owned by a charity. An alternative method, for the profits to be paid up to the charity by means of a dividend, is not recommended since not all the tax suffered by the company is recovered (see generally *Trading by Charities*, IR booklet CS2).   [**42.41**]-[**42.60**]

III   EXPENDITURE BY A CHARITABLE BODY

To qualify for the tax benefits set out in [**42.41**], the charity must spend its money *only for charitable purposes*. Such expenditure will, of course, include the cost of its own charitable activities; buying assets to be used in activities; administrative and fund-raising costs; and the payment of money to bodies established to carry out the work of the charity. It is crucial to bear in mind, however, that spending money non-charitably will not only result in a withdrawal of tax relief so far as both the charity and (in certain cases) its donors are concerned, but may also involve the appropriate trustees in committing a breach of trust and in a criminal offence (see [**42.101**]).

In *IRC v Educational Grants Association Ltd* (1967), the Educational Grants Association had been established for the advancement of education and had a close relationship with the Metal Box Company Ltd in that the bulk of its income came from a deed of covenant executed in its favour by that company. On a repayment claim for income tax deducted at source being made, it transpired that between 76% and 85% of the income of the charity was applied for the education of children of persons connected with the Metal Box Company Ltd. Accordingly the claim for repayment failed since the court was not convinced that the income of the charity was being applied for 'charitable purposes only'. In deciding that the organisation had expended money for non-charitable purposes, the judge accepted that this involved concluding that the managers had acted *ultra vires* in spending the Association's income: he therefore concluded: 'it is of course open to a comparable body to frame its objects so as to make clear that its income may be applied for private as well as public purposes, but in that case it may not obtain tax relief. It does not seem to me that such a body can have it both ways'. **[42.61]**–**[42.80]**

IV EFFECTIVE CHARITABLE GIVING

1 **Deeds of covenant**

Sums paid under deed of covenant are tax effective (ie they reduce the income of the payer) provided that the covenant is *capable of lasting for more than three years* (TA 1988 ss 347(A)(7) and 660A(9)(b)). This requirement can, therefore, be satisfied if *either* a fixed period in excess of three years is chosen (hence the popularity of the four-year covenant) *or*, alternatively, if a period of uncertain duration is chosen which *might* exceed three years. The duration of an annual payment must be considered in the light of circumstances prevailing at the start: so long as capable of lasting more than three years at that time, subsequent events are therefore ignored. If, however, a covenant reserves to the covenantor (or any other person) a power of revocation which could be exercised to bring it to an end before the expiration of four years, the annual payment is caught by TA 1988 s 347A and rendered ineffective. When such a power can only be exercised after that period has ended tax relief continues until such time as the power of revocation is, in fact, exercised. For an example of the position of charitable covenants entered into by companies, see **[28.57]**. Reference should be made to SP 4/90 for the Revenue's practice on charitable covenants and to *Royal College of Veterinary Surgeons Trust Fund v Meldrum* (1996) for an illustration of the problems that can result from a defectively drafted deed of covenant.

[42.81]

2 **Deposit covenants**

In recent years deposit covenants have proved popular: they are particularly beneficial to the taxpayer who wishes to give a lump sum to the relevant charity but who also wishes to obtain the normal income tax benefits associated with covenanted payments. In essence, the arrangement involves a covenant to pay annually one-quarter of a stated capital sum over a four-year period. That entire capital sum, however, is handed over to the charity at once and is therefore said to be held by the charity 'on deposit'. Thereafter, each year, a fraction of that sum is released in satisfaction of the covenant (see further SP 4/90). Although these arrangements smack of artificiality and could conceivably fall within the *Ramsay* principle, the Revenue has expressly stated that they will not be challenged provided that they are made in favour of charity (see **[36.36]**). **[42.82]**

3 **Payroll giving**

The so called 'payroll deduction scheme' has been discussed at **[5.172]**. In broad terms, it involves employers who wish to set up a scheme for their employees entering into a contract with an agency approved by the Inland Revenue. Employees who wish to join the scheme authorise their employer to deduct the relevant amount from their pay before calculating PAYE tax due and to pay over the relevant amount to the agency. The function of the agency is to act as a clearing house, distributing the appropriate sums to the individual charities which have been nominated by the employees. **[42.83]**

4   Gift Aid (FA 1990 ss 25–26)

An innovation of recent years has been the introduction of tax reliefs for one-off cash gifts to charity. From 1986 companies (other than close companies) were able to obtain corporation tax reliefs for single gifts to charities up to a limit equivalent to 3% of the dividends paid by the company in the same accounting period. 'Gift Aid' (single gifts by individuals and companies) came into effect on 1 October 1990 and extended this relief to single gifts of £600 or more subject to a maximum limit of £5m on total qualifying gifts by any company or individual in any relevant year. *The upper* limits have now been abolished and companies and individuals can now claim tax relief on gifts to charity with no ceiling, provided, of course, that the gift does not exceed the total income or profits of the individual or company concerned in the relevant year. The lower limit is now £250 *except* for non-close companies—in this case single gifts of any amount qualify for relief.

Such gifts will be made subject to deduction of basic rate income tax at source which must be accounted for by the relevant individual or corporation to the Revenue and then refunded to the charity on an appropriate claim being made. For the payer (whether individual or company) full tax relief will be available for the gross sum paid. For example, if the donor is an individual who gives £7,700 to charity net of basic rate income tax, in the year 1997/98 the charity will be able to claim a tax repayment of £2,300 (23% of the gross equivalent of the sum paid: ie £10,000). If that individual is a higher rate tax payer his taxable income will be reduced by £10,000.

Gift Aid is unlikely wholly to replace the deed of covenant as the most popular method of charitable giving since, although covenants bind the payer for a number of years, they enable smaller sums to be paid to charity.

It had been thought that Gift Aid could be employed to achieve a 'cake and eat it' result. For IHT purposes there are certain situations where 'reading back fictions' are available. For instance, a deed of variation falling within IHTA 1984 s 142 may be read back into the will of the testator (and therefore taxed as if that testator had made the relevant disposition of property: see [**22.118**]) and, similarly, a precatory gift, falling within IHTA 1984 s 143, attracts reading back. The fiction in both these cases holds good for IHT but not for income tax where the analysis remains that the original gift became the property of the named beneficiary who then in turn transferred that property to another person.

Assume, therefore, that Berta, who has just died, has left £250,000 to her daughter Janice. Janice now wishes to make a substantial donation to charitable causes. She enters into an instrument of variation whereby Berta's will is amended to provide for a gift of £50,000 to the charity (IHT free: if the tax has been paid a refund is in order) with the remaining £200,000 being paid to Janice. She may seek full income tax relief for the £50,000 under Gift Aid. Janice has tried to combine Gift Aid with an instrument of variation and she may, if she so wishes, claim a second slice of this particular cake in the next year since a will can be varied more than once within the relevant two-year period. Unfortunately the Revenue has now successfully challenged the availability of Gift Aid relief on the basis that to qualify 'neither the donor or any person connected with him [must] receive a benefit in consequence of making [the gift]'. In an unsatisfactory judgment a Special Commissioner has decided that the saving in IHT amounts to such a benefit thereby preventing relief (*St Dunstan's v Major* (1997)).   [**42.84**]

5 Capital gifts

TCGA 1992 s 257 provides that for CGT purposes gifts to charity shall be at no gain no loss (compare the similar rule for inter-spouse gifts under TCGA 1992 s 58). In appropriate cases it may be better, however, to sell the asset (thereby attracting a CGT charge) and then gift the cash to charity taking advantage of the Gift Act rules. For IHT purposes, charitable gifts are exempt transfers of value under IHTA 1984 s 23. **[42.85]**

6 Business gifts to educational establishments

TA 1988 s 84 provides relief for gifts of equipment by businesses to schools and other educational establishments. The relief applies to gifts by companies and unincorporated businesses of items of equipment either manufactured, sold or used in the course of their trade. It applies where such equipment is given to educational establishments, whether schools or higher educational institutions.

The company or unincorporated business is allowed a deduction for the cost of acquiring or manufacturing the item of plant and machinery in calculating its taxable profits. This means that the business will be given full relief for the cost of the item and there will be no charge on the profit foregone by reason of the gift. Further, items of equipment used in the course of the donor's trade, and on which capital allowances have been given, are treated as having been disposed of at nil value, so that the balance of allowances due on the asset will be given to the business in the normal way.

This relief brings the tax treatment of gifts of equipment into line with the treatment of gifts of cash used by the recipient to purchase equipment. **[42.86]–[42.100]**

V RESTRICTION ON TAX RELIEF

In cases where a charity spends money on non-charitable purposes or invests or lends money in ways which are not for the benefit of the charitable objects, tax relief on the income or gains so employed may be withdrawn. The charity may therefore be taxed on the income or gains misused. In addition, under provisions introduced in 1986, larger charities are subject to more detailed rules in such circumstances which may result in tax relief given in earlier years being withdrawn.

So far as donors are concerned, in cases where that donation has not been applied for charitable purposes, tax relief at higher rate may be lost. **[42.101]**

PART C   APPENDICES

APPENDIX I: THE BASIS OF ASSESSMENT: SCHEDULE D CASES I AND II (INCLUDING PARTNERSHIPS)

I BACKGROUND

A taxpayer can commence or cease his business at any time, but he should normally draw up his accounts over a 12-month period known as the 'accounting year' which need not coincide with the tax year (6 April to 5 April). This gives rise to two difficulties:

(1) the actual profits made in each year of assessment can only be arrived at by splitting two accounting years and taking the proportions which fall into the assessment year;

(2) the calculation of the taxpayer's liability has to await the completion and agreement of the accounts with the inspector of taxes.

As an incentive to businesses, assessments had, since 1926, been made on the 'preceding year basis'. FA 1994 ss 200–218 (and Sch 20), however, under the title 'Changes for facilitating self-assessment' laid down a new legislative framework which has become operational as follows:

(1) for *new* businesses (ie those set up on or after 6 April 1994) the new rules applied at once;

(2) for *existing* businesses (those in existence on 5 April 1994) the new rules came into effect from the tax year 1997–98 with a transitional year in 1996–97;

(3) if an existing partnership suffered a deemed discontinuance (typically as the result of a partner either leaving or joining) and a continuation election (see [**I.46**]) was not made the new rules thereafter applied to the firm.

This appendix is divided as follows:

First, a consideration of the old (pre-self-assessment) rules for sole traders etc;
Secondly, the old rules insofar as they affect partnerships;
Thirdly, the new rules for sole traders etc;
Finally, the new rules for partnerships. [**I.1**]–[**I.20**]

II THE PRECEDING YEAR BASIS FOR SOLE TRADERS/PRACTITIONERS (THE 'OLD' RULES)

1 The normal basis

The preceding year basis of assessment meant that in any year of assessment tax was charged on the profits of the 12-month accounting period which ended in the previous year of assessment (TA 1988 s 60(1)).

EXAMPLE I.1

Ernest's accounting year runs from 6 October to 5 October following. He had made the following profits:

Accounting year ending	Profits
5 October 1992	£ 5,000
5 October 1993	£ 8,000
5 October 1994	£10,000
5 October 1995	£12,000

In the year of assessment 1995–96 Ernest was assessed on the profits of the 12-month accounting period ending in the preceding year of assessment (ie ending between 6 April 1994 and 5 April 1995). This was the accounting year to 5 October 1994 which showed £10,000 profit. Assessments on Ernest for the earlier years were:

Year of assessment	Assessment
1994–95	£8,000
1993–94	£5,000

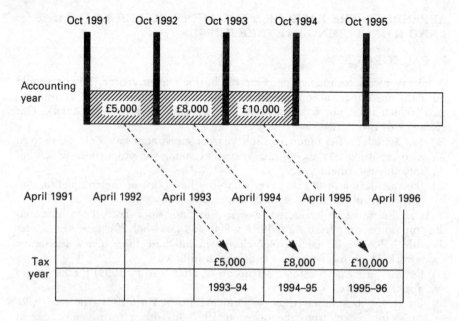

For 1996–97 Ernie was taxed under the transitional year rules: see [**I.71**].

The taxpayer's duty to produce annual accounts was imposed indirectly. No time limit was provided in the legislation for making up accounts. However, if the taxpayer had not made up accounts in the three years preceding the relevant year of assessment, the Revenue took his accounting period to be the previous tax year (ie 6 April to 5 April) and made an estimated assessment (TA 1988 s 60(4)). The only way for the taxpayer to appeal successfully against such an assessment was to render accurate accounts. The taxpayer had to submit accounts over a 12-month period; if he produced accounts which related to a period other than 12 months, the Revenue could assess him to tax on the profits of any 12-month period ending in the previous year of assessment (TA 1988 s 60(4)). This provision did not apply to the first or second year of a business.

Tax was assessed directly on the taxpayer under Schedule D Cases I and II and, as a general rule, was payable in two equal instalments on 1 January in the year of assessment and on 1 July following (TA 1988 s 5(2)).(In the transitional year—1996–97—the payment dates were 31 January and 31 July.) The preceding year basis made possible an assessment raised on the basis of accounts agreed before 1 December in that tax year. If, however, the assessment was not made until after 1 December, but before 1 June following, the first instalment of tax was due 30 days after the assessment and the second instalment on 1 July following; if the assessment was not made until after 1 June in the following year of assessment, all the tax was payable 30 days after the assessment.

To maximise the delay in paying tax, a taxpayer was advised to choose his accounting period carefully. If that period coincided with the tax year, it formed the basis of charge for the tax year immediately following so that there was a delay of only 9 and 15 months between the end of the accounting period and the payment of tax. If he chose an accounting period which ran from 7 April to 6 April following, however, the maximum possible delay of 21 and 27 months applied. Delay in paying tax was especially attractive when the profits of the business were rising. Not only would the taxpayer have the use of the tax for a considerable period of time but, additionally, he would be able to avoid immediate taxation on the current (higher) profits. If profits were constant the advantage was much reduced whilst, if they were falling, a large tax bill had to be met out of current (smaller) profits.   [**I.21**]

2 Exceptions to the normal basis

It was impossible to apply the normal preceding year basis in the opening years of the business and where the taxpayer changed his accounting date. In the closing years of the business an exceptional basis applied to prevent the closure being manipulated to avoid tax. **[I.22]**

a) *The opening years for businesses commencing before 6 April 1994 (TA 1988 ss 61, 62)*

For the year of assessment in which the business commenced, the taxpayer was charged on his actual profits from the date of commencement to the end of the tax year (TA 1988 s 61(1)). If his accounting period straddled the end of the tax year, the profits were apportioned on a time (straight-line) basis.

In the second year of assessment the taxpayer was taxed on the profits of his first 12 months' trading.

In the third and subsequent years of assessment, the normal basis of assessment under TA 1988 s 60 applied so he was taxed on the profits of the accounting period ending in the previous year of assessment.

EXAMPLE I.2

Popeye began trading on 6 October 1992 and made the following profits:

Accounting period	Profit
6 October 1992–5 October 1993	£ 3,000
6 October 1993–5 October 1994	£ 9,000
6 October 1994–5 October 1995	£12,000

His first year of assessment was 1992–93 in which he was taxed on his actual profits from 6 October 1992 to 5 April 1993

ie $\frac{6}{12} \times £3,000 = £1,500$

In his second year (1993–94) Popeye was taxed on his first 12 months of trading: ie on profits from 6 October 1992 to 5 October 1993 = £3,000.

In his third year (1994–95) Popeye was taxed on the preceding year basis on the profits from 6 October 1992–5 October 1993 = £3,000 (again).

In 1995–96 he was taxed on £9,000.

1996–97 was Popeye's transitional year: see **[I.71]**.

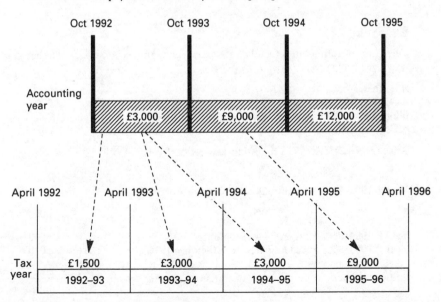

If the taxpayer's first accounting period was longer or shorter than 12 months (which may well have been the case) this did not affect the assessment of his first and second years. However, in the third year, the normal basis could not be applied, because there was no 12-month accounting period ending in the previous year of assessment. The Revenue could, therefore, take any period of 12 months ending in the previous year of assessment. In practice, they took the 12 months ending on the taxpayer's chosen accounting date.

EXAMPLE I.3

Pluto began trading on 6 August 1993 and made up his first accounts to 5 October 1994 (14 months). The accounts showed a profit of £14,000.

In 1993–94 (first year) Pluto was assessed on his actual profits for the eight-month period ending 5 April 1994, ie £8,000. In 1994–95 (second year), Pluto was assessed on his profit of the first 12 months of trading to 5 August 1994, ie £12,000.

In 1995–96 (third year), as Pluto intended to make up accounts to 5 October each year, the assessment was on the intended 12-month period ending 5 October 1994, ie £12,000.

The effect of TA 1988 s 61 (the opening year rule) was to use the profits of the first 12 months of trading as the basis for the tax assessment in each of the first three years of assessment. This was not, however, double (or even triple) taxation because those profits were *deemed* to be the profits of the years of assessment. The taxpayer was content with this duplication where the profits were low in relation to current profits, but not where the first year profits were higher than current profits. TA 1988 s 62 therefore allowed him to elect to have the assessments of the second and third years made on the basis of *actual* profits earned in those years. The election had to cover both years and be made within seven years of the end of the second year of assessment. It could be withdrawn within that period to cover the case where the taxpayer made low profits in year two, elected for the actual basis, but then discovered that because of high profits in the third year, the election had made him worse off.   **[I.23]**

EXAMPLE I.4

Olive began trading on 6 October 1993 and made up accounts to 5 October each year. Her profits were (*see diagram following*):

Accounting period	Profits
6 October 1993–5 October 1994	£12,000
6 October 1994–5 October 1995	£ 4,000
6 October 1995–5 October 1996	£ 2,000

Assessment under TA 1988 s 61 produced profits of £30,000:

Tax year	Basic period	Profits £
Year 1 1993–94	Actual: 6 October 1993–5 April 1994	
	$\frac{6}{12} \times £12,000 =$	6,000
Year 2 1994–95	12 months to 5 October 1994	12,000
Year 2 1995–96	Preceding year to 5 October 1994	12,000
		£30,000

An election under TA 1988 s 62 produces profits of £17,000:

Tax year	Basic period	£	Profits £
Year 1 1993–94	Actual: (no change)		6,000
Year 2 1994–95	Actual: 6 April 1994–5 April 1995		
	ie $\frac{6}{12} \times £12,000 =$	6,000	
	Plus $\frac{6}{12} \times £4,000 =$	2,000	
			8,000
Year 3 1995–96	Actual: 6 April 1995–5 April 1996		
	ie $\frac{6}{12} \times £4,000 =$	2,000	
	Plus $\frac{6}{12} \times £2,000 =$	1,000	
			3,000
			£17,000

Olive would make a s 62 election. Whenever profits were falling the election should have been made. When the trend is upwards it would be ignored.

b) *Change of accounting date*

If the taxpayer decided to change his accounting date, there would be at least one year which did not fit the normal assessment basis since he had to make up a set of accounts for one period of less or more than 12 months in order to effect that change.

In this case, the Revenue were able to take 'any period of 12 months ending in the preceding year of assessment' as the basis period *and* if it thought that the year before that should be dealt with on the same basis it had the power to do so (TA 1988 s 60(4), (5)). As a matter of practice, the Revenue normally took as a basis the period of 12 months ending on the date in the preceding year which the taxpayer had chosen as his new year-end date.

EXAMPLE I.5

In 1993 Unlucky changed his accounting date from 5 October to 31 December. His profits were:

Accounting period	Profits £
Year ended 5 October 1991	20,000
Year ended 5 October 1992	6,000
14 months ended 31 December 1993	21,000
Year ended 31 December 1994	10,000

Assessments		Profits £
1992–93	(Normal Basis) Year ended 5 October 1991	20,000
*1993–94	(Normal Basis) Year ended 5 October 1992	6,000
1994–95	(No Normal Basis) Revenue will take 12 months to 31 December 1993	
	ie $\frac{12}{14} \times £21,000 =$	18,000
1995–96	(Normal Basis) Year ended 31 December 1994	10,000

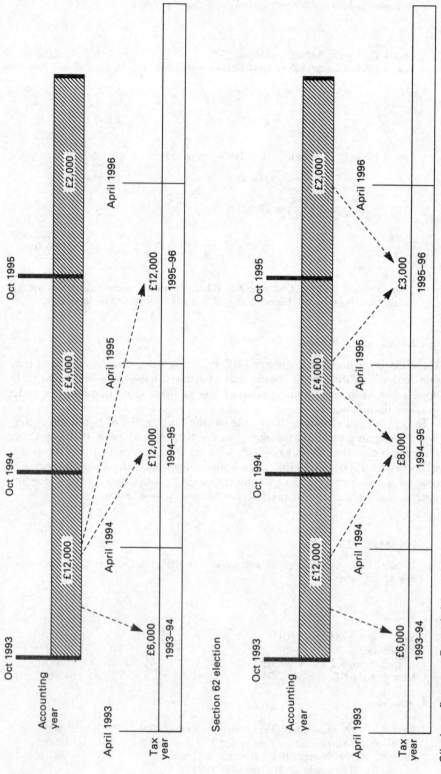

Section 62 election

Olive's profits — see Example I.4

* The Revenue were able to revise the last normal assessment before the change (1993-94) to an assessment based on the new accounting date which results in tax on additional profits of £2,000:

		£
1993-94	Twelve months to 31 December 1992	
	ie $\frac{10}{12}$ × £6,000	5,000
	Plus $\frac{2}{14}$ × £21,000	3,000
		£8,000

The taxpayer was able to appeal against the revised assessment under TA 1988 s 60(6). The principles on which the commissioners acted in considering such appeals were considered in *IRC v Helical Bar Ltd* (1972). An appeal would not succeed merely because the Revenue was assessing profits of the same period twice since that was the effect of the legislation. In practice, the Revenue operated an 'averaging procedure' (see IR 26) which affected the revision year only (ie 1993-94 in *Example I.5*) and aimed to be fair to both parties. Much of IR 26 was made statutory under the new rules: see [**I.65**]. [**I.24**]

c) *Closing year rules (TA 1988 s 63(1))*

In the year of assessment in which the business terminated, the taxpayer was assessed on his actual profits from the beginning of that tax year (6 April) to the date of discontinuance. This normally involved apportioning the profits of an accounting period on a time basis (TA 1988 s 72). The two years of assessment preceding the final year (penultimate and pre-penultimate years of assessment) were taxed on the normal basis. However, the Revenue could elect under TA 1988 s 63 to assess the taxpayer on his actual profits of those years. The election was needed since under the preceding year basis the actual profits of those years would never be charged, so that taxpayers could have ensured that large profits were channelled into that period (on the Revenue's election, see *Baylis v Roberts* (1989)).

EXAMPLE I.6 *(see diagram following)*

B ceased to trade on 5 July 1995. His profits for years ended 31 December were:
$$£\ 9,000 \text{ for } 1991$$
$$£15,000 \text{ for } 1992$$
$$£12,000 \text{ for } 1993$$
$$£18,000 \text{ for } 1994$$
$$\text{and } £6,000 \text{ to 5 July 1995}$$

Tax year	*Basis period*	£	*Profits* £
1995-96	Actual: 6 April 1995–5 July 1995		
Final	ie $= \frac{3}{6}$ × £6,000		3,000
1994-95	Preceding year: year ended 31 December 1993		12,000
Penultimate			
1993-94	Preceding year: year ended 31 December 1992		15,000
Pre-penultimate			
1992-93	Preceding year: year ended 31 December 1991		9,000
			£39,000

TA 1988 s 63 Revenue election:

1995–96	Actual: (as above)	3,000
Final		
1994–95	Actual: 6 April 1994–5 April 1995	
Penultimate		

$$\text{ie} = \frac{3}{6} \times \pounds 6,000 \qquad\qquad 3,000$$

$$\text{Plus} = \frac{9}{12} \times \pounds 18,000 \qquad\qquad \underline{13,500}$$

16,500

1993–94   Actual: 6 April 1993–5 April 1994
Pre-penultimate

$$\text{ie} = \frac{3}{12} \times \pounds 18,000 \qquad\qquad 4,500$$

$$\text{Plus} = \frac{9}{12} \times \pounds 12,000 \qquad\qquad 9,000$$

		13,500
1992–93	Preceding year (as above)	9,000
		$\underline{\underline{\pounds 42,000}}$

The Revenue would have exercised its option to amend the assessments of 1993–94 and 1994–95 to an actual basis. Otherwise, the higher profits of the period from 1 January 1994 to 5 April 1995 escaped tax completely.

The Revenue had to exercise its election for both years. Therefore (as with the s 62 taxpayer's election), it would only be made if the total profit of both years on an actual basis was higher than the total on the preceding year basis. Generally, if profits were rising the election would be made, if falling it was not.   [**I.25**]

3 When to apply opening and closing year rules

a) *Commencement of a business*

The taxpayer had to apply the opening year rules from the date that he commenced business. *Napier v Griffiths* (1989) illustrates the importance of precise dating. Had the taxpayer succeeded in arguing that his business commenced in May 1980 the sum of £1,296 would have been taxed (in total) in the first three tax years. However, because the court decided that the business commenced one year later the sum taxed in the first three years became £30,024!

When a business commenced was a question of fact and acts preparatory to carrying on the business did not constitute commencement. For example, in *Birmingham and District Cattle By-Products Co Ltd v IRC* (1919) the construction of a factory, the purchase of machinery, and the making of contracts to purchase raw materials were preparatory acts. Business only commenced once the machinery was installed and the raw materials received. In practice, it was thought that renting premises, engaging staff, opening a bank account, and advertising were all evidence that a business has begun. Expenditure was normally only deductible after that date, although expenses incurred in the seven years before the business starts were treated as incurred on the date when the business commenced (TA 1988 s 401).

When the taxpayer who already ran an existing business took up new business activities, it was a question of fact whether he was merely extending his existing business or starting a new one (see *Seldon v Croom-Johnson* (1932) where a barrister who took silk was held to be continuing his existing profession and *Maidment v Kibby* (1993) where a continuing trade (in fish and chips) was expanded by

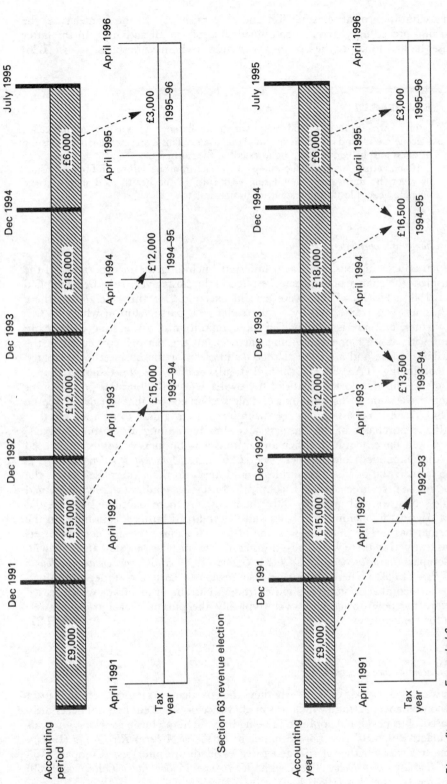

Section 63 revenue election

B's profits — see Example I.6

the acquisition of an existing fish and chip business). In the former case, the normal preceding year basis continued to apply to all activities. In the latter case, he had to apply the opening year rules to the new business.   **[I.26]**

EXAMPLE I.7

Lenny owns a health food shop which he extends to serve morning coffee (decaffeinated) and brown sugar (only) doughnuts. This is an extension of his existing business and he continues to be assessed on the normal basis.

If Lenny turns his health food shop into a restaurant specialising in French cuisine, however, he must apply the closing year rules to the health food shop and the opening year rules to the restaurant business.

b) *Change of ownership*

When an existing business was transferred (including the incorporation of the business) the change of ownership resulted in the closing year rules being applied (TA 1988 s 113(1)). There were certain exceptions to this rule. *First,* where a business was transferred by a sole trader to a partnership in which he was a partner, or there is a change in the composition of an existing partnership (but with at least one continuing partner), all the persons concerned in the business before and after the change could elect for the business to be treated as continuing (TA 1988 s 113(2) and **[I.46]**). *Secondly,* by concession, a change of ownership due to the death of the owner where the business passed to his spouse was not a discontinuance, unless claimed by that surviving spouse (ESC A7: this concession has been withdrawn from a date to be announced).

If the purchaser of the business was already running an existing business, he would have acquired either an entirely new business or assets to be used in the (expanded) old business (see **[I.26]** and *Maidment v Kibby* (1993)). If the former, the opening year rules would apply to that enterprise but, at the end of the first three years of account, the businesses could normally be merged unless they were of a totally different nature. A mere purchase of assets did not trigger the opening year rules and the enlarged business continued on the normal basis. The question was one of fact. If a business and not just assets was transferred there would be a transfer of, *inter alia,* custom, staff and goodwill. (Compare *Reynolds Sons & Co Ltd v Ogston* (1930) and *Thomson and Balfour v Le Page* (1923).) There cannot be a succession to part of a trade; or through the accidental acquisition of another trader's custom; or to a trade which ceased before the new owner took over (typically the purchase of a trader's assets on his bankruptcy).   **[I.27]**

c) *Discontinuance of a business*

It was a question of fact whether the particular change resulted in a discontinuance. A trade which was in abeyance or quiescent had not necessarily ceased. 'Business is not confined to being busy; in many businesses long intervals of inactivity occur' (see Lord Sumner in *IRC v South Behar Rly Co Ltd* (1925)). One test was whether it still generated expenditure and loss. (Compare *Kirk and Randall Ltd v Dunn* (1924) with *JG Ingram & Son Ltd v Callaghan* (1969) and see *Watts v Hart* (1984).)

If a business was discontinued within two to five years of its commencement so that the opening and closing year rules overlaped, the closing year rules prevailed (TA 1988 s 63(1)).   **[I.28]-[I.40]**

III THE OLD RULES AS THEY AFFECTED PARTNERSHIPS

1 **General**

For the purposes of assessing and collecting income tax a partnership was to some extent treated as a separate entity under the pre-1994 rules. A trading partnership is taxed under the rules of Schedule D Case I, a professional partnership under Schedule D Case II. In both cases, the precedent partner (which means the senior partner or the partner whose name appears first in the partnership deed) had to make a return of partnership income. Each individual partner then made his own separate tax return in which he claimed his personal allowances (TA 1988 s 277). The Revenue then made joint assessment to tax in the partnership name. This tax bill, which was simply the aggregate tax for which each partner was liable, was based upon each partner's share of profits for the current tax year and took into account his personal reliefs, charges on income etc. The Revenue supplied information to the senior partner as to how the bill was calculated so that individual accountability could be established between the partners. The assessment could be appealed by *any* partner even if his co-partners objected (*Re Sutherland & Partners' Appeal* (1994)). Tax was due in two equal instalments, on 1 January in the appropriate tax year, and on 1 July following the tax year (for 1996–97 *et seq* the payment dates became 31 January and 31 July). **[I.41]**

2 **Liability for the tax**

The tax could be paid either by each partner remitting his own share, or by the firm discharging the bill when arrangements would be made to charge individual partners with their proportion, normally by debiting their current account. Liability of the partners for the assessment was joint, but not several, so that if the bill was not paid the Revenue could proceed for the entire sum against any one of the partners who could join his fellow partners as co-defendants (RSC Ord 15 r 6). On the death of a partner his estate was released from liability to the Revenue for any unpaid tax, except where the deceased was the last surviving partner when his estate was liable for all the tax, with the right of contribution from his former partners' estates (see *Harrison v Willis Bros* (1965)). Thus, if one partner was bankrupt, the Revenue was not affected since it could proceed against the other (solvent) partners for the full amount of tax; it was the other partners who suffered because of that bankruptcy.

The nature of the partnership tax bill was illustrated in *Stevens v Britten* (1954) where a retiring partner was to be indemnified by the continuing partners for all partnership liabilities outstanding at the date of his retirement. Since the partnership's liabilities included the income tax bill presented after his retirement, but in respect of a period before his retirement, the retiring partner was entitled to be indemnified against his share of that bill. **[I.42]**

3 **Division of taxed profit**

Although the partnership's income tax was charged on profits calculated on the preceding year basis, those profits were allocated between the partners in accordance with the profit sharing ratio in force for the tax year when the profits were assessed and *not* by reference to any arrangement in force for the accounting year when the profits were earned (contrast the position under the new rules: see **[I.72]**). **[I.43]**

EXAMPLE I.8

Zea and Co made up their accounts to 31 December. For the year ending 31 December 1994 profits were £60,000 divided equally between Z and E. On 6 April 1995 a new arrangement was entered into whereby Z agreed to take 60% and E 40% of the profit.

£60,000 was the assessable profits for 1995–96 (preceding year basis). Tax was assessed according to the profit sharing ratio in force *for that tax year* (1995–96).

Hence:
Z's share = 60% × £60,000 = £36,000
E's share = 40% × £60,000 = £24,000

Notice that Z was, therefore, taxed on £6,000 profits which E had received in 1994. If the changed sharing ratio came into force on a day other than the first day of the tax year it was necessary to divide the profits on a time basis and then to apply the different sharing ratios to those divided profits. Say, for instance, that the change occurred on 5 October 1995:

Profits from 6 April to 5 October 1995 = £30,000 (½ × £60,000) divided between Z and E in the ratio 50:50. Therefore, Z's share was £15,000 and E's share was £15,000.

Profits from 6 October 1995 to 5 April 1996 = £30,000 (½ × £60,000) divided between Z and E in the ratio 60:40. Therefore, Z's share was £18,000 and E's share was £12,000.

Thus, of the total taxable profits for 1995–96 of £60,000, Z's share was £33,000 (£15,000 + £18,000) and E's share was £27,000 (£15,000 + £12,000).

4   Changes in the partnership

a) *Basic income tax rule: a deemed discontinuance*

This section is concerned with a change in the partners not with an alteration in the profit sharing ratios in a case where the partners of the firm remain the same. The following examples all represent changes in the partners of a firm:

	old firm	the change	new firm
(1)	AB	take in C	ABC
(2)	ABC	C leaves	AB
(3)	ABC	replace C with D	ABD
(4)	ABC	death of C	AB
*(5)	A	creates partnership	AB
*(6)	AB	dissolution of partnership	A

(5) and (6) although not examples of changes in a continuing partnership were subject to similar rules.

Any change in the ownership of a business, eg the taking in of a new partner, resulted, under the pre-1994 rules, in a deemed discontinuance of the old business. Hence, in the above examples the old firm was treated as discontinued and a new firm as commencing the business (TA 1988 s 113). As a result, the old partners were subject to the closing year rules (which have been considered at [**I.25**]) and the new partners were assessed in accordance with opening year rules. So far as the opening year rules were concerned the position was as follows:

(1) Prior to 19 March 1985 the 'normal' opening year rules (ie those discussed at [**I.23**]) were applied to all partnership changes (thus they applied in the six illustrations listed above).

(2) For changes of partners *within a continuing partnership*, new opening rules

were, however, introduced in 1985. Notice therefore that these new rules did not apply in *Illustrations* (5) and (6) above since the changes did not occur within a continuing partnership.

It is not proposed to discuss further the closing year rules nor the 'normal' opening rules but the new rules are considered at [**I.45**].

Although a deemed discontinuance was provided for, it was possible to prevent this from happening in cases where at least one person continued to be engaged in the business before and after the change and *all* those engaged in the business before and after the change made the necessary election. This election for a continuance, which ensured that the closing and opening rules did not apply, is considered at [**I.46**]. In the case of deemed discontinuances occurring after 5 April 1994, failure to exercise the election resulted in the 1994 rules (the new rules) applying to the business thereafter. At [**I.47**] the effect of changes in the partners when losses were being made by the firm is considered.   [**I.44**]

b) *Special opening year rules for continuing partnerships*

These opening year rules applied where there is at least one common partner in the old and the new partnership and the same business continued to be carried on (ie as in (1)–(4) above).

In contrast to the ordinary opening year rules which displaced the normal (ie preceding year) basis for only two years with the result that the new firm's first 12 months of profit formed the basis for its assessments to tax in its first three years, these special rules displaced the normal basis for the year in which the change occurred and the *three* following years of assessment.

In the year of assessment in which the change occurred the firm was taxed on its actual profits from the date of the change to the end of the tax year. In the second, third and fourth years of assessment, the firm was assessed on its actual profits earned in those tax years. In the fifth and subsequent years of assessment, the normal (preceding year) basis of assessment applied, although the firm had an election (under TA 1988 s 62) in respect of the fifth and sixth years to be taxed on the actual profits of those years. The election had to be made within seven years after the end of the fifth year of assessment for both the fifth and sixth years. The election could be withdrawn within that same period.   [**I.45**]

c) *Electing for a continuance (TA 1988 s 113(2))*

The deemed discontinuance rules of TA 1988 s 113(1) did not apply if all the partners (or their PRs) before and after the change made a written election (within two years of that change) that the firm should continue to be taxed on the preceding year basis. As a result the closing and opening year rules were excluded. The same trade had to be carried on before and after the change.

The continuing partners needed to ensure that all necessary consents for an election could be obtained. Hence, new partners were usually only admitted to the partnership if they agreed (often in a recital to the partnership deed) to join in making a TA 1988 s 113 election if required to do so by the other partners. Provision was also be made in the partnership deed to ensure that a partner who left could be required to join in any election and for the PRs of a deceased partner to be under a duty to sign the notice of election if required to do so by the continuing partners.

Where an election was made so that the firm continued to be taxed on the preceding year basis, the new partnership was assessed on profits earned by the old partnership.

EXAMPLE I.9

For the year ended 31 December 1994 Zea and Co's adjusted profits were £100,000 divided equally between Z and E. On 6 April 1995 A became a partner receiving 20% of the profits and joined in a s 113(2) election.

£100,000 was the taxable profits for 1995–96 (preceding year basis). Profits were allocated on a *current year* basis—ie in accordance with the profit sharing agreement of the partners in 1995–96. As A was then a partner the allocation was:

Total profits	=	£100,000
A's 20%	=	£20,000
Balance	=	£80,000
Z and E (40% each)	=	£40,000 each

Although Z and E each received £50,000 of the profits earned in 1994, they were taxed only on £40,000 of those profits. A, on the other hand, was taxed on £20,000 but received none of the 1994 profits!

It was common for an incoming partner, the PRs of a deceased partner and outgoing partners to be given an indemnity in the partnership deed for any extra tax occasioned by their joining in the election.

Where a partnership change occurred on a day other than the first day of the tax year, the tax assessment was divided into two: one on the old partners, and one on the new with the profits being apportioned on a 'just' basis. In practice, time-apportionment was employed.

EXAMPLE I.10

If in *Example I.9* A had joined the firm on 5 October 1995, the income tax was calculated thus:

Profits for tax year 1995–96 = £100,000 (preceding year basis)

Profits from 6 April–5 October = £50,000 (6 months)

Z's share (50%) = £25,000
E's share (50%) = £25,000

Profits from 6 October–5 April = £50,000 (6 months)

A's share (20%) = £10,000
Z's share (40%) = £20,000
E's share (40%) = £20,000

The total profits for 1995–96 of £100,000 was, therefore, allocated as to £45,000 to each of Z and E and £10,000 to A.

There was nothing to prevent a whole series of elections being made at short intervals. Indeed the operation of large professional partnerships made such elections commonplace. Special provision was, however, made for the case where two changes occurred within two years of each other and the election for a continuance was made on the first, but not on the second of those changes (TA 1988 s 113(3)(b)). In this case, on the second change (the discontinuance), the closing rules applied as if the first change had never occurred. Hence, although the earlier change was not treated as a discontinuance, the operation of the closing rules could increase the liability of a partner who left the firm at the time of the election for a continuance.

It should be remembered, however, that the special opening rules did not apply to *actual* discontinuances: eg on a merger (or demerger) where there was a change in the nature of the business carried on by the two firms comprised in the merger (or demerger) (see *George Humphries Ltd v Cook* (1934) and, for the Revenue view, SP 9/86). Nor did the special opening rules apply to the dissolution of a firm where one partner only was left to continue the business.

EXAMPLE I.11

(1) Firm A and firm B, both estate agents, agree to a merger. Given that the new firm, AB, will carry on the same business (albeit on an expanded scale) the Revenue view is that AB has succeeded to the businesses of both the old firms. Accordingly, the choices facing the partners were; *first*, to elect in respect of both businesses; *secondly*, to elect in respect of one only (the election might be that AB continues the business of A); or, *thirdly*, to accept a discontinuance in which event the special opening rules applied to AB. (SP 9/86 para 3.)

(2) Firm AB splits into its component parts, partnership A and partnership B. It is a question of fact whether A or B has succeeded to the trade of AB but this will often not be the case so that there will be discontinuance of the business of AB and two new businesses (subject to the normal opening rules) will have commenced. The Revenue accepts that a succession may occur if 'one of the businesses carried on after the division was so large in relation to the rest as to be recognisably "the business" as previously carried on'. (SP 9/86 para 5.) (See *C Connelly & Co v Wilbey* (1992)—a case concerned with the now defunct stock relief.)

It should also be remembered that if the election was not exercised in respect of a deemed discontinuance occurring on or after 6 April 1994 the new rules would apply to the firm from the date of the discontinuance.   **[I.46]**

d) *The deemed discontinuance and loss relief*

The deemed discontinuance rules did not affect entitlement to loss relief. Instead, the loss provisions looked to what actually happened to the individual partners. Hence,

(1) Relief under TA 1988 s 380 and FA 1991 s 72 (carry-across) and TA 1988 s 385 (carry-forward) was available so long as the taxpayer remained engaged in the same business as a partner before and after the change. In *Illustration (1)* at [**I.44**], for instance, A and B would be able to utilise these loss provisions.

(2) Relief under TA 1988 s 388 (terminal relief) was only available to an outgoing partner and only if the continuation election was not made. The continuing partners could not take advantage of the deemed discontinuance to claim terminal relief. In *Illustration (2)*, therefore, C was able to take advantage of s 388 (he was, of course, not be able to claim relief under TA 1988 s 380, FA 1991 s 72 or TA 1988 s 385), but A and B were unable to do so. (Note the different rules that apply under the new rules: see [**I.72**]).

(3) Relief under TA 1988 s 381 (new businesses and professions) was available only to new partners. Thus, in *Illustration (1)*, C was entitled to use s 381; and, in *Illustration (3)*, D.   **[I.47]**

e) *The well-timed departure!*

A well-timed departure (typically by the senior partner) could, as a result of the firm making a continuation election, result in a substantial tax holiday. Note, in the following example, the contrast between the share of profits taken by that partner (£156,000) and the sum on which he is actually taxed (£66,000)!   **[I.48]-[I.60]**

EXAMPLE I.12

The accounts of the firm are made up to 6 April each year and the senior partner retires on 6 April 1994. The election for a continuance is made.

Year ended	Adjusted profits	Senior partner's 30%	Year of assessment	Senior partner pays tax on
6.4.92	100,000	30,000	1993–94	30,000
6.4.93	120,000	36,000	1994–95	36,000
6.4.94	140,000	42,000	1995–96	Nil
6.4.95 *	160,000	48,000	1996–97	Nil
6.4.96 *	180,000	Nil	1996–97	Nil
	£156,000			£66,000

* Transitional year: see [**I.71**].

IV   THE CURRENT YEAR BASIS OF ASSESSMENT

1   **When does it apply?**

(1) To new businesses (trades, professions etc) commencing on or after 6 April 1994.
(2) To existing businesses and sources of income falling under Schedule D from 6 April 1997 (ie for tax years 1997–98ff).
(3) In the case of partnership changes occurring in the period from 6 April 1994 to 5 April 1997, *if no election for a continuance was made,* a new business was treated as commenced immediately after the change.   [**I.61**]

2   **How the current year basis operates**

a) *The position of a continuing business*

EXAMPLE I.13

Bob makes his accounts up to 30 April each year. For the accounting year ending 30 April 1997 his profits are £50,000. As that accounting period ends in the tax year 1997–98, those profits will be assessed to tax in that year. The tax is payable in three instalments: two being estimated on the basis of the previous year's tax on 31 January 1998 and 31 July 1998 with a balancing payment (or refund) payable on submission of the tax return on 31 January 1999.   [**I.62**]

b) *Opening years of a new business*

EXAMPLE I.14

Assume that Thelma begins her millinery business on 1 June 1998 making up her accounts to the following 31 May. Her profits are as follows:

	£
y/e 31.5.99	6,000
y/e 31.5.00	9,500
y/e 31.5.01	12,650

For the *first tax year* of the business (1998–99) Thelma is taxed on her profits from the date of commencement (1 June 1998) to the following 5 April, ie:

$$^9/_{12} \times £6,000 = £4,500$$

(Note that this rule is the same as that which applied under the old system: see [**I.23**]).

For the *second year* (1999–2000) the current year basis applies so that the first year's profit of £6,000 is subject to tax.

When the accounting date chosen is not 5 April (as in *Example I.14*) the first year's profits are used as the basis for part of the tax charge in both the first and second years (in this case £4,500). This is contrary to the principle that profits taxed must equal profits earned and accordingly a limited relief is available for these doubly taxed profits (*'overlap relief'*: see below). If there is an accounting date in the second year which falls less than 12 months after the commencement, the basis period for this year is the profits from the first 12 months of trading. For the third (and subsequent) years of assessment tax is calculated on a current year basis. **[I.63]**

c)   *The closing years of a business*

In the final tax year, profits from the end of the basis period of the preceding year until the date of cessation are taxed.

EXAMPLE I.15

Assume that Louise ceases trading on 30 September 2002. Her final accounts are as follows:

	£
to 30.4.2001	10,000
to 30.4.2002	4,500
to 30.9.2002	1,500

Her tax position is as follows:

Tax year	*Taxed profits (£)*
2001–2002	10,000 (current year basis)
2002–2003	6,000 (final year)

Note that Louise may be entitled to 'overlap relief' (see *Example I.14* above); this will reduce the taxable profit in her final year (for the computation, see [**I.70**]).

If the business ceases in its second tax year, the assessment is on profit from the end of the commencement year until cessation. If the business starts and finishes in the same tax year the basis period is the actual profits earned. **[I.64]**

3   Accounting dates

A taxpayer is free to choose whatever accounting date he wishes. There are, however, statutory provisions concerning *changes* of accounting date which replicate to some extent the Revenue practice formerly set out in IR 26 (see [**I.24**]).

First, a change of accounting date in the second or third year of a business is permitted without restriction thereby enabling a business to make suitable adjustments when the original date turns out to be impractical.

Secondly, in all other cases a change will only have a *fiscal* effect if certain prescribed conditions are satisfied. Otherwise the change is disregarded and tax computations continue on the basis of the old date (thereby necessitating apportionments). There are four conditions: both conditions I and II must be satisfied together with *either* condition III *or* condition IV.

Condition I: The first accounting period ending on the new (changed) date must not exceed 18 months (s 62A(2)).

Condition II: Notice of the change must be given to the inspector by 31 January following the year of change (s 62A(3)). The 'year of change' is the first year in which accounts are made up to the new date or, if there is a year without an accounting date, it is that year.

Condition III: Either no accounting date change occurred in any of the five preceding tax years *or* any such change was fiscally ineffective (ie because these conditions were not met) *or* the change took place before 1996–97.

Condition IV: The notice under condition II must set out the reasons for the change and the inspector then has 60 days to decide whether he is satisfied that the change is for '*bona fide* commercial reasons'. If he is not so satisfied he must give the taxpayer notice of the fact: if he does not respond at all within this period the change is (presumably) deemed to be effective. The taxpayer can appeal against an inspector's notice of dissatisfaction within 30 days and the commissioners then have to decide if there are *bona fide* commercial reasons for the change. 'Obtaining a tax advantage' is *not* regarded as a *bona fide* commercial reason for a change (s 62A(9)) and the Revenue has indicated that this will include the obtaining of a cashflow benefit as well as a reduction in liability. Bearing in mind, however, that condition IV is irrelevant if condition III is satisfied it is possible to make one change *for purely fiscal reasons* every five years.

How are effective changes of date treated for income tax purposes? Consider the following situations.   **[I.65]**

Situation 1. If the accounting period of change is under 12 months (or the change occurs in the second year of business) the basis period is 12 months to the new accounting date (s 62(2)(a)).   **[I.66]**

EXAMPLE I.16

Hank's business, having made up its accounts to 30 September, changes its accounting date to 30 April in 2001. Its profits are as follows:

		£
y/e 30.9.2000		8,500
y/e 30.4.2001		4,500
y/e 30.4 2002		10,500

The tax assessments are:

Tax year	Accounting period	£
2000–2001	y/e 30.9.2000	8,500
2001–2002	y/e to 30.4.2001	
	(ie six months' account to 30.4.2001 + $^6/_{12}$ of profit to 30.9.2000)	8,750
2002–2003	y/e 30.4.2002	10,500

Situation 2. If, as a result of the change, no account ends in the next financial year, this is the year in which the change is deemed to take effect and the basis period is 12 months to the new accounting date.　　　　**[I.67]**

EXAMPLE I.17

If Hank had prepared an 18-month account to 30.4.2002 the position would be:

		£
y/e 30.9.2000		8,500
y/e 30.4.2002		15,000

and the tax assessment would be:

Tax year	Accounting period	£
2000–2001	y/e 30.9.2000	8,500
2001–2002	12-month period to 30.4.2001 (ie $^6/_{12}$ of £8,500 (as before) + $^6/_{18}$ of £15,000)	9,250
2002–2003	12-month period to 30.4.2002, (ie $^{12}/_{18}$ of £15,000)	10,000

Situation 3. If the accounting period exceeds 12 months but ends in the next tax year, profits of that accounting period are assessed (s 62(2)(b)). If, for instance, Hank had made up accounts to 30 December 2001, profits of the period from 30 September 2000 to that date would be taxed in the tax year 2001–2002.　　　　**[I.68]**

Situation 4. If the new period is a short one so that there are two accounting periods ending in the same tax year, the two are treated as a single period ending on the new date (s 60(5)).　　　　**[I.69]**

EXAMPLE I.18

Having made accounts up to 30.9.2001, Hawk makes up his next account to 31.3.2002. His profits are:

	£
y/e 30.9.2000	8,500
y/e 30.9.2001	11,000
y/e 31.3.2002	4,000
y/e 31.3.2003	14,000

which gives tax assessments of:

Tax year	Accounting period	£
2000–2001	y/e 30.9.2000	8,500
2001–2002	y/e 31.3.2002	15,000
2002–2003	y/e 31.3.2003	14,000

4　Overlap relief

This is given where the same profits are used twice as the basis of assessment (as for instance in *Example I.15*). The relief for the overlap, which is calculated in money terms and is not index-linked, is given on the earlier of:

(1) a change of accounting date which results in an assessment for a period of *more than* 12 months; or

(2) a cessation of the trade or business.

If none or not all the overlap is used in (1) above, then it can be carried forward for use in (2).   **[I.70]**

5   Transitional rules for existing businesses

For businesses trading at 5 April 1994 there was a transition to the new rules over three tax years. The transitional year was 1996–97. For that year the assessable profit was a 12-month average of the profits since the year that was taxed on the old (preceding year) basis in 1995–96 and the beginning of the year to be assessed on the new basis in 1997–98 (which will be on the current year basis—ie on the profits for the accounting period ending in that year of assessment in *Example I.13*).

EXAMPLE I.19

A business makes up accounts to 30 June and the profits assessable are as follows:

	£
y/e 30.6.94	50,000
y/e 30.6.95	54,000
y/e 30.6.96	60,000
y/e 30.6.97	66,000

	£
1995/96 (PY)	50,000
1996/97 transitional	57,000
1997/98 (CY)	66,000

Assessable profit for the transitional year is calculated as:

$$12/24 \times (£54,000 + £60,000) = £57,000$$

Overlap relief is available in respect of the nine months' profit from 1 July 1996 to 5 April 1997, ie on $^9/_{12} \times £66,000$ ($£49,500$).

For existing businesses the old rules for cessation applied up to 5 April 1997. On a cessation in 1997–98 the Revenue has the option of applying the pre-1994 legislation, ie to revise the assessments for 1995–96 and 1996–97 to actual. On a cessation in 1998–99 the Revenue has the option of applying the actual basis for 1996–97 rather than the 12-month average. The following *example* is taken from *Tax Bulletin*, February 1994:   **[I.71]**

EXAMPLE I.20

(1) A long standing business, making up accounts annually to 30 June, ceases trading on 30 June 1996. Basis periods will be as follows:

1994–95—Year ended 30 June 1993
1995–96—Year ended 30 June 1994
1996–97—Period from 6 April 1996 to 30 June 1996

It will be possible for 1994–95 and 1995–96 to be adjusted to actual basis under TA 1988 s 63.

(2) Alternatively the business ceases trading on 30 April 1997:

1995–96—Year ended 30 June 1994
1996–97—12/24 × 2 years to 30 June 1996
1997–98—Period from 1 July 1996 to cessation on 30 April 1997. (Transitional relief relating to the period 1 July 1996 to 5 April 1997 will be given.)

Here the Revenue has a right to direct that the new rules be disapplied if the old rules would lead to higher aggregate profits being charged to tax for 1995–96 and 1996–97. 1997–98 will be unaffected by this direction.

(3)   As before but the business ceases trading on 30 April 1998:

1996–97—12/24 × 2 years ended 30 June 1996
1997–98—Year ended 30 June 1997
1998–99—Period 1 July 1997 to 30 April 1998. (Transitional relief due as for 1997–98 in (2) above.)

The Revenue's right to make a direction disapplying the new rules extends only to 1996–97 if the old rules would result in a higher assessment for that year.

6   Taxing partners and the position of partners joining the firm

TA 1988 s 113(3) allocates taxable profits (losses) amongst partners according to their interest during the accounting period *not* according to the shares in the tax year for which that period is the basis period (contrast *Example I.8*). Each partner is treated as carrying on a notional sole trade which begins when he becomes a partner and ends when he ceases to be a partner. As a result initial overlap relief can be given on leaving and terminal loss relief is likewise available on leaving the partnership even though the business itself may continue (contrast [**I.47**]). [**I.72**]

EXAMPLE I.21

Firm ABC makes up accounts to 30 June each year. On 1 January 2002 D joined the firm. Assume profits always split equally.

(1)   *Tax year 2001–2002*
ABC taxed on profits of the accounts to 30 June 2001: profits divided equally.

D taxed on his share of the profits when he became a partner (1 January 2002) to following 5 April. Hence profits for the year ended 30 June 2002 must be divided as follows:
(a)   1 July 2001 to 1 January 2002 ($^6/_{12}$) divided equally between ABC and taxed in the year 2002/2003.
(b)   1 January to 5 April ($^3/_{12}$) divided equally between ABCD and D's share taxed in the year 2001/2002.

(2)   *Tax year 2002/2003*
ABC taxed on their profit share for year to 30 June 2002: being one-third each to 1 January 2002 and thereafter one-quarter each.
   D will be taxed on his share of the profits to 30 June 2002 (being one-half of one-quarter) and in addition on his share of the profit for the following six months to 31 December 2002 (this will be one-half of one-quarter of the profits to 30 June 2003).

(3)   *D's position*
(a)   He will receive credit for profits doubly taxed on commencement, ie on his profit of the year to 30 June 2002 (taxed in 2001–2002) plus a six-month share of profits for the year to 30 June 2003 (since those profits will be taxed in full in the year 2003–2004).
   He will receive overlap relief on the earlier of:
   (i)   when he leaves the firm;
   (ii)   when the firm's business ceases;
   (iii)   on a change to a later accounting date (relief may only be partial).
(b)   For D no accounting period fell within the period of 12 months from the date when his notional trade began: hence he only reaches the current year basis in the third tax year (being 2003–2004).

7 Partners leaving the firm

Given that each partner is treated as carrying on a notional sole trade, the usual principles apply. **[I.73]**

EXAMPLE I.22

XYZ make up their accounts to 30 June each year. Profits are divided equally. On 31 December 2002 Z retires and X and Y continue the business splitting the profits equally.

Position of Z
He is taxed on the basis of his share of the profits from the end of the basis period of the preceding year until 31 December 2002, ie profits from 30 June 2001 to 31 December 2002 (18 months).

But assuming that he joined the firm on 1 January 1998 overlap relief will be due. This will amount to approximately nine months: in theory therefore he is taxed on retirement on the nine-month period from 5 April to 31 December 2002 (but note that there is no necessary link between profits in the start and at the end and there is no index-linking of overlap relief).

8 Partnership changes

TA 1988 s 113(2) is amended so that when there is a change in the persons carrying on a trade and at least one person was a member of the firm before and after the change, there is a continuance, ie there is no deemed discontinuance and recommencement. Accordingly, it is only *actual* discontinuances which have tax consequences. These occur when:

(1) all the partners sell out;
(2) on the death of a sole trader;
(3) on an actual discontinuance: for instance on a merger (or demerger) when there results a change in the nature of the business carried on by the two firms engaged in the merger (or demerger): see for instance *George Humphries Ltd v Cook* (1934); SP 9/86 and **[I.28]**. **[I.74]–[I.110]**

VI TAX PLANNING

The switch to the current year basis marked a revolution in the income tax treatment of the self-employed. Careful thought should be given to the consequences of this change: consider for instance the following:

(1) With the ending of partnership joint and several liability will partnership tax reserves become a thing of the past?
(2) To eliminate overlap relief a change of accounting date to a date close after 5 April should be considered. Note, however, that making up accounts to 5 April will result in the business being assessed on a true current year basis thereafter and thereby remove any element of delay in the payment of tax: by contrast a firm adopting 30 June has 19 months in which to prepare computations, sort out problems etc.

Not surprisingly, legislation was introduced in FA 1995 s 123 and Sch 22 to counter avoidance of tax through the manipulation of the rules during the transition from the preceding year to the current year basis of assessment. **[I.111]**

APPENDIX II: INHERITANCE TAX FORMS: COMPLETING THE IHT 200

1 Introduction

The full list of IHT forms is as follows:

Subject	Form
(a) *Death*	
Account to lead to grant of representation of transferor who died domiciled in the UK.	IHT 200
Alternative where deceased died domiciled out of the UK	IHT 201
Deceased died domiciled in the UK, but the net estate does not exceed the IHT threshold at the time of death; the gross estate does not exceed twice the threshold and certain other conditions are met	IHT 202
[Instructions for completion of IHT 200 and IHT 201]	[IHT 210]
(b) *Lifetime transfers*	
Transfers of value including:	IHT 100
(i) potentially exempt transfers ('PETs') chargeable on death of the transferor within seven years;	
(ii) gifts of property with reservation;	
(iii) terminations of interests in possession in settled property; and	
(iv) other chargeable lifetime transfers.	
[Instructions for completion of IHT 100]	[IHT 110]
(c) *Discretionary trusts*	
Chargeable events involving settlements without an interest in possession	IHT 101
[Instructions for completion of IHT 101]	[IHT 111]
	[II.1]

2 Completing the IHT Account 200

General

IHT Form 200 is the appropriate form for PRs to use when applying for a grant of representation to the estate of a deceased person who dies domiciled in the UK where the estate is not an excepted estate and where IHT Form 202 is inapplicable. For a description of how to complete the form, see the booklet (Form 210). IHT Form 200 contains 12 pages and should be accompanied, in appropriate circumstances, by Form IHT 40 (schedule of shares and securities) and Form IHT 37B (land owned by the deceased). The Account divides into the following parts:

(1) Page 1 contains the personal details of the deceased.
(2) Section 1 comprises questions designed to discover whether the deceased made chargeable lifetime transfers or gifts subject to a reservation.
(3) Pages 3–9 comprise sections 2–7 of the Account.

Section 2 is concerned with nominated and joint property. It is divided into two parts: Part A for a property on which the tax cannot be paid by instalments and Part B for property with the instalment option. It should be noted that although in the early part of the form the questions relate to all jointly held property (ie whether held as beneficial joint tenants or tenants in common) the final portion of the form is concerned only with property held as beneficial

827

joint tenants: ie which passes by survivorship and so does not pass through the hands of the personal representatives. Property held as beneficial tenants in common must be listed in *section 3* since the relevant interest of the deceased passes under his will and therefore the property passes through the hands of his personal representatives.

Section 3   lists all property of the deceased in the UK which he owned solely and beneficially before his death and which now vests in his personal representatives (excluding property over which he had a general power of appointment exercisable by will which should be included in *section 5*). It is divided into two parts:

(a) Part A is for property on which tax cannot be paid by instalments (eg chattels) and on which PRs must pay IHT on delivery of the form.
(b) Part B is for property subject to the instalment option (eg land). In both parts the gross value of the property must be entered, any liabilities which reduce that value being shown separately.

Section 4   is concerned with foreign property: again it is divided into the two familiar Parts A and B. This property does not pass through the hands of personal representatives and will normally bear its own IHT on death.

Section 5   combines settled property and gifts with a reservation (not a particularly happy combination!). So far as settled property is concerned the interest of the deceased in a discretionary trust is not relevant: accordingly the only settled property that should be entered here is property in which the deceased had enjoyed a beneficial interest in possession. The interest of a reversionary beneficiary should be entered in *section 3* (an 'interest in expectancy'). Turning to property subject to a reservation, notice that the original gift should be entered in section 1 but if the property was still subject to a reservation retained by the deceased at the date of the death, its value must be included in this section and will therefore be ignored in *section 1*.

Section 6   is concerned with IHT exemptions and reliefs (eg spouse exemption; business relief; charity exemption). This section applies to all such reliefs in relation to any of the property falling within the previous *sections 2-5*.

Section 7   is concerned with artificial debts arising under FA 1986 s 103 (see [**22.13**]).

(4) Pages 10 and 11 are the assessment of tax pages to which the total value from the preceding sections must be transferred. These pages provide a format for calculating the total tax (if any) that is due and the tax (if any) that is payable on delivery of the account. At the bottom of page 11 there is a summary for probate purposes (the figures here determine the amount of probate fees chargeable).
(5) Page 12 contains a declaration to be signed by the personal representatives confirming that to the best of their knowledge the form has been correctly completed.   [**II.2**]

3 Completion of the form—case illustration

Siegfried George Lomax deceased

The following information is taken from the file of Mallet & Co (solicitors) of 11 Ducks Lane, Cooknam, Northamptonshire—solicitors for the PRs of the deceased.

Full name of the deceased	Siegfried George Lomax
Last residential address	Church View, Resurrection Lane, Cooknam, Northamptonshire
Occupation	Company director
Date of birth	5 November 1911
Date of death	4 July 1997
Surviving relatives	Two children and brother
Will	Dated 1 January 1984
Executors	(1) George Siegfried Lomax (son), 15 Gun Street, Hardwick, Yorkshire
	(2) Elspeth Georgina Pollax (daughter), The Range, Horseshoe Close, Barrowmouth, Devon

Terms of the will

Pecuniary legacy of £5,000 to the RSPCA
Specific legacy of shares in Buttons Ltd to son,
   George Lomax
Residue to children equally

Assets

	£
Cash	100
Midshire Bank, Cooknam:	
Current account	740
Deposit account	420
Interest to date of death (net)	16
Personal chattels, household goods etc valued at	5,960
Director's fees to date of death	1,000
Policy of assurance payable to the estate by	
Moon Life Assurance Co	25,000
Thrifty Building Society account	17,900
Interest to date of death (net)	64
Minority holdings of listed shares as valued (all 'cum div')	20,765
Freehold property	
(1) Church View (above) owned solely and beneficially by deceased, but subject to a mortgage to the Thrifty Building Society (below). House valued at	145,000
(2) Primrose Cottage, Rosetree Lane, Bangor, Wales owned by the deceased as a joint tenant with his brother Siegmund Earnest Lomax of the same address. The whole is valued at	70,000
Unquoted shares: 99% holding in Buttons Ltd, which manufactures buttons. The holding comprises 10,000 unquoted shares, the valuation of which has been agreed between the Revenue and the deceased's accountants, Prigmore & Co at £10 per share, ie	100,000

Liabilities

Electricity account outstanding	80
Housekeeper's wages (Annie Pringle)	100
British Telecom	32
Income tax (estimated)	1,225
Mark Cole & Sons (butchers)	12
Chinns up (victuallers)	120
Funeral expenses (excluding tombstone)	560
Mortgage on Church View	10,125

Other relevant information

(1) On 25 December 1990 the deceased made a potentially exempt transfer to his daughter, Elspeth of £20,000.

(2) The deceased was life tenant in the Lomax Will Trust established by the will of his father Tristan Lomax who died on 8 April 1960. The settled funds now pass to the deceased's son George. They consist of:

Investments valued at	48,640
Cash (uninvested)	400
Income accrued due	80
Income subsequently apportioned to deceased life tenant	60

(3) In 1990 the deceased gave his country cottage ('Wye Knot') to his daughter, Elspeth. He has continued to occupy the cottage during the summer months and the PRs have been advised that the cottage falls within the gift with reservation rules. The value of the cottage in 1990 was £25,000: at death it was worth £40,000.   **[II.3]**

Method of payment

The PRs will take out a loan to pay the IHT due on delivery of the form. They will elect wherever possible to pay IHT by instalments so as to reduce the amount that they have to borrow (see *Howarth's Executors v IRC* (1997)). Once probate has been obtained, they propose to sell Church View to pay off the loan and the remaining IHT.   **[II.4]**

4 Page by page analysis

The IHT Form 200 will now be completed for this estate. Note that for the purpose of this exercise, it is assumed that the valuations of all the deceased's assets have been agreed with the Revenue. In practice, however, this is unlikely in the case of certain assets (eg land and unquoted shareholdings) and PRs submit the form on the basis of estimated valuations and complete a corrective account when the valuations are agreed.   **[II.5]**

Inland **Revenue**
Capital Taxes Office

Inland Revenue Account for Inheritance Tax

This Account is for use only where the deceased died on or after 18 March 1986 and was domiciled in the United Kingdom.

If the deceased died before 18 March 1986 or you need any further help or information, contact the Capital Taxes Office where the staff will be pleased to help you.

Before you start to fill in this Account, read the Guidance Notes in booklet IHT 210. The marginal notes on this Account refer to the relevant paragraphs of the booklet. They will help you to fill it in quickly and correctly. If you need more space use a separate sheet of paper showing to which section of the Account it relates.

Insert 'Principal', or the name of the District and 'District'

In the High Court of Justice Family Division (Probate), The (1) Carlshire **Registry**

Please give your full name and address including postcode, using capital letters, even if the DX code is given

Solicitor(s) or Agent(s)

(2) Mallet & Co
Ducks Lane
Cooknam
Northamptonshire
NR2 4PQ

In the estate of

Please give the full name and title of the deceased using CAPITAL letters

Surname

(3) LOMAX

Title and Forenames

Mr Siegfried George

All communications concerning Inheritance Tax will be sent to the solicitors or agents unless the executors or administrators request otherwise

DX Code

-

Show, for example, 9 January 1993 as 09 Jan 1993

Date of birth	**Date of death**
0 5 N O V 1 9 1 1	0 4 J U L 1 9 9 7

Marital Status

Married   Single   Divorced   Widowed   X

Surviving relatives

Husband   Wife   Child(ren) X   Parent(s)

Your reference

LH

Domicile

You may wish to give the name of the person dealing with this estate

Contact

-

(4) **England and Wales** X   Scotland   N. Ireland

Address

Telephone

Cooknam 451

Give the last known usual address of the deceased including postcode

Church View
Resurrection Lane
Cooknam
Northamptonshire
NR2 1PO

Fax

-

If available, please give this information

Tax District and reference

Salford 16 TG/767/LOM

National Insurance No

-

Please give the occupation of the deceased

Occupation

Company Director

Date of Grant (For official use only)

Executors or intending administrators

Give the full names and permanent addresses including postcode of the executors or intending administrators

(5) George Siegfried Lomax
15 Gun Street
Hardwick
Yorkshire
YS3 1LP

Elspeth Georgina Pollax
The Range
Horseshoe Close
Barrowmouth
Devon
DL1 2BS

-

(1) Accounts should be sent to the Inland Revenue, Finance Division (Cashier), Barrington Road, Worthing, West Sussex so that they can be properly receipted *before* presentation of the relevant papers to the Probate Registries.

(2) Details of the PRs' solicitors with whom the Capital Taxes Office will communicate.

(3) Personal details of the deceased.

(4) If the deceased had died domiciled outside the UK, IHT Form 201 would be the appropriate form to use.

(5) The deceased's executors complete the declaration on page 12.

Section 1 - Lifetime gifts or transfers of value

Did the deceased within 7 years of death

		Yes	No	For Official use only
Note 1	(6) make any gift, settlement, or other transfer of value? (See Note 1 as to the transfers you should not include)	X		
Note 2	pay any premium on a policy of life assurance not included on Page 4 Section 3A of this form?		X	
Note 3	cease to be entitled to any beneficial interest in possession in settled property?		X	

Note 4 (7) Did the deceased at any time on or after 18 March 1986 dispose of any property by way of gift where

	Yes	No
possession and enjoyment of the property was not bona fide assumed by the donee?		X
the property was not enjoyed to the entire exclusion of the deceased?	X	
any benefit was retained by contract or otherwise?		X

Details of lifetime gifts or transfers of value

Please enter in chronological order details of each lifetime gift or transfer of value. You should deduct any exemptions and reliefs due (See Note 5). Enter the chargeable value showing how you have calculated this

Date of disposition	To whom given (name and address)	Description of asset(s) at date of transfer	Value
25 December 1990	Elspeth Georgina Pollax The Range Horseshoe Close Barrowmouth Devon DL1 2BS	Cash	£20,000
(8) 1990	Elspeth Georgina Pollax (as above)	Wye Knot Cottage (valued at date of death)	£40,000

Carry the total chargeable value of lifetime transfers to Page 10 Box A unless the property given was subject to a reservation retained by the deceased at the date of death, in which case it should be included in Section 5 on Page 8

Total chargeable value of gifts made within 7 years of death	£20,000

Show on a schedule details of all gifts made within 7 years of the earliest transfer but do not carry the value of these gifts to Page 10 (See Note 54).

Note 6 (9) **Superannuation benefits**

	Yes	No
Was any provision, apart from State Pension, made by the deceased, the deceased's employers or otherwise for retirement, pension, or other superannuation benefits?		X
If 'Yes' were any benefits payable, or dispositions made as described in Note 6?		

2

(6)   The gift of £20,000 to the deceased's daughter was made within seven years of the death. Accordingly, it must be cumulated for the purpose of calculating the rate at which the deceased's estate will be charged on death, although it does not form part of the deceased's taxable estate on death (see page 10). Although this gift attracts taper relief (see [**22.22**]), because that relief operates by reducing the tax payable (and not the value of the gift) it is of no value where, as here, the gift falls within the taxpayer's IHT nil rate band.

(7)   Property given away subject to a reservation is included in the donor's estate at death if the reserved benefit is still continuing: if the benefit came to an end during the donor's life a deemed PET would have occurred at that time (see [**21.182**]).

(8)   Full details of the gift of 'Wye Knot' must be given. The Double Charges Regulations (see Appendix III) ensure that *either* the value of the cottage in 1990 at the time of the gift *or* its value at death are charged and, because of the substantial increase in the value of the cottage, it is assumed that the latter applies.

(9)   If a lump sum benefit is payable to the deceased's personal representatives on his death or was subject to a power of nomination at the time of death it must be included as part of the deceased's free estate on page 5. It is standard tax planning to ensure that this sum is settled *inter vivos* to prevent such a charge from arising.

				Yes	No	

You must answer the first two questions in this Section

Section 2 - Nominated and Joint Property

		Yes	No	

Note 7
If 'Yes', please give full particulars in Section 2A

(10) Did the deceased nominate any Savings Bank Account, Savings Certificates or other assets in favour of any person? — No: X

Note 8

(11) Was the deceased joint owner of any property of any description or did the deceased hold any money on a joint account? — Yes: X

On a separate sheet of paper state for each item of joint property

• the name(s) of the other joint owner(s)

• when the joint ownership began or when the joint account was opened

Note 9

• by whom and from what source the joint property was provided and, if it or its purchase price was contributed by more than one of the joint owners, the extent of the contribution made by each

Note 10

• how any income was dealt with and enjoyed.

If 'Yes', include the value in Section 4A or 4B

Was any joint property situated outside the UK? — No: X

If 'Yes', include the value in Section 2A or 2B if the property was situated in the UK

Did any joint property pass by survivorship? — Yes: X

If 'Yes', include the value in Section 3A or 3B if the property was situated in the UK

Did any joint property pass under the deceased's Will or intestacy? — No: X

Section 2A - Nominated and Joint Property without the Instalment Option

Note 11
All claims for exemptions or reliefs should be made in Section 6 on Page 9

Particulars of the property   Gross value at date of death
-   -

See Note 24 and first paragraph of Note 46 before continuing

Deceased's share of liabilities in respect of the property

Name of creditor	Description of liability	Amount
-	-	-

Carry the net value forward to Page 10 Box 1

Net value | - |

Section 2B - Joint Property with the Instalment Option

(12) Particulars of the property   Gross value at date of death
    Primrose Cottage   £31,500
    Rosetree Lane
    Bangor
    Wales

All claims for exemptions or reliefs should be made in Section 6 on Page 9

See Note 24 and first paragraph of Note 46 before continuing

Deceased's share of liabilities in respect of the property

Name of creditor	Description of liability	Amount
-	-	-

Carry the net value forward to Page 10 Box 8

Net value | £31,500 |

	Yes	No

Note 12

(13) Is tax to be paid by instalments? — Yes: X

For Official use only

3

(10) A nomination in the prescribed form takes effect in the same way as a disposition by will and the property remains comprised in the estate at death. By contrast, a mere request to trustees of a company pension scheme is not a nomination and property in the pension fund is not therefore included in the death estate.

(11) Although the deceased's joint tenancy in Primrose Cottage passes by right of survivorship to his brother and does not vest in his PRs, the value of his interest immediately before death forms part of his estate. Notice that all joint property is covered by this question not just beneficial joint tenancies passing by right of survivorship.

(12) The deceased had no nominated property. The only property which he owned jointly (and which passes to his brother by right of survivorship) is Primrose Cottage. The instalment option is available for tax attributable to the value of the deceased's half share. Although the property is worth £70,000 the value of the deceased's half share (£35,000) will be discounted (usually by about 10%) to (say) £31,500 to allow for the fact that it does not carry the right to exclusive occupation of any portion of the house.

(13) The instalment option will be exercised to ensure that the least amount of tax is payable in order to obtain the grant of probate. The entire tax liability can be paid off once the grant is obtained: see further [**22.49**].

Note 13	**Section 3 - Free Estate in the UK**		
All claims for exemptions or reliefs should be made in Section 6 on Page 9	**All the property of the deceased in respect of which the grant is required**		For Official use only
	Section 3A - Property without the Instalment Option		
Notes 14, 15 and 16 (14)	Stocks, shares, debentures and other securities as set out on IHT 40:	Value at date of death	
	quoted or listed in the Stock Exchange Daily Official List except so far as included in Section 3B	£20,750	
	others, except so far as included in Section 3B	-	
	Uncashed dividends and interest received, dividends declared, and interest accrued due to the date of death in respect of the above investments, as statement attached	-	
	Premium Savings Bonds	-	
Note 17	National Savings Certificates including interest to the date of death	-	
(15)	Bank accounts including interest to the date of death, as statement attached	£1,176	
	Money with the National Savings Bank, a building society, a co-operative or friendly society, including interest to the date of death, as statement attached	£17,964	
	Cash (other than cash at banks, etc)	£100	
	Money out on mortgage including interest to the date of death, as statement attached	-	
Note 18	Debts due to the deceased including interest to the date of death (except book debts included in section 3B) as statement attached	-	
	Rents including apportionment of rents of the deceased's own real and leasehold property to the date of death	-	
Note 19	Income arising, but not received before the death, from real and personal property in which the deceased had a life or other limited interest		
Please state the source	(16) LOMAX WILL TRUST Accrued	£80	
	Apportioned	£60	
(17)	Any other income, apportioned where necessary, to which the deceased was entitled at the date of death (for example pensions, annuities, director's fees, etc), as statement attached	£1,000	
Note 20 (18)	Policies of insurance and bonuses thereon (if any) on the life of the deceased, as statement attached	£25,000	
	Saleable value of policies of insurance and bonuses (if any) on the life of any other person, as statement attached	-	
	Amounts payable under private health insurance schemes	-	
	Income Tax repayable	-	
Note 21 (19) Please attach a valuation if one has been obtained	Household and personal goods, including pictures, china, clothes, books, jewellery, stamp, coin and other collections, motor cars, boats etc		
	Sold, realised gross	-	
	Unsold, estimated	£5,960	
Note 22 (20) Please state the name and date of death of the testator or intestate	Interest in an unadministered estate	-	
	Carried forward	**£72,105**	

4

(14) The instalment option is not available for the deceased's listed shares because none of the holdings constitutes a controlling shareholding (see IHTA 1984 s 228(1)(a) and Chapter 22). The holdings must be listed (with values) on Form 40. If shares are listed 'ex div' at the date of death, the dividend must be added to this figure.

(15) Net interest on the deposit account which has accrued to the date of death is included in the deceased's estate for IHT purposes.

(16) Any income which accrued to the trustees of the Lomax Will Trust before the deceased's death forms part of his estate for IHT purposes, even though the trustees have not paid it over (ie £80). Also, income paid to the trustees after the deceased's death and apportioned to him forms part of his estate (ie £60).

(17) The director's fees to which the deceased was entitled form part of his estate.

(18) The value of the policy forms part of the deceased's estate on death. Notice that if the policy had been written in trust for a third party it would not be included in the estate; details would, however, be given on page 2 because the payment of the premiums might have been chargeable transfers of value.

(19) Self-explanatory. In practice, a valuation would have to accompany the IHT form (not shown here). Details and individual values of items valued at £500 and upwards should be given.

(20) The value of the *chose in action* should be entered. In the case of a valuable estate this may result in a substantial IHT liability arising even though there is no prospect of an early completion of administration.

Section 3A - Property without the Instalment Option - continued

Brought forward	£72,105	For Official use only

Interest in expectancy

Note 23
Please state how the deceased acquired the interest and the estimated value at the date of the deceased's death

(21) -

	–

Other personal property as listed below or as statement attached

–

	–

Carry the total forward to the Probate Summary on Page 11 Box L

Gross value of property without the Instalment Option | £72,105

See Note 24 and first paragraph of Note 46 before continuing

Liabilities at the date of death and funeral expenses

Note 25

Name of creditor	Description of liability	Amount
(22)		
Electricity Board	Electricity Account	£80
British Telecom	Telephone Account	£32
Annie Pringle	Housekeeper's wages	£100
Mark Cole & Sons	Butcher	£12
Chinns Up	Wine	£120
Inland Revenue	Income tax (estimated)	£1,225

Note 26

Funeral expenses

(23) S Toomay & Bros, Cooknam | £560

Note 27
Carry the total forward to the Probate Summary on Page 11 Box Q

Total liabilities | £2,129

Carry the net total (24) forward to Page 10 Box 2

Value of property without the Instalment Option less liabilities | £69,976

5

(21)   For the treatment of reversionary interests, see [**25.61**].

(22)   The deceased's debts which are not attributable to items of particular property are included here.

(23)   Funeral expenses are deductible if reasonable (see [**22.5**]).

(24)   The value of the deceased's section 3A property less debts (ie £69,976) is taken to page 10.

NB: all the expenses deducted satisfy the requirements of FA 1986 s 103 since consideration for those debts was not property derived from the deceased (see further section 7, page 9).

Section 3B - Property with the Instalment Option

	Value at date of death

Note 28   (25)   Land etc owned by the deceased in the UK (not being settled land) as described on IHT 37 attached — **£145,000**

Note 29   **Business interests**

(26)   Net value of deceased's interest in the business(es), as statement or balance sheet attached — **-**

Note 30   Net value of the deceased's interest as partner in the firm of

Please give the name of the firm   -   **-**

as statement or balance sheet attached

Note 31   Stocks, shares, debentures and other securities, as set out on IHT40

Shares or securities which gave the deceased control of the company immediately before the death *(Section 228(1)(a) Inheritance Tax Act 1984)* — **£100,000**

Unquoted shares or securities within Section 228(1) (b), (c) or (d) Inheritance Tax Act 1984 *(All other unquoted shares or securities should be included in Section 3A)* — **-**

Gross value of property with the Instalment Option — **£245,000**

Liabilities charged at the date of the deceased's death on the property included above other than those already reflected in the net value of Business interests

Name of creditor	Description of liability and property on which charged	Amount
(27) Thrifty Building Society	Mortgage on Church View Resurrection Lane Cooknam Northamptonshire	£10,125

Total liabilities — **£10,125**

(28) **Value of property with the Instalment Option less liabilities** — **£234,875**

	Yes	No

Note 33   (29) **Is tax to be paid by instalments?** — **X** |

6

For Official use only

(25)   The gross value of Church View is shown here. Full details of the property must be set out on Form IHT 37 (not reproduced).

(26)   The shareholding and its value must be detailed with the deceased's quoted shares on Form IHT 40 (not reproduced). Business property relief on the value of the holding is claimed elsewhere (see (33)).

(27)   The mortgage is a deductible liability.

(28)   The deduction is given against the total value of the section 3B property. As all the IHT is a testamentary expense this is irrelevant. If, however, Church View had been the subject of a specific tax-bearing devise, the devisee would only be liable for IHT on the value of Church View less the mortgage, ie on £134,875.

(29)   As far as possible, the PRs elect to pay IHT by ten yearly instalments. (They hope to discharge the IHT liability before the first instalment falls due on 1 February 1998 by realising assets in the estate once they have obtained the grant of probate.) Instalment option property owned solely and beneficially by the deceased comprises Church View. Note the problems that may arise in the future for PRs if the instalments are not duly paid: see *Howarth's Executors v IRC* (1997)

Section 4 - Foreign Property

For Official use only

Note 34

Section 4A - Property without the Instalment Option

Note 35

All claims for exemptions or reliefs should be made in Section 6 on Page 9

Particulars of the property

Value at date of death

Gross Value

Note 36

Liabilities in respect of the property above or due outside the UK

Name and address of creditor	Description of liability	Amount

Total liabilities

Carry the net total forward to Page 10 Box 3

Value of property without the Instalment Option less liabilities

Section 4B - Property with the Instalment Option

Note 35

Particulars of the property

Value at date of death

All claims for exemptions or reliefs should be made in Section 6 on Page 9

Gross Value

Liabilities in respect of the property above or due outside the UK

Name and address of creditor	Description of liability	Amount

Total liabilities

Carry the net total forward to Page 10 Box 10

Value of property with the Instalment Option less liabilities

Note 37

Is tax to be paid by instalments?

Yes   No

7

[*Notes to IHT Form 200 continue on page 846*]

Note 38

Section 5 - Settled Property and Gifts with Reservation

All other property to which the deceased was beneficially entitled or was treated as beneficially entitled.

For Official use only

You must answer the question opposite

Was the deceased, at the date of death, entitled to a life interest, annuity or other interest in possession in settled property whether as beneficiary under a settlement or otherwise? See Note 39.

Yes No

Note 39

If so, please state below the name(s) of the settlement(s), the trustees and their solicitors.

(30) Lomax Will Trust (CTO L 4590)
The deceased was the life tenant under the will of his father (died 8 April 1960)

Note 40
Please note that the value of any property within Section 5 **must** be included on Page 10 even if you are not liable for the tax on that property.
Enter the value in Box 15 and/or Box 16 unless you are paying tax on delivery, in which case enter it in Box 4 and/or Box 11.

All claims for exemptions or reliefs should be made in Section 6 on Page 9

Section 5A - Property without the Instalment Option

Particulars of the property	Value at date of death
Investments	£48,640
Cash - capital	£400

Liabilities in respect of the property above	Amount
-	-

Carry the net value forward to Page 10 Box 4

Property on which tax is being paid now on delivery of this Account	Net value	-

Carry the net value forward to Page 10 Box 15

Property on which tax is not being paid now	Net value	£49,040

Section 5B - Property with the Instalment Option

All claims for exemptions or reliefs should be made in Section 6 on Page 9

Particulars of the property	Value at date of death
(31) Wye Knot, Nr Tinertn, Gloucestershire Transferred to Elspeth Pollax by Instrument of Transfer dated 30 October 1990	£40,000

Liabilities in respect of the property above	Amount
-	-

Carry the net value forward to Page 10 Box 11

Property on which tax is being paid now on delivery of this Account	Net value	-

Carry the net value forward to Page 10 Box 16

Property on which tax is not being paid now	Net value	£40,000

Note 41

	Yes	No
Is tax to be paid by instalments?	X	

8

(30) The value of the whole settled fund at the date of the deceased's death must be included. Either (as here) the trustee(s) will account separately for the tax attributable to the settled property; or, if the trustee(s) provide the deceased's PRs with the necessary funds to do so, the PRs can elect to pay this tax on the delivery of the Form together with the tax on the deceased's free estate. As the settled property does not consist of instalment option property, the tax will be payable by the trustee(s) in one lump sum six months after the date of the deceased's death (ie by 1 February 1998). Insofar as the settled fund comprises shares and securities, these must be set out on Form IHT 40 (not reproduced). As there have been no advances or property taken out of settlement (which affect the calculation of the IHT bill) there must be a statement to this effect. The trustee and the trust's solicitors must be identified as the Revenue will need to communicate with them. The settlement has a CTO reference as a result of the admission of Tristan Lomax's will to probate.

(31) Property subject to a reservation of benefit ('Wye Knot') should be entered here. It is the donee who is primarily liable for payment of the IHT on this property: hence tax will not be paid on delivery of the Account on this property.

See Notes
42, 43, 44
and 45

Section 6 - Exemptions, Exclusions and Reliefs against Capital

For Official
use only

Property without the Instalment Option on which tax is being paid on delivery of this Account

Property in Sections:
2A, 3A, 4A, and 5A

Description of property and Section of Account in which included	Nature of relief claimed	Net value of property	Amount of relief claimed
(32) Pecuniary legacy	Charity	£5,000	£5,000

Carry this total
forward to Page 10
Box 6

Total of reliefs etc £5,000

Property with the Instalment Option on which tax is being paid on delivery of this Account

Property in Sections:
2B, 3B, 4B, and 5B

Description of property and Section of Account in which included	Nature of relief claimed	Net value of property	Amount of relief claimed
-		-	-

Carry this total
forward to Page 10
Box 13

Total of reliefs etc -

Property on which tax is not being paid on delivery of this Account

Property in Sections:
2B, 3B, 4B, 5A and 5B

Description of property and Section of Account in which included	Nature of relief claimed	Net value of property	Amount of relief claimed
(33) Unquoted shares in Buttons Ltd	Business Property Relief (100%)	£100,000	£100,000

Carry this total
forward to Page 10
Box 18

Total of reliefs etc £100,000

(34)
Section 7 - Liabilities within Section 103, Finance Act 1986

If the reply to either
question is 'Yes' see
Note 46

In the case of any liability for which a deduction has been taken in this Account

	Yes	No
did the consideration for any such debt or incumbrance incurred or created on or after 18 March 1986 consist of property derived from the deceased?		X
was the consideration given by any person who was at any time entitled to, or amongst whose resources there was at any time, any property derived from the deceased?		X

Any deduction claimed may be disallowed for Inheritance Tax purposes

9

(32) The pecuniary legacy to charity is exempt from IHT. As the exemption does not relate to specific property it is claimed against section 1A property.

(33) The value of the deceased's controlling shareholding in Buttons Ltd (£100,000) is eligible for 100% business property relief.

(34) Artificial debts (see **[22.13]**) must be itemised here.

Note 47   (35)   **Calculation of Inheritance Tax**

The tax calculated to be due is payable prior to lodging the application for the grant.
The Account will be fully examined after the grant has been issued.

You may use the reliefs box to show against which property a particular exemption, exclusion or relief has been taken

Summary for determining the chargeable estate

(36) **Section 1**   Total of chargeable transfers from Page 2 | A | £20,000

Part 1.   Property without the Instalment Option

Section	Net Total	Reliefs	Value after Reliefs
Bring forward the totals from Sections 2A, 3A, 4A, 5A and 6			
2A	1 -	-	
3A	2 £69,976	£5,000	
4A	3 -	-	
5A	4 -		
Sub-total	5 £69,976	6 £5,000	7 £64,976

Part 2.   Property with the Instalment Option

Section			
Bring forward the totals from Sections 2B, 3B, 4B, 5B and 6			
2B	8 £31,500		
3B	9 £234,875	£100,000	
4B	10 -		
5B	11 -		
Sub-total	12 £266,375	13 £100,000	14 £166,375

Part 3.   Other Property on which tax is not being paid on this Account

Section			
Bring forward the totals from Sections 5A, 5B and 6			
5A	15 £49,040		
5B	16 £40,000		
Sub-total	17 £89,040	18 -	19 £89,040

	Box 5 + 12 + 17	Box 6 + 13 + 18	Box 7 + 14 + 19
Totals	£425,391	£105,000	B £320,391

(37)   Aggregate chargeable transfers A + B = | C | (37) £340,391

Note 48   **Calculation of Tax**

Tax on C on first   £   £215,000   - | -

(38) **Plus balance of** £   (38) £125,391   @   40 % =   £50,156 | 40

     Total   £50,156 | 40

There will be no tax chargeable on A unless it exceeds the date of death threshold

Less tax on A at death rate

on first   £   £20,000   - | -

Plus balance of £   -   @   - % =   - | -

     Total   50,156 | 40

Note 49
Please attach a schedule showing how you have calculated the relief

Less Quick Succession Relief   - | -

Total tax chargeable on B above = | D | £50,156 | 40

(35) Pages 10 and 11 are the assessment pages. The purpose of page 10 is to calculate the tax payable on the deceased's estate. However, not all that tax is necessarily payable on delivery of the form or by the PRs. The purpose of page 11, therefore, is to calculate the amount of tax payable on delivery of the IHT Form.

(36) The £20,000 lifetime gift only forms part of the deceased's chargeable transfers for the purpose of calculating the rate at which tax is to be charged on death. Accordingly, a sum equal to the tax at table rates on a gift of £20,000 must be deducted from the tax bill. As the gift fell within the deceased's nil rate band, no tax is, or was, payable on this figure, so there is nothing to deduct. (Notice that the chargeable estate on death is £320,391, ie £340,391–£20,000.)

(37) A and B together yield the value of the deceased's total gross cumulative transfers (£340,391) made up of the transfer on death (being the net value of property from sections 2, 3 and 5 less any exemptions or reliefs), plus the value of any chargeable transfers made within seven years before death (ie £20,000 to daughter Elspeth).

(38) The tax on a chargeable transfer of £340,391 is calculated from the IHT table, ie £50,156.4.

(39) For quick succession relief see [**22.113**].

(40) The total tax payable on this estate (£320,391) is £50,156.4. This tax is attributable to the four types of property comprised in the estate:
   (1) the value of the non-instalment option property, ie £64,976, on which the PRs are to pay tax at once;
   (2) the value of the instalment option property, ie £166,375 made up of Church View (£134,875) and Primrose Cottage (£31,500). The shareholding in Buttons Ltd benefits from 100% business property relief and is therefore excluded from charge;
   (3) the value of the settled fund (£49,040) on which the trustees are responsible for the tax;
   (4) the value of the property subject to a reservation ('Wye Knot') which is £40,000: the donee, Elspeth, is liable for the tax.
       The tax (£50,156.4) is allocated between these four groups of property *pro rata.*

Note 50

Any capital figure multiplied by $\frac{D}{B}$ gives the proportion of tax assessable on the capital

From Page 10 Box 7

(41) Property without the Instalment Option   £   £64,976   × $\frac{D}{B}$ =   10,168 | 74

Note 51
Please attach a schedule showing how you have calculated the relief

Less reliefs against tax other than Quick Succession Relief   - | -

Net tax **E**   - | -

Note 52
Tax becomes due 6 months after the end of the month during which the death occurred. Unpaid tax including tax being paid by instalments carries interest from and including the day after the due date irrespective of the reason for the late payment

Add Interest on net tax from   -   19 -   to   -   19 -

  -   years   -   days   @   - %   =   - | -

(42) Total tax and interest on property without the Instalment Option   **F**   10,168 | 74

Carry this total forward to Box F below

That part of Box 14 opposite on which tax is to be paid now either in full or by instalments

(43) Property with the Instalment Option   £   -   × $\frac{D}{B}$ =   - | -

Less reliefs against tax other than Quick Succession Relief   - | -

Net tax **G**   - | -

Add Interest on net tax from   -   19 -   to   -   19 -

  -   years   -   days   @   - %   =   - | -

Note 33

include the date the last instalment became due

Instalments   -   tenths of net tax   **H**   - | -

Add Interest on instalments now assessed from: -   19 -   to   -   19 -

  -   days   @   - %   =   - | -

If the due date for the second or subsequent instalment has now passed and interest relief is not appropriate, add here interest on the whole of the net tax on property with the Instalment Option up to the due date of the last instalment

Add Interest on whole of net tax on instalment property from   -   19 -   to   -   19 -

  -   years   -   days   @   - %   =   - | -

Note 53
Carry this total forward to Box J below

Total tax and interest on property with the Instalment Option   **J**   - | -

For official use only

EDP

Financial Services Office

Total tax and interest - Property without the Instalment Option   **F**   10,168 | 74

Total tax and interest - Property with the Instalment Option   **J**   - | -

Total tax and interest payable now on this Account   **K**   10,168 | 74

Signature of Solicitor(s) or agent(s) for the applicant(s)   Date

-

If tax is payable, send the Account for receipting to Inland Revenue Financial Services Office by post at Barrington Road Worthing West Sussex BN12 4XH or by DX 90950 Worthing 3 or take it by hand to Room G21 West Wing Somerset House Strand London WC2

Aggregate Gross Value which in law devolves on and vests in the personal representatives of the deceased, for and in respect of which the grant is to be made.	Section 3A	**L**	72,105
	Section 3B	**M**	£245,000
	Section 5	**N**	-
(44) Total to be carried to the Probate papers		**P**	£317,105
Deduct			
Section 3A, total of liabilities and funeral expenses		**Q**	£2,129
Section 3B, total of liabilities		**R**	£10,125
(45) Net estate for Probate purposes		**S**	£304,851

Only include at N general power property

(41) The tax attributable to the non-instalment option property is the proportion of the total tax (£50,156.4) that the value of that property (£64,976) bears to the total chargeable estate (£320,391). The tax payable on delivery of the form is £10,168.74. Note that this property is charged at an effective estate rate of 15.65%, ie:

$$\frac{\text{Tax}}{\text{Chargeable estate}} = \frac{£50,156.40}{£320,391} \times 100\%$$

(42) Interest is charged only on tax that is outstanding six months after the end of the month of the deceased's death. As he died on 4 July 1997 and this account is delivered on 1 August 1997, no interest is payable.

(43) The value of the instalment option property is £166,375. No tax is payable on the delivery of this account as the first instalment only becomes due six months after the end of the month of death. Tax on this sum is calculated as:

$$\frac{£166,375}{£320,391} \times 50,156.4 = \text{total tax of } £26,037.69$$

The first instalment due on 1 February 1998 will be £2,603.77 (£26,037.69 ÷ 10). It carries interest from the date the first instalment is due (1 February 1998) to the date of payment.

Subsequent instalments given that the tax payable is wholly attributable to the value of land (ie Church View and Primrose Cottage) carry interest on the whole of the unpaid IHT (and on the whole of the current instalment, if it is overdue).

If any of the property is sold, the balance of the outstanding tax attributable to that property (with interest if applicable) becomes payable immediately. Remember that in this case, the PRs hope to sell Church View and discharge all the outstanding tax, ie £26,037.69 before the first instalment becomes due.

The total tax payable on the deceased's free estate is:

$$£10,168.74 + £26,037.69 = £36,206.42.$$

The balance of the tax attributable to the settled fund and 'Wye Knot' and payable by the Trustees and Elspeth is:

$$\frac{£89,040}{£320,391} \times 50,156.4 = £13,934.76$$

(44) This figure is entered in the executor's oath as the gross value of the estate which vests in the PRs and for which they are applying for a grant of probate. Section 2 and 5 property is excluded because it does not vest in the PRs; the fact that they may be liable for tax on it is irrelevant for probate purposes.

(45) Probate fees are calculated on this figure.

Note 55   (46)   I/We wish to apply for a • Grant of Probate   x

Tick the appropriate box

                           • Grant of Letters of Administration   –

                           • Grant of Letters of Administration with Will annexed   –

                           • Grant of _____   –

(47)   To the best of my/our knowledge and belief all the statements made and particulars given in this Account and its accompanying schedules are true and complete.

(48)   I/We have made the fullest enquiries that are reasonably practicable in the circumstances to ascertain the value of all assets, interests, liabilities, etc.
- Where it has been possible to obtain exact values these have been included.
- Where exact values have not been obtained the values included are the best estimates which could be made on the information available, and

     I/We undertake, as soon as the final values are obtained, to deliver a further Account, and to pay any additional tax and interest for which I/we may be liable.

I/We have aggregated on Pages 10 and 11 the value of chargeable gifts and settled property.

(49)   So far as the tax on property disclosed in this Account may be paid by instalments, I/we elect to pay ~~or not to pay~~ by instalments as indicated in the Sections, and I/we understand that interest may be payable on unpaid tax in accordance with the statutory rules.

Notes 56 and 57   I/We understand that the issue of the Grant does not imply acceptance by the Inland Revenue of any of the statements made or values included in this Account.

(50)   An executor or intending administrator who fails to make the fullest enquiries that are reasonably practicable in the circumstances may be liable to penalties.

     Name   George Siegfried Lomax

     Signature

     Date

You may be liable to penalties or prosecution if you fail to disclose, in this Account and in your answers to the questions on Pages 2, 3, 8 and 9, all the property in respect of which tax may be payable.

     Name   Elspeth Georgina Pollax

     Signature

     Date

     Name

     Signature

     Date

     Name

     Signature

     Date

12

(46) The executors want a grant of probate as opposed to a grant of letters of administration with or without will annexed.

(47) The declaration made by the PRs requires them to take all practicable steps to ensure that the form is correct.

(48) There are no items in this estate that the PRs have been unable to value. (Notice that any valuations referred to should accompany the form.)

(49) So far as possible the PRs elect to pay the tax by instalments.

(50) Declaration signed by the PRs. Before signing the declaration, the 'warning' in the right hand box should be brought to the PRs' attention to emphasise the seriousness of their task.   **[II.6]**

APPENDIX III: RELIEF AGAINST DOUBLE CHARGES TO IHT

The risk of a double charge to IHT arises in a number of situations and FA 1986 s 104 enabled the Board to make regulations to give relief to taxpayers in certain cases. The Regulations were made on 30 June 1987 and came into force on 22 July 1987, although the relief is given for transfers of value made, and other events occurring on or after 18 March 1986 (the Inheritance Tax (Double Charges Relief) Regulations 1987: SI 1987/1130).   **[III.1]**

Case 1—PETs and death

The first case is concerned with the area of mutual transfers, ie where property is transferred (by a PET which becomes chargeable) but at the death of the donor he has received back property from his donee (either the original property or property which represents it) which is included in the donor's death estate. The position is illustrated in the following example: all the examples in this Appendix are based on illustrations given in the Regulations themselves. It is assumed that current IHT rates apply throughout; grossing up does not apply to lifetime transfers; and that no exemptions or reliefs are available.

EXAMPLE III.1

July 1995	A makes a gift of a Matthew Smith oil painting (value £100,000) to B (a PET)	
July 1996	A makes a gift into a discretionary trust of £265,000	IHT paid £10,000
Jan 1997	A makes a further gift into the same trust of £30,000	IHT paid £6,000
Jan 1998	B dies and the Smith picture returns to A	
Apr 1999	A dies. His death estate of £400,000 includes the picture returned to him in 1997 which is still worth £100,000	

If no relief were available, A in *Example III.1* would be subject to IHT on the value of the picture twice: once when it was given away in 1995 (the chargeable PET) and a second time on its value in 1999 (as part of his death estate). In addition A's cumulative total would be increased by the 1995 PET, thereby necessitating a recalculation of the tax charged on the 1996 and 1997 transfers and resulting in a higher charge on his death estate.

Regulation 4 affords relief in this situation and provides for two alternative IHT calculations to be made and for the lower amount of tax produced by those calculations to be payable. The alternative calculations may be illustrated as follows:

EXAMPLE III.1 continued

First calculation:

Charge the picture as part of a death estate and ignore the 1995 PET.

July 1995	PET £100,000 ignored	Tax nil
July 1996	Gift £265,000: tax £20,000 less £10,000 already paid	Tax payable £10,000
Jan 1997	Gift £30,000: tax £12,000 *Less:* £6,000 already paid	Tax payable £6,000

Apr 1999   Death estate £400,000   Tax payable
                                                           £160,000
Total tax due as result of A's death   £176,000

(*Note* that because the 1995 PET is ignored A's cumulative total is unaltered and a recalculation of tax on the 1996 and 1997 transfers is unnecessary.)

Second calculation:
Charge the 1995 PET and ignore the value of the picture on A's death
July 1995   PET £100,000: tax   £nil
July 1996   Gift £265,000: tax £60,000
            Less: £10,000 already paid   £50,000
Jan 1997   Gift £30,000: tax £12,000
            Less: £6,000 already paid   £6,000
Apr 1999   Death estate £300,000   £120,000

Total tax due as result of A's death   £176,000

Tax payable
The tax payable is equal in amount under the two calculations: see *Example III.3* below.

It may be that reg 4 is capable of being exploited to the benefit of the taxpayer as can be seen from the following illustration. Assume that Adam gives property worth £100,000 to his daughter Berta in 1994 and buys the property back for £75,000 (which represents less than full consideration) in 1995. He then dies in 1997. Under reg 4 the value of the property (£100,000) will remain subject to IHT but Adam's estate has been reduced by the £75,000 paid for the property (see especially reg 4(3)(a)).

[**III.2**]

Case 2—Gifts with a reservation and subsequent death

This case covers the situation where a gift with a reservation (either immediately chargeable or a chargeable PET) is followed by the death of the donor at a time when he still enjoys a reserved benefit or within seven years of that benefit ceasing (ie within seven years of the deemed PET: see [21.41])). The situation is illustrated in *Example III.2*.

EXAMPLE III.2

Jan 1996   A makes a PET of £150,000 to B
Mar 2000   A makes a gift of a house worth £265,000 into a   IHT paid
            discretionary trust but continues to live in the   £10,000
            property. The gift is of property subject to a
            reservation
Feb 2003   A dies still living in the house. His death estate is
            valued at £415,000 including the house which is
            then worth £300,000

Regulation 5 prevents double taxation of the house in this example by providing for two separate IHT calculations to be made as follows: [**III.3**]

EXAMPLE III.2 continued

First calculation:
Charge the house as part of A's death estate and ignore the gift with reservation:

		Tax
Jan 1996	PET	Nil
Mar 2000	Gift with reservation ignored	Nil
Feb 2003	Death estate £415,000: tax £80,000	
	Less: £10,000 already paid	£70,000
Total tax due as a result of A's death		£70,000

(*Note:* credit for tax already paid on the gift with reservation cannot exceed the amount of death tax attributable to that property. In this example the tax so attributable is £57,831 (ie £80,000 × 300,000/415,000)—hence credit is given for the full amount of £10,000.)

Second calculation:
The gift with reservation is charged and the value of the gifted property is ignored in taxing the death estate:

		Tax
Jan 1996	PET	Nil
Mar 2000	Gift of house £265,000: tax £20,000	
	Less: £10,000 already paid	£10,000
Feb 2003	Death estate £115,000 (ignoring house)	£46,000
Total tax due as result of A's death:		£56,000

Tax payable: the first calculation yields a higher amount of tax. Therefore the gift of the house in 2000 is ignored and tax on death is charged as in the first calculation giving credit for IHT already paid.

Case 3—Artificial debts and death

Relief is afforded under reg 6 when a chargeable transfer (or chargeable PET) is followed by the transferor incurring a liability to his transferee which falls within FA 1986 s 103 (the artificial debt rules).

EXAMPLE III.3

Nov 1995	X makes a PET of cash (£95,000) to Y
Dec 1995	Y makes a loan to X of £95,000
May 1996	X makes a gift into a discretionary trust of £20,000
Apr 2001	X dies. His death estate is worth £228,000 and the
	loan from Y remains outstanding

Under s 103 the deduction of £95,000 would be disallowed so that the 1995 PET and the disallowed debt would both attract an IHT charge. Relief is provided, however, under reg 6 on the basis of the following alternative calculations: **[III.4]**

EXAMPLE III.3 continued

First calculation:
Ignore the 1995 gift but do not allow the debt to be deducted in the death estate.

		Tax
Nov 1995	PET ignored	Nil
May 1996	£20,000	Nil
Apr 2001	Death estate £235,000	£16,000
Total tax due as result of X's death:		£16,000

Second calculation:
Charge the 1995 PET but allow the debt to be deducted from the estate at death.

		Tax
Nov 1995	PET £95,000: tax	£nil
May 1996	Gift £20,000: tax	£nil
Apr 2001	Death estate (£235,000 – loan of £95,000)	£16,000
Total tax due as result of X's death:		£16,000

Tax payable: The total tax chargeable is equal in amount under the two calculations and reg 8 provides that in such cases the first calculation shall be treated as producing a higher amount: accordingly the debt is disallowed against the death estate and the PET of £95,000 is not charged.

Case 4—Chargeable transfers and death

Under FA 1986 s 104(1)(d) regulations can be made to prevent a double charge to IHT in circumstances 'similar' to those dealt with in the first three cases above.

Regulation 7, made in pursuance of this power, applies when an individual makes a chargeable transfer of value to a *person* after 17 March 1986, and dies within seven years of that transfer, at a time when he was beneficially entitled to property which either directly or indirectly represented the property which had been transferred by the original chargeable transfer.

For relief to be given under this regulation it is important to realise that the lifetime transfer must have been chargeable when made. The majority of transfers to individuals will not therefore fall within its ambit since they will be PETs. Accordingly, the regulation is only of importance in the following cases:

(1) When the chargeable transfer is to a discretionary trust which subsequently returns all or part of the property to settlor.
(2) When the chargeable transfer is to a company with, again, that property being returned to the transferor.
(3) Between 18 March 1986 and 17 March 1987 the creation of an interest in possession trust was immediately chargeable and therefore if such a trust was created during that period and property is later returned to the settlor the regulation would, *prima facie,* be applicable.

It should be noted that the regulation does not afford relief in cases where the chargeable transfer occurred before *18 March 1986* and the gift-back after that date. In such cases, the repeal of the CTT mutual transfer rules in 1986 means that the gift-back may be subject to charge without the possibility of any relief.

As with the other cases, relief under reg 7 is given on the basis of two alternative calculations. The first includes the returned property in the death estate but ignores the original chargeable transfer (although there is no question of any refund of tax paid at that time). The second calculation taxes the original chargeable transfer (ie it may be subject to a supplementary charge on death and remains in the taxpayer's cumulative total) but ignores the returned property in taxing the transferor's death estate.   **[III.5]**

APPENDIX IV: PENSIONS

1 Introduction

The provision of financial security in old age is a major concern not only for an individual and his dependants but also for the state. The state discharges its duty in this area by providing a statutory pension scheme which is available to all who make national insurance contributions. As this provides relatively small benefits, occupational pension schemes (private schemes provided by an employer for his employees) are crucially important and represent a significant (albeit hidden) part of an employee's remuneration. The self-employed and others who either cannot or chose not to benefit from an occupational scheme can make their own arrangements through a personal pension scheme. [**IV.1**]

2 The state scheme

a) *State pensions*

The state scheme is funded by national insurance contributions. It is in two parts. The first part is the flat rate pension (the old age pension) payable from the age of 65 for men and 60 for women. To qualify for a full basic state pension a person has to have paid (or been credited with) Class 1 national insurance contributions for 90% of their working life. For 1997–98 the full basic state pension is £62.45 per week for a single person and £99.80 per week for a married couple.

The second part is the state earnings-related pension ('SERPs') which is an additional pension related to individual employees' earnings. A SERPs pension is provided to all employees who are not 'contracted-out' (see below). The amount of pension received depends on earnings (in each tax year after 5 April 1978) between the 'upper earnings limit' (currently £465 per week or £24,180 per year) and the 'lower earnings limit' (currently £62 per week or £3,224 per year). When calculating the pension due, each year's earnings are revalued annually until retirement in accordance with movements in national average earnings. The maximum SERPs pension that can be received is 20% of the employee's average revalued earnings: for these purposes earnings are averaged over all of an employee's working life and not just the years actually worked.

National insurance contributions paid by employers and employees are not set aside to fund pensions when they come into payment. Instead the national insurance fund at the time of payment funds the pensions then payable. As a result, pressure on the national insurance fund increases as the number of pensioners increases proportionate to the number of workers paying national insurance contributions (cf the effect of increasing unemployment). The government has, therefore, been anxious to encourage people to 'contract-out' of SERPs. [**IV.2**]

b) *Contracting-out*

An employee can contract-out of SERPs by reference either to an occupational scheme or a personal pension scheme. Contracted-out schemes used to be supervised by the Occupational Pensions Board but on 6 April 1977 its functions were divided between various bodies, the Contributions Agency assuming responsibility for all contracting-out matters.

Occupational schemes are of two types — 'money purchase' or 'final salary' (otherwise known as 'defined benefit').

Under the former, a certain amount is contributed to be invested for the benefit of the employee. The pot of money is then used to provide retirement benefits for the employee. No level of benefit is guaranteed. Under a final salary scheme a member is promised a pension based on his earnings at the time of retirement (for instance, he may receive 1/60th of his final earnings for each year he has been in service). The scheme is then funded to ensure that there will be sufficient moneys to provide the benefits promised.

Personal pension schemes are effected by the individual employee and benefits are provided on a money purchase basis: the accumulated savings are used to fund the benefits on retirement.

When a person 'contracts-out' of SERPs through a private scheme, the scheme pension then in effect replaces the lost SERPs one. Originally only members of final salary occupational schemes could contract-out of SERPs but now money purchase occupational and personal pension schemes can be used as well.

The Pensions Act 1995 and regulations made thereunder substantially altered the contracting-out arrangements with effect from 6 April 1997 as part of the government's continuing drive to encourage more people to contract-out. That encouragement comes in the form of reducing the rate at which Class 1 national insurance contributions are paid by employers and employees and/or the government paying an age-related rebate into the scheme: the form of the incentive differs according to the type of scheme. The quid pro quo for these incentives is that contracted-out schemes have to provide a certain level of benefit to replace the foregone SERPs (again, how this is calculated depends on the type of scheme) and are subject to a range of controls to ensure these replacement benefits will be provided.

Whilst these are all important changes, increasing the ability to contract-out may not be a radical enough answer to the problems that will arise from state pensions being funded on a 'pay-as-you-go' basis. The investment return shown by personal pension plans (thought to be too much affected by the level of commission and charges, including those for investment managers who fail to outperform the market)and the detrimental effect that moving jobs still has on occupational schemes have recently been highlighted by an OFT report. The new Labour government has announced a wide-ranging review of pension provision, including the underlying theory: whose responsibility is it to ensure retired persons (including those who have not been employed because they are carers) do not live in poverty? It seems we may be moving towards a different type of top-up pension, perhaps a compulsory one for those not in occupational schemes, with contributions paid by the state for carers.   **[IV.3]**

c) *Sex equality*

Following ECJ rulings that pensions are 'pay' and, therefore, must be provided equally to men and women to comply with the equality provisions in the Treaty of Rome, occupational pension schemes became obliged to equalise pension benefits. However, the unequal state retirement ages create substantial barriers to placing men and women in the same overall financial position between ages 60 and 65; and they make it virtually impossible for a contracted-out scheme to comply with the Treaty of Rome because some of the scheme benefits are inextricably linked with SERPs.

These issues were also addressed in the Pensions Act 1995. State pension age will be equalised at 65. This will not affect women born before 6 April 1950 and for those born between then and 6 April 1955 the state pension age will depend on how long after 5 April 1950 they were born. Further, the link between contracting-out and SERPs is broken, thus better enabling schemes to provide equal benefits.   **[IV.4]**

d) *The need for private arrangements*

The state scheme has the following main disadvantages:
(1) the retirement age is not flexible (although payment of pension can be deferred);
(2) although the employer's national insurance contributions are not taxed as emoluments of the employee, there is no income tax relief for the employee's own contributions;
(3) for the tax year 1997–98, earnings above £24,180 are unpensionable;
(4) there is no right to commute part of the pension for a tax-free lump sum.

As a result of these limits on state provision, many people participate in private arrangements, either occupational schemes or personal pension schemes.   [**IV.5**]

3 Occupational pension schemes

a) *Types of employer provision*

An employer could provide pension benefits merely through a contractual promise: the employer could contract to pay a pension on retirement according to a formula or at a set rate. Alternatively, the promised benefits could be pre-funded (ie set aside to meet the employee's claims).

Some sort of arrangement whereby the security of the contractual promise does not depend on the company still being in existence and solvent when they retire is obviously preferable for employees. Traditionally this security has been provided by pension benefits being pre-funded through a trust. If contributions are held on trust for the employees, they will be protected from the company's creditors.

From a tax viewpoint, only pension schemes established under irrevocable trusts can be granted exempt approved status and benefit from the various tax reliefs (TA 1988 s 592(1)).

Given the trust structure, scheme members have generally had to rely on trust law to protect their interests. Recent scandals led to the establishment of the Pension Law Review Committee (the Goode Committee) which, *inter alia*, considered whether statute should replace trust law as the basis for occupational schemes. The key recommendation made was that: 'Trust law should continue to provide the foundation for interests, rights and duties arising in connection with occupational pension schemes but should be reinforced by a Pensions Act administered by a Pensions Regulator' (see generally Cmnd 2342). The Pensions Act 1995 seeks to provide greater security for pension scheme members, for instance by replacing the OPB by the Occupational Pensions Regulatory Authority, which has much wider powers of investigation and regulation; and by introducing member-nominated trustees of schemes, new minimum funding requirements and the Pensions Compensation Board. While trust law will continue to govern the rights and duties arising in relation to schemes, the Act does clarify the powers and duties of a scheme's trustees and its professional advisers.   [**IV.6**]

b) *Types of benefits*

Benefits from an occupational scheme can be provided on a 'money purchase' or 'final salary' ('defined benefits') basis—see [**IV.3**]   [**IV.7**]

c) *Types of funding*

Occupational schemes may be funded by contributions from both the employer and the employee. If the employee is not obliged to contribute to the scheme it is a 'non-contributory' scheme; if he is, it is 'contributory'.

An employee may wish to contribute to the scheme even though not obliged to do so and every exempt approved scheme must provide facilities to enable members to make voluntary contributions ('AVCs').

An employee would make AVCs in order to improve the benefits he will eventually receive from the scheme: his contributions (plus investment return—sometimes this will include capital appreciation but often the contributions are invested in such a way that interest only is received) will be accumulated and the 'pot' used to buy extra benefits on retirement.

Instead of making additional contributions to his employer's scheme, he may make them to a 'free-standing additional voluntary contributions scheme' (FSAVC). This type of scheme is completely separate from the employer's scheme and is run by a bank, insurance company, etc. By choosing the FSAVC provider, the employee is able to choose the investment medium for his contributions and may opt for an arrangement providing capital appreciation as well as income.   **[IV.8]**

4 Exempt approved occupational pension schemes

a) *Securing approval*

Most schemes are approved by the Pension Schemes Office (PSO) so that they may take advantage of the tax benefits discussed below. If a scheme complies with the benefit limits in TA 1988 s 590 the PSO must approve it. However, the requirements of s 590 are restrictive and normally schemes seek discretionary approval under s 591. Approval is normally granted to schemes which satisfy the requirements set out in IR12 (1991); many of these relate to the level of benefits that may be provided. Only schemes approved under s 590 or s 591 may be granted exempt approved status and normally they will only be granted such status if they are established under irrevocable trusts (s 592(1)). Normally an approved scheme will be established by a trust.   **[IV.9]**

b) *Funding*

Employer contributions are not taxed as emoluments of the employee (TA 1988 s 596) and are deductible in arriving at the profits of the employer: accordingly they represent a valuable tax-free fringe benefit. Further, because of the high level of employers' national insurance contributions in the case of higher paid employees (10% of salary in the case of employees earning £210 or more per week), increased contributions by the employer to such a scheme (which are not subject to NICs) may prove more attractive than paying a higher wage or bonus.

Although there is no fixed upper limit on an employer's contribution to an occupational scheme, the essential requirement is that contributions must be adequate to ensure the appropriate pension benefits. To prevent funds which are not needed to provide benefits being rolled-up tax free in an approved pension scheme and then returned to an employer when he has sufficient losses to avoid paying tax on the refund, pension schemes must keep the surplus of assets over liabilities within a prescribed limit. If this limit is exceeded, the surplus must then be reduced in one or more of the following ways: by improving benefits; by giving contribution holidays to employees and/or employers; by a refund to the employer (TA 1988 Sch 22 para 3). Any such refund is, however, subject to a 40% tax charge deducted at source (TA 1988 s 601) and this tax is charged whatever the tax position of the recipient employer (ie even if he has trading losses).

Following the introduction of this tax charge some small self-administered schemes ('SSASs') devised a new way of taking advantage of the tax-free roll-up of funds. SSASs are, basically, schemes with fewer than 12 members, usually established to provide benefits to directors with controlling interests. Some SSASs deliberately took action to breach the conditions which have to be complied with to maintain the scheme's approved status. Approval was then withdrawn with the result that the accumulated pension fund could be paid out immediately (either to the members or as an investment in the (cash-strapped) company); in certain cases no tax would be payable on the distributed funds.

Not surprisingly, FA 1995 introduced a tax charge in these circumstances. The charge applies not only to traditional SSASs but also to schemes with 12 or more members if they included (in the 12 months prior to withdrawal of approval) a person who was or had been a controlling director of a company which had at any time participated in the scheme. Section 61 introduced TA 1988 s 591C under which tax is charged when approval of such schemes is withdrawn. Tax is charged at 40% under Case VI of Schedule D on the value of the scheme assets. Section 61 also made a consequential amendment to TCGA 1992: s 239A provides that the assets shall be deemed to have been reacquired by the trustees at the value on which tax is charged under s 591C, but there is no deemed disposal (and hence no CGT payable on the reacquisition).

Tax Bulletin, December 1995, p 266 addresses the attempts that have been made to avoid this new 40% tax charge by the original SSAS paying a transfer value to a new scheme established by a different (probably newly formed) company which then transfers the new scheme offshore where it operates as a non-approved scheme. The *Bulletin* indicates that, if the arrangement is considered to be artificial, then tax approval could be withdrawn from the original SSAS with effect from the day the transfer value was paid, leading to a 40% charge on the value of its assets before the transfer (see *R v IRC ex parte Roux Waterside Inn Ltd* (1997) for an example of the Revenue successfully claiming this tax). The sponsoring company is ultimately responsible for payment of the s 591C charge.

If the benefits to be provided by a scheme already equal the Inland Revenue limits set out in IR12, an employee cannot make, or must cease making, AVCs. Excess contributions are refunded to the employee. Tax at [33%] is deducted from the refund and this satisfies the employee's basic rate liability on the refund (the extra 10% reflects the benefit received from the contributions having grown tax free when within the fund): higher rate taxpayers must pay higher rate tax on the amount of the repayment grossed up at [23%] (s 599A). If an employee's ordinary contributions are refunded for any reason, then s 598 imposes a 20% tax charge on the trustees of the scheme.   **[IV.10]**

c) *Tax treatment*

Retirement benefits schemes (schemes for the provision of 'relevant benefits') are governed for tax purposes by a code originally introduced in FA 1970.

The term 'relevant benefits' is widely defined to cover virtually any kind of payment to any employee or to his widow, children or dependants made as a result of his retirement or death (TA 1988 s 612). Most occupational schemes are governed by this code, but only if the scheme is 'exempt-approved' will it enjoy the following tax advantages:

(1) The employer's contributions will not be taxed as the employee's income (s 596(1)(a)).
(2) An employer may claim a tax deduction for ordinary annual contributions (s 592(4)). Deductions for contributions in excess of these must be spread over a number of years (s 592(6), IR12 (1991) paras 5.6–5.8 for contributions made in chargeable periods ending on or before 31 May 1996 and *Tax Bulletin*, August 1996, p 342 for those made thereafter). In *Kelsall v Investments Chartwork Ltd* (1994) the High Court held that the commissioners had no

power to review the exercise of the Inland Revenue's discretion to require spreading as no criteria are given as to how the discretion should be exercised, so that it is wholly at large. FA 1993 by amending s 592(4) made it clear that the deduction under s 592 may only be claimed for actual payments into a scheme: it cannot be claimed when a provision for such payments is made in the employer's accounts. The costs of establishing and running a scheme are not deductible under s 592 but they will be allowed as an expense of the chargeable period in which they are paid (IR12 para 5.11).

(3) The employee obtains income tax relief on his own contributions subject to a limit of 15% of his remuneration (s 592(7)-(8E) and note that certain emoluments are excluded from the definition of remuneration by s 612(1)).

A major change introduced by FA 1989 was the introduction of an *earnings limit* (£84,000 for 1997-98). This ceiling applies for the purpose of calculating certain benefits paid and contribution levels in the case of tax approved pension schemes established on or after 14 March 1989 and also applies to new entrants to existing schemes who join on or after 1 June 1989. Generally the ceiling has been increased each year by reference to movements in prices. Since traditionally earnings increase at a faster rate than prices, eventually a higher proportion of scheme members will be affected by the earnings cap.

EXAMPLE IV.1

Gerontius's salary is £150,000 pa and he is subject to the earnings ceiling. The maximum pension is two-thirds of £84,000 (ie £56,000—the two-thirds limit is imposed by the PSO (see IR12)). This is reduced if he has less than 20 years' service.

(4) Pensions payable under an approved scheme are taxable under Schedule E and subject to PAYE (TA 1988 ss 19 and 597).

(5) A member may, on retirement, elect to commute part of his pension for a tax-free lump sum (s 189). The maximum sum that can, generally, be received is 1½ times the employee's final remuneration: again, this is reduced if he has less than 20 years' service. For members joining a scheme on or after 17 March 1987, the maximum tax-free lump sum is limited to £150,000. If a member is subject to the earnings cap, then this applies to the lump sum payment as well as the pension.

EXAMPLE IV.2

The maximum tax-free lump sum Gerontius could receive is £126,000 (1.5 × £84,000).

Benefits based on remuneration in excess of £84,000 may be provided under unapproved 'top-up schemes'—see 5 below.

(6) Refunds to employers and employees are taxed: see b) above.

(7) Lump sum payments made to the employee's dependants on his death will not be charged to IHT provided that they are made at the trustees' discretion (in practice, an employee may make a 'declaration of wishes' indicating who he would like to benefit on his death, and the trustees pay particular attention to this when exercising their discretion). Pensions will be taxable in the hands of the recipient.

(8) The pension fund is not subject to income tax on the investments (except for any income produced from commercial trading) nor to CGT on a disposal of investments—(TA 1988 s 592(2) and TCGA 1992 s 271(1)(g))—but note that in certain cases income tax may be charged on the value of the fund when approval is withdrawn (see b) above)). Pension funds are not able

to claim a refund of the tax credit on distributions made by UK companies after 1 July 1997 (F(No 2)A 1997).   **[IV.11]**

d) *The wider picture*

The company pension fund is generally administered by trustees who are responsible for making the investments and paying the pensions (a self-administered scheme). Alternatively, responsibility for providing the pensions may be passed to an insurance company which receives premiums in the form of employer/employee contributions: the scheme is still established under trust.

Self-administered schemes provide flexibility and can be more cost effective than insurance company schemes. Small self-administered schemes (broadly those with less than 12 members) ('SSASs') are particularly suited to controlling shareholders of private companies. Directors of the relevant company may be appointed trustees of the pension fund together with one professional trustee and, as they will be given wide investment powers, may employ the fund for the benefit of the company itself. For instance, they can purchase the business premises and then lease them back to the company at a commercial rent. The rent will be tax deductible by the company and tax free in the hands of the pension fund trustees. Additionally, the trustees may be given the power to make loans to the company or may choose to invest in the company's shares (any type of employer-related investment is generally known as self-investment). There are, however, restrictions on the freedom of pension scheme trustees to self-invest and over time the restrictions are becoming more extensive, even in relation to SSASs (see eg SI 1991/1614 and IR12 (1991)). The latest changes relate to larger schemes and follow from Goode Committee (see **[IV.6]**) recommendations: see Pensions Act 1995 s 40 and regulations made thereunder. Subject to these restrictions, the following example illustrates the type of arrangement trustees of an SSAS may contemplate.

EXAMPLE IV.3

A small family company trades profitably. Mr and Mrs A themselves own the property from which the business is conducted (current value £80,000) and all the shares in the company. The business is now run by their three daughters. A small self-administered pension scheme is established and the following events occur:

(1) A contribution of £40,000 is made by the company to the scheme. In practice, this sum will be deducted in arriving at the profits of the business (probably by spreading over a number of years: see c) (2) above).
(2) The fund is loaned £40,000 by a bank.
(3) The trustees of the scheme pay Mr and Mrs A £80,000 for the property.
(4) The trustees lease the property to the company charging a rent of £8,000 pa. This is an allowable expense for corporation tax purposes so far as the company is concerned and the rental income is tax free so far as the fund is concerned.

Note: (a) in the future the bank loan can be repaid out of pension contributions and rental income; (b) the property has been taken out of the estates of Mr and Mrs A and will therefore be tax free when they die; (c) as and when pensions become payable the property may have to be sold to raise funds to purchase life annuities.

[IV.12]

5 Unapproved occupational pension schemes

a) *Uses*

Prior to the introduction of the earnings cap (see 4c)(3) above) there were few (if any) unapproved occupational pension schemes: if the total benefits provided under an employer's schemes exceeded the Inland Revenue limits for approved schemes, then *none* of the schemes could be approved. The 1989 changes, however, have led to a much greater interest in such schemes: although the earnings cap does not apply to executives in pensionable service at the time it was introduced, new recruits are affected by it and employers may feel that they need to make some sort of provision to keep 'old' and 'new' employees on equal terms. This aim has been helped by FA 1989 which provided that only benefits granted under approved schemes need to be aggregated in calculating whether the benefit limits have been reached. This has left employers free to introduce 'top-up' schemes for executives subject to the earnings cap. The current NIC exemption for employer contributions may make such schemes attractive even for employees not subject to the cap but this is to be removed (DSS Press Release of 22 July 1997). **[IV.13]**

b) *Choices*

Unapproved schemes will normally be 'retirement benefits schemes' (as defined in s 611): these are any arrangement or scheme for providing benefits consisting of or including 'relevant benefits' for employees or their families and so include benefits provided under the contract of employment as well as those provided under separately constituted schemes. It is worth noting that unapproved schemes do *not* escape entirely from the regulatory framework governing approved schemes.

'Relevant benefits' are widely defined in s 612: the width of the definition means that most unapproved occupational pension schemes will be 'retirement benefits schemes'; indeed the Inland Revenue booklet *The Tax Treatment of Top-Up Pension Schemes* (issued August 1991) points out that schemes which were not intended to be retirement benefits schemes could be caught (eg a sick pay scheme which provided for a lump sum to be paid on death of a member).

Unapproved benefits may be provided by a funded scheme or through an unfunded contractual promise. **[IV.14]**

c) *Tax treatment*

Unapproved retirement benefits schemes give rise to the following tax consequences:

(1) When an employer 'pays a sum with a view to the provision of relevant benefits to any employee', the employee is taxed on the amount of the sum paid (s 595(1)). So, if the scheme is funded the employee will be taxable when the employer makes a payment to a trust fund or an insurance policy to fund the *benefits,* even though he has not actually received any cash (separate contributions for the establishment and running costs of the scheme do not give rise to this charge). If the scheme is unfunded, the charge under s 595 would arise when the benefit was paid to the employee: however note that, in the case of a pension, the charge is under s 19 rather than s 595 (see s 595(1)(a)) and in the case of a lump sum benefit the charge arises under s 596A(2) (and see ESC A62, reissued 17 July 1996, for an income tax exclusion where extra pension is provided through non-approved arrangements when a person has to retire because of work-related injury or illness).

If the scheme is funded, then *pensions* are still taxable in the hands of the employee even though the contributions to fund the pension have already been taxed on him (s 596A(6) and s 19(1)). The taxation of lump sum payments is less straightforward. Prior to FA 1994 lump sum benefits paid from funded unapproved retirement benefits schemes (FURBS) were normally tax free in the hands of the recipient. However, to avoid the tax charges on the fund and thus enable a larger lump sum to be paid for the same contributions, some FURBS were established offshore or contributions to on-shore FURBS were invested offshore. FA 1994 therefore introduced a new tax regime for lump sums received from FURBS. The new regime only applies to schemes entered into on or after 1 December 1993 or pre-existing schemes which are varied on or after that date 'with a view to the provision of the benefit' (FA 1994 s 108(6)).

The major change introduced by FA 1994 s 108(5) (by amending TA 1988 s 596A) is to tax a lump sum if any of the FURBS' income or gains are not brought into the tax charge (but note that the Inland Revenue practice is not to tax the lump sum where the investments are UK tax-exempt ones—*Taxation*, 24 November 1994, p 191). The Revenue view is that the 40% tax payable under s 591C when certain approved schemes have their approval withdrawn (see 4b) above) is not a charge on the scheme's 'income and gains' and, therefore, tax remains payable under s 596A (*Tax Bulletin*, August 1995, pp 232 and 233). Where s 596A applies, the whole lump sum is taxable subject to a deduction for any sums on which the employee was taxed under s 595(1) and any employee contributions which, in either case, were paid as a contribution to the provision of the lump sum. There are apportionment provisions to deal with the position where the lump sum is provided on part disposal of an asset (or the surrender of any part of or share in any rights in an asset) if the employee or someone connected with him has a right to receive, or an expectation of receiving, further lump sums on a further disposal of any part of the asset (or further surrender of rights).

The taxation of FURBS was further changed in 1994 by the introduction of a new sub-s (8) to TA 1988 s 596A. The previous sub-s (8) exempted a benefit from tax if it was 'attributable to the payment of a sum which is deemed to be the income of a person by virtue of s 595(1) and in respect of which that person has been assessed to tax'. The exemption given by the new sub-s (8) is both narrower and wider than the previous one.

First, it only applies where a *lump sum* is paid whereas previously it applied when a *benefit* was received.

Secondly, under the old provision lump sum benefits funded by employee contributions did not escape the s 596A charge but now they seem to do so (see (3) below).

Thirdly, even where the employee has paid tax on the employer contributions, the lump sum now only escapes the s 596A charge if it is provided to the employee, any person falling within s 595(5) or any individual designated by the employee. Trust deeds would normally contain a wider class of beneficiaries than those set out in s 595(5)—for instance, a common law spouse who was not a dependant—and such persons could, therefore, only benefit without giving rise to a tax charge if they had been designated by the employee. Unfortunately, the reference to 'individual' seems to exclude designating trustees for minor beneficiaries or charities. Further, it is to be hoped that 'designation' will cover a non-binding letter of wishes, which is the usual procedure for establishing an employee's wishes in relation to the discretionary trust on which lump sum benefits on death are normally held: requiring a binding nomination would have adverse IHT consequences.

In the absence of the tax charge on pre-funding under s 595, employees would obviously prefer a pre-funded scheme where the assets are held on trust, in order to provide security against the employer's creditors. There has been, therefore, much debate about how top-up arrangements should be structured: advocates of the funded scheme suggest that the employer should pay the tax due under s 595 and point out the advantages of a funded scheme as opposed to, say, increasing an employee's salary to compensate him for only receiving limited benefits under the approved scheme (eg no NICs on contributions, (but this is to be changed—see [**IV.13**]); basic rate tax only on investment income).

(2) Employers cannot claim a tax deduction for contributions unless either the employee receives a benefit on which he is then taxed or the employee is taxable under s 595(1) on the money paid (FA 1989 s 76—and see *Tax Bulletin*, June 1995, pp 224 and 225, for the Revenue's view that this section successfully ensures that there is timing symmetry between when the company can claim the relief and when the employee is charged to tax). The Inland Revenue booklet referred to above appears to indicate that there is a right to a deduction if the payments result in a tax charge on the employee: the employer does not also need to show that the payments have been made 'wholly and exclusively' for the purposes of the trade. Payments to meet establishment and running costs will only be deductible if they are deductible under normal principles.

(3) There is no tax deduction for employee contributions. Indeed, where the scheme was established before 1 December 1993 and has not been varied so as to fall within FA 1994 s 108(6), such contributions should not generally be made: the tax exemption for lump sum payments from such schemes only applies if the contribution was taxed under s 595(1); as the employee's income would have been taxed under other provisions, the exemption will not apply and the benefit financed by his contributions will be taxable under s 596A, resulting in a double tax charge. However, where the amended provisions of TA 1988 s 596A apply it appears employee contributions can be made without giving rise to a double tax charge (see (1) above).

(4) Refunds to employers will be taxed as a trading expense and losses may be used to reduce the charge. However, if the scheme was ever exempt approved, s 601 will continue to apply to refunds to employers and ss 598 and 599A to those to employees (see 4b) above).

(5) Lump sum payments from a funded scheme made to the employee's dependants on his death will normally be IHT free: if the employer pays the establishment and running costs then the scheme will be a sponsored superannuation scheme under IHTA 1984 s 151. There will be an IHT charge if the benefit is payable only to the deceased's estate; there will not usually be an IHT charge if the benefit is held on discretionary trust, if the employee's estate is not a discretionary beneficiary; if the estate is a potential beneficiary, there may be an IHT charge under the gifts with reservation regime (the Inland Revenue Press Release of 9 July 1986 does not apply to unapproved schemes).

(6) An on-shore FURBS will be subject to income tax and capital gains tax at the basic rate only if the scheme provides only 'relevant benefits'—(TA 1988 s 686(2)(c)(1) and TCGA 1992 s 5). Pension funds are not able to claim a refund of the tax credit on distributions made by UK companies after 1 July 1997 (F(No 2)A 1997).   [**IV.15**]

6 Personal pension schemes

Personal pensions replaced retirement annuity contracts from 1 July 1988 as the means by which the self-employed and employees in non-pensionable employment could make provision for their retirement (but existing contracts can be maintained—see the 10th edition of this work for a discussion of their tax treatment). Benefits are provided on a money-purchase basis (see below). Normally the scheme will be approved under Chapter IV of TA 1988 Part XIV. A scheme can also be contracted-out (see 2 above): it is then known as an 'appropriate' personal pension scheme. A person cannot normally be a member of both an occupational scheme and a personal scheme in relation to the same period of employment. However, if the occupational scheme is not contracted-out, a personal pension scheme can be established to receive the national insurance rebate.

Contributions to a personal pension scheme up to the permitted level (see below) qualify for income tax relief at the individual's highest rate (but note the Revenue's view (see *Taxation*, 15 June 1995, p 275) that an *employee* can only obtain basic rate tax relief by deduction from his contributions (see TA 1989 s 639)). Those contributions are held and invested through a tax exempt fund. As this fund is not subject to investment controls, the individual may choose to pay his contributions into a high risk fund. Unlike the majority of occupational pension schemes, therefore, personal pensions are money purchase contracts: in other words it is the accumulated savings from the chosen fund which will eventually be used to buy an annuity (the pension) from a life insurance company. Accordingly, the eventual pension payable is not limited to a fraction of the individual's earnings at any particular time. Other features of personal pensions worthy of note include the following:

(1) The maximum contributions are computed by reference to a percentage of the individual's 'net relevant earnings' (defined in TA 1988 s 644). For 1997–98 the relevant percentage which can be contributed, dependent upon the taxpayer's age, is set out in the following table.

Age	Max contribution
Up to 36	17.5%
36 to 45	20%
46 to 50	25%
51 to 55	30%
56 to 60	35%
61 or more	40%

(2) As with occupational pensions, the tax relief available will, however, be restricted to contributions on earnings up to £84,000 pa. Assume, therefore, that Gerontius in *Example IV.1* above was paying into a personal pension and was aged 57. The maximum contribution that will attract tax relief in 1997–98 is limited to 35% × £84,000.

(3) If the individual's contributions fall short of the maximum permitted, there are rules allowing unused relief to be carried forward. In certain circumstances excess contributions can be carried back.

The interaction of these rules when a person has both a retirement annuity contract and a personal pension plan (taking into account the maximum contribution under TA 1988 s 655) is complicated and has been made more so with the introduction of self-assessment. These problems have been widely discussed (see *Taxation*, 6 July 1995, p 358 and 14 March 1996, p 614 and *Tax Bulletin*, April 1996, p 298), but for now a Special Commissioner's decision (*Brock v O'Conner* (1997)) may have settled the debate (though see *Taxation*, 26 June 1997, p 335 and another can of worms it may have opened!)

The *means* by which relief actually due is to be given when a claim is made to carry back pension contributions under self-assessment has also been subject to much debate: the Revenue's view as to how it should give effect to such claims has been stated in detail in the December 1996 issue of the *Tax Bulletin* (see the February 1997 issue p 396 and June 1997 issue p 443 for additional comments).

(4) The maximum tax-free lump sum permitted at retirement is 25% of the total fund excluding 'protected rights' (the benefits provided to replace SERPs) but including the value of dependants' benefits. Any annuity payable

under an approved personal pension scheme is treated as earned income (TA 1988 s 643).

Prior to FA 1995, if the personal pension scheme member wished to take a tax free lump sum on his retirement, his annuity also had then to be purchased and come into payment. Annuity rates can vary significantly over time and if they were low at the time of retirement, this could have a profound effect on the member's financial position throughout retirement. FA 1995, by amending TA 1988, gave the member power, even if he took the lump sum, to defer purchase of the annuity (up to the age of 75, if he wishes) and in the meantime withdraw income from the fund: the Pensions Act 1995 extended these provisions to contracted-out personal pensions. Income must be withdrawn at the rate of 35–100% of the annuity that would have been payable (reviewed every three years) and is taxed under Schedule E and within the PAYE system (TA 1988 s 643(5)).

During this deferral period the income and capital gains of the fund will continue to build up tax free. If the member dies, any surviving spouse or dependant will be able either to continue making income withdrawals and then purchase an annuity before the earlier of his 75th birthday or the member's or to purchase an immediate annuity or take the fund in cash no later than two years after the death of the member; a surviving spouse under 60 will also have the option of deferring annuity purchase until he is 60 (but will not be able to withdraw income in the meantime and he will not be able to take the fund in cash). If the spouse or dependant withdraws the fund in cash, tax at [35%] will be charged (TA 1988 s 648B)—as with refunded AVCs, this was originally intended to recoup the benefit received from the fund having grown tax free (although at the time of waiting it has not been reduced to reject the two subsequent falls in base rate). In the absence of a spouse or dependant, the lump sum will still be subject to income tax at [35%] and payable within two years of the member's death: normally there will not also be an IHT charge.

Formerly if there was a spouse or dependant but he did not take the fund in cash nor purchase an annuity during the two years following the member's death, then when he subsequently died any funds remaining in the plan were lost. FA 1996 s 172 now provides that the remaining funds can pass as a lump sum to the deceased spouse's (or dependant's) heirs even if more than two years have elapsed since the member's death.   **[IV.16]**

APPENDIX V: FOREIGN EXCHANGE GAINS AND LOSSES AND FINANCIAL INSTRUMENTS FOR MANAGING INTEREST RATE AND CURRENCY RISK

1 Introduction

A uniform system of taxation for foreign exchange gains and losses (FOREX) was contained in FA 1993 ss 125–170 and Schs 15–18 subject to amendments in FA 1994 and FA 1995. The legislation provided for exchange gains and losses of companies on monetary assets, liabilities, and currency contracts to be taxed or relieved as *income* and as they accrued (further detail is contained in seven sets of regulations: SI 1994/3226–3232). Meanwhile FA 1994 ss 147–177 and Sch 18 introduced provisions reforming the tax treatment of financial instruments used by companies for managing interest rate and currency risk (see also SI 1994/3233). As with FOREX the law which applied in this area preceded the development of new types of financial instrument and produced a confusing and, in some cases, uncertain result. These provisions interleave with the FOREX legislation. The entire legislative package came into effect for companies on the first day of their first accounting period to begin on or after 23 March 1995. The Inland Revenue published a useful explanatory statement 'Exchange Gains and Losses and Financial Instruments' in December 1994.   **[V.1]**

2 Exchange gains and losses

The legislation is concerned with the gain whether of an income or a capital nature arising solely from currency fluctuations.

EXAMPLE V.1

May 1997: X Co borrows DM750,000 when the exchange rate is £1: DM3.00.
    In sterling, the value of the debt is £250,000.
November 1997: X Co repays the debt; the exchange rate is now £1: DM2.50, so the sterling cost to X Co is £300,000.
    Because of the currency fluctuation X Co has had to pay an additional £50,000 on its debt. This is known as the *exchange difference*, and in this case is an *exchange loss*.

The system applies to companies that are UK resident, or non-resident with UK interests; it does not apply to partnerships or individuals. Charities, unit trusts and investment trusts are also excluded, while a separate set of rules apply to insurance companies.

Exchange gains and losses are assessed upon the following assets which are generally removed from the CGT regime:
(1) *qualifying assets*, ie foreign currency, debts and bank balances;
(2) *qualifying liabilities*, ie debts: whether or not on security;
(3) *foreign currency contracts*: these are contracts to purchase an amount of foreign currency in exchange for a fixed amount of sterling at a predetermined date in the future.

On acquiring a qualifying asset or becoming subject to a qualifying liability a company is obliged to calculate the exchange gain or loss arising at each *translation time*. This is defined as (i) the date on which the asset or liability is acquired or disposed of and, for retained assets, (ii) the company's accounting date.

EXAMPLE V.2

T Co borrows DM750,000 in January 1996 and repays the loan in September 1997. Its accounting period ends on 31 March.

Translation time	Exchange rate	Sterling value	Exchange difference
Jan 1996	£1: DM2.50	£300,000	–
March 1996	£1: DM2.80	£268,000	£32,000 gain
March 1997	£1: DM3.00	£250,000	£18,000 gain
Sept 1997	£1: DM2.75	£273,000	£23,000 loss

The significance of the new system is that at the end of each accounting period the company is assessed to tax on its exchange gain even though the gain is unrealised, ie the asset has not yet been disposed of.

All exchange differences arising on qualifying assets and liabilities are treated as income. However, a distinction is retained between the differences arising on trading and non-trading items, which are treated as income arising under Cases I and V respectively. In each case exchange gains and losses for the tax year are aggregated and any overall gain is taxed. But while trading exchange losses can be carried back or forward against all profits, non-trading losses can be offset against exchange gains only.   **[V.2]**

3 Non-sterling currency

UK companies operating abroad may elect to calculate their tax liability on foreign exchange gains and losses in a non-sterling currency, provided that the following criteria are met:
(1) that the non-sterling currency is the currency of the primary economic environment of the company; and
(2) the whole (or substantially the whole) of the expenses and receipts of the trade are in that currency; and
(3) the company's accounts are maintained in that currency.
The final foreign currency profit/loss is then translated into sterling for taxation by the Inland Revenue. The rate of exchange is at either the average rate throughout the accounting period or the closing rate of exchange at the end of that period. A company must choose which method to use when it elects for its tax liabilities to be assessed in a non-sterling currency and must then use that method consistently (see SI 1994/3230).   **[V.3]**

4 Deferral of unrealised gains on long-term capital items

If a capital item is being held for one year or longer, and the exchange gains arising from it are unrealised, it is possible for the company to defer payment of tax on part of the gain if one of the following conditions is satisfied:
(1) the unrealised exchange gain exceeds 10% of the company's annual profits; or
(2) (if lower than (1)) the aggregate of unrealised *and* realised exchange gains and losses exceeds 10% of the company's annual accounts.
The excess can be deferred for one year (see SI 1994/3228).

EXAMPLE V.3

Z Co has a number of foreign currency assets and liabilities. One of these is a five-year loan which has given rise to an unrealised exchange gain of £500,000. The aggregate of realised and unrealised exchange differences on all the assets and liabilities gives rise to an exchange gain of £475,000 for the same tax year. Z Co's annual profits for the year are £4m.

The aggregate figure of £475,000 is the lower of the two figures. As it exceeds 10% of the annual profits (ie £400,000) the excess of £75,000 is deducted from Z Co's profits for this accounting period and can be carried forward into the next.

Special provisions apply to a group of companies. To assess the amount of tax that can be deferred for any given company within the group, it is necessary to aggregate the unrealised exchange differences for all the companies in the group and to apportion a share of this gain to the particular company. A similar process is carried out with the net realised and unrealised exchange differences. The lower of the two figures is used to ascertain any excess over 10% of the individual company's profits.   **[V.4]**

5 Matching

Under the new regime it will be possible to match certain non-qualifying assets to the qualifying liabilities with which they were acquired, thus enabling exchange losses to be offset against the corresponding exchange gains. The non-qualifying assets to which matching is permissible are shares in an overseas subsidiary, net investment in an overseas branch, ships and aircraft.

EXAMPLE V.4

March 1997: Co borrows $10m to buy shares in its US subsidiary when the exchange rate is £1: $1.50. The loan is a qualifying liability, the shares are an asset with which matching is permissible. Both are worth £6.6m.

December 1997: The exchange rate is £1: $2, so that the value of both asset and liability is now £5 million. In other words, the loan/liability has acquired an exchange gain of £1.6 million, while the shares/asset has experienced a corresponding exchange loss of equal value.

Without the matching facility, the exchange gain would be taxable but the exchange loss on the shares, which are not a qualifying asset, could not be offset against it.

Matching enables the gain and the loss to cancel each other out until the asset is disposed of (or matching ceases for some other reason) at which point the tax liability must be satisfied.   **[V.5]**

6 Transitional measures

As already noted, the rules applied to the company's first accounting period beginning on or after 23 March 1995. Any qualifying asset or liability already belonging to the company was treated as having been acquired on the date of commencement.

The method by which the item's initial value was assessed depended upon the manner in which it was previously taxed (see SI 1994/3226).   **[V.6]**

a) *Trading assets/liabilities*

Items whose exchange gains were assessed under Case I were subject to a deemed disposal and reacquisition at the value in the last set of accounts. Any resulting exchange difference could be held over until the following year's accounts.   **[V.7]**

b) *Capital assets/liabilities*

These would previously have been assessed for CGT on realisation only and were subjected to a deemed disposal and reacquisition at the market value on the date of commencement of the FOREX regime. The resulting exchange difference could also be held over until the following year's accounts.   **[V.8]**

c) *'Nothings'*

This was the name given to assets and liabilities whose exchange differences were simply ignored under the old system.   **[V.9]**

Fixed debts and borrowings   Liabilities of a fixed nature were treated as having been acquired on the date of commencement of the FOREX regime and valued as stated in the company's previous set of accounts. A 'kink test' was applied at each translation time to determine whether the gain/loss should be assessable to tax:

> A = the overall exchange gain/loss arising on the liability since the day it was acquired;
> B = the overall exchange gain/loss arising on the liability since the date of commencement of the new regime.

If A was greater than B, the exchange gain/loss would not be recognised for that accounting period. If B was greater than A, the difference would be assessed to tax.   **[V.10]**

EXAMPLE V.5

1988: M Co borrows DM10m.
1995: FOREX tax regime commences.
1996: M Co prepares its accounts for the accounting period just ended.
  A = overall exchange difference on loan, 1988–96 = £100,000 gain;
  B = overall exchange difference on loan, 1995–96 = £120,000 gain.

B is greater than A, so the difference (£20,000) *is* treated as an exchange gain for the purpose of that accounting period.

Note: If A is a gain and B is a loss, or vice versa, the exchange gain/loss is not recognised for that accounting period.

Fluctuating debts and borrowings   Fluctuating liabilities were excluded from the FOREX regime for six years after the commencement date ('grandfathering'), although a company can elect otherwise.   **[V.11]**

7   Anti-avoidance provisions

The Inland Revenue has outlined some of the tax avoidance measures that it will act against:
(1) where the main intention of a foreign currency loan is the creation of an offsettable exchange loss;
(2) loans and foreign currency contracts that are not entered into at arm's length;
(3) attempts by a company to change its accounting period in order to minimise its exchange gains or maximise its exchange losses.   **[V.12]**

8 Instruments for managing interest rate and currency risk

These provisions became effective at the same time as the FOREX legislation. The key provisions are as follows:

(1) The rules apply only to companies within the charge to corporation tax: authorised unit trusts are excluded and insurance and mutual trading companies subject to special rules (see FA 1994 Sch 18).

(2) The rules only apply to 'qualifying contracts' defined as interest rate contracts or options or currency contracts or options (*interest rate instruments* include swaps, caps, floors, forward rate agreements and options to enter into these agreements; *exchange rate instruments* comprise forward currency contracts, including currency swaps, and options to enter into these contracts).

Profits and losses from such contracts are treated as income so that if the contract is held for the purposes of a trade those profits and losses form part of the trading calculation. In the case of non-trading profits or losses from qualifying contracts, the amount is treated as a non trading credit/loss under the loan relationship rules (see FA 1994 s 160).

(3) Profits and losses arising from qualifying contracts may either be computed on the basis of full mark to market accounting or on an acceptable accruals basis. There are anti-avoidance provisions designed to prevent transfers of value between associated companies through financial instruments and denying relief for losses on transactions entered into otherwise than at arm's length. **[V.13]**

Index